# DATE DUE

| | |
|---|---|
| APR 13 2012 | |
| OCT 29 2014 | |
| NOV 12 2014 | |
| | |
| NOV 24 2014 | |
| | |
| APR 04 2016 | |
| | |
| | |
| | |
| | |
| | |
| | |
| | |

# THE COMPLETE

# DOG BOOK

# THE COMPLETE

# DOG BOOK

## 20th Edition

*Official Publication of*

## THE AMERICAN KENNEL CLUB

BALLANTINE BOOKS
NEW YORK

Published in the United States by Ballantine Books, an imprint of The Random House Publishing Group, a division of Random House, Inc., New York.

BALLANTINE and colophon are registered trademarks of Random House, Inc. AKC is a registered trademark of The American Kennel Club, Inc.

Library of Congress Cataloging-in-Publication Data

Purebred dogs.
The complete dog book / American Kennel Club.—20th ed.
    p.    cm.
Originally published: Purebred dogs. New York: G.H. Watt, 1929.
ISBN 0-345-47626-3
1. Dog breeds.    2. Dogs.    3. Dogs—Standards—United States.
I. American Kennel Club.    II. Title.
SF426.C66 2006
636.7'1—dc22        2005048263

Printed in the United States of America on acid-free paper

www.ballantinebooks.com

9 8 7 6 5 4

# CONTENTS

## THE BREEDS: HISTORIES AND OFFICIAL STANDARDS

## THE GROUPS

### GROUP I: SPORTING BREEDS   14

## GROUP II: HOUND BREEDS  132

## GROUP III: WORKING BREEDS  227

# GROUP IV: TERRIER BREEDS   340

# GROUP V: TOY BREEDS   446

# GROUP VI: NON-SPORTING BREEDS   524

## GROUP VII: HERDING BREEDS  606

## THE MISCELLANEOUS CLASS  694

# LIVING WITH YOUR DOG  715

# CANINE HEALTH AND FIRST AID  759

# GLOSSARY  803

# INDEX  853

# CREDITS

Breed standards effective January 1, 2006.

New standards, and revisions of standards, are published when approved in the American Kennel Club's official monthly magazine, the AKC GAZETTE.

Each breed standard is owned by the breed's national parent club, with full use granted to the American Kennel Club.

The American Kennel Club thanks the many members of the dog fancy, officers of breed, companion and performance clubs, and our own staff members who have contributed their knowledge, photographs, expertise, and enthusiasm to make the compilation of this book possible.

We offer special thanks to the AKC parent clubs for their invaluable contributions, and to George Berger, Bud Buccone, Russell Bianca, Kimberly Silva, and Marcy Zingler.

# NOTICE

# INTRODUCTION TO THE TWENTIETH EDITION

*From time immemorial, the dog—of all animals—has been most closely associated with man. By his service and devotion, he has earned himself the sobriquet of "man's best friend," a title acquired by no other member of the animal kingdom. His loyalty, affection and heroism have been extolled in many tongues in prose and poetry, and scarcely a day passes that some example of his courage, sagacity and devotion to man is not in the press.*

*Dr. John E. DeMund, AKC President, 1923–1932*

Those words, written by Dr. DeMund in 1929, are as true today—seventy-six years later—as they were back then. A dog cares not who you are or what you are, just that you are at his side to be showered with unquestioning love and devotion. In exchange, dog owners everywhere serve as protectors of their beloved pets. They see to it that their dogs are properly fed, housed, and provided with veterinary attention. They freely give of themselves and their time to take care of their four-legged companions. The love they give is received and reflected many times over. Dog owners like to share their love of animals with others of like minds. They enjoy the camaraderie, the good sportsmanship, the partaking of experiences, and the competitive spirit.

The American Kennel Club is pleased to present this twentieth edition of *The Complete Dog Book* for the enjoyment of everyone who owns a dog or is thinking about owning a dog; who participates in AKC events or is thinking about participating in such events. This edition of *The Complete Dog Book* features the breed standards for all breeds recognized by the AKC, including all the breeds added to our registry and the Miscellaneous class since the nineteenth edition was published in 1998.

The AKC's newest sport, Rally, has been added to the long list of AKC participatory events included in this book. The American Kennel Club encourages all readers to consider participating in some of the many opportunities offered by AKC shows, obedience trials, and performance events. All events, their titles and purposes, are fully explained in depth and detail.

With this twentieth edition, the AKC is meeting its obligation and responsibility to provide all dog lovers with the premier sourcebook covering purebred dogs. The AKC is proud of its heritage and its commitment to preserve, protect, and nurture those dogs for generations to come.

Find a comfortable chair, sit back, and enjoy reading about the world of purebred dogs. *The Complete Dog Book* was created by and for fanciers from all walks of life, all levels of interest. It serves as a valued reference book with something for everyone contained within its pages.

—Dennis B. Sprung, President/
Chief Executive Officer
The American Kennel Club

# THE AMERICAN KENNEL CLUB

*T*he American Kennel Club is a not-for-profit organization devoted to the advancement of purebred dogs.

Established in 1884, the AKC comprises 579 autonomous dog clubs nationwide. In addition, approximately 4,050 affiliated clubs hold AKC events and use AKC rules to conduct dog shows, performance and companion events, educational programs, training classes, and health clinics. In 2005, there were 18,542 AKC events in the United States, including 5,218 matches and sweepstakes, 3,684 dog shows, 5,750 companion events, and 3,890 performance events.

Each member club exercises its voting privilege through a representative known as a delegate. Only dog clubs may be AKC members. The delegates make up the legislative body of the AKC; they set the rules of the sport and elect a thirteen-member Board of Directors. The directors are responsible for managing the AKC, electing AKC officers, and making regulations and policies in conformity with the rules prescribed by the delegates.

The staff of the American Kennel Club is divided between headquarters in New York City and operations in Raleigh, North Carolina. All registration functions are administered in North Carolina. The AKC records the parentage of more than one million dogs annually but is not itself involved in the sale of dogs and cannot, therefore, guarantee the health and quality of dogs in its registry. Some employees, including the AKC field representatives and kennel inspectors, work outside the office and report back to their respective department heads.

Also located in New York City is the AKC reference library. Containing more than 18,000 volumes, the library has one of the most complete collections of its kind in existence. It includes many rare and antique editions, as well as modern works, international publications, and studbooks from around the world. It is open to the public Monday through Friday from 9 A.M. to 4 P.M. The library can also help with questions over the phone (call 212-696-8245), and its catalog is online at *www.akc.org.*

## The AKC Mission Statement

The American Kennel Club is dedicated to upholding the integrity of its Registry, promoting the sport of purebred dogs, and breeding for type and function. Founded in 1884, the AKC and its affiliate organizations advocate for the purebred dog as a family companion, advance canine health and well-being, work to protect the rights of all dog owners, and promote responsible dog ownership.

The AKC works to inform the public about the pleasures and responsibilities of owning purebred dogs. The web site at *akc.org* brings the AKC message to 1.4 million unique visitors monthly. Visitors can register dogs and litters online; acquire AKC goods, services, and educational materials; track breaking news; and generally rely upon the site as their one-stop authority for all things canine.

The AKC mission is also furthered through print and television ads, seminars, publications, and school teaching aids.

The AKC works for the passage of laws that protect the rights of dog owners. The Canine Legislation department supports local and regional dog organizations in their efforts to ensure that new laws are fair, enforceable, and nondiscriminatory.

The AKC Canine Health Foundation, founded in 1994 as a separate entity, raises and distributes funds for canine health research and helps to coordinate research worldwide. The AKC also offers annual scholarships for veterinary students with a special interest in dogs.

AKC Companion Animal Recovery is a national database service committed to reuniting lost pets with their owners. For more information, contact AKC Companion Animal Recovery, 5580 Centerview Drive, Suite 250, Raleigh, NC 27606-3394; 800-252-7894; fax 919-233-1290; *akc.org*.

The American Kennel Club Museum of the Dog houses the nation's finest collection of artwork on the dog, including paintings, sculptures, and porcelains. It is open to the public daily, except Mondays and holidays. For more information, contact The American Kennel Club Museum of the Dog, 1721 S. Mason Road, St. Louis, MO 63131; 314-821-DOGS.

The AKC Stud Book is the recorded ancestry of every dog and bitch who has produced a litter registered with the AKC since its inception. To date, more than 40 million dogs have been registered with the AKC, and approximately one million individual registrations are added each year.

The AKC publishes an award-winning magazine for breeders and enthusiasts. The AKC GAZETTE, continuously published since 1889, offers a wide range of articles and photographs, as well as news of the various breed clubs, AKC activities and forthcoming events, and actions taken by the AKC Board of Directors. Its companion publication, the EVENTS CALENDAR, is a supplement that lists all AKC-licensed shows and events for the coming months. An official record of awards and titles given at AKC events is published in a separate monthly, *AKC Awards.* In addition, the AKC publishes the NEW PUPPIES HANDBOOK, which is sent to all new purebred puppy registrants, and the bimonthly AKC FAMILY DOG, a magazine devoted to the purebred-pet owner.

For more than a century, the AKC's name has been synonymous with purebred dogs and the sport of dogs in this country. The AKC continues to be an important source of information for anyone interested in breeding, registering, studying, exhibiting, or raising purebred dogs.

# Selecting the Right Purebred Dog

*P*urebred dogs are found in an impressive variety of sizes, shapes, colors, and personalities. Some breeds are old, others are new, and all have been molded over time to serve humanity in some capacity. Thus we have hunters, guards, trackers, shepherds, sled dogs, and above all, companions. We have energetic dogs, sedate dogs, extroverted dogs, and those that prefer the fellowship of one or a few familiar faces.

Choosing the purebred dog that's right for you requires some work. There is no substitute for making a careful study of each breed's characteristics and narrowing down the field until you are left with the one that best suits your temperament, lifestyle, accommodations, and taste. Unfortunately, many people purchase their puppy on impulse, without pausing to consider its eventual size, appearance, and personality—traits that are well established and largely predetermined by breed. Before you buy any puppy, be sure you fully understand what the future holds in store. Will the adult dog be large or require extensive grooming? Is it likely to need lots of outdoor exercise? Don't forget to ask yourself whether its temperament will be appropriate for your family, especially the children.

Once you've decided what pleases you in a dog, turn to the section of this book that describes each breed with a photograph, a historical account, and the official AKC standard. The all-important standard is a detailed description of the ideal breed specimen. For example, if you are interested in Labrador Retrievers, the standard describes color (yellow, black, and chocolate), size (sixty-five to seventy pounds at maturity for males), and general temperament (kind, outgoing). The breed history explains why Labrador Retrievers have a special affinity for water. Additionally, the photograph shows you a typical dog of that breed—handsome, strongly built, shorthaired, and alert.

A visit to one or more dog shows, companion events, or field trials is very helpful when selecting a breed. These events offer an opportunity to compare good representatives of various breeds, and you will also be able to talk with breeders, owners, and handlers. Other options include visiting kennels to interact with puppies and adult dogs and to discuss them with a knowledgeable breeder. It is also helpful to ask the advice of a veterinarian.

A fundamental decision is which sex you plan to buy. Males are typically larger than females. For this reason, some people prefer to own a bitch. On the other hand, a bitch that has not been spayed will come into season approximately twice each year, at which time you must take measures to isolate her from males and prevent staining in your home. If you do not expect to breed or exhibit your dog at shows, we recommend having it spayed or neutered. These procedures do not change a dog's personality, but they can help preserve its health.

Another major consideration in choosing a breed is what you envision doing with the dog. If you anticipate entering it in shows or field trials someday, or if you plan to breed, the pedigree of the puppy you select takes on greater significance and you should learn as much as possible about the dog's ancestry.

Today some people want to own a good watchdog. Certain breeds were specifically bred to guard their owner's home and property, but in fact, most dogs naturally bark at unusual sights or sounds. If, however, you want a specially trained guard or apprehension dog, such as those used for police work, be aware that a dog trained to this extent is safe *only* in the custody of a person who is equally well trained.

Once you've decided on the right breed, you should make every attempt to find the right breeder, someone you can communicate with and trust. The right breeder will advise you on your choice (perhaps even point you in another direction) and will guide you through the selection process. The breeder will also continue to provide information and support as your dog matures, and should be able to answer your questions and address your concerns about issues such as housebreaking, leash training, grooming, and feeding. Someday this same person may guide you through your first effort at whelping or applaud your dog's first venture in the show ring.

How do you find a quality breeder? By attending dog events, reading breed publications, contacting local breed clubs and veterinarians, asking other owners for recommendations, and visiting the "Breeder Referral" page at *akc.org*. If you call a breeder for information and discover you are answering as many questions as you ask, that's probably a good sign. *Responsible breeders screen buyers very carefully because they want to ensure that their puppies go to suitable homes.*

Many puppies are sent to their new homes when they are about eight weeks old. Your puppy should be fully weaned, appear healthy and alert, and be clearly ready for independence from its mother. Do not select a puppy that appears ill (signs include nasal discharge or watery eyes) or one whose littermates seem unhealthy. A cowering, trembling, shy puppy, or one that seems snappy and bad-tempered, should be avoided. As soon as possible, bring the new puppy to your own veterinarian for a complete physical examination and any necessary inoculations or dewormings.

# THE AKC AND REGISTRATION

## *Registering a Litter*

A litter is eligible for registration if it is the result of a mating between an AKC-registered sire (male) and an AKC-registered dam (female) of the same breed, and if it is whelped (born) in the United States or its possessions or territories (Puerto Rico, Virgin Islands, Guam, and the Mariana Islands).

To register a litter, the litter owner should complete an AKC Litter Registration Application.

The application requires basic information such as the date of birth, number of males and females born, and the registered names and numbers of the sire and dam. The application must be signed by all the owners and co-owners of the dam and by one owner of the sire. Failure to complete the application properly will result in processing delays.

Processing fees are nonrefundable, and all fees are subject to change without notice.

When completed, the application should be submitted to the AKC with the proper fee. Applications can be mailed. You can also register your litter online at *akc.org*. The AKC will mail the litter owner a "litter kit." The litter kit will include an individual registration application for each puppy in the litter, as well as a form for record keeping. The litter owner should examine the kit thoroughly for errors before issuing the papers to puppy buyers.

Each person or firm who owns, breeds, or sells dogs that are AKC registrable must keep accurate, up-to-date records of all transactions involving these dogs. There must be no doubt as to the identity of any individual dog or as to the parentage of a particular dog or litter.

The AKC recommends commonsense practices for those who regularly have multiple dogs or litters on their premises, including:

- Permanent identification of each dog, with tattoos, microchips, marking, or tagging.
- Isolation of bitches in season.
- Segregation of litters whelped near the same date.

The AKC requires that the owner of an AKC-registered dog maintain the following information on the dog:

- Breed.
- Registered name and number (or litter number if not registered).
- Sex, color, and markings.

- Date of birth.
- Names and numbers of sire and dam.
- Name of breeder.
- Name and address of person from whom directly acquired.
- Date of acquisition.
- Date and duration of lease, if any.

The owner of a dog that is bred must record:

- Date and place of mating.
- Names of persons handling mating.
- Registered name and number of dog to which mated.
- Name and address of its owner.

The owner of a litter must record:

- Date of whelping.
- Number of puppies whelped by sex and by color and markings.
- Litter registration number.
- Date of sale, gift, or death of each puppy so described.
- Name and address of person acquiring each puppy so described.
- Kinds of papers and date supplied.
- Registered name and number of each puppy registered by breeder.

Failure to uphold proper record-keeping procedures could lead to penalties, including the suspension of AKC privileges. See the "AKC Procedures for Registration Matters" at *akc.org* for complete information.

## Registering a Dog

A purebred dog is eligible for AKC registration if its litter has been registered. When you purchase a dog said to be AKC registrable, you should get an individual Dog Registration Application from the seller. Once the application has been completed, you should submit it to the AKC with the proper fee. You can also register a dog online at *akc.org*.

The Dog Registration Application must be filled out jointly by the litter owner and the new owner of the dog. The litter owner must fill out most of the application, including the following information:

- Sex of dog.
- Color and markings of dog.

- Registration type (Full or Limited).
- Transfer date.
- Name and address of all new owners and co-owners.
- Signatures of all litter owners.

The new owner of the dog must fill out the following:

- Name of dog.
- Signatures of all owners and co-owners.
- Payment information.
- Registration options (for purchasing pedigrees and videos).

Processing fees are nonrefundable, and all fees are subject to change without notice.

Please note that each litter owner and each new owner must sign the application individually. It is crucial that all sections of the application are filled out correctly. Failure to properly complete the application will result in processing delays.

If you did not acquire the dog directly from the litter owner(s), you must include a Supplemental Transfer Statement for each intermediate transfer with the application.

When the application has been received and processed by the AKC, a Registration Certificate will be mailed to the owner. The owner should examine the certificate carefully and report any errors to the AKC.

# THE BREEDS:
# HISTORIES AND OFFICIAL
# STANDARDS

# THE AKC BREEDS

*T*HE BREEDS CURRENTLY RECOGNIZED FOR REGISTRATION BY THE AMERI-can Kennel Club are presented in this section in the order in which they appear in dog show catalogs. A representative photograph, history, and official AKC standard are included for each breed.

AKC breeds are organized into seven groups: Sporting, Hound, Working, Terrier, Toy, Non-Sporting, and Herding. The members of each group often share similar characteristics, such as physical appearance, ancestry, temperament, and function.

An understanding of any breed must begin with its standard. This applies to all dogs, not just those intended for showing. Standards are written by breed experts, and they depict the ideal specimen of each breed. They describe perfect type, structure, gait, and temperament, information that describes the ideal dog. Rarely does a dog measure up to every specification of its standard. Instead, the standard is a conceptualization—one that guides the imaginations of breeders, dog show judges, and students of the breed.

The official standard for each breed and any revision of the standard originates with the parent club, which is the national organization for each respective breed. The membership of the parent club must vote on and approve the standard or revision before it is submitted to the AKC Board of Directors for approval. The date shown at the end of each standard is the date the latest revision was approved. Where no date is shown, the standard has remained unchanged since the first AKC *Complete Dog Book* was published in 1929.

The AKC does not wish to do anything to encourage the indiscriminate breeding of dogs of any breed, and quality is always considered more important than quantity. If proponents of a breed would like to apply for full AKC registration status, the parent club must approach the AKC and demonstrate that it has met certain criteria. Before the AKC considers adding a breed to its registry (the final decision is made by the AKC Board of Directors), there must be clear and categorical proof that substantial, sustained nationwide interest and activity in the breed exist. This includes an active parent club, with serious and expanding breeding activity over a wide geographic area.

When, in the judgment of the AKC Board of Directors, such interest and activity exists, a breed is admitted into the Miscellaneous class. Breeds in the Miscellaneous class may compete and earn titles in AKC companion events. They may compete at conformation shows, but here are limited to competition in the Miscellaneous class and are not eligible for championship points. Dogs of the Miscellaneous class may also be shown in Juniors competition.

When the Board of Directors is satisfied that a breed is continuing a healthy, dynamic growth in the Miscellaneous class, it may be admitted to registration in the AKC Stud Book and have the opportunity to compete in regular classes.

(Photo courtesy of the New Bedford Standard–Times)

*The first dog to appear in the AKC Stud Book was Adonis, an English Setter whelped in 1875. Adonis was owned and bred by George Delano, of New Bedford, Massachusetts.*

# DISQUALIFICATIONS APPLYING TO ALL BREEDS

*S*PAYED AND NEUTERED DOGS ARE LIMITED IN COMPETITION AT CONFORMA-tion events (they may compete only in the Stud Dog and Brood Bitch classes and in the Veterans classes at independent specialty shows), but they are eligible to compete in obedience trials and *all* performance events except Beagle field trials.

In addition to the disqualifications found in each individual standard, the following disqualifications apply to all breeds at conformation shows.

A dog that is blind, deaf, castrated, spayed, or that has been changed in appearance by artificial means except as specified in the standard for its breed, or a male that does not have two normal testicles normally located in the scrotum, may not compete at any show and will be disqualified except that a castrated male may be entered as a Stud Dog in the Stud Dog class and a spayed bitch may be entered as a Brood Bitch in the Brood Bitch class. Neutered dogs and spayed bitches would be allowed to compete in Veterans classes only at independent specialties or those all-breed shows that do not offer any competitive classes beyond Best of Breed.

A dog will not be considered to have been changed by artificial means because of removal of dewclaws or docking of tail if it is of a breed in which such removal or docking is a regularly approved practice not contrary to the standard. Procedures that would in and of themselves be considered a change in appearance by artificial means and make a dog ineligible for shows include, but are not limited to, the following:

1. Correction of entropion, ectropion, trichiasis, or distichiasis.
2. Trimming, removal, or tattooing of the third eyelid (nictitating membrane).
3. Insertion of an eye prosthesis.
4. Correction of harelip, cleft palate, stenotic nares, or an elongated soft palate resection.
5. Procedures to change ear set or carriage other than that permitted by the breed standard.
6. Dental procedures for restoration, the use of bands or braces on teeth or any alteration of the dental arcade.

7. The removal of excess skin folds or the removal of skin patches to alter markings.
8. Correction of inguinal, scrotal, or perineal hernias.
9. Surgery for hip dysplasia, OCD, patellar luxation, or femoral head resection.
10. Alteration of the location of the testes or the insertion of an artificial testicle.
11. Alteration of the set or carriage of the tail.

Any dog whose ears have been cropped or cut in any way shall be ineligible to compete at any show in any state where the laws prohibit the same, except subject to the provisions of such laws.

A dog that is lame at any show may not compete and shall not receive any award at that show. It shall be the judge's responsibility to determine whether a dog is lame.

No dog shall be eligible to compete at any show and no dog shall receive any award at any show in the event the natural color or shade of natural color or the natural markings of the dog have been altered or changed by the use of any substance, whether such substance may have been used for cleaning purposes or for any other reason. Such cleaning substances are to be removed before the dog enters the ring.

No dog shall be eligible to compete at any show, no dog shall be brought onto the grounds or premises of any dog show, and any dog that may have been brought onto the grounds or premises of a dog show shall immediately be removed, if it:

1. Shows clinical symptoms of distemper, infectious hepatitis, leptospirosis, or any other communicable disease.
2. Is known to have been in contact with distemper, infectious hepatitis, leptospirosis, or any other communicable disease within thirty days before the opening of the show.
3. Has been kenneled within thirty days before the opening of the show at premises on which there existed distemper, infectious hepatitis, leptospirosis, or any other communicable disease.

# How Height and Length
# Are Measured on a Dog

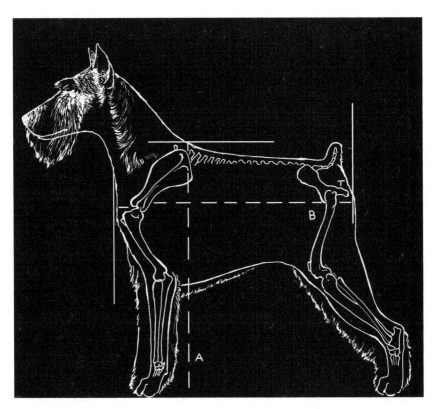

*A dog's height is measured from the highest point of the shoulder blade to the ground (line A). In most breeds a dog's length is measured from the point of shoulder to point of buttock (line B).*

*(Reproduced, with permission, from* Illustrated Discussion of the Miniature Schnauzer Standard. *Drawing by Loraine L. Bush.)*

# Inaugural AKC Registrations

| BREED | YEAR | NAME AND NUMBER OF FIRST DOG |
|---|---|---|
| Affenpinscher | 1936 | Nollie v Anwander   A-107711 |
| Afghan Hound | 1926 | Tezin   544928 |
| Airedale Terrier | 1888 | Pin   9087 |
| Akita | 1972 | Akita Tani's Terukoshi   WC-292650 |
| Alaskan Malamute | 1935 | Rowdy of Nome   998426 |
| American Eskimo Dog | 1994 | Kuddly's Kansas Storm   NM503995/01 |
| American Staffordshire Terrier | 1936 | Wheeler's Black Dinah   A-86066 |
| Anatolian Shepherd | 1996 | Keechi's Sandy Dusty   WP69124801 |
| Australian Cattle Dog | 1980 | Glen Iris Boomerang, CDX   WE-507650 |
| Australian Shepherd | 1991 | Hi-Cotton's Vamp of Savanna DL390226/01 |
| Australian Terrier | 1960 | Canberra Kookaburra   R-258126 |
| Basenji | 1944 | Phemister's Bois   A-738970 |
| Basset Hound | 1885 | Bouncer   3234 |
| Beagle | 1885 | Blunder   3188 |
| Bearded Collie | 1976 | Cannamoor Cartinka   WD-439250 |
| Bedlington Terrier | 1886 | Ananias   4475 |
| Belgian Malinois (*Registered as Belgian Sheepdog until 1959*) | | |
| Belgian Sheepdog | 1912 | Rumford Dax   160405 |
| Belgian Tervuren (*Registered as Belgian Sheepdog until 1959*) | | |
| Bernese Mountain Dog | 1937 | Quell v Tiergarten   A-156752 |
| Bichon Frise | 1972 | Sha-Bob's Nice Girl Missy   NS-077900 |
| Black Russian Terrier | 2004 | Czar Nicholas Li   WP69789101 |
| Black and Tan Coonhound | 1945 | Grand Mere Big Rock Molly   A-898800 |

| BREED | YEAR | NAME AND NUMBER OF FIRST DOG |
|---|---|---|
| Bloodhound | 1885 | Carodoc   3237 |
| Border Collie | 1995 | Darkwind Drift   DL562522/01 |
| Border Terrier | 1930 | Netherbyers Ricky   719372 |
| Borzoi (*Originally registered as Russian Wolfhound*) | 1891 | Princess Irma   20716 |
| Boston Terrier | 1893 | Hector   28814 |
| Bouvier des Flandres | 1931 | Hardix   780160 |
| Boxer | 1904 | Arnulf Grandenz   78043 |
| Briard | 1928 | Dauphine de Montjoye   635613 |
| Brittany (*Registered as Brittany Spaniel until 1982*) | 1934 | Edir du Mesnil   949896 |
| Brussels Griffon | 1910 | Dolley's Biddy   137219 |
| Bulldog | 1886 | Bob   4982 |
| Bullmastiff | 1934 | Fascination of Felons Fear   914895 |
| Bull Terrier | 1885 | Nellie II   3308 |
| Canaan Dog | 1997 | Reva Me Patpatan   DL684793/01 |
| Cairn Terrier | 1913 | Sandy Peter out of the West   173555 |
| Cavalier King Charles Spaniel | 1995 | Regis Lido's Sunne in Splendour   TN196410/01 |
| Chihuahua | 1904 | Midget   82291 |
| Chinese Crested | 1991 | Maya of Rivercrest   D 413100 |
| Chinese Shar-Pei | 1992 | Shir Du Moo Cho   NM844828/01 |
| Chow Chow | 1903 | Yen How   74111 |
| Collie | 1885 | Black Shep   3249 |
| Dachshund | 1885 | Dash   3223 |
| Dalmatian | 1888 | Bessie   10519 |
| Dandie Dinmont Terrier | 1886 | Bonnie Britton   4472 |
| Doberman Pinscher | 1908 | Doberman Intelectus   122650 |
| English Toy Spaniel | 1886 | Mildmay Park Beauty   4456 |
| Finnish Spitz | 1991 | Hammerfest's Loveable Sister   D87106/01 |
| Foxhound (American) | 1886 | Lady Stewart   4320 |
| Foxhound (English) | 1909 | Auditor   129533 |
| Fox Terrier | 1885 | Cricket   3289 |
| French Bulldog | 1898 | Guguss II   49705 |
| German Shepherd Dog | 1908 | Queen of Switzerland   115006 |
| Giant Schnauzer | 1930 | Bella v Fuchspark Potzhauss   721736 |
| Glen of Imaal Terrier | 2004 | Liberty's Darby O'Gill   RM20342707 |
| Great Dane | 1887 | Don Caesar   6046 |
| Great Pyrenees | 1933 | Blanchette   866751 |

| BREED | YEAR | NAME AND NUMBER OF FIRST DOG |
|---|---|---|
| Greater Swiss Mountain Dog | 1995 | Flyer Cat's a Tiny Tuxedo   WP616061/01 |
| Greyhound | 1885 | Baron Walkeen   3241 |
| German Pinscher | 2001 | Sea Breeze's Splash   WP66050505 |
| Harrier | 1885 | Jolly   3236 |
| Havanese | 1995 | Havana's Elske O'Jimka   TN30161001 |
| Ibizan Hound | 1978 | Asuncion HC   522350 |
| Irish Terrier | 1885 | Aileen   3306 |
| Irish Wolfhound | 1897 | Ailbe   45994 |
| Italian Greyhound | 1886 | Lilly   4346 |
| Japanese Chin (*Registered as Japanese Spaniel until 1977*) | 1888 | Jap   9216 |
| Keeshond | 1930 | Bella v Trennfeld   751187 |
| Kerry Blue Terrier | 1922 | Brian of Muchia   349159 |
| Komondor | 1937 | Andrashazi Dorka   A-199838 |
| Kuvasz | 1931 | Tamar v Wuermtal   791292 |
| Lakeland Terrier | 1934 | Egton What a Lad of Howtown   938424 |
| Lhasa Apso | 1935 | Empress of Kokonor   987979 |
| Löwchen | 1996 | Ketara's Whoopi   NM64909703 |
| Maltese | 1888 | Topsy   12056 |
| Manchester Terrier (Standard) | 1887 | Lever   7585 |
| Manchester Terrier (Toy) (*Toys and Standards were considered separate breeds until 1959*) | 1886 | Gypsy   4485 |
| Mastiff | 1885 | Bayard   3271 |
| Miniature Bull Terrier | 1991 | Navigation Pinto   RM023801 |
| Miniature Pinscher | 1925 | Asta von Sandreuth   454601 |
| Miniature Schnauzer | 1926 | Schnapp v Dornbusch of Hitofa   551063 |
| Neapolitan Mastiff | 2004 | Fruit D'Amour Quaterna   WR0000610 |
| Newfoundland | 1886 | Fly   4447 |
| Norfolk Terrier (*Registered as Norwich Terrier until 1979*) | 1979 | Bar Sinister Little Ruffian   RA475550 |
| Norwegian Elkhound | 1913 | Koik   170389 |
| Norwich Terrier | 1936 | Witherslack Sport   A-58858 |
| Nova Scotia Duck Tolling Retriever | 2003 | Kilcreek's Coppertone Kid   SN66644502 |
| Old English Sheepdog | 1888 | Champion of Winkleigh   9252 |

| BREED | YEAR | NAME AND NUMBER OF FIRST DOG |
|---|---|---|
| Otterhound | 1909 | Hartland Spokesman    124965 |
| Papillon | 1915 | Joujou    192537 |
| Parson Russell Terrier | 1997 | Heza Handsome Jack    RM20004901 |
| Pekingese | 1906 | Rascal    95459 |
| Petit Basset Griffon Vendéen | 1990 | Axmos Babette de la Garonne    HDB93000 |
| Pharaoh Hound | 1983 | Fqira    HD-027750 |
| Pointer | 1878 | Ace of Spades    1187 |
| Pointer (German Shorthaired) | 1930 | Grief v.d. Fliegerhalde    723642 |
| Pointer (German Wirehaired) | 1959 | Eiko vom Schultenhof    S-963376 |
| Pomeranian | 1888 | Dick    10776 |
| Poodle | 1887 | Czar    7597 |
| Portuguese Water Dog | 1983 | Renascenca do Al-Gharb    WF-382950 |
| Pug | 1885 | George    3286 |
| Puli | 1936 | Torokvesz Sarika    A-107734 |
| Retriever (Chesapeake Bay) | 1878 | Sunday    1408 |
| Retriever (Curly-Coated) | 1924 | Knysna Conjurer    398399 |
| Retriever (Flat-Coated) | 1915 | Sand Bridge Jester    190223 |
| Retriever (Golden) | 1925 | Lomberdale Blondin    490685 |
| Retriever (Labrador) | 1917 | Brocklehirst Floss    223339 |
| Rhodesian Ridgeback | 1955 | Tchaika of Redhouse    H-520551 |
| Rottweiler | 1931 | Stina v Felsenmeer    805867 |
| Saint Bernard | 1885 | Chief    3280 |
| Saluki | 1929 | Jinniyat of Grevel    674570 |
| Samoyed | 1906 | Moustan of Argenteau    102896 |
| Schipperke | 1904 | Snowball    83461 |
| Scottish Deerhound | 1886 | Bonnie Robin    4345 |
| Scottish Terrier | 1885 | Prince Charlie    3310 |
| Sealyham Terrier | 1911 | Harfats Pride    151623 |
| Setter (English) | 1878 | Adonis    1 |
| Setter (Gordon) | 1878 | Bank    793 |
| Setter (Irish) | 1878 | Admiral    534 |
| Shetland Sheepdog | 1911 | Lord Scott    148760 |
| Shiba Inu | 1992 | Minamoto Shogun    NM334598/01 |
| Shih Tzu | 1969 | Choo Lang of Telota    TA-573228 |
| Siberian Husky | 1930 | Fairbanks Princess Chena    758529 |
| Silky Terrier | 1959 | Winsome Beau Ideal    T-610051 |
| Skye Terrier | 1887 | Romach    6184 |

| BREED | YEAR | NAME AND NUMBER OF FIRST DOG |
|---|---|---|
| Soft Coated Wheaten Terrier | 1973 | Holmenocks Gramachree, CD   RA-44600 |
| Spaniel (American Water) | 1940 | Tidewader Teddy   A-426838 |
| Spaniel (Clumber) | 1878 | Bustler   1353 |
| Spaniel (Cocker) | 1878 | Capt   1354 |
| Spaniel (English Cocker) (*Separated from Cocker Spaniel in 1946*) | | |
| Spaniel (English Springer) | 1910 | Denne Lucy   142641 |
| Spaniel (Field) | 1894 | Colehill Rufus   33395 |
| Spaniel (Irish Water) | 1878 | Bob   1352 |
| Spaniel (Sussex) | 1878 | Jack (alias Toby)   1363 |
| Spaniel (Welsh Springer) | 1914 | Faircroft Bob   185938 |
| Spinone Italiano | 2000 | Mal's-About's Salvatore Riga SN57589605 |
| Staffordshire Bull Terrier | 1974 | Tinkinswood Imperial   RA-161150 |
| Standard Schnauzer | 1904 | Norwood Victor   77886 |
| Tibetan Spaniel | 1983 | Tritou Charlotte   NS-789150 |
| Tibetan Terrier | 1973 | Amanda Lamleh of Kalai   NS-107000 |
| Toy Fox Terrier | 2001 | Windy Acres Jessica's Casanova TN33580801 |
| Vizsla | 1960 | Rex Z Arpadvar   SA-63201 |
| Weimaraner | 1943 | Adda v Schwarzen Kamp   646165 |
| Welsh Corgi (Cardigan) | 1935 | Blodwen of Robinscroft   965012 |
| Welsh Corgi (Pembroke) | 1934 | Little Madam   939536 |
| Welsh Terrier | 1888 | T'Other   9171 |
| West Highland White Terrier | 1908 | Talloch   116076 |
| Whippet | 1888 | Jack Dempsey   9804 |
| Wirehaired Pointing Griffon (*Registered as a Russian Setter*) | 1887 | Zolette   6773 |
| Yorkshire Terrier | 1885 | Belle   3307 |

Breeding records existed in the United States long before the American Kennel Club was founded in 1884, but most were kept by private individuals. In 1886, the AKC decided that a reliable record of pedigrees was vital to the advancement of the sport of purebred dogs, and it began negotiating with the two existing studbooks, the American Kennel Register and the National American Kennel Club. Although the former declined the AKC's offer, Dr. N. Rowe (who had published Volumes II and III of the *National American Kennel Club Stud Book* at his own expense) agreed to hand over the National American Kennel Club's three volumes. Containing a list of 5,397 dogs, these volumes became the basis of the AKC Stud Book, kept continuously since 1887.

# THE GROUPS

# GROUP I: SPORTING BREEDS

BRITTANY

POINTER

GERMAN SHORTHAIRED POINTER

GERMAN WIREHAIRED POINTER

CHESAPEAKE BAY RETRIEVER

CURLY-COATED RETRIEVER

FLAT-COATED RETRIEVER

GOLDEN RETRIEVER

LABRADOR RETRIEVER

NOVA SCOTIA DUCK TOLLING
   RETRIEVER

ENGLISH SETTER

GORDON SETTER

IRISH SETTER

AMERICAN WATER SPANIEL

CLUMBER SPANIEL

COCKER SPANIEL

ENGLISH COCKER SPANIEL

ENGLISH SPRINGER SPANIEL

FIELD SPANIEL

IRISH WATER SPANIEL

SUSSEX SPANIEL

WELSH SPRINGER SPANIEL

SPINONE ITALIANO

VIZSLA

WEIMARANER

WIREHAIRED POINTING GRIFFON

# BRITTANY

*N*AMED FOR THE FRENCH PROVINCE IN WHICH IT ORIGINATED, THE BRIT-
tany was first registered by the American Kennel Club as the Brittany
Spaniel in 1934. Although called a spaniel, by its manner of working game the Brittany belongs with the pointing breeds. In appearance, the breed is smaller than the
setters but leggier than the spaniels, having a short tail and characteristic high earset. On September 1, 1982, the breed's official AKC name became Brittany, to
more correctly identify their hunting style.

Though it is generally conceded that the basic stock for all bird dogs is the
same, most of the facts concerning the development and spread of the various
breeds are lost in antiquity. The first accurate records to pinpoint the actual
Brittany-type dog are seventeenth-century paintings and tapestries. The frequency
with which these appear suggests this type of dog was fairly common. Paintings by
Jean-Baptiste Oudry (1686–1755) show a liver-and-white dog pointing partridge.
This same type of dog is common in Flemish paintings from the school of Jan
Steen. Still other artists show this type of bird dog, so it would appear that it was
common throughout the northern coast of France and in Holland.

Still, there is nothing written before 1850 that can be unequivocally interpreted as a reference to the Brittany. In that year, the English clergyman Reverend
Davies wrote of hunting in Carhaix with small, bobtailed dogs. They were not as
smooth as the Pointer, but worked well in the brush. They pointed, retrieved game

well, and were particularly popular with poachers, as the nature of that occupation required that the dogs be easy to handle. The description fits the Brittany to perfection.

It was speculated, and in at least one case confirmed, that around 1900 some native spaniels of Brittany were mated with English pointing dogs, whose owners vacationed in France, for woodcock shooting. These matings intensified the pointing qualities of the breed while the basic features remained essentially Breton. The Brittany was an all-purpose dog, a family pet, and a guard dog as well as a hunting dog for the thrifty French peasant. This certainly influenced its shape, size, and disposition. The climate, the nature of the terrain hunted, the manner of hunting, and even its popularity with poachers all had an effect on the type of coat, keenness of nose, and retrieving ability that was developed over the years.

Legend has it that the first tailless ancestor of the modern Brittany emerged in the mid-1800s at Pontou, a little town in the valley of Douron. It resulted from a cross between a white-and-mahogany bitch owned by a hunter in the region and a lemon-and-white dog brought to Brittany for woodcock shooting by an English sportsman. Of two tailless puppies in this litter, one proved outstanding. His work in the field has been described as wonderful, and he became a popular stud. All of his litters produced puppies either without tails or with short stubs.

The Brittany became a recognized breed in 1907, when Boy, an orange-and-white, was registered in France as the first l'épagneul Breton queue courte naturelle. This name was soon shortened to l'épagneul Breton, or Brittany Spaniel. Before 1907, Brittanys had competed in classes for Miscellaneous French spaniels.

In the same year, an outline for the first breed standard was written. This early standard required that the tail be short at birth and that, in order to discourage further crossbreeding, black and white be disqualified. The requirement for the natural bobtail was soon dropped.

The breed was introduced in the United States in 1931 and was officially recognized by the American Kennel Club in 1934. The first standard was a direct translation from the French and not particularly comprehensible. The first major accomplishment of the American Brittany Club after its formation in 1942 was to replace the original standard with a clear and concise one.

An early gain in popularity was due largely to the Brittany's merits as a shooting dog. A superb nose and desire to please, coupled with relatively small size, endeared the breed to rural and urban hunters alike.

The last fifty years have seen a tremendous growth in both field trials and hunt tests sponsored by the American Brittany Club under the auspices of the AKC. Brittany competition in AKC dog shows has grown equally, and the majority of Brittany owners and breeders are today dedicated to the Dual Champion (field and show champion). Now, seventy years since first recognition, more than 500 Brittanys have gained the ultimate title, that of Dual Champion.

# OFFICIAL STANDARD FOR THE BRITTANY

**General Appearance**—A compact, closely knit dog of medium size, a leggy dog having the appearance, as well as the agility, of a great ground coverer. Strong, vigorous, energetic and quick of movement. Ruggedness, without clumsiness, is a characteristic of the breed. He can be tailless or has a tail docked to approximately four inches.

**Size, Proportion, Substance**—*Height*—17½ to 20½ inches, measured from the ground to the highest point of the shoulders. Any Brittany measuring under 17½ inches or over 20½ inches shall be disqualified from dog show competition. *Weight*—Should weigh between 30 and 40 pounds.

*Proportion*—So leggy is he that his height at the shoulders is the same as the length of his body.

*Body Length*—Approximately the same as the height when measured at the shoulders. Body length is measured from the point of the forechest to the rear of the rump. A long body should be heavily penalized. *Substance*—Not too light in bone, yet never heavy-boned and cumbersome.

**Head**—*Expression*—Alert and eager, but with the soft expression of a bird dog. *Eyes*—Well set in head. Well protected from briers by a heavy, expressive eyebrow. A prominent, full or popeye should be heavily penalized. It is a serious fault in a dog that must face briers. Skull well chiseled under the eyes, so that the lower lid is not pulled back to form a pocket or haw that would catch seeds, dirt and weed dust. Preference should be for the darker colored eyes, though lighter shades of amber should not be penalized. Light and mean-looking eyes should be heavily penalized. *Ears*—Set high, above the level of the eyes. Short and triangular, rather than pendulous, reaching about half the length of the muzzle. Should lie flat and close to the head, with the tip rounded very slightly. Ears well covered with dense, but relatively short hair, and with little fringe. *Skull*—Medium length, rounded, very slightly wedge-shaped, but evenly made. Width, not quite as wide as the length and never so broad as to appear coarse, or so narrow as to appear racy. Well defined, but gently sloping stop. Median line rather indistinct. The occiput only apparent to the touch. Lateral walls well rounded. The Brittany should never be "apple-headed" and he should never have an indented stop. *Muzzle*—Medium length, about two thirds the length of the skull, measuring the muzzle from the tip to the stop, and the skull from the occiput to the stop. Muzzle should taper gradually in both horizontal and vertical dimensions as it approaches the nostrils. Neither a Roman nose nor a dishface is desirable. Never broad, heavy or snipy. *Nose*—Nostrils well open to permit deep breathing of air and adequate scenting. Tight nostrils should be penalized. Never shiny. Color: fawn, tan, shades of brown or deep pink. A black nose is a disqualification. A two-tone or butterfly nose should be penalized. *Lips*—Tight, the upper lip overlapping the lower jaw just to cover the lower lip. Lips dry, so that feathers will not stick. Drooling to be heavily penalized. Flews to be penalized. *Bite*—A true scissors bite. Overshot or undershot jaw to be heavily penalized.

**Neck, Topline, Body**—*Neck*—Medium length. Free from throatiness, though not a serious fault unless accompanied by dewlaps, strong without giving the impression of being overmuscled. Well set into sloping shoulders. Never concave or ewe-necked. *Topline*—Slight slope from the highest point of the shoulders to the root of the tail. *Chest*—Deep, reaching the level of the elbow. Neither so wide nor so rounded as to disturb the placement of the shoulders and elbows. Ribs well sprung. Adequate heart room provided by depth as well as width. Narrow or slab-sided chests are a fault. *Back*—Short and straight. Never hollow, saddle, sway or roach-backed. Slight drop from the hips to the root of the tail. *Flanks*—Rounded. Fairly full. Not extremely tucked up, or flabby and falling. Loins short and strong. Distance from last rib to upper thigh short, about three to four finger widths. Narrow and weak loins are a fault. In motion, the loin should not sway sideways, giving a zig-zag motion to the back, wasting energy. *Tail*—Tailless to approximately four inches, natural or docked. The tail not to be so long as to affect the overall balance of the dog. Set on high, actually an extension of the spine at about the same level. Any tail substantially more than four inches shall be severely penalized.

**Forequarters**—*Shoulders*—Shoulder blades should not protrude too much, not too wide apart, with perhaps two thumbs' width between. Sloping and muscular. Blade and upper arm should form nearly a ninety-degree angle. Straight shoulders are a fault. At the shoulders the Brittany is slightly higher than at the rump. *Front Legs*—Viewed from the front, perpendicular, but not set too wide. Elbows and feet turning neither in nor out. Pasterns slightly sloped. Down in pasterns is a serious fault. Leg bones clean, graceful, but not too fine. Extremely heavy bone is as much a fault as spindly legs. One must look for substance and suppleness. Height at elbows should approximately equal distance from elbow to withers. *Feet*—Should be strong, proportionately smaller than the spaniels', with close-fitting, well-arched toes and thick pads. The Brittany is "not up on his toes." Toes not heavily feathered. Flat feet, splayed feet, paper feet, etc., are to be heavily penalized. An ideal foot is halfway between the hare and the cat foot. Dewclaws may be removed.

**Hindquarters**—Broad, strong and muscular, with powerful thighs and well-bent stifles, giving the angulation necessary for powerful drive. *Hind Legs*—Stifles well bent. The stifle should not be so angulated as to place the hock joint far out behind the dog. A Brittany should not be condemned for straight stifle until the judge has checked the dog in motion from the side. The stifle joint should not turn out making a cowhock. Thighs well feathered but not profusely, halfway to the hock. Hocks, that is, the back pasterns, should be moderately short, pointing neither in nor out, perpendicular when viewed from the side. They should be firm when shaken by the judge. *Feet*—Same as front feet.

**Coat**—Dense, flat or wavy, never curly. Texture neither wiry nor silky. Ears should carry little fringe. The front and hind legs should have some feathering, but too little is definitely preferable to too much. Dogs with long or profuse feathering or furnishings shall be so severely penalized as to effectively eliminate them from competition. *Skin*—Fine and fairly loose. A loose skin rolls with briers and sticks, thus diminishing punctures or tearing. A skin so loose as to form pouches is undesirable.

**Color**—Orange and white or liver and white in either clear or roan patterns. Some ticking is desirable. The orange or liver is found in the standard parti-color or piebald patterns. Washed-out colors are not desirable. Tri-colors are allowed but not preferred. A tri-color is a liver and white dog with classic orange markings on eyebrows, muzzle and cheeks; inside the ears and under the tail; freckles on the lower legs are orange. Anything exceeding the limits of these markings shall be severely penalized. Black is a disqualification.

**Gait**—When at a trot the Brittany's hind foot should step into or beyond the print left by the front foot. Clean movement, coming and going, is very important, but most important is side gait, which is smooth, efficient and ground covering.

**Temperament**—A happy, alert dog, neither mean nor shy.

## DISQUALIFICATIONS

*Any Brittany measuring under 17½ inches or over 20½ inches.*
*A black nose.*
*Black in the coat.*

**Approved April 10, 1990**
**Effective May 31, 1990**

# POINTER

*T*HE POINTER COMES BY HIS NAME HONESTLY. HE WAS THE FIRST DOG, SO far as we know, used to stand game in the sense in which we use the term today, and was developed as a distinct breed much earlier than any of the setters. For years it was believed the first Pointers used in England were importations from Spain and Portugal, but that theory has been pretty thoroughly disproved. It seems far more likely that Pointers came into general use in Spain, Portugal, throughout Eastern Europe, and in the British Isles at approximately the same time. Whether or not the dogs from which they sprung were native to all these places no one can say, but it can be stated with confidence that the *development* of the English Pointer took place within the confines of Great Britain, most probably in England itself. Later on, Spanish Pointers were brought in, but from the first they were considered as a different strain, if not a different breed, from the English dogs.

The first Pointers of which there is any dependable record appeared in England in about 1650, some years before the era of wing-shooting with guns. The use to which they were put is interesting. Coursing with Greyhounds was a favorite sport of those times, and the earliest accounts of Pointers reveal that they were taken afield to locate and point hares. When the hare had been found, the Greyhounds were brought up and unleashed, the game was kicked from cover, and the fun began. But early in the eighteenth century, at least by 1711, wing-shooting had come into vogue, and from that day on, the "shorthair" has been considered by the majority of sportsmen the equal, if not the superior, of any of the gundogs.

As to the Pointer's lineage, as usual we find it something of an enigma, but there is no question that the Foxhound, Greyhound, and Bloodhound all had a share in his making. Individuals of the three breeds were probably crossed with the inevitable "setting spaniel," which played such a prominent part in the creation of all our modern bird dogs.

During the first years of the eighteenth century the Spanish Pointer began to appear in England, and he, too, was used for a cross. But, as he was exceedingly heavy and very slow in comparison with the English, French, and German Pointers, subsequent breeding operations not only left him out but definitely attempted to correct the faults he had introduced. It appears that his real value was not to improve type but to fix and intensify the pointing instinct, in which, we are told, he was peculiarly strong.

If this was the purpose, it seems to have been successful. Remarkable (and, incidentally, quite unbelievable) stories are to be found in British sporting papers of the early nineteenth century, relating the prodigies performed by certain English Pointers of a former day. Colonel Thornton's Pluto and Juno, for example, are said to have held a point on a covey of partridges for an hour and a quarter by a watch. But when we find so solid an authority as Stonehenge telling as gospel truth the now famous yarn of the sportsman who lost his Pointer on the moors and, returning a year later, discovered the skeleton of the dog pointing a skeleton bird, we realize that the statements of these pre-Victorian worthies must be taken with considerably more than a pinch of salt.

During the nineteenth century the English Pointer was repeatedly crossed with the various setters as they came into existence and favor. This, it seems, was partly to improve his disposition, for an old-time writer, commenting on the breed, says: "They have a ferocity of temper which will not submit to correction or discipline, unless taken in hand very young." While the Pointer of today is anything but ferocious, it may be that this characteristic, tempered by judicious breeding and in combination with the natural independence that made him object to correction and discipline, has made him the superlative field-trial dog he is today. He certainly possesses the competitive spirit to a greater degree than is usually found in the other bird dogs, a quality that makes him especially suited to public performance.

The modern Pointer is a specialist and looks the part. He is every inch a gundog. Clean-limbed, lithe, and muscular without being coarse, full of nervous energy and "hunt," put together for speed and endurance, courageous, and with the ability to concentrate on his job, he is an ideal dog for the man or woman who is looking for results when afield. His short hair makes him neat and clean around the house, and his disposition makes him adaptable for the kennel. He requires less personal attention than some other gundogs, and he is willing to work satisfactorily for someone other than his own master and handler.

In addition to all this, he has another characteristic: tendency toward early development. As a breed, Pointers seem to acquire the hunting instinct at a tender age, puppies of two months frequently pointing and even backing. For this reason they are especially suited for derby and puppy stakes.

For show purposes, the Pointer's short coat makes his outline, conformation, and quality easily seen at a glance, and he is a superb poser. Today's Pointer can be seen in all four colors and on occasion a solid black or liver. His gentle disposition makes him an ideal conformation dog. Lemon and white, orange and white, black and white, and sometimes solid black are other colorings.

The Pointer is peculiarly fortunate in one all-important respect. He has always been bred for type as well as field ability, hence we have in this case no divergence between the two insofar as appearance goes. From the beginning, type has been carefully developed and intelligently preserved. An illustration for Colonel Thornton's book *A Tour Through Scotland* shows Captain Fleming of Barochan out hawking. This picture was drawn or painted about 1786, yet a Pointer among the dogs shown would pass muster today as an excellent specimen.

The modern-day Pointer is commonly seen in many other competitive events, including obedience and agility. The Pointer is also for many people a wonderful therapy dog.

# OFFICIAL STANDARD FOR THE POINTER

**General Appearance**—The Pointer is bred primarily for sport afield; he should unmistakably look and act the part. The ideal specimen gives the immediate impression of compact power and agile grace; the head noble, proudly carried; the expression intelligent and alert; the muscular body bespeaking both staying power and dash. Here is an animal whose every movement shows him to be a wide-awake, hard-driving hunting dog possessing stamina, courage, and the desire to go. And in his expression are the loyalty and devotion of a true friend of man.

**Temperament**—The Pointer's even temperament and alert good sense make him a congenial companion both in the field and in the home. He should be dignified and should never show timidity toward man or dog.

**Head**—The skull of medium width, approximately as wide as the length of the muzzle, resulting in an impression of length rather than width. Slight furrow between the eyes, cheeks cleanly chiseled. There should be a pronounced stop. From this point forward the muzzle is of good length, with the nasal bone so formed that the nose is slightly higher at the tip than the muzzle at the stop. Parallel planes of the skull and muzzle are equally acceptable. The muzzle should be deep without pendulous flews. Jaws ending square and level, should bite evenly or as scissors. Nostrils well developed and wide open. *Ears*—Set on at eye level. When hanging naturally, they should reach just below the lower jaw, close to the head, with little or no folding. They should be somewhat pointed at the tip—never round—and soft and thin in leather. *Eyes*—Of ample size, rounded and intense. The eye color should be dark in contrast with the color of the markings, the darker the better.

**Neck**—Long, dry, muscular and slightly arched, springing cleanly from the shoulders.

**Shoulders**—Long, thin and sloping. The top of blades close together.

**Front**—Elbows well let down, directly under the withers and truly parallel so as to work just clear of the body. Forelegs straight and with oval bone. Knee joint never to knuckle over. Pasterns of moderate length, perceptibly finer in bone than the leg, and slightly slanting. Chest, deep rather than wide, must not hinder free action of forelegs. The breastbone bold, without being unduly prominent. The ribs well sprung, descending as low as the elbow-point.

**Back**—Strong and solid with only a slight rise from croup to top of shoulders. Loin of moderate length, powerful and slightly arched. Croup falling only slightly to base of tail. Tuck-up should be apparent, but not exaggerated.

**Tail**—Heavier at the root, tapering to a fine point. Length no greater than to hock. A tail longer than this or docked must be penalized. Carried without curl, and not more than 20 degrees above the line of the back; never carried between the legs.

**Hindquarters**—Muscular and powerful with great propelling leverage. Thighs long and well developed. Stifles well bent. The hocks clean; the legs straight as viewed from behind. Decided angulation is the mark of power and endurance.

**Feet**—Oval, with long, closely set, arched toes, well padded and deep. Catfoot is a fault. Dewclaws on the forelegs may be removed.

**Coat**—Short, dense, smooth with a sheen.

**Color**—Liver, lemon, black, orange; either in combination with white or solid-colored. A good Pointer cannot be a bad color. In the darker colors, the nose should be black or brown; in the lighter shades it may be lighter or flesh-colored.

**Gait**—Smooth, frictionless, with a powerful hindquarters' drive. The head should be carried high, the nostrils wide, the tail moving from side to side rhythmically with the pace, giving the impression of a well-balanced, strongly built hunting dog capable of top speed combined with great stamina. Hackney gait must be faulted.

**Balance and Size**—Balance and overall symmetry are more important in the Pointer than size. A smooth, balanced dog is to be more desired than a dog with strongly contrasting good points and faults. Hound or terrier characteristics are most undesirable. Because a sporting dog must have both endurance and power, great variations in size are undesirable, the desirable height and weight being within the following limits:

| | |
|---|---|
| **Dogs:** | **Height**—25–28 inches |
| | **Weight**—55–75 pounds |
| **Bitches:** | **Height**—23–26 inches |
| | **Weight**—45–65 pounds |

**Approved November 11, 1975**

# German Shorthaired Pointer

THE GERMAN SHORTHAIRED POINTER COMBINES IN FIELD-DOG REQUIRE-
ments those qualities which have long popularized the various breeds of
hunting dogs. So successfully have keen scenting powers, linked with high intelligence, been fused into the breed through judicious crossing of the descendants of
the old Spanish Pointer, English Foxhound, and local German tracking hounds, and
so varied are this dog's field accomplishments, that it has been called an all-purpose
dog. In fact, the term was applied to the breed by the Germans before American
sportsmen began importing it to any extent in the early 1920s.

It is indeed rare to find wrapped up in one package a staunchly pointing bird
dog; a keen-nosed night trailer; a proven duck dog; a natural retriever on land and
water, with pleasing conformation and markings and great powers of endurance;
and an intelligent family watchdog and companion. Indicative of this dog's versatility is its successful work on pheasant, quail, grouse, partridge, jacksnipe, woodcock,
duck, rabbits, coon, and possum. It is also used to trail and handle deer. With a
water-repellent coat and webbed feet, it retrieves well from rough terrain or icy
waters.

The origin of the German Shorthaired Pointer, as indeed with most breeds,
cannot be described precisely. Few records were kept before the establishment of
the Klub Kurzhaar studbook in the 1870s, though the German hunting fraternity
had already spent many years attempting to produce a truly versatile utility dog-of-

all-work, using of necessity the stock that was locally available. The main source of foundation stock seems to have been the German Bird Dog, a not very admirable step down by inheritance from the old Spanish Pointer. Its utility was further improved by introducing local types of scenthounds, track and trail dogs that were also dependable in water and that were used by the German foresters. These Schweiss-hunde (*schweiss*—"scent"; *hunde*—"dogs") were of many and diverse types. They had originated principally down through the centuries from the hounds introduced from Eastern countries after the Crusades, and had been developed particularly in France, so that they became the forebears of practically all present-day scenting hounds.

The Germans still were not satisfied. Since obedience was of paramount importance, these early dogs were selectively bred for biddability. Steps were taken later to improve stance, style, and, above all, nose. Fine Pointers were brought from England and were used to lend elegance to the manner of working—*die hohe nase* ("the high nose") being the major aim. This was accomplished, and the breeders then had only the problem of ridding their developing Kurzhaar of its unwanted Pointer characteristics—aversion to water and lack of aggressiveness toward predators. These objectives were achieved long before the turn of the twentieth century. A dog breeding true to type was developed, giving the world at long last a magnificent utility dog combining these virtues with the good looks, sound temperament, and longevity that have made the German Shorthaired Pointer a favorite with sportsmen everywhere.

The German Shorthaired Pointer was first admitted to the American Kennel Club Stud Book in March 1930. The first AKC-licensed specialty show for German Shorthaired Pointers was held by the German Shorthaired Pointer Club of America at the 1941 International Kennel Club show in Chicago; the first AKC-licensed field trial for the breed was also held by the parent club at Anoka, Minnesota, on May 21, 1944.

# OFFICIAL STANDARD FOR
# THE GERMAN SHORTHAIRED POINTER

**General Appearance**—The German Shorthaired Pointer is a versatile hunter, an all-purpose gundog capable of high performance in field and water. The judgment of Shorthairs in the show ring reflects this basic characteristic. The overall picture created in the observer's eye is that of an aristocratic, well-balanced, symmetrical animal with conformation indicating power, endurance, and agility and a look of intelligence and animation. The dog is neither unduly small nor conspicuously large. It gives the impression of medium size but is like the proper hunter, "with a short back, but standing over plenty of ground." Symmetry and field quality are most essential. A dog in hard and lean field condition is not to be penalized; however, overly fat or poorly muscled dogs are to be penalized. A dog well balanced in all points is preferable to one with outstanding good qualities and defects. Grace of outline, clean-cut head, sloping shoulders, deep chest, powerful back, strong quarters, good bone composition, adequate muscle, well carried tail and taut coat produce a look of nobility and indicate a heritage of purposefully conducted breeding. Further evidence of this heritage is movement which is balanced, alertly coordinated and without wasted motion.

**Size, Proportion, Substance**—*Size*—Height of dogs, measured at the withers, 23 to 25 inches. Height of bitches, measured at the withers, 21 to 23 inches. Deviations of one inch above or below the described heights are to be severely penalized. Weight of dogs 55 to 70 pounds. Weight of bitches 45 to 60 pounds. *Proportion*—Measuring from the forechest to the rearmost projection of the rump and from the withers to the ground, the Shorthair is permissibly either square or slightly longer than he is tall. *Substance*—Thin and fine bones are by no means desirable in a dog which must possess strength and be able to work over any type of terrain. The main importance is not laid so much on the size of bone, but rather on the bone being in proper proportion to the body. Bone structure too heavy or too light is a fault. Tall and leggy dogs, dogs which are ponderous because of excess substance, doggy bitches, and bitchy dogs are to be faulted.

**Head**—The *head* is clean-cut, is neither too light nor too heavy, and is in proper proportion to the body. The *eyes* are of medium size, full of intelligence and expression, good-humored and yet radiating energy, neither protruding nor sunken. The eye is almond shaped, not circular. The preferred color is dark brown. Light yellow eyes are not desirable and are a fault. Closely set eyes are to be faulted. China or wall eyes are to be disqualified. The *ears* are broad and set fairly high, lie flat and never hang away from the head. Their placement is just above eye level. The ears when laid in front without being pulled, should extend to the corner of the mouth. In the case of heavier dogs, the ears are correspondingly longer. Ears too long or fleshy are to be faulted. The *skull* is reasonably broad, arched on the side and slightly round on top. Unlike the Pointer, the median line between the eyes at the forehead is not too deep and the occipital bone is not very conspicuous. The foreface rises gradually from nose to forehead. The rise is more strongly pronounced in the dog than in the bitch. The jaw is powerful and the muscles well developed. The line to the forehead rises gradually and never has a definite stop as that of the Pointer, but rather a stop-effect when viewed from the side, due to the position of the eyebrows. The *muzzle* is sufficiently long to enable the dog to seize game properly and be able to carry it for a long time. A pointed muzzle is not desirable. The depth is in the right proportion to the length, both in the muzzle and in the skull proper. The length of the muzzle should equal the length of skull. A dish-shaped muzzle is a fault. A definite Pointer stop is a serious fault. Too many wrinkles in the forehead is a fault. The *nose* is brown, the larger the better, and with nostrils well opened and broad. A spotted nose is not desirable. A flesh colored nose disqualifies. The chops fall away from the somewhat projecting nose. Lips are full and deep yet are never flewy. The *teeth* are strong and healthy. The molars intermesh properly. The bite is a true scissors bite. A perfect level bite is not desirable and must be penalized. Extreme overshot or undershot disqualifies.

**Neck, Topline, Body**—The *neck* is of proper length to permit the jaws reaching game to be retrieved, sloping downward on beautifully curving lines. The nape is rather muscular, becoming gradually larger toward the shoulders. Moderate throatiness is permitted. The *skin* is close and tight. The *chest* in general gives the impression of depth rather than breadth; for all that, it is in correct proportion to the other parts of the body. The chest reaches down to the elbows, the ribs forming the thorax show a rib spring and are not flat or slab-sided; they are not perfectly round or barrel-shaped. The back ribs reach well down. The circumference of the thorax immediately behind the elbows is smaller than that of the thorax about a hand's breadth behind elbows, so that the upper arm has room for movement. Tuck-up is apparent. The *back* is short, strong and straight with a slight rise from the root of the tail to the withers. The loin is strong, is of moderate length, and is slightly arched. An excessively long, roached or swayed back must be penalized. The hips are broad with hip sockets wide apart and fall slightly toward the tail in a graceful curve. A steep croup is a fault. The *tail* is set high and firm, and must be docked, leaving approximately 40% of its length. The tail hangs down when the dog is quiet and is held horizontally when he is walking. The tail must never be curved over the back toward the head when the dog is moving. A tail curved or bent toward the head is to be severely penalized.

**Forequarters**—The *shoulders* are sloping, movable, and well covered with muscle. The shoulder blades lie flat and are well laid back, nearing a 45 degree angle. The upper arm (the bones between the shoulder and elbow joint) is as long as possible, standing away somewhat from the trunk so that the straight and closely muscled legs, when viewed from the front, appear to be parallel. Elbows which stand away from the body or are too close result in toes turning inwards or outwards and must be faulted. *Pasterns* are strong, short and nearly vertical with a slight spring. Loose, short-bladed or straight shoulders must be faulted. Knuckling over is to be faulted. Dewclaws on the forelegs may be removed. The *feet* are compact, close-knit and round to spoon-shaped. The toes are sufficiently arched and heavily nailed. The pads are strong, hard and thick.

**Hindquarters**—Thighs are strong and well muscled. Stifles are well bent. Hock joints are well angulated and strong with straight bone structure from hock to pad. Angulation of both stifle and hock joint is such as to achieve the optimal balance of drive and traction. Hocks turn neither in nor out. Cowhocked legs are a serious fault.

**Coat**—The hair is short and thick and feels tough to the hand; it is somewhat longer on the underside of the tail and the back edges of the haunches. The hair is softer, thinner and shorter on the ears and the head. Any dog with long hair in the body coat is to be severely penalized.

**Color**—The coat may be of solid liver or a combination of liver and white such as liver and white ticked, liver patched and white ticked, or liver roan. A dog with any area of black, red, orange, lemon or tan or a dog solid white will be disqualified.

**Gait**—A smooth lithe gait is essential. It is to be noted that as gait increases from the walk to a faster speed, the legs converge beneath the body. The tendency to single track is desirable. The forelegs reach well ahead as if to pull in the ground without giving the appearance of a hackney gait. The hindquarters drive the back legs smoothly and with great power.

**Temperament**—The Shorthair is friendly, intelligent, and willing to please. The first impression is that of a keen enthusiasm for work without indication of nervous or flighty character.

## DISQUALIFICATIONS

*China or wall eyes.*
*Flesh colored nose.*
*Extreme overshot or undershot.*
*A dog with any area of black, red, orange, lemon, or tan, or a dog solid white.*

**Approved August 11, 1992**
**Effective September 30, 1992**

# GERMAN WIREHAIRED POINTER

*H*UNTING HAS BEEN CALLED OUR EARLIEST SPORT, BUT IT IS MORE THAN that. It was a way of life in prehistoric times when the ax, the club, and the spear were the sole weapons man had with which to find food for himself and his brood. Over time he hunted with traps and pitfalls, hawks and falcons, nets and snares, bows and arrows. Later, the princes, nobles, and big landowners hunted not for food but for sport. To all others, such privilege was denied.

Around 1850, however, the incidence of political revolt, together with improvements in the shotgun and the cartridge, spurred the business of hunting to such degree that everybody, regardless of class distinction, took to the hunt. The number of sportsmen more than doubled, as game-bird shooting grew popular. More dogs were needed, hence more were bred. And slowly but surely the hunting dog became something of a specialist. One kind grew adept at ranging woods and fields where it pointed birds for the huntsman to shoot, others learned to retrieve from land and from water; and as time went on each attained proficiency in its special department.

Continental sportsmen were hard to please; they were not satisfied with a gundog that would hunt only one kind of game. They envisioned an all-purpose dog, and so it happened that in various European countries retrieving pointers began to emerge. One of these, native to Germany, was the Deutsch-Drahthaar which, literally translated, means German Wirehair.

In order to understand the heritage of this breed we must bear in mind that there existed abroad a wide variety of retrieving pointers, all of them more or less interbred. The early Deutsch-Drahthaar Klub, in fact, at first catered to all varieties of wirehaired pointing dogs. Later, however, they thought it best to separate their activities into four subdivisions catering to the advancement of the Deutsch-Drahthaar, the Pudelpointer, the Stichelhaar, and the Griffon.

Most of the early wirehaired pointers represented a combination of Griffon, Stichelhaar, Pudelpointer, and German Shorthair. The Pudelpointer was a cross between a Poodle dog and an English Pointer bitch; the Griffon and the Stichelhaar were composed of Pointer, Foxhound, Pudelpointer, and a Polish water dog. Thus it is easy to appreciate the different hunting skills incorporated in the wirehaired pointers of a century or more ago.

Admirable breeders and trainers, the Germans demanded a great deal of their sporting dogs. They had no patience with specialists, preferring instead an extra-rugged hunter capable of working on any kind of game and on any terrain. In the German Wirehaired Pointer, this is exactly what they got, for they molded into the one breed the distinctive traits of pointer, foxhound, and Poodle. Through these avenues of diversified accomplishment they created an all-purpose dog approximating their ideal. He pointed and retrieved equally well on land and in water. He was keen nosed and constitutionally tough. What is more, he had the courage as well as the coat fit to brave any sort of cover.

Coat has always been emphasized throughout the development of the breed, as indicated by a statement made by members of the Drahthaar Klub back in 1902, when they said: "*The breeding of a correct wire coat is the most important feature.*" There was ample reason for this emphasis on coat, considering the work that the German Wirehair was called upon to do. In short, he was designed as an all-weather as well as an all-purpose dog, and he had to negotiate underbrush that would have punished severely any dog not so characteristically armored.

The coat is weather resistant in every sense of the term, and it is to large extent water-repellent. It is straight, harsh, wiry, and quite flat lying. One and one-half to two inches in length, it is long enough to shield the body from rough cover, yet not so long as to hide the outline. A heavy growth on the brow guards the eyes from injury, and a short beard and whiskers combine to save the foreface from laceration by brush and brier. A very dense undercoat insulates the body against the cold of winter, but it sheds out to such a degree as to be almost invisible in summertime.

Although it had become a favored sporting dog in Germany many years earlier, the Drahthaar was not admitted into the German Kartell for dogs until 1928. The breed was imported to the United States in the 1920s. In 1953, the German Drahthaar Club of America was formed. The breed was admitted into the AKC Stud Book in 1959 as the German Wirehaired Pointer, and the name of the national club was changed to the German Wirehaired Pointer Club of America.

# OFFICIAL STANDARD FOR THE GERMAN WIREHAIRED POINTER

**General Appearance**—The German Wirehaired Pointer is a well-muscled, medium sized dog of distinctive appearance. Balanced in size and sturdily built, the breed's most distinguishing characteristics are its weather resistant, wire-like coat and its facial furnishings. Typically Pointer in character and style, the German Wirehaired Pointer is an intelligent, energetic and determined hunter.

**Size, Proportion, Substance**—The *height* of males should be from 24 to 26 inches at the withers. Bitches are smaller but not under 22 inches. To insure the working quality of the breed is maintained, dogs that are either over or under the specified height must be severely penalized. The body is a little longer than it is high, as ten is to nine. The German Wirehaired Pointer is a versatile hunter built for agility and endurance in the field. Correct size and balance are essential to high performance.

**Head**—The head is moderately long. *Eyes* are brown, medium in size, oval in contour, bright and clear and overhung with medium length eyebrows. Yellow eyes are not desirable. The *ears* are rounded but not too broad and hang close to the head. The *skull* broad and the occipital bone not too prominent. The *stop* is medium. The *muzzle* is fairly long with nasal bone straight, broad and parallel to the top of the skull. The *nose* is dark brown with nostrils wide open. A spotted or flesh colored nose is to be penalized. The *lips* are a trifle pendulous but close to the jaw and bearded. The *jaws* are strong with a full complement of evenly set and properly intermeshing teeth. The incisors meet in a true *scissors bite.*

**Neck, Topline, Body**—The *neck* is of medium length, slightly arched and devoid of dewlap. The entire *back line* showing a perceptible slope down from withers to croup. The skin throughout is notably tight to the body. The *chest* is deep and capacious with ribs well sprung. The *tuck-up* apparent. The back is short, straight and strong. Loins are taut and slender. Hips are broad with the croup nicely rounded. The *tail* is set high, carried at or above the horizontal when the dog is alert. The tail is docked to approximately two-fifths of its original length.

**Forequarters**—The shoulders are well laid back. The forelegs are straight with elbows close. Leg bones are flat rather than round, and strong, but not so heavy or coarse as to militate against the dog's natural agility. Dewclaws are generally removed. Round in outline, the feet are webbed, high arched with toes close, pads thick and hard, and nails strong and quite heavy.

**Hindquarters**—The angulation of the hindquarters balances that of the forequarters. The thighs are strong and muscular. The hind legs are moderately angulated at the stifle and hock and, as viewed from behind, parallel to each other. Dewclaws are generally removed. Feet as in front.

**Coat**—The functional wiry coat is the breed's most distinctive feature. A dog must have a correct coat to be of correct type. The coat is weather resistant and, to some extent, water-repellent. The undercoat is dense enough in winter to insulate against the cold but is so thin in summer as to be almost invisible. The distinctive outer coat is straight, harsh, wiry and flat lying, and is from one to two inches in length. The outer coat is long enough to protect against the punishment of rough cover, but not so long as to hide the outline of the dog. On the lower legs the coat is shorter, and between the toes it is of softer texture. On the skull the coat is naturally short and close fitting. Over the shoulders and around the tail it is very dense and heavy. The tail is nicely coated, particularly on the underside, but devoid of feather. Eyebrows are of strong, straight hair. Beard and whiskers are medium length. The hairs in the liver patches of a liver and white dog may be shorter than the white hairs. A short smooth coat, a soft woolly coat, or an excessively long coat is to be severely penalized. While maintaining a harsh, wiry texture, the puppy coat may be shorter than that of an adult coat. Coats may be neatly groomed to present a dog natural in appearance. Extreme and excessive grooming to present a dog artificial in appearance should be severely penalized.

**Color**—The coat is liver and white, usually either liver and white spotted, liver roan, liver and white spotted with ticking and roaning or solid liver. The head is liver, sometimes with a white blaze. The ears are liver. Any black in the coat is to be severely penalized.

**Gait**—The dog should be evaluated at a moderate gait. The movement is free and smooth with good reach in the forequarters and good driving power in the hindquarters. The topline should remain firm.

**Temperament**—Of sound, reliable temperament, the German Wirehaired Pointer is at times aloof but not unfriendly toward strangers; a loyal and affectionate companion who is eager to please and enthusiastic to learn.

**Approved July 9, 1985**
**Reformatted May 14, 1989**

# CHESAPEAKE BAY RETRIEVER

*T*HE CHESAPEAKE BAY RETRIEVER IS ONE OF THE FEW BREEDS TO BE CREATED and developed in the United States.

In 1807, a British brig was wrecked off the coast of Maryland. An American ship, the *Canton,* rescued the crew and cargo. Among those plucked from the water were two Newfoundlands, a dingy red dog and a black bitch. The two dogs, Sailor and Canton, were presented to local landowners John Mercer and Dr. James Stewart. Later, Governor Lloyd of Maryland acquired Sailor and took him to the Eastern Shore. The dog's progeny later became well known on both shores as the "Sailor" breed. Whether Sailor and Canton themselves were ever paired is unknown, but the superior qualities of both resulted in an improvement of the local duck-hunting dogs being bred for waterfowl work.

Wealthy owners of duck clubs that lined both shores of the Chesapeake Bay set the breed's basic type. Yellow and tan hounds were outcrosses used to help fix the brown and sedge color and provide superior water-scenting ability. Irish Water Spaniels contributed to the Chesapeake's coat and water zeal. These crosses helped enhance the natural attributes of the original Newfoundland pair. By the time the AKC was established in 1884, a definite Chesapeake Bay Retriever type had been developed.

"Bay dogs" were expected to have the determination and perseverance to retrieve birds from the icy, rough waters of the Chesapeake Bay, often as many as 100 or 200 ducks in one day. A harsh, oily double coat helped to repel water, allowing the dog to work for long periods in adverse weather conditions. All of the colors seen in the breed today were present from the beginning: brown, sedge (red), dead-grass (varying shades of blond, including tan), and ash (a diluted shade of brown that is gray to taupe in color). The deadgrass color was favored in the American Midwest and in western Canada for hunting on the grain fields and prairie potholes common to those areas.

The Chesapeake Bay Retriever is a remarkable water dog. The American Chesapeake Club, the breed's AKC parent club, was founded in 1918 and held its first licensed retriever trial in 1932. To those Chesapeakes that pass retrieving tests on land and water, the club issues certificates and titles: Working Dog (WD), Working Dog Excellent (WDX), and Working Dog Qualified (WDQ). The breed is active in all areas of AKC Competition and more. While still primarily a working gundog breed, Chesapeakes compete successfully in field trials, dog shows, companion events, and hunt tests.

Chesapeakes have also made excellent therapy, search-and-rescue, and drug- and bomb-detection dogs. The breed is valued for its bright and happy disposition; intelligence; quiet good sense; and affectionate, protective nature. They are physically tough dogs but can often be mentally soft. Whether they live in a house or an apartment, Chesapeakes do best and thrive when they spend most of the time with their family. It is recommended that this breed be well socialized from puppyhood and obedience trained for a correct owner-dog relationship.

# OFFICIAL STANDARD FOR THE CHESAPEAKE BAY RETRIEVER

**General Appearance**—Equally proficient on land and in the water, the Chesapeake Bay Retriever was developed along the Chesapeake Bay to hunt waterfowl under the most adverse weather and water conditions, often having to break ice during the course of many strenuous multiple retrieves. Frequently the Chesapeake must face wind, tide and long cold swims in its work. The breed's characteristics are specifically suited to enable the Chesapeake to function with ease, efficiency and endurance. In head, the Chesapeake's skull is broad and round with a medium stop. The jaws should be of sufficient length and strength to carry large game birds with an easy, tender hold. The double coat consists of a short, harsh, wavy outer coat and a dense, fine, woolly undercoat containing an abundance of natural oil and is ideally suited for the icy rugged conditions of weather the Chesapeake often works in. In body, the Chesapeake is a strong, well-balanced, powerfully built animal of moderate size and medium length in body and leg, deep and wide in chest, the shoulders built with full liberty of movement, and with no tendency to weakness in any feature, particularly the rear. The power though, should not be at the expense of agility or stamina. Size and substance should not be excessive as this is a working retriever of an active nature.

Distinctive features include eyes that are very clear, of yellowish or amber hue, hindquarters as high or a trifle higher than the shoulders, and a double coat which tends to wave on shoulders, neck, back and loins only.

The Chesapeake is valued for its bright and happy disposition, intelligence, quiet good sense and affectionate protective nature. Extreme shyness or extreme aggressive tendencies are not desirable in the breed either as a gun dog or companion.

*Disqualifications:* Specimens that are lacking in breed characteristics should be disqualified.

**Size, Proportion, Substance**—*Height*—Males should measure 23 to 26 inches; females should measure 21 to 24 inches. *Oversized* or *undersized* animals are to be *severely penalized. Proportion*—Height from the top of the shoulder blades to the ground should be slightly less than the body length from the breastbone to the point of buttocks. Depth of body should extend at least to the elbow. Shoulder to elbow and elbow to ground should be equal. *Weight*—Males should weigh 65 to 80 pounds; females should weigh 55 to 70 pounds.

**Head**—The Chesapeake Bay Retriever should have an intelligent expression. *Eyes* are to be medium large, very clear, of yellowish or amber color and wide apart. *Ears* are to be small, set well up on the head, hanging loosely, and of medium leather. *Skull* is broad and round with a medium stop. *Nose* is medium short. *Muzzle* is approximately the same length as the skull, tapered, pointed but not sharp. *Lips* are thin, not pendulous. *Bite*—Scissors is preferred, but a level bite is acceptable.

*Disqualifications:* Either undershot or overshot bites are to be disqualified.

**Neck, Topline, Body**—*Neck* should be of medium length with a strong muscular appearance, tapering to the shoulders. *Topline* should show the hindquarters to be as high as or a trifle higher than the shoulders. *Back* should be short, well coupled and powerful. *Chest* should be strong, deep and wide. Rib cage barrel round and deep. *Body* is of medium length, neither cobby nor roached, but rather approaching hollowness from underneath as the flanks should be well tucked up. *Tail* of medium length; medium heavy at the base. The tail should be straight or slightly curved and should not curl over back or side kink.

**Forequarters**—There should be no tendency to weakness in the forequarters. *Shoulders* should be sloping with full liberty of action, plenty of power and without any restrictions of movement. *Legs* should be medium in length and straight, showing good bone and muscle. Pasterns slightly bent and of medium length. The front legs should appear straight when viewed from front or rear. Dewclaws on the forelegs may be removed. Well webbed hare feet should be of good size with toes well-rounded and close.

**Hindquarters**—Good hindquarters are essential. They should show fully as much power as the forequarters. There should be no tendency to weakness in the hindquarters. Hindquarters should be especially powerful to supply the driving power for swimming. Legs should be medium length and straight, showing good bone and muscle. Stifles should be well angulated. The distance from hock to ground should be of medium length. The hind legs should look straight when viewed from the front or rear. Dewclaws, if any, must be removed from the hind legs.

*Disqualifications:* Dewclaws on the hind legs are a disqualification.

**Coat**—Coat should be thick and short, nowhere over 1½ inches long, with a dense fine woolly undercoat. Hair on the face and legs should be very short and straight with a tendency to wave on the shoulders, neck, back and loins only. Moderate feathering on rear of hindquarters and tail is permissible.

The texture of the Chesapeake's coat is very important, as the Chesapeake is used for hunting under all sorts of adverse weather conditions, often working in ice and snow. The oil in the harsh outer coat and woolly undercoat is of extreme value in preventing the cold water from reaching the Chesapeake's skin and aids in quick drying. A Chesapeake's coat should resist the water in the same way that a duck's feathers do. When the Chesapeake leaves the water and shakes, the coat should not hold water at all, being merely moist.

*Disqualifications:* A coat that is curly or has a tendency to curl all over the body must be disqualified. Feathering on the tail or legs over 1¾ inches long must be disqualified.

**Color**—The color of the Chesapeake Bay Retriever must be as nearly that of its working surroundings as possible. Any color of brown, sedge or deadgrass is acceptable, self-colored Chesapeakes being preferred. One color is not to be preferred over another. A white spot on the breast, belly, toes or back of the feet (immediately above the large pad) is permissible, but the smaller the spot the better, solid colored preferred. The color of the coat and its texture must be given every consideration when judging on the bench or in the ring. Honorable scars are not to be penalized.

*Disqualifications:* Black colored; white on any part of the body except breast, belly, toes or back of feet must be disqualified.

**Gait**—The gait should be smooth, free and effortless, giving the impression of great power and strength. When viewed from the side, there should be good reach with no restrictions of movement in the front and plenty of drive in the rear, with good flexion of the stifle and hock joints. Coming at you, there should be no sign of elbows being out. When the Chesapeake is moving away from you, there should be no sign of cowhockness from the rear. As speed increases, the feet tend to converge toward a center line of gravity.

**Temperament**—The Chesapeake Bay Retriever should show a bright and happy disposition with an intelligent expression. Courage, willingness to work, alertness, nose, intelligence, love of water, general quality and, most of all, disposition should be given primary consideration in the selection and breeding of the Chesapeake Bay Retriever.


## DISQUALIFICATIONS

1. *Specimens lacking in breed characteristics.*
2. *Teeth overshot or undershot.*
3. *Dewclaws on the hind legs.*
4. *Coat curly or with a tendency to curl all over the body.*
5. *Feathering on the tail or legs over 1¾ inches long.*
6. *Black colored.*
7. *White on any part of the body except breast, belly, toes, or back of feet.*

The question of coat and general type of balance takes precedence over any scoring table which could be drawn up. The Chesapeake should be well proportioned, an animal with a good coat and well balanced in other points being preferable to one excelling in some but weak in others.

## POSITIVE SCALE OF POINTS

| | |
|---|---|
| Head, including lips, ears and eyes | 16 |
| Neck | 4 |
| Shoulders and body | 12 |
| Hindquarters and stifles | 12 |
| Elbows, legs and feet | 12 |
| Color | 4 |
| Stern and tail | 10 |
| Coat and texture | 18 |
| General conformation | 12 |
| **Total** | **100** |

## APPROXIMATE MEASUREMENTS

| | INCHES |
|---|---|
| Length head, nose to occiput | 9½ to 10 |
| Girth at ears | 20 to 21 |
| Muzzle below eyes | 10 to 10½ |
| Length of ears | 4½ to 5 |
| Width between eyes | 2½ to 2¾ |
| Girth neck close to shoulder | 20 to 22 |
| Girth at flank | 24 to 25 |
| Length from occiput to tail base | 34 to 35 |
| Girth forearms at shoulders | 10 to 10½ |
| Girth upper thigh | 19 to 20 |
| From root to root of ear, over skull | 5 to 6 |
| Occiput to top shoulder blades | 9 to 9½ |
| From elbow to elbow over the shoulders | 25 to 26 |

**Approved November 9, 1993**
**Effective December 31, 1993**

# Curly-Coated Retriever

*I*N THE ABSENCE OF VERY EARLY RECORDS, THE ORIGIN OF THE CURLY-COATED Retriever must remain a matter of conjecture, but there appears little doubt that he is one of the oldest of all breeds now classified as retrievers. He is popularly believed to be descended from the sixteenth-century English Water Spaniel and from the Retrieving Setter. Some maintain the Irish Water Spaniel was his ancestor and it is more than probable that a cross was made with this breed from time to time.

Whichever spaniel was his progenitor, it is certain that added to the mixture of Water Spaniel and Retrieving Setter was the small or St. John's Newfoundland, which, according to records, first arrived in England in 1835 as a ship's dog aboard the boats that brought salted cod from Newfoundland. The St. John's dog, curiously enough, is sometimes called a Labrador by early writers, a fact which has given rise to some confusion with respect to the modern Labrador.

In the early 1880s, the Curly is said to have been crossed again with the Poodle (the one-time retriever of France), this cross taken with the object of giving his coat a tight curl.

The popular gundog following the Old English Water Spaniel, the Curly was first exhibited in 1860 at Birmingham. In 1889, specimens were exported to New Zealand, where they have long been used for retrieving duck and California quail. In Australia, too, where they are used on duck in the swamps and lagoons of the

Murray River, they are much admired as steady and tender-mouthed retrievers quite unsurpassed in the water.

The first breed club for the Curly-Coated Retriever was formed in England in 1896. The breed was introduced to the United States as early as 1907, but the first AKC registration was in 1924.

Many assert that the Curly Retriever is temperamentally easy to train. He is affectionate, enduring, hardy, and will practically live in the water. Moreover, his thick coat enables him to face the most punishing covert. He is a charming and faithful companion and an excellent guard.

# OFFICIAL STANDARD FOR THE CURLY-COATED RETRIEVER

**General Appearance**—This smartly upstanding, multi-purpose hunting retriever is recognized by most canine historians as one of the oldest of the retrieving breeds. Developed in England, the Curly was long a favorite of English gamekeepers. Prized for innate field ability, courage and indomitable perseverance, a correctly built and tempered Curly will work as long as there is work to be done, retrieving both fur and feather in the heaviest of cover and the iciest of waters. To work all day a Curly must be balanced and sound, strong and robust, and quick and agile. Outline, carriage and attitude all combine for a grace and elegance somewhat uncommon among the other retriever breeds, providing the unique, upstanding quality desired in the breed. In outline, the Curly is moderately angulated front and rear and, when comparing height to length, gives the impression of being higher on leg than the other retriever breeds. In carriage, the Curly is an erect, alert, self-confident dog. In motion, all parts blend into a smooth, powerful, harmonious symmetry. The coat, a hallmark of the breed, is of great importance for all Curlies, whether companion, hunting or show dogs. The perfect coat is a dense mass of small, tight, distinct, crisp curls. The Curly is wickedly smart and highly trainable and, as such, is cherished as much for his role as loyal companion at home as he is in the field.

**Size, Proportion, Substance**—Ideal height at withers: dogs, 25 to 27 inches; bitches, 23 to 25 inches. A clearly superior Curly falling outside of this range should not be penalized because of size. The body proportions are slightly off square, meaning that the dog is slightly longer from prosternum to buttocks as he is from withers to ground. The Curly is both sturdy and elegant. The degree of substance is sufficient to ensure strength and endurance without sacrificing grace. Bone and substance are neither spindly nor massive and should be in proportion with weight and height and balanced throughout.

**Head**—The head is a longer-than-wide wedge, readily distinguishable from that of all other retriever breeds, and of a size in balance with the body. Length of foreface is equal, or nearly equal, to length of backskull and, when viewed in profile, the planes are parallel. The stop is shallow and sloping. At the point of joining, the width of foreface may be slightly less than the width of the backskull but blending of the two should be smooth. The head has a nearly straight, continuous taper to the nose and is clean-cut, not coarse, blocky or cheeky. *Expression*—Intelligent and alert. *Eyes*—Almond-shaped, rather large but not too prominent. Black or brown in black dogs and brown or amber in liver dogs. Harsh yellow eyes and loose haws are undesirable. *Ears*—Rather small, set on a line slightly above the corner of the eye, and lying close to the head. *Backskull*—Flat or nearly flat. *Foreface*—Muzzle is wedge-shaped with no hint of snipiness. The taper ends mildly, neither acutely pointed nor bluntly squared-off but rather slightly rounding at the bottom. Mouth is level and never wry. Jaws are long and strong. A scissors bite is preferred. Teeth set straight and even. The lips are tight and clean, not pendulous. The nose is fully pigmented; black on black dogs, brown on liver dogs. Nostrils are large.

**Neck, Topline, Body**—*Neck*—Strong and slightly arched, of medium length, free from throatiness and flowing freely into moderately laid-back shoulders. *Backline*—The back, that portion of the body from the rear point of the withers to the beginning of the loin, is strong and level. The loin, that part of the body extending from the end of the rib cage to the start of the pelvis, is short and muscular. The croup, that portion of the body from the start of the pelvis to the tail set-on, is only slightly sloping. *Body*—Chest is decidedly deep and not too wide, oval in cross-section, with brisket reaching elbow. While the impression of the chest should be of depth not width, the chest is not pinched or narrow. The ribs are well-sprung, neither barrel-shaped nor slab-sided, and extend well back into a deep, powerful loin with a moderate tuck-up of flank. *Tail*—Carried straight or fairly straight, never docked, and reaching approximately to the hock. Never curled over the back and should not be kinked or crooked. Covered with curls and, if trimmed, tapering toward the point.

**Forequarters**—Shoulder blades are very long, well covered with muscle, and are moderately laid back at about a 55-degree angle. The width between shoulder blades is adequate to allow enough flexibility to easily retrieve game. Upper arm bones are about equal in length with shoulder blades and laid back at approximately the same angle as the blades, meaning the forelegs are set under the withers. The equal length of shoulder blade and upper arm bone and the balanced angulation between the two allows for good extension of the front legs. The forelegs are straight with strong, true pasterns. Feet are round and compact, with well-arched toes and thick pads. Front dewclaws are generally removed.

**Hindquarters**—Strong and in balance with front angulation. Thighs are powerful with muscling carrying well down into the second thigh. Stifle is of moderate bend. The hocks are strong and true, turning neither in nor out, with hock joint well let down. Rear dewclaws are generally removed.

**Coat**—The coat is a distinguishing characteristic and quite different from that of any other breed. The body coat is a thick mass of small, tight, crisp curls, lying close to the skin, resilient, water resistant, and of sufficient density to provide protection against weather, water and punishing cover. Curls also extend up the entire neck to the occiput, down the thigh and back leg to at least the hock, and over the entire tail. Elsewhere, the coat is short, smooth and straight, including on the forehead, face, front of forelegs, and feet. A patch of uncurled hair behind the withers or bald patches anywhere on the body, including bald strips down the back of the legs or a triangular bald patch on the throat, should be severely penalized. A looser, more open curl is acceptable on the ears. Sparse, silky, fuzzy or very harsh, dry or brittle hair is a fault. *Trimming*—Feathering may be trimmed from the ears, belly, backs of forelegs, thighs, pasterns, hocks and feet. On the tail, feathering should be removed. Short trimming of the coat on the ear is permitted but shearing of the body coat is undesirable.

**Color**—Black or liver. Either color is correct. A prominent white patch is undesirable but a few white hairs are allowable in an otherwise good dog.

**Gait**—The dual function of the Curly as both waterfowl retriever and upland game hunter demands a dog who moves with strength and power yet is quick and agile. The ground-covering stride is a well-coordinated melding of grace and power, neither mincing nor lumbering. The seemingly effortless trot is efficient and balanced front to rear. When viewed from the side, the reach in front and rear is free-flowing, not stilted or hackneyed. When viewed from the front or rear, movement is true: the front legs turn neither in nor out and the rear legs do not cross. Well-developed, muscular thighs and strong hocks do their full share of work, contributing to rear thrust and drive. The extension in front is strong and smooth and in balance with rear action. Balance in structure translates to balance in movement and is of great importance to ensure soundness and endurance; extremes of angulation and gait are not desirable.

**Temperament**—Self-confident, steadfast and proud, this active, intelligent dog is a charming and gentle family companion and a determined, durable hunter. The Curly is alert, biddable and responsive to family and friends, whether at home or in the field. Of independent nature and discerning intelligence, a Curly sometimes appears aloof or self-willed, and, as such, is often less demonstrative, particularly toward strangers, than the other retriever breeds. The Curly's independence and poise should not be confused with shyness or a lack of willingness to please. In the show ring, a correctly-tempered Curly will steadily stand his ground, submit easily to examination, and might or might not wag his tail when doing so. In the field, the Curly is eager, persistent and inherently courageous. At home, he is calm and affectionate. Shyness is a fault and any dog who shies away from show ring examination should be penalized. Minor allowances can be made for puppies who misbehave in the show ring due to overexuberance or lack of training or experience.

**Approved October 12, 1993**
**Effective November 30, 1993**

# FLAT-COATED RETRIEVER

*W*HEN IT BECAME POSSIBLE FOR MAN TO KILL GAME ON THE WING MANY different breeds of dogs were used to find and retrieve it, and any such dog was regarded a retriever. Eventually, by selective breeding for the perfection of this skill, the Retriever Proper, a large black dog, had come into existence in Britain by the early part of the nineteenth century. It was not accepted as a pure breed, but regarded as a mongrel because of its crossbred origin from various breeds—the Large Newfoundland, the setter, the sheepdog, spaniel-like water dogs.

The last named were invaluable as retrievers to fishermen and were the subjects of trade between Britain and North America, particularly with the cod fishery off Newfoundland during the nineteenth century. It was at this time that the term "Labrador" dog came into use and was applied indiscriminately to a number of different types of dogs associated with this area. These dogs, found in St. John's, Newfoundland, and called the Small Labrador Dog, the Lesser Newfoundland, or St. John's Newfoundland, contributed toward the Wavy-Coated (and subsequently the Flat-Coated) Retriever, but they must have had considerable British stock as ancestors. They should not be confused with the modern-day Labrador Retriever as they differed in coat, size, and structure.

The first British dog show was held in 1859, but classification for retrievers, comprising Curly-Coated and Wavy or Smooth-Coated, was not available until the following year. Records of awards and pedigrees, if known, were kept from the beginning of shows and published in the Kennel Club studbook in 1874.

From 1864 on, two bitches of a working strain of retrievers belonging to J. Hull, a gamekeeper, figured in the awards. These were Old Bounce, out of his bitch Boss and by Blaydon's Black Sailor; and Young Bounce, her daughter, by Mr. Chattock's Cato. It was this stock that produced an important nucleus to the development of the breed. The greatest credit for the integration of these retrievers into a stable type goes to S. E. Shirley, founder of the Kennel Club in 1873.

The breed gained enormous popularity, and numerous important breeders made their contribution to the quality and elegance of the Flat-Coated Retriever as well as to his excellent working abilities. The most famous patron was H. R. Cooke, who for more than seventy years kept the breed in his fabulous Riverside kennel—a kennel perhaps unique among those for any breed of dog in numbers, quality, and awards won in the field and on the show bench.

The liver-colored Flat-Coat became more popular after J. H. Abbott's liver-colored dog Rust won at the Retriever Society's official field trials in 1900. His prestigious win proved that this color was finally considered acceptable.

The Flat-Coated Retriever was admitted to the AKC Stud Book in 1915. By 1918 the breed's popularity was overtaken by the modern Labrador Retriever, and by the end of the 1920s by the Golden Retriever. At times, particularly during the two world wars, registrations dwindled to dangerous levels. After World War II it was not easy to pick up the threads of disappearing lines. Stanley O'Neill, one of the greatest authorities on the breed, must be credited with a valuable contribution to this end. He showed selfless devotion in putting the breed on as sound a footing as possible and in advising new patrons on correct type. Stock continued to build up gradually until about the mid-1960s, when an appreciable increase in number and popularity took place in Britain and a keen demand for the breed appeared in Europe and America.

The parent club in the United States is the Flat-Coated Retriever Society of America, a flourishing and well-integrated club, whose members are very enthusiastic and anxious to further the best interests of the breed.

His fall from popularity has kept the Flat-Coat out of the hands of the commercial breeder and under control of those interested in retaining his great natural working abilities. He is unafraid of thick covert and cold water, shows drive and perseverance when out hunting, and retrieves tenderly to hand. He has a delightful and inimitable character and temperament, is highly intelligent and companionable, and retains his youthful outlook on life into old age, tail-wagging being the hallmark of the breed. In addition to these virtues, he is a handsome fellow.

# OFFICIAL STANDARD FOR
# THE FLAT-COATED RETRIEVER

**General Appearance**—The Flat-Coated Retriever is a versatile family companion hunting retriever with a happy and active demeanor, intelligent expression, and clean lines. The Flat-Coat has been traditionally described as showing "*power without lumber and raciness without weediness.*"

The distinctive and most important features of the Flat-Coat are the silhouette (both moving and standing), smooth effortless movement, head type, coat and character. In silhouette the Flat-Coat has a long, strong, clean, "one piece" head, which is unique to the breed. Free from exaggeration of stop or cheek, the head is set well into a moderately long neck which flows smoothly into well laid back shoulders. A level topline combined with a deep, long rib cage tapering to a moderate tuck-up create the impression of a blunted triangle. The brisket is well developed and the forechest forms a prominent prow. This utilitarian retriever is well balanced, strong, but elegant; never cobby, short legged or rangy. The coat is thick and flat lying, and the legs and tail are well feathered. A proud carriage, responsive attitude, waving tail and overall look of functional strength, quality, style and symmetry complete the picture of the typical Flat-Coat.

Judging the Flat-Coat moving freely on a loose lead and standing naturally is more important than judging him posed. Honorable scars should not count against the dog.

**Size, Proportion, Substance**—*Size*—Individuals varying more than an inch either way from the preferred height should be considered not practical for the types of work for which the Flat-Coat was developed. Preferred height is 23 to 24½ inches at the withers for dogs, 22 to 23½ inches for bitches. Since the Flat-Coat is a working hunting retriever he should be shown in lean, hard condition, free of excess weight.

*Proportion*—The Flat-Coat is not cobby in build. The length of the body from the point of the shoulder to the rearmost projection of the upper thigh is slightly more than the height at the withers. The female may be slightly longer to better accommodate the carrying of puppies. **Substance**—Moderate. Medium bone is flat or oval rather than round; strong but never massive, coarse, weedy or fine. This applies throughout the dog.

**Head**—The long, clean, well-molded head is adequate in size and strength to retrieve a large pheasant, duck or hare with ease. **Skull and Muzzle**—The impression of the skull and muzzle being "cast in one piece" is created by the fairly flat skull of moderate breadth and flat, clean cheeks, combined with the long, strong, deep muzzle which is well filled in before, between and beneath the eyes. Viewed from above, the muzzle is nearly equal in length and breadth to the skull. *Stop*—There is a gradual, slight, barely perceptible stop, avoiding a down or dish-faced appearance. Brows are slightly raised and mobile, giving life to the expression. Stop must be evaluated in profile so that it will not be confused with the raised brow. *Occiput* not accentuated, the skull forming a gentle curve where it fits well into the neck. **Expression** alert, intelligent and kind. **Eyes** are set widely apart. Medium-sized, almond-shaped, dark brown or hazel; not large, round or yellow. Eye rims are self-colored and tight. **Ears** relatively small, well set on, lying close to the side of the head and thickly feathered. Not low set (houndlike or setterish). **Nose**—Large open nostrils. Black on black dogs, brown on liver dogs. **Lips** fairly tight, firm, clean and dry to minimize the retention of feathers. **Jaws** long and strong, capable of carrying a hare or a pheasant. **Bite**—Scissors bite preferred, level bite acceptable. Broken teeth should not count against the dog. **Severe Faults**—Wry and undershot or overshot bites with a noticeable gap must be severely penalized.

**Neck, Topline, Body**—*Neck* strong and slightly arched for retrieving strength. Moderately long to allow for easy seeking of the trail. Free from throatiness. Coat on neck is untrimmed. **Topline** strong and level. **Body**—*Chest (Brisket)*—Deep, reaching to the elbow and only moderately broad. *Forechest*—Prow prominent and well developed. *Rib cage* deep, showing good length from forechest to last rib (to allow ample space for all body organs), and only moderately broad. The foreribs fairly flat showing a gradual spring, well arched in the center of the body but rather lighter towards the loin. *Underline*—Deep chest tapering to a moderate *tuck-up. Loin* strong, well muscled and long enough to allow for agility, freedom of movement and length of stride, but never weak or loosely coupled. *Croup* slopes very slightly; rump moderately broad and well muscled. **Tail** fairly straight, well set on, with bone reaching approximately to the hock joint. When the dog is in motion, the tail is carried happily but without curl as a smooth extension of the topline, never much above the level of the back.

**Forequarters**—*Shoulders* long, well laid back shoulder blade with *upper arm* of approximately equal length to allow for efficient reach. Musculature wiry rather than bulky. *Elbows* clean, close to the body and set well back under the withers. *Forelegs* straight and strong with medium bone of good quality. *Pasterns* slightly sloping and strong. *Dewclaws*—Removal of dewclaws is optional. *Feet* oval or round. Medium-sized and tight with well-arched toes and thick pads.

**Hindquarters**—Powerful with angulation in balance with the front assembly. *Upper thighs* powerful and well muscled. *Stifle*—Good turn of stifle with sound, strong joint. *Second thighs* (Stifle to hock joint)—Second or lower thigh as long as or only slightly longer than upper thigh. *Hock*—Hock joint strong, well let down. *Dewclaws*—There are no hind dewclaws. *Feet* oval or round. Medium-sized and tight with well-arched toes and thick pads.

**Coat**—Coat is of moderate length, density and fullness, with a high luster. The ideal coat is straight and flat lying. A slight waviness is permissible but the coat is not curly, woolly, short, silky or fluffy. The Flat-Coat is a working retriever and the coat must provide protection from all types of weather, water and ground cover. This requires a coat of sufficient texture, length and fullness to allow for adequate insulation. When the dog is in full coat the ears, front, chest, back of forelegs, thighs and underside of tail are thickly feathered without being bushy, stringy or silky. Mane of longer, heavier coat on the neck extending over the withers and shoulders is considered typical, especially in the male dog, and can cause the neck to appear thicker and the withers higher, sometimes causing the appearance of a dip behind the withers. Since the Flat-Coat is a hunting retriever, the feathering is not excessively long. **Trimming**—The Flat-Coat is shown with as natural a coat as possible and must not be penalized for lack of trimming, as long as the coat is clean and well brushed. Tidying of ears, feet, underline and tip of tail is acceptable. Whiskers serve a specific function and it is preferred that they not be trimmed. Shaving or barbering of the head, neck or body coat must be severely penalized.

**Color**—Solid black or solid liver. *Disqualification*—Yellow, cream or any color other than black or liver.

**Gait**—Sound, efficient movement is of critical importance to a hunting retriever. The Flat-Coat viewed from the side covers ground efficiently and movement appears balanced, free-flowing and well coordinated, never choppy, mincing or ponderous. Front and rear legs reach well forward and extend well back, achieving long clean strides. Topline appears level, strong and supple while dog is in motion.

**Summary**—The Flat-Coat is a strong but elegant, cheerful hunting retriever. Quality of structure, balance and harmony of all parts both standing and in motion are essential. As a breed whose purpose is of a utilitarian nature—structure, condition and attitude should give every indication of being suited for hard work.

**Temperament**—Character is a primary and outstanding asset of the Flat-Coat. He is a responsive, loving member of the family, a versatile working dog, multi-talented, sensible, bright and tractable. In competition the Flat-Coat demonstrates *stability* and a desire to please with a confident, happy and outgoing attitude characterized by a wagging tail. Nervous, hyperactive, apathetic, shy or obstinate behavior is undesirable. *Severe Fault*—Unprovoked aggressive behavior toward people or animals is *totally* unacceptable.

**Character**—Character is as important to the evaluation of stock by a potential breeder as any other aspect of the breed standard. The Flat-Coat is primarily a family companion hunting retriever. He is keen and birdy, flushing within gun range, as well as a determined, resourceful retriever on land and water. He has a great desire to hunt with self-reliance and an uncanny ability to adapt to changing circumstances on a variety of upland game and waterfowl.

As a family companion he is sensible, alert and highly intelligent; a lighthearted, affectionate and adaptable friend. He retains these qualities as well as his youthful good-humored outlook on life into old age. The adult Flat-Coat is usually an adequate alarm dog to give warning, but is a good-natured, optimistic dog, basically inclined to be friendly to all.

The Flat-Coat is a cheerful, devoted companion who requires and appreciates living with and interacting as a member of his family. To reach full potential in any endeavor he absolutely must have a strong personal bond and affectionate individual attention.


## DISQUALIFICATION

*Yellow, cream or any color other than black or liver.*

**Approved September 11, 1990**
**Effective October 30, 1990**

# GOLDEN RETRIEVER

*I*N THE 1800S, WITH GAME PLENTIFUL IN SCOTLAND AND ENGLAND, HUNTING was both a sport and a practical way of obtaining food. Retrievers became popular when the use of breech-loading shotguns demanded an efficient retrieving dog for both waterfowl and upland game. All retriever breeds begin with the water-loving Saint John's dog of Newfoundland, ancestor of the wavy-coated retriever that contributed to both the Flat-Coated and Golden retrievers.

The most complete records of the Golden Retriever's origin as a specific strain are included in a record book kept from about 1840 to 1890 by Dudley Marjoribanks, the first Lord Tweedmouth, at his Guisachan estate in the Highlands, Inverness-shire, Scotland. These records were made public in 1952 by Tweedmouth's great-nephew, the sixth Lord Ilchester. Further information from the original record book, and additional pedigree research, was published by Elma Stonex.

In 1865, Tweedmouth bought Nous (Greek for *wisdom*), the single yellow pup in a litter of black wavy-coated retrievers. Photos of Nous show a handsome, sturdy dog with a wavy coat, quite recognizably a Golden. Nous was bred to Belle, a Tweed Water Spaniel, resulting in four yellow pups that became the foundation of the breed. Two of these, Cowslip and Primrose, were retained at Guisachan; Crocus went to Tweedmouth's eldest son, Edward, and Ada to his cousin the fifth Lord Ilchester. Through several generations of clever breeding, Tweedmouth created a consistent line of exceptional working retrievers. Always keeping the main line from Nous and Belle, he blended in another Tweed Water Spaniel, a couple of black wavy-coated retrievers, and a red setter, primarily retaining the yellow pups. Working ability and retrieving aptitude were paramount, requiring a strong, biddable dog that could withstand cold and the punishing topography of the Highlands.

The Tweed Water Spaniel, now extinct, was native to the east coast of southern Scotland, particularly in the Tweed River area near Berwick. The breed was used both to retrieve game and assist fishermen. According to Hugh Dalziel, Tweed spaniels were "light liver" in color, with a fairly short, close-curled coat only slightly feathered, and a head "conical" in shape. Stanley O'Neill, the Flat-Coat historian, described them as more retriever than spaniel in appearance. *Liver* at that time could be used to describe anything from dark brown to light sandy color.

Some of the Tweedmouth retrievers were given to friends and relatives, but the strain remained largely unknown until after 1900. In 1904, a Tweedmouth dog sired the winner of the first field trial for retrievers. A few "yellow retrievers" were registered with The Kennel Club (England) as "Retrievers (Wavy or Flat-Coated)." They finally appeared at dog shows in 1908, entered in classes for Flat-Coats "of any other color." One of the earliest exhibitors, Mrs. W. M. Charlesworth, was nearly single-handedly responsible for recognition in 1913 of "Goldens" in their own right as "Retrievers (Yellow or Golden)." Mrs. Charlesworth always advocated the romantic story of the breed being based on a group of Russian circus dogs bought by Lord Tweedmouth, but there is no evidence whatever to substantiate this charming story.

Some Goldens were brought to North America before either the American Kennel Club or the Canadian Kennel Club officially recognized the breed, and the AKC registered its first Golden in 1925. But the real Golden Retriever foundation sire was Am./Can. Ch. Speedwell Pluto, whelped in 1929 in England. Through further imports and family connections, Goldens became established in several areas of the United States before World War II. After the war, the breed grew steadily in popularity, with a pronounced surge of registrations in the 1970s.

The Golden's kindly expression and distinctive double golden coat are appealing, but their natural qualities of amiable temperament, trainability, willingness, useful size, and sturdy physique have equipped them for a variety of practical uses. In addition to serving as personal hunting dogs, they are excellent as guide dogs for the blind, assistance and service dogs, search-and-rescue dogs, and tracking and scenting specialists. In organized dog sports, the breed is widely popular in obedience trials (the first three Obedience Trial Champions were Goldens), hunt tests, and agility. Golden registrations have remained in the top ten of all breeds for years, attesting to their popularity as companions and family dogs as well as workers.

The Golden Retriever Club of America was organized in 1938. It is one of the strongest AKC parent clubs, with approximately 5,000 members and approximately fifty local specialty clubs, many of which hold specialty events. The GRCA sponsors an extensive array of programs, including the Working and Versatility Certificates, a very large national specialty and three regional specialties yearly, and the philanthropic Golden Retriever Foundation.

# OFFICIAL STANDARD FOR THE GOLDEN RETRIEVER

**General Appearance**—A symmetrical, powerful, active dog, sound and well put together, not clumsy nor long in the leg, displaying a kindly expression and possessing a personality that is eager, alert and self-confident. Primarily a hunting dog, he should be shown in hard working condition. Overall appearance, balance, gait and purpose to be given more emphasis than any of his component parts. *Faults*—Any departure from the described ideal shall be considered faulty to the degree to which it interferes with the breed's purpose or is contrary to breed character.

**Size, Proportion, Substance**—Males 23 to 24 inches in height at withers; females 21½ to 22½ inches. Dogs up to one inch above or below standard size should be proportionately penalized. Deviation in height of more than one inch from the standard shall *disqualify*. Length from breastbone to point of buttocks slightly greater than height at withers in a ratio of 12:11. Weight for dogs, 65 to 75 pounds; bitches, 55 to 65 pounds.

**Head**—Broad in *skull,* slightly arched laterally and longitudinally without prominence of frontal bones (forehead) or occipital bones. *Stop* well defined but not abrupt. *Foreface* deep and wide, nearly as long as skull. *Muzzle* straight in profile, blending smooth and strongly into skull; when viewed in profile or from above, slightly deeper and wider at stop than at tip. No heaviness in flews. Removal of whiskers is permitted but not preferred. *Eyes* friendly and intelligent in expression, medium large with dark, close-fitting rims, set well apart and reasonably deep in sockets. Color preferably dark brown; medium brown acceptable. Slant eyes and narrow, triangular eyes detract from correct expression and are to be faulted. No white or haw visible when looking straight ahead. Dogs showing evidence of functional abnormality of eyelids or eyelashes (such as, but not limited to, trichiasis, entropion, ectropion, or distichiasis) are to be excused from the ring. *Ears* rather short with front edge attached well behind and just above the eye and falling close to cheek. When pulled forward, tip of ear should just cover the eye. Low, hound-like ear set to be faulted. *Nose* black or brownish black, though fading to a lighter shade in cold weather not serious. Pink nose or one seriously lacking in pigmentation to be faulted. *Teeth* scissors bite, in which the outer side of the lower incisors touches the inner side of the upper incisors. Undershot or overshot bite is a *disqualification*. Misalignment of teeth (irregular placement of incisors) or a level bite (incisors meet each other edge to edge) is undesirable, but not to be confused with undershot or overshot. Full dentition. Obvious gaps are serious faults.

**Neck, Topline, Body**—*Neck* medium long, merging gradually into well laid back shoulders, giving sturdy, muscular appearance. No throatiness. *Backline* strong and level from withers to slightly sloping croup, whether standing or moving. Sloping backline, roach or sway back, flat or steep croup to be faulted. *Body* well balanced, short coupled, deep through the chest. Chest between forelegs at least as wide as a man's closed hand including thumb, with well developed forechest. Brisket extends to elbow. Ribs long and well sprung but not barrel shaped, extending well towards hindquarters. Loin short, muscular, wide and deep, with very little tuck-up. Slab-sidedness, narrow chest, lack of depth in brisket, excessive tuck-up to be faulted. *Tail* well set on, thick and muscular at the base, following the natural line of the croup. Tail bones extend to, but not below, the point of hock. Carried with merry action, level or with some moderate upward curve; never curled over back nor between legs.

**Forequarters**—Muscular, well coordinated with hindquarters and capable of free movement. *Shoulder blades* long and well laid back with upper tips fairly close together at withers. *Upper arms* appear about the same length as the blades, setting the elbows back beneath the upper tip of the blades, close to the ribs without looseness. *Legs,* viewed from the front, straight with good bone, but not to the point of coarseness. *Pasterns* short and strong, sloping slightly with no suggestion of weakness. Dewclaws on forelegs may be removed, but are normally left on. *Feet* medium size, round, compact, and well knuckled, with thick pads. Excess hair may be trimmed to show natural size and contour. Splayed or hare feet to be faulted.

**Hindquarters**—Broad and strongly muscled. Profile of croup slopes slightly; the pelvic bone slopes at a slightly greater angle (approximately 30 degrees from horizontal). In a natural stance, the femur joins the pelvis at approximately a 90-degree angle; *stifles* well bent; *hocks* well let down with short, strong *rear pasterns. Feet* as in front. *Legs* straight when viewed from rear. Cow-hocks, spread hocks, and sickle hocks to be faulted.

**Coat**—Dense and water-repellent with good undercoat. Outer coat firm and resilient, neither coarse nor silky, lying close to body; may be straight or wavy. Untrimmed natural ruff; moderate feathering on back of forelegs and on underbody; heavier feathering on front of neck, back of thighs and underside of tail. Coat on head, paws, and front of legs is short and even. Excessive length, open coats, and limp, soft coats are very undesirable. Feet may be trimmed and stray hairs neatened, but the natural appearance of coat or outline should not be altered by cutting or clipping.

**Color**—Rich, lustrous golden of various shades. Feathering may be lighter than rest of coat. With the exception of graying or whitening of face or body due to age, any white marking, other than a few white hairs on the chest, should be penalized according to its extent. Allowable light shadings are not to be confused with white markings. Predominant body color which is either extremely pale or extremely dark is undesirable. Some latitude should be given to the light puppy whose coloring shows promise of deepening with maturity. Any noticeable area of black or other off-color hair is a serious fault.

**Gait**—When trotting, gait is free, smooth, powerful and well coordinated, showing good reach. Viewed from any position, legs turn neither in nor out, nor do feet cross or interfere with each other. As speed increases, feet tend to converge toward centerline of balance. It is recommended that dogs be shown on a loose lead to reflect true gait.

**Temperament**—Friendly, reliable, and trustworthy. Quarrelsomeness or hostility towards other dogs or people in normal situations, or an unwarranted show of timidity or nervousness, is not in keeping with Golden Retriever character. Such actions should be penalized according to their significance.

## DISQUALIFICATIONS

*Deviation in height of more than one inch from the standard either way.*
*Undershot or overshot bite.*

**Approved October 13, 1981**
**Reformatted August 18, 1990**

# LABRADOR RETRIEVER

*T*HE LABRADOR RETRIEVER DID NOT, AS HIS NAME IMPLIES, COME FROM Labrador, but from Newfoundland, although there is no indication of by what means he reached the latter place. However, in 1822 a traveler in that region reported a number of small water dogs: "The dogs are admirably trained as retrievers in fowling, and are otherwise useful. . . . The smooth or short-haired dog is preferred because in frosty weather the long-haired kind become encumbered with ice on coming out of the water."

Early in the nineteenth century, the Earl of Malmesbury reputedly saw one of the dogs that had been carried to England by fishermen and immediately arranged to have some imported. In 1830 the noted British sportsman Colonel Hawker referred to the ordinary Newfoundland and what he called the St. John's breed of water dog, mentioning the former as "very large, strong of limb, rough hair, and carrying his tail high." Referring to what is known now as the Labrador, he said they were "by far the best for any kind of shooting. He is generally black and no bigger than a Pointer, very fine in legs, with short, smooth hair, and does not carry his tail so much curled as the other; is extremely quick running, swimming and fighting . . . and their sense of smell is hardly to be credited. . . ."

The dogs were not at first generally known in England as Labradors. In fact, the origin of the name is shown in a letter written in 1887 by the Earl of Malmesbury: "We always call mine Labrador dogs, and I have kept the breed as pure as I could from the first I had from Poole, at that time carrying on a brisk trade with New-foundland. The real breed may be known by its close coat which turns the water off like oil and, above all, a tail like an otter."

The Labrador gradually died out in Newfoundland on account of a heavy dog tax that, with the English quarantine law, practically stopped the importations into England. Thereafter many Labradors were interbred with other types of retrievers. Fortunately, however, the Labrador characteristics predominated. And finally fanciers, desiring to stop the interbreeding, drew up a standard so as to discourage crossing with other retrievers.

There is a studbook of the Duke of Buccleuch's Labrador Retrievers which made it possible to work out pedigrees of the two dogs that did most to produce the modern Labrador, Mr. A. C. Butter's Peter of Faskally, and Major Portal's Flapper. These pedigrees go back as far as 1878.

The Labrador Retriever was first recognized as a separate breed by The Kennel Club (England) in 1903. The first registration of Labradors by the American Kennel Club was in 1917—Brocklehirst Nell, a Scottish bitch import. From the late 1920s through the 1930s, there was a great influx of British dogs (and Scottish retriever trainers) that was to form the backbone of the breed in this country.

In England, no Labrador can become a show champion unless he has a working certificate, too—testament that he has also qualified in the field. In America, the Labrador became primarily a retriever trial and shooting dog, but the dual concept of retriever excellence combined with good looks, style, and proper type was established early. The fanciers of the 1930s who started the retriever trials—the Labrador Retriever Club (U.S.) was organized in 1931—also exhibited their field dogs at the bench shows with marked success.

The Labrador Retriever's capabilities, fine temperament, and dependability have established it as one of the prime breeds for service as a guide dog for the blind or for search-and-rescue work.

# OFFICIAL STANDARD FOR THE LABRADOR RETRIEVER

**General Appearance**—The Labrador Retriever is a strongly built, medium-sized, short-coupled dog possessing a sound, athletic, well-balanced conformation that enables it to function as a retrieving gun dog; the substance and soundness to hunt waterfowl or upland game for long hours under difficult conditions; the character and quality to win in the show ring; and the temperament to be a family companion. Physical features and mental characteristics should denote a dog bred to perform as an efficient retriever of game with a stable temperament suitable for a variety of pursuits beyond the hunting environment.

The most distinguishing characteristics of the Labrador Retriever are its short, dense, weather-resistant coat; an "otter" tail; a clean-cut head with broad back skull and moderate stop; powerful jaws; and its "kind," friendly eyes, expressing character, intelligence and good temperament.

Above all, a Labrador Retriever must be well balanced, enabling it to move in the show ring or work in the field with little or no effort. The typical Labrador possesses style and quality without over refinement, and substance without lumber or cloddiness. The Labrador is bred primarily as a working gun dog; structure and soundness are of great importance.

**Size, Proportion and Substance**—*Size*—The height at the withers for a dog is 22½ to 24½ inches; for a bitch it is 21½ to 23½ inches. Any variance greater than one-half inch above or below these heights is a disqualification. Approximate weight of dogs and bitches in working condition: dogs 65 to 80 pounds; bitches 55 to 70 pounds.

The minimum height ranges set forth in the paragraph above shall not apply to dogs or bitches under twelve months of age.

*Proportion*—Short-coupled; length from the point of the shoulder to the point of the rump is equal to or slightly longer than the distance from the withers to the ground. Distance from the elbow to the ground should be equal to one-half of the height at the withers. The brisket should extend to the elbows, but not perceptibly deeper. The body must be of sufficient length to permit a straight, free and efficient stride; but the dog should never appear low and long or tall and leggy in outline. *Substance*—Substance and bone proportionate to the overall dog. Light, "weedy" individuals are definitely incorrect; equally objectionable are cloddy lumbering specimens. Labrador Retrievers shall be shown in working condition well-muscled and without excess fat.

**Head**—*Skull*—The skull should be wide; well developed but without exaggeration. The skull and foreface should be on parallel planes and of approximately equal length. There should be a moderate stop—the brow slightly pronounced so that the skull is not absolutely in a straight line with the nose. The brow ridges aid in defining the stop. The head should be clean-cut and free from fleshy cheeks; the bony structure of the skull chiseled beneath the eye with no prominence in the cheek. The skull may show some median line; the occipital bone is not conspicuous in mature dogs. Lips should not be squared off or pendulous, but fall away in a curve toward the throat. A wedge-shape head, or a head long and narrow in muzzle and back skull is incorrect as are massive, cheeky heads. The jaws are powerful and free from snippiness—the muzzle neither long and narrow nor short and stubby. *Nose*—The nose should be wide and the nostrils well-developed. The nose should be black on black or yellow dogs, and brown on chocolates. Nose color fading to a lighter shade is not a fault. A thoroughly pink nose or one lacking in any pigment is a disqualification. *Teeth*—The teeth should be strong and regular with a scissors bite; the lower teeth just behind, but touching the inner side of the upper incisors. A level bite is acceptable, but not desirable. Undershot, overshot, or misaligned teeth are serious faults. Full dentition is preferred. Missing molars or premolars are serious faults. *Ears*—The ears should hang moderately close to the head, set rather far back, and somewhat low on the skull; slightly above eye level. Ears should not be large and heavy, but in proportion with the skull and reach to the inside of the eye when pulled forward. *Eyes*—Kind, friendly eyes imparting good temperament, intelligence and alertness are a hallmark of the breed. They should be of medium size, set well apart, and neither protruding nor deep-set. Eye color should be brown in black and yellow Labradors, and brown or hazel in chocolates. Black or yellow eyes give a harsh expression and are undesirable. Small eyes, set close together, or round prominent eyes are not typical of the breed. Eye rims are black in black and yellow Labradors; and brown in chocolates. Eye rims without pigmentation is a disqualification.

**Neck, Topline and Body**—*Neck*—The neck should be of proper length to allow the dog to retrieve game easily. It should be muscular and free from throatiness. The neck should rise strongly from the shoulders with a moderate arch. A short, thick neck or a "ewe" neck is incorrect. *Topline*—The back is strong and the topline is level from the withers to the croup when standing or moving. However, the loin should show evidence of flexibility for athletic endeavor. *Body*—The Labrador should be short-coupled, with good spring of ribs tapering to a moderately wide chest. The Labrador should not be narrow chested; giving the appearance of hollowness between the front legs, nor should it have a wide spreading, Bulldog-like front. Correct chest conformation will result in tapering between the front legs that allows unrestricted forelimb movement. Chest breadth that is either too wide or too narrow for efficient movement and stamina is incorrect. Slab-sided individuals are not typical of the breed; equally objectionable are rotund or barrel chested specimens. The underline is almost straight, with little or no tuck-up in mature animals. Loins should be short, wide and strong; extending to well-developed, powerful hindquarters. When viewed from the side, the Labrador Retriever shows a well-developed, but not exaggerated forechest. *Tail*—The tail is a distinguishing feature of the breed. It should be very thick at the base, gradually tapering toward the tip, of medium length, and extending no longer than to the hock. The tail should be free from feathering and clothed thickly all around with the Labrador's short, dense coat, thus having that peculiar rounded appearance that has been described as the "otter" tail. The tail should follow the topline in repose or when in motion. It may be carried gaily, but should not curl over the back. Extremely short tails or long thin tails are serious faults. The tail completes the balance of the Labrador by giving it a flowing line from the top of the head to the tip of the tail. Docking or otherwise altering the length or natural carriage of the tail is a disqualification.

**Forequarters**—Forequarters should be muscular, well coordinated and balanced with the hindquarters. *Shoulders*—The shoulders are well laid-back, long and sloping, forming an angle with the upper arm of approximately 90 degrees that permits the dog to move his forelegs in an easy manner with strong forward reach. Ideally, the length of the shoulder blade should equal the length of the upper arm. Straight shoulder blades, short upper arms or heavily muscled or loaded shoulders, all restricting free movement, are incorrect. *Front Legs*—When viewed from the front, the legs should be straight with good strong bone. Too much bone is as undesirable as too little bone, and short legged, heavy-boned individuals are not typical of the breed. Viewed from the side, the elbows should be directly under the withers, and the front legs should be perpendicular to the ground and well under the body. The elbows should be close to the ribs without looseness. Tied-in elbows or being "out at the elbows" interfere with free movement and are serious faults. Pasterns should be strong and short and should slope slightly from the perpendicular line of the leg. Feet are strong and compact, with well-arched toes and well-developed pads. Dew claws may be removed. Splayed feet, hare feet, knuckling over, or feet turning in or out are serious faults.

**Hindquarters**—The Labrador's hindquarters are broad, muscular and well developed from the hip to the hock with well-turned stifles and strong short hocks. Viewed from the rear, the hind legs are straight and parallel. Viewed from the side, the angulation of the rear legs is in balance with the front. The hind legs are strongly boned, muscled with moderate angulation at the stifle, and powerful, clearly defined thighs. The stifle is strong and there is no slippage of the patellae while in motion or when standing. The hock joints are strong, well let down and do not slip or hyper-extend while in motion or when standing. Angulation of both stifle and hock joint is such as to achieve the optimal balance of drive and traction. When standing the rear toes are only slightly behind the point of the rump. Over angulation produces a sloping topline not typical of the breed. Feet are strong and compact, with well-arched toes and well-developed pads. Cowhocks, spread hocks, sickle hocks and over-angulation are serious structural defects and are to be faulted.

**Coat**—The coat is a distinctive feature of the Labrador Retriever. It should be short, straight and very dense, giving a fairly hard feeling to the hand. The Labrador should have a soft, weather-resistant undercoat that provides protection from water, cold, and all types of ground cover. A slight wave down the back is permissible. Woolly coats, soft silky coats, and sparse slick coats are not typical of the breed, and should be severely penalized.

**Color**—The Labrador Retriever coat colors are black, yellow and chocolate. Any other color or a combination of colors is a disqualification. A small white spot on the chest is permissible, but not desirable. White hairs from aging or scarring are not to be misinterpreted as brindling. *Black*—Blacks are all black. A black with brindle markings or a black with tan markings is a disqualification. *Yellow*—Yellows may range in color from fox-red to light cream, with variations in shading on the ears, back, and underparts of the dog. *Chocolate*—Chocolates can vary in shade from light to dark chocolate. Chocolate with brindle or tan markings is a disqualification.

*Movement*—Movement of the Labrador Retriever should be free and effortless. When watching a dog move toward oneself, there should be no sign of elbows out. Rather, the elbows should be held neatly to the body with the legs not too close together. Moving straight forward without pacing or weaving, the legs should form straight lines, with all parts moving in the same plane. Upon viewing the dog from the rear, one should have the impression that the hind legs move as nearly as possible in a parallel line with the front legs. The hocks should do their full share of the work, flexing well, giving the appearance of power and strength. When viewed from the side, the shoulders should move freely and effortlessly, and the foreleg should reach forward close to the ground with extension. A short, choppy movement or high knee action indicates a straight shoulder; paddling indicates long, weak pasterns; and a short, stilted rear gait indicates a straight rear assembly; all are serious faults. Movement faults interfering with performance including weaving; side-winding; crossing over; high knee action; paddling; and short, choppy movement, should be severely penalized.

**Temperament**—True Labrador Retriever temperament is as much a hallmark of the breed as the "otter" tail. The ideal disposition is one of a kindly, outgoing, tractable nature; eager to please and non-aggressive toward man or animal. The Labrador has much that appeals to people; his gentle ways, intelligence and adaptability make him an ideal dog. Aggressiveness toward humans or other animals, or any evidence of shyness in an adult should be severely penalized.

## DISQUALIFICATIONS

1. *Any deviation from the height prescribed in the Standard.*
2. *A thoroughly pink nose or one lacking in any pigment.*
3. *Eye rims without pigment.*
4. *Docking or otherwise altering the length or natural carriage of the tail.*
5. *Any other color or a combination of colors other than black, yellow or chocolate as described in the Standard.*

**Approved February 12, 1994**
**Effective March 31, 1994**

# Nova Scotia Duck Tolling Retriever

THE NOVA SCOTIA DUCK TOLLING RETRIEVER, COMMONLY CALLED THE
Toller, is a medium-sized, powerful, compact, balanced dog and the small-est of the retrievers. The height at the withers for males is 18 to 21 inches, with the ideal being 19. Corresponding height for females is 17 to 20 inches, with the ideal at 18 inches. Weight is in proportion to the height and bone of the dog. The Toller's attitude and bearing suggest strength with a high degree of agility. They are alert, determined, and quick, with a keen desire to work and please.

This breed was developed in Nova Scotia in the early nineteenth century to toll (or lure) and retrieve waterfowl. The tolling dog runs, jumps, and plays along the shoreline, occasionally disappearing from sight, then quickly reappearing in full view of a flock of ducks. The hunter, who throws a ball or small sticks for the dog, aids this action. The dog's playful actions arouse the curiosity of ducks swimming offshore, which are then lured within gunshot range. The Toller is subsequently sent out to retrieve any dead or wounded birds.

The Nova Scotia Duck Tolling Retriever has broken free from the constraints of the hunting technique for which it is named. Today, the Toller is multifaceted. You get the ideal dog—a retriever, hunter, loyal watchdog, competition dog, and wonderful loving pet—all rolled into one breed that has more simple zest and joy for life than most others. Tollers wholly involve themselves in everything. Whether stealing from the counter, chasing a ball, breaking ice to get a bird, or curling up on the couch, everything is done 100 percent.

Toller owners love their dogs but know that it is not the breed for everyone. Tollers are ardent observers of life and as young dogs are full of energy and easily distracted. This breed can be mischievous, wild, or even take over the household. They are not always ideal, loving companions. Toller energy needs to be channeled in constructive ways. Though they learn quickly, they also bore quickly. Training sessions must be kept short, light, fun, and challenging.

People choose Tollers after months of research for many reasons. They fell in love with the breed and may have done so because the dogs are not couch potatoes. Most people were looking for a dog with high intelligence, one that would be a companion but would also think for itself. They were looking for a dog that could keep up with the family's outdoor activities and still have lots of get-up-and-go at the end of the day. Some were looking for a dog that would challenge them and their training abilities. In the Toller you get it all!

This personality may not be what everyone is looking for. Consider the whole breed, not just one dog you see in a given situation. The dogs you see may not be themselves or may have been trained to be calm and responsive. People who are looking for a smaller version of a Golden or Labrador in obedience, field trials, or hunting will find major differences in the personalities of this breed. Tollers have a special spark.

What makes the Toller different from other retrievers? Size is the biggest difference. They may be the smallest of the retrievers, but they have a spirit and attitude bigger than life. Tollers are happy and a bit full of themselves. They have fun and goof off a little. You won't see that quiet "ho-hum, well, here we are" attitude. What you will see is, "Well, what's *next*?"

Tollers are working retrievers with no excessive coat. They are well-muscled and athletic. The breed is well-balanced and sports an air of confidence. Toller movement should appear powerful, smooth, and effortless. They are ready to spring into action at any time, or with any indication that retrieving is right around the corner!

# OFFICIAL STANDARD FOR
# THE NOVA SCOTIA DUCK TOLLING RETRIEVER

**General Appearance**—The Nova Scotia Duck Tolling Retriever (Toller) was developed in the early nineteenth century to toll, lure, and retrieve waterfowl. The playful action of the Toller retrieving a stick or ball along the shoreline arouses the curiosity of the ducks offshore. They are lured within gunshot range, and the dog is sent out to retrieve the dead or wounded birds.

This medium sized, powerful, compact, balanced dog is the smallest of the retrievers. The Toller's attitude and bearing suggest strength with a high degree of agility. He is alert, determined, and quick, with a keen desire to work and please.

Many Tollers have a slightly sad or worried expression when they are not working. The moment the slightest indication is given that retrieving is required, they set themselves for springy action with an expression of intense concentration and excitement. The heavily feathered tail is held high in constant motion while working.

The Nova Scotia Duck Tolling Retriever Club (USA) feels strongly that all Tollers should have these innate abilities, and encourages all Tollers to prove them by passing an approved Nova Scotia Duck Tolling Retriever Club (USA) field test.

**Size, Proportion and Substance**—*Size:* Height at the withers-males, 18–21 inches. The ideal is 19 inches. Females, 17–20 inches. The ideal is 18 inches. *Bone:* is medium. Weight is in proportion to height and bone of the dog. The dog's length should be slightly longer than height, in a ratio of 10 to 9, but should not give the impression of a long back.

**Head**—*Skull:* The head is clean-cut and slightly wedge shaped. The broad skull is only slightly rounded, giving the appearance of being flat when the ears are alert. The occiput is not prominent. The cheeks are flat. The length of the skull from the occiput to the stop is slightly longer than the length of the muzzle from the stop to the tip of the nose. The head must be in proportion to body size. *Expression:* The expression is alert, friendly, and intelligent. Many Tollers have a slightly sad expression until they go to work, when their aspect changes to intense concentration and desire. *Eyes:* The eyes are set well apart, slightly oblique and almond in shape. Eye color blends with the coat or is darker. Eye rims must be self-colored or black, matching the nose and lips. *Faults:* Large round eyes. Eye rims and/or eyes not of prescribed color. *Ears:* The high set ears are triangular in shape with rounded tips, set well back on the skull, framing the face, with the base held slightly erect. Ear length should reach approximately to the inside corners of the eyes. Ears should be carried in a drop fashion. Ears are short-coated, and well feathered only on the back of the fold. *Stop:* The stop is Moderate. *Muzzle:* The muzzle tapers in a clean line from stop to nose, with the lower jaw not overly prominent. The jaws are strong enough to carry a sizable bird, and softness in the mouth is essential. The underline of the muzzle is strong and clean. *Fault:* dish face. *Nose:* The nose is fairly broad with the nostrils well open, tapering at the tip. The color should blend with that of the coat, or be black. *Fault:* bright pink nose. *Disqualification:* butterfly nose. *Lips and flews:* Lips fit fairly tightly, forming a gentle curve in profile, with no heaviness in the flews. *Bite:* The correct bite is tight scissors. Full dentition is required. *Disqualifications:* undershot bite. Wry mouth. Overshot by more than ⅛ inch.

**Neck, Backline, Body**—*Neck:* The neck is strongly muscled and well set on, of medium length, with no indication of throatiness. *Backline:* level. *Faults:* roached or sway back. *Body:* The body is deep in chest, with good spring of rib, the brisket reaching to the elbow. Ribs are neither barrel shaped nor flat. The back is strong, short and straight. The loins are strong and muscular, with moderate tuck-up. *Fault:* slack loins. *Tail:* The tail follows the natural very slight slope of the croup, is broad at the base, and is luxuriant and well feathered, with the last vertebra reaching at least to the hock. The tail may be carried below the level of the back except when the dog is alert, when it is held high in a curve, though never touching the body. *Faults:* tail too short, kinked, or curled over touching the back. Tail carried below the level of the back when the dog is gaiting.

**Forequarters**—The shoulder should be muscular, strong, and well angulated, with the blade roughly equal in length to the upper arm. The elbows should work close to the body, cleanly and evenly. When seen from the front, the forelegs' appearance is that of parallel columns. The pasterns are strong and slightly sloping. *Fault:* down in the pasterns. *Feet:* The feet are strongly webbed, slightly oval medium in size, and tight, with well-arched toes and thick pads. Front dewclaws may be removed. *Faults:* splayed or paper feet.

**Hindquarters**—The hindquarters are muscular, broad, and square in appearance. The croup is very slightly sloped. The rear and front angulation should be in balance. The upper and lower thighs are very muscular and equal in length. The stifles are well bent. The hocks are well let down, turning neither in nor out. Rear dewclaws must not be present. *Disqualification:* rear dewclaws.

**Coat**—The Toller was bred to retrieve from icy waters and must have a water-repellent double coat of medium length and softness, and a soft dense undercoat. The coat may have a slight wave on the back but is otherwise straight. Some winter coats may form a long loose curl at the throat. Featherings are soft and moderate in length. The hair on the muzzle is short and fine. Seasonal shedding is to be expected. Over-coated specimens are not appropriate for a working dog and should be faulted. While neatening of the feet, ears, and hocks for the show ring is permitted, the Toller should always appear natural, never barbered. Whiskers must be present. *Faults:* coat longer than medium length. Open coat.

**Color**—Color is any shade of red, ranging from a golden red through dark coppery red, with lighter featherings on the underside of the tail, pantaloons, and body. Even the lighter shades of golden red are deeply pigmented and rich in color. *Disqualifications:* brown coat, black areas in coat, or buff. Buff is bleached, faded, or silvery. Buff may also appear as faded brown with or without silver tips. *Markings:* the Toller has usually at least one of the following white markings—tip of tail, feet (not extending above the pasterns), chest and blaze. A dog of otherwise high quality is not to be penalized for lack of white. *Disqualifications:* white on the shoulders, around the ears, back of neck, or across the flanks.

**Gait**—The Toller combines an impression of power with a springy gait, showing good reach in front and a strong driving rear. Feet should turn neither in nor out, and legs travel in a straight line. In its natural gait at increased speeds, the dog's feet tend to converge towards a center line, with the backline remaining level.

**Temperament**—The Toller is highly intelligent, alert, outgoing, and ready for action, though not to the point of nervousness or hyperactivity. He is affectionate and loving with family members and is good with children, showing patience. Some individuals may display reserved behavior in new situations, but this is not to be confused with shyness. Shyness in adult classes should be penalized. The Toller's strong retrieving desire coupled with his love of water, endurance and intense birdiness, is essential for his role as a tolling retriever.

# DISQUALIFICATIONS

*Butterfly nose.*

*Undershot bite, wry mouth, overshot by more than ⅛ inch.*

*Rear dewclaws.*

*Brown coat, black areas in coat, or buff. Buff is bleached, faded or silvery. Buff may also appear as faded brown, with or without silver tips.*

*White on the shoulders, around the ears, back of the neck, or across the flanks.*

**Approved June 11, 2001**
**Effective September 1, 2001**

# ENGLISH SETTER

*T*HE BEST AUTHORITIES ON THE SUBJECT TELL US THAT THE ENGLISH SETTER was a trained bird dog in England more than 400 years ago. A perusal of some old writings leads us to believe the English Setter evolved from some of the older land spaniels that originated in Spain. We are indebted to Hans Bols, who, in *Partridge Shooting and Partridge Hawking* (1852), presented quite definite pictorial evidence that the setter and the spaniel breeds were quite different in appearance. Even at that time, the tails of the spaniels appeared to have been docked as they are today, and the tails of setters were left as nature intended them.

There is some evidence in the earlier writings of sportsmen to suggest that the old English Setter was originally produced from crosses of the Spanish Pointer, the large Water Spaniel, and the Springer Spaniel. By careful cultivation, breeders produced dogs that attained a high degree of proficiency in finding and pointing game in open country. We can see from examination of the sketches in many of the old writings, that this setter-spaniel was an extremely handsome dog. Many had a head much longer with a more classical cut than that of the spaniel, while others had the short spaniel-like head, lacking the well-defined profile of the skull and foreface of modern dogs. Also, most of these older setters had coats that were quite curly, particularly at the thighs. It can be seen from this brief review that even our oldest authorities were not entirely in accord as to the origin of the breed.

There is little doubt that the major credit for developing the modern setter goes to Edward Laverack. In about 1825, he obtained Pronto and Old Moll from Reverend A. Harrison. Reverend Harrison had apparently kept this breed pure for thirty-five years or more. From these two setters, Edward Laverack produced Prince, Countess, Nellie, and Fairy, which were marvelous specimens of the English Setter. This was accomplished through a remarkable process of inbreeding.

The first show for English Setters was held at Newcastle-on-Tyne on January 28, 1859. From then on, dog shows flourished throughout England, gradually increasing in popularity.

In 1874, Laverack sold a pair of dogs to Charles H. Raymond, of Morris Plains, New Jersey. During the next ten years, the English Setter became increasingly popular.

About this time, many setters bred by R. L. Purcell Llewellin were imported to the United States and Canada. In considering the so-called Llewellin strain, Dr. William A. Bruette recorded that when the Laverack was at its zenith in England, Llewellin purchased a number of Laverack's best show dogs. These were from Laverack's pure Dash-Moll and Dash-Hill lines. They were crossed with some entirely new blood, which Llewellin obtained from the north of England. This new blood was from Mr. Statter's and Sir Vincent Corbet's strain, since referred to as the Duke-Rhoebes, so named for the two most prominent members of the strain. The results of these crosses were eminently successful, particularly at field trials. Llewellin's primary focus was to breed a dog that could win field trials. His dogs' reputation spread to North America. Many were purchased by sportsmen in different sections of the United States and Canada, firmly establishing Llewellin's line on this side of the Atlantic.

During the last hundred years, a divergence in type has appeared and has constantly widened, so that in the United States and Canada there are now two distinct types of English Setters being bred, each having its own devotees. The Llewellin type is the field trial dog, and the Laverack type is the show dog. Both, however, can be excellent gundogs.

Primarily because of both usefulness and beauty, the English Setter thrives in this country. As a result of intelligent breeding, it has been brought to a high state of perfection. A representative entry can usually be found at both conformation shows and field trials.

The mild, sweet disposition characteristic of this breed, combined with the beauty, intelligence, and aristocratic appearance, both in the field and in the home, has endeared it to gundog owners as well as all lovers of a beautiful, active, and rugged outdoor dog. A lovable disposition makes the English Setter truly an ideal companion.

# OFFICIAL STANDARD FOR THE ENGLISH SETTER

**General Appearance**—An elegant, substantial and symmetrical gun dog suggesting the ideal blend of strength, stamina, grace and style. Flat-coated with feathering of good length. Gaiting freely and smoothly with long forward reach, strong rear drive and firm topline. Males decidedly masculine without coarseness. Females decidedly feminine without over-refinement. Overall appearance, balance, gait, and purpose to be given more emphasis than any component part. Above all, extremes of anything distort type and must be faulted.

**Head**—Size and proportion in harmony with body. Long and lean with a well-defined stop. When viewed from the side, head planes (top of muzzle, top of skull and bottom of lower jaw) are parallel. *Skull*—Oval when viewed from above, of medium width, without coarseness, and only slightly wider at the earset than at the brow. Moderately defined occipital protuberance. Length of skull from occiput to stop equal in length of muzzle. *Muzzle*—Long and square when viewed from the side, of good depth with flews squared and fairly pendant. Width in harmony with width of skull and equal at nose and stop. Level from eyes to tip of nose. *Nose*—Black or dark brown, fully pigmented. Nostrils wide apart and large. *Foreface*—Skeletal structure under the eyes well chiseled with no suggestion of fullness. Cheeks present a smooth and clean-cut appearance. *Teeth*—Close scissors bite preferred. Even bite acceptable. *Eyes*—Dark brown, the darker the better. Bright, and spaced to give a mild and intelligent expression. Nearly round, fairly large, neither deep-set nor protruding. Eyelid rims dark and fully pigmented. Lids fit tightly so that haw is not exposed. *Ears*—Set well back and low, even with or below eye level. When relaxed carried close to the head. Of moderate length, slightly rounded at the ends, moderately thin leather, and covered with silky hair.

**Neck and Body**—*Neck*—Long and graceful, muscular and lean. Arched at the crest and clean-cut where it joins the head at the base of the skull. Larger and more muscular toward the shoulders, with the base of the neck flowing smoothly into the shoulders. Not too throaty. *Topline*—In motion or standing appears level or sloping slightly downward without sway or drop from withers to tail forming a graceful outline of medium length. *Forechest*—Well developed, point of sternum projecting slightly in front of point of shoulder/upper arm joint. *Chest*—Deep, but not so wide or round as to interfere with the action of the forelegs. Brisket deep enough to reach the level of the elbow. *Ribs*—Long, springing gradually to the middle of the body, then tapering as they approach the end of the chest cavity. *Back*—Straight and strong at its junction with loin. *Loin*—Strong, moderate in length, slightly arched. Tuck-up moderate. *Hips*—Croup nearly flat. Hip bones wide apart, hips rounded and blending smoothly into hind legs. *Tail*—A smooth continuation of the topline. Tapering to a fine point with only sufficient length to reach the hock joint or slightly less. Carried straight and level with the back. Feathering straight and silky, hanging loosely in a fringe.

**Forequarters**—*Shoulder*—Shoulder blade well laid back. Upper arm equal in length to and forming a nearly right angle with the shoulder blade. Shoulders fairly close together at the tips. Shoulder blades lie flat and meld smoothly with contours of body. *Forelegs*—From front or side, forelegs straight and parallel. Elbows have no tendency to turn in or out when standing or gaiting. Arm flat and muscular. Bone substantial but not coarse and muscles hard and devoid of flabbiness. *Pasterns*—Short, strong and nearly round with the slope deviating very slightly forward from the perpendicular. *Feet*—Face directly forward. Toes closely set, strong and well arched. Pads well developed and tough. Dewclaws may be removed.

**Hindquarters**—Wide, muscular thighs and well-developed lower thighs. Pelvis equal in length to and forming a nearly right angle with upper thigh. In balance with forequarter assembly. Stifle well bent and strong. Lower thigh only slightly longer than upper thigh. Hock joint well bent and strong. Rear pastern short, strong, nearly round and perpendicular to the ground. Hind legs, when seen from the rear, straight and parallel to each other. Hock joints have no tendency to turn in or out when standing or gaiting.

**Coat**—Flat without curl or woolliness. Feathering on ears, chest, abdomen, underside of thighs, back of all legs and on the tail of good length but not so excessive as to hide true lines and movement or to affect the dog's appearance or function as a sporting dog.

**Markings and Color**—*Markings*—White ground color with intermingling of darker hairs resulting in belton markings varying in degree from clear distinct flecking to roan shading, but flecked all over preferred. Head and ear patches acceptable, heavy patches of color on the body undesirable. *Color*—Orange belton, blue belton (white with black markings), tricolor (blue belton with tan on muzzle, over the eyes and on the legs), lemon belton, liver belton.

**Movement and Carriage**—An effortless graceful movement demonstrating endurance while covering ground efficiently. Long forward reach and strong rear drive with a lively tail and a proud head carriage. Head may be carried slightly lower when moving to allow for greater reach of forelegs. The back strong, firm, and free of roll. When moving at a trot, as speed increases, the legs tend to converge toward a line representing the center of gravity.

**Size**—Dogs about 25 inches; bitches about 24 inches.

**Temperament**—Gentle, affectionate, friendly, without shyness, fear or viciousness.

**Approved November 11, 1986**

# GORDON SETTER

$\mathcal{B}$EAUTY, BRAINS, AND BIRD SENSE ARE THE OUTSTANDING QUALITIES OF THIS handsome black-and-tan setter from Scotland. Breed lineage dates back at least to 1620 when a writer of the time praised the "black and fallow setting dog" as "hardest to endure labor."

Popular among hunters in Scotland for decades, the black-and-tan (or occasionally black, white, and tan) setter came into prominence in the kennels of the fourth Duke of Gordon in the late 1820s. Commenting on this kennel, a writer familiar with the duke's setters described them much as a sportsman would describe a Gordon of today:

> The Castle Gordon Setters are, as a rule, easy to break and naturally back well. They are not fast dogs but they have good staying powers and can keep on steadily from morning until night. Their noses are first-class and they seldom make a false point on what is called at field trials a sensational stand. . . . When they stand you may be sure there are birds.

A later and illustrious authority, Idstone, wrote: "I have seen better Setters of the black and tan, than of any other breed."

In 1842, George Blunt, attracted by the Gordon's beauty and superior hunting ability, imported a brace from Castle Gordon to America. Drawings of the pair,

Rake and Rachel, show Rake to be a mostly white, curly-coated dog with a black saddle; Rachel was black with tan markings, and was given to Daniel Webster. Other imports from Great Britain and Scandinavia followed, and the perfecting of the American strains helped the Gordon achieve great popularity as a pet and faithful gundog. This was particularly true in the period when game was marketed commercially, and a real "meat dog" assured a full bag at the end of the day's shooting.

With the arrival of field trial competition Gordon popularity waned for a time, as the dog's habit of quartering thoroughly and working close to the gun placed the breed at a disadvantage where flashing speed was demanded. The comment that their coloring makes Gordons difficult to see in the field has doubtless been made by those who have never seen them there. Against the tan sedge grass of fall or an early snow, a black dog is highly conspicuous. When it is difficult to distinguish this black dog against the background, it is then too dark to shoot with safety. As a personal shooting dog, the Gordon Setter knows no peer.

Characteristic eagerness to work for a loving owner has never changed over the centuries, nor have the Gordon's keen intellect and retentive memory, which enable this breed to improve with age without the need for retraining each season. Gordon breeders, backed by a strong national club, make no distinction between field or show types in their breed standard.

In many countries, benched-show champions are used regularly for hunting and give a good account of themselves in the field, as do the field trial winners at a benched show. The Gordon Setter Club of America and several independent Gordon clubs hold approximately fifteen field trials, thirty hunt tests, and twenty-two specialty shows each year. Several of these specialties offer obedience or agility competition. Gordons excel in all of these endeavors.

A true setter, the Gordon is a distinctive breed, resembling English or Irish setters in general type only. In field trial competition the smaller but not light-boned Gordon has been more favored, while the larger dog is preferred for benched-show competition. The official breed standard allows considerable range in size primarily because individual hunters from various corners of the nation prefer their Gordons of a size to suit the local hunting terrain. There is general agreement, however, on the aristocratic beauty of Gordon Setters: They are sturdy but stylish with a silky black coat, rich mahogany markings, and well-feathered legs. The finely chiseled, somewhat heavy head with long, low-set ears is distinctive for its intelligent expression. A good-sized, sturdy build with plenty of bone and substance combined with an upstanding, stylish gait give the necessary stamina to match the breed's enthusiasm for long days in the field.

The quality that most endears Gordon Setters to pet owners or sensitive sportsmen is their devotion and loyalty to family members. Gordons and their families are happiest when they have adequate exercise. Suspicious of unwanted intruders, Gordons are not chums to every passerby, but live for the pleasure of being near their owners. This almost fanatic devotion has not only helped make Gordons responsive gundogs but also mannerly, eager-to-please dogs in the home. Slow to mature, Gordons are like puppies well into their middle years but retain stamina and function well into old age.

# OFFICIAL STANDARD FOR THE GORDON SETTER

*General Appearance*—The Gordon Setter is a good-sized, sturdily built, black and tan dog, well muscled, with plenty of bone and substance, but active, upstanding and stylish, appearing capable of doing a full day's work in the field. He has a strong, rather short back, with well sprung ribs and a short tail. The head is fairly heavy and finely chiseled. His bearing is intelligent, noble, and dignified, showing no signs of shyness or viciousness. Clear colors and straight or slightly waved coat are correct. He suggests strength and stamina rather than extreme speed. Symmetry and quality are most essential. A dog well balanced in all points is preferable to one with outstanding good qualities and defects. A smooth, free movement, with high head carriage, is typical.

**Size, Proportion, Substance**—*Size*—Shoulder height for males, 24 to 27 inches; females, 23 to 26 inches. Weight for males, 55 to 80 pounds; females, 45 to 70 pounds. Animals that appear to be over or under the prescribed weight limits are to be judged on the basis of conformation and condition. Extremely thin or fat dogs are discouraged on the basis that under or overweight hampers the true working ability of the Gordon Setter. The weight-to-height ratio makes him heavier than other Setters. *Proportion*—The distance from the forechest to the back of the thigh is approximately equal the height from the ground to the withers. The Gordon Setter has plenty of bone and substance.

*Head*—Head deep, rather than broad, with plenty of brain room. *Eyes* of fair size, neither too deep-set nor too bulging, dark brown, bright and wise. The shape is oval rather than round. The lids are tight. *Ears* set low on the head approximately on line with the eyes, fairly large and thin, well folded and carried close to the head. *Skull* nicely rounded, good-sized, broadest between the ears. Below and above the eyes is lean and the cheeks as narrow as the leanness of the head allows. The head should have a clearly indicated stop. *Muzzle* fairly long and not pointed, either as seen from above or from the side. The flews are not pendulous. The muzzle is the same length as the skull from occiput to stop and the top of the muzzle is parallel to the line of the skull extended. *Nose* broad, with open nostrils and black in color. The lip line from the nose to the flews shows a sharp, well-defined, square contour. *Teeth* strong and white, meeting in front in a scissors bite, with the upper incisors slightly forward of the lower incisors. A level bite is not a fault. Pitted teeth from distemper or allied infections are not penalized.

**Neck, Topline, Body**—*Neck*—long, lean, arched to the head, and without throatiness. *Topline* moderately sloping. *Body* short from shoulder to hips. Chest deep and not too broad in front; the ribs well sprung, leaving plenty of lung room. The chest reaches to the elbows. A pronounced forechest is in evidence. Loins short and broad and not arched. Croup nearly flat, with only a slight slope to the tailhead. *Tail* short and not reaching below the hocks, carried horizontal or nearly so, not docked, thick at the root and finishing in a fine point. The placement of the tail is important for correct carriage. When the angle of the tail bends too sharply at the first coccygeal bone, the tail will be carried too gaily or will droop. The tail placement is judged in relationship to the structure of the croup.

**Forequarters**—Shoulders fine at the points, and laying well back. The tops of the shoulder blades are close together. When viewed from behind, the neck appears to fit into the shoulders in smooth, flat lines that gradually widen from neck to shoulder. The angle formed by the shoulder blade and upper arm bone is approximately 90 degrees when the dog is standing so that the foreleg is perpendicular to the ground. Forelegs big-boned, straight and not bowed, with elbows free and not turned in or out. Pasterns are strong, short and nearly vertical with a slight spring. Dewclaws may be removed. Feet catlike in shape, formed by close-knit, well arched toes with plenty of hair between; with full toe pads and deep heel cushions. Feet are not turned in or out.

**Hindquarters**—The hind legs from hip to hock are long, flat and muscular; from hock to heel, short and strong. The stifle and hock joints are well bent and not turned either in or out. When the dog is standing with the rear pastern perpendicular to the ground, the thighbone hangs downward parallel to an imaginary line drawn upward from the hock. Feet as in front.

**Coat**—Soft and shining, straight or slightly waved, but not curly, with long hair on ears, under stomach and on chest, on back of the fore and hind legs, and on the tail. The feather which starts near the root of the tail is slightly waved or straight, having a triangular appearance, growing shorter uniformly toward the end.

**Color and Markings**—Black with tan markings, either of rich chestnut or mahogany color. Black penciling is allowed on the toes. The borderline between black and tan colors is clearly defined. There are not any tan hairs mixed in the black. The tan markings are located as follows: (1) Two clear spots over the eyes and not over three-quarters of an inch in diameter; (2) On the sides of the muzzle. The tan does not reach to the top of the muzzle, but resembles a stripe around the end of the muzzle from one side to the other; (3) On the throat; (4) Two large clear spots on the chest; (5) On the inside of the hind legs showing down the front of the stifle and broadening out to the outside of the hind legs from the hock to the toes. It must not completely eliminate the black on the back of the hind legs; (6) On the forelegs from the carpus, or a little above, downward to the toes; (7) Around the vent; (8) A white spot on the chest is allowed, but the smaller the better. Predominantly tan, red or buff dogs which do not have the typical pattern of markings of a Gordon Setter are ineligible for showing and undesirable for breeding. Predominantly tan, red or buff dogs are ineligible for showing and undesirable for breeding.

**Gait**—A bold, strong, driving free-swinging gait. The head is carried up and the tail "flags" constantly while the dog is in motion. When viewed from the front the forefeet move up and down in straight lines so that the shoulder, elbow and pastern joints are approximately in line. When viewed from the rear the hock, stifle and hip joints are approximately in line. Thus the dog moves in a straight pattern forward without throwing the feet in or out. When viewed from the side the forefeet are seen to lift up and reach forward to compensate for the driving hindquarters. The hindquarters reach well forward and stretch far back, enabling the stride to be long and the drive powerful. The overall appearance of the moving dog is one of smooth-flowing, well balanced rhythm, in which the action is pleasing to the eye, effortless, economical and harmonious.

**Temperament**—The Gordon Setter is alert, gay, interested, and confident. He is fearless and willing, intelligent and capable. He is loyal and affectionate, and strong-minded enough to stand the rigors of training.

## DISQUALIFICATION

*Predominantly tan, red or buff dogs.*

### Scale of Points

To be used as a guide when judging the Gordon Setter:

| | |
|---|---|
| Head and neck (include ears and eyes) | 10 |
| Body | 15 |
| Shoulders, forelegs, forefeet | 10 |
| Hind legs and feet | 10 |
| Tail | 5 |
| Coat | 8 |
| Color and markings | 5 |
| Temperament | 10 |
| Size, general appearance | 15 |
| Gait | 12 |
| **Total** | **100** |

**Approved October 7, 2002**
**Effective November 27, 2002**

# IRISH SETTER

HE IRISH SETTER FIRST CAME INTO POPULAR NOTICE EARLY IN THE EIGH-
teenth century and less than a hundred years later his reputation was firmly
established, not only in his native Ireland but throughout the British Isles. Specula-
tions as to his origin are little more than guesswork. Various breeds have been
named as his progenitors, but none can boast a clear title to the honor. Among the
conjectures is that he was developed from an Irish Water Spaniel–Irish Terrier cross,
but it is far more believable that an English Setter–spaniel-pointer combination,
with a dash of Gordon thrown in, was the true formula.

The Irish Red Setter was the name originally chosen by the Irish Setter Club
of America to designate the breed in this country. His earliest ancestors in the
Emerald Isle, on the contrary, were rarely self-colored dogs. By far the larger number were red and white, the white frequently predominating over the red, and even
today many individuals across the water are parti-colored. In America, however,
solid reds or reds with small and inconspicuous white markings are the only ones
accepted as typical. The Irishman's rich mahogany coat is thoroughly distinctive
and has done much to make its wearer the show-ring favorite he is today.

The solid-red setter, as distinguished from the red and white, first appeared in
Ireland in the nineteenth century. Jason Hazzard of Timaskea, County Fermanagh,
Sir St. George Gore, and the Earl of Enniskillen all bred self-colored dogs, and it is

a matter of record that in 1812 the earl would have nothing else in his kennels. A few years later Stonehenge wrote:

> The blood red, or rich chestnut or mahogany color is the color of an Irish Setter of high mark. This color must be unmixed with black; and studied in a strong light, there must not be black shadows or waves, much less black fringes to the ears, or to the profile of the form.

The mention of black in the above is significant as indicating the possibility of the Gordon cross already mentioned. Today, this color is absolutely taboo and even a few black hairs are faulted at the shows.

So much for the external appearance of the Irish Setter. Now for more important if less obvious characteristics. The breed is essentially a sporting one, and it is as a gundog, after all, that this flashy red fellow must stand or fall. The first individuals imported into this country were brought over for use on game and, in spite of the fact that our ruffed grouse, quail, and prairie chicken were new and strange to them, they made good immediately. Elcho, imported in 1875 and one of the first of his breed to make a reputation for himself and his progeny in the United States, was not only a sensational success on the bench, but a thoroughly trained and capable shooting dog. To quote A. F. Hochwalt, in his book *The Modern Setter,* "All through the early field-trial records we find the Irish Setter holding his own with the 'fashionable blue bloods.' Had the Irish Setter fanciers continued on, their favorite breed would no doubt now be occupying a place as high in field trials as the other two breeds"; by which he means, of course, the English Setter and Pointer.

But the Irish Setter men didn't continue on, insofar as field trials were concerned, with the result that the Llewellin Setter and the Pointer have practically cornered the market in public competition in that field. Yet, in spite of this handicap, the red dog from Erin has lost none of the attributes of the good hunting companion, and given a fair chance, can and does demonstrate his quality as a high–class gundog on all kinds of game. Strange as it may seem, his good looks have been his undoing in a way. His fatal gift of beauty, together with his gaiety, courage, and personality, have made him an ideal show dog. For this reason many fanciers have yielded to the temptation to breed for the ring only and to sacrifice to this most worthwhile object, field ability equally worthwhile and in no way incompatible with proper color, good size, and correct breed type.

Just a word regarding the characteristic personality of the red dog. There is a devil-may-care something about him that not only makes him tremendously likeable but also adds to his value as a bird dog in rough country and briers. He is bold and at the same time gentle and lovable and loyal. He is tough—good and tough. He can stand continued work in the brush, is almost never stiff or sore, has the best of feet and running gear, and almost never gets "sour" when corrected in his work.

He is not an early developer and frequently requires more training than some other breeds, but he is not as a rule headstrong in the sense that he is hard to handle in the brush. His outstanding fault as a field-trial performer is that he is not independent enough and pays too much attention to his handler. In reply to the criticism that he develops slowly, it is only fair to say that, once trained on birds, he is trained for the rest of his life and does not require a repetition of the process every fall. When you own a good Irishman, you own him for many years, every day of which you can be proud of his appearance, his personality, and his performance.

# OFFICIAL STANDARD FOR THE IRISH SETTER

**General Appearance**—The Irish Setter is an active, aristocratic bird dog, rich red in color, substantial yet elegant in build. Standing over two feet tall at the shoulder, the dog has a straight, fine, glossy coat, longer on ears, chest, tail and back of legs. Afield, the Irish Setter is a swift-moving hunter; at home, a sweet natured, trainable companion.

At their best, the lines of the Irish Setter so satisfy in overall balance that artists have termed it the most beautiful of all dogs. The correct specimen always exhibits balance, whether standing or in motion. Each part of the dog flows and fits smoothly into its neighboring parts without calling attention to itself.

**Size, Proportion, Substance**—There is no disqualification as to size. The make and fit of all parts and their overall balance in the animal are rated more important. 27 inches at the withers and a show weight of about 70 pounds is considered ideal for the dog; the bitch 25 inches, 60 pounds. Variance beyond an inch up or down is to be discouraged. *Proportion*—Measuring from the breastbone to rear of thigh and from the top of the withers to the ground, the Irish Setter is slightly longer than it is tall. *Substance*—All legs sturdy with plenty of bone. Structure in the male reflects masculinity without coarseness. Bitches appear feminine without being slight of bone.

**Head**—Long and lean, its length at least double the width between the ears. Beauty of head is emphasized by delicate chiseling along the muzzle, around and below the eyes, and along the cheeks. *Expression* soft, yet alert. *Eyes* somewhat almond shaped, of medium size, placed rather well apart, neither deep-set nor bulging. Color, dark to medium brown. *Ears* set well back and low, not above level of eye. Leather thin, hanging in a neat fold close to the head, and nearly long enough to reach the nose. The *skull* is oval when viewed from above or front; very slightly domed when viewed in profile. The brow is raised, showing a distinct stop midway between the tip of the nose and the well-defined occiput (rear point of skull). Thus the nearly level line from occiput to brow is set a little above, and parallel to, the straight and equal line from eye to nose. *Muzzle* moderately deep, jaws of nearly equal length, the underline of the jaws being almost parallel with the topline of the muzzle. *Nose* black or chocolate; nostrils wide. Upper lips fairly square but not pendulous. The *teeth* meet in a scissors bite in which the upper incisors fit closely over the lower, or they may meet evenly.

**Neck, Topline, Body**—*Neck* moderately long, strong but not thick, and slightly arched; free from throatiness and fitting smoothly into the shoulders. *Topline* of body from withers to tail should be firm and incline slightly downward without sharp drop at the croup. The *tail* is set on nearly level with the croup as a natural extension of the topline, strong at root, tapering to a fine point, nearly long enough to reach the hock. Carriage straight or curving slightly upward, nearly level with the back. *Body* sufficiently long to permit a straight and free stride. *Chest* deep, reaching approximately to the elbows with moderate forechest, extending beyond the point where the shoulder joins the upper arm. Chest is of moderate width so that it does not interfere with forward motion and extends rearward to well sprung ribs. *Loins* firm, muscular, and of moderate length.

**Forequarters**—Shoulder blades long, wide, sloping well back, fairly close together at the withers. Upper arm and shoulder blades are approximately the same length, and are joined at sufficient angle to bring the elbows rearward along the brisket in line with the top of the withers. The elbows moving freely, incline neither in nor out. *Forelegs* straight and sinewy. Strong, nearly straight pastern. *Feet* rather small, very firm, toes arched and close.

**Hindquarters**—Hindquarters should be wide and powerful with broad, well-developed thighs. Hind legs long and muscular from hip to hock; short and perpendicular from hock to ground; well angulated at stifle and hock joints, which, like the elbows, incline neither in nor out. Feet as in front. Angulation of the forequarters and hindquarters should be balanced.

**Coat**—Short and fine on head and forelegs. On all other parts of moderate length and flat. Feathering long and silky on ears; on back of forelegs and thighs long and fine, with a pleasing fringe of hair on belly and brisket extending onto the chest. Fringe on tail moderately long and tapering. All coat and feathering as straight and free as possible from curl or wave. The Irish Setter is trimmed for the show ring to emphasize the lean head and clean neck. The top third of the ears and the throat nearly to the breastbone are trimmed. Excess feathering is removed to show the natural outline of the foot. All trimming is done to preserve the natural appearance of the dog.

**Color**—Mahogany or rich chestnut red with no black. A small amount of white on chest, throat or toes, or a narrow centered streak on skull is not to be penalized.

**Gait**—At the trot the gait is big, very lively, graceful and efficient. At an extended trot the head reaches slightly forward, keeping the dog in balance. The forelegs reach well ahead as if to pull in the ground without giving the appearance of a hackney gait. The hindquarters drive smoothly and with great power. Seen from front or rear, the forelegs, as well as the hind legs below the hock joint, move perpendicularly to the ground, with some tendency toward a single track as speed increases. Structural characteristics which interfere with a straight, true stride are to be penalized.

**Temperament**—The Irish Setter has a rollicking personality. Shyness, hostility or timidity are uncharacteristic of the breed. An outgoing, stable temperament is the essence of the Irish Setter.

**Approved August 14, 1990**
**Effective September 30, 1990**

# AMERICAN WATER SPANIEL

*E*XACTLY HOW, WHEN, AND WHERE THE AMERICAN WATER SPANIEL ORIGInated is something of a mystery. Nevertheless, the virtues of the breed have long been appreciated by sportsmen in many parts of the United States. It is principally in the Midwest, however, that the present-day specimen evolved, since the dogs from that section had been known to breed true to type for countless generations. Color, coat, and conformation combine to suggest the Irish Water Spaniel and the Curly-Coated Retriever, together with the latter's forebear the old English Water Spaniel, as progenitors, although this cannot be advanced categorically.

Before recognition by the American Kennel Club in 1940, the American Water Spaniel had been purely a working gundog. He had never been introduced to the show ring since his admirers evidently feared that bench shows might damage his prowess as a hunter. But they were soon to learn that selective breeding along with show-ring competition actually enhances the value of a dog no matter how well that dog may have been endowed by nature.

As a retriever the American Water Spaniel leaves little to be desired. He will watch the huntsman drop perhaps four or five birds, then work swiftly and merrily until every one is brought in. Rabbits, chickens, grouse, quail, pheasant, ducks—he handles all with unfailing dispatch and tender care. He swims "like a seal," hence few wounded waterfowl escape him; his tail serves as a rudder to aid him, especially in turbulent water.

He is, as well, an all-around shooting dog possessed of an excellent nose; he works thicket, rough ground, or covert depending on body scent for location of game. His enthusiasm and thoroughness are an inspiration to the huntsman, while his desire to please makes him easily taught. He learns quickly to drop to shot and wing, although occasionally his eagerness may render him overanxious. He does not point game; instead, he springs it. In addition, he is an efficient watchdog who fits agreeably into the family circle.

# OFFICIAL STANDARD FOR THE AMERICAN WATER SPANIEL

**General Appearance**—The American Water Spaniel was developed in the United States as an all-around hunting dog, bred to retrieve from skiff or canoes and work ground with relative ease. The American Water Spaniel is an active muscular dog, medium in size with a marcel to curly coat. Emphasis is placed on proper size and a symmetrical relationship of parts, texture of coat and color.

**Size, Proportion, Substance**—15 to 18 inches for either sex. Males weighing 30 to 45 lbs. Females weighing 25 to 40 lbs. Females tend to be slightly smaller than the males. There is no preference for size within the given range of either sex providing correct proportion, good substance and balance are maintained. *Proportion* is slightly longer than tall, not too square or compact. However, exact proportion is not as important as the dog being well-balanced and sound, capable of performing the breed's intended function. *Substance,* a solidly built and well-muscled dog full of strength and quality. The breed has as much substance and bone as necessary to carry the muscular structure but not so much as to appear clumsy.

**Head**—The head must be in proportion to the overall dog. Moderate in length. *Expression* is alert, self-confident, attractive and intelligent. Medium size *eyes* set well apart, while slightly rounded, should not appear protruding or bulging. Lids tight, not drooping. Eye color can range from a light yellowish brown to brown, hazel or of dark tone to harmonize with coat. Disqualify yellow eyes. Yellow eyes are a bright color like that of lemon, not to be confused with the light yellowish brown. *Ears* set slightly above the eye line but not too high on the head, lobular, long and wide with leather extending to nose.

*Skull* rather broad and full, *stop* moderately defined, but not too pronounced. *Muzzle* moderate in length, square with good depth. No inclination to snipiness. The lips are clean and tight without excess skin or flews. Nose dark in color, black or dark brown. The nose sufficiently wide and with well-developed nostrils to insure good scenting power. *Bite* either scissors or level.

**Neck, Topline, Body**—*Neck* round and of medium length, strong and muscular, free of throatiness, set to carry head with dignity, but arch not accentuated. *Topline* level or slight, straight slope from withers. *Body* well-developed, sturdily constructed but not too compactly coupled. Well-developed brisket extending to elbow neither too broad nor too narrow. The ribs well-sprung, but not so well-sprung that they interfere with the movement of the front assembly. The loins strong, but not having a tucked-up look. *Tail* is moderate in length, curved in a rocker fashion, can be carried either slightly below or above the level of the back. The tail is tapered, lively and covered with hair with moderate feathering.

**Forequarters**—Shoulders sloping, clean and muscular. Legs medium in length, straight and well-boned but not so short as to handicap for field work or so heavy as to appear clumsy. Pasterns strong with no suggestion of weakness. Toes closely grouped, webbed and well-padded. Size of feet to harmonize with size of dog. Front dewclaws are permissible.

**Hindquarters**—Well-developed hips and thighs with the whole rear assembly showing strength and drive. The hock joint slightly rounded, should not be small and sharp in contour, moderately angulated. Legs from hock joint to foot pad moderate in length, strong and straight with good bone structure. Hocks parallel.

**Coat**—Coat can range from marcel (uniform waves) to closely curled. The amount of waves or curls can vary from one area to another on the dog. It is important to have undercoat to provide sufficient density to be of protection against weather, water or punishing cover, yet not too coarse or too soft. The throat, neck and rear of the dog well-covered with hair. The ear well-covered with hair on both sides with ear canal evident upon inspection. Forehead covered with short smooth hair and without topknot. Tail covered with hair to tip with moderate feathering. Legs have moderate feathering with waves or curls to harmonize with coat of dog. Coat may be trimmed to present a well-groomed appearance; the ears may be shaved; but neither is required.

**Color**—Color either solid liver, brown or dark chocolate. A little white on toes and chest permissible.

**Gait**—The American Water Spaniel moves with well-balanced reach and drive. Watching a dog move toward one, there should be no signs of elbows being out. Upon viewing the dog from the rear, one should get the impression that the hind legs, which should be well-muscled and not cow-hocked, move as nearly parallel as possible, with hocks doing their full share of work and flexing well, thus giving the appearance of power and strength.

**Temperament**—Demeanor indicates intelligence, eagerness to please and friendly. Great energy and eagerness for the hunt yet controllable in the field.

## DISQUALIFICATION

*Yellow eyes.*

**Approved March 13, 1990**
**Effective May 1, 1990**

# CLUMBER SPANIEL

*T*HE HISTORY OF THE CLUMBER SPANIEL HAS BEEN MARKED BY COLORFUL tales of dukes, escapes across the English Channel from the French Revolution, and fanciful crossbreeding. There is, however, no factual basis for the previously most prevalent story and only speculation about the true origin of the breed. We do hope that in the near future DNA analysis will determine from what canine combinations this wonderful breed has evolved. It is the current thinking that those who actually dealt with and hunted with the dogs in the latter part of the eighteenth and first half of the nineteenth century, such as the gamekeepers, combined dogs whose functions fit their demands.

It is true that the breed name derives from the Duke of Newcastle's estate at Clumber Park in Nottinghamshire, England. A number of titled families and landed gentry living in that area, known as the Dukeries, hunted with these Clumber Spaniels. Certainly there are records of Clumber breedings between these owners' dogs. It has been theorized that the duke's gamekeeper was himself responsible for the development of this breed. It is known that he and his descendants worked in that area for many years with a significant number of hunting spaniels.

Many vintage paintings feature Clumbers in hunting situations. It is interesting to note that the dogs closely resemble today's, with a little less bone and smaller heads. The color pattern evident in almost all old pictorial records is white and orange, even though early standards and written descriptions mention a preference for lemon.

Clumber Spaniels were first shown in England in 1859. The breed arrived in North America relatively early, entering Canada in 1844 with Lieutenant Venables of Her Majesty's 97th Regiment, stationed in Halifax, Nova Scotia. The first Clumber Spaniel registered with the American Kennel Club is recorded for 1878, six years before the establishment of the AKC. (The records of dog breeding in the United States existed long before the AKC's founding, and three volumes of studbooks were accepted by the AKC as the basis for its Stud Book Register, maintained continuously since 1887.)

The Clumber Spaniel is described as dignified, charming, loving, entertaining, inquisitive, affectionate, intelligent, gentle, mischievous, stubborn, determined, self-willed, appealing, and naughty. The Clumber is a loyal dog, good with children and amiable with other animals. His happy personality and perceptive intelligence make him a much-loved member of the family. The hallmark of the breed is his sweet and gentle temperament.

The Clumber thrives on attention. Most Clumbers love to fetch, so they are not difficult to exercise or keep amused. They also like to carry things in their mouths, often picking something off the floor when greeting, all the while dancing a little jig. While Clumbers like nothing better than a walk with their master, they are not the breed of choice for people who wish to run or jog long distances with their pet.

The Clumber Spaniel responds to positive reinforcement and praise. Most Clumbers are readily trained, but harsh training methods are usually ineffective with this sensitive breed.

Some important consideration should be given to shedding and slobbering in the Clumber. You should be aware that males develop luxurious coats on the belly and in front of the rear legs (not to mention the skirt around the rear and the ruff on the chest). Females are often less coated in the chest, but they have abundant skirting and belly hair. They will grow a profuse coat (especially in cold temperatures), and that coat will shed moderately all year round. Also, the correct Clumber has a big head with a broad topskull, well-developed flews, and plenty of lip. That often means many Clumbers slobber and drool, not as much as a Mastiff or Saint Bernard, but certainly more than many other breeds with tighter lips.

Some Clumbers run to meet every visitor, but occasionally you may find them initially reticent with strangers—never shy or aggressive, but dignified. They tend to be poor watchdogs because they generally do not bark at everything. Their friendly, all-accepting personality makes them poor candidates for guarding.

The Clumber is a rather slow worker, moving with a distinctive rolling, comfortable gait that can be maintained at steady trot for a day's work in the field without exhaustion. He is particularly adaptable for use in heavy cover; he generally hunts mute and is able to come up very close to the game. He is a sure finder and a splendid retriever when trained.

# OFFICIAL STANDARD FOR THE CLUMBER SPANIEL

**General Appearance**—The Clumber Spaniel is a long, low, substantial dog. His heavy brow, deep chest, straight forelegs, powerful hindquarters, massive bone and good feet all give him the power and endurance to move through dense underbrush in pursuit of game. His white coat enables him to be seen by the hunter as he works within gun range. His stature is dignified, his expression pensive, but at the same time he shows great enthusiasm for work and play.

**Size, Proportion, Substance**—The Clumber is rectangular in shape possessing massive bone structure and has the appearance of great power. The ideal height for dogs is 18 to 20 inches at the withers and for bitches is 17 to 19 inches at the withers. The ideal length to height is 11 to 9 measured from the withers to the base of the tail and from the floor to the withers. Dogs weigh between 70 and 85 pounds and bitches weigh between 55 and 70 pounds.

**Head**—The head is massive with a marked stop and heavy brow. The top skull is flat with a pronounced occiput. A slight furrow runs between the eyes and up through the center of the skull. The *muzzle* is broad and deep to facilitate retrieving many species of game. The *nose* is large, square and colored shades of brown, which include beige, rose and cherry. The *flews* of the upper jaw are strongly developed and overlap the lower jaw to give a square look when viewed from the side. A scissors bite is preferred. The *eyes* are dark amber in color, large, soft in expression, and deep set in either a diamond shaped rim or a rim with a "V" on the bottom and a curve on the top. Some haw may show but excessive haw is undesirable. Prominent or round shaped eyes are to be penalized. Excessive tearing or evidence of entropion or ectropion is to be penalized. *Ears* are broad on top with thick ear leather. The ears are triangular in shape with a rounded lower edge, set low and attached to the skull at approximately eye level.

**Neck, Topline, Body**—The Clumber should have a long neck with some slackness of throat or presence of dewlap not to be faulted. The *neck* is strong and muscular, fitting into a well laid back shoulder. The *back* is straight, firm, long and level. The brisket is deep and the ribs well sprung. The *chest* is deep and wide. The loin arches slightly. The *tail* is well feathered and set on just below the line of back; its trimming minimal, serving to tidy the feathering to allow for a natural appearance and outline. The tail is normally carried level with the topline or slightly elevated, never down between the rear legs. The tail may be docked or left natural, both being of equal value. If docked, the tail's length should be in keeping with the overall proportion of the adult dog. If natural, the tailbone should extend to the point of hock, but should not extend to the ground.

**Forequarters**—The Clumber *shoulder* is well laid back. The *upper arm* is of sufficient length to place the elbow under the highest point of the shoulder. The *forelegs* are short, straight and heavy in bone, with elbows held close to the body. *Pasterns* are strong and only slightly sloped. The front *feet* are large, compact and have thick pads that act as shock absorbers. Removal of dewclaws is optional.

**Hindquarters**—The *thighs* are heavily muscled and, when viewed from behind, the rear is round and broad. The *stifle* shows good functional angulation, and hock to heel is short and perpendicular to the ground. Lack of angulation is objectionable. The *rear feet* are not as large or as round as on the front feet but compact, with thick pads and are of substantial size.

**Coat**—The body coat is dense, straight and flat. It is of good weather resistant texture, which is soft to the touch, not harsh. Ears are slightly feathered with straight hair. Feathering on the legs and belly is moderate. The Clumber has a good neck frill and on no condition should his throat be shaved. Evidence of shaving is to be penalized. The hair on the feet should be trimmed neatly to show their natural outline and for utility in the field. The rear legs may be trimmed up to the point of the hock. Tail feathering may be tidied. Trimming of whiskers is optional.

**Color and Markings**—The Clumber is primarily a white dog with lemon color or orange color markings. Markings are frequently seen on one or both ears and the face. Facial markings include color around one or both eyes, freckling on the muzzle and a spot on top of the head. A head with lemon/orange markings and an all-white head are of equal value. Freckles on the legs and/or a spot near the root of the tail are also frequently seen and acceptable. The body should have as few markings as possible.

**Gait**—The Clumber moves easily and freely with good reach in front and strong drive from behind, neither crossing over nor elbowing out. The hocks drive in a straight line without rocking or twisting. Because of his wide body and short legs he tends to roll slightly. The proper Clumber roll occurs when the dog, with the correct proportion, reaches forward with the rear leg toward the centerline of travel and rotates the hip downward while the back remains level and straight. The gait is comfortable and can be maintained at a steady trot for a day of work in the field without exhaustion.

**Temperament**—The Clumber Spaniel is a gentle, loyal and affectionate dog. He possesses an intrinsic desire to please. An intelligent and independent thinker, he displays determination and a strong sense of purpose while at work. A dog of dignity, the Clumber Spaniel may sometimes seem aloof with people unknown to him, but in time he will display his playful and loving nature. The Clumber Spaniel should never be hostile or aggressive; neither is acceptable and should not be condoned.

**Approved January 8, 2001**
**Effective March 28, 2001**

# COCKER SPANIEL

*Black*

---

$\mathscr{T}$ HE COCKER SPANIEL IS THE SMALLEST OF THE SPORTING SPANIELS. TRAINABLE, with stamina and intelligence, Cockers have a unique capacity to connect with humans. This deep sensitivity is reflected in their dark eyes, which quickly capture the imagination and hearts of people everywhere.

The breed emerged from a general spaniel population in the late 1800s. Early English dog shows presented them as "Field Spaniels" and subsequently offered classes for "other small breeds of Spaniels," where "Cocker Spaniels" were then shown.

In 1883, the Ashton show in England included a class for Cocker Spaniels for the first time. This is where the breed founders were exhibited. Soon after, The Kennel Club (England) recognized Cocker Spaniels in their studbooks and, based on weight, distinguished them from other spaniels. Cockers could be any color but could not exceed twenty-five pounds.

During this period Cocker Spaniels were imported to the United States and Canada, and were shown in North America for the first time at Massachusetts in 1875. Since then, the breed has evolved from a longer-backed, shorter-legged dog to one with a shorter back and longer leg. The slightly taller, shorter-backed dog was developed to provide more flexibility in the field.

The Cocker Spaniel is a flushing dog, one that works closely with a hunter. The breed's function is to find and flush game birds into the air so they can be shot. The dog then finds the fallen bird and gently brings it back to the hunter. Using its

*ASCOB*

*Parti-Color*

nose and compact body, the Cocker probes into brush and grasses too thick for larger spaniels. Cockers are often used to work the edges of woods, but are also fine flushers on savannas. Cocker Spaniels quarter land, using wind and ground scents to find game. As capable swimmers, Cockers will retrieve from the water or cross water and land barriers in order to find and bring back a fallen bird.

The multifaceted Cocker Spaniel is seen performing well in many sports. From the exquisite conformation dog to the fine gundog and competitor in field trials, Cocker Spaniels truly exemplify form following function. They are also good contenders in companion events, and are increasingly seen as therapy dogs at rehabilitation centers, schools, and nursing homes.

From the moment the Cocker Spaniel appeared as a distinct breed, its playful, affectionate personality; soft, silky coat; and large, dark eyes captured hearts. The breed's intelligent, gentle nature, together with an impish playfulness, continue to enchant and delight people who pause to experience the depth reflected in those wonderful Cocker Spaniel eyes.

# OFFICIAL STANDARD FOR THE COCKER SPANIEL

**General Appearance**—The Cocker Spaniel is the smallest member of the Sporting Group. He has a sturdy, compact body and a cleanly chiseled and refined head, with the overall dog in complete balance and of ideal size. He stands well up at the shoulder on straight forelegs with a topline sloping slightly toward strong, moderately bent, muscular quarters. He is a dog capable of considerable speed, combined with great endurance. Above all, he must be free and merry, sound, well balanced throughout and in action show a keen inclination to work. A dog well balanced in all parts is more desirable than a dog with strongly contrasting good points and faults.

**Size, Proportion, Substance**—*Size*—The ideal height at the withers for an adult dog is 15 inches and for an adult bitch, 14 inches. Height may vary one-half inch above or below this ideal. A dog whose height exceeds 15½ inches or a bitch whose height exceeds 14½ inches shall be disqualified. An adult dog whose height is less than 14½ inches and an adult bitch whose height is less than 13½ inches shall be penalized. Height is determined by a line perpendicular to the ground from the top of the shoulder blades, the dog standing naturally with its forelegs and lower hind legs parallel to the line of measurement. *Proportion*—The measurement from the breast bone to back of thigh is slightly longer than the measurement from the highest point of withers to the ground. The body must be of sufficient length to permit a straight and free stride; the dog never appears long and low.

**Head**—To attain a well proportioned head, which must be in balance with the rest of the dog, it embodies the following: *Expression*—The expression is intelligent, alert, soft and appealing. *Eyes*—Eyeballs are round and full and look directly forward. The shape of the eye rims gives a slightly almond shaped appearance; the eye is not weak or goggled. The color of the iris is dark brown and in general the darker the better. *Ears*—Lobular, long, of fine leather, well feathered, and placed no higher than a line to the lower part of the eye. *Skull*—Rounded but not exaggerated with no tendency toward flatness; the eyebrows are clearly defined with a pronounced stop. The bony structure beneath the eyes is well chiseled with no prominence in the cheeks. The muzzle is broad and deep, with square even jaws. To be in correct balance, the distance from the stop to the tip of the nose is one half the distance from the stop up over the crown to the base of the skull. *Nose*—Of sufficient size to balance the muzzle and foreface, with well developed nostrils typical of a sporting dog. It is black in color in the blacks, black and tans, and black and whites; in other colors it may be brown, liver or black, the darker the better. The color of nose harmonizes with the color of the eye rim. *Lips*—The upper lip is full and of sufficient depth to cover the lower jaw. *Teeth*—Teeth strong and sound, not too small and meet in a scissors bite.

**Neck, Topline, Body**—*Neck*—The neck is sufficiently long to allow the nose to reach the ground easily, muscular and free from pendulous "throatiness." It rises strongly from the shoulders and arches slightly as it tapers to join the head. *Topline*—Sloping slightly toward muscular quarters. *Body*—The chest is deep, its lowest point no higher than the elbows, its front sufficiently wide for adequate heart and lung space, yet not so wide as to interfere with the straightforward movement of the forelegs. Ribs are deep and well sprung. Back is strong and sloping evenly and slightly downward from the shoulders to the set-on of the docked tail. The docked tail is set on and carried on a line with the topline of the back, or slightly higher; never straight up like a Terrier and never so low as to indicate timidity. When the dog is in motion the tail action is merry.

**Forequarters**—The shoulders are well laid back forming an angle with the upper arm of approximately 90 degrees, which permits the dog to move his forelegs in an easy manner with forward reach. Shoulders are clean-cut and sloping without protrusion and so set that the upper points of the withers are at an angle which permits a wide spring of rib. When viewed from the side with the forelegs vertical, the elbow is directly below the highest point of the shoulder blade. Forelegs are parallel, straight, strongly boned and muscular and set close to the body well under the scapulae. The pasterns are short and strong. Dewclaws on forelegs may be removed. Feet compact, large, round and firm with horny pads; they turn neither in nor out.

**Hindquarters**—Hips are wide and quarters well rounded and muscular. When viewed from behind, the hind legs are parallel when in motion and at rest. The hind legs are strongly boned, and muscled with moderate angulation at the stifle and powerful, clearly defined thighs. The stifle is strong and there is no slippage of it in motion or when standing. The hocks are strong and well let down. Dewclaws on hind legs may be removed.

**Coat**—On the head, short and fine; on the body, medium length, with enough undercoating to give protection. The ears, chest, abdomen and legs are well feathered, but not so excessively as to hide the Cocker Spaniel's true lines and movement or affect his appearance and function as a moderately coated sporting dog. The texture is most important. The coat is silky, flat or slightly wavy and of a texture which permits easy care. Excessive coat or curly or cottony textured coat shall be severely penalized. Use of electric clippers on the back coat is not desirable. Trimming to enhance the dog's true lines should be done to appear as natural as possible.

**Color and Markings**—*Black Variety*—Solid color black to include black with tan points. The black should be jet; shadings of brown or liver in the coat are not desirable. A small amount of white on the chest and/or throat is allowed; white in any other location shall disqualify.

*Any Solid Color Other than Black (ASCOB)*—Any solid color other than black, ranging from lightest cream to darkest red, including brown and brown with tan points. The color shall be of a uniform shade, but lighter color of the feathering is permissible. A small amount of white on the chest and/or throat is allowed; white in any other location shall disqualify.

*Parti-Color Variety*—Two or more solid, well broken colors, one of which must be white; black and white, red and white (the red may range from lightest cream to darkest red), brown and white, and roans, to include any such color combination with tan points. It is preferable that the tan markings be located in the same pattern as for the tan points in the Black and ASCOB varieties. Roans are classified as parti-colors and may be of any of the usual roaning patterns. Primary color which is ninety percent (90%) or more shall disqualify.

*Tan Points*—The color of the tan may be from the lightest cream to the darkest red and is restricted to ten percent (10%) or less of the color of the specimen; tan markings in excess of that amount shall disqualify. In the case of tan points in the Black or ASCOB variety, the markings shall be located as follows:

1) A clear tan spot over each eye;
2) On the sides of the muzzle and on the cheeks;
3) On the underside of the ears;
4) On all feet and/or legs;
5) Under the tail;
6) On the chest, optional; presence or absence shall not be penalized.

Tan markings which are not readily visible or which amount only to traces, shall be penalized. Tan on the muzzle which extends upward, over and joins shall also be penalized. The absence of tan markings in the Black or ASCOB variety in any of the specified locations in any otherwise tan-pointed dog shall disqualify.

**Gait**—The Cocker Spaniel, though the smallest of the sporting dogs, possesses a typical sporting dog gait. Prerequisite to good movement is balance between the front and rear assemblies. He drives with strong, powerful rear quarters and is properly constructed in the shoulders and forelegs so that he can reach forward without constriction in a full stride to counterbalance the driving force from the rear. Above all, his gait is coordinated, smooth and effortless. The dog must cover ground with his action; excessive animation should not be mistaken for proper gait.

**Temperament**—Equable in temperament with no suggestion of timidity.

## DISQUALIFICATIONS

*Height*—Males over 15½ inches; females over 14½ inches.
*Color and Markings*—The aforementioned colors are the only acceptable colors or combination of colors. Any other colors or combination of colors to disqualify.

*Black Variety—White markings except on chest and throat.*
*Any Solid Color Other than Black Variety—White markings except on chest and throat.*
*Parti-color Variety—Primary color ninety percent (90%) or more.*
*Tan Points—(1) Tan markings in excess of ten percent (10%); (2) Absence of tan markings in Black or ASCOB Variety in any of the specified locations in an otherwise tan pointed dog.*

**Approved May 12, 1992**
**Effective June 30, 1992**

# ENGLISH COCKER SPANIEL

$\mathcal{O}$NE OF THE OLDEST KNOWN TYPES OF LAND SPANIELS, THE COCKER SPANIEL descended from the original spaniels of Spain as one of a family of breeds destined to become highly diversified in size, type, coloring, and hunting ability.

Before the seventeenth century, all members of this group were designated merely as spaniels, whether they were large or small, long bodied or short, fast or slow on their feet. Gradually, the marked size difference began to impress those who used these dogs for hunting. Soon, the larger dogs were springing game and the smaller ones were hunting woodcock. The names Springer Spaniel, and Cocker or Woodcock Spaniel, naturally followed. In 1892, The Kennel Club (England) finally recognized them as separate breeds. The larger dog is the English Cocker Spaniel.

The Springers and Cockers described above, both before and after the date of their official separation in England, appeared in the same litters. Size alone was the dividing line between them. They enjoyed the same heritage, the same colorings, the same hunting skill, and much the same general type. Cocker and Springer developed side by side. In fact, Springer inheritance, naturally incorporated in the Cocker, was a fortunate directive for the success of English Cockers, for it enabled them to become one of the finest of the smaller hunting dogs.

Exhaustive research disclosed that during the nineteenth century there were two other lines of Cocker development. One involved the dogs known as Field or Cocker Spaniels. These eventually branched out into Sussex, Field, and Cocker

Spaniels, the latter weighing less than twenty-five pounds and usually being black in color. The other line involved spaniels from the House of Marlborough, of which there were two types: a small, round-headed, short-nosed, red-and-white dog and a slightly larger dog with shorter ears and a longer foreface. The Marlborough Cocker eventually became the English Toy Spaniel, but before they emerged as a distinct breed, they were combined with smaller cockers of partial Field Spaniel derivation. From these two lines came a spaniel approximating the size and type fancied by American importers of that time.

The English Cocker Spaniel Club of America was formed June 20, 1936, "to foster the interests of the English Cocker Spaniel." The English Cocker had already been recognized as a variety of the Cocker Spaniel by action of the AKC Board of Directors on May 12, 1936, but not as a separate breed in its own right. The breed standard from England was adopted here as well. The club's first specialty show was held in conjunction with the 1937 Morris & Essex Kennel Club show.

The immediate aim of the club was to discourage interbreeding of the English and American varieties, which English Cocker fanciers considered detrimental to the type they sponsored. Separate classes for the English variety were provided at shows. Nevertheless, for some time, interbred English and American Cockers continued to compete side by side with pure English and pure American specimens. In fact, many an American Cocker was entered in the show ring as an English Cocker on the basis of larger size alone. The resulting confusion worked against the best interests of both varieties, but nothing could be done because no one knew which dogs were pure English, which were American, and which were a combination of the two.

Geraldine R. Dodge, then the parent club president, directed that an extensive pedigree search be made of Cockers in England, Canada, and the United States, going back to the beginning of official Cocker history abroad in 1892. This was done to distinguish the pure English lines of descent that were entirely devoid of American Cocker mixtures. In 1941, this information was finally obtained, and the English Cocker Spaniel Club was in a position to advise authoritatively on the problems of selection and breeding.

In 1940, the Canadian Kennel Club recognized the English Cocker Spaniel as a separate breed, as did the American Kennel Club in 1946. But because there was much to be done in order to comply with the provisions laid down for official certification of pedigrees, breed registrations did not appear in the AKC Stud Book under their own heading until January 1947.

# OFFICIAL STANDARD FOR THE ENGLISH COCKER SPANIEL

**General Appearance**—The English Cocker Spaniel is an active, merry sporting dog, standing well up at the withers and compactly built. He is alive with energy; his gait is powerful and frictionless, capable both of covering ground effortlessly and penetrating dense cover to flush and retrieve game. His enthusiasm in the field and the incessant action of his tail while at work indicate how much he enjoys the hunting for which he was bred. His head is especially characteristic. He is, above all, a dog of balance, both standing and moving, without exaggeration in any part, the whole worth more than the sum of its parts.

**Size, Proportion, Substance**—*Size*—Height at withers: males 16 to 17 inches; females 15 to 16 inches. Deviations to be penalized. The most desirable weights: males, 28 to 34 pounds; females, 26 to 32 pounds. Proper conformation and substance should be considered more important than weight alone. *Proportion*—Compactly built and short-coupled, with height at withers slightly greater than the distance from withers to set-on of tail. *Substance*—The English Cocker is a solidly built dog with as much bone and substance as is possible without becoming cloddy or coarse.

**Head**—General appearance: strong, yet free from coarseness, softly contoured, without sharp angles. Taken as a whole, the parts combine to produce the expression distinctive of the breed. *Expression*—Soft, melting, yet dignified, alert, and intelligent. *Eyes*—The eyes are essential to the desired expression. They are medium in size, full and slightly oval; set wide apart; lids tight. Haws are inconspicuous; may be pigmented or unpigmented. Eye color dark brown, except in livers and liver parti-colors where hazel is permitted, but the darker the hazel the better. *Ears*—Set low, lying close to the head; leather fine, extending to the nose, well covered with long, silky, straight or slightly wavy hair. *Skull*—Arched and slightly flattened when seen both from the side and from the front. Viewed in profile, the brow appears not appreciably higher than the back-skull. Viewed from above, the sides of the skull are in planes roughly parallel to those of the muzzle. Stop definite, but moderate, and slightly grooved. *Muzzle*—Equal in length to skull; well cushioned; only as much narrower than the skull as is consistent with a full eye placement; cleanly chiseled under the eyes. Jaws strong, capable of carrying game. Nostrils wide for proper development of scenting ability; color black, except in livers and parti-colors of that shade where they will be brown; reds and parti-colors of that shade may be brown, but black is preferred. Lips square, but not pendulous or showing prominent flews. *Bite*—Scissors. A level bite is not preferred. Overshot or undershot to be severely penalized.

**Neck, Topline and Body**—*Neck*—Graceful and muscular, arched toward the head and blending cleanly, without throatiness, into sloping shoulders; moderate in length and in balance with the length and height of the dog. *Topline*—The line of the neck blends into the shoulder and backline in a smooth curve. The backline slopes very slightly toward a gently rounded croup, and is free from sagging or rumpiness. *Body*—Compact and well-knit, giving the impression of strength without heaviness. Chest deep; not so wide as to interfere with action of forelegs, nor so narrow as to allow the front to appear narrow or pinched. Forechest well developed, prosternum projecting moderately beyond shoulder points. Brisket reaches to the elbow and slopes gradually to a moderate tuck-up. Ribs well sprung and springing gradually to mid-body, tapering to back ribs which are of good depth and extend well back. Back short and strong. Loin short, broad and very slightly arched, but not enough to affect the topline appreciably. Croup gently rounded, without any tendency to fall away sharply. *Tail*—Docked. Set on to conform to croup. Ideally, the tail is carried horizontally and is in constant motion while the dog is in action. Under excitement, the dog may carry his tail somewhat higher, but not cocked up.

**Forequarters**—The English Cocker is moderately angulated. Shoulders are sloping, the blade flat and smoothly fitting. Shoulder blade and upper arm are approximately equal in length. Upper arm set well back, joining the shoulder with sufficient angulation to place the elbow beneath the highest point of the shoulder blade when the dog is standing naturally. *Forelegs*—Straight, with bone nearly uniform in size from elbow to heel; elbows set close to the body; pasterns nearly straight, with some flexibility. *Feet*—Proportionate in size to the legs, firm, round and catlike; toes arched and tight; pads thick.

**Hindquarters**—Angulation moderate and, most importantly, in balance with that of the forequarters. Hips relatively broad and well rounded. Upper thighs broad, thick and muscular, providing plenty of propelling power. Second thighs well muscled and approximately equal in length to the upper. Stifle strong and well bent. Hock to pad short. Feet as in front.

**Coat**—On head, short and fine; of medium length on body; flat or slightly wavy; silky in texture. The English Cocker is well-feathered, but not so profusely as to interfere with field work. Trimming is permitted to remove overabundant hair and to enhance the dog's true lines. It should be done so as to appear as natural as possible.

**Color**—Various. Parti-colors are either clearly marked, ticked or roaned, the white appearing in combination with black, liver or shades of red. In parti-colors it is preferable that solid markings be broken on the body and more or less evenly distributed; absence of body markings is acceptable. Solid colors are black, liver or shades of red. White feet on a solid are undesirable; a little white on throat is acceptable; but in neither case do these white markings make the dog a parti-color. Tan markings, clearly defined and of rich shade, may appear in conjunction with black, livers and parti-color combinations of those colors. Black and tans and liver and tans are considered solid colors.

**Gait**—The English Cocker is capable of hunting in dense cover and upland terrain. His gait is accordingly characterized more by drive and the appearance of power than by great speed. He covers ground effortlessly and with extension both in front and in rear, appropriate to his angulation. In the ring, he carries his head proudly and is able to keep much the same topline while in action as when standing for examination. Going and coming, he moves in a straight line without crabbing or rolling, and with width between both front and rear legs appropriate to his build and gait.

**Temperament**—The English Cocker is merry and affectionate, of equable disposition, neither sluggish nor hyperactive, a willing worker and a faithful and engaging companion.

**Approved October 11, 1988**
**Effective November 30, 1988**

# ENGLISH SPRINGER SPANIEL

*F*OR MANY CENTURIES, SPANIELS HAVE BEEN ORGANIZED IN ART AND LITER-
ature as a clearly defined type of dog. They were originally used to flush
game for the net and the falcon, but the seventeenth-century invention of the
wheel-lock firearm forever transformed the English Springer Spaniel into the excellent upland game hunter that remains today.

First recognized as a distinct breed in 1902 by The Kennel Club (England), this
is "the gamekeeper's dog," whose purpose is to find, flush, and fetch game. Many
historic writings tell us that these great dogs worked, and still should work, tirelessly
in the field all day and then retire to the easy companionship of family, hearth, and
home after a good day's hunt.

Importation of English Springer Spaniels from England to Canada and the
United States began in earnest in the 1920s. The breed became better known after
1924, when the English Springer Spaniel Field Trial Association was formed and
field trials were inaugurated. Three years later, the ESSFTA became the breed's parent club.

In those early days, it was not unusual for Springers to compete successfully in
a field trial one day and the show ring the next. (It is to be hoped that such versatility might someday return.) Widely diverging competition goals have succeeded
in creating a "field" Springer and a "show" Springer. There is one breed standard,
and it describes the ideal conformation and unique traits of *all* English Springers.

Those new to the breed should study the differences in function and appearance that distinguish "field" from "show."

The English Springer Spaniel Field Trial Association promotes the breed in the field and in hunting tests, obedience trials, agility trials, and conformation competition. As the parent club, it maintains the AKC breed standard, which was most recently updated and approved in 1994. An illustrated standard that presents key aspects of breed history, type, and character has also been published. In 1996 the ESSFTA Foundation was founded as a tax-exempt charity with a separate board of directors. Since then, the foundation has raised significant funds from hundreds of Springer enthusiasts to address breed health and genetic issues. The foundation sponsors and presents educational programs and seminars on breed health and genetic issues. A joint committee of the parent club and the foundation has recently been established to collaborate on maintaining and preserving archival materials and items of importance to the breed's history.

Many of the English Springer Spaniel's unique type characteristics have continued unchanged through the centuries. Those characteristics include the breed's moderate size, substance, and overall balance; its beautifully chiseled and well-proportioned head, with lovely eye and expression; and a structure that supports a hard day's hunting. True spaniel character is the ideal hardy, efficient upland game hunter and the ideal kind, trusting family dog.

Coat texture is also of a unique type, having a firm topcoat and a protective undercoat. The breed's familiar colors are white coupled with black or liver. Either of those two colors may have tan points (tricolor). There is no preferred pattern of markings, and ticking is characteristic. Lemon, red, and orange do occur occasionally, but these colors are not preferred and should not place in conformation competition. English Springers have docked tails; a natural tail is considered a conformation fault, though not a disqualification.

Britain is the country of origin, though it is believed that the word *spaniel* may indicate that the breed had Spanish origins. The English Springer Spaniel Field Trial Association and the ESSFTA Foundation both enjoy a warm friendship and frequent exchanges with their counterparts in Britain, recognizing that common roots have given us this beautiful breed, and common goals will protect and preserve the breed for the future. All English Springer Spaniel enthusiasts, present and future, must thoroughly understand and appreciate the breed's true purpose as both companion and hunter, a member of the ancient and distinguished family of spaniels.

# OFFICIAL STANDARD FOR THE ENGLISH SPRINGER SPANIEL

**General Appearance**—The English Springer Spaniel is a medium-sized sporting dog, with a compact body and a docked tail. His coat is moderately long, with feathering on his legs, ears, chest and brisket. His pendulous ears, soft gentle expression, sturdy build and friendly wagging tail proclaim him unmistakably a member of the ancient family of Spaniels. He is above all a well-proportioned dog, free from exaggeration, nicely balanced in every part. His carriage is proud and upstanding, body deep, legs strong and muscular, with enough length to carry him with ease. Taken as a whole, the English Springer Spaniel suggests power, endurance and agility. He looks the part of a dog that can go, and keep going, under difficult hunting conditions. At his best, he is endowed with style, symmetry, balance and enthusiasm, and is every inch a sporting dog of distinct spaniel character, combining beauty and utility.

**Size, Proportion, Substance**—The Springer is built to cover rough ground with agility and reasonable speed. His structure suggests the capacity for endurance. He is to be kept to medium size. Ideal height at the shoulder for dogs is 20 inches; for bitches, it is 19 inches. Those more than one inch under or over the breed ideal are to be faulted. A 20-inch dog, well-proportioned and in good condition, will weigh approximately 50 pounds; a 19-inch bitch will weigh approximately 40 pounds. The length of the body (measured from point of shoulder to point of buttocks) is slightly greater than the height at the withers. The dog too long in body, especially when long in the loin, tires easily and lacks the compact outline characteristic of the breed. A dog too short in body for the length of his legs, a condition which destroys balance and restricts gait, is equally undesirable. A Springer with correct substance appears well-knit and sturdy with good bone, however, he is never coarse or ponderous.

**Head**—The head is impressive without being heavy. Its beauty lies in a combination of strength and refinement. It is important that its size and proportion be in balance with the rest of the dog. Viewed in profile, the head appears approximately the same length as the neck and blends with the body in substance. The stop, eyebrows and chiseling of the bony structure around the eye sockets contribute to the Springer's beautiful and characteristic expression, which is alert, kindly and trusting. The eyes, more than any other feature, are the essence of the Springer's appeal. Correct size, shape, placement and color influence expression and attractiveness. The eyes are of medium size and oval in shape, set rather well-apart and fairly deep in their sockets. The color of the iris harmonizes with the color of the coat, preferably dark hazel in the liver and white dogs and black or deep brown in the black and white dogs. Eye rims are fully pigmented and match the coat in color. Lids are tight with little or no haw showing. Eyes that are small, round or protruding, as well as eyes that are yellow or brassy in color, are highly undesirable. Ears are long and fairly wide, hanging close to the cheeks with no tendency to stand up or out. The ear leather is thin and approximately long enough to reach the tip of the nose. Correct ear set is on a level with the eye and not too far back on the skull. The skull is medium-length and fairly broad, flat on top and slightly rounded at the sides and back. The occiput bone is inconspicuous. As the skull rises from the foreface, it makes a stop, divided by a groove, or fluting, between the eyes. The groove disappears as it reaches the middle of the forehead. The amount of stop is moderate. It must not be a pronounced feature; rather it is a subtle rise where the muzzle joins the upper head. It is emphasized by the groove and by the position and shape of the eyebrows, which are well-developed. The muzzle is approximately the same length as the skull and one half the width of the skull. Viewed in profile, the toplines of the skull and muzzle lie in approximately parallel planes. The nasal bone is straight, with no inclination downward toward the tip of the nose, the latter giving an undesirable downfaced look. Neither is the nasal bone concave, resulting in a "dish-faced" profile; nor convex, giving the dog a Roman nose. The cheeks are flat, and the face is well-chiseled under the eyes. Jaws are of sufficient length to allow the dog to carry game easily: fairly square, lean and strong. The upper lips come down full and rather square to cover the line of the lower jaw, however, the lips are never pendulous or exaggerated. The nose is fully-pigmented, liver or black in color, depending on the color of the coat. The nostrils are well-opened and broad. Teeth are strong, clean, of good size and ideally meet in a close scissors bite. An even bite or one or two incisors slightly out of line are minor faults. Undershot, overshot and wry jaws are serious faults and are to be severely penalized.

**Neck, Topline, Body**—The neck is moderately long, muscular, clean and slightly arched at the crest. It blends gradually and smoothly into sloping shoulders. The portion of the topline from withers to tail is firm and slopes very gently. The body is short-coupled, strong and compact. The chest is deep, reaching the level of the elbows, with well-developed forechest; however, it is not so wide or round as to interfere with the action of the front legs. Ribs are fairly long, springing gradually to the middle of the body, then tapering as they approach the end of the ribbed section. The underline stays level with the elbows to a slight upcurve at the flank. The back is straight, strong and essentially level. Loins are strong, short and slightly arched. Hips are nicely rounded, blending smoothly into the hind legs. The croup slopes gently to the set of the tail, and tail-set follows the natural line of the croup. The tail is carried horizontally or slightly elevated and displays a characteristic lively, merry action, particularly when the dog is on game. A clamped tail (indicating timidity or undependable temperament) is to be faulted, as is a tail carried at a right angle to the backline in Terrier fashion.

**Forequarters**—Efficient movement in front calls for proper forequarter assembly. The shoulder blades are flat and fairly close together at the tips, molding smoothly into the contour of the body. Ideally, when measured from the top of the withers to the point of the shoulder to the elbow, the shoulder blade and upper arm are of apparent equal length, forming an angle of nearly 90 degrees; this sets the front legs well under the body and places the elbows directly beneath the tips of the shoulder blades. Elbows lie close to the body. Forelegs are straight with the same degree of size continuing to the foot. Bone is strong, slightly flattened, not too round or too heavy. Pasterns are short, strong and slightly sloping, with no suggestion of weakness. Dewclaws are usually removed. Feet are round or slightly oval. They are compact and well-arched, of medium size with thick pads, and well-feathered between the toes.

**Hindquarters**—The Springer should be worked and shown in hard, muscular condition with well-developed hips and thighs. His whole rear assembly suggests strength and driving power. Thighs are broad and muscular. Stifle joints are strong. For functional efficiency, the angulation of the hindquarter is never greater than that of the forequarter, and not appreciably less. The hock joints are somewhat rounded, not small and sharp in contour. Rear pasterns are short (about one-third the distance from the hip joint to the foot) and strong, with good bone. When viewed from behind, the rear pasterns are parallel. Dewclaws are usually removed. The feet are the same as in front, except that they are smaller and often more compact.

**Coat**—The Springer has an outer coat and an undercoat. On the body, the outer coat is of medium length, flat or wavy, and is easily distinguishable from the undercoat, which is short, soft and dense. The quantity of undercoat is affected by climate and season. When in combination, outer coat and undercoat serve to make the dog substantially waterproof, weatherproof and thornproof. On ears, chest, legs and belly the Springer is nicely furnished with a fringe of feathering of moderate length and heaviness. On the head, front of the forelegs, and below the hock joints on the front of the hind legs, the hair is short and fine. The coat has the clean, glossy, "live" appearance indicative of good health. It is legitimate to trim about the head, ears, neck and feet, to remove dead undercoat, and to thin and shorten excess feathering as required to enhance a smart, functional appearance. The tail may be trimmed, or well fringed with wavy feathering. Above all, the appearance should be natural. Overtrimming, especially the body coat, or any chopped, barbered or artificial effect is to be penalized in the show ring, as is excessive feathering that destroys the clean outline desirable in a sporting dog. Correct quality and condition of coat is to take precedence over quantity of coat.

**Color**—All the following combinations of colors and markings are equally acceptable: (1) Black or liver with white markings or predominantly white with black or liver markings; (2) Blue or liver roan; (3) Tricolor: black and white or liver and white with tan markings, usually found on eyebrows, cheeks, inside of ears and under the tail. Any white portion of the coat may be flecked with ticking. Off colors such as lemon, red or orange are not to place.

**Gait**—The final test of the Springer's conformation and soundness is proper movement. Balance is a prerequisite to good movement. The front and rear assemblies must be equivalent in angulation and muscular development for the gait to be smooth and effortless. Shoulders which are well laid-back to permit a long stride are just as essential as the excellent rear quarters that provide driving power. Seen from the side, the Springer exhibits a long, ground-covering stride and carries a firm back, with no tendency to dip, roach or roll from side to side. From the front, the legs swing forward in a free and easy manner. Elbows have free action from the shoulders, and the legs show no tendency to cross or interfere. From behind, the rear legs reach well under the body, following on a line with the forelegs. As speed increases, there is a natural tendency for the legs to converge toward a center line of travel. Movement faults include high-stepping, wasted motion; short, choppy stride; crabbing; and moving with the feet wide, the latter giving roll or swing to the body.

**Temperament**—The typical Springer is friendly, eager to please, quick to learn and willing to obey. Such traits are conducive to tractability, which is essential for appropriate handler control in the field. In the show ring, he should exhibit poise and attentiveness and permit himself to be examined by the judge without resentment or cringing. Aggression toward people and aggression toward other dogs is not in keeping with sporting dog character and purpose and is not acceptable. Excessive timidity, with due allowance for puppies and novice exhibits, is to be equally penalized.

**Summary**—In evaluating the English Springer Spaniel, the overall picture is a primary consideration. One should look for *type,* which includes general appearance and outline, and also for *soundness,* which includes movement and temperament. Inasmuch as the dog with a smooth easy gait must be reasonably sound and well-balanced, he is to be highly regarded, however, not to the extent of forgiving him for not looking like an English Springer Spaniel. An atypical dog, too short or long in leg length or foreign in head or expression, may move well, but he is not to be preferred over a good all-round specimen that has a minor fault in movement. It must be remembered that the English Springer Spaniel is first and foremost a sporting dog of the Spaniel family, and he must *look, behave* and *move* in character.

**Approved February 12, 1994**
**Effective March 31, 1994**

# FIELD SPANIEL

$\mathcal{T}$HE FIELD SPANIEL, TO PROBABLY GREATER EXTENT THAN ANY VARIETY within the great spaniel group, has been taken over the hurdles of man's fancy for exaggerations in type, and as a result the breed suffered greatly.

Phineas Bullock of England is credited with perpetuating a dog of tremendous body length and lowness to the ground, which together with phenomenal bone, culminated for a time in a grotesque caricature of a spaniel. Apparently the type was established by repeated crosses of the Welsh Cocker with the Sussex Spaniel. Later, largely through the efforts of Mortimer Smith, the breed was improved—it took on a type that all who like sporting spaniels can really admire.

Considerable difficulty was encountered in establishing the modern Field Spaniel in the United States due to the necessity for introducing Springer and Cocker crosses in order to eliminate the exaggerations, and this, of course, rendered many individuals ineligible for registration with the American Kennel Club. In fact, in the early 1880s when the Cocker was introduced to America and until 1901, the sole distinction between the Cockers and the Field Spaniels for show purposes was one of size—with any over twenty-five pounds designated as a Field, and twenty-five pounds or under as a Cocker.

Usually black in color, the Field Spaniel became a useful and handsome breed, sound, straight in the forelegs, and with a height more nearly in balance to length.

When built along these lines, he is a dog possessed of endurance, moderate speed, and agility. He is level-headed and intelligent, and a dog of great perseverance.

# OFFICIAL STANDARD FOR THE FIELD SPANIEL

**General Appearance**—The Field Spaniel is a combination of beauty and utility. It is a well balanced, substantial hunter-companion of medium size, built for activity and endurance in a heavy cover and water. It has a noble carriage; a proud but docile attitude; is sound and free moving. Symmetry, gait, attitude and purpose are more important than any one part.

**Size, Proportion, Substance**—Balance between these three components is essential. *Size*—Ideal height for mature adults at the withers is 18 inches for dogs and 17 inches for bitches. A one inch deviation either way is acceptable. *Proportion*—A well balanced dog, somewhat longer than tall. The ratio of length to height is approximately 7:6. (Length is measured on a level from the foremost point of the shoulder to the rearmost point of the buttocks.) *Substance*—Solidly built, with moderate bone, and firm smooth muscles.

**Head**—Conveys the impression of high breeding, character and nobility, and must be in proportion to the size of the dog. *Expression*—Grave, gentle and intelligent. *Eyes*—Almond in shape, open and of medium size; set moderately wide and deep. Color: dark hazel to dark brown. The lids are tight and show no haw; rims comparable to nose in color. *Ears*—Moderately long (reaching the end of the muzzle) and wide. Set on slightly below eye level: pendulous, hanging close to the head; rolled and well feathered. Leather is moderately heavy, supple, and rounded at the tip. *Skull*—The crown is slightly wider at the back than at the brow and lightly arched laterally; sides and cheeks are straight and clean. The occiput is distinct and rounded. Brows are slightly raised. The stop is moderate, but well defined by the brows. The face is chiseled beneath the eyes. *Muzzle*—Strong, long and lean, neither snipy nor squarely cut. The nasal bone is straight and slightly divergent from parallel, sloping downward toward the nose from the plane of the top skull. In profile, the lower plane curves gradually from the nose to the throat. Jaws are level. *Nose*—Large, fleshy and well developed with open nostrils. Set on as an extension of the muzzle. Color: solid: light to dark brown or black as befits the color of the coat. *Lips*—Close fitting, clean, and sufficiently deep to cover the lower jaw without being pendulous. *Bite*—Scissors or level, with complete dentition. Scissors preferred.

**Neck, Topline, Body**—*Neck*—Long, strong, muscular, slightly arched, clean, and well set into shoulders. *Topline*—The neck slopes smoothly into the withers; the back is level, well muscled, firm and strong; the croup is short and gently rounded. *Body*—The prosternum is prominent and well fleshed. The depth of chest is roughly equal to the length of the front leg from elbow to ground. The rib cage is long and extending into a short loin. Ribs are oval, well sprung and curve gently into a firm loin. *Loin*—Short, strong, and deep, with little or no tuck up. *Tail*—Set on low, in line with the croup, just below the level of the back with a natural downward inclination. Docked tails preferred, natural tails are allowed. The tail whether docked or natural length should be in balance with the overall dog.

**Forequarters**—Shoulder blades are oblique and sloping. The upper arm is closed-set; elbows are directly below the withers, and turn neither in nor out. Bone is flat. Forelegs are straight and well boned to the feet. Pasterns are moderately sloping but strong. Dewclaws may be removed. Feet face forward and are large, rounded, and webbed, with strong, well arched relatively tight toes and thick pads.

**Hindquarters**—Strong and driving; stifles and hocks only moderately bent. Hocks well let down; pasterns relatively short, strong and parallel when viewed from the rear. Hips moderately broad and muscular; upper thigh broad and powerful; second thigh well muscled. Bone corresponds to that of the forelegs. No dewclaws.

**Coat**—Single; moderately long; flat or slightly wavy; silky; and glossy; dense and water-repellent. Moderate setter-like feathering adorns the chest, underbody, backs of the legs, buttocks, and may also be present on the second thigh and underside of the tail. Pasterns have clean outlines to the ground. There is short, soft hair between the toes. Overabundance of coat, or cottony texture, impractical for field work should be penalized. Trimming is limited to that which enhances the natural appearance of the dog. Amount of coat or absence of coat should not be faulted as much as structural faults.

**Color**—Black, liver, golden liver or shades thereof, in any intensity (dark or light); either self-colored or bi-colored. Bi-colored dogs must be roaned and/or ticked in white areas. Tan points are acceptable on the aforementioned colors and are the same as any normally tan pointed breed. White is allowed on the throat, chest, and/or brisket, and may be clear, ticked, or roaned on a self color dog.

**Gait**—The head is carried alertly, neither so high nor so low as to impede motion or stride. There is good forward reach that begins in the shoulder, coupled with strong drive from the rear, giving the characteristic effortless, long, low majestic stride. When viewed from front and/or rear elbows and hocks move parallel. The legs move straight, with slight convergence at increased speed. When moving, the tail is carried inclined slightly downward or level with the back, and with a wagging motion. Tail carried above the back is incorrect. Side movement is straight and clean, without energy wasting motions. Overreaching and single tracking are incorrect. The Field Spaniel should be shown at its own natural speed in an endurance trot, preferably on a loose lead, in order to evaluate its movement.

**Temperament**—Unusually docile, sensitive, fun-loving, independent and intelligent, with a great affinity for human companionship. They may be somewhat reserved in initial meetings. Any display of shyness, fear, or aggression is to be severely penalized.

**Approved September 14, 1998**
**Effective October 30, 1998**

# Irish Water Spaniel

*T*HAT THE IRISH WATER SPANIEL IS A DOG OF VERY ANCIENT LINEAGE IS supported by the research made by Alan J. Stern and reported upon in four articles in *Pure-Bred Dogs—American Kennel Gazette,* January–April 1965.

The articles noted that a Harvard archaeological expedition to Ireland in 1934–36, excavating a lake dwelling of Lagore near Dunshaughlin, unearthed among other dog remains an Irish Water Spaniel–type skull—medium sized, with clearly defined stop and a more pronounced dome—identified to dogs living in the seventh or eighth century A.D. The same type of skull was found in the Lake Districts of Central Europe, dating from later Stone and Bronze ages. Old Roman ruins bear carvings which most resemble the Irish Water Spaniel.

In the late 1100s, before the days of King McCarthy II, dogs found in southern Ireland below the River Shannon were called Shannon Spaniels, Irish Water Spaniels, Rat-Tail Spaniels, or Whip-Tail Spaniels. Ireland's Sir Robert Cecil is recorded as having sent the King of France an Irish Water Spaniel in 1598. In 1607, Topsell, in his *Historie of the four-footed Beastes,* tells of the Water Spagnel with his long, rough, curled hair and a tail somewhat bare and naked. Captain Thomas Brown, in the mid-1700s, remarks on the long ears of the Irish Water Spaniel and the crisp, curly texture of the coat.

These evidences indicate that the dog known as the Southern Irish Water Spaniel was well established centuries before the legendary Boatswain (1834–52), the famous sire of many outstanding gundogs and bench champions who is often credited as having been the first of the breed as it is known today. Boatswain (pedigree unknown) was bred by Justin McCarthy.

However disputable the breed's development before him, in Boatswain's wake a clear type was bred, exhibited, and accepted by kennel club officialdom. In 1849 he sired Jack, whose name appears in many early pedigrees. The first special class for Irish Water Spaniels was provided in 1859. In 1866, Doctor—a great grandson of Boatswain—won first (Best of Breed) at Birmingham. An oil painting of Rake, bred in 1864 of Boatswain's bloodlines, shows the contemporary Irish Water Spaniel.

In America, we note that there was an entry of four Irish Water Spaniels at the first Westminster Kennel Club show in 1877. One of these was listed as having been imported from Ireland in 1873.

The Irish Water Spaniel is often called the clown of the spaniel family, possibly due to the unique appearance of a characteristic topknot together with a peak of curly hair between the eyes. He is likewise the tallest of our spaniels. Ordinarily he is loyal to those he knows, but forbidding to strangers. He is a grand water dog, not only because he likes water, but because his coat is naturally water-shedding. For this reason he is used in some parts of the country as a duck retriever, although he is not quite as adaptable for upland work because his coat tends to catch on briers.

# OFFICIAL STANDARD FOR THE IRISH WATER SPANIEL

**General Appearance**—The Irish Water Spaniel presents a picture of a smart, up-standing strongly built sporting dog. Great intelligence is combined with rugged endurance and a bold, dashing eagerness of temperament. Distinguishing characteristics are a topknot of long, loose curls, a body covered with a dense, crisply curled liver colored coat, contrasted by a smooth face and a smooth "rat" tail.

**Size, Proportion, Substance**—Strongly built and well boned, the Irish Water Spaniel is a dog of medium length, slightly rectangular in appearance. He is well balanced and shows no legginess or coarseness. Dogs 22 to 24 inches, bitches 21 to 23 inches, measured at the highest point of the shoulder. Dogs 55 to 65 pounds, bitches 45 to 58 pounds.

**Head**—The head is cleanly chiseled, not cheeky, and should not present a short, wedge shaped appearance. The skull is rather large and high in the dome, with a prominent occiput and a gradual stop. The muzzle is square and rather long, with a deep mouth opening and lips fine in texture. The nose large and liver in color. Teeth strong and regular with a scissors or level bite. The hair on the face is short and smooth, except for a beard which grows in a narrow line at the back of the jaw. *Topknot*—A characteristic of the breed, consists of long, loose curls growing down into a well-defined peak between the eyes and falling like a shawl over the tops of the ears and occiput.

Trimming of this breed characteristic in an exaggerated manner is highly objectionable. *Eyes*—Medium in size, slightly almond shaped with tight eyelids. Eyes are hazel in color, preferably of a dark shade. The expression is keenly alert, intelligent, direct and quizzical. *Ears*—Long, lobular, set low, with leathers reaching about to the end of the nose when extended forward, and abundantly covered with long curls, extending two or more inches below the tips of the leathers.

**Neck, Topline, Body**—The neck is long, arching, strong and muscular; smoothly set into cleanly sloping shoulders. *Topline*—Strong and level, or slightly higher in the rear; never descending, or showing sag or roach. *Body*—The body is of medium length, slightly rectangular. Chest deep, with brisket extending to the elbows. Ribs well sprung and carried well back. Immediately behind the shoulders ribs are flattened enough to allow free movement of the forelegs, becoming rounder behind. Loin short, wide and muscular. The body should not present a tucked-up appearance.

**Forequarters**—The entire front gives the impression of strength without heaviness. Shoulders are sloping and clean. Forelegs well boned, muscular, medium in length; with sufficient length of upper arm to ensure efficient reach. Elbows close set. Forefeet are large, thick and somewhat spreading; well clothed with hair both over and between the toes.

**Hindquarters**—Sound hindquarters are of great importance to provide swimming power and drive. They should be as high or slightly higher than the shoulders, powerful and muscular, with well developed upper and second thighs. Hips wide, stifles moderately bent, hocks low set and moderately bent. Rear angulation is moderate, and balance of front and rear angulation is of paramount importance. Rear feet are large, thick and somewhat spreading; well clothed with hair. Tail should be set on low enough to give a rather rounded appearance to the hindquarters and should be carried nearly level with the back.

**Tail**—The so-called rat tail is a striking characteristic of the breed. At the root it is thick and covered for two or three inches with short curls. It tapers to a fine point at the end; and from the root curls is covered with short, smooth hair so as to look as if it had been clipped. The tail should not be long enough to reach the hock joint.

**Coat**—Proper double coat is of vital importance to protect the dog while working. The neck, back, sides, and rear are densely covered with tight, crisp ringlets, with the hair longer underneath the ribs. Forelegs are well covered with abundant curls or waves. The hind legs should also be abundantly covered by hair falling in curls or waves, except that the hair should be short and smooth on the front of the legs below the hocks. The hair on the throat is very short and smooth, forming a V-shaped patch. All curled areas should be clearly defined by curls of sufficient length to form a sharp contrast with the smooth coat on face, throat, tail, and rear legs below the hocks. Fore and hind feet should be well clothed with hair both over and between the toes. Dogs may be shown in natural coat or trimmed. However, no dog should be groomed or trimmed so excessively as to obscure the curl or texture of the coat.

**Color**—Solid liver. With the exception of graying due to age, white hair or markings objectionable.

**Gait**—The Irish Water Spaniel moves with a smooth, free, ground covering action that, when viewed from the side, exhibits balanced reach and drive. True and precise coming and going. When walking or standing, the legs are perpendicular to the ground, toeing neither in nor out.

**Temperament**—Very alert and inquisitive, the Irish Water Spaniel is often reserved with strangers. However, aggressive behavior or excessive shyness should be penalized. A stable temperament is essential in a hunting dog.

## FAULTS

*The foregoing description is that of the ideal Irish Water Spaniel in hard working condition. Any deviation from the above described dog must be penalized to the extent of the deviation, keeping in mind the importance of the various features toward the basic original purpose of the breed.*

**Approved June 12, 1990**
**Effective August 1, 1990**

# SUSSEX SPANIEL

*T*WO BOOKS PRINTED IN THE 1850S PROVIDE THE FIRST CLEAR REFERENCE TO the Sussex Spaniel as a distinct breed. One of the two books credited Augustus Elliot Fuller, owner of Rosehill estate in Brightling, Sussex County, England, with breeding the two Sussex whose illustration was used in the book. Twenty years later, writers began embellishing the Fuller connection to the breed. By the 1880s, Rosehill was the proclaimed birthplace of the Sussex Spaniel, and the Fuller legend was born.

This premise was repeated in nearly every book written on dog breeds for the next hundred years. Several details about the Fullers and their Sussex Spaniels, however, contain inaccuracies. Despite the factual errors, the early accounts were written while contemporaries of the Fullers were still living. No account disputes that Sussex Spaniels once resided at Rosehill estate. While the Fullers may not deserve all the credit for the existence of the Sussex Spaniel, there is little doubt that Rosehill estate played a key role in the early days of the breed.

Photographs show that by the 1880s, the Sussex possessed the unmistakable type unique among spaniels. During this decade, the two men who would shepherd the Sussex into the twentieth century came into possession of the breed.

Moses Woolland obtained his first Sussex Spaniel in 1882, twenty-five years after A. E. Fuller's death. Within a few short years, dogs he bred under the Bridford prefix monopolized the show ring. Woolland was equally successful with his kennel of Field Spaniels. A study of the pedigrees shows that his Fields were mostly of Sussex Spaniel ancestry, and were very similar in type to the Sussex except for color and head properties. These Sussex-bred Fields from the Bridford kennels appear in the lineage of all modern descendants of both breeds.

Campbell Newington began his involvement with the breed in 1887. Capitalizing on the association of the breed with the Fuller estate, Newington chose Rosehill as his kennel name. Through the efforts of Woolland and Campbell, the breed attained a consistency in type and quality that remains unmatched even today. During this time, the first breed standard was written. The low, long, and level outline, the golden-liver color, and the massive head with the short, square muzzle became trademarks of the breed. Woolland's eventual departure left Newington almost solely in the care of the breed, until J. E. Kerr bred his first litter of Sussex in 1909 at Harviestoun Castle in Scotland. Kerr was a renowned breeder of Shetland ponies and various breeds of livestock. He also had a successful kennel of Cairn Terriers. These two men single-handedly kept the breed alive during the 1910s. The pedigrees from this time show names of dogs either with the Harviestoun or Rosehill prefix.

The years following World War I were perhaps the darkest for the breed. The war had brought about profound changes in British society as well as the hunting practices that once were in vogue on the large estates. The need for a specialized hunting breed was no longer there. What replaced it was the desire for a utilitarian spaniel. Such a spaniel required speed in the field, and speed required a tall spaniel of square proportions. In 1921, after thirty-four years of dedication to the breed, Newington whelped the last Sussex Spaniel carrying the Rosehill name.

The old breed traits proved tenacious, and by the late 1930s good specimens with the hallmark traits of the breed began to replace off-type examples common in the 1920s. Before the Great Depression, the first examples of the breed arrived in the United States. Further imports occurred in the years just before the start of World War II. One of the last Sussex to have made the crossing to America was rescued from a ship torpedoed by a German U-boat. The war nearly sounded the death knell for the breed in the United Kingdom. Of all the British breeds, the Sussex perhaps suffered the most. But for the efforts of Joy Freer, the breed surely would have been lost.

Mrs. Freer's involvement with the breed spanned an astonishing sixty years. After obtaining her first Sussex Spaniel in 1923, Mrs. Freer established her Fourclover kennels and quickly became a strong competitor at the shows. By 1925, she bred her first champion, whom many considered to be the best example of the breed since the demise of the Bridford kennels. Several other people had become very active in breeding Sussex, and by the outbreak of hostilities the Sussex population had peaked. By the end of 1939, however, the breed's fortunes quickly changed and breeding activity had virtually ceased in England.

The revival of the breed in America began with three imports in 1969, followed by eleven more Sussex over the next three years. While still considered an extremely rare breed, the threat of extinction no longer exists. The breed in America has gained many longtime supporters interested in all aspects of the sport. Sussex have not only won top awards at the most prestigious dog shows but have also earned titles in all AKC performance events open to sporting dogs. Two characteristics have steadfastly remained with the breed: acute hunting instincts and correct historical type. The breed's docile nature, cheerful disposition, and overall good health will surely guarantee the Sussex Spaniel a bright future.

# OFFICIAL STANDARD FOR THE SUSSEX SPANIEL

**General Appearance**—The Sussex Spaniel was among the first ten breeds to be recognized and admitted to the Stud Book when the American Kennel Club was formed in 1884, but it has existed as a distinct breed for much longer. As its name implies, it derives its origin from the county of Sussex, England, and it was used there since the eighteenth century as a field dog. During the late 1800s the reputation of the Sussex Spaniel as an excellent hunting companion was well known among the estates surrounding Sussex County. Its short legs, massive build, long body, and habit of giving tongue when on scent made the breed ideally suited to penetrating the dense undergrowth and flushing game within range of the gun. Strength, maneuverability, and desire were essential for this purpose. Although it has never gained great popularity in numbers, the Sussex Spaniel continues today essentially unchanged in character and general appearance from those 19th century sporting dogs.

The Sussex Spaniel presents a long and low, rectangular and rather massive appearance coupled with free movements and nice tail action. The breed has a somber and serious expression. The rich golden liver color is unique to the breed.

**Size, Proportion, Substance**—*Size*—The height of the Sussex Spaniel as measured at the withers ranges from 13 to 15 inches. Any deviation from these measurements is a minor fault. The weight of the Sussex Spaniel ranges between 35 and 45 pounds. *Proportion*—The Sussex Spaniel presents a rectangular outline as the breed is longer in body than it is tall. *Substance*—The Sussex Spaniel is muscular and rather massive.

**Head**—Correct head and expression are important features of the breed. *Eyes*—The eyes are hazel in color, fairly large, soft and languishing, but do not show the haw overmuch. *Expression*—The Sussex Spaniel has a somber and serious appearance, and its fairly heavy brows produce a frowning expression. *Ears*—The ears are thick, fairly large, and lobe-shaped and are set moderately low, slightly above the outside corner of the eye. *Skull and Muzzle*—The skull is moderately long and also wide with an indentation in the middle and with a full stop. The brows are fairly heavy, the occiput is full but not pointed, the whole giving an appearance of heaviness without dullness. The muzzle should be approximately three inches long, broad, and square in profile. The skull as measured from the stop to the occiput is longer than the muzzle. The nostrils are well-developed and liver colored. The lips are somewhat pendulous. *Bite*—A scissors bite is preferred. Any deviation from a scissors bite is a minor fault.

**Neck, Topline, Body**—*Neck*—The neck is rather short, strong, and slightly arched, but does not carry the head much above the level of the back. There should not be much throatiness about the skin. *Topline and Body*—The whole body is characterized as low and long with a level topline. The chest is round, especially behind the shoulders, and is deep and wide which gives a good girth. The back and loin are long and very muscular both in width and depth. For this development, the back ribs must be deep. *Tail*—The tail is docked from 5 to 7 inches and set low. When gaiting the Sussex Spaniel exhibits nice tail action, but does not carry the tail above the level of the back.

**Forequarters**—The shoulders are well laid back and muscular. The upper arm should correspond in length and angle of return to the shoulder blade so that the legs are set well under the dog. The forelegs should be very short, strong, and heavily boned. They may show a slight bow. Both straight and slightly bowed constructions are proper and correct. The pasterns are very short and heavily boned. The feet are large and round with short hair between the toes.

**Hindquarters**—The hindquarters are full and well-rounded, strong, and heavily boned. They should be parallel with each other and also set wide apart—about as wide as the dog at the shoulders. The hind legs are short from the hock to the ground, heavily boned, and should seem neither shorter than the forelegs nor much bent at the hocks. The hindquarters must correspond in angulation to the forequarters. The hocks should turn neither in nor out. The rear feet are like the front feet.

**Coat**—The body coat is abundant, flat or slightly waved, with no tendency to curl. The legs are moderately well-feathered, but clean below the hocks. The ears are furnished with soft, wavy hair. The neck has a well-marked frill in the coat. The tail is thickly covered with moderately long feather. No trimming is acceptable except to shape foot feather, or to remove feather between the pads or between the hock and the feet. The feather between the toes must be left in sufficient length to cover the nails.

**Color**—Rich golden liver is the only acceptable color and is a certain sign of the purity of the breed. Dark liver or puce is a major fault. White on the chest is a minor fault. White on any other part of the body is a major fault.

**Gait**—The round, deep and wide chest of the Sussex Spaniel coupled with its short legs and long body produce a rolling gait. While its movement is deliberate, the Sussex Spaniel is in no sense clumsy. Gait is powerful and true with perfect coordination between the front and hind legs. The front legs do not paddle, wave, or overlap. The head is held low when gaiting. The breed should be shown on a loose lead so that its natural gait is evident.

**Temperament**—Despite its somber and serious expression, the breed is friendly and has a cheerful and tractable disposition.

## FAULTS

The standard ranks features of the breed into three categories. The most important features of the breed are color and general appearance. The features of secondary importance are the head, ears, back and back ribs, legs, and feet. The features of lesser importance are the eyes, nose, neck, chest and shoulders, tail, and coat. Faults also fall into three categories. Major faults are color that is too light or too dark, white on any part of the body other than the chest, and a curled coat. Serious faults are a narrow head, weak muzzle, the presence of a topknot, and a general appearance that is sour and crouching. Minor faults are light eyes, white on chest, the deviation from proper height ranges, lightness of bone, shortness of body or a body that is flat-sided, and a bite other than scissors. There are no disqualifications in the Sussex Spaniel standard.

**Approved April 7, 1992**
**Effective May 27, 1992**

# WELSH SPRINGER SPANIEL

*T*HE HISTORY OF THE WELSH SPRINGER SPANIEL BEGINS AS FAR BACK AS 7000 B.C., when the first hunting dogs were employed by man. The likely ancestors of most of today's domestic hunting dogs, these canines accompanied man on his hunting sojourns on the coastlines of Brittany, Cornwall, Wales, Ireland, and Scotland during the Mesolithic Age.

By approximately 250 B.C., the ancestors of the Welsh Springer had developed into the Agassian hunting dog, belonging to the wild tribes of Roman-occupied Briton. Writings of the time include mention of the dog's "springing" action while on the hunt. Oppian, a Greek poet of the second century, also described the dog in detail.

During the Renaissance, the Land Spaniel, a Welsh Springer–type dog with red and white markings, was used for retrieving. The dog was used when hunting with the falcon, gun, and bow, as these were all means employed at the time. Tapestries woven during the period show the Land Spaniel as having nearly the same colorings and physical characteristics as today's Welsh.

In the 1700s, the British masters included the red-and-white spaniel in a number of their oil paintings. According to some experts, the stance, color, and conformation of the dogs depicted in this art are those of the modern Welsh. This spaniel gained some popularity in eighteenth-century England and was a favorite hunting dog of many well-to-do individuals.

By the 1800s, however, the breed had been primarily replaced by liver-and-white or black-and-white spaniels. During this lapse in the breed's popularity in England, it is thought that the dog was still maintained in the region of South Wales, notably in the Neath Valley.

A trend in selective breeding, spurred by the newly popularized Darwinian theory, eventually brought the red-and-white spaniel back to Victorian England. Emphasis was put on breeding dogs for color and, subsequently, the popularity of the breed grew during this time. The Kennel Club (England) was formed in 1873, and the red-and-white spaniel was shown at the club's first competition, along with other spaniels. Both the Welsh Springer and the English Springer were judged together since their only differences at the time were in color. The breeds were eventually separated in the classes.

Welsh Springer Spaniels apparently gained popularity in the late 1800s in America, since the American Kennel Club officially recognized them in 1906. The first dog, Faircroft Bob, was registered in 1914, and was soon followed by five others, all in the same year. Between the years of 1926 and 1948, however, there were no Welsh Springers registered by the AKC. Many believe that by the time World War II had ended, no Welsh Springers were alive in the United States. Importing soon changed this situation, and in 1949 eleven dogs were registered with the AKC. The Welsh Springer Spaniel Club of America was formed in 1961.

The Welsh Springer is an excellent water dog, a keen, hardworking dog—no day is too long, no country too rough—and under all circumstances he is a faithful and willing worker for man. He has an excellent nose. He can be used on any kind of game; the well-trained Welshman compares with any gundog. As a companion, the Welsh Springer is a true pal of handy size, larger and stronger than the Cocker, but smaller than the English Springer. He makes a good guard, too, yet is ordinarily gentle with children and other animals.

# OFFICIAL STANDARD FOR
# THE WELSH SPRINGER SPANIEL

**General Appearance**—The Welsh Springer Spaniel is a dog of distinct variety and ancient origin, who derives his name from his hunting style and not his relationship to other breeds. He is an attractive dog of handy size, exhibiting substance without coarseness. He is compact, not leggy, obviously built for hard work and endurance. The Welsh Springer Spaniel gives the impression of length due to obliquely angled forequarters and well developed hindquarters. Being a hunting dog, he should be shown in hard muscled working condition. His coat should not be so excessive as to hinder his work as an active flushing spaniel, but should be thick enough to protect him from heavy cover and weather.

**Size, Proportion, Substance**—A dog is ideally 18 to 19 inches in height at the withers and a bitch is 17 to 18 inches at the withers. Any animal above or below the ideal to be proportionately penalized. Weight should be in proportion to height and overall balance. Length of body from the withers to the base of the tail is very slightly greater than the distance from the withers to the ground. This body length may be the same as the height but never shorter, thus preserving the rectangular silhouette of the Welsh Springer Spaniel.

**Head**—The Welsh Springer Spaniel head is unique and should in no way approximate that of other spaniel breeds. Its overall balance is of primary importance. Head is in proportion to body, never so broad as to appear coarse nor so narrow as to appear racy. The skull is of medium length, slightly domed, with a clearly defined stop. It is well chiseled below the eyes. The top plane of the skull is very slightly divergent from that of the muzzle, but with no tendency toward a down-faced appearance. A short chubby head is most objectionable.

*Eyes* should be oval in shape, dark to medium brown in color with a soft expression. Preference is for a darker eye though lighter shades of brown are acceptable. Yellow or mean-looking eyes are to be heavily penalized. Medium in size, they are neither prominent, nor sunken, nor do they show haw. Eye rims are tight and dark pigmentation is preferred.

*Ears* are set on approximately at eye level and hang close to the cheeks. Comparatively small, the leather does not reach to the nose. Gradually narrowing toward the tip, they are shaped somewhat like a vine leaf and are lightly feathered.

The length of the *muzzle* is approximately equal to, but never longer than that of the skull. It is straight, fairly square, and free from excessive flew. Nostrils are well developed and black or any shade of brown in color. A pink nose is to be severely penalized. A scissors *bite* is preferred. An undershot jaw is to be severely penalized.

**Neck, Topline, Body**—The *neck* is long and slightly arched, clean in throat, and set into long, sloping shoulders. *Topline* is level. The loin is slightly arched, muscular, and close-coupled. The croup is very slightly rounded, never steep nor falling off. The topline in combination with proper angulation fore and aft presents a silhouette that appears rectangular. The *chest* is well developed and muscular with a prominent forechest, the ribs well sprung and the brisket reaching to the elbows. The *tail* is an extension of the topline. Carriage is nearly horizontal or slightly elevated when the dog is excited. The tail is generally docked and displays a lively action.

**Forequarters**—The shoulder blade and upper arm are approximately equal in length. The upper arm is set well back, joining the shoulder blade with sufficient angulation to place the elbow beneath the highest point of the shoulder blade when standing. The forearms are of medium length, straight and moderately feathered. The legs are well boned but not to the extent of coarseness. The Welsh Springer Spaniel's elbows should be close to the body and its pasterns short and slightly sloping. Height to the elbows is approximately equal to the distance from the elbows to the top of the shoulder blades. Dewclaws are generally removed. Feet should be round, tight and well arched with thick pads.

**Hindquarters**—The hindquarters must be strong, muscular, and well boned, but not coarse. When viewed in profile the thighs should be wide and the second thighs well developed. The angulation of the pelvis and femur corresponds to that of the shoulder and upper arm. Bend of stifle is moderate. The bones from the hocks to the pads are short with a well angulated hock joint. When viewed from the side or rear they are perpendicular to the ground. Rear dewclaws are removed. Feet as in front.

**Coat**—The coat is naturally straight flat and soft to the touch, never wiry or wavy. It is sufficiently dense to be waterproof, thornproof, and weatherproof. The back of the forelegs, the hind legs above the hocks, chest and underside of the body are moderately feathered. The ears and tail are lightly feathered. Coat so excessive as to be a hindrance in the field is to be discouraged. Obvious barbering is to be avoided as well.

**Color**—The color is rich red and white only. Any pattern is acceptable and any white area may be flecked with red ticking.

**Gait**—The Welsh Springer moves with a smooth, powerful, ground covering action that displays drive from the rear. Viewed from the side, he exhibits a strong forward stride with a reach that does not waste energy. When viewed from the front, the legs should appear to move forward in an effortless manner with no tendency for the feet to cross over or interfere with each other. Viewed from the rear, the hocks should follow on a line with the forelegs, neither too widely nor too closely spaced. As the speed increases the feet tend to converge towards a center line.

**Temperament**—The Welsh Springer Spaniel is an active dog displaying a loyal and affectionate disposition. Although reserved with strangers, he is not timid, shy nor unfriendly. To this day he remains a devoted family member and hunting companion.

**Approved June 13, 1989**
**Effective August 1, 1989**

# SPINONE ITALIANO

$\mathscr{T}$HE SPINONE ITALIANO IS A VERSATILE HUNTING DOG OF ANCIENT HERITAGE. The name Spinone evolved from Bracco Spinoso ("prickly pointer") or Bracco Spinone, to simply Spinone in its country of origin. The breed is known as the Italian Spinone in the United Kingdom. Some say the name refers to the coat's harsh texture, while others say it is derived from the dense, thorny bushes where these hunting dogs excelled.

One of the oldest griffon varieties in existence, the Spinone is descended from an ancient hunting breed originating in Italy's Piedmont region. Although the exact origin is uncertain, it is believed that the Spinone's ancestors can be traced to approximately 500 B.C., as attested by Senofonte in his work *Cynegetica* (*On Hunting*). Senofonte described a rough, bristly-haired dog, with great physical endurance and exceptional ability for pointing game. Other historical references include a fifteenth-century fresco by Andrea Mantegna in the Ducal Palace at Mantua, depicting a dog that in all probability is a Spinone. References also appear later, in other works by celebrated artists such as Titian and Tiepolo. Literary works from the mid-thirteenth to early fifteenth century indicate that a dog with characteristics of today's Spinone was held in great esteem for its indefatigable stamina, as well as increasingly tight contact with the owner during a hunt. Modern Spinone history can be divided into two parts: the early 1800s to World War II, and the postwar period until now.

In various regions of Italy in the early nineteenth century there were several groups of dogs with similar characteristics, both in the white-and-orange and brown roan colors, but having different coat textures. Although these dogs were most likely not directly related, they probably had some common origin. In 1828, characteristics of a breed described as a "soft-coated pointer" were detailed in *Trattato della Caccia,* a book by Bonoventura Crippa.

The first breed standard was written by the Società Braccofila in 1897. Several subsequent standards appeared. These evolved from numerous sources: canine author Signor Angelo Vecchio (1904); Società Braccofila (again, in 1923); the Italian Kennel Club (1928); the breed club of the period, Società Amici dello Spinone (1936); and Giuseppe Solario (1939). This last standard was revised and approved by Ente Nazionale della Cinofilia Italiana (ENCI) in 1944. The most important characteristics of the breed—including head, topline, skin, and coat—were outlined in each of these standards.

During the war, there were few Spinoni available for breeding, and some crossbreeding was done with breeds such as the German Wirehaired Pointer, the Wirehaired Pointing Griffon, and the Bracco Italiano. Fortunately, a small group of serious enthusiasts selectively bred the dogs after the war, retaining the Spinone's conformation and working ability. La Famiglia dello Spinone was formed in the 1950s and was recognized by ENCI as the Italian national breed club.

In 1931, Dr. Nicola Gigante imported the first known pair of Spinoni in the United States, Bella and Tris. A Spinone Italiano was entered in the Miscellaneous class at the Westminster Kennel Club show in 1932 and 1933, but the breed was not officially accepted into that class until March 1955. It remained there until September 2000, when it became eligible to compete in the Sporting Group. The AKC parent club, the Spinone Club of America, was founded in 1987.

The Spinone's hunting characteristics have remained consistent through the ages. Suited for work in all climates and all terrain, these are dogs that do not hunt for themselves but for their masters. They are not too fast while searching out game and move with an easy, loose trot geared for endurance. Spinoni are excellent swimmers and model retrievers.

Their harsh coat and very resistant, thick skin protect them in the field, in water, and in freezing temperatures. Coat color can be solid white, white with orange-roan or orange patches, or white with brown-roan or brown patches. No color is preferred over any other. The appearance of the Spinone is that of a large, rugged dog with a unique head and topline. The eyebrows, beard, and mustache protect the face and give the Spinone its distinctive "grouchy" look, while the eyes, described as humanlike, are impossible to resist.

A gentle disposition and docile temperament make them excellent companions for the right family. Tireless in the field, they are affectionate and calm in the house. They can also be clownish, stubborn, and demanding of attention, "talking" to their owners with a variety of growls, moans, and whines. Today, Spinoni are successful as personal hunting or therapy dogs; in competitions, such as hunt tests, obedience, agility, and tracking; and as personal companions. This is a breed that will hunt with you all day in the field or lie on your feet at home, happy as long as they can be with you.

# OFFICIAL STANDARD FOR THE SPINONE ITALIANO

**General Appearance**—Muscular dog with powerful bone. Vigorous and robust, his purpose as hardworking gundog is evident. Naturally sociable, the docile and patient Spinone is resistant to fatigue and is an experienced hunter on any terrain. His hard textured coat is weather resistant. His wiry, dense coat and thick skin enable the Spinone to negotiate underbrush and endure cold water that would severely punish any dog not so naturally armored. He has a remarkable tendency for an extended and fast trotting gait. The Spinone is an excellent retriever by nature.

**Size, Proportion, Substance**—*Height:* The height at the withers is 23 to 27 inches for males and 22 to 25 inches for females. *Weight:* In direct proportion to size and structure of dog. *Proportion:* His build tends to fit into a square. The length of the body, measured from sternum to point of buttocks, is approximately equal to the height at the withers with tolerance of no more than 1 inch in length compared to height. *Substance:* The Spinone is a solidly built dog, robust with powerful bone.

**Head**—Long. The profile of the Spinone is unique to this breed. Expression is of paramount importance to the breed. It should denote intelligence and gentleness. *Skull* of oval shape, with sides gently sloping. With occipital protuberance well developed, medial-frontal furrow is very pronounced. *Muzzle:* Square when viewed from the front. Muzzle length is equal to that of backskull. The planes of the skull and muzzle are diverging, downfaced. Its width measured at its midpoint is a third of its length. Stop is barely perceptible. Bridge of the muzzle is preferably slightly Roman, however, straight is not to be faulted. *Lips* fitting tightly to the jawline. Convergence of planes of the skull and muzzle or a dish-faced muzzle is to be faulted so severely as to eliminate from further competition. *Eyes:* Must have a soft sweet expression. Ocher (yellowish brown) in color, darker eyes with darker colored dogs, lighter eyes with lighter colored dogs. Large, well opened, set well apart, the eye is almost round, the lids closely fitting the eye, to protect the eye from gathering debris while the dog is hunting, loose eye lids must be faulted. Which is neither protruding nor deep set. Eye rim clearly visible, color will vary with coat color from flesh colored to brown. *Disqualification:* Walleye. *Nose:* Bulbous and spongy in appearance with upper edge rounded. Nostrils are large and well opened. In profile, the nose protrudes past the forward line of the lips. (Pigment is flesh colored in white dogs, darker in white and orange dogs, brown in brown or brown roan dogs.) *Disqualification:* Any pigment other than described or incomplete pigment of the nose. *Teeth:* Jaw is powerful. Teeth are positioned in a scissors or level bite. *Disqualification:* Overshot or undershot bite. *Ears:* Practically triangular shape. Set on a level just below the eye, carried low, with little erectile power. The leather is fine, covered with short, thick hair mixed with a longer sparser hair, which becomes thicker along edges. Length, if measured along the head would extend to tip of nose and no more than 1 inch beyond the tip. The forward edge is adherent to the cheek, not folded, but turned outward; the tip of the ear is slightly rounded.

**Neck, Topline, Body**—*Neck:* Strong, thick, and muscular. Clearly defined from the nape, blending in to the shoulders in a harmonious line. The throat is moderate in skin with a double dewlap. *Chest:* Broad, deep, well muscled and well rounded; extending at least to the elbow. The ribs are well sprung. The distance from ground to the elbow is equal to ½ the height at the withers. *Back:* The topline consists of two segments. The first slopes slightly downward in a nearly straight line from the withers to the 11th thoracic vertebrae, approximately 6 inches behind the withers. The second rises gradually and continues into a solid and well-arched loin. The underline is solid and should have minimal tuck up. *Croup:* Well muscled, long. The hipbones fall away from the spinal column at an angle of about 30 degrees, producing a lightly rounded, well filled-out croup. *Tail:* Follows the line of the croup, thick at the base, carried horizontally or down; flicking from side to side while moving is preferred. The tail should lack fringes. It is docked to a length of 5½ to 8 inches. Tail habitually carried above the level of the back or straight up when working is to be penalized.

**Forequarters**—*Shoulders:* Powerful and long, withers not too prominent; forming an angle with the upper arm of approximately 105 degrees. With well-developed muscles, the points of the shoulder blades are not close together. The ideal distance between the shoulder blades is approximately two inches or more. Angulation of shoulder is in balance with angulation in the rear. *Forelegs:* The forelegs are straight when viewed from the front angle with strong bone and well-developed muscles; elbows set under the withers and close to the body. Pasterns are long, lean and flexible following the vertical line of the forearm. In profile, they are slightly slanted. *Feet:* Large compact, rounded with well-arched toes, which are close together, covered with short, dense hair, including between the toes. Pads are lean and hard with strong nails curving toward the ground, well pigmented, but never black. Dewclaws may be removed.

**Hindquarters**—Thighs are strong and well muscled, stifles show good function angulation, lower thigh to be well developed and muscled with good breadth. The hock, with proportion of ⅓ the distance from the hip joint to foot being ideal, is strong, lean and perpendicular to the ground. *Fault:* Cow hocks. *Feet:* Slightly more oval than the forefoot with the same characteristics. Dewclaws may be removed.

**Skin**—The skin must be very thick, closely fitting the body. The skin is thinner on the head, throat, groin, under the legs and in the folds of the elbows is soft to the touch. Pigmentation is dependent upon the color or markings of the coat. *Disqualification:* Any black pigmentation.

**Coat**—A Spinone must have a correct coat to be of correct type. The ideal coat length is 1½ to 2½ inches on the body, with a tolerance of ½ inch over or under the ideal length. Head, ears, muzzle and front sides of legs and feet are covered by shorter hair. The hair on the backsides of the legs forms a rough brush, but there are never any fringes. The eyes and lips are framed by stiff hair forming eyebrows, mustache and tufted beard, which combine to save foreface from laceration by briar and bush. The coat is dense, stiff and flat or slightly crimped, but not curly, with an absence of undercoat. The

Spinone is exhibited in a natural state. The appearance of the Spinone may not be altered. The dog must present the natural appearance of a functional field dog. Dogs with a long, soft or silky coat, the presence of undercoat, or any deviation of the coat as defined in this as well as excessive grooming—i.e., scissoring, clipping, or setting of pattern—shall be severely penalized as to eliminate them from further competition.

**Color**—The accepted colors are: solid white; white and orange; orange roan with or without orange markings; white with brown markings; brown roan with or without brown markings. The most desired color of brown is chestnut brown, "monks habit," however, varying colors of brown are acceptable. *Disqualification*—Any black in the coat, tan, tri-color in any combination, or any color other than accepted colors.

**Gait**—The Spinone is first and foremost a functional working gun dog. Its purpose as a versatile hunting dog must be given the utmost consideration. Easy and loose trot geared for endurance. Maximum ground is covered with least amount of effort, which his purpose as a versatile working gun dog demands. Profile of the topline kept throughout the trotting gait, light body roll in mature bitches is characteristic of the breed. While hunting, an extended fast trot with intermittent paces of a gallop allows the Spinone to cover ground quickly and thoroughly. Any characteristics that interfere with the accomplishment of the function of the Spinone shall be considered as a serious fault.

*Faults*—Any departure from the foregoing points constitutes a fault which when judging must be penalized according to its seriousness and extension.

## DISQUALIFICATION

*Wall Eye.*
*Any pigment other than described or incomplete pigment of the nose.*
*Overshot or undershot bite.*
*Any black pigmentation.*
*Any black in the coat; tan; tri-color markings in any combination; or any color other than accepted colors.*

**Approved February 11, 2000**
**Effective September 28, 2000**

# VIZSLA

THE ORIGIN OF THE VIZSLA, OR HUNGARIAN POINTER, HAS BEEN OBSCURED through the centuries, but it is fair to assume that breed ancestors were hunters and companions for the Magyar hordes that swarmed over Central Europe more than a thousand years ago, finally settling in what became Hungary. Primitive tenth-century stone etchings show a Magyar huntsman with a falcon and a dog resembling the Vizsla. A fourteenth-century manuscript of early Hungarian codes carried a chapter on falconry illustrated with a picture of a dog reasonably identified as a Vizsla. The breed became a favorite of barons and warlords, who either deliberately or accidentally preserved the breed's purity through the years.

The Vizsla's continued existence resulted from its innate hunting ability. Before the twentieth century, Hungarian territory included fertile plains surrounded by forested mountains. In the agricultural grasslands, partridge and other game birds were plentiful, as was the Hungarian hare. The forests were home to deer and wild boar. Before the invention of firearms, hunting dogs were used to drive birds into nets and to track game in the forests. In falconry, dogs found and flushed prey for the falcons.

With the advent of firearms, different hunting styles developed. What the huntsman required and selected for was a dog swift of foot yet cautious enough not to alert the quarry. Hunters wanted a close-working companion with a superior nose and generally high-class hunting ability. In short, they developed a dog that combined the duties of the specialists as both pointer and retriever.

The two world wars interfered markedly with what otherwise would have been normal breed progress. The close of World War I found the Vizsla all but extinct, preserved in only a small way by just a few of its firmest friends. The years between the two wars were difficult, but those who loved the breed refused to let it die out. Hungarians who fled before the Russian occupation in 1945 took their dogs with them into Austria, Italy, and Germany. Likewise, there were some Vizslas in Czechoslovakia, Turkey, and southern Russia.

Importation into the United States began in the 1950s. In 1954, the organization that would eventually become the Vizsla Club of America, the AKC parent club, held its first meeting. The breed was admitted to the AKC Stud Book in 1960. Vizslas are active in all AKC competitions open to the breed, including conformation events; hunt tests; obedience, field, and agility trials; and tracking tests. The versatility of the breed is demonstrated by its success in these venues. The Vizsla produced the first AKC Triple Champion, a dog with field, obedience, and conformation championships. The first AKC quintuple champion was a Field Champion, Amateur Field Champion, Obedience Trial Champion, and Agility Trial Champion, as well as a conformation champion and a Master Hunter.

Essentially pointer in type, the Vizsla is a clean, distinguished-looking dog of aristocratic bearing, with a short, smooth coat in a striking golden-rust color. Vizslas are powerfully built, but lithe and well balanced, with a gait that is far-reaching, light-footed, and smooth. The Vizsla is a multipurpose hunting dog, developed for pointing and retrieving fur or feather on land and in water. A robust, enduring hunter, the Vizsla is also a versatile, demonstrative, affectionate, friendly companion who thrives on human attention and activity.

A gentle disposition, eagerness to please, and willingness to learn make the Vizsla exceptionally well suited to serve in many capacities. Vizslas have participated in everything from archaeological excavations to the search at Ground Zero in New York following the September 11, 2001, terrorist attacks. They are used as therapy dogs, guide dogs for the blind, service dogs for the disabled, narcotics- and explosives-detection dogs, and search-and-rescue dogs.

# OFFICIAL STANDARD FOR THE VIZSLA

**General Appearance**—That of a medium-sized short-coated hunting dog of distinguished appearance and bearing. Robust but rather lightly built; the coat is an attractive solid golden rust. This is a dog of power and drive in the field yet a tractable and affectionate companion in the home. It is strongly emphasized that field-conditioned coats, as well as brawny or sinewy muscular condition and honorable scars indicating a working and hunting dog are never to be penalized in this dog. The qualities that make a "dual" dog are always to be appreciated, not deprecated.

**Head**—Lean and muscular. *Skull* moderately wide between the ears with a median line down the forehead. Stop between skull and foreface is moderate, not deep. Foreface or *muzzle* is of equal length or slightly shorter than skull when viewed in profile, should taper gradually from stop to tip of nose. Muzzle square and deep. It must not turn up as in a "dish" face nor should it turn down. Whiskers serve a functional purpose; their removal is permitted but not preferred. Nostrils slightly open. *Nose* brown. Any other color is faulty. *A totally black nose is a disqualification.* Ears, thin, silky and proportionately long, with rounded-leather ends, set fairly low and hanging close to cheeks. *Jaws* are strong with well-developed white teeth meeting in a scissors bite. *Eyes* medium in size and depth of setting, their surrounding tissue covering the whites. Color of the iris should blend with the color of the coat. Yellow or any other color is faulty. Prominent pop-eyes are faulty. Lower eyelids should neither turn in nor out, since both conditions allow seeds and dust to irritate the eye. *Lips* cover the jaws completely but are neither loose nor pendulous.

**Neck and Body**—*Neck* strong, smooth and muscular, moderately long, arched and devoid of dewlap, broadening nicely into shoulders which are moderately laid back. This is mandatory to maintain balance with the moderately angulated hindquarters. *Body* is strong and well proportioned. Back short. Withers high and the *topline* slightly rounded over the loin to the set-on of the tail. *Chest* moderately broad and deep reaching down to the elbows. Ribs well-sprung; underline exhibiting a slight tuck-up beneath the loin. *Tail* set just below the level of the croup, thicker at the root and docked one-third off. Ideally, it should reach to the back of the stifle joint and be carried at or near the horizontal. An undocked tail is faulty.

**Forequarters**—*Shoulder* blades proportionately long and wide sloping moderately back and fairly close at the top. *Forelegs* straight and muscular with elbows close. Feet cat-like, round and compact with toes close. Nails brown and short. Pads thick and tough. Dewclaws, if any, to be removed on front and rear feet. Hare feet are faulty.

**Hindquarters**—*Hind legs* have well-developed thighs with moderately angulated stifles and hocks in balance with the moderately laid back shoulders. They must be straight as viewed from behind. Too much angulation at the hocks is as faulty as too little. The hocks are let down and parallel to each other.

**Coat**—Short, smooth, dense and close-lying without woolly undercoat. *A distinctly long coat is a disqualification.*

**Color**—Solid golden rust in different shadings. Solid dark mahogany red and pale yellow are *faulty.* White on the forechest, preferably as small as possible, and white on the toes are permissible. *Solid white extending above the toes or white anywhere else on the dog except the forechest is a disqualification.* When viewing the dog from the front, white markings on the forechest must be confined to an area from the top of the sternum to a point between the elbows when the dog is standing naturally. *White extending on the shoulders or neck is a disqualification.* White due to aging shall not be faulted. Any noticeable area of black in the coat is a serious fault.

**Gait**—Far reaching, light footed, graceful and smooth. When moving at a fast trot, a properly built dog single tracks.

**Size**—The ideal male is 22 to 24 inches at the highest point over the shoulder blades. The ideal female is 21 to 23 inches. Because the Vizsla is meant to be a medium-sized hunter, any dog measuring more than 1½ inches over or under these limits must be disqualified.

**Temperament**—A natural hunter endowed with a good nose and above-average ability to take training. Lively, gentle-mannered, demonstrably affectionate and sensitive though fearless with a well-developed protective instinct. Shyness, timidity or nervousness should be penalized.

## DISQUALIFICATIONS

*Completely black nose.*

*Solid white extending above the toes or white anywhere else on the dog except the forechest.*

*White extending on the shoulders or neck.*

*A distinctly long coat.*

*Any male over 25½ inches, or under 20½ inches and any female over 24½ inches or under 19½ inches at the highest point over the shoulder blades.*

**Approved December 11, 1995**
**Effective January 31, 1996**

# WEIMARANER

*A*S HISTORY IS RECKONED, THE WEIMARANER IS A YOUNG DOG, DATING only to the early nineteenth century. The Bloodhound is believed to be among its ancestors, if not in direct line of descent, then certainly in a collateral way. In their breed investigations, historians stopped when they got as far back as the Red Schweisshund, but it is difficult to imagine that any of the several varieties of Schweisshund did not trace to the Bloodhound, which was well established in Europe at the time of the Crusades. Indeed, the red-tan Schweisshund found in the vicinity of Hanover is described as having "many of the characteristics of the Bloodhound." It was, however, a breed measuring about twenty-one inches at the shoulder, compared with the Bloodhound's average height of twenty-six inches and the Weimaraner's top of twenty-seven inches.

The Weimaraner that we know today is the product of selective breeding, of judicious crosses followed by generations of linebreeding to fix type and quality. It came from the same general stock which has produced a number of Germany's hunting breeds, one of its cousins being the German Shorthaired Pointer. In fact, in its early days, the Weimaraner was known simply as the Weimar Pointer. Since then height and weight have both been increased, but the distinctive coat color, described as silver grizzle or mouse gray, was approximately the same.

Throughout its early career the Weimaraner was sponsored by the sportsmen nobles in the court of Weimar. Long accustomed to many types of hunting, these men determined to meld into one breed all the qualities they had found worthwhile in their forays against the then abundant game of Germany. In short, the dog had to have good scenting ability, speed, courage, and intelligence.

Formerly the Weimaraner had been a big-game dog used on such quarry as wolves, wildcats, deer, mountain lion, and bear. By the time big game in Germany became a rarity, the breed was supported by a club originally started by a few of the men who had drawn up the dog's specifications. They were amateur sportsmen who desired to breed for sport rather than for profit. Accordingly, it was not easy to purchase a Weimaraner in Germany and practically impossible in any foreign country. One had to become a member of the club before purchasing, while gaining admittance to the club meant that the applicant's previous record of sportsmanship must assure proper maintenance of the club's breeding rules. One of these rules demanded that litters resulting from matings deemed unsuitable by a breed survey were not given place in the studbook; another, that specimens, even from approved litters, which did not measure up physically and temperamentally were to be destroyed. Hence there was no chance of a boom in the breed.

America came to know the Weimaraner back in 1929, when an American sportsman and dog breeder, Howard Knight, was made a member of Germany's Weimaraner Club. Permitted to bring back two specimens, he helped found the club in this country and served as its first president. The club has made every effort to carry out the same principles that mapped the career of the breed in its native land.

It should be mentioned in passing that with the demise of big-game hunting in Germany, the Weimaraner was trained as a bird dog used on various types of game in upland shooting and as a water retriever noted for its soft mouth. Both in Germany and in America, however, the dog has been used more as a personal hunting companion than as a field-trial competitor.

Obedience trials incited the first interest in the breed over here, even before recognition was granted in 1943 by the American Kennel Club. A bitch qualified for her CD in three straight shows in 1941. Later, another specimen went through all the degrees except the tracking test before reaching his tenth month. Curiously enough, the Weimaraner has seen more actual competition of various kinds in America than it did in all its decades in Germany.

As for temperament, this dog is not happy when relegated to the kennel. He is accustomed to being a member of the family and accepts the responsibilities which that entails.

# OFFICIAL STANDARD FOR THE WEIMARANER

**General Appearance**—A medium-sized gray dog, with fine aristocratic features. He should present a picture of grace, speed, stamina, alertness and balance. Above all, the dog's conformation must indicate the ability to work with great speed and endurance in the field.

**Height**—Height at the withers: dogs, 25 to 27 inches; bitches, 23 to 25 inches. One inch over or under the specified height of each sex is allowable but should be penalized. Dogs measuring less than 24 inches or more than 28 inches and bitches measuring less than 22 inches or more than 26 inches shall be disqualified.

**Head**—Moderately long and aristocratic, with moderate stop and slight median line extending back over the forehead. Rather prominent occipital bone and trumpets well set back, beginning at the back of the eye sockets. Measurement from tip of nose to stop equals that from stop to occipital bone. The flews should be straight, delicate at the nostrils. Skin drawn tightly. Neck clean-cut and moderately long. Expression kind, keen and intelligent. *Ears*—Long and lobular, slightly folded and set high. The ear when drawn snugly alongside the jaw should end approximately 2 inches from the point of the nose. *Eyes*—In shades of light amber, gray or blue-gray, set well enough apart to indicate good disposition and intelligence. When dilated under excitement the eyes may appear almost black. *Teeth*—Well set, strong and even; well-developed and proportionate to jaw with correct scissors bite, the upper teeth protruding slightly over the lower teeth but not more than $\frac{1}{16}$ of an inch. Complete dentition is greatly to be desired. *Nose*—Gray. *Lips* and *Gums*—Pinkish flesh shades.

**Body**—The back should be moderate in length, set in a straight line, strong, and should slope slightly from the withers. The chest should be well developed and deep with shoulders well laid back. Ribs well sprung and long. Abdomen firmly held; moderately tucked-up flank. The brisket should extend to the elbow.

**Coat and Color**—Short, smooth and sleek, solid color, in shades of mouse-gray to silver-gray, usually blending to lighter shades on the head and ears. A small white marking on the chest is permitted, but should be penalized on any other portion of the body. White spots resulting from injury should not be penalized. A distinctly long coat is a disqualification. A distinctly blue or black coat is a disqualification.

**Forelegs**—Straight and strong, with the measurement from the elbow to the ground approximately equaling the distance from the elbow to the top of the withers.

**Hindquarters**—Well-angulated stifles and straight hocks. Musculation well developed.

**Feet**—Firm and compact, webbed, toes well arched, pads closed and thick, nails short and gray or amber in color. *Dewclaws*—Should be removed.

**Tail**—Docked. At maturity it should measure approximately 6 inches with a tendency to be light rather than heavy and should be carried in a manner expressing confidence and sound temperament. A non-docked tail shall be penalized.

**Gait**—The gait should be effortless and should indicate smooth coordination. When seen from the rear, the hind feet should be parallel to the front feet. When viewed from the side, the topline should remain strong and level.

**Temperament**—The temperament should be friendly, fearless, alert and obedient.

**Minor Faults**—Tail too short or too long. Pink nose.

**Major Faults**—Doggy bitches. Bitchy dogs. Improper muscular condition. Badly affected teeth. More than four teeth missing. Back too long or too short. Faulty coat.

Neck too short, thick or throaty. Low-set tail. Elbows in or out. Feet east and west. Poor gait. Poor feet. Cowhocks. Faulty backs, either roached or sway. Badly overshot, or undershot bite. Snipy muzzle. Short ears.

**Very Serious Faults**—White, other than a spot on the chest. Eyes other than gray, blue-gray or light amber. Black mottled mouth. Non-docked tail. Dogs exhibiting strong fear, shyness or extreme nervousness.

## DISQUALIFICATIONS

*Deviation in height of more than one inch from standard either way.*
*A distinctly long coat. A distinctly blue or black coat.*

**Approved December 14, 1971**

# Wirehaired Pointing Griffon

$\mathcal{T}$HE ORIGIN OF THE WIREHAIRED POINTING GRIFFON WAS SHORTLY AFTER Gregor Mendel (1822–84) published his experiments on genetic heredity, which inspired many Europeans to try their skills at breeding.

It cannot be said for certain where the griffon originated in the time before "purebred" dogs arose. The Greek historian Xenophon made mention of the griffon as early as the fifth century B.C. From the sixteenth century there are further references to various regional strains of griffon-like dogs throughout Europe. Indeed, even today there are many different kinds of purebred griffons. We can, however, trace for certain the development of the Wirehaired Pointing Griffon.

Eduard K. Korthals, born in 1851, was the son of a wealthy Amsterdam ship outfitter. He was an avid hunter in the marshes and swamps of the polders of his Dutch homeland. As his passion for hunting grew, so did his quest for a dog that could hunt not only in the marshes but also in other terrains. Korthals had been exposed to the effectiveness of selective breeding by his father, who had already succeeded in developing a strain of cattle with unusual markings.

As a young man, Korthals began to assemble the dogs from which he was to establish a new, more versatile sporting breed than the single-purpose specialists or the slow Continental dogs used at that time. The ideal dog would be robust, and have a swift and efficient ground-covering stride and the endurance for an all-day hunt. It would possess the keen game-finding nose of the pointing breeds, and have the cooperative nature and willingness of the retrievers to recover upland game and waterfowl. In addition, it was to be resistant to heat and cold and endowed with a harsh, water-repellant coat.

In 1873, Korthals was hired by Prince Albrecht zu Solms-Braunfels to run his large kennel in Germany. There, Korthals continued his breeding program in earnest. He purchased dogs from the Netherlands, Germany, Belgium, and France. According to Korthals's detailed records, the dogs in his kennels were largely griffon types, along with Barbets, Boulets, pointers from France and Germany, spaniels, and retrievers. Korthals bred extensively, selecting only those dogs that contributed the desired attributes he was seeking in a versatile hunting dog. In less than two decades, Korthals succeeded in fixing the new breed that he called the Wirehaired Pointing Griffon. In 1886 he wrote the standard and just two years later formed the international Griffon Club.

It was not until many years later in his breeding program that Korthals realized the prepotent impact of eight dogs, in particular, that came to be known as the "patriarchs" of the breed. The first six were purchased while Korthals was in Holland: Mouche, Janus, Hector, Satan, Junon, and Banco. The other two, Donna and Vesta, were German dogs.

Korthals was a man of wide acquaintance among the European sporting fraternity, and invariably he was present at any major field activity connected with dogs, and later the bench shows, where he sought to popularize the strain of griffon he had developed. Korthals had a loyal following throughout Europe and especially in France, where the majority of the modern-day development has taken place. Some proponents of the new breed honored him, after his untimely death, by renaming it the Korthals Griffon.

In 1887 the first Griffon arrived in the United States from Europe and was registered by the American Kennel Club as Zolette, a Russian Setter (Griffon). The sire, Guerre, was a grandson of Donna, one of the eight patriarchs. So started the American Griffon legacy.

In August of 1916, the Griffon Club of America was formed. Unfortunately, the two world wars interrupted club activity. In 1951, with renewed interest, the Wirehaired Pointing Griffon Club of America was formed. During the 1980s, this club decided to crossbreed the Cesky Fousek with the Wirehaired Pointing Griffon. This resulted in the formation of a new club, the American Wirehaired Pointing Griffon Association, devoted to the purebred griffon and recognized in 1991 as the breed's official AKC parent club.

The modern Wirehaired Pointing Griffon still possesses the qualities that Korthals envisioned over a century ago. It is a medium-sized dog with a functional double coat and distinctive facial furnishings. A versatile gundog with a high degree of trainability, the griffon excels in hunting upland birds, waterfowl, and furred game.

It is a deliberate, thorough, and tireless worker with a strong desire to please its master. This sporting dog needs plenty of exercise to keep it physically and mentally fit.

The Griffon is a loyal, affectionate family companion and is easily adaptable to any task its master asks it to perform.

# OFFICIAL STANDARD FOR
# THE WIREHAIRED POINTING GRIFFON

**General Appearance**—Medium sized, with a noble, square-shaped head, strong of limb, bred to cover all terrain encountered by the walking hunter. Movement showing an easy catlike gracefulness. Excels equally as a pointer in the field, or a retriever in the water. Coat is hard and coarse, never curly or woolly, with a thick undercoat of fine hair, giving an unkempt appearance. His easy trainability, devotion to family, and friendly temperament endear him to all. The nickname of "supreme gundog" is well earned.

**Size, Proportion, Substance**—*Size*—22 to 24 inches for males, 20 to 22 inches for females. Correct size is important. Oversize to be *severely penalized*. **Proportion**— Slightly longer than tall, in a ratio of 10 to 9. Height from withers to ground; length from point of shoulder to point of buttocks. The Griffon must not evolve towards a square conformation. **Substance** medium, reflecting his work as an all-terrain hunting dog.

**Head**—The **head** is to be in proportion to the overall dog. The **skull** is of medium width with equal length from nose to stop and from stop to occiput. The skull is slightly rounded on top, but from the side the **muzzle** and head are square. The *stop* and *occiput* are only slightly pronounced. The required abundant mustache and eyebrows contribute to the friendly **expression.** The **eyes** are large and well open, more rounded than elliptical. They have an alert, friendly, and intelligent expression. Eye color ranges in all shades of yellow and brown. Haws should not show nor should there be protruding eyes. The **ears** should be of medium size, lying flat and close to the head, set high, at the height of the eye line. **Nose**—Well open nostrils are essential. Nose color is always brown. Any other color is a *disqualification*. **Bite** scissors. Overshot or undershot bite is a *serious fault*.

**Neck, Topline, Body**—**Neck** rather long, slightly arched, no dewlap. **Topline**— The back is strong and firm, descending in a gentle slope from the slightly higher withers to the base of the tail. **Body-Chest**—The *chest* must descend to the level of the elbow, with a moderate spring of rib. The chest must neither be too wide nor too narrow, but of medium width to allow freedom of movement. The **loin** is strong and well developed, being of medium length. The croup and rump are stoutly made with adequate length to favor speed. The **tail** extends from the back in a continuation of the topline. It may be carried straight or raised slightly. It is docked by one-third to one-half length.

**Forequarters**—*Shoulders* are long, with good angulation, and well laid back. The *forelegs* are straight and vertical from the front and set well under the shoulder from the side. *Pasterns* are slightly sloping. Dewclaws should be removed. *Feet* are round, firm, with tightly closed webbed toes. Pads are thick.

**Hindquarters**—The *thighs* are long and well muscled. Angulation in balance with the front. The legs are vertical with the hocks turning neither in nor out. The *stifle* and *hock joints* are strong and well angulated. *Feet* as in front.

**Coat**—The coat is one of the distinguishing features of the breed. It is a double coat. The outer coat is medium length, straight and wiry, never curly or woolly. The harsh texture provides protection in rough cover. The obligatory undercoat consists of a fine, thick down, which provides insulation as well as water resistance. The undercoat is more or less abundant, depending upon the season, climate, and hormone cycle of the dog. It is usually lighter in color. The head is furnished with a prominent mustache and eyebrows. These required features are extensions of the undercoat, which gives the Griffon a somewhat untidy appearance. The hair covering the ears is fairly short and soft, mixed with longer harsh hair from the coat. The overall feel is much less wiry than the body. The legs, both front and rear, are covered with denser, shorter, and less coarse hair. The coat on the tail is the same as the body; any type of plume is prohibited. The breed should be exhibited in full body coat, not stripped short in pattern. Trimming and stripping are only allowed around the ears, top of head, cheeks and feet.

**Color**—Preferably steel gray with brown markings, frequently chestnut brown, or roan, white and brown; white and orange also acceptable. A uniformly brown coat, all white coat, or white and orange are less desirable. A black coat *disqualifies.*

**Gait**—Although close working, the Griffon should cover ground in an efficient, tireless manner. He is a medium-speed dog with perfect coordination between front and rear legs. At a trot, both front and rear legs tend to converge toward the center line of gravity. He shows good extension both front and rear. Viewed from the side, the topline is firm and parallel to the line of motion. A smooth, powerful ground-covering ability can be seen.

**Temperament**—The Griffon has a quick and intelligent mind and is easily trained. He is outgoing, shows a tremendous willingness to please and is trustworthy. He makes an excellent family dog as well as a meticulous hunting companion.

## DISQUALIFICATIONS

*Nose any color other than brown.*
*Black coat.*

**Approved October 8, 1991**
**Effective November 28, 1991**

# GROUP II: HOUND BREEDS

AFGHAN HOUND
BASENJI
BASSET HOUND
BEAGLE
BLACK AND TAN COONHOUND
BLOODHOUND
BORZOI
DACHSHUND
AMERICAN FOXHOUND
ENGLISH FOXHOUND
GREYHOUND

HARRIER
IBIZAN HOUND
IRISH WOLFHOUND
NORWEGIAN ELKHOUND
OTTERHOUND
PETIT BASSET GRIFFON VENDÉEN
PHARAOH HOUND
RHODESIAN RIDGEBACK
SALUKI
SCOTTISH DEERHOUND
WHIPPET

# AFGHAN HOUND

$\mathcal{T}$HE AFGHAN HOUND WAS DISCOVERED BY THE WESTERN WORLD IN Afghanistan and surrounding regions during the nineteenth century. The first specimens of the breed were brought to England in the latter part of that century, and the earliest known pictorial representation of an unmistakable, full-coated Afghan Hound is a drawing reproduced in some copies of a volume of letters written in India in 1809 and published in London in 1813.

Of the breed's origin and its history before then, little is known for certain. A vast amount of research, however, has turned up no basis for the once popular belief that the Afghan Hound existed in Egypt thousands of years ago, or for the theory that the breed evolved on the steppes of Asia and represents the original sighthound.

The basic structure of the dog beneath the coat is that of a relatively sturdy coursing hound of a type which might have evolved or been created from other canine types almost anytime, anywhere. The extremely fine, longhaired coat, however, is of a sort found among animals native to high altitudes, and the desired coat pattern of contrasting short hair on the foreface, back, and dorsal surface of the tail may also be related to climate.

A problem in any study of the breed is that, like so many other breeds recognized today, the Afghan Hound represents a blending of dogs of more than one type. Some sources in Afghanistan divide the breed as found there into a half-dozen or more varieties based on locality, color, and so on. Although intermediate variations undoubtedly exist, it has been more common to speak in terms of two extremes in type—the hounds of the southern and western desert regions, which tend to be relatively rangy in build, light in color, and sparse in outer coat; and the hounds of the northern mountain regions, which tend to be more compact in structure, darker in color, and more heavily coated. These and other variations represent logical adaptations to the wide diversity of climate and terrain in the area of Afghanistan.

Among other things, this diversity in the breed—plus the diversity in the Afghan people, their culture, and their country—helps explain the apparent conflicts among accounts of how the breed was utilized in its native land. Some tell of Afghan Hounds serving as guard dogs and herd dogs, which are within the capabilities of the breed as we know it. The major role of these dogs, however, was undoubtedly that of hunting. The kings of Afghanistan maintained a kennel of hunting hounds for many generations.

The breed is primarily a coursing hound, pursuing its quarry by sight and followed by the huntsman on horseback. Because these dogs tended to outdistance the horses, the Afghan Hounds hunted on their own, without direction by the huntsman, giving rise to the independence of thought and spirit still typical of the breed.

The Afghan Hound could and quite certainly was employed to hunt whatever animals the locality provided and the huntsman wanted to hunt. In the truest coursing-hound sense, they ran down game such as mountain deer, plains antelopes, and hares wherever they might be found. They could be used to bring to bay such predators as wolves, jackals, wild dogs, and snow leopards. They were also used to flush quail and partridge for the falcon or gun. And they are the equal to any terrier for dispatching marmots, greatly prized by the mountain people for their fur and flesh.

As coursing dogs Afghan Hounds excel, not so much in straightaway speed—although they have considerable—as in the ability to traverse rough terrain swiftly and sure-footedly. This requires agility in leaping and quickness in turning, plus the stamina to maintain such a strenuous chase for as long as it may take to close on the quarry.

The first recorded appearance of the Afghan Hound in the West was in the latter part of the nineteenth century, when British officers and others returning from the Indian-Afghanistan border wars brought dogs from that area back to England, some of which were exhibited at dog shows as "Afghan Hounds." These aroused some interest but no real enthusiasm until 1907, when Captain John Barff brought from Persia via India his dog Zardin—a typey, well-coated dog with a dark mask and a great deal of style. This, English dog fanciers decided, was what an Afghan Hound should be! There was some breeding of Afghan Hounds in Great Britain at this time, and some specimens from there or Afghanistan may have reached America before World War I.

During that war, however, the breed literally disappeared in the Western world, and the start of the Afghan Hounds we have today dates to 1920, when Major and Mrs. G. Bell Murray and Miss Jean C. Manson brought to Scotland a group of Afghan Hounds they had acquired or bred during an eight-year stay in Baluchistan, today a part of Pakistan. Most of these dogs were of the "desert" type—racy, fine headed, and light in coat. Breeding from these imports, Miss Manson, the major, and others further developed the "Bell-Murray strain" throughout the 1920s.

In 1925, Mrs. Mary Amps shipped to England the first of a group of Afghan Hounds from the kennel she had maintained in Kabul. These were mainly of the "mountain" type—sturdily built, relatively short-coupled, and more or less full-coated. From these imports—the most successful of which as a show dog and sire was the English champion Sirdar of Ghazni—Mrs. Amps and others developed what is called (from her kennel name) the "Ghazni strain."

During the 1920s, a number of Bell-Murray Afghan Hounds were exported to the United States, and when the AKC Stud Book was opened to the breed, some of these were registered, beginning in October 1926. From two of them came the first registered American-bred Afghan Hound in 1927.

The real start of the breed in this country, however, dates to the first Ghazni imports in 1931, when Zeppo Marx and his wife brought from England a bitch, Asra of Ghazni, and a dog, Westmill Omar. Asra and Omar were later acquired by Q. A. Shaw McKean's Prides Hill kennels in Massachusetts. McKean soon added a young English champion, Badshah of Ainsdart, a bitch of pure Bell-Murray breeding. These three—Asra, Omar, and Badshah—formed the cornerstone of the breed in America.

Although the Afghan Hound was admitted to the AKC Stud Book in 1926, there was no parent club for the breed until a group of leading fanciers met at the 1937 Westminster Kennel Club show and organized what, after a reorganization the following year, became the Afghan Hound Club of America. In 1940, the club was admitted to AKC membership and held its first specialty show.

There being no parent club in 1926, the AKC had adopted a standard which was an expanded version of one then in use by an English breed club. This standard, in turn, was little more than a description of Zardin written some twenty years earlier. One of the first tasks assigned to the AHCA, therefore, was the drafting of a "clarified standard." A new and quite original standard was drafted and approved by the AHCA membership without dissent in 1948 and adopted by the AKC later that year.

Much of the Afghan Hound's popularity here has been generated by the breed's spectacular qualities as a show dog. The Afghan Hound also excels in lure coursing, and although its tendency to think for itself makes for something less than perfect precision in executing set exercises and commands, the breed has also done well in obedience work.

Over and beyond their success in such fields, however, Afghan Hounds are prized and loved by their owners as companions and members of the family. With its highly individual personality and with its coat which requires regular care and grooming, it is not the breed for all would-be dog owners, but where the dog and owner combination is right, there is no animal which can equal the Afghan Hound as a pet.

# OFFICIAL STANDARD FOR THE AFGHAN HOUND

**General Appearance**—The Afghan Hound is an aristocrat, his whole appearance one of dignity and aloofness with no trace of plainness or coarseness. He has a straight front, proudly carried head, eyes gazing into the distance as if in memory of ages past. The striking characteristics of the breed—exotic, or "Eastern," expression, long silky topknot, peculiar coat pattern, very prominent hipbones, large feet, and the impression of a somewhat exaggerated bend in the stifle due to profuse trouserings—stand out clearly, giving the Afghan Hound the appearance of what he is, a king of dogs, that has held true to tradition throughout the ages.

**Head**—The head is of good length, showing much refinement, the skull evenly balanced with the foreface. There is a slight prominence of the nasal bone structure causing a slightly Roman appearance, the center line running up over the foreface with little or no stop, falling away in front of the eyes so there is an absolutely clear outlook with no interference; the underjaw showing great strength, the jaws long and punishing; the mouth level, meaning that the teeth from the upper jaw and lower jaw match evenly, neither overshot nor undershot. This is a difficult mouth to breed. A scissors bite is even more punishing and can be more easily bred into a dog than a level mouth, and a dog having a scissors bite, where the lower teeth slip inside and rest against the teeth of the upper jaw, should not be penalized. The occipital bone is very prominent. The head is surmounted by a topknot of long silky hair. *Ears*—The ears are long, set approximately on level with outer corners of the eyes, the leather of the ear reaching nearly to the end of the dog's nose, and covered with long silky hair. *Eyes*—The eyes are almond-shaped (almost triangular), never full or bulgy, and are dark in color. *Nose*— Nose is of good size, black in color. *Faults*—Coarseness; snipiness; overshot or undershot; eyes round or bulgy or light in color; exaggerated Roman nose; head not surmounted by topknot.

**Neck**—The neck is of good length, strong and arched, running in a curve to the shoulders which are long and sloping and well laid back. *Faults*—Neck too short or too thick; a ewe neck; a goose neck; a neck lacking in substance.

**Body**—The back line appearing practically level from the shoulders to the loin. Strong and powerful loin and slightly arched, falling away toward the stern, with the hipbones very pronounced; well ribbed and tucked up in flanks. The height at the shoulders equals the distance from the chest to the buttocks; the brisket well let down, and of medium width. *Faults*—Roach back, swayback, goose rump, slack loin; lack of prominence of hipbones; too much width of brisket, causing interference with elbows.

**Tail**—Tail set not too high on the body, having a ring, or a curve on the end;

should never be curled over, or rest on the back, or be carried sideways; and should never be bushy.

**Legs**—Forelegs are straight and strong with great length between elbow and pastern; elbows well held in; forefeet large in both length and width; toes well arched; feet covered with long thick hair; fine in texture; pasterns long and straight; pads of feet unusually large and well down on the ground. Shoulders have plenty of angulation so that the legs are well set underneath the dog. Too much straightness of shoulder causes the dog to break down in the pasterns, and this is a serious fault. All four feet of the Afghan Hound are in line with the body, turning neither in nor out. The hind feet are broad and of good length; the toes arched, and covered with long thick hair; hindquarters powerful and well muscled, with great length between hip and hock; hocks are well let down; good angulation of both stifle and hock; slightly bowed from hock to crotch. *Faults*—Front or back feet thrown outward or inward; pads of feet not thick enough; or feet too small; or any other evidence of weakness in feet; weak or broken down pasterns; too straight in stifle; too long in hock.

**Coat**—Hindquarters, flanks, ribs, forequarters, and legs well covered with thick, silky hair, very fine in texture; ears and all four feet well feathered; from in front of the shoulders; and also backwards from the shoulders along the saddle from the flanks and the ribs upwards, the hair is short and close, forming a smooth back in mature dogs— this is a traditional characteristic of the Afghan Hound. The Afghan Hound should be shown in its natural state; the coat is not clipped or trimmed; the head is surmounted (in the full sense of the word) with a topknot of long, silky hair—that is also an outstanding characteristic of the Afghan Hound. Showing of short hair on cuffs on either front or back legs is permissible. *Fault*—Lack of shorthaired saddle in mature dogs.

**Height**—Dogs, 27 inches, plus or minus one inch; bitches, 25 inches, plus or minus one inch.

**Weight**—Dogs, about 60 pounds; bitches, about 50 pounds.

**Color**—All colors are permissible, but color or color combinations are pleasing; white markings, especially on the head, are undesirable.

**Gait**—When running free, the Afghan Hound moves at a gallop, showing great elasticity and spring in his smooth, powerful stride. When on a loose lead, the Afghan can trot at a fast pace; stepping along, he has the appearance of placing the hind feet directly in the footprints of the front feet, both thrown straight ahead. Moving with head and tail high, the whole appearance of the Afghan Hound is one of great style and beauty.

**Temperament**—Aloof and dignified, yet gay. *Faults*—Sharpness or shyness.

**Approved September 14, 1948**

# BASENJI

HE BASENJI, POPULARLY KNOWN AS THE "BARKLESS DOG," IS ONE OF THE oldest breeds. The first specimens were brought from the source of the Nile as presents to the Pharaohs of ancient Egypt. Later, when the civilization of Egypt declined and fell, the Basenji lapsed into obscurity. It was, however, still valued and preserved in its native Central Africa, where it was highly prized for its intelligence, speed, hunting power, and silence.

Centuries later an English explorer rediscovered the Basenji and a pair were brought to England in 1895. Unfortunately, these little dogs contracted distemper and shortly thereafter died. Aside from that abortive attempt to make the breed known, the "outside" world in general did not hear of the Basenji until 1937, when it was successfully introduced to England. At the same time, a pair were brought to America by Mrs. Byron Rogers, of New York City. Unfortunately for America, this pair and a litter of puppies produced from mating these specimens contracted distemper. All died except the older male dog, Bois.

In 1941 a young female Basenji was brought from Africa to Boston; Alexander Phemister, of Kingston, Massachusetts, obtained her and shortly afterward also acquired Bois. The young female, Congo, and Bois, both African-bred, were mated, resulting in the first litter of Basenji puppies to be raised to maturity in America. Later, other Basenjis were imported from the Canadian kennels of Dr. A.R.B. Richmond, and still others were brought over from England.

Dog lovers all over the country became interested in this breed—so old, yet so new in America—and later purchased young specimens as foundation breeding stock. The Basenji Club of America was formed in 1942 and accepted the breed standard as drawn up by the Basenji Club of England. In 1943, the American Kennel Club accepted the breed for registration in the AKC Stud Book, and approved the standard. Within a few months, there were 59 Basenjis registered. Several dedicated Basenji breeders went to the Congo/Zaire in 1987 and 1988 and brought back new stock, with the goal of increasing the very limited gene pool.

The Basenji is about the size and build of a Fox Terrier. The first impression one gets of a Basenji is that he is a proud little dog, and then one is impressed with his beauty, grace, and intelligence. In fact, he has often been compared to a little deer.

The coat of the Basenji is one of his most beautiful features. Appropriate to its native tropical climate, the coat is short and fine and shines in the sun. In colder countries the coat tends to become more coarse, but it never loses its brilliant luster. Other distinctive features include the lack of bark; the forehead deeply furrowed with wrinkles; the prick ears; the dark, intelligent, far-seeing eyes; and the tail curled forward to one side.

The Basenji's intelligence and courage stands proven by his use in his native habitat. The natives use him for pointing, retrieving, for driving game into nets, and for hunting wounded quarry. He is also used for hunting the reed rats—vicious long-toothed creatures weighing from 12 to 20 pounds—and here his silence is a particularly valuable asset.

Those in America as well as England, Europe, and Australia who have had the opportunity to know the little Basenji have found him to be an interesting companion. He is a fascinating and endearing fellow, full of play, curious and active. His fastidious, dainty habits, such as cleaning himself all over as does a cat and his lack of doggy odor, are assets in a house dog.

The Basenji's distinctive sound of happiness fairly thrills one, yet it is a sound hard to describe. It is somewhere between a chortle and a yodel. He is usually very happy when he makes it and one can't help but share the happiness with him.

For uncounted thousands of years the Basenji survived as a hunting dog. Great importance must have been given to intelligence and adaptability, for the dogs often worked out of sight of the hunters. At times the Basenji can still be quite independent and aloof. It is alert and careful with strangers, open and calm with friends, loving and solicitous with children. When meeting strangers, Basenjis prefer to make the first overtures and should not be approached from behind. Although not high-strung, the Basenji should be an alert, active, curious dog.

# OFFICIAL STANDARD FOR THE BASENJI

**General Appearance**—The Basenji is a small, short haired hunting dog from Africa. It is short backed and lightly built, appearing high on the leg compared to its length. The wrinkled head is proudly carried on a well arched neck and the tail is set high and curled. Elegant and graceful, the whole demeanor is one of poise and inquiring alertness. The balanced structure and the smooth musculature enables it to move with ease and agility. The Basenji hunts by both sight and scent. **Characteristics**—The Basenji should not bark but is not mute. The wrinkled forehead, tightly curled tail and swift, effortless gait (resembling a racehorse trotting full out) are typical of the breed. **Faults**—Any departure from the following points must be considered a fault, and the seriousness with which the fault is regarded is to be in exact proportion to its degree.

**Size, Proportion, Substance**—Ideal height for dogs is 17 inches and bitches 16 inches. Dogs 17 inches and bitches 16 inches from front of chest to point of buttocks. Approximate weight for dogs, 24 pounds and bitches, 22 pounds. Lightly built within this height to weight ratio.

**Head**—The head is proudly carried. **Eyes**—Dark hazel to dark brown, almond shaped, obliquely set and farseeing, rims dark. **Ears**—Small, erect and slightly hooded, of fine texture and set well forward on top of head. The skull is flat, well chiseled and of medium width, tapering toward the eyes. The foreface tapers from eye to muzzle with a perceptible stop. Muzzle shorter than skull, neither coarse nor snipy, but with rounded cushions. Wrinkles appear upon the forehead when ears are erect, and are fine and profuse. Side wrinkles are desirable, but should never be exaggerated into dewlap. Wrinkles are most noticeable in puppies, and because of lack of shadowing, less noticeable in blacks, tricolors and brindles. **Nose**—Black greatly desired. **Teeth**—Evenly aligned with a scissors bite.

**Neck, Topline, Body**—Neck of good length, well crested and slightly full at base of throat. Well set into shoulders. **Topline**—Back level. **Body**—Balanced with a short back, short coupled and ending in a definite waist. Ribs moderately sprung, deep to elbows and oval. Slight forechest in front of point of shoulder. Chest of medium width. **Tail** is set high on topline, bends acutely forward and lies well curled over to either side.

**Forequarters**—Shoulders moderately laid back. Shoulder blade and upper arm of approximately equal length. Elbows tucked firmly against brisket. Legs straight with clean fine bone, long forearm and well defined sinews. Pasterns of good length, strong and flexible. **Feet**—Small, oval and compact with thick pads and well arched toes. Dewclaws are usually removed.

**Hindquarters**—Medium width, strong and muscular, hocks well let down and turned neither in nor out, with long second thighs and moderately bent stifles. **Feet**—Same as in "Forequarters."

**Coat and Color**—Coat short and fine. Skin very pliant.

**Color**—Chestnut red; pure black; tricolor (pure black and chestnut red); or brindle (black stripes on a background of chestnut red); all with white feet, chest and tail tip. White legs, blaze and collar optional. The amount of white should never predominate over primary color. Color and markings should be rich, clear and well-defined, with a distinct line of demarcation between the black and red of tricolors and the stripes of brindles.

**Gait**—Swift, tireless trot. Stride is long, smooth, effortless and the topline remains level. Coming and going, the straight column of bones from shoulder joint to foot and from hip joint to pad remains unbroken, converging toward the centerline under the body. The faster the trot, the greater the convergence.

**Temperament**—An intelligent, independent, but affectionate and alert breed. Can be aloof with strangers.

**Approved May 8, 1990**
**Effective June 28, 1990**

# BASSET HOUND

*S*INCE THE 1950S THE BASSET HOUND HAS EMERGED FROM RELATIVE OBSCU-
rity to become one of the most publicized and characterized breeds. Actually,
the Basset Hound is an old, aristocratic breed. Originally of French lineage, it has
flourished for centuries in Europe, primarily in France and Belgium, where it was
used chiefly for the slow trailing of rabbits, hares, deer, and any other game that can
be trailed on foot or taken to ground.

The foremost use of the Basset Hound in the United States is for the hunting
of rabbits, but it is possible to train them for hunting other game such as raccoons
and for the trailing, flushing, and retrieving of wounded pheasants and other game
birds. The Basset is a sturdy, accurate trailer; his tongue is loud and distinctive. The
shortness of his legs and his tight, close coat makes him particularly useful in dense
cover. In trailing ability, the accuracy of his nose makes him second only to the
Bloodhound. His slow-going ways and appealing, clownish appearance belie great
intelligence.

Gentle in disposition, the Basset is agreeable to hunting in packs as well as
singly. Medium as to size, loyal and devoted to his master and family, not requiring
extensive coat care or trimming, considered an "easy keeper"—these attributes
make the Basset an ideal family pet and housedog.

The first mention of the word *basset* as applied to a breed of dog appears to have
been in an early text on hunting written by Fouilloux in 1585. This book is illus-

trated with what is considered the first drawing of a Basset, a woodcut showing a sportsman going out in his *charette de chasse* accompanied by his "badger dog," and Fouilloux gives advice on training the dogs for the purpose of badger hunting.

It is thought that the friars of the French Abbey of St. Hubert were instrumental in selective breeding from various other strains of French hounds to produce a lower-set, hence slower-moving dog that could be followed on foot. The word *basset,* derived from the French adjective *bas,* means a "low thing" or "dwarf." Since hunting was a royal pastime in medieval France, it is not surprising that many of the thoroughly efficient small hounds found their way into the kennels of the aristocracy, only to be dispersed with the changing lifestyle brought on by the Revolution. But the breed was not lost, and we find them mentioned again by M. Blaze in his 1850 sporting book *Le Chasseur.* About the same time, in his book *Chiens de Chasse,* M. Robert wrote: "The Basset will hunt all animals, even boar and wolf, but he is especially excellent for the *chasse à tir* (shooting with the aid of hounds) of rabbits and hares."

By the mid-nineteenth century, the two largest breeders of Bassets in France were producing dogs of slightly different type, especially in head and eye, the two types being identified by the names of their respective breeders. M. Lane's hounds were broader of skull and shorter of ear, with a rounder and more prominent eye. They were generally lemon and white in marking and had a tendency to knuckling. Count Le Couteulx produced hounds that had more narrow heads, more doming in topskull, a softer, more sunken eye, with prominent jaw and a down-faced look that created more facial expression. The more glamorous tricolors of the Le Couteulx hounds made them preferred.

In 1866, Lord Galway imported a pair of French Bassets of the Le Couteulx type to England. The following year a mating of these two produced a litter of five pups, but as there was no public exposure of them, no interest in the breed was stirred. It was not until 1874, when Sir Everett Millais imported from France the hound Model, that real activity with the breed began in England. For his support of the breed and continued drive on a breeding program within his own kennel as well as cooperation with breeding programs established by Lord Onslow and George Krehl, Millais has to be considered the "father of the breed" in England. He first exhibited a Basset at an English dog show in 1875, but it was not until he helped make up a large entry for the Wolverhampton show in 1880 that a great deal of public attention was drawn to the breed. A few years later, further interest was created when Queen Alexandra kept Basset Hounds in the royal kennels.

In the United States, it is thought that George Washington was the owner of Basset Hounds presented to him as a gift by the Marquis de Lafayette after the American Revolution. In 1883 and 1884, English importations were made by American fanciers of the breed. In 1884, Westminster Kennel Club held a class for the Basset Hound and the English import Nemours made his debut before the American public. After subsequent entries at Eastern shows, he completed his championship at Boston in 1886. The American Kennel Club registered its first Basset Hounds in 1885.

Gradually the breed began to find favor. By the 1920s, Gerald Livingston was making multiple importations for his Kilsyth Kennels on Long Island. About the same time, Erastus Tefft brought over to his kennels a number of English Bassets, drawing heavily from the Walhampton Pack. Carl Smith imported two French Bassets, one a French champion. Bassets were being seen regularly at larger shows.

Further attention was drawn to the breed when the February 27, 1928, cover of *Time* magazine carried the picture of a Basset puppy. The accompanying story was a write-up of the 52nd annual Westminster show at Madison Square Garden as if it were attended and observed by the puppy.

In 1935, a national parent breed club was organized in the United States, the Basset Hound Club of America. The club holds annual national shows that bring together the various fields of activity for this capable breed: conformation, field trialing, pack hunting, obedience, and tracking.

By the 1950s, the Basset Hound was synonymous with TV's "Cleo" to Americans, and in England cartoonist Alex Graham's "Fred Basset" was an almost human Everyman. But the dependable and multipurpose qualities of the breed can never be completely obscured behind a droll facade.

# OFFICIAL STANDARD FOR THE BASSET HOUND

**General Appearance**—The Basset Hound possesses in marked degree those characteristics which equip it admirably to follow a trail over and through difficult terrain. It is a short-legged dog, heavier in bone, size considered, than any other breed of dog, and while its movement is deliberate, it is in no sense clumsy. In temperament it is mild, never sharp or timid. It is capable of great endurance in the field and is extreme in its devotion.

**Head**—The head is large and well proportioned. Its length from occiput to muzzle is greater than the width at the brow. In overall appearance the head is of medium width. The *skull* is well domed, showing a pronounced occipital protuberance. A broad flat skull is a fault. The length from nose to stop is approximately the length from stop to occiput. The sides are flat and free from cheek bumps. Viewed in profile the top lines of the muzzle and skull are straight and lie in parallel planes, with a moderately defined stop. The skin over the whole of the head is loose, falling in distinct wrinkles over the brow when the head is lowered. A dry head and tight skin are faults. The *muzzle* is deep, heavy, and free from snipiness. The *nose* is darkly pigmented, preferably black, with large wide-open nostrils. A deep liver-colored nose conforming to the coloring of the head is permissible but not desirable. The *teeth* are large, sound, and regular, meeting in either a scissors or an even bite. A bite either overshot or undershot is a serious fault. The *lips* are darkly pigmented and are pendulous, falling squarely in front and, toward the back, in loose hanging flews. The *dewlap* is very pronounced. The **neck** is powerful, of good length, and well arched. The *eyes* are soft, sad, and slightly sunken, showing a prominent haw, and in color are brown, dark brown preferred. A somewhat lighter-colored eye conforming to the general coloring of the dog is acceptable but not desirable. Very light or protruding eyes are faults. The *ears* are extremely long, low set, and when drawn forward, fold well over the end of the nose. They are velvety in texture, hanging in loose folds with the ends curling slightly inward. They are set far back on the head at the base of the skull and, in repose, appear to be set on the neck. A high set or flat ear is a serious fault.

**Forequarters**—The *chest* is deep and full with prominent sternum showing clearly in front of the legs. The *shoulders* and elbows are set close against the sides of the chest. The distance from the deepest point of the chest to the ground, while it must be adequate to allow free movement when working in the field, is not to be more than one-third the total height at the withers of an adult Basset. The shoulders are well laid back and powerful. Steepness in shoulder, fiddle fronts, and elbows that are out, are serious faults. The *forelegs* are short, powerful, heavy in bone, with wrinkled skin. Knuckling over of the front legs is a disqualification. The *paw* is massive, very heavy with tough heavy pads, well rounded and with both feet inclined equally a trifle outward, balancing the width of the shoulders. Feet down at the pastern are a serious fault. The *toes* are neither pinched together nor splayed, with the weight of the forepart of the body borne evenly on each. The dewclaws may be removed.

**Body**—The rib structure is long, smooth, and extends well back. The ribs are well sprung, allowing adequate room for heart and lungs. Flatsidedness and flanged ribs are faults. The topline is straight, level, and free from any tendency to sag or roach, which are faults.

**Hindquarters**—The hindquarters are very full and well rounded, and are approximately equal to the shoulders in width. They must not appear slack or light in relation to the overall depth of the body. The dog stands firmly on its hind legs showing a well-let-down stifle with no tendency toward a crouching stance. Viewed from behind, the hind legs are parallel, with the hocks turning neither in nor out. Cowhocks or bowed legs are serious faults. The hind feet point straight ahead. Steep, poorly angulated hindquarters are a serious fault. The dewclaws, if any, may be removed.

**Tail**—The tail is not to be docked, and is set in continuation of the spine with but slight curvature, and carried gaily in hound fashion. The hair on the underside of the tail is coarse.

**Size**—The height should not exceed 14 inches. Height over 15 inches at the highest point of the shoulder blade is a disqualification.

**Gait**—The Basset Hound moves in a smooth, powerful, and effortless manner. Being a scenting dog with short legs, it holds its nose low to the ground. Its gait is absolutely true with perfect coordination between the front and hind legs, and it moves in a straight line with hind feet following in line with the front feet, the hocks well bent with no stiffness of action. The front legs do not paddle, weave, or overlap, and the elbows must lie close to the body. Going away, the hind legs are parallel.

**Coat**—The coat is hard, smooth, and short, with sufficient density to be of use in all weather. The skin is loose and elastic. A distinctly long coat is a disqualification.

**Color**—Any recognized hound color is acceptable and the distribution of color and markings is of no importance.


## DISQUALIFICATIONS

*Height of more than 15 inches at the highest point of the shoulder blade.*
*Knuckled over front legs.*
*Distinctly long coat.*

**Approved January 14, 1964**

# BEAGLE

*T*HE ORIGIN OF THE BEAGLE IS LOST IN THE MISTS OF ANCIENT DAYS AND NO research, it seems, can ever bring its true history to light. Several well-known beaglers have written their opinions on the origin of the breed, and the following remarks are by Captain J. Otho Paget, of Melton Mowbray, England, who was, perhaps, the dean of all beaglers.

According to Xenophon there were hounds that hunted by scent in his day and the Romans acquired many of the sports of ancient Greece. There were, however, in England, packs of hounds before the time of the Romans and it is on record that Pwyll, Prince of Wales, a contemporary of King Arthur, had a special breed of white hounds of great excellence. Wales, to this day is still celebrated for its hounds, generally of a light color. Admirers of shooting dogs, setters, spaniels and other kinds, have asserted that these animals were used in building up the hound. By exercise of a little thought it will seem that this must be wrong and that in fact it is the other way about. The hound was the original progenitor of all sporting dogs, and the two distinct breeds would be the "Gaze" or "Greyhound" that hunted by sight alone, and the hound, probably the Bloodhound, that relied entirely on its nose. By the time of good Queen Bess, nearly every country gentleman in England kept a pack of hounds of some sort and hunted the animal of his choice. The fox was not at that time an honored beast of the chase. Hounds in those days seem to have been divided into two classes, the large and the small. The large sort were called "Buck Hounds" and hunted the deer, and the smaller variety were called "Beagles" from the French "Begle" and were hunted on hare.

Coming down to the middle of the eighteenth century, we find fox hunting popular with the younger generations, who wanted something quicker and more exhilarating than watching hounds puzzling out the intricate windings of a hare. The Foxhound was undoubtedly evolved from a mixture of Buck Hound and Beagle. By this time the vagaries of breeders had produced two distinct types of hare-hunting hounds, one of which was called the Southern Hound and the other the North Country Beagle. The former was slow and ponderous, with long ears and deep voice, while the other was the exact opposite. According to a writer of that day the North Country Beagle was nimble and vigorous and did his business as furiously "as Jehu himself could wish him."

At mid-nineteenth century, Parson Honeywood got together a good pack and showed some excellent sport in Essex. His pack marks the beginning of the modern Beagle, and nearly every well-known pack of subsequent date owed its origin to that inheritance. We can accept it as true that the Beagle is one of the oldest breeds in history and, with the Bloodhound and perhaps the Otterhound, closest to the original breed of hounds.

In the United States little hunting hounds called Beagles were popular in the antebellum South, but they were more of the type of straight-legged Bassets or Dachshunds with weaker heads than the Basset. They were mostly white with few dark markings and were said to be snappy, tireless hunters, full of vim and quick at a turn, but not handsome in outline. The importations of General Richard Rowett, of Carlinsville, Illinois, in the 1860s are the turning point in the history of the American strain, or strains, of Beagle. They brought to this country an acquisition of canine beauty little thought of by the huntsman. From what packs in England General Rowett obtained his hounds is not known.

About 1880, Mr. Arnold, of Providence, Rhode Island, imported a pack from the Royal Rock Beagles in the North of England, and this also had a good deal of influence on the development of American Beagles. In 1896, James L. Kernochan imported a pack from England. From then on a great many high-class hounds were brought over.

In 1888, the National Beagle Club was formed and held the first field trial. From that time on field trials carrying championship points sprang up all over the United States, and as many more clubs were sanctioned to hold informal trials. At all these, packs are run in single classes for hounds 13 to 15 inches in height and classes for those under 13 inches, and at the national trials the pack classes are an important feature. There are single classes, called derbies, for young hounds and all-age classes for large and small dogs and bitches. At the national there are, in addition to these single classes, four pack classes which, of course, cannot be run against each other at the same time, as are the hounds in the single classes. Each pack is hunted separately and scored by the judges.

In addition to the regular all-breed AKC shows, almost all the field-trial clubs conduct specialty shows in connection with their events, and in addition to this again, there are hound shows limited to the various breeds of hounds.

Those who are interested in hunting Beagles as a pack generally enjoy hunting the larger hares, rather than cottontail rabbits. Hares do not go to ground and spoil a hunt, and they give much longer, straighter, and faster runs. The white hare, or snowshoe rabbit, is found in northern swamps and provides excellent sport for a pack, but these hares will not do well when imported to other communities and disappear immediately.

There are thousands of people all over the United States who keep a few Beagles and hunt them individually. In addition, there are many packs recorded with the National Beagle Club. They are all hunted in the legitimate manner with a regular hunt staff, in hunt liveries, with their own distinctive colored collar and accessories.

The height limit of a Beagle in the United States is 15 inches and in England 16 inches. Hounds above this height cannot be entered in field trials or shows.

The soft brown eyes of the Beagle betray his warm personality but do not instantly reveal his admirable courage and stamina. The latter qualities are especially important while the Beagle is at work in the field, but in the home no gentler, more trustworthy friend could be found.

# OFFICIAL STANDARD FOR THE BEAGLE

**Head**—The skull should be fairly long, slightly domed at occiput, with cranium broad and full. *Ears*—Ears set on moderately low, long, reaching when drawn out nearly, if not quite, to the end of the nose; fine in texture, fairly broad—with almost entire absence of erectile power—setting close to the head, with the forward edge slightly inturning to the cheek—rounded at tip. *Eyes*—Eyes large, set well apart—soft and houndlike—expression gentle and pleading; of a brown or hazel color. ***Muzzle***— Muzzle of medium length—straight and square-cut—the stop moderately defined. *Jaws*—Level. Lips free from flews; nostrils large and open. *Defects*—A very flat skull, narrow across the top; excess of dome, eyes small, sharp and terrier-like, or prominent and protruding; muzzle long, snipy or cut away decidedly below the eyes, or very short. Roman-nosed, or upturned, giving a dish-face expression. Ears short, set on high or with a tendency to rise above the point of origin.

**Body**—*Neck and Throat*—Neck rising free and light from the shoulders strong in substance yet not loaded, of medium length. The throat clean and free from folds of skin; a slight wrinkle below the angle of the jaw, however, may be allowable. *Defects*—

A thick, short, cloddy neck carried on a line with the top of the shoulders. Throat showing dewlap and folds of skin to a degree termed "throatiness."

**Shoulders and Chest**—Shoulders sloping—clean, muscular, not heavy or loaded—conveying the idea of freedom of action with activity and strength. Chest deep and broad, but not broad enough to interfere with the free play of the shoulders. *Defects*—Straight, upright shoulders. Chest disproportionately wide or with lack of depth.

**Back, Loin and Ribs**—Back short, muscular and strong. Loin broad and slightly arched, and the ribs well sprung, giving abundance of lung room. *Defects*—Very long or swayed or roached back. Flat, narrow loin. Flat ribs.

**Forelegs and Feet**—*Forelegs*—Straight, with plenty of bone in proportion to size of the hound. Pasterns short and straight. *Feet*—Close, round and firm. Pad full and hard. *Defects*—Out at elbows. Knees knuckled over forward, or bent backward. Forelegs crooked or Dachshundlike. Feet long, open or spreading.

**Hips, Thighs, Hind Legs and Feet**—Hips and thighs strong and well muscled, giving abundance of propelling power. Stifles strong and well let down. Hocks firm, symmetrical and moderately bent. Feet close and firm. *Defects*—Cowhocks, or straight hocks. Lack of muscle and propelling power. Open feet.

**Tail**—Set moderately high; carried gaily, but not turned forward over the back; with slight curve; short as compared with size of the hound; with brush. *Defects*—A long tail. Teapot curve or inclined forward from the root. Rat tail with absence of brush.

**Coat**—A close, hard, hound coat of medium length. *Defects*—A short, thin coat, or of a soft quality.

**Color**—Any true hound color.

**General Appearance**—A miniature Foxhound, solid and big for his inches, with the wear-and-tear look of the hound that can last in the chase and follow his quarry to the death.

## SCALE OF POINTS

| Head | | | Running Gear | | |
|---|---|---|---|---|---|
| Skull | 5 | | Forelegs | 10 | |
| Ears | 10 | | Hips, thighs and | | |
| Eyes | 5 | | hind legs | 10 | |
| Muzzle | 5 | 25 | Feet | 10 | 30 |
| Body | | | Coat | 5 | |
| Neck | 5 | | Stern | 5 | 10 |
| Chest and shoulders | 15 | | | | |
| Back, loin and ribs | 15 | 35 | TOTAL | | 100 |

**Varieties**—There shall be two varieties:

*Thirteen Inch*—Which shall be for hounds not exceeding 13 inches in height.

*Fifteen Inch*—Which shall be for hounds over 13 but not exceeding 15 inches in height.

# DISQUALIFICATION

*Any hound measuring more than 15 inches shall be disqualified.*

## PACKS OF BEAGLES
## SCORE OF POINTS FOR JUDGING

*Hounds*

| | |
|---|---|
| General levelness of pack | 40% |
| Individual merit of hounds | 30% |
| | **70%** |
| Manners | 20% |
| Appointments | 10% |
| Total | **100%** |

**Levelness of Pack**—The first thing in a pack to be considered is that they present a unified appearance. The hounds must be as near to the same height, weight, conformation and color as possible.

**Individual Merit of the Hounds**—Is the individual bench-show quality of the hounds. A very level and sporty pack can be gotten together and not a single hound be a good Beagle. This is to be avoided.

**Manners**—The hounds must all work gaily and cheerfully, with flags up—obeying all commands cheerfully. They should be broken to heel up, kennel up, follow promptly and stand. Cringing, sulking, lying down to be avoided. Also, a pack must not work as though in terror of master and whips. In Beagle packs it is recommended that the whip be used as little as possible.

**Appointments**—Master and whips should be dressed alike, the master or huntsman to carry horn—the whips and master to carry light thong whips. One whip should carry extra couplings on shoulder strap.

## RECOMMENDATIONS FOR SHOW LIVERY

*Black velvet cap, white stock, green coat, white breeches or knickerbockers, green or black stockings, white spats, black or dark brown shoes. Vest and gloves optional. Ladies should turn out exactly the same except for a white skirt instead of white breeches.*

**Approved September 10, 1957**

# BLACK AND TAN COONHOUND

*T*HE BLACK AND TAN COONHOUND IS ONE OF THE FEW TRULY AMERICAN breeds. It was developed in the Deep South by hunters who blended the unique traits of several early hound breeds.

While wealthy landowners were conducting organized fox hunts with imported pedigreed hounds, settlers were developing their own trailing hounds for the purpose of putting meat on the table and running off varmints that threatened crops and livestock. These pioneers were more concerned with performance than appearance. Nevertheless, a distinct type of hound emerged from crosses among various lines of accomplished hunting dogs. Dedicated hunters developed a medium-sized hound capable of independently locating and tracking its own prey, following cold trails for long distances when necessary—with joyful, beautiful voices all during the chase. Combining powerful scenting ability with great stamina and fierce desire to hunt, today's Black and Tan has been used across North America on many types of game, including raccoons, bobcat, cougar, deer, elk, wild boar, and even bear. The breed works equally well whether hunting alone or with a pack, on open level ground or in the most rugged terrain.

The Black and Tan once again demonstrated its exceptional versatility as rural hunting areas have given way to urban development in recent years. Always a devoted companion and family dog, in many instances this breed has adapted remarkably well to city life and become a willing participant in all aspects of human activity. From jogging companion to camping buddy, vocal watchdog to tender babysitter, marathon runner to couch potato, the Coonhound is most content when included in the family's daily routine.

As good a pet as a Black and Tan can be, his keen hunting instinct warrants special consideration. As a rule, all exercise must be either on lead or in a securely fenced area. Even the best-trained hound can give in to the irresistible urge to chase an errant cat, squirrel, or deer—a chase that can go for miles or lead into the path of a car. The Black and Tan's bugling call is music to the hunter but can be quite a disturbance in a residential neighborhood.

In 1945, the Black and Tan became the first coonhound breed fully recognized by the American Kennel Club. Since then, the breed has proven to be a worthy competitor in all types of AKC events. In the conformation ring, numerous Black and Tans have been successful at the highest levels, receiving Hound Group and Best in Show awards. The breed's willingness to please has led to success in the obedience ring. The Companion Dog title is quite attainable, and advanced titles are routinely earned by hounds and dedicated owners. Exceptional scenting ability makes tracking tests a natural venue for these hounds, although they can be distracted when the track crosses a path left by small furry game. Coonhounds are enthusiastic participants in agility and rally, enjoying the opportunity to work as a team with their owners.

The Black and Tan is exceptionally tolerant of children but is equally happy as the only family pet or one of several. Aside from routine attention to teeth, nails, and ears, there is little special grooming required other than bathing. A Black and Tan Coonhound's combination of independent spirit and loyal dedication can make him an ideal addition to a household that appreciates these qualities.

# OFFICIAL STANDARD FOR THE BLACK AND TAN COONHOUND

**General Appearance**—The Black and Tan Coonhound is first and fundamentally a working dog, a trail and tree hound, capable of withstanding the rigors of winter, the heat of summer, and the difficult terrain over which he is called upon to work. Used principally for trailing and treeing raccoon, the Black and Tan Coonhound runs his game entirely by scent. The characteristics and courage of the Coonhound also make him proficient on the hunt for deer, bear, mountain lion and other big game. Judges are asked by the club sponsoring the breed to place great emphasis upon these facts when evaluating the merits of the dog. The general impression is that of power, agility and alertness. He immediately impresses one with his ability to cover the ground with powerful rhythmic strides.

**Size, Proportion, Substance**—*Size* measured at the shoulder—males 25 to 27 inches; females 23 to 25 inches. Oversized dogs should not be penalized when general soundness and proportion are in favor. *Penalize* undersize. **Proportion**—Measured from the point of shoulder to the buttocks and from withers to ground the length of body is equal to or slightly greater than the height of the dog at the withers. Height is in proportion to general conformation so that dog appears neither leggy nor close to the ground. *Substance*—Considering their job as a hunting dog, the individual should exhibit moderate bone and good muscle tone. Males are heavier in bone and muscle tone than females.

**Head**—The head is cleanly modeled. From the back of the skull to the nose the head measures from 9 to 10 inches in males and from 8 to 9 inches in females. *Expression* is alert, friendly and eager. The skin is devoid of folds. Nostrils well open and always black. The flews are well developed with typical hound appearance. *Penalize* excessive wrinkles. **Eyes** are from hazel to dark brown in color, almost round and not deeply set. *Penalize* yellow or light eyes. **Ears** are low set and well back. They hang in graceful folds, giving the dog a majestic appearance. In length they extend naturally well beyond the tip of the nose and are set at eye level or lower. *Penalize* ears that do not reach the tip of the nose and are set too high on the head. **Skull** tends toward oval outline. Medium stop occurring midway between occiput bone and nose. Viewed from profile the line of the skull is on a practically parallel plane to the foreface or muzzle. **Teeth** fit evenly with scissors bite. *Penalize* excessive deviation from scissors bite.

**Neck, Topline, Body**—The neck is muscular, sloping, medium length. The skin is devoid of excess dewlap. The back is level, powerful and strong. The dog possesses full, round, well sprung ribs, avoiding flatsidedness. Chest reaches at least to the elbows. The **tail** is strong, with base slightly below level of backline, carried free and when in action at approximately right angle to back.

**Forequarters**—Powerfully constructed shoulders. The forelegs are straight, with elbows turning neither in nor out; pasterns strong and erect. **Feet** are compact, with well knuckled, strongly arched toes and thick, strong pads. *Penalize* flat or splayed feet.

**Hindquarters**—Quarters are well boned and muscled. From hip to hock long and sinewy, hock to pad short and strong. Stifles and hocks well bent and not inclining either in or out. When standing on a level surface, the hind feet are set back from under the body and the leg from pad to hock is at right angles to the ground. *Fault*—Rear dewclaws.

**Coat**—The coat is short but dense to withstand rough going.

**Color**—As the name implies, the color is coal black with rich tan markings above eyes, on sides of muzzle, chest, legs and breeching, with black pencil markings on toes. *Penalize* lack of rich tan markings, excessive areas of tan markings, excessive black coloration. *Faults*—White on chest or other parts of body is highly undesirable, and a solid patch of white which extends more than one inch in any direction is a disqualification.

**Gait**—When viewed from the side, the stride of the Black and Tan Coonhound is easy and graceful with plenty of reach in front and drive behind. When viewed from the front the forelegs, which are in line with the width of the body, move forward in an effortless manner, but never cross. Viewed from the rear the hocks follow on a line with the forelegs, being neither too widely nor too closely spaced, and as the speed of the trot increases the feet tend to converge toward a centerline or single track indicating soundness, balance and stamina. When in action, his head and tail carriage is proud and alert; the topline remains level.

**Temperament**—Even temperament, outgoing and friendly. As a working scent hound, must be able to work in close contact with other hounds. Some may be reserved but never shy or vicious. Aggression toward people or other dogs is most undesirable.

Note—Inasmuch as this is a hunting breed, scars from honorable wounds shall not be considered faults.

## DISQUALIFICATION

*A solid patch of white which extends more than one inch in any direction.*

**Approved December 11, 1990**
**Effective January 30, 1991**

# BLOODHOUND

WHEN CLAUDIUS AELIANUS, OR AELIAN, WROTE HIS FAMOUS *HISTORIA Animalium* in the third century A.D., he mentioned in especially glowing terms a hound unrivaled for scenting powers, possessed of such great determination that he would not leave the trail until he had his quarry. Thus the early Italian scholar gives us a picture of the dog known today as the Bloodhound, a breed improved considerably in appearance but which still retains its peculiarly intensified ability to follow the faintest scent.

There is little known of Bloodhound origins, but some authorities say the breed was known throughout the ancient Mediterranean. It is the oldest race of hounds that hunt by scent, indicating, of course, that selective breeding over many centuries has made it outwardly changed from the breed the ancients extolled. Yet, its characteristics are so distinctive that cynologists can trace it through the centuries.

The Bloodhound made its appearance in Europe long before the Crusades, the first specimens being brought from Constantinople. There were two strains, black and white. The blacks were the famed St. Huberts of the eighth century, while the whites later became known as the Southern Hounds. It was from the black stock that importations were made to England. Both varieties have played big parts in the development of other hounds and hound-type dogs.

In the twelfth century, when even bishops rode to hounds, dignitaries of the church were among the foremost in fostering the development of the Bloodhound.

A number of high ecclesiastics maintained packs, and the kennel was an important part of every monastery. To them goes a great deal of the credit for keeping the strain clean. In fact, so much care was taken in the breeding of this hound that it came to be called the "blooded hound," meaning aristocratic.

Nearly four centuries later that noted English physician and dog lover John Caius gives us a different explanation of the name, but his description is interesting:

> . . . The larger class remain to be mentioned; these too have drooping lips and ears, and it is well known that they follow their prey not only while alive but also after death when they have caught the scent of blood. For whether the beasts are wounded alive and slip out of the hunter's hands, or are taken dead out of the warren (but with a profusion of blood in either case), these hounds perceive it at once by smell and follow the trail. For that reason they are properly called Sanguinaraii.
>
> Frequently, however, an animal is stolen, and owing to the cleverness of thieves there is no effusion of blood; but even so they are clever enough to follow dry human footsteps for a huge distance, and can pick a man out of a crowd however large, pressing on through the densest thickets, and they will still go on even though they have to swim across a river. When they arrive at the opposite bank, by a circular movement, they find out which way a man has gone, even if at first they do not hit on the track of the thief.

The purebred Bloodhound is one of the most docile of all breeds. His trailing is more for his own sport than for anything else. Unlike the police-trained dog, he does not apprehend the man he is trailing. The Bloodhound's task ends once he has followed the trail to its termination. But so accurate is he in following a trail that his evidence has been accepted in a court of law.

Some of the great Bloodhounds of the United States have brought about more convictions for police departments than the best human detectives. One dog was credited with more than 600 actual convictions. The famous hound Nick Carter (b. 1899) picked up a trail that was 105 hours old and followed it to a subsequent conviction. This record has since been more than doubled. Owners have proven that a good Bloodhound can be a show champion and a working man-trailer, and the law officers of the National Police Bloodhound Association and volunteer search-and-rescue clubs throughout the country utilize him in his traditional work. The breed's stamina and determination are apparent in the great distances it will travel. Several specimens have followed human quarry for more than 50 miles, and one led the detectives 138 miles—all with success.

In obedience, Bloodhounds are quick to learn but may prove obstinate unless taught to enjoy this type of work. Many have earned their Companion Dog degrees, and a few have gone on to Companion Dog Excellent and Utility.

Bloodhounds have been exhibited in the United States almost from the beginning of organized dog shows in America. The American Bloodhound Club, a national breed organization, enables fanciers to conduct specialty shows nationwide.

# OFFICIAL STANDARD FOR THE BLOODHOUND

**General Character**—The Bloodhound possesses, in a most marked degree, every point and characteristic of those dogs which hunt together by scent (Sagaces). He is very powerful, and stands over more ground than is usual with hounds of other breeds. The skin is thin to the touch and extremely loose, this being more especially noticeable about the head and neck, where it hangs in deep folds.

**Height**—The mean average height of adult dogs is 26 inches, and of adult bitches 24 inches. Dogs usually vary from 25 inches to 27 inches, and bitches from 23 inches to 25 inches; but, in either case, the greater height is to be preferred, provided that character and quality are also combined.

**Weight**—The mean average weight of adult dogs, in fair condition, is 90 pounds, and of adult bitches 80 pounds. Dogs attain the weight of 110 pounds, bitches 100 pounds. The greater weights are to be preferred, provided (as in the case of height) that quality and proportion are also combined.

**Expression**—The expression is noble and dignified, and characterized by solemnity, wisdom and power.

**Temperament**—In temperament he is extremely affectionate, neither quarrelsome with companions nor with other dogs. His nature is somewhat shy, and equally sensitive to kindness or correction by his master.

**Head**—The head is narrow in proportion to its length, and long in proportion to the body, tapering but slightly from the temples to the end of the muzzle, thus (when viewed from above and in front) having the appearance of being flattened at the sides and of being nearly equal in width throughout its entire length. In profile the upper outline of the skull is nearly in the same plane as that of the foreface. The length from end of nose to stop (midway between the eyes) should be not less than that from stop to back of occipital protuberance (peak). The entire length of head from the posterior part of the occipital protuberance to the end of the muzzle should be 12 inches, or more, in dogs, and 11 inches, or more, in bitches. *Skull*—The skull is long and narrow, with the occipital peak very pronounced. The brows are not prominent, although, owing to the deep-set eyes, they may have that appearance. *Foreface*—The foreface is long, deep, and of even width throughout, with square outline when seen in profile. *Eyes*—The eyes are deeply sunk in the orbits, the lids assuming a lozenge or diamond shape, in consequence of the lower lids being dragged down and everted by the heavy flews. The eyes correspond with the general tone of color of the animal, varying from deep hazel to yellow. The hazel color is, however, to be preferred, although very seldom seen in liver-and-tan hounds. *Ears*—The ears are thin and soft to the touch, extremely long, set very low, and fall in graceful folds, the lower parts curling inward and backward. *Mouth*—A scissors bite is preferred, level bite accepted.

**Wrinkle**—The head is furnished with an amount of loose skin, which in nearly every position appears superabundant, but more particularly so when the head is carried low; the skin then falls into loose, pendulous ridges and folds, especially over the forehead and sides of the face. *Nostrils*—The nostrils are large and open. ***Lips, Flews, and Dewlap***—In front the lips fall squarely, making a right angle with the upper line of the foreface; whilst behind they form deep, hanging flews, and, being continued into the pendant folds of loose skin about the neck, constitute the dewlap, which is very pronounced. These characters are found, though to a lesser degree, in the bitch.

**Neck, Shoulders and Chest**—The neck is long, the shoulders muscular and well sloped backwards; the ribs are well sprung; and the chest well let down between the forelegs, forming a deep keel.

**Legs and Feet**—The forelegs are straight and large in bone, with elbows squarely set; the feet strong and well knuckled up; the thighs and second thighs (gaskins) are very muscular; the hocks well bent and let down and squarely set.

**Back and Loin**—The back and loins are strong, the latter deep and slightly arched. *Stern*—The stern is long and tapering, and set on rather high, with a moderate amount of hair underneath.

**Gait**—The gait is elastic, swinging and free, the stern being carried high, but not too much curled over the back.

**Color**—The colors are black and tan, liver and tan, and red; the darker colors being sometimes interspersed with lighter or badger-colored hair, and sometimes flecked with white. A small amount of white is permissible on chest, feet and tip of stern.

**Approved January 9, 1996**
**Effective February 29, 1996**

# BORZOI

*T*HE BORZOI, KNOWN HERE BEFORE 1936 AS THE RUSSIAN WOLFHOUND, IS a sighthound dependent on his extreme speed, agility, and courage to pursue, overtake, and hold quarry. Today these beautiful and intelligent dogs are as at home in our living rooms as they are in the field.

With a history clouded by the misty past of Czarist Russia, we know the dogs were bred by the Russian aristocracy for hundreds of years. There are, in fact, accounts of hunting expeditions of several Mongol rulers from the time of the conqueror Genghis Khan in the thirteenth century, in which long hounds were mentioned as principal coursing dogs. In Russia, the precursors of the Borzoi were thought to be of several different types including the long-coated, smooth-faced bearhound of early Russia; the coursing hounds of the Tatars; the Owtchar, a tall Russian sheepdog; as well as other ancient sighthound types. Whatever the Borzoi origin, by 1260 the coursing of hare for sport is mentioned in connection with the Court of the Grand Duke of Novgorod, and in 1650 the first Borzoi standard was written (reportedly it did not differ greatly from the standard of today). From the time of Ivan the Terrible in the mid-1500s to the abolition of serfdom in 1861, hunting with Borzoi was the national sport of the aristocracy.

Great rural estates, thousands of acres in extent, with hundreds of serfs, were given over to the breeding and training of, and hunting with, Borzois. In fact, it is difficult today to even imagine the grand scale and magnificence to which the gentle Borzoi is heir. Before 1861, and to a lesser extent after that time up to the Russian Revolution in 1917, the time, effort, and money expended on these "hunts," as they were called, is surely unequaled in the development of any breed.

Dmitri Walzoff, writing in his 1912 monograph on the Perchino Hunt, says a special hunting train used to transport the people, horses, dogs, tents, kitchens, and carriages to a hunting ground consisted of forty freight cars, one first- and one second-class passenger car, with the grand duke and guests arriving on another special train. The hunting party itself would consist of more than a hundred Borzoi, as many foxhounds, and as many people to assist. Often all the horses of a hunt were matched, as well as the leashes of the Borzoi and the foxhound packs. Once the team arrived at the spot where wolves were known to be, plans were drawn, preparations made, and the hunting commenced. The beaters accompanying a pack of foxhounds would dislodge the game, most notably the wolf, from the forest into the open field where awaiting them at a respectable distance were the mounted huntsmen, each with a trio of Borzoi consisting of a bitch and two dogs. When game was sighted, the dogs were slipped by the huntsman. With the Borzoi in pursuit of the wolf, and the mounted huntsmen in pursuit of the Borzoi, a hair-raising ride ensued, and if the wolf did not escape, the Borzoi were required to capture, pin, and hold the creature until the arrival of the huntsmen. The approved style was for the huntsmen to leap headlong into the fray, gag and bind the wolf, after which the wolf was often set free—surely wiser and much more wary for the next time. A moving account of such a hunt can be read in Tolstoy's *War and Peace* (Book II, Part 4, Chapter 3).

From after the Napoleonic Wars to the abolition of serfdom, there was a period of uncertainty which seemed to result in many experimental outcrosses in the breed. By 1873, only a few Borzoi of the old type existed, and in that year the Imperial Association was formed to protect and promote this ancient type. This association is of great interest to the present-day Borzoi fancier as many bloodlines of Borzoi in America today, if not most, can be traced back to breeders who were its members. Most notable among these was the Grand Duke Nicholas, uncle to the Czar and field marshal of the Russian armies. Second in importance was Artem Boldareff, a wealthy landowner. With these two men in the foreground, members of the association found, bred, and protected the old-type Borzoi. And it is to their hunts at Perchino and Woronzova that many of today's Borzoi owe their heritage.

As far as is known, the first Borzoi that came to America was brought over from England in 1889 by William Wade, of Hulton, Pennsylvania. This hound, purchased from Freeman Lloyd, was a bitch named Elsie, described in *The English Stockkeeper* as "nothing much to look at, being small, light and weedy, with no bone, straight back, very curly tail and too much bent in stifles."

The first American to visit Russia and import Borzoi directly from that country (including two who became AKC champions) was C. Steadman Hanks, of Massachusetts, who established the Seacroft Kennels in the 1890s.

Beginning in 1903, Joseph B. Thomas (acting for the Valley Farm Kennels) made three trips to Russia, the importations from which were to play a very important part in the establishment of American Borzoi bloodlines. Included in these importations were Borzoi from the Perchino Kennels owned by the Grand Duke Nicholas, and from the Woronzova Kennels owned by Artem Boldareff.

The Borzoi today remains largely unchanged from his Russian ancestors, both in terms of his appearance, his quiet, gentle nature, and his abilities. He is a mainstay of the AKC lure coursing program. His intelligence and easy training have resulted in many obedience titles. While the hunt has been the primary purpose of the Borzoi, his beauty and temperament were also always of prime importance. He was always a companion *par excellence* and the *amourment* of the salon. Today, this noble breed easily finds its way to the heart of its owner and, while the circumstances of the breed have changed from those of Czarist Russia, Borzoi remain true aristocrats.

# OFFICIAL STANDARD FOR THE BORZOI

**General Appearance**—The Borzoi was originally bred for the coursing of wild game on more or less open terrain, relying on sight rather than scent. To accomplish this purpose, the Borzoi needed particular structural qualities to chase, catch and hold his quarry. Special emphasis is placed on sound running gear, strong neck and jaws, courage and agility, combined with proper condition. The Borzoi should always possess unmistakable elegance, with flowing lines, graceful in motion or repose. Males, masculine without coarseness; bitches, feminine and refined.

**Head**—Skull slightly domed, long and narrow, with scarcely any perceptible stop, inclined to be Roman-nosed. Jaws long, powerful and deep, somewhat finer in bitches but not snippy. Teeth strong and clean with either an even or a scissors bite. Missing teeth should be penalized. Nose large and black.

**Ears**—Small and fine in quality, lying back on the neck when in repose with the tips when thrown back almost touching behind occiput; raised when at attention.

**Eyes**—Set somewhat obliquely, dark in color, intelligent but rather soft in expression; never round, full nor staring, nor light in color; eye rims dark; inner corner midway between tip of nose and occiput.

**Neck**—Clean, free from throatiness; slightly arched, very powerful and well set on.

**Shoulders**—Sloping, fine at the withers and free from coarseness or lumber.

**Chest**—Rather narrow, with great depth of brisket.

**Ribs**—Only slightly sprung, but very deep, giving room for heart and lung play.

**Back**—Rising a little at the loins in a graceful curve.

**Loins**—Extremely muscular, but rather tucked up, owing to the great depth of chest and comparative shortness of back and ribs.

**Forelegs**—Bones straight and somewhat flattened like blades, with the narrower edge forward. The elbows have free play and are turned neither in nor out. Pasterns strong.

**Feet**—Hare-shaped, with well-arched knuckles, toes close and well padded.

**Hindquarters**—Long, very muscular and powerful with well bent stifles; somewhat wider than the forequarters; strong first and second thighs; hocks clean and well let down; legs parallel when viewed from the rear.

**Dewclaws**—Dewclaws, if any, on the hind legs are generally removed; dewclaws on the forelegs may be removed.

**Tail**—Long, set on and carried low in a graceful curve.

**Coat**—Long, silky (not woolly), either flat, wavy or rather curly. On the head, ears and front of legs it should be short and smooth; on the neck the frill should be profuse and rather curly. Feather on hindquarters and tail, long and profuse, less so on chest and back of forelegs.

**Color**—Any color, or combination of colors, is acceptable.

**Size**—Mature males should be at least 28 inches at the withers and mature bitches at least 26 inches at the withers. Dogs and bitches below these respective limits should be severely penalized; dogs and bitches above the respective limits should not be penalized as long as extra size is not acquired at the expense of symmetry, speed and staying quality. Range in weight for males from 75 to 105 pounds and for bitches from 15 to 20 pounds less.

**Gait**—Front legs must reach well out in front with pasterns strong and springy. Hackneyed motion with mincing gait is not desired nor is weaving and crossing. However, while the hind legs are wider apart than the front, the feet tend to move closer to the center line when the dog moves at a fast trot. When viewed from the side there should be a noticeable drive with a ground-covering stride from well-angulated stifles and hocks. The overall appearance in motion should be that of effortless power, endurance, speed, agility, smoothness and grace.

## FAULTS

*The foregoing description is that of the ideal Borzoi. Any deviation from the above described dog must be penalized to the extent of the deviation, keeping in mind the importance of the contribution of the various features toward the basic original purpose of the breed.*

**Approved June 13, 1972**

# DACHSHUND

Smooth

Wirehaired

Longhaired

*D*ACHSHUND IS A GERMAN WORD MEANING "BADGER DOG" (*DACHS,* "BADGER"; *hund,* "dog"). In medieval books on hunting, dogs possessing the tracking skills of hounds and the proportions and temperament of terriers, and that were used to follow badgers to earth, were called badger-dogs or *dachs-hunds.* This terminology is similar to the use of the description "rabbit dog" for dogs of various sorts used to hunt rabbits.

Illustrations from the fifteenth through seventeenth centuries show badgers hunted by dogs with elongated bodies, short legs, and houndlike ears. Some had the bent front legs of the Basset, some had the heads of terriers, and some had indications of smooth and long coats. These illustrations were made before the days of photography, and woodcuts do not lend themselves to fine reproductions of dog anatomy or coat distinctions. At best, the pictures and descriptive words can be interpreted with certainty only to define the functions of dogs used to hunt badgers.

The preponderance of available evidence indicates that selective breeding separated smooth and longhaired coats long before there were recorded registrations. Documented history has established that the wirehaired coat was produced for protection against brier and thorn by breeding in harsh, wiry terrier coats and then breeding out incompatible conformation characteristics. Early in the seventeenth century, *Dachshund* became the name for a breed with smooth and longhaired coat varieties. Since 1890, wirehairs have been registered as the third variety. Early on, German breeders barred registration of dogs resulting from crossbreeding coat varieties. Although coat variety crossing is permitted in the United States, it is not done as a matter of course.

The badger was a formidable adversary, at twenty-five to forty pounds. Badger dogs needed strength and stamina, keenness and courage, both above and below ground. Therefore, dogs weighing thirty to thirty-five pounds were not uncommon. Packs of Dachshunds were often used against wild boar. As time went on, the breed was adapted for hunting other game. A smaller sixteen-to-twenty-two-pound Dachshund proved effective against foxes and for trailing wounded deer. Still smaller twelve-pound Dachshunds were used for ermine, weasel, and hare. Today, in the United States, miniatures compete in a conformation class division for "11 pounds and under at 12 months of age and older." Weight of standard Dachshunds is usually between sixteen and thirty-two pounds.

A German Standard describing Dachshund breed type was set in 1879, and registration of Dachshunds was included in an all-breed studbook, the *Deutsche Hunde-Stammbuch,* before the German Dachshund Club or Deutsche Teckelklub was founded in 1888. Since World War II, management of the breed has reverted to the Deutsche Teckelklub and the Gebrauchsteckelklub. Before the war, the balance between breeding for hunting and conformation advanced the breed for twenty-five years. After the war, hunting was emphasized, and this produced a more terrierlike conformation.

In this country, those prewar objectives have continued to direct the breed standard. Field trials under AKC rules were instituted in 1935, promoting hunting ability, exemplary conformation, and temperament.

In 1885, eleven Dachshunds were included in AKC Stud Book, Vol. II. During the late 1800s and early 1900s, Dachshunds rapidly gained in popularity. The Dachshund Club of America was founded in 1895, and by 1914 Dachshunds were among the top ten breeds exhibited at the Westminster Kennel Club show. With the start of World War I, the association between Dachshunds and Germany resulted in an abrupt reversal of fortune for the breed in America. During this time, German breeding stock became almost nonexistent. Fortunately, there were dedicated individuals under whose guidance Dachshund breeding was reestablished in the United States. The popularity of the breed reemerged and extends to the present day, with Dachshunds consistently among the top ten breeds registered.

Not many Dachshunds are used for hunting in the United States, but understanding the function, origin, and development of the breed helps us appreciate the elegant, streamlined proportions and adds significance to application of the breed standard. Dachshunds are participating in field trials and earthdog tests in great numbers, aptly demonstrating keen hunting instincts and utilizing their go-to-ground hunting ability.

Dachshunds are small enough to live in a house or an apartment, yet sturdy enough for street, suburb, or country. Outdoors, Dachshunds are hardy, vigorous, and tireless. Indoors, they are affectionate and responsive, companionable in restful moods, hilarious in play, eager to please, and alert in announcing strangers. The breed offers three coat varieties, as well as standard and miniature sizes in each coat. In addition to the familiar red or black-and-tan colors, Dachshunds come in several patterns and other colors.

# OFFICIAL STANDARD FOR THE DACHSHUND

**General Appearance**—Low to ground, long in body and short of leg with robust muscular development, the skin is elastic and pliable without excessive wrinkling. Appearing neither crippled, awkward, nor cramped in his capacity for movement, the Dachshund is well-balanced with bold and confident head carriage and intelligent, alert facial expression. His hunting spirit, good nose, loud tongue and distinctive build make him well-suited for below-ground work and for beating the bush. His keen nose gives him an advantage over most other breeds for trailing.

**Note**—Inasmuch as the Dachshund is a hunting dog, scars from honorable wounds shall not be considered a fault.

**Size, Proportion, Substance**—Bred and shown in two sizes, standard and miniature, miniatures are not a separate classification but compete in a class division for "11 pounds and under at 12 months of age and older." Weight of the standard size is usually between 16 and 32 pounds.

**Head**—Viewed from above or from the side, the head tapers uniformly to the tip of the nose. The eyes are of medium size, almond-shaped and dark-rimmed, with an energetic, pleasant expression; not piercing; very dark in color. The bridge bones over the eyes are strongly prominent. Wall eyes, except in the case of dappled dogs, are a serious fault. The ears are set near the top of the head, not too far forward, of moderate length, rounded, not narrow, pointed, or folded. Their carriage, when animated, is with the forward edge just touching the cheek so that the ears frame the face. The skull is slightly arched, neither too broad nor too narrow, and slopes gradually with little perceptible stop into the finely formed, slightly arched muzzle. Black is the preferred color of the nose. Lips are tightly stretched, well covering the lower jaw. Nostrils well open. Jaws opening wide and hinged well back of the eyes, with strongly developed bones and teeth. *Teeth*—Powerful canine teeth; teeth fit closely together in a scissors bite. An even bite is a minor fault. Any other deviation is a serious fault.

**Neck**—Long, muscular, clean-cut, without dewlap, slightly arched in the nape, flowing gracefully into the shoulders.

**Trunk**—The trunk is long and fully muscled. When viewed in profile, the back lies in the straightest possible line between the withers and the short very slightly arched loin. A body that hangs loosely between the shoulders is a serious fault. *Abdomen*—Slightly drawn up.

**Forequarters**—For effective underground work, the front must be strong, deep, long and cleanly muscled. Forequarters in detail: *Chest*—The breastbone is strongly prominent in front so that on either side a depression or dimple appears. When viewed from the front, the thorax appears oval and extends downward to the mid-point of the forearm. The enclosing structure of well-sprung ribs appears full and oval to allow, by its ample capacity, complete development of heart and lungs. The keel merges gradually into the line of the abdomen and extends well beyond the front legs. Viewed in profile, the lowest point of the breast line is covered by the front leg. *Shoulder Blades*—Long, broad, well-laid back and firmly placed upon the fully developed thorax, closely fitted at the withers, furnished with hard yet pliable muscles. *Upper Arm*—Ideally the same length as the shoulder blade and at right angles to the latter, strong of bone and hard of muscle, lying close to the ribs, with elbows close to the body, yet capable of free movement. *Forearm*—Short; supplied with hard yet pliable muscles on the front and outside, with tightly stretched tendons on the inside and at the back, slightly curved inwards. The joints between the forearms and the feet (wrists) are closer together than the shoulder joints, so that the front does not appear absolutely straight. Knuckling over is a disqualifying fault. *Feet*—Front paws are full, tight, compact, with well-arched toes and tough, thick pads. They may be equally inclined a trifle outward. There are five toes, four in use, close together with a pronounced arch and strong, short nails. Front dewclaws may be removed.

**Hindquarters**—Strong and cleanly muscled. The pelvis, the thigh, the second thigh, and the metatarsus are ideally the same length and form a series of right angles. From the rear, the thighs are strong and powerful. The legs turn neither in nor out. *Metatarsus*—Short and strong, perpendicular to the second thigh bone. When viewed from behind, they are upright and parallel. *Feet—Hind Paws*—Smaller than the front paws with four compactly closed and arched toes with tough, thick pads. The entire foot points straight ahead and is balanced equally on the ball and not merely on the toes. Rear dewclaws should be removed. *Croup*—Long, rounded and full, sinking *slightly* toward the tail. *Tail*—Set in continuation of the spine, extending without kinks, twists, or pronounced curvature, and not carried too gaily.

**Gait**—Fluid and smooth. Forelegs reach well forward, without much lift, in unison with the driving action of hind legs. The correct shoulder assembly and well-fitted elbows allow the long, free stride in front. Viewed from the front, the legs do not move in exact parallel planes, but incline slightly inward to compensate for shortness of leg and width of chest. Hind legs drive on a line with the forelegs, with hocks (metatarsus) turning neither in nor out. The propulsion of the hind leg depends on the dog's ability to carry the hind leg to complete extension. Viewed in profile, the forward reach of the hind leg equals the rear extension. The thrust of correct movement is seen when the rear pads are clearly exposed during rear extension. Feet must travel parallel to the line of motion with no tendency to swing out, cross over, or interfere with each other. Short, choppy movement, rolling or high-stepping gait, close or overly wide coming or going are incorrect. The Dachshund must have agility, freedom of movement, and endurance to do the work for which he was developed.

**Temperament**—The Dachshund is clever, lively and courageous to the point of rashness, persevering in above and below ground work, with all the senses well-developed. Any display of shyness is a serious fault.

## SPECIAL CHARACTERISTICS OF THE THREE COAT VARIETIES

The Dachshund is bred with three varieties of coat: (1) Smooth; (2) Wirehaired; (3) Longhaired, and is shown in two sizes: standard and miniature. All three varieties and both sizes must conform to the characteristics already specified. The following features are applicable for each variety.

**Smooth Dachshund**—*Coat*—Short, smooth and shining. Should be neither too long nor too thick. Ears not leathery. *Tail*—Gradually tapered to a point, well but not too richly haired. Long sleek bristles on the underside are considered a patch of strong-growing hair, not a fault. A brush tail is a fault, as is also a partly or wholly hairless tail.

*Color of Hair*—Although base color is immaterial, certain patterns and basic colors predominate. One-colored Dachshunds include red (with or without a shading of interspersed dark hairs or sable) and cream. A small amount of white on the chest is acceptable, but not desirable. Nose and nails—black.

Two-colored Dachshunds include black, chocolate, wild boar, gray (blue) and fawn (Isabella), each with tan markings over the eyes, on the sides of the jaw and underlip, on the inner edge of the ear, front, breast, inside and behind the front legs, on the paws and around the anus, and from there to about one-third to one-half of the length of the tail on the underside. Undue prominence or extreme lightness of tan markings is undesirable. A small amount of white on the chest is acceptable but not desirable. Nose and nails—in the case of black dogs, black; for chocolate and all other colors, dark brown, but self-colored is acceptable.

*Dappled Dachshunds*—The "single" dapple pattern is expressed as lighter-colored areas contrasting with the darker base color, which may be any acceptable color. Neither the light nor the dark color should predominate. Nose and nails are the same as for one and two-colored Dachshunds. Partial or wholly blue (wall) eyes are as acceptable as dark eyes. A large area of white on the chest of a dapple is permissible.

A "double" dapple is one in which varying amounts of white coloring occur over the body in addition to the dapple pattern. Nose and nails: as for one and two-color Dachshunds; partial or wholly self-colored is permissible.

Brindle is a pattern (as opposed to a color) in which black or dark stripes occur over the entire body although in some specimens the pattern may be visible only in the tan points.

**Wirehaired Dachshund**—*Coat*—With the exception of jaw, eyebrows, and ears, the whole body is covered with a uniform tight, short, thick, rough, hard, outer coat but with finer, somewhat softer, shorter hairs (undercoat) everywhere distributed between the coarser hairs. The absence of an undercoat is a fault. The distinctive facial furnishings include a beard and eyebrows. On the ears the hair is shorter than on the body, almost smooth. The general arrangement of the hair is such that the wirehaired Dachshund, when viewed from a distance, resembles the smooth. *Any sort of soft hair in the outer coat, wherever found on the body, especially on the top of the head, is a fault.* The same is true of long, curly, or wavy hair, or hair that sticks out irregularly in all directions. *Tail*—Robust, thickly haired, gradually tapering to a point. A flag tail is a *fault. Color of Hair*—While the most common colors are wild boar, black and tan, and various shades of red, all colors are admissible. A small amount of white on the chest, although acceptable, is not desirable. Nose and nails—same as for the smooth variety.

**Longhaired Dachshund**—*Coat*—The sleek, glistening, often slightly wavy hair is longer under the neck and on the forechest, the underside of the body, the ears, and behind the legs. The coat gives the dog an elegant appearance. Short hair on the ear is not desirable. Too profuse a coat which masks type, equally long hair over the whole body, a curly coat, or a pronounced parting on the back are faults. *Tail*—Carried gracefully in prolongation of the spine; the hair attains its greatest length here and forms a veritable flag. *Color of Hair*—Same as for the smooth Dachshund. Nose and nails—same as for the smooth.

The foregoing description is that of the ideal Dachshund. Any deviation from the above described dog must be penalized to the extent of the deviation, keeping in mind the importance of the contribution of the various features toward the basic original purpose of the breed.

## DISQUALIFICATION

*Knuckling over of front legs.*

**Approved April 7, 1992**
**Effective May 27, 1992**

# AMERICAN FOXHOUND

*A*S THE NAME IMPLIES, THE AMERICAN FOXHOUND WAS DEVELOPED IN THE
United States or, more accurately, in the original thirteen colonies and the
western frontier of Kentucky and Tennessee. In 1650, Robert Brooks and his foxhounds arrived from England in the colony that became Maryland. From that time
forward, this hound has been an integral part of America and of her history.
Brooks's hounds were, of course, English. Young George Washington's original
English hounds came from his patron, Lord Fairfax, around 1750, and the future
first president developed his pack from these. Washington kept hounds all his life,
and his records and pedigrees on the early hounds of Virginia were some of the best.
In 1785, the general received a gift of several pairs of French hounds from the Marquis de Lafayette. The most notable of these hounds was named Vulcan.

In the late 1700s, Dr. Thomas Walker took some of his hounds into the Ken-
tucky region. Later, Wash Maupin and William Walker bred two strains of hounds
that had a profound effect on hunting through the centuries to the present day.
Maupin crossed his hounds on one particular hound brought out of Tennessee.
Known as Tennessee Lead, he was the first hound to catch a red fox in Kentucky.
From this cross came the Walker Hound, which is today's most popular strain of
American Foxhound.

In 1814 two Irish hounds were imported by Bolton Jackson, of Maryland. This
proved to be a most important cross, as it increased the speed of the American

hound. From this cross of Irish-Maryland hounds, the Birdsong and Henry hounds of Virginia and Georgia were developed, along with the hounds of Hayden Trigg, of Kentucky.

The American Foxhound has provided generations of Americans with a sport that attracts men and women to open fields, woodlands, and river valleys. The gray fox was native to our land, and after its importation to Maryland's Eastern Shore the red fox migrated to our warmer climes. The sport of foxhunting promoted the fox from the status of vermin to that of game animal. From Revolutionary times until the Civil War, foxhunting was the principal field sport of the gentry, and its devotees read like a who's who of early America: from Virginia, Fairfax, Washington, Jefferson, the Lees, and the Custises. (Virginia, the birthplace of American Foxhounds, was also the birthplace of eight American presidents.) From Maryland, we acknowledge Robert Brooks, Charles Carroll, John Stuart Skinner, the Dorseys, and the Hammonds.

One can follow the history of the United States by reading the stories and biographies of the men who hunted the fox and continued to move a little farther west across the mountains. The independence of thought and determination that one finds in American Foxhounds are the same admirable qualities found in the American people, from our nation's earliest times to the present day.

Today, American Foxhounds are still used as night hunters, as field trial hounds, and as pack hounds for hunt clubs. It is probably one of the most popular hound breeds in the country. When not hunting, their temperament and laid-back personality make them ideal family pets. Not only will they tolerate toddlers nicely but also they have the boundless energy to roughhouse and explore the great outdoors with older children and lovers of nature. The Foxhound is an easy hound to keep, requiring only proper feeding, regular exercise, and minimal grooming.

# OFFICIAL STANDARD FOR THE AMERICAN FOXHOUND

**Head**—*Skull*—Should be fairly long, slightly domed at occiput, with cranium broad and full. *Ears*—Ears set on moderately low, long, reaching when drawn out nearly, if not quite, to the tip of the nose; fine in texture, fairly broad, with almost entire absence of erectile power—setting close to the head with the forward edge slightly inturning to the cheek—round at tip. *Eyes*—Eyes large, set well apart—soft and hound-like—expression gentle and pleading; of a brown or hazel color. *Muzzle*—Muzzle of fair length—straight and square-cut—the stop moderately defined. *Defects*—A very flat skull, narrow across the top; excess of dome; eyes small, sharp and terrierlike, or prominent and protruding; muzzle long and snipy, cut away decidedly below the eyes, or very short. Roman-nosed, or upturned, giving a dish-face expression. Ears short, set on high, or with a tendency to rise above the point of origin.

**Body**—*Neck and Throat*—Neck rising free and light from the shoulders, strong in substance yet not loaded, of medium length. The throat clean and free from folds of skin, a slight wrinkle below the angle of the jaw, however, is allowable. *Defects*—A thick, short, cloddy neck carried on a line with the top of the shoulders. Throat showing dewlap and folds of skin to a degree termed "throatiness."

**Shoulders, Chest and Ribs**—Shoulders sloping—clean, muscular, not heavy or loaded—conveying the idea of freedom of action with activity and strength. Chest should be deep for lung space, narrower in proportion to depth than the English hound—28 inches (*girth*) in a 23-inch hound being good. Well-sprung ribs—back ribs should extend well back—a three-inch flank allowing springiness.

**Back and Loins**—Back moderately long, muscular and strong. Loins broad and slightly arched. *Defects*—Very long or swayed or roached back. Flat, narrow loins.

**Forelegs and Feet**—*Forelegs*—Straight, with fair amount of bone. Pasterns short and straight. *Feet*—Fox-like. Pad full and hard. Well-arched toes. Strong nails. *Defects*—Straight, upright shoulders, chest disproportionately wide or with lack of depth. Flat ribs. Out at elbow. Knees knuckled over forward, or bent backward. Forelegs crooked. Feet long, open or spreading.

**Hips, Thighs, Hind Legs and Feet**—Hips and thighs, strong and muscled, giving abundance of propelling power. Stifles strong and well let down. Hocks firm, symmetrical and moderately bent. Feet close and firm. *Defects*—Cowhocks, or straight hocks. Lack of muscle and propelling power. Open feet.

**Tail**—Set moderately high; carried gaily, but not turned forward over the back; with slight curve; with very slight brush. *Defects*—A long tail, Teapot curve or inclined forward from the root. Rat tail, entire absence of brush.

**Coat**—A close, hard, hound coat of medium length. *Defects*—A short thin coat, or of a soft quality.

**Height**—Dogs should not be under 22 or over 25 inches. Bitches should not be under 21 or over 24 inches measured across the back at the point of the withers, the hound standing in a natural position with his feet well under him.

**Color**—Any color.

## SCALE OF POINTS

| Head | | | Running Gear | | |
|---|---|---|---|---|---|
| Skull | 5 | | Forelegs | 10 | |
| Ears | 5 | | Hips, thighs and | | |
| Eyes | 5 | | hind legs | 10 | |
| Muzzle | 5 | 20 | Feet | 15 | 35 |
| Body | | | Coat and Tail | | |
| Neck | 5 | | Coat | 5 | |
| Chest and shoulders | 15 | | Tail | 5 | __10__ |
| Back, loin and ribs | 15 | 35 | | Total | 100 |

# ENGLISH FOXHOUND

OXHUNTING IN THE UNITED STATES IS ALMOST CONTEMPORANEOUS WITH the sport in Great Britain. The foxhound with which we are dealing is known in the United States in dog shows and elsewhere as the *English* Foxhound, though why it should be so designated any more than a fox terrier should be called an *English* Fox Terrier, is hard to understand. The English Foxhound has been bred along careful lines for over 150 years. The studbooks published by the Masters of Foxhounds Association (England) date before 1800, and it is an easy matter for any owner of any English Foxhound to trace its pedigree. The breeding of foxhounds in England has always been in the hands of masters of hounds, who kept the most careful records of their breeding operations.

For the benefit of those who may be interested in knowing how long the English Foxhound in his pure state has been in the United States, we find that there are records which establish that the first Lord Fairfax imported hounds from England in 1738, and there are unauthenticated records of even earlier importations. The *English Foxhound Stud Book of America,* published by the Masters of Foxhounds Association of America, dates its earliest entries to 1890, but there are earlier records which would incline one to the belief that there were many earlier importations. Certainly the blood of the Genesee Valley pack must date at least twenty years before that time, records having been kept of it with fair accuracy ever since.

In England, as in America, these hounds have always been used for foxhunting as followed in the English fashion of riding to hounds. There have been over 250 packs of hounds in Great Britain, all of which used English Hounds, while in America we have over a hundred packs, of which not over 10 percent use hounds which would be eligible for the English Foxhound Stud Book, although the blood has been freely mixed with the American Foxhound.

In appearance the English hound is far stouter than his American cousin, and perhaps no better description of his general appearance can be given than to quote a passage from Cuthbert Bradley's *Reminiscences of Frank Gillard,* in which he describes Belvoir Gambler '85, one of the greatest hounds ever bred:

> Although Belvoir Gambler cannot be bred from rule of thumb, the proportions of this remarkable Foxhound are worth preserving as an example of what symmetry should be. Standing twenty-three inches at the shoulder, from the extreme point of his shapely shoulders to the outer curve of his well-fumed quarters, he measured twenty-seven and a half inches in length whilst from elbow to ground his height was only twelve inches. Possessing great depth of rib and room round the heart, he girthed thirty-one inches, and his arm below was eight and a quarter inches round. Below the knee he measured eight and a quarter inches of solid bone, while round the thigh he spanned full nine and a quarter inches. The extended neck was ten inches from cranium to shoulder and the head ten inches and a half long. His color was of the richest, displaying all of the beautiful "Belvoir tan," and his head had that brainy appearance expressive of the highest intelligence. Gambler might have inspired that earnest poet, Cannon Kingsley, when he described the modern Foxhound, "The result of nature not limited, but developed by high civilization. Next to an old Greek statue there are few such combinations of grace and strength as in a fine Foxhound."

Although the tendency today is to breed hounds a little bigger, the above description cannot be equaled.

# OFFICIAL STANDARD FOR THE ENGLISH FOXHOUND

**Head**—Should be of full size, but by no means heavy. Brow pronounced, but not high or sharp. There should be a good length and breadth, sufficient to give in a dog hound a girth in front of the ears of fully 16 inches. The nose should be long (4½ inches) and wide, with open nostrils. Ears set on low and lying close to the cheeks. Most English hounds are "rounded" which means that about 1½ inches is taken off the end of the ear. The teeth must meet squarely, either a *pig-mouth* (overshot) or undershot being a disqualification.

**Neck**—Must be long and clean, without the slightest throatiness, not less than 10 inches from cranium to shoulder. It should taper nicely from shoulders to head, and the upper outline should be slightly convex.

**The Shoulders** should be long and well clothed with muscle, without being heavy, especially at the points. They must be well sloped, and the true arm between the front and the elbow must be long and muscular, but free from fat or lumber. ***Chest and Back Ribs***—The chest should girth over 31 inches in a 24-inch hound, and the back ribs must be very deep.

**Back and Loin**—Must both be very muscular, running into each other without any contraction between them. The couples must be wide, even to raggedness, and the topline of the back should be absolutely level, the ***Stern*** well set on and carried gaily but not in any case curved over the back like a squirrel's tail. The end should taper to a point and there should be a fringe of hair below. The ***Hindquarters*** or propellers are required to be very strong, and as endurance is of even greater consequence than speed, straight stifles are preferred to those much bent as in a Greyhound. ***Elbows*** set quite straight, and neither turned in nor out are a *sine qua non*. They must be well let down by means of the long true arm above mentioned.

**Legs and Feet**—Every Master of Foxhounds insists on legs as straight as a post, and as strong; size of bone at the ankle being especially regarded as all important. The desire for straightness had a tendency to produce knuckling-over, which at one time was countenanced, but in recent years this defect has been eradicated by careful breeding and intelligent adjudication, and one sees very little of this trouble in the best modern Foxhounds. The bone cannot be too large, and the feet in all cases should be round and catlike, with well-developed knuckles and strong horn, which last is of the greatest importance.

**Color and Coat**—Not regarded as very important, so long as the former is a good "hound color," and the latter is short, dense, hard, and glossy. Hound colors are black, tan, and white, or any combination of these three, also the various "pies" compounded of white and the color of the hare and badger, or yellow, or tan. The ***Symmetry*** of the Foxhound is of the greatest importance, and what is known as "quality" is highly regarded by all good judges.

## SCALE OF POINTS

| | |
|---|---|
| Head | 5 |
| Neck | 10 |
| Shoulders | 10 |
| Chest and back ribs | 10 |
| Back and loin | 15 |
| Hindquarters | 10 |
| Elbows | 5 |

| | | |
|---|---|---:|
| Legs and feet | | 20 |
| Color and coat | | 5 |
| Stern | | 5 |
| Symmetry | | <u>5</u> |
| | **Total** | **100** |

## DISQUALIFICATION

*Pig-mouth (overshot) or undershot.*

**Approved 1935**

# GREYHOUND

*S*WIFT AS A RAY OF LIGHT, GRACEFUL AS A SWALLOW, AND WISE AS SOLOMON: This poetically describes this breed of great antiquity that can be traced to the varying terrains of almost every country on every continent. This was the type of dog the ancients knew, and from time immemorial it has been a symbol of aristocracy. The first evidence of the Greyhound appears in Egyptian tombs, about 2900 to 2751 B.C., where carvings portray dogs of unmistakable Greyhound type. Centuries later, both Greeks and Romans favored Greyhounds and hunted an assortment of game with them. Greyhounds were adaptable enough to be successful in each new environment, and thus the breed spread throughout the ancient world. Hunt scenes on tapestries, in illuminated manuscripts, and in paintings portray packs of Greyhounds in pursuit of large and small game: deer, stag, rabbit, fox, and the occasional bear and boar. Royalty kept large kennels of hunting Greyhounds and had special favorites as pets. Portraits of royal families posing with beloved Greyhounds grace many castles in Europe.

When there were no longer enormous estates, royal hunts, and forests reserved for the exclusive use of nobility, it was natural that the Greyhound's most popular quarry was the one that was also the most prevalent. Hare coursing became increasingly popular in Elizabethan England, where fanciers have organized such events for over two centuries. In these coursing events, dogs are matched against each other and against the hare, testing speed, agility, and endurance in the open field.

Europeans brought Greyhounds with them to the New World long before 1776, and by the 1800s they were being used on wild game in the American West. Most of today's show Greyhounds descend from English and European coursing dogs imported during the 1900s.

The ancients knew what we still know today: Greyhounds make delightful companions. Centuries as treasured companions have produced a sweet, personable, and tractable nature. They are affectionate with their families and friends. The way they have been kept through the centuries have made them, like many hounds, a pack breed. Greyhounds thrive in the company of other dogs and often dislike being solitary.

Though generally quiet by nature, they need daily exercise including long walks or a good run to stay in optimum condition, both physically and mentally. To deny Greyhounds their heritage of running is to deny their very reason for existence. Greyhounds are members of the sighthound family and have a passion for galloping, as well as keen instinct for the chase. They are best kept where they have the opportunity to run, especially with others that can play games at high speed. A safely fenced yard is a must for this breed.

They can live harmoniously with cats or smaller dogs, but this may require some training. Greyhounds can be good with children, but they should also be able to remove themselves if they tire and prefer peace and quiet. Like most hounds, they can have an independent air that should be acknowledged and respected. Essentially, Greyhounds are more interested in doing something with you than for you.

Greyhounds are a natural breed; they need no cropping or special trimming. Grooming their short, fine coat is as simple as routine brushing with a soft bristle brush or rubber curry in addition to bathing when needed. With no body fat or heavy coat, the breed is best suited as a house dog. Because they are athletes, Greyhounds can be subject to sports injuries, such as pulled muscles, broken toes, or split pads, and their fine, taut skin can be prone to tears and lacerations. Their long, whiplike tails can split or break from impact.

Greyhounds were among the first breeds registered with the AKC, appearing in the 1885 second edition of the Stud Book. They were also among the earliest breeds exhibited at American dog shows, and in 1877 the first Westminster Kennel Club show catalog included an entry of eighteen Greyhounds. The invention of the mechanical lure led to the pari-mutuel dog-racing industry in the 1920s. Racing Greyhounds have been adapted to racing at top speed in a single direction around an oval track. They have a separate registry under the auspices of the National Greyhound Association.

There are many activities to enjoy with today's traditional Greyhounds, including competition in the conformation show ring. Coursing trials are exciting and appeal to their instincts and desire for the chase. Greyhounds are independent by nature, but they are very clever and can be fun to train in obedience for those with patience and a sense of humor. They are active, lively, and nimble enough to enjoy agility training and competition. Best of all, though, is the joy of a Greyhound's calm, sweet, and sunny presence in daily family life.

# OFFICIAL STANDARD FOR THE GREYHOUND

**Head**—Long and narrow, fairly wide between the ears, scarcely perceptible stop, little or no development of nasal sinuses, good length of muzzle, which should be powerful without coarseness. Teeth very strong and even in front.

**Ears**—Small and fine in texture, thrown back and folded, except when excited, when they are semi-pricked.

**Eyes**—Dark, bright, intelligent, indicating spirit.

**Neck**—Long, muscular, without throatiness, slightly arched, and widening gradually into the shoulder.

**Shoulders**—Placed as obliquely as possible, muscular without being loaded.

**Forelegs**—Perfectly straight, set well into the shoulders, neither turned in nor out, pasterns strong.

**Chest**—Deep, and as wide as consistent with speed, fairly well-sprung ribs.

**Back**—Muscular and broad.

**Loins**—Good depth of muscle, well arched, well cut up in the flanks.

**Hindquarters**—Long, very muscular and powerful, wide and well let down, well-bent stifles. Hocks well bent and rather close to ground, wide but straight fore and aft.

**Feet**—Hard and close, rather more hare than catfeet, well knuckled up with good strong claws.

**Tail**—Long, fine and tapering with a slight upward curve.

**Coat**—Short, smooth and firm in texture.

**Color**—Immaterial.

**Weight**—Dogs, 65 to 70 pounds; bitches 60 to 65 pounds.

## SCALE OF POINTS

| | |
|---|---|
| General symmetry and quality | 10 |
| Head and neck | 20 |
| Chest and shoulders | 20 |
| Back | 10 |
| Quarters | 20 |
| Legs and feet | 20 |
| **Total** | **100** |

# HARRIER

*P*ROBABLY THE OLDEST WORK ON HARE HUNTING IS THE FAMOUS ESSAY BY the Greek historian Xenophon in about 400 B.C., and with that as a basis, hare hunting has been a favorite subject of the greatest authorities on the dog for the past 2,300 years. But there is a striking unanimity of doubt concerning the direct ancestors of this old breed of scent hound.

The Harrier, as he exists today, was unknown in Xenophon's time, although he describes two types of hounds that were used with equal success in the early hunting of the hare. One he calls the Castorean, the favorite of the demigod Castor. The other is designated as the fox-breed, which is explained as a product of the fox and the dog. On the other hand, Xenophon has listed the qualities of a hound suitable for the purposes, and they bear amazing similarity to the desirable points of modern times.

This early treatise on hunting is no fragmentary remnant of a scholarly mind, but one of the most definite and minute portrayals of a sport that ever has been written. Perhaps the only real difference between the way the Greeks hunted the hare and the manner accepted in England and other countries is that in 400 B.C. the hares were driven into nets. This practice would bring great censure on hunters of today. Still, sportsmanship was given some consideration in ancient times, for Xenophon says: "In tracking the hare, no delay should be made, for it is sportsmanlike, as well as a proof of fondness for exertion, to use every means to capture the animals speedily."

Even the great English authority on all breeds, Stonehenge, was a little mystified by the origin of the Harrier. The theory he advances rather cautiously is that it springs from the old Southern Hound, with an infusion of a little Greyhound blood.

Undoubtedly the Southern Hound has played a great part in the development of all scenthound breeds in the British Isles, yet there is little or no mention of the origin of this basic breed. The most logical supposition appears to be that it was brought to England by the Normans, for hunting is of great antiquity on the Continent.

The first pack of Harriers in England was the Penistone, established by Sir Elias de Midhope in 1260. These Harriers were held together for at least five hundred years, and it is recorded that in the fourteenth, seventeenth, and the eighteenth centuries, the masters were supplied by the Wilsons of Broomhead Hall. Hunting the hare has always had great popularity in the British Isles, and in some ways enjoyed greater favor than foxhunting. One great cause of its popularity was that a pack of Harriers could be followed on foot. This enlisted the interest of many, and among the hundred-odd packs that hunted regularly in England, many were scratch packs. A scratch pack was made up of hounds owned by various individuals—thus bringing the sport down to the level of the poorer man. However, horses are used in most cases today.

In support of the Norman origin of this and other hound breeds, there has been an interesting bit of information supplied by Wynn in regard to the word *harrier.* He shows that this may have come from the Norman *harier,* denoting Saxon *raches,* or hounds. Further, *harier* was used down to 1750 for all hounds, not necessarily hare-hounds. And back in 1570, Dr. Caius mentioned stag- and fox-harriers.

The studbooks for Harriers published by the association of Masters of Harriers and Beagles (AMHB in England) began in March 1891 and continues to this day. In America, the Harrier has been present as long as any other scent hound and has been used for hunting since Colonial times. Being one of the oldest British breeds, the Harrier in 1885 became the fourth hound breed to be registered by the American Kennel Club.

Although their origin is that of a hunting pack hound, today they are equally at home in the conformation ring, in performance events, and as family companions.

# OFFICIAL STANDARD FOR THE HARRIER

**General Appearance**—Developed in England to hunt hare in packs, Harriers must have all the attributes of a scenting pack hound. They are very sturdily built with large bone for their size. They must be active, well balanced, full of strength and quality, in all ways appearing able to work tirelessly, no matter the terrain, for long periods. Running gear and scenting ability are particularly important features. The Harrier should, in fact, be a smaller version of the English Foxhound.

**Size, Proportion, Substance**—*Size*—19 to 21 inches for dogs and bitches, variation of one inch in either direction is acceptable. *Proportion* is off-square. The Harrier is slightly longer from point of shoulder to rump than from withers to ground. *Substance*—Solidly built, full of strength and quality. The breed has as much substance and bone as possible without being heavy or coarse.

**Head**—The head is in proportion to the overall dog. No part of the head should stand out relative to the other parts. The expression is gentle when relaxed, sensible yet alert when aroused. *Eyes* are medium size, set well apart, brown or hazel color in darker dogs, lighter hazel to yellow in lighter dogs, though darker colors are always desired. *Ears* are set on low and lie close to the cheeks, rounded at the tips.

The *skull* is in proportion to the entire animal, with good length and breadth and a bold forehead. The *stop* is moderately defined. The *muzzle* from stop to tip of nose is approximately the same length as the skull from stop to occiput. The muzzle is substantial with good depth, and the *lips* complete the square, clean look of the muzzle, without excess skin or flews. A good *nose* is essential. It must be wide, with well opened nostrils. Teeth meet in a scissors *bite* or they may be level. Overshot or undershot bites faulted to the degree of severity of the misalignment.

**Neck, Topline, Body**—The *neck* is long and strong with no excess skin or throatiness, sweeping smoothly into the muscling of the forequarters. The *topline* is level. Back muscular with no dip behind the withers or roach over the loin. *Body*—Chest deep, extending to the elbows, with well sprung ribs that extend well back, providing plenty of heart and lung room. The ribs should not be so well sprung that they interfere with the free, efficient movement of the front assembly. The loin is short, wide and well muscled.

The *tail* is long, set on high and carried up from 12 o'clock to 3 o'clock, depending on attitude. It tapers to a point with a brush of hair. The tail should not be curled over the back.

**Forequarters**—Moderate angulation, with long shoulders sloping into the muscles of the back, clean at the withers. The shoulders are well clothed with muscle without being excessively heavy or loaded, giving the impression of free, strong action. Elbows are set well away from the ribs, running parallel with the body and not turning outwards. Good straight legs with plenty of bone running well down to the toes, but not overburdened, inclined to knuckle over very slightly but not exaggerated in the slightest degree. *Feet* are round and catlike, with toes set close together turning slightly inwards. The pads are thick, well developed and strong.

**Hindquarters**—Angulation in balance with the front assembly, so that rear drive is in harmony with front reach. Well developed muscles, providing strength for long hours of work, are important. Endurance is more important than pure speed, and as such, the stifles are only moderately angulated. *Feet* point straight ahead, are round and catlike with toes set close together, and thick, well developed pads.

**Coat**—Short, dense, hard and glossy. Coat texture on the ears is finer than on the body. There is a brush of hair on the underside of the tail.

**Color**—Any color, not regarded as very important.

**Gait**—Perfect coordination between the front and hind legs. Reach and drive are consistent with the desired moderate angulation. Coming and going, the dog moves in a straight line, evidencing no sign of crabbing. A slight toeing-in of the front feet is acceptable. Clean movement coming and going is important, but not nearly as important as side gait, which is smooth, efficient and ground-covering.

**Temperament**—Outgoing and friendly, as a working pack breed, Harriers must be able to work in close contact with other hounds. Therefore, aggressiveness towards other dogs cannot be tolerated.

**Approved December 13, 1988**
**Effective February 1, 1989**

# IBIZAN HOUND

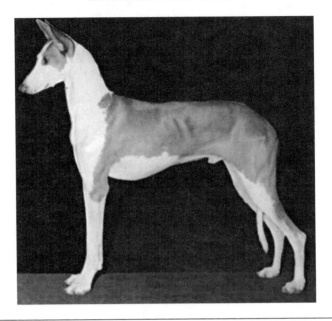

*I*BIZAN HOUND HISTORY IS TRACEABLE TO APPROXIMATELY 3400 B.C. THE glory that was ancient Egypt was a most fitting setting for this regal hound, owned and hunted by the pharaohs.

Numerous artifacts found in the tombs of the pharaohs now reinforce the existence of such a dog in those long-past times. Hemako, who reigned in the period of the First Dynasty (3100–2700 B.C.), was buried near Saggara. When this site was unearthed many artifacts were uncovered, one of which was a carved dish bearing the image of the Ibizan. These dogs, which are also referred to as Galgo Hounds, are quite distinct in their appearance; therefore, no other could be mistaken as being represented. Nevermat of the Fourth Dynasty, who lived at approximately 2600 B.C., Tutankhamen of the Eighteenth Dynasty, and the Ptolemies of the Thirtieth and final Dynasty, all have tombs which have yielded further proof of the hound's ancient and proud heritage. Cleopatra was an ardent devotee of the Galgo, and her reign was the twilight of the pharaohs' time in Egypt.

The tomb of Tutankhamen proved a treasure trove when discovered in 1922. Anubis, "The Watchdog of the Dead," a long-honored deity, was well represented by a full-sized true-to-life statue, which is the identical duplicate of the Ibizan Hound of today. This marvelously preserved piece of carved statuary was coated with resins and varnishes. The eyes are of obsidian (a volcanic variety of rock that has a very glassy look and is deep black) and are rimmed with gold leaf, as are the insides of the ears. Anubis also bears a beautiful collar of gold, but time had not deteriorated his beauty nor the fact that the original model could only have been the Greyhound-type, prick-eared, sickle-tailed dog now known as the Ibizan. It was originally thought that the jackal had been the original model, this miscalculation due to the fact that the Ibizan was extinct in its land of origin at the time of these numerous discoveries.

We can but surmise the movement of the breed from Egypt to the island from which it now derives its name. The hardy sea-traders of Phoenicia were well traveled in those days and had entree to many lands. It is thought that they are basically responsible for the survival of this breed. It was the Phoenicians who discovered the island now known as Ibiza in the eighth or ninth century B.C. Now belonging to Spain, Ibiza has been ruled and conquered by many—Egyptians, Chaldeans, Carthaginians, Romans, Vandals, and Arabs. Roman coins bear the head of an Ibizan Hound, and Hasdrubal once ruled this land. Conejera, a member of this Balearic grouping, was a small off island also which claims historical fame by being the birthplace of the famed Hannibal. It is said that the Ibizan Hound was the dog which accompanied him with his mighty elephants on that long trek over the Alps.

This breed has survived even the hard life that the Ibizan group of islands has imposed on it. Only the fittest could survive, as food is scarce, and the islanders used these dogs to assist in providing the necessary food to sustain their lives. As a result, these dogs have learned to hunt with great skill, tenacity, and patience. The owners of these hounds also culled their litters diligently, for only the strongest and most perfect specimens could survive the hardships. We must give our thanks to those early owners and breeders, for through their dedication we have seen a breed travel through centuries unmarked by numerous problems evident in many other breeds. These animals are as strong, fit, and vigorous today as they were in the days of the pharaohs.

The first Ibizans reached the United States in mid-1956, imported by Colonel and Mrs. Seoane, of Rhode Island. Hannibal (Stop) and Certera (Tanit) created quite a stir, and soon it was known that the first litter would arrive in the fall. Eight pups were the result of the first breeding and the four males and four females (Asuncion, Malchus V, Denia, Heulalia, Granada, Mago, Gisco, and Sertorius), along with several other imports and their parents, form the foundations of the breed here.

Over the years the breed has flourished in this country. Ibizans are respected by all who have come into intimate contact with them as lively companions, pets, watchdogs, hunters, and friends. They lend themselves well to family life and the ever-changing American lifestyles. Their temperament is excellent, and their health has proven superior. Structurally they are extremely strong and resilient. The Ibizan Hound Club of the United States has been most stringent in impressing upon owners and breeders the importance of fully retaining the fine qualities of this dog first and foremost, and has kept its pledge to preserve it true to form.

The Ibizan Hound was admitted to AKC Stud Book registration effective October 1, 1978, and became eligible for show competition January 1, 1979.

# OFFICIAL STANDARD FOR THE IBIZAN HOUND

**General Appearance**—The Ibizan's clean-cut lines, large prick ears and light pigment give it a unique appearance. A hunting dog whose quarry is primarily rabbits, this ancient hound was bred for thousands of years with function being of prime importance. Lithe and racy, the Ibizan possesses a deerlike elegance combined with the power of a hunter. Strong, without appearing heavily muscled, the Ibizan is a hound of moderation. With the exception of the ears, he should not appear extreme or exaggerated.

In the field the Ibizan is as fast as top coursing breeds and without equal in agility, high jumping and broad jumping ability. He is able to spring to great heights from a standstill.

**Size, Proportion, Substance**—*Size*—The height of dogs is 23½ inches to 27½ inches at the withers. Bitches are 22½ to 26 inches at the withers. There is no preference for size within this range. Sizes slightly over or under the norms are not to be regarded as demerits when other qualities are good. *Weight*—Average weight of dogs is 50 pounds; bitches, 45 pounds. *Proportion*—Slightly longer than tall. *Substance*—The Ibizan possesses clean, fine bone. The muscling is strong, yet flat, with no sign of heaviness.

**Head**—Long and narrow in the form of a sharp cone truncated at its base. Finely chiseled and extremely dry fleshed.

*Expression*—The Ibizan has an elegant, deer-like look. The *eyes* are oblique and small, ranging in color from clear amber to caramel. The rims are the color of the nose and are fully or partially pigmented. The appearance of the eye is intelligent, alert and inquisitive. The *ears* are large, pointed, and natural. On alert the ear should never droop, bend, or crease. Highly mobile, the ear can point forward, sideways, or be folded backward, according to mood. On alert, the lowest point of the base is at level of the eye. On frontal examination, the height of the ear is approximately 2½ times that of the widest point of the base. *Skull*—Long and flat, prominent occipital bone, little defined *stop;* narrow brow. The *muzzle* is elongated, fine, and slender with a very slight Roman convex. The length from the eyes to point of nose is equal to the distance from eyes to occiput. The muzzle and skull are on parallel *planes.* The *nose* is prominent, extending beyond the lower jaw. It is of a rosy flesh color, never black or liver, and tends to harmonize with that of the coat. Pigment is solid or butterfly. Nostrils are open. *Lips* are thin and tight and the color of the nose. Flews are tight and dry fleshed. *Bite*—The teeth are perfectly opposed in a scissors bite; strong and well set.

**Neck, Topline, Body**—The *neck* is long, slender, slightly arched and strong, yet flat muscled. The *topline,* from ears to tail, is smooth and flowing. The *back* is level and straight. *Body*—The chest is deep and long with the breastbone sharply angled and prominent. The ribs are slightly sprung. The brisket is approximately 2½ inches above the elbow. The deepest part of the chest, behind the elbow, is nearly to or to the elbow. The abdomen is well tucked up, but not exaggerated. The *loin* is very slightly arched, of medium breadth and well muscled. The *croup* is very slightly sloping. The *tail* is set low, highly mobile, and reaches at least to the hock. It is carried in a sickle, ring, or saber position, according to the mood and individual specimen.

**Forequarters**—*Angulation* is moderate. The *shoulders* are elastic but never loose with moderate breadth at the withers. The shoulder blades are well laid back. At the *point of the shoulder* they join to a rather upright *upper arm.* The *elbow* is positioned in front of the deepest part of the chest. It is well held in but not so much as to restrict movement. *Legs*—The forearms are very long, strong, straight, and close, lying flat on the chest and continuing in a straight line to the ground. Bone is clean and fine. The *pasterns* are strong and flexible, slightly sloping, with well developed tendons. *Dewclaw* removal is optional. *Feet*—Hare-foot. The toes are long, closed and very strong. Interdigital spaces are well protected by hair. Pads are durable. Nails are white.

**Hindquarters**—*Angulation* is moderate with the hindquarters being set under the body. *Legs*—The thighs are very strong with flat muscling. The hocks are straight when viewed from the rear. Bone is clean and fine. There are no rear dewclaws. The *feet* are as in front.

**Coat**—There are two types of coat; both untrimmed. *Short*—Shortest on head and ears and longest at back of the thighs and under the tail. *Wire-haired* can be from one to three inches in length with a possible generous mustache. There is more hair on the back, back of thighs, and tail. Both types of coat are hard in texture and neither coat is preferable to the other.

**Color**—White or red (from light, yellowish-red called "lion" to deep red), solid or in any combination. No color or pattern is preferable to the other. *Disqualify* any color other than white or red.

**Gait**—An efficient, light and graceful single tracking movement. A suspended trot with joint flexion when viewed from the side. The Ibizan exhibits smooth reach in front with balanced rear drive, giving the appearance of skimming over the ground.

**Temperament**—The Ibizan Hound is even-tempered, affectionate and loyal. Extremely versatile and trainable, he makes an excellent family pet, and is well suited to the breed ring, obedience, tracking and lure coursing. He exhibits a keen, natural hunting instinct with much determination and stamina in the field.

**Disqualification**—Any color other than white or red.

**Approved September 11, 1989**
**Effective November 1, 1989**

# IRISH WOLFHOUND

$\mathcal{E}$ ARLY IRISH LITERATURE ABOUNDS WITH REFERENCES TO THESE DOGS, INTER-changeably called Irish dogs, Big Dogs of Ireland, Greyhounds (or *Grehounds*) of Ireland, Wolfdogs of Ireland, or Great Hounds of Ireland. Irish Wolfhound is the modern name.

The breed was known in Rome by A.D. 391, when the Roman consul received seven of them as a gift, which "all Rome viewed with wonder." Through the ensuing centuries, Irish Wolfhounds inspired poets and authors. In 1790, an anonymous sportsman wrote: "The Irish Greyhound is the largest of dogkind and its appearance the most beautiful. He is about 3 feet high, somewhat like a Greyhound, but more robust. His aspect is mild, his disposition is peaceable yet his strength is so great that in combat the Mastiff or Bulldog is far from being equal to him."

Wolfhounds were coveted for their hunting prowess, particularly in pursuing the wolf and the gigantic Irish elk, which stood six feet at the shoulder. With the disappearance of these animals from Ireland, and excessive exportation of dwindling Wolfhound ranks, the breed almost became extinct.

In 1862, Captain George A. Graham, a Scotsman in the British army, gathered the remaining specimens and restored the breed. Twenty-three years later, under his supervision, the first breed standard was written. Meeting this standard remains the goal every conscientious breeder strives to attain.

The Irish Wolfhound is a large, rough-coated, browed, and bearded hound built on galloping lines. Whether lying by a modern hearth, galloping in a meadow, romping on a fenced lawn or along a beach, it is easy to imagine Wolfhounds as the prominent figures they once were in the Middle Ages.

Because of their great size and the amount of exercise essential to their well-being, the Irish Wolfhound should not be acquired without serious forethought. The ideal home is one with sufficient fenced property to accommodate the galloping nature of this athletic sighthound.

Most Irish Wolfhounds bred in this century have enjoyed private homes where their quiet manners, gentle nature, and comfortable sense of companionship have flourished. The Irish Wolfhound does best when human companionship is the core of daily life. Wolfhounds do not thrive in a harsh, demanding environment or respond well to loud, abrasive treatment. At maturity, despite their size, the typical Wolfhound is a calm, dignified, and responsive presence within the home. That is not to say Wolfhounds need no management, for a large, unruly animal can be unpleasant for family and visitors alike. Early training for basic manners is essential.

Though alert, Irish Wolfhounds are not suspicious by nature and will usually assume visitors are friends. Though courageous, they are not aggressive. Aggressive behavior would be atypical of the breed and should never be encouraged in a dog of this size. A kind nature makes the typical Wolfhound totally unsuited to be a guard dog. As an incidental function, their very appearance is a formidable deterrent to intruders, but they are more likely to serenade the moon than bark at noises and people.

A Wolfhound puppy takes a year or more to mature, and left to its own devices can demolish a room per hour and injure itself in the process. Six-month-old Irish Wolfhounds weigh about 100 pounds, yet are not through teething, nor are their body functions ready for prolonged containment.

An occasional Irish Wolfhound is successfully raised and kept under less than ideal conditions by owners who have the wish, will, and stamina to provide extensive leash walking and cope with sidewalks, traffic, close neighbors, and pedestrians. The hygienic responsibility of owners with giant breeds is awesome. Typically, Irish Wolfhounds have only the kindest intentions toward children. Common sense, however, precludes the mingling of a small child and a large dog without supervision.

A completely natural breed, Wolfhound ears are uncropped, and tails are undocked. No part of the breed should appear styled, clipped, or scissored. Their typically harsh coats can be well maintained by regular brushing and plucking to tidy them up a bit.

Bringing their natural qualities to perfection is the goal of responsible, modern-day breeders. Some Irish Wolfhounds are entered in dog shows, where they compete based on physical excellence in relation to the official breed standard. Most owners, however, have a hound simply for the pleasure of their company. Although the chase is not a Wolfhound preoccupation, we must never forget it is their natural sport. The sight of them in characteristic gallop, swiftly covering the ground, is exhilarating and leaves no doubt of their need to exercise this birthright. Lure coursing, therefore, is great adventure and sport for Irish Wolfhounds. It gives them an opportunity to run full out harmlessly and chase an inanimate object without the risk encountered in hunting their natural prey, the wolf.

# OFFICIAL STANDARD FOR THE IRISH WOLFHOUND

**General Appearance**—Of great size and commanding appearance, the Irish Wolfhound is remarkable in combining power and swiftness with keen sight. The largest and tallest of the galloping hounds, in general type he is a rough-coated, Greyhound-like breed; very muscular, strong though gracefully built; movements easy and active; head and neck carried high, the tail carried with an upward sweep with a slight curve towards the extremity. The minimum height and weight of dogs should be 32 inches and 120 pounds; of bitches, 30 inches and 105 pounds; these to apply only to hounds over 18 months of age. Anything below this should be debarred from competition. Great size, including height at shoulder and proportionate length of body, is the desideratum to be aimed at, and it is desired to firmly establish a race that shall average from 32 to 34 inches in dogs, showing the requisite power, activity, courage and symmetry.

**Head**—Long, the frontal bones of the forehead very slightly raised and very little indentation between the eyes. Skull, not too broad. Muzzle, long and moderately pointed. Ears, small and Greyhound-like in carriage.

**Neck**—Rather long, very strong and muscular, well arched, without dewlap or loose skin about the throat.

**Chest**—Very deep. Breast, wide.

**Back**—Rather long than short. Loins arched.

**Tail**—Long and slightly curved, of moderate thickness, and well covered with hair.

**Belly**—Well drawn up.

**Forequarters**—Shoulders, muscular, giving breadth of chest, set sloping. Elbows well under, neither turned inwards nor outwards.

**Leg**—Forearm muscular, and the whole leg strong and quite straight.

**Hindquarters**—Muscular thighs and second thigh long and strong as in the Greyhound, and hocks well let down and turning neither in nor out.

**Feet**—Moderately large and round, neither turned inwards nor outwards. Toes, well arched and closed. Nails, very strong and curved.

**Hair**—Rough and hard on body, legs and head; especially wiry and long over eyes and underjaw.

**Color and Markings**—The recognized colors are gray, brindle, red, black, pure white, fawn, or any other color that appears in the Deerhound.

## FAULTS

*Too light or heavy a head, too highly arched frontal bone; large ears and hanging flat to the face; short neck; full dewlap; too narrow or too broad a chest; sunken or hollow or quite straight back; bent forelegs; overbent fetlocks; twisted feet; spreading toes; too curly a tail; weak hindquarters and a general want of muscle; too short in body. Lips or nose liver-colored or lacking pigmentation.*

## LIST OF POINTS IN ORDER OF MERIT

1. *Typical.* The Irish Wolfhound is a rough-coated Greyhound-like breed, the tallest of the coursing hounds and remarkable in combining power and swiftness.
2. *Great size* and commanding appearance.
3. Movements easy and active.
4. Head, long and level, carried high.
5. Forelegs, heavily boned, quite straight; elbows well set under.
6. Thighs long and muscular; second thighs, well muscled, stifles nicely bent.
7. Coat, rough and hard, especially wiry and long over eyes and under jaw.
8. Body, long, well-ribbed up, with ribs well sprung, and great breadth across hips.
9. Loins arched, belly well drawn up.
10. Ears, small, with Greyhound-like carriage.
11. Feet, moderately large and round; toes, close, well arched.
12. Neck, long, well arched and very strong.
13. Chest, very deep, moderately broad.
14. Shoulders, muscular, set sloping.
15. Tail, long and slightly curved.
16. Eyes, dark.

**Note**—The above in no way alter the Standard of Excellence, which must in all cases be rigidly adhered to; they simply give the various points in order of merit. If in any case they appear at variance with Standard of Excellence, it is the latter which is correct.

**Approved September 12, 1950**

# NORWEGIAN ELKHOUND

*C*OMRADE TO THE VIKINGS, GUARDIAN OF LONELY FARMS AND *SAETERS,* HERDER of flocks and defender from wolves and bear, a hunter always and roamer with hardy men, the Norwegian Elkhound comes down to us through more than six millennia with all his Nordic traits untainted, a fearless dog and friendly, devoted to man and the chase. We read of him in sagas, we find his remains by the side of his Viking master along with the Viking's weapons—sure proof of the esteem in which he was held; and in the Viste Cave at Jaeren, in western Norway, his skeleton was uncovered among the stone implements in a stratum dating from 4000 to 5000 B.C.

Selected and bred for his ability to accomplish a definite purpose, the Elkhound achieved his distinctive type by natural methods. No form was imposed upon him; he was not squeezed into a preconceived standard; his structure and rare beauty, like those of the Thoroughbred horse, were evolved from the tests of performance. Every physical characteristic is the expression of a need. His compactness, his muscled robustness, his squareness, his width and depth are true expressions of nature's requirements for a dog that would hunt day after day, all day long, in rugged country, where stamina counts more than extreme speed.

For though the Elkhound has become known and loved chiefly, perhaps, for his engaging and sensitive qualities as a comrade of man and his reliability and quickness to learn and adapt himself to any circumstances and conditions, it should never be forgotten that from first to last he has been at all times the peerless hunter of big game.

Many years ago, bear were still common in Norway, but today they are almost extinct, and the native dog's main use is the hunting of elk. (*Elk* is incorrectly used in the United States for the wapiti, *Cervus canadensis*; our *moose* is a true elk.) A century ago, Captain Lloyd, an English sportsman, a mighty hunter, and a fascinating writer, devoted his leisure to the description of bear hunting in Norway; and from that time on, everyone that has seen the Elkhound work in the forests of his native land has added to his praise.

The Elkhound's highly developed senses amount almost to intuition. It is common to read of, or—if one is fortunate—experience such incidents as seeing a seasoned dog take body scent at from two to three miles or to hear him indicating to his master by a slight whimpering that the elk has become alarmed and has begun to run, at a time when no human senses can apprehend any sign by which the hound ascertains this fact.

Equally subtle is his method of engaging a bull. Knowing well that an elk can outfoot him, he holds the animal by just enough barking to attract his attention. Even with a skillful dog, however, the elk often moves on before the hunter can get up over the steep countryside; and in that case, the dog, aware that the bull, if not excited by sound or scent, will soon pause, work silently and very carefully upwind until he is once more with his quarry. After a while, the bull, becoming angry at the small beast annoying him, begins to attack with a wide sweeping movement of the great antlers and by striking with his deadly forefeet. But now, the Elkhound, shortbacked so that he can, to use Herr Aarflot's apt expression, "bounce like a rubber ball," jumps nimbly in and out, while giving full and furious tongue so that his high-pitched voice will reach his master.

The Elkhound is well adapted to the hunting of any other four-footed game and soon becomes expert on lynx, mountain lion, and raccoon. Sir Henry Pottinger declares that he is also an excellent tracker of fox. The same authority states: "There is no more deadly way of approaching capercailzie, black game, and other forest birds than with a dog of the breed under discussion, held or fastened to the belt by a long leash and allowed to precede the hunter."

The Elkhound, then, is an exceedingly versatile dog developed through constant contact with man in pursuit of game. It was not until 1877 that he began to be considered from an exhibition point of view. In that year the Norwegian Hunters' Association held its first show, and, shortly thereafter, pedigrees, which had been handed down, were checked and traced as far back as feasible, a studbook (*Norsk Hundestambak*) was published, and a standard drawn up. Before that time, there had been some confusion of type owing to different developments in different parts of the country; but if we study the photograph of such a grand dog as that pillar of the studbook, known as Gamle Bamse Gram, we shall see that all the essential elements of the modern show dog were already there, requiring only a little refinement, a little emphasis.

At any rate, by the turn of the twentieth century the breed was making very rapid progress, and though there were few or no really large kennels, there were many expert breeders devoted to the Elkhound's improvement. When the Norwegian Kennel Club (Norsk Kennelklub) inaugurated its annual shows at Oslo, the Elkhound came into his own as Norway's great contribution to dogdom. Since then, he has been exported in ever-increasing numbers. His friendly disposition, his intelligence, his staunchness, his absolute dependability and trustworthiness, his eagerness to please, his sensitivity, and his fearless confidence have gained for him everywhere a popularity based even more on his comradely character than on his unsurpassed abilities as a hunting dog.

# OFFICIAL STANDARD OF THE NORWEGIAN ELKHOUND

**General Appearance**—The Norwegian Elkhound is a hardy gray hunting dog. In appearance, a typical northern dog of medium size and substance, square in profile, close-coupled and balanced in proportions. The head is broad with prick ears, and the tail is tightly curled and carried over the back. The distinctive gray coat is dense and smooth lying. As a hunter, the Norwegian Elkhound has the courage, agility and stamina to hold moose and other big game at bay by barking and dodging attack, and the endurance to track for long hours in all weather over rough and varied terrain.

**Size, Proportion, Substance**—*Height* at the withers for dogs is 20½ inches, for bitches 19½ inches. *Weight* for dogs about 55 pounds, for bitches about 48 pounds.

Square in profile and close coupled. Distance from brisket to ground appears to be half the height at the withers. Distance from forechest to rump equals the height at the withers. Bone is substantial, without being coarse.

**Head**—*Head* broad at the ears, wedge shaped, strong and dry (without loose skin). *Expression* keen, alert, indicating a dog with great courage. *Eyes* very dark brown, medium in size, oval, not protruding. *Ears* set high, firm and erect, yet very mobile. Comparatively small; slightly taller than their width at the base with pointed (not rounded) tips. When the dog is alert, the orifices turn forward and the outer edges are vertical. When relaxed or showing affection, the ears go back, and the dog should not be penalized for doing this during the judge's examination.

Viewed from the side, the forehead and back of the *skull* are only slightly arched; the *stop* not large, yet clearly defined. The *muzzle* is thickest at the base and, seen from above or from the side, tapers evenly without being pointed. The bridge of the *nose* is straight, parallel to and about the same length as the skull. *Lips* are tightly closed and *teeth* meet in a scissors bite.

**Neck, Topline, Body**—*Neck* of medium length, muscular, well set up with a slight arch and with no loose skin on the throat. *Topline*—The back is straight and strong from its high point at the withers to the root of the tail. The *body* is short and close-coupled with the rib cage accounting for most of its length. **Chest** deep and moderately broad; brisket level with points of elbows; and ribs well sprung. **Loin** short and wide with very little tuck-up. **Tail** set high, tightly curled, and carried over the centerline of the back. It is thickly and closely haired, without brush, natural and untrimmed.

**Forequarters**—Shoulders sloping with elbows closely set on. **Legs** well under body and medium in length; substantial, but not coarse, in bone. Seen from the front, the legs appear straight and parallel. Single dewclaws are normally present. **Feet**—Paws comparatively small, slightly oval with tightly closed toes and thick pads. Pasterns are strong and only slightly bent. Feet turn neither in nor out.

**Hindquarters**—Moderate angulation at stifle and hock. **Thighs** are broad and well muscled. Seen from behind, legs are straight, strong and without dewclaws. **Feet** as in front.

**Coat**—Thick, hard, weather resisting and smooth lying; made up of soft, dense, woolly undercoat and coarse, straight covering hairs. Short and even on head, ears, and front of legs; longest on back of neck, buttocks and underside of tail. The coat is not altered by trimming, clipping or artificial treatment. Trimming of whiskers is optional. In the show ring, presentation in a natural, unaltered condition is essential.

**Color**—Gray, medium preferred, variations in shade determined by the length of black tips and quantity of guard hairs. Undercoat is clear light silver as are legs, stomach, buttocks, and underside of tail. The gray body color is darkest on the saddle, lighter on the chest, mane and distinctive harness mark (a band of longer guard hairs from shoulder to elbow). The muzzle, ears and tail tip are black. The black of the muzzle shades to lighter gray over the forehead and skull.

Yellow or brown shading, white patches, indistinct or irregular markings, "sooty" coloring on the lower legs and light circles around the eyes are undesirable. Any overall color other than gray as described above, such as red, brown, solid black, white or other solid color, disqualifies.

**Gait**—Normal for an active dog constructed for agility and endurance. At a trot the stride is even and effortless; the back remains level. As the speed of the trot increases, front and rear legs converge equally in straight lines toward a centerline beneath the body, so that the pads appear to follow in the same tracks (single track). Front and rear quarters are well balanced in angulation and muscular development.

**Temperament**—In temperament, the Norwegian Elkhound is bold and energetic, an effective guardian yet normally friendly, with great dignity and independence of character.

**Summary**—The Norwegian Elkhound is a square and athletic member of the northern dog family. His unique coloring, weather resistant coat and stable disposition make him an ideal multipurpose dog at work or at play.

# DISQUALIFICATIONS

*An overall color other than gray.*

**Approved December 13, 1988**
**Effective February 1, 1989**

# OTTERHOUND

*A*LTHOUGH THERE ARE REFERENCES TO OTTERHOUNDS AND OTTER HUNT-ing during the reign of Britain's King John (1199–1216), the dogs themselves were not described until the time of Edward II (1307–1327). Fortunately, a hunter of that era, William Twici, described the Otterhound as a "rough sort of dog, between a hound and a terrier."

Otter hunting, never a major sport in Britain, nonetheless appears to have existed from very early times. It was first intended to stop otters from preying on fish in rivers, streams, and stocked ponds. Later, the activity became more popular because it was the only kind of hunting possible from April to September.

The actual origin of the Otterhound is unknown, but some early writers have advanced logical opinions on the subject. Stonehenge (J. H. Walsh) believed that the Otterhound's ancestors were the Southern Hound and the Welsh Harrier. Indeed, large numbers of Otterhounds were found in Wales and in Devonshire, which was the chief stronghold of the Southern Hound. E. Buckley attributed the Otterhound's coat to the Water Spaniel, a somewhat different type from the breed known today, and credits the Otterhound's hardiness to the Bulldog. Other writers mention the Bloodhound, citing the domed shape of the skull and the length of the ears. In fact, as early as 1575, John Turberville made no distinction between the Bloodhound and the Otterhound in his description of otter hunting. One of the most reasonable opinions about Otterhound origin came from Marples, who noted the strong similarity between the Otterhound and the old Vendéen Hound of France. Both breeds are alike in coat and body conformation.

The heyday of the Otterhound in Britain extended from the middle to the end of the nineteenth century. During those years, as many as eighteen to twenty packs hunted regularly throughout the season. Authorities agree that the best-trained pack of Otterhounds ever hunted belonged to Squire Lomax of Clitheroe. The squire was a stickler for the fine points of game, and though the results interested him, his major concern was the manner in which his pack worked. According to legend, the pack was so well trained that Lomax's hand signals could be given with a casual wave. His pack reached its peak of perfection about 1868.

By the mid-nineteenth century the breed was identical in appearance to the modern Otterhound, but the hunting packs of Great Britain continued to cross-breed to other hounds, including the Bloodhound, Griffon Nivernais, and fox-hounds until the mid-twentieth century.

The Otterhound is a big dog, standing 24 to 27 inches tall and weighing from 75 to 115 pounds. Its hard, crisp, close coat is oily and repels water. The breed is found in many color combinations, the most common being grizzled black and tan. They are peerless swimmers, greatly aided by their webbed feet.

In Britain, the working qualities of the Otterhound breed have been empha-sized to such an extent that they had never been common as benched-show speci-mens until the late twentieth century. Still, a few dogs from some of the great packs were customarily sent to major shows. The Carlisle and Kendal packs were noted for their show dogs.

Otterhounds made their first appearance in the United States around 1900. In 1907 they made their benched-show debut in Claremont, Oklahoma. In that same year, registrations were recorded for Hartland Moss Trooper and Hartland States-man, both owned by H. S. Wardner, of New York City. Wardner was one of two exhibiters of the breed at the Claremont show, and he was undoubtedly America's first Otterhound breeder.

While Otterhounds have never achieved wide popularity in the United States, their sagacity and character have earned them many steadfast friends. Their tousled appearance may not appeal to some, but their working ability and cheerful approach to life are more than adequate compensation. Though few Otterhounds now hunt, their scenting ability and determination have made them very successful as tracking dogs. In recent years, their athleticism has been used to earn advanced agility and obedience titles.

# OFFICIAL STANDARD FOR THE OTTERHOUND

**General Appearance**—The Otterhound is a large, rough-coated hound with an imposing head showing great strength and dignity, and the strong body and long striding action fit for a long day's work. It has an extremely sensitive nose, and is inquisitive and perseverant in investigating scents. The Otterhound hunts its quarry on land and water and requires a combination of characteristics unique among hounds—most notably a rough, double coat; and substantial webbed feet. Otterhounds should not be penalized for being shown in working condition (lean, well muscled, with a naturally stripped coat). Any departure from the following points should be considered a fault; its seriousness should be regarded in exact proportion to its degree.

**Size, Proportion, Substance**—Males are approximately 27 inches at the withers, and weigh approximately 115 lbs. Bitches are approximately 24 inches at the withers, and weigh approximately 80 lbs. This is not an absolute, but rather a guideline. The Otterhound is *slightly* rectangular in body; the length from point of shoulder to buttocks is slightly greater than the height at the withers. The Otterhound has good substance with strongly boned legs and broad muscles, without being coarse. Balance, soundness and type are of greater importance than size.

**Head**—The head is large, fairly narrow, and well covered with hair. The head should measure 11 to 12 inches from tip of nose to occiput in a hound 26 inches at the withers, with the muzzle and skull approximately equal in length. This proportion should be maintained in larger and smaller hounds. The *expression* is open and amiable. The *eyes* are deeply set. The haw shows only slightly. The eyes are dark, but eye color and eye rim pigment will complement the color of the hound. Dogs with black pigmented noses and eye rims should have darker eyes, while those with liver or slate pigment may have hazel eyes. The *ears,* an essential feature of this breed, are long, pendulous, and folded (the leading edge folds or rolls to give a draped appearance). They are set low, at or below eye level, and hang close to the head, with the leather reaching at least to the tip of the nose. They are well covered with hair. The *skull* (cranium) is long, fairly narrow under the hair, and only slightly domed. The *stop* is not pronounced. The *muzzle* is square, with no hint of snipiness; the jaws are powerful with deep flews. From the side, the planes of the muzzle and skull should be parallel. The *nose* is large, dark, and completely pigmented, with wide nostrils. The *jaws* are powerful and capable of a crushing grip. A *scissors bite* is preferred.

**Neck, Topline, Body**—The *neck* is powerful and blends smoothly into well laid back, clean shoulders, and should be of sufficient length to allow the dog to follow a trail. It has an abundance of hair; a slight dewlap is permissible. The *topline* is level from the withers to the base of tail. The *chest* is deep reaching at least to the elbows on a mature hound. *Forechest* is evident, there is sufficient width to impart strength and endurance. There should be no indication of narrowness or weakness. The well sprung, oval *rib cage* extends well towards the rear of the body. The *loin* is short, broad and strong. The *tail* is set high, and is long reaching at least to the hock. The tail is thicker at the base, tapers to a point, and is feathered (covered and fringed with hair). It is carried saber fashion (not forward over the back) when the dog is moving or alert, but may droop when the dog is at rest.

**Forequarters**—*Shoulders* are clean, powerful, and well sloped with moderate angulation at shoulders and elbows. *Legs* are strongly boned and straight, with strong, slightly sprung *pasterns.* Dewclaws on the forelegs may be removed. *Feet*—Both front and rear feet are large, broad, compact when standing, but capable of spreading. They have thick, deep pads, with arched toes; they are web-footed (membranes connecting the toes allow the foot to spread).

**Hindquarters**—*Thighs* and *second thighs* are large, broad, and well muscled. *Legs* have moderately bent stifles with well-defined hocks. *Hocks* are well let down, turning neither in nor out. Legs on a standing hound are parallel when viewed from the rear. Angulation front and rear must be balanced and adequate to give forward reach and rear drive. Dewclaws, if any, on the hind legs are generally removed. Feet are as previously described.

**Coat**—The coat is an essential feature of the Otterhound. Coat texture and quality are more important than the length. The outer coat is dense, rough, coarse and crisp, of broken appearance. Softer hair on the head and lower legs is natural. The outer coat is two to four inches long on the back and shorter on the extremities. A water-resistant undercoat of short wooly, slightly oily hair is essential, but in the summer months may be hard to find except on the thighs and shoulders. The ears are well covered with hair, and the tail is feathered (covered and fringed with hair). A naturally stripped coat lacking length and fringes is correct for an Otterhound that is being worked. A proper hunting coat will show a hard outer coat and wooly undercoat. The Otterhound is shown in a natural coat, with no sculpturing or shaping of the coat. *Faults*—A soft outer coat is a *very* serious fault, as is a wooly textured outer coat. Lack of undercoat is a serious fault. An outer coat much longer than six inches becomes heavy when wet and is a fault. Any evidence of stripping or scissoring of coat to shape or stylize should be *strongly* penalized as a fault.

**Color**—Any color or combination of colors is acceptable. There should be no discrimination on the basis of color. The nose should be dark and fully pigmented, black, liver, or slate, depending on the color of the hound. Eye rim pigment should match the nose.

**Gait**—The Otterhound moves freely with forward reach and rear drive. The gait is smooth, effortless, and capable of being maintained for many miles. Characteristic of the Otterhound gait is a very loose, shambling walk, which springs immediately into a loose and very long striding, sound, active trot with natural extension of the head. The gallop is smooth and exceptionally long striding. Otterhounds single track at slow speeds. Otterhounds do not lift their feet high off the ground and may shuffle when they walk or move at a slow trot. The Otterhound should be shown on a loose lead.

**Temperament**—The Otterhound is amiable, boisterous and even-tempered.

**Approved October 10, 1995**
**Effective November 30, 1995**

# PETIT BASSET GRIFFON VENDÉEN

HE PETIT BASSET GRIFFON VENDÉEN IS OF ANCIENT ORIGIN, A PROUD member of some twenty-eight hound breeds that even today are bred in France to serve their original purpose. The breed can be traced to the sixteenth century and to the Griffon Vendéen, a larger, more powerful ancestor. The name in French reveals much: *Petit*—"small," *Basset*—"low to the ground," *Griffon*—"rough or wire-coated," and *Vendéen*—referring to the breed's area of origin in France. In the United States, the breed is often referred to as the PBGV or Petit.

This small hunting dog has an intriguing and charming personality. First and foremost, however, the Petit Basset Griffon Vendéen is a hound developed to hunt game by scent. Furthermore, their physical evolution is directly related to the environment and terrain on the western coast of France. That area, the Vendée, is characterized by thick underbrush, rocks, thorns, and brambles. This difficult terrain demanded a hardy, alert, bold, determined, intelligent hunter, with mental and physical stamina as well as a rough coat to serve as protection from the harsh elements of the environment. The desired type of hunting also required an independent personality.

Most French hounds come in large and small versions and are used for different prey. The Griffon Vendéen is the only breed to come in four distinct sizes. Each is used to hunt different game. The Grand Griffon Vendéen, twenty-five inches or more at the withers, was used for large game such as roe deer and wolf, which are hunted from horseback. The Briquet Griffon Vendéen, at approximately twenty inches tall at the withers, is next in size. Then come the two *basset* breeds: the Grand Basset Griffon Vendéen and the smallest, the Petit Basset Griffon Vendéen. The PBGV is used to trail and drive smaller quarry, such as rabbit, hare, and sometimes even feathered game, hunted on foot in France and other European countries, as well as in the United States and Canada.

The attempt to standardize breed type was not undertaken seriously until the latter half of the nineteenth century. Until 1898, when the first official standard for Basset Griffon Français was adopted, judges made their placements without an official standard. In 1907, Paul Dezamy became the first president of the newly founded Club du Griffon Vendéen. Dezamy devised the breed's first standard, and his family would preside over the club for three generations. Dezamy's standard described both the Petit and Grand, which at the time came from the same litters. In 1909, a standard for the Basset Griffon Vendéen recognized two types: one standing thirty-four to thirty-eight centimeters (approximately thirteen to fifteen inches) at the shoulder, and the other thirty-eight to forty-two centimeters (fifteen to seventeen inches). The Petit was distinguished by smaller size and sometimes semicrooked front legs. The Grand always had straight legs.

It was not until the 1950s that the Société de Venerie published a new book of standards. The Petit Basset Griffon Vendéen was given an official standard of its own and thereby was considered a separate breed. But the earlier practice of interbreeding Petits and Grands made it common for offspring from the same litter to be entered, some as Petit and some as Grand, at the French Exhibition. Paul Dezamy II wrote the standard, even though he did not breed Petits. He became famous for his forty-two-centimeter Grands, referred to as "forty-two Dezamys," and was responsible for devising both standards.

Finally, in 1975, through the efforts of Hubert Dezamy, the interbreeding of the Grand and Petit Basset was disallowed. As a result of longtime interbreeding, though, Petits today both manifest Grand and Petit characteristics and are likely to continue to do so for generations to come. For this reason, heavy emphasis is placed on type and size. It is hoped that breeders and judges will learn to recognize the features unique to a Petit so that the desired characteristics will be encouraged.

The ideal PBGVs are busy, active, alert, often vocal, and outgoing dogs that require regular daily exercise to remain at their best. They have a good voice, purposefully and freely used. As pack hounds, they get along well with other dogs and are often happiest in their company. Distinctive characteristics of the breed include a compact, casual, and unrefined appearance, featuring the definitive long eyebrows, beard, and mustache, and a strong, tapered tail carried like the blade of a saber. At heart, this breed remains a working hound whose typical active temperament is often not suitable for those desiring a calm, quiet dog.

The Petit Basset Griffon Vendéen Club of America was founded at the AKC Centennial Show in 1984 to protect and promote the breed in this country. The

PBGV was approved for AKC registration effective December 1, 1990, and became eligible to compete at AKC-licensed shows February 1, 1991.

# OFFICIAL STANDARD FOR
# THE PETIT BASSET GRIFFON VENDÉEN

**General Appearance**—The Petit Basset Griffon Vendéen is a French scent hound developed first and foremost to hunt small game over the rough and difficult terrain of the Vendéen region. To function efficiently, he must be equipped with certain characteristics. He is bold and vivacious in character; compact, tough and robust in construction. He has an alert outlook, lively bearing and a good voice freely and purposefully used.

The most distinguishing characteristics of this bold hunter are: his rough, unrefined outline; his proudly carried head, displaying definitive long eyebrows, beard, and moustache; his strong, tapered tail carried like a saber, alert and in readiness. Important to breed type is the compact, casual, rather tousled appearance, with no feature exaggerated and his parts in balance.

Any deviation from the ideal described in the standard should be penalized to the extent of the deviation. Structural faults common to all breeds are as undesirable in the PBGV as in any other breed, regardless of whether they are specifically mentioned.

**Size, Proportion, Substance**—*Size*—Both sexes should measure between 13 and 15 inches at the withers. Height of adult dogs over 15 inches or under 13 inches at the withers is a disqualification. *Proportion*—When viewed in profile, the body is somewhat longer than tall when measured from point of shoulder to buttocks, as compared to the height from withers to ground. *Substance*—Strong bone with substance in proportion to overall dog.

**Head**—The head is carried proudly and, in size, must be in balance with the overall dog. It is longer than its width in a ratio of approximately two to one. A coarse or overly large head is to be penalized. *Expression* alert, friendly and intelligent. *Eyes* large and dark with good pigmentation, somewhat oval in shape, showing no white. The red of the lower eyelid should not show. The eyes are surmounted by long eyebrows, standing forward, but not obscuring the eyes. *Ears* supple, narrow and fine, covered with long hair, folding inward and ending in an oval shape. The leathers reach almost to the end of the nose. They are set on low, below the line of the eyes. An overly long or high-set ear should be penalized.

**Skull** domed, oval in shape when viewed from the front. It is well cut away under the eyes and has a well developed occipital protuberance. *Stop* clearly defined. *Muzzle*—The length of the muzzle from nose to stop is slightly shorter than the length from the stop to occiput. The underjaw is strong and well developed. *Nose* black and large, with wide nostrils. A somewhat lighter shading is acceptable in lighter colored dogs. A butterfly nose is a fault. *Lips*—The lips are covered by long hair forming a beard and moustache. **Bite**—It is preferable that the teeth meet in a scissors bite, but a level bite is acceptable.

**Neck, Topline, Body**—**Neck**—The neck is long and strong, without throatiness, and flows smoothly into the shoulders. **Topline**—The back is visibly level from withers to croup. There is a barely perceptible rise over a strong loin. Viewed in profile, the withers and the croup should be equidistant from the ground. **Body** muscular, somewhat longer than tall. Compact, casual in appearance, with no feature exaggerated and his parts in balance. *Chest* rather deep, with prominent sternum. *Ribs* moderately rounded, extending well back. *Loin* short, strong, and muscular. There is but little tuck-up. **Tail** of medium length, set on high, it is strong at the base and tapers regularly. It is well furnished with hair, has but a slight curve and is carried proudly like the blade of a saber; normally pointing at about two o'clock. In a curved downward position the tip of the tail bone should reach no further than the hock joint.

**Forequarters**—**Shoulders** clean and well laid back. *Upper arm* approximately equal in length to the shoulder blade. *Elbows* close to the body. **Legs**—The length of leg from elbow to ground should be slightly more than one half the height from withers to ground. Viewed from the front, it is desirable that the forelegs be straight, but a slight crook is acceptable. In either case, the leg appears straight, is strong and well boned, but never coarse nor weedy. Improperly constructed front assemblies, including poor shoulder placement, short upper arms, out at elbows, lack of angulation and fiddle fronts, are all serious faults. *Pasterns* strong and slightly sloping. Any tendency to knuckle over is a serious fault. *Dewclaws* may, or may not, be removed. **Feet** not too long, between hare and cat foot, with hard, tight pads. The nails are strong and short.

**Hindquarters**—Strong and muscular with good bend of stifle. A well-defined second thigh. Hips wide, thighs well muscled. Hocks are short and well angulated, perpendicular from hock to ground. Feet are as in front, except that they must point straight ahead.

**Coat**—The coat is rough, long without exaggeration and harsh to the touch, with a thick shorter undercoat. It is never silky or woolly. The eyes are surmounted by long eyebrows, standing forward but not obscuring the eyes. The ears are covered by long hair. The lips are covered by long hair forming a beard and moustache. The tail is well furnished with hair. The overall appearance is casual and tousled.

The natural, casual and tousled appearance of the breed is vitally important. While some neatening is occasionally necessary, he should be shown naturally. Dogs whose coat has been altered by excessive grooming, sculpting, clipping, or by artificial means shall be so severely penalized as to be effectively eliminated from competition.

**Color**—White with any combination of lemon, orange, black, sable, tricolor or grizzle markings, providing easy visibility in the field.

**Gait**—The movement should be free at all speeds. Front action is straight and reaching well forward. Going away, the hind legs are parallel and have great drive. Convergence of the front and rear legs towards his center of gravity is proportional to the speed of his movement. Gives the appearance of an active hound, capable of a full day's hunting.

**Temperament**—Confident, happy, extroverted, independent yet willing to please, never timid nor aggressive.

## DISQUALIFICATION

*Height, of both sexes at one year of age or older, over 15 inches or under 13 inches at the withers is a disqualification.*

**Approved July 12, 2005**
**Effective August 31, 2005**

# Pharaoh Hound

$\mathscr{T}$HE PHARAOH HOUND, ONE OF THE OLDEST DOMESTICATED DOGS, TRACES his lineage to roughly 3000 B.C. Fortunately, the history of Egyptian civilization was well documented and preserved through paintings and hieroglyphics. From these we learn that this unique dog was treasured for his great hunting ability and his affinity for close family relationships.

King Tutankhamen loved to watch his graceful hound Abuwitiyuw leap with joy at the sight of a gazelle. When the hound died, he commanded the dog to be buried as would be fitting of a nobleman; he was laid in a coffin with fine linen, perfumed ointment, and incense so that he might be honored before the god Anubis. A striking model of a dog was found at the entrance to Tutankhamen's tomb during the excavations.

Reliefs of these hounds hunting can be found in the tomb chapel of Mereruwka and in the tomb chapel of Senbi. Both the Pharaoh Hound Club of England and the Pharaoh Hound Club of America use as their emblem the dog depicted on the tomb of Antefa II, Eleventh Dynasty, about 3000 B.C. The dogs are described in a translation of a letter of the Nineteenth Dynasty: "The red, long-tailed dog goes at night into the stalls of the hills, he is better than the long-faced dog. He makes no delay in hunting, his face glows like a god and he delights to do his work." This "blushing" trait has not been lost through the ages. It is beautiful to see a Pharaoh Hound glow with excitement or happiness—the nose and ears fuming a deep rose color, and the lovely amber eyes further enriched with a deep rose hue.

It seems reasonably certain that the origins of this dog lie in Egypt and they were carried by Phoenician traders to the island of Malta well before the birth of Christ. The breeders of Malta maintained a purity of breed type over a period of 2,000 years, for the dog today still closely resembles his Egyptian fore-bears.

In Malta, the Pharaoh Hound was bred to hunt rabbit and only the best hunters were used in selective breeding programs. The high esteem in which these dogs have been held was evidenced in 1979, when a silver coin bearing the likeness of a standing Pharaoh Hound was minted to commemorate the occasion of the dog being declared the national dog of Malta.

Pharaoh Hounds were apparently first imported into England in the early 1930s, but records are inconclusive. In 1963, Pauline Block, who had become an admirer of the breed while living in Malta, returned home to England with Bahri of Twinley. This Pharaoh Hound was the first to be shown in England at the Hound Show at Alexandria Palace in London.

In 1967 Mrs. Ruth Taft Harper brought the first Pharaoh Hound to the United States. It was a bitch secured with the help of Mrs. Block and her husband, General Adam Block. The first litter of Pharaoh Hounds was whelped in the United States in 1970. Another of the earliest champions of the breed in America was Rita Laventhall Sacks, who imported Pharaohs from England and Malta to enrich the gene pool.

The American Kennel Club admitted Pharaoh Hounds into the Miscellaneous class in January 1979. Then, effective August 1, 1983, the breed was recognized for registration in the AKC Stud Book, and on January 1, 1984, became eligible to compete in the Hound Group.

The Pharaoh Hound gives a striking impression of elegance, power, and grace. He is intelligent, friendly, and affectionate. His great speed combined with his alertness and agility give him a marked keenness for hunting both by sight and by scent.

An outstanding feature of the breed is their haunting, beautiful amber eyes. Their nose, eye rims, and lips are flesh-colored, blending with the coat. Many Pharaoh Hounds display a marvelous trait of smiling, showing their pearly white scissors bite. They are particularly fond of children and never lose their fondness for romping and playing, as they crave human attention. Their short, glossy coats tend to make them most enjoyable as house dogs, and another desirable feature is that they have no doggy odor, even when wet. Their willingness to please allows them to be trained swiftly, which makes them excellent candidates for hunting, obedience, and coursing.

# OFFICIAL STANDARD FOR THE PHARAOH HOUND

**General Appearance**—General Appearance is one of grace, power and speed. The Pharaoh Hound is medium sized, of noble bearing with hard clean-cut lines— graceful, well balanced, very fast with free easy movement and alert expression.

The following description is that of the ideal Pharaoh Hound. Any deviation from the below described dog must be penalized to the extent of the deviation.

**Size, Proportion, Substance**—*Height*—Dogs 23 inches–25 inches. Bitches 21 inches–24 inches. All-over balance must be maintained. Length of body from breast to haunch bone slightly longer than height of withers to ground. Lithe.

**Head**—Alert *expression. Eyes* amber colored, blending with coat; oval, moderately deep set with keen intelligent expression. *Ears* medium high set, carried erect when alert, but very mobile, broad at the base, fine and large. *Skull* long, lean and chiseled. Only slight stop. Foreface slightly longer than the skull. Top of the skull parallel with the foreface representing a blunt wedge. *Nose* flesh colored, blending with the coat. No other color. Powerful jaws with strong teeth. Scissors *bite.*

**Neck, Topline, Body**—*Neck* long, lean and muscular with a slight arch to carry the head on high. Clean throat line. Almost straight *topline.* Slight slope from croup to root of tail. *Body* lithe. Deep brisket almost down to point of elbow. Ribs well sprung. Moderate tuck-up. *Tail* medium set—fairly thick at the base and taper-ing whip-like, reaching below the point of hock in repose. Well carried and curved when in action. The tail should not be tucked between the legs. A screw tail is a fault.

**Forequarters**—*Shoulders* long and sloping and well laid back. Strong without being loaded. *Elbows* well tucked in. *Forelegs* straight and parallel. Pasterns strong. Dew-claws may be removed. *Feet* neither cat nor hare but strong, well knuckled and firm, turning neither in nor out. Paws well padded.

**Hindquarters**—Strong and muscular. Limbs parallel. Moderate sweep of stifle. Well developed second thigh. Dewclaws may be removed. *Feet* as in front.

**Coat**—Short and glossy, ranging from fine and close to slightly harsh with no feathering. Accident blemishes should not be considered as faults.

**Color**—Ranging from tan/rich, tan/chestnut with white markings allowed as fol-lows: White tip on tail strongly desired. White on chest (called "the Star"). White on toes and slim white snip on centerline of face permissible. Flecking or other white un-desirable, except for any solid white spot on the back of neck, shoulder, or any part of the back or sides of the dog, which is a *disqualification.*

**Gait**—Free and flowing; the head should be held fairly high and the dog should cover the ground well without any apparent effort. The legs and feet should move in line with the body; any tendency to throw the feet sideways, or a high stepping "hack-ney" action is a definite fault.

**Temperament**—Intelligent, friendly, affectionate and playful. Alert and active. Very fast with a marked keenness for hunting, both by sight and scent.

## DISQUALIFICATION

*Any solid white spot on the back of neck, shoulder, or any part of the back or sides of the dog.*

**Approved May 10, 1983**
**Reformatted April 3, 1989**

# RHODESIAN RIDGEBACK

$\mathcal{T}$HE FIRST PICTURES OF AFRICAN DOGS WERE MADE ALL OVER SOUTHERN Africa thousands of years ago in the caves of the San (Bushmen), the region's oldest existing people. The Bushmen obtained their dogs from the nomadic, pastoralist Khoi people (known by the Dutch as the Hottentot) and from Bantu-speaking agriculturalists. The Khoi originated in the north and migrated southward with dogs, which they also obtained from Bantu-speaking people.

Many of the Khoi and Bushmen dogs were jackal-like in appearance, approximately forty pounds, reddish brown or tan in color, with a distinguishing ridge that ran along their backs. These dogs hunted, herded, and protected the Khoi's cattle, goats, and sheep from wild predators, such as jackal, hyena, leopard, and lion. They were particularly faithful when their masters were threatened by such predators and were therefore highly valued and sought after.

In 1652 Jan van Riebeck, a Dutch merchant, landed in South Africa. As early as 1685 European settlers were bartering their cattle for Khoi dogs to which they bred Mastiffs, Great Danes, Bloodhounds, Pointers, Staghounds, Irish Wolfhounds, and Greyhounds, among others. These Dutch, German, and French settlers intermarried and became Boers, with their own Afrikaans language. The Boers (Afrikaans for *farmers*) needed a dog that was resistant to local diseases; able to thrive in spite of extreme temperatures, limited water, rough bush, and relentless ticks; and an extraordinarily brave and cunning hunter, all while being a loyal family dog.

Mating European breeds to native ridged Khoi hunting stock, the Boers produced unique dogs that hunted by both sight and scent and were devoted family guardians.

Through such interbreeding came the next generation of the Ridgeback ancestry, including the Steekbaard ("prickly beard") and Vuilbaard ("dirty beard" or "wooly beard") Afrikaans farm dogs. These evolved into the Boerhounds ("farmer's dog"), which became distinct and were found, with their noticeable ridge, on almost every farm.

To escape British rule of the Cape Colony, many Boers moved north in the 1830s and took their dogs with them. In 1873, the Reverend Charles Helm began his trek north and passed through the Naauwpoort area, which had a concentrated source of ridged dogs belonging to a displaced population of Khoi and Bushmen. Helms acquired two Greyhound-type bitches of these ridged dogs in 1875 and continued his trek.

It was in Rhodesia where renowned big-game hunter Cornelius Van Rooyen, a farmer at Plumtree in Southern Rhodesia, used the Helms dogs and selectively bred them with his own to produce a hunter with courage, intelligence, and the natural tendency to hold lion at bay. His pack included Greyhounds, Irish Terriers, English Pointers, Bulldogs, Rough Collies, Great Danes, and mixes thereof. The ridged dogs became known as Van Rooyen's Lion Dogs. They used their unique ability for tracking and then holding lions at bay, relying on a protective instinct activated when threatened by lion and leopard. This trait was unique among dogs and contributed greatly to the success of these fearless hunters, whose distinctive ridge became a trademark passed on from their very beginnings.

By the 1920s, there were so many different variations of the Lion Dogs that a meeting was held under the leadership of Francis Richard Barnes to elucidate the most desirable points of the breed. These points became the basis for the current standard, adopted in 1922 and virtually unchanged to this day. Dogs meeting the standard criteria came to be known as Rhodesian Ridgebacks. Today, the Rhodesian Ridgeback is the national dog of South Africa and is depicted on the emblem of the Kennel Club of the Union of Southern Africa.

The breed was introduced into England in the 1930s and America soon after. In both countries, it gained recognition in the 1950s and quickly attracted admirers. The AKC conferred official recognition upon the breed in 1955. On March 9, 1971, the AKC formally admitted the Rhodesian Ridgeback Club of the United States. In 1992, the breed received recognition as a sighthound eligible to compete in AKC coursing trials.

The Rhodesian Ridgeback is not only a keen and versatile hunter but also a loyal guardian. It is good with children, especially protective of those in its family, but might be too rambunctious in play for small children. The Ridgeback is strong willed and powerful; some can become domineering. Reserved with strangers, the Ridgeback can, if not properly socialized, be aggressive toward strange dogs and animals.

The Ridgeback is athletic. It loves to run and needs daily mental and physical exercise to keep from becoming bored. Ridgebacks have strong prey drive—which means, basically, if they see it, they go for it! When off leash, Ridgebacks should be in a fenced-in area.

Moderate exercise programs can be started after the age of twelve months, if the dog is in good physical condition and not exercised in excessive heat. Harder exercise should wait until the age of eighteen months, to allow proper bone and joint development. The Ridgeback is a family member and house dog, and prefers sleeping indoors and dividing time between the house and yard during the day. Grooming is minimal, consisting only of occasional bathing and brushing the coat to remove dead hair, and regular nail trimming, which should begin in puppyhood.

(The writings of Sian Hall, including her book *Dogs of Africa,* have been a helpful source in this history of the Rhodesian Ridgeback.)

# OFFICIAL STANDARD FOR THE RHODESIAN RIDGEBACK

**General Appearance**—The Ridgeback represents a strong, muscular and active dog, symmetrical and balanced in outline. A mature Ridgeback is a handsome, upstanding and athletic dog, capable of great endurance with a fair (good) amount of speed. Of even, dignified temperament, the Ridgeback is devoted and affectionate to his master, reserved with strangers. The peculiarity of this breed is the *ridge* on the back. The ridge must be regarded as the characteristic feature of the breed.

**Size, Proportion, Substance**—A mature Ridgeback should be symmetrical in outline, slightly longer than tall but well balanced. Dogs—25 to 27 inches in height; Bitches—24 to 26 inches in height. Desirable weight: Dogs—85 pounds; Bitches—70 pounds.

**Head**—Should be of fair length, the skull flat and rather broad between the ears and should be free from wrinkles when in repose. The stop should be reasonably well defined. *Eyes*—Should be moderately well apart and should be round, bright and sparkling with intelligent expression, their color harmonizing with the color of the dog. *Ears*—Should be set rather high, of medium size, rather wide at the base and tapering to a rounded point. They should be carried close to the head. *Muzzle*—Should be long, deep and powerful. The lips clean, closely fitting the jaws. *Nose*—Should be black, brown or liver, in keeping with the color of the dog. No other colored nose is permissible. A black nose should be accompanied by dark eyes, a brown or liver nose with amber eyes. *Bite*—Jaws level and strong with well-developed teeth, especially the canines or holders. Scissors bite preferred.

**Neck, Topline, Body**—The neck should be fairly strong and free from throatiness. The chest should not be too wide, but very deep and capacious, ribs moderately well sprung, never rounded like barrel hoops (which would indicate want of speed). The back is powerful and firm with strong loins which are muscular and slightly arched. The tail should be strong at the insertion and generally tapering towards the end, free from coarseness. It should not be inserted too high or too low and should be carried with a slight curve upwards, never curled or gay.

**Forequarters**—The shoulders should be sloping, clean and muscular, denoting speed. Elbows close to the body. The forelegs should be perfectly straight, strong and heavy in bone. The feet should be compact with well-arched toes, round, tough, elastic pads, protected by hair between the toes and pads. Dewclaws may be removed.

**Hindquarters**—In the hind legs the muscles should be clean, well defined and hocks well down. Feet as in front.

**Coat**—Should be short and dense, sleek and glossy in appearance but neither woolly nor silky.

**Color**—Light wheaten to red wheaten. A little white on the chest and toes permissible but excessive white there, on the belly or above the toes is undesirable.

**Ridge**—The hallmark of this breed is the *ridge* on the back which is formed by the hair growing in the opposite direction to the rest of the coat. The ridge must be regarded as the characteristic feature of the breed. The ridge should be clearly defined, tapering and symmetrical. It should start immediately behind the shoulders and continue to a point between the prominence of the hips and should contain two identical crowns (whorls) directly opposite each other. The lower edge of the crowns (whorls) should not extend further down the ridge than one third of the ridge.

Disqualification: Ridgelessness. Serious Fault: One crown (whorl) or more than two crowns (whorls).

**Gait**—At the trot, the back is held level and the stride is efficient, long, free and unrestricted. Reach and drive expressing a perfect balance between power and elegance. At the chase, the Ridgeback demonstrates great coursing ability and endurance.

**Temperament**—Dignified and even tempered. Reserved with strangers.

## SCALE OF POINTS

| | |
|---|---|
| General appearance, size, symmetry and balance | 20 |
| Ridge | 20 |
| Head | 15 |
| Legs and feet | 15 |
| Neck and shoulders | 10 |
| Body, back, chest and loin | 10 |
| Coat and color | 5 |
| Tail | 5 |
| **Total** | **100** |

## DISQUALIFICATION

*Ridgelessness*

**Approved August 11, 1992**
**Effective September 30, 1992**

# SALUKI

*Feathered*

*Smooth*

HE SALUKI IS PERHAPS THE OLDEST KNOWN DOMESTICATED DOG BREED, SAID to be as old as the earliest known civilization. Historians identified the Saluki as a distinct breed and type as long ago as 329 B.C., when Alexander the Great invaded India. This claim is based on hounds depicted in the earliest carvings, which look more like Salukis than any other breed. They have Greyhound-type bodies with long-leathered ears; some are smooth coated and some with feathering, just as we have today. Similar hound images appear on the Egyptian tombs of 2100 B.C. More recent excavations of the still-older Sumerian empire, estimated at 7000 to 6000 B.C., have unearthed carvings with striking resemblance to the Saluki.

The Saluki was declared sacred and called the "noble one" given by Allah for people's amusement and benefit, despite the Islamic teaching that dogs are unclean and unfit to touch anything that Moslems touch. This permitted Moslems to eat the meat brought down in the chase.

Salukis were the only dog of the time allowed to sleep on the carpets in the sheikh's tent. In Egypt, these dogs were held in such great esteem that their bodies were often mummified along with the pharaohs themselves. The remains of numerous specimens have been found in the ancient tombs of the Upper Nile region. It is claimed that whenever one sees the word *dog* in the Bible, it means Saluki.

Desert tribes were nomadic. Therefore, the Saluki's habitat was the region stretching from the Caspian Sea to the Sahara, including Egypt, Arabia, Palestine, Syria, Mesopotamia, Anatolia, and Persia. Naturally, the types in this vast area varied somewhat, mostly in size and coat. The Arabian-bred Saluki was smaller than the Persian-bred, with less furnishings in the feathered variety.

Salukis were brought into England in 1840. The first imports included a bitch owned by Sir Hamilton Smith, a dog placed in the Regents Park Zoological Gardens, and a dog owned by the Duke of Devonshire at Chatsworth. They were known as Persian Greyhounds, since these three came from Persia. In the twentieth century, England learned more about Salukis from army officers stationed in the Middle East during World War I. Other specimens, either prizes of war or the gifts of friendly tribes, were brought home at that time.

It was not until 1895 that real interest in the breed developed in the West. The Honorable Florence Amherst imported the first Arabians from the kennels of Prince Abdulla in Transjordania. It is recorded that the pharaohs rode to the chase with hawks on their wrists and Salukis on lead. Because of their tremendous speed, Salukis were used by the Arabs to bring down gazelle, the fastest of antelopes. We also believe Salukis were used on jackals, foxes, and hare. A cut published in 1852 even shows a wild boar hunt in Algeria with Salukis tackling the boar! Today in England, the breed is used largely on hare. Regular coursing meets are held, with judging based on the dog's ability to turn quickly and overtake the hare in the best possible time. Salukis hunt largely by sight, although they have a fair nose.

The sport of racing Salukis, with a mechanical rabbit and hurdles at intervals, is enjoyed in England and on the Continent. In the United States, Salukis exercise their love of the chase in lure coursing, in which an artificial lure is pulled through a simulated live game course, with hounds in pursuit. In some areas, live game coursing is permitted.

The Saluki's sight is remarkable. Related hereditary traits are often seen in Salukis lying on the sand watching an eagle soaring for prey but paying no attention to a nearby gull. Soon after his arrival in America, one famous dog, Sarona Dhole, chased a fox and registered a kill within a few seconds after sighting the quarry.

In their native wasteland, Salukis get no pampering. They live hard, and it's survival of the fittest. This is one reason for the breed's strong constitution and sturdy frame, which enables it to tolerate extreme temperatures and withstand any climate. Their feet are hard and firm, and the hair between the toes is great protection. In running and dodging over the roughest terrain and rocky country, they rarely damage their pads or toes.

The Saluki's beauty is like that of the Arabian horse, with grace and symmetry of form, and clean-cut pleasing lines, proportion, and movement. Completing the image is characteristic short, silky hair, except on ears, legs, and tail in the feathered variety. A slender, well-muscled neck, shoulder, and thigh, with arched loins, a long tail carried naturally in a curve with silky hair hanging from the underside, arched toes, and the rather long head with deep, farseeing eyes and an expression of dignity mixed with gentleness all are physical properties of this ancient breed.

Salukis come in a wide variety of colors, including white, cream, fawn, gold, red, grizzle and tan, black and tan, and tri-color (white, black, and tan). They show great attachment to their owners and are affectionate without being demonstrative. Salukis are good watchdogs, but are not aggressive. The Saluki was a well-established breed in England for many years before coming into their own in this country. It was not until November 1927 that the Saluki was officially recognized by the American Kennel Club. In 2002 the breed came full circle, with certified descendants of Salukis imported from countries of origin again becoming eligible for AKC registration.

# OFFICIAL STANDARD FOR THE SALUKI

**Head**—Long and narrow, skull moderately wide between the ears, not domed, stop not pronounced, the whole showing great quality. Nose black or liver. *Ears*—Long and covered with long silky hair hanging close to the skull and mobile. *Eyes*—Dark to hazel and bright; large and oval, but not prominent. *Teeth*—Strong and level.

**Neck**—Long, supple and well muscled.

**Chest**—Deep and moderately narrow.

**Forequarters**—Shoulders sloping and set well back, well muscled without being coarse. *Forelegs*—Straight and long from the elbow to the knee.

**Hindquarters**—Strong, hipbones set well apart and stifle moderately bent, hocks low to the ground, showing galloping and jumping power.

**Loin and Back**—Back fairly broad, muscles slightly arched over loin.

**Feet**—Of moderate length, toes long and well arched, not splayed out, but at the same time not cat-footed; the whole being strong and supple and well feathered between the toes.

**Tail**—Long, set on low and carried naturally in a curve, well feathered on the underside with long silky hair, not bushy.

**Coat**—Smooth and of a soft silky texture, slight feather on the legs, feather at the back of the thighs and sometimes with slight woolly feather on the thigh and shoulder.

**Colors**—White, cream, fawn, golden, red, grizzle and tan, tricolor (white, black and tan) and black and tan.

**General Appearance**—The whole appearance of this breed should give an impression of grace and symmetry and of great speed and endurance coupled with strength and activity to enable it to kill gazelle or other quarry over deep sand or rocky mountains. The expression should be dignified and gentle with deep, faithful, far-seeing eyes. Dogs should average in height from 23 to 28 inches and bitches may be considerably smaller, this being very typical of the breed.

**The Smooth Variety**—In this variety the points should be the same with the exception of the coat, which has no feathering.

# Scottish Deerhound

$\mathcal{T}$HE ORIGIN OF THE BREED IS OF SUCH ANTIQUITY, AND THE EARLIEST descriptive names bestowed on it so inextricably mixed, that no sound conclusion can be arrived at as to whether the Deerhound was at one time identical with the ancient Irish Wolfdog and, in the course of centuries, bred to a type better suited to hunt deer, or whether, as some writers claim, he is the descendant of the hounds of the Picts. Very early descriptive names were used to identify the purpose of the dog rather than to identify species. We find such names as Irish Wolf Dog, Scotch Greyhound, Rough Greyhound, Highland Deerhound. John Caius, in *Of Englishe Dogges* (1576), describing Greyhounds, wrote, "Some are of a greater sorte, some of a lesser; some are smoothe skynned and some curled, the bigger therefore are appointed to hunt the bigger beastes, the duck, the hart, the doe."

All this is relatively unimportant when we can definitely identify the breed as Deerhounds as early as the sixteenth and seventeenth centuries. From there on the word *deerhound* has been applied to the breed, which of all dogs has been found best suited for the pursuit and killing of the deer.

At all times great value has been set on the Deerhound. The history of the breed teems with romance increasing in splendor right down through the Age of Chivalry, when no one of rank lower than an earl might possess these dogs. A leash of Deerhounds was held the fine whereby a noble lord condemned to death might purchase his reprieve. Medieval documents allude repeatedly to the delightful attributes of this charming hound, his tremendous courage in the chase, his gentle dignity in the home.

So highly has the Deerhound been esteemed that the desire for exclusive ownership has at many times endangered the continuance of the breed. As the larger beasts of the chase became extinct or rare in England and southern Scotland, the more delicate, smooth Greyhound took the place of the larger Deerhound. The Highlands of Scotland, the last territory wherein the stag remained numerous in a wild state, became the last stronghold of this breed. Here again the Highland chieftains assumed exclusive proprietorship to such an extent that it was rare to find a good specimen south of the River Forth. So severely was this policy pursued that in 1769 the breed physically and numerically ran very low. This, of course, must be attributed in great measure to the collapse of the clan system after the failed Jacobite rebellion at Culloden Moor in 1745. It was not until about 1825, when the restoration of the breed was undertaken very successfully by Archibald and Duncan McNeill (the latter afterward Lord Colonsay), that the Deerhound regained his place of preeminence and former perfection. World War I had considerable effect on the breed, as many of the large estates in Scotland and England were broken up. Although this "Royal Dog of Scotland" is represented at English shows in good numbers and to an extent at shows in this country, the Deerhound remains a rare dog of such historical interest and character that ownership should give anyone great pride of possession.

The high valuation of the Deerhound is not the result of rarity so much as the fact that as a hunter he is preeminent, with a high aggregate of desirable characteristics. He has a keen scent, which may be used in tracking, but it is that combination of strength and speed necessary to cope with the large Scottish deer (often weighing 250 pounds) that is most valued. The hounds are usually hunted singly or in pairs. Centuries of hunting as the companions and guards of Highland chieftains have given the Deerhound an insatiable desire for human companionship. For this reason the best Deerhounds are seldom raised as kennel dogs. In character the Deerhound is quiet and dignified, keen and alert, and although not aggressive, has great persistence and indomitable courage when necessary. While it might be an exaggeration to claim that the Deerhound of today is identical with the dog of early history, descriptions of which are mostly legendary, it is nevertheless a well-established fact that in type, size, and character he closely conforms to authentic records of the eighteenth and nineteenth centuries.

The hunting of antlered game with dogs is not permitted in the United States, but the Deerhound has been used very successfully on wolves, coyotes, and rabbits, and is keen to match his speed with anything that runs. As a companion the Deerhound is ideal, being tractable and easy to train and possessing the most dependable loyalty and utmost devotion to his master. The best descriptions of the breed are found in nineteenth-century British dog books.

The grace, dignity, and beauty of the Deerhound have been faithfully depicted in many of Landseer's paintings and drawings, and Sir Walter Scott, who owned the famous Deerhound Maida, wrote many enthusiastic allusions to the breed, which he described as "the most perfect creature of Heaven."

# OFFICIAL STANDARD FOR THE SCOTTISH DEERHOUND

**Head**—Should be broadest at the ears, narrowing slightly to the eyes, with the muzzle tapering more decidedly to the nose. The muzzle should be pointed, but the teeth and lips level. The head should be long, the skull flat rather than round with a very slight rise over the eyes but nothing approaching a stop. The hair on the skull should be moderately long and softer than the rest of the coat. The nose should be black (in some blue fawns—blue) and slightly aquiline. In lighter colored dogs the black muzzle is preferable. There should be a good mustache of rather silky hair and a fair beard.

**Ears**—Should be set on high; in repose, folded back like a Greyhound's, though raised above the head in excitement without losing the fold, and even in some cases semierect. A prick ear is bad. Big thick ears hanging flat to the head or heavily coated with long hair are bad faults. The ears should be soft, glossy, like a mouse's coat to the touch and the smaller the better. There should be no long coat or long fringe, but there is sometimes a silky, silvery coat on the body of the ear and the tip. On all Deerhounds, irrespective of color of coat, the ears should be black or dark colored.

**Neck and Shoulders**—The neck should be long—of a length befitting the Greyhound character of the dog. Extreme length is neither necessary nor desirable. Deerhounds do not stoop to their work like the Greyhounds. The mane, which every good specimen should have, sometimes detracts from the apparent length of the neck. The neck, however, must be strong as is necessary to hold a stag. The nape of the neck should be very prominent where the head is set on, and the throat clean cut at the angle and prominent. Shoulders should be well sloped; blades well back and not too much width between them. Loaded and straight shoulders are very bad faults.

**Tail**—Should be tolerably long, tapering and reaching to within 1½ inches of the ground and about 1½ inches below the hocks. Dropped perfectly down or curved when the Deerhound is still, when in motion or excited, curved, but in no instance lifted out of line of the back. It should be well covered with hair, on the inside, thick and wiry, underside longer and towards the end a slight fringe is not objectionable. A curl or ring tail is undesirable.

**Eyes**—Should be dark—generally dark brown, brown or hazel. A very light eye is not liked. The eye should be moderately full, with a soft look in repose, but a keen, far away look when the Deerhound is roused. Rims of eyelids should be black.

**Body**—General formation is that of a Greyhound of larger size and bone. Chest deep rather than broad but not too narrow or slab-sided. Good girth of chest is indicative of great lung power. The loin well arched and drooping to the tail. A straight back is not desirable, this formation being unsuited for uphill work, and very unsightly.

**Legs and Feet**—Legs should be broad and flat, and good broad forearms and elbows are desirable. Forelegs must, of course, be as straight as possible. Feet close and compact, with well-arranged toes. The hindquarters drooping, and as broad and powerful as possible, the hips being set wide apart. A narrow rear denotes lack of power. The stifles should be well bent, with great length from hip to hock, which should be broad and flat. Cowhocks, weak pasterns, straight stifles and splay feet are very bad faults.

**Coat**—The hair on the body, neck and quarters should be harsh and wiry about 3 or 4 inches long; that on the head, breast and belly much softer. There should be a slight fringe on the inside of the forelegs and hind legs but nothing approaching the "feather" of a Collie. A woolly coat is bad. Some good strains have a mixture of silky coat with the hard which is preferable to a woolly coat. The climate of the United States tends to produce the mixed coat. The ideal coat is a thick, close-lying ragged coat, harsh or crisp to the touch.

**Color**—Is a matter of fancy, but the dark blue-gray is most preferred. Next come the darker and lighter grays or brindles, the darkest being generally preferred. Yellow and sandy red or red fawn, especially with black ears and muzzles, are equally high in estimation. This was the color of the oldest known strains—the McNeil and Chesthill Menzies. White is condemned by all authorities, but a white chest and white toes, occurring as they do in many of the darkest-colored dogs, are not objected to, although the less the better, for the Deerhound is a self-colored dog. A white blaze on the head, or a white collar, should entirely disqualify. The less white the better but a slight white tip to the stern occurs in some of the best strains.

**Height**—*Height of Dogs*—From 30 to 32 inches, or even more if there by symmetry without coarseness, which is rare. *Height of Bitches*—From 28 inches upwards. There is no objection to a bitch being large, unless too coarse, as even at her greatest height she does not approach that of the dog, and therefore could not be too big for work as overbig dogs are.

**Weight**—From 85 to 110 pounds in dogs, and from 75 to 95 pounds in bitches.

## POINTS OF THE DEERHOUND, ARRANGED IN ORDER OF IMPORTANCE

1. *Typical*—A Deerhound should resemble a rough-coated Greyhound of larger size and bone.
2. *Movements*—Easy, active and true.
3. As tall as possible consistent with quality.
4. *Head*—Long, level, well balanced, carried high.
5. *Body*—Long, very deep in brisket, well-sprung ribs and great breadth across hips.
6. *Forelegs*—Strong and quite straight, with elbows neither in nor out.
7. *Thighs*—Long and muscular, second thighs well muscled, stifles well bent.
8. *Loins*—Well arched, and belly well drawn up.
9. *Coat*—Rough and hard, with softer beard and brows.
10. *Feet*—Close, compact, with well-knuckled toes.
11. *Ears*—Small (dark) with Greyhoundlike carriage.

12. *Eyes*—Dark, moderately full.
13. *Neck*—Long, well arched, very strong with prominent nape.
14. *Shoulders*—Clean, set sloping.
15. *Chest*—Very deep but not too narrow.
16. *Tail*—Long and curved slightly, carried low.
17. *Teeth*—Strong and level.
18. *Nails*—Strong and curved.

## DISQUALIFICATION

*White blaze on the head, or a white collar.*

**Approved March 1935**

# WHIPPET

$\mathcal{T}$HE WHIPPET, A MEDIUM-SIZED MEMBER OF THE SIGHTHOUND FAMILY, IS Greyhound-like in appearance. Although their origin is uncertain, small Greyhound-type dogs have been depicted in art throughout the ages; the breed evolved with the English working class as a utility dog, to provide companionship, rabbits for the table, and racing sport in leisure time. Whippets came to America with British immigrants and were recognized by the AKC in 1888, ironically three years before Kennel Club (England) recognition.

Whippets, born athletes, excel at coursing and racing, but unlike Greyhound racing, Whippet racing is purely sport, not involving gambling or prize money. Whippets, one of the most popular show dogs competing in the Hound Group, are a versatile breed and can compete in agility, obedience, flyball, and Frisbee, and, with their gentle demeanor, they excel at therapy work.

Ranging in size from eighteen to twenty-two inches at the shoulder and twenty-eight to thirty-eight pounds in weight, Whippets are capable of attaining speeds of thirty-five miles per hour and are genetically programmed to run, jump, and chase. They are energetic puppies that can be destructive when bored. A properly socialized and trained puppy will mature into a well-behaved, confident competitor and companion.

Intelligent, sensitive, and affectionate, Whippets are uniquely individual in temperament. They make excellent indoor companions, but with their lean build and short, close coat they do not tolerate long exposure to extreme cold. Whippets require vigorous, safe exercise almost daily and, because they are visually oriented, if they see something interesting to chase, they will run, oblivious to danger and the calls of their owners. It is ideal to provide access and exercise in a fenced yard or take your Whippet on lead to a secure park or field.

The Whippet, extraordinarily keen when racing or on game, thrives on human contact and companionship. When treated as a member of the family, the Whippet is quiet, dignified, unobtrusive, and, above all, highly decorative on your living room furniture. Contrary to external appearances, he is by no means delicate or difficult to care for. All in all, he makes an ideal dual-purpose medium-sized dog for an owner of discrimination.

# OFFICIAL STANDARD FOR THE WHIPPET

**General Appearance**—A medium size sighthound giving the appearance of elegance and fitness, denoting great speed, power and balance without coarseness. A true sporting hound that covers a maximum of distance with a minimum of lost motion. Should convey an impression of beautifully balanced muscular power and strength, combined with great elegance and grace of outline. Symmetry of outline, muscular development and powerful gait are the main considerations; the dog being built for speed and work, all forms of exaggeration should be avoided.

**Size, Proportion, Substance**—Ideal height for dogs, 19 to 22 inches; for bitches, 18 to 21 inches, measured at the highest point of the withers. More than one-half inch above or below the stated limits will disqualify. Length from forechest to buttocks equal to or slightly greater than height at the withers. Moderate bone throughout.

**Head**—Keen, intelligent, alert expression. *Eyes* large and dark. Both eyes must be of the same color. Yellow or light eyes should be strictly penalized. Blue or wall eyes shall disqualify. Fully pigmented eyelids are desirable.

Rose *ears,* small, fine in texture; in repose, thrown back and folded along neck. Fold should be maintained when at attention. Erect ears should be severely penalized.

*Skull* long and lean, fairly wide between the ears, scarcely perceptible stop.

*Muzzle* should be long and powerful, denoting great strength of bite, without coarseness. Lack of underjaw should be strictly penalized. Nose entirely black.

*Teeth* of upper jaw should fit closely over teeth of lower jaw creating a scissors bite. Teeth should be white and strong. Undershot shall disqualify. Overshot one-quarter inch or more shall disqualify.

**Neck, Topline, Body**—*Neck* long, clean and muscular, well arched with no suggestion of throatiness, widening gracefully into the top of the shoulder. A short thick neck, or a ewe neck, should be penalized. The *back* is broad, firm and well muscled, having length over the loin. The backline runs smoothly from the withers with a graceful natural arch, not too accentuated, beginning over the loin and carrying through over the croup; the arch is continuous without flatness. A dip behind shoulder blades, wheel-back, flat back, or a steep or flat croup should be penalized. *Brisket* very deep, reaching as nearly as possible to the point of the elbow. *Ribs* well sprung but with no suggestion of barrel shape. The space between the forelegs is filled in so that there is no appearance of a hollow between them. There is a definite tuck-up of the underline. The *tail* long and tapering, reaching to the hipbone when drawn through between the hind legs. When the dog is in motion, the tail is carried low with only a gentle upward curve; tail should not be carried higher than top of back.

**Forequarters**—*Shoulder blade* long, well laid back, with flat muscles, allowing for moderate space between shoulder blades at peak of withers. Upper arm of equal length, placed so that the elbow falls directly under the withers.

The points of the elbows should point neither in nor out, but straight back. A steep shoulder, short upper arm, a heavily muscled or loaded shoulder, or a very narrow shoulder, all of which restrict low free movement, should be strictly penalized. *Forelegs* straight, giving appearance of strength and substance of bone. Pasterns strong, slightly bent and flexible. Bowed legs, tied-in elbows, legs lacking substance, legs set far under the body so as to create an exaggerated forechest, weak or upright pasterns should be strictly penalized.

Both front and rear feet must be well formed with hard, thick pads. Feet more hare than cat, but both are acceptable. Flat, splayed or soft feet without thick hard pads should be strictly penalized. Toes should be long, close and well arched. Nails strong. Dewclaws may be removed.

**Hindquarters**—Long and powerful. The thighs are broad and muscular, stifles well bent; muscles are long and flat and carry well down toward the hock. The hocks are well let down and close to the ground. Sickle or cow hocks should be strictly penalized.

**Coat**—Short, close, smooth and firm in texture. Any other coat shall be a disqualification. Old scars and injuries, the result of work or accident, should not be allowed to prejudice the dog's chance in the show ring.

**Color**—Color immaterial.

**Gait**—Low, free moving and smooth, with reach in the forequarters and strong drive in the hindquarters. The dog has great freedom of action when viewed from the side; the forelegs move forward close to the ground to give a long, low reach; the hind legs have strong propelling power. When moving and viewed from front or rear, legs should turn neither in nor out, nor should feet cross or interfere with each other. Lack of front reach or rear drive, or a short, hackney gait with high wrist action, should be strictly penalized. Crossing in front or moving too close should be strictly penalized.

**Temperament**—Amiable, friendly, gentle, but capable of great intensity during sporting pursuits.

## DISQUALIFICATIONS

*More than one-half inch above or below stated height limits.*
*Blue or wall eyes.*

*Undershot, overshot one-quarter inch or more.*
*Any coat other than short, close, smooth and firm in texture.*

**Approved August 10, 1993**
**Effective September 29, 1993**

# GROUP III: WORKING BREEDS

AKITA

ALASKAN MALAMUTE

ANATOLIAN SHEPHERD DOG

BERNESE MOUNTAIN DOG

BLACK RUSSIAN TERRIER

BOXER

BULLMASTIFF

DOBERMAN PINSCHER

GERMAN PINSCHER

GIANT SCHNAUZER

GREAT DANE

GREAT PYRENEES

GREATER SWISS MOUNTAIN DOG

KOMONDOR

KUVASZ

MASTIFF

NEAPOLITAN MASTIFF

NEWFOUNDLAND

PORTUGUESE WATER DOG

ROTTWEILER

SAINT BERNARD

SAMOYED

SIBERIAN HUSKY

STANDARD SCHNAUZER

# AKITA

*T*HE AKITA IS ONE OF SEVEN BREEDS DESIGNATED AS A NATIONAL MONUMENT in his native Japan. Bred as a versatile hunting dog in the rugged mountains of northern Japan, the breed is a wonderful combination of dignity with good nature, alert courage, and docility.

There is a spiritual significance attached to the Akita. In Japan they are affectionately regarded as loyal companions and pets, protectors of the home and a symbol of good health. When a child is born, the proud family will usually receive a small statue of an Akita signifying health, happiness, and a long life. If a person is ill, friends will send a small statue of an Akita to express their wish for a speedy recovery.

The Akita is very affectionate with family members and friends and thrives on human companionship. Since times long past, Japanese mothers have left their children in the trusted care of the family Akita. Typically reserved in demeanor, he will stand to the defense of his family whenever a threatening stranger or animal arouses his protective instinct.

The Akita today is the large-sized descendant of the ancient Japanese dog whose likeness has been found carved in the tombs of the early Japanese people. The upright ears and tail curled over the back are unmistakable.

Historical records cite the breed's development early in the seventeenth century. A famous nobleman was exiled to Akita prefecture, the northernmost province of the island of Honshu and ordered to live out his days as a provincial ruler. The nobleman had an ardent interest in dogs and encouraged the land barons in his domain to compete in the breeding of a large, versatile, intelligent hunting dog. Through generations of selective breeding there evolved the Akita, of superior size and frame, with keen hunting abilities, powerful working attributes, and a fearless spirit.

The ancient Japanese word *matagi* means "esteemed hunter," an honor applied to the men of a village having the best hunting skills. Akita is a rugged mountainous area with cold snowy winters. There the Akita was known as *matagiinu,* "esteemed dog hunter," and used to hunt bear, deer, and wild boar. The Yezo, largest and fiercest of Old World bears, was typically held at bay by a team of Akitas, a male and a female, awaiting the arrival of the hunter with arrow or spear.

The Akita's hunting abilities include great strength, keen eye and nose, silence, and speed in a durable, sturdy body suitable for hunting in deep snows. His hard, intelligent, never-give-in attitude in the field was prized by his masters. His soft mouth enabled him to retrieve waterfowl after they had been brought down by the hunter's arrow. The breed is said to have been used to drive fish at sea into the fisherman's nets.

Once, ownership was restricted to the imperial family and the ruling aristocracy. Care and feeding of the Akita were detailed in elaborate ceremony, and special leashes were used to denote the Akita's rank and the standing of his owner. A special vocabulary was used to address the Akita and in speaking about them. Each dog became the charge of a specially appointed caretaker who wore an ornate costume commensurate with the esteem in which the individual Akita was held.

Over the centuries the breed suffered near extinction as interest in the continuity of selective breeding surged and waned, depending on the inclination of the then ruling class. Fortunately, periodic favor managed to perpetuate the breed through the Meiji and Taisho eras. As the twentieth century drew near and Japan was exposed to other societies, being a dog devotee became very fashionable in emulation of European culture.

In 1927, the Akitainu Hozankai Society of Japan was established to preserve the purity of the breed. In July 1931, the government designated the Akita as a national monument and as one of Japan's national treasures. So highly regarded is the breed that the Japanese government will subsidize the care and feeding of an Akita champion if the owner is unable to do so.

Each year at a solemn ceremony in Tokyo's Shibuya railroad station hundreds of dog lovers do homage to the loyalty and devotion of an Akita dog, Hachiko, faithful pet of Dr. Eisaburo Ueno, a professor at Tokyo University.

It was the daily habit of Hachiko to accompany his master to the train station to see him off. Every afternoon Hachiko would return to the station to greet his master. On a May evening in 1925, Professor Ueno did not return; he had died that afternoon at the university. The loyal Akita waited at the station until midnight.

The next day and for the next nine years Hachiko returned to the station and waited for his beloved master before walking home, alone. Nothing and no one could discourage Hachiko from maintaining his nightly vigil. It was not until he followed his master in death, in March 1934, that Hachiko failed to appear in his place at the railroad station.

The fidelity of Hachiko was known throughout Japan. Upon his death, newspaper stories led to the suggestion that a statue be erected in the station. Contributions from the United States and other countries were received. Today the statue of Hachiko pays silent tribute to the breed's faithfulness and loyalty.

Helen Keller is credited with bringing the first Akitas into the United States. While visiting the prefecture of Akita in June 1937, she was presented with a two-month-old puppy by the Ministry of Education. Later, after the death of the puppy, the ministry forwarded a second Akita to Miss Keller.

The breed's popularity in the United States following World War II may be attributed to American servicemen of the occupational forces, who so admired the noble dogs that they took them home to their families. They were attracted to the Akita because of the breed's intelligence and adaptability to different situations.

The Akita Club of America was founded in 1956. The breed was admitted to registration in the American Kennel Club Stud Book in October 1972, and to regular show classification in the Working Group at AKC shows beginning April 4, 1973.

# OFFICIAL STANDARD FOR THE AKITA

**General Appearance**—Large, powerful, alert, with much substance and heavy bone. The broad head, forming a blunt triangle, with deep muzzle, small eyes and erect ears carried forward in line with back of neck, is characteristic of the breed. The large, curled tail, balancing the broad head, is also characteristic of the breed.

**Head**—Massive but in balance with body; free of wrinkle when at ease. Skull flat between ears and broad; jaws square and powerful with minimal dewlap. Head forms a blunt triangle when viewed from above. *Fault*—Narrow or snipy head. *Muzzle*—Broad and full. Distance from nose to stop is to distance from stop to occiput as 2 is to 3. *Stop*—Well defined, but not too abrupt. A shallow furrow extends well up forehead. *Nose*—Broad and black. Liver permitted on white Akitas, but black always preferred. *Disqualification*—Butterfly nose or total lack of pigmentation on nose. *Ears*—The ears of the Akita are characteristic of the breed. They are strongly erect and small in relation to rest of head. If ear is folded forward for measuring length, tip will touch upper eye rim. Ears are triangular, slightly rounded at tip, wide at base, set wide on head but not too low, and carried slightly forward over eyes in line with back of neck. *Disqualification*—Drop or broken ears. *Eyes*—Dark brown, small, deep-set and triangular in shape. Eye rims black and tight. *Lips and Tongue*—Lips black and not pendulous; tongue pink. *Teeth*—Strong with scissors bite preferred, but level bite acceptable. *Disqualification*—Noticeably undershot or overshot.

**Neck and Body**—*Neck*—Thick and muscular; comparatively short, widening gradually toward shoulders. A pronounced crest blends in with base of skull. *Body*—Longer than high, as 10 is to 9 in males; 11 to 9 in bitches. Chest wide and deep; depth of chest is one-half height of dog at shoulder. Ribs well sprung, brisket well developed. Level back with firmly-muscled loin and moderate tuck-up. Skin pliant but not loose. *Serious Faults*—Light bone, rangy body.

**Tail**—Large and full, set high and carried over back or against flank in a three-quarter, full, or double curl, always dipping to or below level of back. On a three-quarter curl, tip drops well down flank. Root large and strong. Tail bone reaches hock when let down. Hair coarse, straight and full, with no appearance of a plume. *Disqualification*—Sickle or uncurled tail.

**Forequarters and Hindquarters**—*Forequarters*—Shoulders strong and powerful with moderate layback. Forelegs heavy-boned and straight as viewed from front. Angle of pastern 15 degrees forward from vertical. *Faults*—Elbows in or out, loose shoulders. *Hindquarters*—Width, muscular development and bone comparable to forequarters. Upper thighs well developed. Stifle moderately bent and hocks well let down, turning neither in nor out. *Dewclaws*—On front legs generally not removed; dewclaws on hind legs generally removed. *Feet*—Cat feet, well knuckled up with thick pads. Feet straight ahead.

**Coat**—Double-coated. Undercoat thick, soft, dense and shorter than outer coat. Outer coat straight, harsh and standing somewhat off body. Hair on head, legs and ears short. Length of hair at withers and rump approximately two inches, which is slightly longer than on rest of body, except tail, where coat is longest and most profuse. *Fault*—Any indication of ruff or feathering.

**Color**—Any color including white; brindle; or pinto. Colors are brilliant and clear and markings are well balanced, with or without mask or blaze. White Akitas have no mask. Pinto has a white background with large, evenly placed patches covering head and more than one-third of body. Undercoat may be a different color from outer coat.

**Gait**—Brisk and powerful with strides of moderate length. Back remains strong, firm and level. Rear legs move in line with front legs.

**Size**—Males 26 to 28 inches at the withers; bitches 24 to 26 inches. *Disqualification*—Dogs under 25 inches; bitches under 23 inches.

**Temperament**—Alert and responsive, dignified and courageous. Aggressive toward other dogs.

## DISQUALIFICATIONS

*Butterfly nose or total lack of pigmentation on nose.*
*Drop or broken ears.*
*Noticeably undershot or overshot.*
*Sickle or uncurled tail.*
*Dogs under 25 inches; bitches under 23 inches.*

**Approved December 12, 1972**

# ALASKAN MALAMUTE

*T*HE ALASKAN MALAMUTE IS ONE OF THE OLDEST ARCTIC SLED-DOG BREEDS. The breed name was taken from the Mahlemuts, an Inuit tribe that settled along the shores of Kotzebue Sound in northwestern Alaska. Long before Alaska became a possession of the United States, native people were living on "Alyeska" land when Asiatic mariners visited this northern expanse. Returning to their homeland, the sailors told stories about seeing indigenous people using dogs to haul sledges.

The origin of these people and their dogs has never been completely determined. We know that they had been in Alaska for generations, but where they originated is not definitely known. The Alaskan Arctic sledge-dog breed native to the territory is now called the Alaskan Malamute.

The Mahlemut people are never mentioned in early writings without reference to their dogs. A traveling missionary, who had journeyed thousands of miles by dog team, wrote:

> These Malamutes . . . are peaceful, happy, hard workers, believe in one wife, are able guides and have wonderful dogs. Even though uncivilized, they have realized that it is important to have fine animals to pull sledges, that without them, means of travel in this sort of country would be impossible at times.

The dogs are powerful looking, have thick dense double coats (outer coat of thick coarse fur and inner coat of fuzzy down lying close to skin) called weather coats, erect ears, magnificently bushy tails carried over their backs like waving plumes, tough feet, colors varying but mostly wolf grey or black and white. The dogs have remarkable endurance and fortitude. The Malamute people and their dogs are much respected among other Inuits.

When white men settled Alaska, the Arctic breeds were mingled with outside dogs. During the Alaskan Sweepstakes, the lure of racing became so popular that many drivers experimented with mixing Arctic breeds with outside strains. This period, 1909 to 1918, was considered the "age of decay of the Arctic sledge dog."

Fortunately, the sport of sled-dog racing became popular in the United States. Interest in developing a pure strain of the native Alaskan Malamute began in 1926. Malamutes were being bred for expedition work, including vital roles as pack dogs, freight dogs, and rescue dogs. They served important missions during World War II.

The Alaskan Malamute was fully recognized by the AKC in 1935, and the breed's first championship was awarded that same year. As pets they have become popular among those who enjoy sledding, weight pulling, skijoring, backpacking, and other winter activities, and Malamutes have earned titles in the obedience ring and at agility trials.

The Malamute is a true pack animal with the natural instinct to lead or be led. As a result, training must begin as early as three to five months of age. These dogs must be raised in an atmosphere of controlled socialization with humans and other animals, as they can dominate people they don't respect and become quite aggressive with other dogs of the same sex. A sensible combination of love and discipline will result in a devoted, trustworthy, and valuable companion.

# OFFICIAL STANDARD FOR THE ALASKAN MALAMUTE

**General Appearance**—The Alaskan Malamute, one of the oldest Arctic sled dogs, is a powerful and substantially built dog with a deep chest and strong, well-muscled body. The Malamute stands well over the pads, and this stance gives the appearance of much activity and a proud carriage, with head erect and eyes alert showing interest and curiosity. The head is broad. Ears are triangular and erect when alerted. The muzzle is bulky, only slight diminishing in width from root to nose. The muzzle is not pointed or long, yet not stubby. The coat is thick with a coarse guard coat of sufficient length to protect a woolly undercoat. Malamutes are of various colors. Face markings are a distinguishing feature. These consist of a cap over the head, the face either all white or marked with a bar and/or mask. The tail is well furred, carried over the back, and has the appearance of a waving plume.

The Malamute must be a heavy boned dog with sound legs, good feet, deep chest and powerful shoulders, and have all of the other physical attributes necessary for the efficient performance of his job. The gait must be steady, balanced, tireless and totally efficient. He is not intended as a racing sled dog designed to compete in speed trials. The Malamute is structured for strength and endurance, and any characteristic of the individual specimen, including temperament, which interferes with the accomplishment of this purpose, is to be considered the most serious of faults.

**Size, Proportion, Substance**—There is a natural range in size in the breed. The desirable freighting sizes are males, 25 inches at the shoulders, 85 pounds; females, 23 inches at the shoulders, 75 pounds. However, size consideration should not outweigh that of type, proportion, movement and other functional attributes. When dogs are judged equal in type, proportion, movement, the dog nearest the desirable freighting size is to be preferred. The depth of chest is approximately one half the height of the dog at the shoulders, the deepest point being just behind the forelegs. The length of the body from point of shoulder to the rear point of pelvis is longer than the height of the body from ground to top of the withers. The body carries no excess weight, and bone is in proportion to size.

**Head**—The head is broad and deep, not coarse or clumsy, but in proportion to the size of the dog. The expression is soft and indicates an affectionate disposition. The *eyes* are obliquely placed in the skull. Eyes are brown, almond shaped, and of medium size. Dark eyes preferred. *Blue eyes are a disqualifying fault.* The *ears* are of medium size, but small in proportion to the head. The ears are triangular in shape and slightly rounded at the tips. They are set wide apart on the outside back edges of the skull on line with the upper corner of the eye, giving ears the appearance, when erect, of standing off from the skull. Erect ears point slightly forward, but when the dog is at work, the ears are sometimes folded against the skull. High set ears are a fault.

The *skull* is broad and moderately rounded between the ears, gradually narrowing and flattening on top as it approaches the eyes, rounding off to cheeks that are moderately flat. There is a slight furrow between the eyes. The topline of the skull and the topline of the muzzle show a slight break downward from a straight line as they join. The *muzzle* is large and bulky in proportion to the size of the skull, diminishing slightly in width and depth from junction with the skull to the nose. In all coat colors, except reds, the *nose, lips,* and *eye rims' pigmentation* is black. Brown is permitted in red dogs. The lighter-streaked "snow nose" is acceptable. The lips are close fitting. The upper and lower jaws are broad with large teeth. The incisors meet with a scissors grip. Overshot or undershot is a fault.

**Neck, Topline, Body**—The *neck* is strong and moderately arched. The chest is well developed. The *body* is compactly built but not short coupled. The *back* is straight and gently sloping to the hips. The *loins* are hard and well muscled. A long loin that may weaken the back is a fault. The *tail* is moderately set and follows the line of the spine at the base. The tail is carried over the back when not working. It is not a snap tail or curled tight against the back, nor is it short furred like a fox brush. The Malamute tail is well furred and has the appearance of a waving plume.

**Forequarters**—The shoulders are moderately sloping; forelegs heavily boned and muscled, straight to the pasterns when viewed from the front. Pasterns are short and strong and slightly sloping when viewed from the side. The feet are of the snowshoe type, tight and deep, with well-cushioned pads, giving a firm, compact appearance. The feet are large, toes tight fitting and well arched. There is a protective growth of hair between the toes. The pads are thick and tough; toenails short and strong.

**Hindquarters**—The rear legs are broad and heavily muscled through the thighs; stifles moderately bent; hock joints are moderately bent and well let down. When viewed from the rear, the legs stand and move true in line with the movement of the front legs, not too close or too wide. Dewclaws on the rear legs are undesirable and should be removed shortly after puppies are whelped.

**Coat**—The Malamute has a thick, coarse guard coat, never long and soft. The undercoat is dense, from one to two inches in depth, oily and woolly. The coarse guard coat varies in length as does the undercoat. The coat is relatively short to medium along the sides of the body, with the length of the coat increasing around the shoulders and neck, down the back, over the rump, and in the breeching and plume. Malamutes usually have a shorter and less dense coat during the summer months. The Malamute is shown naturally. Trimming is not acceptable except to provide a clean cut appearance of feet.

**Color**—The usual colors range from light gray through intermediate shadings to black, sable, and shadings of sable to red. Color combinations are acceptable in undercoats, points, and trimmings. The only solid color allowable is all white. White is always the predominant color on underbody, parts of legs, feet, and part of face markings. A white blaze on the forehead and/or collar or a spot on the nape is attractive and acceptable. The Malamute is mantled, and broken colors extending over the body or uneven splashing are undesirable.

**Gait**—The gait of the Malamute is steady, balanced and powerful. He is agile for his size and build. When viewed from the side, the hindquarters exhibit strong rear drive that is transmitted through a well-muscled loin to the forequarters. The forequarters receive the drive from the rear with a smooth reaching stride. When viewed from the front or from the rear, the legs move true in line, not too close or too wide. At a fast trot, the feet will converge toward the centerline of the body. A stilted gait, or any gait that is not completely efficient and tireless, is to be penalized.

**Temperament**—The Alaskan Malamute is an affectionate, friendly dog, not a "one man" dog. He is a loyal, devoted companion, playful in invitation, but generally impressive by his dignity after maturity.

**Summary**—IMPORTANT: In judging Malamutes, their function as a sledge dog for heavy freighting in the Arctic must be given consideration above all else. The degree to which a dog is penalized should depend upon the extent to which the dog deviates from the description of the ideal Malamute and the extent to which the particular fault would actually affect the working ability of the dog. The legs of the Malamute must indicate unusual strength and tremendous propelling power. Any indication of unsoundness in legs and feet, front or rear, standing or moving, is to be considered a *serious fault*. *Faults* under this provision would be splay-footedness, cowhocks, bad pasterns, straight shoulders, lack of angulation, stilted gait (or any gait that isn't balanced, strong and steady), ranginess, shallowness, ponderousness, lightness of bone, and poor overall pro-portion.

## DISQUALIFICATION

*Blue eyes.*

**Approved April 12, 1994**
**Effective May 31, 1994**

# ANATOLIAN SHEPHERD DOG

T HE ANATOLIAN SHEPHERD DOG IS A GUARDIAN BREED WITH ITS ORIGIN IN Turkey. Quite probably more than 6,000 years old, the breed is impressive in size, serving as the Turkish shepherd's frontline defense from predators. Developed to withstand Turkey's harsh climate, the Anatolian Shepherd has evolved to endure the nomadic lifestyle of the shepherds.

Loyalty, independence, and hardiness are the three factors most appreciated by fanciers of the breed. First entering the United States in the 1950s, the Anatolian Shepherd is a fiercely loyal guard dog, not considered a "glamour breed." Faithful to its job, the Anatolian is highly intelligent and responsive to its master. However, its independent nature means it can be slow to respond to commands.

## OFFICIAL STANDARD FOR THE ANATOLIAN SHEPHERD DOG

**General Appearance**—Large, rugged, powerful and impressive, possessing great endurance and agility. Developed through a set of very demanding circumstances for a purely utilitarian purpose; he is a working guard dog without equal, with a unique ability to protect livestock. *General impression*—Appears bold, but calm, unless challenged. He possesses size, good bone, a well-muscled torso with a strong head. Reserve out of its territory is acceptable. Fluid movement and even temperament is desirable.

**Size, Proportion, Substance**—General balance is more important than absolute size. Dogs should be from 29 inches and weighing from 110 to 150 pounds proportionate to size and structure. Bitches should be from 27 inches, weighing from 80 to 120 pounds, proportionate to size and structure. Neither dog nor bitch appear fat. Both dog and bitch should be rectangular, in direct proportion to height. Measurements and weights apply at age 2 or older.

**Head**—*Expression* should be intelligent. *Eyes* are medium size, set apart, almond shaped and dark brown to light amber in color. *Blue eyes or eyes of two different colors are a disqualification.* Eye rims will be black or brown and without sag or looseness of haw. Incomplete pigment is a serious fault. *Ears* should be set on no higher than the plane of the head. V-shaped, rounded apex, measuring about four inches at the base to six inches in length. The tip should be just long enough to reach the outside corner of the eyelid. Ears dropped to sides. *Erect ears are a disqualification. Skull* is large but in proportion to the body. There is a slight centerline furrow, fore and aft, from apparent stop to moderate occiput. Broader in dogs than in bitches. *Muzzle* is blockier and stronger for the dog, but neither dog nor bitch would have a snipey head or muzzle. *Nose* and flews must be solid black or brown. Seasonal fading is not to be penalized. Incomplete pigment is a serious fault. Flews are normally dry but pronounced enough to contribute to "squaring" the overall muzzle appearance. *Teeth* and gums strong and healthy. Scissors bite preferred, level bite acceptable. Broken teeth are not to be faulted. *Overshot, undershot or wry bite are disqualifications.*

**Neck, Topline, Body**—*Neck* slightly arched, powerful, and muscular, moderate in length with more skin and fur than elsewhere on the body, forming a protective ruff. The dewlap should not be pendulous and excessive. *Topline* will appear level when gaiting. *Back* will be powerful, muscular, and level, with drop behind withers and gradual arch over loin, sloping slightly downward at the croup. *Body* well proportioned, functional, without exaggeration. Never fat or soft. *Chest* is deep (to the elbow) and well-sprung with a distinct tuck up at the loin. *Tail* should be long and reaching to the hocks. Set on rather high. When relaxed, it is carried low with the end curled upwards. When alert, the tail is carried high, making a "wheel." Both low and wheel carriage are acceptable, when gaiting. "Wheel" carriage preferred. The tail will not necessarily uncurl totally.

**Forequarters**—Shoulders should be muscular and well developed, blades long, broad and sloping. *Elbows* should be neither in nor out. *Forelegs* should be relatively long, well-boned and set straight with strong pasterns. The feet are strong and compact with well-arched toes, oval in shape. They should have stout nails with pads thick and tough. Dewclaws may be removed.

**Hindquarters**—Strong, with broad thighs and heavily muscled. Angulation at the stifle and hock are in proportion to the forequarters. As seen from behind, the legs are parallel. The feet are strong and compact with well-arched toes, oval in shape. Double dewclaws may exist. Dewclaws may be removed.

**Coat**—Short (one inch minimum, not tight) to Rough (approximately 4 inches in length) with neck hair slightly longer. Somewhat longer and thicker at the neck and mane. A thick undercoat is common to all. Feathering may occur on the ear fringes, legs, breeching and tail.

**Color**—All color patterns and markings are equally acceptable.

**Gait**—At the trot, the gait is powerful yet fluid. When viewed from the front or rear, the legs turn neither in nor out, nor do feet cross or interfere with each other. With increased speed, footfall converges toward the center line of gravity. When viewed from the side, the front legs should reach out smoothly with no obvious pounding. The withers and backline should stay nearly level with little rise or fall. The rear assembly should push out smoothly with hocks doing their share of the work and flexing well.

**Temperament**—Alert and intelligent, calm and observant. Instinctively protective, he is courageous and highly adaptable. He is very loyal and responsive. Highly territorial, he is a natural guard. Reserve around strangers and off its territory is acceptable. Responsiveness with animation is not characteristic of the breed. Overhandling would be discouraged.

## DISQUALIFICATIONS

*Blue eyes or eyes of two different colors.*
*Erect ears.*
*Overshot, undershot or wry bite.*

**Approved June 1995**
**Effective June 1, 1996**

# BERNESE MOUNTAIN DOG

*A*RISTOCRATIC IN APPEARANCE, ANCIENT IN LINEAGE, THE BERNESE MOUN-
tain Dog has long been at home on the farms in the midland of Switzerland. The Bernese, known in its homeland as the Berner Sennenhund, is one of
four varieties of Swiss mountain dogs, along with the Appenzeller Sennenhund, the
Entlebucher Sennenhund, and the Greater Swiss Mountain Dog. The breed shares
similar distinctive coloring with the others but is the only one of the four to have a
long, silky coat. In size, it is the second largest of the four. Bernese Mountain Dogs
worked mainly in the canton of Berne as farmer's dogs, companions, drovers, and
draft dogs, as well as farmyard watchdogs. The ancestors of these dogs were working farm dogs in other areas of Switzerland.

Until the late nineteenth century, Bernese Mountain Dogs had been almost
forgotten by all except the oldest inhabitants of Berne. They were still found in the
area of Duerrbach, but the breed had degenerated to such an extent as to be practically unrecognizable. In 1892 the Swiss fancier Franz Schertenleib attempted to
find good specimens for use as breeding stock, and his search was a long one. He
was ultimately successful, however, and several other fanciers became interested as
well. The rehabilitation and comeback had begun. This effort succeeded under the
knowledgeable leadership of geologist, canine researcher, and judge Professor Albert Heim. In 1907, a specialty club was formed, and the Bernese Mountain Dog

breed was exhibited. They found favor with many Swiss, who developed them as home companions, although their old working roles on farms continued.

A handsome, longhaired, large, and sturdily built dog, the Bernese is jet black in color with rich russet markings on the legs, cheeks, over each eye, and on either side of the snowy white chest. A white blaze adorns the muzzle and forehead, and it is highly desirable that the dogs have white feet and a white tip on the tail. The coat is thick, moderately long, and slightly wavy or straight. The broad, firm back; deep chest; well-sprung ribs; and strong loins advertise the Bernese as a breed well suited to hard work.

The Bernese Mountain Dog is an extremely hardy dog that thrives in cold weather. Bernese need but little daily grooming to look well kept, but they depend on human companionship for emotional development and overall well-being. Although they are generally low-energy dogs, Bernese are willing and quick learners, self-confident, and exceptionally faithful.

First brought to the United States in 1926, the breed achieved AKC recognition in 1937. The parent club, the Bernese Mountain Dog Club of America (BMDCA), was formed in 1968 and became an AKC member club in 1981. Draft and carting tests are sponsored by the BMDCA to test the natural ability of this breed for its working function.

Berner-Garde, an open health registry, was established in 1989 to safeguard the breed's future. All Bernese Mountain Dog breeders and owners are encouraged to utilize it.

# OFFICIAL STANDARD FOR THE BERNESE MOUNTAIN DOG

**General Appearance**—The Bernese Mountain Dog is a striking, tri-colored, large dog. He is sturdy and balanced. He is intelligent, strong and agile enough to do the draft and droving work for which he was used in the mountainous regions of his origin. Dogs appear masculine, while bitches are distinctly feminine.

**Size, Proportion, Substance**—Measured at the withers, dogs are 25 to 27½ inches; bitches are 23 to 26 inches. Though appearing square, Bernese Mountain Dogs are slightly longer in body than they are tall. Sturdy bone is of great importance. The body is full.

**Head**—*Expression* is intelligent, animated and gentle. The *eyes* are dark brown and slightly oval in shape with close-fitting eyelids. Inverted or everted eyelids are serious faults. Blue eye color is a disqualification. The *ears* are medium sized, set high, triangular in shape, gently rounded at the tip, and hang close to the head when in repose. When the Bernese Mountain Dog is alert, the ears are brought forward and raised at the base; the top of the ear is level with the top of the skull. The *skull* is flat on top and broad, with a slight furrow and a well-defined but not exaggerated stop. The *muzzle* is strong and straight. The *nose* is always black. The *lips* are clean and, as the Bernese Mountain Dog is a dry-mouthed breed, the flews are only slightly developed. The *teeth* meet in a scissors bite. An overshot or undershot bite is a serious fault. Dentition is complete.

**Neck, Topline, Body**—The *neck* is strong, muscular and of medium length. The *topline* is level from the withers to the croup. The chest is deep and capacious with well-sprung, but not barrel-shaped, ribs and brisket reaching at least to the elbows. The back is broad and firm. The *loin* is strong. The *croup* is broad and smoothly rounded to the tail insertion. The *tail* is bushy. It should be carried low when in repose. An upward swirl is permissible when the dog is alert, but the tail may never curl or be carried over the back. The bones in the tail should feel straight and should reach to the hock joint or below. A kink in the tail is a fault.

**Forequarters**—The shoulders are moderately laid back, flat-lying, well-muscled and never loose. The *legs* are straight and strong and the *elbows* are well under the shoulder when the dog is standing. The *pasterns* slope very slightly, but are never weak. *Dewclaws* may be removed. The *feet* are round and compact with well-arched toes.

**Hindquarters**—The *thighs* are broad, strong and muscular. The *stifles* are moderately bent and taper smoothly into the hocks. The *hocks* are well let down and straight as viewed from the rear. *Dewclaws* should be removed. *Feet* are compact and turn neither in nor out.

**Coat**—The *coat* is thick, moderately long and slightly wavy or straight. It has a bright natural sheen. Extremely curly or extremely dull-looking coats are undesirable. The Bernese Mountain Dog is shown in natural coat and undue trimming is to be discouraged.

**Color and Markings**—The Bernese Mountain Dog is tri-colored. The ground color is jet black. The markings are rich rust and clear white. Symmetry of markings is desired. Rust appears over each eye, on the cheeks reaching to at least the corner of the mouth, on each side of the chest, on all four legs, and under the tail. There is a white blaze and muzzle band. A white marking on the chest typically forms an inverted cross. The tip of the tail is white. White on the feet is desired but must not extend higher than the pasterns. Markings other than described are to be faulted in direct relationship to the extent of the deviation. White legs or a white collar are serious faults. Any ground color other than black is a disqualification.

**Gait**—The natural working gait of the Bernese Mountain Dog is a slow trot. However, in keeping with his use in draft and droving work, he is capable of speed and agility. There is good reach in front. Powerful drive from the rear is transmitted through a level back. There is no wasted action. Front and rear legs on each side follow through in the same plane. At increased speed, legs tend to converge toward the center line.

**Temperament**—The *temperament* is self-confident, alert and good-natured, never sharp or shy. The Bernese Mountain Dog should stand steady, though may remain aloof to the attentions of strangers.

# DISQUALIFICATIONS

*Blue eye color.*
*Any ground color other than black.*

**Approved February 10, 1990**
**Effective March 28, 1990**

# BLACK RUSSIAN TERRIER

*T*HE BLACK RUSSIAN TERRIER (BRT) IS ONE OF THE NEWEST BREEDS IN the world, created after World War II and recognized by the Fédération Cynologique Internationale in 1984. (First a member of the FCI Terrier Group, the Black Russian Terrier was later moved into the Working Group because it is not a true terrier.)

Russia's Central School of Cynology Specialists, founded in 1924, made a great contribution in development of canine science through its creation of Krasnaya Zvezda ("Red Star"), a kennel factory outside Moscow devoted to working dogs. The Black Terrier was cultivated at this facility.

World War II drastically decreased the number of working dogs in Russia, but demand for them at military installations, prisons, and other government sites remained high. The Soviets needed a powerful guard dog with a good sense of smell, a well-balanced nervous system, and the ability to withstand a wide range of climates.

Red Star set out to address these needs. The staff began a series of crossbreedings, giving special attention to such working breeds as the Rottweiler, Giant Schnauzer, and the Airedale Terrier, the basic ancestors of the Blackie. The result was large dogs with heavy bone and strong muscles. Their nervous systems were much more stable than the Schnauzer's, and their reactions to situations were much quicker. The black color and long wire coats, with considerable amount of hair on face and legs, became inherited traits.

Offspring of the first and second generation were shown at the 1955 USSR Agricultural Exhibition. Many of those dogs received high grades from the judges. In 1957, forty-three Black Terriers were exhibited in All-USSR Working and Hunting Dog shows. They attracted the attention of dog lovers, and after Stalin's death Red Star began selling puppies to be raised in private homes. This was the beginning of breeding BRTs in working-dog clubs all over the country.

Up to the 1990s, breeding of all working dogs had been under strict control of club specialists, who wrote the breeding plan for a whole year and a perspective plan for five years. The only dogs considered for breeding were those with very good to excellent ratings in conformation and which had passed obedience and protection trials. Many of the working dogs along with their owners were used in the community to assist police and to guard different sites.

The Black Russian Terrier gained attention at the World Show in Helsinki and started on its way to international attention. When you see a Blackie you will think of a Giant Schnauzer or a Bouvier des Flandres. The BRT is a large, strong, massive dog. The color is solid black, with some gray hairs on the back. It possesses a thick undercoat with a coarse, wavy guard hair on top. Soft, very curly hair is not acceptable. Sex type must be well expressed, males being much bigger and more masculine than females.

The BRT is a confident dog with a strong personality and a will of his own. He is very protective and willing to guard his house and family. He should be guided in the right direction in his early education, beginning from when he first enters his new home. If you have any doubt about your ability to handle a big, powerful, determined dog, or if you have never raised a dog before, it is in the best interest of all concerned to look for another breed that best fits your family needs. A well-trained BRT is a faithful and devoted family member whose personality will provide the right owner with years of enjoyment.

Since entering the AKC Working Group in July 2004, the Black Russian Terrier has gained popularity in the United States. The Black Russian Terrier Club of America was founded in 1994.

# OFFICIAL STANDARD FOR THE BLACK RUSSIAN TERRIER

**General Appearance**—The Black Russian Terrier (BRT) is a robust, large and powerful dog. The dog has large bone and well-developed muscles. The breed was developed in Russia and used as guard dogs for protection. They must be balanced, have a good temperament and be reliable. The dogs have great courage and strength. They are capable of endurance. Dogs must have a large frame and heavy bone. Bitches are definitely to appear feminine but never lacking in substance.

**Size, Proportion, Substance**—*Size*—Dogs at maturity are between 27 inches and 30 inches. Bitches at maturity are to be between 26 and 29 inches. A deviation from the ideal height is to be faulted. *Any dog or bitch under 26 inches is a disqualification. Proportion*—The Black Russian Terrier is slightly longer than tall. The most desired proportions are 9½ to 10. The length is measured from breastbone to rear edge of the pelvis.

**Head**—The head must be in proportion to the body. It should give the appearance of power and strength. *Eyes*—The eyes should be of medium size and dark. Eye rims are to be black without sagging or prominent haw. The eye is to be oval shaped. Light eyes are a serious fault. *Ears*—The ears are set high and are rather small and triangular in shape. The front edge of the ear should lie close to the cheek. The length of the ear should reach the outside corner of the eye. Ears set low on the skull are to be faulted. Cropped ears are not acceptable. The head should be powerfully built with a moderately broad and blocky *skull*. Viewed from the side it should appear balanced. The head is made of two parallel planes. The back skull to muzzle is measured from the corner of the eye. Occiput should be well developed. The *muzzle* should be slightly shorter than the back skull. The length of the muzzle to the back skull is approximately a ratio of 4:5. The forehead must be flat with a marked but not pronounced stop. The head of the male is distinctly masculine, and that of the bitch, distinctly feminine. *Nose*—The nose must be large and black. *Disqualification*—*Nose other than black. Lips* are full, tight and black. There are to be no flews. The gums have dark pigmentation. Black mark on the tongue is allowed. *Teeth*—The teeth are large and white. There should be full dentition. The incisors form a straight line at the base. The bite should be scissors. Any missing teeth are a serious fault. *Undershot or overshot bites are a disqualification.*

**Neck, Topline, and Body**—*Neck*—The neck should be thick, muscular and powerful. Length is not to be excessive. There should be no pendulous or excessive dewlap. The length of the neck and the length of the head should be approximately the same. An excessively thick neck is considered a fault. *Body*—The whole structure of the body should give the impression of strength. The chest is deep and wide. The shape should be oval and reach to the elbows or a little below. The withers are high, pronounced and well developed. The topline is level and straight. The *loin* is short. The abdomen is well tucked up and firm. Withers are higher than and sloping into the level back. *Croup* is wide, muscular, moderately long slightly sloping toward the high tail set. *Tail* is set high, thick and docked with 3 to 5 vertebrae left. An undocked tail is not to be penalized.

**Forequarters**—Shoulders should be large and muscular, well developed with blades broad and sloping. The shoulders should be well laid back. The angle between the shoulder blades and the upper arm is 100 to 110 degrees. Shoulders are well muscled. The forelegs are straight and well boned. The elbows must turn neither in nor out while standing or moving. The forelegs are straight and muscular. Pasterns are short and almost vertical. Length of the front leg to the elbow should be about 53 to 54 percent of the dog's height. *Feet* are large, compact, and rounded in shape. The pads of the feet are thick and firm. Nails are short and dark. Rear dewclaws could be removed.

**Hindquarters**—Viewed from the rear the legs are straight and parallel, set slightly wider than the forelegs. The hindquarters are well boned and muscular with good angulation. The stifle is long and sloping. The thighs are muscular. The hocks are well let down, long and vertical when standing.

**Coat**—Tousled, double coat. The texture of the outer coat is coarse. The undercoat is thick and soft. Length of coat should vary from 1½ to 4 inches and cover the entire body. It is a pronounced, tousled coat rather than wiry or curly.

**Presentation**—In the show ring, the dog's outline is clearly defined. The dogs will be trimmed but should not appear to be sculpted. *Ears*—hair should be trimmed inside and outside the ear. The ears will lie flat to the side of the head. *Forehead*—Just behind the eyebrows the hair is to be shaved or cut very short so as to make what appears to be a platform. The rest of the forehead is trimmed so that the shorter hairs will blend with the longer hairs of the muzzle. This forms a "cap" which should help define length of backskull. Looking from the top of the head it should give the appearance of a "brick." The fringe from the eyebrows is brushed forward and blends with the beard and muzzle. This blending of hair should look from the side like a "triangle." *Neck*—The front of the neck from the throat to the point of shoulder should be shaved or scissored short. The hair on the back of the neck should appear to have a mane down to the withers. *Topline* is trimmed from the withers to the tail so that when viewed from the side it appears level. The hair from the back should then blend down the sides of the dog. It is stressed that there should be no distinct lines or scissors marks.

**Color**—The only acceptable colors for the Black Russian Terrier is black or black with a few gray hairs. *Any other color is to be considered a disqualification.*

**Gait**—A Black Russian Terrier should move freely with a smooth easy springy motion. The motion should be well-balanced and fluid. As the Black Russian Terrier moves faster the feet will converge toward a centerline. The topline should remain level.

**Temperament**—The character and temperament of the Black Russian Terrier is of utmost importance. The Black Russian Terrier is a calm, confident, and courageous dog with a self-assurance which sometimes is rather aloof toward strangers. They are highly intelligent, extremely reliable. They were bred to guard and protect. The behavior in the show ring should be controlled, willing, adaptable, and trained to submit to examination.

## DISQUALIFICATIONS

*Any dog or bitch under 26 inches.*
*Nose other than black.*
*Undershot or overshot bite.*
*Any color other than black.*

**Approved June 11, 2001**
**Effective September 1, 2001**

# BOXER

*T*HE BOXER WE KNOW TODAY IS A PRODUCT OF MANY GENERATIONS OF selective breeding. Although as early as 2500 B.C. the breed's progenitors in Assyria were heavily built, short-muzzled, courageous dogs, the modern Boxer was largely defined in Germany in the late nineteenth and early twentieth centuries.

The Boxer itself was developed from stocky Bullenbeissers ("bull biters"), which were held in great esteem. According to one authority, "Throughout the Middle Ages, the Bullenbeisser was Germany's only hunting hound." They were used to run down, catch, and hold fierce wild game—boar, bear, and bison. The Bullenbeisser had a wide, short muzzle that distinguished the breed from all others, both then and now. After the Napoleonic Wars (1803–1815) many of Germany's ducal estates were broken up and hunting became a less popular pursuit among the gentry. The last recorded boar hunt was held at Kurhesser Courts in 1865, after which the hunting dogs were sold.

During the time that hunting was declining in popularity, the English exported a dog to Germany they called a Bulldog, which actually resembled a small Mastiff, square in proportion and with long legs. Seventy years later, some of the pioneering Boxer breeders in Germany used two descendants of these Bulldogs in their breeding programs. These descendants, Trutzel and Tom, appear in the pedigrees of early German Boxers.

It becomes evident that in selecting for type and function, German breeders were developing a smaller and lighter dog from the heavy dogs of the purest old Bullenbeisser lines. Though it has been conjectured that the breed resulted from crosses with several other breeds, the mastiff like English Bulldog seems likely to be the only significant cross. Through ensuing generations, the Boxer evolved to satisfy some very specific needs of late–nineteenth century human society.

Bullbaiting, a terribly cruel pursuit, was considered great sport in early-nineteenth century England. A dog was encouraged to attack and hang on to the bull's nose, no matter what the consequences. Dogs were kicked, tossed, and killed, and the bulls were terrified and exhausted. Of course, wagering accompanied these events, and a good bull baiter was prized by owner and gallery alike. There are a number of contemporary etchings and lithographs (by Henry Alken, most notably) that recorded these events, popular throughout England, Germany, and elsewhere in Europe. Mercifully, bullbaiting was eventually outlawed.

It is not surprising that a dog used to bait bulls would be adopted into the households of cattle dealers and butchers, and Boxers saw duty as cattle dogs because of their success with bulls. Even today, on America's western plains, there are ranchers who use Boxers to control cattle. The breed also gained favor as an excellent circus performer—obedient, extremely intelligent, and agile.

German pioneers who developed the Boxer were careful and conscientious. They recorded their efforts in studbooks and formalized their work in 1896 by founding the first German club devoted to the breed, the Deutsche Boxer Club, in Munich. Other clubs followed, and the first German breed standard was written and adopted in 1902. No one is quite sure how the name Boxer arose, but conjecture suggests that it may have something to do with the characteristic playing gestures using the front feet, still a hallmark of the breed.

The first AKC Boxer was registered in 1904, the first championship was earned in 1915, and the American Boxer Club was formed in 1935. In the ensuing years we have witnessed great popularity of the breed as a guard and companion, one especially devoted to children. The Boxer's noble appearance may tend to camouflage great muscular strength and power, as the breed has been called the "middleweight athlete of dogdom."

High intelligence is not conducive to slavish obedience—the Boxer always wants to know why. During both world wars, Boxers served as military-service and courier dogs. They were one of the pioneering breeds for guiding the blind, and they are used in many avenues of modern police work. Many Boxers have proven to be uncanny seizure-alert dogs. Although they possess the unique ability to mirror the moods of their owners, Boxers are quintessentially playful into oldest age, being bold, exuberant, and utterly loyal to the family they adore.

# OFFICIAL STANDARD FOR THE BOXER

**General Appearance**—The *ideal* Boxer is a medium-sized, square-built dog of good substance with short back, strong limbs, and short, tight-fitting coat. His well-developed muscles are clean, hard, and appear smooth under taut skin. His movements denote energy. The gait is firm yet elastic, the stride free and ground-covering, the carriage proud. Developed to serve as guard, working, and companion dog, he combines strength and agility with elegance and style. His expression is alert and his temperament steadfast and tractable.

The chiseled head imparts to the Boxer a unique individual stamp. It must be in correct proportion to the body. The broad, blunt muzzle is the distinctive feature, and great value is placed upon its being of proper form and balance with the skull.

In judging the Boxer, first consideration is given to general appearance and overall balance. Special attention is then devoted to the head, after which the individual body components are examined for their correct construction and the gait evaluated for efficiency.

**Size**—Adult males, 23 to 25 inches; females, 21½ to 23½ inches at the withers. Proper balance and quality in the individual should be of primary importance since there is no size disqualification.

*Proportion*—The body in profile is square in that a horizontal line from the front of the forechest to the rear projection of the upper thigh should equal the length of a vertical line dropped from the top of the withers to the ground.

*Substance*—Sturdy, with balanced musculature. Males larger boned than females.

**Head**—The beauty of the head depends upon the harmonious proportion of muzzle to skull. The blunt muzzle is ⅓ the length of the head from the occiput to the tip of the nose, and ⅔ the width of the skull. The head should be clean, not showing deep wrinkles (wet). Wrinkles typically appear upon the forehead when ears are erect, and are always present from the lower edge of the stop running downward on both sides of the muzzle.

*Expression*—Intelligent and alert.

*Eyes*—Dark brown in color, frontally placed, generous, not too small, too protruding, or too deep set. Their mood-mirroring character, combined with the wrinkling of the forehead, gives the Boxer head its unique quality of expressiveness. Third eyelids preferably have pigmented rims.

*Ears*—Set at the highest points of the sides of the skull, the ears are customarily cropped, cut rather long and tapering, and raised when alert. If uncropped, the ears should be of moderate size, thin, lying flat and close to the cheeks in repose, but falling forward with a definite crease when alert.

*Skull*—The top of the skull is slightly arched, not rounded, flat, nor noticeably broad, with the occiput not overly pronounced. The forehead shows a slight indentation between the eyes and forms a distinct stop with the topline of the muzzle. The cheeks should be relatively flat and not bulge (cheekiness), maintaining the clean lines of the skull as they taper into the muzzle in a slight, graceful curve.

*Muzzle and Nose*—The muzzle, proportionately developed in length, width, and depth, has a shape influenced first through the formation of both jawbones, second through the placement of the teeth, and third through the texture of the lips. The top of the muzzle should not slant down (down-faced), nor should it be concave (dish-faced); however, the tip of the nose should lie slightly higher than the root of the muzzle. The nose should be broad and black.

*Bite and Jaw Structure*—The Boxer bite is undershot, the lower jaw protruding beyond the upper and curving slightly upward. The incisor teeth of the lower jaw are in a straight line, with the canines preferably up front in the same line to give the jaw the greatest possible width. The upper line of the incisors is slightly convex with the corner upper incisors fitting snugly in back of the lower canine teeth on each side. Neither the teeth nor the tongue should ever show when the mouth is closed.

The upper jaw is broad where attached to the skull and maintains this breadth, except for a very slight tapering to the front. The lips, which complete the formation of the muzzle, should meet evenly in front. The upper lip is thick and padded, filling out the frontal space created by the projection of the lower jaw, and laterally is supported by the canines of the lower jaw. Therefore, these canines must stand far apart and be of good length so that the front surface of the muzzle is broad and squarish and, when viewed from the side, shows moderate layback. The chin should be perceptible from the side as well as from the front. Any suggestion of an overlip obscuring the chin should be penalized.

**Neck**—Round, of ample length, muscular and clean without excessive hanging skin (dewlap). The neck should have a distinctly arched and elegant nape blending smoothly into the withers.

*Back and Topline*—The back is short, straight, muscular, firm, and smooth. The *topline* is slightly sloping when the Boxer is at attention, leveling out when in motion.

*Body*—The chest is of fair width, and the forechest well-defined and visible from the side. The brisket is deep, reaching down to the elbows; the depth of the body at the lowest point of the brisket equals half the height of the dog at the withers. The ribs, extending far to the rear, are well arched but not barrel shaped.

The loins are short and muscular. The lower stomach line is slightly tucked up, blending into a graceful curve to the rear. The croup is slightly sloped, flat and broad. The pelvis is long, and in females especially broad. The tail is set high, docked, and carried upward. An undocked tail should be severely penalized.

**Forequarters**—The shoulders are long and sloping, close-lying, and not excessively covered with muscle (loaded). The upper arm is long, approaching a right angle to the shoulder blade. The elbows should not press too closely to the chest wall nor stand off visibly from it. The forelegs are long, straight, and firmly muscled, and, when viewed from the front, stand parallel to each other. The pastern is strong and distinct, slightly slanting, but standing almost perpendicular to the ground. The dewclaws may be removed. Feet should be compact, turning neither in nor out, with well-arched toes.

**Hindquarters**—The hindquarters are strongly muscled, with angulation in balance with that of the forequarters. The thighs are broad and curved, the breech musculature hard and strongly developed. Upper and lower thigh are long. The legs are well-angulated at the stifle, neither too steep nor over-angulated, with clearly defined, well "let down" hock joints. Viewed from behind, the hind legs should be straight, with hock joints leaning neither in nor out. From the side, the leg below the hock (metatarsus) should be almost perpendicular to the ground, with a slight slope to the rear permissible. The metatarsus should be short, clean, and strong. The Boxer has no rear dewclaws.

**Coat**—Short, shiny, lying smooth and tight to the body.

**Color**—The colors are fawn and brindle. Fawn shades vary from light tan to mahogany. The brindle ranges from sparse but clearly defined black stripes on a fawn background to such a heavy concentration of black striping that the essential fawn background color barely, although clearly, shows through (which may create the appearance of reverse brindling). White markings, if present, should be of such distribution as to enhance the dog's appearance, but may not exceed one-third of the entire coat. They are not desirable on the flanks or on the back of the torso proper. On the face, white may replace part of the otherwise essential black mask, and may extend in an upward path between the eyes, but it must not be excessive, so as to detract from true Boxer expression. The absence of white markings, the so-called "plain" fawn or brindle, is perfectly acceptable, and should not be penalized in any consideration of color.

*Disqualifications*—Boxers that are any color other than fawn or brindle. Boxers with a total of white markings exceeding one-third of the entire coat.

**Gait**—Viewed from the side, proper front and rear angulation is manifested in a smoothly efficient, level-backed, ground covering stride with a powerful drive emanating from a freely operating rear. Although the front legs do not contribute impelling power, adequate reach should be evident to prevent interference, overlap, or sidewinding (crabbing). Viewed from the front, the shoulders should remain trim and the elbows not flare out. The legs are parallel until gaiting narrows the track in proportion to increasing speed, then the legs come in under the body but should never cross. The line from the shoulder down through the leg should remain straight although not necessarily perpendicular to the ground. Viewed from the rear, a Boxer's rump should not roll. The hind feet should dig in and track relatively true with the front. Again, as speed increases, the normally broad rear track will become narrower. The Boxer's gait should always appear smooth and powerful, never stilted or inefficient.

**Character and Temperament**—These are of paramount importance in the Boxer. Instinctively a hearing guard dog, his bearing is alert, dignified, and self-assured. In the show ring his behavior should exhibit constrained animation. With family and friends, his temperament is fundamentally playful, yet patient and stoical with children. Deliberate and wary with strangers, he will exhibit curiosity, but, most importantly, fearless courage if threatened. However, he responds promptly to friendly overtures honestly rendered. His intelligence, loyal affection, and tractability to discipline make him a highly desirable companion. Any evidence of shyness, or lack of dignity or alertness, should be severely penalized.

**The foregoing description is that of the ideal Boxer. Any deviation from the above-described dog must be penalized to the extent of the deviation.**

# DISQUALIFICATIONS

*Boxers that are any color other than fawn or brindle.*
*Boxers with a total of white markings exceeding one-third of the entire coat.*

**Approved February 11, 2005**
**Effective March 30, 2005**

# BULLMASTIFF

*T*HE KNOWN HISTORY OF THE BULLMASTIFF BEGINS ABOUT THE YEAR 1860 in England. It is probable that the breed is really centuries old, but proof is scarce.

Toward the end of the nineteenth century, keeping Britain's large estates and game preserves free from the depredations of poachers was an acute problem. Penalties were severe, yet poaching seemed impossible to eradicate by mere laws. Accordingly, the gamekeeper's life was anything but safe. Poachers would often prefer to shoot it out with the keeper on the chance of escape rather than accept the penalties that they would incur upon apprehension.

It is not surprising, therefore, that the gamekeepers enlisted the aid of the greatest protector nature has given to man—the dog. These men cared nothing for the looks of a dog as long as he served them well. Numerous breeds were therefore tried. The Mastiff, courageous and powerful, was not fast enough and not sufficiently aggressive. The Bulldog—big, strong, and active in those days—was a trifle too ferocious and not large enough for their needs. These men wanted dogs that would remain silent at the approach of poachers. They needed fearless dogs that would attack on command. They wanted the poachers thrown and held, but not mauled. For these needs, they crossed Mastiff and Bulldog, and from this utilitarian birth, the Bullmastiff was founded.

Inevitably came the rivalry between keepers as to the quality of their dogs. Inevitably, also, came the breeding to and from outstanding performers of their time—a true survival of the fittest. For many years, then, after the birth of the breed, its history was wholly a utilitarian one. The only contests in which the Bullmastiffs engaged were against man, either on the moor or in demonstrations. In those days the Bullmastiff was known sometimes by his present name, but more often as the "Gamekeeper's Night-Dog."

During the breed's early years, we find interesting references by contemporary writers. From the book *Dog Breaking,* published in 1885: "Bulldogs have good noses. I have known of the cross between them and the Mastiff being taught to follow the scent of a man almost as truly as a Bloodhound." In *The Field,* August 20, 1901, we find the following:

> Mr. Burton of Thorneywood Kennels brought to the show one Night-Dog (not for competition) and offered any person one pound who could escape from it while securely muzzled. One of the spectators who had had experience with dogs volunteered and amused a large assembly of sportsmen and keepers who had gathered there. The man was given a long start and the muzzled dog slipped after him. The animal caught him immediately and knocked down this man the first spring. The latter bravely tried to hold his own, but was floored every time he got on his feet, ultimately being kept to the ground until the owner of the dog released him. The man had three rounds with the powerful canine, but was beaten each time and was unable to escape.

For this type of work, dogs of a dark brindle color were preferred owing to their lack of visibility. It was inevitable, however, that as the breed gained in popularity and true Mastiff blood was used, a large number of light fawns should appear. With the gradual disappearance of poaching and the continued demand for Bullmastiffs as guards and watchdogs, this color became popular. The black mask and densely colored ears were often inherited from the Mastiff.

Finally, owing to the increasing popularity of the breed, a number of pioneers started, on a scientific basis, to breed to type in an effort to set a goal which purebred dog breeders might seek. This type finally became sufficiently distinct for The Kennel Club (England) to grant recognition of the Bullmastiff as a purebred dog in 1924. At this time The Kennel Club differentiated between the Bullmastiff, crossbred, and the Bullmastiff, purebred, the latter being, of necessity, the descendant of three generations of dogs which were neither pure Mastiff nor pure Bulldog. Classes were then provided at a few shows and the dogs were finally awarded Challenge Certificates in 1928. In time the breed became known in many countries, exported to Siam, India, the Federated Malay States, Africa, and America. The short coat has proved convenient in warm climates, and yet the dog can live in the open in inclement weather.

The AKC granted recognition to the Bullmastiff in October 1933, and since then the breed has made numerous friends in this country.

# OFFICIAL STANDARD FOR THE BULLMASTIFF

**General Appearance**—That of a symmetrical animal, showing great strength, endurance, and alertness; powerfully built but active. The foundation breeding was 60% Mastiff and 40% Bulldog. The breed was developed in England by gamekeepers for protection against poachers.

**Size, Proportion, Substance**—*Size*—Dogs, 25 to 27 inches at the withers, and 110 to 130 pounds weight. Bitches, 24 to 26 inches at the withers, and 100 to 120 pounds weight. Other things being equal, the more substantial dog within these limits is favored. *Proportion*—The length from tip of breastbone to rear of thigh exceeds the height from withers to ground only slightly, resulting in a nearly square appearance.

**Head**—*Expression*—Keen, alert, and intelligent. *Eyes*—Dark and of medium size. *Ears*—V-shaped and carried close to the cheeks, set on wide and high, level with occiput and cheeks, giving a square appearance to the skull; darker in color than the body and medium in size. *Skull*—Large, with a fair amount of wrinkle when alert; broad, with cheeks well developed. Forehead flat. *Stop*—Moderate. *Muzzle*—Broad and deep; its length, in comparison with that of the entire head, approximately as 1 is to 3. Lack of foreface with nostrils set on top of muzzle is a reversion to the Bulldog and is very undesirable. A dark muzzle is preferable. *Nose*—Black, with nostrils large and broad. *Flews*—Not too pendulous. *Bite*—Preferably level or slightly undershot. Canine teeth large and set wide apart.

**Neck, Topline, Body**—*Neck*—Slightly arched, of moderate length, very muscular, and almost equal in circumference to the skull. *Topline*—Straight and level between withers and loin. *Body*—Compact. Chest wide and deep, with ribs well sprung and well set down between the forelegs. *Back*—Short, giving the impression of a well balanced dog. *Loin*—Wide, muscular, and slightly arched, with fair depth of flank. *Tail*—Set on high, strong at the root, and tapering to the hocks. It may be straight or curved, but never carried hound fashion.

**Forequarters**—*Shoulders*—Muscular but not loaded, and slightly sloping. *Forelegs*—Straight, well boned, and set well apart; elbows turned neither in nor out. *Pasterns* straight, feet of medium size, with round toes well arched. *Pads* thick and tough, nails black.

**Hindquarters**—Broad and muscular, with well developed second thigh denoting power, but not cumbersome. Moderate angulation at hocks. Cowhocks and splay feet are *serious* faults.

**Coat**—Short and dense, giving good weather protection.

**Color**—Red, fawn, or brindle. Except for a very small white spot on the chest, white marking is considered a fault.

**Gait**—Free, smooth, and powerful. When viewed from the side, reach and drive indicate maximum use of the dog's moderate angulation. Back remains level and firm.

Coming and going, the dog moves in a straight line. Feet tend to converge under the body, without crossing over, as speed increases. There is no twisting in or out at the joints.

**Temperament**—Fearless and confident yet docile. The dog combines the reliability, intelligence, and willingness to please required in a dependable family companion and protector.

**Approved February 8, 1992**
**Effective March 31, 1992**

# DOBERMAN PINSCHER

*W*ITH ITS ROOTS SOMEWHAT OBSCURE, THE DOBERMAN PINSCHER BECAME within a comparatively short time a dog of fixed type, whose characteristics of both body and spirit have extended its popularity in many lands. Originating in Apolda, in Thueringen, Germany, around 1890, the breed was officially recognized in 1900. It takes its name from Louis Dobermann, of Apolda.

Of medium size and clean-cut appearance, the dog at first glance does not give evidence of its great muscular power. So compact is its structure, so dense the laying on of muscle under the short coat, and so elegant and well-chiseled the outline, that the novice would probably underestimate the weight by 15 to 20 pounds. Weight is the only particular, however, in which the Doberman is deceptive. Its qualities of alertness, agility, muscularity, and temperamental fire stand patent for any eye to see. It is an honest dog, uncamouflaged by superfluous coat or the wiles of the artful conditioner. One gains at once the impression of sinewy nimbleness, of the quick coordination of the well-trained athlete.

There is also an air of nobility about the Doberman Pinscher that is part of its birthright. More than most other breeds, it gives the impression of a blue-blooded animal, or aristocrat. From the strong muzzle and wedge-shaped head to the clearly defined stifle, the outline is definite and sharply etched. The fearless and inquisitive expression of the dark eye is in harmony with the bodily characteristics. The Doberman looks upon the stranger boldly and judges him with unerring instinct.

He is ready, if need be, to give prompt alarm and to back his warning with defense of his master and his master's goods. Yet he is affectionate, obedient, and loyal.

Traditionally compounded of the old shorthaired shepherd-dog stock, with admixtures of Rottweiler, Black and Tan Terrier, and smooth-haired German Pinscher, the Doberman has been fortunate, with the aid of selective breeding, to have absorbed the good qualities of the breeds which have contributed to its heritage. It has been from the beginning a working dog devoted to the service of mankind.

The properly bred and trained Doberman has proved itself as friend and guardian. As it developed, its qualities of intelligence and ability to absorb and retain training brought it into demand as a police and war dog. In this service its agility and courage make it highly prized. An excellent nose adapted the dog to criminal trailing; it has also led to its use as a hunting dog.

In the United States the breed's popularity has been fostered by the Doberman Pinscher Club of America, which was founded in February 1921.

# OFFICIAL STANDARD FOR THE DOBERMAN PINSCHER

**General Appearance**—The appearance is that of a dog of medium size, with a body that is square. Compactly built, muscular and powerful, for great endurance and speed. Elegant in appearance, of proud carriage, reflecting great nobility and temperament. Energetic, watchful, determined, alert, fearless, loyal and obedient.

**Size, Proportion, Substance**—*Height* at the withers: *Dogs* 26 to 28 inches, ideal about 27½ inches; *Bitches* 24 to 26 inches, ideal about 25½ inches. The height, measured vertically from the ground to the highest point of the withers, equaling the length measured horizontally from the forechest to the rear projection of the upper thigh. Length of head, neck and legs in proportion to length and depth of body.

**Head**—Long and dry, resembling a blunt wedge in both frontal and profile views. When seen from the front, the head widens gradually toward the base of the ears in a practically unbroken line. *Eyes* almond shaped, moderately deep-set, with vigorous, energetic expression. Iris, of uniform color, ranging from medium to darkest brown in black dogs; in reds, blues, and fawns the color of the iris blends with that of the markings, the darkest shade being preferable in every case. *Ears* normally cropped and carried erect. The upper attachment of the ear, when held erect, is on a level with the top of the skull.

Top of skull flat, turning with slight stop to bridge of muzzle, with muzzle line extending parallel to topline of skull. Cheeks flat and muscular. *Nose* solid black on black dogs, dark brown on red ones, dark gray on blue ones, dark tan on fawns. Lips lying close to jaws. Jaws full and powerful, well filled under the eyes.

*Teeth* strongly developed and white. Lower incisors upright and touching inside of upper incisors—a true scissors bite. 42 correctly placed teeth, 22 in the lower, 20 in the upper jaw. Distemper teeth shall not be penalized. *Disqualifying Faults:* Overshot more than ³⁄₁₆ of an inch. Undershot more than ⅛ of an inch. Four or more missing teeth.

**Neck, Topline, Body**—*Neck*—proudly carried, well muscled and dry. Well arched, with nape of neck widening gradually toward body. Length of neck proportioned to body and head. *Withers* pronounced and forming the highest point of the body. Back short, firm, of sufficient width, and muscular at the loins, extending in a straight line from withers to the slightly rounded croup.

*Chest* broad with forechest well defined. *Ribs* well sprung from the spine, but flattened in lower end to permit elbow clearance. *Brisket* reaching deep to the elbow. *Belly* well tucked-up, extending in a curved line from the brisket. *Loins* wide and muscled. *Hips* broad and in proportion to body, breadth of hips being approximately equal to breadth of body at rib cage and shoulders. *Tail* docked at approximately second joint, appears to be a continuation of the spine, and is carried only slightly above the horizontal when the dog is alert.

**Forequarters**—*Shoulder Blade*—sloping forward and downward at a 45-degree angle to the ground meets the upper arm at an angle of 90 degrees. Length of shoulder blade and upper arm are equal. Height from elbow to withers approximately equals height from ground to elbow. *Legs* seen from front and side, perfectly straight and parallel to each other from elbow to pastern; muscled and sinewy, with heavy bone. In normal pose and when gaiting, the elbows lie close to the brisket. *Pasterns* firm and almost perpendicular to the ground. Dewclaws may be removed. *Feet* well arched, compact, and catlike, turning neither in nor out.

**Hindquarters**—The angulation of the hindquarters balances that of the forequarters. *Hip Bone* falls away from spinal column at an angle of about 30 degrees, producing a slightly rounded, well filled-out croup. *Upper Shanks* at right angles to the hip bones, are long, wide, and well muscled on both sides of thigh, with clearly defined stifles. Upper and lower shanks are of equal length. While the dog is at rest, hock to heel is perpendicular to the ground. Viewed from the rear, the legs are straight, parallel to each other, and wide enough apart to fit in with a properly built body. Dewclaws, if any, are generally removed. *Cat feet* as on front legs, turning neither in nor out.

**Coat**—Smooth-haired, short, hard, thick and close lying. Invisible gray undercoat on neck permissible.

**Color and Markings**—*Allowed Colors:* Black, red, blue, and fawn (Isabella). *Markings:* Rust, sharply defined, appearing above each eye and on muzzle, throat and forechest, on all legs and feet, and below tail. White patch on chest, not exceeding ½ inch square, permissible. *Disqualifying Fault:* Dogs not of an allowed color.

**Gait**—Free, balanced and vigorous, with good reach in the forequarters and good driving power in the hindquarters. When trotting, there is strong rear-action drive. Each rear leg moves in line with the foreleg on the same side. Rear and front legs are thrown neither in nor out. Back remains strong and firm. When moving at a fast trot, a properly built dog will single-track.

**Temperament**—Energetic, watchful, determined, alert, fearless, loyal and obedient. *The judge shall dismiss from the ring any shy or vicious Doberman.*

*Shyness:* A dog shall be judged fundamentally shy if, refusing to stand for examination, it shrinks away from the judge; if it fears an approach from the rear; if it shies at sudden and unusual noises to a marked degree.

*Viciousness:* A dog that attacks or attempts to attack either the judge or its handler, is definitely vicious. An aggressive or belligerent attitude toward other dogs shall not be deemed viciousness.

## FAULTS

*The foregoing description is that of the ideal Doberman Pinscher. Any deviation from the above described dog must be penalized to the extent of the deviation.*

## DISQUALIFICATIONS

*Overshot more than ³⁄₁₆ of an inch, undershot more than ⅛ of an inch. Four or more missing teeth.*
*Dogs not of an allowed color.*

**Approved February 6, 1982**
**Reformatted November 6, 1990**

# GERMAN PINSCHER

*T*HE GERMAN PINSCHER—A MEDIUM-SIZED, SHORT-COATED, MUSCULAR, and powerful working dog—originated in Germany and was officially recognized as a distinct breed in 1895. The first breed standard was written in 1884 and revised in 1895. At that time, coat colors were quite varied. Today, acceptable colors are shades of red, black with red markings, blue with tan markings, and fawn.

The German Pinscher was one of the foundation breeds in the development of the Doberman Pinscher and Miniature Pinscher breeds in Germany during the late 1800s. Both German Pinschers and Standard Schnauzers, which were also being bred for coat type at that time, are descendants of the Rat Catcher, Great Rattler, or Rat Pinscher, which became extinct in the 1800s.

The German Pinscher is a dog selectively bred to be territorial and protective, and to seek out and kill vermin. This is a working breed and, as with many members of this group, they work independently of man.

The breed came close to extinction following both world wars. Only one litter was whelped in West Germany in 1949, and no litters were born for nine years thereafter. Werner Jung saved the breed in West Germany in 1958 with a dedicated breeding program.

The German Pinscher excels as a home guardian. He generally accepts friends of the family but is wary of strangers and warns them with a strong voice. As for the intruder or attacker: Beware!

The German Pinscher insists on being part of the family and its activities, and does not do well as an outside dog. He is a wonderful companion because of his devotion to his human family. But children must be taught to respect these independent-thinking dogs, and adults should supervise interactions between them. The German Pinscher is a high-energy dog who loves to play, and he requires a lot of exercise. A fenced yard is necessary for an unsupervised dog.

From its strong terrier background, the German Pinscher is strong willed, determined, manipulative, and assertive, and can be possessive of his owner. Willing learners and highly intelligent, German Pinschers make wonderful companions with firm but gentle and consistent discipline. Early and frequent socialization that includes obedience training is strongly encouraged. They are long-lived and keep their puppy playfulness well into adulthood. German Pinschers love to travel and enjoy adventure in any form. Their elegant looks can be maintained with minimal grooming.

The German Pinscher was admitted to the AKC Working Group in 2001.

# OFFICIAL STANDARD FOR THE GERMAN PINSCHER

**General Appearance**—The German Pinscher is a medium size, short coated dog, elegant in appearance with a strong square build and moderate body structure, muscular and powerful for endurance and agility. Energetic, watchful, alert, agile, fearless, determined, intelligent and loyal, the German Pinscher has the prerequisites to be an excellent watchdog and companion. The German Pinscher is examined on the ground.

**Size, Proportion, Substance**—*Size*—the ideal height at the highest point of the withers for a dog or bitch is 17–20 inches. Size should be penalized in accordance with the degree it deviates from the ideal. Quality should always take precedence over size. *Faults*—under 17 inches or over 20 inches. *Proportion*—squarely built in proportion of body length to height. The height at the highest point of the withers equals the length of the body from the prosternum to the rump. *Substance*—muscular with moderate bone.

**Head and Skull**—Powerful, elongated without the occiput being too pronounced and resembles a blunt wedge in both frontal and profile views. The total length of the head from the tip of the nose to the occiput is one half the length from the withers to the base of the tail resulting in a ratio of approximately 1:2. *Expression*—sharp, alert and responsive. *Eyes*—medium size, dark, oval in shape without the appearance of bulging. The eyelid should be tight and the eyeball non-protruding. *Ears*—set high, symmetrical, and carried erect when cropped. If uncropped, they are V-shaped with a folding pleat, or small standing ears carried evenly upright. *Skull*—flat, unwrinkled from occiput to stop when in repose. The stop is slight but distinct. *Muzzle*—parallel and equal in length to the topskull and ends in a blunt wedge. The *cheeks* are muscled and flat. *Nose*—full, and black. *Lips*—black, close fitting. *Bite*—strong, scissors bite with complete dentition and white teeth.

**Neck, Topline, Body**—*Neck*—elegant and strong, of moderate thickness and length, nape elegantly arched. The skin is tight, closely fitting to the dry throat without wrinkles, sagging, or dewlaps. *Topline*—the withers form the highest point of the topline, which slopes slightly toward the rear, extending in a straight line from behind the withers, through the well-muscled loin to the faintly curved croup. *Back*—short, firm, and level, muscular at the loins. *Faults*—long back, not giving the appearance of squarely built, roach back, sway back. *Body*—compact and strong, so as to permit greater flexibility and agility, with the length of leg being equal to the depth of body. *Loin*—is well-muscled. The distance from the last rib to the hip is short. *Chest*—moderately wide with well-sprung ribs, and when viewed from the front, appears to be oval. The forechest is distinctly marked by the prosternum. The brisket descends to the elbows and ascends gradually to the rear with the belly moderately drawn up. *Fault*—excessive tuck up. *Tail*—moderately set and carried above the horizontal. Customarily docked between the second and third joints.

**Forequarters**—The sloping shoulder blades are strongly muscled, yet flat and well laid back, forming an angle of approximately 45 degrees to the horizontal. They are well angled and slope forward, forming an approximately 90 degree angle to the upper arm, which is equal in length to the shoulder blade. Such angulation permits the maximum forward extension of the forelegs without binding or effort. *Forelegs*—straight and well boned, perfectly vertical when viewed from all sides, set moderately apart with elbows set close to the body. Dewclaws on the forelegs may be removed. *Pasterns*—firm and almost perpendicular to the ground. *Feet*—short, round, compact with firm dark pads and dark nails. The toes **are** well closed and arched like cat feet.

**Hindquarters**—The thighs are strongly muscled and in balance with forequarters. The stifles are well bent and well boned, with good angulation. When viewed from the rear, the hocks are parallel to each other.

**Coat**—Short and dense, smooth and close lying. Shiny and covers the body without bald spots. A hard coat should not be penalized.

**Color**—Isabella (fawn), to red in various shades to stag red (red with intermingling of black hairs), black and blues with red/tan markings. In the reds, a rich vibrant medium to dark shade is preferred. In bi-colored dogs, sharply marked dark and rich red/tan markings are desirable. Markings distributed as follows: at cheeks, lips, lower jaw, above eyes, at throat, on forechest as two triangles distinctly separated from each other, at metatarsus or pasterns, forelegs, feet, inner side of hind legs and below tail. Pencil marks on the toes are acceptable. Any white markings on the dog are undesirable. A few white hairs do not constitute a marking. **Disqualification:** *Dogs not of an allowable color.*

**Gait**—The ground covering trot is relaxed, well balanced, powerful and uninhibited with good length of stride, strong drive and free front extension. At the trot the back remains firm and level, without swaying, rolling or roaching. When viewed from the front and rear, the feet must not cross or strike each other. *Fault*—hackney gait.

**Temperament**—The German Pinscher has highly developed senses, intelligence, aptitude for training, fearlessness, and endurance. He is alert, vigilant, deliberate and watchful of strangers. He has fearless courage and tenacity if threatened. A very vivacious dog but not an excessive barker. He should not show viciousness by unwarranted or unprovoked attacks.

★*Note*—Great consideration should be given to a dog giving the desired alert, highly intelligent, vivacious character of the German Pinscher. Aggressive behavior towards another dog is not deemed viciousness. *Fault*—shy.

The foregoing description is that of the ideal German Pinscher. Any deviation from this is to be penalized to the extent of the deviation.

## DISQUALIFICATION

*Dogs not of an allowable color.*

**Approved November 7, 2005**
**Effective January 1, 2006**

# GIANT SCHNAUZER

$\mathcal{F}$EW NATIONS HAVE BEEN MORE PROLIFIC IN THEIR DEVELOPMENT OF NEW breeds of dog than the Germanic peoples. Not only have they evinced rare patience in tracing ancestries, but they have proven their ability to fix type. One of the most notable examples of their breeding skill is the Schnauzer, for here is a dog not only brought to splendid physical conformation and keen mental development, but reproduced in three distinct sizes. The one under consideration here is the *Riesenschnauzer*—the Giant.

It is important to realize that the Miniature, the Standard, and the Giant Schnauzers are three separate and distinct breeds. Schnauzer breeding has been remarkable in that it has produced, from various sources that intermingled only in rare instances, if at all, three breeds which have developed toward one comparable standard of perfection.

Of the three, the dog now known in America as the Standard Schnauzer, which is the medium-sized specimen, is without doubt the oldest. He is the one apparently portrayed in paintings by Dürer, dating from 1492, and he is also the one of the *Nachtwächter-Brunnen,* the statue of a night watchman and his dog erected in a square in Stuttgart, Württemberg, in 1620. These instances are important only as they indicate the antiquity of the type of dog perfected at those dates and still retained today.

In unearthing the history of this breed it must be remembered that occupations of men had a great deal to do with all development in dogs. There were no dog shows in those days, and when a new breed was produced, it was aimed at a specific work. Also, its characteristics were governed to large extent by weather and living conditions.

All Schnauzers had their origin in the neighboring kingdoms of Württemberg and Bavaria. These are agricultural sections where the raising of sheep, cattle, and other livestock has been a major occupation for years. Since railroads were not known, sheep and cattle had to be driven to market, which meant that dogs were necessary to help the shepherds.

There is little doubt that when Bavarian cattlemen went to Stuttgart they came across the medium-sized Schnauzer. Here was a dog to catch anyone's attention, for even then it was sound, while it showed power throughout its trim lines. The Bavarians liked the dog, but they were not satisfied with its size. The sheepmen could use this size of dog, but the drovers needed a larger specimen for cattle.

The first attempts to produce a drover's dog on terrier lines, with a wiry coat, were no doubt by crossings between the medium-sized Schnauzer and some of the smooth-coated driving and dairymen's dogs then in existence. Later there were crossings with the rough-haired sheepdogs, and much later, with the black Great Dane. There is also reason to believe that the Giant Schnauzer is closely related to the Bouvier des Flandres, which was the driving dog of Flanders.

For many years the Giant Schnauzer was called the Münchener, and it was widely known as a great cattle and driving dog. Von Stephanitz places its origin as Swabia—in the south of Bavaria, and it was found in a state of perfection in the region between Munich and Augsburg.

The Giant Schnauzer was practically unknown outside of Bavaria until nearly the end of the first decade of this century. Cattle-driving was then a thing of the past, but the breed was still found in the hands of butchers, at stockyards, and at breweries. The breweries maintained the dogs as guards, at which duty they were preeminently successful.

Not until just before World War I did the Giant Schnauzer begin to come to nationwide attention in Germany as a suitable subject to receive police training at the schools in Berlin and other principal cities. He proved such an intelligent pupil that police work has been his main occupation since that time. His progress in this capacity in the United States has been very slow. Making his appearance here at the time when the German Shepherd was reaching its peak, the Bavarian dog had little chance to make headway against such well-established, direct competition.

# OFFICIAL STANDARD FOR THE GIANT SCHNAUZER

**General Description**—The Giant Schnauzer should resemble, as nearly as possible, in general appearance, a larger and more powerful version of the Standard Schnauzer, on the whole a bold and valiant figure of a dog. Robust, strongly built, nearly square in proportion of body length to height at withers, active, sturdy, and well muscled. Temperament which combines spirit and alertness with intelligence and reliability. Composed, watchful, courageous, easily trained, deeply loyal to family, playful, amiable in repose, and a commanding figure when aroused. The sound, reliable temperament, rugged build, and dense weather-resistant wiry coat make for one of the most useful, powerful, and enduring working breeds.

**Head**—Strong, rectangular in appearance, and elongated; narrowing slightly from the ears to the eyes, and again from the eyes to the tip of the nose. The total length of the head is about one-half the length of the back (withers to set-on of tail). The head matches the sex and substance of the dog. The top line of the muzzle is parallel to the top line of the skull; there is a slight stop which is accentuated by the eyebrows. *Skull*—(Occiput to Stop). Moderately broad between the ears: occiput not too prominent. Top of skull flat; skin unwrinkled. *Cheeks*—Flat, but with well-developed chewing muscles; there is no "cheekiness" to disturb the rectangular head appearance (with beard). *Muzzle*—Strong and well filled under the eyes; both parallel and equal in length to the topskull; ending in a moderately blunt wedge. The nose is large, black, and full. The lips are tight, and not overlapping, black in color. *Bite*—A full complement of sound white teeth (6/6 incisors, 2/2 canines, 8/8 premolars, 4/6 molars) with a scissors bite. The upper and lower jaws are powerful and well formed. *Disqualifying Faults*—Overshot or undershot. *Ears*—When cropped, identical in shape and length with pointed tips. They are in balance with the head and are not exaggerated in length. They are set high on the skull and carried perpendicularly at the inner edges with as little bell as possible along the other edges. When uncropped, the ears are V-shaped button ears of medium length and thickness, set high and carried rather high and close to the head. *Eyes*—Medium size, dark brown, and deep-set. They are oval in appearance and keen in expression with lids fitting tightly. Vision is not impaired nor eyes hidden by too long eyebrows. *Neck*—Strong and well arched, of moderate length, blending cleanly into the shoulders, and with the skin fitting tightly at the throat; in harmony with the dog's weight and build.

**Body**—Compact, substantial, short-coupled and strong, with great power and agility. The height at the highest point of the withers equals the body length from breastbone to point of rump. The loin section is well developed, as short as possible for compact build.

**Forequarters**—The forequarters have flat, somewhat sloping shoulders and high withers. Forelegs are straight and vertical when viewed from all sides with strong pasterns and good bone. They are separated by a fairly deep brisket which precludes a pinched front. The elbows are set close to the body and point directly backwards. *Chest*—Medium in width, ribs well sprung but with no tendency toward a barrel chest; oval in cross section; deep through the brisket. The breastbone is plainly discernible, with strong forechest; the brisket descends at least to the elbows, and ascends gradually toward the rear with the belly moderately drawn up. The ribs spread gradually from the first rib so as to allow space for the elbows to move close to the body. *Shoulders*—The sloping shoulder blades (scapulae) are strongly muscled, yet flat. They are well laid back so that from the side the rounded upper ends are in a nearly vertical line above the elbows. They slope well forward to the point where they join the upper arm (humerus), forming as nearly as possible a right angle. Such an angulation permits the maximum forward extension of the forelegs without binding or effort. Both shoulder blades and upper arm are long, permitting depth of chest at the brisket.

**Back**—Short, straight, strong and firm.

**Tail**—The tail is set moderately high and carried high in excitement. It should be docked to the second or not more than the third joint (approximately one and one-half to about three inches long at maturity).

**Hindquarters**—The hindquarters are strongly muscled, in balance with the forequarters; upper thighs are slanting and well bent at the stifles, with the second thighs (tibiae) approximately parallel to an extension of the upper neckline. The legs from the hock joint to the feet are short, perpendicular to the ground while the dog is standing naturally, and from the rear parallel to each other. The hindquarters do not appear over-built or higher than the shoulders. Croup full and slightly rounded. *Feet*—Well-arched, compact and catlike, turning neither in nor out, with thick tough pads and dark nails. *Dewclaws*—Dewclaws, if any, on hind legs should be removed; on the forelegs, may be removed.

**Gait**—The trot is the gait at which movement is judged. Free, balanced and vigorous, with good reach in the forequarters and good driving power in the hindquarters. Rear and front legs are thrown neither in nor out. When moving at a fast trot, a properly built dog will single-track. Back remains strong, firm, and flat.

**Coat**—Hard, wiry, very dense; composed of a soft undercoat and a harsh outer coat which, when seen against the grain, stands slightly up off the back, lying neither smooth nor flat. Coarse hair on top of head; harsh beard and eyebrows, the Schnauzer hallmark.

**Color**—Solid black or pepper and salt. *Black*—A truly pure black. A small white spot on the breast is permitted; any other markings are *disqualifying faults. Pepper and Salt*—Outer coat of a combination of banded hairs (white with black and black with white) and some black and white hairs, appearing gray from a short distance. *Ideally;* an intensely pigmented medium gray shade with "peppering" evenly distributed throughout the coat, and a gray undercoat. *Acceptable;* all shades of pepper and salt from dark iron-gray to silver-gray. Every shade of coat has a dark facial mask to emphasize the expression; the color of the mask harmonizes with the shade of the body coat. Eyebrows, whiskers, cheeks, throat, chest, legs, and under tail are lighter in color but include "peppering." Markings are disqualifying faults.

**Height**—The height at the withers of the male is 25½ to 27½ inches, and of the female, 23½ to 25½ inches, with the mediums being desired. Size alone should never take precedence over type, balance, soundness, and temperament. It should be noted that too small dogs generally lack the power and too large dogs, the agility and maneuverability, desired in the working dog.

## FAULTS

The foregoing description is that of the ideal Giant Schnauzer. Any deviation from the above described dog must be penalized to the extent of the deviation.

*The judge shall dismiss from the ring any shy or vicious Giant Schnauzer.*

*Shyness*—A dog shall be judged fundamentally shy if, refusing to stand for examination, it repeatedly shrinks away from the judge; if it fears unduly any approach from the rear; if it shies to a marked degree at sudden and unusual noises.

*Viciousness*—A dog that attacks or attempts to attack either the judge or its handler, is definitely vicious. An aggressive or belligerent attitude toward other dogs shall not be deemed viciousness.

## DISQUALIFICATIONS

*Overshot or undershot.*
*Markings other than specified.*

**Approved October 11, 1983**

# GREAT DANE

*J*N APPEARANCE AND NATURE THE GREAT DANE IS ONE OF THE MOST ELEGANT
and distinguished varieties of giant-type dog.

The name of the breed is a translation of an old French designation, *grand Danois,* meaning "big Danish." This was only one of half a dozen names which had been used for centuries in France. Why the English adopted the name Great Dane from the French is a mystery. At the same time, the French were also calling it *dogue allemand* or "German mastiff." *Mastiff* in English, *dogge* in the Germanic, *dogue* or *dogo* in the Latin languages, all meant the same thing: a giant dog with heavy head for fighting or hunting purposes. It was one of the dozen varieties of dog recognized as distinctive enough at that time to have a name of its own.

There is no known reason for connecting Denmark with either the origin or the development of the breed. It was "made in Germany," and it was German fanciers who led the world in breeding most of the finest specimens.

If the reader is susceptible to the charms of antiquity, he will be interested in Cassel's claim that on Egyptian monuments of about 3000 B.C. there are drawings of dogs much like the Great Dane. Also, the earliest written description of a dog resembling the breed may be found in Chinese literature of 1121 B.C., according to an article by Dr. G. Ciaburri in a Great Dane Club of Italy publication of 1929.

Eminent zoologists believe that the mastiff breeds originated in Asia. They think the modern Tibetan Mastiff, occasionally shown in England, is the most direct descendant of the prototype.

The great naturalist Georges Buffon (1707–88) claimed the Irish Wolfhound as the principal ancestor of our Great Dane. The comparative anatomist Georges Cuvier (1769–1832) found more evidence in favor of the old English Mastiff as the root from which it sprang. Both Irish and English breeds are known to have been carefully bred for 1,300 years and more. Today, most students favor the idea that the Great Dane, or Deutsche dogge, resulted from a mixture of both these ancient types.

This is not to say that the German Mastiff or Great Dane is a new breed. It is, indeed, a very old one that has been cultivated as a distinct type for probably 400 years, if not longer. Like all old varieties of dog, it was developed for a useful purpose. The Germans used the Great Dane as a boar hound. Europe's erstwhile boar was one of the most savage, swift, powerful, and well armed of all big game on the Continent. To tackle the wild boar required a superdog, and that is precisely what the Germans developed. Breed fanciers speak of him as the king of dogs.

In common with all other breeds, the Great Dane's history of and development to a modern standard type began in the latter nineteenth century. In 1880 at Berlin, a Dr. Bodinus called a meeting of Great Dane judges who declared that the breed should be known as Deutsche dogge and that all other designations, especially the term Great Dane, should be abolished thereafter. So far as the German people are concerned this declaration has been observed, but English-speaking people have paid no heed. The Italians, who have a large Great Dane fancy, have also failed to give Germany credit for the name selected: *Alano.* This word means "a mastiff," consequently the name of their organization translates to "Mastiff Club of Italy." This, however, has not prevented close cooperation between fanciers of the two countries. The leading Italian breeders have based their operation on nothing but German imported stock or its descendants.

In 1891, the Great Dane Club of Germany adopted a precise standard, or official description of the ideal specimen. In 1885, there was a Great Dane Club in England, and in 1889, at Chicago, the German Mastiff or Great Dane Club of America was founded, with Gustav Muss-Arnolt as first delegate. Two years later, the club reorganized as the Great Dane Club of America. At that time, its membership was mostly of Eastern fanciers.

The Great Dane has developed steadily in popularity all over the world. Breeders have kept before them the image of the boar hound and the special qualities it called for. A merely "pretty" dog has not been enough. He must have size and weight, nobility and courage, speed and endurance. What more can one ask for in a dog?

# OFFICIAL STANDARD FOR THE GREAT DANE

**General Appearance**—The Great Dane combines, in its regal appearance, dignity, strength and elegance with great size and a powerful, well-formed, smoothly muscled body. It is one of the giant working breeds, but is unique in that its general conformation must be so well balanced that it never appears clumsy, and shall move with a long reach and powerful drive. It is always a unit—the Apollo of dogs. A Great Dane must be spirited, courageous, never timid; always friendly and dependable. This physical and mental combination is the characteristic which gives the Great Dane the majesty possessed by no other breed. It is particularly true of this breed that there is an impression of great masculinity in dogs, as compared to an impression of femininity in bitches. Lack of true Dane breed type, as defined in this standard, is a serious fault.

**Size, Proportion, Substance**—The male should appear more massive throughout than the bitch, with larger frame and heavier bone. In the ratio between length and height, the Great Dane should be square. In bitches, a somewhat longer body is permissible, providing she is well proportioned to her height. Coarseness or lack of substance are equally undesirable. The male shall not be less than 30 inches at the shoulders, but it is preferable that he be 32 inches or more, providing he is well proportioned to his height. The female shall not be less than 28 inches at the shoulders, but it is preferable that she be 30 inches or more, providing she is well proportioned to her height. Danes under minimum height must be disqualified.

**Head**—The head shall be rectangular, long, distinguished, expressive, finely chiseled, especially below the eyes. Seen from the side, the Dane's forehead must be sharply set off from the bridge of the nose (a strongly pronounced stop). The plane of the skull and the plane of the muzzle must be straight and parallel to one another. The skull plane under and to the inner point of the eye must slope without any bony protuberance in a smooth line to a full square jaw with a deep muzzle (fluttering lips are undesirable). The masculinity of the male is very pronounced in structural appearance of the head. The bitch's head is more delicately formed. Seen from the top, the skull should have parallel sides and the bridge of the nose should be as broad as possible. The cheek muscles should not be prominent. The length from the tip of the nose to the center of the stop should be equal to the length from the center of the stop to the rear of the slightly developed occiput. The head should be angular from all sides and should have flat planes with dimensions in proportion to the size of the Dane. Whiskers may be trimmed or left natural. *Eyes* shall be medium size, deep set, and dark, with a lively intelligent expression. The eyelids are almond-shaped and relatively tight, with well developed brows. Haws and mongolian eyes are serious faults. In harlequins, the eyes should be dark; light colored eyes, eyes of different colors and walleyes are permitted but not desirable. *Ears* shall be high set, medium in size and of moderate thickness, folded forward close to the cheek. The top line of the folded ear should be level with the skull. If cropped, the ear length is in proportion to the size of the head and the ears are carried uniformly erect. *Nose* shall be black, except in the blue Dane, where it is a dark blue-black. A black spotted nose is permitted on the harlequin; a pink colored nose is not desirable. A split nose is a disqualification. **Teeth** shall be strong, well developed, clean and with full dentition. The incisors of the lower jaw touch very lightly the bottoms of the inner surface of the upper incisors (scissors bite). An undershot jaw is a very *serious fault.* Overshot or wry bites are serious faults. Even bites, misaligned or crowded incisors are minor faults.

**Neck, Topline, Body**—The neck shall be firm, high set, well arched, long and muscular. From the nape, it should gradually broaden and flow smoothly into the withers. The neck underline should be clean. Withers shall slope smoothly into a short level back with a broad loin. The chest shall be broad, deep and well muscled. The forechest should be well developed without a pronounced sternum. The brisket extends to the elbow, with well sprung ribs. The body underline should be tightly muscled with a well-defined tuck-up.

The croup should be broad and very slightly sloping. The tail should be set high and smoothly into the croup, but not quite level with the back, a continuation of the spine. The tail should be broad at the base, tapering uniformly down to the hock joint. At rest, the tail should fall straight. When excited or running, it may curve slightly, but never above the level of the back. A ring or hooked tail is a serious fault. A docked tail is a disqualification.

**Forequarters**—The forequarters, viewed from the side, shall be strong and muscular. The shoulder blade must be strong and sloping, forming, as near as possible, a right angle in its articulation with the upper arm. A line from the upper tip of the shoulder to the back of the elbow joint should be perpendicular. The ligaments and muscles holding the shoulder blade to the rib cage must be well developed, firm and securely attached to prevent loose shoulders. The shoulder blade and the upper arm should be the same length. The elbow should be one-half the distance from the withers to the ground. The strong pasterns should slope slightly. The feet should be round and compact with well-arched toes, neither toeing in, toeing out, nor rolling to the inside or outside. The nails should be short, strong and as dark as possible, except that they may be lighter in harlequins. Dewclaws may or may not be removed.

**Hindquarters**—The hindquarters shall be strong, broad, muscular and well angulated, with well let down hocks. Seen from the rear, the hock joints appear to be perfectly straight, turned neither toward the inside nor toward the outside. The rear feet should be round and compact, with well-arched toes, neither toeing in nor out. The nails should be short, strong and as dark as possible, except they may be lighter in harlequins. Wolf claws are a serious fault.

**Coat**—The coat shall be short, thick and clean with a smooth glossy appearance.

**Color, Markings and Patterns**—*Brindle*—The base color shall be yellow gold and always brindled with strong black cross stripes in a chevron pattern. A black mask is preferred. Black should appear on the eye rims and eyebrows, and may appear on the ears and tail tip. The more intensive the base color and the more distinct and even the brindling, the more preferred will be the color. Too much or too little brindling are equally undesirable. White markings at the chest and toes, black-fronted, dirty colored brindles are not desirable.

*Fawn*—The color shall be yellow gold with a black mask. Black should appear on the eye rims and eyebrows, and may appear on the ears and tail tip. The deep yellow gold must always be given the preference. White markings at the chest and toes, black-fronted dirty colored fawns are not desirable.

*Blue*—The color shall be a pure steel blue. White markings at the chest and toes are not desirable.

*Black*—The color shall be a glossy black. White markings at the chest and toes are not desirable.

*Harlequin*—Base color shall be pure white with black torn patches irregularly and well distributed over the entire body; a pure white neck is preferred. The black patches should never be large enough to give the appearance of a blanket, nor so small as to give a stippled or dappled effect. Eligible, but less desirable, are a few small gray patches, or a white base with single black hairs showing through, which tend to give a salt and pepper or dirty effect.

*Mantle*—The color shall be black and white with a solid black blanket extending over the body; black skull with white muzzle; white blaze is optional; whole white collar is preferred; a white chest; white on part or whole of forelegs and hind legs; white tipped black tail. A small white marking in the blanket is acceptable, as is a break in the white collar.

**Any variance in color or markings as described above shall be faulted to the extent of the deviation. Any Great Dane which does not fall within the above color classifications must be disqualified.**

**Gait**—The gait denotes strength and power with long, easy strides resulting in no tossing, rolling or bouncing of the topline or body. The backline shall appear level and parallel to the ground. The long reach should strike the ground below the nose while the head is carried forward. The powerful rear drive should be balanced to the reach. As speed increases, there is a natural tendency for the legs to converge toward the center-line of balance beneath the body. There should be no twisting in or out at the elbow or hock joints.

**Temperament**—The Great Dane must be spirited, courageous, always friendly and dependable, and never timid or aggressive.


## DISQUALIFICATIONS

*Danes under minimum height.*
*Split nose. Docked tail.*
*Any color other than those described under "Color, Markings and Patterns."*

**Approved March 8, 1999**
**Effective April 28, 1999**

# GREAT PYRENEES

*P*ERHAPS NO OTHER BREED CAN BOAST SUCH A COLORFUL HISTORY OF association with, and service to, mankind through as many centuries as can the Great Pyrenees, Le Grande Chien des Montagnes, Le Chien des Pyrenees, or, as he is known in England and on the Continent, the Pyrenean Mountain Dog, the dog of French royalty and nobility and working associate of the peasant shepherds high on the slopes of the Pyrenees Mountains. His remains are found in the fossil deposits of the Bronze Age, which roughly dates his appearance in Europe between 1800 and 1000 B.C., although it is believed that he came originally from Central Asia or Siberia and followed the Aryan migration into Europe. It is also generally accepted that he is a descendant of the mastiff type whose remains are found in the kitchen-middens of the Baltic and North Sea coasts in the oldest strata containing evidence of the domestic dog, and which appear in Babylonian art about the close of the third millennium B.C. in the size and general appearance resembling the Great Pyrenees.

Once in Europe, the Great Dog of the Mountains developed under climatic conditions similar to those of his habitat and there remained isolated in the high mountainous areas until medieval times, when we find him gracing bas reliefs at Carcassone, bearing the royal arms of France, approximately some five hundred years before his adoption as the court dog in the seventeenth century. As early as 1407, the historian Bourdet describes the regular guard of Pyrenees dogs owned by the Château of Lourdes. These dogs were given a special place in the sentry boxes along with the armed guards; they also accompanied the jailers on their daily rounds. Their use for these purposes became very general and each large château boasted its band of Great Pyrenees. It was not until the young Dauphin, accompanied by Mme. de Maintenon in 1675 on a visit to Barreges, fell in love with a beautiful *patou* (a generic name for the breed, meaning "shepherd") and insisted on taking it back to the Louvre with him, and not until the Marquis de Louvois also succumbed to their charm, that the dog of the Pyrenees shepherd became the companion and pet of nobility. Once accepted at court, every noble wanted one, and the breed gained prominence.

It was, however, in the isolation of the lonely mountain pastures that the Pyrenean Mountain Dog developed his inherent traits of devotion, fidelity, sense of guardianship, and intelligent understanding of mankind. Here, in the days when packs of wild animals roamed the mountain slopes freely, he was the official guardian of the flocks. Having a precocious sense of smell and keen sight, he was an invaluable companion of the shepherd, his worth being counted equal to that of two men. Armed by nature with a long, heavy coat that rendered him invulnerable against attack except for the point of the chin and the base of the brain, and armed by his masters with a broad iron collar from which protruded spikes an inch and a half long, the Pyrenees dog was an almost unbeatable foe which won such glory and fame as a vanquisher of wolves and bears that he became known as the Pyrenean Wolf Dog and the Pyrenean Bearhound.

By disposition and profession, no better dog could have been chosen to assume the role of protector and friend of the early settlements of the Biscay fisherfolk on Newfoundland Island. By 1662, when their first permanent colony at Rougnoust was made, it was the Great Pyrenees dog which had become the companion of the people. Here he was crossed with the black English Retriever, brought over by the English settlers, and from this cross resulted the Newfoundland. The old Landseer type, with its black-and-white coat, showed the cross far more markedly because of his coloring than the black Newfoundland, although the resemblance in general type is quite noticeable in both.

For a while, with the diminution of the wild beasts in the Pyrenees, the breed seemed destined to extinction. Moreover, it was eagerly sought after by the breeders of continental Europe and great numbers were exported from France. But thanks to the efforts of some gentlemen sportsmen, as well as to the fact that dogs were of use about the peasants' farms in winter (when their services were not required on the mountain slopes), they were bred in increasing numbers. Today, the breed is well established in its habitat once again. The dogs are not infrequently referred to as "mat dogs" because of their habit of lying outside the cottage doors when not busying themselves with menial chores such as pulling carts.

The Great Pyrenees has come into general prominence only since its recognition by the AKC in February 1933. It seems hard to realize that the first pair were brought over by General Lafayette for his friend, J. S. Skinner, in 1824, being "recommended by him from personal experience as of inestimable value to woolgrowers in all regions exposed to the depredations of wolves and sheepkilling dogs." Thus writes Mr. Skinner in his book *The Dog and the Sportsman*. Following this a few scattered specimens were imported, but not until 1933 was the actual breeding of the dogs launched in America. Today, he ranks in the top half of the AKC annual breed registrations.

The nearer his appearance approaches that of the brown bear, except for the color and the drooping ears, the closer he is to the perfect type. Certainly, no more picturesque animal could be found; he has been aptly called an "animated snowdrift of the Pyrenees Mountains." Preeminently a watchdog and companion, the Great Pyrenees holds promise also as a dog suited for the sportsman. His love of pulling carts makes him amenable to sled work in winter, and his instinct for feeling out soft places in the snow makes him ideal for pack and guide work on ski trips. He was used during World War I for pack service and for many years for running contraband goods over the Franco-Spanish border by similar methods. Taking dangerous byways impossible for man to travel, he ran the circuit regularly, successfully avoiding the customs officials. His beauty also recommends him for use in the film industry, especially as he has been used with success for this purpose in France.

# OFFICIAL STANDARD FOR THE GREAT PYRENEES

**General Appearance**—The Great Pyrenees dog conveys the distinct impression of elegance and unsurpassed beauty combined with great overall size and majesty. He has a white or principally white coat that may contain markings of badger, gray, or varying shades of tan. He possesses a keen intelligence and a kindly, while regal, expression. Exhibiting a unique elegance of bearing and movement, his soundness and coordination show unmistakably the purpose for which he has been bred, the strenuous work of guarding the flocks in all kinds of weather on the steep mountain slopes of the Pyrenees.

**Size, Proportion, Substance**—*Size*—The height at the withers ranges from 27 inches to 32 inches for dogs and from 25 inches to 29 inches for bitches. A 27 inch dog weighs about 100 pounds and a 25 inch bitch weighs about 85 pounds. Weight is in proportion to the overall size and structure. **Proportion**—The Great Pyrenees is a balanced dog with the height measured at the withers being somewhat less than the length of the body measured from the point of the shoulder to the rearmost projection of the upper thigh (buttocks). These proportions create a somewhat rectangular dog, slightly longer than it is tall. Front and rear angulation are balanced. **Substance**—The Great Pyrenees is a dog of medium substance whose coat deceives those who do not feel the bone and muscle. Commensurate with his size and impression of elegance there is sufficient bone and muscle to provide a balance with the frame. **Faults**—Size—Dogs and bitches under minimum size or over maximum size. **Substance**—Dogs too heavily boned or too lightly boned to be in balance with their frame.

**Head**—Correct head and expression are essential to the breed. The head is not heavy in proportion to the size of the dog. It is wedge shaped with a slightly rounded crown. **Expression**—The expression is elegant, intelligent and contemplative. **Eyes**—Medium sized, almond shaped, set slightly obliquely, rich dark brown. Eyelids are close fitting with black rims. **Ears**—Small to medium in size, V-shaped with rounded tips, set on at eye level, normally carried low, flat, and close to the head. There is a characteristic meeting of the hair of the upper and lower face which forms a line from the outer corner of the eye to the base of the ear. **Skull and Muzzle**—The muzzle is approximately equal in length to the back skull. The width and length of the skull are approximately equal. The muzzle blends smoothly with the skull. The cheeks are flat. There is sufficient fill under the eyes. A slight furrow exists between the eyes. There is no apparent stop. The bony eyebrow ridges are only slightly developed. Lips are tight fitting with the upper lip just covering the lower lip. There is a strong lower jaw. The nose and lips are black. **Teeth**—A scissors bite is preferred, but a level bite is acceptable. It is not unusual to see dropped (receding) lower central incisor teeth. **Faults**—Too heavy head (Saint Bernard or Newfoundland-like). Too narrow or small skull. Foxy appearance. Presence of an apparent stop. Missing pigmentation on nose, eye rims, or lips. Eyelids round, triangular, loose or small. Overshot, undershot, wry mouth.

**Neck, Topline, Body**—**Neck**—Strongly muscled and of medium length, with minimal dewlap. **Topline**—The backline is level. **Body**—The chest is moderately broad. The rib cage is well sprung, oval in shape, and of sufficient depth to reach the elbows. Back and loin are broad and strongly coupled with some tuck-up. The croup is gently sloping with the tail set on just below the level of the back. **Tail**—The tailbones are of sufficient length to reach the hock. The tail is well plumed, carried low in repose and may be carried over the back, "making the wheel," when aroused. When present, a "shepherd's crook" at the end of the tail accentuates the plume. When gaiting, the tail may be carried either over the back or low. Both carriages are equally correct. **Fault**—Barrel ribs.

**Forequarters**—**Shoulders**—The shoulders are well laid back, well muscled and lie close to the body. The upper arm meets the shoulder blade at approximately a right angle. The upper arm angles backward from the point of the shoulder to the elbow and is never perpendicular to the ground. The length of the shoulder blade and the upper arm is approximately equal. The height from the ground to the elbow appears approximately equal to the height from the elbow to the withers. **Forelegs**—The legs are of sufficient bone and muscle to provide a balance with the frame. The elbows are close to the body and point directly to the rear when standing and gaiting. The forelegs, when viewed from the side, are located directly under the withers and are straight and vertical to the ground. The elbows, when viewed from the front, are set in a straight line from the point of shoulder to the wrist. Front pasterns are strong and flexible. Each foreleg carries a single dewclaw. **Front Feet**—Rounded, close-cupped, well padded, toes well arched.

**Hindquarters**—The angulation of the hindquarters is similar in degree to that of the forequarters. **Thighs**—Strongly muscular upper thighs extend from the pelvis at right angles. The upper thigh is the same length as the lower thigh, creating moderate stifle joint angulation when viewed in profile. The rear pastern (metatarsus) is of medium length and perpendicular to the ground as the dog stands naturally. This produces a moderate degree of angulation in the hock joint, when viewed from the side. The hindquarters from the hip to the rear pastern are straight and parallel, as viewed from the rear. The rear legs are of sufficient bone and muscle to provide a balance with the frame. Double dewclaws are located on each rear leg. *Rear Feet*—The rear feet have a structural tendency to toe out slightly. This breed characteristic is not to be confused with cow-hocks. The rear feet, like the forefeet, are rounded, close-cupped, well padded with toes well arched. *Fault*—Absence of double dewclaws on each rear leg.

**Coat**—The weather resistant double coat consists of a long, flat, thick, outer coat of coarse hair, straight or slightly undulating, and lying over a dense, fine, woolly undercoat. The coat is more profuse about the neck and shoulders where it forms a ruff or mane which is more pronounced in males. Longer hair on the tail forms a plume. There is feathering along the back of the front legs and along the back of the thighs, giving a "pantaloon" effect. The hair on the face and ears is shorter and of finer texture. Correctness of coat is more important than abundance of coat. *Faults*—Curly coat. Stand-off coat (Samoyed type).

**Color**—White or white with markings of gray, badger, reddish brown, or varying shades of tan. Markings of varying size may appear on the ears, head (including a full face mask), tail and as a few body spots. The undercoat may be white or shaded. All of the above described colorings and locations are characteristic of the breed and equally correct. *Fault*—Outer coat markings covering more than one third of the body.

**Gait**—The Great Pyrenees moves smoothly and elegantly, true and straight ahead, exhibiting both power and agility. The stride is well balanced with good reach and strong drive. The legs tend to move toward the center line as speed increases. Ease and efficiency of movement are more important than speed.

**Temperament**—Character and temperament are of utmost importance. In nature, the Great Pyrenees is confident, gentle, and affectionate. While territorial and protective of his flock or family when necessary, his general demeanor is one of quiet composure, both patient and tolerant. He is strong willed, independent and somewhat reserved, yet attentive, fearless and loyal to his charges both human and animal.

**Although the Great Pyrenees may appear reserved in the show ring, any sign of excessive shyness, nervousness, or aggression to humans is unacceptable and must be considered an extremely serious fault.**

**Approved June 12, 1990**
**Effective August 1, 1990**

# GREATER SWISS MOUNTAIN DOG

$\mathcal{A}$S STATED IN THE NAME, THIS NATIVE OF SWITZERLAND IS ONE OF THE earliest descendants of the large mastiff-type dogs introduced to the Alpine by the ancient Romans. Developed in the remote and isolated areas of Switzerland, the Greater Swiss Mountain Dog was adapted to general farm use as a herding dog, guard dog, and utilitarian draft dog. Of the four Sennenhund breeds developed in Switzerland, the Greater Swiss Mountain Dog is both the largest and the oldest. Though little known outside its country of origin for many years, the Greater Swiss was instrumental in the early development of both the Saint Bernard and the Rottweiler.

In the late nineteenth century, much of the work previously done by the Greater Swiss Mountain Dog was either supplied by other breeds of dogs or replaced by machines. In 1908, a Greater Swiss was shown to the famous dog expert Dr. Albert Heim, of Zurich. It had been assumed that the Greater Swiss Mountain Dog had already died out. With the urging of Heim, other specimens were located, and he called upon breeders to save this ancient Alpine dog. By 1910, the Greater Swiss Mountain Dog was recognized by the Swiss Kennel Club.

J. Frederick and Patricia Hoffman imported the first of this breed to the United States after seeing them exhibited at a show in Frankfurt, Germany.

While growth of interest in the breed has been slow, it has been steady. In 1968, the Greater Swiss Mountain Dog Club of America was formed for the express purpose of obtaining AKC recognition. The GSMDCA studbook was transferred to the AKC on March 17, 1993, with an initial 1,300 dogs as foundation stock. The Greater Swiss Mountain Dog was given Working Group designation and became eligible for full recognition status on July 1, 1995.

# OFFICIAL STANDARD FOR THE GREATER SWISS MOUNTAIN DOG

**General Appearance**—The Greater Swiss Mountain Dog is a Draft and Drover breed and should structurally appear as such. It is a striking, tri-colored, large, powerful, confident dog of sturdy appearance. It is a heavy boned and well muscled dog which, in spite of its size and weight, is agile enough to perform the all-purpose farm duties of the mountainous regions of its origin.

**Size, Proportion and Substance**—Height at the highest point of the shoulder is ideally: Dogs: 25.5 to 28.5 inches. Bitches 23.5 to 27 inches. Body length to height is approximately a 10 to 9 proportion, thus appearing slightly longer than tall. It is a heavy boned and well muscled dog of sturdy appearance.

**Head**—*Expression* is animated and gentle. The *eyes* are almond shaped and brown, dark brown preferred, medium sized, neither deep set nor protruding. Blue eye or eyes is a disqualification. Eyelids are close fitting and eyerims are black. The *ears* are medium sized, set high, triangular in shape, gently rounded at the tip, and hang close to the head when in repose. When alert, the ears are brought forward and raised at the base. The top of the ear is level with the top of the skull. The *skull* is flat and broad with a slight stop. The backskull and muzzle are of approximately equal length. The backskull is approximately twice the width of the muzzle. The *muzzle* is large, blunt and straight, not pointed and most often with a slight rise before the end. In adult dogs the nose leather is always black. The *lips* are clean and as a dry-mouthed breed, flews are only slightly developed. The *teeth* meet in a scissors bite.

**Neck, Topline and Body**—The neck is of moderate length, strong, muscular and clean. The topline is level from the withers to the croup. The chest is deep and broad with a slight protruding breastbone. The ribs are well-sprung. Depth of chest is approximately one half the total height of the dog at the withers. Body is full with slight tuck up. The loins are broad and strong. The croup is long, broad and smoothly rounded to the tail insertion. The tail is thick from root to tip, tapering slightly at the tip, reaching to the hocks, and carried down in repose. When alert and in movement, the tail may be carried higher and slightly curved upwards, but should not curl, or tilt over the back. The bones of the tail should feel straight.

**Forequarters**—The shoulders are long, sloping, strong and moderately laid back. They are flat and well-muscled. Forelegs are straight and strong. The pasterns slope very slightly, but are not weak. Feet are round and compact with well arched toes, and turn neither in nor out. The dewclaws may or may not be present.

**Hindquarters**—The thighs are broad, strong and muscular. The stifles are moderately bent and taper smoothly into the hocks. The hocks are well let down and straight when viewed from the rear. Feet are round and compact with well arched toes, and turn neither in nor out. Dewclaws should be removed.

**Coat**—Topcoat is dense, approximately 1¼ to 2 inches in length. Undercoat must be present and may be thick and sometimes showing, almost always present at neck but may be present throughout. Color of undercoat ranges from the preferred dark gray to light gray to tawny. Total absence of undercoat is undesirable and should be penalized.

**Color**—The topcoat is black. The markings are rich rust and white. Symmetry of markings is desired. On the head, rust typically appears over each eye, on each cheek and on the underside of the ears. On the body, rust appears on both sides of the forechest, on all four legs and underneath the tail. White markings appear typically on the head (blaze) and muzzle. The blaze may vary in length and width. It may be a very thin stripe or wider band. The blaze may extend just barely to the stop or may extend over the top of the skull and may meet with white patch or collar on the neck. Typically, white appears on the chest, running unbroken from the throat to the chest, as well as on all four feet and on the tip of the tail. White patches or collar on the neck is acceptable. Any color other than the "Black, Red and White" tri-colored dog described above, such as "Blue/Charcoal, Red and White" or "Red and White" is considered a disqualification. When evaluating the Greater Swiss Mountain Dog, markings and other cosmetic factors should be considered of lesser importance than other aspects of type which directly affect working ability.

**Gait**—Good reach in front, powerful drive in rear. Movement with a level back.

**Temperament**—Bold, faithful, willing worker. Alert and vigilant. Shyness or aggressiveness shall be severely penalized.

## SUMMARY

The foregoing is the description of the ideal Greater Swiss Mountain Dog. Defects of both structure and temperament are to be judged more severely than mere lack of elegance because they reduce the animal's capacity to work. Any fault that detracts from the above described working dog should be penalized to the extent of the deviation.

## DISQUALIFICATIONS

*Any color other than the "Black, Red and White" tri-colored dog described above, such as "Blue/Charcoal, Red and White" or "Red and White."*
*Blue eye or eyes.*

**Approved April 8, 2003**
**Effective May 29, 2003**

# KOMONDOR

*O*F THE THREE BREEDS OF WORKING DOG NATIVE FOR TEN CENTURIES TO THE sheep and cattle countries of Hungary, there seems little doubt that the king of them all is the Komondor. This heavily coated dog is an almost direct descendant of the Aftscharka, which the Huns found on the southern steppes when they passed through Russia. Many of today's Komondorok (plural) bear striking resemblance to the massive, long-legged Russian herdsman's dog, but the breed generally has become more compact.

The Komondor is a mighty fellow. His head is impressive in its generous formation, and his general appearance is commanding. At first sight he is likely to create fear. Strangers of evil intent have reason to be fearful, but he is a devoted companion to his master and readily mingles with friends of the family.

One often sees pictures of the Komondor that show him with a heavily matted coat and with his head covered all over with long hair. The dog thus seems unkempt, and this is the way he is found in his habitat, where he lives in the open practically all the time. Under such circumstances, it would be impossible for the Komondor to have a well-groomed appearance, but he responds readily to care. When reared in kennels and prepared for shows, he is a handsome dog.

The Komondor is the chief of the herdsman's dogs, but he is not often utilized for rounding up the herds. He merely accompanies the flocks and herds in exceptional cases, and then more in the capacity of protector than as herder. His vigilance and courage have earned him a rather enviable position of trust, and much of the routine work is left to the smaller dogs.

The Magyars who have bred the Komondor for more than a thousand years attend principally to their herds and flocks and do not concern themselves with keeping pedigrees of their dogs. However, there is no need of pedigrees for them, as the dogs are not permitted to mate outside their own breed.

It is doubtful if any dogs with pedigrees could have been found in the arid grasslands of eastern Hungary, the so-called Puszta, for the shepherds and herdsmen did not look upon dog breeding either as a commercial venture or as a hobby. Still, the crossing of a Komondor and a Kuvasz would have been unimaginable—and also practically impossible.

The history of purebred dog breeding in Hungary is not unlike that of any other country in the world. Definite records go back hardly a century, but those in existence are soundly attested by reliable parties. The Hungarian Kennel Club and the Hungarian Komondor Club maintain a strong control over the interests of the Komondor, these organizations having accepted the standard of the breed as drawn up by a committee made up of members of the two clubs. The American Kennel Club's standard of the breed is a translation of the Hungarian.

In reading the standard, it should be noted that its salient points denote the strength and protective features that have been bred into the Komondor for centuries, and these should be maintained. Today there is not, perhaps, as pressing a need for such a self-reliant dog as there was in the past. In times of old he had to be ready at any moment to fight all manner of beasts of prey, many of which were his superior in size and weight. When the odds were against him, he could depend to some extent on that heavy coat to cover his most vulnerable points, and could call, too, upon an intelligence far superior to that of his wild adversaries.

# OFFICIAL STANDARD FOR THE KOMONDOR

**General Appearance**—The Komondor is characterized by imposing strength, dignity, courageous demeanor and pleasing conformation. He is a large, muscular dog with plenty of bone and substance, covered with an unusual, heavy coat of white cords. The working Komondor lives during the greater part of the year in the open, and his coat serves to help him blend in with his flock and to protect him from extremes of weather and beasts of prey. *Nature and Characteristics:* The Komondor is a flock guardian, not a herder. Originally developed in Hungary to guard large herds of animals on the open plains, the Komondor was charged with protecting the herd by himself, with no assistance and no commands from his master. The mature, experienced dog tends to stay close to his charges, whether a flock or family; he is unlikely to be drawn away from them in chase, and typically doesn't wander far. Though very sensitive to the desires of his master, heavy-handed training will produce a stubborn, unhappy Komondor. While reserved with strangers, the Komondor is demonstrative with those he loves, selflessly devoted to his family and his charges, and will defend them against any attack. The combination of this devotion to all things dear to him and the desire to take responsibility for them produces an excellent guardian of herds or home, vigilant, courageous and very faithful.

**Size, Proportion, Substance**—Dogs 27½ inches and up at the withers; bitches 25½ inches and up at the withers. Dogs are approximately 100 pounds and up, bitches, approximately 80 pounds and up at maturity, with plenty of bone and substance. While large size is important, type, character, symmetry, movement and ruggedness are of the greatest importance and are on no account to be sacrificed for size alone. The body is slightly longer than the height at the withers. Height below the minimum is a fault.

**Head**—The head is large. The length of the head from occiput to tip of nose is approximately two-fifths the height of the dog at the withers. The skin around the eyes and on the muzzle is dark.

*Eyes:* Medium-sized and almond-shaped, not too deeply set. The iris of the eye is dark brown. Edges of the eyelids are gray or black. Light eyes are a fault. Blue eyes are a disqualification. *Ears:* In shape the ear is an elongated triangle with a slightly rounded tip. Medium-set and hanging and long enough to reach to the inner corner of the eye on the opposite side of the head. Erect ears or ears that move toward an erect position are a fault. *Skull:* The skull is broad with well-developed arches over the eyes. The occiput is fairly well-developed and the stop is moderate. *Muzzle:* The muzzle is wide, coarse, and truncated. Measured from inner corner of the eye to tip of nose the muzzle is two-fifths of the total length of the head. The top of the muzzle is straight and is parallel to the top of the skull. Underjaw is well-developed and broad. Lips are tight and are black in color. Ideally gums and palate are dark or black. *Nose:* Nose is wide and the front of the nose forms a right angle with the top of the muzzle. The nostrils are wide. The nose is black. A dark gray or dark brown nose is not desirable but is acceptable. A flesh-colored nose is a disqualification. *Bite:* Bite is scissors; a level bite is acceptable. A distinctly overshot or undershot bite is a *fault*. Any missing teeth is a serious fault. Three or more missing teeth is a disqualification.

**Neck**—Muscular, of medium length, moderately arched, with no dewlap. The head erect.

**Topline**—The back is level and strong.

**Body**—Characterized by a powerful, deep chest, which is muscular and proportionately wide. The breast is broad and well-muscled. The belly is somewhat drawn up at the rear. The rump is wide, muscular, and slopes slightly toward the root of the tail. Softness or lack of good muscle tone is a fault.

**Tail**—A continuation of the rump line, hanging, and long enough to reach the hocks. Slightly curved upwards and/or to one side at its end. Even when the dog is moving or excited, the greater part of the tail is raised no higher than the level of the back. A short or curly tail is a fault.

**Forequarters**—Shoulders are well laid back. Forelegs straight, well-boned, and muscular. Viewed from any side, the legs are like vertical columns. The upper arms are carried close to the body, without loose elbows.

**Feet**—Strong, rather large, and with close, well-arched toes. Pads are hard, elastic, and black or gray. Ideally, nails are black or gray, although light nails are acceptable.

**Hindquarters**—The steely, strong bone structure is covered with highly-developed muscles. The legs are straight as viewed from the rear. Stifles are well-bent. Rear dewclaws must be removed.

**Coat**—Characteristic of the breed is the dense, protective coat. The puppy coat is relatively soft, but it shows a tendency to fall into cord-like curls. The young adult coat, or intermediate coat, consists of very short cords next to the skin which may be obscured by the sometimes lumpy looking fluff on the outer ends of the cords. The mature coat consists of a dense, soft, woolly undercoat much like the puppy coat, and a coarser outer coat that is wavy or curly. The coarser hairs of the outer coat trap the softer undercoat, forming permanent, strong cords that are felt-like to the touch. A grown dog is entirely covered with a heavy coat of these tassel-like cords, which form naturally. It must be remembered that the length of the Komondor's coat is a function of age, and a younger dog must never be penalized for having a shorter coat. Straight or silky coat is a *fault*. Failure of the coat to cord by two years of age is a disqualification. Short, smooth coat on both head and legs is a disqualification.

**Color**—Color of the coat is white, but not always the pure white of a brushed coat. A small amount of cream or buff shading is sometimes seen in puppies, but fades with maturity. In the ideal specimen the skin is gray. Pink skin is not desirable but is acceptable. Color other than white, with the exception of small amounts of cream or buff in puppies, is a disqualification.

**Gait**—Light, leisurely and balanced. The Komondor takes long strides, is very agile and light on his feet. The head is carried slightly forward when the dog trots.

*The foregoing is a description of the ideal Komondor. Any deviation should be penalized in direct proportion to the extent of that deviation. Extreme deviation in any part should be penalized to the extent that the dog is effectively eliminated from competition.*


## DISQUALIFICATIONS

*Blue eyes.*
*Flesh-colored nose.*
*Three or more missing teeth.*
*Failure of the coat to cord by two years of age.*
*Short, smooth coat on both head and legs.*
*Color other than white, with the exception of small amounts of cream or buff in puppies.*

**Approved June 13, 1994**
**Effective July 31, 1994**

# KUVASZ

ROM TIBET, THAT EXOTIC HIGH-FLUNG DOMAIN OF THE LAMAS, CAME THE ancestors of the breed that today is known as the Kuvasz (plural, Kuvaszok). Yet this is not a new name for the breed. It is merely a corrupted spelling of Turkish and Arabian words that signified the unexcelled guarding instincts of this big dog.

The Turkish word is *kawasz,* which means "armed guard of the nobility." In the Arabian this appears as *kawwasz,* which signifies "archer," an expression that probably was a mere figure of speech to denote the high esteem in which the dog was held, since many centuries ago an archer was regarded with great respect. Words with nearly the same spelling and meaning are found throughout all the countries whose languages originate in Tibet.

There is little doubt of the part that the Kuvasz played in the history of the kingdoms and empires which flourished throughout Europe five to eight centuries ago. Dogs of this breed were the constant companions of many a ruler of a turbulent country; indeed, none but those within the favor of the royal circles were permitted to own Kuvasz.

Known in many countries, it was in Hungary that the Kuvasz developed into the form in which he is seen today. He still is a big dog, but he is not the giant of ancient times. At present he measures 28 to 30 inches at the withers, but there is every reason to believe that the dog that issued from Tibet stood considerably higher. He was a dog of which the common people stood in awe; his appearance alone was enough to discourage attacks on noblemen by the populace.

The first great period in the Hungarian history of the Kuvasz seemed to reach a climax during the second half of the fifteenth century. His renown reached far and wide. There were numerous big estates that bred the dog and kept their own stud-books. Many were trained for hunting, and they proved very successful on the big game of those times.

King Matthias I, who reigned from 1458 to 1490, had at least one Kuvasz with him whenever he traveled, and there were numerous specimens about his palace and the surrounding grounds. Few other rulers have had to strive so hard to hold his domains together. Plots and political intrigue were the rule rather than the exception, while assassinations were not uncommon. It is said that Matthias was reluctant to place any great trust in even the members of his own household, and his court was filled with ambitious noblemen.

It is no wonder that Matthias relied more upon his dogs than upon his human guards. He knew that in this big, sturdy fellow he had, perhaps, the only true security that was possible. Often, when the tumultuous day was over—and he waged wars almost continually—the king would spend half the night poring over his books and maps, preparing his orders for the following day, and while he worked, a big white Kuvasz sprawled just inside the door.

Matthias became so impressed with the Kuvasz that he developed a large pack to be used for hunting. His kennels on his large estates in Siebenbuergen were among the most impressive in Europe, and the scope of his breeding did a great deal toward perpetuating a splendid strain of the breed. Surplus puppies were presented only to noblemen and visiting dignitaries.

Eventually, many specimens got into the hands of commoners, but this was long after the time of Matthias I, when herders found them suitable for work with sheep and cattle. It was in this later period that the name of the breed was corrupted to its present spelling. Incidentally, this spelling is rather unfortunate, because it changes the meaning rather ridiculously to "mongrel."

According to von Stephanitz, the great German authority on all Central European breeds, the Kuvasz is related to the Komondor, which had been brought from the Russian steppes by the Huns. He ventured the opinion that the Kawasz or Kawwasz was crossed with the indigenous country dog of Hungary. While this is something of a conjecture, there is strong evidence that points to truth. At any rate, the original type has proved dominant, and the Kuvasz of today—perhaps a little smaller—is very similar to his earliest progenitors.

# OFFICIAL STANDARD FOR THE KUVASZ

**General Appearance**—A working dog of larger size, sturdily built, well balanced, neither lanky nor cobby. White in color with no markings. Medium boned, well muscled, without the slightest hint of bulkiness or lethargy. Impresses the eye with strength and activity combined with light-footedness, moves freely on strong legs. The following description is that of the ideal Kuvasz. Any deviation must be penalized to the extent of the deviation.

**Size, Proportion, Substance**—*Height* measured at the withers: Dogs, 28 to 30 inches; bitches, 26 to 28 inches. *Disqualifications:* Dogs smaller than 26 inches. Bitches smaller than 24 inches. *Weight:* Dogs approximately 100 to 115 pounds, bitches approximately 70 to 90 pounds. Trunk and limbs form a horizontal rectangle slightly deviated from the square. *Bone* in proportion to size of body. Medium, hard. Never heavy or coarse. Any tendency to weakness or lack of substance is a decided fault.

**Head**—Proportions are of great importance as the head is considered to be the most beautiful part of the Kuvasz. Length of head measured from tip of nose to occiput is slightly less than half the height of the dog at the withers. Width is half the length of the head. *Eyes* almond-shaped, set well apart, somewhat slanted. In profile, the eyes are set slightly below the plane of the muzzle. Lids tight, haws should not show. Dark brown, the darker the better. *Ears* V-shaped, tip is slightly rounded. Rather thick, they are well set back between the level of the eye and the top of the head. When pulled forward the tip of the ear should cover the eye. Looking at the dog face to face, the widest part of the ear is about level to the eye. The inner edge of the ear lies close to the cheek, the outer edge slightly away from the head forming a V. In the relaxed position, the ears should hold their set and not cast backward. The ears should not protrude above the head. The *skull* is elongated but not pointed. The stop is defined, never abrupt, raising the forehead gently above the plane of the muzzle. The longitudinal midline of the forehead is pronounced, widening as it slopes to the muzzle. Cheeks flat, bony arches above the eyes. The skin is dry. *Muzzle:* length in proportion to the length of the head, top straight, not pointed, underjaw well developed. Inside of the mouth preferably black. *Nose* large, black nostrils well opened. *Lips* black, closely covering the teeth. The upper lip covers tightly the upper jaw only; no excess flews. Lower lip tight and not pendulous. *Bite:* dentition full, scissors bite preferred. Level bite acceptable. *Disqualifications:* overshot bite; undershot bite.

**Neck, Topline, Body**—*Neck* muscular, without dewlap, medium length, arched at the crest. *Back* is of medium length, straight, firm and quite broad. The loin is short, muscular and tight. The croup well muscled, slightly sloping. Forechest is well developed. When viewed from the side, the forechest protrudes slightly in front of the shoulders. Chest deep with long, well-sprung ribs reaching almost to the elbows. The brisket is deep, well developed and runs parallel to the ground. The stomach is well tucked up. *Tail* carried low, natural length reaching at least to the hocks. In repose it hangs down resting on the body, the end but slightly lifted. In state of excitement, the tail may be elevated to the level of the loin, the tip slightly curved up. Ideally there should not be much difference in the carriage of the tail in state of excitement or in repose.

**Forequarters**—*Shoulders*—muscular and long. *Topline*—withers are higher than the back. The scapula and humerus form a right angle, are long and of equal length. Elbows neither in nor out. *Legs* are medium boned, straight and well muscled. The joints are dry, hard. Dewclaws on the forelegs should not be removed. *Feet* well padded. *Pads* resilient, black. Feet are closed tight, forming round "cat feet." Some hair between the toes, the less the better. Dark nails are preferred.

**Hindquarters**—The portion behind the hip joint is moderately long, producing wide, long and strong muscles of the upper thigh. The femur is long, creating well-bent stifles. Lower *thigh* is long, dry, well muscled. Metatarsus is short, broad and of great strength. Dewclaws, if any, are removed. *Feet* as in front, except the rear paws somewhat longer.

**Coat**—The Kuvasz has a double coat, formed by guard hair and fine undercoat. The texture of the coat is medium coarse. The coat ranges from quite wavy to straight. Distribution follows a definite pattern over the body regardless of coat type. The head, muzzle, ears and paws are covered with short, smooth hair. The neck has a mane that extends to and covers the chest. Coat on the front of the forelegs up to the elbows and the hind legs below the thighs is short and smooth. The backs of the forelegs are feathered to the pastern with hair 2 to 3 inches long. The body and sides of the thighs are covered with a medium length coat. The back of the thighs and the entire tail are covered with hair 4 to 6 inches long. It is natural for the Kuvasz to lose most of the long coat during hot weather. Full luxuriant coat comes in seasonally, depending on climate. Summer coat should not be penalized.

**Color**—White. The skin is heavily pigmented. The more slate gray or black pigmentation the better.

**Gait**—Easy, free and elastic. Feet travel close to the ground. Hind legs reach far under, meeting or even passing the imprints of the front legs. Moving toward an observer, the front legs do not travel parallel to each other, but rather close together at the ground. When viewed from the rear, the hind legs (from the hip joint down) also move close to the ground. As speed increases, the legs gradually angle more inward until the pads are almost single-tracking. Unless excited, the head is carried rather low at the level of the shoulders. Desired movement cannot be maintained without sufficient angulation and firm slimness of body.

**Temperament**—A spirited dog of keen intelligence, determination, courage and curiosity. Very sensitive to praise and blame. Primarily a one-family dog. Devoted, gentle and patient without being overly demonstrative. Always ready to protect loved ones even to the point of self-sacrifice. Extremely strong instinct to protect children. Polite to accepted strangers, but rather suspicious and very discriminating in making new friends. Unexcelled guard, possessing ability to act on his own initiative at just the right moment without instruction. Bold, courageous and fearless. Untiring ability to work and cover rough terrain for long periods of time. Has good scent and has been used to hunt game.

## DISQUALIFICATIONS

*Overshot bite. Undershot bite.*
*Dogs smaller than 26 inches. Bitches smaller than 24 inches.*

**Approved July 12, 1999**
**Effective August 30, 1999**

# Mastiff

HE BREED COMMONLY CALLED MASTIFF IN ENGLISH-SPEAKING COUNTRIES is more properly described as the *Old English* Mastiff. It is a giant short-haired dog, with heavy head and short muzzle, which has been bred as a watchdog in England for over two thousand years. The word *mastiff* describes a group of giant varieties of dog rather than a single breed. They are supposed to have originated in Asia.

So little is known about dogs of any sort before the nineteenth century that almost all theories of ancestry are of small importance. Every partisan would like to claim the greatest antiquity for his particular sort of mastiff, as well as to say that the other sorts sprang from it. There is very little proof one way or the other.

Cassel finds drawings on Egyptian monuments of typical mastiffs dating about 3000 B.C. In literature, the earliest reference is in Chinese about 1121 B.C. This evidence supports the undoubted antiquity of the mastiff group's ancestry.

So far as the mastiff is concerned, it has a longer history than most. Julius Caesar describes them in his account of invading Britain in 55 B.C., when they fought beside their masters against the Roman legions with such courage and power as to make a great impression. Soon afterward we find several different accounts of the huge British fighting dogs brought back to Rome, where they defeated all other varieties in combat in the arena. They were also matched against human gladiators as well as against bulls, bears, lions, and tigers.

Today we are likely to think of such cruel spectacles as belonging only to antiquity, but this is not true. Dogfights, bullbaiting, and bearbaiting were respectable and popular forms of amusement in England and America less than two hundred years ago. Such brutal events were patronized by nobility and clergy in England, while public-spirited citizens left legacies so that the common folk might be entertained in this way on holidays.

Dogfighting and animal-baiting were made illegal in England in 1835, but for twenty years longer the law was little obeyed. American dog fanciers are interested in the word *fancier*, which was synonymous with *bettor*—meaning especially a bettor on a dog or prizefight—and are interested also in the name of one of the most fashionable sporting establishments in London, over a hundred years ago, called the Westminster Pit, with 300 seats. *Westminster* meant *dogs* even then—but fighting dogs!

The Mastiff was always in front rank as a fighting dog, but this does not account for his popularity in England for two thousand years. It was as bandogs, or tiedogs (tied by day but loose at night), that they were found everywhere. In fact, long ago, keeping of these Mastiffs was compulsory for the peasants. During Anglo-Saxon times there had to be kept at least one Mastiff for each two villeins. By this means, wolves and other savage game were kept under control. They were also used in hunting packs by the nobility. It was as protectors of the home, however, that they were most used, and probably as a result of centuries of such service the Mastiff has acquired unique traits as a family dog.

That the Mastiff has long been numerous is indicated by the development of the English language itself. The ancient word in Anglo-Saxon and in over a score of kindred languages for a member of the canine race is *hound,* or something very similar. A rather modern word coming from the Latin languages is like *dog,* but in all but English it means a mastiff sort. So we can believe that when the Normans conquered the Anglo-Saxons in 1066 and made Norman-French the official language of England, *dogues* (or mastiffs) were so plentiful that people forgot eventually there was any other name for a canine creature. This is the only explanation a dog fancier can offer for such a peculiar change in a language.

Anecdotes extolling the power and agility of Mastiffs as well as their devotion to their masters would fill a large volume of marvels. Herodotus tells of Cyrus the Great, founder of the Persian Empire who, about 550 B.C., received a Mastiff as a gift from the King of Albania. Cyrus matched the dog against another and also set it against a bull. But the Mastiff was meek, so Cyrus, in disgust, had it killed. News of this reception of his gift came back to the King of Albania. He sent messengers with another Mastiff—a bitch—to Cyrus, telling him that a Mastiff was no ordinary cur and that it scorned to notice such common creatures as a Persian dog or a bull. He urged him to select a worthy opponent such as a lion or even an elephant. The King of Albania concluded by saying Mastiffs were rare and royal gifts and that he would not send Cyrus another. Whereupon, says Herodotus, the Mastiff bitch was set to attack an elephant and did so with such fury and efficiency that she worried the elephant down to the ground and would have killed it.

That is probably the tallest Mastiff tale on record! It does, however, give proof of the reputation of Mastiffs as powerful, agile, and courageous dogs. It is even more interesting to know that Albania was the land of the people known as Alani, an Asiatic people. Also that similar names stand for *mastiffs,* e.g., *Alano, Alan,* and *Alaunt.*

The story of Sir Peers Legh, Knight of Lyme Hall (near Stockport, Cheshire), at the Battle of Agincourt, October 25, 1415, is well known. He had brought his favorite Mastiff—also a bitch—to France, and when he fell, she stood over him and defended him many hours until he was picked up by English soldiers and carried to Paris, where he died of his wounds. The faithful Mastiff was returned to England and from her is descended the famous Lyme Hall strain which the family has bred over a period of over five centuries. In the drawing room of the castle is still to be seen an old stained-glass window portraying the gallant Sir Peers and his devoted Mastiff.

The present-day English Mastiff is based on the strains of Lyme Hall and that of the Duke of Devonshire's Kennels at Chatsworth. Chaucer, writing in Middle English (a language resulting from a cross between old Anglo-Saxon and Norman-French) 300 years after the Norman Conquest, described the Old English Mastiff in his "Knight's Tale." He tried to use the Italian-French word for Mastiff, *Alan,* which is still used in English heraldry to describe the figure of a "mastiff with cropped ears" on a coat of arms:

> *Aboute his char ther wenten white Alaunts*
> *Twenty and mo, as gret as any stere*
> *To hunten at the leon or the dere.*

So, here is proof that 600 years ago Mastiffs were hunted in packs in England on such different game as lion or deer. Chaucer says they were as large as steer! Even though cattle were much smaller in those days, this is hard to credit. The white color is authentic. We have plenty of pictures and descriptions of white and piebald Mastiffs, often with long coats, of about a century ago.

The American Mastiff Club was formed in 1879, and some time thereafter disbanded. In 1920, the first Mastiff Club of America was founded. The present club was established in 1929.

# OFFICIAL STANDARD FOR THE MASTIFF

**General Appearance**—The Mastiff is a large, massive, symmetrical dog with a well-knit frame. The impression is one of grandeur and dignity. Dogs are more massive throughout. Bitches should not be faulted for being somewhat smaller in all dimensions while maintaining a proportionally powerful structure. A good evaluation considers positive qualities of type and soundness with equal weight.

**Size, Proposition, Substance**—*Size*—Dogs, minimum, 30 inches at the shoulder. Bitches, minimum, 27½ inches at the shoulder. *Fault*—Dogs or bitches below the minimum standard. The farther below standard, the greater the fault.

*Proportion*—Rectangular, the length of the dog from forechest to rump is somewhat longer than the height at the withers. The height of the dog should come from depth of body rather than from length of leg.

*Substance*—Massive, heavy boned, with a powerful muscle structure. Great depth and breadth desirable. *Fault*—Lack of substance or slab-sided.

**Head**—In general outline giving a massive appearance when viewed from any angle. Breadth greatly desired.

*Eyes* set wide apart, medium in size, never too prominent. *Expression* alert but kindly. Color of eyes brown, the darker the better, and showing no haw. Light eyes or a predatory expression is undesirable. *Ears* small in proportion to the skull, V-shaped, rounded at the tips. Leather moderately thin, set widely apart at the highest points on the sides of the skull continuing the outline across the summit. They should lie close to the cheeks when in repose. Ears dark in color, the blacker the better, conforming to the color of the muzzle.

*Skull* broad and somewhat flattened between the ears, forehead slightly curved, showing marked wrinkles which are particularly distinctive when at attention. Brows (superciliary ridges) moderately raised. Muscles of the temples well developed, those of the cheeks extremely powerful. Arch across the skull a flattened curve with a furrow up the center of the forehead. This extends from between the eyes to halfway up the skull. The *stop* between the eyes well marked but not too abrupt.

*Muzzle* should be half the length of the skull, thus dividing the head into three parts—one for the foreface and two for the skull. In other words, the distance from the tip of the nose to stop is equal to one-half the distance between the stop and the occiput. Circumference of the muzzle (measured midway between the eyes and nose) to that of the head (measured before the ears) is as 3 is to 5. *Muzzle* short, broad under the eyes and running nearly equal in width to the end of the nose. Truncated, i.e., blunt and cut off square, thus forming a right angle with the upper line of the face. Of great depth from the point of the nose to the underjaw. Underjaw broad to the end and slightly rounded. Muzzle dark in color, the blacker the better. *Fault*—Snipiness of the muzzle.

*Nose* broad and always dark in color, the blacker the better, with spread flat nostrils (not pointed or turned up) in profile. *Lips* diverging at obtuse angles with the septum and sufficiently pendulous so as to show a modified square profile. *Canine Teeth* healthy and wide apart. Jaws powerful. Scissors *bite* preferred, but a moderately undershot jaw should not be faulted providing the teeth are not visible when the mouth is closed.

**Neck, Topline, Body**—*Neck* powerful, very muscular, slightly arched, and of medium length. The neck gradually increases in circumference as it approaches the shoulder. Neck moderately "dry" (not showing an excess of loose skin). *Topline*—In profile the topline should be straight, level, and firm, not swaybacked, roached, or dropping off sharply behind the high point of the rump. *Chest* wide, deep, rounded, and well let down between the forelegs, extending at least to the elbow. Forechest should be deep and well defined with the breastbone extending in front of the foremost point of the shoulders. Ribs well rounded. False ribs deep and well set back. *Underline*—There should be a reasonable, but not exaggerated, tuck-up. Back muscular, powerful and straight. When viewed from the rear, there should be a slight rounding over the rump. *Loins* wide and muscular.

*Tail* set on moderately high and reaching to the hocks or a little below. Wide at the root, tapering to the end, hanging straight in repose, forming a slight curve, but never over the back when the dog is in motion.

**Forequarters**—*Shoulders* moderately sloping, powerful and muscular, with no tendency to looseness. Degree of front angulation to match correct rear angulation. *Legs* straight, strong and set wide apart, heavy boned. *Elbows* parallel to body. *Pasterns* strong and bent only slightly. *Feet* large, round, and compact with well arched toes. Black nails preferred.

**Hindquarters**—*Hindquarters* broad, wide and muscular. *Second thighs* well developed, leading to a strong hock joint. *Stifle joint* is moderately angulated matching the front. *Rear legs* are wide apart and parallel when viewed from the rear. When the portion of the leg below the hock is correctly "set back" and stands perpendicular to the ground, a plumb line dropped from the rearmost point of the hindquarters will pass in front of the foot. This rules out straight hocks, and since stifle angulation varies with hock angulation, it also rules out insufficiently angulated stifles. *Fault*—Straight stifles.

**Coat**—Outer coat straight, coarse, and of moderately short length. Undercoat dense, short, and close lying. Coat should not be so long as to produce "fringe" on the belly, tail, or hind legs. *Fault*—Long or wavy coat.

**Color**—Fawn, apricot, or brindle. Brindle should have fawn or apricot as a background color which should be completely covered with very dark stripes. Muzzle, ears and nose must be dark in color, the blacker the better, with similar color tone around the eye orbits and extending upward between them. A small patch of white on the chest is permitted.

*Faults*—Excessive white on the chest or white on any other part of the body. Mask, ears or nose lacking dark pigment.

**Gait**—The gait denotes power and strength. The rear legs should have drive, while the forelegs should track smoothly with good reach. In motion, the legs move straight forward; as the dog's speed increases from a walk to a trot, the feet move in toward the centerline of the body to maintain balance.

**Temperament**—A combination of grandeur and good nature, courage and docility. Dignity, rather than gaiety, is the Mastiff's correct demeanor. Judges should not condone shyness or viciousness. Conversely, judges should also beware of putting a premium on showiness.

**Approved November 12, 1991**
**Effective December 31, 1991**

# Neapolitan Mastiff

ROM THE BEGINNING OF MAN'S RELATIONSHIP WITH *CANIS FAMILIARIS,* ancient cultures all over the world created giant dogs of heavy bone with a large head and short muzzle. While in times past they were used in battle, these breeds have evolved to protect and guard and today serve as family companions. The Neapolitan Mastiff, or Mastino, is one of these dogs—the giant guard dog of Italy. Like its cousin, the English Mastiff, the modern Neapolitan Mastiff is an estate guard dog.

Instrumental in creating this breed was none other than Alexander the Great. In the fourth century B.C., Alexander was known to have crossed the giant Macedonian and Epirian war dogs with shorthaired Indian dogs to create the Molossus. The Molossus was a notable creature characterized by a wide, short muzzle and a heavy dewlap. Alexander used it to fight tigers, lions, elephants, and men in battle.

When the Romans set out to conquer the world, they adopted the Molossus and used them in battle, on the hunt, and in the arena. The Roman conquest of Britain in 54 B.C. gave them access to the even larger giant dogs there. The several different breeds descended from these dogs have many traits in common: They are large, powerful animals; are devoted to their masters; and are superior defenders of person and property.

Over the centuries, the farmers in the Neapolitan area of southern Italy focused on breeding Mastini that retained the giant size; heavy, loose skin; and dewlap of their ancestors. They created an animal that was a stay-at-home type and was good with the family, although still adept at detecting unwanted intruders and deterring. Indeed, many say that the Neapolitan Mastiff was developed purposely as an alarmingly ugly dog, whose looks alone were enough to repulse any intruder.

After World War II this breed was recognized as a national treasure, and several Italians began to organize the breed. Six Neapolitan Mastiffs were presented at the first exhibition in Naples in 1946. Dr. Piero Scanziani codified the standard in 1948, and in the following year the breed was first officially recognized. By the early 1970s the breed had representatives in most European countries and had acquired significant footholds in America, where a few fanciers became fascinated by the art of breeding this distinctive-looking and uniquely moving dog.

The first and possibly most important feature of the Neapolitan Mastiff is that it must appear massive—so much so that even though physically smaller than the English Mastiff, it often appears more massive because of the heaviness of the bones, the width of the trunk, and the awe-inspiring head.

Next most important is the head, which is massive in and of itself, and which must appear large in relation to the rest of the dog. Covered with wrinkles and folds, eyes deep set with the haw drooping, the lips sagging pendulously below the chin, and a characteristic dewlap, the head is simply astonishing.

The third key to Neapolitan Mastiff breed type is the wrinkles and loose skin over the whole body. The thick skin can be seen sloshing and rolling as the dog moves. While the skin is most obviously abundant over the head, it is also loose and plentiful over the whole body. When the dog sits, the skin can be seen to sag toward the buttocks and tail.

The most common color of the Mastino is blue (light or dark gray). Also acceptable are black, tawny, and mahogany, all colors with or without a slight tan brindling. Small white marks are allowed on the chest and on the feet. The ears are often cropped short, and the tail is usually cropped by one-third. These practices, begun in ancient times, are traditional but not required for show dogs. The Mastino was created by common folk of Italy who treasured their guard dogs and wanted to make sure that everyone else would be astonished upon seeing them, too. And so they created a dog that draws the eye. The observer should never be bored or left unmoved upon seeing these dogs!

When protecting home and family and repelling unwanted intruders, the dog often walks in a typically slow and shuffling gait and may deceptively appear indolent and lazy. Yet, also typical of the Mastino is that, lethargic though it may seem, it can when needed explode into the action necessary to do his job.

# OFFICIAL STANDARD FOR THE NEAPOLITAN MASTIFF

**General Appearance**—An ancient breed, rediscovered in Italy in the 1940's, the Neapolitan Mastiff is a heavy-boned, massive, awe inspiring dog bred for use as a guard and defender of owner and property. He is characterized by loose skin, over his entire body, abundant, hanging wrinkles and folds on the head and a voluminous dewlap. The essence of the Neapolitan is his bestial appearance, astounding head and imposing size and attitude. Due to his massive structure, his characteristic movement is rolling and lumbering, not elegant or showy.

**Size, Proportion, Substance**—A stocky, heavy boned dog, massive in substance, rectangular in proportion. Length of body is 10%–15% greater than height. *Height:* Dogs: 26 to 31 inches, Bitches: 24 to 29 inches. Average weight of mature Dogs: 150 pounds; Bitches: 110 pounds; but greater weight is usual and preferable as long as correct proportion and function are maintained. The absence of massiveness is to be so severely penalized as to eliminate from competition.

**Head**—Large in comparison to the body. Differentiated from that of other mastiff breeds by more extensive wrinkling and pendulous lips which blend into an ample dewlap. Toplines of cranium and the muzzle must be parallel. The face is made up of heavy wrinkles and folds. Required folds are those extending from the outside margin of the eyelids to the dewlap, and from under the lower lids to the outer edges of the lips. Severe Faults: Toplines of the cranium and muzzle not parallel. Disqualifications: Absence of wrinkles and folds. Expression: Wistful at rest, intimidating when alert. Penetrating stare. Eyes: Set deep and almost hidden beneath drooping upper lids. Lower lids droop to reveal haw. Eye Color: Shades of amber or brown, in accordance with coat color. Pigmentation of the eye rims same as coat color. Severe Faults: Whitish-blue eyes; incomplete pigmentation of the eye rims. Ears: Set well above the cheekbones. May be cropped or uncropped, but are usually cropped to an equilateral triangle for health reasons. If uncropped, they are medium sized, triangular in shape, held tight to the cheeks, and not extending beyond the lower margin of the throat. Skull: Wide flat between the ears, slightly arched at the frontal part, and covered with wrinkled skin. The width of the cranium between the cheekbones is approximately equal to its length from occiput stop. The brow is very developed. Frontal furrow is marked. Occiput is barely apparent. Stop: Very defined, forming a right angle at the junction of muzzle and frontal bones, and the sloping back at a greater angle where the frontal bones meet the frontal furrow of the forehead. Nose: Large with well-opened nostrils, and in color the same as the coat. The nose is an extension of the topline of the muzzle and should not protrude beyond nor recede behind the front plane of the muzzle. Severe Faults: Incomplete pigmentation of the nose. Muzzle: It is ⅓ the length of the whole head and is as broad as it is long. Viewed from the front, the muzzle is very deep with the outside borders parallel giving it a "squared" appearance. The top plane of the muzzle from stop to tip of nose is straight, but is ridged due to heavy folds of skin covering it. Severe Faults: Top plane of the muzzle curved upward or downward. Lips: Heavy, thick, and long, the upper lips join beneath the nostrils to form an inverted "V." The upper lips form the lower, outer borders of the muzzle, and the lowest part of these borders is made by the corners of the lips. The corners turn outward to reveal the flews, and are in line with the outside corners of the eyes. Bite: Scissors bite or pincer bite is standard; slight undershot is allowed. Dentition is complete. Faults: More than 1 missing premolar. Severe Faults: Overshot jaw: pronounced undershot jaw which disrupts the outline of the front plane of the muzzle; more than 2 missing teeth.

**Neck, Topline, and Body**—Neck: Slightly arched, rather short, stocky and well-muscled. The voluminous and well-divided dewlap extends from the lower jaw to the lower neck. Disqualification: Absence of dewlap. Body: The length of the dog, measured from the point of the shoulder to the point of buttock is 10–15 percent greater than the height of the dog measured from the highest point of the shoulder to the ground. Depth of the ribcage is equal to half the total height of the dog. Ribs are long and well sprung. Chest: Broad and deep, well muscled. Underline and tuckup: The underline of the abdomen is practically horizontal. There is little or no tuckup. Back: Wide and strong. Highest part of shoulder blade barely rising above the strong, level topline of the back. Loin: well-muscled, and harmoniously joined to the back. Croup: Wide, strong, muscular and slightly sloped. The top of the croup rises slightly and is level with the highest point of the shoulder. Tail: Set on slightly lower than the topline, wide and thick at the root, tapering gradually toward the tip. It is docked by ⅓. At rest, the tail hangs straight or in slight "S" shape. When in action, it is raised to the horizontal or a little higher than the back. Severe Fault: Tail carried straight up or curved over the back. Kinked tail. Disqualification: Lack of tail or short tail, which is less than ⅓ the length from point of insertion of the tail to the hock-joint.

**Forequarters**—Heavily built, muscular, and in balance with the hindquarters. Shoulders: Long, well-muscled, sloping and powerful. Upper arms: Strongly muscled, powerful. In length, almost ⅓ the height of the dog. Elbows: Covered with abundant and loose skin; held parallel to the ribcage, neither tied in nor loose. Forelegs: Thick, straight, heavy bone, well muscled, exemplifying strength. About the same length as the upper arms. Set well apart. Pasterns: Thick and flattened from front to back, moderately sloping forward from the leg. Dewclaws: Front dewclaws are not removed. Feet: Round and noticeably large with arched, strong toes. Nails strong, curved and preferably dark-colored. Slight turn out of the front feet is characteristic.

**Hindquarters**—As a whole, they must be powerful and strong, in harmony with the forequarters. Thighs: About the same length as the forearms, broad, muscular. Stifles: Moderate angle, strong. Legs: Heavy and thick boned, well-muscled. Slightly shorter than thigh bones. Hocks: Powerful and long. Rear pasterns: (metatarsus) Heavy thick bones. Viewed from the side, they are perpendicular to the ground. Viewed from the rear, parallel to each other. Rear dewclaws: Any dewclaws must be removed. Hind feet: Same as the front feet but slightly smaller.

**Coat**—The coat is short, dense and of uniform length and smoothness all over the body. The hairs are straight and not longer than 1 inch. No fringe anywhere.

**Color**—Solid coats of gray (blue), black, mahogany and tawny, and the lighter and darker shades of these colors. Some brindling allowable in all colors. When present, brindling must be tan (reverse brindle). There may be solid white markings on the chest, throat area from chin to chest, underside of the body, penis sheath, backs of the pasterns, and on the toes. There may be white hairs at the back of the wrists. Disqualifications: White markings on any part of the body not mentioned as allowed.

**Gait**—The Neapolitan Mastiff's movement is not flashy, but rather slow and lumbering. Normal gaits are the walk, trot, gallop, and pace. The strides are long and elastic, at the same time, powerful, characterized by a long push from the hindquarters and extension of the forelegs. Rolling motion and swaying of the body at all gaits is characteristic. Pacing in the show ring is not to be penalized. Slight paddling movement of the front feet is normal. The head is carried level with or slightly above the back.

**Temperament**—The Neapolitan Mastiff is steady and loyal to his owner, not aggressive or apt to bite without reason. As a protector of his property and owners, he is always watchful and does not relish intrusion by strangers into his personal space. His attitude is calm yet wary. In the show ring he is majestic and powerful, but not showy.

**Faults**—The foregoing description is that of the ideal Neapolitan Mastiff. Any deviation from the above described dog must be penalized to the extent of the deviation.

## DISQUALIFICATIONS

*Absence of wrinkles and folds.*
*Absence of dewlap.*
*Lack of tail or short tail, which is less than ⅓ the length from point of insertion of the tail to the hock.*
*White markings on any part of the body not mentioned.*

**Approved January 13, 2004**
**Effective May 1, 2004**

# NEWFOUNDLAND

THERE IS MUCH UNCERTAINTY ABOUT THE ORIGIN OF THE NEWFOUNDLAND breed. Some say that the ancestors are a combination of indigenous Indian dogs interbred with others such as the Great Pyrenees dogs brought to the coast of Newfoundland by the Basque fishermen or dogs brought to North America by the Vikings. At any rate, a breed evolved that was particularly suited to its island of origin.

Newfoundlands were large dogs, with sufficient size and strength to perform the tasks required of them. They had heavy coats for protection against the long winters and icy waters surrounding their native island. Strong and partially webbed feet have enabled them to travel easily over marshes and shores. The breed was admired for its physical prowess and attractive disposition, and as a result, some specimens were taken to England where they were bred extensively. Most Newfoundlands, even those in Newfoundland, are descended from forebears born in England. Today's Newfoundland is admired and bred in many countries worldwide.

The breed standard describes a true working dog, one that is essentially as much at home in water as on land. Canine literature gives us stories of brave Newfoundlands that have rescued men and women from the sea. There are also stories of shipwrecks made less terrible by dogs that carried lifelines to stricken vessels and of Newfoundlands rescuing children who had fallen into deep water. We find other accounts of dogs whose work was less spectacular but equally valuable, as they helped fishermen with heavy nets and performed other tasks necessary to the owners' occupations. Although this is a superior water dog, Newfoundlands have been and are still used as working dogs, pulling carts or carrying burdens as a pack animal.

In order to perform these duties, Newfoundlands must be large dogs, big enough to bring even a drowning adult to shore. They must have powerful hindquarters and lung capacity enabling them to swim great distances. Their heavy coat is needed for protection from the icy waters. In short, they must be strong, muscular, and sound so that they are able to do the work for which they have become justly famous. Above all, Newfoundlands must have intelligence, loyalty, and a sweet nature, which are their best-known traits. Upon command, they must be willing and able to help their owners perform any necessary tasks, and they must also have the intelligence to act independently with responsibility when rescue work demands it.

In this country, where the Newfoundland is kept not as an active worker but largely as a companion, we particularly appreciate the sterling traits of the true Newfoundland disposition. Here we have the great size and strength that make the breed an effective guardian, combined with the gentleness that makes them safe companions. For generations, Newfoundlands have been the traditional children's protector and playmate. Not as easily hurt by small tugging fingers—as a small dog may be—of their own accord Newfoundlands undertake without training the duties of nursemaid.

We know of no better description of Newfoundland character than the famous epitaph on the monument at Lord Byron's estate, at Newstead Abbey, England:

*Near this spot*
*Are deposited the Remains of one*
*Who possessed Beauty without Vanity,*
*Strength without Insolence,*
*Courage without Ferocity,*
*And all the Virtues of Man without his Vices.*
*This Praise, which would be unmeaning Flattery*
*If inscribed over human Ashes,*
*Is but a just tribute to the Memory of*
*Boatswain, a Dog,*
*Who was born in Newfoundland May 1803*
*And died at Newstead Nov. 18th, 1808.*

# OFFICIAL STANDARD FOR THE NEWFOUNDLAND

**General Appearance**—The Newfoundland is a sweet-dispositioned dog that acts neither dull nor ill-tempered. He is a devoted companion. A multipurpose dog, at home on land and in water, the Newfoundland is capable of draft work and possesses natural lifesaving abilities.

The Newfoundland is a large, heavily coated, well balanced dog that is deep-bodied, heavily boned, muscular, and strong. A good specimen of the breed has dignity and proud head carriage.

The following description is that of the ideal Newfoundland. Any deviation from this ideal is to be penalized to the extent of the deviation. Structural and movement faults common to all working dogs are as undesirable in the Newfoundland as in any other breed, even though they are not specifically mentioned herein.

**Size, Proportion, Substance**—Average height for adult dogs is 28 inches, for adult bitches, 26 inches. Approximate weight of adult dogs ranges from 130 to 150 pounds, adult bitches from 100 to 120 pounds. The dog's appearance is more massive throughout than the bitch's. Large size is desirable, but never at the expense of balance, structure, and correct gait. The Newfoundland is slightly longer than tall when measured from the point of shoulder to point of buttocks and from withers to ground. He is a dog of considerable substance which is determined by spring of rib, strong muscle, and heavy bone.

**Head**—The head is massive, with a broad *skull*, slightly arched crown, and strongly developed occipital bone. Cheeks are well developed. *Eyes* are dark brown. (Browns and Grays may have lighter eyes and should be penalized only to the extent that color affects expression.) They are relatively small, deep-set, and spaced wide apart. Eyelids fit closely with no inversion. *Ears* are relatively small and triangular with rounded tips. They are set on the skull level with, or slightly above, the brow and lie close to the head. When the ear is brought forward, it reaches to the inner corner of the eye on the same side. *Expression* is soft and reflects the characteristics of the breed: benevolence, intelligence and dignity.

Forehead and face are smooth and free of wrinkles. Slope of the stop is moderate but, because of the well developed brow, it may appear abrupt in profile. The *muzzle* is clean-cut, broad throughout its length, and deep. Depth and length are approximately equal, the length from tip of nose to stop being less than that from stop to occiput. The top of the muzzle is rounded, and the bridge, in profile, is straight or only slightly arched. Teeth meet in a scissors or level *bite*. Dropped lower incisors, in an otherwise normal bite, are not indicative of a skeletal malocclusion and should be considered only a minor deviation.

**Neck, Topline, Body**—The *neck* is strong and well set on the shoulders and is long enough for proud head carriage. The *back* is strong, broad, and muscular and is level from just behind the withers to the croup. The chest is full and deep with the brisket reaching at least down to the elbows. Ribs are well sprung, with the anterior third of the rib cage tapered to allow elbow clearance. The flank is deep. The croup is broad and slopes slightly. *Tail*—Tail set follows the natural line of the croup. The tail is broad at the base and strong. It has no kinks, and the distal bone reaches to the hock. When the dog is standing relaxed, its tail hangs straight or with a slight curve at the end. When the dog is in motion or excited, the tail is carried out, but it does not curl over the back.

**Forequarters**—Shoulders are muscular and well laid back. Elbows lie directly below the highest point of the withers. Forelegs are muscular, heavily boned, straight, and parallel to each other, and the elbows point directly to the rear. The distance from elbow to ground equals about half the dog's height. Pasterns are strong and slightly sloping. Feet are proportionate to the body in size, webbed, and cat foot in type. Dewclaws may be removed.

**Hindquarters**—The rear assembly is powerful, muscular and heavily boned. Viewed from the rear, the legs are straight and parallel. Viewed from the side, the thighs are broad and fairly long. Stifles and hocks are well bent and the line from hock to ground is perpendicular. Hocks are well let down. Hind feet are similar to the front feet. Dewclaws should be removed.

**Coat**—The adult Newfoundland has a flat, water-resistant, double coat that tends to fall back into place when rubbed against the nap. The outer coat is coarse, moderately long, and full, either straight or with a wave. The undercoat is soft and dense, although it is often less dense during the summer months or in warmer climates. Hair on the face and muzzle is short and fine. The backs of the legs are feathered all the way down. The tail is covered with long dense hair. Excess hair may be trimmed for neatness. Whiskers need not be trimmed.

**Color**—Color is secondary to type, structure and soundness. Recognized Newfoundland colors are black, brown, gray, and white and black.

*Solid Colors*—Blacks, Browns, and Grays may appear as solid colors or solid colors with white at any, some, or all, of the following locations: chin, chest, toes and tip of tail. Any amount of white found at these locations is typical and is not penalized. Also typical are a tinge of bronze on a black or gray coat and lighter furnishings on a brown or gray coat.

*Landseer*—White base coat with black markings. Typically, the head is solid black, or black with white on the muzzle, with or without a blaze. There is a separate black saddle and black on the rump extending onto a white tail.

Markings, on either Solid Colors or Landseers, might deviate considerably from those described and should be penalized only to the extent of the deviation. Clear white or white with minimal ticking is preferred. Beauty of markings should be considered only when comparing dogs of otherwise comparable quality and never at the expense of type, structure and soundness.

*Disqualifications*—Any colors or combinations of colors not specifically described are disqualified.

**Gait**—The Newfoundland in motion has good reach, strong drive, and gives the impression of effortless power. His gait is smooth and rhythmic, covering the maximum amount of ground with the minimum number of steps. Forelegs and hind legs travel straight forward. As the dog's speed increases, the legs tend toward single tracking. When moving, a slight roll of the skin is characteristic of the breed. Essential to good movement is the balance of correct front and rear assemblies.

**Temperament**—Sweetness of temperament is the hallmark of the Newfoundland; this is the most important single characteristic of the breed.

## DISQUALIFICATIONS

*Any colors or combinations of colors not specifically described are disqualified.*

**Approved May 8, 1990**
**Effective June 28, 1990**

# PORTUGUESE WATER DOG

*Lion clip*

*Working clip*

HE PORTUGUESE WATER DOG ONCE EXISTED ALL ALONG PORTUGAL'S coast, where it was taught to herd fish into the nets, to retrieve lost tackle or broken nets, and to act as a courier from ship to ship, or ship to shore. Portuguese Water Dogs rode in bobbing trawlers as they worked their way from the warm Atlantic waters of Portugal to the frigid fishing waters off the coast of Iceland, where the fleets caught saltwater codfish to bring home.

In Portugal, the breed is called Cao de Agua (pronounced *Kown-d'Ahgwa*). *Cao* means dog, *de Agua* means of water. In his native land, the dog is also known as the Portuguese Fishing Dog. Cao de Agua de Pelo Ondulado is the name given the wavy-coated variety, and Cao de Agua de Pelo Encaradolado is the name for the curly-coated variety.

A spirited, intelligent breed of fine temperament, rugged and robust, with a profuse waterproof coat (sometimes tolerated by individuals with allergies) and webbed feet, he is an ideal outdoor dog, capable of limitless work. He stands 20 to 23 inches (17 to 21 for bitches) and weighs between 42 and 60 pounds (35 and 50 for bitches)—a variation explained for by the fact that small dogs were more practical for small boats, and larger dogs for the larger boats.

He is shown in either of two clips—the lion clip, with the middle, hindquarters, and muzzle clipped short and the rest of the coat left long, and in the working-retriever clip. Adherents of the lion clip say it shows off a good rear and displays the muscles better, while advocates of the retriever clip like the fact that it is easy to care for, and prepares the dog for all sorts of outdoor adventure.

Some belief exists that the breed traces as far back as 700 B.C. to the wild Central-Asian steppes, near the Chinese-Russian border, terrains and waters guaranteed to encourage ruggedness. The early people who lived here raised cattle, sheep, camels, or horses, depending upon where they lived. They also raised dogs to herd them. Isolated from the rest of the world, these dogs developed into a definite type very much like the heavier long-coated Portuguese Water Dog.

One theory of these long-perished times is that some of the rugged Asian herding dogs were captured by the fierce Berbers. The Berbers spread slowly across the face of North Africa to Morocco. Their descendants, the Moors, arrived in Portugal in the eighth century, bringing the water dogs with them.

Another theory purports that some of the dogs left the Asian steppes with the Goths, a confederation of German tribes. Some (the Ostrogoths) went west and their dogs became the German *pudel*. Others (the Visigoths) went south to fight the Romans, and their dogs became the Lion Dog. In A.D. 400, the Visigoths invaded Spain and Portugal (then known only as Iberia) and the dogs found their homeland.

These theories explain how the Poodle and the Portuguese Water Dog may have developed from the same ancient genetic pool. At one time the Poodle was a longer-coated dog, as is one variety of the Portuguese Water Dog. The possibility also exists that some of the long-coated water dogs grew up with the ancient Iberians. In early times, Celtiberians migrated from lands which now belong to southwestern Germany. Swarming over the Pyrenees, circulating over the whole of Western Europe, they established bases in Iberia, as well as in Ireland, Wales, and Brittany. The Irish Water Spaniel is believed to be a descendant of the Portuguese Water Dog.

Cloistered along remote cliffs of the rugged coast of southern Portugal, the breed remained in its rough form for centuries. But early in the twentieth century, as the agricultural country experienced social upheaval, the dog shared the fate of the Portuguese fishermen who were quickly vanishing from the coastline.

In the 1930s, a wealthy Portuguese shipping magnate and dog fancier, Dr. Vasco Bensuade, took it upon himself to save the breed. The Clube dos Cacadores Portuguese was reorganized, the breed was exhibited in shows, a standard was written, and the breed was classified as a Working Dog by the Clube Portuguese de Caniculture.

In 1954, a few Portuguese Water Dogs were exported from Portugal to England. The Kennel Club (England) recognized the breed as a Working Dog. Though accepted, the breed languished in the British Isles and there were no registrations after 1957.

Interest began in the United States in 1958, when Mr. and Mrs. Harrington, of New York, received a pair from England as part of a trade of rare breeds. Among those taking an early interest in the breed were Mr. and Mrs. Herbert Miller, of Connecticut, who acquired the first direct import to this country from Portugal— a puppy bitch purchased from Senhora Branco, a former lady bullfighter who had inherited Dr. Bensuade's kennels in Portugal.

On August 13, 1972, sixteen people involved with the breed met at the Miller home to form the Portuguese Water Dog Club of America. At the time there were only twelve known dogs of the breed in America, but the breeders worked dedicatedly, and by September 1982 the number of dogs had grown to over 650, located in forty-one states, and there were over fifty serious breeders. The Portuguese Water Dog was admitted to the AKC Miscellaneous class on June 3, 1981. Three months later, the breed had its first obedience champion, Spindrift Kedge. The Portuguese Water Dog was accepted for AKC registration on August 1, 1983, and became eligible to compete as a member of the Working Group, on January 1, 1984.

# OFFICIAL STANDARD FOR THE PORTUGUESE WATER DOG

**General Appearance**—Known for centuries along Portugal's coast, this seafaring breed was prized by fishermen for a spirited, yet obedient nature, and a robust, medium build that allowed for a full day's work in and out of the water. The Portuguese Water Dog is a swimmer and diver of exceptional ability and stamina, who aided his master at sea by retrieving broken nets, herding schools of fish, and carrying messages between boats and to shore. He is a loyal companion and alert guard. This highly intelligent utilitarian breed is distinguished by two coat types, either curly or wavy; an impressive head of considerable breadth and well proportioned mass; a ruggedly built, well-knit body; and a powerful, thickly based tail, carried gallantly or used purposefully as a rudder. The Portuguese Water Dog provides an indelible impression of strength, spirit and soundness.

**Size, Proportion, Substance**—*Size*—*Height* at the withers: Males, 20 to 23 inches. The ideal is 22 inches. Females, 17 to 21 inches. The ideal is 19 inches. *Weight*—For males, 42 to 60 pounds; for females, 35 to 50 pounds. *Proportion*—Off square; slightly longer than tall when measured from prosternum to rearmost point of the buttocks, and from withers to ground. *Substance*—Strong, substantial bone; well developed, neither refined nor coarse, and a solidly built, muscular body.

**Head**—An essential characteristic; distinctively large, well proportioned and with exceptional breadth of topskull. *Expression*—Steady, penetrating, and attentive. *Eyes*—Medium in size; set well apart, and a bit obliquely. Roundish and neither prominent nor sunken. Black or various tones of brown in color. Darker eyes are preferred. Eye rims fully pigmented with black edges in black, black and white, or white dogs; brown edges in brown dogs. Haws are dark and not apparent. *Ears*—Set well above the line of the eye. Leather is heart shaped and thin. Except for a small opening at the back, ears are held nicely against the head. Tips should not reach below the lower jaw.

*Skull*—In profile, it is slightly longer than the muzzle, its curvature more accentuated at the back than in the front. When viewed head-on, the top of the skull is very broad and appears domed, with a slight depression in the middle. The forehead is prominent, and has a central furrow, extending two-thirds of the distance from stop to occiput. The occiput is well defined. *Stop*—Well defined. *Muzzle*—Substantial; wider at the base than at the nose. *Jaws*—Strong and neither over nor undershot. *Nose*—Broad, well flared nostrils. Fully pigmented; black in dogs with black, black and white, or white coats; various tones of brown in dogs with brown coats. *Lips*—Thick, especially in front; no flew. Lips and mucous membranes of the roof of the mouth, under tongue, and gums are quite black, or well ticked with black in dogs with black, black and white, or white coats; various tones of brown in dogs with brown coats. *Bite*—Scissors or level. *Teeth*—Not visible when the mouth is closed. Canines strongly developed.

**Neck, Topline, Body**—*Neck*—Straight, short, round, and held high. Strongly muscled. No dewlap. *Topline*—Level and firm. *Body*—Chest is broad and deep, reaching down to the elbow. *Ribs* are long and well-sprung to provide optimum lung capacity. *Abdomen* well held up in a graceful line. *Back* is broad and well muscled. Loin is short and meets the croup smoothly. *Croup* is well formed and only slightly inclined with hip bones hardly apparent. *Tail*—Not docked; thick at the base and tapering; set on slightly below the line of the back; should not reach below the hock. When the dog is attentive the tail is held in a ring, the front of which should not reach forward of the loin. The tail is of great help when swimming and diving.

**Forequarters**—*Shoulders* are well inclined and very strongly muscled. *Upper arms* are strong. *Forelegs* are strong and straight with long, well muscled forearms. *Carpus* is heavy-boned, wider in front than at the side. *Pasterns* are long and strong. Dewclaws may be removed. *Feet* are round and rather flat. Toes neither knuckled up nor too long. Webbing between the toes is of soft skin, well covered with hair, and reaches the toe tips. Central pad is very thick, others normal. Nails held up slightly off the ground. Black, brown, white, and striped nails are allowed.

**Hindquarters**—Powerful; well balanced with the front assembly. *Legs,* viewed from the rear, are parallel to each other, straight and very strongly muscled in upper and lower thighs. *Buttocks* are well developed. *Tendons* and hocks are strong. *Metatarsus* long, no dewclaws. *Feet* similar in all respects to forefeet.

**Coat**—A profuse, thickly planted coat of strong, healthy hair, covering the whole body evenly, except where the forearm meets the brisket and in the groin area, where it is thinner. No undercoat, mane or ruff.

There are *two varieties of coat:*

*Curly*—Compact, cylindrical curls, somewhat lusterless. The hair on the ears is sometimes wavy.

*Wavy*—Falling gently in waves, not curls, and with a slight sheen.

**No preference will be given to coat type, either curly or wavy.**

**Clip**—Two clips are acceptable:

*Lion Clip*—As soon as the coat grows long, the middle part and hindquarters, as well as the muzzle, are clipped. The hair at the end of the tail is left at full length.

*Retriever Clip*—In order to give a natural appearance and a smooth unbroken line, the entire coat is scissored or clipped to follow the outline of the dog, leaving a short blanket of coat no longer than one inch in length. The hair at the end of the tail is left at full length.

**No discrimination will be made against the correct presentation of a dog in either Lion Clip or Retriever Clip.**

**Color**—Black, white, and various tones of brown; also combinations of black or brown with white. A white coat does not imply albinism provided nose, mouth, and eyelids are black. In animals with black, white, or black and white coats, the skin is decidedly bluish.

**Gait**—Short, lively steps when walking. The trot is a forward striding, well balanced movement.

**Temperament**—An animal of spirited disposition, self-willed, brave, and very resistant to fatigue. A dog of exceptional intelligence and a loyal companion, it obeys its master with facility and apparent pleasure. It is obedient with those who look after it or with those for whom it works.

**Summary Statement**—The Portuguese Water Dog is spirited yet obedient, robust, and of unexaggerated, functional conformation; sure, substantially boned and muscled, and able to do a full day's work in and out of the water.

**Faults**—Any deviation from the described ideal is a fault. However, those inherent characteristics that are imperative for the maintenance of proper type, and therefore cannot be overlooked, are listed as Major Faults.

## MAJOR FAULTS

1. **Temperament**—*Shy, vicious or unsound behavior.*
2. **Head**—*Unimpressive; small in overall size; narrow in topskull; snipy in muzzle.*
3. **Substance**—*Light or refined in bone; lacking in muscle.*
4. **Coat**—*Sparse; naturally short, close-lying hair, partially or over all; wispy or wiry in texture; brittle; double-coated.*
5. **Tail**—*Other than as described. Extremely low set. Heavy or droopy in action.*
6. **Pigment**—*Any deviation from described pigmentation; other than black or various tones of brown eye color; pink or partial pigmentation in nose, lips, eyes, or eye rims.*
7. **Bite**—*Overshot or undershot.*

**Approved January 15, 1991**
**Effective February 27, 1991**

# Rottweiler

HE ORIGIN OF THE ROTTWEILER IS NOT DOCUMENTED. ACTUAL HISTORY, tempered by reasonable supposition, indicates the likelihood that this breed is descended from one of the drover dogs indigenous to ancient Rome. This drover has been described by various accredited sources as being of the mastiff type: a dependable, rugged, willing worker, possessing great intelligence and a strong guarding instinct.

The transition from Roman herding dog to the Rottweiler we know today can be attributed to the desire of Roman emperors to conquer Europe. Vast armies were required for these expeditions, and the logistics of feeding the legions became a major consideration. No refrigeration existed, so meat had to be on the hoof and travel with the troops. A dog had to keep the herd intact during the long march, and the mastiff type described above was admirably suited to that job and the additional responsibility of guarding the supply dumps at night.

Roman military campaigns varied in scope, but the one of concern to us took place in approximately A.D. 74. Its route across the Alps terminated in what is now southern Germany. There is much evidence supporting the vital role played by the fearless Roman drover dog on this trek from Rome to the banks of the Neckar River.

We have no reason to doubt that through the next two centuries, descendants of the original Roman drover dogs continued to guard the herds. Agriculture and trading cattle remained prime occupations, ensuring further need for the dogs.

In about 700, the local duke ordered that a Christian church be built on the site of the former Roman baths. Excavations unearthed the red tiles of Roman villas. The site was named das Rote Wil ("the red tile"). This, of course, is recognizable as the derivation of the present name, Rottweil. Rottweil's dominance as a cultural and trade center increased unabated. In the middle of the twelfth century an all-new town with elaborate fortifications was built. This security attracted and increased commerce in cattle. Butchers concentrated in the area, and more dogs were needed to drive the cattle to and from market.

The descendants of the Roman drover dog plied their trade without interruption until the middle of the nineteenth century, at which time cattle driving was outlawed. The Rottweiler Metzgerhund, or Butcher Dog, then fell on hard times, as their function had been severely curtailed. In those days, dogs earned their keep or there was no reason for their existence. The number of Rottweilers declined so radically that in 1882 the dog show in Heilbronn, Germany, reported just one poor example of the breed.

The annals of cynology make no further mention of the breed until 1901, when a combined Rottweiler and Leonberger club was formed. This club was short-lived but important because it produced the first Rottweiler standard. It is noteworthy that the general type advocated in that standard has not changed substantially, and the character called for has not changed at all.

From 1901 to 1907, the Rottweiler again found favor as a police dog. Several clubs were organized, as dissension was common. In 1921, the Allgemeiner Deutscher Rottweiler Klub (ADRK) was formed. By then, 3,400 Rottweilers had been registered by three or four separate clubs. Duplications and confusion ended in 1924, when the ADRK published its first studbook. The ADRK has remained intact since its inception, despite the difficulties encountered during and in the aftermath of World War II.

The Rottweiler was admitted to the AKC Stud Book in 1931, and the standard was adopted in 1935. An American Rottweiler won an obedience title for the first time in 1939, and the first championship was earned in 1948. The American Rottweiler Club (ARC), organized in 1971, is the AKC parent club for the breed. The ARC was approved for its first specialty show in 1981.

The standard calls for a compact and muscular dog, with a medium- to large-size body that enables Rottweilers to efficiently perform their original functions: pull carts, herd stock for farmers, and assist police in apprehending criminals. The short, docked tail is a distinctive characteristic of the Rottweiler. The only acceptable color is solid black with tan- to rust-colored markings. Rottweilers must be calm, confident, and courageous, but not unduly aggressive. This strong-willed, powerful breed is not for everyone, but with proper breeding, socializing, and training Rottweilers are very gentle and totally devoted to their families.

# OFFICIAL STANDARD FOR THE ROTTWEILER

**General Appearance**—The ideal Rottweiler is a medium large, robust and powerful dog, black with clearly defined rust markings. His compact and substantial build denotes great strength, agility and endurance. Dogs are characteristically more massive throughout with larger frame and heavier bone than bitches. Bitches are distinctly feminine, but without weakness of substance or structure.

**Size, Proportion, Substance**—Dogs—24 inches to 27 inches. Bitches—22 inches to 25 inches, with preferred size being mid-range of each sex. Correct proportion is of primary importance, as long as size is within the standard's range.

The length of body, from prosternum to the rearmost projection of the rump, is slightly longer than the height of the dog at the withers, the most desirable proportion of the height to length being 9 to 10. The Rottweiler is neither coarse nor shelly. Depth of chest is approximately fifty percent (50%) of the height of the dog. His bone and muscle mass must be sufficient to balance his frame, giving a compact and very powerful appearance.

*Serious Faults*—Lack of proportion, undersized, oversized, reversal of sex characteristics (bitchy dogs, doggy bitches).

**Head**—Of medium length, broad between the ears; forehead line seen in profile is moderately arched; zygomatic arch and stop well developed with strong broad upper and lower jaws. The desired ratio of backskull to muzzle is 3 to 2. Forehead is preferred dry, however, some wrinkling may occur when dog is alert. *Expression* is noble, alert, and self-assured. *Eyes* of medium size, almond shaped with well fitting lids, moderately deep-set, neither protruding nor receding. The desired color is a uniform dark brown. *Serious Faults*—Yellow (bird of prey) eyes, eyes of different color or size, hairless eye rim. *Disqualification*—Entropion. Ectropion. *Ears* of medium size, pendant, triangular in shape; when carried alertly the ears are level with the top of the skull and appear to broaden it. Ears are to be set well apart, hanging forward with the inner edge lying tightly against the head and terminating at approximately mid-cheek. *Serious Faults*—Improper carriage (creased, folded or held away from cheek/head). *Muzzle*—Bridge is straight, broad at base with slight tapering towards tip. The end of the muzzle is broad with well developed chin. Nose is broad rather than round and always black. Lips—Always black; corners closed; inner mouth pigment is preferred dark. *Serious Faults*—Total lack of mouth pigment (pink mouth). *Bite and Dentition*—Teeth 42 in number (20 upper, 22 lower), strong, correctly placed, meeting in a scissors bite—lower incisors touching inside of upper incisors. *Serious Faults*—Level bite; any missing tooth. *Disqualifications*—Overshot, undershot (when incisors do not touch or mesh); wry mouth; two or more missing teeth.

**Neck, Topline, Body**—*Neck*—Powerful, well muscled, moderately long, slightly arched and without loose skin. *Topline*—The back is firm and level, extending in a straight line from behind the withers to the croup. The back remains horizontal to the ground while the dog is moving or standing. *Body*—The chest is roomy, broad and deep, reaching to elbow, with well pronounced forechest and well sprung, oval ribs. Back is straight and strong. Loin is short, deep and well muscled. Croup is broad, of medium length and only slightly sloping. Underline of a mature Rottweiler has a slight tuck-up. Males must have two normal testicles properly descended into the scrotum. *Disqualification*—Unilateral cryptorchid or cryptorchid males. *Tail*—Tail docked short, close to body, leaving one or two tail vertebrae. The set of the tail is more important than length. Properly set, it gives an impression of elongation of topline; carried slightly above horizontal when the dog is excited or moving.

**Forequarters**—Shoulder blade is long and well laid back. Upper arm equal in length to shoulder blade, set so elbows are well under body. Distance from withers to elbow and elbow to ground is equal. Legs are strongly developed with straight, heavy bone, not set close together. Pasterns are strong, springy and almost perpendicular to the ground. Feet are round, compact with well arched toes, turning neither in nor out. Pads are thick and hard. Nails short, strong and black. Dewclaws may be removed.

**Hindquarters**—Angulation of hindquarters balances that of forequarters. Upper thigh is fairly long, very broad and well muscled. Stifle joint is well turned. Lower thigh is long, broad and powerful, with extensive muscling leading into a strong hock joint. Rear pasterns are nearly perpendicular to the ground. Viewed from the rear, hind legs are straight, strong and wide enough apart to fit with a properly built body. Feet are somewhat longer than the front feet, turning neither in nor out, equally compact with well arched toes. Pads are thick and hard. Nails short, strong, and black. Dewclaws must be removed.

**Coat**—Outer coat is straight, coarse, dense, of medium length and lying flat. Undercoat should be present on neck and thighs, but the amount is influenced by climatic conditions. Undercoat should not show through outer coat. The coat is shortest on head, ears and legs, longest on breeching. The Rottweiler is to be exhibited in the natural condition with no trimming. *Fault*—Wavy coat. *Serious Faults*—Open, excessively short, or curly coat; total lack of undercoat; any trimming that alters the length of the natural coat. *Disqualification*—Long coat.

**Color**—Always black with rust to mahogany markings. The demarcation between black and rust is to be clearly defined. The markings should be located as follows: a spot over each eye; on cheeks; as a strip around each side of muzzle, but not on the bridge of the nose; on throat; triangular mark on both sides of prosternum; on forelegs from carpus downward to the toes; on inside of rear legs showing down the front of the stifle and broadening out to front of rear legs from hock to toes, but not completely eliminating black from rear of pasterns; under tail; black penciling on toes. The undercoat is gray, tan or black. Quantity and location of rust markings is important and should not exceed ten percent of body color. *Serious Faults*—Straw-colored, excessive, insufficient or sooty markings; rust marking other than described above; white marking any place on dog (a few rust or white hairs do not constitute a marking). *Disqualifications*—Any base color other than black; absence of all markings.

**Gait**—The Rottweiler is a trotter. His movement should be balanced, harmonious, sure, powerful and unhindered, with strong forereach and a powerful rear drive. The motion is effortless, efficient and ground-covering. Front and rear legs are thrown neither in nor out, as the imprint of hind feet should touch that of forefeet. In a trot the forequarters and hindquarters are mutually coordinated while the back remains level, firm and relatively motionless. As speed increases the legs will converge under body towards a center line.

**Temperament**—The Rottweiler is basically a calm, confident and courageous dog with a self-assured aloofness that does not lend itself to immediate and indiscriminate friendships. A Rottweiler is self-confident and responds quietly and with a wait-and-see attitude to influences in his environment. He has an inherent desire to protect home and family, and is an intelligent dog of extreme hardness and adaptability with a strong willingness to work, making him especially suited as a companion, guardian and general all-purpose dog.

The behavior of the Rottweiler in the show ring should be controlled, willing and adaptable, trained to submit to examination of mouth, testicles, etc. An aloof or reserved dog should not be penalized, as this reflects the accepted character of the breed. An aggressive or belligerent attitude towards other dogs should not be faulted.

A judge shall excuse from the ring any shy Rottweiler. A dog shall be judged fundamentally shy if, refusing to stand for examination, it shrinks away from the judge. A dog that in the opinion of the judge menaces or threatens him/her, or exhibits any sign that it may not be safely approached or examined by the judge in the normal manner, shall be excused from the ring. A dog that in the opinion of the judge attacks any person in the ring shall be disqualified.

**Summary**—*Faults*—The foregoing is a description of the ideal Rottweiler. Any structural fault that detracts from the above described working dog must be penalized to the extent of the deviation.


## DISQUALIFICATIONS

*Entropion, ectropion. Overshot, undershot (when incisors do not touch or mesh); wry mouth; two or more missing teeth. Unilateral cryptorchid or cryptorchid males. Long coat. Any base color other than black; absence of all markings. A dog that in the opinion of the judge attacks any person in the ring.*

**Approved May 8, 1990**
**Effective June 28, 1990**

# SAINT BERNARD

*Shorthaired Dog*                    *Longhaired Dog*

*S*HROUDED IN LEGEND AND THE MISTS OF TIME, THE ORIGIN OF THE SAINT Bernard is subject to many theories.

It seems most probable that the Saint Bernard developed from stock that resulted from the breeding of heavy Asian Molosser (*Canis molossus*), brought to Helvetia (Switzerland) by Roman armies during the first two centuries A.D., with native dogs which undoubtedly existed in the region at the time of the Roman invasions.

During the following centuries, these dogs were widely used in the valley farms and Alpine dairies for a variety of guarding, herding, and drafting duties. Referred to as Talhund (Valley Dog) or Bauernhund (Farm Dog), they were apparently well established by 1050, when Archdeacon Bernard de Menthon founded the famous hospice in the Swiss Alps as a refuge for travelers crossing the treacherous passes between Switzerland and Italy.

Just when dogs were first brought to the hospice is debatable, since the building was destroyed by fire in the late sixteenth century, and, soon after, a large part of the hospice archives were lost. The first notation concerning the dogs was not until 1707. This, however, was merely a casual reference to dogs at the hospice and carried the implication that their rescue work at the Saint Bernard Pass was a fact well known at the time. From a digest of early references, it appears that the dogs were first brought to the hospice sometime between 1660 and 1670. It is likely that the monks recruited large dogs from the valley to serve as watchdogs and companions during the long winter months, when the hospice was almost completely isolated.

This isolation of the hospice no doubt resulted in inbreeding of the original stock which soon produced the distinctive strain of Hospice Dog. It also follows that only those animals with the strongest instincts for survival in the extremely adverse conditions at the hospice were to leave their genetic imprint upon the breed during those early years.

The lonely monks, who took the dogs along on their trips of mercy, soon discovered the animals were excellent pathfinders in the drifting snow, and the dogs' highly developed sense of smell made them invaluable in locating helpless travelers overcome during storms. Thus began this working together of monk and dog which made many pages of romantic canine history.

During the three centuries that Saint Bernards were used in rescue work at the hospice, it is estimated that they were responsible for the saving of well over 2,500 human lives. Although the building of railroad tunnels through the Alps has lessened foot and vehicular travel across the Saint Bernard Pass, the monks continued until 2004 to maintain these fine dogs for companionship and in the honor of the hospice tradition.

We are told that Saint Bernards required no training for their work since generations of service in this capacity seemed to have stamped the rescuing instinct indelibly upon their character. It would be more accurate to say that the dogs' rescue instincts were used as the basis for training by the monks. In the company of the monks, young dogs were taken on patrols with a pack of older dogs in search of possible traveler casualties. When the dogs came upon a victim, they would lie down beside him to provide warmth and lick the person's face to restore consciousness. In the meantime, one of the patrol dogs would be on his way back to the hospice to give the alarm and guide a rescue party to the scene.

In addition to their pathfinding capabilities and keen sense of smell that enables them to locate human beings buried under the snow, the dogs are reputed to possess an uncanny sixth sense which warns them of approaching avalanches. Instances have been reported where a dog would suddenly change position for no apparent reason a few seconds before an avalanche came hurtling down across the spot where he had stood, burying it under tons of snow and ice.

Although it was well known that a special type of dog did rescue work at the hospice by 1800, the breed at that time had been given no name other than Hospice Dogs. Between 1800 and 1810, Barry, perhaps the most celebrated dog in history, lived at the hospice. For fully half a century after his death, the hospice dogs in certain parts of Switzerland were called Barryhund (Barry dog) in his honor.

Barry is credited with saving forty lives. Although legend has it that he was killed by the forty-first person he attempted to rescue, who mistook his bulk for that of a wolf, this tale is only an interesting story. As a matter of fact, Barry was given a painless death in Bern, Switzerland, in 1814, after he had attained a ripe old age. His mounted remains are preserved in the Natural History Museum in Bern.

The years 1816 to 1818 were seasons of uncommonly severe weather at the hospice, and, as a result, many of the leading hospice strains perished. It was easy at that time, however, to get good animals of like breeding from the lower valleys, and within a few years, the dog situation at the hospice was again satisfactory. Confronted by a similar situation in 1830, coupled with the fact that their breed was considerably weakened by inbreeding and disease, the monks resorted to an out-cross to give added size and new vigor to their dogs. The Newfoundland, which at that time was larger than the Saint Bernard and shared strong rescuing instincts, was the breed decided upon to give the new blood. Results of this cross showed all of the desired objectives and, at the same time, did not destroy the Saint Bernard type and characteristics. Due to this crossing, however, the first longhaired Saint Bernards appeared—before 1830 all Saint Bernards were shorthaired.

At first it was believed that the longhaired variety might have an advantage in the snow and icy conditions existing at the hospice. Unfortunately, ice clung to the coat and made the longhaired dogs unsuited to the tasks of the rescue. The monks gave the longhaired dogs as gifts to friends and benefactors in the valley areas, and only the shorthaired dogs were kept at the hospice.

The English, who as early as 1810 imported some of the hospice dogs to replenish their Mastiff blood, referred to the breed for a number of years as Sacred Dogs. In Germany, around 1828, the name Alpendog was proposed. In 1833, writer Daniel Wilson first spoke of the so-called Saint Bernard dog, but it was not until 1865 that this name definitely appeared, and only since 1880 has it been recognized as the official designation for the breed.

During the last half of the 1800s, breeding of both the longhaired and shorthaired Saint Bernards continued in the valleys of Switzerland, and eventually the breed spread across Germany and other continental European countries and England.

In 1887 at Zurich, an International Congress was guided by Swiss authorities on the breed. At this congress, an international standard for the perfection of the breed was developed.

The Saint Bernard Club of America was organized in the year following the Zurich Congress, and the international standard was adopted by it. This club continues to function for the interests of the Saint Bernard and is one of the oldest specialty clubs in the United States.

# OFFICIAL STANDARD FOR THE SAINT BERNARD

## Shorthaired

**General**—Powerful, proportionately tall figure, strong and muscular in every part, with powerful head and most intelligent expression. In dogs with a dark mask the expression appears more stern, but never ill-natured.

**Head**—Like the whole body, very powerful and imposing. The massive skull is wide, slightly arched and the sides slope in a gentle curve into the very strongly developed, high cheek bones. Occiput only moderately developed. The supra-orbital ridge is very strongly developed and forms nearly a right angle with the long axis of the head. Deeply imbedded between the eyes and starting at the root of the muzzle, a furrow runs over the whole skull. It is strongly marked in the first half, gradually disappearing toward the base of the occiput. The lines at the sides of the head diverge considerably from the outer corner of the eyes toward the back of the head. The skin of the forehead, above the eyes, forms rather noticeable wrinkles, more or less pronounced, which converge toward the furrow. Especially when the dog is alert or at attention, the wrinkles are more visible without in the least giving the impression of morosity. Too strongly developed wrinkles are not desired. The slope from the skull to the muzzle is sudden and rather steep.

The *muzzle* is short, does not taper, and the vertical depth at the root of the muzzle must be greater than the length of the muzzle. The bridge of the muzzle is not arched, but straight; in some dogs, occasionally, slightly broken. A rather wide, well-marked, shallow furrow runs from the root of the muzzle over the entire bridge of the muzzle to the nose. The flews of the upper jaw are strongly developed, not sharply cut, but turning in a beautiful curve into the lower edge, and slightly overhanging. The flews of the lower jaw must not be deeply pendant. The teeth should be sound and strong and should meet in either a scissors or an even bite; the scissors bite being preferable. The undershot bite, although sometimes found with good specimens, is not desirable. The overshot bite is a *fault*. A black roof to the mouth is desirable.

*Nose (Schwamm)*—Very substantial, broad, with wide open nostrils, and, like the lips, always black.

*Ears*—Of medium size, rather high set, with very strongly developed burr (*Muschel*) at the base. They stand slightly away from the head at the base, then drop with a sharp bend to the side and cling to the head without a turn. The flap is tender and forms a rounded triangle, slightly elongated toward the point, the front edge lying firmly to the head, whereas the back edge may stand somewhat away from the head, especially when the dog is at attention. Lightly set ears, which at the base immediately cling to the head, give it an oval and too little marked exterior, whereas a strongly developed base gives the skull a squarer, broader and much more expressive appearance.

*Eyes*—Set more to the front than the sides, are of medium size, dark brown, with intelligent, friendly expression, set moderately deep. The lower eyelids, as a rule, do not close completely and, if that is the case, form an angular wrinkle toward the inner corner of the eye. Eyelids which are too deeply pendant and show conspicuously the lachrymal glands, or a very red, thick haw, and eyes that are too light, are objectionable.

**Neck**—Set high, very strong and when alert or at attention is carried erect. Otherwise horizontally or slightly downward. The junction of head and neck is distinctly marked by an indentation. The nape of the neck is very muscular and rounded at the sides which makes the neck appear rather short. The dewlap of throat and neck is well pronounced: too strong development, however, is not desirable.

**Shoulders**—Sloping and broad, very muscular and powerful. The withers are strongly pronounced.

**Chest**—Very well arched, moderately deep, not reaching below the elbows.

**Back**—Very broad, perfectly straight as far as the haunches, from there gently sloping to the rump, and merging imperceptibly into the root of the tail.

**Hindquarters**—Well-developed. Legs very muscular.

**Belly**—Distinctly set off from the very powerful loin section, only little drawn up.

**Tail**—Starting broad and powerful directly from the rump is long, very heavy, ending in a powerful tip. In repose it hangs straight down, turning gently upward in the lower third only, which is not considered a fault. In a great many specimens the tail is carried with the end slightly bent and therefore hangs down in the shape of an "f." In action all dogs carry the tail more or less turned upward. However it may not be carried too erect or by any means rolled over the back. A slight curling of the tip is sooner admissible.

**Upper Arms**—Very powerful and extraordinarily muscular.

**Lower Leg**—Straight, strong.

**Hind legs**—Hocks of moderate angulation. Dewclaws are not desired; if present, they must not obstruct gait.

**Feet**—Broad, with strong toes, moderately closed, and with rather high knuckles. The so-called dewclaws which sometimes occur on the inside of the hind legs are imperfectly developed toes. They are of no use to the dog and are not taken into consideration in judging. They may be removed by surgery.

**Coat**—Very dense, shorthaired (*stockhaarig*), lying smooth, tough, without however feeling rough to the touch. The thighs are slightly bushy. The tail at the root has longer and denser hair which gradually becomes shorter toward the tip. The tail appears bushy, not forming a flag.

**Color**—White with red or red with white, the red in its various shades; brindle patches with white markings. The colors red and brown-yellow are of entirely equal value. Necessary markings are: white chest, feet and tip of tail, noseband, collar or spot on the nape; the latter and blaze are very desirable. Never of one color or without white. Faulty are all other colors, except the favorite dark shadings on the head (mask) and ears. One distinguishes between mantle dogs and splash-coated dogs.

**Height at Shoulder**—Of the dog should be 27½ inches minimum, of the bitch 25½ inches. Female animals are of finer and more delicate build.

**Considered as Faults**—Are all deviations from the Standard, as for instance a swayback and a disproportionately long back, hocks too much bent, straight hindquarters, upward growing hair in spaces between the toes, out at elbows, cowhocks and weak pasterns.

## Longhaired

The longhaired type completely resembles the shorthaired type except for the coat which is not shorthaired (*stockhaarig*) but of medium length plain to slightly wavy, never rolled or curly and not shaggy either. Usually, on the back, especially from the region of the haunches to the rump, the hair is more wavy, a condition, by the way, that is slightly indicated in the shorthaired dogs. The tail is bushy with dense hair of moderate length. Rolled or curly hair or a flag tail, is faulty. Face and ears are covered with short and soft hair; longer hair at the base of the ear is permissible. Forelegs only slightly feathered; thighs very bushy.

**Approved April 13, 1998**
**Effective May 31, 1998**

# SAMOYED

*D*OG OF THE AGES, WITH A HISTORY AND TRADITION AS FASCINATING AS THE breed itself! The legend runs that from the plateau of Iran, man's first earthly habitat, as the sons of man multiplied, the mightier tribes drove the lesser ones, with their families, their herds, and their dogs, farther and farther away in order that the natural food found there might be ample for those remaining. Onward and still farther north through Mongolia, then the center of the world's culture, on and on, went the lesser tribes, until eventually the Samoyed peoples, of the family of Sayantsi, reliably described as in the "transition stages between the Mongol pure and the Finn," found themselves safely entrenched behind bulwarks of snow and ice in the vast stretches of tundra reaching from the White Sea to the Yenisei River. Here for generations they lived a nomadic life, dependent upon their reindeer herds and upon their dogs as reindeer shepherds, sledge dogs, and household companions.

Here, through the centuries, the Samoyed has bred true. Of all modern breeds, the Samoyed is most nearly akin to the primitive dog—no admixture of wolf or fox runs in the Samoyed strain. The Arctic suns and snows have bleached the harsh stand-off coat and tipped the hairs with an icy sheen. The constant companionship with man through the years has given an almost uncanny "human" understanding, while generations of guarding reindeer, requiring always a protector, never a killer, has developed through the ages in the breed a disposition unique in the canine world.

Nor has the long human association made the stalwart Samoyed a pampered pet. As work dogs, Samoyeds of the great Arctic and Antarctic expeditions have a record of achievement unexcelled in the canine world. The sledge dogs of early polar explorer Fridtjof Nansen (nineteen males averaging 58.7 pounds each, and nine bitches averaging 50.5 pounds), working day after day under conditions of utmost hardship, drew one and a half times their own weight of supplies and worked with the joyous abandon and carefree air typical of the breed. Each new expedition—Jackson-Harmsworth, the Duc d'Abruzzi, Borchgrevink, Shackleton, Scott, and, most notably, Roald Amundsen in his successful reach of the South Pole in 1911—added new luster to the breed's history.

Introduced in England about a hundred years ago, practically every show sees the Samoyeds in the forefront. Queen Alexandra was an ardent fancier, and the descendants of her dogs are found today in many English and American kennels. The dog is found in every region—Samoyeds born in northern Siberia have safely crossed the equator and remained in healthy condition to work in Antarctic snows. Dogs from Antarctic expeditions have survived the suns of Australia to return to England and start great kennels there.

Excitingly eye-arresting, the big white dog with the "smiling face" and dark, intelligent eyes, with a strong, sturdy, muscular body on legs built for speed—the Samoyed is for many the most beautiful breed in existence. An excellent watchdog, yet gentle and companionable. Never a troublemaker, yet able to hold his own when forced into a fight. With an independence born of unusual intelligence, yet marked with a loyalty to a loved owner that wins hearts.

His noble characteristics evidence themselves even in puppies—the "little white teddy bears." Dependable guardian, gentle, kind, sturdy, adaptable, the Samoyed carries in its face and heart the spirit of Christmas the whole year through.

# OFFICIAL STANDARD FOR THE SAMOYED

**General Conformation**

(a) *General Appearance*—The Samoyed, being essentially a working dog, should present a picture of beauty, alertness and strength, with agility, dignity and grace. As his work lies in cold climates, his coat should be heavy and weather-resistant, well groomed, and of good quality rather than quantity. The male carries more of a "ruff" than the female. He should not be long in the back as a weak back would make him practically useless for his legitimate work, but at the same time, a close-coupled body would also place him at a great disadvantage as a draft dog. Breeders should aim for the happy medium, a body not long but muscular, allowing liberty, with a deep chest and well-sprung ribs, strong neck, straight front and especially strong loins. Males should be masculine in appearance and deportment without unwarranted aggressiveness; bitches feminine without weakness of structure or apparent softness of temperament. Bitches may be slightly longer in back than males. They should both give the appearance of being capable of great endurance but be free from coarseness. Because of the depth of chest required, the legs should be moderately long. A very short-legged dog is to be deprecated. Hindquarters should be particularly well developed, stifles well bent and any suggestion of unsound stifles or cowhocks severely penalized. General appearance should include movement and general conformation, indicating balance and good substance.

(b) *Substance*—Substance is that sufficiency of bone and muscle which rounds out a balance with the frame. The bone is heavier than would be expected in a dog of this size but not so massive as to prevent the speed and agility most desirable in a Samoyed. In all builds, bone should be in proportion to body size. The Samoyed should never be so heavy as to appear clumsy nor so light as to appear racy. The weight should be in proportion to the height.

(c) *Height*—Males—21 to 23½ inches; females—19 to 21 inches at the withers. An oversized or undersized Samoyed is to be penalized according to the extent of the deviation.

(d) *Coat (Texture and Condition)*—The Samoyed is a double-coated dog. The body should be well covered with an undercoat of soft, short, thick, close wool with longer and harsh hair growing through it to form the outer coat, which stands straight out from the body and should be free from curl. The coat should form a ruff around the neck and shoulders, framing the head (more on males than on females). Quality of coat should be weather resistant and considered more than quantity. A droopy coat is undesirable. The coat should glisten with a silver sheen. The female does not usually carry as long a coat as most males and it is softer in texture.

(e) *Color*—Samoyeds should be pure white, white and biscuit, cream, or all biscuit. Any other colors disqualify.

**Movement**

(a) *Gait*—The Samoyed should trot, not pace. He should move with a quick agile stride that is well timed. The gait should be free, balanced and vigorous, with good reach in the forequarters and good driving power in the hindquarters. When trotting, there should be a strong rear action drive. Moving at a slow walk or trot, they will not single-track, but as speed increases the legs gradually angle inward until the pads are finally falling on a line directly under the longitudinal center of the body. As the pad marks converge the forelegs and hind legs are carried straight forward in traveling, the stifles not turned in nor out. The back should remain strong, firm and level. A choppy or stilted gait should be penalized.

(b) *Rear End*—Upper thighs should be well developed. Stifles well bent—approximately 45 degrees to the ground. Hocks should be well developed, sharply defined and set at approximately 30 percent of hip height. The hind legs should be parallel when viewed from the rear in a natural stance, strong, well developed, turning neither in nor out. Straight stifles are objectionable. Double-jointedness or cowhocks are a fault. Cowhocks should only be determined if the dog has had an opportunity to move properly.

(c) *Front End*—Legs should be parallel and straight to the pasterns. The pasterns should be strong, sturdy and straight, but flexible with some spring for proper let-down of feet. Because of depth of chest, legs should be moderately long. Length of leg from the ground to the elbow should be approximately 55 percent of the total height at the withers—a very short-legged dog is to be deprecated. Shoulders should be long and sloping, with a layback of 45 degrees and be firmly set. Out at the shoulders or out at the elbows should be penalized. The withers separation should be approximately 1 to 1½ inches.

(d) *Feet*—Large, long, flattish—a hare-foot, slightly spread but not splayed; toes arched; pads thick and tough, with protective growth of hair between the toes. Feet should turn neither in nor out in a natural stance but may turn in slightly in the act of pulling. Turning out, pigeon-toed, round or cat-footed or splayed are faults. Feathers on feet are not too essential but are more profuse on females than on males.

**Head**

(a) *Conformation*—Skull is wedge-shaped, broad, slightly crowned, not round or apple-headed, and should form an equilateral triangle on lines between the inner base of the ears and the central point of the stop. *Muzzle*—Muzzle of medium length and medium width, neither coarse nor snipy; should taper toward the nose and be in proportion to the size of the dog and the width of skull. The muzzle must have depth. Whiskers are not to be removed. *Stop*—Not too abrupt, nevertheless, well defined. *Lips*—Should be black for preference and slightly curved up at the corners of the mouth, giving the "Samoyed smile." Lip lines should not have the appearance of being coarse nor should the flews drop predominately at corners of the mouth. *Ears*—Strong and thick, erect, triangular and slightly rounded at the tips; should not be large or pointed, nor should they be small and "bear-eared." Ears should conform to head size and the size of the dog; they should be set well apart but be within the border of the outer edge of the head; they should be mobile and well covered inside with hair; hair full and stand-off before the ears. Length of ear should be the same measurement as the distance from inner base of ear to outer corner of eye. *Eyes*—Should be dark for preference; should be placed well apart and deep-set; almond shaped with lower lid slanting toward an imaginary point approximately the base of ears. Dark eye rims for preference. Round or protruding eyes penalized. Blue eyes *disqualifying. Nose*—Black for preference but brown, liver, or Dudley nose not penalized. Color of nose sometimes changes with age and weather. *Jaws and Teeth*—Strong, well-set teeth, snugly overlapping with scissors bite. Undershot or overshot should be penalized.

(b) *Expression*—The expression, referred to as "Samoyed expression," is very important and is indicated by sparkle of the eyes, animation and lighting up of the face when alert or intent on anything. Expression is made up of a combination of eyes, ears and mouth. The ears should be erect when alert; the mouth should be slightly curved up at the corners to form the "Samoyed smile."

**Torso**

(a) *Neck*—Strong, well muscled, carried proudly erect, set on sloping shoulders to carry head with dignity when at attention. Neck should blend into shoulders with a graceful arch.

(b) *Chest*—Should be deep, with ribs well sprung out from the spine and flattened at the sides to allow proper movement of the shoulders and freedom for the front legs. Should not be barrel-chested. Perfect depth of chest approximates the point of elbows, and the deepest part of the chest should be back of the forelegs—near the ninth rib. Heart and lung room are secured more by body depth than width.

*(c) Loin and Back*—The withers forms the highest part of the back. Loins strong and slightly arched. The back should be straight to the loin, medium in length, very muscular and neither long nor short coupled. The dog should be "just off square"—the length being approximately five percent more than the height. Females allowed to be slightly longer than males. The belly should be well shaped and tightly muscled and, with the rear of the thorax, should swing up in a pleasing curve (tuck-up). Croup must be full, slightly sloping, and must continue imperceptibly to the tail root.

*Tail*—The tail should be moderately long with the tail bone terminating approximately at the hock when down. It should be profusely covered with long hair and carried forward over the back or side when alert, but sometimes dropped when at rest. It should not be high or low set and should be mobile and loose—not tight over the back. A double hook is a fault. A judge should see the tail over the back once when judging.

*Disposition*—Intelligent, gentle, loyal, adaptable, alert, full of action, eager to serve, friendly but conservative, not distrustful or shy, not overly aggressive. Unprovoked aggressiveness is to be severely penalized.


# DISQUALIFICATIONS

*Any color other than pure white, cream, biscuit, or white and biscuit.*
*Blue eyes.*

**Approved August 10, 1993**
**Effective September 29, 1993**

# SIBERIAN HUSKY

*T*HE SIBERIAN HUSKY WAS ORIGINATED BY THE CHUKCHI PEOPLE OF NORTH-eastern Asia as an endurance sled dog. When changing conditions forced these seminomads to expand their hunting grounds, they responded by developing a unique breed of sled dog, which met their special requirements and upon which their very survival depended. The Chukchis required a sled dog capable of traveling great distances at a moderate speed, carrying a light load in low temperatures, with a minimum expenditure of energy. Research indicates that the Chukchis maintained the purity of their sled dogs through the nineteenth century and that these dogs were the sole and direct ancestors of the breed known in the United States today as the Siberian Husky.

Shortly after 1900, Americans in Alaska began to hear accounts of this superior strain of sled dog in Siberia. The first team of Siberian Huskies made its appearance in the All-Alaska Sweepstakes Race of 1909. The same year, a large number of them were imported to Alaska by Charles Fox Maule Ramsay. His team, driven by John "Iron Man" Johnson, won the grueling 400-mile Sweepstakes in 1910. For the next decade, Siberian Huskies, particularly those bred and raced by Leonhard Seppala, captured most of the racing titles in Alaska, where the rugged terrain was ideally suited to the endurance capabilities of the breed.

In 1925, the city of Nome was stricken by a diphtheria epidemic. Supplies of antitoxin were urgently needed. Many sled dog drivers, including Seppala, were called upon to relay the lifesaving serum to Nome by dog team. This heroic "serum run" focused attention upon Siberian Huskies, and Seppala brought his dogs to the United States on a personal appearance tour. While here, he was invited to compete in sled dog races in New England, where the sport had already been introduced. The superior racing ability and delightful temperament of Seppala's Siberian Huskies won the respect and the hearts of sportsmen from Alaska to New England. It was through the efforts of these pioneer fanciers that the breed was established in the United States and that AKC recognition was granted in 1930. Many Siberian Huskies were assembled and trained at Chinook Kennels in New Hampshire for use on the Byrd Antarctic Expeditions. Dogs of the breed also served valiantly in the Army's Arctic Search and Rescue Unit during World War II.

The Siberian Husky is naturally friendly and gentle in temperament. He possesses at times an independent nature, and although very alert, in many cases he lacks the aggressive or protective tendencies of a watchdog. He is by nature fastidiously clean and free from the body odors that many dense-coated breeds have. Although remarkable for his adaptability to all kinds of living conditions, his natural desire to roam makes a measure of control necessary at all times. The understanding owner will find the Siberian Husky an enjoyable companion in country or city. He has endeared himself to dog fanciers everywhere by his versatility, striking beauty, and amiable disposition.

# OFFICIAL STANDARD FOR THE SIBERIAN HUSKY

**General Appearance**—The Siberian Husky is a medium-sized working dog, quick and light on his feet and free and graceful in action. His moderately compact and well furred body, erect ears and brush tail suggest his Northern heritage. His characteristic gait is smooth and seemingly effortless. He performs his original function in harness most capably, carrying a light load at a moderate speed over great distances. His body proportions and form reflect this basic balance of power, speed and endurance. The males of the Siberian Husky breed are masculine but never coarse; the bitches are feminine but without weakness of structure. In proper condition, with muscle firm and well developed, the Siberian Husky does not carry excess weight.

**Size, Proportion, Substance**—*Height*—Dogs, 21 to 23½ inches at the withers. Bitches, 20 to 22 inches at the withers. *Weight*—Dogs, 45 to 60 pounds. Bitches, 35 to 50 pounds. Weight is in proportion to height. The measurements mentioned above represent the extreme height and weight limits with no preference given to either extreme. Any appearance of excessive bone or weight should be penalized. In profile, the length of the body from the point of the shoulder to the rear point of the croup is slightly longer than the height of the body from the ground to the top of the withers. *Disqualification*—Dogs over 23½ inches and bitches over 22 inches.

**Head**—*Expression* is keen, but friendly; interested and even mischievous. *Eyes* almond shaped, moderately spaced and set a trifle obliquely. Eyes may be brown or blue in color; one of each or parti-colored are acceptable. *Faults*—Eyes set too obliquely; set too close together. *Ears* of medium size, triangular in shape, close fitting and set high on the head. They are thick, well furred, slightly arched at the back, and strongly erect, with slightly rounded tips pointing straight up. *Faults*—Ears too large in proportion to the head; too wide set; not strongly erect. *Skull* of medium size and in proportion to the body; slightly rounded on top and tapering from the widest point to the eyes. *Faults*—Head clumsy or heavy; head too finely chiseled. *Stop*—The stop is well-defined and the bridge of the nose is straight from the stop to the tip. *Fault*—Insufficient stop. *Muzzle* of medium length; that is, the distance from the tip of the nose to the stop is equal to the distance from the stop to the occiput. The muzzle is of medium width, tapering gradually to the nose, with the tip neither pointed nor square. *Faults*—Muzzle either too snipy or too coarse; muzzle too short or too long. *Nose* black in gray, tan or black dogs; liver in copper dogs; may be flesh-colored in pure white dogs. The pink-streaked "snow nose" is acceptable. *Lips* are well pigmented and close fitting. *Teeth* closing in a scissors bite. *Fault*—Any bite other than scissors.

**Neck, Topline, Body**—*Neck* medium in length, arched and carried proudly erect when dog is standing. When moving at a trot, the neck is extended so that the head is carried slightly forward. *Faults*—Neck too short and thick; neck too long. *Chest* deep and strong, but not too broad, with the deepest point being just behind and level with the elbows. The ribs are well sprung from the spine but flattened on the sides to allow for freedom of action. *Faults*—Chest too broad; "barrel ribs"; ribs too flat or weak. *Back*—The back is straight and strong, with a level topline from withers to croup. It is of medium length, neither cobby nor slack from excessive length. The loin is taut and lean, narrower than the rib cage, and with a slight tuck-up. The croup slopes away from the spine at an angle, but never so steeply as to restrict the rearward thrust of the hind legs. *Faults*—Weak or slack back; roached back; sloping topline.

**Tail**—The well furred tail of fox-brush shape is set on just below the level of the topline, and is usually carried over the back in a graceful sickle curve when the dog is at attention. When carried up, the tail does not curl to either side of the body, nor does it snap flat against the back. A trailing tail is normal for the dog when in repose. Hair on the tail is of medium length and approximately the same length on top, sides and bottom, giving the appearance of a round brush. *Faults*—A snapped or tightly curled tail; highly plumed tail; tail set too low or too high.

**Forequarters**—*Shoulders*—The shoulder blade is well laid back. The upper arm angles slightly backward from point of shoulder to elbow, and is never perpendicular to the ground. The muscles and ligaments holding the shoulder to the rib cage are firm and well developed. *Faults*—Straight shoulders; loose shoulders. *Forelegs*—When standing and viewed from the front, the legs are moderately spaced, parallel and straight, with the elbows close to the body and turned neither in nor out. Viewed from the side, pasterns are slightly slanted, with the pastern joint strong, but flexible. Bone is substantial but never heavy. Length of the leg from elbow to ground is slightly more than the distance from the elbow to the top of withers. Dewclaws on forelegs may be removed.

*Faults*—Weak pasterns; too heavy bone; too narrow or too wide in the front; out at the elbows. *Feet* oval in shape but not long. The paws are medium in size, compact and well furred between the toes and pads. The pads are tough and thickly cushioned. The paws neither turn in nor out when the dog is in natural stance. *Faults*—Soft or splayed toes; paws too large and clumsy; paws too small and delicate; toeing in or out.

**Hindquarters**—When standing and viewed from the rear, the hind legs are moderately spaced and parallel. The upper thighs are well muscled and powerful, the stifles well bent, the hock joint well-defined and set low to the ground. Dewclaws, if any, are to be removed. *Faults*—Straight stifles, cow-hocks, too narrow or too wide in the rear.

**Coat**—The coat of the Siberian Husky is double and medium in length, giving a well furred appearance, but is never so long as to obscure the clean-cut outline of the dog. The undercoat is soft and dense and of sufficient length to support the outer coat. The guard hairs of the outer coat are straight and somewhat smooth lying, never harsh nor standing straight off from the body. It should be noted that the absence of the undercoat during the shedding season is normal. Trimming of whiskers and fur between the toes and around the feet to present a neater appearance is permissible. Trimming the fur on any other part of the dog is not to be condoned and should be severely penalized. *Faults*—Long, rough, or shaggy coat; texture too harsh or too silky; trimming of the coat, except as permitted above.

**Color**—All colors from black to pure white are allowed. A variety of markings on the head is common, including many striking patterns not found in other breeds.

**Gait**—The Siberian Husky's characteristic gait is smooth and seemingly effortless. He is quick and light on his feet, and when in the show ring should be gaited on a loose lead at a moderately fast trot, exhibiting good reach in the forequarters and good drive in the hindquarters. When viewed from the front to rear while moving at a walk the Siberian Husky does not single-track, but as the speed increases the legs gradually angle inward until the pads are falling on a line directly under the longitudinal center of the body. As the pad marks converge, the forelegs and hind legs are carried straightforward, with neither elbows nor stifles turned in or out. Each hind leg moves in the path of the foreleg on the same side. While the dog is gaiting, the topline remains firm and level. *Faults*—Short, prancing or choppy gait, lumbering or rolling gait; crossing or crabbing.

**Temperament**—The characteristic temperament of the Siberian Husky is friendly and gentle, but also alert and outgoing. He does not display the possessive qualities of the guard dog, nor is he overly suspicious of strangers or aggressive with other dogs. Some measure of reserve and dignity may be expected in the mature dog. His intelligence, tractability, and eager disposition make him an agreeable companion and willing worker.

**Summary**—The most important breed characteristics of the Siberian Husky are medium size, moderate bone, well balanced proportions, ease and freedom of movement, proper coat, pleasing head and ears, correct tail and good disposition. Any appearance of excessive bone or weight, constricted or clumsy gait, or long, rough coat should be penalized. The Siberian Husky never appears so heavy or coarse as to suggest a freighting animal; nor is he so light and fragile as to suggest a sprint-racing animal. In both sexes the Siberian Husky gives the appearance of being capable of great endurance. In addition to the faults already noted, the obvious structural faults common to all breeds are as undesirable in the Siberian Husky as in any other breed, even though they are not specifically mentioned herein.

## DISQUALIFICATION

*Dogs over 23½ inches and bitches over 22 inches.*

**Approved October 9, 1990**
**Effective November 28, 1990**

# STANDARD SCHNAUZER

*O*F THE THREE SCHNAUZER BREEDS, THE MEDIUM-SIZED STANDARD SCHNAUZER is the oldest. It is the prototype for the Miniature and Giant. Originating in the farming and cattle-raising area of Bavaria, now part of Germany, the breed's roots can be traced to the Middle Ages, and breed likenesses can be found in paintings and statues from that period. During the following centuries dogs much like today's Standard Schnauzer performed household and farm duties in Germany: guarding the family and its possessions, ridding the farmyard of vermin, driving livestock, and protecting owners as they traveled to market. These rough-coated, medium-sized dogs descended from early European herding and guarding breeds and should not be confused with the superficially similar but unrelated terriers of Britain.

In the mid-nineteenth century, German dog fanciers began to take an interest in this useful native breed. Crosses were made with the gray Wolfspitz and black German Poodle to produce the distinctive salt-and-pepper and black colors seen in today's Schnauzers. At this time, the medium-sized dogs were also crossed with other breeds to develop the Miniature and, later, the Giant Schnauzer.

The breed was originally known as the Wire-haired Pinscher, and was first exhibited in Germany in the mid-1870s. By the turn of the century, the breed was becoming universally known as the Schnauzer. We do not know whether this name is a reference to the breed's hallmark, a muzzle (*schnauze* in German) sporting a bristly beard and mustache, or to an early show winner of that same name. In 1907, the German Schnauzer Klub published a breed standard that described a dog remarkably similar to today's Standard Schnauzer.

Standard Schnauzers first entered the United States around 1900, but it was not until after World War I that the breed reached significant numbers here. In 1925, the Schnauzer Club of America was formed to include both Standard and Miniature Schnauzers, and the first national specialty show was held two years later. The first breed standard, for both varieties, was adopted in 1929. In 1933, the AKC parent club separated into the Standard Schnauzer Club of America and the American Miniature Schnauzer Club. At that time, the AKC approved a written standard of perfection describing the ideal Standard Schnauzer. This standard has been revised several times since to further clarify the picture of the ideal dog.

Today's Standard Schnauzer is a working breed in the Schnauzer-Pinscher family. A robust, square, athletic build and a dense, harsh, wiry coat of black or salt-and-pepper, which sheds only minimally, characterize the breed. Standard Schnauzers have an energetic, intelligent temperament and are sociable, alert, affectionate, protective, and reliable, with a good sense of humor. Standard Schnauzers are generally healthy, sturdy, and long-lived, with few hereditary illnesses. The breed is of true medium size. Males stand 18 to 20 inches at the shoulder and weigh 40 to 45 pounds. Females are 17 to 19 inches and weigh 35 to 40 pounds. The AKC standard allows dogs to be shown with either cropped or natural ears.

Standard Schnauzers are not for those who want a slow, placid dog or one that can be fed and forgotten. Schnauzers insist on being part of family activities and develop best when treated in this manner. Outstanding companions known for their devotion and love of family, they are not one-person dogs but rather become true family members. Standard Schnauzers, being playful and tolerant, are particularly good with children. At the same time, they are alert to any intruder who might threaten their home and family. But Standards are very intelligent and can be strong willed and determined. Owners must be prepared to train the new puppy from the beginning. Kindergarten puppy training, and regular obedience classes later on, are the best approach.

Many Standards participate in conformation as well as obedience and agility events, where their trainability, alertness, and enthusiasm serve them well. These same characteristics also allow Standards to serve successfully as therapy dogs, service dogs for the disabled, search-and-rescue dogs, and drug- or bomb-detection dogs. One growing interest among Standard Schnauzer owners is herding, for which most dogs show considerable talent. The AKC has recently accepted Standard Schnauzers for competition in herding trials.

# OFFICIAL STANDARD FOR THE STANDARD SCHNAUZER

**General Appearance**—The Standard Schnauzer is a robust, heavy-set dog, sturdily built with good muscle and plenty of bone; square-built in proportion of body length to height. His rugged build and dense harsh coat are accentuated by the hallmark of the breed, the arched eyebrows and the bristly mustache and whiskers. *Faults*—Any deviation that detracts from the Standard Schnauzer's desired general appearance of a robust, active, square-built, wire-coated dog. Any deviation from the specifications in the Standard is to be considered a fault and should be penalized in proportion to the extent of the deviation.

**Size, Proportion, Substance**—Ideal height at the highest point of the shoulder blades, 18½ to 19½ inches for males and 17½ inches to 18½ inches for females. Dogs measuring over or under these limits must be faulted in proportion to the extent of the deviation. Dogs measuring more than one half inch over or under these limits must be disqualified. The height at the highest point of the withers equals the length from breastbone to point of rump.

**Head**—*Head* strong, rectangular and elongated; narrowing slightly from the ears to the eyes and again to the tip of the nose. The total length of the head is about one half the length of the back measured from the withers to the set-on of the tail. The head matches the sex and substance of the dog. *Expression* alert, highly intelligent, spirited. *Eyes* medium size; dark brown; oval in shape and turned forward; neither round nor protruding. The brow is arched and wiry, but vision is not impaired nor eyes hidden by too long an eyebrow. *Ears* set high, evenly shaped with moderate thickness of leather and carried erect when cropped. If uncropped, they are of medium size, V-shaped and mobile so that they break at skull level and are carried forward with the inner edge close to the cheek. *Faults*—Prick, or hound ears. *Skull* (Occiput to Stop) moderately broad between the ears with the width of the skull not exceeding two thirds the length of the skull. The skull must be flat; neither domed nor bumpy; skin unwrinkled. There is a slight stop which is accentuated by the wiry brows. *Muzzle* strong, and both parallel and equal in length to the topskull; it ends in a moderately blunt wedge with wiry whiskers accenting the rectangular shape of the head. The topline of the muzzle is parallel with the topline of the skull. *Nose* is large, black and full. The lips should be black, tight and not overlapping. *Cheeks*—Well developed chewing muscles, but not so much that "cheekiness" disturbs the rectangular head form.

**Bite**—A full complement of white teeth, with a strong, sound scissors bite. The canine teeth are strong and well developed with the upper incisors slightly overlapping and engaging the lower. The upper and lower jaws are powerful and neither overshot nor undershot. *Faults*—A level bite is considered undesirable but a lesser fault than an overshot or undershot mouth.

**Neck, Topline, Body**—*Neck* strong, of moderate thickness and length, elegantly arched and blending cleanly into the shoulders. The skin is tight, fitting closely to the dry throat with no wrinkles or dewlaps. The *topline* of the back should not be absolutely horizontal, but should have a slightly descending slope from the first vertebra of the withers to the faintly curved *croup* and set-on of the tail. *Back* strong, firm, straight and short. *Loin* well developed, with the distance from the last rib to the hips as short as possible.

**Body** compact, strong, short-coupled and substantial so as to permit great flexibility and agility. *Faults*—Too slender or shelly; too bulky or coarse.

**Chest** of medium width with well-sprung ribs, and if it could be seen in cross section would be oval. The breastbone is plainly discernible. The brisket must descend at least to the elbows and ascend gradually to the rear with the belly moderately drawn up. *Fault*—Excessive tuck-up. *Croup* full and slightly rounded. *Tail* set moderately high and carried erect. It is docked to not less than one inch nor more than two inches. *Fault*—Squirrel tail.

**Forequarters—Shoulders**—The sloping shoulder blades are strongly muscled, yet flat and well laid back so that the rounded upper ends are in a nearly vertical line above the elbows. They slope well forward to the point where they join the upper arm, forming as nearly as possible a right angle when seen from the side. Such an angulation permits the maximum forward extension of the forelegs without binding or effort. *Forelegs* straight, vertical, and without any curvature when seen from all sides; set moderately far apart; with heavy bone; elbows set close to the body and pointing directly to the rear. Dewclaws on the forelegs may be removed. *Feet* small and compact, round with thick pads and strong black nails. The toes are well closed and arched (cat's paws) and pointing straight ahead.

**Hindquarters**—Strongly muscled, in balance with the forequarters, never appearing higher than the shoulders. Thighs broad with well bent stifles. The second thigh, from knee to hock, is approximately parallel with an extension of the upper neck line. The legs, from the clearly defined hock joint to the feet, are short and perpendicular to the ground and, when viewed from the rear, are parallel to each other. Dewclaws, if any, on the hind legs are generally removed. Feet as in front.

**Coat**—Tight, hard, wiry and as thick as possible, composed of a soft, close undercoat and a harsh outer coat which, when seen against the grain, stands up off the back, lying neither smooth nor flat. The outer coat (body coat) is trimmed (by plucking) only to accent the body outline.

As coat texture is of the greatest importance, a dog may be considered in show coat with back hair measuring from ¾ to 2 inches in length. Coat on the ears, head, neck, chest, belly and under the tail may be closely trimmed to give the desired typical appearance of the breed. On the muzzle and over the eyes the coat lengthens to form the beard and eyebrows; the hair on the legs is longer than that on the body. These "furnishings" should be of harsh texture and should not be so profuse as to detract from the neat appearance or working capabilities of the dog. *Faults*—Soft, smooth, curly, wavy, or shaggy; too long or too short; too sparse or lacking undercoat; excessive furnishings; lack of furnishings.

**Color**—Pepper and salt or pure black.

**Pepper and Salt**—The typical pepper and salt color of the topcoat results from the combination of black and white hairs, and white hairs banded with black. Acceptable are all shades of pepper and salt and dark iron gray to silver gray. Ideally, pepper and salt Standard Schnauzers have a gray undercoat, but a tan or fawn undercoat is not to be penalized. It is desirable to have a darker facial mask that harmonizes with the particular shade of coat color. Also, in pepper and salt dogs, the pepper and salt mixture may fade out to light gray or silver white in the eyebrows, whiskers, cheeks, under throat, across chest, under tail, leg furnishings, under body, and inside legs.

*Black*—Ideally the black Standard Schnauzer should be a true rich color, free from any fading or discoloration or any admixture of gray or tan hairs. The undercoat should also be solid black. However, increased age or continued exposure to the sun may cause a certain amount of fading and burning. A small white smudge on the chest is not a fault. Loss of color as a result of scars from cuts and bites is not a fault.

*Faults*—Any colors other than specified, and any shadings or mixtures thereof in the topcoat such as rust, brown, red, yellow or tan; absence of peppering; spotting or striping; a black streak down the back; or a black saddle without typical salt and pepper coloring—and gray hairs in the coat of a black; in blacks, any undercoat color other than black.

**Gait**—Sound, strong, quick, free, true and level gait with powerful, well-angulated hindquarters that reach out and cover ground. The forelegs reach out in a stride balancing that of the hindquarters. At a trot, the back remains firm and level, without swaying, rolling or roaching. When viewed from the rear, the feet, though they may appear to travel close when trotting, must not cross or strike. Increased speed causes feet to converge toward the centerline of gravity.

*Faults*—Crabbing or weaving; paddling, rolling, swaying; short, choppy, stiff, stilted rear action; front legs that throw out or in (east and west movers); hackney gait, crossing over or striking in front or rear.

**Temperament**—The Standard Schnauzer has highly developed senses, intelligence, aptitude for training, fearlessness, endurance and resistance against weather and illness. His nature combines high-spirited temperament with extreme reliability.

*Faults*—In weighing the seriousness of a fault, greatest consideration should be given to deviation from the desired alert, highly intelligent, spirited, reliable character of the Standard Schnauzer. Dogs that are shy or appear to be highly nervous should be seriously faulted and dismissed from the ring. Vicious dogs shall be disqualified.

## DISQUALIFICATIONS

*Males under 18 inches or over 20 inches in height. Females under 17 inches or over 19 inches in height.*
*Vicious dogs.*

**Approved February 9, 1991**
**Effective March 27, 1991**

# Group IV: Terrier Breeds

Airedale Terrier
American Staffordshire Terrier
Australian Terrier
Bedlington Terrier
Border Terrier
Bull Terrier
Cairn Terrier
Dandie Dinmont Terrier
Smooth Fox Terrier
Wire Fox Terrier
Glen of Imaal Terrier
Irish Terrier
Kerry Blue Terrier
Lakeland Terrier

Manchester Terrier
Miniature Bull Terrier
Miniature Schnauzer
Norfolk Terrier
Norwich Terrier
Parson Russell Terrier
Scottish Terrier
Sealyham Terrier
Skye Terrier
Soft Coated Wheaten Terrier
Staffordshire Bull Terrier
Welsh Terrier
West Highland White Terrier

# AIREDALE TERRIER

*A*IREDALE ORIGIN IS SHROUDED IN THE SAME THEORY AND CONJECTURE AS that of many other breeds.

The Airedale is a "manufactured breed," having been created in England's Aire Valley, located less than a hundred miles south of the Scottish border. This was an industrial center, with many mills and factories, so the Airedale was created by workingmen, not aristocrats. There is not much written on the breed's early development, but it is generally believed Airedales first emerged near the Aire and Wharfe rivers in Yorkshire around 1840. It is said the breed was created to be a large, fearless, hardy duck-and-rat hunter of the terrier type. Airedales were probably meant to be good poachers and strong, intelligent guards and companions. It is also generally stated that Otterhounds and old English Black and Tan Terriers were mainstays in the mix.

In 1900, Airedale scholars concluded that the breed was largely composed of the Otterhound, contributing size and bone, combined with the old English Black and Tan, or Rat Catcher Terrier, giving ears, harder coat, and expression. The Irish Terrier was also evident in head development. Sporting breeds, such as retrievers and setters; sheepdogs, such as the Yorkshire Collie; and Bedlington Terriers were all used. In fact, any breed enhancing the sporting value of Bingley or Waterside terriers, as Airedales were then called, may have been used.

The publication of "Genetic Structure of the Purebred Domestic Dog" in the spring 2004 issue of *Science Magazine* was the most thorough DNA analysis of pure-bred dogs to date. Airedales were found to be in the "Hunting Cluster." Other terriers were included, such as the Soft Coated Wheaten, Irish, Kerry Blue, and Cairn. Also named were traditional gundog breeds: the Golden, Chesapeake Bay, Flat Coated, and Labrador retrievers; the Pointer and German Shorthaired Pointer; and the American Cocker, Clumber, and Welsh springer spaniels. Others were hounds, such as the Beagle and Bloodhound, and herding dogs, such as Border Collies and Old English Sheepdogs. No wonder Airedale fanciers feel they have the most versatile dogs on the planet.

The breed is unique, having been working dogs, war dogs, and sporting dogs. Before World War I, Lieutenant Colonel Edwin Hautonville Richardson bred, trained, and provided working dogs in the British Isles and for several heads of state and armies worldwide. He touted Airedales as the world's number one working breed. Their work as watchdogs and police dogs is legendary.

After the outbreak of war, Richardson headed the British war-dog program. Again, Airedales rose to the occasion, serving as messengers, sentries, and guards. They were Red Cross dogs, carrying medical supplies, searching out wounded, and helping place signal wire for communication. This is documented in Richardson's *Fifty Years with Dogs, British War Dogs,* and *Watch-Dogs.*

The Airedale's big break came when they were imported to North America, where Airedales developed into the original three-in-one gundog, equally able to handle upland game birds, waterfowl, and fur. During the first quarter of the twentieth century, Airedales went west and their numbers grew. They became first-choice farm and ranch dogs because of their versatility and grit. Their do-it-all skills included guarding the farm or ranch against two- and four-legged predators; babysitting toddlers; herding sheep and cattle; and being a gundog when there was time for upland bird, waterfowl, or fur hunts. Through the 1950s, Airedales were the first choice of most serious hunters because of their versatility. During this time, there were thousands of references to Airedales' hunting prowess in the mainstream press. To cite one example, William L. Barkley, a founding member of the Airedale Terrier Club of America, confirms their use in his article "What Can't an Airedale Do?" for the April 1924 *American Kennel Gazette.* He wrote: "It is said about the first Airedales, and it is as true today as it was then, that they could do the work of any breed their size, and do it better. . . . The dogs principally were used as hunting and working dogs. . . . On Chesapeake Bay, they have done the work of a retriever."

Stability of type is attained by those who adhere to the ideal of the breed standard, and is illustrated by Airedales being judged Best in Show at the most prestigious shows in England and America.

Today's Airedale, when bred to the standard, is still prized as a first-rate hunting partner by countless devotees who hunt all manner of game, and is the dog of choice for many in police and search-and-rescue work. They are also well suited as therapy and assistance dogs and are adept at herding, sledding, carting, and backpacking. When it comes to fun, many of them enjoy the obedience ring as well as agility and flyball. Finally, they are great family companions.

# OFFICIAL STANDARD FOR THE AIREDALE TERRIER

**Head**—Should be well balanced with little apparent difference between the length of skull and foreface.

**Skull**—Should be long and flat, not too broad between the ears and narrowing very slightly to the eyes. Scalp should be free from wrinkles, stop hardly visible and cheeks level and free from fullness.

**Ears**—Should be V-shaped with carriage rather to the side of the head, not pointing to the eyes, small but not out of proportion to the size of the dog. The topline of the folded ear should be above the level of the skull.

**Foreface**—Should be deep, powerful, strong and muscular. Should be well filled up before the eyes.

**Eyes**—Should be dark, small, not prominent, full of terrier expression, keenness and intelligence.

**Lips**—Should be tight.

**Nose**—Should be black and not too small.

**Teeth**—Should be strong and white, free from discoloration or defect. Bite either level or viselike. A slightly overlapping or scissors bite is permissible without preference.

**Neck**—Should be of moderate length and thickness gradually widening towards the shoulders. Skin tight, not loose.

**Shoulders and Chest**—Shoulders long and sloping well into the back. Shoulder blades flat. From the front, chest deep but not broad. The depth of the chest should be approximately on a level with the elbows.

**Body**—Back should be short, strong and level. Ribs well sprung. Loins muscular and of good width. There should be but little space between the last rib and the hip joint.

**Hindquarters**—Should be strong and muscular with no droop.

**Tail**—The root of the tail should be set well up on the back. It should be carried gaily but not curled over the back. It should be of good strength and substance and of fair length.

**Legs**—Forelegs should be perfectly straight, with plenty of muscle and bone. Elbows should be perpendicular to the body, working free of sides. Thighs should be long and powerful with muscular second thigh, stifles well bent, not turned either in or out, hocks well let down parallel with each other when viewed from behind. Feet should be small, round and compact with a good depth of pad, well cushioned; the toes moderately arched, not turned either in or out.

**Coat**—Should be hard, dense and wiry, lying straight and close, covering the dog well over the body and legs. Some of the hardest are crinkling or just slightly waved. At the base of the hard very stiff hair should be a shorter growth of softer hair termed the undercoat.

**Color**—The head and ears should be tan, the ears being of a darker shade than the rest. Dark markings on either side of the skull are permissible. The legs up to the thighs and elbows and the underpart of the body and chest are also tan and the tan frequently runs into the shoulder. The sides and upper parts of the body should be black or dark grizzle. A red mixture is often found in the black and is not to be considered objectionable. A small white blaze on the chest is a characteristic of certain strains of the breed.

**Size**—Dogs should measure approximately 23 inches in height at the shoulder; bitches, slightly less. Both sexes should be sturdy, well muscled and boned.

**Movement**—Movement or action is the crucial test of conformation. Movement should be free. As seen from the front the forelegs should swing perpendicular from the body free from the sides, the feet the same distance apart as the elbows. As seen from the rear the hind legs should be parallel with each other, neither too close nor too far apart, but so placed as to give a strong well-balanced stance and movement. The toes should not be turned either in or out.

## FAULTS

*Yellow eyes, hound ears, white feet, soft coat, being much over or under the size limit, being undershot or overshot, having poor movement, are faults which should be severely penalized.*

### SCALE OF POINTS

| | |
|---|---|
| Head | 10 |
| Neck, shoulders and chest | 10 |
| Body | 10 |
| Hindquarters and tail | 10 |
| Legs and feet | 10 |
| Coat | 10 |
| Color | 5 |
| Size | 10 |
| Movement | 10 |
| General characteristics and expression | 15 |
| **Total** | **100** |

**Approved July 14, 1959**

# AMERICAN STAFFORDSHIRE TERRIER

$\mathcal{T}$O CORRECTLY GIVE THE ORIGIN AND HISTORY OF THE AMERICAN STAFFORD-shire Terrier, it is necessary to comment briefly on two other dogs, namely the Bulldog and the terrier.

Until the early part of the nineteenth century, the Bulldog was bred with great care in England for the purpose of baiting bulls. The Bulldog of that day was vastly different from our present-day "sourmug." Pictures from as late as 1870 represent the Bulldog as agile and as standing straight on his legs—his front legs in particular. In some cases he was even possessed of a muzzle, and long rat tails were not uncommon. The Bulldog of that day, with the exception of the head, looked more like the present-day American Staffordshire Terrier than like the present-day Bulldog.

Some writers contend it was the White English Terrier, or the Black-and-Tan Terrier, that was used as a cross with the Bulldog to perfect the Staffordshire Terrier. It seems easier to believe that any game terrier, such as the fox terrier of the early 1800s, was used in this cross, since some of the foremost authorities on dogs of that time state that the Black-and-Tan and the White English Terrier were none too game, but these same authorities go on to stress the gameness of the fox terrier. It is reasonable to believe that breeders attempting to perfect a dog that would combine the spirit and agility of the terrier with the courage and tenacity of the Bulldog would not use a terrier which was not game. In analyzing the three above-mentioned terriers at that time, we find that there was not a great deal of difference in body conformation, the greatest differences being in color, aggressiveness, and spirit.

In any event, it was the cross between the Bulldog and the terrier that resulted in the Staffordshire Terrier, which was originally called the Bull-and-Terrier Dog, Half and Half, and at times Pit Dog or Pit Bullterrier. Later, it assumed the name in England of Staffordshire Bull Terrier.

These dogs began to find their way into America as early as 1870, where they became known as Pit Dog, Pit Bull Terrier, later American Bull Terrier, and still later as Yankee Terrier.

In 1936, they were accepted for registration in the AKC Stud Book as Staffordshire Terriers. The name of the breed was revised effective January 1, 1972, to American Staffordshire Terrier. Breeders in this country had developed a type which is heavier in weight than the Staffordshire Bull Terrier of England and the name change was to distinguish them as separate breeds.

The American Staffordshire Terrier's standard allows a variance in weight, but it should be in proportion to size. The dog's chief requisites should be strength unusual for his size, soundness, balance, a strong powerful head, a well-muscled body, and courage that is proverbial.

To clarify the confusion that may exist, even in the minds of dog fanciers, as to the difference between the American Staffordshire Terrier and the Bull Terrier, a comment on the latter may be helpful. The Bull Terrier was introduced by James Hinks, of Birmingham, who had been experimenting for several years with the old Bull-and-Terrier Dog, now known as Staffordshire. It is generally conceded that he used the Staffordshire, crossed with the white English Terrier, and some writers contend that a dash of Pointer and Dalmatian blood was also used to help perfect the all-white Bull Terrier.

In mentioning the gameness of the Staffordshire, it is not the intention to tag him as a fighting machine or to praise this characteristic. These points are discussed because they are necessary in giving the correct origin and history of the breed. The good qualities of the dogs are many, and it would be difficult for anyone to overstress them. In appearance they are flashy-looking and they attract much attention on the show bench. As to character, they are game for anything; nevertheless, they should not be held in ill repute merely because some have been taking advantage of this rare courage to use them in the pit as gambling tools. These dogs are docile, and with a little training are even tractable around other dogs. They are intelligent, excellent guardians, and they protect their masters' property with an air of authority that counts; they easily discriminate between strangers who mean well and those who do not. They have another characteristic that is unusual: When they are sold, or change hands, they accept their new master in a comparatively short time.

# OFFICIAL STANDARD FOR
# THE AMERICAN STAFFORDSHIRE TERRIER

**General Impression**—The American Staffordshire Terrier should give the impression of great strength for his size, a well put-together dog, muscular, but agile and graceful, keenly alive to his surroundings. He should be stocky, not long-legged or racy in outline. His courage is proverbial.

**Head**—Medium length, deep through, broad skull, very pronounced cheek muscles, distinct stop; and ears are set high. *Ears*—Cropped or uncropped, the latter preferred. Uncropped ears should be short and held rose or half prick. Full drop to be penalized. *Eyes*—Dark and round, low down in skull and set far apart. No pink eyelids. *Muzzle*—Medium length, rounded on upper side to fall away abruptly below eyes. Jaws well defined. Underjaw to be strong and have biting power. Lips close and even, no looseness. Upper teeth to meet tightly outside lower teeth in front. Nose definitely black.

**Neck**—Heavy, slightly arched, tapering from shoulders to back of skull. No looseness of skin. Medium length.

**Shoulders**—Strong and muscular with blades wide and sloping.

**Back**—Fairly short. Slight sloping from withers to rump with gentle short slope at rump to base of tail. Loins slightly tucked.

**Body**—Well-sprung ribs, deep in rear. All ribs close together. Forelegs set rather wide apart to permit chest development. Chest deep and broad.

**Tail**—Short in comparison to size, low set, tapering to a fine point; not curled or held over back. Not docked.

**Legs**—The front legs should be straight, large or round bones, pastern upright. No resemblance of bend in front. Hindquarters well-muscled, let down at hocks, turning neither in nor out. Feet of moderate size, well-arched and compact. Gait must be springy but without roll or pace.

**Coat**—Short, close, stiff to the touch, and glossy.

**Color**—Any color, solid, parti, or patched is permissible, but all white, more than 80 percent white, black and tan, and liver not to be encouraged.

**Size**—Height and weight should be in proportion. A height of about 18 to 19 inches at shoulders for the male and 17 to 18 inches for the female is to be considered preferable.

**Faults**—Faults to be penalized are: Dudley nose, light or pink eyes, tail too long or badly carried, undershot or overshot mouths.

**Approved June 10, 1936**

# AUSTRALIAN TERRIER

$\mathcal{T}$HE AUSTRALIAN TERRIER WAS THE FIRST AUSTRALIAN BREED TO BE RECOGnized and shown in its native land, and was also the first Australian breed to be accepted officially in other countries. An Australian native-bred, broken-coated terrier made its first appearance on the show bench at Melbourne in 1868. In 1899 the breed was exhibited specifically as "Australian Terriers, Rough-Coated," and both sandy/red and blue/tan colors are noted in show records of that year. An Australian Rough-Coated Terrier Club, founded at Melbourne in 1887, made the first attempt at standardizing the breed, and by 1896 a standard for the breed had been established. Exports to England and the United States soon followed, and in 1933 breed status was granted in England. The American Kennel Club admitted the breed to its registry in 1960, its first terrier addition in 24 years and the 114th breed entered in the AKC Stud Book.

In 1977, the Australian Terrier Club of America joined the AKC. The breed is officially recognized and shown in many countries worldwide.

This dog, one of the smallest of the working terriers, was bred to be both helper and companion in rough times and terrain. A native dog known as the Rough-Coated Terrier, a close relative of the old Scotch Dog of Great Britain (not the present-day Scottish Terrier), had been in Tasmania since the early 1880s. These terriers are believed to have been crossbred with a number of other breeds of British terrier stock to produce the fast, sturdy, rough, weatherproof, fearless little dog which the settlers needed as they expanded the frontiers of their country—helping to control rodents and snakes on the waterfronts, farms, and sheep and cattle stations in the outback, sometimes tending flocks, sounding an alarm when intruders appeared, and being a companion. The breeds chosen for crossbreeding were selected to promote specific desired traits. Although there are differences among writers of the histories of the Australian Terrier, there is consensus of opinion that the breeds used in its development included the precursors of the Dandie Dinmont, Skye, Yorkshire terriers, and the old Black-and-Tan Terrier (today's Manchester), with perhaps the Irish and Cairn terriers. Fortunately, the various crossbreedings produced a handsome dog that prosperous settlers were proud to show at home or in public.

The Australian Terrier is an excellent choice for show, city, home, or farm. He is very spirited, with an air of self-assurance and inquiry into all that goes on about him. His excellent hearing and good eyesight make him a fine watch-alert dog to warn of any kind of disturbance. He is generally adaptable to any climate and terrain, and his weatherproof double coat, which sheds little, keeps him comfortable year-round.

He continues to be a natural and tireless ratter and sporting terrier. Perhaps because he was developed in close association with man under often stressful conditions, he has a very strong sense of devotion and affection for his humans and accepts full responsibility for his household. He is a good family dog and also a fine companion for the single person. He indeed seems to have fulfilled the dream of early breeders to produce a dog who was tough, smart, and able to withstand a full day's work outdoors and yet small and biddable enough to come into the home at night.

# OFFICIAL STANDARD FOR THE AUSTRALIAN TERRIER

**General Appearance**—A small, sturdy, medium-boned working terrier, rather long in proportion to height with pricked ears and docked tail. Blue and tan, solid sandy or solid red in color, with harsh-textured outer coat, a distinctive ruff and apron, and a soft, silky topknot. As befits their heritage as versatile workers, Australian Terriers are sound and free moving with good reach and drive. Their expression keen and intelligent; their manner spirited and self-assured.

The following description is that of the ideal Australian Terrier. Any deviation from this description must be penalized to the extent of the deviation.

**Size, Proportion, Substance**—*Size*—Height 10 to 11 inches at the withers. Deviation in either direction is to be discouraged. *Proportion*—The body is long in proportion to the height of the dog. The length of back from withers to the front of the tail is approximately 1 to 1½ inches longer than from withers to the ground. *Substance*—Good working condition, medium bone, correct body proportions, symmetry and balance determine proper weight.

**Head**—The head is long and strong. The length of the muzzle is equal to the length of the skull. *Expression*—Keen and intelligent. *Eyes*—Small, dark brown to black (the darker the better), keen in expression, set well apart. Rims are black, oval in shape. *Faults:* Light-colored or protruding eyes. *Ears*—Small, erect and pointed; set high on the skull yet well apart, carried erect without any tendency to flare obliquely off the skull. *Skull*—Viewed from the front or side is long and flat, slightly longer than it is wide and full between the eyes, with slight but definite stop. *Muzzle*—Strong and powerful with slight fill under the eyes. The jaws are powerful. *Nose*—Black. A desirable breed characteristic is an inverted V-shaped area free of hair extending from the nose up the bridge of the muzzle, varying in length in the mature dog. *Lips*—Tight and dark brown- or black-rimmed. *Bite*—Scissors with teeth of good size.

**Neck, Topline, Body**—*Neck*—Long, slightly arched and strong, blending smoothly into well laid back shoulders. *Topline*—Level and firm. *Body*—The body is of sturdy structure with ribs well-sprung but not rounded, forming a chest reaching slightly below the elbows with a distinct keel. The loin is strong and fairly short with slight tuck-up. *Faults:* Cobbiness, too long in loin. *Tail*—Set on high and carried erect at a twelve to one o'clock position, docked in balance with the overall dog leaving slightly less than one half, a good hand-hold when mature.

**Forequarters**—*Shoulders*—Long blades, well laid back with only slight space between the shoulder blades at the withers. The length of the upper arm is comparable to the length of the shoulder blade. The angle between the shoulder and the upper arm is 90 degrees. *Faults:* Straight, loose and loaded shoulders. *Elbows*—Close to the chest. *Forelegs*—Straight, parallel when viewed from the front; the bone is round and medium in size. They should be set well under the body, with definite body overhang (keel) before them when viewed from the side. *Pasterns*—Strong, with only slight slope. *Fault*—Down on pasterns. *Dewclaws*—Removed. *Feet*—Small, clean, catlike; toes arched and compact, nicely padded turning neither inward nor outward. *Nails*—Short, black and strong.

**Hindquarters**—Strong; legs well angulated at the stifles and hocks, short and perpendicular from the hocks to the ground. Upper and lower thighs are well muscled. Viewed from behind the rear legs are straight from the hip joints to the ground and in the same plane as the forelegs. *Faults:* Lack of muscular development or excessive muscularity. *Feet*—(See under Forequarters.)

**Coat**—*Outer Coat*—Harsh and straight; 2½ inches all over body except the tail, pasterns, rear legs from the hocks down, and the feet which are kept free of long hair. Hair on the ears is kept very short. *Undercoat*—Short and soft. *Furnishings*—Softer than body coat. The neck is well furnished with hair, which forms a protective ruff blending into the apron. The forelegs are slightly feathered to the pasterns. *Topknot*—Covering only the top of the skull; of finer and softer texture than the rest of the coat.

**Color and Markings**—*Colors:* Blue and tan, solid sandy and solid red. *Blue and Tan*—Blue: dark blue, steel-blue, dark gray-blue, or silver-blue. In silver-blues, each hair carries blue and silver alternating with the darker color at the tips. Tan markings (not sandy or red), as rich as possible, on face, ears, underbody, lower legs and feet, and around vent. The richer the color and more clearly defined the better. *Topknot*—Silver or a lighter shade than head color. *Sandy or Red*—Any shade of solid sandy or solid red, the clearer the better. ***Topknot***—Silver or a lighter shade of body coat. ***Faults:*** All black body coat in the adult dog. Tan smut in the blue portion of the coat, or dark smut in sandy/red coated dogs. In any color, white markings on chest or feet are to be penalized.

**Gait**—As seen from the front and from the rear, the legs are straight from the shoulder and hip joints to the pads, and move in planes parallel to the centerline of travel. The rear legs move in the same planes as the front legs. As the dog moves at a faster trot, the front and rear legs and feet may tend to converge toward the centerline of travel, but the legs remain straight even as they flex or extend. Viewed from the side, the legs move in a ground-covering stride. The rear feet should meet the ground in the same prints as left by the front feet, with no gap between them. Topline remains firm and level, without bounce.

**Temperament**—The Australian Terrier is spirited, alert, courageous and self-confident, with the natural aggressiveness of a ratter and hedge hunter; as a companion, friendly and affectionate. ***Faults:*** Shyness or aggressiveness toward people.

**Approved August 9, 1988**

# BEDLINGTON TERRIER

*T*HE BEDLINGTON TERRIER TAKES HIS NAME FROM A MINING SHIRE IN THE county of Northumberland, England. Purely a Northumbrian production, he first came to be known as the Rothbury Terrier, having originated in the Hannys hills, where the sporting squires loved a game terrier.

Going back to 1820, we find that a Joseph Ainsley of Bedlington acquired a bitch, Coates Phoebe. In 1825 Phoebe was mated to a Rothbury dog, Anderson's Piper, also acquired by Ainsley, and the fruit of this union was a dog referred to as Ainsley's Piper—the first dog known to have been called a Bedlington Terrier.

About this time there flourished in Bedlington a colony of nailers who took to the breed and became noted for their plucky terriers. Of this dog's gameness there was not the slightest doubt—he never shirked at any kind of vermin and could more than hold his own at drawing a badger or at ratting in or out of Wales.

Both Piper and his mother, Phoebe, were considerably lighter in weight and smaller in stature than the dogs of the present day. But it is on record that Piper was set on a badger at eight months old and was constantly at work, more or less on badgers, foxes, otters, and other vermin. He drew a badger after he was fourteen years old, when toothless and nearly blind, after several other terriers had failed.

Although many crosses were introduced, there was always a band of enthusiastic admirers who kept to the original breed. In 1877, the National Bedlington Terrier Club (England) was formed by a few influential fanciers who made themselves responsible for bringing him to the notice of the public by exhibiting him on the show bench. Since then the Bedlington has made vast improvement in type.

Many tales have been told by the older generation of matches made by the miners and nailers of that period, where large sums were at stake on the result of a fight between terriers of their respective fancies. The Bedlington was never a mischief seeker, but once he started fighting, it was to the death.

As time went on, he was taken into the homes of the elite, who found him a tractable and first-class companion. He was not long in developing into a pet, his great heart and lovable nature endearing him to all fortunate enough to own him.

There are two distinct colors, liver and blue, and it is only a question of fancy as to which is preferred. In the early days the liver was much in evidence, and some great dogs were of that color; in fact, the liver dog was preferred to the blue which is now so fashionable. Whether the former shade has become rarer from a change of tastes on the part of Bedlington breeders, or whether it is merely a coincidence that so few good liver-colored specimens happen to be shown at the present time, we are unable to say, but the fact remains that, of late, high-class blue Bedlingtons far outnumber good liver specimens. While there have been many good specimens of both colors, it is noticeable that the mother of the celebrated Piper was a blue-black bitch, possessing a light-colored topknot, a characteristic which has been meticulously preserved.

One reason there were fewer Bedlingtons at one time than their desirability warranted was the trimming necessary for exhibition in the show ring. Known only to a few so-called experts, this trimming seemed difficult. Gradually, however, the knack was mastered so that now most owners trim their own dogs and find it quite easy. It is only necessary to see it done by someone who knows how, after which, with a little practice, the novice becomes expert. The dog is hardy and not difficult to raise, and his feeding is the same as that required for other terriers of like weight.

# OFFICIAL STANDARD FOR THE BEDLINGTON TERRIER

**General Appearance**—A graceful, lithe, well-balanced dog with no sign of coarseness, weakness or shelliness. In repose the expression is mild and gentle, not shy or nervous. Aroused, the dog is particularly alert and full of immense energy and courage. Noteworthy for endurance, Bedlingtons also gallop at great speed, as their body outline clearly shows.

**Head**—Narrow, but deep and rounded. Shorter in skull and longer in jaw. Covered with a profuse topknot which is lighter than the color of the body, highest at the crown, and tapering gradually to just back of the nose. There must be no stop and the unbroken line from crown to nose end reveals a slender head without cheekiness or snipiness. Lips are black in the blue and tans and brown in all other solid and bi-colors.
*Eyes*—Almond-shaped, small, bright and well sunk with no tendency to tear or water.

Set is oblique and fairly high on the head. Blues have dark eyes; blues and tans, less dark with amber lights; sandies, sandies and tans, light hazel; livers, livers and tans, slightly darker. Eye rims are black in the blue and blue and tans, and brown in all other solid and bi-colors. *Ears*—Triangular with rounded tips. Set on low and hanging flat to the cheek in front with a slight projection at the base. Point of greatest width approximately 3 inches. Ear tips reach the corners of the mouth. Thin and velvety in texture, covered with fine hair forming a small silky tassel at the tip. *Nose*—Nostrils large and well defined. Blues and blues and tans have black noses. Livers, livers and tans, sandies, sandies and tans have brown noses. *Jaws*—Long and tapering. Strong muzzle well filled up with bone beneath the eye. Close-fitting lips, no flews. *Teeth*—Large, strong and white. Level or scissors bite. Lower canines clasp the outer surface of the upper gum just in front of the upper canines. Upper premolars and molars lie outside those of the lower jaw.

**Neck and Shoulders**—Long, tapering neck with no throatiness, deep at the base and rising well up from the shoulders which are flat and sloping with no excessive musculature. The head is carried high.

**Body**—Muscular and markedly flexible. Chest deep. Flat-ribbed and deep through the brisket, which reaches to the elbows. Back has a good natural arch over the loin, creating a definite tuck-up of the underline. Body slightly greater in length than height. Well-muscled quarters are also fine and graceful.

**Legs and Feet**—Lithe and muscular. The hind legs are longer than the forelegs, which are straight and wider apart at the chest than at the feet. Slight bend to pasterns which are long and sloping without weakness. Stifles well angulated. Hocks strong and well let down, turning neither in nor out. Long hare feet with thick, well-closed-up, smooth pads. Dewclaws should be removed.

**Coat**—A very distinctive mixture of hard and soft hair standing well out from the skin. Crisp to the touch but not wiry, having a tendency to curl, especially on the head and face. When in show trim must not exceed 1 inch on body; hair on legs is slightly longer.

**Tail**—Set low, scimitar-shaped, thick at the root and tapering to a point which reaches the hock. Not carried over the back or tight to the underbody.

**Color**—Blue, sandy, liver, blue and tan, sandy and tan, liver and tan. In bi-colors the tan markings are found on the legs, chest, under the tail, inside the hindquarters and over each eye. The topknots of all adults should be lighter than the body color. Patches of darker hair from an injury are not objectionable, as these are only temporary. Darker body pigmentation of all colors is to be encouraged.

**Height**—The preferred Bedlington Terrier dog measures 16½ inches at the withers, the bitch 15½ inches. Under 16 inches or over 17½ inches for dogs and under 15 inches or over 16½ inches for bitches are serious faults. Only where comparative superiority of a specimen outside these ranges clearly justifies it, should greater latitude be taken.

**Weight**—To be proportionate to height within the range of 17 to 23 pounds.

**Gait**—Unique lightness of movement. Springy in the slower paces, not stilted or hackneyed. Must not cross, weave or paddle.

**Approved September 12, 1967**

# Border Terrier

*A*S THE NAME SUGGESTS, THE BORDER TERRIER HAS ITS ORIGIN ON EITHER side of the Cheviot Hills which form the border country, and may be regarded as one of the oldest kinds of terrier in Great Britain. As a purely "working terrier," border farmers, shepherds, and sportsmen for generations carefully preserved a particular strain of this dog, which could be found in almost every border homestead.

With the hills at their disposal and miles from habitation, stock was subjected to the ravages of the powerful hill foxes, and to hunt and kill them the border farmer and shepherd required a game terrier with length of leg sufficient to follow a horse, yet small enough to follow a fox to ground. The dogs had to be active, strong, and tireless; they had to have weather-resistant coats in order to withstand prolonged exposure to drenching rains and mists in the hills.

The Border Terrier is a tireless hard-worker for his size, and he is full of pluck. There is no wall he cannot get over or wire entanglement he cannot scramble through. Should the fox run to earth, he will bolt him every time, or stay the night in the earth until the matter is settled. It may therefore be gathered that in order to meet these requirements the Border Terrier, as now known, was evolved by a process of judicious selection from the native hill terriers.

Until Kennel Club (England) recognition was given, the Border Terrier was unknown to the great majority but was always exhibited in considerable numbers at most of the Agricultural Societies' shows in the border country. Following recognition by the English Kennel Club and the formation of the Border Terrier Club in 1920, the breed has been catered to at many of the important shows in the British Isles. The first registration of the breed in the United States was in 1930.

# OFFICIAL STANDARD FOR THE BORDER TERRIER

**General Appearance**—He is an active terrier of medium bone, strongly put together, suggesting endurance and agility, but rather narrow in shoulder, body and quarter. The body is covered with a somewhat broken though close-fitting and intensely wiry jacket. The characteristic "otter" head with its keen eye, combined with a body poise which is "at the alert," gives a look of fearless and implacable determination characteristic of the breed.

Since the Border Terrier is a working terrier of a size to go to ground and able, within reason, to follow a horse, his conformation should be such that he be ideally built to do his job. No deviations from this ideal conformation should be permitted, which would impair his usefulness in running his quarry to earth and in bolting it therefrom. For this work he must be alert, active and agile, and capable of squeezing through narrow apertures and rapidly traversing any kind of terrain. His head, "like that of an otter," is distinctive, and his temperament ideally exemplifies that of a terrier. By nature he is good-tempered, affectionate, obedient, and easily trained. In the field he is hard as nails, "game as they come" and driving in attack. It should be the aim of Border Terrier breeders to avoid such overemphasis of any point in the Standard as might lead to unbalanced exaggeration.

**Size, Proportion, Substance**—*Weight*—Dogs, 13–15½ pounds, bitches, 11½–14 pounds, are appropriate weights for Border Terriers in hard-working condition. The *proportions* should be that the height at the withers is slightly greater than the distance from the withers to the tail, i.e., by possibly 1–1½ inches in a 14-pound dog. Of medium bone, strongly put together, suggesting endurance and agility, but rather narrow in shoulder, body and quarter.

**Head**—Similar to that of an otter. *Eyes* dark hazel and full of fire and intelligence. Moderate in size, neither prominent nor small and beady. *Ears* small, V-shaped and of moderate thickness, dark preferred. Not set high on the head but somewhat on the side, and dropping forward close to the cheeks. They should not break above the level of the skull. Moderately broad and flat in *skull* with plenty of width between the eyes and between the ears. A slight, moderately broad curve at the *stop* rather than a pronounced indentation. Cheeks slightly full. *Muzzle* short and "well filled." A dark muzzle is characteristic and desirable. A few short whiskers are natural to the breed. *Nose* black, and of a good size. *Teeth* strong, with a scissors bite, large in proportion to size of dog.

**Neck, Topline, Body**—*Neck* clean, muscular and only long enough to give a well-balanced appearance. It should gradually widen into the shoulder. *Back* strong but laterally supple, with no suspicion of a dip behind the shoulder. *Loin* strong. *Body* deep, fairly narrow and of sufficient length to avoid any suggestions of lack of range and agility. The body should be capable of being spanned by a man's hands behind the shoulders. Brisket not excessively deep or narrow. Deep ribs carried well back and not oversprung in view of the desired depth and narrowness of the body. The *underline* fairly straight. *Tail* moderately short, thick at the base, then tapering. Not set on too high. Carried gaily when at the alert, but not over the back. When at ease, a Border may drop his stern.

**Forequarters**—*Shoulders* well laid back and of good length, the blades converging to the withers gradually from a brisket not excessively deep or narrow. *Forelegs* straight and not too heavy in bone and placed slightly wider than in a Fox Terrier. *Feet* small and compact. Toes should point forward and be moderately arched with thick pads.

**Hindquarters**—Muscular and racy, with *thighs* long and nicely molded. *Stifles* well bent and *hocks* well let down. *Feet* as in front.

**Coat**—A short and dense undercoat covered with a very wiry and somewhat broken topcoat which should lie closely, but it must not show any tendency to curl or wave. With such a coat a Border should be able to be exhibited almost in his natural state, nothing more in the way of trimming being needed than a tidying up of the head, neck and feet. *Hide* very thick and loose fitting.

**Color**—Red, grizzle and tan, blue and tan, or wheaten. A small amount of white may be allowed on the chest but white on the feet should be penalized. A dark muzzle is characteristic and desirable.

**Gait**—Straight and rhythmical before and behind, with good length of stride and flexing of stifle and hock. The dog should respond to his handler with a gait which is free, agile and quick.

**Temperament**—His temperament ideally exemplifies that of a terrier. By nature he is good-tempered, affectionate, obedient and easily trained. In the field he is hard as nails, "game as they come" and driving in attack.

## Scale of Points

| | |
|---|---|
| Head, ears, neck and teeth | 20 |
| Legs and feet | 15 |
| Coat and skin | 10 |
| Shoulders and chest | 10 |
| Eyes and expression | 10 |
| Back and loin | 10 |
| Hindquarters | 10 |
| Tail | 5 |
| General Appearance | 10 |
| **Total** | **100** |

**Approved March 14, 1950**
**Reformatted July 13, 1990**

# BULL TERRIER

*Colored*

*White*

*T*HE BULL TERRIER BREED DATES BACK TO ABOUT 1835. THERE ARE TWO varieties, white and colored. It is almost unanimously believed that this breed was established by mating a Bulldog to the now-extinct White English Terrier. The results were known as the Bull-and-Terrier. Some few years later, the Bull-and-Terrier was crossed with the Spanish Pointer to gain size. To this day, evidence of pointer inheritance is occasionally seen.

In approximately 1860, fanciers decided that an entirely white dog would be more attractive, so James Hinks produced such a specimen. Breeding all-white dogs was most fashionable and was enthusiastically taken up by youngbloods of the day.

The Bull Terrier was a dog for sportsmen in a time when life in general was more strenuous and of rougher, coarser fiber. Because this breed was developed for sport as well as to be the gentleman's companion, it had to be athletic and possess great strength, agility, and courage. The Bull Terrier was bred by gentlemen for gentlemen, for those who had a great sense of fair play. These dogs were taught to courageously defend themselves and their masters yet to never seek or provoke a fight. As a result the white variety became known as "The White Cavalier," a nickname the breed bears with distinction to this day. The colored Bull Terrier, in accordance with the standard, must be any color other than white or any color *with* white, just so long as the white does not predominate. In 1936, it was voted that the colored Bull Terrier would be a separate variety of the Bull Terrier breed.

Contrary to the belief of those who evaluate the breed only by its powerful physical presence, Bull Terriers are exceedingly friendly dogs. They thrive on affection yet are always ready for a frolic. As youngsters, Bull Terriers' exuberance and ebullient nature require families with active lifestyles. It should be remembered that the Bull Terrier comes from the Terrier Group. As such, this is an independent free-thinker with a higher commitment to sports and games than to the traditional work ethic. The desire is for a well-balanced animal, not extreme in any aspect, but well put together, active, and agile—that is, an athlete of perfect form.

# OFFICIAL STANDARD FOR THE BULL TERRIER

## White

The Bull Terrier must be strongly built, muscular, symmetrical and active, with a keen, determined and intelligent expression, full of fire but of sweet disposition and amenable to discipline.

**Head**—Should be long, strong and deep right to the end of the muzzle, but not coarse. Full face it should be oval in outline and be filled completely up giving the impression of fullness with a surface devoid of hollows or indentations, i.e., egg shaped. In profile it should curve gently downwards from the top of the skull to the tip of the nose. The forehead should be flat across from ear to ear. The distance from the tip of the nose to the eyes should be perceptibly greater than that from the eyes to the top of the skull. The underjaw should be deep and well defined.

**Lips**—Should be clean and tight.

**Teeth**—Should meet in either a level or in a scissors bite. In the scissors bite the upper teeth should fit in front of and closely against the lower teeth, and they should be sound, strong and perfectly regular.

**Ears**—Should be small, thin and placed close together. They should be capable of being held stiffly erect, when they should point upwards.

**Eyes**—Should be well sunken and as dark as possible, with a piercing glint and they should be small, triangular and obliquely placed; set near together and high up on the dog's head. Blue eyes are a disqualification.

**Nose**—Should be black, with well-developed nostrils bent downward at the tip.

**Neck**—Should be very muscular, long, arched and clean, tapering from the shoulders to the head and it should be free from loose skin.

**Chest**—Should be broad when viewed from in front, and there should be great depth from withers to brisket, so that the latter is nearer the ground than the belly.

**Body**—Should be well rounded with marked spring of rib, the back should be short and strong. The back ribs deep. Slightly arched over the loin. The shoulders should be strong and muscular but without heaviness. The shoulder blades should be wide and flat and there should be a very pronounced backward slope from the bottom edge of the blade to the top edge. Behind the shoulders there should be no slackness or dip at the withers. The underline from the brisket to the belly should form a graceful upward curve.

**Legs**—Should be big boned but not to the point of coarseness; the forelegs should be of moderate length, perfectly straight, and the dog must stand firmly upon them. The elbows must turn neither in nor out, and the pasterns should be strong and upright. The hind legs should be parallel viewed from behind. The thighs very muscular with hocks well let down. Hind pasterns short and upright. The stifle joint should be well bent with a well-developed second thigh.

**Feet**—Round and compact with well-arched toes like a cat.

**Tail**—Should be short, set on low, fine, and ideally should be carried horizontally. It should be thick where it joins the body, and should taper to a fine point.

**Coat**—Should be short, flat, harsh to the touch and with a fine gloss. The dog's skin should fit tightly.

**Color**—Is white though markings on the head are permissible. Any markings elsewhere on the coat are to be severely faulted. Skin pigmentation is not to be penalized.

**Movement**—The dog shall move smoothly, covering the ground with free, easy strides; fore and hind legs should move parallel each to each when viewed from in front or behind. The forelegs reaching out well and the hind legs moving smoothly at the hip and flexing well at the stifle and hock. The dog should move compactly and in one piece but with a typical jaunty air that suggests agility and power.

## FAULTS

Any departure from the foregoing points shall be considered a fault and the seriousness of the fault shall be in exact proportion to its degree, i.e., a very crooked front is a very bad fault; a rather crooked front is a rather bad fault; and a slightly crooked front is a slight fault.

## DISQUALIFICATION

*Blue eyes.*

## *Colored*

The Standard for the Colored Variety is the same as for the White except for the sub-head "Color" which reads: *Color.* Any color other than white, or any color with white markings. Other things being equal, the preferred color is brindle. A dog which is predominantly white shall be disqualified.

## DISQUALIFICATIONS

*Blue eyes.*
*Any dog which is predominantly white.*

**Approved July 9, 1974**

# Cairn Terrier

*T*HE HISTORY OF THE CAIRN TERRIER IS ENHANCED BY THE FACT THAT THE modern Cairn is an attempt to preserve in typical form the old-time working terrier of the Isle of Skye.

From Martin's 1845 *History of the Dog*, Captain McDonald's description and measurements of the ideal Cairn in 1876, from Ross's *Cairn Terrier*, Darley Matheson's *Terriers*, and from many other sources, it is plain that these were working terriers, with courage for the bolting of otter, foxes, and other vermin from rocks, cliffs, and ledges on the wild shores of their misty isle.

Scotland's terriers had been grouped together as Scotch Terriers until 1873, when they were separated into two classifications—Dandie Dinmont Terriers and Skye Terriers. The breeds we now know as the Scottish Terrier, West Highland White Terrier, and Cairn Terrier were included in classes for Skye Terriers. The Scottish, West Highland, and Cairn had developed from the same stock, originating in the islands and highlands of western Scotland. The three often were found in the same litter, distinguished only by color. A club for Hard-Haired Scotch Terriers embracing the three was formed in 1881, and a standard was approved in 1882. White markings were considered a fault, though an all-white dog was valued.

Toward the end of the nineteenth century, fanciers of the Scottish Terrier type (who were in the majority) began to breed along separate lines. The Kennel Club (England) was petitioned by a group known as the White Scottish Terrier Club for separate classes for whites in 1899. The request originally had been denied, but at Crufts in 1907 separate classes were available for white terriers. The studbooks were opened to West Highland White Terriers as a separate breed, with the first registrations listed as 1908.

In 1909, the show at Inverness offered classes for Short-Haired Skyes. At a meeting of the Skye Terrier Club, fanciers protested the use of the name. The confusion over the classification of these "Short-Haired Skyes" was once again apparent when they were entered in classes for Skye Terriers at Crufts in 1910, even though classes for Short-Haired Skyes were provided. The judge refused to judge these dogs as entered and marked her book "wrong class." A change of name to the Cairn Terrier of Skye was suggested for the Short-Haired Skye. (Cairns were piles of stones which served as landmarks or memorials. Common throughout much of Scotland, cairns were frequent hiding places for small mammals. Farmers used small terriers to bolt the animals from their rocky lairs.) The shortened name, Cairn Terrier, was agreed upon, and in 1912 the breed was permitted to compete for Challenge Certificates.

The Cairn Terrier standard in England permitted white as a color until 1923. The interbreeding of Cairns and West Highland White Terriers had occurred in both England and the United States. However, the AKC (which had given the breed official recognition in 1913) in 1917 barred any Cairn from registration if it was a product of "such a mixed breeding practice."

The modern Cairn should have the hardiness to meet the performance of his old-time prototype. Utility should be the aim of the fancier, since the expressed object of Cairn Terrier clubs is to preserve the breed in its best old working-type.

The height of the Cairn, which differs from that of other terriers, is important in giving the breed the distinctive conformation that has been called "Cairnishness." He is not so low to ground, in proportion to his size, as the Sealyham and the Scottish Terrier. There is one, and only one, correct size for the Cairn Terrier—fourteen pounds for dogs, thirteen pounds for bitches, and the dogs should be in proper proportion to those weights.

If the breed is to resist passing fads and the inroads of modernization, the first consideration in judging should be given to those qualities which are unique in the Cairn.

# OFFICIAL STANDARD FOR THE CAIRN TERRIER

**General Appearance**—That of an active, game, hardy, small working terrier of the short-legged class; very free in its movements, strongly but not heavily built, standing well forward on its forelegs, deep in the ribs, well coupled with strong hindquarters and presenting a well-proportioned build with a medium length of back, having a hard, weather-resisting coat; head shorter and wider than any other terrier and well furnished with hair giving a general foxy expression.

**Head:**

*Skull*—Broad in proportion to length with a decided stop and well furnished with hair on the top of the head, which may be somewhat softer than the body coat. *Muzzle*—Strong but not too long or heavy. *Teeth*—Large, mouth neither overshot nor undershot. *Nose*—Black. *Eyes*—Set wide apart, rather sunken, with shaggy eyebrows, medium in size, hazel or dark hazel in color, depending on body color, with a keen terrier expression. *Ears*—Small, pointed, well carried erectly, set wide apart on the side of the head. Free from long hairs.

**Tail**—In proportion to head, well furnished with hair but not feathery. Carried gaily but must not curl over back. Set on at back level.

**Body**—Well-muscled, strong, active body with well-sprung, deep ribs, coupled to strong hindquarters, with a level back of medium length, giving an impression of strength and activity without heaviness.

**Shoulders, Legs and Feet**—A sloping shoulder, medium length of leg, good but not too heavy bone; forelegs should not be out at elbows, and be perfectly straight, but forefeet may be slightly turned out. Forefeet larger than hind feet. Legs must be covered with hard hair. Pads should be thick and strong and dog should stand well up on its feet.

**Coat**—Hard and weather-resistant. Must be double-coated with profuse harsh outer coat and short, soft, close furry undercoat.

**Color**—May be of any color except white. Dark ears, muzzle and tail tip are desirable.

**Ideal Size**—Involves the weight, the height at the withers and the length of body. Weight for bitches, 13 pounds; for dogs, 14 pounds. Height at the withers—bitches, 9½ inches; dogs, 10 inches. Length of body from 14¼ to 15 inches from the front of the chest to back of hindquarters. The dog must be of balanced proportions and appear neither leggy nor too low to ground; and neither too short nor too long in body. Weight and measurements are for matured dogs at two years of age. Older dogs may weigh slightly in excess and growing dogs may be under these weights and measurements.

**Condition**—Dogs should be shown in good hard flesh, well muscled and neither too fat or thin. Should be in full good coat with plenty of head furnishings, be clean, combed, brushed and tidied up on ears, tail, feet and general outline. Should move freely and easily on a loose lead, should not cringe on being handled, should stand up on their toes and show with marked terrier characteristics.


## FAULTS

1. *Skull*—Too narrow in skull.
2. *Muzzle*—Too long and heavy a foreface; mouth overshot or undershot.
3. *Eyes*—Too large, prominent, yellow, and ringed are all objectionable.
4. *Ears*—Too large, round at points, set too close together, set too high on the head; heavily covered with hair.
5. *Legs and Feet*—Too light or too heavy bone. Crooked forelegs or out at

elbow. Thin, ferrety feet; feet let down on the heel or too open and spread. Too high or too low on the leg.

6. **Body**—Too short back and compact a body, hampering quickness of movement and turning ability. Too long, weedy and snaky a body, giving an impression of weakness. Tail set on too low. Back not level.

7. **Coat**—Open coats, blousy coats, too short or dead coats, lack of sufficient undercoat, lack of head furnishings, lack of hard hair on the legs. Silkiness or curliness. A slight wave permissible.

8. **Nose**—Flesh or light-colored nose.

9. **Color**—White on chest, feet or other parts of body.

**Approved May 10, 1938**

# DANDIE DINMONT TERRIER

FIRST RECORDED AS A DISTINCT BREED ABOUT 1700, THE DANDIE DINMONT Terrier was bred from selected specimens of the rough native terrier owned by border hunters in the Cheviot Hills between England and Scotland. The breed was distinguished as preeminent in hunting otter and badger. A direct line of these dogs descended to dogs of the farmers in the Teviotdale Hills, where Sir Walter Scott chanced upon them and made them famous in his 1815 novel, *Guy Mannering*. One of Scott's characters, the farmer Dandie Dinmont, was believed to be patterned after James Davidson, of Hindlee, near Hawick, who kept the immortal six: Old Pepper, Old Mustard, Young Pepper, Young Mustard, Little Pepper, and Little Mustard. During the popularity of *Guy Mannering*, the breed was referred to as "Dandie Dinmont's terriers." Over the years the name was slightly modified to Dandie Dinmont Terriers.

Terriers recognizable as Dandies appear in paintings by Ansdell and Landseer before 1850. King Louis Philippe of France owned a pair of the breed in 1845. Today the hunting ability of the Dandie is not so often required, but other qualities make this an excellent house dog. They are intelligent, fond of children, and often alert the family with a deep bark. They have a will of their own and will sometimes obey a command reluctantly with a look that seems to say, "I'll do it, but please don't make me."

The physical characteristics of Dandies are quite the opposite from those of the average terrier, as they are mostly a set of curves. The head is large, with a full, domed skull. Their very deep hazel eyes are large and luminous, the darker the better. The jaw is strong, deep, and punishing. Dandies' bodies are long. The topline of the back is rather low at the shoulder with a corresponding arch over the loins and a slight drop at the root of the tail. The Dandie has a broad, deep, and powerful chest; the front legs are short and the feet may be turned slightly out. The hind legs are longer, and the tail is set low, slightly curved, and carried at an angle of about 45 degrees, coming up like a scimitar. There are two distinct colors. One is pepper, which is blue-gray to light silver, with tan or silver points and a very light gray or white topknot on the skull. The other is mustard, a dark ocher to cream color, with white points and topknot. The Dandie has a rough double coat, made up of both hard and soft hair, in a ratio of about 2 to 1. This type of coat easily sheds water and feels crisp to the touch but does not have the harsh feel of a wire-coated dog. The head is covered with soft, silky hair that should not be confined to a mere topknot. When groomed and properly shaped, this forms one of the characteristic features of the show Dandie. Dandies require regular coat care. Frequent plucking (pulling out) will improve both the texture and color of the coat. In doing so, only the longest hairs should be removed to keep the double coat and appearance of penciling. If the coat is neglected for a long period, it may be necessary to strip it down close to the skin. This will leave only undercoat and the Dandie may appear white. After stripping, it can take months for the coat to grow in to a proper length and texture.

Dandies fit in anywhere, either in a rough-and-tumble country life or the confines of a city. They are ideally between eighteen and twenty-four pounds, small enough to be comfortable in an apartment, but a dog big in character.

# OFFICIAL STANDARD FOR
# THE DANDIE DINMONT TERRIER

**General Appearance**—Originally bred to go to ground, the Dandie Dinmont Terrier is a long, low-stationed working terrier with a curved outline. The distinctive head with silken topknot is large but in proportion to the size of the dog. The dark eyes are large and round with a soft, wise expression. The sturdy, flexible body and scimitar shaped tail are covered with a rather crisp double coat, either mustard or pepper in color.

**Size, Proportion, Substance**—*Height* is from 8 to 11 inches at the top of the shoulders. *Length* from top of shoulders to root of tail is one to two inches less than twice the height. For a dog in good working condition, the preferred *weight* is from 18 to 24 pounds. Sturdily built with ample bone and well developed muscle, but without coarseness. The overall balance is more important than any single specification.

**Head**—The *head* is strongly made and large, but in proportion to the dog's size. Muscles are well developed, especially those covering the foreface. The *expression* shows great determination, intelligence and dignity. The *eyes* are large, round, bright and full, but not protruding. They are set wide apart and low, and directly forward. Color, a rich dark hazel. Eye rims dark. The *ears* are set well back, wide apart and low on the skull, hanging close to the cheek, with a very slight projection at the fold. The shape is broad at the base, coming almost to a point. The front edge comes almost straight down from base to tip; the tapering is primarily on the back edge. The cartilage and skin of the ear are rather thin. The ear's length is from three to four inches. The *skull* is broad between the ears, gradually tapering toward the eyes, and measures about the same from stop to occiput as it does from ear to ear. Forehead (brow) well domed. Stop well defined. The *cheeks* gradually taper from the ears toward the muzzle in the same proportion as the taper of the skull. The *muzzle* is deep and strong. In length, the proportions are a ratio of three (muzzle) to five (skull). The *nose* is moderately large and black or dark colored. The lips and inside of the mouth are black or dark colored. The *teeth* meet in a tight scissors bite. The teeth are very strong, especially the canines, which are an extraordinary size for a small dog. The canines mesh well with each other to give great holding and punishing power. The incisors in each jaw are evenly spaced and six in number.

**Neck, Topline, Body**—The *neck* is very muscular, well developed and strong, showing great power of resistance. It is well set into the shoulders and moderate in length. The *topline* is rather low at the shoulder, having a slight downward curve and a corresponding arch over the loins, with a very slight gradual drop from the top of the loins to the root of the tail. Both sides of the backbone well muscled. The outline is a continuous flow from the crest of the neck to the tip of the tail. The *body* is long, strong and flexible. *Ribs* are well sprung and well rounded. The *chest* is well developed and well let down between the forelegs. The underline reflects the curves of the topline. The *tail* is 8 to 10 inches in length, rather thick at the root, getting thicker for about four inches, then tapering off to a point. The set-on of the tail is a continuation of the very slight gradual drop over the croup. The tail is carried a little above the level of the body in a curve like a scimitar. Only when the dog is excited may the tip of the tail be aligned perpendicular to its root.

**Forequarters**—There should be sufficient layback of *shoulder* to allow good reach in front; angulation in balance with hindquarters. *Upper arms* nearly equal in length to the shoulder blades, elbows lying close to the ribs and capable of moving freely. The *forelegs* are short with good muscular development and ample bone, set wide apart. Feet point forward or very slightly outward. Pasterns nearly straight when viewed from the side. Bandy legs and fiddle front are objectionable.

**Hindquarters**—The *hind legs* are a little longer than the forelegs and are set rather wide apart, but not spread out in an unnatural manner. The upper and lower thighs are rounded and muscular and approximately the same length; stifles angulated, in balance with forequarters. The hocks are well let down and rear pasterns perpendicular to the ground.

**Feet**—The *feet* are round and well cushioned. Dewclaws preferably removed on forelegs. Rear feet are much smaller than the front feet and have no dewclaws. Nails strong and dark; nail color may vary according to the color of the dog. White nails are permissible. Flat feet are objectionable.

**Coat**—This is a very important point: The hair should be about two inches long; the body coat is a mixture of about ⅔ hardish hair with about ⅓ soft hair, giving a sort of crisp texture. The hair is not wiry. The body coat is shortened by plucking. The coat is termed pily or penciled, the effect of the natural intermingling of the two types of hair. The hair on the underpart of the body is softer than on the top.

The head is covered with very soft, silky hair, the silkier the better. It should not be confined to a mere topknot but extends to cover the upper portion of the ears, including the fold, and frames the eyes. Starting about two inches from the tip, the ear has a thin feather of hair of nearly the same color and texture as the topknot, giving the ear the appearance of ending in a distinct point. The body of the ear is covered with short, soft, velvety hair. The hair on the muzzle is of the same texture as the foreleg feather. For presentation, the hair on the top of the muzzle is shortened. The hair behind the nose is naturally more sparse for about an inch. The forelegs have a feather about two inches long, the same texture as the muzzle. The hind leg hair is of the same texture but has considerably less feather. The upper side of the tail is covered with crisper hair than that on the body. The underside has a softer feather about two inches long, gradually shorter as it nears the tip, shaped like a scimitar. Trimming for presentation is to appear entirely natural; exaggerated styling is objectionable.

**Color**—The color is pepper or mustard.

***Pepper*** ranges from dark bluish black to a light silvery gray, the intermediate shades preferred. The topknot and ear feather are silvery white, the lighter the color the better. The hair on the legs and feet should be tan, varying according to the body color from a rich tan to a very pale fawn. ***Mustard*** varies from a reddish brown to a pale fawn. The topknot and ear feather are a creamy white. The hair on the legs and feet should be a darker shade than the topknot.

In both colors the body color comes well down the shoulders and hips, gradually merging into the leg color. Hair on the underpart of the body is lighter in color than on the top. The hair on the muzzle (beard) is a little darker shade than the topknot. Ear color harmonizes with the body color. The upper side of the tail is a darker shade than the body color, while the underside of the tail is lighter, as the legs. Some white hair on the chest is common.

**Gait**—Proper movement requires a free and easy stride, reaching forward with the front legs and driving with evident force from the rear. The legs move in a straight plane from shoulder to pad and hip to pad. A stiff, stilted, hopping or weaving gait and lack of drive in the rear quarters are faults to be penalized.

**Temperament**—Independent, determined, reserved and intelligent. The Dandie Dinmont Terrier combines an affectionate and dignified nature with, in a working situation, tenacity and boldness.

**Approved February 9, 1991**
**Effective March 27, 1991**

# SMOOTH FOX TERRIER

*T*HE FOX TERRIER IS AN OLD ENGLISH BREED. FOR ALMOST 100 YEARS IT WAS registered and shown in the United States as one breed with two varieties, smooth and wire. However, in 1984 the American Kennel Club approved separate standards for the Smooth Fox Terrier and the Wire Fox Terrier; this ruling became effective on June 1, 1985.

Authorities believe the two fox terriers probably originated from very different sources. The ancestor of the Wire is thought to be the old rough-coated, black-and-tan working terrier of Wales, Derbyshire, and Durham. The important ancestors of the Smooth are believed to include the smooth-coated black-and-tan terrier, the Bull Terrier, the Greyhound, and the Beagle.

One of the first records of the breed was made in 1790, when Colonel Thornton's Pitch—a smooth-coated white fox terrier—was immortalized in print and paintings.

Smooth Fox Terriers preceded the Wires in the show ring by 15 to 20 years. At first they were classified with sporting dogs, a tribute to their keen nose, remarkable eyesight, and stamina in driving foxes from their hole.

Early breeders liberally crossed Wire Fox Terriers with Smooths to give the former predominantly white pigmentation, a cleaner-cut head, and a more classical outline. However, interbreeding has been almost universally discontinued for many years.

The original breed standard was so well drawn in 1876 by the Fox Terrier Club in Great Britain that, with the exception of reducing the weight of a male dog in show condition from 20 pounds to 18 pounds, changes were unnecessary for many decades. The American Fox Terrier Club, the parent club of the breed in this country, adopted this standard when the club was founded in 1885.

# OFFICIAL STANDARD FOR THE SMOOTH FOX TERRIER

**General Appearance**—The dog must present a generally gay, lively and active appearance; bone and strength in a small compass are essentials; but this must not be taken to mean that a Fox Terrier should be cloddy, or in any way coarse—speed and endurance must be looked to as well as power, and the symmetry of the Foxhound taken as a model. The Terrier, like the Hound, must on no account be leggy, nor must he be too short in the leg. He should stand like a cleverly made hunter, covering a lot of ground, yet with a short back, as stated below. He will then attain the highest degree of propelling power, together with the greatest length of stride that is compatible with the length of his body. Weight is not a certain criterion of a Terrier's fitness for his work—general shape, size and contour are the main points; and if a dog can gallop and stay, and follow his fox up a drain, it matters little what his weight is to a pound or so.

**N.B.** Old scars or injuries, the result of work or accident, should not be allowed to prejudice a Terrier's chance in the show ring, unless they interfere with its movement or with its utility for work or stud.

**Size, Proportion, Substance**—According to present-day requirements, a full-sized, well balanced dog should not exceed 15½ inches at the withers—the bitch being proportionately lower—nor should the length of back from withers to root of tail exceed 12 inches, while to maintain the relative proportions, the head should not exceed 7¼ inches or be less than 7 inches. A dog with these measurements should scale 18 pounds in show condition—a bitch weighing some two pounds less—with a margin of one pound either way. *Balance*—This may be defined as the correct proportions of a certain point, or points, when considered in relation to a certain other point or points. It is the keystone of the Terrier's anatomy. The chief points for consideration are the relative proportions of skull and foreface; head and back; height at withers and length of body from shoulder point to buttock—the ideal of proportion being reached when the last two measurements are the same. It should be added that, although the head measurements can be taken with absolute accuracy, the height at withers and length of back and coat are approximate, and are inserted for the information of breeders and exhibitors rather than as a hard-and-fast rule.

**Head**—*Eyes* and *rims* should be dark in color, moderately small and rather deep set, full of fire, life and intelligence and as nearly possible circular in shape. Anything approaching a yellow eye is most objectionable. *Ears* should be V-shaped and small, of moderate thickness, and dropping forward close to the cheek, not hanging by the side of the head like a Foxhound. The topline of the folded ear should be well above the level of the skull. *Disqualifications*—Ears prick, tulip or rose.

The **skull** should be flat and moderately narrow, gradually decreasing in width to the eyes. Not much "stop" should be apparent, but there should be more dip in the profile between the forehead and the top jaw than is seen in the case of a Greyhound. It should be noticed that although the foreface should gradually taper from eye to muzzle and should tip slightly at its junction with the forehead, it should not "dish" or fall away quickly below the eyes, where it should be full and well made up, but relieved from "wedginess" by a little delicate chiseling. There should be apparent little difference in length between the skull and foreface of a well balanced head. *Cheeks* must not be full.

**Jaws,** upper and lower, should be strong and muscular and of fair punishing strength, but not so as in any way to resemble the Greyhound or modern English Terrier. There should not be much falling away below the eyes. This part of the head should, however, be moderately chiseled out, so as not to go down in a straight slope like a wedge. The **nose,** toward which the muzzle must gradually taper, should be black. **Disqualifications**—Nose white, cherry or spotted to a considerable extent with either of these colors.

The **teeth** should be as nearly as possible together, i.e., the points of the upper (incisors) teeth on the outside of or slightly overlapping the lower teeth. **Disqualifications**—Much undershot, or much overshot.

**Neck, Topline, Body**—*Neck* should be clean and muscular, without throatiness, of fair length, and gradually widening to the shoulders. **Back** should be short, straight (i.e., level), and strong, with no appearance of slackness. *Chest* deep and not broad. *Brisket* should be deep, yet not exaggerated. The foreribs should be moderately arched, the back ribs deep and well sprung, and the dog should be well ribbed up. *Loin* should be very powerful, muscular and very slightly arched. **Stern** should be set on rather high, and carried gaily, but not over the back or curled, docked to leave about three quarters of the original length of the tail. It should be of good strength, anything approaching a "Pipestopper" tail being especially objectionable.

**Forequarters**—*Shoulders* should be long and sloping, well laid back, fine at the points, and clearly cut at the withers. The elbows should hang perpendicular to the body, working free of the sides. The forelegs viewed from any direction must be straight with bone strong right down to the feet, showing little or no appearance of ankle in front, and being short and straight in pastern. Both fore and hind legs should be carried straight forward in traveling. *Feet* should be round, compact, and not large; the soles hard and tough; the toes moderately arched, and turned neither in nor out.

**Hindquarters**—Should be strong and muscular, quite free from droop or crouch; the thighs long and powerful, stifles well curved and turned neither in nor out; hocks well bent and near the ground should be perfectly upright and parallel each with the other when viewed from behind, the dog standing well up on them like a Foxhound, and not straight in the stifle. The worst possible form of hindquarters consists of a short second thigh and a straight stifle. Both fore and hind legs should be carried straight forward in traveling, the stifles not turning outward. Feet as in front.

**Coat**—Should be smooth, flat, but hard, dense and abundant. The belly and underside of the thighs should not be bare.

**Color**—White should predominate; brindle, red or liver markings are objectionable. Otherwise this point is of little or no importance.

**Gait**—Movement, or action, is the crucial test of conformation. The Terrier's legs should be carried straight forward while traveling, the forelegs hanging perpendicular and swinging parallel with the sides, like the pendulum of a clock. The principal propulsive power is furnished by the hind legs, perfection of action being found in the Terrier possessing long thighs and muscular second thighs well bent at the stifles, which admit of a strong forward thrust or "snatch" of the hocks. When approaching, the forelegs should form a continuation of the straight line of the front, the feet being the same distance apart as the elbows. When stationary it is often difficult to determine whether a dog is slightly out at shoulder, but, directly he moves, the defect—if it exists—becomes more apparent, the forefeet having a tendency to cross, "weave," or "dish." When, on the contrary, the dog is tied at the shoulder, the tendency of the feet is to move wider apart, with a sort of paddling action. When the hocks are turned in— cow-hocks—the stifles and feet are turned outwards, resulting in a serious loss of propulsive power. When the hocks are turned outward the tendency of the hind feet is to cross, resulting in an ungainly waddle.

**Temperament**—The dog must present a generally gay, lively and active appearance.


## DISQUALIFICATIONS

*Ears prick, tulip or rose.*
*Nose white, cherry or spotted to a considerable extent with either of these colors.*
*Mouth much undershot, or much overshot.*

**Approved July 8, 2002**
**Effective August 28, 2002**

# WIRE FOX TERRIER

THE FOX TERRIER IS AN OLD ENGLISH BREED. FOR ALMOST 100 YEARS IT WAS registered and shown in the United States as one breed with two varieties, Smooth and Wire. However, in 1984 the American Kennel Club approved separate standards for the Smooth Fox Terrier and the Wire Fox Terrier; this ruling became effective on June 1, 1985.

For more information on the history and characteristics of the breed, see the entry for the Smooth Fox Terrier.

## OFFICIAL STANDARD FOR THE WIRE FOX TERRIER

**General Appearance**—The Terrier should be alert, quick of movement, keen of expression, on the tip-toe of expectation at the slightest provocation. Character is imparted by the expression of the eyes and by the carriage of ears and tail.

Bone and strength in a small compass are essential, but this must not be taken to mean that a Terrier should be "cloddy," or in any way coarse—speed and endurance being requisite as well as power. The Terrier must on no account be leggy, nor must he be too short on the leg. He should stand like a cleverly made, short-backed hunter, covering a lot of ground.

**N.B.** Old scars or injuries, the result of work or accident, should not be allowed to prejudice a Terrier's chance in the show ring, unless they interfere with its movement or with its utility for work or stud.

**Size, Proportion, Substance**—According to present-day requirements, a full-sized, well balanced dog should not exceed 15½ inches at the withers—the bitch being proportionately lower—nor should the length of back from withers to root of tail exceed 12 inches, while to maintain the relative proportions, the head—as mentioned below—should not exceed 7¼ inches or be less than 7 inches. A dog with these measurements should scale 18 pounds in show condition—a bitch weighing some two pounds less—with a margin of one pound either way.

The dog should be balanced and this may be defined as the correct proportions of a certain point or points, when considered in relation to a certain other point or points. It is the keystone of the Terrier's anatomy. The chief points for consideration are the relative proportions of skull and foreface; head and back; height at withers; and length of body from shoulder point to buttock—the ideal of proportion being reached when the last two measurements are the same. It should be added that, although the head measurements can be taken with absolute accuracy, the height at withers and length of back are approximate, and are inserted for the information of breeders and exhibitors rather than as a hard-and-fast rule.

**Head**—The length of the *head* of a full-grown well developed dog of correct size—measured with calipers—from the back of the occipital bone to the nostrils—should be from 7 to 7¼ inches, the bitch's head being proportionately shorter. Any measurement in excess of this usually indicates an oversized or long-backed specimen, although occasionally—so rarely as to partake of the nature of a freak—a Terrier of correct size may boast a head 7½ inches in length. In a well balanced head there should be little apparent difference in length between skull and foreface. If, however, the foreface is noticeably shorter, it amounts to a fault, the head looking weak and "unfinished." On the other hand, when the eyes are set too high up in the skull and too near the ears, it also amounts to a fault, the head being said to have a "foreign appearance."

Keen of *expression.* **Eyes** should be dark in color, moderately small, rather deep-set, not prominent, and full of fire, life, and intelligence; as nearly as possible circular in shape, and not too far apart. Anything approaching a yellow eye is most objectionable. **Ears** should be small and V-shaped and of moderate thickness, the flaps neatly folded over and dropping forward close to the cheeks. The topline of the folded ear should be well above the level of the skull. A pendulous ear, hanging dead by the side of the head like a Hound's, is uncharacteristic of the Terrier, while an ear which is semierect is still more undesirable. **Disqualifications**—Ears prick, tulip or rose.

The topline of the **skull** should be almost flat, sloping slightly and gradually decreasing in width toward the eyes, and should not exceed 3½ inches in diameter at the widest part—measuring with the calipers—in the full-grown dog of correct size, the bitch's skull being proportionately narrower. If this measurement is exceeded, the skull is termed "coarse," while a full-grown dog with a much narrower skull is termed "bitchy" in head.

Although the *foreface* should gradually taper from eye to muzzle and should dip slightly at its juncture with the forehead, it should not "dish" or fall away quickly below the eyes, where it should be full and well made up, but relieved from "wedginess" by a little delicate chiseling. While well developed *jaw bones,* armed with a set of strong, white teeth, impart that appearance of strength to the foreface which is so desirable, an excessive bony or muscular development of the jaws is both unnecessary and unsightly, as it is partly responsible for the full and rounded contour of the cheeks to which the term "cheeky" is applied.

*Nose* should be black. *Disqualifications*—Nose white, cherry or spotted to a considerable extent with either of these colors. *Mouth*—Both upper and lower jaws should be strong and muscular, the *teeth* as nearly as possible level and capable of closing together like a vise—the lower canines locking in front of the upper and the points of the upper incisors slightly overlapping the lower. *Disqualifications*—Much undershot, or much overshot.

**Neck, Topline, Body**—*Neck* should be clean, muscular, of fair length, free from throatiness and presenting a graceful curve when viewed from the side. The *back* should be short and level with no appearance of slackness—the *loins* muscular and very slightly arched. The term "slackness" is applied both to the portion of the back immediately behind the withers when it shows any tendency to dip, and also the flanks when there is too much space between the back ribs and hipbone. When there is little space between the ribs and hips, the dog is said to be "short in couplings," "short-coupled," or "well ribbed up." A Terrier can scarcely be too short in back, provided he has sufficient length of neck and liberty of movement. The bitch may be slightly longer in couplings than the dog.

*Chest* deep and not broad, a too narrow chest being almost as undesirable as a very broad one. Excessive depth of chest and brisket is an impediment to a Terrier when going to ground. The *brisket* should be deep, the front ribs moderately arched, and the back ribs deep and well sprung. *Tail* should be set on rather high and carried gaily but not curled. It should be of good strength and substance and of fair length—a three-quarters dock is about right—since it affords the only safe grip when handling working Terriers. A very short tail is suitable neither for work nor show.

**Forequarters**—*Shoulders* when viewed from the front should slope steeply downwards from their juncture, with the neck towards the points, which should be fine. When viewed from the side they should be long, well laid back, and should slope obliquely backwards from points to withers, which should always be clean-cut. A shoulder well laid back gives the long forehand which, in combination with a short back, is so desirable in Terrier or Hunter. The elbows should hang perpendicular to the body, working free of the sides, carried straight through in traveling. Viewed from any direction the legs should be straight, the bone of the forelegs strong right down to the feet. *Feet* should be round, compact, and not large—the pads tough and well cushioned, and the toes moderately arched and turned neither in nor out. A Terrier with good-shaped forelegs and feet will wear his nails down short by contact with the road surface, the weight of the body being evenly distributed between the toe pads and the heels.

**Hindquarters**—Should be strong and muscular, quite free from droop or crouch; the thighs long and powerful; the stifles well curved and turned neither in nor out; the hock joints well bent and near the ground; the hocks perfectly upright and parallel with each other when viewed from behind. The worst possible form of hindquarters consists of a short second thigh and a straight stifle, a combination which causes the hind legs to act as props rather than instruments of propulsion. The hind legs should be carried straight through in traveling. Feet as in front.

**Coat**—The best coats appear to be broken, the hairs having a tendency to twist, and are of dense, wiry texture—like coconut matting—the hairs growing so closely and strongly together that, when parted with the fingers, the skin cannot be seen. At the base of these stiff hairs is a shorter growth of finer and softer hair—termed the undercoat. The coat on the sides is never quite so hard as that on the back and quarters. Some of the hardest coats are "crinkly" or slightly waved, but a curly coat is very objectionable. The hair on the upper and lower jaws should be crisp and only sufficiently long to impart an appearance of strength to the foreface. The hair on the forelegs should also be dense and crisp. The coat should average in length from ¾ to one inch on shoulders and neck, lengthening to 1½ inches on withers, back, ribs, and quarters. These measurements are given rather as a guide to exhibitors than as an infallible rule, since the length of coat depends on the climate, seasons, and individual animal. The judge must form his own opinion as to what constitutes a "sufficient" coat on the day.

**Color**—White should predominate; brindle, red, liver or slaty blue are objectionable. Otherwise, color is of little or no importance.

**Gait**—The movement or action is the crucial test of conformation. The Terrier's legs should be carried straight forward while traveling, the forelegs hanging perpendicular and swinging parallel to the sides, like the pendulum of a clock. The principal propulsive power is furnished by the hind legs, perfection of action being found in the Terrier possessing long thighs and muscular second thighs well bent at the stifles, which admit of a strong forward thrust or "snatch" of the hocks. When approaching, the forelegs should form a continuation of the straight of the front, the feet being the same distance apart as the elbows. When stationary it is often difficult to determine whether a dog is slightly out at shoulder but, directly he moves, the defect—if it exists—becomes more apparent, the forefeet having a tendency to cross, "weave," or "dish." When, on the contrary, the dog is tied at the shoulder, the tendency of the feet is to move wider apart, with a sort of paddling action. When the hocks are turned in—cow-hocks—the stifles and feet are turned outwards, resulting in a serious loss of propulsive power. When the hocks are turned outwards the tendency of the hind feet is to cross, resulting in an ungainly waddle.

**Temperament**—The Terrier should be alert, quick of movement, keen of expression, on the tip-toe of expectation at the slightest provocation.

## DISQUALIFICATIONS

*Ears prick, tulip or rose.*
*Nose white, cherry or spotted to a considerable extent with either of these colors.*
*Mouth much undershot, or much overshot.*

**Approved February 9, 1991**
**Effective March 27, 1991**

# Glen of Imaal Terrier

"THERE IS A GLEN, IMAAL, IN THE WICKLOW MOUNTAINS THAT HAS ALWAYS been, and still is, celebrated for its terriers." This is an early–nineteenth century reference to the fascinating breed we know now as the Glen of Imaal Terrier.

The valley where the breed was developed is one of Ireland's most remote regions, helping to explain why this rough-and-ready terrier bearing the valley's name has been so little known. The Glen of Imaal evolved along different lines from the three other terrier breeds indigenous to Ireland: the Kerry Blue, Soft Coated Wheaten, and Irish terriers. Until recently, geographic isolation has defined the history and evolution of the Glen of Imaal Terrier. Because of this unique breed's specific place of origin, there is considerable information on how it probably came into existence.

Around 1570, Elizabeth I faced what nearly every British monarch has faced: trouble in Ireland. She hired Flemish and Lowland soldiers to do her fighting, and as payment for their services she offered them tracts of land in the largely barren Wicklow mountains of Ireland.

The soldiers did Elizabeth's bidding effectively and proceeded to settle the Glen of Imaal and its environs. We know from several sources that they brought their dogs with them. Among these was a low-slung, harsh-coated "French" hound. These dogs mingled with several different native Irish canines, including hounds and emerging terrier types. Over time, these settlers began to develop a breed of terrier that would not only perform the traditional terrier tasks of dispatching vermin, as well as hunting fox and badger, but also would perform a most unique function.

These prototype Glens were meant to be turnspit dogs. The turnspit was a large wheel rigged with a pulley that was connected to a rotisserie-like device over the hearth. The dog was put into the wheel, and when he began to paddle away, dinner was cooked over the fire.

Some controversy exists about the veracity of the turnspit portion of Glen history. This is largely due to a fanciful and widely published artist's rendering depicting a Glen in such a device. Indeed, the device illustrated could never have fit in the average Irish cottage of the day. Further research reveals that smaller devices were common throughout Ireland and used largely to churn butter. For several centuries these hardy dogs performed their unique task in this quiet and distant corner of Ireland, largely unknown elsewhere in the country, let alone the rest of the world.

The advent of dog shows in the 1860s brought the breed wider appreciation. By 1933, enthusiasm had grown sufficiently that the Irish Kennel Club recognized the Glen of Imaal Terrier, the third of Ireland's four terrier breeds to be so recognized.

In the United States we know of several Glens arriving in the 1930s, when families emigrated from Ireland with their dogs. The breed did not gain a true foothold here, however, until the early 1980s, when several breed pioneers led by Frank and Mary Murphy, of Kansas City, Missouri, imported foundation stock from the United Kingdom, Ireland, and Finland. Shortly thereafter, they founded the Glen of Imaal Terrier Club of America. The breed became eligible for the AKC Miscellaneous class on September 1, 2001. Glens were admitted to full AKC registration effective July 1, 2004, and became eligible for Terrier Group competition in October of that year.

Hardy and resilient to the point of stoicism, the Glen is very much a big dog on short legs, which speaks both to its conformation and its approach to life. An understanding of terrier temperament, and the rigors of hand-stripping a harsh-coated breed, are essential considerations for the prospective Glen owner. A superb earthdog and loyal companion, the Glen of Imaal Terrier has been unaltered by fashion. The Glens of today are true descendants, in form and spirit, of their celebrated ancestors in County Wicklow.

# OFFICIAL STANDARD FOR THE GLEN OF IMAAL TERRIER

**General Appearance**—The Glen of Imaal Terrier, named for the region in the Wicklow Mountains of Ireland where it was developed long ago, is a medium-sized working terrier. Longer than tall and sporting a double coat of medium length, the Glen possesses great strength and should always convey the impression of maximum substance for size of dog. Unrefined to this day, the breed still possesses "antique" features once common to many early terrier types; its distinctive head with rose or half-prick ears, its bowed forequarters with turned out feet, its unique outline and topline are hallmarks of the breed and essential to the breed type.

**Size, Proportion, Substance**—*Height*—The maximum height is 14 inches with a minimum of 12½ inches, measured at the highest point of the shoulder blades. *Weight*—Weight is approximately 35 pounds, bitches somewhat less; however, no Glen in good condition and otherwise well-balanced shall be penalized for being slightly outside the suggested weight. *Length*—The length of body, measured from sternum to buttocks, and height measured from the highest point of the shoulder blades to ground, to be in a ratio of approximately 5 (length) to 3 (height). The overall balance is more important than any single specification.

*Head*—The head must be powerful and strong with no suggestion of coarseness. Impressive in size yet in balance with, and in proportion to, the overall size and symmetry of the dog. *Eyes*—Brown, medium size, round and set well apart. Light eyes should be penalized. *Ears*—Small, rose or half pricked when alert, thrown back when in repose. Set wide apart and well back on the top outer edge of the skull. Full drop or prick ears undesirable. *Skull*—Broad and slightly domed; tapering slightly toward the brow. Of fair length, distance from stop to occiput being approximately equal to distance between ears. *Muzzle*—Foreface of power, strong and well filled below the eyes, tapering toward the nose. Ratio of length of muzzle to length of skull is approximately three (muzzle) to five (skull). Bottle head or narrow foreface undesirable. *Stop*—Pronounced. *Nose*—Black. *Teeth*—Set in a strong jaw, sound, regular, and of good size. Full dentition. Scissors bite preferred; level mouth accepted.

**Neck, Topline, Body**—*Neck*—Very muscular and of moderate length. *Topline*—Straight, slightly rising to a very strong well-muscled loin with no drop-off at the croup. *Body*—Deep, long and fully muscled. Longer than high with the ideal ratio of body length to shoulder height approximately five (length) to three (height). *Chest*—Wide, strong and deep, extending below the elbows. *Ribs*—Well sprung with neither a flat nor a barrel appearance. *Loins*—Strong and well muscled. *Tail*—Docked to approximately half-length, in balance with the overall dog and long enough to allow a good handhold. Strong at root, well set on and carried gaily. Dogs with undocked tails not to be penalized.

**Forequarters**—*Shoulder*—Well laid back, broad and muscular. *Forelegs*—Short, bowed and well boned. Forearm should curve slightly around the chest. Upper arm (humerus) nearly equal in length to the shoulder blades (scapula). Feet to turn out slightly but perceptibly from pasterns. *Feet*—Compact and strong with rounded pads.

**Hindquarters**—Strong and well muscled, with ample bone and in balance with forequarters. Good bend of stifle and a well-defined second thigh. Hocks turn neither in nor out, are short, well let down and perpendicular from hock to ground. *Feet*—As front, except they should point forward.

**Coat**—Medium length, of harsh texture with a soft undercoat. The coat may be tidied to present a neat outline characteristic of a rough-and-ready working terrier. Overtrimming of dogs is undesirable.

**Color**—Wheaten, blue or brindle. Wheaten includes all shades from cream to red wheaten. Blue may range from silver to deepest slate but not black. Brindle may be any shade but is most commonly seen as blue brindle, a mixture of dark blue, light blue, and tan hairs in any combination or proportion.

**Gait**—The action should be free and even, covering the ground effortlessly with good reach in front and good drive behind. This is a working terrier, which must have the agility, freedom of movement and endurance to do the work for which it was developed.

**Temperament**—Game and spirited with great courage when called upon, otherwise gentle and docile. Although generally less easily excited than other terriers, the Glen is always ready to give chase. When working they are active, agile, silent and dead game.

*Faults*—Any departure from the foregoing points should be considered a fault and the seriousness with which the fault should be regarded should be in exact proportion to its degree.

**Approved June 11, 2001**
**Effective September 1, 2001**

# IRISH TERRIER

T HE MODERN IRISH TERRIER SERVES PRIMARILY AS A LOYAL FAMILY COMPANION but has a rich heritage as a hardworking farm dog. Affectionate to family members, reserved with strangers, and challenging to enemies, this strong-willed breed was highly valued by rural Irish families. Bred to control vermin, Irish Terriers were the watchful guardians of farm and family, and also served as hunting companions, capable on land and in the water.

The existence of an Irish sporting terrier was referred to for centuries in ancient manuscripts now archived in the Dublin Museum. One old-time Irish writer referred to these dogs as the poor-man's sentinel, the farmer's friend, and the gentleman's favorite. A generally accepted theory traces the origin of the breed to the wirehaired black-and-tan terriers that existed in Great Britain more than 300 years ago.

The Irish Terrier emerged as a recognized breed in the 1870s. Separate classes for Irish Terriers were first provided at a Dublin dog show in 1873. In 1879, the first Irish Terrier Club was founded in Dublin. A standard was adopted to provide breeders with a description of an ideal Irish Terrier. In 1897, the Irish Terrier Club of America was formed. Every breed has defining characteristics. For the Irish Terrier they are good temper, a graceful racing outline, keen expression, and a dense, wiry coat with a distinctive broken appearance.

The original breed standard describes Irish Terriers as remarkably good tempered, notably so with mankind. When off duty, they are characterized by a quiet, caress-inviting appearance, and when one sees them endearingly, timidly pushing their heads into their master's hands, it is difficult to realize that on occasion, at the set-on, they can prove they have the courage of a lion and will fight with their last breath. The average Irish Terrier today continues to exhibit this wonderful personality, being both gentle and game.

The Irish Terrier is built on lines of speed. His moderately long back gives him a graceful racing outline and sets him apart from the other terriers. In 1906, F. M. Jowett, a prominent English breeder and the author of the first book on the breed, wrote:

> A true Irish Terrier should not be a short-backed dog, but well up on his legs, a shade long in the body, a dog that looks like galloping, but still with plenty of bone and substance, and not whippety; a dog, in short, that even if he were white could not possibly be mistaken for a Wirehaired Fox Terrier.

Dr. E. S. Montgomery reflected on the breed's keen expression in his book *The Complete Irish Terrier:*

> By his head, the Irish Terrier is first recognized and last remembered, because the challenging piercing expression is unlike the expression of any other member of the canine kingdom. All exhibitors, all judges, but more important, all breeders must always carry in their minds the hard-bitten devil-may-care expression which is so necessary and so desirable in this breed.

The wiry and dense coat of an Irish Terrier hugs the body and creates a tight water-resistant jacket. After a walk in light rain, a correctly coated dog just needs a couple of good shakes to dry off. Underneath the stiff outer coat, a dense undercoat of softer, finer hair traps body heat on a cool, damp day. Dried mud on a good-coated dog knocks off easily with a quick brushing.

The Irish Terrier is not born with a propensity to obey. The breed's heritage as a strong-willed, independent worker can get in the way at times. Some owners refer to this as willfulness, others as stubbornness. "Let's try it my way first" is an Irish Terrier's natural response to a challenge, including obedience training.

Although willful, the Irish Terrier is a loyal family companion and ultimately wants to please. Channeling this trait and leveraging the breed's intelligence, owners routinely train dogs that distinguish themselves at obedience and agility trials. The pluck and devotion of an Irish Terrier provides the opportunity for a companion you'll never forget.

# OFFICIAL STANDARD FOR
# THE IRISH TERRIER

**Head**—Long, but in nice proportion to the rest of the body; the skull flat, rather narrow between the ears, and narrowing slightly toward the eyes; free from wrinkle, with the stop hardly noticeable except in profile. The jaws must be strong and muscular, but not too full in the cheek, and of good punishing length. The foreface must not fall away appreciably between or below the eyes; instead, the modeling should be delicate. An exaggerated foreface, or a noticeably short foreface, disturbs the proper balance of the head and is not desirable. The foreface and the skull from occiput to stop should be approximately equal in length. Excessive muscular development of the cheeks, or bony development of the temples, conditions which are described by the fancier as "cheeky," or "strong in head," or "thick in skull" are objectionable. The "bumpy" head, in which the skull presents two lumps of bony structure above the eyes, is to be *faulted*. The hair on the upper and lower jaws should be similar in quality and texture to that on the body, and of sufficient length to present an appearance of additional strength and finish to the foreface. Either the profuse, goat-like beard, or the absence of beard, is unsightly and undesirable.

**Teeth**—Should be strong and even, white and sound; and neither overshot nor undershot.

**Lips**—Should be close and well-fitting, almost black in color.

**Nose**—Must be black.

**Eyes**—Dark brown in color; small, not prominent; full of life, fire and intelligence, showing an intense expression. The light or yellow eye is most objectionable, and is a bad fault.

**Ears**—Small and V-shaped; of moderate thickness; set well on the head, and dropping forward closely toward the outside corner of the eye. The top of the folded ear should be well above the level of the skull. A "dead" ear, hound-like in appearance, must be severely penalized. It is not characteristic of the Irish Terrier. The hair should be much shorter and somewhat darker in color than that on the body.

**Neck**—Should be of fair length and gradually widening toward the shoulders; well and proudly carried, and free from throatiness. Generally there is a slight frill in the hair at each side of the neck, extending almost to the corner of the ear.

**Shoulders and Chest**—Shoulders must be fine, long, and sloping well into the back. The chest should be deep and muscular, but neither full nor wide.

**Body**—The body should be moderately long. The short back is not characteristic of the Irish Terrier, and is extremely objectionable. The back must be strong and straight, and free from an appearance of slackness or "dip" behind the shoulders. The loin should be strong and muscular, and slightly arched, the ribs fairly sprung, deep rather than round, reaching to the level of the elbow. The bitch may be slightly longer than the dog.

**Hindquarters**—Should be strong and muscular; thighs powerful; hocks near the ground; stifles moderately bent.

**Stern**—Should be docked, taking off about one quarter. It should be set on rather high, but not curled. It should be of good strength and substance; of fair length and well covered with harsh, rough hair.

**Feet and Legs**—The feet should be strong, tolerably round, and moderately small; toes arched and turned neither out nor in, with dark toenails. The pads should be deep, and must be perfectly sound and free from corns. Cracks alone do not necessarily indicate unsound feet. In fact, all breeds have cracked pads occasionally, from various causes.

Legs moderately long, well set from the shoulders, perfectly straight, with plenty of bone and muscle; the elbows working clear of the sides; pasterns short, straight, and hardly noticeable. Both fore and hind legs should move straight forward when traveling; the stifles should not turn outward. "Cowhocks"—that is, the hocks turned in and the feet turned out—are intolerable. The legs should be free from feather and covered with hair of similar texture to that on the body to give proper finish to the dog.

**Coat**—Should be dense and wiry in texture, rich in quality, having a broken appearance, but still lying fairly close to the body, the hairs growing so closely and strongly together that when parted with the fingers the skin is hardly visible; free of softness or silkiness, and not so long as to alter the outline of the body, particularly in the hindquarters. On the sides of the body the coat is never as harsh as on the back and quarters, but it should be plentiful and of good texture. At the base of the stiff outer coat there should be a growth of finer and softer hair, lighter in color, termed the undercoat. Single coats, which are without any undercoat, and wavy coats are undesirable; the curly and the kinky coats are most objectionable.

**Color**—Should be whole-colored: bright red, golden red, red wheaten, or wheaten. A small patch of white on the chest, frequently encountered in all whole-colored breeds, is permissible but not desirable. White on any other part of the body is most objectionable. Puppies sometimes have black hair at birth, which should disappear before they are full grown.

**Size**—The most desirable weight in show condition is 27 pounds for the dog and 25 pounds for the bitch. The height at the shoulder should be approximately 18 inches. These figures serve as a guide to both breeder and judge. In the show ring, however, the informed judge readily identifies the oversized or undersized Irish Terrier by its conformation and general appearance. Weight is not the last word in judgment. It is of the greatest importance to select, insofar as possible, terriers of moderate and generally accepted size, possessing the other various characteristics.

**General Appearance**—The overall appearance of the Irish Terrier is important. In conformation he must be more than a sum of his parts. He must be all-of-a-piece, a balanced vital picture of symmetry, proportion and harmony. Furthermore, he must convey character. This terrier must be active, lithe and wiry in movement, with great animation; sturdy and strong in substance and bone structure, but at the same time free from clumsiness, for speed, power and endurance are most essential. The Irish Terrier must be neither "cobby" nor "cloddy," but should be built on lines of speed with a graceful, racing outline.

**Temperament**—The temperament of the Irish Terrier reflects his early background: he was family pet, guard dog, and hunter. He is good tempered, spirited and game. It is of the utmost importance that the Irish Terrier show fire and animation. There is a heedless, reckless pluck about the Irish Terrier which is characteristic, and which, coupled with the headlong dash, blind to all consequences, with which he rushes at his adversary, has earned for the breed the proud epithet of "Daredevil." He is of good temper, most affectionate, and absolutely loyal to mankind. Tender and forbearing with those he loves, this rugged, stout-hearted terrier will guard his master, his mistress and children with utter contempt for danger or hurt. His life is one continuous and eager offering of loyal and faithful companionship and devotion. He is ever on guard, and stands between his home and all that threatens.

**Approved December 10, 1968**

# KERRY BLUE TERRIER

*T*HE KERRY BLUE TERRIER ORIGINATED IN IRELAND, HAVING BEEN NOTICED first in the mountainous regions of County Kerry, hence the name. The dogs had been purebred in that section for more than a hundred years.

Gentle, lovable, and intelligent, the Kerry is an all-round working and utility terrier, used in Ireland and England for hunting small game and birds, and for retrieving from land and water. He is used quite successfully, too, for herding sheep and cattle and ridding the farm of vermin. This overall working and sporting terrier is a faithful companion to the family, showing great personality, drive, and energy.

After the formation of the Republic, they began to appear on the show bench and met with quick favor. The first few came out at the Dublin show. Fostered by the Irish Blue Terrier Club of Dublin, organized by H. G. Fotterell.

English fanciers were quick to realize the Blues' possibilities once groomed, and the Kennel Club there provided regular classification for them. Their rise to popularity was almost instant, and each show brought out increasing numbers of entries.

The Blue Terrier Club of England, organized by Captain Watts Williams, is the supporting organization back of the Blues for England. The English standard is with a few minor exceptions identical with the American standard in that coats must be trimmed.

There is more or less conjecture in America as to who imported the first Kerry and where it was originally shown, but it appears that the first important show at which the breed appeared was Westminster in 1922. For two years following their initial exhibition at Madison Square Garden they resided in the Miscellaneous class, but in 1924 they were officially recognized by the American Kennel Club as a breed and given championship rating.

During the Westminster show of 1926, a group of fanciers met at the Waldorf-Astoria and organized the Kerry Blue Terrier Club of America. At about the same time another club, the United States Kerry Blue Terrier Club, Inc., was formed, and in 1938 both clubs joined membership to form the parent club under the title of the United States Kerry Blue Terrier Club, as it remains today. As the national representative and guardian of the breed, the USKBTC encourages and promotes responsible and ethical ownership and breeding of the purebred Kerry Blue Terrier and fosters both the utilitarian and sporting qualities of the breed.

The Kerry is a dog of many-sided accomplishment and can be seen in many performance events. He is an instinctive trailer and retrieves well. He is adaptable to all manner of farm work, for which he is easily trained. He is an indomitable foe and cannot be surpassed as a watchdog and companion. In some instances in England he has even been used for police work. With proper treatment, food, and exercise, the Kerry Blue Terrier is very long-lived and will usually retain his activeness until the end; in fact, at six and eight years of age they might be taken for young dogs.

# OFFICIAL STANDARD FOR THE KERRY BLUE TERRIER BREED

**General Appearance**—The typical Kerry Blue Terrier should be upstanding well knit and in good balance, showing a well-developed and muscular body with definite terrier style and character throughout. Correct coat and color are important. A low-slung Kerry is not typical.

**Size, Proportion, Substance**—The ideal Kerry should be 18 inches at the withers for a dog, slightly less for a bitch. In judging Kerries, a height of 18–19 inches for a dog, and 17–19 inches for a bitch, should be given primary preference. Only where the comparative superiority of a specimen outside of the ranges noted clearly justifies it should greater latitude be taken. In no case should it extend to a dog over 20 inches or under 17 inches, or to a bitch over 19 inches or under 17 inches. The minimum limits do not apply to puppies. The most desirable weight for a fully developed dog is from 33–40 pounds, bitches weighing proportionately less. A well-developed and muscular body. Legs moderately long with plenty of bone and muscle.

**Head**—Long, but not exaggerated, and in good proportion to the rest of the body. Well balanced. *Eyes*—Dark, small, not prominent, well placed and with a keen terrier expression. Anything approaching a yellow eye is very undesirable. *Ears*—V-shaped, small but not out of proportion to the size of the dog, of moderate thickness, carried forward close to the cheeks with the top of the folded ear slightly above the level of the skull. A "dead" ear, houndlike in appearance, is very undesirable. *Skull*—Flat, with very slight stop, of moderate breadth between the ears, and narrowing very slightly to the eyes. Foreface full and well made up, not falling away appreciably below the eyes but moderately chiseled out to relieve the foreface from wedginess. Little apparent difference between the length of the skull and foreface. Jaws deep, strong and muscular. *Cheeks*—Clean and level, free from bumpiness. *Nose*—Black, nostrils large and wide. *Teeth*—Strong, white and either level or with the upper (incisors) teeth slightly overlapping the lower teeth. An undershot mouth should be strictly penalized.

**Neck, Topline, Body**—*Neck*—Clean and moderately long, gradually widening to the shoulders upon which it should be well set and carried proudly. Back short, strong and straight (i.e., level), with no appearance of slackness. Chest deep and of moderate breadth. Ribs fairly well sprung, deep rather than round. A slight tuck-up. Loin short and powerful. Tail should be set on high, of moderate length and carried gaily erect, the straighter the tail the better.

**Forequarters**—Shoulders fine, long and sloping, well laid back and well knit. The elbows hanging perpendicularly to the body and working clear of the side in movement. The forelegs should be straight from both front and side view. The pasterns short, straight and hardly noticeable. Feet should be strong, compact, fairly round and moderately small, with good depth of pad free from cracks, the toes arched, turned neither in nor out, with black toenails.

**Hindquarters**—Strong and muscular with full freedom of action, free from droop or crouch, the thighs long and powerful, stifles well bent and turned neither in nor out, hocks near the ground and, when viewed from behind, upright and parallel with each other, the dog standing well up on them.

**Coat**—Correct coat is important it is soft, dense and wavy. A harsh, wire or bristle coat should be severely penalized. In show trim the body should be well covered but tidy, with the head (except for the whiskers) and the ears and cheeks clear.

**Color**—Color is important. The correct mature color is any shade of blue gray or gray blue from the deep slate to light blue gray, of a fairly uniform color throughout except that distinctly darker to black parts may appear on the muzzle, head, ears, tail and feet. Kerry color, in its process of "clearing," changes from an apparent black at birth to the mature gray blue or blue gray. The color passes through one or more transitions—involving a very dark blue (darker than deep slate), shades or tinges of brown, and mixtures of these, together with a progressive infiltration of the correct mature color. The time needed for this "clearing" process varies with each dog. Small white markings are permissible. Black on the muzzle, head, ears, tail and feet is permissible at any age. A black dog 18 months of age or older is never permissible in the show ring and is to be disqualified. **Disqualification—A black dog 18 months of age or older is to be disqualified. (White markings on a black dog 18 months of age or older does not constitute clearing or mature color and the dog is to be disqualified.)**

**Gait**—Full freedom of action. The elbows hanging perpendicularly to the body and working clear of the sides in movement; both forelegs and hind legs should move straight forward when traveling, the stifles turning neither in nor out.

## DISQUALIFICATIONS

*A black dog 18 months of age or older is to be disqualified. (White markings on a black dog 18 months of age or older does not constitute clearing or mature color and the dog is to be disqualified.)*

Approved October 10, 2005
Effective January 1, 2006

# LAKELAND TERRIER

*T*HE LAKELAND TERRIER IS ONE OF THE OLDEST WORKING TERRIER BREEDS still known today. It was bred, raised, and worked in the Lake District of England long before there was a kennel club or an official studbook. The fact that it has been outstripped by many younger terrier breeds is not so much a reflection on its quality as a tribute to the scope of its working ability. The name Lakeland, indeed, is a modern acquisition for the breed once known as the Patterdale Terrier.

It is said that long before the days of the famous foxhunter John Peel, or before any packs of hounds were formed, the Lakeland was kept by the farmers in the mountain districts, who, at that time, would form a hunt with a couple of hounds and these terriers. Their work was to destroy the foxes found raiding the sheepfolds. There was sport, but it was not sport for sport's sake alone. It was a very practical matter.

The color of these dogs did not matter to their owners; they bred principally for gameness at first. The color was quite secondary as long as the dogs were game enough to withstand the punishment meted out by the foxes in their rocky mountain lairs. Later came the packs of hounds, but there was not a single pack in the lake district that did not have one or two game old terriers that had continually shown their courage with fox or otter. These were coveted as breeding material. None of their puppies were ever destroyed. They were given out among various friends and followers of the hunt, later to be tried and the best workers retained to carry on the traditions of the older dogs.

So great was the courage of the native Lakeland Terriers that they would follow underground for tremendous distances. It is told that, in 1871, Lord Lonsdale had one that crawled 23 feet under rock after an otter. In order to extricate the dog it was necessary to undertake extensive blasting operations. Finally, after three days' work, they reached the dog, and he was gotten out, none the worse for his experience. Still other dogs have been known to be trapped underground for ten or twelve days and have been taken out alive. Others have paid the penalty.

Classes for the likeliest-looking terrier, suitable for fox or otter, were judged in connection with agricultural shows throughout the lake district about 1896, when more interest was evinced in this game old breed. They were judged by masters of hounds or other experienced hunting men. At that time, the color ranged from grizzle to blue and tan, red, or wheaten, with a sprinkling of white terriers. Later these classes were divided in color; for white working terriers and for colored working terriers. Always, working ability was taken into consideration.

Usually the white terriers were found working with the Otterhounds, as in many cases a dark terrier got severely mauled in the muddy waters due to the excitement of the younger hounds when the otter had been dislodged from under tree roots and drains.

It is believed by experienced terrier fanciers that the somewhat remote ancestors of the Lakeland Terrier are similar to the progenitor of the Border Terrier. In fact, there is sound evidence that the Lakeland is an offshoot of the breed known later as the Bedlington, which was closely related to the Dandie Dinmont.

In 1830 or thereabouts, these northern counties of England—Northumberland, Cumberland, and Westmoreland—had many varieties of terrier, each named after the small locality in which it was found in greatest numbers. Many of the old names have been lost since the breeds have gained recognition. This changing of names usually took place when specialist clubs were formed, with breeders unwilling to agree on any of the older names; and, of course, there were cases where the same dog might have been known by half a dozen different names.

Cumberland was the birthplace of the Lakeland Terrier. This is a particularly beautiful county, richly studded with lakes, particularly in the southern part. The Bedlington is attributed to neighboring Northumberland county, but it is not difficult to suppose that there was certain traffic in dogs at that time.

The first organized effort to promote the interest of this Cumberland County breed came at the Kersurck show in 1912, when a terrier club was formed. The new club made considerable headway for two years. Then came the outbreak of World War I, and little or nothing was heard of the Lakeland Terrier again until 1921, when nine fanciers met at Whitehaven, in Cumberland. According to Thomas Hosking, who later came to the United States, and who was one of the fanciers in attendance, the name Lakeland Terrier was chosen at that meeting. The standard was drawn up at that time, and shortly after the breed was made eligible for registration in the studbook of The Kennel Club (England). The Lakeland Terrier was accepted for registration in the AKC Stud Book in 1934.

Although a worker for generations, the Lakeland makes a very good appearance in the ring. He has a dense, weather-resisting coat, strong jaws of moderate length, powerful hindquarters, and good legs and feet on a short, strong back. Despite his gameness and courage, he has an attractive, quiet disposition.

# OFFICIAL STANDARD FOR THE LAKELAND TERRIER

**General Appearance**—The Lakeland Terrier was bred to hunt vermin in the rugged shale mountains of the Lake District of northern England. He is a small, workmanlike dog of square, sturdy build. His body is deep and relatively narrow, which allows him to squeeze into rocky dens. He has sufficient length of leg under him to cover rough ground easily. His neck is long, leading smoothly into high withers and a short topline ending in a high tail set. His attitude is gay, friendly and self-confident, but not overly aggressive. He is alert and ready to go. His movement is lithe and graceful, with a straight-ahead, free stride of good length. His head is rectangular, jaws are powerful and ears are V-shaped. A dense, wiry coat is finished off with longer furnishings on muzzle and legs.

**Size, Proportion, Substance**—The ideal height of the mature dog is 14½ inches from the withers to the ground, with up to a one-half inch deviation either way permissible. Bitches may measure as much as one inch less than dogs. The weight of the well balanced, mature male in hard show condition averages approximately 17 pounds. Dogs of other heights will be proportionately more or less. The dog is squarely built, and bitches may be slightly longer than dogs. Balance and proportion are of primary importance. Short-legged, heavy-bodied dogs or overly refined, racy specimens are atypical and should be penalized. The dog should have sufficient bone and substance, so as to appear sturdy and workmanlike without any suggestion of coarseness.

**Head**—The *expression* depends on the dog's mood of the moment; although typically alert, it may be intense and determined, or gay and even impish. The *eyes,* moderately small and somewhat oval in outline, are set squarely in the skull, fairly wide apart. In liver or liver and tan dogs, the eyes are dark hazel to warm brown and eye rims are brown. In all other colors, the eyes are warm brown to black and eye rims are dark. The *ears* are small, V-shaped, their fold just above the top of the skull, the inner edge close to the side of the head, and the flap pointed toward the outside corner of the eye.

The *skull* is flat on top and moderately broad, the cheeks flat and smooth as possible. The stop is barely perceptible. The *muzzle* is strong with straight nose bridge and good fill-in beneath the eyes. The head is well balanced, rectangular, the length of skull equaling the length of the muzzle when measured from occiput to stop, and from stop to nose tip. The proportions of the head are critical to correct type. An overlong foreface or short, wedge shaped head are atypical and should be penalized. The *nose* is black. A "winter" nose with faded pigment is permitted, but not desired. Liver colored noses and lips are permissible on liver coated dogs only. A pink or distinctly spotted nose is very undesirable. The lips are dark. Jaws are powerful. The **teeth,** which are comparatively large, may meet in either a level, edge to edge bite, or a slightly overlapping scissors bite. Specimens with teeth overshot or undershot are to be disqualified.

**Neck, Topline, Body**—The **neck** is long; refined but strong; clean at the throat; slightly arched, and widening gradually and smoothly into the shoulders. The withers, that point at the back of the neck where neck and body meet, are noticeably higher than the level of the back. The **topline,** measured from the withers to the tail, is short and level. The **body** is strong and supple. The moderately narrow oval *chest* is deep, extending to the elbows. The *ribs* are well sprung and moderately rounded off the vertebrae. The Lakeland Terrier is a breed of moderation. A barrel-chested, big-bodied dog or one which is slab-sided and lacking substance is atypical and should be penalized. The *loins* are taut and short, although they may be slightly longer in bitches. There is moderate *tuck-up.* The **tail** is set high on the back. It is customarily docked so that when the dog is set up in show position, the tip of the tail is level with the occiput. In carriage, it is upright and a slight curve toward the head is desirable. Behind the tail is a well-defined, broad pelvic shelf. It is more developed in dogs than in bitches. The tail tightly curled over the back is a fault.

**Forequarters**—The *shoulders* are well angulated. An imaginary line drawn from the top of the shoulder blade should pass through the elbow. The shoulder blade is long in proportion to the upper arm, which allows for reasonable angulation while maintaining the more upright "terrier front." The musculature of the shoulders is flat and smooth. The *elbows* are held close to the body, standing or moving. The *forelegs* are strong, clean and straight when viewed from the front or side. There is no appreciable bend at the pasterns. The *feet* are round and point forward, the toes compact and strong. The pads are thick and black or dark gray, except in liver colored dogs where they are brown. The nails are strong and may be black or self-colored. Dewclaws are removed.

**Hindquarters**—The *thighs* are powerful and well muscled. The *hind legs* are well angulated, but not so much as to affect the balance between front and rear, which allows for smooth efficient movement. The *stifles* turn neither in nor out. The distance from the hock to the ground is relatively short and the line from the hock to toes is straight when viewed from the side. From the rear the hocks are parallel to each other. *Feet* same as front. Dewclaws, if any, are removed.

**Coat**—Two-ply or double, the *outer coat* is hard and wiry in texture, the *undercoat* is close to the skin and soft and should never overpower the wiry outer coat. The Lakeland is hand stripped to show his outline. (Clipping is inappropriate for the show ring.) The appearance should be neat and workmanlike. The coat on the skull, ears, forechest, shoulders and behind the tail is trimmed short and smooth. The coat on the body is longer (about one-half to one inch) and may be slightly wavy or straight. The furnishings on the legs and foreface are plentiful as opposed to profuse and should be tidy. They are crisp in texture. The legs should appear cylindrical. The face is traditionally trimmed, with the hair left longer over the eyes to give the head a rectangular appearance from all angles, with the eyes covered from above. From the front, the eyes are quite apparent, giving the Lakeland his own unique mischievous expression.

**Color**—The Lakeland Terrier comes in a variety of colors, all of which are equally acceptable. Solid colors include blue, black, liver, red and wheaten. In saddle marked dogs, the saddle covers the back of the neck, back, sides and up the tail. A saddle may be blue, black, liver or varying shades of grizzle. The remainder of the dog (head, throat, shoulders and legs) is a wheaten or golden tan. Grizzle is a blend of red or wheaten intermixed in varying proportions with black, blue or liver.

**Gait**—Movement is straightforward and free, with good reach in front and drive behind. It should be smooth, efficient and ground-covering. Coming and going, the legs should be straight with feet turning neither in nor out; elbows close to the sides in front and hocks straight behind. As the dog moves faster he will tend to converge toward his center of gravity. This should not be confused with close movement.

**Temperament**—The typical Lakeland Terrier is bold, gay and friendly, with a confident, cock-of-the-walk attitude. Shyness, especially shy-sharpness, in the mature specimen is to be heavily penalized. Conversely, the overly aggressive, argumentative dog is not typical and should be strongly discouraged.

## DISQUALIFICATIONS

*Teeth overshot or undershot.*

**Approved January 15, 1991**
**Effective February 27, 1991**

# MANCHESTER TERRIER

$\mathcal{G}$ENERATIONS AGO, BEFORE THE DAYS OF DOG SHOWS, THERE WAS IN ENGLAND a Black-and-Tan Terrier, less graceful in outline and coarser in type than those of today. Those early dogs did not have penciled toes and dotted brows, and their tan was smutty; nevertheless they were sound, game, and useful. They were accomplished rat killers, whether in the pits or along the watercourses. In fact, their value was reckoned not at all upon any consideration of make and shape, but solely upon the number of rats they had killed.

The Black-and-Tan Terrier was one of the breeds mentioned by Dr. John Caius in the famous letter concerning the dogs of England that was sent to Gesner for inclusion in his encyclopedic work on the dogs of all nations. Caius completed his survey in 1570. He described the breed as carrying the essential colors and characteristics, but as being rougher in coat and shorter on the leg.

The Manchester district of England was a noted center for two "poor men's sports," rat killing and rabbit coursing. A fancier by the name of John Hulme, with the idea of producing a dog that could be used at both contests, mated a Whippet bitch with a celebrated rat-killing dog, a crossbred terrier dark brown in color. On this basis the roached back, seldom found in a terrier, is explained. The dogs proved useful, other fanciers took to breeding them, and the Manchester school of terriers was launched.

The name Manchester, however, was regarded as somewhat misleading, for similar dogs were known in many parts of England. Designation of the new breed did not take place until 1860 or thereabouts, at which time the city for which the dog was named had become a breed center. Manchesters soon spread over the British Isles and eventually came to this country in considerable numbers, but years were to pass before the name was stabilized. Actually it was dropped for a time as being too restricted in designation, and the dog was once again known as the Black-and-Tan Terrier. In 1923, however, the newly formed Manchester Terrier Club of America changed the name back to Manchester Terrier, and there it has remained.

Whippet, Greyhound, and Italian Greyhound have all been mentioned (with how much accuracy none can say) as partners of more or less importance in the creation of the Manchester. But supposition regarding heritage does not end there. That intrepid investigator, Edward C. Ash, surmised a bit regarding a Dachshund ancestor. He said it would be interesting to know not whether the Dachshund is related, but how closely it is related to the Manchester Terrier. In substantiation of the conjecture is the 1771 description of the dog of Manchester as a "short-legged, crooked-legged dog." Such a relationship seems fantastic; even so it is not an impossibility since the Dachshund's forebears were not as exaggerated as the modern breed.

As a sagacious, intelligent companion, no dog is superior to the well-bred Manchester. There is a sleek, breedy look about him that no other dog presents. His long, clean head, keen expression, glossy coat, whip tail, and smart, wide-awake appearance always command attention, while his clean habits and short coat admit him to homes which might shut out his rough-haired brothers. Moreover, his weight leaves nothing to be desired, for there is a medium-sized type weighing over twelve and not exceeding twenty-two pounds, and a toy weighing twelve pounds or under.

Until 1959 the Manchester Terrier and the Toy Manchester Terrier were registered as two separate breeds, although interbreeding between the two breeds was permitted. They have since been registered as a single breed, the Manchester Terrier, with two varieties, the Toy and the Standard, for dog-show purposes.

Development of the Toy from the larger dog was first a matter of chance and later a matter of selective breeding. Two of the larger specimens would produce a litter in which all but one puppy attained the same size as the parents. As has happened again and again in the breeding of dogs, the tiny prototype attracted attention to such a degree as to create a demand for more. So naturally the breeders tried to produce more puppies of the smaller size. It had been claimed that the Toy was so highly prized as to prompt surreptitious matings with Italian Greyhounds in order to keep the dog small. Fortunately these crosses were not perpetuated.

At this point excessive inbreeding took its toll. As can be readily understood, there are few toy-size dogs to breed from, so inbreeding became the order of the day. In Victorian times size diminished alarmingly to around two and a half pounds, and the tiny ones were admittedly delicate. Realizing their mistake, breeders endeavored to correct their technique; they aimed for, and got, more normal toy weight together with renewed vigor.

When the anti-cropping edict was passed in England, many of the older fanciers grew discouraged after trying for a time to produce an attractive-looking dog with small button ears, and consequently many ceased breeding. A few staunch devotees, however, kept the breed alive. They loved the game little fellow, whether his ears were up or down, trimmed or untrimmed, and they stayed with him through lean times and good.

No longer are extremes of any sort favored or fostered within the breed, for "the gentleman's terrier," as he was known long ago, has come into his own. He exhibits that true Manchester type, with its flat skull, triangular eyes, accented kiss marks, and sleek ebony coat with clearly delineated markings. The sole difference between the larger dog and the Toy is concerned with the ears. Both varieties have moderately small, thin ears, narrow at the base and pointed at the tips. They are set high on the skull and quite close together. In the Standard variety, ears may be erect or button; if cropped, they are long and carried straight up. In the Toy variety, however, cropping disqualifies. The Toy ear is carried naturally erect, without sidewise flare.

# OFFICIAL STANDARD FOR THE MANCHESTER TERRIER

**General Appearance**—A small, black, short-coated dog with distinctive rich mahogany markings and a taper-style tail. In structure the Manchester presents a sleek, sturdy, yet elegant look, and has a wedge-shaped, long and clean head with a keen, bright, alert expression. The smooth, compact, muscular body expresses great power and agility, enabling the Manchester to kill vermin and course small game.

Except for size and ear options, there are no differences between the Standard and Toy varieties of the Manchester Terrier. The Toy is a diminutive version of the Standard variety.

**Size, Proportion, Substance**—The *Toy variety* shall not exceed 12 pounds. It is suggested that clubs consider dividing the American-bred and Open classes by weight as follows: 7 pounds and under, over 7 pounds and not exceeding 12 pounds.

The *Standard variety* shall be over 12 pounds and not exceeding 22 pounds. Dogs weighing over 22 pounds shall be disqualified. It is suggested that clubs consider dividing the American-bred and Open classes by weight as follows: over 12 pounds and not exceeding 16 pounds, over 16 pounds and not exceeding 22 pounds.

The Manchester Terrier, overall, is slightly longer than tall. The height, measured vertically from the ground to the highest point of the withers, is slightly less than the length, measured horizontally from the point of the shoulders to the rear projection of the upper thigh. The bone and muscle of the Manchester Terrier is of sufficient mass to ensure agility and endurance.

**Head**—The Manchester Terrier has a keen and alert *expression*. The nearly black, almond-shaped *eyes* are small, bright, and sparkling. They are set moderately close together, slanting upwards on the outside. The eyes neither protrude nor sink in the skull. Pigmentation must be black.

Correct *ears* for the *Standard variety* are either the naturally erect ear, the cropped ear or the button ear. No preference is given to any of the ear types. The naturally erect ear, and the button ear, should be wider at the base tapering to pointed tips, and carried well up on the skull. Wide, flaring, blunt tipped, or "bell" ears are a serious fault. Cropped ears should be long, pointed and carried erect.

The only correct *ear* for the *Toy variety* is the naturally erect ear. They should be wider at the base tapering to pointed tips, and carried well up on the skull. Wide, flaring, blunt tipped, or "bell" ears are a serious fault. Cropped, or cut ears are a disqualification in the Toy variety.

The *head* is long, narrow, tight skinned and almost flat, with a slight indentation up the forehead. It resembles a blunted wedge in frontal and profile views. There is a visual effect of a slight *stop* as viewed in profile.

The *muzzle* and *skull* are equal in length. The *muzzle* is well filled under the eyes with no visible cheek muscles. The underjaw is full and well defined and the *nose* is black.

Tight black *lips* lie close to the jaw. The jaws should be full and powerful with full and proper *dentition.* The teeth are white and strongly developed with a true scissors bite. Level bite is acceptable.

**Neck, Topline, Body**—The slightly arched *neck* should be slim and graceful, and of moderate length. It gradually becomes larger as it approaches, and blends smoothly with the sloping shoulders. Throatiness is undesirable.

The *topline* shows a slight arch over the robust loins falling slightly to the tail set. A flat back or roached back is to be severely penalized. The *chest* is narrow between the legs and deep in the brisket. The forechest is moderately defined. The *ribs* are well sprung, but flattened in the lower end to permit clearance of the forelegs. The *abdomen* should be tucked up extending in an arched line from the deep brisket. The taper style *tail* is moderately short reaching no farther than the hock joint. It is set on at the end of the croup. Being thicker where it joins the body, the tail tapers to a point. The tail is carried in a slight upward curve, but never over the back.

**Forequarters**—The *shoulder blades* and the *upper arm* should be relatively the same length. The distance from the elbow to the withers should be approximately the same as the distance from the elbow to the ground. The *elbows* should lie close to the brisket. The *shoulders* are well laid back.

The *forelegs* are straight, of proportionate length, and placed well under the brisket. The pasterns should be almost perpendicular.

The *front feet* are compact and well arched. The two middle toes should be slightly longer than the others. The pads should be thick and the toenails should be jet black.

**Hindquarters**—The *thigh* should be muscular with the length of the upper and lower thighs being approximately equal. The stifle is well turned. The well let down *hocks* should not turn in nor out as viewed from the rear. The *hind legs* are carried well back. The *hind feet* are shaped like those of a cat, with thick pads and jet black nails.

**Coat**—The coat should be smooth, short, dense, tight and glossy; not soft.

**Color**—The coat color should be jet black and rich mahogany tan, which should not run or blend into each other, but abruptly form clear, well defined lines of color. There shall be a very small tan spot over each eye, and a very small tan spot on each cheek. On the head, the muzzle is tanned to the nose. The nose and nasal bone are jet black. The tan extends under the throat, ending in the shape of the letter V. The inside of the ears are partly tan. There shall be tan spots, called "rosettes," on each side of the chest above the front legs. These are more pronounced in puppies than in adults. There should be a black "thumbprint" patch on the front of each foreleg at the pastern. The remainder of the foreleg shall be tan to the carpus joint. There should be a distinct black "pencil mark" line running lengthwise on the top of each toe on all four feet. Tan on the hind leg should continue from the penciling on the toes up the inside of the legs to a little below the stifle joint. The outside of the hind legs should be black. There should be tan under the tail, and on the vent, but only of such size as to be covered by the tail.

White on any part of the coat is a serious fault, and shall disqualify whenever the white shall form a patch or stripe measuring as much as one half inch at its longest dimension.

Any color other than black and tan shall be disqualified.

Color and/or markings should never take precedence over soundness and type.

**Gait**—The gait should be free and effortless with good reach of the forequarters, showing no indication of hackney gait. Rear quarters should have strong, driving power to match the front reach. Hocks should fully extend. Each rear leg should move in line with the foreleg of the same side, neither thrown in nor out. When moving at a trot, the legs tend to converge towards the center of gravity line beneath the dog.

**Temperament**—The Manchester Terrier is neither aggressive nor shy. He is keenly observant, devoted, but discerning. Not being a sparring breed, the Manchester is generally friendly with other dogs. Excessive shyness or aggressiveness should be considered a serious fault.


## DISQUALIFICATIONS

*Standard variety—Weight over 22 pounds.*

*Toy variety—Cropped or cut ears.*

*Both varieties—White on any part of the coat whenever the white shall form a patch or stripe measuring as much as one half inch at its longest dimension.*

*Any color other than black and tan.*

**Approved June 10, 1991**
**Effective July 31, 1991**

# MINIATURE BULL TERRIER

*T*HE MINIATURE BULL TERRIER IS NO NEWCOMER TO THE WORLD OF PURE-
bred dogs. As a matter of fact, for more than eighty years he has been highly
prized as a distinctive small dog noted, among other things, for tenacity and remarkable courage. He is a sturdy chap, muscular, active, and full of fire but withal
good tempered and amenable to discipline.

Miniature beginnings date to the early nineteenth century, when the Bulldog
and the now extinct White English Terrier were interbred to produce the Bull and
Terrier, later known as the Bull Terrier. There are some who say, too, that the
Black-and-Tan played a part in the dog's creation. The original offshoot of the cross
was a rather small dog that was crossed again, this time with the Spanish Pointer to
increase the size.

Possessed of such a heritage, it is small wonder that the earliest specimens came
in a wide range of sizes. There were toys that weighed from four to seven pounds,
medium-sized ones of some fifteen and sixteen pounds, as well as the more usual
sort resembling the full-sized Bull Terrier of this day. The small dog came in various colors; some black-patched, a few blue, and others pure white. Incidentally, the
tiny white ones were known for a while as Coverwood Terriers, after England's
kennel of that name.

The toys were exhibited abroad up to about 1914, but they elicited scant response from the fanciers because their type was poor. Dogs of medium or minia-

ture size fared better since particularly in eyes and foreface they more closely approximated the type desired. This has been exactly what the fanciers have been aiming for, namely, a down-faced, smaller dog weighing around sixteen pounds and identical in make and shape and every single feature to the full-sized Bull Terrier.

The Miniature Bull Terrier became eligible to be shown in the AKC Miscellaneous class in 1963, and was accepted as a breed in 1991.

# OFFICIAL STANDARD FOR
# THE MINIATURE BULL TERRIER

**General Appearance**—The Miniature Bull Terrier must be strongly built, symmetrical and active, with a keen, determined and intelligent expression. He should be full of fire, having a courageous, even temperament and be amenable to discipline.

**Size, Proportion, Substance**—*Height* 10 inches to 14 inches. Dogs outside these limits should be faulted. *Weight* in proportion to height. In *proportion,* the Miniature Bull Terrier should give the appearance of being square.

**Head**—The *head* should be long, strong and deep, right to the end of the muzzle, but not coarse. The *full face* should be oval in outline and be filled completely up, giving the impression of fullness with a surface devoid of hollows or indentations, i.e., egg shaped. The *profile* should curve gently downwards from the top of the skull to the tip of the nose. The *forehead* should be flat across from ear to ear. The distance from the tip of the nose to the eyes should be perceptibly greater than that from the eyes to the top of the skull. The *underjaw* should be deep and well defined.

To achieve a keen, determined and intelligent *expression,* the *eyes* should be well sunken and as dark as possible with a piercing glint. They should be small, triangular and obliquely placed, set near together and high up on the dog's head. The *ears* should be small, thin and placed close together, capable of being held stiffly erect when they point upwards. The *nose* should be black, with well developed nostrils bent downwards at the tip. The *lips* should be clean and tight. The *teeth* should meet in either a *level* or *scissor bite.* In the scissor bite, the top teeth should fit in front of and closely against the lower teeth. The teeth should be sound, strong and perfectly regular.

**Neck, Topline, Body**—The *neck* should be very muscular, long, and arched; tapering from the shoulders to the head, it should be free from loose skin. The *back* should be short and strong with a slight arch over the loin. Behind the shoulders there should be no slackness or dip at the withers. The *body* should be well rounded with marked spring of rib. The back ribs deep. The *chest* should be broad when viewed from in front. There should be great depth from withers to brisket, so that the latter is nearer to the ground than the belly. The *underline,* from the brisket to the belly, should form a graceful upward curve. The *tail* should be short, set on low, fine, and should be carried horizontally. It should be thick where it joins the body, and should taper to a fine point.

**Forequarters**—The *shoulders* should be strong and muscular, but without heaviness. The shoulder blades should be wide and flat and there should be a very pronounced backward slope from the bottom edge of the blade to the top edge. The *legs* should be big boned but not to the point of coarseness. The *forelegs* should be of moderate length, perfectly straight, and the dog must stand firmly up on them. The *elbows* must turn neither in nor out, and the *pasterns* should be strong and upright.

**Hindquarters**—The *hind legs* should be parallel when viewed from behind. The *thighs* are very muscular with *hocks* well let down. The stifle joint is well bent with a well developed second thigh. The *hind pasterns* should be short and upright.

**Feet**—The *feet* are round and compact with well arched toes like a cat.

**Coat**—The *coat* should be short, flat and harsh to the touch with a fine gloss. The dog's skin should fit tightly.

**Color**—For white, pure white coat. Markings on head and skin pigmentation are not to be penalized. For colored, any color to predominate.

**Gait**—The dog shall move smoothly, covering the ground with free, easy strides. Fore and hind legs should move parallel to each other when viewed from in front or behind, with the forelegs reaching out well and the hind legs moving smoothly at the hip and flexing well at the stifle and hock. The dog should move compactly and in one piece but with a typical jaunty air that suggests agility and power.

**Temperament**—The temperament should be full of fire and courageous, but even and amenable to discipline.

**Faults**—Any departure from the foregoing points shall be considered a fault, and the seriousness of the fault shall be in exact proportion to its degree.

**Approved May 14, 1991**
**Effective January 1, 1992**

# MINIATURE SCHNAUZER

THE SCHNAUZER IS OF GERMAN ORIGIN, SAID TO BE RECOGNIZABLE IN pictures of the fifteenth century. The Miniature Schnauzer is derived from the Standard Schnauzer and is said to have come from mixing of Affenpinschers and Poodles with small Standards. The Miniature Schnauzer was exhibited as a distinct breed as early as 1899.

Today's Miniature Schnauzer in the United States is an elegant dog of the Terrier Group. While the breed resembles other dogs in this group, almost all of which were bred in the British Isles to "go to ground" to root out vermin of all kinds, his origin and blood are quite different, giving the Miniature Schnauzer a naturally happy temperament.

The breed is characterized by its stocky build, wiry coat, and abundant whiskers and leg furnishings. A Miniature Schnauzer may be of several colors with salt-and-pepper (gray) being the most common, although blacks and black-and-silvers are now seen in increasing numbers. The salt-and-pepper color is the result of unique light and dark banding of each hair instead of mixing of light and dark hairs. The correct coat can be retained only by stripping and is lost when the coat is clipped. The breed has a soft undercoat that can range from black and dark gray, to very light gray, or beige. If the animal is clipped, in time only the undercoat will remain.

The breed is hardy, healthy, intelligent, and fond of children. It was developed as a small farm dog, used as a ratter. His size (twelve to fourteen inches at the withers) has permitted him to adapt easily to small city quarters. On the other hand, he is still at home in the country and can cover a substantial amount of ground without tiring. As a rule a Miniature Schnauzer is not a fighter, although he will stand up for himself if necessary.

There is no standard weight for the breed, but a grown bitch of about thirteen inches should weigh about fourteen pounds, with a dog weighing somewhat more. The weight depends, to a great extent, on the amount of bone.

The Miniature Schnauzer is now viewed primarily as a charming and attractive companion. He is seldom a wanderer and is devoted to his home and family. He functions very well as a guard dog in that he can give an alarm as well as a larger dog. His good health, good temperament, and attractive appearance combine to fit him admirably for his role as family pet.

Miniature Schnauzers have been bred in the United States since 1925 and have gained steadily in popular favor. The American Miniature Schnauzer Club began its independent operation in August 1933.

# OFFICIAL STANDARD FOR THE MINIATURE SCHNAUZER

**General Appearance**—The Miniature Schnauzer is a robust, active dog of terrier type, resembling his larger cousin, the Standard Schnauzer, in general appearance, and of an alert, active disposition. *Faults—Type*—Toyishness, ranginess or coarseness.

**Size, Proportion, Substance**—*Size*—From 12 to 14 inches. He is sturdily built, nearly square in *proportion* of body length to height with plenty of bone, and without any suggestion of toyishness. *Disqualifications*—Dogs or bitches under 12 inches or over 14 inches.

**Head**—*Eyes*—Small, dark brown and deep-set. They are oval in appearance and keen in *expression. Faults*—Eyes light and/or large and prominent in appearance. *Ears*—When cropped, the ears are identical in shape and length, with pointed tips. They are in balance with the head and not exaggerated in length. They are set high on the skull and carried perpendicularly at the inner edges, with as little bell as possible along the outer edges. When uncropped, the ears are small and V-shaped, folding close to the skull.

*Head* strong and rectangular, its width diminishing slightly from ears to eyes, and again to the tip of the nose. The forehead is unwrinkled. The *topskull* is flat and fairly long. The foreface is parallel to the topskull, with a slight stop, and it is at least as long as the topskull. The *muzzle* is strong in proportion to the skull; it ends in a moderately blunt manner, with thick whiskers which accentuate the rectangular shape of the head. *Faults*—Head coarse and cheeky. The *teeth* meet in a *scissors bite.* That is, the upper front teeth overlap the lower front teeth in such a manner that the inner surface of the upper incisors barely touches the outer surface of the lower incisors when the mouth is closed. *Faults*—Bite—Undershot or overshot jaw. Level bite.

**Neck, Topline, Body**—*Neck*—Strong and well arched, blending into the shoulders, and with the skin fitting tightly at the throat. *Body* short and deep, with the brisket extending at least to the elbows. Ribs are well sprung and deep, extending well back to a short loin. The underbody does not present a tucked-up appearance at the flank. The *backline* is straight; it declines slightly from the withers to the base of the tail. The withers form the highest point of the body. The overall length from chest to buttocks appears to equal the height at the withers. *Faults*—Chest too broad or shallow in brisket. Hollow or roach back.

*Tail* set high and carried erect. It is docked only long enough to be clearly visible over the backline of the body when the dog is in proper length of coat. *Fault*—Tail set too low.

**Forequarters**—Forelegs are straight and parallel when viewed from all sides. They have strong pasterns and good bone. They are separated by a fairly deep brisket which precludes a pinched front. The elbows are close, and the ribs spread gradually from the first rib so as to allow space for the elbows to move close to the body. *Fault*—Loose elbows.

The sloping *shoulders* are muscled, yet flat and clean. They are well laid back, so that from the side the tips of the shoulder blades are in a nearly vertical line above the elbow. The tips of the blades are placed closely together. They slope forward and downward at an angulation which permits the maximum forward extension of the forelegs without binding or effort. Both the shoulder blades and upper arms are long, permitting depth of chest at the brisket.

*Feet* short and round (cat feet) with thick, black pads. The toes are arched and compact.

**Hindquarters**—The hindquarters have strong-muscled, slanting thighs. They are well bent at the stifles. There is sufficient angulation so that, in stance, the hocks extend beyond the tail. The hindquarters never appear overbuilt or higher than the shoulders. The rear pasterns are short and, in stance, perpendicular to the ground and, when viewed from the rear, are parallel to each other. *Faults*—Sickle hocks, cow hocks, open hocks or bowed hindquarters.

**Coat**—Double, with hard, wiry, outer coat and close undercoat. The head, neck, ears, chest, tail, and body coat must be plucked. When in show condition, the body coat should be of sufficient length to determine texture. Close covering on neck, ears and skull. Furnishings are fairly thick but not silky. *Faults*—Coat too soft or too smooth and slick in appearance.

**Color**—The recognized colors are salt and pepper, black and silver and solid black. All colors have uniform skin pigmentation, i.e., no white or pink skin patches shall appear anywhere on the dog.

*Salt and Pepper*—The typical salt and pepper color of the topcoat results from the combination of black and white banded hairs and solid black and white unbanded hairs, with the banded hairs predominating. Acceptable are all shades of salt and pepper, from light to dark mixtures with tan shadings permissible in the banded or unbanded hair of the topcoat. In salt and pepper dogs, the salt and pepper mixture fades out to light gray or silver white in the eyebrows, whiskers, cheeks, under throat, inside ears, across chest, under tail, leg furnishings, and inside hind legs. It may or may not also fade out on the underbody. However, if so, the lighter underbody hair is not to rise higher on the sides of the body than the front elbows.

**Black and Silver**—The black and silver generally follows the same pattern as the salt and pepper. The entire salt and pepper section must be black. The black color in the topcoat of the black and silver is a true rich color with black undercoat. The stripped portion is free from any fading or brown tinge and the underbody should be dark.

**Black**—Black is the only solid color allowed. Ideally, the black color in the topcoat is a true rich glossy solid color with the undercoat being less intense, a soft matting shade of black. This is natural and should not be penalized in any way. The stripped portion is free from any fading or brown tinge. The scissored and clippered areas have lighter shades of black. A small white spot on the chest is permitted, as is an occasional single white hair elsewhere on the body.

**Disqualifications**—Color solid white or white striping, patching, or spotting on the colored areas of the dog, except for the small white spot permitted on the chest of the black.

The body coat color in salt and pepper and black and silver dogs fades out to light gray or silver white under the throat and across the chest. Between them there exists a natural body coat color. Any irregular or connecting blaze or white mark in this section is considered a white patch on the body, which is also a disqualification.

**Gait**—The trot is the gait at which movement is judged. When approaching, the forelegs, with elbows close to the body, move straight forward, neither too close nor too far apart. Going away, the hind legs are straight and travel in the same planes as the forelegs.

*Note—It is generally accepted that when a full trot is achieved, the rear legs continue to move in the same planes as the forelegs, but a very slight inward inclination will occur. It begins at the point of the shoulder in front and at the hip joint in the rear. Viewed from the front or rear, the legs are straight from these points to the pads. The degree of inward inclination is almost imperceptible in a Miniature Schnauzer that has correct movement. It does not justify moving close, toeing in, crossing, or moving out at the elbows.*

Viewed from the side, the forelegs have good reach, while the hind legs have strong drive, with good pickup of hocks. The feet turn neither inward nor outward.

**Faults**—Single tracking, sidegaiting, paddling in front, or hackney action. Weak rear action.

**Temperament**—The typical Miniature Schnauzer is alert and spirited, yet obedient to command. He is friendly, intelligent and willing to please. He should never be overaggressive or timid.

## DISQUALIFICATIONS

*Dogs or bitches under 12 inches or over 14 inches.*
*Color solid white or white striping, patching, or spotting on the colored areas of the dog, except for the small white spot permitted on the chest of the black.*

*The body coat color in salt and pepper and black and silver dogs fades out to light gray or silver white under the throat and across the chest. Between them there exists a natural body coat color. Any irregular or connecting blaze or white mark in this section is considered a white patch on the body, which is also a disqualification.*

**Approved January 15, 1991**
**Effective February 27, 1991**

# Norfolk Terrier

$\mathcal{T}$HE NORFOLK TERRIER IS SMALL AND STURDY, ALERT AND FEARLESS, WITH sporting instincts and an even temperament. Good-natured and gregarious, the Norfolk has proved adaptable under a wide variety of conditions.

In England at the turn of the century, working terriers from stables in Cambridge, Market Harborough, and Norwich were used by Frank "Roughrider" Jones to develop a breed recognized by The Kennel Club (England) in 1932 as the Norwich Terrier. In the early days there was a diversity in type, size, color, coat, and ear carriage. Correct color and ear carriage were constantly argued. When the Norwich breed standard was drawn up, the drop-ear and the prick-ear terriers remained one breed. The Kennel Club, in 1964, recognized them as two breeds—the drop-ear variety as the Norfolk and the prick-ear as the Norwich.

The year that the breed divided in England, an article in *The Field* explained: "Actually there is nothing new about the Norfolk Terrier, but simply the name under which it is registered. The Eastern Counties have always produced these principally wheaten, red, and otherwise black-and-tan or grizzle good-ribbed short-legged terriers, built on the generally accepted lines of a hunt terrier. They go to ground readily and are famous ratters."

In the United States the Norwich was for generations referred to as the Jones Terrier after Frank Jones, from whom many American sportsmen traveling abroad bought their first little red terriers. In 1936, thanks to the efforts of Gordon Massey (who registered the first Norwich Terrier in this country) and Henry Bixby, then executive vice president of the American Kennel Club, the Norwich Terrier was accepted as a breed by the AKC. It remained one breed until 1979, when division by ear carriage became official. The drop-ears are now recognized as the Norfolk, while the prick-ears remain Norwich.

Visually there appears to be a distinct difference between the two breeds, resulting in two slightly different breed standards. Each breed has developed with success since separation.

Today, although as many live in cities as in foxhunting country, the Norfolk should still conform to the standard. The characteristic coat requires regular grooming, but trimming is heavily penalized. The ears should be neatly dropped, slightly rounded at the tip, carried close to the cheek, and not falling lower than the outer corner of the eye.

The Norfolk Terrier is essentially a sporting terrier—not a toy. His chief attributes are gameness, hardiness, loyalty to his master, and great charm. He is affectionate and reasonably obedient. He must be kept small enough to conform with the standard. Above all, the outstanding personality characteristic of the breed must never be subordinated for the sake of appearance and conformation.

# OFFICIAL STANDARD FOR THE NORFOLK TERRIER

**General Appearance**—The Norfolk Terrier, game and hardy, with expressive dropped ears, is one of the smallest of the working terriers. It is active and compact, free-moving, with good substance and bone. With its natural, weather-resistant coat and short legs, it is a "perfect demon" in the field. This versatile, agreeable breed can go to ground, bolt a fox and tackle or dispatch other small vermin, working alone or with a pack. Honorable scars from wear and tear are acceptable in the ring.

**Size, Proportion, Substance**—*Height* at the withers 9 to 10 inches at maturity. Bitches tend to be smaller than dogs. Length of back from point of withers to base of tail should be slightly longer than the height at the withers. Good *substance* and bone. *Weight* 11 to 12 pounds or that which is suitable for each individual dog's structure and balance. Fit working condition is a prime consideration.

**Head**—*Eyes* small, dark and oval, with black rims. Placed well apart with a sparkling, keen and intelligent *expression*. *Ears* neatly dropped, small, with a break at the skull line, carried close to the cheek and not falling lower than the outer corner of the eye. V-shaped, slightly rounded at the tip, smooth and velvety to the touch.

*Skull* wide, slightly rounded, with good width between the ears. *Muzzle* is strong and wedge shaped. Its length is one-third less than a measurement from the occiput to the well-defined *stop*. Jaw clean and strong. Tight-lipped with a scissor *bite* and large teeth.

**Neck, Topline, Body**—*Neck* of medium length, strong and blending into well laid back shoulders. Level *topline*. Good width of *chest*. *Ribs* well sprung, chest moderately deep. Strong *loins*. *Tail* medium docked, of sufficient length to ensure a balanced outline. Straight, set on high, the base level with the topline. Not a squirrel tail.

**Forequarters**—Well laid back *shoulders*. Elbows close to ribs. Short, powerful *legs,* as straight as is consistent with the digging terrier. Pasterns firm. *Feet* round, pads thick, with strong, black nails.

**Hindquarters**—Broad with strong, muscular *thighs*. Good turn of *stifle*. *Hocks* well let down and straight when viewed from the rear. *Feet* as in front.

**Coat**—The protective coat is hard, wiry and straight, about 1½ to 2 inches long, lying close to the body, with a definite undercoat. The mane on neck and shoulders is longer and also forms a ruff at the base of the ears and the throat. Moderate furnishings of harsh texture on legs. Hair on the head and ears is short and smooth, except for slight eyebrows and whiskers. Some tidying is necessary to keep the dog neat, but shaping should be heavily penalized.

**Color**—All shades of red, wheaten, black and tan, or grizzle. Dark points permissible. White marks are not desirable.

**Gait**—Should be true, low and driving. In front, the legs extend forward from the shoulder. Good rear angulation showing great powers of propulsion. Viewed from the side, hind legs follow in the track of the forelegs, moving smoothly from the hip and flexing well at the stifle and hock. Topline remains level.

**Temperament**—Alert, gregarious, fearless and loyal. Never aggressive.

**Approved October 13, 1981**
**Reformatted March 23, 1990**

# Norwich Terrier

$\mathcal{T}$HE ROOTS OF THE NORWICH WERE FIRMLY PLANTED IN EAST ANGLIA, England. By the 1880s owning a small ratting terrier was a fad among the sporting undergraduates of Cambridge University. A popular strain developed of very small red and black-and-tan working crossbreeds from native, Yorkshire, and Irish stock.

By the turn of the twentieth century one of these dogs, then called Trumpington Terriers, was living in a stable near the city of Norwich. Rags was sandy colored, short of leg, stocky, with cropped ears. A prodigious ratter and dominant sire, he is the modern breed's progenitor. For the next two decades various horsemen bred other game terrier types to Rags and his descendants, including a half-sized brindle Staffordshire. So, from companions and barnyard ratters, there gradually developed a line of excellent fox bolters, and one of these introduced the breed to America in 1914.

Bred in Market Harborough by the noted Frank "Roughrider" Jones, Willum became the inseparable companion of a Philadelphia sportsman, Robert Strawbridge. This Jones terrier was also low legged, cropped, and docked. But his very hard coat had black shadings, and his head showed a marked resemblance to a Bull Terrier. Willum proved a charming, muscular twelve-pound ambassador, and a prolific sire of M.F.H. Hunt Terriers in Vermont, New York, Pennsylvania, and Virginia. He died at fourteen years of age defending his hearth from a vicious canine intruder just a few years before the breed was recognized in England in 1932. Though the AKC made Norwich Terriers official in 1936, there are still some Americans who associate Norwich with Willum's breeder and steadfastly call them Jones Terriers.

In 1964 The Kennel Club (England) recognized the drop-ear Norwich as a separate breed, terming them the Norfolk Terrier. The American Kennel Club took the same step effective January 1, 1979. The recognition of the two varieties as separate breeds is now the rule in all English-speaking countries and in Europe and Scandinavia.

Norwich are hardy, happy-go-lucky, weatherproof companions. Though game on vermin, they are usually gregarious with children, adults, and other domestic animals. Today they still weigh about twelve pounds, are short legged, sturdy, and can be any shade from wheaten to dark red, black-and-tan, or grizzle. They are very loyal, alert, and have a sensitive intelligence.

Their body lengths and breadths vary, but their docked tails should be long enough to firmly grasp. Smooth coated and wedge shaped, their heads should have plenty of brain room, with ears spaced well apart. A delineated stop between the wide-set eyes should be just nearer the muzzle than the top of the skull. The small, dark almond eyes coupled with a slightly foxy muzzle give Norwich their typical impish expression.

Most Norwich owners prefer a terrier of sagacious character with a harsh, care-free coat and large close-fitting teeth, and tolerate the variations of color and conformation which befit its heritage. Its unique standard employs horsemen's terms and the breed's characteristic mane calls for coarser, longer protective hair on neck and shoulders. Breeders must remain watchful and guard against show fads, exaggerations, excessive coats, or fancy trimming. To keep personality a priority, the parent club rewards working abilities, obedience, and racing competitions along with show-ring events.

# OFFICIAL STANDARD FOR THE NORWICH TERRIER

**General Appearance**—The Norwich Terrier, spirited and stocky with sensitive prick ears and a slightly foxy expression, is one of the smallest working terriers. This sturdy descendant of ratting companions, eager to dispatch small vermin alone or in a pack, has good bone and substance and an almost weatherproof coat. A hardy hunt terrier—honorable scars from fair wear and tear are acceptable.

**Size, Proportion, Substance**—One of the smallest of the terriers, the ideal *height* should not exceed 10 inches at the withers. Distance from the top of the withers to the ground and from the withers to base of tail are approximately equal. Good bone and substance. *Weight* approximately 12 pounds. It should be in proportion to the individual dog's structure and balance. Fit working condition is a prime consideration.

**Head**—A slightly foxy *expression*. *Eyes* small, dark and oval shaped with black rims. Placed well apart with a bright and keen expression. *Ears* medium size and erect. Set well apart with pointed tips. Upright when alert.

The *skull* is broad and slightly rounded with good width between the ears. The *muzzle* is wedge shaped and strong. Its length is about one-third less than the measurement from the occiput to the well-defined *stop*. The jaw is clean and strong. Nose and lip pigment black. Tight-lipped with large teeth. A scissor *bite*.

**Neck, Topline, Body**—*Neck* of medium length, strong and blending into well laid back shoulders. Level *topline*. *Body* moderately short. Compact and deep. Good width of *chest*. Well-sprung *ribs* and short *loins*. *Tail* medium docked. The terrier's working origin requires that the tail be of sufficient length to grasp. Base level with topline; carried erect.

**Forequarters**—Well laid back *shoulders*. Elbows close to ribs. Short, powerful *legs*, as straight as is consistent with the digging terrier. Pasterns firm. *Feet* round with thick pads. Nails black. The feet point forward when standing or moving.

**Hindquarters**—Broad, strong and muscular with well-turned *stifles*. *Hocks* low set and straight when viewed from the rear. *Feet* as in front.

**Coat**—Hard, wiry and straight, lying close to the body with a definite undercoat. The coat on neck and shoulders forms a protective mane. The hair on head, ears and muzzle, except for slight eyebrows and whiskers, is short and smooth. This breed should be shown with as natural a coat as possible. A minimum of tidying is permissible but shaping should be heavily penalized.

**Color**—All shades of red, wheaten, black and tan or grizzle. White marks are not desirable.

**Gait**—The legs moving parallel, extending forward, showing great powers of propulsion. Good rear angulation with a true, yet driving movement. The forelegs move freely with feet and elbows the same distance apart, converging slightly with increased pace. Hind legs follow in the track of the forelegs, flexing well at the stifle and hock. The topline remains level.

**Temperament**—Gay, fearless, loyal and affectionate. Adaptable and sporting, they make ideal companions.

**Approved October 13, 1981**
**Reformatted March 23, 1990**

# PARSON RUSSELL TERRIER

*T*HE PARSON RUSSELL TERRIER WAS FIRST BRED TO HUNT RED FOX ABOVE
and below the ground in the south of England in the mid-1800s. In the traditional sport of foxhunting, the Parson Russell Terrier followed horse and hound
across the countryside. When the hounds drove the fox to ground, the terrier dug
in and followed, baying to bolt the fox back above ground. Everything about the
breed denotes foxhunting: conformation, character, attitude, and intelligence. The
breed is distinguished by a balanced and flexible build, with straight legs; a narrow
chest; and a harsh, weatherproof double coat. Height ranges from twelve to fifteen
inches at the withers, balance being the main factor. The Parson Russell Terrier is
all white or predominantly white with black, tan, or tricolored markings.

The breed is named for the Reverend John Russell (1795–1883), often referred
to as the father of the Wirehaired Fox Terrier and as the "Sporting Parson." He was
a founding member of The Kennel Club (England) in 1873 and maintained his
own pack of foxhounds. Russell bred a strain of white fox terriers known country-
wide for its distinctive type, harsh weatherproof jacket, and hunting acumen. His
terriers were frequently bred with dogs from notable fox terrier kennels of the day
and can be traced from modern fox terrier pedigrees. The English champion
Carlisle Tack (1884) carried Russell's bloodlines and was said to be indistinguish-
able from the type of terrier bred by the reverend. The breed we recognize today as
the Parson Russell Terrier mirrors Russell's own stock.

Authorities assert that after Russell's death, some of his bloodlines were crossed into various other breeds, which would explain the many specimens seen with short legs, long bodies, and big chests. These crossbred dogs were incorrectly called Jack Russell Terriers, although they were not at all representative of Reverend Russell's terriers. With the approval of the American Kennel Club, in 2003 the Parson Russell Terrier Association of America changed the breed name to Parson Russell Terrier, in order to distinguish the true type terrier.

Still widely used with foxhounds in England, the Parson Russell Terrier is also very popular throughout the world. This is first and foremost a working terrier, one that is single-minded, tenacious, courageous, and clever. Although playful, overwhelmingly affectionate, and an excellent companion, the Parson Russell Terrier is a high-energy terrier with a strong hunting instinct and is not the dog for everyone.

# OFFICIAL STANDARD FOR THE PARSON RUSSELL TERRIER

**General Appearance**—The Parson Russell Terrier was developed in the south of England in the 1800s as a white terrier to work European red fox both above and below ground. The terrier was named for the Reverend John Russell, whose terriers trailed hounds and bolted foxes from dens so the hunt could ride on. To function as a working terrier, he must possess certain characteristics: a ready attitude, alert and confident; balance in height and length; medium in size and bone, suggesting strength and endurance. Important to breed type is a natural appearance: harsh, weatherproof coat with a compact construction and clean silhouette. The coat is broken or smooth. He has a small, flexible chest to enable him to pursue his quarry underground and sufficient length of leg to follow the hounds. Old scars and injuries, the result of honorable work or accident, should not be allowed to prejudice a terrier's chance in the show ring, unless they interfere with movement or utility for work or breeding.

**Size, Substance, Proportion**—*Size*—The ideal height of a mature dog is 14 inches at the highest point of the shoulder blade, and bitches 13 inches. Terriers whose heights measure either slightly larger or smaller than the ideal are not to be penalized in the show ring provided other points of their conformation, especially balance, are consistent with the working aspects of the standard. Larger dogs must remain spannable and smaller dogs must continue to exhibit breed type and sufficient bone to allow them to work successfully. The weight of a terrier in hard working condition is usually between 13–17 pounds. *Proportion*—Balance is the keystone of the terrier's anatomy. The chief points of consideration are the relative proportions of skull and foreface, head and frame, height at withers, and length of body. The height at withers is slightly greater than the distance from the withers to tail, i.e., by possibly 1 to 1½ inches on a 14-inch dog. The measurement will vary according to height. *Substance*—The terrier is of medium bone, not so heavy as to appear coarse or so light as to appear racy. The conformation of the whole frame is indicative of strength and endurance.

*Disqualification*—Height under 12 inches or over 15 inches.

**Head**—*Head*—Strong and in good proportion to the rest of the body, so the appearance of balance is maintained. *Expression*—Keen, direct, full of life and intelligence. *Eyes*—Almond shaped, dark in color, moderate in size, not protruding. Dark rims are desirable, however, where the coat surrounding the eye is white, the eye rim may be pink. *Ears*—Small V-shaped drop ears of moderate thickness carried forward close to the head with the tip so as to cover the orifice and pointing toward the eye. Fold is level with the top of the skull or slightly above. When alert, ear tips do not extend below the corner of the eye. *Skull*—Flat with muzzle and backskull in parallel planes. Fairly broad between the ears, narrowing slightly to the eyes. The stop is well defined but not prominent. *Muzzle*—Length from nose to stop is slightly shorter than the distance from stop to occiput. Strong and rectangular, measuring in width approximately ⅔ that of the backskull between the ears. *Jaws*—Upper and lower are of fair and punishing strength. *Nose*—Must be black and fully pigmented. *Bite*—Teeth are large with complete dentition in a perfect scissors bite, i.e., upper teeth closely overlapping the lower teeth and teeth set square to the jaws. *Faults*—Snipey muzzle, weak or coarse head. Light or yellow eye, round eye. Hound ear, fleshy ear, rounded tips. Level bite, missing teeth. Four or more missing premolars, incisors or canines is a fault. *Disqualifications*—Prick ears. Liver color nose. Overshot, undershot or wry mouth.

**Neck, Topline, Body**—*Neck*—Clean and muscular, moderately arched, of fair length, gradually widening so as to blend well into the shoulders. *Topline*—Strong, straight, and level in motion, the loin of moderate length. *Body*—In overall length-to-height proportion, the dog appears approximately square and balanced. The back is neither short nor long. The back gives no appearance of slackness but is laterally flexible, so that he may turn around in an earth. Tuck-up is moderate. *Chest*—Narrow and of moderate depth, giving an athletic rather than heavily-chested appearance; must be flexible and compressible. The ribs are fairly well sprung, oval rather than round, not extending past the level of the elbow. *Tail*—Docked so the tip is approximately level to the skull. Set on not too high, but so that a level topline, with a very slight arch over the loin, is maintained. Carried gaily when in motion, but when baiting or at rest may be held level but not below the horizontal. *Faults*—Chest not spannable or shallow; barrel ribs. Tail set low or carried low to or over the back, i.e., squirrel tail.

*Forequarters*—*Shoulders*—Long and sloping, well laid back, cleanly cut at the withers. Point of shoulder sits in a plane behind the point of the prosternum. The shoulder blade and upper arm are of approximately the same length; forelegs are placed well under the dog. Elbows hang perpendicular to the body, working free of the sides. Legs are strong and straight with good bone. Joints turn neither in nor out. Pasterns firm and nearly straight. *Feet*—Round, cat-like, very compact, the pads thick and tough, the toes moderately arched pointing forward, turned neither in nor out. *Fault*—Hare feet.

**Hindquarters**—Strong and muscular, smoothly molded, with good angulation and bend of stifle. Hocks near the ground, parallel, and driving in action. Feet as in front.

**Coat**—Smooth and Broken: Whether smooth or broken, a double coat of good sheen; naturally harsh, close and dense, straight with no suggestion of kink. There is a clear outline with only a hint of eyebrows and beard if natural to the coat. No sculptured furnishings. The terrier is shown in his natural appearance not excessively groomed. Sculpturing is to be severely penalized. *Faults*—Soft, silky, woolly, or curly topcoat. Lacking undercoat. Excessive grooming and sculpturing.

**Color**—White, white with black or tan markings, or a combination of these, tricolor. Colors are clear. As long as the terrier is predominantly white, moderate body markings are not to be faulted. Grizzle is acceptable and should not be confused with brindle. *Disqualification*—Brindle markings.

**Gait**—Movement or action is the crucial test of conformation. A tireless ground covering trot displaying good reach in front with the hindquarters providing plenty of drive. Pasterns break lightly on forward motion with no hint of hackney-like action or goose-stepping. The action is straight in front and rear.

**Temperament**—Bold and friendly. Athletic and clever. At work he is a game hunter, tenacious, courageous, and single minded. At home he is playful, exuberant and overwhelmingly affectionate. He is an independent and energetic terrier and requires his due portion of attention. He should not be quarrelsome. Shyness should not be confused with submissiveness. Submissiveness is not a fault. Sparring is not acceptable. *Fault*—Shyness. *Disqualification*—Overt aggression toward another dog.

Spanning—To measure a terrier's chest, span from behind, raising only the front feet from the ground, and compress gently. Directly behind the elbows is the smaller, firm part of the chest. The central part is usually larger but should feel rather elastic. Span with hands tightly behind the elbows on the forward portion of the chest. The chest must be easily spanned by average size hands. Thumbs should meet at the spine and fingers should meet under the chest. This is a significant factor and a critical part of the judging process. The dog cannot be correctly judged without this procedure.

## DISQUALIFICATIONS

*Height under 12 inches or over 15 inches.*
*Prick ears, liver nose.*
*Overshot, undershot or wry mouth.*
*Brindle markings.*
*Overt aggression toward another dog.*

**Approved July 13, 2004**
**Effective September 29, 2004**

# Scottish Terrier

$\mathcal{M}$ OST LOVERS OF THE SCOTTISH TERRIER HAVE A DEEP AND ABIDING BELIEF that this breed is the most ancient of any of the Highland terriers; that the other breeds are only offshoots from this, the parent stem, and that the Scottie is the original, dyed-in-the-wool, simon-pure Highland terrier. They will tell you that the Skye Terrier mentioned in early histories and chronicles was not the Skye as we know it today, but the forerunner of the Scottie and similar in type to it. They will refer you to such early writers as Jacques du Fouilloux, who published *La Venerie* in 1561, Turberville and Dr. Stevens, whose books *The Noble Art of Venerie* and *The Maison Rustique* appeared in 1575 and 1572, respectively. All of these works described an "earth dog used in hunting the fox and the brocke," and these descriptions fit closely to what might have been the forerunner of our present-day Scottie.

In the seventeenth century, when King James VI of Scotland became James I of England, he wrote to Edinburgh to have a half a dozen terriers sent to France as a present and addressed the letter to the Laird of Caldwell, naming the Earl of Montieth as having good ones. Later, the great English authority Rawdon B. Lee wrote:

> The Scottie is the oldest variety of the canine race indigenous to Britain. . . . For generations he had been a popular dog in the Highlands where, strangely enough, he was always known as the Skye Terrier, although

he is different from the long-coated, unsporting-like creature with which that name is now associated.

While all this is very interesting and quite possibly true, the fact remains that it is neither definite nor conclusive.

Leaving the realm of speculation and inference and coming down to history and known facts, the Scottish Terrier as we find it today has been bred in purity for many years. The first show to have a class for Scottish Terriers was at Birmingham, England, in 1860. Later, a number of other shows carried this classification, but the dogs shown in these classes were not Scottish Terriers, but Skyes, Dandie Dinmonts, and Yorkshires.

All the while, however, Scotchmen who saw these dogs winning as Scottish Terriers were indignant, and about 1877 they broke into print in the *Live Stock Journal* with a series of letters protesting the situation and discussing the points and character of the true Scottish Terrier. The discussion waxed so furious that the editors finally called a halt with the statement, "We see no use in prolonging this discussion unless each correspondent described the dog which he holds to be the true type." This challenge was taken up by Captain Gordon Murray, who in a letter to the *Stock Keeper* under the nom de plume "Strathbogie," described in detail his conception of a proper Scottish Terrier. This quieted the warring factions, and about 1880 J. B. Morrison was persuaded to draw up a standard. This was accepted by all parties.

The essentials of this standard have been retained in all the later standards, only minor changes having been introduced. In 1882 the Scottish Terrier Club was organized with joint officers for England and Scotland. Later, as interest in the breed grew, the two countries organized separate clubs, although they have always worked harmoniously together.

John Naylor is credited with being the first to introduce the Scottish Terrier to America; his initial importation in 1883 was of a dog and a bitch, Tam Glen and Bonnie Belle. He showed extensively and continued importing, among his later importations being his famous dogs Glenlyon and Whinstone. The first Scottish Terrier registered in America was Dake, a brindle dog whelped September 15, 1884, bred by O. P. Chandler, of Kokomo, Indiana. His sire was Naylor's Glenlyon. This was in the *American Kennel Register,* published by *Forest and Stream,* at about the time the American Kennel Club was being organized. In December 1887, the bitch Lassie was registered, bred by W. H. Todd, of Vermillion, Ohio. Her sire was Glencoe, by Imp. Whinstone *ex.* Imp. Roxie. Here we find Whinstone figuring as a sire. Now Whinstone was by Allister, which together with Dundee formed the two great fountainheads of the breed. Whinstone sired Ch. Bellingham Baliff, acquired by J. J. Little, founder of the famous Newcastle Kennels. Whinstone therefore was the forerunner and progenitor of the Scottish Terrier in this country.

Since those days there have been thousands of importations and many notable breeders have carried on the work. Probably none of the early blood is to be found today. Nevertheless, these early dogs must take their place in history; and to that pioneer breeder and missionary of the breed, John Naylor, the great popularity of this staunch little breed stands as an enduring monument.

# OFFICIAL STANDARD FOR THE SCOTTISH TERRIER

**General Appearance**—The Scottish Terrier is a small, compact, short-legged, sturdily built dog of good bone and substance. His head is long in proportion to his size. He has a hard, wiry, weather-resistant coat and a thick-set, cobby body which is hung between short, heavy legs. These characteristics, joined with his very special keen, piercing, "varminty" expression, and his erect ears and tail are salient features of the breed. The Scottish Terrier's bold, confident, dignified aspect exemplifies power in a small package.

**Size, Proportion, Substance**—The Scottish Terrier should have a thick body and heavy bone. The principal objective must be symmetry and balance without exaggeration. Equal consideration shall be given to height, weight, length of back and length of head. Height at withers for either sex should be about 10 inches. The length of back from withers to set-on of tail should be approximately 11 inches. Generally, a well-balanced Scottish Terrier dog should weigh from 19 to 22 pounds and a bitch from 18 to 21 pounds.

**Head**—The head should be long in proportion to the overall length and size of the dog. In profile, the skull and muzzle should give the appearance of two parallel planes. The *skull* should be long and of medium width, slightly domed and covered with short, hard hair. In profile, the skull should appear flat. There should be a slight but definite stop between the skull and muzzle at eye level, allowing the eyes to be set in under the brow, contributing to proper Scottish Terrier expression. The skull should be smooth with no prominences or depressions and the cheeks should be flat and clean. The *muzzle* should be approximately equal to the length of skull with only a slight taper to the nose. The muzzle should be well filled in under the eye, with no evidence of snipiness. A correct Scottish Terrier muzzle should fill an average man's hand. The *nose* should be black, regardless of coat color, and of good size, projecting somewhat over the mouth and giving the impression that the upper jaw is longer than the lower. The *teeth* should be large and evenly spaced, having either a scissors or level bite, the former preferred. The jaw should be square, level and powerful. Undershot or overshot bites should be penalized. The *eyes* should be set wide apart and well in under the brow. They should be small, bright and piercing, and almond-shaped not round. The color should be dark brown or nearly black, the darker the better. The *ears* should be small, prick, set well up on the skull and pointed, but never cut. They should be covered with short velvety hair. From the front, the outer edge of the ear should form a straight line up from the side of the skull. The use, size, shape and placement of the ear and its erect carriage are major elements of the keen, alert, intelligent Scottish Terrier expression.

**Neck, Topline, Body**—The *neck* should be moderately short, strong, thick and muscular, blending smoothly into well laid back shoulders. The neck must never be so short as to appear clumsy. The *body* should be moderately short with ribs extending well back into a short, strong loin, deep flanks and very muscular hindquarters. The ribs should be well sprung out from the spine, forming a broad, strong back, then curving down and inward to form a deep body that would be nearly heart-shaped if viewed in cross-section. The *topline* of the back should be firm and level. The *chest* should be broad, very deep and well let down between the forelegs. The forechest should extend well in front of the legs and drop well down into the brisket. The chest should not be flat or concave, and the brisket should nicely fill an average man's slightly cupped hand. The lowest point of the brisket should be such that an average man's fist would fit under it with little or no overhead clearance. The tail should be about seven inches long and never cut. It should be set on high and carried erectly, either vertical or with a slight curve forward, but not over the back. The tail should be thick at the base, tapering gradually to a point and covered with short, hard hair.

**Forequarters**—The shoulders should be well laid back and moderately well knit at the withers. The forelegs should be very heavy in bone, straight or slightly bent with elbows close to the body, and set in under the shoulder blade with a definite forechest in front of them. Scottish Terriers should not be out at the elbows. The forefeet should be larger than the hind feet, round, thick and compact with strong nails. The front feet should point straight ahead, but a slight "toeing out" is acceptable. Dew claws may be removed.

**Hindquarters**—The thighs should be very muscular and powerful for the size of the dog with the stifles well bent and the legs straight from hock to heel. Hocks should be well let down and parallel to each other.

**Coat**—The Scottish Terrier should have a broken coat. It is a hard, wiry outer coat with a soft, dense undercoat. The coat should be trimmed and blended into the furnishings to give a distinct Scottish Terrier outline. The dog should be presented with sufficient coat so that the texture and density may be determined. The longer coat on the beard, legs and lower body may be slightly softer than the body coat but should not be or appear fluffy.

**Color**—Black, wheaten or brindle of any color. Many black and brindle dogs have sprinklings of white or silver hairs in their coats which are normal and not to be penalized. White can be allowed only on the chest and chin and that to a slight extent only.

**Gait**—The gait of the Scottish Terrier is very characteristic of the breed. It is not the square trot or walk desirable in the long-legged breeds. The forelegs do not move in exact parallel planes; rather, in reaching out, the forelegs incline slightly inward because of the deep broad forechest. Movement should be free, agile and coordinated with powerful drive from the rear and good reach in front. The action of the rear legs should be square and true and, at the trot, both the hocks and stifles should be flexed with a vigorous motion. When the dog is in motion, the back should remain firm and level.

**Temperament**—The Scottish Terrier should be alert and spirited but also stable and steady-going. He is a determined and thoughtful dog whose "heads up, tails up" attitude in the ring should convey both fire and control. The Scottish Terrier, while loving and gentle with people, can be aggressive with other dogs. He should exude ruggedness and power, living up to his nickname, the "Diehard."

## PENALTIES

*Soft coat; curly coat; round, protruding or light eyes; overshot or undershot jaws; obviously oversize or undersize; shyness or timidity; upright shoulders; lack of reach in front or drive in rear; stiff or stilted movement; movement too wide or too close in rear; too narrow in front or rear; out at the elbow; lack of bone and substance; low set tail; lack of pigment in the nose; coarse head; and failure to show with head and tail up are faults to be penalized.*
NO JUDGE SHOULD PUT TO WINNERS OR BEST OF BREED ANY SCOTTISH TERRIER NOT SHOWING REAL TERRIER CHARACTER IN THE RING.

### SCALE OF POINTS

| | |
|---|---|
| Skull | 5 |
| Muzzle | 5 |
| Eyes | 5 |
| Ears | 10 |
| Neck | 5 |
| Chest | 5 |
| Body | 15 |
| Legs and feet | 10 |
| Tail | 5 |
| Coat | 15 |
| Size | 10 |
| General appearance | 10 |
| **Total** | **100** |

**Approved October 12, 1993**
**Effective November 30, 1993**

# SEALYHAM TERRIER

THE SEALYHAM TERRIER DERIVES ITS NAME FROM SEALYHAM, HAVERFORD-west, Wales. Sealyham was the estate of Captain John Edwardes. Between 1850 and 1890, Edwardes developed a strain of small white dogs from obscure ancestry, noted for prowess in quarrying badger, otter, and fox. The requisite qualities were extreme gameness and endurance, with as much substance as could be had in a dog that was small and quick enough to dig and battle underground.

As the working ability of Sealyham Terriers drew public interest, they began to take their places with other terrier breeds in prominent homes and at shows. Their first recorded appearance at a dog show was at Haverfordwest in October 1903. In January 1908, a group of Welsh fanciers founded the Sealyham Terrier Club of Haverfordwest. At their first meeting, they drew up the original standard for the breed. The first championship show in which Sealyhams appeared was the English Kennel Club show of October 1910. The Kennel Club (England) recognized the breed in March 1911, and in that year the first Challenge Certificates for Sealyham Terriers were offered at London's Great Joint Terrier Show.

The American Kennel Club recognized the breed in 1911, shortly after its original importation into the United States. Since its American show debut at San Mateo, California, in September of that year, the breed's popularity as a show dog has remained fairly constant.

The American Sealyham Terrier Club was founded on May 15, 1913, to promote the interests of the breed in the United States and to encourage working trials and show exhibiting. More recently, interest has developed in agility, obedience, and tracking. Now, at the beginning of the twenty-first century, Sealyham owners and their dogs enjoy successful participation in AKC-sponsored events in addition to the show ring, and companion and performance titles are becoming more frequent. The ASTC annual specialty show is held as part of the Montgomery County Kennel Club terrier show in Pennsylvania, and the club encourages sponsorship of entries throughout the year at all-breed or all-terrier group conformation events.

The breed has had an illustrious record in AKC show rings through the years. A properly prepared Sealyham showing with typical style and vigor is an impressive dog, providing the excitement of a classic terrier. The Sealyham remains a highly competitive participant in the group ring, in spite of low breed-registration numbers and a sharp decline in the number of Sealyham kennels in many regions of the United States. Because there are not large numbers of Sealyhams registered each year, people who want a puppy have to be particularly determined and persevering in their search for breeders.

Sealyham conformation and temperament may be chiefly characterized by the word *strength*. The word *strong* appears six times in the standard, the words *power* or *powerful* four times. The Sealyham standard also contains the telling phrase, "of extraordinary substance." These words leave no doubt how earlier fanciers wished the breed to be seen.

Sealyhams are eye-catching show dogs as well as loyal and entertaining pets. They serve instinctively and well in therapy assignments with both children and the elderly.

It is an outgoing breed yet a good watchdog, whose big-dog bark discourages intruders. Proper care, food, and training promote the breed's long life. A life span of twelve to sixteen years is not uncommon for the Sealyham.

With terrier temperament and strength of will, the individual dog can be stubborn. That obstinate behavior is tempered, however, by a sly sense of humor. Owners accept and appreciate the Sealyham character, knowing that it includes an immense capacity for loyalty and love of home and family.

As a family pet, the Sealyham is flexible in its requirements, adapting easily to apartment living or to the luxury of acreage. Regular coat care is necessary to keep the Sealyham smart looking, clean, and comfortable. Brushing, plucking, or clipping the hair is necessary. The primary requirement is that Sealyhams be allowed to accompany their owners wherever they go and add their cheerful dispositions to their family's everyday life.

# OFFICIAL STANDARD FOR
# THE SEALYHAM TERRIER

**The Sealyham should be the embodiment of power and determination, ever keen and alert, of extraordinary substance, yet free from clumsiness.**

**Height**—At withers about 10½ inches.

**Weight**—23–24 pounds for dogs; bitches slightly less. It should be borne in mind that size is more important than weight.

**Head**—Long, broad and powerful, without coarseness. It should, however, be in perfect balance with the body, joining neck smoothly. Length of head roughly, three-quarters height at withers, or about an inch longer than neck. Breadth between ears a little less than one-half length of head. *Skull*—Very slightly domed, with a shallow indentation running down between the brows, and joining the muzzle with a moderate stop. *Cheeks*—Smoothly formed and flat, without heavy jowls. *Jaws*—Powerful and square. Bite level or scissors. Overshot or undershot bad faults. *Teeth*—Sound, strong and white, with canines fitting closely together. *Nose*—Black, with large nostrils. White, cherry or butterfly bad faults. *Eyes*—Very dark, deeply set and fairly wide apart, of medium size, oval in shape with keen terrier expression. Light, large or protruding eye bad faults. Lack of eye rim pigmentation not a fault. *Ears*—Folded level with top of head, with forward edge close to cheek. Well rounded at tip, and of length to reach outer corner of eye. Thin, not leathery, and of sufficient thickness to avoid creases. Prick, tulip, rose or hound ears bad faults.

**Neck**—Length slightly less than two-thirds of height of dog at withers. Muscular without coarseness, with good reach, refinement at throat, and set firmly on shoulders.

**Shoulders**—Well laid back and powerful, but not over-muscled. Sufficiently wide to permit freedom of action. Upright or straight shoulder placement highly undesirable.

**Legs**—Forelegs strong, with good bone; and as straight as is consistent with chest being well let down between them. Down on pasterns, knuckled over, bowed, and out at elbow, bad faults. Hind legs longer than forelegs and not so heavily boned. *Feet*—Large but compact, round with thick pads, strong nails. Toes well arched and pointing straight ahead. Forefeet larger, though not quite so long as hind feet. Thin, spread or flat feet bad faults.

**Body**—Strong, short-coupled and substantial, so as to permit great flexibility. Brisket deep and well let down between forelegs. Ribs well sprung.

**Back**—Length from withers to set-on of tail should approximate height at withers, or 10½ inches. Topline level, neither roached nor swayed. Any deviations from these measurements undesirable. *Hindquarters*—Very powerful, and protruding well behind the set-on of tail. Strong second thighs, stifles well bent, and hocks well let down. Cowhocks bad fault.

**Tail**—Docked and carried upright. Set on far enough forward so that spine does not slope down to it.

**Coat**—Weather-resisting, comprised of soft, dense undercoat and hard, wiry top coat. Silky or curly coat bad fault.

**Color**—All white, or with lemon, tan or badger markings on head and ears. Heavy body markings and excessive ticking should be discouraged.

**Action**—Sound, strong, quick, free, true and level.

## SCALE OF POINTS

| | | | | | |
|---|---|---|---|---|---|
| General character, balance and size | | 15 | Shoulders and brisket | 10 | |
| Head | 5 | | Body, ribs and loin | 10 | |
| Eyes | 5 | | Hindquarters | 10 | |
| Mouth | 5 | | Legs and feet | 10 | |
| Ears | 5 | | Coat | 10 | 50 |
| Neck | 5 | 25 | Tail | 5 | |
| | | | Color (body marking & ticking) | 5 | 10 |
| | | | **Total** | | **100** |

**Approved February 9, 1974**

# SKYE TERRIER

*T*HE MAJORITY OF TERRIERS HAVE ATTAINED SOMETHING OF THEIR PRESENT-day form within the last century, but the Skye Terrier of nearly four centuries ago was like the specimens of today.

One may find mention of the Skye Terrier in that historic volume *Of Englishe Dogges,* by John Caius, master of Gonville and Caius College, Cambridge University, and court physician to Edward VI, Queen Mary, and Queen Elizabeth. He was a man of broad education aside from the sciences, and also a great traveler and sportsman. Referring to the breed, he says it was "brought out of barbarous borders fro' the uttermost countryes northward . . . which, by reason of the length of heare, makes showe neither of face nor of body."

Thus we find the Skye Terrier of today. His flowing coat is the same as the one that proved such a grand protection in the days when his only occupation was to challenge vicious animals that otherwise might have crippled him at a single bite. Perhaps this long coat has been a handicap, for all followers of this game old working terrier have witnessed him surpassed in popularity by one after another of the newer breeds. Still they are reluctant to change him in any manner. Indeed, they stand by the motto of the Skye Club of Scotland—"Wha daur meddle wi' me."

The breed takes its name from the chief of those northwestern islands of Scotland that, as far back as he can be traced, formed his native home, and in which he was found in greatest perfection. He is the only terrier distinctively belonging to the northwestern islands that is not common to the whole of Scotland. Those who have the best practical knowledge of the Skye maintain that he is without rival in his own peculiar domain, and that wherever there are rocks, dens, burrow, cairns, or coverts to explore, or waters to take to, his services should be called.

From the nature of Caius's allusion to him, it is evident that the Skye Terrier had become known in the cities of England, especially in the royal palace. The kings and queens of England have always set the styles in that country, and as soon as the Skye had been accepted in court—evidently in the mid-sixteenth century when Caius penned the historic work—he was soon the fashionable pet of all degrees of nobility, and after that of the commoners.

The Skye was the most widely known of all the terriers down to the end of the nineteenth century. Queen Victoria's early interest and Sir Edwin Landseer's paintings featuring the breed helped attract attention. He was kept in all the English-speaking countries. Since then he has slipped quietly into the background, yet his admirers in England and Scotland—where he has maintained his greatest foothold—are happy to point to the time when "a duchess would almost be ashamed to be seen in the park unaccompanied by her long-coated Skye."

The Skye Terrier was first registered with the AKC in 1887 and was one of the most important breeds at American benched shows before the turn of the twentieth century. The rivalry among the leading kennels was exceptionally keen. Although the frontiers of his activities have been somewhat curtailed, the true value of the Skye Terrier is evinced by the tenacious grasp which he has on those who have come in contact with him. Thus, entries may sometimes be small at shows today, but seldom does one find a major show without some specimens of this old terrier breed.

# OFFICIAL STANDARD FOR THE SKYE TERRIER

**General Appearance**—The Skye Terrier is a dog of style, elegance and dignity: agile and strong with sturdy bone and hard muscle. Long, low and level—he is twice as long as he is high—he is covered with a profuse coat that falls straight down either side of the body over oval-shaped ribs. The hair well feathered on the head veils forehead and eyes to serve as protection from brush and briar as well as amid serious encounters with other animals. He stands with head high and long tail hanging and moves with a seemingly effortless gait. He is strong in body, quarter and jaw.

**Size, Proportion, Substance**—*Size*—The ideal shoulder height for dogs is 10 inches and bitches 9½ inches. Based on these heights a 10 inch dog measured from chest bone over tail at rump should be 20 inches. A slightly higher or lower dog of either sex is acceptable. Dogs 9 inches or less and bitches 8½ inches or less at the withers are to be penalized. *Proportion*—The ideal ratio of body length to shoulder height is 2 to 1, which is considered the correct proportion. **Substance**—Solidly built, full of strength and quality without being coarse. Bone is substantial.

**Head**—Long and powerful, strength being deemed more important than extreme length.

*Eyes* brown, preferably dark brown, medium in size, close-set and alight with life and intelligence.

*Ears* symmetrical and gracefully feathered. They may be carried prick or drop. If prick, they are medium in size, placed high on the skull, erect at their outer edges, and slightly wider apart at the peak than at the skull. Drop ears, somewhat larger in size and set lower, hang flat against the skull.

Moderate width at the back of the skull tapers gradually to a strong muzzle. The stop is slight. The dark muzzle is just moderately full as opposed to snipy. Powerful and absolutely true jaws. The nose is always black. A Dudley, flesh-colored or brown nose shall disqualify. Mouth with the incisor teeth closing level, or with upper teeth slightly overlapping the lower.

**Neck, Topline, Body**—*Neck*—Long and gracefully arched, carried high and proudly.

The backline is level.

*Body* pre-eminently long and low, the chest deep, with oval-shaped ribs. The sides appear flattish due to the straight falling and profuse coat.

*Tail* long and well feathered. When hanging, its upper section is pendulous, following the line of the rump, its lower section thrown back in a moderate arc without twist or curl. When raised, its height makes it appear a prolongation of the backline. Though not to be preferred, the tail is sometimes carried high when the dog is excited or angry. When such carriage arises from emotion only, it is permissible. But the tail should not be constantly carried above the level of the back or hang limp.

**Forequarters**—Shoulders well laid back, with tight placement of shoulder blades at the withers, and elbows should fit closely to the sides and be neither loose nor tied. Forearm should curve slightly around the chest. Legs short, muscular and straight as possible. "Straight as possible" means straight as soundness and chest will permit, it does not mean "Terrier straight."

*Feet*—Large hare-feet preferably pointing forward, the pads thick and nails strong and preferably black.

**Hindquarters**—Strong, full, well developed and well angulated. Legs short, muscular and straight when viewed from behind. Feet as in front.

**Coat**—Double. Undercoat short, close, soft and woolly. Outer coat hard, straight and flat. 5½ inches long without extra credit granted for greater length. The body coat hangs straight down each side, parting from head to tail. The head hair, which may be shorter, veils forehead and eyes and forms a moderate beard and apron. The long feathering on the ears falls straight down from the tips and outer edges, surrounding the ears like a fringe and outlining their shape. The ends of the hair should mingle with the coat of the neck. Tail well feathered.

**Color**—The coat must be of one overall color at the skin but may be of varying shades of the same color in the full coat, which may be black, blue, dark or light gray, silver platinum, fawn or cream. The dog must have no distinctive markings except for the desirable black points of ears, muzzle and tip of tail, all of which points are preferably dark even to black. The shade of head and legs should approximate that of the body. There must be no trace of pattern, design or clear-cut color variations, with the exception of the breed's only permissible white which occasionally exists on the chest not exceeding 2 inches in diameter.

The puppy coat may be very different in color from the adult coat. Therefore, as it is growing and clearing, wide variations of color may occur; consequently, this is permissible in dogs under 18 months of age. However, even in puppies there must be no trace of pattern, design or clear-cut variations with the exception of the black band encircling the body coat of the cream colored dog, and the only permissible white which, as in the adult dog, occasionally exists on the chest not exceeding 2 inches in diameter.

**Gait**—The legs proceed straight forward when traveling. When approaching, the forelegs form a continuation of the straight line of the front. The feet being the same distance apart as the elbows. The principal propelling power is furnished by the back legs which travel straight forward. Forelegs should move well forward, without too much lift. The whole movement may be termed free, active and effortless and give a more or less fluid picture.

**Temperament**—That of the typical working terrier capable of overtaking game and going to ground, displaying stamina, courage, strength and agility. Fearless, good-tempered, loyal and canny, he is friendly and gay with those he knows and reserved and cautious with strangers.

## DISQUALIFICATION

*A Dudley, flesh-colored or brown nose shall disqualify.*

**Approved February 10, 1990**
**Effective March 28, 1990**

# Soft Coated Wheaten Terrier

*P*ARTIALLY SHROUDED BY THE MISTS OF TIME, THE HISTORY OF THIS BREED sometimes reflects the Irish people's gift as storytellers rather than historians. Folklore persists that following the defeat of the Spanish Armada in 1588, a dog swam to the shore of Ireland from a sinking ship. Supposedly, he then bred to native terriers to produce the Wheaten, among other breeds.

Most agree that this breed can be traced back 200 years. Many fanciers feel the Soft Coated Wheaten predates and is the progenitor of its closest terrier kin, the Kerry Blue and the Irish, in spite of the fact that the latter was shown for some eighty years before the Wheaten's acceptance by the Irish Kennel Club. There is also reason to surmise a very early link to the Irish Wolfhound.

Long before kennel clubs and official records, Wheatens could be found all over Ireland, but the greatest numbers were in the south and southwest. There are records of numerous Wheatens in County Kerry as far back as 1785. They whelped in barns, hedges, and haystacks, and only the fittest survived. Quite early in Britain's history, the "laws of the forest" were placed in force. These laws allowed only freemen and landowners to own hunting dogs. The poor tenant farmer or fisherman could not legally own any animal of greater value than five British pounds. Also, only wealthy landowners could own a hunting dog or sporting dog more than nineteen inches tall. Further, those dogs with "whole" tails were for the landed gentry. Otherwise a tax was levied, which was not affordable by poor farm folk. Docking was done to provide evidence that these dogs were within the bounds of the law. Thus was born the Soft Coated Wheaten Terrier.

This "poor man's Wolfhound" came to serve as guardians of the tenant farmer's household and as all-purpose farm dogs. They were adept at herding and guarding sheep. They killed vermin and gave their family ample warning of intruders. They were keen of scent and might often be found with their owners, out for the hunt, bringing down small game.

Certainly the need for a dog's companionship is firmly established historically. This versatile breed had a keen desire to please and a willingness to do whatever was asked. Indeed, the poor farmer had myriad chores, which this working, sporting terrier eagerly performed. It is said that they might even have been called upon to perform menial kitchen chores, such as turning the spit. They were hardy easy keepers, not fussy about food and totally indifferent to the hardships of weather.

The Soft Coated Wheaten Terrier was registered with the Irish Kennel Club and made its debut at the Irish Kennel Club championship show on Saint Patrick's Day, 1937.

Wheatens first came to American shores in November 1946, when a litter of six arrived from Belfast. Two of these were assigned to Lydia Vogels, of Springfield, Massachusetts, and were shown at the Westminster Kennel Club show the following year. In total these dogs produced seventeen puppies, but public interest was not forthcoming. Consequently, Vogels' efforts to earn AKC recognition were in vain and would not come to fruition for another twenty-six years.

In 1957 the breed surfaced in the United States once more. Spurred on by the O'Connors (Gramachree kennel name) of Brooklyn, New York, and the Arnolds (Sunset Hills) of Hartford, Connecticut, Wheatens began to appear at dog shows, competing in the Miscellaneous class. In 1962, once again on that most appropriate date, Saint Patrick's Day, the Soft Coated Wheaten Terrier Club of America was formed.

By 1972, the ranks of Wheaten Terrier devotees swelled to 500, with over 1,000 dogs. The breed was admitted to the American Kennel Club Stud Book on May 1, 1973, and on October 3 of that year the Wheatens became eligible to compete in the Terrier Group. That October date auspiciously fell on the weekend of this country's most illustrious terrier showcase, the Montgomery County Kennel Club show, then held in Ambler, Pennsylvania. At the end of this four-show weekend, the Soft Coated Wheaten Terrier breed would celebrate its first champion.

# OFFICIAL STANDARD FOR THE SOFT COATED WHEATEN TERRIER

**General Appearance**—The Soft Coated Wheaten Terrier is a medium-sized, hardy, well balanced sporting terrier, square in outline. He is distinguished by his soft, silky, gently waving coat of warm wheaten color and his particularly steady disposition. The breed requires moderation both in structure and presentation, and any exaggerations are to be shunned. He should present the overall appearance of an alert and happy animal, graceful, strong and well coordinated.

**Size, Proportion, Substance**—A dog shall be 18 to 19 inches at the withers, the ideal being 18½. A bitch shall be 17 to 18 inches at the withers, the ideal being 17½. *Major Faults*—Dogs under 18 inches or over 19 inches; bitches under 17 inches or over 18 inches. Any deviation must be penalized according to the degree of its severity. Square in outline. Hardy, well balanced. Dogs should weigh 35–40 pounds; bitches 30–35 pounds.

**Head**—Well balanced and in proportion to the body. Rectangular in appearance; moderately long. Powerful with no suggestion of coarseness. *Eyes* dark reddish brown or brown, medium in size, slightly almond shaped and set fairly wide apart. Eye rims black. *Major Fault*—Anything approaching a yellow eye. *Ears* small to medium in size, breaking level with the skull and dropping slightly forward, the inside edge of the ear lying next to the cheek and pointing to the ground rather than to the eye. A hound ear or a high-breaking ear is not typical and should be *severely penalized*. *Skull* flat and clean between ears. Cheekbones not prominent. Defined *stop*. *Muzzle* powerful and strong, well filled below the eyes. No suggestion of snipiness. Skull and foreface of equal length. *Nose* black and large for size of dog. *Major Fault*—Any nose color other than solid black. *Lips* tight and black. *Teeth* large, clean and white; scissors or level *bite*. *Major Fault*—Undershot or overshot.

**Neck, Topline, Body**—*Neck* medium in length, clean and strong, not throaty. Carried proudly, it gradually widens, blending smoothly into the body. *Back* strong and level. *Body* compact; relatively short coupled. *Chest* is deep. *Ribs* are well sprung but without roundness. *Tail* is docked and well set on, carried gaily but never over the back.

**Forequarters**—*Shoulders* well laid back, clean and smooth; well knit. *Forelegs* straight and well boned. All *dewclaws* should be removed. *Feet* are round and compact with good depth of pad. *Pads* black. *Nails* dark.

**Hindquarters**—*Hind legs* well developed with well bent *stifles* turning neither in nor out; *hocks* well let down and parallel to each other. All *dewclaws* should be removed. The presence of dewclaws on the hind legs should be *penalized*. *Feet* are round and compact with good depth of pad. *Pads* black. *Nails* dark.

**Coat**—A distinguishing characteristic of the breed which sets the dog apart from all other terriers. An abundant single coat covering the entire body, legs and head; coat on the latter falls forward to shade the eyes. Texture soft and silky with a gentle wave. In both puppies and adolescents, the mature wavy coat is generally not yet evident. *Major Faults*—Woolly or harsh, crisp or cottony, curly or standaway coat; in the adult, a straight coat is also objectionable.

*Presentation*—For show purposes, the Wheaten is presented to show a terrier outline, but coat must be of sufficient length to flow when the dog is in motion. The coat must never be clipped or plucked. Sharp contrasts or stylizations must be avoided. Head coat should be blended to present a rectangular outline. Eyes should be indicated but never fully exposed. Ears should be relieved of fringe, but not taken down to the leather. Sufficient coat must be left on skull, cheeks, neck and tail to balance the proper length of body coat. *Dogs that are overly trimmed shall be severely penalized.*

**Color**—Any shade of wheaten. Upon close examination, occasional red, white or black guard hairs may be found. However, the overall coloring must be clearly wheaten with no evidence of any other color except on ears and muzzle where blue-gray shading is sometimes present. *Major Fault*—Any color save wheaten.

*Puppies and Adolescents*—Puppies under a year may carry deeper coloring and occasional black tipping. The adolescent, under two years, is often quite light in color, but must never be white or carry gray other than on ears and muzzle. However, by two years of age, the *proper* wheaten color should be obvious.

**Gait**—Gait is free, graceful and lively with good reach in front and strong drive behind. Front and rear feet turn neither in nor out. Dogs who fail to keep their tails erect when moving should be *severely penalized*.

**Temperament**—The Wheaten is a happy, steady dog and shows himself gaily with an air of self-confidence. He is alert and exhibits interest in his surroundings; exhibits less aggressiveness than is sometimes encouraged in other terriers. *Major Fault*—Timid or overly aggressive dogs.

**Approved February 12, 1983**
**Reformatted July 20, 1989**

# STAFFORDSHIRE BULL TERRIER

THE STAFFORDSHIRE BULL TERRIER HAD ITS BEGINNINGS IN ENGLAND MANY centuries ago when the Bulldog and Mastiff were closely linked. Bullbaiting and bearbaiting in the Elizabethan era produced large dogs for these sports. Later on the 100- to 120-pound animal gave way to a small, more agile breed of up to 90 pounds.

Early in the nineteenth century the sport of dogfighting gained popularity and a smaller, faster dog was developed. It was called by names such as Bulldog Terrier and Bull-and-Terrier. The Bulldog bred then was a larger dog than we know today and weighed about sixty pounds. This dog was crossed with a small native terrier that appears in the history of the present-day Manchester Terrier. The result, averaging between thirty and forty-five pounds, became the Staffordshire Bull Terrier.

James Hinks, in about 1860, crossed the Old Pit Bull Terrier, now known as the Staffordshire Bull Terrier, and produced the all-white English Bull Terrier. The Bull Terrier obtained recognition by The Kennel Club (England) in the last quarter of the nineteenth century, but the Staffordshire Bull Terrier, due to its reputation as a fighting dog, did not receive this blessing.

In 1935 the Staffordshire Bull Terrier was recognized by The Kennel Club and enthusiasts were able to conduct conformation matches. The sport of dogfighting had long been made illegal, and the Staffordshire Bull Terrier had evolved into a dog of such temperament as to make him a fine pet and companion and a worthy show dog.

Bull-and-Terrier types were believed to have arrived in North America sometime in the mid-1880s. Here they developed along different lines with a heavier, taller dog being the result. Today's American Staffordshire Terrier represents that breeding.

The Staffordshire Bull Terrier was admitted to registration in the AKC Stud Book effective October 1, 1974, and joined the Terrier Group in March 1975.

# OFFICIAL STANDARD FOR THE STAFFORDSHIRE BULL TERRIER

**General Appearance**—The Staffordshire Bull Terrier is a smooth-coated dog. It should be of great strength for its size and, although muscular, should be active and agile.

**Size, Proportion, Substance**—Height at shoulder: 14 to 16 inches. Weight: Dogs, 28 to 38 pounds; bitches, 24 to 34 pounds, these heights being related to weights. Non-conformity with these limits is a fault. In proportion, the length of back, from withers to tail set, is equal to the distance from withers to ground.

**Head**—Short, deep through, broad skull, very pronounced cheek muscles, distinct stop, short foreface, black nose. Pink (Dudley) nose to be considered a serious fault. *Eyes*—Dark preferable, but may bear some relation to coat color. Round, of medium size, and set to look straight ahead. Light eyes or pink eye rims to be considered a fault, except that where the coat surrounding the eye is white the eye rim may be pink. *Ears*—Rose or half-pricked and not large. Full drop or full prick to be considered a serious fault. *Mouth*—A bite in which the outer side of the lower incisors touches the inner side of the upper incisors. The lips should be tight and clean. The badly undershot or overshot bite is a serious fault.

**Neck, Topline, Body**—The neck is muscular, rather short, clean in outline and gradually widening toward the shoulders. The body is close coupled, with a level topline, wide front, deep brisket and well sprung ribs being rather light in the loins. The tail is undocked, of medium length, low set, tapering to a point and carried rather low. It should not curl much and may be likened to an old-fashioned pump handle. A tail that is too long or badly curled is a fault.

**Forequarters**—Legs straight and well boned, set rather far apart, without looseness at the shoulders and showing no weakness at the pasterns, from which point the feet turn out a little. Dewclaws on the forelegs may be removed. The feet should be well padded, strong and of medium size.

**Hindquarters**—The hindquarters should be well muscled, hocks let down with stifles well bent. Legs should be parallel when viewed from behind. Dewclaws, if any, on the hind legs are generally removed. Feet as in front.

**Coat**—Smooth, short and close to the skin, not to be trimmed or de-whiskered.

**Color**—Red, fawn, white, black or blue, or any of these colors with white. Any shade of brindle or any shade of brindle with white. Black-and-tan or liver color to be disqualified.

**Gait**—Free, powerful and agile with economy of effort. Legs moving parallel when viewed from front or rear. Discernible drive from hind legs.

**Temperament**—From the past history of the Staffordshire Bull Terrier, the modern dog draws its character of indomitable courage, high intelligence and tenacity. This, coupled with its affection for its friends, and children in particular, its off-duty quietness and trustworthy stability, makes it a foremost all-purpose dog.

## DISQUALIFICATION

*Black-and-tan or liver color.*

**Approved November 14, 1989**
**Effective January 1, 1990**

# WELSH TERRIER

*J*UDGING FROM THE OLD PAINTINGS AND PRINTS OF THE FIRST KNOWN
terriers, the Welsh Terrier is a very old breed, for these prints show us a
rough-haired black-and-tan terrier.

In the early nineteenth century the breed was more commonly known as the
Old English Terrier or Black-and-Tan Wire Haired Terrier, and as late as 1886 The
Kennel Club (England) allotted one class for "Welsh or Old English Wire Haired
Black and Tan Terriers." Even to this day the color of the Welsh is as it was more
than a hundred years ago.

In other respects, also, the Welsh Terrier has changed very slightly. He is, as he
was then, a sporting dog extensively used in Wales for hunting otter, fox, and
badger, and he possesses the characteristic gameness that one naturally looks for in
such a dog. Although game, he is not quarrelsome; in fact, he is well mannered and
easy to handle.

The first record of Welsh Terriers having a classification of their own in England was in 1884–85 at Carnavon, where there were twenty-one entries. But even
at this time it was not uncommon for dogs to be shown as Old English Terriers and
also as Welsh Terriers. As late as 1893, Dick Turpin, a well-known show dog of
those days, continued in this dual role.

Welsh Terriers were first brought to this country by Prescott Lawrence in 1888,
when he imported a dog and a bitch and showed them at Madison Square Garden

in the Miscellaneous class. No other Welsh, however, were imported for some time. But, about 1901, classification was offered for Welsh at Westminster and four or five dogs were shown; from then on their popularity has steadily increased.

# OFFICIAL STANDARD FOR THE WELSH TERRIER

**General Appearance**—The Welsh Terrier is a sturdy, compact, rugged dog of medium size with a coarse wire-textured coat. The legs, underbody and head are tan; the jacket black (or occasionally grizzle). The tail is docked to length meant to complete the image of a "square dog" approximately as high as he is long. The movement is a terrier trot typical of the long-legged terrier. It is effortless, with good reach and drive. The Welsh Terrier is friendly, outgoing to people and other dogs, showing spirit and courage. The "Welsh Terrier expression" comes from the set, color and position of the eyes combined with the use of the ears.

**Size, Proportion, Substance**—Males are about 15 inches at the withers, with an acceptable range between 15 and 15½. Bitches may be proportionally smaller. Twenty pounds is considered an average weight, varying a few pounds depending on the height of the dog and the density of bone. Both dog and bitch appear solid and of good substance.

**Head**—The entire head is rectangular. The *eyes* are small, dark brown and almond-shaped, well set in the skull. They are placed fairly far apart. The size, shape, color and position of the eyes give the steady, confident but alert expression that is typical of the Welsh Terrier. The *ears* are V-shaped, small, but not too thin. The fold is just above the topline of the skull. The ears are carried forward close to the cheek with the tips falling to, or toward, the outside corners of the eyes when the dog is at rest. The ears move slightly up and forward when at attention. *Skull*—The foreface is strong with powerful, punishing jaws. It is only slightly narrower than the backskull. There is a slight stop. The backskull is of equal length to the foreface. They are on parallel planes in profile. The backskull is smooth and flat (not domed) between the ears. There are no wrinkles between the ears. The cheeks are flat and clean (not bulging).

The *muzzle* is one-half the length of the entire head from tip of nose to occiput. The foreface in front of the eyes is well made up. The furnishings on the foreface are trimmed to complete without exaggeration the total rectangular outline. The muzzle is strong and squared off, never snipy. The nose is black and squared off. The lips are black and tight. A scissors bite is preferred, but a level bite is acceptable. Either one has complete dentition. The teeth are large and strong, set in powerful, vise-like jaws.

**Neck, Topline, Body**—The neck is of moderate length and thickness, slightly arched and sloping gracefully into the shoulders. The throat is clean with no excess of skin.

The topline is level.

The body shows good substance and is well ribbed up. There is good depth of brisket and moderate width of chest. The loin is strong and moderately short. The tail is docked to a length approximately level (on an imaginary line) with the occiput, to complete the square image of the whole dog. The root of the tail is set well up on the back. It is carried upright.

**Forequarters**—The front is straight. The shoulders are long, sloping and well laid back. The legs are straight and muscular with upright and powerful pasterns. The feet are small, round, and catlike. The pads are thick and black. The nails are strong and black; any dewclaws are removed.

**Hindquarters**—The hindquarters are strong and muscular with well-developed second thighs and the stifles well bent. The hocks are moderately straight, parallel and short from joint to ground. The feet should be the same as in the forequarters.

**Coat**—The coat is hard, wiry, and dense with a close-fitting thick jacket. There is a short, soft undercoat. Furnishings on muzzle, legs and quarters are dense and wiry.

**Color**—The jacket is black, spreading up onto the neck, down onto the tail and into the upper thighs. The legs, quarters and head are clear tan. The tan is a deep reddish color, with slightly lighter shades acceptable. A grizzle jacket is also acceptable.

**Gait**—The movement is straight, free and effortless, with good reach in front, strong drive behind, with feet naturally tending to converge toward a median line of travel as speed increases.

**Temperament**—The Welsh Terrier is a game dog—alert, aware, spirited—but at the same time, is friendly and shows self control. Intelligence and desire to please are evident in his attitude. A specimen exhibiting an overly aggressive attitude, or shyness, should be penalized.

## FAULTS

*Any deviation from the foregoing should be considered a fault; the seriousness of the fault depending upon the extent of the deviation.*

**Approved August 10, 1993**
**Effective September 29, 1993**

# WEST HIGHLAND WHITE TERRIER

BY MOST NOTABLE AUTHORITIES, THE TERRIERS OF SCOTLAND—WHICH include the West Highland along with the Scottish, Cairn, Skye, and Dandie Dinmont—are branches of the same tree. The Westie's actual origin, cloaked within the mists of the Scottish hills, may well trace to the early seventeenth century. The West Highland Terrier may be derived from those "earth-dogges" that James I sent from Argyllshire to a friend in France. Artwork of the mid-Victorian era clearly depicts breed representatives.

The Kennel Club (England) recognized the breed's current name in November 1906. Before then, the dog was known by several names, including Roseneath Terrier, from the Duke of Argyll's estate of the same name, and Poltalloch Terrier, after the Malcolm home. Colonel Edward Donald Malcolm (1837–1930), generally credited with developing this robust terrier, attributed this distinction to his father, John Malcolm (1805–1893), and grandfather Neill Malcolm (1769–1837). Colonel Malcolm claimed his contribution was obtaining a place for the breed on the show bench.

Under its modern name, the West Highland was first exhibited at the 1904 Scottish Kennel Club show, although classes for dogs described as "white" were held as early as 1896. The breed was first shown in the United States in 1906, under the then-current Roseneath designation. The name changed to West Highland White Terrier on May 31, 1909, and classes for the breed have been held under that name ever since.

The exact date that the first West Highland was imported is unknown, but it was probably during 1905. Initial AKC registrations fell under the Roseneath name. A bitch, Sky Lady, whelped in England in 1906, became the first of the breed to be registered as a West Highland.

The West Highland is all terrier, with large amounts of Scottish spunk, determination, and devotion crammed into a small body. They are indeed all that can be desired of a pet: faithful, understanding, and devoted, while still gay and light-hearted. Outdoors they are good hunters, exhibiting speed, cunning, and great intelligence. As the breed standard says, the true Highlander is "possessed with no small amount of self-esteem."

One reason West Highland White Terriers are such delightful little dogs is their hardiness. They need no pampering; they love to romp and play, and they enjoy a nice walk. Since by nature Westies will run after anything that moves, the breed does best in a fenced area or on a leash.

This faithful but independent terrier can excel in a variety of canine sports and activities. Still true to their original purpose, they have the instinct to go to ground in either a natural or artificial setting. An excellent nose and boundless determination make West Highlands good trackers. Their enthusiasm, energy, and happy attitude serve them well in agility trials. Under the tutelage of a trainer using modern, inductive methods, the extremely intelligent Westie will do well in obedience competition. In addition, their small size and delight in traveling and meeting new people contribute to their successful participation in therapy-dog programs.

A Westie shown in conformation competition must be properly trained for the ring. The breed requires considerable grooming, with such skill perfected over time. The West Highland's outer coat is hard and stiff and should be kept so by a grooming regimen that includes regular stripping of the coat and an occasional bath. For the companion-dog owner, a few minutes daily spent brushing and combing, as well as professional grooming every six to eight weeks, keeps this terrier in nice condition.

While the highly intelligent, independent, and energetic Westie is not the right dog for every person or family, with time, diligence, and patience, prospective owners can find the right puppy or adult to suit their lifestyle.

# OFFICIAL STANDARD FOR THE WEST HIGHLAND WHITE TERRIER

**General Appearance**—The West Highland White Terrier is a small, game, well-balanced hardy looking terrier, exhibiting good showmanship, possessed with no small amount of self-esteem, strongly built, deep in chest and back ribs, with a straight back and powerful hindquarters on muscular legs, and exhibiting in marked degree a great combination of strength and activity. The coat is about two inches long, white in color, hard, with plenty of soft undercoat. The dog should be neatly presented, the longer coat on the back and sides, trimmed to blend into the shorter neck and shoulder coat. Considerable hair is left around the head to act as a frame for the face to yield a typical Westie expression.

**Size, Proportion, Substance**—The ideal size is eleven inches at the withers for dogs and ten inches for bitches. A slight deviation is acceptable. The Westie is a compact dog, with good balance and substance. The body between the withers and the root of the tail is slightly shorter than the height at the withers. Short-coupled and well boned. *Faults*—Over or under height limits. Fine boned.

**Head**—Shaped to present a round appearance from the front. Should be in proportion to the body.

*Expression*—Piercing, inquisitive, pert. *Eyes*—Widely set apart, medium in size, almond shaped, dark brown in color, deep-set, sharp and intelligent. Looking from under heavy eyebrows, they give a piercing look. Eye rims are black. *Faults*—Small, full or light colored eyes. *Ears*—Small, carried tightly erect, set wide apart, on the top outer edge of the skull. They terminate in a sharp point, and must never be cropped. The hair on the ears is trimmed short and is smooth and velvety, free of fringe at the tips. Black skin pigmentation is preferred. *Faults*—Round-pointed, broad, large, ears set closely together, not held tightly erect, or placed too low on the side of the head.

**Skull**—Broad, slightly longer than the muzzle, not flat on top but slightly domed between the ears. It gradually tapers to the eyes. There is a defined stop, eyebrows are heavy. *Faults*—Long or narrow skull. *Muzzle*—Blunt, slightly shorter than the skull, powerful and gradually tapering to the nose, which is large and black. The jaws are level and powerful. Lip pigment is black. *Faults*—Muzzle longer than skull. Nose color other than black. *Bite*—The teeth are large for the size of the dog. There must be six incisor teeth between the canines of both lower and upper jaws. An occasional missing premolar is acceptable. A tight scissors bite with upper incisors slightly overlapping the lower incisors or level mouth are equally acceptable. *Faults*—Teeth defective or misaligned. Any incisors missing or several premolars missing. Teeth overshot or undershot.

**Neck, Topline, Body**—*Neck*—Muscular and well set on sloping shoulders. The length of neck should be in proportion to the remainder of the dog. *Faults*—Neck too long or too short. *Topline*—Flat and level, both standing and moving. *Faults*—High rear, any deviation from above. *Body*—Compact and of good substance. Ribs deep and well arched in the upper half of rib, extending at least to the elbows, and presenting a flattish side appearance. Back ribs of considerable depth, and distance from last rib to upper thigh as short as compatible with free movement of the body. Chest very deep and extending to the elbows, with breadth in proportion to the size of the dog. Loin short, broad and strong. *Faults*—Back weak, either too long or too short. Barrel ribs, ribs above elbows. *Tail*—Relatively short, with good substance, and shaped like a carrot. When standing erect it is never extended above the top of the skull. It is covered with hard hair without feather, as straight as possible, carried gaily but not curled over the back. The tail is set on high enough so that the spine does not slope down to it. The tail is never docked. *Faults*—Set too low, long, thin, carried at half-mast or curled over back.

**Forequarters**—*Angulation, Shoulders*—Shoulder blades are well laid back and well knit at the backbone. The shoulder blade should attach to an upper arm of moderate length, and sufficient angle to allow for definite body overhang. *Faults*—Steep or loaded shoulders. Upper arm too short or too straight. *Legs*—Forelegs are muscular and well boned, relatively short, but with sufficient length to set the dog up so as not to be too close to the ground. The legs are reasonably straight, and thickly covered with short hard hair. They are set in under the shoulder blades with definite body overhang before them. Height from elbow to withers and elbow to ground should be approximately the same. *Faults*—Out at elbows, light bone, fiddle-front. *Feet*—Forefeet are larger than the hind ones, are round, proportionate in size, strong, thickly padded; they may properly be turned out slightly. Dewclaws may be removed. Black pigmentation is most desirable on pads of all feet and nails, although nails may lose coloration in older dogs.

**Hindquarters**—*Angulation*—Thighs are very muscular, well angulated, not set wide apart, with hock well bent, short, and parallel when viewed from the rear. *Legs*—Rear legs are muscular and relatively short and sinewy. *Faults*—Weak hocks, long hocks, lack of angulation. Cowhocks. *Feet*—Hind feet are smaller than front feet, and are thickly padded. Dewclaws may be removed.

**Coat**—Very important and seldom seen to perfection. Must be double-coated. The head is shaped by plucking the hair, to present the round appearance. The outer coat consists of straight hard white hair, about two inches long, with shorter coat on neck and shoulders, properly blended and trimmed to blend shorter areas into furnishings, which are longer on stomach and legs. The ideal coat is hard, straight and white, but a hard straight coat which may have some wheaten tipping is preferable to a white fluffy or soft coat. Furnishings may be somewhat softer and longer but should never give the appearance of fluff. *Faults*—Soft coat. Any silkiness or tendency to curl. Any open or single coat, or one which is too short.

**Color**—The color is white, as defined by the breed's name. *Faults*—Any coat color other than white. Heavy wheaten color.

**Gait**—Free, straight and easy all around. It is a distinctive gait, not stilted, but powerful, with reach and drive. In front the leg is freely extended forward by the shoulder. When seen from the front the legs do not move square, but tend to move toward the center of gravity. The hind movement is free, strong and fairly close. The hocks are freely flexed and drawn close under the body, so that when moving off the foot the body is thrown or pushed forward with some force. Overall ability to move is usually best evaluated from the side, and topline remains level. *Faults*—Lack of reach in front, and/or drive behind. Stiff, stilted or too wide movement.

**Temperament**—Alert, gay, courageous and self-reliant, but friendly. *Faults*—Excess timidity or excess pugnacity.

**Approved December 13, 1988**
**Effective February 1, 1989**

# GROUP V: TOY BREEDS

AFFENPINSCHER
BRUSSELS GRIFFON
CAVALIER KING CHARLES SPANIEL
CHIHUAHUA
CHINESE CRESTED
ENGLISH TOY SPANIEL
HAVANESE
ITALIAN GREYHOUND
JAPANESE CHIN
MALTESE
MANCHESTER TERRIER (TOY)

MINIATURE PINSCHER
PAPILLON
PEKINGESE
POMERANIAN
POODLE (TOY)
PUG
SHIH TZU
SILKY TERRIER
TOY FOX TERRIER
YORKSHIRE TERRIER

# AFFENPINSCHER

*O*NE OF THE MOST ANCIENT OF TOY DOGS, THE AFFENPINSCHER (TRANSLATED from German as "Monkey-Terrier") originated in Central Europe. During the seventeenth century, small terriers frequently were kept around stables on farms or in shops where they served as ratters. Bred down to size, these small terriers became companions in the home and kept mice from overrunning their mistresses' boudoirs.

A game, alert, intelligent, and sturdy little terrier type, the Affenpinscher is characterized by his "monkeyish" expression, derived from a prominent chin with hair-tuft and mustache. This expression is further accentuated by his bushy eyebrows, shadowing black-bordered eyelids and medium, round, piercing dark eyes. The coat is dense, rough, and harsh on the shoulders and body. He is every inch a real dog despite his small size.

The Affenpinscher is believed to have been a major influence in the development of many of the smaller rough-coated breeds of continental Europe, including the Brussels Griffon and the Miniature Schnauzer.

The area around Munich eventually became the heart of Affenpinscher breeding in Europe. The Pinscher Klub was founded in 1895 at Cologne, and the Bayerischer Schnauzer Klub was formed in 1907. In 1923 these two clubs joined forces as the Pinscher-Schnauzer Klub, which attracted many new breeders.

The breed was admitted to the American Kennel Club Stud Book in 1936.

This quaint little dog's popularity has been overshadowed by that of his descendant, the Brussels Griffon, but more recently he is enjoying a return to favor.

# OFFICIAL STANDARD FOR THE AFFENPINSCHER

**General Appearance**—The Affenpinscher is a balanced, wiry-haired terrier-like toy dog whose intelligence and demeanor make it a good house pet. Originating in Germany, the name Affenpinscher means "monkey-like terrier." The breed was developed to rid the kitchens, granaries, and stables of rodents. In France the breed is described as the "Diablotin Moustachu" or mustached little devil. Both describe the appearance and attitude of this delightful breed. The total overall appearance of the Affenpinscher is more important than any individual characteristic. He is described as having a neat but shaggy appearance.

**Size, Proportion, Substance**—A sturdy, compact dog with medium bone, not delicate in any way. Preferred height at the withers is 9½ to 11½ inches. Withers height is approximately the same as the length of the body from the point of the shoulder to point of the buttocks, giving a square appearance. The female may be slightly longer.

**Head**—The head is in proportion to the body, carried confidently with monkey-like facial expression. *Eyes*—Round, dark, brilliant, and of medium size in proportion to the head but not bulging or protruding. Eye rims are black. *Ears*—Cropped to a point, set high and standing erect; or natural, standing erect, semi-erect or dropped. All of the above types of ears, if symmetrical, are acceptable as long as the monkey-like expression is maintained. *Skull*—Round and domed, but not coarse. *Stop*—Well-defined. *Muzzle*—Short and narrowing slightly to a blunt nose. The length of the muzzle is approximately the same as the distance between the eyes. *Nose*—Black, turned neither up nor down. *Lips*—Black, with prominent lower lip. *Bite*—Slightly undershot. A level bite is acceptable if the monkey-like expression is maintained. An overshot bite is to be severely penalized. A wry mouth is a serious fault. The teeth and tongue do not show when the mouth is closed. The lower jaw is broad enough for the lower teeth to be straight and even.

**Neck, Topline, Body**—*Neck*—Short and straight. *Topline*—straight and level. *Body*—The *chest* is moderately broad and deep; ribs are moderately sprung. Tuckup is slight. The *back* is short and level with a strong loin. The *croup* has just a perceptible curve. *Tail* may be docked or natural. A docked tail is generally between 1 and 2 inches long, set high and carried erect. The natural tail is set high and carried curved gently up over the back while moving. The type of tail is not a major consideration.

**Forequarters**—Front angulation is moderate. *Shoulders*—with moderate layback. The length of the shoulder blade and the upper arm are about equal. *Elbows*—close to the body. *Front legs* straight when viewed from any direction. *Pasterns* short and straight. *Dewclaws* generally removed. *Feet* small, round, and compact with black pads and nails.

**Hindquarters**—Rear angulation is moderate to match the front. *Hindlegs*—straight when viewed from behind. From the side, hindlegs are set under the body to maintain a square appearance. The length of the upper thigh and the second thigh are about equal with moderate bend to the stifle. ***Hocks***—Moderately angulated.

**Coat**—Dense hair, rough, harsh, and about 1 inch in length on the shoulders and body. May be shorter on the rear and tail. Head, neck, chest, stomach and legs have longer, less harsh coat. The mature Affenpinscher has a mane or cape of strong hair which blends into the back coat at the withers area. The longer hair on the head, eyebrows and beard stands off and frames the face to emphasize the monkey-like expression. Hair on the ears is cut very short. A correct coat needs little grooming to blend the various lengths of hair to maintain a neat but shaggy appearance.

**Color**—Black, gray, silver, red, black and tan, or belge are all acceptable. Blacks may have a rusty cast or a few white or silver hairs mixed with the black. Reds may vary from a brownish red to an orangey tan. Belge has black, brown, and/or white hairs mixed with the red. With various colors, the furnishings may be a bit lighter. Some dogs may have black masks. A small white spot on the chest is not penalized, but large white patches are undesirable. Color is not a major consideration.

**Gait**—Light, free, sound, balanced, confident, the Affenpinscher carries itself with comic seriousness. Viewed from the front or rear while walking, the legs move parallel to each other. Trotting, the feet will converge toward a midline as speed increases. Unsound gait is to be heavily penalized.

**Temperament**—General demeanor is game, alert, and inquisitive with great loyalty and affection toward its master and friends. The breed is generally quiet, but can become vehemently excited when threatened or attacked, and is fearless toward any aggressor.

**Approved June 12, 2000**
**Effective July 27, 2000**

# BRUSSELS GRIFFON

$\mathcal{T}$HE BRUSSELS GRIFFON, NAMED FOR THE BELGIAN CITY OF ITS ORIGIN, IS A lively, sturdy little fellow, classified as a member of the Toy Group due to his small size. Adults usually range in weight from six to twelve pounds. During the early 1800s, it was the custom for coachmen to keep small terrier types as ratters in stables, and those of that period in Belgium were Affenpinscher-like, known as *griffons d'ecurie* (wire-coated stable dogs).

Just when or why other breeds were introduced can only be conjecture, as the Brussels stablemen who initiated these crosses apparently kept no records. The Pug, a Victorian favorite from across the Channel, was bred to the native Belgian dog in the mid-1800s. From this cross came a smooth-coated Griffon designated Brabançon after the Belgian national anthem, "La Brabançonne." At about the same time the King Charles (black-and-tan), and Ruby varieties of the English Toy Spaniel were also crossed with the Belgian dogs. From these two crossings not only did two distinct types of coat emerge—the harsh-coated, bewhiskered rough and the smooth-coated Brabançon—but also the rich red color. The English Toy Spaniel ancestry can also be seen to this day in an occasional (and completely acceptable) web-footed, kink-tailed, or tailless Griffon puppy, often the one with the most desirable head properties. These two short-faced, big-headed, large-eyed breeds forever changed the serviceable little ratter into a delightful small companion dog with a strong, broad, upswept underjaw and a very short, uptilted nose placed high between very dark, lustrous eyes, with the high-domed skull of the English Toy Spaniel. All of this together conjures that wonderful "pout" which gives the Griffon that almost-human expression. No longer serving his original function (in itself obsolete), the Brussels Griffon has evolved into a most intriguing-looking, alert, and active companion.

In intelligence, Griffons are second to none. They are unusually sensitive, and demand much attention and love. The Brussels Griffon is strictly a house dog. Be he small or oversized, if relegated to garage or kennel, no matter how well his creature comforts are met, he will pine without love and personal attention, and should always be made to socialize with people lest he withdraw into his shell. The Griffon is peaceable and enjoys the company of other dogs and also cats. A good hiking companion, he loves to romp and play. Playtime over, he relaxes quietly as close to his owner as possible. His intelligence and desire to please make the Griffon fairly easy to train. Leash training must be started early for short periods and made to seem fun, for in this department our little Belgian friend can dig in his heels and show a stubborn streak.

The Griffon is a sturdy dog with a relatively long life span, with ten to fifteen years being usual. Like all short-faced breeds he is sensitive to temperature extremes, making him an indoor dog. Despite his pushed-in nose, he is not a snorer, nor is he prone to eye ailments. In matters of feeding and general health care, the instructions of the breeder from whom the puppy was obtained should be followed. Coat care in the smooth is simple. Regular brushing and occasional baths suffice. The roughs should be hand plucked, about twice yearly, by pulling out the long, dead hairs by their tips a few hairs at a time. This should be enough to keep the dog neat and comfortable, unless he is being kept in show coat, which requires more frequent grooming. Never bathe a rough before stripping or shortly before showing.

Because of his small size and sensitive nature, the Griffon is not recommended as a pet for young children. The Griffon does make an excellent house dog and devoted, lifelong companion.

# OFFICIAL STANDARD FOR THE BRUSSELS GRIFFON

**General Appearance**—A toy dog, intelligent, alert, sturdy, with a thickset, short body, a smart carriage and set-up, attracting attention by an almost human expression. There are two distinct types of coat: rough and smooth. Except for coat, there is no difference between the two.

**Size, Proportion, Substance**—*Size*—Weight usually 8 to 10 pounds, and should not exceed 12 pounds. Type and quality are of greater importance than weight, and a smaller dog that is sturdy and well proportioned should not be penalized. ***Proportion***—Square, as measured from point of shoulder to rearmost projection of upper thigh and from withers to ground. *Substance*—Thickset, compact with good balance. Well boned.

**Head**—A very important feature. An almost human *expression*. *Eyes* set well apart, very large, black, prominent, and well open. The eyelashes long and black. Eyelids edged with black. *Ears* small and set rather high on the head. May be shown cropped or natural. If natural they are carried semi-erect. *Skull* large and round, with a domed forehead. The stop deep. *Nose* very black, extremely short, its tip being set back deeply between the eyes so as to form a lay-back. The nostrils large. *Disqualifications*— Dudley or butterfly nose. *Lips* edged with black, not pendulous but well brought together, giving a clean finish to the mouth. *Jaws* must be undershot. The incisors of the lower jaw should protrude over the upper incisors. The lower jaw is prominent, rather broad with an upward sweep. Neither teeth nor tongue should show when the mouth is closed. A wry mouth is a serious fault. *Disqualifications*—Bite overshot. Hanging tongue.

**Neck, Topline, Body**—*Neck* medium length, gracefully arched. *Topline*—Back level and short. *Body*—A thickset, short body. Brisket should be broad and deep, ribs well sprung. Short-coupled. *Tail*—Set and held high, docked to about one-third.

**Forequarters**—*Forelegs* medium length, straight in bone, well muscled, set moderately wide apart and straight from the point of the shoulders as viewed from the front. *Pasterns* short and strong. *Feet* round, small, and compact, turned neither in nor out. Toes well arched. Black pads and toenails preferred.

**Hindquarters**—*Hind legs* set true, thighs strong and well muscled, stifles bent, hocks well let down, turning neither in nor out.

**Coat**—The *rough coat* is wiry and dense, the harder and more wiry the better. On no account should the dog look or feel woolly, and there should be no silky hair anywhere. The coat should not be so long as to give a shaggy appearance, but should be distinctly different all over from the smooth coat. The head should be covered with wiry hair, slightly longer around the eyes, nose, cheeks, and chin, thus forming a fringe. The rough coat is hand-stripped and should never appear unkempt. Body coat of sufficient length to determine texture. The coat may be tidied for neatness of appearance, but coats prepared with scissors and/or clippers should be severely penalized. The *smooth coat* is straight, short, tight and glossy, with no trace of wiry hair.

**Color**—Either 1) *Red:* reddish brown with a little black at the whiskers and chin allowable; 2) *Belge:* black and reddish brown mixed, usually with black mask and whiskers; 3) *Black and Tan:* black with uniform reddish brown markings, appearing under the chin, on the legs, above each eye, around the edges of the ears and around the vent; or 4) *Black:* solid black. Any white hairs are a serious fault, except for "frost" on the muzzle of a mature dog, which is natural. *Disqualification*—White spot or blaze anywhere on coat.

**Gait**—Movement is a straightforward, purposeful trot, showing moderate reach and drive, and maintaining a steady topline.

**Temperament**—Intelligent, alert and sensitive. Full of self-importance.

## Scale of Points

| Head | | |
|---|---|---|
| Skull | 5 | |
| Nose and stop | 10 | |
| Eyes | 5 | |
| Bite, chin and jaws | 10 | |
| Ears | 5 | 35 |

| Coat | | |
|---|---|---|
| Color | 12 | |
| Texture | 13 | 25 |

| Body and General Conformation | | |
|---|---|---|
| Body (brisket and rib) | 15 | |
| Gait | 10 | |
| Legs and feet | 5 | |
| General appearance (neck, topline and tail carriage) | 10 | 40 |

Total    100

## DISQUALIFICATIONS

*Dudley or butterfly nose.*
*Bite overshot.*
*Hanging tongue.*
*White spot or blaze anywhere on coat.*

**Approved September 11, 1990**
**Effective October 30, 1990**

# CAVALIER KING CHARLES SPANIEL

*T*HERE HAS BEEN MUCH DEBATE ABOUT THE ORIGINS OF THE CAVALIER KING Charles Spaniel, but there is no question that dogs of the small spaniel-type existed for many centuries. These dogs have been recorded in paintings and tapestries depicting the aristocracy, and today's modern Cavalier is directly modeled on its royal ancestors. Paintings from the fifteenth and sixteenth centuries nearly always show representative small spaniels with the children of the court families. Cavaliers were obviously a luxury item, for the average person could not afford to keep and feed a dog that did no work.

The Cavalier or Toy Spaniel became a great favorite of Charles I of Britain, and it is from this source that the name King Charles came into use. Charles II continued this interest in the breed, and their popularity increased until the fall of the house of Stuart. Because the favorite breed of William and Mary was the Pug, it soon became a political liability to be associated with the dogs of King Charles. The Cavalier became quite rare as a consequence.

Even though as a young child Queen Victoria owned a Cavalier named Dash, her lifetime interest in developing and breeding dogs, and the advent of formalized dog shows, helped to change the breed radically from its original form. The breed that we know today as the English Toy Spaniel, with its domed head, short upturned muzzle, and slightly undershot bite, was the result of this activity. This breed became so popular that the original version of the Cavalier all but disappeared.

In the early 1920s, an American named Roswell Eldridge came to England to find a pair of spaniels of the type he had seen in the paintings of Gainsborough and Copley. He was unsuccessful in his search, so in 1926 he offered prizes of twenty-five pounds each for the best dog and best bitch of the "Old Type" at the Cruft's dog show for the next five years. On one hand, the prize generated much ridicule, as any dog entered as a Toy Spaniel which had an old-fashioned head certainly did not possess the correct head for its breed. But on the other hand, the large sum of prize money also generated interest in reviving the original spaniel form. In 1928, the Cavalier King Charles Spaniel Club was founded in England and the breed was given recognition by The Kennel Club (England) in 1944. The first Challenge Certificates in the breed were awarded in 1946. Since that time, the Cavalier has become one of the most popular breeds in Great Britain.

The Cavalier has always had a loyal following in the United States, and the breed was in the Miscellaneous class for many years. The American Kennel Club has recognized the American Cavalier King Charles Spaniel Club as the parent club for the breed, and the Cavalier King Charles Spaniel was given Toy Group designation and became eligible for full recognition on January 1, 1996.

# OFFICIAL STANDARD FOR
# THE CAVALIER KING CHARLES SPANIEL

**General Appearance**—The Cavalier King Charles Spaniel is an active, graceful, well-balanced toy spaniel, very gay and free in action; fearless and sporting in character, yet at the same time gentle and affectionate. It is this typical gay temperament, combined with true elegance and royal appearance, which are of paramount importance in the breed. Natural appearance with no trimming, sculpting or artificial alteration is essential to breed type.

**Size, Proportion, Substance**—*Size*—Height 12 to 13 inches at the withers; weight proportionate to height, between 13 and 18 lbs. A small, well balanced dog within these weights is desirable, but these are ideal heights and weights and slight variations are permissible. *Proportion*—The body approaches squareness, yet if measured from point of shoulder to point of buttock, is slightly longer than the height at the withers. The height from the withers to the elbow is approximately equal to the height from the elbow to the ground. *Substance*—Bone moderate in proportion to size. Weedy and coarse specimens are to be equally penalized.

**Head**—Proportionate to size of dog, appearing neither too large nor too small for the body. *Expression*—The sweet, gentle, melting expression is an important breed characteristic. *Eyes*—Large, round, but not prominent and set well apart; color a warm, very dark brown; giving a lustrous, limpid look. Rims dark. There should be cushioning under the eyes, which contributes to the soft expression. *Faults*—Small, almond-shaped, prominent, or light eyes; white surrounding ring. *Ears*—Set high, but not close, on top of the head. Leather long with plenty of feathering and wide enough so that when the dog is alert, the ears fan slightly forward to frame the face. *Skull*—Slightly rounded, but without dome or peak; it should appear flat because of the high placement of the ears. Stop is moderate, neither filled nor deep. *Muzzle*—Full muzzle slightly tapered. Length from base of stop to tip of nose about 1½ inches. Face well filled below eyes. Any tendency towards snipiness undesirable. Nose pigment uniformly black without flesh marks and nostrils well developed. *Lips* well developed but not pendulous, giving a clean finish. *Faults*—Sharp or pointed muzzles. *Bite*—A perfect, regular and complete scissors bite is preferred, i.e., the upper teeth closely overlapping the lower teeth and set square into the jaws. *Faults*—Undershot bite, weak or crooked teeth, crooked jaws.

**Neck, Topline, Body**—*Neck*—Fairly long, without throatiness, well enough muscled to form a slight arch at the crest. Set smoothly into nicely sloping shoulders to give an elegant look. *Topline*—Level both when moving and standing. *Body*—Short-coupled with ribs well sprung but not barrelled. Chest moderately deep, extending to elbows, allowing ample heart room. Slightly less body at the flank than at the last rib, but with no tucked-up appearance. *Tail*—Well set on, carried happily but never much above the level of the back, and in constant characteristic motion when the dog is in action. Docking is optional. If docked, no more than one third to be removed.

**Forequarters**—*Shoulders* well laid back. *Forelegs* straight and well under the dog with elbows close to the sides. *Pasterns* strong and feet compact with well-cushioned pads. Dewclaws may be removed.

**Hindquarters**—The hindquarters construction should come down from a good broad pelvis, moderately muscled; stifles well turned and hocks well let down. The hindlegs when viewed from the rear should parallel each other from hock to heel. *Faults*—Cow or sickle hocks.

**Coat**—Of moderate length, silky, free from curl. Slight wave permissible. Feathering on ears, chest, legs and tail should be long, and the feathering on the feet is a feature of the breed. No trimming of the dog is permitted. *Specimens where the coat has been altered by trimming, clipping, or by artificial means shall be so severely penalized as to be effectively eliminated from competition.* Hair growing between the pads on the underside of the feet may be trimmed.

**Color**—*Blenheim*—Rich chestnut markings well broken up on a clear, pearly white ground. The ears must be chestnut and the color evenly spaced on the head and surrounding both eyes, with a white blaze between the eyes and ears, in the center of which may be the lozenge or "Blenheim spot." The lozenge is a unique and desirable, though not essential, characteristic of the Blenheim. *Tricolor*—Jet black markings well broken up on a clear, pearly white ground. The ears must be black and the color evenly spaced on the head and surrounding both eyes, with a white blaze between the eyes. Rich tan markings over the eyes, on cheeks, inside ears and on underside of tail. *Ruby*—Whole-colored rich red. *Black and Tan*—Jet black with rich, bright tan markings over eyes, on cheeks, inside ears, on chest, legs, and on underside of tail. *Faults*—Heavy ticking on Blenheims or Tricolors, white marks on Rubies or Black and Tans.

**Gait**—Free moving and elegant in action, with good reach in front and sound, driving rear action. When viewed from the side, the movement exhibits a good length of stride, and viewed from front and rear it is straight and true, resulting from straight-boned fronts and properly made and muscled hindquarters.

**Temperament**—Gay, friendly, non-aggressive with no tendency towards nervousness or shyness. *Bad temper, shyness and meanness are not to be tolerated and are to be so severely penalized as to effectively remove the specimen from competition.*

**Approved January 10, 1995**
**Effective April 30, 1995**

# CHIHUAHUA

*Long Coat*

*Smooth Coat*

# PUREBRED DOGS IN ART

A special feature of the milestone twentieth edition of *The Complete Dog Book* is this portfolio selected from the American Kennel Club and AKC Museum of the Dog collections. Taken together, the collections form the world's most comprehensive gathering of dog-related art and artifacts.

A popular topic among dog breeders is the delicate balance between art and science. Some study art for clues to their breed's original form and function. Others use the painted or sculpted contours of a great champion to help visualize the ideal specimen described in the written breed standard.

And yet, the dog you live with might look different from his ancestors immortalized on canvas. Dog breeds, along with the civilizations that spawn them, evolve. Vast shifts of human populations, technological advances, changing notions of beauty, dogkind's long march from worker to companion—these are just a few factors contributing to a breed's physical development.

Also, the nature of art itself should be considered. Since time immemorial the artist has had license to not just depict a subject, but to interpret it. They say that in any good portrait there is a dash of caricature, and this likely holds true in the following pages.

*I Hear a Voice*
Saint Bernard
Maud Earl (English, 1863–1943)
AKC COLLECTION

*Mike, an Imported Irish Water Spaniel*
Alexander Pope (American, 1849–1924)

*Ch. Merridip Ethel Ann and Ch. Downberry Volunteer*
Old English Sheepdogs
Edwin Megargee (American, 1883–1958)

*Ch. Kay's Don Feleciano-L*
Chihuahua
Roy Andersen (American, contemporary)

*Kerry Blue Terriers*
Edwin Megargee (American, 1883–1958)

AKC COLLECTION

*Scottish Deerhounds in an Interior*
Conradijn Cunaeus (Dutch, 1828–1895)

*Wan Lung*
Chow Chow
Gustav Muss-Arnolt (American, 1858–1927)

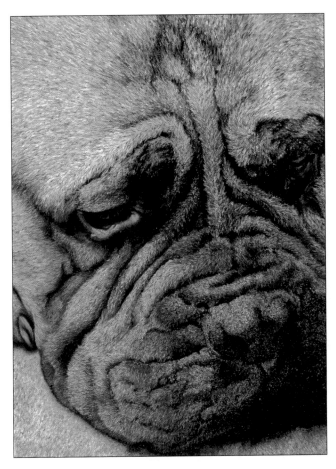

*Bullmastiff*
Christine Truesdale Shreve (American, contemporary)
AKC MUSEUM COLLECTION, GIFT OF JOE MILLER/
ART SHOW AT THE DOG SHOW

*Greyhound Near Stonehenge*
Edmund Bristow (English, 1787–1876)

AKC MUSEUM COLLECTION, GIFT OF J. P. MORGAN & CO.

*Int. Ch. Seedly Sterling*
Collie
F. Sinet (English, circa 1916)

*The Beat of Wings*
Cocker Spaniels
Roy Andersen (American, contemporary)

*Bichon Frise*
Louis-Eugéne Lambert (French, 1825–1900)
AKC MUSEUM COLLECTION, GIFT OF MR. AND MRS. ALVIN E. MAURER JR.

*The Totteridge XI*
Smooth Fox Terriers
Arthur Wardle (English, 1864–1949)
AKC COLLECTION

*Ch. Lancelot of Rowanoaks and Ch. Tynside Taraleeds*
Bedlington Terriers
Edwin Megargee (American, 1883–1958)

*On the Scent*
Bloodhounds
John Sargent Noble (English, 1848–1896)

*Briard*
Edwin Megargee (American, 1883–1958)

AKC MUSEUM COLLECTION, GIFT OF BRIARD CLUB OF AMERICA
THROUGH MARC DELANIER

*Horse, Mastiff, and Newfoundland*
Arthur Batt (English, 1846–1911)

*Dog with a Ball*
Papillon
Malcom S. Tucker (English, circa 1890)
AKC MUSEUM COLLECTION, GIFT OF CATHERINE D. GAUSS

*Ch. Windholme's Market Rose*
Dalmatian
Gustav Muss-Arnolt (American, 1858–1927)

*Pug and Terrier*
John Sargent Noble (English, 1848–1896)

*Maltese*
Arthur Wardle (English, 1864–1949)

*Reynal's Monarch*
Harrier
Edwin Megargee (American, 1883–1958)
AKC COLLECTION, GIFT OF BERNARD V. BURNS JR.,
FROM THE ESTATE OF ALICE HESS

*Ch. Argus von Schloss-Kesselweiher of Giralda*
German Shepherd Dog
Reuben Ward Binks (English, 1880–1940)

*Zillah*
Saluki
Charles Hamilton (English, circa 1830)
AKC MUSEUM COLLECTION, GIFT OF CYNTHIA S. WOOD

*Ch. Bang Away of Sirrah Crest*
Boxer
T. Tashira (American, contemporary)

*Golden Retriever*
Reuben Ward Binks (English, 1880–1940)

*The Intruder*
Wire Fox Terriers, Irish Terrier
Arthur Wardle (English, 1864–1949)
AKC MUSEUM COLLECTION, GIFT OF MR. AND MRS. RONALD MENAKER

*Ch. Estat d'Argeles of Basquaerie*
*and Ch. Estagel d'Argeles of Basquaerie*
Great Pyrenees
Edwin Megargee (American, 1883–1958)

*English Setter, Gordon Setter, and Pointer*
Gustav Muss-Arnolt (American, 1858–1927)

AKC COLLECTION

*Head Study*
White Terrier
Carl Reichert (American, circa 1872)

*French Bulldog*
S. Raphael (American, mid–twentieth century)

HOUGH LITTLE IS KNOWN OF THE CHIHUAHUA'S ORIGIN, RESEARCH HAS uncovered Chihuahua-like images from many times and in many places in the world, including China, Egypt, Malta, Mexico, South America, and parts of Europe. Beginning in the ninth century, historians documented similar little dogs in artifacts, written descriptions, and artwork, including Botticelli's 1482 Sistine Chapel fresco, *Scenes from the Life of Moses.*

A breed called the Techichi was common to the Toltecs, who occupied Mexico for several centuries. Evidence firmly establishing the Techichi in the Toltec period is shown in stone carvings in the monastery of Huejotzingo, found on the highway from Mexico City to Puebla. The carvings give a full head view and picture of an entire dog that closely resembles the modern Chihuahua. The Techichi was silent, small but not tiny, heavy boned, and had a long coat.

When the Aztecs conquered the Toltecs in the twelfth century, they brought with them a small, hairless breed similar to dogs found in China. One theory is that the present-day Chihuahua originated with the crossing of those two early breeds. It is believed the hairless dog was responsible for the reduction in size. Aztec culture flourished for several centuries. Dogs of the rich were highly regarded, and those blue in color were held as sacred. Paradoxical as it seems, the common people found little use for this breed. There are even tales of these dogs being eaten.

Upon the conquest and destruction of Aztec civilization by Cortez beginning in 1519, the treasures of Montezuma II, including his dogs, were lost for centuries. The earlier Toltec civilization was centered close to present-day Mexico City, but evidence of the modern breed's first specimens was discovered in the State of Chihuahua in the mid-1800s. The canine remains were found in ruins close to Casas Grandes, said to be the remains of a palace built by the emperor.

While the Techichi's principal home was Mexico, there is a historic letter written by Christopher Columbus to King Ferdinand of Spain that adds a curious note to knowledge of the breed. Reporting on what is today Cuba, Columbus wrote that he had found a small, domesticated dog that was mute.

Legend and history are rich in tales of a Chihuahua ancestor described as a popular pet and a religious necessity. Archaeologists have discovered the breed's remains in human graves both in Mexico and parts of the United States. It is believed this was because of the dog's role in the religious and mythological life of the Aztecs. Upon the cremation of both dog and human the sins of the human were supposedly transferred to the dog, and the indignation of the deity was thereby averted. The dog was also credited with guiding the human soul through the dark underworld, fighting off evil spirits and leading the soul of the deceased to its ultimate destination.

The breed's history in the United States began about 1850, when Americans acquired these little dogs from Mexico. Many were from the State of Chihuahua, hence the breed name. Both varieties, long coat and smooth coat, were popular. The presence of a *molera* (open fontanel) was a breed characteristic. Modern Chihuahuas are quite different from their early ancestors. American breeders have produced a diminutive dog, one with few peers in size, symmetry, conformation, alertness, or intelligence. Chihuahuas are clannish, recognizing and often preferring their own breed. The two varieties are identical except for coat.

In *This Is the Chihuahua*, Maxwell Riddle wrote, "Whatever its origin, the modern Chihuahua is a purely American dog. The American standard is worldwide and probably every Chihuahua in the world traces to purely American blood." The American Kennel Club recognized the breed in 1904, and the first three registered Chihuahuas were long-coats. The first Chihuahua champion, Beppie, was listed in the 1908 AKC Stud Book. The two coat varieties were recognized in 1952.

Today the Chihuahua is a treasured companion. The terrier-like attitude of this small breed is not only entertaining but also serves as an alarm system for the family. Along with quickness and a self-assured attitude comes the occasional adoring look of love, all of which make the Chihuahua an endearing family member.

The breed has consistently ranked among the top ten in popularity and leads the Toy Group in championships attained each year. The popularity and diminutive size of the Chihuahua require uncompromising adherence by judges and breeders to the descriptions set forth in the breed standard.

# OFFICIAL STANDARD FOR THE CHIHUAHUA

**General Appearance**—A graceful, alert, swift-moving little dog with saucy expression, compact, and with terrier-like qualities of temperament.

**Size, Proportion, Substance**—*Weight*—A well balanced little dog not to exceed 6 pounds. *Proportion*—The body is off-square; hence, slightly longer when measured from point of shoulder to point of buttocks, than height at the withers. Somewhat shorter bodies are preferred in males. *Disqualification*—Any dog over 6 pounds in weight.

**Head**—A well rounded "apple dome" skull, with or without molera. *Expression*—Saucy. *Eyes*—Full, but not protruding, balanced, set well apart—luminous dark or luminous ruby. (Light eyes in blond or white-colored dogs permissible.) *Ears*—Large, erect-type ears, held more upright when alert, but flaring to the sides at a 45-degree angle when in repose, giving breadth between the ears. *Muzzle*—Moderately short, slightly pointed. Cheeks and jaws lean. *Nose*—Self-colored in blond types, or black. In moles, blues, and chocolates, they are self-colored. In blond types, pink nose permissible. *Bite*—Level or scissors. Overshot or undershot bite, or any distortion of the bite or jaw, should be penalized as a serious fault. *Disqualifications*—Broken down or cropped ears.

**Neck, Topline, Body**—*Neck*—Slightly arched, gracefully sloping into lean shoulders. *Topline*—Level. *Body*—Ribs rounded and well sprung (but not too much "barrel-shaped"). *Tail*—Moderately long, carried sickle either up or out, or in a loop over the back, with tip just touching the back. (Never tucked between legs.) ***Disquali-fications***—Cropped tail, bobtail.

**Forequarters**—***Shoulders***—Lean, sloping into a slightly broadening support above straight forelegs that set well under, giving a free play at the elbows. Shoulders should be well up, giving balance and soundness, sloping into a level back. (Never down or low.) This gives a chestiness, and strength of forequarters, yet not of the "Bulldog" chest. ***Feet***—A small, dainty foot with toes well split up but not spread, pads cushioned. (Neither the hare nor the cat foot.) ***Pasterns***—Fine.

**Hindquarters**—Muscular, with hocks well apart, neither out nor in, well let down, firm and sturdy. The feet are as in front.

**Coat**—In the ***Smooth Coats,*** the coat should be of soft texture, close and glossy. (Heavier coats with undercoats permissible.) Coat placed well over body with ruff on neck preferred, and more scanty on head and ears. Hair on tail preferred furry. In ***Long Coats,*** the coat should be of a soft texture, either flat or slightly curly, with undercoat preferred. ***Ears***—Fringed. (Heavily fringed ears may be tipped slightly if due to the fringes and not to weak ear leather, never down.) ***Tail***—Full and long (as a plume). Feathering on feet and legs, pants on hind legs and large ruff on the neck desired and preferred. ***Disqualification***—In Long Coats, too thin coat that resembles bareness.

**Color**—Any color—Solid, marked or splashed.

**Gait**—The Chihuahua should move swiftly with a firm, sturdy action, with good reach in front equal to the drive from the rear. From the rear, the hocks remain parallel to each other, and the foot fall of the rear legs follows directly behind that of the forelegs. The legs, both front and rear, will tend to converge slightly toward a central line of gravity as speed increases. The side view shows good, strong drive in the rear and plenty of reach in the front, with head carried high. The topline should remain firm and the backline level as the dog moves.

**Temperament**—Alert, with terrier-like qualities.


## DISQUALIFICATIONS

*Any dog over 6 pounds in weight.*
*Broken down or cropped ears.*
*Cropped tail, bobtail.*
*In* Long Coats, *too thin coat that resembles bareness.*

**Approved September 11, 1990**
**Effective October 30, 1990**

# CHINESE CRESTED

*Hairless*

*Powderpuff*

*A*LTHOUGH THE EXACT ORIGIN OF THE CHINESE CRESTED IS UNKNOWN, IT is believed to have evolved from African hairless dogs which were reduced in size by the Chinese, who seemed to favor smaller toy breeds. The breed in earlier times was known by several different names, including the Chinese Hairless, the Chinese Edible Dog, the Chinese Ship Dog, and the Chinese Royal Hairless. It also took on local nicknames, depending on where it was found. Thus, in Egypt it was called a Pyramid or Giza Hairless, in southern Africa it was the South African Hairless, and in Turkey a larger version was known as the Turkish Hairless.

It is believed that for centuries Chinese mariners sailed the high seas with the breed on board, and that puppies were frequently traded with local merchants at port cities. It is known that during the time of the plagues that originated in China, hairless dogs were stowed aboard ships to hunt vermin which were heavily infested with fleas carrying disease. Today the breed can still be found in ancient port cities around the world.

Spanish explorers found Chinese Crested dogs in Mexico and other parts of Central and South America as early as the 1500s. British, French, and Portuguese explorers likewise found the breed in various parts of Africa and Asia during the 1700s and 1800s. The diaries of early missionaries, who frequently traveled with the explorers, describe finding the breed in many of these countries.

By the mid-nineteenth century, Cresteds began to appear in numerous European paintings and prints. During the 1850s and 1860s, some dogs of the breed were exhibited at a local zoological show in England, and photos of them were published, but no breeding program was established.

Entries of the breed at American dog shows began in the late 1800s. In the 1800s, Ida Garrett, a young New York newspaper reporter, became interested in Cresteds and other hairless breeds. Over the course of sixty years Garrett bred, exhibited, and wrote extensively about dogs—hairless breeds in particular. She traveled widely and imported several prized Cresteds. In the 1920s she assisted Debra Woods, of Homestead, Florida, in obtaining Chinese Cresteds and other hairless breeds, and the two women became close associates. For nearly forty years they jointly promoted the Chinese Crested—Garrett through her prolific writing, speaking, and dog club activities, and Woods through her extensive breeding, advertising, and registration service.

Mrs. Woods began keeping a log of all of her dogs in the 1930s and by the 1950s it had become a registration service for all hairless breeds and eventually the American Hairless Dog Club. She took great pride in maintaining these studbooks and closely guarded them until her death in 1969. They were maintained for nearly twelve years by Jo Ann Orlik and then became the property of the American Chinese Crested Club, founded in 1979.

Gypsy Rose Lee, the famous exotic dancer, acquired a Crested from her sister, actress June Havoc, in the early 1950s and became an ardent breeder and helped considerably in publicizing the breed.

The Chinese Crested was admitted to the AKC Miscellaneous class in September 1985. It became eligible for AKC registration effective February 1, 1991, and eligible to show at AKC-licensed events on April 1, 1991.

At first sight the two types of Chinese Crested—hairless and powderpuff—may appear to be different breeds. However, as one becomes more familiar with the breed it is easy to see that they are almost exactly the same, except that the coated have more hair. The hairless should have hair on its head, feet, and tail—the powderpuff is born fully coated. Breeding a hairless to a hairless, or a hairless to a powderpuff, can produce either type. But breeding a powderpuff to a powderpuff will always produce the powderpuff type.

A unique feature of hairless dogs is that they have sweat glands. Rather than panting to release body heat as coated dogs do, they simply sweat. Properly cared for, the skin of the hairless remains soft to the touch, yet it is thicker and tougher than that of a coated dog, and it heals very quickly if scratched or cut.

# OFFICIAL STANDARD FOR THE CHINESE CRESTED

**General Appearance**—A toy dog, fine-boned, elegant and graceful. The distinct varieties are born in the same litter. The Hairless with hair only on the head, tail and feet and the Powderpuff, completely covered with hair. The breed serves as a loving companion, playful and entertaining.

**Size, Proportion, Substance**—*Size*—Ideally 11 to 13 inches. However, dogs that are slightly larger or smaller may be given full consideration. *Proportion*—Rectangular—proportioned to allow for freedom of movement. Body length from withers to base of tail is slightly longer than the height at the withers. *Substance*—Fine-boned and slender but not so refined as to appear breakable or alternatively, not a robust, heavy structure.

**Head**—*Expression*—Alert and intense. *Eyes*—Almond-shaped, set wide apart. Dark-colored dogs have dark-colored eyes, and lighter-colored dogs may have lighter-colored eyes. Eye rims match the coloring of the dog. *Ears*—Uncropped large and erect, placed so that the base of the ear is level with the outside corner of the eye. *Skull*—The skull is arched gently over the occiput from ear to ear. Distance from occiput to stop equal to distance from stop to tip of nose. The head is wedge-shaped viewed from above and the side. *Stop*—Slight but distinct. *Muzzle*—Cheeks taper cleanly into the muzzle. *Nose*—Dark in dark-colored dogs; may be lighter in lighter-colored dogs. Pigment is solid. *Lips*—Lips are clean and tight. *Bite*—Scissors or level in both varieties. Missing teeth in the Powderpuff are to be faulted. The Hairless variety is not to be penalized for absence of full dentition.

**Neck, Topline, Body**—*Neck*—Neck is lean and clean, slightly arched from the withers to the base of the skull and carried high. *Topline*—Level to slightly sloping croup. *Body*—Brisket extends to the elbow. Breastbone is not prominent. Ribs are well developed. The depth of the chest tapers to a moderate tuck-up at the flanks. Light in loin. *Tail*—Tail is slender and tapers to a curve. It is long enough to reach the hock. When dog is in motion, the tail is carried gaily and may be carried slightly forward over the back. At rest the tail is down with a slight curve upward at the end resembling a sickle. In the Hairless variety, two-thirds of the end of the tail is covered by long, flowing feathering referred to as a plume. The Powderpuff variety's tail is completely covered with hair.

**Forequarters**—*Angulation*—Layback of shoulders is 45 degrees to point of shoulder allowing for good reach. *Shoulders*—Clean and narrow. *Elbows*—Close to body. *Legs*—Long, slender and straight. *Pasterns*—Upright, fine and strong. Dewclaws may be removed. *Feet*—Hare foot, narrow with elongated toes. Nails are trimmed to moderate length.

**Hindquarters**—*Angulation*—Stifle moderately angulated. From hock joint to ground perpendicular. Dewclaws may be removed. *Feet*—Same as forequarters.

**Coat**—The Hairless variety has hair on certain portions of the body: the head (called a crest), the tail (called a plume) and the feet from the toes to the front pasterns and rear hock joints (called socks). The texture of all hair is soft and silky, flowing to any length. Placement of hair is not as important as overall type. Areas that have hair usually taper off slightly. Wherever the body is hairless, the skin is soft and smooth. Head Crest begins at the stop and tapers off between the base of the skull and the back of the neck. Hair on the ears and face is permitted on the Hairless and may be trimmed for neatness in both varieties. Tail Plume is described under Tail.

The Powderpuff variety is completely covered with a double soft and silky coat. Close examination reveals long thin guard hairs over the short silky undercoat. The coat is straight, of moderate density and length. Excessively heavy, kinky or curly coat is to be penalized. Grooming is minimal, consisting of presenting a clean and neat appearance.

**Color**—Any color or combination of colors.

**Gait**—Lively, agile and smooth without being stilted or hackneyed. Comes and goes at a trot moving in a straight line.

**Temperament**—Gay and alert.

**Approved June 12, 1990**
**Effective April 1, 1991**

# ENGLISH TOY SPANIEL

$S$INCE THE SPREAD OF CIVILIZATION HAS BEEN FROM EAST TO WEST, IT IS ONLY natural that most of our oldest breeds of dog should trace their origin to the eastern countries. Such is the case of the English Toy Spaniel, an affectionate, intelligent little dog that captivated royalty, aristocrats, and the wealthy for at least three centuries.

It has been a widespread fallacy that the toy spaniel made its first appearance in England during the reign of Charles II in the seventeenth century, for it was in honor of this sovereign that the black-and-tan variety took its name. Yet the toy spaniel had been known in England and in Scotland more than a hundred years before.

Just how long the toy spaniel had been known in Europe, particularly the south of Europe, before it was carried to England, must remain a matter of doubt. Yet most authorities are agreed that it goes back to Japan, and possibly China, of very ancient times.

According to Leighton, the English Toy Spaniel had its origin in Japan, was taken from there to Spain, and thence to England. Yet the extremely short nose of the breed might constitute evidence that it went from Spain to Japan, where it developed its present characteristics. There is a story, also, that specimens of this toy breed were brought from Japan by Captain Saris, a British naval officer, in 1613. They were presents from the Emperor of Japan—Japanese royal gifts always included dogs—to King James I.

The tale of Captain Saris seems a logical one, but it cannot be accepted as marking the debut of the toy spaniel into England and Scotland. The breed was known in England long before that, for Dr. John Caius, celebrated professor and the physician to Queen Elizabeth I, included it in his work *Of Englishe Dogges.* He refers to it as the "Spaniell Gentle, otherwise called the Comforter." His other references stamp it as almost the identical dog of today.

It is difficult to associate the toy spaniel with the austere Elizabeth; evidence that the breed was the favorite of the warmer-hearted Mary Queen of Scots, in the same century, is much more acceptable. The early years of Mary, during the first third of the sixteenth century, were spent in France. When she returned to Scotland as queen, she brought specimens of the breed with her, and these dogs remained her favorites up to the time of her execution. In fact, her especial pet refused to leave her, even on the scaffold.

All toy spaniels up to the time of King Charles II (b. 1630) appear to have been of the black-and-tan variety, later called the King Charles. This king's favorites were brought over from France by Henrietta of Orleans, and one is described as a black-and-white.

The development of the other varieties—the Prince Charles, which is a tricolor of white, black, and tan; the Ruby, which is mahogany red; and the Blenheim, which is white and chestnut red—occurred at later times. All are identical in their characteristics, with the exception of color. For a long time they were bred without any reference to color. Often the same litter would produce dogs of several varieties. It is only in modern times that the science of color breeding set the different varieties apart.

The history of the Blenheim variety seems more definite than that of the King Charles, although in some ways incompatible with other data. The development of the Blenheim, or red and white, is credited to John Churchill, the first Duke of Marlborough. Churchill, famous soldier and diplomat, was made an earl in 1689 and became a duke in 1702. At that time he acquired Blenheim, which has been the family seat of the Marlboroughs ever since.

It was written by Edward C. Ash that the first duke received as a present from China a pair of red-and-white Cocker Spaniels, and that these dogs were the basis of his subsequent breeding. The Chinese origin of the breed is mentioned also by Lady de Gex, who claims that during the fifteenth and sixteenth centuries there were carried from China to Italy numerous specimens of both red-and-white and black-and-white spaniels. These dogs subsequently were crossed with Cockers and Springers, intensifying the sporting instincts which the English Toy Spaniel still retains.

The dukes of Marlborough bred the Blenheim variety for many generations, and apparently they did so without the infusion of much outside blood—unless it were that of the Cocker and other varieties of spaniel. It was said by Sir Walter Scott in 1800 that the duke of Marlborough's Blenheims were the smallest and best

Cockers in England. They were used very successfully for woodcock shooting. And writers of a still later period describe the dogs found at Blenheim as larger than other specimens of the red-and-white. Also, the Marlborough strain did not have such exaggerated short noses.

Regardless of the early history of the English Toy Spaniel, it seems certain that many specimens of modern times trace their origin back to various small spaniels of England. Selective breeding has reduced them down to the limits of nine to twelve pounds, but it has not altogether erased their natural hunting instincts.

# OFFICIAL STANDARD FOR THE ENGLISH TOY SPANIEL

**General Appearance**—The English Toy Spaniel is a compact, cobby and essentially square toy dog possessed of a short-nosed, domed head, a merry and affectionate demeanor and a silky, flowing coat. His compact, sturdy body and charming temperament, together with his rounded head, lustrous dark eye, and well cushioned face, proclaim him a dog of distinction and character. *The important characteristics of the breed are exemplified by the head.*

**Size, Proportion, Substance**—*Size*—The most desirable weight of an adult is eight to fourteen pounds. General symmetry and substance are more important than the actual weight; however, all other things being equal, the smaller sized dog is to be preferred.

*Proportion*—Compact and essentially square in shape, built on cobby lines.

*Substance*—Sturdy of frame, solidly constructed.

**Head**—Head large in comparison to size, with a plush, chubby look, albeit with a degree of refinement which prevents it from being coarse.

*Expression*—Soft and appealing, indicating an intelligent nature.

*Eyes*—Large and very dark brown or black, set squarely on line with the nose, with little or no white showing. The eye rims should be black.

*Ears*—Very long and set low and close to the head, fringed with heavy feathering.

*Skull*—High and well domed; from the side, curves as far out over the eyes as possible.

*Stop*—Deep and well-defined.

*Muzzle*—Very short, with the nose well laid back and with well developed cushioning under the eyes.

*Jaw*—Square, broad, and deep, and well turned up, with lips properly meeting to give a finished appearance.

*Nose*—Large and jet black in color, with large, wide open nostrils.

*Bite*—Slightly undershot; teeth not to show. A wry mouth should be penalized; a hanging tongue is extremely objectionable.

**Neck, Topline, Body**—*Neck*—Moderate in length; nicely arched.

*Topline*—Level.

*Body*—Short, compact, square and deep, on cobby lines, with a broad back. Sturdy of frame, with good rib and deep brisket.

*Tail*—The tail is docked to two to four inches in length and carried at or just slightly above the level of the back. The set of the tail is at the back's level. Many are born with a shorter or screw tail which is acceptable. The feather on the tail should be silky and from three to four inches in length, constituting a marked "flag" of a square shape. The tail and its carriage is an index of the breed's attitude and character.

*Forequarters*—Shoulders well laid back; legs well boned and strong, dropping straight down from the elbow; strong in pastern. Feet, front and rear, are neat and compact; fused toes are often seen and are acceptable.

*Hindquarters*—Rear legs are well muscled and nicely angulated to indicate strength, and parallel of hock.

*Coat*—Profusely coated, heavy fringing on the ears, body, and on the chest, and with flowing feathering on both the front and hind legs, and feathering on the feet. The coat is straight or only slightly wavy, with a silken, glossy texture. Although the Blenheim and the Ruby rarely gain the length of coat and ears of the Prince Charles and King Charles, good coats and long ear fringes are a desired and prized attribute. Over-trimming of the body, feet or tail fringings should be penalized.

*Color*—The Blenheim (red and white) consists of a pearly white ground with deep red or chestnut markings evenly distributed in large patches. The ears and the cheeks are red, with a blaze of white extending from the nose up the forehead and ending between the ears in a crescentic curve. It is preferable that there be red markings around both eyes. The Blenheim often carries a thumb mark or "Blenheim Spot" placed on the top and the center of the skull.

The Prince Charles (tricolor) consists of a pearly white ground, with evenly distributed black patches, solid black ears and black face markings. It is preferable that there be black markings around both eyes. The tan markings are of a rich color, and on the face, over the eyes, in the lining of the ears and under the tail.

The King Charles (black and tan) is a rich, glossy black with bright mahogany tan markings appearing on the cheeks, lining of the ears, over the eyes, on the legs and underneath the tail. The presence of a small white chest patch about the size of a quarter, or a few white hairs on the chest of a King Charles Spaniel are not to be penalized; other white markings are an extremely serious fault.

The Ruby is a self-colored, rich mahogany red. The presence of a small white chest patch about the size of a quarter, or a few white hairs on the chest of a Ruby Spaniel are not to be penalized. Other white markings are an extremely serious fault.

*Gait*—Elegant with good reach in the front, and sound, driving rear action. The gait as a whole is free and lively, evidencing stable character and correct construction. In profile, the movement exhibits a good length of stride, and viewed from front and rear it is straight and true, resulting from straight-boned fronts and properly made and muscled hindquarters.

*Temperament*—The English Toy Spaniel is a bright and interested little dog, affectionate and willing to please.

**Approved June 13, 1989**
**Effective August 1, 1989**

# HAVANESE

*Corded*

THE HAVANESE IS AN OLD BREED OF THE BICHON FAMILY. THE EARLIEST references to the ancestors of the modern Havanese go back to Pliny the Elder, who studied the natural history of the Mediterranean region in the first century A.D. The breed may have originated on the island of Malta. Dogs in both Spain and Italy played an integral part in bringing the Havanese to the New World. Also known as the Havana Silk Dog, today's Havanese descended from the dogs that found a permanent home in Cuba, where they were popular among the wealthy Cubans. After the Cuban revolution in 1959, many of these dogs ended up in the United States.

Today the Havanese is a happy, outgoing, sturdy, small dog. Combining an outgoing temperament with their trainability, Havanese are excellent candidates for obedience training.

## OFFICIAL STANDARD FOR THE HAVANESE

**General Appearance**—The Havanese is a small sturdy dog of immense charm. He is slightly longer than tall, and covered with a profuse mantle of untrimmed long, silky, wavy hair. His plumed tail is carried loosely curled over his rump. A native of

Cuba, he has evolved over the centuries from the pampered lapdog of the aristocracy into what he is today—the quintessential family pet of a people living on a small tropical island. His duties traditionally have been those of companion, watchdog, child's playmate and herder of the family poultry flock. His presentation in the show ring should reflect his function—always in excellent condition but never so elaborately coifed as to preclude an impromptu romp in the leaves, as his character is essentially playful rather than decorative.

While historically always a toy dog and therefore never overly large or coarse, he does not appear so fragile as to make him unsuitable as a child's pet. His unique coat reflects centuries in the tropics, and protects against heat. It is remarkably soft and light in texture, profuse without being harsh or woolly. Likewise, the furnishings of the head are believed to protect the eyes from the harsh tropical sun, and have traditionally never been gathered in a topknot for this reason.

In both structure and gait, the Havanese is not easily mistaken for any other breed. His characteristic topline, rising slightly from withers to rump is a result of moderate angulation both fore and aft combined with a typically short upper arm. The resulting springy gait is flashy rather than far-reaching and unique to the breed. The overall impression of the dog on the move is one of agility rather than excessive ability to cover ground. These characteristics of temperament, structure and gait contribute in large part to the character of the breed, and are essential to type.

**Size, Proportion and Substance**—The height range is from 8½ to 11½ inches, with the ideal being between 9 and 10½ inches, measured at the withers, and is slightly less than the length from point of shoulder to point of buttocks, creating a rectangular outline rather than a square one. The Havanese is a sturdy little dog, and should never appear fragile. A coarse dog with excessive bone is likewise contrary to type and therefore equally undesirable. The minimum height ranges set forth in the description above shall not apply to dogs and bitches under twelve months of age. *Disqualification:* Height at withers under 8½ inches or over 11½ inches, except that the minimum height ranges set forth in the description above shall not apply to dogs or bitches under twelve months of age.

**Head**—The expression is soft and intelligent, mischievous rather than cute. The eyes are dark brown, large, almond-shaped, and set rather widely apart. Dark eyes are preferred irrespective of coat color, although the chocolate colored dog may have somewhat lighter eyes. The pigment on the eye-rims is complete, solid black for all colors except for the chocolate dog, which has complete solid, dark chocolate pigment. No other dilution of pigment is acceptable. Ears are of medium length; the leather, when extended, reaches halfway to the nose. They are set high on the skull, slightly above the endpoint of the zygomatic arch, and are broad at the base, showing a distinct fold. When the dog is alert, the ears lift at the base, producing an unbroken shallow arc from the outer edge of each ear across the backskull. The backskull is broad and slightly rounded. The stop is moderate. Length of muzzle is slightly less than length of backskull measured from stop to point of occiput and the planes are level. The nose is broad and squarish, fitting a full and rectangular muzzle, with no indication of snipiness. The pigment on the nose and lips is complete, solid black for all colors except for the chocolate dog which has complete solid, dark chocolate brown pigment. No other dilution of pigment is acceptable. A scissors bite is ideal. Full complement of incisors preferred.

*Disqualification:* Complete absence of black (or chocolate in the chocolate dog) pigmentation on the eye-rims, nose or lips.

**Neck, Topline, and Body**—The neck is of moderate length, in balance with the height and length of the dog. It carries a slight arch and blends smoothly into the shoulders. The topline is straight but not level, rising slightly from withers to rump. There is no indication of a roach back. The body, measured from point of shoulder to point of buttocks, is slightly longer than the height at the withers. This length comes from the ribcage and not from the short, well-muscled loin. The chest is deep, rather broad in front, and reaches the elbow. The ribs are well sprung. There is a moderate tuck-up. The tail is high-set and plumed with long, silky hair. It arcs forward over the back, but neither lies flat on the back nor is tightly curled. On the move the tail is carried loosely curled over the rump. The long plume of the hair may fall straight forward or to either side of the body. The tail may not be docked.

**Forequarters**—Shoulder layback is moderate, lying not more than 40 degrees off vertical. Extreme shoulder layback will negatively affect proper gait, and should be faulted. The tops of the shoulder blades lie in at the withers, allowing the neck to merge smoothly into the back. The upper arm is relatively short, but there is sufficient angle between the shoulder and upper arm to set the legs well under the body with a pronounced forechest. The elbows turn neither in nor out, and are tight to the body. Forelegs are well-boned and straight when viewed from any angle. The distance from the foot to the elbow is equal to the distance from elbow to withers. The pasterns are short, strong and flexible, very slightly sloping. Dewclaws may be removed. The feet are round, with well arched toes, and turn neither in nor out. Pads and nails may be black, white, pink, or a combination of these colors. Chocolate dogs may also have brown pads and nails.

**Hindquarters**—The hind legs are well-boned and muscular through the thigh, with moderate angulation. The hocks are short and turn neither in nor out. In normal stance, the hind legs are parallel to each other from hock to heel and all the joints are in line when viewed from the rear. The rear assembly, in which the rump is slightly higher than the withers, contributes to the breed's unique, springy gait. Dewclaws should be removed. The hind feet fall slightly behind a perpendicular line from point of buttock when viewed from the side. Hind feet have well arched toes and turn neither in nor out. Pads and nails may be black, white, pink or a combination of these colors. Chocolate dogs may also have brown pads and nails.

**Coat**—The coat is double, but without the harsh standoff guard hair and woolly undercoat usually associated with double coats. Rather, it is soft and light in texture throughout, though the outer coat carries slightly more weight. The long hair is abundant and, ideally, wavy. An ideal coat will not be so profuse nor overly long as to obscure the natural lines of the dog. Puppies may have a shorter coat. A single, flat coat or an excessively curly coat are equally contrary to type and should be faulted. *Disqualification:* A coarse, wiry coat. An atypical short coat on an adult dog (atypical would be smooth, flat coat with, or without furnishings).

**Color**—All colors are acceptable, singly or in any combination. No preference is given to one color over another. The skin may be freckled or parti-colored.

**Gait**—The Havanese gait is lively, elegant, resilient, and unique, contributing greatly to the breed's overall essential typiness. The characteristic "spring" is caused by the strong rear drive combined with a "flashy" front action effected by the short upper arm. While a truly typey dog is incapable of exaggerated reach and drive, the action does not appear stilted or hackneyed. The slightly higher rear may cause a correctly built specimen to show a flash of pad coming and going. The front legs reach forward freely. There is good extension in the rear and no tendency toward sickle hocks. The topline holds under movement, neither flattening nor roaching. Head carriage is typically high, even on the move.

**Temperament**—Playful and alert. The Havanese is both trainable and intelligent with a sweet, non-quarrelsome disposition.

**Presentation**—The dog should be shown as naturally as is consistent with good grooming. He may be shown either brushed or corded. His coat should be clean and well conditioned. In mature specimens, the length of the coat may cause it to fall to either side down the back but it should not appear to be artificially parted. The long, untrimmed head furnishings may fall forward over the eyes, naturally and gracefully to either side of the skull, or be held in two small braids beginning above the outer corner of the eyes, secured with plain elastic bands. (No ribbons or bows are permitted.) Corded coats will naturally separate into wavy sections in young dogs and will in time develop into cords. Adult corded dogs will be completely covered with a full coat of tassle-like cords. In either coat, minimal trimming of the hair at the inside corner of the eye is allowed for hygienic purposes only, not an attempt to resculpt the planes of the head. Minimal trimming around the anal and genital areas, for hygienic purposes only, is permissible but should not be noticeable on presentation. The hair on the feet and between the pads should be neatly trimmed for the express purpose of a tidy presentation. Any other trimming or sculpting of the coat is to be severely penalized as to preclude placement. Because correct gait is essential to breed type, the Havanese is presented at natural speed on a loose lead.

**Faults**—The foregoing description is that of the ideal Havanese. Any deviation from the above described dog must be penalized to the extent of the deviation keeping in mind the importance of the contribution of the various features toward the "original purpose of the breed."

# DISQUALIFICATION

*Height at withers under 8½ or over 11½ inches except that the minimum height range shall not apply to dogs or bitches under twelve months of age.*

*Complete absence of black (or chocolate in the chocolate dog) pigmentation on the eye-rims, nose or lips.*

*Coarse, wiry coat.*

*An atypical short coat on an adult. (Atypical refers to a smooth, flat coat with, or without furnishings.)*

**Approved May 7, 2001**
**Effective June 27, 2001**

# ITALIAN GREYHOUND

 HE ITALIAN GREYHOUND IS THE SMALLEST OF THE FAMILY OF GAZEHOUNDS
(dogs that hunt by sight). The breed is believed to have originated more than 2,000 years ago in the Mediterranean basin, possibly in the countries now known as Greece and Turkey. This belief is based on the depiction of miniature Greyhounds in the early decorative arts of these countries and on the archaeological discoveries of small Greyhound skeletons. Though never excessively popular, by the Middle Ages the breed had become distributed throughout southern Europe and was a favorite of the Italians of the sixteenth century, with whom miniature dogs were much in demand. Thus they became known as Italian Greyhounds. As a breed it has survived many centuries, prized for its beauty, small size, and sweet disposition. It appears frequently in the work of such Renaissance artists as Giotto, Carpaccio, Memling, Van de Weyden, Gerard David, and Hieronymus Bosch.

The breed was a favorite of various royal families of Europe, including the consort of England's James I, Anne of Denmark; Mary Beatrice d'Este of Modena, the Italian consort of James II; Frederick the Great of Prussia; Catherine the Great of Russia; and Queen Victoria.

The first volume of The Kennel Club (England) studbook listed forty of the breed. Volume III of the AKC Stud Book (1886) contains the first Italian Greyhound registration in this country. However, it was not until 1950 that as many as fifty were registered in the United States in a single year, and 1957 before an equal number were registered in Great Britain.

Following the world wars, when the breed was in danger of extinction, fresh stock was imported into England from the United States, giving evidence of the high quality to be found in America. Italian Greyhounds have competed successfully in all parts of the country in dog shows, obedience trials, and lure coursing events with a number of Best in Show awards to its credit.

The Italian Greyhound is a true Greyhound in miniature. There is some difference of opinion as to whether he was originally bred for hunting small game or was meant to be simply a pet and companion. It seems most likely that he filled both roles, and for this reason he is very adaptable to both city and country living. He is rather luxury loving and enjoys the comforts of an apartment; at the same time being a true hound, he likes exercise and outdoor activities.

The Italian Greyhound can weigh as little as five pounds or as much as fourteen or fifteen pounds, but the average weight is about eight pounds. His coat is short and smooth and requires little grooming. He is odorless and sheds little. Though he gives the impression of fragility, the breed is hardy, seldom ill, and thrives in such northern countries as Sweden and Scotland. The bitches are easy whelpers and good mothers.

Perhaps the most outstanding characteristic of the Italian Greyhound is his affectionate disposition. He thrives best when this affection is returned, and is happiest with his owner and immediate family, though he may sometimes seem a trifle aloof with strangers. He is sensitive, alert, and intelligent, and remains playful until long past puppyhood. He adapts to most households and gets along well with children and with other pets.

While very similar in appearance to the Greyhound, the Italian Greyhound is considerably smaller and more slender in all proportions. He differs also from his larger relative in his characteristic and elegant gait, high-stepping and free. His coat should be fine, smooth, and glossy, and any color and markings are acceptable, except that a dog with brindle markings or a dog with the tan markings normally found on black-and-tan dogs of other breeds will be disqualified in the show rings.

# OFFICIAL STANDARD FOR THE ITALIAN GREYHOUND

**Description**—The Italian Greyhound is very similar to the Greyhound, but much smaller and more slender in all proportions and of ideal elegance and grace.

**Head**—Narrow and long, tapering to nose, with a slight suggestion of stop.

**Skull**—Rather long, almost flat.

**Muzzle**—Long and fine.

**Nose**—Dark. It may be black or brown or in keeping with the color of the dog. A light or partly pigmented nose is a fault.

**Teeth**—Scissors bite. A badly undershot or overshot mouth is a fault.

**Eyes**—Dark, bright, intelligent, medium in size. Very light eyes are a fault.

**Ears**—Small, fine in texture; thrown back and folded except when alerted, then carried folded at right angles to the head. Erect or button ears severely penalized.

**Neck**—Long, slender and gracefully arched.

**Body**—Of medium length, short coupled; high at withers, back curved and drooping at hindquarters, the highest point of curve at start of loin, creating a definite tuckup at flanks.

**Shoulders**—Long and sloping.

**Chest**—Deep and narrow.

**Forelegs**—Long, straight, set well under shoulder; strong pasterns, fine bone.

**Hindquarters**—Long, well-muscled thigh; hind legs parallel when viewed from behind, hocks well let down, well-bent stifle.

**Feet**—Harefoot with well-arched toes. Removal of dewclaws optional.

**Tail**—Slender and tapering to a curved end, long enough to reach the hock; set low, carried low. Ring tail a serious fault, gay tail a fault.

**Coat**—Skin fine and supple, hair short, glossy like satin and soft to the touch.

**Color**—Any color and markings are acceptable except that a dog with brindle markings and a dog with the tan markings normally found on black-and-tan dogs of other breeds must be disqualified.

**Action**—High stepping and free, front and hind legs to move forward in a straight line.

**Size**—Height at withers, ideally 13 inches to 15 inches.


## DISQUALIFICATIONS

*A dog with brindle markings. A dog with the tan markings normally found on black-and-tan dogs of other breeds.*

**Approved December 14, 1976**

# JAPANESE CHIN

*I*N JAPAN, THERE ARE *INU* ("DOGS") AND THERE ARE CHIN. TO THE JAPANESE, the distinction needs no clarification. Chin are royalty. They are descendants of dogs that warmed the laps of Chinese aristocracy and kept court with the ladies of the Imperial Palace.

The Japanese Chin is a very old toy breed, as witnessed by the fact that renderings of dogs closely resembling them decorate old Chinese temples as well as ancient pottery and embroideries. While the breed origin is basically obscured by time, it is thought that these dogs originated in China centuries ago. Different stories abound concerning when the Chin came to Japan. It is said that Zen Buddhist teachers may have brought the dogs in A.D. 520. Others say that a Korean prince may have taken a pair to Japan as a gift for the Emperor in 732, or that a Chinese emperor may have presented a pair to the Japanese royal family at least 1,000 years ago.

Regardless of their exact origin, the Chin became known as the Japanese Chin to differentiate these parti-colored dogs from their cousin or, as some report, brother, the Pekingese. The Chin were closely kept in the hands of the nobility and frequently given to diplomats and foreigners as gifts of esteem to those who had rendered outstanding service to Japan.

Japan chose to isolate itself from Westerners in the 1600s, when the Tokugawa shogunate took control of the country. Thus, with the exception of a Dutch trading post, Japan was closed to the Western world. This 200-year isolation ended in 1854, with the signing of the Treaty of Kanagawa. Commodore Matthew C. Perry, who led the American expeditionary forces that opened the country, was presented with some of these prized little dogs as a gift. Those that survived the long voyage home reintroduced the breed to the rest of the world. The Chin quickly became a favorite with England's Queen Alexandra, her Marlborough House set, and various other European royals. These dogs were at the feet and in the lap of some of that time's most prominent leaders. Ships heading home from Japan included the Chin among their treasures, and the breed soon found itself in households large and small in Europe and in America. Breeders from around the world helped to establish and maintain the breed for the enjoyment of the dedicated fancier in future generations through world wars, diseases, and natural disasters.

In 1888, the first Chin registered by the American Kennel Club was simply known as Jap, and the breed was registered in America as a Japanese Spaniel. In 1977, however, the breed's parent club successfully convinced the AKC to officially change the breed's name to Japanese Chin.

The Chin is a small breed whose ideal height is eight to eleven inches at the withers. The dogs are aristocratic in appearance and stylish in carriage. They have few health problems, and their biggest drawback is that they tend to shed. Being single coated, their hair seldom mats if they are brushed once a week and bathed once a month. Males tend to have more coat than females.

The Chin can be black and white; white with lemon or red markings, including all shades from pale lemon to deep red as well as sable; and black and white with tan points. In all cases, the nose color must match the markings, and the eyes must be dark. Different colors may appear in the same litter when either the sire or dam is of other than pure black and white inheritance.

Japanese Chin are good companions, bright, alert, smart, and determined. Naturally clean and playful, they make ideal pets for young and old alike, and are happiest when with their owners. The breed is known for being a bit stubborn but is quick to learn, as long as the dogs think it is their idea. The Chin is a sensitive breed with definite likes and dislikes and rarely, if ever, forgets a friend or foe. The dogs love to be on top of things and are often described as being part cat and part dog, ruling their household and all who reside in it.

# OFFICIAL STANDARD FOR THE JAPANESE CHIN

**General Appearance**—The Japanese Chin is a small, well balanced, lively, aristocratic toy dog with a distinctive Oriental expression. It is light and stylish in action. The plumed tail is carried over the back, curving to either side. The coat is profuse, silky, soft and straight. The dog's outline presents a square appearance.

**Size, Proportion, Substance**—*Size*—Ideal size is 8 inches to 11 inches at the highest point of the withers. *Proportion*—Length between the sternum and the buttock is equal to the height at the withers. *Substance*—Solidly built, compact, yet refined. Carrying good weight in proportion to height and body build.

**Head**—*Expression*—Bright, inquisitive, alert and intelligent. The distinctive Oriental expression is characterized by the large broad head, large wide-set eyes, short broad muzzle, ear feathering, and the evenly patterned facial markings. *Eyes*—Set wide apart, large, round, dark in color, and lustrous. A small amount of white showing in the inner corners of the eyes is a breed characteristic that gives the dog a look of astonishment. *Ears*—Hanging, small, V-shaped, wide apart, set slightly below the crown of the skull. When alert, the ears are carried forward and downward. The ears are well feathered and fit into the rounded contour of the head. *Skull*—Large, broad, slightly rounded between the ears but not domed. Forehead is prominent, rounding toward the nose. Wide across the level of the eyes. In profile, the forehead and muzzle touch on the same vertical plane of a right angle whose horizontal plane is the top of the skull. *Stop*—Deep. *Muzzle*—Short and broad with well-cushioned cheeks and rounded upper lips that cover the teeth. *Nose*—Very short with wide, open nostrils. Set on a level with the middle of the eyes and upturned. Nose leather is black in the black and white and the black and white with tan points, and is self-colored or black in the red and white. *Bite*—The jaw is wide and slightly undershot. A dog with one or two missing or slightly misaligned teeth should not be severely penalized. The Japanese Chin is very sensitive to oral examination. If the dog displays any hesitancy, judges are asked to defer to the handler for presentation of the bite.

**Neck, Topline, Body**—*Neck*—Moderate in length and thickness. Well set on the shoulders enabling the dog to carry its head up proudly. *Topline*—Level. *Body*—Square, moderately wide in the chest with rounded ribs. Depth of rib extends to the elbow. *Tail*—Set on high, carried arched up over the back and flowing to either side of the body.

**Forequarters**—*Legs*—Straight, and fine boned, with the elbows set close to the body. Removal of dewclaws is optional. *Feet*—Hare-shaped with feathering on the ends of the toes in the mature dog. Point straight ahead or very slightly outward.

**Hindquarters**—*Legs*—Straight as viewed from the rear and fine boned. Moderate bend of stifle. Removal of dewclaws is optional. *Feet*—Hare-shaped with feathering on the ends of the toes in the mature dog. Point straight ahead.

**Coat**—Abundant, straight, single, and silky. Has a resilient texture and a tendency to stand out from the body, especially on neck, shoulders, and chest areas where the hair forms a thick mane or ruff. The tail is profusely coated and forms a plume. The rump area is heavily coated and forms culottes or pants. The head and muzzle are covered with short hair except for the heavily feathered ears. The forelegs have short hair blending into profuse feathering on the backs of the legs. The rear legs have the previously described culottes, and in mature dogs, light feathering from hock joint to the foot.

**Color**—Either black and white, red and white, or black and white with tan points. The term *tan points* shall include tan or red spots over each eye, inside the ears, on both cheeks, and at the anal vent area if displaying any black. The term *red* shall include all shades of red, orange, and lemon, and sable, which includes any aforementioned shade intermingled or overlaid with black. Among the allowed colors there shall be no preference when judging. A clearly defined white muzzle and blaze are preferable to a solidly marked head. Symmetry of facial markings is preferable. The size, shape, placement or number of body patches is not of great importance. The white is clear of excessive ticking.

**Gait**—Stylish and lively in movement. Moves straight with front and rear legs following in the same plane.

**Temperament**—A sensitive and intelligent dog whose only purpose is to serve man as a companion. Responsive and affectionate with those it knows and loves but reserved with strangers or in new situations.

**Approved December 8, 1992**
**Effective January 27, 1993**

# MALTESE

HE MALTESE, ONCE KNOWN AS "YE ANCIENT DOGGE OF MALTA," HAS FOR more than twenty-eight centuries been an aristocrat of the canine world.

Malta has been prominent in history from earliest times. Though settled by the Phoenicians about 1500 B.C., we know that other Mediterranean races lived there as far back as 3500 B.C. Many writers of old have spoken in glowing terms of the fame and opulence of Malta, justly celebrated for proficiency in the arts and crafts of peace and war as well as for the high state of civilization of its people. Amid these surroundings, among these people, the tiny Maltese lived.

In the first century A.D., Publius, the Roman governor of Malta, had a beloved Maltese named Issa. The poet Martial made this attachment famous in one of his celebrated epigrams:

> Issa is more frolicsome than Catulla's sparrow. Issa is purer than a dove's kiss. Issa is gentler than a maiden. Issa is more precious than Indian gems . . . Lest the last days that she sees light should snatch her from him forever, Publius has had her picture painted.

This last referred to a painting of Issa said to have been so lifelike that it was difficult to tell the picture from the living dog.

Other classical authors discoursed on the beauty, intelligence, and lovable qualities of Maltese dogs, among them Callimachus the Elder, Strabo, Pliny the Elder, Saint Clement of Alexandria, and others equally celebrated.

The Greeks erected tombs to their Maltese, and from the fifth century on, Greek ceramic art shows innumerable paintings of these dogs. A fine model of one was dug up in the Fayum in Egypt—it is not unlikely that this was the kind of dog worshipped by the Egyptians. And it is said that queens of old served the choicest foods out of golden vases to their Maltese.

In 1570, Dr. John Caius, physician to Elizabeth I, wrote:

> There is among us another kind of highbred dogs, but outside the common run those which Callimachus called Melitei from the Island of Melita . . . That kind is very small indeed and chiefly sought after for the pleasure and amusement of women. The smaller the kind, the more pleasing it is; so that they may carry them in their bosoms, in their beds and in their arms while in their carriages.

The Italian scientist Ulysses Aldrovanus (1522–1605) claimed to have seen one of these dogs sold for the equivalent of $2,000. Considering the value of the dollar in the time of Queen Elizabeth, the price paid would be equal to a five-figure sum in this day. Since the time of Good Queen Bess, the Maltese has often been mentioned—writers invariably drawing attention to its small size. In 1607, E. Topsell said they were "not bigger than common ferrets." Almost 200 years later, in 1792, Linnaeus referred to them as being "about the size of squirrels," while Danberton in his *History Naturelle* wrote that "ladies carried them in their sleeves."

The first Maltese exhibited in the United States was white and listed as a Maltese Lion Dog at Westminster's first show in 1877. At the 1879 Westminster show, a colored Maltese was exhibited as a Maltese Skye Terrier. The American Kennel Club accepted the Maltese for registration in 1888.

The fact that for so many centuries Maltese have been the household pets of people of culture, wealth, and fastidious taste may account for their refinement, fidelity, and cleanliness. It should be remembered that they are spaniels, not terriers, and that, as history has long recorded them, they are healthy and spirited even though tiny.

# OFFICIAL STANDARD FOR THE MALTESE

**General Appearance**—The Maltese is a toy dog covered from head to foot with a mantle of long, silky, white hair. He is gentle-mannered and affectionate, eager and sprightly in action, and, despite his size, possessed of the vigor needed for the satisfactory companion.

**Head**—Of medium length and in proportion to the size of the dog. *The skull* is slightly rounded on top, the stop moderate. *The drop ears* are rather low set and heavily feathered with long hair that hangs close to the head. *Eyes* are set not too far apart; they are very dark and round, their black rims enhancing the gentle yet alert expression. *The muzzle* is of medium length, fine and tapered but not snipy. *The nose* is black. *The teeth* meet in an even, edge-to-edge bite, or in a scissors bite.

**Neck**—Sufficient length of neck is desirable as promoting a high carriage of the head.

**Body**—Compact, the height from the withers to the ground equaling the length from the withers to the root of the tail. Shoulder blades are sloping, the elbows well knit and held close to the body. The back is level in topline, the ribs well sprung. The chest is fairly deep, the loins taut, strong, and just slightly tucked up underneath.

**Tail**—A long-haired plume carried gracefully over the back, its tip lying to the side over the quarter.

**Legs and Feet**—Legs are fine-boned and nicely feathered. Forelegs are straight, their pastern joints well knit and devoid of appreciable bend. Hind legs are strong and moderately angulated at stifles and hocks. The feet are small and round, with toe pads black. Scraggly hairs on the feet may be trimmed to give a neater appearance.

**Coat and Color**—The coat is single, that is, without undercoat. It hangs long, flat, and silky over the sides of the body almost, if not quite, to the ground. The long head-hair may be tied up in a topknot or it may be left hanging. Any suggestion of kinkiness, curliness, or woolly texture is objectionable. Color, pure white. Light tan or lemon on the ears is permissible, but not desirable.

**Size**—Weight under 7 pounds, with from 4 to 6 pounds preferred. Overall quality is to be favored over size.

**Gait**—The Maltese moves with a jaunty, smooth, flowing gait. Viewed from the side, he gives an impression of rapid movement, size considered. In the stride, the forelegs reach straight and free from the shoulders, with elbows close. Hind legs to move in a straight line. Cowhocks or any suggestion of hind leg toeing in or out are faults.

**Temperament**—For all his diminutive size, the Maltese seems to be without fear. His trust and affectionate responsiveness are very appealing. He is among the gentlest mannered of all little dogs, yet he is lively and playful as well as vigorous.

**Approved March 10, 1964**

# Manchester Terrier (Toy)

$\mathcal{U}$NTIL 1959, MANCHESTER TERRIERS AND TOY MANCHESTER TERRIERS were registered as separate breeds, although interbreeding was permitted. But since then, they have been registered as a single breed, the Manchester Terrier, with two varieties: Toy and Standard. For more information on the early development of the Manchester Terrier, refer to the Standard Manchester breed history in the Terrier Group.

Development of the Toy from the larger dog was first a matter of chance and later the business of selective breeding. It began when litters produced by larger dogs would include puppies of small stature. People liked them and wanted more, so naturally breeders tried to produce more small puppies. Some say the Toy was so highly prized that surreptitious matings with Italian Greyhounds were done to keep size to a minimum. Fortunately, these crosses were not perpetuated.

Few Toy-size dogs were available for breeding, however, and fanciers apparently resorted to excessive inbreeding. During the Victorian era, weight dropped to an alarming two-and-a-half pounds, and dogs were admittedly delicate. Realizing their mistake, breeders endeavored to correct their technique and succeeded in producing dogs of more normal Toy weight and renewed vigor.

When ear cropping was prohibited in Britain, many older fanciers tried to produce an attractive-looking dog with small, button ears. They became discouraged, however, and consequently many ceased to breed. A few staunch devotees were left to keep the breed alive, and their efforts were rewarded.

The Toy variety of the Manchester Terrier today no longer exhibits extremes of any sort. It has true Manchester type, with a flat skull, triangular eyes, accented kiss marks, and a sleek, ebony coat with clearly delineated markings. The sole difference between the Standard and the Toy (besides size, of course) is ear type. Both varieties have moderately small, thin ears that are narrow at the base and pointed at the tips. The ears are set high on the skull and quite close together. The Standard Manchester Terrier has either erect or button ears; if cropped, the ears are long and carried straight up. Cropping the Toy's ears is cause for disqualification from the show ring. The Toy ear is carried naturally erect without any sideways flare.

# OFFICIAL STANDARD FOR THE MANCHESTER TERRIER

**General Appearance**—A small, black, short-coated dog with distinctive rich mahogany markings and a taper style tail. In structure the Manchester presents a sleek, sturdy, yet elegant look, and has a wedge-shaped, long and clean head with a keen, bright, alert expression. The smooth, compact, muscular body expresses great power and agility, enabling the Manchester to kill vermin and course small game.

Except for size and ear options, there are no differences between the Standard and Toy varieties of the Manchester Terrier. The Toy is a diminutive version of the Standard variety.

**Size, Proportion, Substance**—The *Toy variety* shall not exceed 12 pounds. It is suggested that clubs consider dividing the American-bred and Open classes by weight as follows: 7 pounds and under, over 7 pounds and not exceeding 12 pounds.

The *Standard variety* shall be over 12 pounds and not exceeding 22 pounds. Dogs weighing over 22 pounds shall be disqualified. It is suggested that clubs consider dividing the American-bred and Open classes by weight as follows: over 12 pounds and not exceeding 16 pounds, over 16 pounds and not exceeding 22 pounds.

The Manchester Terrier, overall, is slightly longer than tall. The height, measured vertically from the ground to the highest point of the withers, is slightly less than the length, measured horizontally from the point of the shoulders to the rear projection of the upper thigh.

The bone and muscle of the Manchester Terrier is of sufficient mass to ensure agility and endurance.

**Head**—The Manchester Terrier has a keen and alert *expression.* The nearly black, almond-shaped *eyes* are small, bright, and sparkling. They are set moderately close together, slanting upwards on the outside. The eyes neither protrude nor sink in the skull. Pigmentation must be black.

Correct *ears* for the *Standard variety* are either the naturally erect ear, the cropped ear, or the button ear. No preference is given to any of the ear types. The naturally erect ear, and the button ear, should be wider at the base tapering to pointed tips, and carried well up on the skull. Wide, flaring, blunt tipped, or "bell" ears are a serious fault. Cropped ears should be long, pointed and carried erect.

The only correct *ear* for the *Toy variety* is the naturally erect ear. They should be wider at the base tapering to pointed tips, and carried well up on the skull. Wide, flaring, blunt tipped, or "bell" ears are a serious fault. Cropped, or cut ears are a disqualification in the Toy variety.

The **head** is long, narrow, tight skinned, and almost flat with a slight indentation up the forehead. It resembles a blunted wedge in frontal and profile views. There is a visual effect of a slight *stop* as viewed in profile.

The **muzzle** and **skull** are equal in length. The *muzzle* is well filled under the eyes with no visible cheek muscles. The underjaw is full and well defined and the **nose** is black.

Tight black *lips* lie close to the jaw. The jaws should be full and powerful with full and proper **dentition.** The teeth are white and strongly developed with a true scissors bite. Level bite is acceptable.

**Neck, Topline, Body**—The slightly arched **neck** should be slim and graceful, and of moderate length. It gradually becomes larger as it approaches, and blends smoothly with the sloping shoulders. Throatiness is undesirable.

The **topline** shows a slight arch over the robust loins falling slightly to the tail set. A flat back or roached back is to be severely penalized.

The *chest* is narrow between the legs and deep in the brisket. The forechest is moderately defined.

The *ribs* are well sprung, but flattened in the lower end to permit clearance of the forelegs.

The *abdomen* should be tucked up extending in an arched line from the deep brisket.

The taper style **tail** is moderately short reaching no further than the hock joint. It is set on at the end of the croup. Being thicker where it joins the body, the tail tapers to a point. The tail is carried in a slight upward curve, but never over the back.

**Forequarters**—The *shoulder blades* and the *upper arm* should be relatively the same length. The distance from the elbow to the withers should be approximately the same as the distance from the elbow to the ground. The *elbows* should lie close to the brisket. The *shoulders* are well laid back.

The *forelegs* are straight, of proportionate length, and placed well under the brisket. The pasterns should be almost perpendicular.

The **front feet** are compact and well arched. The two middle toes should be slightly longer than the others. The pads should be thick and the toenails should be jet black.

**Hindquarters**—The *thigh* should be muscular with the length of the upper and lower thighs being approximately equal. The stifle is well turned.

The well let down *hocks* should not turn in nor out as viewed from the rear. The **hind legs** are carried well back.

The *hind feet* are shaped like those of a cat, with thick pads and jet black nails.

**Coat**—The coat should be smooth, short, dense, tight and glossy; not soft.

**Color**—The coat color should be jet black and rich mahogany tan, which should not run or blend into each other, but abruptly form clear, well defined lines of color. There shall be a very small tan spot over each eye, and a very small tan spot on each cheek. On the head, the muzzle is tanned to the nose. The nose and nasal bone are jet black. The tan extends under the throat, ending in the shape of the letter V. The inside of the ears are partly tan. There shall be tan spots, called "rosettes," on each side of the chest above the front legs. These are more pronounced in puppies than in adults. There should be a black "thumbprint" patch on the front of each foreleg at the pastern. The remainder of the foreleg shall be tan to the carpus joint. There should be a distinct black "pencil mark" line running lengthwise on the top of each toe on all four feet. Tan on the hind leg should continue from the pencilling on the toes up the inside of the legs to a little below the stifle joint. The outside of the hind legs should be black. There should be tan under the tail, and on the vent, but only of such size as to be covered by the tail.

White on any part of the coat is a serious fault, and shall disqualify whenever the white shall form a patch or stripe measuring as much as one half inch at its longest dimension.

Any color other than black and tan shall be disqualified.

Color and/or markings should never take precedence over soundness and type.

**Gait**—The gait should be free and effortless with good reach of the forequarters, showing no indication of hackney gait. Rear quarters should have strong, driving power to match the front reach. Hocks should fully extend. Each rear leg should move in line with the foreleg of the same side, neither thrown in nor out. When moving at a trot, the legs tend to converge towards the center of gravity line beneath the dog.

**Temperament**—The Manchester Terrier is neither aggressive nor shy. He is keenly observant, devoted, but discerning. Not being a sparring breed, the Manchester is generally friendly with other dogs. Excessive shyness or aggressiveness should be considered a serious fault.

## DISQUALIFICATIONS

*Standard variety—Weight over 22 pounds.*
*Toy variety—Cropped or cut ears.*
*Both varieties—White on any part of the coat whenever the white shall form a patch or stripe measuring as much as one half inch at its longest dimension.*
*Any color other than black and tan.*

**Approved June 10, 1991**
**Effective July 31, 1991**

# MINIATURE PINSCHER

THE MINIATURE PINSCHER HAS EXISTED FOR SEVERAL CENTURIES. GERMANY, of course, is its native land, but it has been bred as well in the Scandinavian countries for a long time. Real development of the breed abroad began in 1895, when Germany's Pinscher Klub was formed. This club, now called the Pinscher-Schnauzer Klub, gave the breed its initial standard.

From the time of the Pinscher Klub's formation, the breed improved both in type and popularity, but more rapid headway was evident from 1905 up until World War I. That war, of course, handicapped progress in almost everything. Following the Armistice, or in about 1919, fanciers abroad once more started to advance the Miniature Pinscher, and as a result of importations to the United States breeding was undertaken here to a limited extent.

There were few Miniature Pinschers seen at American dog shows before 1928, the impetus to breed advancement dating from 1929 when the Miniature Pinscher Club of America was formed. Previously, the breed had been shown in the Miscellaneous class. The little dog's popularity has increased steadily.

Although the Miniature Pinscher, nicknamed the "Minpin," is similar to a Doberman on a smaller scale, it has a nature and way about it suggestive of a much larger dog. It is especially valuable as a watchdog, sometimes keener even than a dog twice its size. It is a born show dog, too, noted for its lively temperament and intelligence, and it is often used on the stage because of its style, smartness, and energy.

The close, slick coat requires scant attention, hence always looks neat and clean. And last but not least, the Minpin's fondness for home and master is exceptional.

# OFFICIAL STANDARD FOR THE MINIATURE PINSCHER

**General Appearance**—The Miniature Pinscher is structurally a well balanced, sturdy, compact, short-coupled, smooth-coated dog. He naturally is well groomed, proud, vigorous and alert. Characteristic traits are his hackney-like action, fearless animation, complete self-possession, and his spirited presence.

**Size, Proportion, Substance**—*Size*—10 inches to 12½ inches in height allowed, with desired height 11 inches to 11½ inches measured at highest point of the shoulder blades. *Disqualification*—Under 10 inches or over 12½ inches in height. Length of males equals height at withers. Females may be slightly longer.

**Head**—In correct proportion to the body. Tapering, narrow with well fitted but not too prominent foreface which balances with the skull. No indication of coarseness. *Eyes* full, slightly oval, clear, bright and dark even to a true black, including eye rims, with the exception of chocolates, whose eye rims should be self-colored. *Ears* set high, standing erect from base to tip. May be cropped or uncropped.

*Skull* appears flat, tapering forward toward the muzzle. *Muzzle* strong rather than fine and delicate, and in proportion to the head as a whole. Head well balanced with only a slight drop to the muzzle, which is parallel to the top of the skull. *Nose* black only, with the exception of chocolates which should have a self-colored nose. *Lips and Cheeks* small, taut and closely adherent to each other. *Teeth* meet in a scissors bite.

**Neck, Topline, Body**—*Neck* proportioned to head and body, slightly arched, gracefully curved, blending into shoulders, muscular and free from suggestion of dewlap or throatiness. *Topline*—Back level or slightly sloping toward the rear both when standing and gaiting. *Body* compact, slightly wedge-shaped, muscular. *Forechest* well developed. Well-sprung *ribs*. Depth of brisket, the base line of which is level with points of the elbows. Belly moderately tucked up to denote grace of structural form. Short and strong in *loin*. *Croup* level with topline. *Tail* set high, held erect, docked in proportion to size of dog.

**Forequarters**—*Shoulders* clean and sloping with moderate angulation coordinated to permit the hackney-like action. Elbows close to the body. *Legs*—Strong bone development and small clean joints. As viewed from the front, straight and upstanding. *Pasterns* strong, perpendicular. *Dewclaws* should be removed. *Feet* small, catlike, toes strong, well arched and closely knit with deep pads. *Nails* thick, blunt.

**Hindquarters**—Well muscled quarters set wide enough apart to fit into a properly balanced body. As viewed from the rear, the *legs* are straight and parallel. From the side, well angulated. *Thighs* well muscled. *Stifles* well defined. *Hocks* short, set well apart. *Dewclaws* should be removed. *Feet* small, catlike, toes strong, well arched and closely knit with deep pads. *Nails* thick, blunt.

**Coat**—Smooth, hard and short, straight and lustrous, closely adhering to and uniformly covering the body.

**Color**—Solid clear red. Stag red (red with intermingling of black hairs). Black with sharply defined rust-red markings on cheeks, lips, lower jaw, throat, twin spots above eyes and chest, lower half of forelegs, inside of hind legs and vent region, lower portion of hocks and feet. Black pencil stripes on toes. Chocolate with rust-red markings the same as specified for blacks, except brown pencil stripes on toes. In the solid red and stag red a rich vibrant medium to dark shade is preferred. *Disqualifications*—Any color other than listed. Thumb mark (patch of black hair surrounded by rust on the front of the foreleg between the foot and the wrist; on chocolates, the patch is chocolate hair). White on any part of dog which exceeds one-half inch in its longest dimension.

**Gait**—The forelegs and hind legs move parallel, with feet turning neither in nor out. The hackney-like action is a high-stepping, reaching, free and easy gait in which the front leg moves straight forward and in front of the body and the foot bends at the wrist. The dog drives smoothly and strongly from the rear. The head and tail are carried high.

**Temperament**—Fearless animation, complete self-possession, and spirited presence.

## DISQUALIFICATIONS

*Under 10 inches or over 12½ inches in height.*
*Any color other than listed. Thumb mark (patch of black hair surrounded by rust on the front of the foreleg between the foot and the wrist; on chocolates, the patch is chocolate hair). White on any part of dog which exceeds one half (½) inch in its longest dimension.*

**Approved July 8, 1980**
**Reformatted February 21, 1990**

# PAPILLON

*T*HE PAPILLON, KNOWN IN THE SIXTEENTH CENTURY AS THE DWARF SPANIEL, is the modern development of those little dogs often seen pictured in rare old paintings and tapestries. Rubens, Watteau, Fragonard, and Boucher all depicted them, and their popularity was so great that noble ladies of the day did not consider their portraits complete unless one of these elegant little dogs was pictured with them. Madame de Pompadour was the proud possessor of two, Inez and Mimi by name. Marie Antoinette was another ardent admirer, and as early as 1545 there is record of one having been sold to a lady who later ascended the throne of Poland.

It is Spain that we have to thank for the Papillon's primary rise to fame, though Italy, particularly Bologna, probably developed the largest trade. Many were sold to the court of Louis XIV, who had his choice among those brought into France. Prices ran high, and the chief trader, a Bolognese named Filipponi, developed a large business with the court of France and elsewhere. Most of the dogs were transferred from one country to the other upon the backs of mules.

As time went on, a change developed in the Dwarf Spaniel which gave rise to the name Papillon. During the days of Louis the Great, the Dwarf Spaniel possessed large, drooping ears, but gradually there came into being an erect-eared type, the ears being set obliquely on the head and so fringed as to resemble the wings of a butterfly. (*Papillon* is French for *butterfly*.) The causes of this change remain largely theoretical, but whatever they may be, we now have a toy dog whose type of body and coat is about the same as that of the original Dwarf Spaniel of Spain and Italy, but whose ears may be either erect or drooping. Both types may, and often do, appear in the same litter. On the Continent, as well as in Great Britain, the drop-eared variety is called *Phalene,* although the breed as a whole carries the name Papillon, as it does in this country. Here both types are judged together and with equality. Another change concerns color. Originally, almost all were of solid color. Today, white predominates as a ground color, with patches of other colors, and solid-colored dogs are disqualified. In conformation judging, there is no preference between correct ears or correct drop ears.

Papillons are hardy dogs. It is unnecessary to coddle them in winter, and they do not suffer particularly in severe hot weather. They delight in country activities and are equally contented in apartments. As ratters, they are extremely useful. Too small to kill a rat outright, they will worry it until it is exhausted, then dispatch it quickly. As a rule, the bitches whelp easily and give little trouble when raising puppies.

Although they have been exhibited for many years in the United States, it was not until 1935 that Papillons were represented in the American Kennel Club by their own breed club, the Papillon Club of America.

# OFFICIAL STANDARD FOR THE PAPILLON

**General Appearance**—The Papillon is a small, friendly, elegant toy dog of fine-boned structure, light, dainty and of lively action; distinguished from other breeds by its beautiful butterfly-like ears.

**Size, Proportion, Substance**—*Size*—Height at withers, 8 to 11 inches. *Fault*—Over 11 inches. **Disqualification**—Over 12 inches. **Proportion**—Body must be slightly longer than the height at withers. It is not a cobby dog. Weight is in proportion to height. **Substance**—Of fine-boned structure.

**Head**—*Eyes* dark, round, not bulging, of medium size and alert in *expression*. The inner corners of the eyes are on line with the stop. Eye rims black. **Ears**—The ears of either the erect or drop type should be large with rounded tips, and set on the sides and toward the back of the head. (1) Ears of the erect type are carried obliquely and move like the spread wings of a butterfly. When alert, each ear forms an angle of approximately 45 degrees to the head. The leather should be of sufficient strength to maintain the erect position. (2) Ears of the drop type, known as the Phalene, are similar to the erect type, but are carried drooping and must be completely down. *Faults*—Ears small, pointed, set too high; one ear up, or ears partly down.

**Skull**—The head is small. The skull is of medium width and slightly rounded between the ears. A well-defined stop is formed where the muzzle joins the skull. **Muzzle**—The muzzle is fine, abruptly thinner than the head, tapering to the nose. The length of the muzzle from the tip of the nose to stop is approximately one-third the length of the head from tip of nose to occiput. **Nose** black, small, rounded and slightly flat on top. *The following fault shall be severely penalized*—Nose not black. **Lips** tight, thin and black. Tongue must not be visible when jaws are closed. **Bite**—Teeth must meet in a scissors bite. *Faults*—Overshot or undershot.

**Neck, Topline, Body**—*Neck* of medium length. **Topline**—The backline is straight and level. **Body**—The chest is of medium depth with ribs well sprung. The belly is tucked up. **Tail** long, set high and carried well arched over the body. The tail is covered with a long, flowing plume. The plume may hang to either side of the body. *Faults*—Low-set tail; one not arched over the back, or too short.

**Forequarters**—Shoulders well developed and laid back to allow freedom of movement. Forelegs slender, fine-boned and must be straight. Removal of dewclaws on forelegs optional. Front feet thin and elongated (hare-like), pointing neither in nor out.

**Hindquarters**—Well developed and well angulated. The hind legs are slender, fine-boned, and parallel when viewed from behind. Hocks inclined neither in nor out. Dewclaws, if any, must be removed from hind legs. Hind feet thin and elongated (hare-like), pointing neither in nor out.

**Coat**—Abundant, long, fine, silky, flowing, straight with resilient quality, flat on back and sides of body. A profuse frill on chest. There is no undercoat. Hair short and close on skull, muzzle, front of forelegs, and from hind feet to hocks. Ears well fringed, with the inside covered with silken hair of medium length. Backs of the forelegs are covered with feathers diminishing to the pasterns. Hind legs are covered to the hocks with abundant breeches (culottes). Tail is covered with a long, flowing plume. Hair on feet is short, but fine tufts may appear over toes and grow beyond them, forming a point.

**Color**—Always parti-color or white with patches of any color(s). On the head, color(s) other than white must cover both ears, back and front, and extend without interruption from the ears over both eyes. A clearly defined white blaze and nose band are preferred to a solidly marked head. Symmetry of facial markings is desirable. The size, shape, placement and presence or absence of patches of color on the body are without importance. Among the colors there is no preference, provided nose, eye rims and lips are well pigmented black.

*The following faults shall be severely penalized*—Color other than white not covering both ears, back and front, or not extending from the ears over both eyes. A slight extension of the white collar onto the base of the ears, or a few white hairs interspersed among the color, shall not be penalized, provided the butterfly appearance is not sacrificed. *Disqualifications*—An all-white dog or a dog with no white.

**Gait**—Free, quick, easy, graceful, not paddlefooted, or stiff in hip movements.

**Temperament**—Happy, alert and friendly. Neither shy nor aggressive.


# DISQUALIFICATIONS

*Height over 12 inches.*
*An all-white dog or a dog with no white.*

**Approved June 10, 1991**
**Effective July 31, 1991**

# PEKINGESE

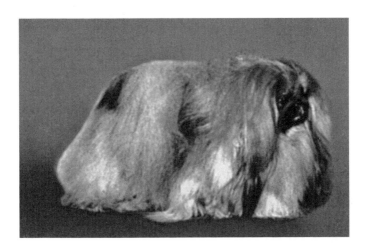

$\mathcal{F}$ASCINATING BY REASON OF ITS EXOTIC BACKGROUND AND DISTINCTIVE personality, the Pekingese holds an honored place in the dog world. In ancient times it was held sacred in China, the land of its origin, and intricately carved Foo Dog idols of varying sizes, ranging in materials from ivory to bronze and jewel-studded wood, have been handed down.

The exact date of origin is debatable, the earliest known record of its existence being traceable to the Tang Dynasty of the eighth century. However, the very oldest strains (held only by the imperial family) were kept pure, and the theft of one of the sacred dogs was punishable by death.

The characteristics we seek to retain and perfect today were in evidence in the earliest Pekingese, as shown by three of the names by which they were designated in ancient China. Some were called Lion Dogs, evidently because of their massive fronts, heavy manes, and tapering hindquarters. We find a second group called Sun Dogs because of their strikingly beautiful golden red coats. Since those early days, many other darker red shades have become identified with certain strains, but even today we see numerous "Sun Dogs" at our shows. A third name was Sleeve Dog, this being given only to those diminutive specimens which were carried about in the voluminous sleeves of the members of the imperial household.

Introduction of Pekingese into the Western world occurred as a result of the looting of the Imperial Palace at Peking by the British in 1860. It is a matter of history that five were found behind some draperies in the apartments of the aunt of the emperor. Apparently they were her particular pets—she committed suicide on the approach of the British troops. It is said that throughout the palace the bodies of many of these dogs were found, the Chinese having killed them rather than have them fall into the hands of the Europeans. The five Pekingese found by the English were of different colors; a fawn and white parti-color was the one presented to Queen Victoria on the troops' return to Great Britain.

Pekingese were not exhibited in England until 1893, when Mrs. Loftus Allen exhibited one at Chester. But the undeniable beauty and interesting history of the breed placed it in the foreground, where it has since remained. The three dogs which were outstanding in the breed's earliest development in the Occident were Ah Cum and Mimosa, called the "pillars of the studbook" in England, followed by a large black-and-tan specimen named Boxer, so-called because he was obtained by a Major Gwayne during the Boxer uprising in 1900. Curiously enough, Boxer had a docked tail and so was never exhibited. He undoubtedly did more for the breed in the early part of the twentieth century than any other Pekingese.

The Pekingese was first registered by the AKC in 1906. That it took quick hold of the American fancy is evidenced by the age of the Pekingese Club of America, which became a member of the American Kennel Club in 1909.

The transplanting of the Pekingese into Western soil has in no way changed his personality. He combines marked dignity with an exasperating stubbornness that serves only to endear him the more to his owners. He is independent and regal in every gesture; it would be a great indignity to attempt to make a lapdog out of him. Calm and good-tempered, the Pekingese employs a condescending cordiality toward the world in general, but in the privacy of his family enjoys nothing better than a good romp. Although never aggressive, he fears not the devil himself and has never been known to turn tail and run. He has plenty of stamina, much more in fact than have a number of the larger breeds, and he is very easy to care for.

Since he has been brought down from his pedestal in Chinese temples, the Pekingese has but one purpose in life, to give understanding companionship and loyalty to his owners. It may be truly said that the Pekingese fulfills his mission to perfection.

# OFFICIAL STANDARD FOR THE PEKINGESE

**General Appearance**—The Pekingese is a well-balanced, compact dog of Chinese origin with a heavy front and lighter hindquarters. Its temperament is one of directness, independence and individuality. Its image is lionlike, implying courage, dignity, boldness and self-esteem rather than daintiness or delicacy.

**Size, Substance, Proportion**—*Size/Substance*—The Pekingese, when lifted, is surprisingly heavy for its size. It has a stocky, muscular body. All weights are correct within the limit of 14 pounds. *Disqualification: Weight over 14 pounds.* **Proportion**—Overall balance is of utmost importance. The head is large in proportion to the body. The Pekingese is slightly longer than tall when measured from the forechest to the buttocks. The overall outline is an approximate ratio of 3 high to 5 long.

**Head**—*Face*—The topskull is massive, broad and flat and, when combined with the wide set eyes, cheekbones and broad lower jaw, forms the correctly shaped face. When viewed from the front, the skull is wider than deep, which contributes to the desired rectangular, envelope-shaped appearance of the head. In profile, the face is flat. When viewed from the side, the chin, nose leather and brow all lie in one plane, which slants very slightly backward from chin to forehead. *Ears*—They are heart-shaped, set on the front corners of the topskull, and lie flat against the head. The leather does not extend below the jaw. Correctly placed ears, with their heavy feathering and long fringing, frame the sides of the face and add to the appearance of a wide, rectangular head. *Eyes*—They are large, very dark, round, lustrous and set wide apart. The look is bold, not bulging. The eye rims are black and the white of the eye does not show when the dog is looking straight ahead. *Nose*—It is broad, short and black. Nostrils are wide and open rather than pinched. A line drawn horizontally over the top of the nose intersects slightly above the center of the eyes. *Wrinkle*—It effectively separates the upper and lower areas of the face. It is a hair-covered fold of skin extending from one cheek over the bridge of the nose in a wide inverted "V" to the other cheek. It is never so prominent or heavy as to crowd the facial features, obscure more than a small portion of the eyes, or fall forward over any portion of the nose leather. *Stop*—It is obscured from view by the over-nose wrinkle. *Muzzle*—It is very flat, broad, and well filled-in below the eyes. The skin is black on all colors. Whiskers add to the desired expression. *Mouth*—The lower jaw is undershot and broad. The black lips meet neatly and neither teeth nor tongue show when the mouth is closed.

**Neck, Body, Tail**—*Neck*—It is very short and thick. *Body*—It is pear-shaped, compact and low to the ground. It is heavy in front with well-sprung ribs slung between the forelegs. The forechest is broad and full without a protruding breastbone. The underline rises from the deep chest to the lighter loin, thus forming a narrow waist. The topline is straight and the loin is short. *Tail*—The high-set tail is slightly arched and carried well over the back, free of kinks or curls. Long, profuse, straight fringing may fall to either side.

**Forequarters**—They are short, thick and heavy-boned. The bones of the forelegs are moderately bowed between the pastern and elbow. The broad chest, wide set forelegs and the closer rear legs all contribute to the correct rolling gait. The distance from the point of the shoulder to the tip of the withers is approximately equal to the distance from the point of the shoulder to the elbow. Shoulders are well laid back and fit smoothly onto the body. The elbows are always close to the body. Front feet are turned out slightly when standing or moving. The pasterns slope gently.

**Hindquarters**—They are lighter in bone than the forequarters. There is moderate angulation of stifle and hock. When viewed from behind, the rear legs are reasonably close and parallel, and the feet point straight ahead when standing or moving.

**Coat & Presentation**—*Coat*—It is a long, coarse-textured, straight, stand-off outer coat, with thick, soft undercoat. The coat forms a noticeable mane on the neck and shoulder area with the coat on the remainder of the body somewhat shorter in length. A long and profuse coat is desirable providing it does not obscure the shape of the body. Long feathering is found on toes, backs of the thighs and forelegs, with longer fringing on the ears and tail. **Presentation**—Presentation should accentuate the natural outline of the Pekingese. Any obvious trimming or sculpting of the coat, detracting from its natural appearance, should be severely penalized.

**Color**—All coat colors and markings are allowable and of equal merit. A black mask or a self-colored face is equally acceptable. Regardless of coat color the exposed skin of the muzzle, nose, lips and eye rims is black.

**Gait**—It is unhurried, dignified, free and strong, with a slight roll over the shoulders. This motion is smooth and effortless and is as free as possible from bouncing, prancing or jarring. The rolling gait results from a combination of the bowed forelegs, well laid back shoulders, full broad chest and narrow light rear, all of which produce adequate reach and moderate drive.

**Temperament**—A combination of regal dignity, intelligence and self-importance make for a good natured, opinionated and affectionate companion to those who have earned its respect.


## DISQUALIFICATION

*Weight over 14 pounds.*
**The foregoing is a description of the ideal Pekingese. Any deviation should be penalized in direct proportion to the extent of that deviation.**

**Approved January 13, 2004**
**Effective March 2, 2004**

# POMERANIAN

*A* MEMBER OF THE FAMILY OF DOGS KNOWN UNOFFICIALLY AS THE SPITZ group, the Pomeranian has descended from the sled dogs of Iceland and Lapland. This heritage is responsible for their breed type. The breed name, of course, traces to Pomerania, not necessarily as a point of origin but possibly because it is there that the breed may have been bred down to size. At any rate, in larger form the breed served as an able sheep-herder. In fact, at about the middle of the nineteenth century, when they first came into notice in Britain, some specimens are said to have weighed as much as thirty pounds and resembled the German Wolfspitz in size, coat, and color.

The Pomeranian was not well known until 1870, when The Kennel Club (England) recognized this so-called spitz dog. In 1888, while visiting Florence, Queen Victoria fell in love with a Pomeranian and brought the dog, Marco, back to England. Since the beloved queen's activities were well chronicled and copied, the breed's popularity grew. Victoria is credited with advocating for and publicizing the trend toward smaller Pomeranians. On her dying day in 1901, the queen requested that her favorite pet, a Pomeranian named Turi, be brought to her bedside. Turi was lying beside Victoria when she died.

Specimens of the breed were shown in the United States in the AKC Miscellaneous class as far back as 1892, but regular classification was not provided until 1900 in New York. In 1911, the American Pomeranian Club held its first specialty show.

The majority of early American Pomeranian winners had heavier bone, larger ears, and usually weighed less than six pounds. Generally speaking, they had good type and coat texture but lacked the profuse coat we see today. Modern American-bred dogs show marked improvement over those early winners, as the patient efforts of fanciers have brought their dogs closer to the standard. Indeed, American-bred Pomeranians have held their own with the best from anywhere and today compete for the highest honors in the show ring.

The glamorous little Pomeranian is now well established as one of the most favored of all breeds in the Toy Group. While small in stature, they are hardy, sturdy, generally healthy, and not at all weak or fragile.

The Pomeranian's magnificent double coat—a soft, dense undercoat topped by a harsh, longer outer coat—is an example of a "stand-off" coat, rather than a flat coat.

Cocky and animated little dogs, they are aptly described as being unaware of their diminutive size. Indeed, the Pomeranian is a very big dog in a very small package. Admired for beauty and temperament, they are attention-getters wherever they go.

While not loud or yappy dogs, Pomeranians are often considered to be excellent guard dogs, instinctively alerting an owner to any intrusion or danger. Although tiny and not able to do much damage to an intruder, they will stand their ground with an amazingly protective demeanor. It is believed that in times past, guarding castles, estates, or other property was actually a desired function of the breed.

The Pomeranian is suitable for most any home or environment. It is the ideal family pet, especially endearing to the elderly and bonding well with children over the age of six. Most are highly energetic, vivacious, and untiring, yet they can be gentle, quiet, soft, and loving, and completely content in someone's lap, thus making them the ideal pet and companion.

# OFFICIAL STANDARD FOR THE POMERANIAN

**General Appearance**—The Pomeranian is a compact, short-backed, active toy dog. He has a soft, dense undercoat with a profuse harsh-textured outer coat. His heavily plumed tail is set high and lies flat on his back. He is alert in character, exhibits intelligence in expression, is buoyant in deportment, and is inquisitive by nature. The Pomeranian is cocky, commanding and animated as he gaits. He is sound in composition and action.

**Size, Proportion, Substance**—The average weight of the Pomeranian is from 3 to 7 pounds, with the ideal weight for the show specimen being 4 to 6 pounds. Any dog over or under the limits is objectionable. However, overall quality is to be favored over size. The distance from the point of shoulder to the point of buttocks is slightly shorter than from the highest point of the withers to the ground. The distance from the brisket to the ground is half the height at the withers. He is medium-boned, and the length of his legs is in proportion to a well-balanced frame. When examined, he feels sturdy.

**Head**—The *head* is in balance with the body. The *muzzle* is rather short, straight, fine, free of lippiness and never snipey. His *expression* is alert and may be referred to as fox-like. The *skull* is closed. The top of the skull is slightly rounded, but not domed. When viewed from the front and side, one sees small *ears* which are mounted high and carried erect. To form a wedge, visualize a line from the tip of the nose ascending through the center of the eyes and the tip of the ears. The *eyes* are dark, bright, medium in size and almond-shaped. They are set well into the skull on either side of a well-pronounced stop. The pigmentation is black on the nose and eye rims except self-colored in brown, beaver, and blue dogs. The *teeth* meet in a scissors bite. One tooth out of alignment is acceptable. *Major Faults*—Round, domed skull; undershot mouth; overshot mouth.

**Neck, Topline, Body**—The *neck* is short with its base set well into the shoulders to allow the head to be carried high. The *back* is short with a level *topline*. The *body* is compact and well-ribbed with brisket reaching the elbow. The plumed *tail* is one of the characteristics of the breed, and lies flat and straight on the back.

**Forequarters**—The Pomeranian has sufficient layback of shoulders to carry the neck and head proud and high. The *shoulders* and *legs* are moderately muscled. The length of the shoulder blade and upper arm are equal. The *forelegs* are straight and parallel to each other. Height from elbows to withers approximately equals height from ground to elbow. The pasterns are straight and strong. The *feet* are well-arched, compact, and turn neither in nor out. He stands well up on his toes. *Dewclaws* may be removed. *Major Fault*—Down in pasterns.

**Gait**—The Pomeranian's gait is smooth, free, balanced and vigorous. He has good reach in his forequarters and strong drive with his hindquarters. Each rear leg moves in line with the foreleg on the same side. To achieve balance, his legs converge slightly inward toward a center line beneath his body. The rear and front legs are thrown neither in nor out. The topline remains level, and his overall balance and outline are maintained.

**Hindquarters**—The angulation of the hindquarters balances that of the forequarters. The buttocks are well behind the set of the tail. The thighs are moderately muscled with *stifles* that are moderately bent and clearly defined. The *hocks* are perpendicular to the ground and the *legs* are straight and parallel to each other. The *feet* are well-arched, compact, and turn neither in nor out. He stands well up on his toes. *Dewclaws,* if any, on the hind legs may be removed. *Major Faults*—Cowhocks or lack of soundness in hind legs or stifles.

**Coat**—A Pomeranian is noted for its double coat. The *undercoat* is soft and dense. The *outer coat* is long, straight, glistening and harsh in texture. A thick undercoat will hold up and permit the guard hair to stand off from the Pomeranian's body. The coat is abundant from the neck and fore part of shoulders and chest, forming a frill which extends over the shoulders and chest. The head and leg coat is tightly packed and shorter in length than that of the body. The forequarters are well-feathered and thighs and hind legs well-feathered to the hock. The tail is profusely covered with long, harsh, spreading straight hair. Trimming for neatness and a clean outline is permissible. *Major Faults*—Soft, flat or open coat.

**Color**—All colors, patterns, and variations thereof are allowed and must be judged on an equal basis. *Patterns: Black and Tan*—Tan or rust sharply defined, appearing above each eye and on muzzle, throat, and forechest, on all legs and feet and below the tail. The richer the tan the more desirable; *Brindle*—The base color is gold, red, or orange-brindled with strong black cross stripes; *Parti-color*—Is white with any other color distributed in patches with a white blaze preferred on the head. *Classifications:* The Open Classes at specialty shows may be divided by color as follows: Open Red, Orange, Cream, and Sable; Open Black, Brown, and Blue; Open Any Other Color, Pattern, or Variation.

**Temperament**—The Pomeranian is an extrovert, exhibiting great intelligence and a vivacious spirit, making him a great companion dog as well as a competitive show dog.

*Even though a Toy dog, the Pomeranian must be subject to the same requirements of soundness and structure prescribed for all breeds, and any deviation from the ideal described in the standard should be penalized to the extent of the deviation.*

**Approved December 9, 1996**
**Effective January 31, 1997**

# POODLE (TOY)

𝓘N POODLES, THE DENOMINATIONS *STANDARD, MINIATURE* AND *TOY* ARE used to describe size only. All are one breed, governed by the same breed standard. All are also known for their innate intelligence and exceptional ability to learn.

For information about the history of this smallest of the three Poodle varieties, refer to the Poodle in the Non-Sporting Group.

## OFFICIAL STANDARD FOR THE POODLE

The Standard for the Poodle (Toy Variety) is the same as for the Standard and the Miniature varieties, except as regards height.

**General Appearance, Carriage and Condition**—That of a very active, intelligent and elegant-appearing dog, squarely built, well proportioned, moving soundly and carrying himself proudly. Properly clipped in the traditional fashion and carefully groomed, the Poodle has about him an air of distinction and dignity peculiar to himself.

**Size, Proportion, Substance**—*Size*—*The Standard Poodle* is over 15 inches at the highest point of the shoulders. Any Poodle which is 15 inches or less in height shall be disqualified from competition as a Standard Poodle.

*The Miniature Poodle* is 15 inches or under at the highest point of the shoulders, with a minimum height in excess of 10 inches. Any Poodle which is over 15 inches or is 10 inches or less at the highest point of the shoulders shall be disqualified from competition as a Miniature Poodle.

*The Toy Poodle* is 10 inches or under at the highest point of the shoulders. Any Poodle which is more than 10 inches at the highest point of the shoulders shall be disqualified from competition as a Toy Poodle.

As long as the Toy Poodle is definitely a Toy Poodle, and the Miniature Poodle a Miniature Poodle, both in balance and proportion for the Variety, diminutiveness shall be the deciding factor when all other points are equal.

*Proportion*—To ensure the desirable squarely built appearance, the length of body measured from the breastbone to the point of the rump approximates the height from the highest point of the shoulders to the ground.

*Substance*—Bone and muscle of both forelegs and hindlegs are in proportion to size of dog.

**Head and Expression**—*(a) Eyes*—Very dark, oval in shape and set far enough apart and positioned to create an alert intelligent expression. *Major fault: eyes round, protruding, large or very light.*

*(b) Ears*—Hanging close to the head, set at or slightly below eye level. The ear leather is long, wide and thickly feathered; however, the ear fringe should not be of excessive length.

*(c) Skull*—Moderately rounded, with a slight but definite stop. Cheekbones and muscles flat. Length from occiput to stop about the same as length of muzzle.

*(d) Muzzle*—Long, straight and fine, with slight chiseling under the eyes. Strong without lippiness. The chin definite enough to preclude snipiness. *Major fault: lack of chin.* **Teeth**—White, strong and with a scissors bite. *Major fault: undershot, overshot, wry mouth.*

**Neck, Topline, Body**—*Neck*—well proportioned, strong and long enough to permit the head to be carried high and with dignity. Skin snug at throat. The neck rises from strong, smoothly muscled shoulders. *Major fault: ewe neck.*

The *topline* is level, neither sloping nor roached, from the highest point of the shoulder blade to the base of the tail, with the exception of a slight hollow just behind the shoulder.

*Body*—*(a)* Chest deep and moderately wide with well sprung ribs. *(b)* The loin is short, broad and muscular. *(c)* Tail straight, set on high and carried up, docked of sufficient length to insure a balanced outline. *Major fault: set low, curled, or carried over the back.*

**Forequarters**—Strong, smoothly muscled shoulders. The shoulder blade is well laid back and approximately the same length as the upper foreleg. *Major fault: steep shoulder.*

*Forelegs*—Straight and parallel when viewed from the front. When viewed from the side the elbow is directly below the highest point of the shoulder. The pasterns are strong. Dewclaws may be removed.

*Feet*—The feet are rather small, oval in shape with toes well arched and cushioned on thick firm pads. Nails short but not excessively shortened. The feet turn neither in nor out. *Major fault: paper or splay foot.*

**Hindquarters**—The angulation of the hindquarters balances that of the forequarters.

Hind legs straight and parallel when viewed from the rear. Muscular with width in the region of the stifles which are well bent; femur and tibia are about equal in length; hock to heel short and perpendicular to the ground. When standing, the rear toes are only slightly behind the point of the rump. *Major fault: cow-hocks.*

**Coat**—*(a) Quality*—(1) Curly: of naturally harsh texture, dense throughout. (2) Corded: hanging in tight even cords of varying length; longer on mane or body coat, head and ears; shorter on puffs, bracelets and pompons.

*(b) Clip*—A Poodle under 12 months may be shown in the "Puppy" clip. In all regular classes, Poodles 12 months or over must be shown in the "English Saddle" or "Continental" clip. In the Stud Dog and Brood Bitch classes and in a non-competitive Parade of Champions, Poodles may be shown in the "Sporting" clip. A Poodle shown in any other type of clip shall be disqualified.

*(1) "Puppy"*—A Poodle under a year old may be shown in the "Puppy" clip with the coat long. The face, throat, feet and base of the tail are shaved. The entire shaven foot is visible. There is a pompon on the end of the tail. In order to give a neat appearance and a smooth unbroken line, shaping of the coat is permissible. *(2) "English Saddle"*—In the "English Saddle" clip the face, throat, feet, forelegs and base of the tail are shaved, leaving puffs on the forelegs and a pompon on the end of the tail. The hindquarters are covered with a short blanket of hair except for a curved shaved area on each flank and two shaved bands on each hindleg. The entire shaven foot and a portion of the shaven leg above the puff are visible. The rest of the body is left in full coat but may be shaped in order to insure overall balance. *(3) "Continental"*—In the "Continental" clip, the face, throat, feet, and base of the tail are shaved. The hindquarters are shaved with pompons (optional) on the hips. The legs are shaved, leaving bracelets on the hindlegs and puffs on the forelegs. There is a pompon on the end of the tail. The entire shaven foot and a portion of the shaven foreleg above the puff are visible. The rest of the body is left in full coat but may be shaped in order to insure overall balance. *(4) "Sporting"*—In the "Sporting" clip, a Poodle shall be shown with face, feet, throat, and base of tail shaved, leaving a scissored cap on the top of the head and a pompon on the end of the tail. The rest of the body and legs are clipped or scissored to follow the outline of the dog leaving a short blanket of coat no longer than one inch in length. The hair on the legs may be slightly longer than that on the body.

In all clips the hair of the topknot may be left free or held in place by elastic bands. The hair is only of sufficient length to present a smooth outline. "Topknot" refers only to hair on the skull, from stop to occiput. This is the only area where elastic bands may be used.

**Color**—The coat is an even and solid color at the skin. In blues, grays, silvers, browns, cafe-au-laits, apricots and creams the coat may show varying shades of the same color. This is frequently present in the somewhat darker feathering of the ears and in the tipping of the ruff. While clear colors are definitely preferred, such natural variation in the shading of the coat is not to be considered a fault. Brown and cafe-au-lait Poodles have liver-colored noses, eye-rims and lips, dark toenails and dark amber eyes. Black, blue, gray, silver, cream and white Poodles have black noses, eye-rims and lips, black or self colored toenails and very dark eyes. In the apricots while the foregoing coloring is preferred, liver-colored noses, eye-rims and lips, and amber eyes are permitted but are not desirable. *Major faults: color of nose, lips and eye-rims incomplete, or of wrong color for color of dog.*

Parti-colored dogs shall be disqualified. The coat of a parti-colored dog is not an even solid color at the skin but is of two or more colors.

**Gait**—A straightforward trot with light springy action and strong hindquarters drive. Head and tail carried up. Sound effortless movement is essential.

**Temperament**—Carrying himself proudly, very active, intelligent, the Poodle has about him an air of distinction and dignity peculiar to himself. *Major fault: shyness or sharpness.*

**Major Faults**—Any distinct deviation from the desired characteristics described in the Breed Standard.

## DISQUALIFICATIONS

*Size*—A dog over or under the height limits specified shall be disqualified.
*Clip*—A dog in any type of clip other than those listed under coat shall be disqualified.
*Parti-colors*—The coat of a parti-colored dog is not an even solid color at the skin but of two or more colors. Parti-colored dogs shall be disqualified.

### VALUE OF POINTS

| | |
|---|---|
| General appearance, temperament, carriage and condition | 30 |
| Head, expression, ears, eyes, and teeth | 20 |
| Body, neck, legs, feet and tail | 20 |
| Gait | 20 |
| Coat, color and texture | 10 |

**Approved August 14, 1984**
**Reformatted March 27, 1990**

# PUG

THE PUG, OR MORE ACCURATELY THE PUG DOG, IS ARGUABLY THE LARGEST of the toy breeds and one of the many companion dog breeds. The Pug originated in the Far East and can be traced to the first century B.C. It was a royal dog in China, owned only by aristocrats and given as treasured gifts to rulers abroad. The oldest surviving breeding records date back to China. They speak of Puglike dogs predominantly with fawn coats, both long and short, as well as of black coats and even parti-colored coats. The fact that records exist telling of dogs with both straight and bowed front legs, suggests some interbreeding with Pekingese, Japanese Chin, and possibly Shih Tzu.

Holland was perhaps the first European country to see Pugs. The Dutch East India Company thrived on commercial ventures in the Orient and Europe. It is highly likely that the company's sailors first brought the Pug to Europe. William III and Mary II came from Holland to Great Britain in 1688 to ascend the throne of England. They brought with them their Pugs, who wore orange ribbons signifying the House of Orange.

Accounts of the Pug's place in history abound. In 1572, a Pug saved the life of William the Silent, Prince of Orange, by barking to warn him of an attack on his camp by Spanish troops. Another refers to a Pug named Fortune who was the beloved companion of Napoleon's Josephine, and who is said to have taken a nip at the general on the couple's wedding night.

The breed suffered rises and falls in popularity, but we are indebted to a few de-voted British fanciers for rescuing them from obscurity and carefully breeding to the type recognized today as proper. Notably among these breeders were a Lady Willoughby d' Eresby and a Charles Morrison. At that time, most Pugs were of the fawn variety. Black Pugs were virtually unknown and had been mongrelized. This changed in 1886, when Britain's Lady Brassey entered a number of her black Pugs in a show at Maidstone, Kent.

Where did the name Pug Dog originate? In France, they are known as *carlin,* in Italy as *carlini,* in Germanic countries as *Mops,* and in the Netherlands as *mophond.* The name Pug seems peculiarly English, but its origin is obscure. Some say the dog's head in profile resembles a clenched fist (*pugnus* in Latin). Others say the Pug's face resembled that of marmoset monkeys, which were a favorite of nineteenth-century ladies and were fondly referred to as mops. These ladies also were known to refer fondly to their husbands as "my mops." Hence, the designation Pug Dog would have distinguished the canine from either husbands or monkeys.

The Pug standard contains the Latin phrase *multum in parvo* ("a lot in a little"). In other words, this is a lot of dog in a little package.

Today's Pugs are a clownish, mischievous, loving, lovable, and devoted breed. They are easy to care for and to groom. Pugs are happy in a city environment or on a country farm, are easily trainable and clean, and love all members of the family, most especially children. They do, however, show partiality toward the hand that feeds them. Pugs demand only one thing: some return of the affection they lavish on their humans.

# OFFICIAL STANDARD FOR THE PUG

**General Appearance**—Symmetry and general appearance are decidedly square and cobby. A lean, leggy Pug and a dog with short legs and a long body are equally ob-jectionable.

**Size, Proportion, Substance**—The Pug should be *multum in parvo,* and this con-densation (if the word may be used) is shown by compactness of form, well knit pro-portions, and hardness of developed muscle. Weight from 14 to 18 pounds (dog or bitch) desirable. *Proportion* square.

**Head**—The *head* is large, massive, round—not apple-headed, with no indentation of the *skull.* The *eyes* are dark in color, very large, bold and prominent, globular in shape, soft and solicitous in *expression,* very lustrous, and, when excited, full of fire. The *ears* are thin, small, soft, like black velvet. There are two kinds—the "rose" and the "button." Preference is given to the latter. The *wrinkles* are large and deep. The *muzzle* is short, blunt, square, but not upfaced. *Bite*—A Pug's bite should be very slightly un-dershot.

**Neck, Topline, Body**—The *neck* is slightly arched. It is strong, thick and with enough length to carry the head proudly. The short *back* is level from the withers to the high tail set. The *body* is short and cobby, wide in chest and well ribbed up. The *tail* is curled as tightly as possible over the hip. The double curl is perfection.

**Forequarters**—The *legs* are very strong, straight, of moderate length, and are set well under. The *elbows* should be directly under the withers when viewed from the side. The *shoulders* are moderately laid back. The *pasterns* are strong, neither steep nor down. The *feet* are neither so long as the foot of the hare, nor so round as that of the cat; well split-up toes, and the nails black. Dewclaws are generally removed.

**Hindquarters**—The strong, powerful hindquarters have moderate bend of *stifle* and short *hocks* perpendicular to the ground. The *legs* are parallel when viewed from behind. The hindquarters are in balance with the forequarters. The *thighs* and *buttocks* are full and muscular. *Feet* as in front.

**Coat**—The coat is fine, smooth, soft, short and glossy, neither hard nor woolly.

**Color**—The colors are silver, apricot-fawn, or black. The silver or apricot-fawn colors should be decided so as to make the contrast complete between the color and the trace and the mask.

**Markings**—The *markings* are clearly defined. The muzzle or mask, ears, moles on cheeks, thumb mark or diamond on forehead, and the back trace should be as black as possible. The mask should be black. The more intense and well defined it is, the better. The trace is a black line extending from the occiput to the tail.

**Gait**—Viewed from the front, the forelegs should be carried well forward, showing no weakness in the pasterns, the paws landing squarely with the central toes straight ahead. The rear action should be strong and free through hocks and stifles, with no twisting or turning in or out at the joints. The hind legs should follow in line with the front. There is a slight natural convergence of the limbs both fore and aft. A slight roll of the hindquarters typifies the gait which should be free, self-assured, and jaunty.

**Temperament**—This is an even-tempered breed, exhibiting stability, playfulness, great charm, dignity, and an outgoing, loving disposition.

**Approved October 8, 1991**
**Effective November 28, 1991**

# SHIH TZU

HE LEGEND OF THE SHIH TZU HAS COME TO US FROM DOCUMENTS, PAINT-
ings, and objets d'art dating from A.D. 624. During the Tang Dynasty, K'iu
T'ai, king of Viqur, gave the Chinese court a pair of dogs, said to have come from
the Fu Lin (assumed to be the Byzantine Empire). Mention of these dogs was again
made in 990–994, when people of the Ho Chou sent dogs as tribute.

Another theory of their introduction to China was recorded in the mid-
seventeenth century, when dogs were brought from Tibet to the Chinese court.
These dogs were bred in the Forbidden City of Peking. Many pictures of them
were kept in *The Imperial Dog Book*. The smallest of these dogs resembled a lion, as
represented in Asian art. In Buddhist belief there is an association between the lion
and their Deity. Shih Tzu means *lion*. The dogs for court breeding were selected
with great care. From these the Shih Tzu known today developed. They were often
called the "chrysanthemum-faced dog" because the hair grows about the face in all
directions.

These dogs were small, intelligent, and extremely docile. It is known that the
breeding of the Shih Tzu was delegated to certain court eunuchs, who vied with
one another to produce specimens which would take the emperor's fancy. Those
selected had their pictures painted on hangings or tapestries, and the eunuchs responsible for the dogs were given gifts by the emperor.

It is known that the Shih Tzu was a house pet during most of the Ming Dynasty and that they were highly favored by the royal family. At the time of the Revolution, many dogs were destroyed and only a few escaped the invaders' knives.

In 1934, the Peking Kennel Club was formed. By 1938 a standard for the Shih Tzu was developed with the help of Madame de Breuil, a Russian refugee.

Breeding of the Shih Tzu began in England after Madelaine Hutchins brought one pair of her own and another of General and Mrs. Douglas Brownrigg's from China in 1930. The breed was first classified as "Apsos," but after a ruling by The Kennel Club (England) that Lhasa Apsos and Shih Tzu were separate breeds, the Shih Tzu Club of England was formed in 1935.

From England, dogs of this breed were sent throughout Europe and to Australia. During World War II, members of the American armed forces stationed in England became acquainted with the breed and on their return brought some back to the United States, thus introducing them to this country. Since then many have been imported.

The Shih Tzu was admitted to registration in the AKC Stud Book in March 1969 and began competing in the Toy Group at AKC shows beginning September of that year.

# OFFICIAL STANDARD FOR THE SHIH TZU

**General Appearance**—The Shih Tzu is a sturdy, lively, alert toy dog with long flowing double coat. Befitting his noble Chinese ancestry as a highly valued, prized companion and palace pet, the Shih Tzu is proud of bearing, has a distinctively arrogant carriage with head well up and tail curved over the back. Although there has always been considerable size variation, the Shih Tzu must be compact, solid, carrying good weight and substance.

Even though a toy dog, the Shih Tzu must be subject to the same requirements of soundness and structure prescribed for all breeds, and any deviation from the ideal described in the standard should be penalized to the extent of the deviation. Structural faults common to all breeds are as undesirable in the Shih Tzu as in any other breed, regardless of whether or not such faults are specifically mentioned in the standard.

**Size, Proportion, Substance**—*Size*—Ideally, height at withers is 9 to 10½ inches; but, not less than 8 inches nor more than 11 inches. Ideally, weight of mature dogs, 9 to 16 pounds. *Proportion*—Length between withers and root of tail is slightly longer than height at withers. *The Shih Tzu must never be so high stationed as to appear leggy, nor so low stationed as to appear dumpy or squatty.* Substance—Regardless of size, the Shih Tzu is *always* compact, solid and carries good weight and substance.

**Head**—*Head*—Round, broad, wide between eyes, its size *in balance* with the overall size of dog being neither too large nor too small. **Fault:** Narrow head, close-set eyes. *Expression*—Warm, sweet, wide-eyed, friendly and trusting. An overall well-balanced and pleasant expression supersedes the importance of individual parts. *Care should be taken to look and examine well beyond the hair to determine if what is seen is the actual head and expression rather than an image created by grooming technique.* *Eyes*—Large, round, not prominent, placed well apart, looking straight ahead. *Very dark.* Lighter on liver pigmented dogs and blue pigmented dogs. *Fault:* Small, close-set or light eyes; excessive eye white. *Ears*—Large, set slightly below crown of skull; heavily coated. *Skull*—Domed. *Stop*—There is a *definite stop.* *Muzzle*—Square, short, unwrinkled, with good cushioning, set no lower than bottom eye rim; never downturned. Ideally, no longer than 1 inch from tip of nose to stop, although length may vary slightly in relation to overall size of dog. Front of muzzle should be flat; lower lip and chin not protruding and definitely never receding. *Fault:* Snipiness, lack of definite stop. *Nose*—Nostrils are broad, wide and open. *Pigmentation*—Nose, lips, eye rims are black on all colors, except liver on liver pigmented dogs and blue on blue pigmented dogs. *Fault:* Pink on nose, lips or eye rims. *Bite*—Undershot. Jaw is broad and wide. A missing tooth or slightly misaligned teeth should not be too severely penalized. Teeth and tongue should not show when mouth is closed. *Fault:* Overshot bite.

**Neck, Topline, Body**—*Of utmost importance is an overall well-balanced dog with no exaggerated features.* *Neck*—Well set-on flowing smoothly into shoulders; of sufficient length to permit natural high head carriage and in balance with height and length of dog. *Topline*—Level. *Body*—Short-coupled and sturdy with no waist or tuck-up. The Shih Tzu is slightly longer than tall. *Fault:* Legginess. *Chest*—Broad and deep with good spring-of-rib, however, not barrel-chested. Depth of ribcage should extend to just below elbow. Distance from elbow to withers is a little greater than from elbow to ground. *Croup*—Flat. *Tail*—Set on high, heavily plumed, carried in curve well over back. Too loose, too tight, too flat, or too low set a tail is undesirable and should be penalized to extent of deviation.

**Forequarters**—*Shoulders*—Well-angulated, well laid-back, well laid-in, fitting smoothly into body. *Legs*—Straight, well-boned, muscular, set well-apart and under chest, with elbows set close to body. *Pasterns*—Strong, perpendicular. *Dewclaws*—May be removed. *Feet*—Firm, well-padded, point straight ahead.

**Hindquarters**—*Angulation of hindquarters should be in balance with forequarters.* *Legs*—Well-boned, muscular, and straight when viewed from rear with well-bent stifles, not close set but in line with forequarters. *Hocks*—Well let down, perpendicular. *Fault:* Hyperextension of hocks. *Dewclaws*—May be removed. *Feet*—Firm, well-padded, point straight ahead.

**Coat**—*Coat*—Luxurious, double-coated, dense, long and flowing. Slight wave permissible. Hair on top of head is tied up. *Fault:* Sparse coat, single coat, curly coat. *Trimming*—Feet, bottom of coat, and anus may be done for neatness and to facilitate movement. *Fault:* Excessive trimming.

**Color and Markings**—*All* are permissible and to be considered *equally.*

**Gait**—The Shih Tzu moves straight and must be shown at its own natural speed, *neither raced nor strung-up,* to evaluate its smooth, flowing, effortless movement with good front reach and equally strong rear drive, level topline, naturally high head carriage, and tail carried in gentle curve over back.

**Temperament**—As the sole purpose of the Shih Tzu is that of a companion and house pet, it is essential that its temperament be outgoing, happy, affectionate, friendly and trusting towards all.

**Approved May 9, 1989**
**Effective June 29, 1989**

# Silky Terrier

*D*EVELOPED AROUND THE TURN OF THE CENTURY IN AUSTRALIA FROM CROSS-ings of native Australian Terriers and imported Yorkshire Terriers, the Silky Terrier encompasses many of the best qualities of both.

A number of Yorkshire Terriers from England were brought into the Australian states of Victoria and New South Wales at the end of the 1800s. In an attempt to improve coat color in the blue and tan Australian Terrier, fanciers bred a few of the larger Yorkie dogs with some of their Australian Terrier bitches. The resulting litters produced individuals, some of which were exhibited as Australian Terriers, some as Yorkies and some as Silkys. The Silkys were then bred together until a recognized type was fixed.

In 1906, a standard was developed for the Silky in Sydney, New South Wales, and a separate standard for the new breed was drawn up at Victoria in 1909. Some discrepancies were apparent between the two standards. The New South Wales standard stated that weights should be over six pounds and under twelve pounds, while the standard in Victoria described two classes, one for weights of under six pounds and the other for six pounds to under twelve pounds. Also, while the New South Wales standard permitted only prick ears, the Victoria standard allowed for both drop and prick ears.

A revised standard was published in 1926 while efforts were being made to stabilize weights. In order to protect the three breeds from further crossings, the Kennel Control Council of Victoria introduced canine legislation in 1932.

Originally known as the Sydney Silky Terrier, in 1955 the official name for the breed in Australia became the Australian Silky Terrier.

The Australian National Kennel Council was formed in 1958 and, aware that the American Kennel Club planned to recognize the breed, one of their first acts was to recommend the development of a national standard for the Australian Silky Terrier. In March 1959, a national standard was approved in which weights were narrowed to "*ideally* from eight to ten pounds."

The first official meeting of the Sydney Silky Terrier Club of America was held on March 25, 1955, and in July the name was changed by a vote of its members to Silky Terrier Club of America.

The Silky Terrier is a lively, friendly, outgoing dog with true terrier temperament and personality. They are devoted to their owners but never forget a familiar face.

# OFFICIAL STANDARD FOR THE SILKY TERRIER

**General Appearance**—The Silky Terrier is a true "toy terrier." He is moderately low set, slightly longer than tall, of refined bone structure, but of sufficient substance to suggest the ability to hunt and kill domestic rodents. His coat is silky in texture, parted from the stop to the tail and presents a well groomed but not sculptured appearance. His inquisitive nature and joy of life make him an ideal companion.

**Size, Proportion, Substance**—*Size*—Shoulder height from nine to ten inches. Deviation in either direction is undesirable. *Proportion*—The body is about one fifth longer than the dog's height at the withers. *Substance*—Lightly built with strong but rather fine bone.

**Head**—The head is strong, wedge-shaped, and moderately long. *Expression* piercingly keen, *eyes* small, dark, almond shaped with dark rims. Light eyes are a serious fault. *Ears* are small, V-shaped, set high and carried erect without any tendency to flare obliquely off the skull. *Skull* flat, and not too wide between the ears. The skull is slightly longer than the muzzle. *Stop* shallow. The *nose* is black. *Teeth* strong and well aligned, scissors bite. An undershot or overshot bite is a serious fault.

**Neck, Topline and Body**—The *neck* fits gracefully into sloping shoulders. It is medium long, fine, and to some degree crested. The *topline* is level. A topline showing a roach or dip is a serious fault. *Chest* medium wide and deep enough to extend down to the elbows. The *body* is moderately low set and about one fifth longer than the dog's height at the withers. The body is measured from the point of the shoulder (or forechest) to the rearmost projection of the upper thigh (or point of the buttocks). A body which is too short is a fault, as is a body which is too long. The *tail* is docked, set high and carried at twelve to two o'clock position.

**Forequarters**—Well laid back shoulders, together with proper angulation at the upper arm, set the forelegs nicely under the body. Forelegs are strong, straight and rather fine-boned. *Feet* small, catlike, round, compact. Pads are thick and springy while nails are strong and dark colored. White or flesh-colored nails are a fault. The feet point straight ahead, with no turning in or out. Dewclaws, if any, are removed.

**Hindquarters**—Thighs well muscled and strong, but not so developed as to appear heavy. Well angulated stifles with low hocks which are parallel when viewed from behind. *Feet* as in front.

**Coat**—Straight, single, glossy, silky in texture. On matured specimens the coat falls below and follows the body outline. It should not approach floor length. On the top of the head, the hair is so profuse as to form a topknot, but long hair on the face and ears is objectionable. The hair is parted on the head and down over the back to the root of the tail. The tail is well coated but devoid of plume. Legs should have short hair from the pastern and hock joints to the feet. The feet should not be obscured by the leg furnishings.

**Color**—Blue and tan. The blue may be silver blue, pigeon blue or slate blue, the tan deep and rich. The blue extends from the base of the skull to the tip of the tail, down the forelegs to the elbows, and half way down the outside of the thighs. On the tail the blue should be very dark. Tan appears on muzzle and cheeks, around the base of the ears, on the legs and feet and around the vent. The topknot should be silver or fawn which is lighter than the tan points.

**Gait**—Should be free, light-footed, lively and straightforward. Hindquarters should have strong propelling power. Toeing in or out is to be faulted.

**Temperament**—The keenly alert air of the terrier is characteristic, with shyness or excessive nervousness to be faulted. The manner is quick, friendly, responsive.

**Approved October 10, 1989**
**Effective November 30, 1989**

# TOY FOX TERRIER

*T*HE TOY FOX TERRIER (TFT) ORIGINATED IN THE UNITED STATES. IT IS truly an American-bred toy dog. Smooth Fox Terriers were the breed's English ancestors, and several small breeds, such as the Toy Manchester Terrier, Italian Greyhound, and quite possibly the Chihuahua, were doubtless intermixed before the Toy Fox Terrier was standardized as the breed we know today. Some believe that the breed's foundation resulted purely from breeding down the Smooth Fox Terrier. Others remain convinced of the influence from the above-mentioned toy breeds. At any rate, the first Toy Fox Terrier was registered at Kalamazoo, Michigan, in 1936.

First recognized and registered by the United Kennel Club, headquartered in Kalamazoo, it was not until January 2003 that the American Kennel Club admitted the Toy Fox Terrier to championship competition in the Toy Group. In the 1970s, there had been some effort put forth to gain AKC recognition, but the goal was not achieved. The first meeting of organizers took place in 1994. From that, a third wave of interested exhibitors pushed forward. There followed a nine-year quest to achieve recognition by the American Kennel Club.

From the beginning, foxhunters liked the gameness of this very small version of the Smooth Fox Terrier. Hunters kept them in saddlebags and released them to chase foxes out of their holes. TFTs serve as mascots for ranches, yachts, and a host of other environments.

Truly a toy as well as a terrier, this animated little bundle of energy is agile, intelligent, and devoted as a companion and family entertainer. The breed is multi-faceted in its ability to go to ground, hunt vermin, and play fetch, as well as conquer fly-ball or agility courses and any number of other competitions. Farmers appreciate their ratting talent, and apartment dwellers find them a perfect match. This is a toy breed to be enjoyed in whatever lifestyle the owner chooses.

The overall appearance of the Toy Fox Terrier is one of a proud, regal, athletic little companion. The basic color is white, with or without body spots matching the primary color of the head. A black head with tan markings may or may not have a moderate blaze of white with white on the muzzle. The body spots would then be black, with or without a small tan fringe on a body spot. Some exhibitors appreciate dogs with completely white bodies. Another color combination is white and tan, with or without body spots, the shades of tan ranging from honey to auburn. A third color combination, white and black, has no tan markings. Fourth, white with chocolate and tan, is similar to the tri-color pattern of white, black, and tan, but with chocolate in place of black. Although there is much in the standard regarding color, it is less important than the correct structure, movement, and type of this little terrier.

Indeed, life is merrier with a Toy Fox Terrier!

# OFFICIAL STANDARD FOR THE TOY FOX TERRIER

**General Appearance**—The Toy Fox Terrier is truly a toy and a terrier and both have influenced his personality and character. As a terrier, the Toy Fox Terrier possesses keen intelligence, courage, and animation. As a toy his is diminutive, and devoted with an endless abiding love for his master. The Toy Fox Terrier is a well-balanced Toy dog of athletic appearance displaying grace and agility in equal measure with strength and stamina. His lithe muscular body has a smooth elegant outline which conveys the impression of effortless movement and endless endurance. He is naturally well groomed, proud, animated, and alert. Characteristic traits are his elegant head, his short glossy and predominantly white coat, coupled with a predominantly solid head, and his short high-set tail.

**Size, Proportion and Substance**—*Size:* 8.5–11.5 inches, 9–11 preferred, 8.5–11.5 acceptable. *Proportion:* The Toy Fox Terrier is square in proportion, with height being approximately equal to length; with height measured from withers to ground and length measured from point of shoulder to buttocks. Slightly longer in bitches is acceptable. *Substance:* Bone must be strong, but not excessive and always in proportion to size. Overall balance is important. *Disqualification:* Any dog under 8.5 inches and over 11.5 inches.

**Head**—The head is elegant, balanced and expressive with no indication of coarseness. *Expression* is intelligent, alert, eager and full of interest. *Eyes:* clear, bright and dark, including eye-rims, with the exception of chocolates whose eye-rims should be self-colored. The eyes are full, round and somewhat prominent, yet never bulging, with a soft intelligent expression. They are set well apart, not slanted, and fit well together into the sockets. *Ears:* The ears are erect, pointed, inverted V-shaped, set high and close together, but never touching. The size is in proportion to the head and body. *Disqualification:* Ears not erect on any dog over six months of age. *Skull:* is moderate in width, slightly rounded and softly wedge shaped. Medium stop, somewhat sloping. When viewed from the front, the head widens gradually from the nose to the base of the ears. The distance from the nose to the stop is equal to the distance from the stop to the occiput. The cheeks are flat and muscular, with the area below the eyes well filled in. *Faults:* Apple head. *Muzzle:* Strong rather than fine, in proportion to the head as a whole and parallel to the top of the skull. *Nose:* Black only with the exception of self-colored in chocolate dogs. *Disqualification:* Dudley nose. *Lips:* are small and tight fitting. *Bite:* a full complement of strong white teeth meeting in a scissors bite is preferred. Loss of teeth should not be faulted as long as the bite can be determined as correct. *Disqualification:* Undershot, wry mouth, overshot more than ⅛ inch.

**Neck, Topline and Body**—The neck is carried proudly erect, well set on, slightly arched, gracefully curved, clean, muscular, and free from throatiness. It is proportioned to the head and body and widens gradually blending smoothly into the shoulders. The length of the neck is approximately the same as that of the head. The *topline* is level when standing and gaiting. The *body* is balanced and tapers slightly from ribs to flank. The *chest* is deep and muscular with well sprung ribs. Depth of chest extends to the point of elbow. The *back* is straight, level, and muscular. Short and strong in loin with moderate tuck-up to denote grace and elegance. The *croup* is level with topline and well-rounded. The *tail* is set high, held erect and in proportion to the size of the dog. Docked to the 3rd or 4th joint.

**Forequarters**—Forequarters are well angulated. The shoulder is firmly set and has adequate muscle, but is not overdeveloped. The shoulders are sloping and well laid back, blending smoothly from neck to back. The forechest is well developed. The elbows are close and perpendicular to the body. The legs are parallel and straight to the pasterns which are strong and straight while remaining flexible. Feet are small and oval, pointing forward turning neither in nor out. Toes are strong, well-arched and closely knit with deep pads.

**Hindquarters**—Hindquarters are well angulated, strong and muscular. The upper and lower thighs are strong, well muscled and of good length. The stifles are clearly defined and well angulated. Hock joints are well let down and firm. The rear pasterns are straight. The legs are parallel from the rear and turn neither in nor out. Dewclaws should be removed from hindquarters if present.

**Coat**—The coat is shiny, satiny, fine in texture and smooth to the touch. It is slightly longer in the ruff, uniformly covering the body.

**Color**—*Tri-Color:* Predominately black head with sharply defined tan markings on cheeks, lips and eye dots. Body is over fifty-percent white, with or without black body spots. *White, Chocolate and Tan:* Predominately chocolate head with sharply defined tan markings on cheeks, lips and eye dots. Body is over fifty-percent white, with or without chocolate body spots. *White and Tan:* Predominately tan head. Body is over fifty-percent white with or without tan body spots. *White and Black:* Predominately black head. Body is over fifty-percent white with or without black body spots. Color should be rich and clear. Blazes are acceptable, but may not touch the eyes or ears. Clear white is preferred, but a small amount of ticking is not to be penalized. Body spots on black headed tri-colors must be black; body spots on chocolate headed tri-colors must be chocolate; both with or without a slight fringe of tan alongside any body spots near the chest and under the tail as seen in normal bi-color patterning. *Faults:* Color, other than ticking, that extends below the elbow or the hock. *Disqualifications:* A blaze extending into the eyes or ears. Any color combination not stated above. Any dog whose head is more than fifty-percent white. Any dog whose body is not more than fifty-percent white. Any dog whose head and body spots are of different colors.

**Gait**—Movement is smooth and flowing with good reach and strong drive. The topline should remain straight and head and tail carriage erect while gaiting. *Fault:* Hackney gait.

**Temperament**—The Toy Fox Terrier is intelligent, alert and friendly, and loyal to its owners. He learns new tasks quickly, is eager to please, and adapts to almost any situation. The Toy Fox Terrier, like other terriers, is self-possessed, spirited, determined and not easily intimidated. He is a highly animated toy dog that is comical, entertaining and playful all of his life. Any individuals lacking good terrier attitude and personality are to be faulted.


## DISQUALIFICATIONS

*Any dog under 8.5 inches or over 11.5 inches.*
*Ears not erect on any dog over six months of age.*
*Dudley nose.*
*Undershot, wry mouth, overshot more than ⅛ inch.*
*A blaze extending into the eye or ears.*
*Any color combination not stated above.*
*Any dog whose head is more than fifty percent white.*
*Any dog whose body is not more than fifty percent white.*
*Any dog whose head and body spots are of different colors.*

**Approved July 8, 2003**
**Effective August 27, 2003**

# YORKSHIRE TERRIER

*T*HE YORKSHIRE TERRIER BECAME A FASHIONABLE PET IN THE LATE VICTORIAN era. But in its beginnings it belonged to the working class, especially the weavers. In fact, it was so closely linked to them that many facetious comments were made regarding the fine texture of its extremely long, silky coat, inferring it was the ultimate product of the looms.

The Yorkshire Terrier made its first appearance at a benched show in England in 1861 as a "broken-haired Scotch Terrier." It became known as a Yorkshire Terrier in 1870 when, after the Westmoreland show, Angus Sutherland—the reporter for *The Field*—wrote, "They ought no longer to be called Scotch Terriers, but Yorkshire Terriers for having been so improved there." For a number of years thereafter classes were offered for the breed as Yorkshire Terriers, as well as Brokenhaired Scotch Terriers. Often members of the same litter were shown in classes of both designations.

The Yorkshire Terrier traces to the Waterside Terrier, a small longish-coated dog, bluish-gray in color, weighing between six and twenty pounds (most commonly ten pounds). A breed common in Yorkshire since early times, the Waterside Terrier—crossed with the old rough-coated Black-and-Tan English Terrier (common in the Manchester area) and with the Paisley and Clydesdale Terriers—was brought to Yorkshire by the Scotch weavers who migrated from Scotland to England in the mid-nineteenth century. All these breeds were bred together to make what is now known as the Yorkshire Terrier.

The earliest record of a Yorkshire Terrier born in the United States dates to 1872. Classes for the breed have been offered at all shows since 1878. At early shows, these classes were divided by weight—under five pounds, and five pounds and over. However, the size soon settled down to an average of between three and seven pounds. Only one class was offered when it became apparent from records that the class for larger dogs was rarely filled as well as the one for smaller dogs.

Modern specimens of the Yorkshire Terrier breed true to type, and their characteristics are well fixed. Coloring is distinctive, with their metallic colors being a dark steel-blue from the occiput to the root of the tail, and a rich golden tan on head, legs, chest, and breeches. Puppies that develop to correct adult colors are always born black with tan markings.

Though a toy, and at times a greatly pampered one, the Yorkshire is a spirited dog that definitely shows its terrier strain. The length of the show dog's coat makes constant care necessary to protect it from damage, but the breed is glad to engage in all the roistering activities of the larger terrier breeds.

# OFFICIAL STANDARD FOR THE YORKSHIRE TERRIER

**General Appearance**—That of a long-haired toy terrier whose blue-and-tan coat is parted on the face and from the base of the skull to the end of the tail and hangs evenly and quite straight down each side of body. The body is neat, compact and well proportioned. The dog's high head carriage and confident manner should give the appearance of vigor and self-importance.

**Head**—Small and rather flat on top, *the skull* not too prominent or round, *the muzzle* not too long, with *the bite* neither undershot nor overshot and teeth sound. Either scissors bite or level bite is acceptable. *The nose* is black. *Eyes* are medium in size and not too prominent; dark in color and sparkling with a sharp, intelligent expression. Eye rims are dark. *Ears* are small, V-shaped, carried erect and set not too far apart.

**Body**—Well proportioned and very compact. The back is rather short, the back line level, with height at shoulder the same as at the rump.

**Legs and Feet**—*Forelegs* should be straight, elbows neither in nor out. *Hind legs* straight when viewed from behind, but stifles are moderately bent when viewed from the sides. *Feet* are round with black toenails. Dewclaws, if any, are generally removed from the hind legs. Dewclaws on the forelegs may be removed.

**Tail**—Docked to a medium length and carried slightly higher than the level of the back.

**Coat**—Quality, texture and quantity of coat are of prime importance. Hair is glossy, fine and silky in texture. Coat on the body is moderately long and perfectly straight (not wavy). It may be trimmed to floor length to give ease of movement and a neater appearance, if desired. The fall on the head is long, tied with one bow in center of head or parted in the middle and tied with two bows. Hair on muzzle is very long. Hair should be trimmed short on tips of ears and may be trimmed on feet to give them a neat appearance.

**Colors**—Puppies are born black and tan and are normally darker in body color, showing an intermingling of black hair in the tan until they are matured. Color of hair on body and richness of tan on head and legs are of prime importance in *adult dogs,* to which the following color requirements apply:

*Blue:* Is a dark steel-blue, not a silver-blue and not mingled with fawn, bronzy or black hairs.

*Tan:* All tan hair is darker at the roots than in the middle, shading to still lighter tan at the tips. There should be no sooty or black hair intermingled with any of the tan.

**Color on Body**—The blue extends over the body from back of neck to root of tail. Hair on tail is a darker blue, especially at end of tail.

**Headfall**—A rich golden tan, deeper in color at sides of head, at ear roots and on the muzzle, with ears a deep rich tan. Tan color should not extend down on back of neck.

**Chest and Legs**—A bright, rich tan, not extending above the elbow on the forelegs nor above the stifle on the hind legs.

**Weight**—Must not exceed seven pounds.

**Approved April 12, 1966**

# GROUP VI:
# NON-SPORTING BREEDS

AMERICAN ESKIMO DOG
BICHON FRISE
BOSTON TERRIER
BULLDOG
CHINESE SHAR-PEI
CHOW CHOW
DALMATIAN
FINNISH SPITZ
FRENCH BULLDOG

KEESHOND
LHASA APSO
LÖWCHEN
POODLE (MINIATURE AND
    STANDARD)
SCHIPPERKE
SHIBA INU
TIBETAN SPANIEL
TIBETAN TERRIER

# AMERICAN ESKIMO DOG

*T*HE AMERICAN ESKIMO DOG, NICKNAMED THE "ESKIE," IS A NORDIC breed that is always white or white with biscuit cream. The American Eskimo dog is bred in three distinct sizes: toy (9 to and including 12 inches); miniature (over 12 to and including 15 inches); and standard (over 15 to and including 19 inches). Sizes under 9 inches or over 19 inches are disqualifications.

The Eskie is a member of the spitz family, or Nordic breeds, as many fanciers prefer to call this group of dogs. The Eskimo Dog is almost certainly descended from the European spitzes, including the white German Spitz, the white Keeshond, the white Pomeranian, and the Volpino Italiano (white Italian Spitz). After World War II, American breeders on the West Coast may even have incorporated some Japanese Spitz into the Eskie.

During the nineteenth century, small, white spitz-type dogs were commonly found in American communities of German immigrants. These dogs were probably descendants of white German Spitz, white Keeshonden, or large white Pomeranians that emigrated with their European masters. The immigrants' dogs could not be recognized in their native countries after reaching the United States. They came to be known collectively as the American Spitz.

Beginning in the late nineteenth century, the American Eskimo Dog was extremely popular for use in trick-dog acts in the many traveling circuses throughout the United States. For the public, this breed has had much appeal because of its sparkling white coat and quickness. Circus trainers favored the breed for this reason and also because of the Eskie's innate intelligence, trainability, and unsurpassed agility. These circus dogs helped develop and spread the popularity of the American Eskimo Dog.

Although the American Spitz was dubbed the American Eskimo in 1917, the exact reason for selecting this name is unknown. One theory is that the word *Eskimo* would associate the breed with various breeds of large, Nordic dogs developed by those Native American peoples. (The Eskie appears to be a miniaturized version of the Eskimos' sled dogs.)

In 1985 the American Eskimo Dog Club of America (AEDCA), the national parent club, was formed to work for AKC recognition for the breed as well as to protect and promote the purebred American Eskimo Dog as set forth by the AKC.

The AEDCA opened its studbook in 1986, and it was transferred to the AKC in November 1993. More than 1,750 American Eskimo Dogs were registered as foundation stock in the AKC Stud Book. The American Eskimo Dog was given Non-Sporting Group status and became eligible for full recognition on July 1, 1995.

# OFFICIAL STANDARD FOR THE AMERICAN ESKIMO DOG

**General Appearance**—The American Eskimo Dog, a loving companion dog, presents a picture of strength and agility, alertness and beauty. It is a small to medium-size Nordic-type dog, always white, or white with biscuit cream. The American Eskimo Dog is compactly built and well balanced, with good substance, and an alert, smooth gait. The face is Nordic type with erect triangular shaped ears, and distinctive black points (lips, nose, and eye rims). The white double coat consists of a short, dense undercoat, with a longer guard hair growing through it forming the outer coat, which is straight with no curl or wave. The coat is thicker and longer around the neck and chest forming a lion-like ruff, which is more noticeable on dogs than on bitches. The rump and hind legs down to the hocks are also covered with thicker, longer hair forming the characteristic breeches. The richly plumed tail is carried loosely on the back.

**Size, Proportion, Substance**—*Size*—There are three separate size divisions of the American Eskimo Dog (all measurements are heights at withers): Toy, 9 inches to and including 12 inches; Miniature, over 12 inches to and including 15 inches; and Standard, over 15 inches to and including 19 inches. There is no preference for size within each division. *Disqualification: Under 9 inches or over 19 inches. Proportion*—Length of back from point of shoulder to point of buttocks is slightly greater than height at withers, an approximate 1.1 to 1 ratio. *Substance*—The American Eskimo Dog is strong and compactly built with adequate bone.

**Head**—*Expression* is keen, intelligent and alert. *Eyes* are not fully round, but slightly oval. They should be set well apart, and not slanted, prominent or bulging. Tear stain, unless severe, is not to be faulted. Presence of tear stain should not outweigh consideration of type, structure or temperament. Dark to medium brown is the preferred eye color. Eye rims are black to dark brown. Eyelashes are white. Faults: amber eye color or pink eye rims. *Disqualification: blue eyes.* Ears should conform to head size and be triangular, slightly blunt-tipped, held erect, set on high yet well apart, and blend softly with the head. *Skull* is slightly crowned and softly wedge-shaped, with widest breadth between the ears. The stop is well defined, although not abrupt. The *muzzle* is broad, with length not exceeding the length of the skull, although it may be slightly shorter. *Nose* pigment is black to dark brown. *Lips* are thin and tight, black to dark brown in color. Faults: pink nose pigment or pink lip pigment. The *jaw* should be strong with a full complement of close fitting teeth. The *bite* is scissors, or pincer.

**Neck, Topline, Body**—The *neck* is carried proudly erect, well set on, medium in length, and in a strong, graceful arch. The *topline* is level. The *body* of the American Eskimo Dog is strong and compact, but not cobby. The chest is deep and broad with well-sprung ribs. Depth of chest extends approximately to point of elbows. Slight tuck-up of belly just behind the ribs. The back is straight, broad, level, and muscular. The loin is strong and well-muscled. The American Eskimo Dog is neither too long nor too short coupled. The *tail* is set moderately high and reaches approximately to the point of hock when down. It is carried loosely on the back, although it may be dropped when at rest.

**Forequarters**—Forequarters are well angulated. The shoulder is firmly set and has adequate muscle but is not overdeveloped. The shoulder blades are well laid back and slant 45° with the horizontal. At the point of shoulder the shoulder blade forms an approximate right angle with the upper arm. The legs are parallel and straight to the pasterns. The pasterns are strong and flexible with a slant of about 20°. Length of leg in proportion to the body. Dewclaws on the front legs may be removed at the owner's discretion; if present, they are not to be faulted. Feet are oval, compact, tightly knit and well padded with hair. Toes are well arched. Pads are black to dark brown, tough and deeply cushioned. Toenails are white.

**Hindquarters**—Hindquarters are well angulated. The lay of the pelvis is approximately 30° to the horizontal. The upper thighs are well developed. Stifles are well bent. Hock joints are well let down and firm. The rear pasterns are straight. Legs are parallel from the rear and turn neither in nor out. Feet are as described for the front legs. Dewclaws are not present on the hind legs.

**Coat**—The American Eskimo Dog has a stand-off, double coat consisting of a dense undercoat and a longer coat of guard hair growing through it to form the outer coat. It is straight with no curl or wave. There is a pronounced ruff around the neck which is more noticeable on dogs than bitches. Outer part of the ear should be well covered with short, smooth hair, with longer tufts of hair growing in front of ear openings. Hair on muzzle should be short and smooth. The backs of the front legs should be well feathered, as are the rear legs down to the hock. The tail is covered profusely with long hair. THERE IS TO BE NO TRIMMING OF THE WHISKERS OR BODY COAT AND SUCH TRIMMING WILL BE SEVERELY PENALIZED. The only permissible trimming is to neaten the feet and the backs of the rear pasterns.

**Color**—Pure white is the preferred color, although white with biscuit cream is permissible. Presence of biscuit cream should not outweigh consideration of type, structure or temperament. The skin of the American Eskimo Dog is pink or gray. *Disqualification: any color other than white or biscuit cream.*

**Gait**—The American Eskimo Dog shall trot, not pace. The gait is agile, bold, well balanced and frictionless, with good forequarter reach and good hindquarter drive. As speed increases, the American Eskimo Dog will single track with the legs converging toward the center line of gravity while the back remains firm, strong and level.

**Temperament**—The American Eskimo Dog is intelligent, alert and friendly, although slightly conservative. It is never overly shy nor aggressive, and such dogs are to be severely penalized in the show ring. At home it is an excellent watchdog, sounding a warning bark to announce the arrival of any stranger. It is protective of its home and family, although it does not threaten to bite or attack people. The American Eskimo Dog learns new tasks quickly and is eager to please.

## DISQUALIFICATIONS

*Any color other than white or biscuit cream*
*Blue eyes*
*Height: under 9 inches or over 19 inches.*

**Approved October 11, 1994**
**Effective November 30, 1994**

# BICHON FRISE

*T*HE BICHON, LIKE HIS COUSIN THE CANICHE, DESCENDED FROM THE Barbet or Water-Spaniel, from which came the name *Barbichon,* later contracted to Bichon. The Bichons were divided into four categories: the Bichon Maltais, the Bichon Bolognais, the Bichon Havanais, and the Bichon Teneriffe. All originated in the Mediterranean region.

Appreciated for their dispositions, the dogs traveled much through antiquity. Frequently offered as items of barter, they were transported by sailors from continent to continent. The dogs found early success in Spain and it is generally felt that Spanish seamen introduced the breed to the Canary Island of Teneriffe. Most sources agree that in this period the name *Teneriffe* was retained mainly because of its slightly exotic nature and the enhanced commercial value the name gave the common Bichon.

In the 1300s, Italian sailors rediscovered the little dogs on their voyages and are credited with returning them to the Continent, where they became great favorites with Italian nobility, and as with other dogs of that era, were often cut "lion style."

The Teneriffe, or Bichon, made its appearance in France under Francis I, the patron of the Renaissance (1515–47). However, its greatest success was in the court of Henry III (1574–89), where it was pampered, perfumed, and beribboned. The breed also enjoyed considerable success in Spain as a favorite of the *infantas* (princesses), and painters of the Spanish school often included them in their works. One finds such a dog in several of the paintings of Goya.

After a brief renewal of interest under Napoleon III, the fate of this aristocratic dog took a new turn. In the late 1800s, it became the "common dog," running the streets, accompanying the organ grinders of Barbary, leading the blind, and doing tricks in circuses and at fairs.

At the end of World War I a few fanciers recognized the potential of the dogs, and in France four breeders began establishing their lines through controlled breeding programs. On March 5, 1933, the official standard of the breed (as written by the president of the Toy Club of France, in conjunction with the Friends of the Belgian Breeds) was adopted by the Société Centrale Canine of France. As the breed was known by two names, "Teneriffe" and "Bichon," the president of the International Canine Federation, Madame Nizet de Leemans, proposed a name based on the characteristics that the dogs presented, and the name Bichon Frise (plural, Bichons Frises) was adopted. *Frise* refers to the dog's soft, curly hair. On October 18, 1934, the Bichon was admitted to the studbook of the French Kennel Club. The International Canine Federation recognizes the Bichon Frise as a "French-Belgian breed having the right to registration in the Book of Origins from all countries." The breed is recognized in France, Belgium, and Italy.

In 1956, Mr. and Mrs. Francois Picault moved to the United States and settled in the Midwest, where Etoile de Steren Vor whelped the first Bichon litter born in this country (sired by Eddie White de Steren Vor). In 1959 and 1960, two breeders in different parts of the United States acquired Bichons, thus providing the origins for breed development in this country.

Accepted for entry in the Miscellaneous class on September 1, 1971, the Bichon Frise was admitted to registration in the AKC Stud Book in October 1972, and to regular show classification in the Non-Sporting Group at AKC shows April 4, 1973.

# OFFICIAL STANDARD FOR THE BICHON FRISE

**General Appearance**—The Bichon Frise is a small, sturdy, white powder puff of a dog whose merry temperament is evidenced by his plumed tail carried jauntily over the back and his dark-eyed inquisitive expression.

This is a breed that has no gross or incapacitating exaggerations, and therefore, there is no inherent reason for lack of balance or unsound movement.

Any deviation from the ideal described in the standard should be penalized to the extent of the deviation. Structural faults common to all breeds are as undesirable in the Bichon Frise as in any other breed, even though such faults may not be specifically mentioned in the standard.

**Size, Proportion, Substance**—*Size*—Dogs and bitches 9½ to 11½ inches are to be given primary preference. Only where the comparative superiority of a specimen outside this range clearly justifies it should greater latitude be taken. In no case, however, should this latitude ever extend over 12 inches or under 9 inches. The minimum limits do not apply to puppies. *Proportion*—The body from the forward-most point of the chest to the point of rump is ¼ longer than the height at the withers. The body from the withers to lowest point of chest represents ½ the distance from withers to ground. *Substance*—Compact and of medium bone throughout; neither coarse nor fine.

**Head**—*Expression*—Soft, dark-eyed, inquisitive, alert. *Eyes* are round, black or dark brown and are set in the skull to look directly forward. An overly large or bulging eye is a fault as is an almond shaped, obliquely set eye. Halos, the black or very dark brown skin surrounding the eyes, are necessary as they accentuate the eye and enhance expression. The eye rims themselves must be black. Broken pigment, or total absence of pigment on the eye rims produce a blank and staring expression, which is a definite fault. Eyes of any color other than black or dark brown are a very serious fault and must be severely penalized. *Ears* are drop and are covered with long flowing hair. When extended toward the nose, the leathers reach approximately halfway the length of the muzzle. They are set on slightly higher than eye level and rather forward on the skull, so that when the dog is alert they serve to frame the face. The *skull* is slightly rounded, allowing for a round and forward looking eye. The *stop* is slightly accentuated. *Muzzle*—A properly balanced head is three parts muzzle to five parts skull, measured from the nose to the stop and from the stop to the occiput. A line drawn between the outside corners of the eyes and to the nose will create a near equilateral triangle. There is a slight degree of chiseling under the eyes, but not so much as to result in a weak or snipy foreface. The lower jaw is strong. The *nose* is prominent and always black. *Lips* are black, fine, never drooping. *Bite* is scissors. A bite which is undershot or overshot should be severely penalized. A crooked or out of line tooth is permissible, however, missing teeth are to be severely faulted.

**Neck, Topline and Body**—The arched *neck* is long and carried proudly behind an erect head. It blends smoothly into the shoulders. The length of neck from occiput to withers is approximately ⅓ the distance from forechest to buttocks. The *topline* is level except for a slight, muscular arch over the loin. *Body*—The chest is well developed and wide enough to allow free and unrestricted movement of the front legs. The lowest point of the chest extends at least to the elbow. The rib cage is moderately sprung and extends back to a short and muscular loin. The forechest is well pronounced and protrudes slightly forward of the point of shoulder. The underline has a moderate tuckup. *Tail* is well plumed, set on level with the topline and curved gracefully over the back so that the hair of the tail rests on the back. When the tail is extended toward the head it reaches at least halfway to the withers. A low tail set, a tail carried perpendicularly to the back, or a tail which droops behind is to be severely penalized. A corkscrew tail is a very serious fault.

**Forequarters**—*Shoulders*—The shoulder blade, upper arm and forearm are approximately equal in length. The shoulders are laid back to somewhat near a forty-five-degree angle. The upper arm extends well back so the elbow is placed directly below the withers when viewed from the side. *Legs* are of medium bone; straight, with no bow or curve in the forearm or wrist. The elbows are held close to the body. The *pasterns* slope slightly from the vertical. The dewclaws may be removed. The *feet* are tight and round, resembling those of a cat and point directly forward, turning neither in nor out. *Pads* are black. *Nails* are kept short.

**Hindquarters**—The hindquarters are of medium bone, well angulated with muscular thighs and spaced moderately wide. The upper and lower thigh are nearly equal in length meeting at a well bent stifle joint. The leg from hock joint to foot pad is perpendicular to the ground. Dewclaws may be removed. Paws are tight and round with black pads.

**Coat**—The texture of the coat is of utmost importance. The undercoat is soft and dense, the outercoat of a coarser and curlier texture. The combination of the two gives a soft but substantial feel to the touch which is similar to plush or velvet and when patted springs back. When bathed and brushed, it stands off the body, creating an overall powder puff appearance. A wiry coat is not desirable. A limp, silky coat, a coat that lies down, or a lack of undercoat are very serious faults. *Trimming*—The coat is trimmed to reveal the natural outline of the body. It is rounded off from any direction and never cut so short as to create an overly trimmed or squared off appearance. The furnishings of the head, beard, mustache, ears and tail are left longer. The longer head hair is trimmed to create an overall rounded impression. The topline is trimmed to appear level. The coat is long enough to maintain the powder puff look which is characteristic of the breed.

**Color**—Color is white, may have shadings of buff, cream or apricot around the ears or on the body. Any color in excess of 10% of the entire coat of a mature specimen is a fault and should be penalized, but color of the accepted shadings should not be faulted in puppies.

**Gait**—Movement at a trot is free, precise and effortless. In profile the forelegs and hind legs extend equally with an easy reach and drive that maintain a steady topline. When moving, the head and neck remain somewhat erect and as speed increases there is a very slight convergence of legs toward the center line. Moving away, the hindquarters travel with moderate width between them and the foot pads can be seen. Coming and going, his movement is precise and true.

**Temperament**—Gentle mannered, sensitive, playful and affectionate. A cheerful attitude is the hallmark of the breed and one should settle for nothing less.

**Approved October 11, 1988**
**Effective November 30, 1988**

# BOSTON TERRIER

*A* TRUE AMERICAN BREED, THE BOSTON TERRIER WAS THE RESULT OF A cross between an English Bulldog and a white English Terrier, later considerably inbred. Incidental peculiarities of the first dogs used as sires are partly responsible for the present type.

About the year 1870 Robert C. Hooper, of Boston, came into the possession of an imported dog named Judge, which he purchased from William O'Brien of the same city. Judge, commonly known as "Hooper's Judge" and destined to be the ancestor of almost all true modern Bostons, was a cross between a Bulldog and an English Terrier, and in type he resembled the former. He was a well-built, high-stationed dog of about thirty-two pounds, of dark brindle color with white blaze. His head was square and blocky and his mouth nearly even. Judge was mated to "Gyp or Kate," as the name appears on old-time pedigrees. This white bitch, owned by Edward Burnett, of Southboro, Massachusetts, weighed around twenty pounds; she was low and square.

From the mating of Judge and Gyp descended Wells' Eph, a dog of strong build and, like his dam, low stationed. He was dark brindle with even white markings and a nearly even mouth. Eph was bred to Tobin's Kate, a comparatively small twenty-pound female with fairly short head and straight three-quarter tail. She was golden brindle in color. From these dogs in the main evolved the Boston Terrier breed.

In the year 1889 about thirty fanciers in and around Boston organized what was known as the American Bull Terrier Club, and they exhibited the dogs as Round Heads or Bull Terriers. As time went on, these fanciers met with considerable opposition from Bull Terrier and Bulldog fanciers who objected to the similarity of breed name, pointing out that this new breed was so unlike their own. The AKC was also not convinced that these dogs would breed true to their type, having been established over such a short time. The Boston Terrier fanciers, however, refused to be discouraged and in 1891 formed the Boston Terrier Club of America. As their dog was bred in Boston, they changed the name to Boston Terrier. After two years of sustained effort to have the Boston recognized as a purebred, they succeeded in persuading the American Kennel Club to admit the breed to the Stud Book in 1893 and the club to membership.

Up to this time, of course, the Boston Terrier was only in its infancy. There was hard work ahead to standardize the breed and to make the Bostons of that day into a more even lot. Great progress has been made, however, since 1900 in developing different strains by careful, selective breeding, which included a certain amount of inbreeding. The result is a clean-cut dog, with short head, snow-white markings, dark, soft eyes, and a body approximately the conformation of the terrier rather than the Bulldog.

The Boston, while not a fighter, is well able to take care of himself. He has a characteristically gentle disposition that has won him the nickname "the American Gentleman." As a companion and house pet, he is eminently suitable.

# OFFICIAL STANDARD FOR THE BOSTON TERRIER

**General Appearance**—The Boston Terrier is a lively, highly intelligent, smooth coated, short-headed, compactly built, short-tailed, well balanced dog, brindle, seal or black in color and evenly marked with white. The head is in proportion to the size of the dog and the expression indicates a high degree of intelligence.

The body is rather short and well knit, the limbs strong and neatly turned, the tail is short and no feature is so prominent that the dog appears badly proportioned. The dog conveys an impression of determination, strength and activity, with style of a high order; carriage easy and graceful. A proportionate combination of "Color and White Markings" is a particularly distinctive feature of a representative specimen.

"Balance, Expression, Color and White Markings" should be given particular consideration in determining the relative value of GENERAL APPEARANCE to other points.

**Size, Proportion, Substance**—Weight is divided by classes as follows: Under 15 pounds; 15 pounds and under 20 pounds; 20 pounds and not to exceed 25 pounds. The length of leg must balance with the length of body to give the Boston Terrier its striking square appearance. The Boston Terrier is a sturdy dog and must not appear to be either spindly or coarse. The bone and muscle must be in proportion as well as an enhancement to the dog's weight and structure. *Fault:* Blocky or chunky in appearance.

*Influence of Sex.* In a comparison of specimens of each sex, the only evident difference is a slight refinement in the bitch's conformation.

**Head**—The *skull* is square, flat on top, free from wrinkles, cheeks flat, brow abrupt and the stop well defined. The ideal Boston Terrier *expression* is alert and kind, indicating a high degree of intelligence. This is a most important characteristic of the breed. The *eyes* are wide apart, large and round and dark in color. The eyes are set square in the skull and the outside corners are on a line with the cheeks as viewed from the front. *Disqualify:* Eyes blue in color or any trace of blue. The *ears* are small, carried erect, either natural or cropped to conform to the shape of the head and situated as near to the corners of the skull as possible.

The *muzzle* is short, square, wide and deep and in proportion to the skull. It is free from wrinkles, shorter in length than in width or depth; not exceeding in length approximately one-third of the length of the skull. The muzzle from stop to end of the nose is parallel to the top of the skull.

The *nose* is black and wide, with a well defined line between the nostrils. *Disqualify:* Dudley nose.

The *jaw* is broad and square with short regular teeth. The bite is even or sufficiently undershot to square the muzzle. The chops are of good depth, but not pendulous, completely covering the teeth when the mouth is closed. *Serious Fault:* Wry mouth.

*Head Faults:* Eyes showing too much white or haw. Pinched or wide nostrils. Size of ears out of proportion to the size of the head. *Serious Head Faults:* Any showing of the tongue or teeth when the mouth is closed.

**Neck, Topline and Body**—The length of *neck* must display an image of balance to the total dog. It is slightly arched, carrying the head gracefully and setting neatly into the shoulders. The *back* is just short enough to square the body. The *topline* is level and the rump curves slightly to the set-on of the tail. The *chest* is deep with good width, ribs well sprung and carried well back to the loins. The body should appear short. The *tail* is set on low, short, fine and tapering, straight or screw and must not be carried above the horizontal. (Note: The preferred tail does not exceed in length more than one-quarter the distance from set-on to hock.) *Disqualify:* Docked tail.

*Body Faults:* Gaily carried tail. *Serious Body Faults:* Roach back, sway back, slab-sided.

**Forequarters**—The *shoulders* are sloping and well laid back, which allows for the Boston Terrier's stylish movement. The *elbows* stand neither in nor out. The *forelegs* are set moderately wide apart and on a line with the upper tip of the shoulder blades. The forelegs are straight in bone with short, strong pasterns. The dewclaws may be removed. The *feet* are small, round and compact, turned neither in nor out, with well arched toes and short nails. *Faults:* Legs lacking in substance; splay feet.

**Hindquarters**—The *thighs* are strong and well muscled, bent at the stifles and set true. The *hocks* are short to the feet, turning neither in nor out, with a well defined hock joint. The *feet* are small and compact with short nails. *Fault:* Straight in stifle.

**Gait**—The gait of the Boston Terrier is that of a sure footed, straight gaited dog, forelegs and hind legs moving straight ahead in line with perfect rhythm, each step indicating grace and power. *Gait Faults:* There will be no rolling, paddling, or weaving, when gaited. Hackney gait. *Serious Gait Faults:* Any crossing movement, either front or rear.

**Coat**—The coat is short, smooth, bright and fine in texture.

**Color and Markings**—Brindle, seal, or black with white markings. Brindle is preferred ONLY if all other qualities are equal. (Note: SEAL DEFINED. Seal appears black except it has a red cast when viewed in the sun or bright light.) *Disqualify:* Solid black, solid brindle or solid seal without required white markings. Gray or liver colors.

*Required Markings:* White muzzle band, white blaze between the eyes, white forechest.

*Desired Markings:* White muzzle band, even white blaze between the eyes and over the head, white collar, white forechest, white on part or whole of forelegs and hind legs below the hocks. (Note: A representative specimen should not be penalized for not possessing "Desired Markings.")

A dog with a preponderance of white on the head or body must possess sufficient merit otherwise to counteract its deficiencies.

**Temperament**—The Boston Terrier is a friendly and lively dog. The breed has an excellent disposition and a high degree of intelligence, which makes the Boston Terrier an incomparable companion.

**Summary**—The clean-cut short backed body of the Boston Terrier coupled with the unique characteristics of his square head and jaw, and his striking markings have resulted in a most dapper and charming American original: The Boston Terrier.

## SCALE OF POINTS

| | |
|---|---|
| General Appearance | 10 |
| Expression | 10 |
| Head (Muzzle, Jaw, Bite, Skull & Stop) | 15 |
| Eyes | 5 |
| Ears | 5 |
| Neck, Topline, Body & Tail | 15 |
| Forequarters | 10 |
| Hindquarters | 10 |
| Feet | 5 |
| Color, Coat & Markings | 5 |
| Gait | 10 |
| **Total** | **100** |

## DISQUALIFICATIONS

*Eyes blue in color or any trace of blue.*
*Dudley nose.*

*Docked tail.*

*Solid black, solid brindle, or solid seal without required white markings.*

*Gray or liver colors.*

**Approved January 9, 1990**
**Effective February 28, 1990**

# BULLDOG

To the best of our knowledge the Bulldog had its origin in the British Isles, the word *bull* being applied because of the dog's use in connection with bullbaiting.

Exactly when this activity began is impossible to say, but in *The Survey of Stamford* the following reference is made to its probable origin:

> William Earl Warren, Lord of this town in the reign of King John (1209), standing upon the walls of his castle at Stamford, saw two bulls fighting for a cow in the castle meadow, till all the butchers' dogs pursued one of the bulls, which was maddened by the noise and multitude, through the town. This so pleased the Earl that he gave the castle meadow where the bulls combat began, for a common to the butchers of the town after the first grass was mowed, on condition that they should find a "mad bull" on a day six weeks before Christmas for the continuance of that sport forever.

Anyone who has read about the "sport" of bullbaiting knows of its extreme cruelty. From this we can gather that the original Bulldog had to be a truly ferocious animal. Beauty and symmetry of form were in no way desirable, the appearance of the dog counting for nothing. The extraordinary courage possessed by these dogs is hardly believable. Bred from a long line of fighting ancestors, they grew to be so savage and so courageous as to be almost insensitive to pain. Such was the Bulldog of British sporting days.

Then came the year 1835, when dogfighting as a sport became illegal in England. To all intents and purposes, therefore, the English Bulldog had outlived his usefulness; his days were numbered. There were, however, dog lovers who felt a deep disappointment at the passing of so fine a breed, so they quickly set themselves the task of preserving it. Though ferocity was no longer necessary or desirable, they wished to retain all the dog's other splendid qualities. With this in mind, they proceeded to eliminate the undesirable characteristics and to preserve and accentuate the finer qualities. Within a few generations the English Bulldog became one of the finest physical specimens, minus its original viciousness.

This is the Bulldog we know today, a breed of which we may be justly proud. At the same time we must express our gratitude to our British cousins, who preserved him for posterity. The modern Bulldog is both docile and very adaptive. He is happy in an apartment or a large yard. He is an excellent family pet and loves children. His short, smooth coat makes him a favorite for owners to show, requiring only a face wash and a nail trimming. His capacious body and short nose make it important to protect him from overheating; however, with common sense, he can live happily even in a warm climate.

# OFFICIAL STANDARD FOR THE BULLDOG

**General Appearance**—The perfect Bulldog must be of medium size and smooth coat; with heavy, thick-set, low-swung body, massive short-faced head, wide shoulders and sturdy limbs. The general appearance and attitude should suggest great stability, vigor and strength. The disposition should be equable and kind, resolute and courageous (not vicious or aggressive), and demeanor should be pacific and dignified. These attributes should be countenanced by the expression and behavior.

**Size, Proportion, Symmetry**—*Size*—The size for mature dogs is about 50 pounds; for mature bitches about 40 pounds. *Proportion*—The circumference of the skull in front of the ears should measure at least the height of the dog at the shoulders. *Symmetry*—The "points" should be well distributed and bear good relation one to the other, no feature being in such prominence from either excess or lack of quality that the animal appears deformed or ill-proportioned. *Influence of Sex*—In comparison of specimens of different sex, due allowance should be made in favor of the bitches, which do not bear the characteristics of the breed to the same degree of perfection and grandeur as do the dogs.

**Head**—*Eyes and Eyelids*—The eyes, seen from the front, should be situated low down in the skull, as far from the ears as possible, and their corners should be in a straight line at right angles with the stop. They should be quite in front of the head, as wide apart as possible, provided their outer corners are within the outline of the cheeks when viewed from the front. They should be quite round in form, of moderate size, neither sunken nor bulging, and in color should be very dark. The lids should cover the white of the eyeball, when the dog is looking directly forward, and the lid should show no "haw." *Ears*—The ears should be set high in the head, the front inner edge of each ear joining the outline of the skull at the top back corner of skull, so as to place them as wide apart, and as high, and as far from the eyes as possible. In size they should be small and thin. The shape termed "rose ear" is the most desirable. The rose ear folds inward at its back lower edge, the upper front edge curving over, outward and backward, showing part of the inside of the burr. (The ears should not be carried erect or prickeared or buttoned and should never be cropped.) *Skull*—The skull should be very large, and in circumference, in front of the ears, should measure at least the height of the dog at the shoulders. Viewed from the front, it should appear very high from the corner of the lower jaw to the apex of the skull, and also very broad and square. Viewed at the side, the head should appear very high, and very short from the point of the nose to occiput. The forehead should be flat (not rounded or domed), neither too prominent nor overhanging the face. *Cheeks*—The cheeks should be well rounded, protruding sideways and outward beyond the eyes. *Stop*—The temples or frontal bones should be very well defined, broad, square and high, causing a hollow or groove between the eyes. This indentation, or stop, should be both broad and deep and extend up the middle of the forehead, dividing the head vertically, being traceable to the top of the skull. *Face and Muzzle*—The face, measured from the front of the cheekbone to the tip of the nose, should be extremely short, the muzzle being very short, broad, turned upward and very deep from the corner of the eye to the corner of the mouth. *Nose*—The nose should be large, broad and black, its tip set back deeply between the eyes. The distance from bottom of stop, between the eyes, to the tip of nose should be as short as possible and not exceed the length from the tip of nose to the edge of underlip. The nostrils should be wide, large and black, with a well-defined line between them. Any nose other than black is objectionable and a brown or liver-colored nose shall **disqualify.** *Lips*—The chops or "flews" should be thick, broad, pendant and very deep, completely overhanging the lower jaw at each side. They join the underlip in front and almost or quite cover the teeth, which should be scarcely noticeable when the mouth is closed. *Bite—Jaws*—The jaws should be massive, very broad, square and "undershot," the lower jaw projecting considerably in front of the upper jaw and turning up. *Teeth:* The teeth should be large and strong, with the canine teeth or tusks wide apart, and the six small teeth in front, between the canines, in an even, level row.

**Neck, Topline, Body**—*Neck*—The neck should be short, very thick, deep and strong and well arched at the back. *Topline*—There should be a slight fall in the back, close behind the shoulders (its lowest part), whence the spine should rise to the loins (the top of which should be higher than the top of the shoulders), thence curving again more suddenly to the tail, forming an arch (a very distinctive feature of the breed), termed "roach back" or, more correctly, "wheel-back." *Body*—The brisket and body should be very capacious, with full sides, well-rounded ribs and very deep from the shoulders down to its lowest part, where it joins the chest. It should be well let down between the shoulders and forelegs, giving the dog a broad, low, short-legged appearance. *Chest*—The chest should be very broad, deep and full. *Underline*—The body should be well ribbed up behind with the belly tucked up and not rotund. *Back and Loin*—The back should be short and strong, very broad at the shoulders and comparatively narrow at the loins. *Tail*—The tail may be either straight or "screwed" (but never curved or curly), and in any case must be short, hung low, with decided downward carriage, thick root and fine tip. If straight, the tail should be cylindrical and of uniform taper. If "screwed," the bends or kinks should be well defined, and they may be abrupt and even knotty, but no portion of the member should be elevated above the base or root.

**Forequarters**—*Shoulders*—The shoulders should be muscular, very heavy, widespread and slanting outward, giving stability and great power. *Forelegs*—The forelegs should be short, very stout, straight and muscular, set wide apart, with well developed calves, presenting a bowed outline, but the bones of the legs should not be curved or bandy, nor the feet brought too close together. *Elbows*—The elbows should be low and stand well out and loose from the body. *Feet*—The feet should be moderate in size, compact and firmly set. Toes compact, well split up, with high knuckles and very short stubby nails. The front feet may be straight or slightly out-turned.

**Hindquarters**—*Legs*—The hind legs should be strong and muscular and longer than the forelegs, so as to elevate the loins above the shoulders. Hocks should be slightly bent and well let down, so as to give length and strength from the loins to hock. The lower leg should be short, straight and strong, with the stifles turned slightly outward and away from the body. The hocks are thereby made to approach each other, and the hind feet to turn outward. *Feet*—The feet should be moderate in size, compact and firmly set. Toes compact, well split up, with high knuckles and short stubby nails. The hind feet should be pointed well outward.

**Coat and Skin**—*Coat*—The coat should be straight, short, flat, close, of fine texture, smooth and glossy. (No fringe, feather or curl.) *Skin*—The skin should be soft and loose, especially at the head, neck and shoulders. *Wrinkles and Dewlap*—The head and face should be covered with heavy wrinkles, and at the throat, from jaw to chest, there should be two loose pendulous folds, forming the dewlap.

**Color of Coat**—The color of coat should be uniform, pure of its kind and brilliant. The various colors found in the breed are to be preferred in the following order: (1) red brindle, (2) all other brindles, (3) solid white, (4) solid red, fawn or fallow, (5) piebald, (6) inferior qualities of all the foregoing. *Note:* A perfect piebald is preferable to a muddy brindle or defective solid color. Solid black is very undesirable, but not so objectionable if occurring to a moderate degree in piebald patches. The brindles to be perfect should have a fine, even and equal distribution of the composite colors. In brindles and solid colors a small white patch on the chest is not considered detrimental. In piebalds the color patches should be well defined, of pure color and symmetrically distributed.

**Gait**—The style and carriage are peculiar, his gait being a loose-jointed, shuffling, sidewise motion, giving the characteristic "roll." The action must, however, be unrestrained, free and vigorous.

**Temperament**—The disposition should be equable and kind, resolute and courageous (not vicious or aggressive), and demeanor should be pacific and dignified. These attributes should be countenanced by the expression and behavior.

## SCALE OF POINTS

| General Properties | | | Body, Legs, etc. | | |
|---|---|---|---|---|---|
| Proportion and symmetry | 5 | | Neck | 3 | |
| Attitude | 3 | | Dewlap | 2 | |
| Expression | 2 | | Shoulders | 5 | |
| Gait | 3 | | Chest | 3 | |
| Size | 3 | | Ribs | 3 | |
| Coat | 2 | | Brisket | 2 | |
| Color of coat | 4 | 22 | Belly | 2 | |
| *Head* | | | Back | 5 | |
| Skull | 5 | | Forelegs and elbows | 4 | |
| Cheeks | 2 | | Hind legs | 3 | |
| Stop | 4 | | Feet | 3 | |
| Eyes and eyelids | 3 | | Tail | 4 | <u>39</u> |
| Ears | 5 | | | | |
| Wrinkle | 5 | | | | |
| Nose | 6 | | | | |
| Chops | 2 | | | | |
| Jaws | 5 | | | | |
| Teeth | 2 | 39 | | | |

Total    100

## DISQUALIFICATION

*Brown or liver-colored nose.*

**Approved July 20, 1976**
**Reformatted November 28, 1990**

# CHINESE SHAR-PEI

Brush Coat

Horse Coat

*A*N ANCIENT AND UNIQUE BREED, THE CHINESE SHAR-PEI IS THOUGHT TO have originated near the small village of Tai Li, in Kwantung province. The breed has existed for centuries in the southern provinces of China, apparently since the Han Dynasty, circa 200 B.C. Statues dating back to the Han Dynasty and bearing strong resemblance to Shar-Pei have been discovered. More recently, a translation of a thirteenth-century Chinese manuscript contains references to a wrinkled dog with characteristics much like those of the Shar-Pei. DNA research confirms that the Chinese Shar-Pei is indeed an ancient breed.

The name Shar-Pei literally means "sand skin" but translates more loosely as "rough, sandy coat" or "sandpaper-like coat." The Shar-Pei coat is short and rough, a unique quality in the dog world. A shiny, longer coat is undesirable. Another distinct characteristic is the solid blue-black tongue, a feature shared with another Chinese breed, the Chow Chow. This would suggest a common ancestor, but with lack of proof such a relationship is difficult to confirm.

Without a recorded history for dogs in China, most of what we know about the Shar-Pei is conjecture or incomplete. We do know that following the establishment of the People's Republic of China, the Communist government systematically eradicated much of the dog population. A few Chinese Shar-Pei were bred and exhibited in British Hong Kong and in the Republic of China (Taiwan). It is believed that the Shar-Pei was a peasant's dog, bred for hunting, guarding, and herding. The breed's intelligence made it a most versatile and valuable asset in early China.

The breed was first recognized by the Hong Kong Kennel Club. Registrations were discontinued in 1968 and then resumed twenty years later, when the Hong Kong and Kowloon Kennel Association (HKKKA) established a dog registry and began registering the Shar-Pei. Most of the early exports carried an HKKKA registration number. The breed's popularity spread throughout the world, and most kennel clubs today recognize the Chinese Shar-Pei.

In the United States the documented history of the breed dates to 1966, when a few dogs were imported from stock registered with the Hong Kong Kennel Club. The American Dog Breeders' Association registered a Chinese Shar-Pei for J. C. Smith on October 8, 1970.

Strong interest in the breed increased in 1973, when Matgo Law, of Down-Homes Kennel in Hong Kong, appealed to dog fanciers in the United States to "save the Chinese Shar-Pei." Law feared breed extinction would come with Communist China's attempt to eliminate dog ownership. The response was enthusiastic. Because of their rarity, a limited number of Shar-Pei arrived in the United States in fall 1973. Recipients of these dogs corresponded with one another and decided to form a national dog club and registry. The Chinese Shar-Pei Club of America (CSPCA), the AKC parent club, held its first organizational meeting in 1974. Its first annual national specialty show was given in 1978, and successive national shows have been held every year since.

The CSPCA maintained a studbook registry and actively promoted this uniquely devoted and appealing family dog noted for its intelligence. By May 1988, when the Shar-Pei was accepted into the AKC Miscellaneous class, there were 29,263 registered. This number grew to 197,215 by July 2004.

The Chinese Shar-Pei was admitted to the AKC Stud Book on June 1, 1992, and became eligible for competition in the Non-Sporting Group two months later.

# OFFICIAL STANDARD FOR THE CHINESE SHAR-PEI

**General Appearance**—An alert, compact dog of medium size and substance; square in profile, close coupled; the well-proportioned head slightly, but not overly large for the body. The short, harsh coat, the loose skin covering the head and body, the small ears, the "hippopotamus" muzzle shape and the high set tail impart to the Shar-Pei a unique look peculiar to him alone. The loose skin and wrinkles covering the head, neck and body are superabundant in puppies but these features may be limited to the head, neck and withers in the adult.

**Size, Proportion, Substance**—The height is 18 to 20 inches at the withers. The weight is 45 to 60 pounds. The dog is usually larger and more square bodied than the bitch but both appear well proportioned. The height of the Shar-Pei from the ground to the withers is approximately equal to the length from the point of breastbone to the point of rump.

**Head and Skull**—The head is large, slightly, but not overly, proudly carried and covered with profuse wrinkles on the forehead continuing into side wrinkles framing the face. *Eyes*—Dark, small, almond-shaped and sunken, displaying a scowling expression. In the dilute colored dogs the eye color may be lighter. *Ears*—Extremely small, rather thick, equilateral triangles in shape, slightly rounded at the tips; edges of the ear may curl. Ears lie flat against the head, are set high, wide apart and forward on the skull, pointing toward the eyes. The ears have the ability to move. *A pricked ear is a disqualification. Skull*—Flat and broad, the stop moderately defined. *Muzzle*—One of the distinctive features of the breed. It is broad and full with no suggestion of snipiness. (The length from nose to stop is approximately the same as from stop to occiput.) *Nose*—Large and wide and darkly pigmented, preferably black but any color conforming to the general coat color of the dog is acceptable. In dilute colors, the preferred nose is self-colored. Darkly pigmented cream Shar-Pei may have some light pigment either in the center of the nose or on the entire nose. The lips and top of muzzle are well-padded and may cause a slight bulge above the nose. *Tongue, roof of mouth, gums and flews*—Solid bluish-black is preferred in all coat colors except in dilute colors, which have a solid lavender pigmentation. A spotted pink tongue is a major fault. *A solid pink tongue is a disqualification.* (Tongue colors may lighten due to heat stress; care must be taken not to confuse dilute pigmentation with a pink tongue.) *Teeth*—Strong, meeting in a scissors bite. Deviation from a scissors bite is a major fault.

**Neck, Topline, Body**—*Neck*—medium length, full and set well into the shoulders. There are moderate to heavy folds of loose skin and abundant dewlap about the neck and throat. The *topline* dips slightly behind the withers, slightly rising over the short, broad loin. A level, roach or swayed topline/backline shall be faulted. *Chest*—Broad and deep with the brisket extending to the elbow and rising slightly under the loin. *Back*—Short and close-coupled. *Croup*—Flat, with the base of the tail set extremely high, clearly exposing an up-tilted anus. *Tail*—The high set tail is a characteristic feature of the Shar-Pei. A low set tail shall be faulted. The tail is thick and round at the base, tapering to a fine point and curling over or to either side of the back. *The absence of a complete tail is a disqualification.*

**Forequarters**—*Shoulders*—Muscular, well laid back and sloping. *Forelegs*—When viewed from the front, straight moderately spaced, with elbows close to the body. When viewed from the side, the forelegs are straight, the pasterns are strong and flexible. The bone is substantial but never heavy and is of moderate length. Removal of front dewclaws is optional. *Feet*—Moderate in size, compact and firmly set, not splayed.

**Hindquarters**—Muscular, strong, and moderately angulated. The metatarsi (hocks) are short, perpendicular to the ground and parallel to each other when viewed from the rear. Hind dewclaws must be removed. Feet as in front.

**Coat**—The extremely harsh coat is one of the distinguishing features of the breed. The coat is absolutely straight and off standing on the main trunk of the body but generally lies somewhat flatter on the limbs. The coat appears healthy without being shiny or lustrous. Acceptable coat lengths may range from extremely short "horse coat" up to the "brush coat," not to exceed one inch in length at the withers. A soft coat, a wavy coat, a coat in excess of one inch at the withers or a coat that has been trimmed is a major fault. The Shar-Pei is shown in its natural state.

**Color**—Only solid colors and sable are acceptable and are to be judged on an equal basis. A solid color dog may have shading, primarily darker, down the back and on the ears. The shading must be variations of the same body color and may include darker hairs throughout the coat. *The following colors are disqualifications: Albino; Not a solid color, i.e., Brindle; Parti-colored; Spotted; Patterned in any combination of colors.*

**Gait**—The movement of the Shar-Pei is to be judged at a trot. The gait is free and balanced with the feet tending to converge on a center line of gravity when the dog moves at a vigorous trot. The gait combines good forward reach and strong drive in the hindquarters. Proper movement is essential.

**Temperament**—Regal, alert, intelligent, dignified, lordly, scowling, sober and snobbish essentially independent and somewhat standoffish with strangers, but extreme in his devotion to his family. The Shar-Pei stands firmly on the ground with a calm, confident stature.

## MAJOR FAULTS

*Deviation from a Scissors Bite.*
*Spotted Tongue.*
*A soft coat, a wavy coat, a coat in excess of one inch in length at the withers or a coat that has been trimmed.*

## DISQUALIFICATIONS

*Pricked ears.*
*Solid pink tongue.*
*Absence of a complete tail.*
*Albino; not a solid color, i.e., Brindle; Parti-colored; Spotted; Patterned in any combination of colors.*

**Approved January 12, 1998**
**Effective February 28, 1998**

# CHOW CHOW

𝒟UE IN GREAT MEASURE TO THE RUTHLESSNESS WITH WHICH CHINESE EMPER-
ors destroyed the works of art and the literature of their predecessors, it is difficult to secure evidence of the antiquity of that lordly, aloof dog, the Chow Chow.
Still, a bas-relief was discovered not so very long ago that dates back to the Han Dynasty, about 150 B.C. This definitely places the Chow as a hunting dog in that period. While this establishes the breed as more than 2,000 years old, it is believed by
many authorities that the Chow goes back much farther; that it is, indeed, one of
the oldest recognizable types of dog.

The theory has been advanced that the Chow originated through a crossing of
the old mastiff of Tibet and the Samoyed, from the northern parts of Siberia. Certainly the Chow evinces some of the characteristics of both breeds. Refutation lies
in the fact that the Chow possesses a blue-black tongue. On this score, some maintain that the Chow is one of the basic breeds, and that he may have been one of the
ancestors of the Samoyed, the Norwegian Elkhound, the Keeshond, and the
Pomeranian, all of which are of somewhat similar type.

In modern times the Chow Chow has become a fashionable pet and guard dog,
but there is plenty of evidence available in China to prove that for centuries he was
the principal sporting dog. Perhaps the most unusual and lavish kennel in all history
was the one maintained by a T'ang emperor in about the seventh century A.D. It
was so extensive that the emperor could not have availed himself of a fraction of the

facilities for sport it afforded. It housed 2,500 couples of "hounds" of the Chow type, and the emperor had a staff of 10,000 huntsmen.

Apparently the Chow has been an unusually gifted breed of dog, since his uses have run the gamut of work done by nearly all recognized breeds. Credited with great scenting powers, with staunchness on point, and with cleverness in hunting tactics, he has been used frequently on Mongolian pheasant, and on the francolin of Yunnan, and on both has received great praise for his speed and stamina.

Undoubtedly the Chow Chow is of far northern origin, but he has always been found in greatest number in the south of China, particularly in the district centering about Canton. In that region of China where he is considered indigenous, he is usually called the "black-tongue," or the "black-mouthed" dog. In the north, as in Peking, he is called *lang kou* (wolf dog), *hsiung kou* (bear dog), or the more sophisticated *hei she-t'ou* (black tongued) or *Kwantung kou,* i.e., the dog of Canton.

The name Chow Chow has little basis for its origin in China; it is believed that expression evolved from the pidgin-English term for articles brought from any part of the Orient during the latter part of the eighteenth century. It meant knickknacks or bric-a-brac, including curios such as porcelain and ivory figurines, and finally what is described today as "mixed pickles," whether of the edible variety or not. It was far easier for the master of a sailing vessel to write "chow chow" than it was to describe all the various items of his cargo. So, in time, the expression came to include the dog.

The first European description of the Chow Chow was penned by the Reverend Gilbert White, rector of Selborne, England, published in his *Natural History and Antiquities of Selbourne.* The description, which is a most complete one, indicates that the dogs were not very different from specimens of modern times. It was a neighbor of the rector who in 1780 brought a brace of Chows from Canton on a vessel of the East India Company.

The importation of Chows into England did not begin, however, until about 1880, and the breed started toward its present popularity after Queen Victoria took an interest in it. The first specialty club was formed in England in 1895. The dog was exhibited for the first time in the United States in 1890, when a specimen named Takya, and identified as a Chinese Chow Chow owned by Miss A. C. Derby, took a third prize in the Miscellaneous class at the Westminster Kennel Club show in New York.

The AKC officially recognized the breed in 1903. The Chow Chow Club of America was admitted as an AKC member club in 1906. Today, it is one of America's firmly established breeds.

# OFFICIAL STANDARD FOR THE CHOW CHOW

**General Appearance**—*Characteristics*—An ancient breed of northern Chinese origin, this all-purpose dog of China was used for hunting, herding, pulling and protection of the home. While primarily a companion today, his working origin must always be remembered when assessing true Chow type. A powerful, sturdy, squarely built, upstanding dog of Arctic type, medium in size with strong muscular development and heavy bone. The body is compact, short coupled, broad and deep, the tail set high and carried closely to the back, the whole supported by four straight, strong, sound legs. Viewed from the side, the hind legs have little apparent angulation and the hock joint and metatarsals are directly beneath the hip joint. It is this structure which produces the characteristic shorter, stilted gait unique to the breed. The large head with broad, flat skull and short, broad and deep muzzle is proudly carried and accentuated by a ruff. Elegance and substance must be combined into a well balanced whole, never so massive as to outweigh his ability to be active, alert and agile. Clothed in a smooth or an offstanding rough double coat, the Chow is a masterpiece of beauty, dignity and naturalness. Essential to true Chow type are his unique blue-black tongue, scowling expression and stilted gait.

**Size, Proportions, Substance**—*Size*—The average height of adult specimens is 17 to 20 inches at the withers but in every case consideration of overall proportions and type should take precedence over size. *Proportions*—Square in profile and close coupled. Distance from forechest to point of buttocks equals height at the highest points of the withers. *Serious Fault*—Profile other than square. Distance from tip of elbow to ground is half the height at the withers. Floor of chest level with tips of elbows. Width viewed from the front and rear is the same and must be broad. It is these proportions that are essential to true Chow type. In judging puppies, no allowance should be made for their failure to conform to these proportions.

*Substance*—Medium in size with strong muscular development and heavy bone. Equally objectionable are snipy, fine boned specimens and overdone, ponderous, cloddy specimens. In comparing specimens of different sex, due allowance must be made in favor of the bitches who may not have as much head or substance as do the males. There is an impression of femininity in bitches as compared to an impression of masculinity in dogs.

**Head**—Proudly carried, large in proportion to the size of the dog but never so exaggerated as to make the dog seem top-heavy or to result in a low carriage. *Expression* essentially scowling, dignified, lordly, discerning, sober and snobbish, one of independence. The scowl is achieved by a marked brow with a padded button of skin just above the inner, upper corner of each eye; by sufficient play of skin to form frowning brows and a distinct furrow between the eyes beginning at the base of the muzzle and extending up the forehead; by the correct eye shape and placement and by the correct ear shape, carriage and placement. Excessive loose skin is not desirable. Wrinkles on the muzzle do not contribute to expression and are not required.

*Eyes* dark brown, deep set and placed wide apart and obliquely, of moderate size, almond in shape. The correct placement and shape should create an Oriental appearance. The eye rims black with lids which neither turn in nor droop and the pupils of the eyes clearly visible. *Serious Faults*—Entropion or ectropion, or pupils wholly or partially obscured by loose skin.

*Ears* small, moderately thick, triangular in shape with a slight rounding at the tip, carried stiffly erect but with a slight forward tilt. Placed wide apart with the inner corner on top of the skull. An ear which flops as the dog moves is very undesirable. *Disqualifying Fault*—Drop ear or ears. A drop ear is one which breaks at any point from its base to its tip or which is not carried stiffly erect but lies parallel to the top of the skull.

*Skull*—The top skull is broad and flat from side to side and front to back. Coat and loose skin cannot substitute for the correct bone structure. Viewed in profile, the toplines of the muzzle and skull are approximately parallel, joined by a moderate stop. The padding of the brows may make the stop appear steeper than it is. The muzzle is short in comparison to the length of the top skull but never less than one-third of the head length. The muzzle is broad and well filled out under the eyes, its width and depth are equal and both dimensions should appear to be the same from its base to its tip. This square appearance is achieved by correct bone structure plus padding of the muzzle and full cushioned lips. The muzzle should never be so padded or cushioned as to make it appear other than square in shape. The upper lips completely cover the lower lips when the mouth is closed but should not be pendulous.

*Nose* large, broad and black in color with well opened nostrils. *Disqualifying Fault*—Nose spotted or distinctly other color than black, except in blue Chows which may have solid blue or slate noses.

*Mouth and Tongue*—Edges of the lips black, tissues of the mouth mostly black, gums preferably black. A solid black mouth is ideal. The top surface and edges of the tongue a solid blue-black, the darker the better. *Disqualifying Fault*—The top surface or edges of the tongue red or pink or with one or more spots of red or pink. *Teeth* strong and even with a scissors bite.

**Neck, Topline, Body**—*Neck* strong, full, well muscled, nicely arched and of sufficient length to carry the head proudly above the topline when standing at attention. *Topline* straight, strong and level from the withers to the root of the tail.

*Body* short, compact, close coupled, strongly muscled, broad, deep and well let down in the flank. The body, back, coupling and croup must all be short to give the required square build. *Chest* broad, deep and muscular, never narrow or slab-sided. The ribs close together and well sprung, not barrel. The spring of the front ribs is somewhat narrowed at their lower ends to permit the shoulder and upper arm to fit smoothly against the chest wall. The floor of the chest is broad and deep extending down to the tips of the elbows. The point of sternum slightly in front of the shoulder points. *Serious Faults*—Labored or abdominal breathing (not to include normal panting), narrow or slab-sided chest. *Loin* well muscled, strong, short, broad and deep. *Croup* short and broad with powerful rump and thigh muscles giving a level croup. *Tail* set high and carried closely to the back at all times, following the line of the spine at the start.

**Forequarters**—*Shoulders* strong, well muscled, the tips of the shoulder blades moderately close together; the spine of the shoulder forms an angle approximately 55 degrees with the horizontal and forms an angle with the upper arm approximately 110 degrees. Length of upper arm never less than length of shoulder blade. Elbow joints set well back alongside the chest wall, elbows turning neither in nor out. *Forelegs* perfectly straight from elbow to foot with heavy bone which must be in proportion to the rest of the dog. Viewed from the front, the forelegs are parallel and widely spaced commensurate with the broad chest. *Pasterns* short and upright. Wrists shall not knuckle over. The dewclaws may be removed. *Feet* round, compact, catlike, standing well upon the thick toe pads.

**Hindquarters**—The rear assembly broad, powerful, and well muscled in the hips and thighs, heavy in bone with rear and front bone approximately equal. Viewed from the rear, the legs are straight, parallel and widely spaced commensurate with the broad pelvis. *Stifle Joint* shows little angulation, is well knit and stable, points straight forward and the bones of the joint should be clean and sharp. *Hock Joint* well let down and appears almost straight. The hock joint must be strong, well knit and firm, never bowing or breaking forward or to either side. The hock joint and metatarsals lie in a straight line below the hip joint. *Serious Faults*—Unsound stifle or hock joints. *Metatarsals* short and perpendicular to the ground. The dewclaws may be removed. *Feet* same as front.

**Coat**—There are two types of coat; rough and smooth. Both are double coated. *Rough*—In the rough coat, the outer coat is abundant, dense, straight and offstanding, rather coarse in texture; the undercoat soft, thick and wooly. Puppy coat soft, thick and wooly overall. The coat forms a profuse ruff around the head and neck, framing the head. The coat and ruff generally longer in dogs than in bitches. Tail well feathered. The coat length varies markedly on different Chows and thickness, texture and condition should be given greater emphasis than length. Obvious trimming or shaping is undesirable. Trimming of the whiskers, feet and metatarsals optional. *Smooth*—The smooth coated Chow is judged by the same standard as the rough coated Chow except that references to the quantity and distribution of the outer coat are not applicable to the smooth coated Chow, which has a hard, dense, smooth outer coat with a definite undercoat. There should be no obvious ruff or feathering on the legs or tail.

**Color**—Clear colored, solid or solid with lighter shadings in the ruff, tail and featherings. There are five colors in the Chow: red (light golden to deep mahogany), black, blue, cinnamon (light fawn to deep cinnamon) and cream. Acceptable colors to be judged on an equal basis.

**Gait**—Proper movement is the crucial test of proper conformation and soundness. It must be sound, straight moving, agile, brief, quick, and powerful, never lumbering. The rear gait shorter and stilted because of the straighter rear assembly. It is from the side that the unique stilted action is most easily assessed. The rear leg moves up and forward from the hip in a straight, stilted pendulum-like line with a slight bounce in the rump, the legs extend neither far forward nor far backward. The hind foot has a strong thrust which transfers power to the body in an almost straight line due to the minimal rear leg angulation. To transmit this power efficiently to the front assembly, the coupling must be short and there should be no roll through the midsection. Viewed from the rear, the line of bone from hip joint to pad remains straight as the dog moves. As the speed increases the hind legs incline slightly inward. The stifle joints must point in the line of travel, not outward resulting in a bowlegged appearance nor hitching in under the dog. Viewed from the front, the line of bone from shoulder joint to pad remains straight as the dog moves. As the speed increases, the forelegs do not move in exact parallel planes, rather, incline slightly inward. The front legs must not swing out in semicircles nor mince or show any evidence of hackney action. The front and rear assemblies must be in dynamic equilibrium. Somewhat lacking in speed, the Chow has excellent endurance because the sound, straight rear leg provides direct, usable power efficiently.

**Temperament**—Keen intelligence, an independent spirit and innate dignity give the Chow an aura of aloofness. It is a Chow's nature to be reserved and discerning with strangers. Displays of aggression or timidity are unacceptable. Because of its deep set eyes the Chow has limited peripheral vision and is best approached from the front.

**Summary**—Faults shall be penalized in proportion to their deviation from the standard. In judging the Chow, the overall picture is of primary consideration. Exaggeration of any characteristic at the expense of balance or soundness shall be severely penalized.

Type should include general appearance, temperament, the harmony of all parts, and soundness especially as seen when the dog is in motion. There should be proper emphasis on movement which is the final test of the Chow's conformation, balance and soundness.

## DISQUALIFICATIONS

*Drop ear or ears. A drop ear is one which breaks at any point from its base to its tip or which is not carried stiffly erect but lies parallel to the top of the skull.*
*Nose spotted or distinctly other color than black, except in blue Chows which may have solid blue or slate noses.*
*The top surface or edges of the tongue red or pink or with one or more spots of red or pink.*

**Approved October 10, 2005**
**Effective January 1, 2006**

# DALMATIAN

*N*O BREED HAS A MORE INTERESTING BACKGROUND OR A MORE DISPUTED heritage than the Dalmatian. Its beginning is buried so deeply in the past that researchers cannot agree as to the true origin. Investigators are in complete agreement, however, regarding the great age of the breed and that it has come through many centuries unchanged.

Models, engravings, paintings, and writings of antiquity have been used to support the claim that the Dalmatian first appeared in Europe, Asia, and Africa. Lack of certainty as to the original home of the Dalmatian can be accounted for by the fact that the breed was frequently found in bands of nomadic gypsies. Therefore, the Dalmatian has been well known but not located definitely in any single place.

Authoritative writers place him first as a positive entry in Dalmatia, a region in the west of the former Yugoslavia, along the Adriatic Sea, which had from 1815 to 1919 been a province of Austria. Some Dalmatian authorities state that the breed originated in England and went from there to Dalmatia. While the breed has been credited with a dozen nationalities and has as many native names, in England it has had several nicknames. These include the English Coach Dog, the Carriage Dog, the Plum Pudding Dog, the Firehouse Dog, and the Spotted Dick.

The breed takes its correct name, Dalmatian, from its first proved and accepted home of the provincial area of Dalmatia. There are references to the breed as a Dalmatian in the mid-eighteenth century. There is no question whatsoever that from then to the present the breed's lineage is a straight and correct record.

The Dalmatian's activities have been extremely varied. It has been a dog of war and a sentinel on the borders of Dalmatia and Croatia. It has been employed as a draft dog and as a shepherd. It is also excellent on rats and vermin. The Dalmatian is well known for its heroic performances as a fire-apparatus follower and as a fire-house mascot. As a sporting dog it has been used on birds, as a trail hound and a retriever, and in packs for boar and stag hunting. The Dalmatian's retentive memory has made it one of the most dependable performers in circuses and on the stage. Through the years, its intelligence and willingness have qualified it for virtually every role that useful dogs are called upon to perform.

Most important among its talents has been its status as the original one and only coaching dog. There is abundant evidence, some of it centuries old, of the Dalmatian with ears entirely cropped away and wearing a padlocked brass collar, using its innate coaching sense as a follower and guardian of the horse-drawn vehicle. (The imaginative might say that the Dalmatian's coaching instincts are depicted in an engraving of a spotted dog following an Egyptian chariot.)

The Dalmatian is physically suited for roadwork associated with the coach. In its correct conformation, appropriate road gait and endurance are essential. Its gait has a beautiful fluidity of motion, and it has the strength, vitality, and fortitude to maintain an effortless stride for extended periods.

The instinct for coaching is bred into the Dalmatian, born into him, and trained into him through years of selective breeding. The Dalmatian takes to a horse as the horse takes to him. It may work in the older way, clearing the path before the Tally-ho coach with dignity and determination, or by following the coach, with his unique markings in full view to add distinction to any rig. The Dalmatian may also coach under the rear axle, the front axle or, most difficult of all, under the pole between the leading and wheeling team of horses.

The Dalmatian's penchant for working is his most renowned characteristic, but it in no way approaches his capacity for friendship. The Dalmatian represents all aspects of loyalty and faithfulness sought for in the companion dog. The breed is exhibited in modern times in conformation and standard performance and companion events. Unique to the breed is the road trial, in which the dog is evaluated upon its ability to perform specific skills and endurance suitable to working with the coach.

The Dalmatian is strong bodied, clean-cut, colorful, and distinctive. There is no dog breed more picturesque than the Dalmatian, with its short white coat highly decorated by clearly defined round spots of jet-black or deep liver brown. The Dalmatian does not look like any other breed, for its markings are uniquely its own. Its flashy appearance is the culmination of centuries of careful breeding.

The Dalmatian's aristocratic bearing does not give a false impression, for the Dalmatian is, first of all, reserved and dignified. It is a quiet, somewhat aloof breed and an ideal sentinel, able to distinguish between barking for fun or for the purpose of indicating intruders. Its courtesy never fails with approved visitors, but its protective instinct is highly developed, making it a sensible and dependable watchdog. A casual admirer will not break its polite reserve, for it has a fine sense of distinction as to whom it belongs.

Modern breeders have developed the Dalmatian to serve more as a family dog than a guard dog. Having outlived the purpose for which it was bred, except for exhibition, the Dalmatian has little opportunity to coach. Therefore, its function as a perfect house companion has been fine-tuned by responsible breeders, and a friendly, confident dog has been the result.

Fashion has not distorted the Dalmatian. It is born pure white, develops quickly, and requires no cropping, docking, stripping, or artifices of any sort. It is ready for sport or the show ring just as nature made it. The Dalmatian is extremely hardy, an easy keeper, and suited for most climates. It requires the minimum of care, for it is both neat and clean.

# OFFICIAL STANDARD FOR THE DALMATIAN

**General Appearance**—The Dalmatian is a distinctively spotted dog; poised and alert; strong, muscular and active; free of shyness; intelligent in expression; symmetrical in outline; and without exaggeration or coarseness. The Dalmatian is capable of great endurance, combined with fair amount of speed.

Deviations from the described ideal should be penalized in direct proportion to the degree of the deviation.

**Size, Proportion, Substance**—Desirable height at the withers is between 19 and 23 inches. Undersize or oversize is a fault. Any dog or bitch over 24 inches at the withers is disqualified.

The overall length of the body from the forechest to the buttocks is approximately equal to the height at the withers.

The Dalmatian has good substance and is strong and sturdy in bone, but never coarse.

**Head**—The head is in balance with the overall dog. It is of fair length and is free of loose skin. The Dalmatian's *expression* is alert and intelligent, indicating a stable and outgoing temperament.

The *eyes* are set moderately well apart, are medium sized and somewhat rounded in appearance, and are set well into the skull. Eye color is brown or blue, or any combination thereof; the darker the better and usually darker in black-spotted than in liver-spotted dogs.

Abnormal position of the eyelids or eyelashes (ectropion, entropion, trichiasis) is a major fault.

Incomplete pigmentation of the eye rims is a major fault.

The *ears* are of moderate size, proportionately wide at the base and gradually tapering to a rounded tip. They are set rather high, and are carried close to the head, and are thin and fine in texture. When the Dalmatian is alert, the top of the ear is level with the top of the skull and the tip of the ear reaches to the bottom line of the cheek.

The top of the skull is flat with a slight vertical furrow and is approximately as wide as it is long. The *stop* is moderately well defined. The cheeks blend smoothly into a powerful *muzzle,* the top of which is level and parallel to the top of the skull. The muzzle and the top of the skull are about equal in length.

The *nose* is completely pigmented on the leather, black in black-spotted dogs and brown in liver-spotted dogs. Incomplete nose pigmentation is a major fault.

The *lips* are clean and close fitting. The teeth meet in a *scissors bite.* Overshot or undershot bites are disqualifications.

**Neck, Topline, Body**—The *neck* is nicely arched, fairly long, free from throatiness, and blends smoothly into the shoulders.

The *topline* is smooth.

The *chest* is deep, capacious and of moderate width, having good spring of rib without being barrel shaped. The brisket reaches to the elbow. The underline of the rib cage curves gradually into a moderate tuck-up.

The *back* is level and strong. The *loin* is short, muscular and slightly arched. The flanks narrow through the loin. The *croup* is nearly level with the back.

The *tail* is a natural extension of the topline. It is not inserted too low down. It is strong at the insertion and tapers to the tip, which reaches to the hock. It is never docked. The tail is carried with a slight upward curve but should never curl over the back. Ring tails and low-set tails are faults.

**Forequarters**—The *shoulders* are smoothly muscled and well laid back. The **upper arm** is approximately equal in length to the shoulder blade and joins it at an angle sufficient to insure that the foot falls under the shoulder. The *elbows* are close to the body. The *legs* are straight, strong and sturdy in bone. There is a slight angle at the *pastern* denoting flexibility.

**Hindquarters**—The *hindquarters* are powerful, having smooth, yet well defined muscles. The *stifle* is well bent. The *hocks* are well let down. When the Dalmatian is standing, the hind legs, viewed from the rear, are parallel to each other from the point of the hock to the heel of the pad. Cowhocks are a major fault.

**Feet**—*Feet* are very important. Both front and rear feet are round and compact with thick, elastic pads and well arched toes. Flat feet are a major fault. Toenails are black and/or white in black-spotted dogs and brown and/or white in liver-spotted dogs. Dewclaws may be removed.

**Coat**—The *coat* is short, dense, fine and close fitting. It is neither woolly nor silky. It is sleek, glossy and healthy in appearance.

**Color and Markings**—*Color and markings* and their overall appearance are very important points to be evaluated.

The ground color is pure white. In black-spotted dogs the spots are dense black. In liver-spotted dogs the spots are liver brown. Any color markings other than black or liver are disqualified.

*Spots* are round and well defined, the more distinct the better. They vary from the size of a dime to the size of a half-dollar. They are pleasingly and evenly distributed. The less the spots intermingle the better. Spots are usually smaller on the head, legs and tail than on the body. Ears are preferably spotted.

*Tri-color* (which occurs rarely in this breed) is a disqualification. It consists of tan markings found on the head, neck, chest, leg or tail of a black- or liver-spotted dog. Bronzing of black spots, and fading and/or darkening of liver spots due to environmental conditions or normal processes of coat change are not tri-coloration.

*Patches* are a disqualification. A patch is a solid mass of black or liver hair containing no white hair. It is appreciably larger than a normal sized spot. Patches are a dense, brilliant color with sharply defined, smooth edges. Patches are present at birth. Large color masses formed by intermingled or overlapping spots are not patches. Such masses should indicate individual spots by uneven edges and/or white hairs scattered throughout the mass.

**Gait**—In keeping with the Dalmatian's historical use as a coach dog, gait and endurance are of great importance. Movement is steady and effortless. Balanced angulation fore and aft combined with powerful muscles and good condition produce smooth, efficient action. There is a powerful drive from the rear coordinated with extended reach in the front. The topline remains level. Elbows, hocks and feet turn neither in nor out. As the speed of the trot increases, there is a tendency to single track.

**Temperament**—Temperament is stable and outgoing, yet dignified. Shyness is a major fault.

## SCALE OF POINTS

| | |
|---|---|
| General appearance | 5 |
| Size, proportion, substance | 10 |
| Head | 10 |
| Neck, topline, body | 10 |
| Forequarters | 5 |
| Hindquarters | 5 |
| Feet | 5 |
| Coat | 5 |
| Color and markings | 25 |
| Gait | 10 |
| Temperament | 10 |
| **Total** | **100** |

# DISQUALIFICATIONS

*Any dog or bitch over 24 inches at the withers.*
*Overshot or undershot bite.*
*Any color markings other than black or liver.*
*Tri-color.*
*Patches.*

**Approved July 11, 1989**
**Effective September 6, 1989**

# FINNISH SPITZ

*S*UOMENPYSTYKORVA, THE FINNISH COCK-EARED DOG, WAS KNOWN IN earlier times as the Finnish Barking Bird Dog. Now called the Finnish Spitz, it is the national dog of Finland.

The history of spitz-type dogs can be traced back several thousand years, to an era when the Finno-Ugrian peoples inhabited central Russia. As various tribes migrated to different areas, they bred their dogs according to need, thus developing separate strains. One clan made its way to the far northern regions where, isolated among 60,000 lakes, the Finnish Spitz emerged as a pure breed and an invaluable asset to the hunter.

As centuries passed and advanced methods of transportation brought diverse populations and their dogs together, the original Finnish Spitz were mated with other breeds, until by 1880 they were nearly extinct. About that time two sportsmen from Helsinki, hunting in the northern forests, observed the pure native dogs, realized their many virtues, and returned home with superior specimens in an effort to salvage the breed.

One of the pioneers, Hugo Roos, became directly involved with the dogs and bred them for over 30 years; later he retired to devote his talents to judging. Another pioneer, Hugo Sandberg, launched an impressive rescue campaign in 1890, though he never actually bred Finnish Spitz himself. At the first Helsinki dog show, held in 1891, five Finnish Spitz were awarded ribbons.

With the advent of dog shows, it became necessary to draw up a standard. Due to the success of Mr. Sandberg's promotion, the Finnish Kennel Club recognized the breed in 1892, with a standard based on his observations. In 1897, when the standard was revised in detail, Finnish Spitz became the official breed name.

In 1927 the first Finnish Spitz arrived in England, a pair brought back by Sir Edward Chichester following a hunting trip to Scandinavia. Among the early British devotees was Lady Kitty Ritson, who was instrumental in forming the breed club. It was she who coined the nickname "Finkie" by which the dogs are affectionately known in several countries. By 1935, the breed had sufficient adherents to warrant registration with The Kennel Club (England). Perhaps the most recognizable name among English supporters is that of Mrs. Griselda Price, whose Cullabine prefix is behind many top-winning dogs worldwide.

A native Finn, Ray Rinta, is credited with piloting the breed to Canadian Kennel Club recognition—the CKC admitted the Finnish Spitz to its studbook in 1974. Mrs. Joan Grant's dogs (Jayenn prefix) have been a major force in the breed's popularity "north of the border."

The first known Finnish Spitz imported to the United States was Cullabine Rudolph, from Mrs. Price's kennel in England, in 1959. It is believed, however, that breeding of the Finnish Spitz in the United States commenced in the mid-1960s from Finnish imports belonging to Henry Davidson, of Minnesota, and Alex Hassel, of Connecticut.

The Finnish Spitz Club of America was founded in 1975 by Richard and Bette Isacoff, with Margaret Koehler. The American standard for the breed was formulated by Mrs. Koehler and Mrs. Isacoff in 1976, based on the standard of the country of origin.

In November 1983, the breed was accepted into the Miscellaneous class. The AKC Board of Directors opened the Stud Book for registration of the Finnish Spitz on August 1, 1987. Assigned to the Non-Sporting Group, the breed became eligible to compete at AKC-licensed shows January 1, 1988.

Except in his native land, the Finnish Spitz is primarily a house dog, a faithful companion with particular fondness for children. In Finland, however, he is still a worker. He has functioned since earliest times as a natural bark pointer, who directs a hunter to the location of tree'd game by a distinctive ringing bark or yodel, and points at the prey with his head and muzzle when the hunter approaches. Ranging far into the forest, he seeks out the *capercaillie* (akin to our wild turkey) using sight, scent, and sound, all the while keeping audio contact with the hunter. Flushing it from the bush, he follows it until it settles into a tree. Soft at first, then building to a crescendo, the dog's vocalizing alerts the hunter and draws him to the site. As he approaches, the dog gently sways his tail to and fro—this has a mesmerizing effect on the bird, which has already been distracted by the barking. In Finland the hunting ability of the breed is so prized that no Finnish Spitz can earn a conformation championship without first proving his worth in the field. Of particular importance is the quality of his bark, and contests are held annually to select a King Barker.

# OFFICIAL STANDARD FOR THE FINNISH SPITZ

**General Appearance**—The Finnish Spitz presents a fox-like picture. The breed has long been used to hunt small game and birds. The pointed muzzle, erect ears, dense coat and curled tail denote his northern heritage. The Finnish Spitz's whole being shows liveliness, which is especially evident in the eyes, ears and tail. Males are decidedly masculine without coarseness. Bitches are decidedly feminine without over-refinement.

The Finnish Spitz's most important characteristics are its square, well-balanced body that is symmetrical with no exaggerated features, a glorious red-gold coat, his bold carriage and brisk movement.

Any deviation from the ideal described in the standard should be penalized to the extent of the deviation. Structural faults common to all breeds are as undesirable in the Finnish Spitz as in any other breed, even though such faults may not be mentioned in the standard.

**Size, Proportion, Substance**—*Size*—Height at the withers in dogs: 17½ to 20 inches; in bitches, 15½ to 18 inches.

*Proportion*—Square: length from forechest to buttocks equal to height from withers to ground. The coat may distort the square appearance.

*Substance*—Substance and bone in proportion to overall dog.

**Head**—Clean cut and fox-like. Longer from occiput to tip of nose than broad at widest part of skull in a ratio of 7:4. More refined with less coat or ruff in females than in males, but still in the same ratio. A muscular or coarse head, or a long or narrow head with snipy muzzle, is to be penalized.

*Expression*—Fox-like and lively.

*Eyes*—Almond-shaped with black rims. Obliquely set with moderate spacing between, neither too far apart nor too close. Outer corners tilted upward. Dark in color with a keen and alert expression. Any deviation, runny, weepy, round or light eyes should be faulted.

*Ears*—Set on high. When alert, upward standing, open to the front with tips directly above the outer corner of the eyes. Small, erect, sharply pointed and very mobile. Ears set too high, too low, or too close together, long or excessive hair inside the ears are faults.

*Skull*—Flat between ears with some minimal rounding ahead of earset. Forehead a little arched. Skull to muzzle ratio is 4:3.

*Stop*—Pronounced.

*Muzzle*—Narrow as seen from the front, above and from the side; of equal width and depth where it insets to the skull, tapering somewhat, equally from all angles.

*Nose*—Black. Any deviation is to be penalized. Circumference of the nose to be 80% of the circumference of the muzzle at its origin.

*Lips*—Black; thin and tight.

*Bite*—Scissors bite. Wry mouth is to be severely faulted.

**Neck, Topline, Body**—*Neck*—Well set; muscular. Clean, with no excess skin below muzzle. Appearing shorter in males due to their heavier ruff.

*Topline*—Level and strong from withers to croup.

*Body*—Muscular, square.

*Chest*—Deep. Brisket reaches to the elbow. Ratio of chest depth to distance from withers to ground is 4:9.

*Ribs*—Well sprung.

*Tuck-up*—Slightly drawn up.

*Loin*—Short.

*Tail*—Set on just below level of topline, forming a single curl falling over the loin with tip pointing towards the thigh. Plumed, curving vigorously from its base in an arch forward, downward, and backward, pressing flat against either thigh with tip extending to middle part of thigh. When straightened, the tip of the tail bone reaches the hock joint. Low or high tail-set, too curly a tail, or a short tail is to be faulted.

**Forequarters**—*Shoulders*—The layback of the shoulders is thirty degrees to the vertical.

*Legs*—Viewed from the front, moderately spaced, parallel and straight with elbows close to the body and turned neither out nor in. Bone strong without being heavy, always in proportion to the dog. Fine bone, which limits endurance, or heavy bone, which makes working movement cumbersome, is to be faulted.

*Pasterns*—Viewed from the side, slope slightly. Weak pasterns are to be penalized.

*Dewclaws*—May be removed.

*Feet*—Rounded, compact foot with well-arched toes, tightly bunched or close-cupped, the two center toes being only slightly longer than those on the outside. The toe pads should be deeply cushioned and covered with thick skin. The impression left by such a foot is rounded in contrast to oval.

**Hindquarters**—Angulation in balance with the forequarters.

*Thighs*—Muscular.

*Hocks*—Moderately let down. Straight and parallel.

*Dewclaws*—Removed.

*Feet*—As in front.

**Coat**—The coat is double with a short, soft, dense undercoat and long, harsh straight guard hairs measuring approximately one to two inches on the body. Hair on the head and legs is short and close; it is longest and most dense on plume of tail and back of thighs. The outer coat is stiffer and longer on the neck and back, and in males considerably more profuse at the shoulder, giving them a more ruffed appearance. Males carry more coat than females. No trimming of the coat except for feet is allowed. Whiskers shall not be trimmed. Any trimming of coat shall be severely faulted. Silky, wavy, long or short coat is to be faulted.

**Color**—Varying shades of golden-red ranging from pale honey to deep auburn are allowed, with no preference given to shades at either extreme so long as the color is bright and clear. As the undercoat is a paler color, the effect of this shading is a coat which appears to glow. White markings on the tips of the toes and a quarter-sized spot or narrow white strip, ideally no wider than ½ inch, on the forechest are permitted.

Black hairs along lipline and sparse, separate black hairs on tail and back permitted. Puppies may have a good many black hairs which decrease with age, black on tail persisting longer. Muddy or unclear color, any white on the body except as specified, is to be penalized.

**Gait**—The Finnish Spitz is quick and light on his feet, steps out briskly, trots with lively grace, and tends to single-track as the speed increases. When hunting he moves at a gallop. The angulation called for permits him to break into a working gait quickly. Sound movement is essential for stamina and agility.

**Temperament**—Active and friendly, lively and eager, faithful; brave, but cautious. Shyness, any tendency toward unprovoked aggression is to be penalized.

**Note**: Finnish Spitz are to be examined on the ground.

**Approved July 12, 1999**
**Effective August 30, 1999**

# FRENCH BULLDOG

*T*HERE HAS BEEN A DIFFERENCE OF OPINION AS TO THE ORIGIN OF THE French Bulldog, but it seems pretty well established that one ancestor must have been the English Bulldog—probably one of the toy variety, of which there were a great number in England around 1860. These toy Bulldogs, not finding favor with the English, were sent in large numbers into France. There they were crossed with various other breeds, and finally became popular in fashionable circles, particularly with women. It was then that they were given the name Boule-Dog Français, although later on England scoffed at the idea of applying the word *Français* to a breed so clearly showing a strong strain of English Bulldog. At that time there was little uniformity of type, and one found dogs with rose ears, while others had bat ears, which have since come to be recognized as an outstanding feature of the French Bulldog.

There are two distinctive features in French Bulldogs: one, the bat ear, as above mentioned; the other, the skull. The correctly formed skull should be level, or flat, between the ears, while directly above the eyes, extending almost across the forehead, it should be slightly curved, giving a domed appearance. Both of these features add much to the unusual appearance of the French Bulldog.

The preservation of the bat ear as a distinct feature has been due to the persistent efforts of American fanciers, since in the early days of breeding these dogs in Europe the tendency was toward the rose ear. Had this movement not been opposed by America, the breed would eventually have lost the feature that so strongly accentuates its individuality, and the result would have been practically a miniature English Bulldog.

This controversy over type was directly responsible for the formation of the French Bulldog Club of America, the first organization in the world devoted to the breed. Fanciers gave a specialty show in the ballroom of the Waldorf-Astoria, New York, in 1898, this being the first of its kind to be held in such deluxe quarters. The affair proved a sensation, and it was due, no doubt, to the resulting publicity that the quaint little chaps became the rage in society. Show entries increased until the peak was reached about 1913, when there were exactly 100 French Bulldogs benched at Westminster, while the following specialty shows had even more.

Unquestionably the dog that did the most toward the establishment of the breed in America was Ch. Nellcote Gamin, imported in 1904 by Mr. and Mrs. Samuel Goldenberg. With the addition of Gamin to the splendid stock already in this country, we were made independent of further importation in order to produce the finest Frenchies in the world.

While bred principally as pets and companions, Frenchies are remarkably intelligent and serve as good watchdogs. They are affectionate, sweet-tempered, and dependable. Alert and playful, they are not noisy and, as a rule, bark very little. Their size is another advantage in considering them as indoor pets, and the smooth, short coat is easily kept clean.

# OFFICIAL STANDARD FOR THE FRENCH BULLDOG

**General Appearance**—The French Bulldog has the appearance of an active, intelligent, muscular dog of heavy bone, smooth coat, compactly built, and of medium or small structure. Expression alert, curious and interested. Any alteration other than removal of dewclaws is considered mutilation and is a *disqualification*.

*Proportion and Symmetry*—All points are well distributed and bear good relation one to the other; no feature being in such prominence from either excess or lack of quality that the animal appears poorly proportioned.

*Influence of Sex*—In comparing specimens of different sex, due allowance is to be made in favor of bitches, which do not bear the characteristics of the breed to the same marked degree as do the dogs.

**Size, Proportion, Substance**—*Weight* not to exceed 28 pounds; over 28 pounds is a *disqualification*. *Proportion*—Distance from withers to ground in good relation to distance from withers to onset of tail, so that animal appears compact, well balanced and in good proportion. *Substance*—Muscular, heavy bone.

**Head**—Head large and square. *Eyes* dark in color, wide apart, set low down in the skull, as far from the ears as possible, round in form, of moderate size, neither sunken nor bulging. In lighter colored dogs, lighter colored eyes are acceptable. No haw and no white of the eye showing when looking forward. **Ears**—Known as the bat ear, broad at the base, elongated, with round top, set high on the head but not too close together, and carried erect with the orifice to the front. The leather of the ear fine and soft. Other than bat ears is a *disqualification*.

The top of the **skull** flat between the ears; the forehead is not flat but slightly rounded. The **muzzle** broad, deep and well laid back; the muscles of the cheeks well developed. The *stop* well defined, causing a hollow groove between the eyes with heavy wrinkles forming a soft roll over the extremely short nose; nostrils broad with a well defined line between them. **Nose** black. Nose other than black is a *disqualification,* except in the case of the lighter colored dogs, where a lighter colored nose is acceptable but not desirable. *Flews* black, thick and broad, hanging over the lower jaw at the sides, meeting the underlip in front and covering the teeth, which are not seen when the mouth is closed. The *underjaw* is deep, square, broad, undershot and well turned up.

**Neck, Topline, Body**—The **neck** is thick and well arched with loose skin at the throat. The **back** is a roach back with a slight fall close behind the shoulders; strong and short, broad at the shoulders and narrowing at the loins. The **body** is short and well rounded. The *chest* is broad, deep, and full; well ribbed with the belly tucked up. The **tail** is either straight or screwed (but not curly), short, hung low, thick root and fine tip; carried low in repose.

**Forequarters**—*Forelegs* are short, stout, straight, muscular and set wide apart. Dewclaws may be removed. *Feet* are moderate in size, compact and firmly set. Toes compact, well split up, with high knuckles and short stubby nails.

**Hindquarters**—*Hind legs* are strong and muscular, longer than the forelegs, so as to elevate the loins above the shoulders. Hocks well let down. *Feet* are moderate in size, compact and firmly set. Toes compact, well split up, with high knuckles and short stubby nails; hind feet slightly longer than forefeet.

**Coat**—Coat is moderately fine, brilliant, short and smooth. Skin is soft and loose, especially at the head and shoulders, forming wrinkles.

**Color**—Acceptable colors—All brindle, fawn, white, brindle and white, and any color except those which constitute disqualification. All colors are acceptable with the exception of solid black, mouse, liver, black and tan, black and white, and white with black, which are *disqualifications.* Black means black without a trace of brindle.

**Gait**—Correct gait is double tracking with reach and drive; the action is unrestrained, free and vigorous.

**Temperament**—Well behaved, adaptable and comfortable companions with an affectionate nature and even disposition; generally active, alert and playful, but not unduly boisterous.

## DISQUALIFICATIONS

*Any alteration other than removal of dewclaws.*
*Over 28 pounds in weight.*
*Other than bat ears.*

*Nose other than black, except in the case of lighter colored dogs, where a lighter colored nose is acceptable.*

*Solid black, mouse, liver, black and tan, black and white, and white with black; black means black without a trace of brindle.*

**Approved June 10, 1991**
**Effective July 31, 1991**

# KEESHOND

$\mathscr{A}$ NATIONAL POLITICAL TURNOVER IN HOLLAND BROUGHT THE KEESHOND (plural, Keeshonden) to wide attention in the latter part of the eighteenth century, but the breed had already been a favorite of the Dutch people for several hundred years. Never used as a hunter, or for any of the specialized work that has characterized so many other breeds, the very force of the Keeshond personality won the breed a high place in the affections of a nation.

Events leading to the Keeshond's recognition as the national dog of Holland were part of the social unrest that seemed to spread like a prairie fire throughout the world in the years immediately preceding the French Revolution. Holland was divided into two great camps, the *Prinsgezinden,* or partisans of the Prince of Orange, and the *Patriotten,* or Patriots.

The Patriots, consisting mainly of the lower and upper-middle class, were led by Kees de Gyselaer, of Dordrecht. Like most of his countrymen, de Gyselaer was a dog lover. At that time he owned a little dog called Kees. This dog gave the breed its name and became the symbol of the Patriots. It appeared in countless pictures and cartoons made during those days of civil strife. Those who belonged to the Patriot party were firmly of the opinion that their own spirit was typified by the dog. Kees was a dog of the people.

History is rather vague as to what name the Keeshond bore before adoption as a symbol of the Patriots, but the breed was mainly known as the "barge dog." The breed had served for countless years on the *rijnaken*, vessels that were found in great numbers on the Rhine. When the Keeshond enjoyed its greatest popularity in Holland, these vessels were relatively small and, consequently, could not accommodate a very large dog. There probably were more Keeshonden kept as pets and watchdogs than as barge dogs throughout the Netherlands. But it was only natural that the barge dogs became better known, for they were continually traveling up and down the river, coming into contact with more people than did the pets.

The origin of the Keeshond type of dog is arctic, or possibly subarctic, and of the same strains that produced the Samoyed, Chow Chow, Norwegian Elkhound, Finnish Spitz, and Pomeranian. It seems most closely related to the Pomeranian, and some authorities believe that the Pomeranian was produced by selective breeding of the Keeshond.

The Keeshond has changed little in the past two centuries, and the earliest descriptions represent it as nearly identical with the dog of today. There also numbers of old paintings and drawings that prove how well the Keeshond type has been preserved. A 1794 drawing shows the children and dog of a burgomaster mourning beside his tomb. The dog clearly resembles today's Keeshonden. Other evidence is found in paintings by the famous Dutch artist Jan Steen.

The close link between the Keeshond and the Patriots was almost the breed's undoing. When the Prince of Orange's party established its dominance, few people wanted the dog that symbolized the opposition of the Patriots. Many who owned Keeshonden disposed of them quietly, and only those most loyal to the breed maintained it. At this point, the vessels used on the rivers began to gradually change. Each year they seemed to get larger, until they were eventually quite spacious, with plenty of room for large dogs. This had a considerable negative effect on Keeshond popularity.

The breed languished at very low ebb until 1920, when the Baroness van Hardenbroek became interested in it and undertook an investigation to determine how much of the old stock remained. The results of this search were surprising. Although the breed was gone from public attention, it was still kept in its original form by certain riverboat captains, farmers, and truck men. There were many excellent specimens. Some owners even maintained their own crude studbooks.

The baroness began breeding Keeshonden and spread their story throughout Europe. Within ten years, she brought the breed to such a solid position that the Dutch Keeshond Club was established. In 1933, De Raad van Beheer op Kynologisch Gebeid in Nederland accepted the standard for judging the breed.

As early as 1905, Keeshonden were making a very good impression in England. In 1930, the American Kennel Club accepted the breed for registration. With few exceptions, early development in this country was based on English imports. These, in turn, were the products of British imports from Holland and Germany.

A well-balanced, handsome dog of medium size, with alert carriage and intelligent expression, the Keeshond is a hardy breed, with a coat easily cared for by brushing. One of the most affectionate and lovable of all dogs, for centuries they have been bred as ideal family companions and sensible watchdogs.

# OFFICIAL STANDARD FOR THE KEESHOND

**General Appearance**—The Keeshond (pronounced *kayz-hawnd*) is a natural, handsome dog of well-balanced, short-coupled body, attracting attention not only by his coloration, alert carriage, and intelligent expression, but also by his stand-off coat, his richly plumed tail well curled over his back, his foxlike expression, and his small pointed ears. His coat is very thick around the neck, fore part of the shoulders and chest, forming a lion-like ruff—more profuse in the male. His rump and hind legs, down to the hocks, are also thickly coated, forming the characteristic "trousers." His head, ears, and lower legs are covered with thick, short hair.

**Size, Proportion, Substance**—The Keeshond is a medium-sized, square-appearing, sturdy dog, neither coarse nor lightly made. The ideal height of fully matured dogs when measured from top of withers to the ground is 18 inches for males and 17 inches for bitches—a one-inch variance either way is acceptable. While correct size is very important, it should not outweigh that of type.

**Head**—*Expression*—Expression is largely dependent on the distinctive characteristic called "spectacles"—a combination of markings and shadings in the orbital area which must include a delicate, dark line slanting from the outer corner of each eye toward the lower corner of each ear coupled with expressive eyebrows. Markings (or shadings) on face and head must present a pleasing appearance, imparting to the dog an alert and intelligent expression. *Very Serious Fault:* Absence of dark lines which form the "spectacles."

*Eyes*—Eyes should be dark brown in color, of medium size, almond shaped, set obliquely and neither too wide apart nor too close together. Eye rims are black. *Faults:* Round and/or protruding eyes or eyes light of color.

*Ears*—Ears should be small, triangular in shape, mounted high on head and carried erect. Size should be proportionate to the head—length approximating the distance from the outer corner of the eye to the nearest edge of the ear. *Fault:* Ears not carried erect when at attention.

*Skull*—The head should be well-proportioned to the body and wedge-shaped when viewed from above—not only the muzzle, but the whole head should give this impression when the ears are drawn back by covering the nape of the neck and the ears with one hand. Head in profile should exhibit a definite stop. *Faults:* Apple head or absence of stop.

*Muzzle*—Of medium length, neither coarse nor snipey, and well proportioned to the skull.

*Mouth*—The mouth should be neither overshot nor undershot. Lips should be black and closely meeting—not thick, coarse or sagging—and with no wrinkle at the corner of the mouth. *Faults:* Overshot, undershot or wry mouth.

*Teeth*—The teeth should be white, sound and strong meeting in a scissors bite. *Fault:* Misaligned teeth.

**Neck, Topline, Body**—The *neck* should be moderately long, well-shaped and well set on shoulders. The body should be compact with a short, straight back sloping slightly downward toward the hindquarters—well ribbed, barrel well rounded, short in loin, belly moderately tucked up, deep and strong of chest.

*Tail*—The tail should be moderately long and well feathered, set on high and tightly curled over the back. It should lie flat and close to the body. The tail must form a part of the "silhouette" of the dog's body, rather than give the appearance of an appendage. *Fault:* Tail not lying close to the back.

*Forequarters*—Forelegs should be straight seen from any angle. Pasterns are strong with a slight slope. Legs must be of good bone in proportion to the overall dog. Shoulder to upper arm angulation is between slight to moderate.

*Hindquarters*—Angulation in rear should be between slight to moderate to complement the forequarters, creating balance and typical gait. Hindquarters are well muscled with hocks perpendicular to the ground.

*Feet*—The feet should be compact, well rounded, cat-like. Toes are nicely arched, with black nails.

*Coat*—The body should be abundantly covered with long, straight, harsh hair standing well out from a thick, downy undercoat. Head, including muzzle, skull and ears, should be covered with smooth, soft, short hair—velvety in texture on the ears. The neck is covered with a mane—more profuse in the male—sweeping from under the jaw and covering the whole of the front part of the shoulders and chest, as well as the top part of the shoulders. The hair on the legs should be smooth and short, except for feathering on the front legs and "trousers" on the hind legs. Hind legs should be profusely feathered down to the hocks—not below. The hair on the tail should form a rich plume. Coat must not part down the back. The Keeshond is to be shown in a natural state with trimming permissible only on feet, pasterns, hocks and—if desired—whiskers. TRIMMING OTHER THAN AS DESCRIBED TO BE SEVERELY PENALIZED. *Faults:* Silky, wavy, or curly coats. Part in coat down the back.

**Color and Markings**—A dramatically marked dog, the Keeshond is a mixture of gray, black and cream. This coloration may vary from light to dark. The hair of the outer coat is black tipped, the length of the black tips producing the characteristic shading of color. Puppies are often less intensely marked. The undercoat is very pale gray or cream, never tawny.

*Head*—The muzzle should be dark in color. "Spectacles" and shadings, as previously described, are characteristic of the breed and must be present to some degree. Ears should be very dark—almost black.

*Ruff, Shoulders and "Trousers"*—The color of the ruff and "trousers" is lighter than that of the body. The shoulder line markings of light gray must be well defined.

*Tail*—The plume of the tail is very light in color when curled on the back, and the tip of the tail should be black.

*Legs and Feet*—Legs and feet are cream.

*Faults:* Pronounced white markings. Black markings more than halfway down the foreleg, penciling excepted. White foot or feet.

*Very Serious Faults*—Entirely black or white or any solid color; any pronounced deviation from the color as described.

**Gait**—The distinctive gait of the Keeshond is unique to the breed. Dogs should move boldly and keep tails curled over the back. They should move cleanly and briskly; the movement should be straight and sharp with reach and drive between slight to moderate.

**Temperament**—Temperament is of primary importance. The Keeshond is neither timid nor aggressive but, instead, is outgoing and friendly with both people and other dogs. The Keeshond is a lively, intelligent, alert and affectionate companion.

**Approved November 14, 1989**
**Effective January 1, 1990**

# LHASA APSO

*O*RIGINATING IN THE LONELY, ISOLATED REACHES OF THE HIMALAYAN MOUN-tains, Lhasa Apsos reflect their Tibetan heritage in many characteristic ways. Fastidious by nature, these sturdy little mountain dogs have remained relatively un-changed for hundreds of years. In Tibet, the breed is referred to as *apso seng kyi,* best translated as "bearded lion dog." The Lhasa's primary function was as a household sentinel, guarding the homes of Tibetan nobility and Buddhist monasteries, partic-ularly in or near the sacred city of Lhasa. Intelligence, acute hearing, and a natural instinct for distinguishing friend from stranger made Lhasas well suited to that role.

Lhasa Apsos were introduced to the United States in 1933 by C. Suydam Cut-ting, who received them as gifts from the thirteenth Dalai Lama. In 1935, the breed was registered by the AKC and is now one of three Tibetan breeds shown in the Non-Sporting Group.

A dog of moderation, each part of Lhasa Apso structure reflects the breed's her-itage and origin in mountainous Tibet. The medium-length muzzle contributes to efficient respiration, while the long rib cage allows for increased lung capacity. Sturdy legs provide necessary agility and stamina. Thick, heavily coated pads help protect the Lhasa's feet from frigid temperatures and rugged surfaces. Although height is an important factor in the breed, consideration must also be given to weight, proportion, and body length, all of which contribute to the breed's overall balance and soundness. Massive bone and body are not desirable characteristics. Slow to mature, Lhasa Apsos do not reach their prime until the third or fourth year. They age gracefully, keeping a youthful attitude and appearance well into their teens.

Distinguishing features of the breed include the coat, tail, and eyes. The Lhasa Apso's beautiful cloak of hair, a necessity in Tibet's harsh climate, is parted in the middle and drapes each side of the body from head to tail. Strong, resilient hair with a moderate amount of undercoat is desirable. When a section of mature Lhasa coat is lifted from the body, it should fall back, immediately blending in with the rest of the coat. When rubbed between the fingers, individual hairs should be felt. The tail, carried over the back, should be well feathered with long hair. A kink in the tail is not uncommon and was once considered a sign of luck. The tail may be carried in a screw or over the back in a curl lying to the side.

Lovely dark brown eyes contribute to the softness of Lhasa expression and are truly mirrors to the soul. Somewhat frontally placed, medium in size, and oval in shape, Lhasa Apso eyes should not protrude. A dark iris fills the eye, with minimal white showing. Black pigment surrounds the eyes.

Not a breed given to being yappy or nervous, the Lhasa Apso is extremely intelligent, often exhibiting a regal attitude, which can be quickly dispelled by a clownish sense of humor and a joy for life. An independent nature ensures that Lhasas seldom need to be entertained. To the contrary, they usually provide the entertainment! However, this same independent (some might call it stubborn) nature requires patient understanding. Rather calm and deliberate, the Lhasa resists harsh or strict discipline, responding best to training with positive reinforcement. Often, being suspicious of strangers is a direct reflection of a long heritage of seclusion in Tibet. They are less protective away from the home environment.

From ancient dwellings in the Himalayas, to homes and apartments in the smallest towns or busiest cities across the United States, Lhasa Apsos continue their service to people as companions and watchdogs. Their joy of life and unwavering devotion to those they love serve only to enhance their physical beauty.

# OFFICIAL STANDARD FOR THE LHASA APSO

**Character**—Gay and assertive, but chary of strangers.

**Size**—Variable, but about 10 inches or 11 inches at shoulder for dogs, bitches slightly smaller.

**Color**—All colors equally acceptable with or without dark tips to ears and beard.

**Body Shape**—The length from point of shoulders to point of buttocks longer than height at withers, well ribbed up, strong loin, well-developed quarters and thighs.

**Coat**—Heavy, straight, hard, not woolly nor silky, of good length, and very dense.

**Mouth and Muzzle**—The preferred bite is either level or slightly undershot. Muzzle of medium length; a square muzzle is objectionable.

**Head**—Heavy head furnishings with good fall over eyes, good whiskers and beard; skull narrow, falling away behind the eyes in a marked degree, not quite flat, but not domed or apple-shaped; straight foreface of fair length. Nose black, the length from tip of nose to eye to be roughly about one-third of the total length from nose to back of skull.

**Eyes**—Dark brown, neither very large and full, nor very small and sunk.

**Ears**—Pendant, heavily feathered.

**Legs**—Forelegs straight; both forelegs and hind legs heavily furnished with hair.

**Feet**—Well feathered, should be round and catlike, with good pads.

**Tail and Carriage**—Well feathered, should be carried well over back in a screw; there may be a kink at the end. A low carriage of stern is a serious fault.

**Approved July 11, 1978**

# LÖWCHEN

*L*ÖWCHEN ARE AN IDEAL FAMILY PET: THEY ARE HYPOALLERGENIC, "NON-shedding," easily trained, and make good companion dogs. Show them a squirrel and they'll bark, but then won't know what to do with it. Show them a stranger, they'll bark, and then be the person's friend. Show them a child, not too young, and they will allow themselves to be picked up and carried gently. If they find an adult who will walk and feed them, and brush them a few times a week, they'll become that person's best friend, never leaving their side.

Löwchen are not meant to be kennel dogs and should be indoors on a bed, not in a yard. They are not, however, couch potatoes. The more exercise this breed is given, the better home companions they will be. Löwchen nature is loving, loyal, bright, and trainable. They are a big dog in a little package. Löwchen bark but do not yip, and will stand up to big dogs and probably intimidate them. This is a breed that can be sensitive to noise and will bark when they hear the doorbell or a shrill sound on television. Because of this alert nature, Löwchen excel in conformation, agility, and obedience competition, and as therapy dogs, too.

The origin of the breed is open to debate. One theory claims Mediterranean antecedents. Another says the breed is related to the Bichon family. Still another source traces the Löwchen background to Belgium, Holland, and Germany. What we certainly do know is that our "little lion dogs" were the pampered pets of royalty, and that the breed was almost completely wiped out during the world wars.

They survived World War II due to the efforts of Madame Bennert, of Belgium, who rescued the surviving lion dogs and shipped them to a veterinarian, Dr. Hans Rickert, in Germany. The Löwchen that eventually arrived in Great Britain and the United States were from Rickert's Von Den Drei kennel.

In 1971, the first Löwchen arrived in the United States from England. At that time, the breed name was Little Lion Dog, although there was no connection with any of the lion dogs from Asia. (The Löwchen is referred to as the little lion dog in art and tapestry dating as early as the mid-fifteenth century. This appellation refers to the style in which the breed is trimmed, with close-cut hindquarters and a full, natural mane resembling that of a lion.) The Löwchen Club of America, founded in 1971, eventually changed the name to Löwchen, German for "little lion dog." Under Fédération Cynologique Internationale registration, the breed is known as the Petite Chien Lion.

The Löwchen was accepted by the American Kennel Club and put into the Non-Sporting Group in 1999. In England and on the Continent, it is shown in the Toy Group.

# OFFICIAL STANDARD FOR THE LÖWCHEN

**General Appearance**—A small, bright and lively dog that originated as a companion breed in pre-Renaissance Europe where ladies of the court groomed it in the likeness of a little lion. Breed characteristics are a compact, balanced body; a relatively short, broad topskull and muzzle; and a proud, lively gait that accentuates the lion cut with a long flowing mane. These quintessential features, combined with an outgoing and positive attitude, result in a dog of great style.

**Size, Proportion, Substance**—Ideally 12" to 14" at the withers. Dogs or bitches above or below these measurements should be faulted to the degree of the variance. The body is just off-square when properly balanced. The distance from the prosternum to the point of buttocks is slightly greater than the distance from the withers to the ground in an 11 to 10 ratio. The Löwchen is strong and sturdy in bone, but never coarse.

**Head**—The head is a hallmark breed characteristic. The *expression* is bright, alert, and lively. The *eyes* are set well into the skull, large, dark and round in shape, set well apart and forward looking. Brown and Champagne coated dogs may have slightly lighter eyes. Full pigmentation is required on the eye rims. The ears are pendant, moderate in length, well fringed, and set on slightly above the level of the eye. *Skull*—The backskull is broad with a moderate stop. The *muzzle* is equal in length or slightly shorter than the backskull and is relatively broad with moderate depth of underjaw resulting in a slightly rounded finish to the muzzle. The *nose* is dark in color. Complete pigmentation is required. Coloration of pigment is black or brown, dependent on the coat color. The *lips* are tight, with color the same as the nose. The *bite* is scissors and the teeth are rather large and well spaced with complete dentition.

**Neck, Topline, Body**—The *neck* is of good length, with a slight arch, fitting smoothly into the shoulders and topline. The head is carried high when the dog is moving. The *topline* is level from withers to tailset. The *body* is slightly off-square when properly balanced. The *loin* is short and strong. The *ribs* are well sprung. The *brisket* is moderate in width and extends approximately to the elbows. The *underline* has a slight tuck-up at the loin. The *tail* is set high and carried in a cup-handle fashion over the back when the dog is moving. A dropped tail while standing is not to be penalized.

**Forequarters**—The *shoulders* are strong and well laid back with smooth musculature. The upper arm is of equal length to the shoulder blade and the two meet in a near 90-degree angle. The *elbows* are held close to the body. *Forearms* are of good length and the distance from the withers to the elbow is slightly less than the distance from the elbow to the ground. From the front the legs are perfectly parallel from the elbow to the feet. The bone is more round than the oval and of medium size with only a slight decrease in size at the pasterns. The *pasterns* are short, parallel from the front and very slightly bent when viewed from the side. The *dewclaws* on the forelegs should be removed. The *forefeet* point straight ahead, and are well arched with deep pads and the two center toes are slightly in advance of the two outer toes. The nails are relatively short. A tight foot is preferred, and a splayed foot is to be penalized.

**Hindquarters**—The pelvic bone projects beyond the set of the tail and is at an approximate 45-degree angle from a perfectly horizontal line. The upper and lower thighs are well muscled and of approximately equal length with medium bone. The *stifles* are well bent. The *hocks* are well let down and perpendicular to the ground from any angle. The rear *dewclaws* should be removed. The *hindfeet* are slightly smaller than the forefeet, and are well arched with deep pads.

**Coat**—The untrimmed coat is long, rather dense and moderately soft in texture. It has a slight to moderate wavy appearance. Wiry, woolly, curly, and flat coat textures are not correct, and are to be penalized to the degree of severity. No scissoring or shaping of the untrimmed coat is permitted. Puppies typically have a softer coat. *Trim*—Trimmed in the Lion Trim, the coat is clipped to about ⅛″ on the following parts of the body: From the last rib back to and including the hindquarters, leaving a ruff or mane which just covers the last rib. The hindquarters are clipped to the hock joint. The front legs are clipped from the elbow to a point above the knee, which is equal to the same distance as from the ground to the hock joint leaving cuffs of hair on all four legs. The tail is clipped from the base to approximately one-half way to the tip leaving a plume at the end of the tail. The feet are clipped to the point where the dewclaws were removed. The unclipped areas must be completely natural and untrimmed. On no account should the unclipped areas be smoothed, shortened, shaped or otherwise tidied with anything other than a comb or brush. *Any trim other than specified or any shaping or scissoring of the long coat are disqualifications.*

**Color**—All colors and color combinations are acceptable, with no preference given to any.

**Gait**—Movement at a trot is effortless with good reach in front and full extension in the rear. From the front, the forelegs move in almost parallel lines, converging slightly as the speed increases. From the rear, the legs move in almost parallel lines and in the same line of motion as the forelegs, converging slightly as the speed increases. From the side, movement is efficient and ground covering. The forelegs reach well out in front in a long, relatively low stride, and the rear legs come well under the body and extend behind to maximize propulsion. The body should remain nearly square in outline, and the topline is held firm and level, with the tail being carried curved over the back and the head is held above the level of the back.

**Temperament**—The Löwchen is alert, intelligent, and affectionate with the overall qualities of a loving companion dog. It has a lively, outgoing and inquisitive personality.

## DISQUALIFICATIONS

*Any trim other than specified.*
*Shaping or scissoring of the long coat.*

**Approved June 1995**
**Effective April 1, 1996**

# POODLE (MINIATURE AND STANDARD)

*F*EW DOGS HAVE CLIMBED TO SUCH HIGH FAVOR IN SO MANY DIFFERENT countries as has the Poodle, but it appeared so early in various parts of the world that there is some doubt as to the land of its origin.

It is supposed to have originated in Germany, where it is known as the Pudel or *canis familiaris aquatius*. However, for years it has been regarded as the national dog of France, where it was commonly used as a retriever as well as a traveling-circus trick dog. In France it was, and is known as, the Caniche, which is derived from *chien canard* or duck dog. Doubtless the English word *poodle* comes from the German *pudel* or *pudelin*, meaning to splash in the water. The expression "French Poodle" was in all probability a somewhat later cognomen, bestowed as a result of the dog's great popularity in France.

At any rate, the Poodle undoubtedly originated as a water retriever. In fact the unclipped Poodle of today bears strong resemblance in type to the old Rough-haired Water Dog of England as painted by Reinagle at the beginning of the nineteenth century; and except that the Irish Water Spaniel is born with short hair on its face and tail, there is little difference between this ancient Irish dog and the Poodle.

Authorities concede that the large, or Standard, Poodle is the oldest of the three varieties, and that the dog gained special fame as a water worker. So widely was it used as retriever that it was shorn of portions of its coat to further facilitate progress in swimming. Thence came the custom of clipping to pattern which so enhanced the style and general appearance that its sponsors, particularly in France, were captivated by it.

All of the Poodle's ancestors were acknowledged to be good swimmers, although one member of the family, the truffle dog (it may have been of Toy or Miniature size), it is said, never went near the water. Truffle hunting was widely practiced in England, and later in Spain and Germany, where the edible fungus has always been considered a great delicacy. For scenting and digging up the fungus, the smaller dogs were favored since they did less damage to the truffles with their feet than the larger kinds. So it is rumored that a terrier was crossed with the Poodle to produce the ideal truffle hunter.

Despite the Standard Poodle's claim to greater age than the other varieties, there is some evidence to show that the smaller types developed only a short time after the breed assumed the general type by which it is recognized today. The smallest, or Toy variety, was known in England in the eighteenth century, when the White Cuban became popular there. This was a sleeve dog attributed to the West Indies from whence it traveled to Spain and then to England. Queen Anne, we are told, admired a troupe of performing dogs that danced to music in almost human fashion. And this penchant, by the way, Poodles of all sizes have carried down the years intact.

But the Continent had known the Poodle long before it came to England. Drawings by Albrecht Dürer establish the breed in the fifteenth and sixteenth centuries. How long the dog had been known in Spain is uncertain, but it was the principal pet dog of the latter eighteenth century, as shown by the paintings of Goya. And France had Toy Poodles as pampered favorites during the reign of Louis XVI, at about the same period.

There is scarcely a purebred dog of this day that can claim so many references in art and literature going back into time. Bas-reliefs dating from the first century, found along the shores of the Mediterranean, portray the Poodle very much as it is in the twentieth century. Clipped to resemble the lion, it is not unlike some of the specimens seen at the earliest dog shows. Possibly long ago there was a link between the dog attributed to the Island of Melita—now known as the Maltese—and the Toy Poodle. Similarly there may have been a relationship between the Poodle and the dog of Spain—the spaniel. If they do not come from the same progenitor, at least the paths of their ancestors must have crossed at some remote time.

The universal esteem in which the Poodle has been held since the beginning of modern history is attested by its interesting variations in size and color. In accordance with present-day show classification, we have three sizes as well as an array of colors to suit almost anyone's taste. We have white ones, black ones, brown, cream, and blue ones, gray, apricot and so on; any solid color is allowed. Some are pink-skinned, some blue- or silver-skinned, others cream-skinned. Hence he who fancies a Poodle is never at a loss: He may choose a big dog to guard and protect, a medium-sized one to fit into restricted quarters, or a tiny tot to serve only as "comforter." And he can pick a color to match whatever his decor may happen to be. Surely such an unusual selection may have played at least some part in the Poodle's continued rise to fame. But even more, the dog's innate intelligence and his ability to learn are considered exceptional.

It should be kept in mind that the words *Standard, Miniature,* and *Toy* are used to denote size only. All are one breed, governed by the same standard of perfection.

In addition to differences in size and color, the Poodle enjoys another unique characteristic, namely, a coat which lends itself to a choice of hair styling. The top coat is very profuse indeed, wiry in texture, and composed of thick, close curls, and the undercoat is woolly and warm. If allowed to grow unhindered the top coat forms thin, cylindrical mats which form a mass of ropelike cords: thus the curly Poodle becomes what used to be known in the old days as the Corded Poodle. This style, though, went out long ago; it was impractical for everyday living and difficult to keep in condition.

The various clips are, of course, a matter of taste insofar as the average owner is concerned. If he plans to exhibit in the show ring, however, he must choose in accordance with the specifications enumerated under "Coat" in the official AKC standard.

# OFFICIAL STANDARD FOR THE POODLE

**General Appearance, Carriage and Condition**—That of a very active, intelligent and elegant-appearing dog, squarely built, well proportioned, moving soundly and carrying himself proudly. Properly clipped in the traditional fashion and carefully groomed, the Poodle has about him an air of distinction and dignity peculiar to himself.

## Size, Proportion, Substance

*Size—The Standard Poodle* is over 15 inches at the highest point of the shoulders. Any Poodle which is 15 inches or less in height shall be disqualified from competition as a Standard Poodle.

*The Miniature Poodle* is 15 inches or under at the highest point of the shoulders, with a minimum height in excess of 10 inches. Any Poodle which is over 15 inches or is 10 inches or less at the highest point of the shoulders shall be disqualified from competition as a Miniature Poodle.

*The Toy Poodle* is 10 inches or under at the highest point of the shoulders. Any Poodle which is more than 10 inches at the highest point of the shoulders shall be disqualified from competition as a Toy Poodle.

As long as the Toy Poodle is definitely a Toy Poodle, and the Miniature Poodle a Miniature Poodle, both in balance and proportion for the Variety, diminutiveness shall be the deciding factor when all other points are equal.

*Proportion*—To insure the desirable squarely built appearance, the length of body measured from the breastbone to the point of the rump approximates the height from the highest point of the shoulders to the ground.

*Substance*—Bone and muscle of both forelegs and hindlegs are in proportion to size of dog.

## Head and Expression

*(a) Eyes*—Very dark, oval in shape and set far enough apart and positioned to create an alert intelligent expression. *Major fault: eyes round, protruding, large or very light.*

*(b) Ears*—Hanging close to the head, set at or slightly below eye level. The ear leather is long, wide and thickly feathered; however, the ear fringe should not be of excessive length.

*(c) Skull*—Moderately rounded, with a slight but definite stop. Cheekbones and muscles flat. Length from occiput to stop about the same as length of muzzle.

*(d) Muzzle*—Long, straight and fine, with slight chiseling under the eyes. Strong without lippiness. The chin definite enough to preclude snipiness. *Major fault: lack of chin.* **Teeth**—White, strong and with a scissors bite. *Major fault: undershot, overshot, wry mouth.*

## Neck, Topline, Body

*Neck*—well proportioned, strong and long enough to permit the head to be carried high and with dignity. Skin snug at throat. The neck rises from strong, smoothly muscled shoulders. *Major fault: ewe neck.*

The *topline* is level, neither sloping nor roached, from the highest point of the shoulder blade to the base of the tail, with the exception of a slight hollow just behind the shoulder.

*Body*—*(a)* Chest deep and moderately wide with well sprung ribs. *(b)* The loin is short, broad and muscular. *(c)* Tail straight, set on high and carried up, docked of sufficient length to insure a balanced outline. *Major fault: set low, curled, or carried over the back.*

## Forequarters

Strong, smoothly muscled shoulders. The shoulder blade is well laid back and approximately the same length as the upper foreleg. *Major fault: steep shoulder.*

*(a) Forelegs*—Straight and parallel when viewed from the front. When viewed from the side the elbow is directly below the highest point of the shoulder. The pasterns are strong. Dewclaws may be removed.

*Feet*—The feet are rather small, oval in shape with toes well arched and cushioned on thick firm pads. Nails short but not excessively shortened. The feet turn neither in nor out. *Major fault: paper or splay foot.*

**Hindquarters**—The angulation of the hindquarters balances that of the forequarters. Hind legs straight and parallel when viewed from the rear. Muscular with width in the region of the stifles which are well bent; femur and tibia are about equal in length; hock to heel short and perpendicular to the ground. When standing, the rear toes are only slightly behind the point of the rump. *Major fault: cow-hocks.*

## Coat

*(a) Quality*—(1) Curly: of naturally harsh texture, dense throughout. (2) Corded: hanging in tight even cords of varying length; longer on mane or body coat, head and ears; shorter on puffs, bracelets, and pompons.

*(b) Clip*—A Poodle under 12 months may be shown in the "Puppy" clip. In all regular classes, Poodles 12 months or over must be shown in the "English Saddle" or "Continental" clip. In the Stud Dog and Brood Bitch classes and in a non-competitive Parade of Champions, Poodles may be shown in the "Sporting" clip. A Poodle shown in any other type of clip shall be disqualified.

*(1) "Puppy"*—A Poodle under a year old may be shown in the "Puppy" clip with the coat long. The face, throat, feet and base of the tail are shaved. The entire shaven foot is visible. There is a pompon on the end of the tail. In order to give a neat appearance and a smooth unbroken line, shaping of the coat is permissible. *(2) "English Saddle"*—In the "English Saddle" clip the face, throat, feet, forelegs and base of the tail are shaved, leaving puffs on the forelegs and a pompon on the end of the tail. The hindquarters are covered with a short blanket of hair except for a curved shaved area on each flank and two shaved bands on each hindleg. The entire shaven foot and a portion of the shaven leg above the puff are visible. The rest of the body is left in full coat but may be shaped in order to insure overall balance. *(3) "Continental"*—In the "Continental" clip, the face, throat, feet, and base of the tail are shaved. The hindquarters are shaved with pompons (optional) on the hips. The legs are shaved, leaving bracelets on the hindlegs and puffs on the forelegs. There is a pompon on the end of the tail. The entire shaven foot and a portion of the shaven foreleg above the puff are visible. The rest of the body is left in full coat but may be shaped in order to insure overall balance. *(4) "Sporting"*—In the "Sporting" clip, a Poodle shall be shown with face, feet, throat and base of tail shaved, leaving a scissored cap on the top of the head and a pompon on the end of the tail. The rest of the body and legs are clipped or scissored to follow the outline of the dog leaving a short blanket of coat no longer than one inch in length. The hair on the legs may be slightly longer than that on the body.

*Puppy Clip*

*Sporting Clip*

*English Saddle Clip*

*Continental Clip*

*Modified Continental Clip*

In all clips the hair of the topknot may be left free or held in place by elastic bands. The hair is only of sufficient length to present a smooth outline. "Topknot" refers only to hair on the skull, from stop to occiput. This is the only area where elastic bands may be used.

**Color**—The coat is an even and solid color at the skin. In blues, grays, silvers, browns, cafe-au-laits, apricots and creams the coat may show varying shades of the same color. This is frequently present in the somewhat darker feathering of the ears and in the tipping of the ruff. While clear colors are definitely preferred, such natural variation in the shading of the coat is not to be considered a fault. Brown and cafe-au-lait Poodles have liver-colored noses, eye-rims and lips, dark toenails and dark amber eyes. Black, blue, gray, silver, cream and white Poodles have black noses, eye-rims and lips, black or self colored toenails and very dark eyes. In the apricots while the foregoing coloring is preferred, liver-colored noses, eye-rims and lips, and amber eyes are permitted but are not desirable. *Major fault: color of nose, lips and eye-rims incomplete, or of wrong color for color of dog.*

Parti-colored dogs shall be disqualified. The coat of a parti-colored dog is not an even solid color at the skin but is of two or more colors.

**Gait**—A straightforward trot with light springy action and strong hindquarters drive. Head and tail carried up. Sound effortless movement is essential.

**Temperament**—Carrying himself proudly, very active, intelligent, the Poodle has about him an air of distinction and dignity peculiar to himself. *Major fault: shyness or sharpness.*

**Major Faults**—Any distinct deviation from the desired characteristics described in the Breed Standard.

**Disqualifications**—*Size*—A dog over or under the height limits specified shall be disqualified. *Clip*—A dog in any type of clip other than those listed under coat shall be disqualified. *Parti-colors*—The coat of a parti-colored dog is not an even solid color at the skin but of two or more colors. Parti-colored dogs shall be disqualified.

## VALUE OF POINTS

| | |
|---|---|
| General appearance, temperament, carriage and condition | 30 |
| Head, expression, ears, eyes, and teeth | 20 |
| Body, neck, legs, feet and tail | 20 |
| Gait | 20 |
| Coat, color and texture | 10 |

**Approved August 14, 1984**
**Reformatted March 27, 1990**

# SCHIPPERKE

$\mathcal{T}$HE SCHIPPERKE ORIGINATED IN THE FLEMISH PROVINCES OF BELGIUM AND is sometimes erroneously described as a Dutch dog, due perhaps to a misconception regarding the location of Flanders (a part of which extends into northern France) and to the fact that before 1832 Belgium and Holland were at times united. A Belgian judge says: "The Schipperke is not derived from the spitz or Pomeranian but is really a diminutive of the black sheepdog commonly called the Leauvenaar, which used to follow the wagons along our old highways in the provinces. The proof of this is that those specimens that are born with a tail carry it like the Groenendael."

In the mid-nineteenth century some of these forty-pound sheepdogs were still herding sheep in the neighborhood of Louvain, and from these both the Schipperke and the Groenendael have descended. The herd dog was gradually bred larger, and the Schipperke bred down to become that "excellent and faithful" little watchdog that we know.

The Schipperke has been known for several hundred years; in fact, it may claim the first known "specialty show" given for any breed. In 1690, a show for Schipperkes of the Guild workmen was held in the Grand Palace of Brussels; the men were invited to bring their dogs and the hammered brass collars which even at that time custom had ordered for the Schipperke.

The breed was called Spits or Spitske then; the name Schipperke was given it only after the forming of the specialty club in 1888. The name is Flemish for "little captain" and is properly pronounced "*sheep-er-ker*" (the last "r" almost silent). It was chosen as being a more distinctive name, and, as a compliment to one Mr. Renssens, known as "the father of the Schipperke" because of his efforts to gain recognition for the breed. He was the owner of a canal boat line operating between Brussels and Antwerp and had observed that there were many Schipperkes used as guards on these boats. Though called a canal boat dog, the Schipperke was as popular with shoemakers and other workmen as it was on the canals.

The legend of the Schipperke relates that the custom of cutting the tails arose in 1609, and it tells the story of a shoemaker who, angered by the repeated thieving of his neighbor's dog, cut off its tail—thereby showing the improved appearance soon copied by others and continued to this day. There is no evidence that the breed was ever born tailless; in fact, it seems that more dogs are born without tails now than earlier in their history. The Belgian Schipperkes Club has an amusing etching illustrating the legend "The Tail of the Schipperke."

The career of the Schipperke as a fashionable pet began in 1885, when Queen Marie Henriette, wife of Leopold II, saw a Schipperke at a Brussels show and acquired it. Before this time it had been the companion of the lower classes.

The first dog in America is believed to have been imported in 1888 by Walter J. Comstock, of Providence. A few years later Frank Dole began showing Schips in the Miscellaneous class. An American specialty club was founded about 1905, but died out during World War I. There was little interest in the breed until, after several years of effort by a few fanciers, the present Schipperke Club of America was founded in 1929.

The general appearance of the Schipperke is very distinctive, resembling no other breed closely. It has a short and thick-set body with foxy head—the whole suggesting a dog with plenty of coat and an outstanding ruff and long culotte. He has an intelligent, keen expression (not at all mean). His close undercoat keeps him warm even in American winters—the latter are far colder than those of his native land—and it sheds water and needs very little attention to keep it in order.

A judge of the breed for fifty years has said that the most important thing in judging is the correct silhouette: "I first look to see if the dog has the correct silhouette. If not, he is nothing and I look no further. If he has, I look into further details beginning with the bone structure."

This curious and energetic breed is usually long-lived for a small one, many instances of dogs living to 15 and 16 years old being recorded; one dog, bred in Rothesay, Scotland, was reputed to have lived 21 years.

The Schipperke is often called "the best house dog" (*le meilleur chien de maison*). Schips are very fond of children and in some cases have served as guards; they have taken the place, to some extent, of human nurses, so devoted are they to their small charges.

The dogs have been used to hunt, and one well-known breeder of the past wrote that he used them with great success on racoons and possums in Minnesota. Though usually an excellent ratter, the Schip is not a powerful fighter but can hold his own with most dogs of his weight and will tackle anything in defense of his household or of his master. He is not aware of the limitations of his size. As Julius Caesar wrote: "The bravest of these were the Belgians."

# OFFICIAL STANDARD FOR THE SCHIPPERKE

**General Appearance**—The Schipperke is an agile, active watchdog and hunter of vermin. In appearance he is a small, thickset, cobby, black, tailless dog, with a fox-like face. The dog is square in profile and possesses a distinctive coat, which includes a standout ruff, cape and culottes. All of these create a unique silhouette, appearing to slope from shoulders to croup. Males are decidedly masculine without coarseness. Bitches are decidedly feminine without over-refinement.

Any deviation from the ideal described in the standard should be penalized to the extent of the deviation. Faults common to all breeds are as undesirable in the Schipperke as in any other breed, even though such faults may not be specifically mentioned in the standard.

**Size, Proportion, Substance**—*Size*—The suggested height at the highest point of the withers is 11 to 13 inches for males and 10 to 12 inches for bitches. Quality should always take precedence over size. *Proportion*—Square in profile. *Substance*—Thickset.

**Head**—*Expression*—The expression is questioning, mischievous, impudent and alert, but never mean or wild. The well proportioned head, accompanied by the correct eyes and ears, will give the dog proper Schipperke expression.

*Skull*—The skull is of medium width, narrowing toward the muzzle. Seen in profile with the ears laid back, the skull is slightly rounded. The upper jaw is moderately filled in under the eyes, so that, when viewed from above, the head forms a wedge tapering smoothly from the back of the skull to the tip of the nose. The stop is definite but not prominent. The length of the muzzle is slightly less than the length of the skull.

*Eyes*—The ideal eyes are small, oval rather than round, dark brown and placed forward on the head.

*Ears*—The ears are small, triangular, placed high on the head, and, when at attention, very erect. A drop ear or ears is a disqualification. *Nose*—The nose is small and black. *Bite*—The bite must be scissors or level. Any deviation is to be severely penalized.

**Neck, Topline, Body**—*Neck*—The neck is of moderate length, slightly arched and in balance with the rest of the dog to give the correct silhouette. *Topline*—The topline is level or sloping slightly from the withers to the croup. The stand-out ruff adds to the slope, making the dog seem slightly higher at the shoulders than at the rump. *Body*—The chest is broad and deep, and reaches to the elbows. The well sprung ribs (modified oval) are wide behind the shoulders and taper to the sternum. The forechest extends in front of the shoulders between the front legs. The loin is short, muscular and moderately drawn up. The croup is broad and well-rounded with the tail docked. No tail is visually discernible.

**Forequarters**—The shoulders are well laid back, with the legs extending straight down from the body when viewed from the front. From the side, legs are placed well under the body. Pasterns are short, thick and strong, but still flexible, showing a slight angle when viewed from the side. Dewclaws are generally removed. Feet are small, round and tight. Nails are short, strong and black.

**Hindquarters**—The hindquarters appear slightly lighter than the forequarters, but are well muscled, and in balance with the front. The hocks are well let down and the stifles are well bent. Extreme angulation is to be penalized. From the rear, the legs extend straight down from the hip through the hock to the feet. Dewclaws must be removed.

**Coat—*Pattern***—The adult coat is highly characteristic and must include several distinct lengths growing naturally in a specific pattern. The coat is short on the face, ears, front of the forelegs and on the hocks; it is medium length on the body, and longer in the ruff, cape, jabot and culottes. The ruff begins in back of the ears and extends completely around the neck; the cape forms an additional distinct layer extending beyond the ruff; the jabot extends across the chest and down between the front legs. The hair down the middle of the back, starting just behind the cape and continuing over the rump, lies flat. It is slightly shorter than the cape but longer than the hair on the sides of the body and sides of the legs. The coat on the rear of the thighs forms culottes, which should be as long as the ruff. Lack of differentiation in coat lengths should be heavily penalized, as it is an essential breed characteristic.

***Texture***—The coat is abundant, straight and slightly harsh to the touch. The softer undercoat is dense and short on the body and is very dense around the neck, making the ruff stand out. Silky coats, body coats over three inches in length or very short harsh coats are equally incorrect.

***Trimming***—As the Schipperke is a natural breed, only trimming of the whiskers and the hair between the pads of the feet is optional. Any other trimming must not be done.

**Color**—The outer coat must be black. Any color other than a natural black is a disqualification. The undercoat, however, may be slightly lighter. During the shedding period, the coat might take on a transitory reddish cast, which is to be penalized to the degree that it detracts from the overall black appearance of the dog. Graying due to age (seven years or older) or occasional white hairs should not be penalized.

**Gait**—Proper Schipperke movement is a smooth, well coordinated and graceful trot (basically double tracking at a moderate speed), with a tendency to gradually converge toward the center of balance beneath the dog as speed increases. Front and rear must be in perfect balance with good reach in front and drive in the rear. The topline remains level or slightly sloping downward from the shoulders to the rump. Viewed from the front, the elbows remain close to the body. The legs form a straight line from the shoulders through the elbows to the toes, with the feet pointing straight ahead. From the rear, the legs form a straight line from the hip through the hocks to the pads, with the feet pointing straight ahead.

**Temperament**—The Schipperke is curious, interested in everything around him, and is an excellent and faithful little watchdog. He is reserved with strangers and ready to protect his family and property if necessary. He displays a confident and independent personality, reflecting the breed's original purpose as watchdog and hunter of vermin.

## DISQUALIFICATIONS

*A drop ear or ears.*
*Any color other than a natural black.*

**Approved November 13, 1990**
**Effective January 1, 1991**

# SHIBA INU

$\mathcal{T}$HE SHIBA INU HAS BEEN WITH THE JAPANESE PEOPLE FOR CENTURIES. THEY are considered the smallest and oldest of Japan's dogs. The ability of these dogs to maneuver through steep hills and mountain slopes, together with their keen senses, have repeatedly shown the Shiba to be a superb hunting dog.

The ancestors of today's Shibas were those hardy survivors of Japan's mountainous regions. Although originally used to hunt large game, they currently are used on smaller animals. Shibas make excellent watchdogs and have established themselves as the number-one companion dog in Japan. They can be seen throughout Japan in the cities, suburbs, and countrysides.

There have been many stories on how the Shiba came about its name. Some are of the opinion that the name Shiba Inu was given because of its skill in going freely through the brushwood bushes. You will hear people refer to the Shiba as the Little Brushwood Dog. Another story has it that the other meaning of the Japanese word *shiba* is "small"; therefore this word has also been attached to these dogs. These stories, however, have not been validated. What is valid is that this small dog called Shiba first came to its name in approximately the 1920s. In December of 1936, through the Cultural Properties Act, the Shiba was designated as a precious natural product of the Japanese nation. Thus, the breed was given official recognition.

Today's Shiba retains many of the characteristics that were essential for its survival as a hunting breed over the centuries: an independent nature coupled with quick reflexes and a strong prey drive. The Shiba often does not regard every stranger as an immediate friend but is loyal and affectionate to those who earn his respect.

Most of the Shibas being shown in the 1930s came from the Yamanashi or San In areas of Japan. These dogs were brought down from the mountains to the more populated areas. As they had been used mostly for hunting, their appearance was somewhat different from the Shiba today. They were large boned and rough looking, unlike the elegant Shibas you now see.

After reaching near extinction during World War II, those Shibas remaining were from three different bloodlines. They were the San In Shiba, the Mino Shiba, and the Shin Shu Shiba—the last being the most popular in Japan past and present. It is from these three lines that the Shiba has evolved into the modern breed.

The first documented Shiba in America was in 1954. It was brought from Japan by an American armed-services family. In the late 1970s, Americans started to import the Shiba for breeding. The first litter born in the United States was in 1979. The sire and dam were imports owned by Julia Cadwell.

The Shiba Inu was admitted to the AKC Stud Book on April 1, 1992, with exhibition in the Miscellaneous class beginning in June of that year, and regular classification in the Non-Sporting Group on June 1, 1993.

# OFFICIAL STANDARD FOR THE SHIBA INU

**General Appearance**—The Shiba is the smallest of the Japanese native breeds of dog and was originally developed for hunting by sight and scent in the dense undergrowth of Japan's mountainous areas. Alert and agile with keen senses, he is also an excellent watchdog and companion. His frame is compact with well-developed muscles. Males and females are distinctly different in appearance: males are masculine without coarseness; females are feminine without weakness of structure.

**Size, Proportion, Substance**—Males, 14½ to 16½ inches. Females, 13½ to 15½ inches. The preferred size is the middle of the range for each sex. Average weight at preferred size is approximately 23 pounds for males, 17 pounds for females. Males have a height to length ratio of 10 to 11, females slightly longer. Bone is moderate. *Disqualification—Males over 16½ and under 14½ inches. Females over 15½ and under 13½ inches.*

**Head**—*Expression* is good natured with a strong and confident gaze. *Eyes* are somewhat triangular in shape, deep set, and upward slanting toward the outside base of the ear. Iris is dark brown. Eye rims are black. *Ears* are triangular in shape, firmly pricked and small, but in proportion to head and body size. Ears are set well apart and tilt directly forward with the slant of the back of the ear following the arch of the neck. *Skull* size is moderate and in proportion to the body. *Forehead* is broad and flat with a slight furrow. *Stop* is moderate. *Muzzle* is firm, full, and round with a strong lower jaw projecting from full *cheeks*. The bridge of the muzzle is straight. Muzzle tapers slightly from stop to nose tip. Muzzle length is 40 percent of the total head length from occiput to nose tip. It is preferred that whiskers remain intact. *Lips* are tight and black. *Nose* is black. *Bite* is scissors, with a full complement of strong, substantial, evenly aligned teeth.

*Serious Fault*—Five or more missing teeth is a very serious fault and must be penalized.

*Disqualification—Overshot or undershot bite.*

**Neck, Topline and Body**—*Neck* is thick, sturdy and of moderate length. *Topline* is straight and level to the base of the tail. *Body* is dry and well muscled without the appearance of sluggishness or coarseness. Forechest is well developed. Chest depth measured from the withers to the lowest point of the sternum is one-half or slightly less than the total height from withers to ground. *Ribs* are moderately sprung. Abdomen is firm and well tucked-up. *Back* is firm. *Loins* are strong. *Tail* is thick and powerful and is carried over the back in a sickle or curled position. A loose single curl or a sickle tail pointing vigorously toward the neck and nearly parallel to the back is preferred. A double curl or sickle tail pointing upward is acceptable. In length the tail reaches nearly to the hock joint when extended. Tail is set high.

**Forequarters**—Shoulder blade and upper arm are moderately angulated and approximately equal in length. Elbows are set close to the body and turn neither in nor out. Forelegs and feet are moderately spaced, straight, and parallel. Pasterns are slightly inclined. Removal of front dewclaws is optional. Feet are catlike with well-arched toes fitting tightly together. Pads are thick.

**Hindquarters**—The angulation of the hindquarters is moderate and in balance with the angulation of the forequarters. Hind legs are strong with a wide natural stance. The hock joint is strong, turning neither in nor out. Upper thighs are long and the second thighs short but well developed. No dewclaws. Feet as in forequarters.

**Coat**—Double coated, with the outer coat being stiff and straight and the undercoat soft and thick. Fur is short and even on face, ears and legs. Guard hairs stand off the body and are about 1½ to 2 inches in length at the withers. Tail hair is slightly longer and stands open in a brush. It is preferred that the Shiba be presented in a natural state. *Trimming of the coat must be severely penalized. Serious Fault*—Long or woolly coat.

**Color**—Coat color is as specified herein, with the three allowed colors given equal consideration. All colors are clear and intense. The undercoat is cream, buff, or gray.

*Urajiro* (cream to white ventral color) is required in the following areas on all coat colors: on the sides of the muzzle, on the cheeks, inside the ears, on the underjaw and upper throat, inside of legs, on the abdomen, around the vent and the ventral side of the tail. On *reds:* commonly on the throat, forechest and chest. On *blacks and sesames:* commonly as a triangular mark on both sides of the forechest. White spots above the eyes permitted on all colors but not required.

Bright orange-red with urajiro lending a foxlike appearance to dogs of this color. Clear red preferred but a very slight dash of black tipping is permitted on the back and tail.

*Black with tan points* and urajiro. Black hairs have a brownish cast, not blue. The undercoat is buff or gray. The borderline between black and tan areas is clearly defined. Tan points are located as follows: two oval spots over the eyes; on the sides of the muzzle between the black bridge of the muzzle and the white cheeks; on the outside of the forelegs from the carpus, or a little above, downward to the toes; on the outside of the hind legs down the front of the stifle broadening from hock joint to toes, but not completely eliminating black from rear of pasterns. Black penciling on toes permitted. Tan hairs may also be found on the inside of the ear and on the underside of the tail.

*Sesame* (black-tipped hairs on a rich red background) with urajiro. Tipping is light and even on the body and head with no concentration of black in any area. Sesame areas appear at least one-half red. Sesame may end in a widow's peak on the forehead, leaving the bridge and sides of the muzzle red. Eye spots and lower legs are also red.

Clearly delineated white markings are permitted but not required on the tip of the tail and in the form of socks on the forelegs to the elbow joint, hind legs to the knee joint. A patch of blaze is permitted on the throat, forechest, or chest in addition to urajiro.

*Serious Fault*—Cream, white, pinto or any other color or marking not specified is a very serious fault and must be penalized.

**Gait**—Movement is nimble, light, and elastic. At the trot, the legs angle in towards a center line while the topline remains level and firm. Forward reach and rear extension are moderate and efficient. In the show ring, the Shiba is gaited on a loose lead at a brisk trot.

**Temperament**—A spirited boldness, a good nature and an unaffected forthrightness, which together yield dignity and natural beauty. The Shiba has an independent nature and can be reserved toward strangers but is loyal and affectionate to those who earn his respect. At times aggressive toward other dogs, the Shiba is always under the control of his handler. Any aggression toward handler or judge or any overt shyness must be severely penalized.

**Summary**—The foregoing is a description of the ideal Shiba. Any deviation from the above standard is to be considered a fault and must be penalized. The severity of the fault is equal to the extent of the deviation. A harmonious balance of form, color, movement and temperament is more critical than any one feature.

## DISQUALIFICATIONS

*Males over 16½ and under 14½ inches. Females over 15½ and under 13½ inches. Overshot or undershot bite.*

**Approved February 7, 1997**
**Effective March 31, 1997**

# TIBETAN SPANIEL

$\mathscr{T}$HE HISTORY OF TIBET IS IMPORTANT TO THE UNDERSTANDING OF THE EARLY Tibetan Spaniel. The country has always been isolated and has little contact with the outside world except for neighboring China and India. The seclusion of Tibetan society, its political isolation, the loneliness of the nomadic life of its people, even the remoteness of villages within the country, together with the rise of Buddhism which did not permit the killing of animals, are all factors leading to the importance of dogs in the lives of the Tibetans.

Independent since 217 B.C., except for short periods of Chinese imperialism, Tibet became a Buddhist country in the seventeenth century. The Tibetans were a deeply religious, peace-loving people, with their own Lamaist form of Buddhism, in which the symbolic lion played an even more important role than it had in the Chinese and Indian interpretations. The lion represented the power of the Lord Buddha over violence and aggression, since Buddha had trained the lion to be tame and to "follow at his heels like a faithful dog." The small monastery dogs, thought to be early representatives of the Tibetan Spaniel, loyally trailed behind their Lama masters and came to be regarded as "little lions," thus giving them even greater value and prestige.

As the breed became more highly regarded, the practice of sending the dogs as gifts to the palaces of China and other Buddhist countries grew significantly, and in reciprocity more "lion dogs" were presented back to Tibet. This practice is believed to have continued until as late as 1908. Through exchange of Tibetan Spaniels between palaces and monasteries, the breed is likely to have common ancestors with a number of the Asian breeds, including the Japanese Chin and the Pekingese.

The villages were a primary location for breeding and these village-bred Tibetan Spaniels varied greatly in size and type, probably because of little understanding of the value of breeding like to like. Size ranged from four to sixteen pounds and the smaller puppies were usually given as gifts to the monasteries. In turn, these smaller dogs used in the monastery breeding programs were probably combined with the more elegant Tibetan Spaniel–type dogs brought from China, eventually producing a more refined dog of greater quality and elegance than their village relatives. Those bred in the monasteries closer to the Chinese borders were characterized by shorter muzzles, similar to the Chinese breeds from which they were descended. The purest ancient Tibetan type was found west of Lhasa, for fewer Chinese dogs had found their way to this area. The tremendous distances between monasteries and villages must account for the great difference in type in the early dog and it is not surprising to find other Tibetan breeds occasionally producing Tibetan Spaniel–type puppies. The true Tibetan Spaniel is the only one of all Tibetan breeds to have a hare foot instead of the round or cat foot. They closely resemble the Tibetan Mastiff in outline.

There is no doubt Buddhism made an impact on the prominence of this breed in Tibetan society. Not only did the religion forbid the killing of animals, but Buddhists had great faith in the doctrine of reincarnation. They believed that in previous lives they may have been animals and may be so again in the future. This theory, in addition to the belief that no essential spiritual differences exist between man and dog, encouraged kindness to and humane treatment of animals in Tibet. To carry this doctrine even further, the Buddhists placed numerous representations of Tibetan Spaniel–type dogs made from pottery and clay within early Chinese tombs. This practice was believed to result in continued service from the dogs in the lives to come.

Not only was the Tibetan Spaniel prized as a pet and companion, but it was considered a very useful animal by all classes of Tibetans. During the day, the dogs would sit on top of the monastery walls keeping a steady watch over the countryside below. Their keen eye and ability to see great distances, as well as their persistent barking, made them exceptionally good watchdogs. The Tibetan Spaniels were always quick to respond to the approach of wolves to the flocks grazing below them, in addition to the arrival of a stranger or an intruder. In this case, the dogs would let out continuous shrill barking, thus alerting a nearby Tibetan Mastiff. The larger dog would then keep watch over the visitors. Evidently, this habit of sitting on high places and surveying the area below is still enjoyed by the Tibetan Spaniel of today.

Sometime in the late 1800s, the Hon. Mrs. McLaren Morris brought the first Tibetan Spaniel to England. In the 1920s, Dr. Agnes R. H. Greig, a medical missionary in the East, sent several of the dogs to her mother, Mrs. A. R. Greig, who exhibited them and started a breeding program. Sadly, the only dog from this line who survived World War II was Skyid, who appears in some of today's pedigrees.

At the start of the war, Sir Edward and Lady Wakefield, an English couple living in Sikkim, received a gift of a bitch in 1938 from Dr. Khanshi Ram, a trade agent in western Tibet. The Wakefields obtained the use of a male, Tashi, from the Tashi Gong monastery for the purpose of breeding their bitch, Mughiwuli. In 1940, the first of several litters of these two Tibetans was whelped. With the help of the King of Sikkim, the Wakefields obtained another bitch puppy, Dolma, who together with Lama, a son of Mughiwuli, formed the nucleus of the English "dynasty" of Tibetans, commencing from 1947. The Tibetan Spaniel Association was formed in 1958, and by 1960 The Kennel Club (England) awarded Challenge Certificates. By 1980, there were 114 recorded English champions.

Recognition moved a bit slower for American devotees. The first authenticated reference we find to Tibetan Spaniels in this country is a litter bred by a Mr. Harrington, of New York State, in 1965 out of two imported dogs from a Tibetan monastery. The first definite step toward popularizing the breed here could be credited to Leo Kearns, the sexton of the Trinity Lutheran Church in New Haven, Connecticut. He purchased a bitch puppy from an antiques dealer who frequented the United Kingdom, and the puppy was such a hit with the parishioners that Kearns ferreted out some of the English breeders. After considerable correspondence, M. C. Hourihane of the Amcross Kennels in Wilts, England, sent him a male, Eng. Ch. Yakrose Chiala of Amcross. This dog was bred to his bitch, Doghouse Dream Baby, and on April 9, 1968, the first known American-bred litter of Tibetan Spaniels was whelped.

Among those who became interested in the breed was Mrs. Jay Child, who purchased an imported bitch from Kearns named Ciceter Norbu (Pandara). Although Kearns had actively imported stock from England, much credit must go to Child for her singular determination to establish the breed in the United States.

In January 1971, the Tibetan Spaniel Club of America was formed, with Child as president. The Tibetan Spaniel was accepted for AKC registration and became eligible to compete in the Non-Sporting Group effective January 1, 1984.

The Tibetan Spaniel possesses a unique personality, described by many as cat-like. The breed is known to be extremely intelligent, sweet-natured, affectionate, family-oriented, and very trusting of other dogs and people.

Litters are small, averaging about three puppies, and the bitches have only one estrus per year. It is a very "natural" breed, presented in the show ring in a completely unaltered condition. Grooming is minimal; they drop their undercoat in late spring and require only occasional brushing and bathing.

Visit the Tibetan Spaniel Club of America web site at *tsca.ws/index.php.*

# OFFICIAL STANDARD FOR THE TIBETAN SPANIEL

**General Appearance**—Should be small, active and alert. The outline should give a well balanced appearance, slightly longer in body than the height at withers. *Fault*—Coarseness of type.

**Size, Proportion, Substance**—*Size*—Height, about 10 inches. Body slightly longer from the point of shoulder to root of tail than the height at withers. Weight 9–15 pounds being ideal.

**Head**—Small in proportion to body and proudly carried, giving an impression of quality. Masculine in dogs but free from coarseness. *Eyes* dark brown in color, oval in shape, bright and expressive, of medium size set fairly well apart but forward looking, giving an apelike *expression*. Eye rims black. *Faults*—Large, full eyes; light eyes; mean expression. *Ears* medium size, pendant, well feathered in the adult and set fairly high. They may have a slight lift from the skull, but should not fly. Large, heavy, low set ears are not typical. *Skull* slightly domed, moderate width and length. *Faults*—Very domed or flat wide skull. *Stop* slight, but defined. Medium length of *muzzle*, blunt with cushioning, free from wrinkle. The *chin* should show some depth and width. *Faults*—Accentuated stop; long, plain down face, without stop; broad flat muzzle; pointed, weak or wrinkled muzzle. Black *nose* preferred. *Faults*—Liver or putty-colored pigmentation.

*Mouth* ideally slightly undershot, the upper incisors fitting neatly inside and touching the lower incisors. *Teeth* should be evenly placed and the lower jaw wide between the canine tusks. Full dentition desired. A level mouth is permissible, providing there is sufficient width and depth of chin to preserve the blunt appearance of the muzzle. Teeth must not show when mouth is closed. *Faults*—Overshot mouth; protruding tongue.

**Neck, Topline, Body**—*Neck* moderately short, strong and well set on. Level *back*. Well ribbed with good depth. *Tail* set high, richly plumed and carried in a gay curl over the back when moving. Should not be penalized for dropping tail when standing.

**Forequarters**—Shoulder well placed. The bones of the forelegs slightly bowed but firm at shoulder. Moderate bone. *Faults*—Very bowed or loose front. Dewclaws may be removed. *Feet* hare-footed, small and neat. *Fault*—Cat feet.

**Hindquarters**—Well made and strong. Stifle well developed, showing moderate angulation. Hocks well let down and straight when viewed from behind. *Faults*—Straight stifle; cow hocks. Dewclaws may be removed. *Feet* as in front.

**Coat**—Double coat, silky in texture, smooth on face and front of legs, of moderate length on body, but lying rather flat. Ears and back of forelegs nicely feathered, tail and buttocks well furnished with longer hair. Neck covered with a mane or "shawl" of longer hair which is more pronounced in dogs than bitches. Feathering between toes often extending beyond the feet. Should not be over-coated and bitches tend to carry less coat and mane than dogs.

*Presentation*—In the show ring it is essential the Tibetan Spaniel be presented in an unaltered condition with the coat lying naturally with no teasing, parting or stylizing of the hair. Specimens where the coat has been altered by trimming, clipping or by artificial means shall be so severely penalized as to be effectively eliminated from competition. Dogs with such a long coat that there is no rectangle of daylight showing beneath, or so profuse that it obstructs the natural outline, are to be severely penalized. Whiskers are not to be removed. Hair growing between the pads on the underside of the feet may be trimmed for safety and cleanliness.

**Color**—All colors, and mixtures of colors allowed. *Feet*—White markings allowed.

**Gait**—Quick moving, straight, free, positive.

**Temperament**—Gay and assertive, highly intelligent, aloof with strangers. *Fault*—Nervousness.

**Approved May 10, 1983**
**Reformatted February 7, 1989**

# TIBETAN TERRIER

*A*S THE NAME INDICATES, TIBETAN TERRIERS CAME FROM TIBET WHERE, SO it is said, they were bred and raised in the monasteries by the Lamas almost 2,000 years ago. Originating in the Lost Valley ("lost" when the access road was destroyed in the fourteenth century by a major earthquake) they were prized as companions and "luck bringers" for those fortunate enough to own them.

So inaccessible was the Lost Valley, so hazardous the journey to and from it, that the occasional visitor was often given a dog to safeguard him on the return trip to the outside world. No dog of this kind was ever sold, as no family would tempt fate by selling part of their "luck," but they were presented as a mark of esteem or a measure of gratitude for favors or services rendered.

Thus it came about that the late Dr. A.R.H. Greig, a practicing physician in India in the 1920s, was given a dog by a grateful Tibetan whose ailing wife she had treated. Greig subsequently bred and raised a number of Tibetan Terriers in India, many of them descended from puppies sent to her by the Dalai Lama in appreciation of her interest in their cherished breed. When Dr. Greig returned to England, she established the famous Lamleh Kennel. Recognized in India in the 1920s and in England in 1937, the breed is now exhibited at shows the world over.

Dr. and Mrs. Henry S. Murphy, of Great Falls, Virginia, brought the first "official" Tibetan Terrier to the United States in 1956, an import from the Lamleh

Kennel in England with a Kennel Club pedigree. Since then the breed has attracted fanciers from Canada to Florida, and from coast to coast.

The Tibetan Terrier is not actually a terrier. He does not have the terrier disposition, nor does he burrow into the earth as terriers were originally expected to do. This breed was called "terrier" because it was of a size widely associated with terriers. The Tibetan people called them Luck Bringers or Holy Dogs, neither of which seemed suitable as a breed name in the Western world.

Tibetan Terriers were neither guard dogs nor herding dogs in Tibet. They were valued as companions and were treated like children of the family. Like children, they eagerly assisted in taking care of the family's property, their flocks, and their herds, but these dogs were not raised for utilitarian purposes. The breed was kept purebred, as any mismating might bring bad luck to the family and might even be blamed for any village misfortune.

This is an exceptionally healthy breed, probably as a result of the rigorous natural selection process in their recent homeland. Tibet has one of the most difficult populated terrains in the world, and one of the most dramatic climates. Lhasa, for example, is exceedingly cold in the winter but often reaches eighty-five degrees in the summer. The Tibetan Terrier is prepared to enjoy a blizzard, thanks to his profuse double coat, facial fur to protect his eyes from snow, and "snowshoe" feet, well furnished and suited for walking on the crust. Surprisingly, they do not seem to be at all upset by a hot, humid summer, simply stopping for a nap during the worst part of such days.

The people of Tibet made no effort to eliminate any of the many colors found in this breed, believing that good health and a delightful temperament were far more important than coat color. It is hoped that Western breeders are continuing this sensible breeding program, and that the Tibetan Terrier will continue to be an exceptional companion and friend of man—healthy, happy, intelligent, and affectionate.

The Tibetan Terrier was admitted to registration in the AKC Stud Book on May 1, 1973, and to the Non-Sporting Group at AKC shows on October 3, 1973.

# OFFICIAL STANDARD FOR THE TIBETAN TERRIER

The Tibetan Terrier evolved over many centuries, surviving in Tibet's extreme climate and difficult terrain. The breed developed a protective double coat, compact size, unique foot construction, and great agility. The Tibetan Terrier served as a steadfast, devoted companion in all of his owner's endeavors.

**General Appearance**—The Tibetan Terrier is a medium-size dog, profusely coated, of powerful build, and square in proportion. A fall of hair covers the eyes and foreface. The well-feathered tail curls up and falls forward over the back. The feet are large, flat and round in shape producing a snowshoe effect that provides traction. The

Tibetan Terrier is well balanced and capable of both strong and efficient movement. The Tibetan Terrier is shown as naturally as possible.

**Head**—*Skull*—Medium length neither broad nor coarse. The length from the eye to the tip of the nose is equal to the length from eye to the occiput. The skull narrows slightly from ear to eye. It is not domed but not absolutely flat between the ears. The head is well furnished with long hair, falling forward over the eyes and foreface. The cheekbones are curved but not so overdeveloped as to bulge. *Muzzle*—The lower jaw has a small amount of beard. *Stop*—There is marked stop but not exaggerated. *Nose*—Black. *Teeth*—White, strong and evenly placed. There is a distinct curve in the jaws between the canines. A tight scissors bite, a tight reverse scissors bite or a level bite are equally acceptable. A slightly undershot bite is acceptable.

*Eyes*—Large, set fairly wide apart, dark brown and may appear black in color, neither prominent nor sunken. Eye rims are dark in color. *Ears*—Pendant, falling not too close to the head, heavily feathered with a "V" shaped leather proportionate to the head.

*Faults*—Weak pointed muzzle. Any color other than a black nose. Overshot bite or a very undershot bite or a wry mouth. Long narrow head. Lack of fall over the eyes and foreface.

**Neck And Body**—*Neck*—Length proportionate to the body and head. *Body*—Compact, square and strong, capable of both speed and endurance. *Topline*—The back is level in motion. *Chest*—Heavily furnished. The brisket extends downward to the top of the elbow in the mature Tibetan Terrier. *Ribs*—The body is well ribbed up and never cloddy or coarse. The rib cage is not too wide across the chest and narrows slightly to permit the forelegs to work free at the sides. *Loin*—Slightly arched. *Tail*—Medium length, heavily furnished, set on fairly high and falls forward over the back, may curl to either side. There may be a kink near the tip.

**Forequarters**—*Shoulders*—Sloping, well muscled and well laid back. *Legs*—Straight and strong when viewed from the front. Heavily furnished. The vertical distance from the withers to the elbow equals the distance from the elbows to the ground. *Feet*—The feet of the Tibetan Terrier are unique in form among dogs. They are large, flat, and round in shape producing a snowshoe effect that provides traction. The pads are thick and strong. They are heavily furnished with hair between the toes and pads. Hair between the toes and pads may be trimmed level with the underside of the pads for health reasons. The dog should stand well down on its pads. *Dewclaws*—May be removed.

**Hindquarters**—*Legs*—Well furnished, with well bent stifles and the hind legs are slightly longer than the forelegs. *Thighs*—Relatively broad and well muscled. *Hocks*—Low set and turn neither in nor out. *Feet*—Same as forefeet. *Dewclaws*—May be removed.

**Coat**—Double coat. Undercoat is soft and woolly. Outer coat is profuse and fine but never silky or woolly. May be wavy or straight. Coat is long but should not hang to the ground. When standing on a hard surface an area of light should be seen under the dog. The coat of puppies is shorter, single and often has a softer texture than that of adults. A natural part is often present over the neck and back. *Fault*—Lack of double coat in adults. Sculpturing, scissoring, stripping or shaving are totally contrary to breed type and are serious faults.

**Color**—Any color or combination of colors including white are acceptable to the breed. There are no preferred colors or combinations of colors.

**Gait**—The Tibetan Terrier has a free, effortless stride with good reach in front and flexibility in the rear allowing full extension. When gaiting the hind legs should go neither inside nor outside the front legs but should move on the same track approaching single tracking when the dog is moved at a fast trot. The dog with the correct foot and leg construction moves with elasticity and drive indicating that the dog is capable of great agility as well as endurance.

**Size**—Average weight is 20 to 24 pounds, but the weight range may be 18 to 30 pounds. Proportion of weight to height is far more important than specific weight and should reflect a well-balanced square dog. The average height in dogs is 15 to 16 inches, bitches slightly smaller. The length, measured from the point of shoulder to the root of tail, is equal to the height measured from the highest point of the withers to the ground. *Faults*—Any height above 17 inches or below 14 inches.

**Temperament**—The Tibetan Terrier is highly intelligent, sensitive, loyal, devoted and affectionate. The breed may be cautious or reserved. *Fault*—Extreme shyness.

**Approved March 10, 1987**

# GROUP VII: HERDING BREEDS

AUSTRALIAN CATTLE DOG
AUSTRALIAN SHEPHERD
BEARDED COLLIE
BELGIAN MALINOIS
BELGIAN SHEEPDOG
BELGIAN TERVUREN
BORDER COLLIE
BOUVIER DES FLANDRES
BRIARD

CANAAN DOG
CARDIGAN WELSH CORGI
COLLIE
GERMAN SHEPHERD DOG
OLD ENGLISH SHEEPDOG
PEMBROKE WELSH CORGI
POLISH LOWLAND SHEEPDOG
PULI
SHETLAND SHEEPDOG

# AUSTRALIAN CATTLE DOG

*A*USTRALIANS OWE A GREAT DEBT TO ALL THOSE INVOLVED IN THE development of the Australian Cattle Dog, for without it the beef industry of Australia would undoubtedly have had great difficulty in growing into the important business it has become.

During the early colonization of Australia, the population was mainly confined to what is now the Sydney metropolitan area, the landholdings were relatively small, and the distances involved in taking stock to market were not very far. The stock contained on these properties were used to seeing men and dogs around them, and so were rather quiet and controllable. Working dogs that were brought out from other countries by the early settlers, although suffering a bit from the warmer climate, are believed to have worked these quiet cattle satisfactorily.

Eventually, settlers began spreading. In 1813, vast grazing lands were opened up to the west. Here, landholdings were often hundreds and even thousands of square miles, and were mostly unfenced. Cattle turned loose on these properties became wild and uncontrollable.

The most popular dog used by the early drovers and cattle owners was a working dog breed brought out from England known as the Smithfield. It was a big, black, square-bodied bobtail dog, with a long, rough coat and a white frill around the neck. The head was shaped like a wedge, with long saddle-flap ears, and the dog had a very cumbersome gait. Like the other working dogs of that time, the Smithfield found the high temperature, rough terrain, and long distances to market more than it could handle. These early working dogs all had a trait of barking and heading while working stock. This is desirable for working sheep and even acceptable with quiet cattle, but made the wild stock on the big cattle stations stampede and run off their condition.

It soon became obvious that a dog with more stamina, that would work quietly but more forcefully, was needed to get the wild cattle to the sale yards in Sydney. Around 1830, a drover named Timmins tried crossing the Smithfield with a native breed, the Dingo, with the aim of producing a silent working dog with more stamina. The progeny from this mating were red, bobtail dogs, which were named Timmins Biters. Unlike the Smithfield, these dogs were silent workers but proved to be too headstrong, and severe with their biting. Although this crossbreed was used for a while, it gradually died out. Other crossbreeding was tried, such as the Rough Collie–Bull Terrier cross, but all these proved to be unsuccessful for working cattle.

In the year 1840, a landowner named Thomas Hall imported a pair of smooth-haired, blue merle Highland Collies from Scotland. They were good workers, but barked and headed. Hall crossed progeny from this pair with the Dingo, which produced silent workers that became known as Hall's Heelers. The color of the dogs from this cross was either red or blue merle, with most of them having pricked ears and a Dingo-shaped head with brown eyes, and were generally of the Dingo type. Hall's dogs were a big improvement on any other available working dogs and became much sought after by cattlemen.

Another landowner, George Elliott, in Queensland, was also experimenting with Dingo-blue merle Collie crosses. Elliott's dogs produced some excellent workers. Cattlemen were impressed with the working ability of these dogs, and purchased pups from them as they became available. Two brothers, Jack and Harry Bagust, of Canterbury in Sydney, purchased some of these dogs and set about improving on them.

Their first step was to cross a bitch with a fine imported Dalmatian dog. This cross changed the merle to red or blue speckle. The pups were born white, developing their coloring at about three weeks of age. The Bagusts' purpose in this cross was to instill the love of horses and faithfulness to master into their dogs. These characteristics were obtained and made these Bagust dogs useful for minding the drover's horse and gear, but some of the working ability was lost. Admiring the working ability of the Black and Tan Kelpie, which is a sheepdog, the Bagusts experimented in crossing them with their speckle dogs.

The result was a compact active dog, identical in type and build to the Dingo, only thicker set and with peculiar markings found on no other dog in the world. The blue dogs had black patches around the eyes, with black ears and brown eyes, with a small white patch in the middle of the forehead. The body was dark blue, evenly speckled with a lighter blue, having the same tan markings on legs, chest, and head as the Black and Tan Kelpie. The red dogs had dark red markings instead of black, with an all-over even red speckle.

Only the pups closest to the ideal were kept, and these became the forebears of the present-day Australian Cattle Dog. The working ability of the Bagusts' dogs was outstanding, retaining the quiet heeling ability and stamina of the Dingo with the faithful protectiveness of the Dalmatian. As the word spread of the ability of these dogs to work cattle, they became keenly sought after by property owners and drovers. The blue-colored dogs proved to be more popular, and became known as Blue Heelers. These cattle dogs became indispensable to the owners of the huge cattle runs in Queensland, where they were given the name tag of Queensland Heelers or Queensland Blue Heelers.

After the Black and Tan Kelpie cross, no other infusion of breeds was practiced with any success. The breeders of the day concentrated on breeding for working ability, type, and color. In 1893 Robert Kaleski took up breeding the Blue Heelers, and he began showing them in 1897.

Kaleski drew up his standard for the Cattle Dog and also for the Kelpie and Barb in 1902. He based the Cattle Dog standard around the Dingo type, believing that this was the type naturally evolved to suit the conditions of this country. Even today the resemblance to the Dingo is evident, except for the color of the blues and the speckle in the reds. After much opposition from careless breeders, Kaleski finally had his standard endorsed by them and all the leading breeders of the time. He then submitted his standard to the Cattle and Sheep Dog Club of Australia and the original Kennel Club of New South Wales for their approval. The standard was approved in 1903.

The breed became known as the Australian Heeler, then later the Australian Cattle Dog, which is now accepted throughout Australia as the official name for this breed. Even today, though, some people can be heard calling them Blue Heelers or Queensland Heelers.

The Australian Cattle Dog was accepted for registration by the American Kennel Club on May 1, 1980, and became eligible to be shown in the Working Group on September 1, 1980. It was transferred to the newly formed Herding Group on January 1, 1983.

# OFFICIAL STANDARD FOR THE AUSTRALIAN CATTLE DOG

**General Appearance**—The general appearance is that of a strong, compact, symmetrically built working dog, with the ability and willingness to carry out his allotted task however arduous. Its combination of substance, power, balance and hard muscular condition must convey the impression of great agility, strength and endurance. Any tendency to grossness or weediness is a serious fault.

**Characteristics**—As the name implies the dog's prime function, and one in which he has no peer, is the control and movement of cattle in both wide open and confined areas. Always alert, extremely intelligent, watchful, courageous and trustworthy, with an implicit devotion to duty making it an ideal dog.

**Temperament**—The Cattle Dog's loyalty and protective instincts make it a self-appointed guardian to the Stockman, his herd and his property. Whilst naturally suspicious of strangers, must be amenable to handling, particularly in the Show ring. Any feature of temperament or structure foreign to a working dog must be regarded as a serious fault.

**Head and Skull**—The head is strong and must be in balance with other proportions of the dog and in keeping with its general conformation. The broad skull is slightly curved between the ears, flattening to a slight but definite stop. The cheeks muscular, neither coarse nor prominent with the underjaw strong, deep and well developed. The foreface is broad and well filled in under the eyes, tapering gradually to form a medium length, deep, powerful muzzle with the skull and muzzle on parallel planes. The lips are tight and clean. Nose black.

*Eyes*—The eyes should be of oval shape and medium size, neither prominent nor sunken and must express alertness and intelligence. A warning or suspicious glint is characteristic when approached by strangers. Eye color, dark brown.

*Ears*—The ears should be of moderate size, preferably small rather than large, broad at the base, muscular, pricked and moderately pointed neither spoon nor bat eared. The ears are set wide apart on the skull, inclining outwards, sensitive in their use and pricked when alert, the leather should be thick in texture and the inside of the ear fairly well furnished with hair.

*Mouth*—The teeth, sound, strong and evenly spaced, gripping with a scissor-bite, the lower incisors close behind and just touching the upper. As the dog is required to move difficult cattle by heeling or biting, teeth which are sound and strong are very important.

**Neck**—The neck is extremely strong, muscular, and of medium length broadening to blend into the body and free from throatiness.

**Forequarters**—The shoulders are strong, sloping, muscular and well angulated to the upper arm and should not be too closely set at the point of the withers. The forelegs have strong, round bone, extending to the feet and should be straight and parallel when viewed from the front, but the pasterns should show flexibility with a slight angle to the forearm when viewed from the side. Although the shoulders are muscular and the bone is strong, loaded shoulders and heavy fronts will hamper correct movement and limit working ability.

**Body**—The length of the body from the point of the breast bone, in a straight line to the buttocks, is greater than the height at the withers, as 10 is to 9. The topline is level, back strong with ribs well sprung and carried well back not barrel ribbed. The chest is deep, muscular and moderately broad with the loins broad, strong and muscular and the flanks deep. The dog is strongly coupled.

**Hindquarters**—The hindquarters are broad, strong and muscular. The croup is rather long and sloping, thighs long, broad and well developed, the stifles well turned and the hocks strong and well let down. When viewed from behind, the hind legs, from the hocks to the feet, are straight and placed parallel, neither close nor too wide apart.

**Feet**—The feet should be round and the toes short, strong, well-arched and held close together. The pads are hard and deep, and the nails must be short and strong.

**Tail**—The set on of tail is moderately low, following the contours of the sloping croup and of length to reach approximately to the hock. At rest it should hang in a very slight curve. During movement or excitement the tail may be raised, but under no circumstances should any part of the tail be carried past a vertical line drawn through the root. The tail should carry a good brush.

**Gait/Movement**—The action is true, free, supple and tireless and the movement of the shoulders and forelegs is in unison with the powerful thrust of the hindquarters. The capability of quick and sudden movement is essential. Soundness is of paramount importance and stiltiness, loaded or slack shoulders, straight shoulder placement, weakness at elbows, pasterns or feet, straight stifles, cow or bow hocks, must be regarded as serious faults. When trotting the feet tend to come closer together at ground level as speed increases, but when the dog comes to rest he should stand four square.

**Coat**—The coat is smooth, a double coat with a short dense undercoat. The outercoat is close, each hair straight, hard, and lying flat, so that it is rain-resisting. Under the body, to behind the legs, the coat is longer and forms near the thigh a mild form of breeching. On the head (including the inside of the ears), to the front of the legs and feet, the hair is short. Along the neck it is longer and thicker. A coat either too long or too short is a fault. As an average, the hairs on the body should be from 2.5 to 4 centimeters (approx. 1–1.5 inches) in length.

**Color (Blue)**—The color should be blue, blue-mottled or blue speckled with or without other markings. The permissible markings are black, blue or tan markings on the head, evenly distributed for preference. The forelegs tan midway up the legs and extending up the front to breast and throat, with tan on jaws; the hindquarters tan on inside of hind legs, and inside of thighs, showing down the front of the stifles and broadening out to the outside of the hind legs from hock to toes. Tan undercoat is permissible on the body providing it does not show through the blue outer coat. Black markings on the body are not desirable.

**Color (Red Speckle)**—The color should be of good even red speckle all over, including the undercoat (neither white nor cream), with or without darker red markings on the head. Even head markings are desirable. Red markings on the body are permissible but not desirable.

**Size**—Height:

**Dogs 46–51 centimeters (approx. 18–20 inches) at withers**
**Bitches 43–48 centimeters (approx. 17–19 inches) at withers**

## FAULTS

Any departure from the foregoing points should be considered a fault and the seriousness with which the fault should be regarded should be in exact proportion to its degree.

**Approved January 11, 1999**
**Effective February 24, 1999**

# AUSTRALIAN SHEPHERD

*A*LTHOUGH THERE ARE MANY THEORIES ABOUT THE ORIGIN OF THE AUS-tralian Shepherd, the modern breed developed exclusively in the United States. It probably originated in the Basque region of the Pyrenees Mountains, between Spain and France, but was dubbed the Australian Shepherd because of its association with Basque shepherds who came to the United States from Australia in the 1800s.

As with most working breeds, the Australian Shepherd was initially called by many names, including Spanish Shepherd, Pastor Dog, Bob-Tail, Blue Heeler, New Mexican Shepherd, and California Shepherd.

The Australian Shepherd's popularity rose rapidly with the boom in Western-style horse riding after World War II. The breed became known to the general public through appearances in rodeos, horse shows, movies, and television programs. Its inherent versatility and trainability made it a useful asset on farms and ranches.

Ranchers continued to develop the breed, maintaining the adaptability, keen intelligence, strong herding instincts, and eye-catching appearance that originally won its admirers. As a herder, the Australian Shepherd is a loose- to medium-eyed dog. ("Eye" is a general term used to describe the way a dog controls stock with its gaze.) It will watch an entire group of animals, but not with an intense gaze. Some dogs use more eye in situations where added power is required to move stubborn or balky animals, while holding off on single animals, as in the shed.

The Aussie (as the breed is nicknamed) is a truly versatile dog. It is so sound minded that it easily adapts to various situations. Today, the Australian Shepherd serves humanity in every imaginable way: as working ranch dogs, guide dogs for the blind, hearing dogs for the deaf, therapy dogs, drug detectors, and search-and-rescue dogs.

The breed is not registered in Australia as a native breed, although Australian Shepherds have been recorded by other registries since the 1950s. The United States Australian Shepherd Association works hard to maintain the breed true to type in its land of origin. The breed entered the AKC Stud Book in 1991 and entered the Herding Group in January 1993.

# OFFICIAL STANDARD FOR THE AUSTRALIAN SHEPHERD

**General Appearance**—The Australian Shepherd is an intelligent working dog of strong herding and guarding instincts. He is a loyal companion and has the stamina to work all day. He is well balanced, slightly longer than tall, of medium size and bone, with coloring that offers variety and individuality. He is attentive and animated, lithe and agile, solid and muscular without cloddiness. He has a coat of moderate length and coarseness. He has a docked or natural bobbed tail.

**Size, Proportion, Substance**—*Size*—The preferred height for males is 20–23 inches, females 18–21 inches. Quality is not to be sacrificed in favor of size. *Proportion*—Measuring from the breastbone to rear of thigh and from top of the withers to the ground the Australian Shepherd is slightly longer than tall. *Substance*—Solidly built with moderate bone. Structure in the male reflects masculinity without coarseness. Bitches appear feminine without being slight of bone.

**Head**—The *Head* is clean-cut, strong and dry. Overall size should be in proportion to the body. The muzzle is equal in length or slightly shorter than the back skull. Viewed from the side the topline of the back skull and muzzle form parallel planes, divided by a moderate, well-defined stop. The muzzle tapers little from base to nose and is rounded at the tip.

*Expression*—Showing attentiveness and intelligence, alert and eager. Gaze should be keen but friendly. *Eyes* are brown, blue, amber or any variation or combination thereof, including flecks and marbling. Almond shaped, not protruding nor sunken. The blue merles and blacks have black pigmentation on eye rims. The red merles and reds have liver (brown) pigmentation on eye rims. *Ears* are triangular, of moderate size and leather, set high on the head. At full attention they break forward and over, or to the side as a rose ear. Prick ears and hanging ears are *severe faults*.

*Skull*—Top flat to slightly domed. It may show a slight occipital protuberance. Length and width are equal. Moderate well-defined stop. *Muzzle* tapers little from base to nose and is rounded at the tip. *Nose*—Blue merles and blacks have black pigmentation on the nose (and lips). Red merles and reds have liver (brown) pigmentation on the nose (and lips). On the merles it is permissible to have small pink spots; however, they should not exceed 25% of the nose on dogs over one year of age, which is a *serious fault*. *Teeth*—A full complement of strong white teeth should meet in a scissors bite or may meet in a level bite. *Disqualifications*—Undershot. Overshot greater than ⅛ inch. Loss of contact caused by short center incisors in an otherwise correct bite shall not be judged undershot. Teeth broken or missing by accident shall not be penalized.

**Neck, Topline, Body**—*Neck* is strong, of moderate length, slightly arched at the crest, fitting well into the shoulders. *Topline*—Back is straight and strong, level and firm from withers to hip joints. The croup is moderately sloped. *Chest* is not broad but is deep with the lowest point reaching the elbow. The ribs are well sprung and long, neither barrel chested nor slab-sided. The underline shows a moderate tuck-up. *Tail* is straight, docked or naturally bobbed, not to exceed four inches in length.

**Forequarters**—*Shoulders*—Shoulder blades are long, flat, fairly close set at the withers and well laid back. The upper arm, which should be relatively the same length as the shoulder blade, attaches at an approximate right angle to the shoulder line with forelegs dropping straight, perpendicular to the ground. *Legs* straight and strong. Bone is strong, oval rather than round. *Pastern* is medium length and very slightly sloped. Front dewclaws may be removed. *Feet* are oval, compact with close knit, well arched toes. Pads are thick and resilient.

**Hindquarters**—The width of the hindquarters is equal to the width of the forequarters at the shoulders. The angulation of the pelvis and upper thigh corresponds to the angulation of the shoulder blade and upper arm, forming an approximate right angle. *Stifles* are clearly defined, hock joints moderately bent. The *hocks* are short, perpendicular to the ground and parallel to each other when viewed from the rear. Rear dewclaws must be removed. *Feet* are oval, compact with close knit, well arched toes. Pads are thick and resilient.

**Coat**—Hair is of medium texture, straight to wavy, weather resistant and of medium length. The undercoat varies in quantity with variations in climate. Hair is short and smooth on the head, ears, front of forelegs and below the hocks. Backs of forelegs and britches are moderately feathered. There is a moderate mane and frill, more pronounced in dogs than in bitches. Non-typical coats are *severe faults*.

**Color**—Blue merle, black, red merle, red—all with or without white markings and/or tan (copper) points, with no order of preference. The hairline of a white collar does not exceed the point of the withers at the skin. White is acceptable on the neck (either in part or as a full collar), chest, legs, muzzle underparts, blaze on head and white extension from underpart up to four inches, measuring from a horizontal line at the elbow. White on the head should not predominate, and the eyes must be fully surrounded by color and pigment. Merles characteristically become darker with increasing age. *Disqualifications*—White body splashes, which means white on body between withers and tail, on sides between elbows and back of hindquarters in all colors.

**Gait**—The Australian Shepherd has a smooth, free and easy gait. He exhibits great agility of movement with a well-balanced, ground covering stride. Fore and hind legs move straight and parallel with the center line of the body. As speed increases, the feet (front and rear) converge toward the center line of gravity of the dog while the back remains firm and level. The Australian Shepherd must be agile and able to change direction or alter gait instantly.

**Temperament**—The Australian Shepherd is an intelligent, active dog with an even disposition; he is good-natured, seldom quarrelsome. He may be somewhat reserved in initial meetings. *Faults*—Any display of shyness, fear or aggression is to be severely penalized.

## DISQUALIFICATIONS

*Undershot. Overshot greater than ⅛ inch.*
*White body splashes, which means white on body between withers and tail, on sides between elbows and back of hindquarters in all colors.*

**Approved May 14, 1991**
**Effective January 1, 1993**

# BEARDED COLLIE

*O*RIGINALLY KNOWN AS THE HIGHLAND COLLIE, THE MOUNTAIN COLLIE, OR the Hairy Mou'ed Collie, the Bearded Collie is one of Britain's oldest breeds. While some have theorized that the Beardie was around to greet the Romans when they invaded Britain in A.D. 43, the current theory is that like most shaggy-haired herding dogs, the Bearded Collie descends from the Magyar Komondor and other herding dogs of Central Europe.

As with most breeds not used by the nobility, there are few early records on this humble herdsman's dog. The earliest known pictures of Bearded Collie types are a 1771 Gainsborough portrait of the Duke of Buccleigh and a 1772 Reynolds portrait of that peer's wife and daughter accompanied by two dogs. With Reinagle's more easily recognizable depiction published in Taplin's 1803 *Sportsman's Cabinet,* and a description of the breed published in an 1818 issue of *Live Stock Journal,* the existence of the breed as we know it was firmly established.

At the end of the Victorian era, Beardies were fairly popular in southern Scotland, both as working and show dogs. When Bearded Collie classes were offered at shows, usually in the area about Peebleshire, they were well supported. But there was then no official standard, since no breed club existed to establish one. Each judge had to adopt his own criteria. The lack of a strong breed club proved quite a misfortune. The local popularity of the breed continued until World War I, during which there were few dog shows. By the 1930s there was no kennel breeding Bearded Collies for show purposes.

That Beardies did not die out rests on their ability as workers and the devotion of the Peebleshire shepherds and drovers to the breed. They are still highly valued as sheepdogs due to their ability to turn in a good day's work in south Scotland's misty, rainy, and cold climate, and their adeptness on the rough, rocky ground.

The Bearded Collie's other major use is as a drover. They work with little direction from the butchers and drovers who find them very valuable in moving troublesome cattle. The shepherds and drovers have valued Beardies to such an extent that they have been more than reluctant to sell any puppies (especially bitches) unless they could be sure the puppies would actually be worked.

After World War II, Mrs. G. O. Willison, of Bothkennar Kennels, saved the Beardie from further chance of extinction when she began to breed them for show purposes. She spearheaded the establishment of the Bearded Collie Club in Britain in 1955. After much travail, in 1959 The Kennel Club (England) allowed Bearded Collies to be eligible for Challenge Certificates and championships and the popularity of the breed began to steadily increase.

Bearded Collies were introduced into the United States in the late 1950s, but none of these dogs were bred. It wasn't until 1967 that the first litter of Bearded Collies was born in this country. By July 1969, there was enough interest for the Bearded Collie Club of America to be founded.

The breed became eligible to be shown in the Miscellaneous class as of June 1, 1974. The AKC Stud Book was opened to Bearded Collie registrations on October 1, 1976, and the breed became eligible to compete in the Working Group on February 1, 1977. It joined the newly formed Herding Group in January 1983.

The Bearded Collie appears in black, brown, blue, and fawn colors, usually with white markings. His beautiful long coat and enthusiastic personality make him appealing in both the show and performance rings. He is a happy fellow and makes a good companion dog.

# OFFICIAL STANDARD FOR THE BEARDED COLLIE

**Characteristics**—The Bearded Collie is hardy and active, with an aura of strength and agility characteristic of a real working dog. Bred for centuries as a companion and servant of man, the Bearded Collie is a devoted and intelligent member of the family. He is stable and self-confident, showing no signs of shyness or aggression. This is a natural and unspoiled breed.

**General Appearance**—The Bearded Collie is a medium sized dog with a medium length coat that follows the natural lines of the body and allows plenty of daylight under the body. The body is long and lean, and, though strongly made, does not appear heavy. A bright inquiring expression is a distinctive feature of the breed. The Bearded Collie should be shown in a natural stance.

**Head**—The head is in proportion to the size of the dog. The skull is broad and flat; the stop is moderate; the cheeks are well filled beneath the eyes; the muzzle is strong and full; the foreface is equal in length to the distance between the stop and occiput. The nose is large and squarish. A snipy muzzle is to be penalized. (See Color section for pigmentation.)

*Eyes:* The eyes are large, expressive, soft and affectionate, but not round nor protruding, and are set widely apart. The eyebrows are arched to the sides to frame the eyes and are long enough to blend smoothly into the coat on the sides of the head. (See Color section for eye color.)

*Ears:* The ears are medium sized, hanging and covered with long hair. They are set level with the eyes. When the dog is alert, the ears have a slight lift at the base.

*Teeth:* The teeth are strong and white, meeting in a scissors bite. Full dentition is desirable.

**Neck**—The neck is in proportion to the length of the body, strong and slightly arched, blending smoothly into the shoulders.

**Forequarters**—The shoulders are well laid back at an angle of approximately 45°; a line drawn from the highest point of the shoulder blade to the forward point of articulation approximates a right angle with a line from the forward point of articulation to the point of the elbow. The tops of the shoulder blades lie in against the withers, but they slope outwards from there sufficiently to accommodate the desired spring of ribs. The legs are straight and vertical, with substantial, but not heavy, bone and are covered with shaggy hair all around. The pasterns are flexible without weakness.

**Body**—The body is longer than it is high in an approximate ratio of five to four, length measured from point of chest to point of buttocks, height measured at the highest point of the withers. The length of the back comes from the length of the ribcage and not that of the loin. The back is level. The ribs are well sprung from the spine but are flat at the sides. The chest is deep, reaching at least to the elbows. The loins are strong. The level back line blends smoothly into the curve of the rump. A flat croup or a steep croup is to be severely penalized.

**Hindquarters**—The hind legs are powerful and muscular at the thighs with well bent stifles. The hocks are low. In normal stance, the bones below the hocks are perpendicular to the ground and parallel to each other when viewed from the rear; the hind feet fall just behind a perpendicular line from the point of buttocks when viewed from the side. The legs are covered with shaggy hair all around.

*Tail:* The tail is set low and is long enough for the end of the bone to reach at least the point of the hocks. It is normally carried low with an upward swirl at the tip while the dog is standing. When the dog is excited or in motion, the curve is accentuated and the tail may be raised but is never carried beyond a vertical line. The tail is covered with abundant hair.

**Feet**—The feet are oval in shape with the soles well padded. The toes are arched and close together, and well covered with hair including between the pads.

**Coat**—The coat is double with the undercoat soft, furry and close. The outercoat is flat, harsh, strong and shaggy, free from wooliness and curl, although a slight wave is permissible. The coat falls naturally to either side but must never be artificially parted.

The length and density of the hair are sufficient to provide a protective coat and to enhance the shape of the dog, but not so profuse as to obscure the natural lines of the body. The dog should be shown as naturally as is consistent with good grooming but the coat must not be trimmed in any way. On the head, the bridge of the nose is sparsely covered with hair which is slightly longer on the sides to cover the lips. From the cheeks, the lower lips and under the chin, the coat increases in length towards the chest, forming the typical beard. An excessively long, silky coat or one which has been trimmed in any way must be severely penalized.

**Color**—*Coat:* All Bearded Collies are born either black, blue, brown or fawn, with or without white markings. With maturity, the coat color may lighten, so that a born black may become any shade of gray from black to slate to silver, a born brown from chocolate to sandy. Blues and fawns also show shades from dark to light. Where white occurs, it only appears on the foreface as a blaze, on the skull, on the tip of the tail, on the chest, legs and feet and around the neck. The white hair does not grow on the body behind the shoulder nor on the face to surround the eyes. Tan markings occasionally appear and are acceptable on the eyebrows, inside the ears, on the cheeks, under the root of the tail, and on the legs where the white joins the main color.

*Pigmentation:* Pigmentation on the Bearded Collie follows coat color. In a born black, the eye rims, nose and lips are black, whereas in the born blue, the pigmentation is a blue-gray color. A born brown dog has brown pigmentation and born fawns a correspondingly lighter brown. The pigmentation is completely filled in and shows no sign of spots.

*Eyes:* Eye color will generally tone with the coat color. In a born blue or fawn, the distinctively lighter eyes are correct and must not be penalized.

**Size**—The ideal height at the withers is 21–22 inches for adult dogs and 20–21 inches for adult bitches. Height over and under the ideal is to be severely penalized. The express objective of this criterion is to insure that the Bearded Collie remains a medium sized dog.

**Gait**—Movement is free, supple and powerful. Balance combines good reach in forequarters with strong drive in hindquarters. The back remains firm and level. The feet are lifted only enough to clear the ground, giving the impression that the dog glides along making minimum contact. Movement is lithe and flexible to enable the dog to make the sharp turns and sudden stops required of the sheepdog. When viewed from the front and rear, the front and rear legs travel in the same plane from the shoulder and hip joint to pads at all speeds. Legs remain straight, but feet move inward as speed increases until the edges of the feet converge on a center line at a fast trot.

## SERIOUS FAULTS:

—*Snipy muzzle*
—*Flat croup or steep croup*
—*Excessively long, silky coat*
—*Trimmed or sculptured coat*
—*Height over or under the ideal*

**Approved August 9, 1978**

# BELGIAN MALINOIS

*T*HE BELGIAN MALINOIS IS ONE OF FOUR TYPES OF BELGIAN SHEEPHERDING dogs registered in Belgium and France as the Chien de Berger Belge. It shares a common foundation with the Belgian Sheepdog and Belgian Tervuren, whose historical sections in this book provide additional information on the beginnings of the breed. One of the first short-coated Belgian shepherds registered by the Société Royale Saint-Hubert was Charlot, born in 1891. The Belgian artist Alexandre Clarys would later use this dog as a model of the Belgian Malinois. The short-haired fawn dog with black mask we know today as the Belgian Malinois shared the beginnings with many coat colors and lengths, but it quickly established itself as an identifiable type. Bred basically around the city of Malines, from whence the breed name is derived, the Belgian Malinois was bred by a dedicated group of trainers and working competitors. They prized the capabilities of this breed and concerned themselves with breeding dogs with excellent working character. Because of this, the Belgian Malinois has historically been the favorite type of Belgian shepherd in its native Belgium. Professor Adolphe Reul, one of the dedicated leaders in the breed's formation, owned and bred many fine subjects, including the famous Mastock.

Because the early breeders were concerned with type and character, many cross-variety breedings took place. The Belgian Malinois was the superior competition dog, and many used it to add strength to their varieties. We still see the effects of those breedings today when longhaired puppies are born in registered Belgian

Malinois litters. Through the offspring with long hair and from cross-variety breedings, Belgian Malinois history is intertwined with that of other Belgian Sheepdogs. The Belgian Tervuren, especially, owes a great deal to the function of Belgian Malinois blood.

There have been two major periods of Belgian Malinois activity in the United States. Beginning in 1911, when the first shorthaired Belgian Shepherds (Belgian Blackie and Belgian Mouche) were registered with the AKC until World War II, the Belgian Malinois enjoyed American popularity. Many subjects from the best Belgian bloodlines were imported and bred. There was some renewed interest after the war, but the breed did not flourish. Before 1959, the Belgian Malinois was relegated to the Miscellaneous class (even though it enjoyed individual AKC Stud Book registration) because there were not enough subjects to provide competition for championships.

The second period of importation and popular support began in 1963. Progressing slowly, the first ten years saw only 107 individual Belgian Malinois registrations. By June 1965, however, sufficient numbers had been registered by the AKC so the Belgian Malinois was moved into the Working Group and was eligible to compete for championships. Importations from Belgium, France, and Switzerland, as well as increased breeding activity since 1973, have given rise to a new era of relative popularity. While still one of the AKC's least populous breeds, the Belgian Malinois is making its presence felt in the Herding Group. The main qualities that make the Belgian Malinois such a desirable breed are the easy-care coat, the medium size, and the keen intelligence and versatility. It is an alert and highly trainable breed that can herd a flock with inexhaustible energy and is sharp enough to protect the flock and farm. Since World War I the Malinois has contributed much to our society, and continues to distinguish itself as a police, military, and service dog. Today many owners are finding pleasure in training their family companion Belgian Malinois for conformation, obedience, schutzhund, herding, sledding, agility, therapy, and tracking. The Breed standards recognized by the AKC differ somewhat for each of the three Belgian shepherd breeds, but the basic dog is the same. In Europe and elsewhere in the world, they share a common standard, differentiated only by coat.

# OFFICIAL STANDARD FOR THE BELGIAN MALINOIS

**General Appearance**—The Belgian Malinois is a well balanced, square dog, elegant in appearance with an exceedingly proud carriage of the head and neck. The dog is strong, agile, well muscled, alert and full of life. He stands squarely on all fours, and viewed from the side, the topline, forelegs, and hind legs closely approximate a square. The whole conformation gives the impression of depth and solidity without bulkiness. The male is usually somewhat more impressive and grand than his female counterpart, which has a distinctly feminine look.

**Size, Proportion, Substance**—Males are 24 to 26 inches in height; females are 22 to 24 inches; measurement to be taken at the withers. Males under 23 inches or over 27 inches and females under 21 inches or over 25 inches are to be *disqualified*. The length, measured from the point of the breastbone to the point of the rump, should equal the height, but bitches may be slightly longer. A square dog is preferred. Bone structure is moderately heavy in proportion to height so that the dog is well balanced throughout and neither spindly or leggy nor cumbersome and bulky.

**Head**—The head is clean-cut and strong without heaviness; overall size is in proportion to the body. The *expression* should indicate alertness, attention and readiness for activity, and the gaze is intelligent and questioning. The *eyes* are brown, preferably dark brown, medium size, slightly almond shaped, not protruding. Eye rims are black. The *ears* approach the shape of an equilateral triangle and are stiff, erect, and in proportion to the head in size. The outer corner of the ear should not come below the center of the eye. Ears hanging as on a hound, or semi-prick ears are disqualifications. The top of the *skull* is flattened rather than rounded with the width approximately the same as the length but no wider. The stop is moderate. The *muzzle* is moderately pointed, avoiding any tendency to snipiness, and approximately equal in length to the topskull. The planes of the muzzle and topskull are parallel. The jaws are strong and powerful. The nose is black without discolored areas. The lips are tight and black with no pink showing on the outside. The Belgian Malinois has a full complement of strong, white teeth, that are evenly set and meet in a scissors or level *bite.* Overshot and undershot bites are a fault. An undershot bite in which two or more of the upper incisors lose contact with two or more of the lower incisors is a disqualification. One or more missing teeth is a serious fault.

**Neck, Topline, Body**—The *neck* is round and of sufficient length to permit the proud carriage of the head. It should taper from the body to the head. The *topline* is generally level. The withers are slightly higher and slope into the back which must be level, straight and firm from withers to hip joint. The croup is medium long, sloping gradually. The *body* should give the impression of power without bulkiness. The chest is not broad but is deep with the lowest point reaching the elbow. The underline forms a smooth ascendant curve from the lowest point of the chest to the abdomen. The abdomen is moderately developed, neither tucked up nor paunchy. The loin section, viewed from above, is relatively short, broad and strong, and blends smoothly into the back. The *tail* is strong at the base, the bone reaching to the hock. In action it is raised with a curve, which is strongest towards the tip, without forming a hook. A cropped or stumped tail is a disqualification.

**Forequarters**—The forequarters are muscular without excessive bulkiness. The shoulder is long and oblique, laid flat against the body, forming a sharp angle with the upper arm. The legs are straight, strong, and parallel to each other. The bone is oval rather than round. Length and substance are well in proportion to the size of the dog. The pastern is of medium length, strong, and very slightly sloped. Dewclaws may be removed. The feet are round (cat footed) and well padded with the toes curved close together. The nails are strong and black except that they may be white to match white toe tips.

**Hindquarters**—Angulation of the hindquarters is in balance with the forequarters; the angle at the hock is relatively sharp, although the Belgian Malinois should not have extreme angulation. The upper and lower thigh bones should approximately parallel the shoulder blade and upper arm respectively. The legs are in proportion to the size of the dog; oval bone rather than round. Legs are parallel to each other. The thighs should be well muscled. Dewclaws, if any, should be removed. Metatarsi are of medium length, strong, and slightly sloped. The hind feet may be slightly elongated, with toes curved close together and well padded. Nails are strong and black except that they may be white to match white toe tips.

**Coat**—The coat should be comparatively short, straight, hard enough to be weather resistant, with dense undercoat. It should be very short on the head, ears, and lower legs. The hair is somewhat longer around the neck where it forms a collarette, and on the tail and backs of the thighs. The coat should conform to the body without standing out or hanging down.

**Color**—The basic coloring is a rich fawn to mahogany, with black tips on the hairs giving an overlay appearance. The mask and ears are black. The underparts of the body, tail and breeches are lighter fawn, but washed-out fawn color on the body is a fault. Color should be considered a finishing point, not to take precedence over structure or temperament. The tips of the toes may be white, and a small white spot on the breastbone/prosternum is permitted, not to extend to the neck. White markings, except as noted, are faulted.

**Gait**—The movement is smooth, free and easy, seemingly never tiring, exhibiting facility of movement rather than a hard driving action. The Belgian Malinois single tracks at a fast gait, the legs, both front and rear, converging toward the center line of gravity, while the topline remains firm and level, parallel to the line of motion with no crabbing. The breed shows a marked tendency to move in a circle rather than a straight line.

**Temperament**—Correct temperament is essential to the working character of the Belgian Malinois. The breed is confident, exhibiting neither shyness nor aggressiveness in new situations. The dog may be reserved with strangers but is affectionate with his own people. He is naturally protective of his owner's person and property without being overly aggressive. The Belgian Malinois possesses a strong desire to work and is quick and responsive to commands from his owner. Faulty temperament is strongly penalized.

**Faults**—The degree to which a dog is penalized should depend upon the extent to which the dog deviates from the standard and the extent to which the particular fault would actually affect the working ability of the dog.

## DISQUALIFICATIONS

*Males under 23 inches or over 27 inches and females under 21 inches or over 25 inches. Ears hanging as on a hound, or semi-prick ears. An undershot bite in which two or more of the upper incisors lose contact with two or more of the lower incisors. A cropped or stumped tail.*

**Approved July 10, 1990**
**Effective August 29, 1990**

# BELGIAN SHEEPDOG

THE BELGIAN SHEEPDOG IS KNOWN AS THE GROENENDAEL, OR CHIEN DE Berger Belge in most parts of the world. Its origin can be traced to the late 1800s when it was listed, both in studbooks and at dog shows, among many other shepherds as the Chien de Berger de Races Continentales (Continental Shepherds). By pedigree we can identify many of the Continental Shepherds not only as the Belgian Shepherds (Groenendael, Malinois, Tervuren, and Laekenois), but also as German Shepherd Dogs, Hollander Herders, Beauceron, Bouviers des Flandres, and Briards.

As European countries developed a sense of pride and a spirit of nationalism, many individuals worked to develop animals which would be identified with their own countries. In Belgium, in the late 1800s, efforts were made to determine if there was a true shepherd dog representative only of Belgium, and in September 1891, the Club du Chien de Berger Belge (Belgian Shepherd Club) was formed for this purpose. A commission of club members was established which contacted veterinarians and others throughout the provinces. In November 1891, under the direction of veterinarian Professor Adolphe Reul, a gathering was held at Cureghem, on the outskirts of Brussels, to examine the shepherd dogs of that area. From the 117 dogs exhibited, Reul and his panel of judges concluded that for this Brabant Province there was a consistent type of sheepdog. They were anatomically identical but differed in hair textures, colors, and hair lengths. What Reul described was a square, medium-sized sheepdog, with well-set triangular ears and very dark brown eyes. The Club du Chien du Berger Belge devoted its efforts to similar exhibitions in the remaining eight provinces, and found similar results. Between 1891 and 1901, when the Belgian Shepherd was registered as a breed by the Société Royale Saint-Hubert, efforts were directed toward developing a standard, improving type, and exhibiting.

The longhaired black Belgian Shepherds primarily owe their existence to Nicolas Rose, restaurateur and owner of the Chateau Groenendael, outside of Brussels. He purchased what are considered to be the foundation couple of the longhaired blacks, Picard d'Uccle and Petite, and established a thriving kennel which can be traced to 1893, the year the Club du Chien de Berger Belge adopted the first standard for the Belgian Shepherds. Picard d'Uccle was bred to Petite, producing the outstanding Pitt, Baronne, and Duc de Groenendael, as well as to his daughters and others in the area, who are to be found in the pedigrees of our current dogs. This stock formed the basis of these beautiful longhaired blacks, officially given the name Groenendael in 1910.

Interest in the Belgian Shepherds developed very quickly after they were recognized as a breed. Before World War I it had become apparent that, although called a shepherd or sheepdog, the Groenendael was a versatile animal, and with its keen intelligence and easy trainability, it could perform a variety of functions. The Paris police utilized the Groenendael in the first decade of the twentieth century, as did the New York City police who, in 1908, imported four Belgian Sheepdogs to work alongside an American-bred Groenendael.

In the same period, Belgian customs officers employed the Groenendael for border patrols, and their efforts in capturing smugglers were greatly praised. The Groenendael were also used as herders, watchdogs, faithful companions, and became outstanding participants in the popular European "working trials," from the local trial through international competitions. The Groenendael Jules du Moulin demonstrated this versatility by earning his World Championship at the defense trials in France in 1908. Repeating his victories in 1909, 1910, and 1912, he also earned his International Championship at the police trials of Belgium and France for four straight years, 1909–1912.

During World War I, Belgian Sheepdogs distinguished themselves as message carriers, ambulance dogs, and even pulling machine guns. Although first registered in the United States as early as 1911, their fame really took hold after the war. The Belgian Sheepdog Club of America was formed in 1919, and it was not uncommon to see ten or twelve Belgian Sheepdogs exhibited at the larger Eastern shows in the 1920s. By 1926, the Belgian Sheepdog was ranked 42 out of 100 breeds recognized by the AKC.

The Great Depression had a marked effect on the Belgian Sheepdog. Its popularity declined, and the American club ceased to function. World War II again found the Belgian Sheepdog serving as a war and defense dog, and many were utilized to guard military installations. Interest in the breed was rekindled after the war, and the current Belgian Sheepdog Club of America was formed in 1949. Since then, many Groenendael have been imported and the interest in the breed has continued to grow.

In 1959, the AKC Board of Directors mandated that only the Groenendael would be registered as Belgian Sheepdogs and that these dogs must have three generations of Groenendael ancestors.

Throughout their history Belgian Sheepdogs have earned their reputation as truly well-rounded dogs, and to this day they continue to captivate our hearts. Their elegance of carriage and balanced movement are a pleasure to behold. Their talents in obedience, tracking, schutzhund, and herding, and as sled dogs, have kept even the most activity-minded of us satisfied. Their skills in police work and search and rescue, and as guide and therapy dogs, have proven very valuable to society. These dogs have found their greatest value, however, in the hearts of their owners as gentle and devoted companions willing to give all to those they love.

# OFFICIAL STANDARD FOR THE BELGIAN SHEEPDOG

**General Appearance**—The first impression of the Belgian Sheepdog is that of a well balanced, square dog, elegant in appearance, with an exceedingly proud carriage of the head and neck. He is a strong, agile, well muscled animal, alert and full of life. His whole conformation gives the impression of depth and solidity without bulkiness. The male dog is usually somewhat more impressive and grand than his female counterpart. The bitch should have a distinctly feminine look.

*Faults*—Any deviation from these specifications is a fault. In determining whether a fault is minor, serious, or major, these two factors should be used as a guide: 1. The extent to which it deviates from the standard. 2. The extent to which such deviation would actually affect the working ability of the dog.

**Size, Proportion, Substance**—Males should be 24–26 inches in height and females 22–24 inches, measured at the withers.

Males under 22½ or over 27½ inches in height and females under 20½ or over 25½ inches in height shall be disqualified.

The length, measured from point of breastbone to point of rump, should equal the height. Bitches may be slightly longer. Bone structure should be moderately heavy in proportion to his height so that he is well balanced throughout and neither spindly or leggy nor cumbersome and bulky. The Belgian Sheepdog should stand squarely on all fours. Side view—The topline, front legs, and back legs should closely approximate a square.

**Head**—Clean-cut and strong, overall size should be in proportion to the body. *Expression* indicates alertness, attention, readiness for activity. Gaze should be intelligent and questioning. *Eyes* brown, preferably dark brown. Medium size, slightly almond shaped, not protruding. *Ears* triangular in shape, stiff, erect, and in proportion to the head in size. Base of the ear should not come below the center of the eye. Ears hanging (as on a hound) shall disqualify.

*Skull*—Top flattened rather than rounded. The width approximately the same, but not wider than the length. *Stop* moderate. *Muzzle* moderately pointed, avoiding any tendency to snipiness, and approximately equal in length to that of the topskull. The jaws should be strong and powerful. *Nose* black without spots or discolored areas. The *lips* should be tight and black, with no pink showing on the outside. *Teeth*—A full complement of strong, white teeth, evenly set. Should not be overshot or undershot. Should have either an even bite or a scissors bite.

**Neck, Topline, Body**—*Neck* round and rather outstretched, tapered from head to body, well muscled, with tight skin. *Topline*—The withers are slightly higher and slope into the back, which must be level, straight, and firm from withers to hip joints. *Chest* not broad, but deep. The lowest point should reach the elbow, forming a smooth ascendant curve to the abdomen. *Abdomen*—Moderate development. Neither tucked up nor paunchy. The *loin* section, viewed from above, is relatively short, broad and strong, but blending smoothly into the back. The *croup* is medium long, sloping gradually. *Tail* strong at the base, bone to reach hock. At rest the dog holds it low, the tip bent back level with the hock. When in action he raises it and gives it a curl, which is strongest toward the tip, without forming a hook. Cropped or stump tail shall disqualify.

**Forequarters**—*Shoulder* long and oblique, laid flat against the body, forming a sharp angle (approximately 90°) with the upper arm. *Legs* straight, strong and parallel to each other. Bone oval rather than round. Development (length and substance) should be well proportioned to the size of the dog. Pastern medium length, strong, and very slightly sloped. *Feet* round (cat footed), toes curved close together, well padded. Nails strong and black, except that they may be white to match white toe tips.

**Hindquarters**—*Legs*—Length and substance well proportioned to the size of the dog. Bone oval rather than round. Legs are parallel to each other. *Thighs* broad and heavily muscled. The upper and lower thigh bones approximately parallel the shoulder blade and upper arm respectively, forming a relatively sharp angle at stifle joint. The angle at the hock is relatively sharp, although the Belgian Sheepdog does not have extreme angulation. Metatarsus medium length, strong and slightly sloped. Dewclaws, if any, should be removed. *Feet* slightly elongated. Toes curved close together, well padded. Nails strong and black, except that they may be white to match white toe tips.

**Coat**—The guard hairs of the coat must be long, well fitting, straight and abundant. They should not be silky or wiry. The texture should be a medium harshness. The undercoat should be extremely dense, commensurate, however, with climatic conditions. The Belgian Sheepdog is particularly adaptable to extremes of temperature or climate. The hair is shorter on the head, outside of the ears, and lower part of the legs. The opening of the ear is protected by tufts of hair.

*Ornamentation*—Especially long and abundant hair, like a collarette, around the neck; fringe of long hair down the back of the forearm; especially long and abundant hair trimming the hindquarters, the breeches; long, heavy and abundant hair on the tail.

**Color**—Black. May be completely black, or may be black with white, limited as follows: Small to moderate patch or strip on forechest. Between pads of feet. On *tips of* hind toes. On chin and muzzle (frost—may be white or gray). On *tips* of front toes— allowable, but a fault.

   *Disqualification*—Any color other than black, except for white in specified areas. Reddening due to climatic conditions in an otherwise correct coat should not be grounds for disqualification.

   **Gait**—Motion should be smooth, free and easy, seemingly never tiring, exhibiting facility of movement rather than a hard driving action. He tends to single track on a fast gait; the legs, both front and rear, converging toward the center line of gravity of the dog. The backline should remain firm and level, parallel to the line of motion, with no crabbing. He shows a marked tendency to move in a circle rather than a straight line.

   **Temperament**—The Belgian Sheepdog should reflect the qualities of intelligence, courage, alertness and devotion to master. To his inherent aptitude as a guardian of flocks should be added protectiveness of the person and property of his master. He should be watchful, attentive, and always in motion when not under command. In his relationship with humans, he should be observant and vigilant with strangers, but not apprehensive. He should not show fear or shyness. He should not show viciousness by unwarranted or unprovoked attack. With those he knows well, he is most affectionate and friendly, zealous of their attention, and very possessive. Viciousness is a disqualification.

## DISQUALIFICATIONS

*Males under 22½ or over 27½ inches in height and females under 20½ or over 25½ inches in height.*
*Ears hanging (as on a hound).*
*Cropped or stump tail.*
*Any color other than black.*
*Viciousness.*

**Approved December 11, 1990**
**Effective January 30, 1991**

# BELGIAN TERVUREN

HE BELGIAN TERVUREN IS KNOWN IN ITS COUNTRY OF ORIGIN AS THE
Chien de Berger Belge. This variety is distinguished by its coat color and
length as "longhaired other than black" in comparison to the Groenendael with
long black hair, the Malinois with a short coat, and the wirehaired Laekenois. The
variety designation, Tervuren, owes its name to the Belgian village of Tervuren, the
home of M. F. Corbeel, an early devotee of the breed. Mr. Corbeel bred the fawn-
colored Tom and Poes, commonly considered the foundation couple of the breed,
to produce the fawn-colored Miss. In turn, Miss was bred to the black Duc de
Groenendael, to produce the famous fawn Milsart, who in 1907 became the first
Tervuren champion.

Before the Industrial Age, the rural farmers of Belgium had a great need for a
general purpose herding and guard dog. The protective instinct of these dogs provided security for the farm and the family, and their herding abilities assisted with
the daily maintenance of the stock. The mental development of the breed as a versatile helper and attentive companion paralleled the physical evolution of a
medium-sized, well-balanced animal with strength and stamina. With industrializa-
tion, the rural farm dog became less important, but the beauty and loyalty of the
breed made them well appreciated as family companions.

Very little written information is available on the origins of the breed before the establishment of the Belgian Shepherd Club in 1891. Professor Adolphe Reul's documentation of the exhibitions held to determine breed type, leading to the first written standard in 1893, and the breed's recognition by the Société Royale Saint-Hubert in 1901, are considered the important historical landmarks in the development of the Belgian Shepherd. In May 1892, the first Belgian Shepherd specialty show was held in Cureghem, Belgium, and was won by a registered Tervuren, Duc II, owned by Arthur Meul. This same Duc, a brown-brindle born in 1890, served as the model for the Belgian Tervuren in the famous painting done by Alexandre Clarys in 1910.

In these early years, differing opinions as to the color of the Tervuren allowed for a range of colors. The breed was established without regard for color, but the development of varieties led to some advocating a charcoaled fawn with a black mask, others preferring a plain fawn with no mask, and still others breeding for the silver color. Currently, any longhaired Belgian Shepherd that is not black is considered a Tervuren. In the United States the preferred colors range from fawn to mahogany, all with a black masking and a blackened overlay, as detailed in the breed standard.

The efforts of a few dedicated breeders continued on a modest scale until after World War II. The outstanding reproducers of the 1900s were General, a direct descendant of Milsart, as well as Minox and Colette ex Folette, who were from Malinois parents, and who produced Jinox, Noisette, and Lakme. These dogs figure heavily in the ancestry of the Belgian Shepherds of the 1940s and 1950s who brought about the revival of the Tervuren as we know it today.

In 1948, at the kennel of P. Daniel in Normandy, the pale fawn Willy de la Garde Noire was born, of Groenendael parents. As a pup he was sold to Gilbert Fontaine, of the Clos St. Clair kennel. Although the longhaired fawns were generally not preferred at the time, Willy was of such excellent type and structure that he competed equally with the best Groenendael and Malinois. He won numerous CACIBs in both Belgium and France, including the 1950, 1953, and 1954 Paris shows. His record as a producer was no less spectacular, and it is because of Willy that the renaissance of the Tervuren began, primarily in France, but eventually extending to the rest of Europe and the United States. The development of the Tervuren during this time is a distinct reminder of the intricate interweavings of the genetics of the Belgian Shepherd. The Tervuren was created after World War II from the longhaired puppies in Malinois litters and the fawn-gray puppies in the Groenendael litters. These dogs were eventually bred to a few remaining postwar Tervuren, producing what is now the most popular variety of Belgian Shepherd in parts of Europe and America.

The first Tervuren was registered with the AKC in 1918. Registrations at this time were sparse, and by the Depression the variety had disappeared from the AKC Stud Book. It was not until 1953 that the blackened fawn longhaired dogs were again imported, through the efforts of Rudy Robinson, Robert and Barbara Krohn, and Marge Coyle. Before 1959, these dogs were registered and shown as Belgian Sheepdogs. In that year, the AKC granted the separate breed classification designating the Belgian Tervuren as a distinct breed.

Belgian Tervurens retain the working characteristics so valued in times past. By virtue of their quick intelligence and unwavering devotion they are precious personal companions. Their versatility is still highly appreciated, as is their graceful elegance and eye-catching appearance. They have remained useful in herding and are now exhibiting their talents as therapy dogs and companions to the disabled. It is not at all unusual for them to compete equally in conformation and companion rings, and many breed champions earn obedience degrees. They have been trained in sports as diverse as schutzhund and sledding. Truly, they have earned our respect, and captivate our hearts, with their adaptability, their exuberant personalities, and their distinctive beauty.

# OFFICIAL STANDARD FOR THE BELGIAN TERVUREN

**General Appearance**—The first impression of the Belgian Tervuren is that of a well balanced, medium size dog, elegant in appearance, standing squarely on all fours, with proud carriage of head and neck. He is strong, agile, well muscled, alert and full of life. He gives the impression of depth and solidity without bulkiness. The male should appear unquestionably masculine; the female should have a distinctly feminine look and be judged equally with the male. The Belgian Tervuren is a *natural* dog and there is no need for excessive posing in the show ring.

The Belgian Tervuren reflects the qualities of intelligence, courage, alertness and devotion to master. In addition to his inherent ability as a herding dog, he protects his master's person and property without being overtly aggressive. He is watchful, attentive, and usually in motion when not under command.

The Belgian Tervuren is a herding dog, and faults which affect his ability to herd under all conditions, such as poor gait, bite, coat or temperament, should be particularly penalized.

**Size, Proportion, Substance**—The ideal male is 24 to 26 inches in height and female 22 to 24 inches in height measured at the withers. Dogs are to be penalized in accordance to the degree they deviate from the ideal. Males under 23 inches or over 26.5 inches or females under 21 inches or over 24.5 inches are to be disqualified. The body is square; the length measured from the point of shoulder to the point of the rump approximates the height. Females may be somewhat longer in body. Bone structure is medium in proportion to height, so that he is well balanced throughout and neither spindly or leggy nor cumbersome and bulky.

**Head**—Well chiseled, skin taut, long without exaggeration. *Expression*—intelligent and questioning, indicating alertness, attention and readiness for action. *Eyes*—

dark brown, medium size, slightly almond shape, not protruding. Light, yellow or round eyes are a fault. *Ears*—triangular in shape, well cupped, stiff, erect, height equal to width at base. Set high, the base of the ear does not come below the center of the eye. Hanging ears, as on a hound, are a disqualification. *Skull* and *muzzle*—measuring from the stop are of equal length. Overall size is in proportion to the body, top of skull flattened rather than rounded, the width approximately the same as, but not wider than the length. *Stop*—moderate. The topline of the muzzle is parallel to the topline of the skull when viewed from the side. Muzzle moderately pointed, avoiding any tendency toward snippiness or cheekiness. *Jaws* strong and powerful. *Nose* black without spots or discolored areas. *Nostrils* well defined. *Lips* tight and black, no pink showing on the outside when mouth is closed. *Teeth*—Full complement of strong white teeth, evenly set, meeting in a scissors or a level bite. Overshot and undershot teeth are a fault. Undershot teeth such that contact with the upper incisors is lost by two or more of the lower incisors is a disqualification. Loss of contact caused by short center incisors in an otherwise correct bite shall not be judged undershot. Broken or discolored teeth should not be penalized. Missing teeth are a fault.

**Neck, Topline, Body**—*Neck* round, muscular, rather long and elegant, slightly arched and tapered from head to body. Skin well fitting with no loose folds. *Withers* accentuated. *Topline* level, straight and firm from withers to croup. *Croup* medium long, sloping gradually to the base of the tail. *Chest* not broad without being narrow, but deep; the lowest point of the brisket reaching the elbow, forming a smooth ascendant curve to the abdomen. *Abdomen* moderately developed, neither tucked up nor paunchy. Ribs well sprung but flat on the sides. *Loin section* viewed from above is relatively short, broad and strong, but blending smoothly into the back. *Tail* strong at the base, the last vertebra to reach at least to the hock. At rest the dog holds it low, the tip bent back level with the hock. When in action, he may raise it to a point level with the topline giving it a slight curve, but not a hook. Tail is not carried above the backline nor turned to one side. A cropped or stump tail is a disqualification.

**Forequarters**—*Shoulders* long, laid back 45 degrees, flat against the body, forming a right angle with the upper arm. Top of the shoulder blades roughly two thumbs width apart. *Upper arms* should move in a direction exactly parallel to the longitudinal axis of the body. *Forearms* long and well muscled. *Legs* straight and parallel, perpendicular to the ground. Bone oval rather than round. *Pasterns* short and strong, slightly sloped. Dewclaws may be removed. *Feet* rounded, cat footed, turning neither in nor out, toes curved close together, well padded, strong nails.

**Hindquarters**—*Legs* powerful without heaviness, moving in the same pattern as the limbs of the forequarters. Bone oval rather than round. *Thighs* broad and heavily muscled. *Stifles* clearly defined, with upper shank at right angles to hip bones. *Hocks* moderately bent. *Metatarsi* short, perpendicular to the ground, parallel to each other when viewed from the rear. Dewclaws are removed. *Feet* slightly elongated, toes curved close together, heavily padded, strong nails.

**Coat**—The Belgian Tervuren is particularly adaptable to extremes of temperature or climate. The guard hairs of the coat must be long, close fitting, straight and abundant. The texture is of medium harshness, not silky or wiry. Wavy or curly hair is undesirable. The undercoat is very dense, commensurate, however, with climatic conditions. The hair is short on the head, outside the ears, and on the front part of the legs. The opening of the ear is protected by tufts of hair. **Ornamentation** consists of especially long and abundant hair, like a collarette around the neck, particularly on males; fringe of long hair down the back of the forearm; especially long and abundant hair trimming the breeches; long, heavy and abundant hair on the tail. *The female rarely has as long or as ornamented a coat as the male. This disparity must not be a consideration when the female is judged against the male.*

**Color**—*Body* rich fawn to russet mahogany with black overlay. The coat is characteristically double pigmented wherein the tip of each fawn hair is blackened. Belgian Tervuren characteristically becomes darker with age. On mature males, this blackening is especially pronounced on the shoulders, back and rib section. Blackening in patches is undesirable. Although allowance should be made for females and young males, absence of blackening in mature dogs is a serious fault. Washed out, predominant color, such as cream or gray is to be severely penalized.

*Chest* is normally black, but may be a mixture of black and gray. A single white patch is permitted on the chest, not to extend to the neck or breast. *Face* has a black mask and the ears are mostly black. A face with a complete absence of black is a serious fault. Frost or white on chin or muzzle is normal. The underparts of the body, tail, and *breeches* are cream, gray, or light beige. The *tail* typically has a darker or black tip. *Feet*—The tips of the toes may be white. Nail color may vary from black to transparent. Solid black, solid liver or any area of white except as specified on the chest, tips of the toes, chin and muzzle are disqualifications.

**Gait**—Lively and graceful, covering the maximum ground with minimum effort. Always in motion, seemingly never tiring, he shows ease of movement rather than hard driving action. He single tracks at a fast gait, the legs both front and rear converging toward the center line of gravity of the dog. Viewed from the side he exhibits full extension of both fore and hindquarters. The backline should remain firm and level, parallel to the line of motion. His natural tendency is to move in a circle, rather than a straight line. Padding, hackneying, weaving, crabbing and similar movement faults are to be penalized according to the degree to which they interfere with the ability of the dog to work.

**Temperament**—In his relationship with humans he is observant and vigilant with strangers, but not apprehensive. He does not show fear or shyness. He does not show viciousness by unwarranted or unprovoked attack. He must be approachable, standing his ground and showing confidence to meet overtures without himself making them. With those he knows well, he is most affectionate and friendly, zealous for their attention and very possessive.

## DISQUALIFICATIONS

*Males under 23 inches or over 26.5 inches or females under 21 inches or over 24.5 inches. Hanging ears, as on a hound.*
*Undershot teeth such that contact with the upper incisors is lost by two or more of the lower incisors.*

*A cropped or stump tail.*

*Solid black, solid liver or any area of white except as specified on the chest, tips of the toes, chin and muzzle.*

**Approved September 11, 1990**
**Effective October 30, 1990**

# BORDER COLLIE

*W*HEN THE ROMANS INVADED BRITAIN IN THE FIRST CENTURY B.C., THEY brought dogs to herd their livestock. These dogs were black, tan, and white, and large, with heavy bone. Romans and their indispensable dogs were a part of British life for centuries. When the empire crumbled, Viking raiders brought with them the spitz-type dogs they used for herding. These were eventually cross-bred with Roman herding dogs, decreasing size and increasing agility. This proved to be an advantage in the hilly, rocky highlands of Scotland and Wales.

One of the earliest written descriptions of sheepdogs in the British Isles is attributed to Hywel Dda in 943. He described a black sheepdog taking a flock of sheep to graze in the hills and coming home with them in the evening.

In the 1576 *Of English Dogges,* by John Caius, we find a description that could apply to our modern-day working Border Collie:

> Our Shepherd's dogge is not huge, vaste, or bigge, but of indifferent stature and growth, because it hath not to deale with the blood thirsty wolf, sythence there be none in England, which happy and fortunate benefit is to be ascribed to the puifaunt Prince Edgar. This dogge, either at the hearing of his master's voice or at the shrill hissing, bringeth the wandering weathers and straying sheep into the self same place where his master's will and wish is to have them, whereby the shepherd reapeth this benefite, namely that with lit-

tle labour nor tyole or moving of his feete he may rule and guide his flocke, according to his own desire.

The sheepdog continued to develop, being bred not for the seemingly artificial criteria of appearance but rather for how well the dog worked. With the arrival of mechanization, many farmers began handling larger flocks. Since less manpower was required for most tasks, an efficient herding dog became a real asset.

Sheepdog trials played an important role in the development of these herders by testing their merit and capabilities in a uniform environment. The first recorded sheepdog trial was held on October 9, 1873, in Bala, Wales. The winner was William Thomson and his Scottish-bred dog, Tweed. A compact dog, Tweed had a black coat with tan and white markings, and was also the winner of the beauty prize!

All modern Border Collies trace to a single dog, Old Hemp, pictured on the previous page. Born in 1893, Old Hemp's appearance is typical of what you would see at a working trial today. It is remarkable that this Renaissance breed has changed little in over a century. Old Hemp, bred by Adam Telfer, of Northumberland, England, stood approximately twenty-one inches tall and weighed about forty-five pounds. He was rough coated, black with some white, and had semi-erect ears. He began in sheepdog trials at age one and was undefeated in his lifetime. This record has never been matched.

Other influential early sires were Isaac Herdman's Tommy #16 (International Sheepdog Society number), Thomas Armstrong's Sweep (both grandsons of Old Hemp), and J. M. Wilson's Craig. The best known was Wilson's Wartime Cap #3036 because of his influence in the pedigree of John Richardson's Wiston Cap, where he appears more than sixteen times. Wiston Cap is perhaps the dog with the greatest influence on the breed in recent history. Cap was the 1965 International Champion. He was a big, handsome, tri-colored, rough-coated dog who produced some excellent progeny. He died in 1979 at 15½ years.

The ability to succeed as a herding dog was what made these early dogs successful stud dogs. All had won important herding championships, were good-natured and biddable, and exhibited a certain style of working, usually well off the stock with wide outruns. Many excellent specimens were exported to the United States, beginning in the 1880s.

The International Sheepdog Society (ISDS) was founded in Scotland in 1906 and played an important role in maintaining pedigrees and registration information. In 1918, ISDS secretary James Reid coined the name Border Collie. There is little doubt that this organization has had tremendous influence on the development of sheepherding and of the dogs used in this activity, whether it be for sport or farmwork. The ISDS, now headquartered in Bedford, England, is still very active in maintaining a registry and governing body for working Border Collies the world over.

Border Collies continue as an invaluable helper to stockmen and a standout in the herding trials of many different societies and registries. Their success in agility competition is prodigious.

Recognized as the premier sheepherding dog worldwide, and known for its obedience, trainability, and natural appearance, the Border Collie entered the AKC Miscellaneous class in 1955. The breed was admitted to the Herding Group and became eligible for full AKC recognition on October 1, 1995.

# OFFICIAL STANDARD FOR THE BORDER COLLIE

**Preamble**—The Border Collie originated in the border country between Scotland and England where the shepherds' breeding selection was based on biddable stock sense and the ability to work long days on rugged terrain. As a result of this selective breeding, the Border Collie developed the unique working style of gathering and fetching the stock with wide sweeping outruns. The stock is then controlled with an intense gaze known as "eye," coupled with a stalking style of movement. This selective breeding over hundreds of years developed the Border Collie's intensity, energy and trainability which are features so important that they are equal to physical size and appearance. The Border Collie has extraordinary instinct and an uncanny ability to reason. One of its greatest assets is the ability to work out of sight of its master without commands. Breeding based on this working ability has made this breed the world's premier sheep herding dog, a job the Border Collie is still used for worldwide.

**General Appearance**—The Border Collie is a well balanced, medium-sized dog of athletic appearance, displaying style and agility in equal measure with soundness and strength. Its hard, muscular body conveys the impression of effortless movement and endless endurance. The Border Collie is extremely intelligent, with its keen, alert expression being a very important characteristic of the breed. Any aspect of structure or temperament that would impede the dog's ability to function as a herding dog should be severely faulted. The Border Collie is, and should remain, a natural and unspoiled true working sheep dog whose conformation is described herein. Honorable scars and broken teeth incurred in the line of duty are acceptable.

**Size, Proportion, Substance**—The height at the withers varies from 19 to 22 inches for males, 18 to 21 inches for females. The body, from prosternum to point of buttocks, is slightly longer than the height at the withers with the length to height ratio being approximately 10:9. Bone must be strong, medium being correct but lighter bone is preferred over heavy. Overall balance between height, length, weight and bone is crucial and is more important than any absolute measurement. Dogs must be presented in hard working condition. Excess body weight is not to be mistaken for muscle or substance. Any single feature of size appearing out of proportion should be considered a fault.

**Head**—Expression is intelligent, alert, eager, and full of interest. *Eyes* are set well apart, of moderate size, oval in shape. The color encompasses the full range of brown eyes, dogs having body colors other than black may have noticeably lighter eye color. Blue eyes (with one, both or part of one or both eyes being blue) in dogs other than merle, are acceptable but not preferred. Eye rims should be fully pigmented, lack thereof considered a fault according to degree. *Ears* are of medium size, set well apart, one or both carried erect and/or semi-erect (varying from ¼ to ¾ of the ear erect). When semi-erect, the tips may fall forward or outward to the side. Ears are sensitive and mobile. *Skull* is relatively flat and moderate in width. The skull and muzzle are approximately equal in length. In profile the top of the skull is parallel with the top of the muzzle. *Stop* moderate, but distinct. The *muzzle* is strong, tapering slightly to the nose. The underjaw is strong and well developed. A domed, blocky or very narrow skull is faulty according to degree, as is cheekiness and a snipy muzzle. *Nose* color matches the primary body color. Nostrils are well developed. Lack of nose pigmentation is a fault according to degree. *Bite*—Teeth and jaws are strong, meeting in a scissors bite. Complete dentition is required. Missing molars or pre-molars are serious faults as is an undershot or overshot bite.

**Neck, Topline, Body**—*Neck* is of proportional length to the body, strong and muscular, slightly arched and blending smoothly into the shoulders. *Topline*—Back is level from behind the withers to the slightly arched, muscular loins, falling to a gently sloping croup. *Body* is athletic in appearance with a deep, moderately broad chest reaching no further than the point of the elbow. The rib cage is moderately long with well sprung ribs. Loins moderately deep and short, muscular, slightly arched and with a slight but distinct tuck up. The tail is set on low and is moderately long with the bone reaching at least to the hock. The ideal tail carriage is low when the dog is concentrating on a given task and may have a slight upward swirl at the end like a shepherd's crook. In excitement, it may be raised proudly and waved like a banner, showing a confident personality. A tail curled over the back is a fault.

**Forequarters**—Forelegs should be parallel when viewed from front, pasterns slightly sloping when viewed from side. Because sufficient length of leg is crucial for the type of work the breed is required to do, the distance from the wither to the elbow is slightly less than from the elbow to the ground and legs that are too short in proportion to the rest of the body are a serious fault. The shoulder blades are long, well laid back and well-angulated to the upper arm. Shoulder blades and upper arms are equal in length. There is sufficient width between the tops of the shoulder blades to allow for the characteristic crouch when approaching and moving stock. The elbows are neither in nor out. Feet are compact, oval in shape; pads deep and strong, toes moderately arched and close together with strong nails of moderate length. Dewclaws may be removed.

**Hindquarters**—Broad and muscular, in profile sloping gracefully to the low set tail. The thighs are long, broad, deep and muscular. Stifles are well turned with strong hocks that may be either parallel or very slightly turned in. Dewclaws should be removed. Feet, although slightly smaller, are the same as front.

**Coat**—Two varieties are permissible, both having close-fitting, dense, weather resistant double coats with the top coat either straight or wavy and coarser in texture than the undercoat which is soft, short and dense. The rough variety is medium in length without being excessive. Forelegs, haunches, chest and underside are feathered and the coat on face, ears, feet, fronts of legs is short and smooth. The smooth variety is short over entire body, is usually coarser in texture than the rough variety and may have slight feathering on forelegs, haunches, chest and ruff. Neither coat type is preferred over the other. Seasonal shedding is normal and should not be penalized. The Border Collie's purpose as an actively working herding dog shall be clearly evident in its presentation. Excess hair on the feet, hock and pastern areas may be neatened for the show ring. Whiskers are untrimmed. Dogs that are overly groomed (trimmed and/or sculpted) should be penalized according to the extent.

**Color**—The Border Collie appears in all colors or combination of colors and/or markings. Solid color, bi-color, tri-color, merle and sable dogs are to be judged equally with no one color or pattern preferred over another. White markings may be clear white or ticked to any degree. Random white patches on the body and head are permissible but should not predominate. Color and markings are always secondary to physical evaluation and gait.

**Gait**—The Border Collie is an agile dog, able to suddenly change speed and direction while maintaining balance and grace. Endurance is its trademark. The Border Collie's most used working gaits are the gallop and a moving crouch (stealth) which convert to a balanced and free trot, with minimum lift of the feet. The head is carried level with or slightly below the withers. When shown, Border Collies should move on a loose lead and at moderate speed, never raced around the ring with the head held high. When viewed from the side the trot is not long striding, yet covers the ground with minimum effort, exhibiting facility of movement rather than a hard-driving action. Exaggerated reach and drive at the trot are not useful to the Border Collie. The topline is firm. Viewed from the front, action is forward and true without wasted motion. Viewed from the rear, hindquarters drive with thrust and flexibility with hocks turning neither in nor out, moving close together but never touching. The legs, both front and rear, tend to converge toward the center line as speed increases. Any deficiency that detracts from efficient movement is a fault.

**Temperament**—The Border Collie is energetic, intelligent, keen, alert, and responsive. An intense worker of great tractability, it is affectionate towards friends but may be sensibly reserved towards strangers. When approached, the Border Collie should stand its ground. It should be alert and interested, never showing fear, dullness or resentment. Any tendencies toward viciousness, nervousness or shyness are very serious faults.

**Faults**—Any deviation from the foregoing should be considered a fault, the seriousness of the fault depending upon the extent of the deviation.

**Approved January 13, 2004**
**Effective March 2, 2004**

# Bouvier des Flandres

D R. ADOLPHE REUL, OF THE VETERINARY SCHOOL OF BRUSSELS, WAS THE first to call attention to the Bouvier's many good qualities. This large dog with a heavy, cylindrical body; rough, gray, dark hair; and a rough appearance was found in southwest Flanders and on the French northern plain. It was a dog owned by people with cattle, for the dog's chief aptitude seemed to be cattle driving. Most of the early Bouvier breeders were farmers, butchers, or cattle merchants whose interest was not breeding pedigreed dogs but rather in having help with their work. The earliest Bouviers were not absolutely uniform in size, weight, or color and were often known by different names, such as *vuilbaard* ("dirty beard"), *koehond* ("cow dog"), *toucheur de boeuf or pic* ("cattle driver"). Nevertheless, they all had enough characteristics in common to be recognized as Bouviers des Flandres.

The Société Royale Saint-Hubert became aware of the breed in 1910, when two Bouviers belonging to M. Paret of Ghent—Nelly and Rex—appeared on the show benches at the international dog show in Brussels. It was not until 1912 that a standard for Bouvier type was adopted. That was accomplished by a Frenchman, M. Fontaine, vice president of the Club Saint-Hubert du Nord. In August of that year, a society of Bouvier breeders, founded in Roules (West) Flanders, invited famous Belgian experts to a meeting. They drew up a "Standard of Perfection," the first official standard to be recognized by the Société Royale Saint-Hubert, and the breed entered the society's studbook.

After the outbreak of World War I, areas where the Bouvier was rapidly becoming popular were entirely destroyed and, as the population fled, most Bouviers were lost. A few people succeeded, however, in keeping their dogs throughout the war. The dog whose progeny did much afterward to revive the Bouvier in Belgium lived with the Belgian army as the property of veterinarian Captain Barbry. This dog, Ch. Nic de Sottegem, was shown in Antwerp at the Olympic show in 1920. Show judge Charles Huge reported: "Nic is the ideal type of Bouvier. He has a short body, with well-developed ribs, short flanks, strong legs, and good feet, long and oblique shoulders. His head is of a good shape, with somber eyes and an ideal courageous expression. His hair is dry and dark. I hope that this dog will have numerous progeny."

Nic died in 1926. He had many descendants whose names appear in almost every pedigree. These dogs were subsequently gathered together at Ghent. After examining and measuring each one carefully, a group of experts, including Charles Huge, V. Tenret, V. Taeymans, Count de Hemptinne, Captain Binon, and A. Gevaert, established a comprehensive standard based on these descendants.

There is little doubt that a few dogs were brought to the Americas during this formative period early in the twentieth century. But it was not until 1929 that the Bouvier des Flandres was first recognized by the American Kennel Club, and not until 1931 that the breed was admitted to the AKC Stud Book. Just a few American fanciers imported these dogs from Europe before World War II. After the war, the Bouvier in Europe was near extinction. A small number of Western European expatriates brought with them a few Bouviers as well as a great understanding of the breed. Interest in this remarkable breed was revived.

The 1950s and 1960s proved to be pivotal for the Bouvier in America. New fanciers established kennel names and reputations that survive to this day. After at least one unsuccessful attempt to form an active Bouvier club, the American Bouvier des Flandres Club was established in 1963 and continues as the breed's AKC parent club. The club is not only active in conformation and various other dog events but also takes a proactive stance on several aspects of Bouvier health and welfare.

The Bouvier is an incredibly versatile breed, one that displays strength of body and character. It is a dog neither to be taken lightly nor relegated to a life lacking interaction with its human family. This is a breed that needs a job or an active responsibility.

If the Bouvier has an ancestral vocation, it is either as a working farm dog that herds, or that manages and protects, livestock and other farm inhabitants. But this is a dog with the structure and temperament to be successful in a number of other activities. In fact, with American urbanization, most Bouviers "work" in obedience, agility, tracking, herding, search and rescue, police service, carting, therapy, personal assistance, and protection. Training in these activities offers the opportunity for owner-and-dog teams to participate in competitions based on real-life tasks.

The Bouvier des Flandres is a strong-willed dog. While definitely not for the faint of heart, the Bouvier will become a trusted friend for one who leads fairly. Those who willingly include a Bouvier in the family will be rewarded many times over from the heart of this great companion.

# OFFICIAL STANDARD FOR BOUVIER DES FLANDRES

**General Appearance**—The Bouvier des Flandres is a powerfully built, compact, short-coupled, rough-coated dog of notably rugged appearance. He gives the impression of great strength without any sign of heaviness or clumsiness in his overall makeup. He is agile, spirited and bold, yet his serene, well behaved disposition denotes his steady, resolute and fearless character. His gaze is alert and brilliant, depicting his intelligence, vigor and daring. By nature he is an equable dog. His origin is that of a cattle herder and general farmer's helper, including cart pulling. He is an ideal farm dog. His harsh double coat protects him in all weather, enabling him to perform the most arduous tasks. He has been used as an ambulance and messenger dog. Modern times find him as a watch and guard dog as well as a family friend, guardian and protector. His physical and mental characteristics and deportment, coupled with his olfactory abilities, his intelligence and initiative enable him to also perform as a tracking dog and a guide dog for the blind. The following description is that of the ideal Bouvier des Flandres. Any deviation from this is to be penalized to the extent of the deviation.

**Size, Proportion, Substance**—*Size*—The height as measured at the withers: Dogs, from 24½ to 27½ inches; bitches, from 23½ to 26½ inches. In each sex, the ideal height is the median of the two limits, i.e., 26 inches for a dog and 25 inches for a bitch. Any dog or bitch deviating from the minimum or maximum limits mentioned shall be severely penalized. *Proportion*—The *length* from the point of the shoulder to the tip of the buttocks is equal to the height from the ground to the highest point of the withers. A long-bodied dog should be seriously faulted. *Substance*—Powerfully built, strong boned, well muscled, without any sign of heaviness or clumsiness.

**Head**—The head is impressive in scale, accentuated by beard and mustache. It is in proportion to body and build. The *expression* is bold and alert. *Eyes* neither protrude nor are sunken in the sockets. Their shape is oval with the axis on the horizontal plane, when viewed from the front. Their color is a dark brown. The eye rims are black without lack of pigment and the haw is barely visible. Yellow or light eyes are to be strongly penalized, along with a walleyed or staring expression. *Ears* placed high and alert. If cropped, they are to be a triangular contour and in proportion to the size of the head. The inner corner of the ear should be in line with the outer corner of the eye. Ears that are too low or too closely set are serious faults. *Skull* well developed and flat, slightly less wide than long. When viewed from the side, the top lines of the skull and the muzzle are parallel. It is wide between the ears, with the frontal groove barely marked. The *stop* is more apparent than real, due to upstanding eyebrows. The proportions of length of skull to length of muzzle are 3 to 2. *Muzzle* broad, strong, well filled out, tapering gradually toward the nose without ever becoming snipy or pointed. A narrow, snipy muzzle is faulty. *Nose* large, black, well developed, round at the edges, with flared nostrils. A brown, pink or spotted nose is a serious fault. The cheeks are flat and lean, with the lips being dry and tight fitting. The jaws are powerful and of equal length. The teeth are strong, white and healthy, with the incisors meeting in a scissors bite. Overshot or undershot bites are to be severely penalized.

**Neck, Topline, and Body**—The *neck* is strong and muscular, widening gradually into the shoulders. When viewed from the side, it is gracefully arched with proud carriage. A short, squatty neck is faulty. No dewlap. *Back* short, broad, well muscled with firm level topline. It is supple and flexible with no sign of weakness. *Body* or *trunk* powerful, broad and short. The chest is broad, with the brisket extending to the elbow in depth. The ribs are deep and well sprung. The first ribs are slightly curved, the others well sprung and very well sloped nearing the rear, giving proper depth to the chest. Flat ribs or slabsidedness is to be strongly penalized. *Flanks* and *loins* short, wide and well muscled, without weakness. The abdomen is only slightly tucked up. The horizontal line of the back should mold unnoticeably into the curve of the rump, which is characteristically wide. A sunken or slanted croup is a serious fault. *Tail* is to be docked, leaving 2 or 3 vertebrae. It must be set high and align normally with the spinal column. Preferably carried upright in motion. Dogs born tailless should not be penalized.

**Forequarters**—Strong boned, well muscled and straight. The *shoulders* are relatively long, muscular but not loaded, with good layback. The shoulder blade and humerus are approximately the same length, forming an angle slightly greater than 90 degrees when standing. Steep shoulders are faulty. *Elbows* close to the body and parallel. Elbows which are too far out or in are faults. *Forearms* viewed either in profile or from the front are perfectly straight, parallel to each other and perpendicular to the ground. They are well muscled and strong boned. *Carpus* exactly in line with the forearms. Strong boned. *Pasterns* quite short, slightly sloped. *Dewclaws* may be removed. Both forefeet and hind feet are rounded and compact turning neither in nor out; the toes close and well arched; strong black nails; thick tough pads.

**Hindquarters**—Firm, well muscled with large, powerful hams. They should be parallel with the front legs when viewed from either front or rear. *Legs* moderately long, well muscled, neither too straight nor too inclined. *Thighs* wide and muscular. The upper thigh must be neither too straight nor too sloping. There is moderate angulation at the stifle. *Hocks* strong, rather close to the ground. When standing and seen from the rear, they will be straight and perfectly parallel to each other. In motion, they must turn neither in nor out. There is a slight angulation at the hock joint. Sickle or cow-hocks are serious faults. *Metatarsi* hardy and lean, rather cylindrical and perpendicular to the ground when standing. If born with dewclaws, they are to be removed. *Feet* as in front.

**Coat**—A tousled, double coat capable of withstanding the hardest work in the most inclement weather. The outer hairs are rough and harsh, with the undercoat being fine, soft and dense. The coat may be trimmed slightly only to accent the body line. Overtrimming which alters the natural rugged appearance is to be avoided. *Topcoat* must be harsh to the touch, dry, trimmed, if necessary, to a length of approximately 2½ inches. A coat too long or too short is a fault, as is a silky or woolly coat. It is tousled without being curly. On the skull, it is short, and on the upper part of the back, it is particularly close and harsh always, however, remaining rough. *Ears* are rough-coated.

*Undercoat* a dense mass of fine, close hair, thicker in winter. Together with the topcoat, it will form a water-resistant covering. A flat coat, denoting lack of undercoat is a serious fault. *Mustache* and *beard* very thick, with the hair being shorter and rougher on the upper side of the muzzle. The upper lip with its heavy mustache and the chin with its heavy and rough beard gives that gruff expression so characteristic of the breed. *Eyebrows,* erect hairs accentuating the shape of the eyes without ever veiling them.

**Color**—From fawn to black, passing through salt and pepper, gray and brindle. A small white star on the chest is allowed. Other than chocolate brown, white, or particolor, which are to be severely penalized, no one color is to be favored.

**Gait**—The whole of the Bouvier des Flandres must be harmoniously proportioned to allow for a free, bold and proud gait. The reach of the forequarters must compensate for and be in balance with the driving power of the hindquarters. The back, while moving in a trot, will remain firm and flat. In general, the gait is the logical demonstration of the structure and build of the dog. It is to be noted that while moving at a fast trot, the properly built Bouvier will tend to single-track.

**Temperament**—The Bouvier is an equable dog, steady, resolute and fearless. Viciousness or shyness is undesirable.

**Approved January 10, 2000**
**Effective February 23, 2000**

# BRIARD

𝒯HE BRIARD IS AN OLD BREED OF FRENCH WORKING DOG. DEPICTED IN tapestries as early as the eighth century, the breed was accurately described in writing by the fourteenth century. Briards initially defended their charges against wolves and poachers, but the land division and population increase following the French Revolution gradually transformed their work into the more peaceful tasks of keeping sheep within unfenced pastures and guarding their masters' flocks and property.

An article in 1809 referred to the breed as Chien Berger de Brie (Shepherd Dog of Brie), but Briards did not necessarily originate in the Brie province. Many authorities claim that Chien de Brie is a distortion of Chien d'Aubry, from the fourteenth-century legend in which the principal role was played by Aubry de Montdidier's dog, believed to be a Briard.

They were first entered in dog shows at the end of the nineteenth century. The first known Briard standard was written in 1897 by a club of shepherd dog breeders. In 1909, Les Amis du Briard (Friends of the Briard) was founded. This club, disbanded during World War I and re-formed in 1923, established a more precise Briard standard in 1925. The Briard Club of America, recognized as the AKC parent club in 1928, adopted this standard with some modification. Except for slight elaboration in 1975, the standard has remained essentially unchanged.

The American history of the Briard is not well documented. Some credit the

Marquis de Lafayette with introducing the breed to America in the late eighteenth century, but the writings of Thomas Jefferson indicate that he also imported Briards at about the same time.

The characteristics of the Briard have helped the breed withstand the test of time. The French shepherd, practical and frugal, kept only dogs with superior abilities. Briard breeders today strive to preserve traditional abilities along with the traits of intelligence, loyalty, and obedience for which the breed has been valued. Briards still display the herding ability for which they were prized. Even today's companion Briards will display the instinct to herd whatever is at hand, giving head nudges to their owners to direct them, alerting them to anything unusual, and enthusiastically carrying out any task owners have given them. Briards are not generally inclined to wander from their property and may decide that children must also remain within these boundaries.

The Briard's distinctive appearance includes eyebrows and beard, which give the breed its typical expression. At the end of the tail is a small crook, called a crochet. The correct coat is slightly wavy, of moderate length, with texture such that mud and dirt do not cling to it. Two dewclaws on each rear foot are another distinctive characteristic, a trait shared by most French sheepdog breeds.

Briards learn readily, and training should begin early. Trainers familiar with the breed believe that consistency, verbal reinforcement, and lavish praise work better than harsh methods. Briards do their utmost to please, once they know what is expected. They have an excellent memory, and once a lesson is learned it is seldom forgotten.

Although Briards have been used primarily as guarding and herding dogs, they are versatile. They have served as tracking, disaster, and avalanche dogs, and during World War I were the official French army dog. In this capacity, they were sentries, work for which their acute hearing proved invaluable. They accompanied patrols and carried food, supplies, and munitions to the front. Medical corps reports describe the Briard's ability to find wounded soldiers on the battlefield, saying that the dogs would even instinctively bypass those beyond hope. They were also used for pulling carts, but this type of work does not suit the Briard. Their eagerness to please causes them to overwork, not seeming to sense their physical limitations. As a result, war service severely reduced their numbers and threatened the breed's existence. Credit belongs to devoted breeders who saved the breed from extinction, carefully preserving the Briard's many cherished qualities.

The Briard is not for every home. Only those willing to devote time and affection to the dog can develop the breed's true character. The coat requires regular grooming or matting will occur. Briards are likely to view themselves more as companions than servants and can be somewhat independent. By nature they are reserved with strangers and can be overprotective. Therefore, owners must take the time to introduce young Briard puppies to various situations and people if they are to become calm, self-assured adults. This is a breed that must have human companionship to reach full potential. They are happiest at the side (or on the feet) of the people they love.

Briards have been described as a heart wrapped in fur, companions who understand every mood and will spend a lifetime trying to please. For those who have time and love to give, a Briard is a loyal and unselfish friend who returns every kindness many times over.

# OFFICIAL STANDARD FOR THE BRIARD

**General Appearance**—A dog of handsome form. Vigorous and alert, powerful without coarseness, strong in bone and muscle, exhibiting the strength and agility required of the herding dog. Dogs lacking these qualities, however concealed by the coat, are to be penalized.

**Size, Proportions**—*Size*—Males 23 to 27 inches at the withers; bitches 22 to 25½ inches at the withers. *Disqualification*—All dogs or bitches under the minimum. *Proportions*—The Briard is not cobby in build. In males the length of the body, measured from the point of the shoulder to the point of the buttock, is equal to or slightly more than his height at the withers. The female may be a little longer.

**Head**—The head of a Briard always gives the impression of length, having sufficient width without being cumbersome. The correct length of a good head, measured from the occiput to the tip of the nose, is about 40 percent (40%) of the height of the dog at the withers. There is no objection to a slightly longer head, especially if the animal tends to a longer body line. Viewed from above, from the front or in profile, the fully-coated silhouette gives the impression of two rectangular forms, equal in length but differing in height and width, blending together rather abruptly. The larger rectangle is the skull and the other forms the muzzle. The head joins the neck in a right angle and is held proudly alert. The head is sculptured in clean lines, without jowls or excess flesh on the sides, or under the eyes or temples. *Expression*—The gaze is frank, questioning and confident. *Eyes*—The eyes set well apart with the inner corners and outer corners on the same level. Large, well opened and calm, they must never be narrow or slanted. The color must be black or black-brown with very dark pigmentation of the rim of the eyelids, whatever the color of the coat. *Disqualification*—yellow eyes or spotted eyes. *Ears*—The ears should be attached high, have thick leather and be firm at the base. Low-set ears cause the head to appear to be too arched. The length of the natural ear should be equal to or slightly less than one-half the length of the head, always straight and covered with long hair. The natural ear must not lie flat against the head and, when alert, the ears are lifted slightly, giving a square look to the top of the skull. The ears when cropped should be carried upright and parallel, emphasizing the parallel lines of the head; when alert, they should face forward, well open with long hair falling over the opening. The cropped ear should be long, broad at the base, tapering gradually to a rounded tip. *Skull*—The width of the head, as measured across the skull, is slightly less than the length of the skull from the occiput to the stop. Although not clearly visible on the fully-coated head, the occiput is prominent and the forehead is very slightly rounded. *Muzzle*—The muzzle with mustache and beard is somewhat wide and terminates in a right angle. The muzzle must not be narrow or pointed. *Planes*—The topline of the muzzle is parallel to the topline of the skull, and the junction of the two forms a well-marked stop, which is midway between the occiput and the tip of the nose, and on a level with the eyes. *Nose*—Square rather than round, always black with nostrils well opened. *Disqualification*—any color other than black. *Lips*—The lips are of medium thickness, firm of line and fitted neatly, without folds or flews at the corners. The lips are black. *Bite, Teeth*—Strong, white and adapting perfectly in a scissors bite.

**Neck, Topline and Body**—*Neck*—Strong and well constructed. The neck is in the shape of a truncated cone, clearing the shoulders well. It is strongly muscled and has good length. *Topline*—The Briard is constructed with a very slight incline, downward from the prominent withers to the back which is straight, to the broad loin and the croup which is slightly inclined. The croup is well muscled and slightly sloped to give a well-rounded finish. The topline is strong, never swayed nor roached. *Body*—The chest is broad and deep with moderately curved ribs, egg-shaped in form, the ribs not too rounded. The breastbone is moderately advanced in front, descending smoothly to the level of the elbows and shaped to give good depth to the chest. The abdomen is moderately drawn up but still presents good volume. *Tail*—Uncut, well feathered, forming a crook at the extremity, carried low and not deviating to the right or to the left. In repose, the bone of the tail descends to the point of the hock, terminating in the crook, similar in shape to the printed "J" when viewed from the dog's right side. In action, the tail is raised in a harmonious curve, never going above the level of the back, except for the terminal crook. *Disqualification*—tail non-existent or cut.

**Forequarters**—Shoulder blades are long and sloping forming a 45-degree angle with the horizontal, firmly attached by strong muscles and blending smoothly with the withers. *Legs*—The legs are powerfully muscled with strong bone. The forelegs are vertical when viewed from the side except the pasterns are very slightly inclined. Viewed from the front or rear, the legs are straight and parallel to the median line of the body, never turned inward or outward. The distance between the front legs is equal to the distance between the rear legs. The construction of the legs is of utmost importance, determining the dog's ability to work and his resistance to fatigue. *Dewclaws*—Dewclaws on the forelegs may or may not be removed. *Feet*—Strong and rounded, being slightly oval in shape. The feet travel straight forward in the line of movement. The toes are strong, well arched and compact. The pads are well developed, compact and elastic, covered with strong tissue. The nails are always black and hard.

**Hindquarters**—The hindquarters are powerful, providing flexible, almost tireless movement. The pelvis slopes at a 30-degree angle from the horizontal and forms a right angle with the upper leg bone. *Legs*—Viewed from the side, the legs are well angulated with the metatarsus slightly inclined, the hock making an angle of 135 degrees. *Dewclaws*—Two dewclaws are required on each rear leg, placed low on the leg, giving a wide base to the foot. Occasionally the nail may break off completely. The dog shall not be penalized for the missing nail so long as the digit itself is present. Ideally the dewclaws form additional functioning toes. *Disqualification*—anything less than two dewclaws on each rear leg. *Feet*—If the rear toes turn out very slightly when the hocks and metatarsus are parallel, then the position of the feet is correct.

**Coat**—The outer coat is coarse, hard and dry (making a dry rasping sound between the fingers). It lies down flat, falling naturally in long, slightly waving locks, having the sheen of good health. On the shoulders the length of the hair is generally six inches or more. The undercoat is fine and tight on all the body. The head is well covered with hair which lies down, forming a natural part in the center. The eyebrows do not lie flat, but instead, arch up and out in a curve that lightly veils the eyes. The hair is never so abundant that it masks the form of the head or completely covers the eyes.

**Color**—All uniform colors are permitted except white. The colors are black, various shades of gray and various shades of tawny. The deeper shades of each color are preferred. Combinations of two of these colors are permitted, provided there are no marked spots and the transition from one color to another takes place gradually and symmetrically. The only permissible white: white hairs scattered throughout the coat and/or a white spot on the chest not to exceed one inch in diameter at the root of the hair. *Disqualification*—white coat, spotted coat, white spot on chest exceeding one inch in diameter.

**Gait**—The well-constructed Briard is a marvel of supple power. His movement has been described as "quicksilver," permitting him to make abrupt turns, springing starts and sudden stops required of the sheepherding dog. His gait is supple and light, almost like that of a large feline. The gait gives the impression that the dog glides along without touching the ground. Strong, flexible movement is essential to the sheepdog. He is above all a trotter, single-tracking, occasionally galloping and he frequently needs to change his speed to accomplish his work. His conformation is harmoniously balanced and strong to sustain him in the long day's work. Dogs with clumsy or inelegant gait must be penalized.

**Temperament**—He is a dog at heart, with spirit and initiative, wise and fearless with no trace of timidity. Intelligent, easily trained, faithful, gentle and obedient, the Briard possesses an excellent memory and an ardent desire to please his master. He retains a high degree of his ancestral instinct to guard home and master. Although he is reserved with strangers, he is loving and loyal to those he knows. Some will display a certain independence.

## DISQUALIFICATIONS

*All dogs or bitches under the minimum size limits.*
*Yellow eyes or spotted eyes.*
*Nose any color other than black.*
*Tail non-existent or cut.*
*Less than two dewclaws on each rear leg.*
*White coat.*
*Spotted coat.*
*White spot on chest exceeding one inch in diameter.*

**Approved February 8, 1975**
**Reformatted January 12, 1992**

# CANAAN DOG

*T*HE CANAAN DOG, THE NATIONAL BREED OF ISRAEL, DATES TO BIBLICAL times. Drawings found on the tombs at Beni-Hassan, from 2200 to 2000 B.C., depict dogs that show an unmistakable resemblance to the Canaan Dog of today. The Canaan Dog was the sentry and herd dog of the ancient Israelites, and in recent times they could be found performing the same functions with nomadic Bedouins, in various Israeli communities, and among the Druze religious sect on Mount Carmel. They were plentiful in the region until the Romans drove the Israelites out of the Holy Land more than 1,900 years ago. Dogs sought refuge in the Negev Desert, a natural reservoir of Israeli wildlife, where they survived and, for the most part, remained undomesticated for centuries.

In 1934, Dr. Rudolphina Menzel, a noted Austrian cynologist, immigrated to what was then Palestine and was asked by the Haganah (a Jewish defense organization) to develop a sentry dog for the isolated Jewish settlements and supervise the buildup of war dogs for Israel's War of Independence. Remembering the semiwild dogs living in the desert, she knew only the fittest would have survived such hardships and began to acquire puppies and adult dogs for redomestication in her breeding program. Naming the breed after the land in which it originated, she found the Canaan Dog proved to be highly intelligent and easily trainable. These dogs soon began to serve as sentry dogs, messengers, Red Cross service dogs, and land-mine locators. During World War II, Dr. Menzel recruited and trained more than 400 of the best dogs as mine detectors for the Middle East forces; these dogs proved superior to mechanical detectors, saving many lives in the process.

After the war, Dr. Menzel dedicated her time to helping the blind. In 1949, she founded the Institute for Orientation and Mobility of the Blind, the only one of its kind in the Middle East. The entire Canaan Dog breeding program was soon concentrated within the institute and established under the kennel name of B'nei Habitatchon. The breed was first recognized by the Palestine Kennel Club, the forerunner of the Israel Kennel Club, and by 1948 approximately 150 Canaan Dogs were registered in their studbook.

On September 7, 1965, Ursula Berkowitz, of Oxnard, California, imported the first four Canaan Dogs with the idea of establishing the breed in the United States. Several more Canaan Dogs were soon imported and the breed slowly began to promulgate its existence in the United States. The Canaan Dog Club of America was formed in 1965 and kept the studbook records until the breed's full recognition into the AKC Herding Group.

The Canaan Dog, while easily trainable and adaptable to situations, still retains some of its natural, reactive qualities. They are territorial and highly suspicious of strangers. They are not a true guard dog, but rather one that will give an alarm if anything is wrong within their territory. Some Canaan Dogs do not regard fences as a barrier or perimeter to their territory. A "thinking breed," the Canaan Dog must be thoroughly socialized and obedience training is highly recommended, though the breed will balk at repetitive training. Loyal to their family, the Canaan Dog regards the human-dog relationship as a partnership. Physically, the Canaan Dog will retain its puppy qualities for a very brief time as its survival in the desert depended upon its fast adult growth; however, its mental and emotional maturity will require another three to four years, testing an owner's patience and loyalty to the breed.

A versatile and agile breed, the Canaan Dog can be found in many companion events, such as agility, tracking, obedience, and rally. Many Canaan Dogs have distinguished themselves in several AKC performance trial–level venues, such as herding. While not specifically bred to herd, the Canaan Dog does exhibit herding instinct and has a 70 to 80 percent pass rate in the Canaan Dog Club of America's annual herding-instinct tests under AKC judges.

The Canaan Dog entered the Miscellaneous class in June 1989, was registered in the AKC Stud Book as of June 1, 1997, and was eligible, in August of that year, to compete in conformation.

# OFFICIAL STANDARD FOR THE CANAAN DOG

**General Appearance**—The Canaan Dog is a herding and flock guardian dog native to the Middle East. He is aloof with strangers, inquisitive, loyal and loving with his family. His medium-size, square body is without extremes, showing a clear, sharp outline. The Canaan Dog moves with athletic agility and grace in a quick, brisk, ground-covering trot. He has a wedge-shaped head with low-set erect ears, a bushy tail that curls over the back when excited, and a straight, harsh, flat-lying double coat.

**Size, Proportion, Substance**—*Size*—Height at the withers is 20 to 24 inches for dogs and 19 to 23 inches for bitches. The ideal Canaan Dog lies in the middle of the stated ranges. *Disqualifications*—*Dogs less than 20 inches or more than 25 inches. Bitches less than 18 inches or more than 23 inches.* Proportion—Square when measured from the point of the withers to the base of the tail and from the point of the withers to the ground. *Substance*—Moderate. Dogs generally weigh 45 to 55 pounds and bitches approximately 35 to 45 pounds. Dogs distinctly masculine without coarseness and bitches feminine without over-refinement.

**Head**—Elongated, the length exceeding the breadth and depth considerably. Wedge-shaped, when viewed from above. Slightly arched when viewed from the side, tapering to stop. The region of the forehead is of medium width, but appearing broader through ears set low to complete an alert expression, with a slight furrow between the eyes. *Expression*—Alert, watchful and inquisitive. Dignified. *Eyes*—Dark, almond-shaped, slightly slanted. Varying shades of hazel with liver-pointed dogs. Eye rims darkly pigmented or of varying shades of liver harmonizing with coat color. *Fault*—Unpigmented eye rims. *Ears*—Erect, medium to large, set moderately low, broad at the base, tapering to a very slightly rounded tip. Ears angled very slightly forward when excited. A straight line from the inner corner of the ear to the tip of the nose should just touch the inner corner of the eye and a line drawn from the tip of the ear to the tip of the nose should just touch the outer corner of the eye. Ear motion contributes to expression and clearly defines the mood of the dog. Major Fault—In the adult dog, other than erect ears. *Stop*—Slightly accentuated. *Muzzle*—Tapering to complete the wedge shape of the head. Length equal to or slightly longer than the length of the skull from the occiput to stop. Whisker trimming optional. *Nose*—Darkly pigmented or varying shades of liver, harmonizing with coat color. *Lips*—Tight with good pigmentation. *Bite*—Scissors.

**Neck, Topline, Body**—*Neck*—Well-arched. Balance to body and head and free from throatiness. *Topline*—Level with slight arch over the loins. *Body*—Strong, displaying athletic agility and trimness. *Chest*—Moderately broad and deep, extending to the elbows, with well-sprung ribs. *Loin*—Well tucked-up. Short, muscled flanks. *Tail*—Set moderately high. May be carried curled over the back when excited; limited to one full curl. When extended, the bone must reach to the hocks. Fault—Tail which falls over to either side of the back.

**Forequarters**—Shoulders moderately angulated. Legs straight. Pasterns flexible with very slight slope when viewed from the side. Dewclaws may be removed. *Feet*—Catlike, pads hard, pigmentation harmonizing with nose and eye rims. Nails strong, hard, pigmentation harmonizing with either nose and eye rims or coat.

**Hindquarters**—Moderately angulated. In balance with forequarters. Straight when viewed from the rear. Thigh musculature well-developed, moderately broad. Hocks well let-down. Dewclaws must be removed. Feet and nails as in forequarters.

**Coat**—Double coat. Outer coat—straight, harsh, flat-lying, with slight ruff. Ruff more pronounced on males. Length of outer coat ½ to 1½ inches; longer on ruff and back of thighs, shorter on body, legs and head. Undercoat—straight, soft, short, flat-lying, density varying with climate. Tail bushy, increasing in plumage from set to end of bones, then tapering to pointed tip. *Faults*—Excessively long guard coat that masks the clean outline of the dog. Any trimming that alters the natural appearance of the dog.

**Color**—There are two color patterns. Pattern 1) Predominantly white with mask and with or without additional patches of color (large body patches are desirable). Pattern 2) Solid colored with or without white trim. Color may range from black through all shades of brown—sandy to red or liver. Shadings of black on a solid brown or tan dog are frequently seen. The trim on a solid colored dog may include chest, undercarriage, feet and lower part of leg and tip of tail. In all color patterns self-ticking may be present. *Disqualifications—a) Gray and/or brindle. b) All white.*

**Mask**—The mask is a desired and distinguishing feature of the predominantly white Canaan Dog. The mask is the same color(s) as the body patches on the dog. The basically symmetrical mask must completely cover the eyes and ears or can completely cover the head as in a hood. The only allowed white in the mask or hood is a white blaze of any size or shape and/or white on the muzzle below the mask. Faults—On predominantly white dogs: absence of mask, half mask, or grossly asymmetrical mask.

**Gait**—Movement is very important. Good reach and drive. Quick, brisk natural trot, apparently tireless, indicating an animal capable of trotting for hours. Covers ground more quickly than expected. Agile, able to change directions almost instantaneously. Tends to single-track at high speed. Fault—Anything that detracts from efficient movement.

**Temperament**—Alert, vigilant, devoted and docile with his family. Reserved and aloof with strangers. Highly territorial, serving as a responsive companion and natural guardian. Very vocal, persistent. Easily trained. Faults—Shyness or dominance toward people.

## DISQUALIFICATIONS

*Dogs less than 20 inches or more than 25 inches. Bitches less than 18 inches or more than 23 inches. Gray and/or brindle. All white.*

**Approved June 10, 1996**
**Effective August 12, 1997**

# CARDIGAN WELSH CORGI

*T*HE CARDIGAN WELSH CORGI, THE CORGI WITH THE TAIL, IS THE OLDER of the two Corgi breeds, and one of the earliest breeds of the British Isles. (The data upon which this summarized history is written was collected over a period of twenty years by W. Lloyd-Thomas, of Mabws Hall, Llanrhystyd, Cardiganshire, South Wales.)

In the beginning, the Corgi came to the high country now known as Cardiganshire with the tall, tawny-headed Celts from central Europe. The migration of this warrior tribe to Wales is placed, roughly, at about 1200 B.C., which means that the Corgi has been known in the land of its origin for more than 3,000 years. The dog was a member of the same family that has produced the Dachshund.

The village of Bronant in Mid-Cardiganshire became the special stronghold of those early Celts. The vigilance and intelligence of the Corgi must have been a great asset to the Celts, and tales handed down from father to son for generations identify him always as a valued member of the family circle. His uses were many and varied, not the least of which were his guardianship of the children and his aid in beating out game, which in those times was of more than ordinary importance.

Still, the occupation which made the Corgi worth his weight in gold to those Welsh hill men came at a much later period, but still hundreds of years ago. This was when the crown owned practically all land, and the tenant farmers, or crofters, were permitted to fence off only a few acres surrounding their dooryards. The rest was open country, known as common land, on which the crofter was permitted to graze his cattle, one of the chief sources of his meager income. It can be imagined that there was great competition among the crofters to secure as much as possible of this pastureland for their own uses, and the task would have been difficult had it not been for the Corgi. The little dog which had been with this Celtic people so long, and which had come to be of almost human intelligence, was trained to perform a service the opposite of that done by the herding dog.

Instead of herding the cattle, the Corgi would nip at their heels and drive them as far afield as desired. Often the crofter called upon his dog to clear "his" ground of the neighbor's cattle. The dog worked the same way in either case. The crofter would stand by his gate and give a soft whistle of two notes, one high, one low. Many times the dog could not see the cattle he was to chase, but he would keep going as long as he could hear that whistle. His speed was remarkable, considering his short legs with their out-turned feet, but the length of his back gave him added spring. When the dog had scattered the cattle by biting their hocks—avoiding death only by ducking close to the ground when they kicked—the crofter would give the recall signal, a shrill, long-drawn-out whistle made by placing the fingers in the mouth. The dog would return at once.

The division of the crown lands, their subsequent sale to the crofters, and the appearance of fences, removed the usefulness of the Corgi. He was still retained as guard and companion by some of the hill men, but to most he was a luxury they could not afford. In many instances he was succeeded by the red herder and by the brindle herder. The original type of Corgi known in Bronant since time immemorial became very scarce, and it is due only to the greatest care on the part of modern breeders that the old strains have been preserved.

Needless to say, studbooks were unknown to the Celts and to the early Welsh farmer-descendants of the old warrior tribe. But if there were no records, there was a rigid policy of selective breeding unsurpassed in this present day. The original Corgis had to be proficient workers, and no mating was consummated without due consideration.

After the breaking up of the crown lands, and the introduction of the new breeds, there was a certain amount of experimentation with crosses. The ancient dog of Bronant was crossed with the red herder, but it did not prove very successful and was not attempted many times. The brindle herder, however, made a rather fortuitous cross. The progeny followed the dominant characteristics of the Corgi, and gained a little through the finer coat and the color of the brindle herder. Crossed later with the Collie, there was produced the breed known as the heeler.

The principal strains of the Cardigan Welsh Corgi of today go back to the old Bronant Corgi with a slight infusion of brindle herder blood. This dog approximates as nearly as possible the dog that enjoyed his greatest popularity in Cardiganshire a century and more ago.

The two Corgi breeds were regarded officially in England as one breed divided into two types until 1934, when they were recognized as separate breeds. Up until that time they had been interbred to some extent, and sorting out the two breeds became a difficult task. In 1934, two hundred and fifty Pembrokes were registered to only fifty-nine Cardigans. The Cardigan was considered to be less uniform in type at that time and the breed nearly disappeared in its native Wales.

The first pair of Cardigans imported to the United States (by Mrs. Robert Bole, of Boston) arrived in June 1931. The breed was admitted to AKC registration in 1935.

# OFFICIAL STANDARD FOR
# THE CARDIGAN WELSH CORGI

**General Appearance**—Low set with moderately heavy bone and deep chest. Overall silhouette long in proportion to height, culminating in a low tail set and foxlike brush. *General Impression*—A handsome, powerful, small dog, capable of both speed and endurance, intelligent, sturdily built but not coarse.

**Size, Proportion, Substance**—Overall balance is more important than absolute size. Dogs and bitches should be from 10.5 to 12.5 inches at the withers when standing naturally. The ideal length/height ratio is 1.8 to 1 when measuring from the point of the breast bone (prosternum) to the rear of the hip (ischial tuberosity) and measuring from the ground to the point of the withers. Ideally, dogs should be from 30 to 38 pounds; bitches from 25 to 34 pounds. Lack of overall balance, oversized or undersized are *serious faults.*

**Head**—The *head* should be refined in accordance with the sex and substance of the dog. It should never appear so large and heavy nor so small and fine as to be out of balance with the rest of the dog. *Expression* alert and gentle, watchful, yet friendly. *Eyes* medium to large, not bulging, with dark rims and distinct corners. Widely set. Clear and dark in harmony with coat color. Blue eyes (including partially blue eyes), or one dark and one blue eye permissible in blue merles, and in any other coat color than blue merle are a *disqualification. Ears* large and prominent in proportion to size of dog. Slightly rounded at the tip, and of good strong leather. Moderately wide at the base, carried erect and sloping slightly forward when alert. When erect, tips are slightly wide of a straight line drawn from the tip of the nose through the center of the eye. Small and/or pointed ears are *serious faults.* Drop ears are a *disqualification.*

*Skull*—Top moderately wide and flat between the ears, showing no prominence of occiput, tapering towards the eyes. Slight depression between the eyes. *Cheeks* flat with some chiseling where the cheek meets the foreface and under the eye. There should be no prominence of cheekbone. *Muzzle* from the tip of the nose to the base of the stop should be shorter than the length of the skull from the base of the stop to the high point of the occiput, the proportion being about three parts muzzle to five parts skull; rounded but not blunt; tapered but not pointed. In profile the plane of the muzzle should parallel that of the skull, but on a lower level due to a definite but moderate *stop.*

*Nose* black, except in blue merles where black noses are preferred but butterfly noses are tolerated. A nose other than solid black in any other color is a *disqualification*. *Lips* fit cleanly and evenly together all around. *Jaws* strong and clean. Underjaw moderately deep and well formed, reaching to the base of the nose and rounded at the chin. *Teeth* strong and regular. Scissors bite preferred; i.e., inner side of upper incisors fitting closely over outer side of lower incisors. Overshot, undershot, or wry bite are *serious faults*.

**Neck, Topline, Body**—*Neck* moderately long and muscular without throatiness. Well developed, especially in males, and in proportion to the dog's build. Neck well set on; fits into strong, well shaped shoulders. *Topline* level. *Body* long and strong. *Chest* moderately broad with prominent breastbone. Deep brisket, with well sprung ribs to allow for good lungs. Ribs extending well back. *Loin* short, strong, moderately tucked up. Waist well defined. *Croup*—Slight downward slope to the tail set.

*Tail* set fairly low on body line and reaching well below hock. Carried low when standing or moving slowly, streaming out parallel to ground when at a dead run, lifted when excited, but never curled over the back. High tail set is a *serious fault*.

**Forequarters**—The moderately broad chest tapers to a deep brisket, well let down between the forelegs. *Shoulders* slope downward and outward from the withers sufficiently to accommodate desired rib-spring. Shoulder blade (scapula) long and well laid back, meeting upper arm (humerus) at close to a right angle. Humerus nearly as long as scapula. *Elbows* should fit close, being neither loose nor tied. The *forearms* (ulna and radius) should be curved to fit spring of ribs. The curve in the forearm makes the wrists (carpal joints) somewhat closer together than the elbows. The *pasterns* are strong and flexible. Dewclaws removed.

The *feet* are relatively large and rounded, with well filled pads. They point slightly outward from a straight-ahead position to balance the width of the shoulders. This outward point is not to be more than 30 degrees from center line when viewed from above. The toes should not be splayed.

*The correct Cardigan front* is neither straight nor so crooked as to appear unsound. Overall, the bone should be heavy for a dog of this size, but not so heavy as to appear coarse or reduce agility. Knuckling over, straight front, fiddle front are *serious faults*.

**Hindquarters**—Well muscled and strong, but slightly less wide than shoulders. Hipbone (pelvis) slopes downward with the croup, forming a right angle with the femur at the hip socket. There should be moderate angulation at stifle and hock. *Hocks* well let down. Metatarsi perpendicular to the ground and parallel to each other. Dewclaws removed. *Feet* point straight ahead and are slightly smaller and more oval than front. Toes arched. Pads well filled.

Overall, the hindquarters must denote sufficient power to propel this low, relatively heavy herding dog efficiently over rough terrain.

**Coat**—Medium length but dense as it is double. Outer hairs slightly harsh in texture; never wiry, curly or silky. Lies relatively smooth and is weather resistant. The insulating undercoat is short, soft and thick. A correct coat has short hair on ears, head, the legs; medium hair on body; and slightly longer, thicker hair in ruff, on the backs of the thighs to form "pants," and on the underside of the tail. The coat should not be so exaggerated as to appear fluffy. This breed has a shedding coat, and seasonal lack of undercoat should not be too severely penalized, providing the hair is healthy. Trimming is not allowed except to tidy feet and, if desired, remove whiskers. Soft guard hairs, uniform length, wiry, curly, silky, overly short and/or flat coats are not desired. A distinctly long or fluffy coat is an extremely *serious fault*.

**Color**—All shades of red, sable and brindle. Black with or without tan or brindle points. Blue merle (black and gray; marbled) with or without tan or brindle points. There is no color preference. White flashings are usual on the neck (either in part or as a collar), chest, legs, muzzle, underparts, tip of tail and as a blaze on head. White on the head should not predominate and should never surround the eyes. Any color other than specified and/or body color predominantly white are *disqualifications*.

**Gait**—Free and smooth. Effortless. Viewed from the side, forelegs should reach well forward when moving at a trot, without much lift, in unison with driving action of hind legs. The correct shoulder assembly and well fitted elbows allow for a long free stride in front. Viewed from the front, legs do not move in exact parallel planes, but incline slightly inward to compensate for shortness of leg and width of chest. Hind legs, when trotting, should reach well under body, move on a line with the forelegs, with the hocks turning neither in nor out, and in one continuous motion drive powerfully behind, well beyond the set of the tail. Feet must travel parallel to the line of motion with no tendency to swing out, cross over, or interfere with each other. Short choppy movement, rolling or high-stepping gait, close or overly wide coming or going, are incorrect. This is a herding dog which must have the agility, freedom of movement, and endurance to do the work for which he was developed.

**Temperament**—Even-tempered, loyal, affectionate, and adaptable. Never shy nor vicious.


## DISQUALIFICATIONS

*Blue eyes, or partially blue eyes, in any coat color other than blue merle.*
*Drop ears.*
*Nose other than solid black except in blue merles.*
*Any color other than specified.*
*Body color predominantly white.*

**Approved December 13, 1994**
**Effective January 31, 1995**

# COLLIE

*Rough*

*Smooth*

*T*HERE ARE TWO VARIETIES OF COLLIE. THE ROUGH-COATED IS FAR MORE familiar, but many fanciers have increased their breeding of the smooth-coated variety and many smooths of excellent type are now being exhibited.

Although the exact origin of the Collie remains an enigma, both varieties existed long ago in the unwritten history of the herding dogs of Scotland and northern England.

Since sheepherding is one of the world's oldest occupations, the Collie's ancestors date far back in the history of dogs. The smooth Collie, which for as long as there have been written standards for the breed has been bred to the same standard except for coat, was considered principally as a drover's dog used for guiding cows and sheep to market, not for standing over and guarding them at pasture. Until the last two centuries, both varieties were strictly working dogs without written pedigrees. Their untutored masters saw no need for pedigrees, if indeed they were capable of keeping studbooks.

The earliest illustrations known to bear a resemblance to both varieties are found as woodcuts in *The History of Quadrupeds,* by Thomas Bewick, antedating 1800. The rough dog was described as a "Shepherd's Dog" and the smooth as a "ban dog." The rough was described as being only fourteen inches at the shoulder, and the smooth was said to be much larger and descended from the mastiff. (*Mastiff* in this sense does not refer to the breed we know today by that name but was something of a generic term used basically to describe a common type dog.) It is well established that the roughs at that time were not only much smaller but had shorter, broader heads and were usually black, or black and white, in color.

From early in the nineteenth century, when some dog fanciers began to take interest in these dogs, and the keeping of written pedigrees began, the breed progressed rapidly, becoming not only larger in stature but also more refined. The dog Old Cockie was born in 1867. He not only stamped characteristic type on the rough Collie, but he is believed by usually reliable authorities to be responsible for introducing to the breed the factors which led to the development of the sable coat color in the Collie. A short time later Collies were seen of almost every imaginable color, including red, buff, mottle of various shades, and a few sables. At that time the most frequently seen colors were black, tan and white, black and white (without tan), and what are now called blue merles, but which were known then as tortoiseshell.

The early pedigrees were very much abbreviated, as compared with our present breed records. In fact, the first volume of the English studbook showed seventy-eight "sheep dogs and Scotch Collies" registered up to 1874. Fifteen of them had written pedigrees but only three extended beyond sire and dam. Serving as proof that pride of ownership was given priority over written records, it was in 1860 that the first classes for "Scotch Sheep Dogs" were offered at the second dog show ever held in England, that of the Birmingham Dog Society. Both varieties competed in the same classes.

Shortly thereafter, Queen Victoria visited Balmoral and saw her first Collies.

They captivated her and she enthusiastically began to sponsor them. There was a marked surge in the popularity of the breed, which found itself not only the indispensable helpmate of the humble shepherd but the treasure and the playmate of the elite.

Collie type was well enough fixed by 1886 so that the English breeders have never seen fit to change the height and weight established in their standard at that time. Clarifying changes have been made in the United States standard over the ensuing years but, except for recognizing that the Collie has become slightly larger and heavier on this side of the Atlantic, there is no fundamental difference, even today, from that 1886 description of the ideal Collie.

Many of the early settlers in the New World brought dogs with them to herd their sheep and cattle in the Colonies, but it was not until May 1877, seventeen years after their show ring debut in England, that they were shown here, at the second show of the Westminster Kennel Club, in New York. Classes were offered for "Shepherd Dogs, or Collie Dogs" and a few were entered. The next year, however, was to see great interest and excitement. Two Collies imported from Victoria's Royal Balmoral Kennel had been entered! Soon Collies were to be found as prized possessions of the wealthy and socially elite. Kennels were established by the well-known financier J. P. Morgan and his contemporaries, and many fashionable estates up the Hudson River and on Long Island had Collie kennels. English dogs were imported for what were then considered to be exorbitant prices. It is interesting to note that about a half century later almost the reverse situation was occurring. The Collie became a highly desired breed in Japan and there was great persuasion to convince some of the American breeders to export some of their top dogs. By this time, the importation of Collies from England had become exceedingly rare.

Being no longer in great demand as a herder, today's Collie has transferred these abilities to serving as a devoted family dog where he shows a particular affinity for small children. For many years his general popularity has placed him in the top half of AKC registration rankings. Elegant and beautiful in appearance, loyal and affectionate in all his actions, self-appointed guardian of everything he can see or hear, the Collie represents, to his many admirers, the ideal family companion.

The Collie Club of America was organized in 1886, two years after the establishment of the American Kennel Club, and was the second parent club to join the AKC. Very active in promoting the interest of the breed, the parent club now has a membership numbering well over 3,500 and its annual specialty show attracts over 400 Collies from all over the United States.

The Collie has been the beneficiary of "good press." Great impetus to the breed's popularity was provided by the famous Collie stories of Albert Payson Terhune. His *Lad: A Dog* was followed by many more volumes, eagerly read by several generations of Americans. And, of course, the literary, film, and television exploits of Lassie spark in children and their parents a strong desire to have for their very own a "lovely dog like that."

# OFFICIAL STANDARD FOR THE COLLIE

## Rough

**General Character**—The Collie is a lithe, strong, responsive, active dog, carrying no useless timber, standing naturally straight and firm. The deep, moderately wide chest shows strength, the sloping shoulders and well-bent hocks indicate speed and grace, and the face shows high intelligence. The Collie presents an impressive, proud picture of true balance, each part being in harmonious proportion to every other part and to the whole. Except for the technical description that is essential to this Standard and without which no Standard for the guidance of breeders and judges is adequate, it could be stated simply that no part of the Collie ever seems to be out of proportion to any other part. Timidity, frailness, sullenness, viciousness, lack of animation, cumbersome appearance and lack of overall balance impair the general character.

**Head**—The head properties are of great importance. When considered in proportion to the size of the dog the head is inclined to lightness and never appears massive. A heavy-headed dog lacks the necessary bright, alert, full-of-sense look that contributes so greatly to expression. Both in front and profile view the head bears a general resemblance to a well-blunted lean wedge, being smooth and clean in outline and nicely balanced in proportion. On the sides it tapers gradually and smoothly from the ears to the end of the black nose, without being flared out in backskull ("cheeky") or pinched in muzzle ("snipy"). In profile view the top of the backskull and the top of the muzzle lie in two approximately parallel, straight planes of equal length, divided by a very slight but perceptible stop or break. A midpoint between the inside corners of the eyes (which is the center of a correctly placed stop) is the center of balance in length of head.

The end of the smooth, well-rounded muzzle is blunt but not square. The underjaw is strong, clean-cut and the depth of skull from the brow to the under part of the jaw is not excessive. The teeth are of good size, meeting in a scissors bite. *Overshot or undershot jaws are undesirable, the latter being more severely penalized.* There is a very slight prominence of the eyebrows. The backskull is flat, without receding either laterally or backward and the occipital bone is not highly peaked. The proper width of backskull necessarily depends upon the combined length of skull and muzzle and the width of the backskull is less than its length. Thus the correct width varies with the individual and is dependent upon the extent to which it is supported by length of muzzle. Because of the importance of the head characteristics, *prominent head faults are very severely penalized.*

**Eyes**—Because of the combination of the flat skull, the arched eyebrows, the slight stop and the rounded muzzle, the foreface must be chiseled to form a receptacle for the eyes and they are necessarily placed obliquely to give them the required forward outlook. Except for the blue merles, they are required to be matched in color. They are almond-shaped, of medium size and never properly appear to be large or prominent. The color is dark and the eye does not show a yellow ring or a sufficiently prominent haw to affect the dog's expression. The eyes have a clear, bright appearance, expressing intelligent inquisitiveness, particularly when the ears are drawn up and the dog is on the alert. In blue merles, dark brown eyes are preferable, but either or both eyes may be merle or china in color without specific penalty. A large, round, full eye seriously detracts from the desired "sweet" expression. *Eye faults are heavily penalized.*

**Ears**—The ears are in proportion to the size of the head and, if they are carried properly and unquestionably "break" naturally, are seldom too small. Large ears usually cannot be lifted correctly off the head, and even if lifted, they will be out of proportion to the size of the head. When in repose the ears are folded lengthwise and thrown back into the frill. On the alert they are drawn well up on the backskull and are carried about three-quarters erect, with about one-fourth of the ear tipping or "breaking" forward. *A dog with prick ears or low ears cannot show true expression, and is penalized accordingly.*

**Neck**—The neck is firm, clean, muscular, sinewy and heavily frilled. It is fairly long, carried upright with a slight arch at the nape and imparts a proud, upstanding appearance showing off the frill.

**Body**—The body is firm, hard and muscular, a trifle long in proportion to the height. The ribs are well-rounded behind the well-sloped shoulders and the chest is deep, extending to the elbows. The back is strong and level, supported by powerful hips and thighs and the croup is sloped to give a well-rounded finish. The loin is powerful and slightly arched. *Noticeably fat dogs, or dogs in poor flesh, or with skin disease, or with no undercoat are out of condition and are moderately penalized accordingly.*

**Legs**—The forelegs are straight and muscular, with a fair amount of bone, considering the size of the dog. A cumbersome appearance is undesirable. *Both narrow and wide placement are penalized.* The forearm is moderately fleshy and the pasterns are flexible but without weakness. The hind legs are less fleshy, muscular at the thighs, very sinewy and the hocks and stifles are well bent. *A cowhocked dog or a dog with straight stifles is penalized.* The comparatively small feet are approximately oval in shape. The soles are well padded and tough, and the toes are well arched and close together. When the Collie is not in motion the legs and feet are judged by allowing the dog to come to a natural stop in a standing position so that both the forelegs and the hind legs are placed well apart, with the feet extending straight forward. Excessive "posing" is undesirable.

**Gait**—Gait is sound. When the dog is moved at a slow trot toward an observer its straight front legs track comparatively close together at the ground. The front legs are not out at the elbows, do not "crossover," nor does the dog move with a choppy, pacing or rolling gait. When viewed from the rear the hind legs are straight, tracking comparatively close together at the ground. At a moderate trot the hind legs are powerful and propelling. Viewed from the side the reasonably long, "reaching" stride is smooth and even, keeping the back line firm and level.

As the speed of the gait is increased the Collie single tracks, bringing the front legs inward in a straight line from the shoulder toward the center line of the body and the hind legs inward in a straight line from the hip toward the center line of the body. The gait suggests effortless speed combined with the dog's herding heritage, requiring it to be capable of changing its direction of travel almost instantaneously.

**Tail**—The tail is moderately long, the bone reaching to the hock joint or below. It is carried low when the dog is quiet, the end having an upward twist or "swirl." When gaited or when the dog is excited it is carried gaily but not over the back.

**Coat**—The well-fitting, proper-textured coat is the crowning glory of the rough variety of Collie. It is abundant except on the head and legs. The outer coat is straight and harsh to the touch. *A soft, open outer coat or a curly outer coat, regardless of quantity is penalized.* The undercoat, however, is soft, furry and so close together that it is difficult to see the skin when the hair is parted. The coat is very abundant on the mane and frill. The face or mask is smooth. The forelegs are smooth and well feathered to the back of the pasterns. The hind legs are smooth below the hock joints. Any feathering below the hocks is removed for the show ring. The hair on the tail is very profuse and on the hips it is long and bushy. The texture, quantity and the extent to which the coat "fits the dog" are important points.

**Color**—The four recognized colors are "Sable and White," "Tri-color," "Blue Merle" and "White." There is no preference among them. The "Sable and White" is predominantly sable (a fawn sable color of varying shades from light gold to dark mahogany) with white markings usually on the chest, neck, legs, feet and the tip of the tail. A blaze may appear on the foreface or backskull or both. The "Tri-color" is predominantly black, carrying white markings as in a "Sable and White" and has tan shadings on and about the head and legs. The "Blue Merle" is a mottled or "marbled" color predominantly blue-grey and black with white markings as in the "Sable and White" and usually has tan shadings as in the "Tri-color." The "White" is predominantly white, preferably with sable, tri-color or blue merle markings.

**Size**—Dogs are from 24 to 26 inches at the shoulder and weigh from 60 to 75 pounds. Bitches are from 22 to 24 inches at the shoulder, weighing from 50 to 65 pounds. *An undersize or an oversize Collie is penalized according to the extent to which the dog appears to be undersize or oversize.*

**Expression**—Expression is one of the most important points in considering the relative value of Collies. *Expression,* like the term "character" is difficult to define in words. It is not a fixed point as in color, weight or height and it is something the uninitiated can properly understand only by optical illustration. In general, however, it may be said to be the combined product of the shape and balance of the skull and muzzle, the placement, size, shape and color of the eye and the position, size and carriage of the ears. An expression that shows sullenness or which is suggestive of any other breed is entirely foreign. The Collie cannot be judged properly until its expression has been carefully evaluated.

## Smooth

The Smooth Variety of Collie is judged by the same Standard as the Rough Variety, except that the references to the quantity and distribution of the coat are not applicable to the Smooth Variety, which has a short, hard, dense, flat coat of good texture, with an abundance of undercoat.

**Approved May 10, 1977**

# GERMAN SHEPHERD DOG

ERIVED FROM THE OLD HERDING AND FARM DOG BREEDS, AND FAMOUS FOR centuries as both servant and companion, today's German Shepherd Dog is the result of intensive development orchestrated by those who valued the breed.

Founded by Captain Max von Stephanitz in 1899, and molded by the Verein für Deutsche Schäferhunde (the German Shepherd Dog Club of Germany) is recognized as the breed's original parent club. From about 1914, the popularity of the German Shepherd Dog spread rapidly throughout the world. Interest in the breed has been fostered worldwide by specialty clubs in many countries, just as it has in the United States by the German Shepherd Dog Club of America.

The German Shepherd Dog is first, last, and always a working dog, whose temperament and physical structure have been developed through selective breeding, judging, and specialized training.

The most important attribute of the breed is its character. German Shepherd Dogs are distinguished by the loyalty, courage, and ability to assimilate and retain training for an amazing number of specialized services. They should be of even disposition, poised, and unexcitable, with restrained and composed confidence. For typical work as a herding sheepdog, they must not be gun-shy and must have the courage to protect the flock from attacks by other animals or humans. For police work, narcotics detection, or search and rescue, they must have courage and stability coupled with excellent scenting capabilities. As guide dogs for the blind, German Shepherd Dogs must and do exhibit a high order of intelligence and discrimination, as this work requires observation, patience, faithfulness, watchfulness, and good judgment. All this is possible because of the German Shepherd Dog's natural aptitude for training.

These qualities have endeared German Shepherd Dogs to a wide public in practically every country in the world. They serve as assistants for the disabled, therapy dogs for the infirm, home guardians, and companions and friends to children and families. They are protectors of livestock and partners to police officers and soldiers. German Shepherd Dogs are not pugnacious brawlers but bold and punishing fighters, if the need arises. With humans, they do not give affection lightly. They are dignified and may be indifferent to strangers, but friendship, once given, is for life.

Physically, the German Shepherd Dog breed has been developed to almost an ideal fitness for the work they do. They are a dog of middle size, strong and well muscled, with enough weight to be effective as a herder of sheep or a dog on patrol, but still agile and not awkward or coarse.

By careful selective breeding, the natural, easy trot of the German Shepherd Dog has evolved to a nearly effortless motion. Essentially a trotting breed, the dog's structure has been developed to increase the power, elasticity, and length of gait. Other things being equal, the best-moving German Shepherd Dog is the one that covers the maximum amount of ground with the minimum expenditure of energy. So well coordinated and harmonious is this gait, that when properly demonstrated, the dog seems to glide forward without visible effort. One might think that the dog is suspended from a firm beam in the back.

The impression of the dog as a whole is one of ruggedness combined with nobility, and power combined with agility. There should be a sense of balance, with forequarters and hindquarters complementing each other. The outline should be smooth and flowing, and the topline, from the tip of the ear to the tip of the tail, should be a single sweeping succession of unbroken curves. The German Shepherd Dog is a natural breed and should not be altered for the ever-changing whims of the show ring.

# OFFICIAL STANDARD FOR THE GERMAN SHEPHERD DOG

**General Appearance**—The first impression of a good German Shepherd Dog is that of a strong, agile, well muscled animal, alert and full of life. It is well balanced, with harmonious development of the forequarter and hindquarter. The dog is longer than tall, deep-bodied, and presents an outline of smooth curves rather than angles. It looks substantial and not spindly, giving the impression, both at rest and in motion, of muscular fitness and nimbleness without any look of clumsiness or soft living. The ideal dog is stamped with a look of quality and nobility—difficult to define, but unmistakable when present. Secondary sex characteristics are strongly marked, and every animal gives a definite impression of masculinity or femininity, according to its sex.

**Size, Proportion, Substance**—The desired *height* for males at the top of the highest point of the shoulder blade is 24 to 26 inches; and for bitches, 22 to 24 inches.

The German Shepherd Dog is longer than tall, with the most desirable *proportion* as 10 to 8½. The length is measured from the point of the prosternum or breastbone to the rear edge of the pelvis, the ischial tuberosity. The desirable long proportion is not derived from a long back, but from overall length with relation to height, which is achieved by length of forequarter and length of withers and hindquarter, viewed from the side.

**Head**—The *head* is noble, cleanly chiseled, strong without coarseness, but above all not fine, and in proportion to the body. The head of the male is distinctly masculine, and that of the bitch distinctly feminine.

The *expression* keen, intelligent and composed. *Eyes* of medium size, almond shaped, set a little obliquely and not protruding. The color is as dark as possible. *Ears* are moderately pointed, in proportion to the skull, open toward the front, and carried erect when at attention, the ideal carriage being one in which the center lines of the ears, viewed from the front, are parallel to each other and perpendicular to the ground. A dog with cropped or hanging ears must be *disqualified*.

Seen from the front the forehead is only moderately arched, and the *skull* slopes into the long, wedge-shaped muzzle without abrupt stop. The *muzzle* is long and strong, and its topline is parallel to the topline of the skull. *Nose* black. A dog with a nose that is not predominantly black must be *disqualified*. The lips are firmly fitted. Jaws are strongly developed. *Teeth*—42 in number—20 upper and 22 lower—are strongly developed and meet in a scissors bite in which part of the inner surface of the upper incisors meet and engage part of the outer surface of the lower incisors. An overshot jaw or a level bite is undesirable. An undershot jaw is a *disqualifying fault*. Complete dentition is to be preferred. Any missing teeth other than first premolars is a *serious fault*.

**Neck, Topline, Body**—The *neck* is strong and muscular, clean-cut and relatively long, proportionate in size to the head and without loose folds of skin. When the dog is at attention or excited, the head is raised and the neck carried high; otherwise typical carriage of the head is forward rather than up and but little higher than the top of the shoulders, particularly in motion.

*Topline*—The *withers* are higher than and sloping into the level back. The *back* is straight, very strongly developed without sag or roach, and relatively short.

The whole structure of the *body* gives an impression of depth and solidity without bulkiness.

*Chest*—Commencing at the prosternum, it is well filled and carried well down between the legs. It is deep and capacious, never shallow, with ample room for lungs and heart, carried well forward, with the prosternum showing ahead of the shoulder in profile. *Ribs* well sprung and long, neither barrel-shaped nor too flat, and carried down to a sternum which reaches to the elbows. Correct ribbing allows the elbows to move back freely when the dog is at a trot. Too round causes interference and throws the elbows out; too flat or short causes pinched elbows. Ribbing is carried well back so that the loin is relatively short. *Abdomen* firmly held and not paunchy. The bottom line is only moderately tucked up in the loin.

*Loin*—Viewed from the top, broad and strong. Undue length between the last rib and the thigh, when viewed from the side, is undesirable. *Croup* long and gradually sloping.

*Tail* bushy, with the last vertebra extended at least to the hock joint. It is set smoothly into the croup and low rather than high. At rest, the tail hangs in a slight curve like a saber. A slight hook—sometimes carried to one side—is faulty only to the extent that it mars general appearance. When the dog is excited or in motion, the curve is accentuated and the tail raised, but it should never be curled forward beyond a vertical line. Tails too short, or with clumpy ends due to ankylosis, are *serious faults.* A dog with a docked tail must be *disqualified.*

**Forequarters**—The shoulder blades are long and obliquely angled, laid on flat and not placed forward. The upper arm joins the shoulder blade at about a right angle. Both the upper arm and the shoulder blade are well muscled. The forelegs, viewed from all sides, are straight and the bone oval rather than round. The pasterns are strong and springy and angulated at approximately a 25-degree angle from the vertical. Dewclaws on the forelegs may be removed, but are normally left on.

The *feet* are short, compact with toes well arched, pads thick and firm, nails short and dark.

**Hindquarters**—The whole assembly of the thigh, viewed from the side, is broad, with both upper and lower thigh well muscled, forming as nearly as possible a right angle. The upper thigh bone parallels the shoulder blade while the lower thigh bone parallels the upper arm. The metatarsus (the unit between the hock joint and the foot) is short, strong and tightly articulated. The dewclaws, if any, should be removed from the hind legs. Feet as in front.

**Coat**—The ideal dog has a double coat of medium length. The outer coat should be as dense as possible, hair straight, harsh and lying close to the body. A slightly wavy outer coat, often of wiry texture, is permissible. The head, including the inner ear and foreface, and the legs and paws are covered with short hair, and the neck with longer and thicker hair. The rear of the forelegs and hind legs has somewhat longer hair extending to the pastern and hock, respectively. *Faults* in coat include soft, silky, too long outer coat, woolly, curly, and open coat.

**Color**—The German Shepherd Dog varies in color, and most colors are permissible. Strong rich colors are preferred. Pale, washed-out colors and blues or livers are *serious faults.* A white dog must be *disqualified.*

**Gait**—A German Shepherd Dog is a trotting dog, and its structure has been developed to meet the requirements of its work. *General Impression*—The gait is outreaching, elastic, seemingly without effort, smooth and rhythmic, covering the maximum amount of ground with the minimum number of steps. At a walk it covers a great deal of ground, with long stride of both hind legs and forelegs. At a trot the dog covers still more ground with even longer stride, and moves powerfully but easily, with coordination and balance so that the gait appears to be the steady motion of a well-lubricated machine. The feet travel close to the ground on both forward reach and backward push. In order to achieve ideal movement of this kind, there must be good muscular development and ligamentation. The hindquarters deliver, through the back, a powerful forward thrust which slightly lifts the whole animal and drives the body forward. Reaching far under, and passing the imprint left by the front foot, the hind foot takes hold of the ground; then hock, stifle and upper thigh come into play and sweep back, the stroke of the hind leg finishing with the foot still close to the ground in a smooth follow-through. The overreach of the hindquarter usually necessitates one hind foot passing outside and the other hind foot passing inside the track of the forefeet, and such action is not faulty unless the locomotion is crabwise with the dog's body sideways out of the normal straight line.

*Transmission*—The typical smooth, flowing gait is maintained with great strength and firmness of back. The whole effort of the hindquarter is transmitted to the forequarter through the loin, back and withers. At full trot, the back must remain firm and level without sway, roll, whip or roach. Unlevel topline with withers lower than the hip is a *fault*. To compensate for the forward motion imparted by the hindquarters, the shoulder should open to its full extent. The forelegs should reach out close to the ground in a long stride in harmony with that of the hindquarters. The dog does not track on widely separated parallel lines, but brings the feet inward toward the middle line of the body when trotting, in order to maintain balance. The feet track closely but do not strike or cross over. Viewed from the front, the front legs function from the shoulder joint to the pad in a straight line. Viewed from the rear, the hind legs function from the hip joint to the pad in a straight line. Faults of gait, whether from front, rear or side, are to be considered very *serious faults*.

**Temperament**—The breed has a distinct personality marked by direct and fearless, but not hostile, expression, self-confidence and a certain aloofness that does not lend itself to immediate and indiscriminate friendships. The dog must be approachable, quietly standing its ground and showing confidence and willingness to meet overtures without itself making them. It is poised, but when the occasion demands, eager and alert; both fit and willing to serve in its capacity as companion, watchdog, blind leader, herding dog or guardian, whichever the circumstances may demand. The dog must not be timid, shrinking behind its master or handler; it should not be nervous, looking about or upward with anxious expression or showing nervous reactions, such as tucking of tail, to strange sounds or sights. Lack of confidence under any surroundings is not typical of good character. Any of the above deficiencies in character which indicate shyness must be penalized as very *serious faults* and any dog exhibiting pronounced indications of these must be excused from the ring. It must be possible for the judge to observe the teeth and to determine that both testicles are descended. Any dog that attempts to bite the judge must be *disqualified*. The ideal dog is a working animal with an incorruptible character combined with body and gait suitable for the arduous work that constitutes its primary purpose.

## DISQUALIFICATIONS

*Cropped or hanging ears.*
*Dogs with noses not predominantly black.*

*Undershot jaw.*
*Docked tail.*
*White dogs.*
*Any dog that attempts to bite the judge.*

**Approved February 11, 1978**
**Reformatted July 11, 1994**

# OLD ENGLISH SHEEPDOG

*C*OMPARED WITH SOME OTHER KINDS OF DOGS THE OLD ENGLISH SHEEPDOG cannot boast the same antiquity, but there is nevertheless ample evidence that it can trace its origin to the early nineteenth century or at least 150 years back, thus proving that among recognized breeds it is no mere upstart. As to its real origin, there are conflicting ideas based on premises obscured by the passage of time. A painting by Gainsborough of a duke of Buccleuch, from which engravings were struck in 1771, shows the peer with his arms clasped about the neck of what appears to be a fairly good specimen of present-day Old English Sheepdog. This is the earliest picture known that in any manner depicts the breed. What, however, the pictured dog was supposed to be at that period is not certain.

In all probability the breed was first developed in the west of England, in the counties of Devon and Somerset and the Duchy of Cornwall, although from what breeds it was produced is a matter of conjecture. Some maintain that the Scotch Bearded Collie had a large part in its making; others claim for one of its progenitors the Russian Owtchar.

At all events, in the beginning of the eighteenth century, we read of a "drover's dog" which was used largely for driving sheep and cattle into the markets of the metropolis. These drover's dogs were exempt from taxes and, to prove their occupation, they were docked. Some believe that the nicknames "bob" and "bobtail" trace to this custom. It is not true, of course, that the practice of removing the tail has produced a breed naturally bobtailed or tailless. In fact, few specimens of the breed are whelped without tails, or with tails long or comparatively short. According to the standard, the tail should be removed at the first joint when the puppy is three or four days old, and it should never be longer than one and one-half or two inches in length at maturity. Seldom is an Old English Sheepdog seen in the show ring today with more than a mere thickening of the skin where the tail has been removed. Since this dog has been used more for driving than for herding, the lack of a tail to serve as a rudder, so to speak, has in no way affected its working ability with heavier kinds of sheep and cattle.

For years after the breed's introduction into this country, fanciers did considerable harm by misinterpreting "profuseness" of coat as "excessiveness." This misled the public into believing that the Old English Sheepdog was difficult to care for, when as a matter of fact a dog with typical coat of the right texture is no harder to keep in shape than is any other longhaired dog. Furthermore, it is home loving, not given to roaming and fighting, and it is extremely agile; because of its intelligence, affection, and lack of boisterousness, it makes an ideal house dog. It has a tender mouth and can be trained as a retriever; it makes a first-class sledge dog, and is satisfactory as a companion equally at home in an apartment, large house, drawing room, and practically anywhere else.

In seeking a good representative of the breed, points to look for include a body practically square; good bone, deep brisket, chest, and spring of rib; strong foreface, dark or walleyes, level teeth; straight forelegs, well-let-down hocks; and a hard coat with good underjacket. Markings are not important. The dogs do well under almost any climatic conditions, their coats serving as insulation against heat, cold, and dampness. A marked characteristic of the breed is its gait, which is quite like the shuffle of a bear.

The Old English Sheepdog Club of America was started by W. A. Tilley in 1904, and received official recognition by the AKC the following year.

# OFFICIAL STANDARD FOR THE OLD ENGLISH SHEEPDOG

**General Appearance**—A strong, compact, square, balanced dog. Taking him all around, he is profusely, *but not excessively coated,* thickset, muscular and able-bodied. These qualities, combined with his agility, fit him for the demanding tasks required of a shepherd's or drover's dog. Therefore, *soundness is of the greatest importance.* His bark is loud with a distinctive "pot-casse" ring in it.

**Size, Proportion, Substance**—Type, character and balance are of greater importance and are on no account to be sacrificed to size alone.

*Size*—Height (measured from top of withers to the ground)—Dogs: 22 inches (55.8 cm) and upward. Bitches: 21 inches (53.3 cm) and upward.

*Proportion*—Length (measured from point of shoulder to point of ischium [tuberosity]) practically the same as the height. Absolutely free from legginess or weaselness.

**Substance**—Well muscled with plenty of bone.

**Head**—A most intelligent expression.

*Eyes*—Brown, blue or one of each. If brown, very dark is preferred. If blue, a pearl, china or wall-eye is considered typical. An amber or yellow eye is most objectionable.

*Ears*—Medium sized and carried flat to the side of the head.

*Skull*—Capacious and rather squarely formed giving plenty of room for brain power. The parts over the eyes (supra-orbital ridges) are well arched. The whole well covered with hair.

*Stop*—Well defined.

*Jaw*—Fairly long, strong, square and truncated. *Attention is particularly called to the above properties as a long, narrow head or snipy muzzle is a deformity.*

*Nose*—Always black, large and capacious.

*Teeth*—Strong, large and evenly placed. The bite is level or tight scissors.

**Neck, Topline, Body**—*Neck*—Fairly long and arched gracefully.

*Topline*—Stands lower at the withers than at the loin with no indication of softness or weakness. *Attention is particularly called to this topline, as it is a distinguishing characteristic of the breed.*

*Body*—Rather short and very compact, broader at the rump than at the shoulders, ribs well sprung and brisket deep and capacious. Neither slab-sided nor barrel-chested. The loin is very stout and gently arched.

*Tail*—Docked close to the body, when not naturally bob tailed.

**Forequarters**—Shoulders well laid back and narrow at the points. The forelegs dead straight with plenty of bone. The measurements from the withers to the elbow and from the elbow to the ground are practically the same.

**Hindquarters**—Round and muscular with well let down hocks. When standing, the metatarses are perpendicular to the ground when viewed from any angle.

**Feet**—Small and round, toes well arched, pads thick and hard, feet pointing straight ahead.

**Coat**—Profuse, but not so excessive as to give the impression of the dog being overly fat, and of a good hard texture; not straight, but shaggy and free from curl. *Quality and texture of coat to be considered above mere profuseness.* Softness or flatness of coat to be considered a *fault*. The undercoat is a waterproof pile when not removed by grooming or season. Ears coated moderately. The whole skull well covered with hair. The neck well coated with hair. The forelegs well coated all around. The hams densely coated with a thick, long jacket in excess of any other part. Neither the natural outline nor the natural texture of the coat may be changed by any artificial means except that the feet and rear may be trimmed for cleanliness.

**Color**—Any shade of gray, grizzle, blue or blue merle with or without white markings or in reverse. *Any shade of brown or fawn to be considered distinctly objectionable and not to be encouraged.*

**Gait**—When trotting, movement is free and powerful, seemingly effortless, with good reach and drive, and covering maximum ground with minimum steps. Very elastic at a gallop. May amble or pace at slower speeds.

**Temperament**—An adaptable, intelligent dog of even disposition, with no sign of aggression, shyness or nervousness.

**Approved February 10, 1990**
**Effective March 28, 1990**

# Pembroke Welsh Corgi

$\mathcal{A}$LTHOUGH ALL EVIDENCE SEEMS TO POINT TO THE FACT THAT THE Pembroke Welsh Corgi is a much younger dog than the Cardigan Welsh Corgi, it is still true that the Corgi from Pembrokeshire is a breed of considerable antiquity. No breed that traces its origin back to A.D. 1107 can be regarded as an especially new type of dog.

In modern times there has been an effort to link the two types of Corgi under the heading of a single breed. This is far from the truth, according to W. Lloyd-Thomas, the Welsh authority who has spent so many years digging out the history of these small cattle dogs. He has given some interesting information, that, while it tends to divorce the two Corgis definitely, still gives the Pembroke a colorful past.

The direct ancestors of the Pembroke were brought across the Channel by the Flemish weavers who had been induced by Henry I of England to take up their abode in Wales. This occurred in 1107, and it stands as a sturdy cornerstone upon which the development of a breed has been built. While weaving was one of their occupations, these Flemish people were also of an agrarian nature, and they soon had transferred to the southwest corner of Wales, at Haverfordwest, the replicas of the model homes and farms in their native land. The dog fitted into this scheme.

This early progenitor of the Pembroke Welsh Corgi of today has been described as having a noticeable resemblance to the old Schipperkes. It sprang from the same family that includes the Keeshond, the Pomeranian, the Samoyed, the Chow Chow, the Norwegian Elkhound, and the Finnish Spitz. It has little or nothing of the Dachshund characteristics.

In relation to the Cardigan, the Pembroke is shorter in body; the legs are straighter and lighter boned, while the coat is of finer texture. Two of the most noticeable differences are in the ears and the tail. Cardigan ears are rounded, while the Pembroke's are pointed at the tip and stand erect. The Cardigan has a long tail, and the Pembroke a short one. In disposition, the Pembroke is more restless, more easily excited. If one could see specimens of the early members of both breeds at the same time, the differences would be very marked. In modern times they have become more similar. The whole development of the Pembroke evinces a desire on the part of its breeders to produce a lower, stockier dog. It also may be noted that the head has grown stronger, while in these times, good-sized, round-tipped ears are not unusual.

The manner in which the Pembroke and the Cardigan have approached each other in appearance is not merely a matter of chance or of selective breeding. It is known, rather definitely, that the two were crossed before the middle of the nineteenth century.

The story comes direct from one of the old crofters, a man of nearly ninety years, who spent his whole lifetime in Bronant. It seems that in his youth, many of the young people in that village found a manner of increasing their pocket money. There were always plenty of the Cardigan puppies; in fact, the majority were a burden on the poor tenant farmers. If these puppies were retained, they would cost money to feed. One day an enterprising young man tucked a couple of Corgi puppies under his arm and set forth into a neighboring shire. When he returned there was the jingle of coins in his pocket. Thereafter, other young men followed the example. The old hill man who relates this incident says that he sold puppies to the farmers in Carmarthenshire and in Pembrokeshire.

It is not known whether any Cardigan Corgis had gone into Pembrokeshire at an earlier date, but it is quite possible, and it is only logical that if the two breeds were in the same section they would be bred together at some time. So far as is known, the Pembroke was not taken into Cardiganshire up to the time of World War I, although since then there have been many instances of intermatings.

The two breeds of Corgi were mated together frequently at the time when these dogs first came to the consciousness of the show fanciers. Little was known about either dog, and crossings were common. This practice has been stopped, and breeders today are determined to keep the Pembroke distinct from the Cardigan.

The Pembroke is one of the most agreeable of small house dogs. It has an affectionate nature but does not force its attentions upon those unwilling to accept them. Its intelligence is undoubted, and it is a remarkably alert, ever-vigilant home guardian.

# OFFICIAL STANDARD FOR THE PEMBROKE WELSH CORGI

**General Appearance**—Low-set, strong, sturdily built and active, giving an impression of substance and stamina in a small space. Should not be so low and heavy-boned as to appear coarse or overdone, nor so light-boned as to appear racy. Outlook bold, but kindly. Expression intelligent and interested. Never shy nor vicious.

Correct type, including general balance and outline, attractiveness of headpiece, intelligent outlook and correct temperament is of primary importance. Movement is especially important, particularly as viewed from the side. A dog with smooth and free gait has to be reasonably sound and must be highly regarded. A minor fault must never take precedence over the above desired qualities.

A dog must be very seriously penalized for the following faults, regardless of whatever desirable qualities the dog may present: oversized or undersized; button, rose or drop ears; overshot or undershot bite; fluffies, whitelies, mismarks or bluies.

**Size, Proportion, Substance**—*Height* (from ground to highest point on withers) should be 10 to 12 inches. *Weight* is in proportion to size, not exceeding 30 pounds for dogs and 28 pounds for bitches. In show condition, the preferred medium-sized dog of correct bone and substance will weigh approximately 27 pounds, with bitches approximately 25 pounds. Obvious oversized specimens and diminutive toylike individuals must be very severely penalized.

*Proportions*—Moderately long and low. The distance from the withers to the base of the tail should be approximately 40 percent greater than the distance from the withers to the ground. *Substance*—Should not be so low and heavy-boned as to appear coarse or overdone, nor so light-boned as to appear racy.

**Head**—The head should be foxy in shape and appearance. *Expression*—Intelligent and interested, but not sly. *Skull*—should be fairly wide and flat between the ears. Moderate amount of stop. Very slight rounding of cheek, not filled in below the eyes, as foreface should be nicely chiseled to give a somewhat tapered muzzle. Distance from occiput to center of stop to be greater than the distance from stop to nose tip, the proportion being five parts of total distance for the skull and three parts for the foreface. Muzzle should be neither dish-faced nor Roman-nosed. *Eyes*—Oval, medium in size, not round, nor protruding, nor deepset and piglike. Set somewhat obliquely. Variations of brown in harmony with coat color. Eye rims dark, preferably black. While dark eyes enhance the expression, true black eyes are most undesirable, as are yellow or bluish eyes. *Ears*—Erect, firm, and of medium size, tapering slightly to a rounded point. Ears are mobile, and react sensitively to sounds. A line drawn from the nose tip through the eyes to the ear tips, and across, should form an approximate equilateral triangle. Bat ears, small catlike ears, overly large weak ears, hooded ears, ears carried too high or too low, are undesirable. Button, rose or drop ears are very serious faults. *Nose*—Black and fully pigmented.

*Mouth*—Scissors bite, the inner side of the upper incisors touching the outer side of the lower incisors. Level bite is acceptable. Overshot or undershot bite is a very serious fault. *Lips*—Black, tight with little or no fullness.

**Neck, Topline, Body**—*Neck*—Fairly long. Of sufficient length to provide overall balance of the dog. Slightly arched, clean and blending well into the shoulders. A very short neck giving a stuffy appearance and a long, thin or ewe neck are faulty. *Topline*—Firm and level, neither riding up to nor falling away at the croup. A slight depression behind the shoulders caused by heavier neck coat meeting the shorter body coat is permissible. *Body*—Rib cage should be well sprung, slightly egg-shaped and moderately long. Deep chest, well let down between the forelegs. Exaggerated lowness interferes with the desired freedom of movement and should be penalized. Viewed from above, the body should taper slightly to end of loin. Loin short. Round or flat rib cage, lack of brisket, extreme length or cobbiness, are undesirable. *Tail*—Docked as short as possible without being indented. Occasionally a puppy is born with a natural dock, which if sufficiently short, is acceptable. A tail up to two inches in length is allowed, but if carried high tends to spoil the contour of the topline.

**Forequarters**—*Legs*—Short, forearms turned slightly inward, with the distance between wrists less than between the shoulder joints, so that the front does not appear absolutely straight. Ample bone carried right down into the feet. Pasterns firm and nearly straight when viewed from the side. Weak pasterns and knuckling over are serious faults. Shoulder blades long and well laid back along the rib cage. Upper arms nearly equal in length to shoulder blades. Elbows parallel to the body, not prominent, and well set back to allow a line perpendicular to the ground to be drawn from tip of the shoulder blade through to elbow. *Feet*—Oval, with the two center toes slightly in advance of the two outer ones. Turning neither in nor out. Pads strong and feet arched. Nails short. Dewclaws on both forelegs and hindlegs usually removed. Too round, long and narrow, or splayed feet are faulty.

**Hindquarters**—Ample bone, strong and flexible, moderately angulated at stifle and hock. Exaggerated angulation is as faulty as too little. Thighs should be well muscled. Hocks short, parallel, and when viewed from the side are perpendicular to the ground. Barrel hocks or cowhocks are most objectionable. Slipped or double-jointed hocks are very faulty. *Feet*—as in front.

**Coat**—Medium length; short, thick, weather-resistant undercoat with a coarser, longer outer coat. Overall length varies, with slightly thicker and longer ruff around the neck, chest and on the shoulders. The body coat lies flat. Hair is slightly longer on back of forelegs and underparts and somewhat fuller and longer on rear of hindquarters. The coat is preferably straight, but some waviness is permitted. This breed has a shedding coat, and seasonal lack of undercoat should not be too severely penalized, providing the hair is glossy, healthy and well groomed. A wiry, tightly marcelled coat is very faulty, as is an overly short, smooth and thin coat. *Very Serious Faults*—*Fluffies*—A coat of extreme length with exaggerated feathering on ears, chest, legs and feet, underparts and hindquarters. Trimming such a coat does not make it any more acceptable. The Corgi should be shown in its natural condition, with no trimming permitted except to tidy the feet, and, if desired, remove the whiskers.

**Color**—The outer coat is to be of self colors in red, sable, fawn, black and tan with or without white markings. White is acceptable on legs, chest, neck (either in part or as a collar), muzzle, underparts and as a narrow blaze on head. *Very Serious Faults: Whitelies*—Body color white, with red or dark markings. *Bluies*—Colored portions of the coat have a distinct bluish or smoky cast. This coloring is associated with extremely light or blue eyes, liver or gray eye rims, nose and lip pigment. *Mismarks*—Self colors with any area of white on the back between withers and tail, on sides between elbows and back of hindquarters, or on ears. Black with white markings and no tan present.

**Gait**—Free and smooth. Forelegs should reach well forward without too much lift, in unison with the driving action of the hind legs. The correct shoulder assembly and well-fitted elbows allow a long, free stride in front. Viewed from the front, legs do not move in exact parallel planes, but incline slightly inward to compensate for shortness of leg and width of chest. Hind legs should drive well under the body and move on a line with the forelegs, with hocks turning neither in nor out. Feet must travel parallel to the line of motion with no tendency to swing out, cross over or interfere with each other. Short, choppy movement, rolling or high-stepping gait, close or overly wide coming or going, are incorrect. This is a herding dog, which must have the agility, freedom of movement and endurance to do the work for which he was developed.

**Temperament**—Outlook bold, but kindly. Never shy or vicious. The judge shall dismiss from the ring any Pembroke Welsh Corgi that is excessively shy.

**Approved June 13, 1972**
**Reformatted January 28, 1993**

# Polish Lowland Sheepdog

*T*HE POLISH LOWLAND SHEEPDOG, ALSO KNOWN BY ITS POLISH ACRONYM PON (Polski Owczarek Nizinny), is neither an ancient breed nor a new one. While the origin of the PON is obscured by time, it is commonly held that the breed evolved from breeding native dogs of Poland to shaggy-haired dogs accompanying Hun migrations from central Asia.

Polish herders needed a robust, tough, harsh-coated, highly intelligent, agile, and fearless dog to use as a sheepherder by day and a guard dog by night. It was these characteristics that were bred for selectively and are still found in today's PON.

An indigenous, medium-sized, longhaired herding dog in Poland was first mentioned in the thirteenth century. A sixteenth-century reference mentions a Polish merchant traveling to Scotland to exchange a shipload of grain for sheep. The Scottish sheep breeder, impressed by the work of the sheepdogs accompanying the Polish merchant, offered to exchange two additional sheep for one male and two female sheepdogs. It is generally believed that these dogs contributed to the development of the Bearded Collie. In the eighteenth century, a medium-sized dog that could easily be the ancestor of the modern PON was said to be "most clever, having almost human intelligence."

When Poland regained her independence from Russia after World War I, there began an interest in purebred Polish animals. Considerable progress was made in developing breed type during this period. This work was almost undone when World War II all but led to the breed's extinction, as only a handful of these dogs survived the conflict. The Polish Kennel Club's 1950 appeal for information on surviving PONs included a mention of the German military's use of PONs from one of the premier prewar kennels. These PONs, which accompanied the German army during the invasion of Norway, were awarded the Iron Cross for their service.

Dr. Danuta Hryniewicz, a veterinarian from northern Poland, is generally credited as the person most responsible for bringing today's PON back from the brink of extinction. Her PON Smok (named for the storybook dragon of Poland), is considered the father of the post–World War II PON. The 1970s saw PON popularity spread throughout Europe, and in 1979 the first PONs were imported into the United States.

The breakthrough in America occurred when Betty and Kaz Augustowski acquired their first PONs in 1982 and established Elzbieta Kennels. The breed entered the AKC Stud Book in 1999 and began competition in the Herding Group in August 2001 after it was officially recognized by the AKC.

PONs must be socialized from a very young age, as they can be suspicious of strangers. They are self-controlled, perceptive, and are endowed with an excellent memory but can be stubborn in order to get their own way. They do well in several environments and are very good companion dogs in the city. PONs are intelligent and learn quickly when given positive reinforcement, and perform well in obedience, agility, herding, and tracking as well as in the conformation ring. They are lively, friendly, family dogs, who are good-natured and gentle with children. The breed is not plagued by any pervasive hereditary health problems and can lead a productive life for twelve to fourteen years.

Today's PONs have not lost the characteristics sought by Polish shepherds centuries ago. Strong and hardy, with a long, thick double coat and hanging hair that covers the eyes, PONs are the quintessential "shaggy dog."

# OFFICIAL STANDARD FOR THE POLISH LOWLAND SHEEPDOG

**General Appearance**—Medium-sized, cobby, strong and muscular, with a long, thick coat and hanging hair that covers the eyes. His herding and working ability is attributed to an intense desire to please and compatible nature. He is lively but self-controlled, clever and perceptive and well known for an excellent memory.

**Size, Proportion, Substance**—Well balanced due to a strong skeleton. Height measured at the withers for an adult dog is 18–20 inches, and 17–19 inches for a bitch. It is not desirable to diminish the size below the Standard, making the dog too delicate for a strong working dog. The silhouette is rectangular rather than square. The ratio of height to length is 9–10, meaning that the height at the withers should equal ⁹⁄₁₀ths of its length. *Fault:* Long legs.

**Head and Skull**—The medium-sized head is in proportion to the body. The profuse hair on the forehead, cheeks and chin make the head look bigger than it actually is. *Expression* should be lively with a penetrating gaze. *Eyes* are of medium size and oval. *Fault:* Protruding eyes. *Colors* are brown or hazel. The edges of the lids are as dark as possible within the coat color. *Ears* are heart-shaped, drop, and set moderately high. *Fault:* Ears set too high. They are medium size in proportion to the head and should be fully covered with long hair. *Skull* is moderately broad and slightly domed. The forehead furrow and occiput are palpable. The stop has a pronounced indentation, but never as pronounced as a round-skull breed. *Faults:* A round head, apple shaped head. The ratio of muzzle to skull is 1:1. A little shorter muzzle is acceptable. The topline of the muzzle is straight. *Fault:* Convex or concave muzzles. The jaws are strong. *Teeth* a full compliment of strong white teeth meet in a scissors or level bite. *Nose* should be large and black or brown, depending on the coat color. A pink nose or a nose partially lacking pigment should be penalized.

**Neck, Topline, Body**—*Neck* is muscular and strong. It is broad, without dewlap and held horizontally when moving. *Faults:* Neck held too high or too narrow. The *back* should be neither too long or too short for proper balance and movement. *Withers* are well pronounced and broad. The *chest* is deep and broad. The *topline* is level. The *loin* is well muscled and broad. The *croup* is slightly cut, but only to a small degree. The belly is slightly drawn up. *Tail* should be short, set low and no longer than two vertebrae. It should not change the shape of the body. Tails are docked on puppies born with long or partial tails.

**Forequarters**—The *shoulders* are heavily muscled, and well laid back at an angle of approximately 45°. A line drawn from the highest point of the shoulder blade to the forward point of articulation approximates a right angle with a line from the forward point of articulation to the point of the elbow. The *legs* are straight and vertical, with heavy bone. The *pasterns* are flexible without weakness. The *feet* are oval, thick and compact, with the front feet larger than the rear feet.

**Hindquarters**—Large, heavily boned, and well muscled. Hocks are parallel when viewed from the rear. *Fault:* Cowhocks. *Feet* are oval with tight arched toes. Pads are hard. Nails are dark.

**Coat**—It is doubled coated. The entire body is covered with a long, dense, shaggy, thick coat that is reasonably straight. The undercoat is soft and dense. Characteristically, long hanging hair covers the eyes. A slight wavy coat is acceptable. *Faults:* A curly coat, lack of undercoat and short coats. The Polish Lowland Sheepdog must be shown naturally—no scissoring is allowed.

**Color**—All coat colors are acceptable. The most common colors are white with either black, gray or sandy patches and gray with white, or chocolate. Most carry a dominant fading factor genetically, which results in puppies being born darker in coat color than they will appear as adults, with the exception of those puppies born white.

**Gait**—The gait is fluid motion. He is often an ambler. With the correct shoulder angulation, he is capable of swinging his front legs forward with great reach of stride, extending out before his body in a long flat arch. The stride propels the body forward, rather than upward, with less fatigue. When viewed from the front, the legs should move parallel from the elbows to the pasterns. Toeing in is considered natural. *Fault:* Toeing out. The greatest source of his forward drive is derived from good rear angulation. When viewed from behind, the back legs should be parallel to each other and not too close. *Fault:* Close rear movement.

**Temperament**—He is stable and self confident. He needs a dominant master and consistent training from the time he is very young. If this is not provided, he will tend to dominate the master. When not used as a herding or working dog, he can be a magnificent companion as he seems to fit into any type of lifestyle. He is extremely loyal, but somewhat aloof and suspicious of strangers. *Faults:* Nervous, cowardly, or extreme vicious behavior.

**Approved January 11, 1999**
**Effective July 1, 1999**

# PULI

*Brushed coat*

*Corded coat*

$\mathcal{T}$HE PULI (*POO LEE,* THE PLURAL IS PULIK), OR DROVER, HAS BEEN AN INTE-gral part of the lives of Hungarian shepherds for more than 1,000 years. For many years, accepted wisdom was that Pulik migrated with the Magyars as they crossed into Hungary from Asia and India. Some now believe, though, that the Puli originated with the Cuman people in western China, near Tibet. Many have noticed a striking resemblance between the Puli and the Tibetan Terrier. It is possible that early dogs of the two breeds share some common root stock.

Nomadic shepherds on the Hungarian plains valued their herding dogs, paying as much as a year's income for a Puli. Hungarian shepherds used the Puli as a drover to move the flock over many miles into the plains and as a herder for large flocks of several hundred sheep. Shepherds were ruthless in maintaining their dogs' working abilities and would eliminate dogs that did not show these qualities. To survive, the Puli had to be physically sound, mentally capable, agile, and willing to work.

Appearance and performance could not be divided. Indeed, the Puli coat is unique. A corded coat protected the Puli against the brutal winter frost and provided insulation against the summer heat when working on the open plains of the Hungarian Puszta. The undercoat is soft, woolly, and dense, the outer coat long and profuse. The puppy coat is tufted, but as it grows the outer and under coats tangle, first forming clumps and then cords.

Color also played a role in the development of Hungary's sheepdogs. The small, dark-colored Puli often worked in tandem with the large, white Komondor, which was easily seen at night while protecting the flock from wild animals and robbers. In contrast, the Puli's dark color was effective because sheep take direction more readily from darker-colored dogs. Moreover, the dark Puli was distinctive to the shepherd's eye as the dog worked the flock, rounding them up, even jumping on the sheep or running over their backs to cut off or turn back a runaway. The Puli has truly earned the distinction as the acrobat of the dog world.

The black color of the Puli is unlike that of any other breed. It is dull: in some cases rusty tinged, in others gray as a weatherworn old coat faded by the sun. The coat of a black dog who worked outdoors in all weather is robbed of its intensity and sheen by the glaring sun. Pulik are also found in gray and white, and any shade of gray is allowed as long as it is solid gray. The Puli must always be a solid-colored dog.

Turkish invaders decimated Hungary during the sixteenth century. Subsequently, herdsmen from Western Europe, looking for greener pastures, repopulated the country. The introduction of French and German sheepherding dogs resulted in interbreeding. Two Hungarian herding breeds, the Pumi and the Mudi, emerged. By the late 1800s, the names Pumi and Puli were used almost interchangeably, although the breeds each maintained several distinct characteristics. In 1912, Dr. Emil Raitsits began a program to revive the Puli breed, fearing it would become extinct during the rapid modernization of agriculture. The first Puli standard was written in 1915 and was approved by the Fédération Cynologique Internationale in 1924. In an effort to popularize the breed in the 1930s, the standard included the large police Puli (19 inches), the working or medium Puli (16 to 19 inches), the small Puli (12 to 16 inches), and the dwarf or toy Puli (11 inches). Time revealed that the breed was not popular enough to warrant so many varieties, and only the medium size was retained.

Pulik were first imported to the United States in 1935 for a USDA project to evaluate sheepherding dogs. The Puli excelled in tests for intelligence. The breed was accepted for AKC registration in 1936, and the Puli Club of America was formed in 1951. The current AKC Puli standard describes a medium-sized dog averaging sixteen to seventeen inches in height, with so striking an appearance that it would be impossible to confuse it with any other breed. The Puli's shaggy, corded coat covers the head like an umbrella and forms a profuse cover for the body, right down to the tip of the tail. Pulik may also be kept in a brushed coat, which demands frequent grooming to prevent cords from forming naturally.

Today's Pulik have adapted well to home or apartment living. They retain the agility, herding instinct, and willingness to work that endeared them to Hungarian shepherds. Pulik are extremely intelligent, deeply loyal dogs, wary of strangers. Quick and keen, when frustrated or excited they can resemble a bouncing ball and bubble with an energy they can scarcely control at times. They are often clowns for their owners, but they are always capable of the dazzling footwork that evoked the admiration of shepherds so long ago.

# OFFICIAL STANDARD FOR THE PULI

**General Appearance**—The Puli is a compact, square appearing, well balanced dog of medium size. He is vigorous, alert and active. Striking and highly characteristic is the shaggy coat which, combined with his light-footed, distinctive movement, has fitted him for the strenuous work of herding flocks on the plains of Hungary. Agility, combined with soundness of mind and body, is of prime importance for the proper fulfillment of this centuries-old task.

**Size, Proportion, Substance**—Ideally, males are 17 inches measured from the withers to the ground; bitches, 16 inches. An inch over or under these measurements is acceptable. The tightly knit body approximates a square measured from withers to ground and point of shoulder to point of buttock. Medium boned.

**Head**—The *head* is of medium size in proportion to the body. The almond shaped *eyes* are deep set, rather large, and dark brown with black or slate gray eye rims. The *ears,* set on somewhat higher than the level of the eyes, are hanging, of medium size, V-shape, and about half the head length. The *skull* slightly domed and medium broad. The *stop* is defined, but not abrupt. The *muzzle* is strong and straight, a third of the head length, and ends in a nose of good size. The *nose* is always black. Flews and gums are black or slate gray. Flews are tight. A full complement of *teeth,* comparatively large, meet in a scissors bite.

**Neck, Topline, Body**—The *neck* is strong, muscular, of medium length and free of throatiness. The *back* is level and strong, of medium length, with croup sloping slightly. The *chest* is moderately broad and deep—the ribs well sprung. The *loin* is short, strong and moderately tucked up. The *tail* is carried over, and blends into the backline.

**Forequarters**—The shoulders are well laid back. Upper arm and scapula are approximately equal in length and form an angle of 90 degrees. The forelegs are straight, strong and medium boned with strong and flexible pasterns. Dewclaws, if any, may be removed. The round, compact *feet* have well arched toes and thick cushioned pads. The Puli stands well up on his pads. The pads and nails are black or slate gray.

**Hindquarters**—The hindquarters are well developed and muscular with well bent stifles, the rear assembly balancing that of the front. The hocks are perpendicular to the ground and well let down. Dewclaws, if any, may be removed. Feet as in front.

**Coat**—The dense, weather resistant coat is profuse on all parts of the body. The outer coat is wavy or curly, but never silky. The undercoat is soft, wooly and dense. The coat clumps together easily, and if allowed to develop naturally, will form cords in the adult. The cords are wooly, varying in shape and thickness, either flat or round, depending on the texture of the coat and the balance of undercoat to outer coat. The Puli may be shown either corded or brushed. It is essential that the proper double coat with correct texture always be apparent. With age the coat can become quite long, even reaching to the ground; however, only enough length to properly evaluate quality and texture is considered necessary so as not to penalize the younger or working specimens.

**Color**—Only the solid colors of rusty black, black, all shades of gray, and white are acceptable; however, on the chest a white spot of not more than 2 inches is permissible. In the black and the gray dogs an intermixture of some gray, black or white hairs is acceptable as long as the overall appearance of a solid color is maintained. The fully pigmented skin has a bluish or gray cast whatever the coat color.

**Gait**—The Puli is typically a lively, acrobatic dog; light, quick, agile and able to change directions instantly. At a collected, or contained trot the gait is distinctive: quick-stepping and animated, not far reaching, yet in no way mincing or stilted. When at a full trot, the Puli covers ground smoothly and efficiently with good reach and drive, the feet naturally tending to converge toward a median line of travel as speed increases. His distinctive movement is essential to the Puli's herding style.

**Temperament**—By nature an affectionate, intelligent and home-loving companion, the Puli is sensibly suspicious and therefore an excellent watchdog. Extreme timidity or shyness are *serious faults.*

**Faults**—Any deviation from the foregoing should be considered a fault, the seriousness of the fault depending upon the extent of the deviation.

**Approved February 12, 1983**
**Reformatted June 19, 1990**

# SHETLAND SHEEPDOG

*T*HE SHETLAND SHEEPDOG, AS ITS NAME IMPLIES, IS A WORKING COLLIE IN miniature. There is little doubt that the small working Collie, from which came the modern show Collie evolving on larger lines, was likewise the progenitor of the Shetland Sheepdog evolving on smaller ones. It was assisted in the process by the environment of the Shetland Islands, which produced diminutiveness in all its stock, and by crosses with other breeds residing in, if not indigenous to, the islands.

The Shetland Islands themselves are not conducive to abundance of fodder or flock, made up as they are of rugged rocks on which only meager vegetation can survive and surrounded by the sea, which brews frequent and severe storms. Small wonder that only the hardiest of both man and beast, and the smaller, could find subsistence. The actual origin of the breed cannot be traced by reference to records, as none were ever written. Tradition makes the dogs as old as the working Collies of Scotland, which frequently came to Shetland as the breed's forebears, and as old as the islands themselves.

As the islands were isolated from the trend of travel, the little dogs were a long time coming to the ken of dog-loving folk. Thus the breed did not take its place on the show bench until well along in the present century. The year 1909 marked the initial recognition of the Sheltie by The Kennel Club (England). Not until 1914 did the breed obtain separate classification as Shetland Sheepdogs, not Shetland Collies, because of pressure brought to bear by the Collie breeders. The first Challenge Certificate was awarded to the breed in 1915, after which World War I put a stop to all progress for the next few years.

The first Shetland Sheepdog registered by the American Kennel Club, in 1911, was Lord Scott, imported from Shetland by John G. Sherman Jr. of New York. The American Shetland Sheepdog Association, parent club of the breed, was organized at the Westminster Kennel Club show in 1929, and held its first specialty show in 1933.

The history of the several clubs catering to the breed reflects the struggle of breeders to fix and perpetuate the proper type and size. The Shetland Sheepdog Club in the Shetland Islands, founded in 1908, is, of course, the oldest. They asked for a rough Collie in miniature, height not exceeding 15 inches. The Scottish Shetland Sheepdog Club, a year later, asked for first an "ordinary Collie in miniature" and finally a "modern show Collie in miniature," ideal height 12 inches, and eventually 13½ inches. The English Shetland Sheepdog Club, founded in 1914, was an offshoot of the Scottish, requiring "approximately a show Collie in miniature," height (ideal) first 12 inches and finally from 12 to 15, the ideal being 13½ inches. The British Breeders' Association came into being for a time as the offspring of the English Club and asked for a "show Collie in miniature," maintaining the same heights. In 1930 the Scottish and English Clubs revised their standards jointly to read "should resemble a Collie (Rough) in miniature." The American Shetland Sheepdog Association, youngest in years, tried to profit by the experience of its predecessors by combining the best of each in its standard.

On the subject of size, the current American standard specifies that the Shetland Sheepdog should stand between 13 and 16 inches at the shoulder. Importantly, it calls for disqualification for heights above or below this range.

The breed characteristics common to all Shelties can be used for two purposes pertaining to their working propensities or their companionship qualities. It is their nature to obey, willingly and naturally, with few or no lessons needed, an instinct coming no doubt from the many generations of obediently trained dogs behind them. This responsiveness has helped to make them one of the most successful of all breeds in obedience competition and a dominating presence on the agility course. The instinct to guard property or places and to give watchdog warning makes them invaluable for work as farm helpers or home protectors, a heritage of the constant vigilance required to protect the crofters' cottages, flocks, and herds from invaders of all kinds. Their ability to run swiftly and gracefully, and jump with agility over obstacles, makes them a delight in fields and woods as well as in farmwork. But what most endears them to everybody is their devoted, docile natures and their keen and all but human intelligence and understanding.

# OFFICIAL STANDARD FOR THE SHETLAND SHEEPDOG

**General Appearance**—*Preamble*—The Shetland Sheepdog, like the Collie, traces to the Border Collie of Scotland, which, transported to the Shetland Islands and crossed with small, intelligent, longhaired breeds, was reduced to miniature proportions. Subsequently crosses were made from time to time with Collies. This breed now bears the same relationship in size and general appearance to the Rough Collie as the Shetland Pony does to some of the larger breeds of horses. Although the resemblance between the Shetland Sheepdog and the Rough Collie is marked, there are differences which may be noted. The Shetland Sheepdog is a small, alert, rough-coated, longhaired working dog. He must be sound, agile and sturdy. The outline should be so symmetrical that no part appears out of proportion to the whole. Dogs should appear masculine; bitches feminine.

**Size, Proportion, Substance**—The Shetland Sheepdog should stand between 13 and 16 inches at the shoulder. Note: Height is determined by a line perpendicular to the ground from the top of the shoulder blades, the dog standing naturally, with forelegs parallel to line of measurement.

*Disqualifications*—Heights below or above the desired size range are to be disqualified from the show ring.

In overall appearance, the body should appear moderately long as measured from shoulder joint to ischium (rearmost extremity of the pelvic bone), but much of this length is actually due to the proper angulation and breadth of the shoulder and hindquarter, as the back itself should be comparatively short.

**Head**—The *head* should be refined and its shape, when viewed from top or side, should be a long, blunt wedge tapering slightly from ears to nose.

*Expression*—Contours and chiseling of the head, the shape, set and use of ears, the placement, shape and color of the eyes combine to produce expression. Normally the expression should be alert, gentle, intelligent and questioning. Toward strangers the eyes should show watchfulness and reserve, but no fear.

*Eyes* medium size with dark, almond-shaped rims, set somewhat obliquely in skull. Color must be dark, with blue or merle eyes permissible in blue merles only. *Faults*—Light, round, large or too small. Prominent haws. *Ears* small and flexible, placed high, carried three-fourths erect, with tips breaking forward. When in repose the ears fold lengthwise and are thrown back into the frill. *Faults*—Set too low. Hound, prick, bat, twisted ears. Leather too thick or too thin.

*Skull and Muzzle*—Top of skull should be flat, showing no prominence at nuchal crest (the top of the occiput). Cheeks should be flat and should merge smoothly into a well-rounded muzzle. Skull and muzzle should be of equal length, balance point being inner corner of eye. In profile the topline of skull should parallel the topline of muzzle, but on a higher plane due to the presence of a slight but definite stop. Jaws clean and powerful. The deep, well-developed underjaw, rounded at chin, should extend to base of nostril. *Nose* must be black. *Lips* tight. Upper and lower lips must meet and fit smoothly together all the way around. Teeth level and evenly spaced. Scissors *bite*.

*Faults*—Two-angled head. Too prominent stop, or no stop. Overfill below, between, or above eyes. Prominent nuchal crest. Domed skull. Prominent cheekbones.

Snipy muzzle. Short, receding, or shallow underjaw, lacking breadth and depth. Overshot or undershot, missing or crooked teeth. Teeth visible when mouth is closed.

**Neck, Topline, Body**—*Neck* should be muscular, arched, and of sufficient length to carry the head proudly. *Faults*—Too short and thick.

*Back* should be level and strongly muscled. *Chest* should be deep, the brisket reaching to point of elbow. The ribs should be well sprung, but flattened at their lower half to allow free play of the foreleg and shoulder. Abdomen moderately tucked up. *Faults*— Back too long, too short, swayed or roached. Barrel ribs. Slab-side. Chest narrow and/or too shallow. There should be a slight arch at the loins, and the *croup* should slope gradually to the rear. The hipbone (pelvis) should be set at a 30-degree angle to the spine. *Faults*—Croup higher than withers. Croup too straight or too steep.

The *tail* should be sufficiently long so that when it is laid along the back edge of the hind legs the last vertebra will reach the hock joint. Carriage of tail at rest is straight down or in a slight upward curve. When the dog is alert the tail is normally lifted, but it should not be curved forward over the back. *Faults*—Too short. Twisted at end.

**Forequarters**—From the withers, the shoulder blades should slope at a 45-degree angle forward and downward to the shoulder joints. At the withers they are separated only by the vertebra, but they must slope outward sufficiently to accommodate the desired spring of rib. The upper arm should join the shoulder blade at as nearly as possible a right angle. Elbow joint should be equidistant from the ground and from the withers. Forelegs straight viewed from all angles, muscular and clean, and of strong bone. Pasterns very strong, sinewy and flexible. Dewclaws may be removed. *Faults*— Insufficient angulation between shoulder and upper arm. Upper arm too short. Lack of outward slope of shoulders. Loose shoulders. Turning in or out of elbows. Crooked legs. Light bone.

*Feet* should be oval and compact with the toes well arched and fitting tightly together. Pads deep and tough, nails hard and strong. *Faults*—Feet turning in or out. Splay feet. Hare feet. Cat feet.

**Hindquarters**—The thigh should be broad and muscular. The thighbone should be set into the pelvis at a right angle corresponding to the angle of the shoulder blade and upper arm. Stifle bones join the thighbone and should be distinctly angled at the stifle joint. The overall length of the stifle should at least equal the length of the thighbone, and preferably should slightly exceed it. Hock joint should be clean-cut, angular, sinewy, with good bone and strong ligamentation. The hock (metatarsus) should be short and straight viewed from all angles. Dewclaws should be removed. *Faults*— Narrow thighs. Cow-hocks. Hocks turning out. Poorly defined hock joint.

*Feet* as in forequarters.

**Coat**—The coat should be double, the outer coat consisting of long, straight, harsh hair; the undercoat short, furry, and so dense as to give the entire coat its "stand-off" quality. The hair on face, tips of ears and feet should be smooth. Mane and frill should be abundant, and particularly impressive in males. The forelegs well feathered, the hind legs heavily so, but smooth below the hock joint. Hair on tail profuse. *Note:* Excess hair on ears, feet, and on hocks may be trimmed for the show ring. *Faults*—Coat short or flat, in whole or in part; wavy, curly, soft or silky. Lack of undercoat. Smooth-coated specimens.

**Color**—Black, blue merle, and sable (ranging from golden through mahogany); marked with varying amounts of white and/or tan. *Faults*—Rustiness in a black or a blue coat. Washed-out or degenerate colors, such as pale sable and faded blue. Self-color in the case of blue merle, that is, without any merling or mottling and generally appearing as a faded or dilute tri-color. Conspicuous white body spots. Specimens with more than 50 percent white shall be so severely penalized as to effectively eliminate them from competition. *Disqualification*—Brindle.

**Gait**—The trotting gait of the Shetland Sheepdog should denote effortless speed and smoothness. There should be no jerkiness, nor stiff, stilted, up-and-down movement. The drive should be from the rear, true and straight, dependent upon correct angulation, musculation, and ligamentation of the entire hindquarter, thus allowing the dog to reach well under his body with his hind foot and propel himself forward. Reach of stride of the foreleg is dependent upon correct angulation, musculation and ligamentation of the forequarters, together with correct width of chest and construction of rib cage. The foot should be lifted only enough to clear the ground as the leg swings forward. Viewed from the front, both forelegs and hindlegs should move forward almost perpendicular to ground at the walk, slanting a little inward at a slow trot, until at a swift trot the feet are brought so far inward toward center line of body that the tracks left show two parallel lines of footprints actually touching a center line at their inner edges. *There should be no crossing of the feet nor throwing of the weight from side to side.*

*Faults*—Stiff, short steps, with a choppy, jerky movement. Mincing steps, with a hopping up and down, or a balancing of weight from side to side (often erroneously admired as a "dancing gait" but permissible in young puppies). Lifting of front feet in hackney-like action, resulting in loss of speed and energy. Pacing gait.

**Temperament**—The Shetland Sheepdog is intensely loyal, affectionate, and responsive to his owner. However, he may be reserved toward strangers but not to the point of showing fear or cringing in the ring. *Faults*—Shyness, timidity or nervousness. Stubbornness, snappiness or ill temper.

## Scale of Points

| General Appearance | | | Forequarters | | |
|---|---|---|---|---|---|
| Symmetry | 10 | | Shoulder | 10 | |
| Temperament | 10 | | Forelegs and feet | 5 | 15 |
| Coat | 5 | 25 | Hindquarters | | |
| *Head* | | | Hip, thigh and stifle | 10 | |
| Skull and stop | 5 | | Hocks and feet | 5 | 15 |
| Muzzle | 5 | | *Gait* | | |
| Eyes, ears and expression | 10 | 20 | Gait—smoothness and | | |
| *Body* | | | lack of wasted motion | | |
| Neck and back | 5 | | when trotting | 5 | <u>5</u> |

| | | |
|---|---|---|
| Chest, ribs and brisket | 10 | |
| Loin, croup and tail | 5 | 20 |

**TOTAL   100**

## DISQUALIFICATIONS

*Heights below or above the desired size range, i.e., 13–16 inches. Brindle color.*

**Approved May 12, 1959**
**Reformatted July 18, 1990**

# THE MISCELLANEOUS CLASS

*T*HERE ARE SEVERAL HUNDRED DISTINCT BREEDS OF PUREBRED DOG. Those officially recognized for registration in the Stud Book of the American Kennel Club are presented in the body of this book. The AKC, however, provides for a regular path of development for a new breed, which may result in that breed's full recognition.

Briefly stated, the requirement for admission to the Stud Book is clear and categorical proof that a substantial, sustained nationwide interest and activity in the breed exists. This includes an active parent club, with serious and expanding breeding activity over a wide geographic area.

When, in the judgment of the AKC Board of Directors, such interest and activity exists, a breed is admitted to the Miscellaneous class. Breeds in the Miscellaneous class may compete in AKC obedience trials and earn obedience titles. They may also compete at conformation shows, but here they are limited to competition in the Miscellaneous class and are not eligible for championship points.

When the Board of Directors is satisfied that a breed is continuing a healthy, dynamic growth in the Miscellaneous class, it may be admitted to registration in the Stud Book and compete in regular classes.

Currently, the breeds in the Miscellaneous class are:

BEAUCERON

PLOTT

REDBONE COONHOUND

SWEDISH VALLHUND

TIBETAN MASTIFF

# BEAUCERON

$\mathcal{T}$HE BEAUCERON, ALSO KNOWN AS BERGER DE BEAUCE AND BAS ROUGE, IS the largest of the French sheepdogs and was developed solely in France, with no foreign crosses. The Beauceron is closely related to the longhaired Briard, or Berger de Brie.

In the early nineteenth century, large flocks of sheep were common and the Beauceron was indispensable to the shepherds of France; two dogs were sufficient to tend flocks of two to three hundred sheep.

Sheep production experienced a sharp decline during the latter 1800s and by the mid-twentieth century was only a phantom of its past. With the decline in sheep raising and advent of corralling rather than moving them to graze, sheepdogs became for the most part obsolete.

In an effort to preserve the breed, the French breed club for the Beauceron, Club Les Amis du Beauceron, promoted the breed in other fields, specifically in the area of protection of home and family. The breed served valiantly during both world wars as messenger and mine-detection dogs and experienced a significant increase in popularity after World War II.

Today, the breed is still utilized as a herding dog, working both sheep and cattle, but is also used as a personal-protection dog; for tracking, police, and military service; and in search-and-rescue work. Obedience enthusiasts in Europe and in the United States, looking for a true athlete with agility, a steady disposition, and an uncanny ability to focus on the task at hand have successfully turned to the Beauceron as a competition partner.

The Beauceron is a working dog of substance, active and serious, with exceptional endurance and keen intelligence and obedience. Loyal and strongly devoted to his master, he is also a faithful family companion. Since the Beauceron has a well-developed guarding instinct and is naturally distrusting of strangers, he lends himself well as a protector of house and home. His build, bearing, and frank and unwavering expression demand respect wherever he goes.

Although easily trainable and obedient, the Beauceron is not a dog for novice owners. These dogs have strong personalities and, coupled with a strong need for both physical and mental outlets, this breed more often than not requires an experienced, dedicated, and active owner. Dogs lacking stimulation become difficult to live with and destructive. The decision to add a Beauceron to one's household should be a well-contemplated one, and though puppies are not readily available, it is advisable to remain patient when selecting a breeder and puppy.

The first mention of a dog that matches the Beauceron's description is found in a manuscript dated 1587. In 1809, Abbé Rozier wrote an article on French herding dogs. It was he who first described the differences in type and used the terms *Berger de la Brie* for long-coated dogs and *Berger de la Beauce* for short-coated dogs. The name Beauceron was used for the first time in 1888, and the first Berger de Beauce was registered with the Société Central Canine in September 1893.

Today's Beaucerons bear little physical resemblance to the dogs of the late 1800s. The Beauceron of yesteryear was more petite in its build, with a shorter, hard, and close-lying outer coat. Next to black and rust and harlequins, a variety of coat colors existed, such as reds. Today's standard recognizes only black-and-tan and harlequin as coat colors. Although the breed has added substance to its build, it remains a natural athlete, without bulk or heaviness, moving effortlessly and with a noble carriage.

The French novelist Colette was a devotee of the breed and labeled the Beauceron the "country gentleman." She described them as affectionate, playful, superb with children, absolutely and deeply attached to their masters. But at the same time, there is something mysterious about a Beauceron. They are like some people who don't talk much but have a strong presence. They have a dimension, a depth, rarely found in other dogs. This is the essence of the Beauceron, then and now.

# OFFICIAL STANDARD FOR THE BEAUCERON

**General Appearance**—The Beauceron is a distinct French breed of herding dog. Though almost unknown outside of France, the Beauceron has a long history. It is a very old breed developed solely in France with no foreign crosses. The earliest record found so far of what is thought to be this breed dates back to a Renaissance manuscript of 1578. In 1809, the Abbé Rozier reported plain dogs guarding flocks and herds. In 1863, Pierre Megnin differentiated, with precision, two types of these sheepdogs: one with a long coat, which became known as the Berger de Brie (Briard), the other with a short coat, which is known as the Berger de Beauce (Beauceron). The Beauceron is a well balanced, solid dog of good height and well muscled without heaviness or coarseness. The dog is alert and energetic with a noble carriage. The whole conformation gives the impression of depth and solidity without bulkiness, exhibiting the strength, endurance and agility required of the herding dog. Dogs are characteristically larger throughout with large frame and heavier bone than bitches. Bitches are distinctly feminine, but without weakness of substance or structure. The Beauceron should be easily approached without showing signs of fear.

**Size, Proportion, Substance**—*Size:* males 25½ to 27½ inches; bitches 24 to 26½ inches, measurement to be taken at the highest point of the shoulder blades. *Disqualification:* Height outside of maximum or minimum limits. *Proportion:* The conformation of the Beauceron is that of a mid-line, that is, harmoniously built with none of its regions exaggerated in shortness or length. The length of body, measured from the point of the shoulder to the point of the buttock, is slightly greater than the height at the highest point of the shoulder blade. Correct proportion is of primary importance, as long as size is within the standard's range.

**Head**—*Long* (⅖ of the dog's height at the highest point of the shoulder blade). The head must be proportionate to the body. Well-chiseled head with harmonious lines. *Skull:* the width of the head, as measured across the skull, is slightly less than the length of the skull from the occiput to the stop. The occiput is prominent and the forehead is very slightly rounded. The skull of the Beauceron viewed from the side or from above should form a rectangle, slightly longer than it is wide. The occiput is prominent. The back of the skull should not drop off and the forehead is very slightly rounded. *Nose:* not hooked, but nonetheless slightly curved (convex) toward the end. The nose in relation to the muzzle must be neither too narrow nor too large, nevertheless well developed; always black with nostrils well opened. View in profile, the nose must be in line with the extension of the upper lip. *Disqualification:* any color other than black. *Planes:* the topline of the muzzle is parallel to the topline of the skull, and the junction of the two forms a well-marked stop, which is midway between the occiput and the tip of the nose, and on a level with the eyes. *Muzzle:* Neither narrow nor pointed; lips lie close to jaws, dry, without folds or flews at the corners. *Lips:* well pigmented. Jaws full and powerful well filled under the eyes. *Teeth:* Strong, well-developed, white. The teeth of the upper jaw covering the teeth of the lower jaw without ever losing contact. The Beauceron should have a full complement of teeth, meeting perfectly in a scissors bite. *Fault:* 1 or 2 missing teeth. *Serious Fault:* 3 missing teeth. *Disqualification:* 4 or more missing teeth; Overshot or Undershot mouths with loss of contact. *Eyes:* Horizontal (the head being held horizontally). The eyes set well apart with the inner corners and outer corners on the same level. Large, slightly oval, well opened and calm, they must never be narrow or slanted. The eyes must always be dark brown, never lighter than dark hazel even if the accents are light tan with very dark pigmentation of the rim of the eyelids, whatever the color of the coat. *Disqualification:* yellow eyes or spotted eyes.

*Expression:* Frank, Confident. *Ears:* Should be attached high, with thick ear leather. The Beauceron ear is usually cropped; however, a natural ear is acceptable. No preference should be given to the natural or cropped ear. If cropped, they should stand straight. The cropped ear should be carried upright and parallel, emphasizing the parallel lines of the head; when alert, they should face forward, well open. The well-held ear is one in which the middle passes through an imaginary line prolonging the sides of the neck. The natural ear must not lie flat against the head and, when alert, the ears are lifted slightly, giving a square look to the top of the skull. The length of the natural ear must be equal to the length of the head always straight and covered with short hair.

**Neck, Topline, Body**—*Neck:* neck muscled and smoothly blended into the bodyline, enabling the head to be carried proudly while standing at attention. *Topline:* straight back; strong, never swayed nor roached. *Body:* The length of the body from the point of the shoulder to the point of the buttock must be slightly more than the height of the dog. *Chest,* wide and deep; Sternum descending to the point of the elbow; top of shoulder blade well defined, wide and well fused to the rest of the body; rib cage extended well back; croup with little sloping and only in the direction of the attachment to the tail. The abdomen is moderately drawn up but still presents good volume. *Tail:* never docked; carried down and not deviating to the right or left; descending at least to the point of the hock, without curvation, forming a slight J-hook. In action, the tail is raised in a harmonious curve, never going above the level of the back, except for the terminal crook. *Disqualification:* Tail lacking or docked.

**Forequarters**—*Shoulder:* Medium length, sloping, forming a 45-degree angle with the horizontal, firmly attached by strong muscles and blending smoothly with the withers; *Legs:* The legs are powerfully muscled with strong bone. The legs are vertical when viewed from the side and from the front. The distance between the front legs equal to the distance between the rear legs. The construction of the legs is of the utmost importance, determining the dog's ability to work and his resistance to fatigue. *Feet:* Strong, round, nails always black; pads firm but still supple. The feet travel straightforward in the line of movement. Some dogs may have multiple dewclaws on the front legs.

**Hindquarters**—The angulation of the hindquarters is to be in balance with the forequarters. The hindquarters are powerful, providing flexible, almost tireless movement. The pelvis slopes at a 30-degree angle from the horizontal and forms a right angle with the upper leg bone. *Leg:* The legs are well angulated with metatarsus slightly inclined, the hock making an angle of 135 degrees. *Feet:* if the rear toes turn out very slightly when the hocks and metatarsus are parallel, then the position of the feet is correct. *Dewclaws:* Double dewclaw on the rear leg; dewclaws placed on the inside, forming "thumbs" well separated one from the other ideally; close to the foot to create a larger weight-bearing surface. *Faults:* Double dewclaw placed too high on the leg or represented by two superimposed stumps; *Disqualification:* Anything less than double dewclaws on each rear leg.

**Coat**—Outer coat is straight, coarse, and dense, of medium length and lying flat, never soft and fine to the touch. The coat should be comparatively short, straight, hard enough to be weather resistant, with dense undercoat. It should be shortest on the head, ears and lower legs. The hair is somewhat longer around the neck, tail and back of thighs where "fringe" will be present. The Beauceron is to be exhibited in the natural condition with no trimming. *Fault:* Wavy coat; *Severely Penalize:* Long Hair, Coat Open or Curly.

**Colors**—Black and Tan (BICOLOR): Red feet (stockings); the black being very pure; the color of the tan must be (squirrel red); the tan marks are found: lozenges over the eyes; on the sides of the muzzle, lessening on the cheeks, never reaching the underside of the ears; two spots on the chest are preferred to a breastplate; on the throat; under the tail; on the legs, the tan extends to the feet, to the pasterns, progressively lessening in ascending, though never covering more than ⅓ of the leg; ascending a little higher on the inside of the leg; some white hairs at the breast are tolerated.

Black, Gray and Tan (TRICOLOR): A color pattern involving Blue/Gray splotches on a Black Background with red points, including stockings as described in the BiColor. *Disqualification:* absence of markings; white spot on the chest exceeding 1″ in diameter in Bi-Color or Tri-Color; In Tri-Color the gray should not exceed half the background color (black).

**Gait**—Movement should be fluid, effortless and covering ground in long strides, permitting him to make abrupt turns, springing starts, and sudden stops required of the sheep herding dog. The gait gives the impression that the dog glides along without touching the ground. Strong, flexible movement is essential to the sheepdog. His conformation harmoniously balanced and strong to sustain him in the long day's work. In movement the head should lower approaching the level of the topline like any other herding breed. Dogs with clumsy or inelegant gait must be penalized.

**Temperament**—He is a dog at heart, with spirit and initiative, wise and fearless with no trace of timidity. Intelligent, easily trained, faithful, gentle and obedient, the Beauceron possesses an excellent memory and an ardent desire to please his master. He retains a high degree of his ancestral instinct to guard home and master. Although he is reserved with strangers, he is loving and loyal to those he knows. Some will display a certain independence.

## DISQUALIFICATIONS

*Height outside of maximum or minimum limits.*
*Nose any color other than black.*
*4 or more missing teeth.*
*Overshot or Undershot mouths with loss of contact.*
*Yellow eyes or spotted eyes.*
*Tail lacking or docked.*
*Anything less than double dewclaws on each rear leg.*
*Absence of markings.*
*White spot on the chest exceeding 1″ in diameter in Bi-Color or Tri-Color.*
*In Tri-Color the gray should not exceed half the background color (black).*

**Approved June 11, 2001**
**Effective September 1, 2001**

# PLOTT

*T*HE PLOTT HOUND, OR SIMPLY THE PLOTT, IS UNIQUE AMONG COON-hounds. Unlike other such breeds and varieties, the Plott is not descended from imported English foxhounds but rather from Germanic stock, notably the Hannoverischer Schweisshund (Hanover Hound).

The breed's history begins in 1750, when sixteen-year-old German immigrant Johannes Plott landed in Philadelphia, finally settling in North Carolina with five German-bred brindle- and buckskin-colored hunting dogs he brought from the Old World. In what is now the county of Cabarrus (formerly a part of Mecklenburg County), Plott hunted his dogs on bear, deer, and smaller game. But it was the son of Johannes, Henry, who is the true founder of the family's eponymous breed. Breed historian John R. Jackson, of Boone, North Carolina, describes Henry Plott's contribution to the breed:

> In the mountainous western section of North Carolina lay the frontier, then a virtual game-laden paradise. Deer hides, especially, and other animal pelts could be harvested in great quantity. It was here to this wilderness area (now Haywood County) that Henry Plott settled and concentrated his efforts in establishing a highly successful big-game dog, a dog especially adept at hunting bears. Exactly what Plott integrated with his father's original stock is

unknown. Be that as it may, however, breedings were carefully maintained, accounting for the best trackers, fighters, and tree dogs available.

Henry Plott's pack possessed an unparalleled ability to run, fight, and tree bears and mountain lions, as well as bay wild boar. Since Henry's time, many small-game hunters have utilized the Plott's courage and versatility to trail and tree raccoons and bobcats.

By the time in the mid-nineteenth century when Henry Plott bequeathed his pack to his sons, John, Amos, Enos, and David, the Plott was already a widely known hunting breed in the region and something of a local legend, figuring prominently in the folklore and tall tales of western North Carolina. The hound that Henry Plott left to posterity was not only a bold trail-and-tree dog but also a multitalented canine of remarkable native intelligence—the loyal, obedient, and tenacious hunter it remains to this day.

# OFFICIAL STANDARD FOR THE PLOTT

The Plott may have an identification mark on the rump used to identify the dog when out hunting. Such a mark is not to be penalized when evaluating the dog.

**General Appearance**—A hunting hound of striking color that traditionally brings big game to bay or tree, the Plott is intelligent, alert and confident. Noted for stamina, endurance, agility, determination and aggressiveness when hunting, the powerful, well muscled, yet streamlined Plott combines courage with athletic ability.

**Size, Proportion, Substance**—Size—Height—Males—20 to 25 inches at the withers. Females 20 to 23 inches at the withers. Proportion—General conformation and height in proportion. Faults: Extremely leggy or close to the ground. Weight—(in hunting condition) Males—50 to 60 pounds. Females 40 to 55 pounds. Substance—Moderately boned. Strong, yet quick and agile. Faults: Overdone. Carrying too much weight and or too much bone to display speed and dexterity.

**Head**—Head—Carried well up with skin fitting moderately tight. Faults: Folds, dewlap, skin stretched too tightly. Expression—Confident, inquisitive, determined. Fault: Sad expression. Eyes—Brown or hazel, prominent rather than deeply set. Faults: Drooping eyelids, red haw. Ears—Medium length, soft textured, fairly broad, set moderately high to high. Hanging gracefully with the inside part rolling forward toward the muzzle. Ear spread in males—18 to 20 inches. Ear spread in females—17 to 19 inches. When attentive or inquisitive, some Plotts display a semi-erectile power in their ears and lift them enough so a noticeable crease occurs on line with the crown. Disqualification: Length of ear extending beyond the tip of the nose or hanging bloodhound-like, in long, pendulous fashion. Skull—Moderately flat. Rounded at the crown with sufficient width between and above the eyes. Faults: Narrow-headed, square, oval or excessively domed. Muzzle—Moderate length, flews give it a squarish appearance. Faults: Bluntly squared. Pointed. Pigmentation—Eye rims, lips and nose are black. Flews—Black. Fault: Pendulous flews. Bite—Teeth-Scissors. Fault: Overshot or undershot.

**Neck, Topline and Body**—Neck—Medium length and muscular. Clean and free of ponderous dewlap. Fault: Loose, wrinkled or folded skin. Topline—Gently sloping, slightly higher at the withers than at the hips. Fault: Roached. Body—Chest—Deep. Ribs—Deep, moderately wide, well sprung. Back—Well muscled, strong, level. Loin—Slightly arched. Tail—Root is slightly below level of topline. Rather long, carried free, well up, saber like. Moderately heavy in appearance and strongly tapered. Sometimes typified by a slight brush.

**Forequarters**—Shoulders—Clean, muscular and sloping, indicating speed and strength. Elbow—Squarely set. Forelegs—Straight, smooth, well muscled. Pasterns—Strong and erect. Feet—Firm, tight, wellpadded and knuckled, with strong toes. Set directly under the leg. Disqualification—Splayed feet. Nails—Usually black, although shades of reddish brown matching the brindle body color are permissible and buckskin colored dogs have light red nails. May be white when portions of the feet are white.

**Hindquarters**—Angulation—Well bent at stifles and at the hocks. Hips—Smooth, round, and proportionally wide, indicating efficient propulsion. Legs—Long and muscular from hip to hock. From hock to pad short, strong and at right angles to the ground. Upper and second thigh—Powerful and well-muscled. Feet—Set back from under the body. Firm and tight. Toes—Strong.

**Coat**—Smooth, fine, glossy, but thick enough to provide protection from wind and water. Rare specimens are double coated, with a short, soft, thick inner coat concealed by a longer, smoother and stiffer outer coat.

**Color**—Any shade of brindle (a streaked or striped pattern of dark hair imposed on a lighter background) is preferred. This includes the following brindle factors: yellow, buckskin, tan, brown, chocolate, liver, orange, red, light or dark gray, blue or Maltese, dilute black, and black. Other acceptable Plott colors are solid black, any shade of brindle, with black saddle, and black with brindle trim. A rare buckskin, devoid of any brindle, sometimes appears among litters; ranging from red fawn, sandy red, light cream, and yellow ochre, to dark fawn and golden tan. Some white on chest and feet is permissible, as is a graying effect around the jaws and muzzle.

**Gait**—Dexterous and graceful, rhythmic footfall. With ample reach in front and drive behind, the Plott easily traverses various terrains with agility and speed. Legs converge to single track at speed.

**Temperament**—Eager to please, loyal, intelligent, alert. Aggressive, bold, and fearless hunter. Disposition generally even, but varies among strains, with a distinction sometimes appearing between those bred for big game and those bred as coonhounds.

## DISQUALIFICATIONS

*Length of ear extending beyond the tip of the nose or hanging bloodhound-like, in long, pendulous fashion. Splayed feet.*

**Approved June 1998**
**Effective October 1, 1998**

# REDBONE COONHOUND

WHEN COLONISTS CAME TO AMERICA, THE FUR-BEARING ANIMALS THEY found became important sources of food and clothing as well as valuable commodities for trade. Because fur-bearing animals typically seek refuge in trees, survival depended on hunting dogs that followed the animal's scent-trail to the tree and barked until the hunter arrived. Early breeders developed such hunting dogs from foundation stock available in the fairly common foxhound packs imported from England and France. The treeing behavior was fine-tuned and the American coonhound was born. From these beginnings six distinctive breeds evolved, one of the first of which was the Redbone, a descendant of foxhound packs in the Deep South. Other American breeds that developed in similar fashion were the Black and Tan, the Bluetick, the English, the Plott, and the Treeing Walker.

Early efforts at breeding a Southern tree hound for hunting raccoon, opossum, and squirrel were based upon stock from George Birdsong and Thomas Henry in the mid-nineteenth century. The earliest of these hounds were red in color with black saddles, and often with white markings on the feet and brisket. An occasional solid coat of deep red occurred and rapidly became the color of choice. Selective breeding over the decades produced the rich red coloring that became the benchmark of today's Redbone Coonhound.

Early Redbones were fleet of foot and showed extreme endurance—obvious by-products of foxhound influence—and were naturally suited for the competition of early coonhound field trials. Dogs were required to run a scent course with great speed and to locate the scented lure in a tree at course's end. In 1927 a Redbone named Little Sheik won the inaugural Leafy Oaks, a coonhound field trial that endured as the premier event of its type well into the last decade of the century.

With the advent of night trials, known as wild coon hunts in the mid-1950s, a Redbone named Red Bud, born in 1949 at Miamisburg, Ohio, was the first to achieve the title of champion in what has become the signature event in modern coonhound competition. Another notable competitor was the famed Midnight Flyer, born in 1918, whose illustrious field-trial career was ended by an accident before his fourth birthday. Perhaps one of the most famous Redbones of all time, a male named Jungle Jim, was a great-great grandson of Midnight Flyer.

Redbones, perhaps more than other coonhound breeds, have gained popularity as companions as well as hunting dogs. This is largely due to a combination of a natural affection for people, and the national exposure gained from the writings of Wilson Rawls, whose 1961 classic *Where the Red Fern Grows,* the tale of an Oklahoma boy and his coon dogs, features two Redbones, Old Dan and Little Ann. The novel, made into a motion picture in 1974, has become a mainstay of elementary-school teachers wishing to emphasize the love and care that can be shared between a child and a dog.

# OFFICIAL STANDARD FOR THE REDBONE COONHOUND

**General Appearance**—Hunted from swamplands to mountains, the Redbone is surefooted and swift, even on the most difficult terrain. Well-balanced, with a flashy red coat and excellent cold nose, the powerfully built Redbone mingles handsome looks with a confident air and fine hunting talents.

**Size, Proportion, Substance**—Size—Males—22 to 27 inches. Females—21 to 26 inches. Proportion Length well proportioned to height. Should be equal in height from highest point of the shoulder blade to the ground as long measured from sternum to the buttocks. Slightly taller at shoulder than at hips. Substance—Weight should be in proportion with height and bone structure. Working dogs not to be penalized for being slightly underweight. Well boned according to size of dog.

**Head**—Expression—Pleading. Eyes—Dark brown to hazel in color, dark preferred. Set well apart. No drooping eyelids. Eyes round in shape. Faults—Yellow eyes, drooping eyelids. Ears—Set moderately low, fine in texture. Reaching near the end of the nose when stretched out. Proportioned to head. Faults—Stiff to the touch. Appearing to be attached only to the skin, instead of firmly attached to the head. Skull—Moderately broad. Shape is flat. Faults—Narrow across top, excess of dome, pointed dome. Muzzle—Square. Well balanced with other features of the head. Faults—Dished or upturned muzzle. Not in proportion with head. Nose—Nostrils large and open, black in color, never pink. Faults—Any color other than black. Teeth—Scissors bite preferred. Even bite acceptable. Faults—Overshot or undershot.

**Neck, Topline, and Body**—Neck—Medium in length, strong, slightly arched and held erect, denoting proudness. Throat clean. Slight fold of skin below the angle of jaw is permissible. Faults—Too long, too thick, not in proportion with head and body. Topline—slightly taller at the withers than at the hips. Fault—Hips higher than withers. Body—Chest—Deep, broad. Ribs—Well sprung to provide optimal lung capacity, denoting stamina. Back—Strong. Faults—Roach or sway back. Loin—Slightly arched. Tail—Medium length, very slight brush, and saber-like. Faults—Not strong at root, heavy brush, Setter-like plume.

**Forequarters**—Shoulders—Clean and muscular. Shoulder angulation should have a perfect 90-degree angle or close. Legs—Straight, well-boned. The forelegs will be set under dog and feet under his withers, not under ears. Pasterns—Straight, well set, clean and muscular, denoting both speed and strength. Faults—Forelegs crooked, out at elbows. Feet—Cat-paw type, compact, well padded. Toes—Stout, strong and well-arched. Nails—Well-set. Faults—Flat feet, open feet, hind dewclaws.

**Hindquarters**—Thighs—Clean and muscular. Fault—Cowhocked. Hindquarters should have same. Well boned.

**Coat**—Short, smooth, coarse enough to provide protection.

**Color**—Solid red preferred. Dark muzzle and small amount of white on brisket and feet permissible. Faults: White on feet extending beyond toes. More white on brisket than an open hand will cover. White stockings on legs.

**Gait**—Determined, steady, and proud, with good reach and drive.

**Temperament**—Even-tempered at home but an aggressive hunter. Amenable to formal training. A good family dog that likes to please.

**Approved June 11, 2001**
**Effective September 1, 2001**

# SWEDISH VALLHUND

𝒯HE SWEDISH VALLHUND (SV) IS AN ANCIENT SWEDISH SPITZ BREED DATING back over one thousand years to the time of the Vikings, when it may have been known as the "Vikingarnas Dog." For centuries the SV had been kept as a farm dog and used for herding cattle. Historians believe that during the eight or ninth century the Vikings either brought the Swedish Vallhund to the coast of Wales or took the Pembroke Corgi back to Sweden and interbred them, hence the similarities between the two breeds. The historian Clifford Hubbard considered the Swedish Vallhund the older of the two.

By 1942, the breed was almost extinct with only a few still seen working on farms in the province of Västergötland, Sweden. In this year, Bjorn von Rosen, who had worked to save several old Swedish breeds from extinction, remembered the SV from his boyhood and decided to try and save it. He placed an advertisement in the papers regarding these beloved dogs from his childhood. K. G. Zettersten responded to his advertisement. Together, these two dedicated men worked to save the breed. They scoured the country and found a few representative SVs, and thus began a breeding program to revive this old breed which had been common prior to World War I. They started with one male named Mopsen and three females named Vivi, Lessi, and Topsy. According to Nicky Gascoigne in her book, *The Swedish Vallhund*, (Dalsetter Designs, 1989), Mopsen and Lessi produced a dog, Jerry 265OTT; a breeding of Mopsen and Vivi produced a female, Tessan 3999VV; and a breeding of possibly Topsy with Mopsen produced Borgalls Mopsan 7871VV. Together these five Swedish Vallhunds were the foundation of their new breeding program.

In 1943, after a year of exhibition at the shows, the Swedish Kennel Club recognized the breed. At this time, the SV was known as Svensk Vallhund (Swedish Vallhund), where "Vallhund" meant "herding dog." In 1964, with the Swedish standard revised, the breed became known as *Västgötaspets* after the Swedish province Västergötland where the revived breeding program originated.

In 1974, the first SV came to England. In 1980, Ms. Nicky Gascoigne helped organize the Breed Society, and the Kennel Club of the United Kingdom granted Championship Status for the breed in 1985. That same year, Marilyn Thell of Rhode Island, USA, being of Swedish decent, visited England and brought two Swedish Vallhunds home to the United States. The first American SV litter was whelped at Thell's Jonricker Kennel in 1986. In 1987, Mrs. Thell founded the Swedish Vallhund Club of America, first known as the Swedish Vallhund Enthusiasts of America. The Swedish Vallhund is now recognized and found in many countries: Sweden, Britain, Finland, USA, France, Netherlands, Canada, Australia, New Zealand, Ireland, Holland, Denmark, and Switzerland.

This is a breed that exhibits many original canine behaviors such as long cycles between seasons, natural mating, easy births, and good maternal instinct. It is hardy, resistant to disease, patient to hardship, long-lived, and able to find food and take initiatives on its own. The teeth are large for the size of the skull. Moreover, Vallhunds intrinsically have variations in many attributes such as color and size. It is interesting to note that within a given litter, Swedish Vallhund puppies may be born with different tail lengths—from none at all to a full Spitz tail.

The Swedish Vallhund is watchful, energetic, fearless, alert, intelligent, friendly, adaptable, active and steady, thus making a good herding and companion animal. While the SV is easily trained, he requires consistent positive reinforcement and leadership from his owner from an early age. The Swedish Vallhund is neither shy nor vicious. Spirited and athletic, with a ready-for-anything attitude, he is a "big dog in a smaller body." The breed has a wonderful sense of humor, and is often chatty in nature. These dogs do not hesitate to announce strangers or their joy of living. The SV was used as an all purpose farm dog capable of guarding home and family, controlling rodents and herding cattle. They also can herd sheep and other farm animals. The SV successfully participates in obedience, agility, tracking, fly ball, and conformation.

# OFFICIAL STANDARD FOR THE SWEDISH VALLHUND

**General Appearance**—The Swedish Vallhund (SV) is a very old Spitz-type breed known since the time of the Vikings. For centuries the SV has been kept as a farm dog and used for herding cattle. The SV is a small, powerful, fearless, sturdily build Spitz herding dog. The correct relationship of height to length of body is 2:3. The SV has a wedge-shaped head, prick ears, and a close-fitting hard coat of medium length and sable coloring. The double coat and the characteristic "harness markings" are essential features of this breed. Tail may be natural (long, stub, or bob) or docked. The appearance of the Swedish Vallhund conveys intelligence, alertness and energy. Balance, outline, temperament and movement are of overriding importance. The SV is a thoroughly sound animal, versatile in its desire to do traditional herding or with proper training compete in companion events such as obedience, tracking and agility, and/or serve as a family companion.

**Size, Proportion, Substance**—Height—Height at withers for dogs ranges from 12.5–13.5 inches and bitches 11.5–12.5 inches. Minor variations may be seen; however, more important is the proportion. Proportion—The relationship of height to length of body, as measured from prosternum to the rearmost portion of the buttocks, should be 2:3. Substance—Strong, well boned, well developed, neither refined nor coarse, and a solidly built, muscular body.

**Head**—Rather long and clean. Viewed from above, the head forms an even wedge from skull to tip of nose and is well filled-in under the eyes. Eyes—Medium size, oval in shape and dark brown with black eye rims. Ears—Medium size, pointed, prick. Set at the outer edge of the skull above a line drawn from the corner of the eye. Ear leather should be firm from base to tip, smooth-haired and mobile. The dog should make good use of them. Skull—Broad and almost flat. Stop—Well defined. Muzzle—Viewed from the side, the muzzle should look rather square, slightly shorter than the skull. Planes—The top line of the muzzle and skull are parallel with each other. Nose—In profile, the nose is on the same line as the muzzle and does not extend beyond the forepart of the muzzle. Pigmentation—Black. Lips—Black and tight with no noticeable flews. Teeth—Strong, well developed, with full dentition in a scissors bite. Any deviation is a serious fault.

**Neck, Topline and Body**—Neck—Long, strongly muscled with good reach. Topline—Level when standing or moving. Chest—Good depth. The ribcage is long with fairly well sprung ribs. Viewed from the front, the chest should be oval; from the side, elliptical. In a mature dog it should reach down two-fifths of the length of the forelegs and, when viewed from the side, the lowest point of the chest is immediately behind the back part of the foreleg. The prosternum is visible and not excessively pronounced. Underline—Slightly tucked up. Back—Well muscled. Loin—Short and strong. Croup—Broad and slightly sloping. Tails—Tails may be long, stub, or bob. May be shown natural or docked. All tail types are equally acceptable.

**Forequarters**—Shoulders—Strongly muscled. Shoulder blades—Long and well laid back. Upper Arms—Slightly shorter than the shoulder blades, set at an approximate 90 degree angle, close fitting to ribs, but still very mobile. A line perpendicular to the ground can be drawn from the tip of the shoulder blade through the elbow to the ground. Elbows—Move parallel to the body, turning neither in nor out. Forearms—When viewed from the front, slightly curved to give free action against the lower part of the chest; the pasterns and feet are parallel. Viewed from the side the forearms are straight. The height from ground to elbow is almost half the height from ground to withers. Legs—Well boned. Pasterns—Slightly sloping, elastic. Dewclaws—May be removed. Feet—Medium sized, short, oval, pointing straight forward. Toes—Tightly knit and well knuckled. Pads—Thick and strong.

**Hindquarters**—Angulation—To balance the front. Well angulated at stifle and hock. Legs—Well boned. Upper and lower thighs are strongly muscled. Lower thigh is slightly longer than the distance from hock to ground. Stifles—Well bent. Hocks (Metatarsal bones)—Perpendicular to the ground and viewed from the rear, parallel. Feet, toes and pads—Same as forefeet.

**Coat**—Medium length hair; harsh, close and tight. Undercoat is soft and dense. Hair is short on the head and the foreparts of the legs and slightly longer on neck, chest and back parts of the hind legs. Dogs are to be shown in an untrimmed, natural state. Faults include wooly, curly, or open coats. Fluffy coats (longer hair on body and furnishings, with ear fringes) are a serious fault.

**Color**—A sable pattern seen in colors of grey through red and combinations of these colors in various shades. All are equally acceptable. Lighter shades of these colors are desirable on the chest, belly, buttocks, lower legs, feet and hocks, with darker hairs on back, neck and sides of the body. Lighter harness markings are essential. Although a dark muzzle is acceptable, a well-defined mask with lighter hair around eyes, on muzzle and under the throat, giving a distinct contrast to head color is highly desirable. White is permitted as a narrow blaze, neck spot, slight necklace, and white markings on the legs, and chest. White in excess of one third of the dog's total color is a very serious fault. Any color other than described above is a very serious fault.

**Gait**—Sound with strong reach and drive. The Swedish Vallhund is a herding dog requiring agility and endurance. Viewed from the front, the legs do not move in exact parallel planes, but incline slightly inward to compensate for shortness of leg and width of chest. The forelegs should reach forward in a free stride without too much lift. Hind legs should drive well under the body and move on a line with forelegs, with hocks turning neither in nor out. Feet should travel parallel to the line of motion with no tendency to swing out, cross over or interfere with each other. Short, choppy movement and overly close or wide movement is faulty.

**Temperament**—The breed is watchful, energetic, fearless, alert, intelligent, friendly, eager to please, active and steady, making for a good herding and companion dog. Sound temperament, neither vicious or shy.

**Any departure from the foregoing points should be considered a fault, and the seriousness of the fault should be in exact proportion to its degree.**

**The following faults are to be so severely penalized as to effectively eliminate the dog from competition: Fluffy coat, any color other than described above, nose not predominantly black, more than one-third white, any bit other than scissors.**

**Approved October 18, 2004**
**Effective September 1, 2005**

# TIBETAN MASTIFF

*T*HE HISTORY OF THE TIBETAN MASTIFF—THE LARGE GUARDIAN DOG OF Tibet—is hidden in the mists of legend, along with the people of the high Himalayan Mountains and the plains of Central Asia. Accurate records of the genetic heritage of the dogs are nonexistent. Even so, history has reserved a special place for the Tibetan Mastiff. They are considered by many to be the basic stock from which most modern large working breeds, including all mastiffs and mountain dogs, have developed.

Earliest written accounts place a large dog around 1100 B.C. in China. Skulls of large dogs date to the Stone and Bronze ages. Ancestors of today's mastiff breeds are believed to have accompanied the armies of the Assyrians, Persians, Greeks, and Romans and later traveled with Attila the Hun and Genghis Khan into Europe. During these centuries of upheaval, it is believed that the Tibetan Mastiff remained isolated on the high plateaus and valleys of the Himalaya and developed into the magnificent animal so highly prized by the people of Tibet.

Today in Himalayan regions, a pure Tibetan Mastiff is hard to find, though they are still bred by the nomads of the Chang Tang plateau. They are bred and live at an average altitude of 16,000 feet, and some are brought to be sold to the Barkhor, the market that surrounds the Jokhang Temple, the holiest site for Tibetan Buddhists. Although Tibetan Mastiffs are traditionally kept tied to the gates of the house or monastery, or tied to stakes in the nomad camps, they are let loose at night. When the flocks are moved to higher pasture, the Tibetan Mastiffs were traditionally left behind to guard the tents and the children. The dogs were expected to defend the flocks of goats, sheep, and yaks, and the women and the children and the tents of their masters against predators such as wolves and snow leopards, as well as human intruders.

Before the early 1800s, few Westerners were allowed into Tibet and little was known about Tibetan dogs. In accounts of visits to Tibet by early travelers, they rarely mentioned the dogs they encountered. Marco Polo wrote of the dogs in Tibet being as large as donkeys, and Jesuit missionaries of the eighteenth century wrote of the ferocious, huge dogs ("Many of the Thibetan dogs are uncommon and extraordinary. They are black with rather long glossy hair, very big and sturdily built, and their bark is most alarming"—I. Desideri, 1712). In 1800 Captain Samuel Turner, in his *Account of an Embassy to the Court of the Teshoo Lama in Tibet,* recorded an encounter with huge dogs:

> The mansion stood upon the right; on the left was a row of wooden cages, containing a number of huge dogs, tremendously fierce, strong and noisy. They were natives of Tibet; and whether savage by nature, or soured by confinement, they were so impetuously furious, that it was unsafe, unless the keepers were near, even to approach their dens.

In 1847, Lord Hardinge, viceroy of India, sent a "large dog from Tibet" called Siring to Queen Victoria. England had its first dog show in 1859; and in 1873, The Kennel Club (England) was formed, with the first studbook containing pedigrees of 4,027 dogs. In the official classification made by The Kennel Club, the "large dog from Tibet" was designated the Tibetan Mastiff for the first time.

Two more Tibetan Mastiffs were brought into England in 1874 by the then Prince of Wales (later King Edward VII). They were exhibited at the Alexandra Palace Show in December 1875. There was a trickle of imports into England and Europe until 1928, when Colonel and Mrs. Bailey imported four Tibetan Mastiffs obtained while the colonel was a political officer in Sikkim, Nepal, and Tibet. In 1931, Mrs. Bailey formed the Tibetan Breeds Association in England and the first official standard for the breed was adopted by The Kennel Club. It was also the standard adopted by the Fédération Cynologique Internationale.

In the late 1950s, two Tibetan Mastiffs were sent from Tibet to President Eisenhower. They were taken to a farm in the Midwest and nothing more was heard of them. Beginning in 1969, several were imported from Nepal and India into the United States. The American Tibetan Mastiff Association was formed in 1974, with a dog imported from Nepal, Jumla's Kalu of Jumla, as dog number 001. The first American national specialty match was held in connection with the California Rare Breeds Dog Association in October 1979, and the first national specialty show was held in 1983.

The close relationship of the Tibetan Mastiff with man through the centuries has given it an almost uncanny "human" understanding. Generations of working as a guardian of yaks, sheep, and, more important, women and children, requiring them to be always a protector and never a killer, has produced a disposition and temperament of controlled strength, initiative, and fearlessness, tempered with patience, loyalty, and gentleness.

# OFFICIAL STANDARD FOR THE TIBETAN MASTIFF

**General Appearance**—Noble and impressive: a large, powerful, heavy, well built dog, well muscled, with much substance and bone, and of solemn but kindly appearance. The Tibetan Mastiff stands well up on the pasterns, with strong, tight, cat feet, giving an alert appearance. The body is slightly longer than tall. The head is broad and impressive, with massive back skull, the eyes deep-set and almond shaped, slightly slanted, the muzzle broad and well-padded, giving a square appearance. The typical expression of the breed is one of watchfulness. The tail is well feathered and carried over the back in a single curl falling over the loin, balancing the head. The coat and heavy mane are thick, with coarse guard hair and a wooly undercoat. The tail and britches are well feathered.

The Tibetan Mastiff has been used primarily as a family and property guardian for many millennia, and is aloof and watchful of strangers, and highly protective of its people and property.

**Size, Proportion, Substance**—Size: Dogs—minimum of 26 inches at the withers. Bitches—minimum of 24 inches at the withers. Dogs and bitches that are more than one inch below the minimum heights to be severely faulted. Proportion: Slightly longer than tall (9–10), (i.e., the height to length, measured from sternum to ischium should be slightly greater than the distance from withers to ground). Substance: The Tibetan Mastiff should have impressive substance, both in bone and structure, as well as strength. When dogs are judged equal in type, proportion and movement, the more substantial dog, in terms of substance and bone, not merely height, is to be given preference.

**Head**—Broad, heavy and strong. Some wrinkling in maturity, extending from above eyes down to corner of mouth. A correct head and expression is essential to the breed. Expression: Noble, intelligent, watchful and aloof. Eyes: Very expressive, medium size, any shade of brown. Rims to be black except in blue/grey, blue/grey and tan dogs and brown dogs, the darkest possible shade of grey or brown. Eyes deep-set, well apart, almondshaped, and slightly slanting. Any other color or shape to be severely faulted since it detracts from the typical expression. Ears: Medium size, V-shaped, pendant, set-on high, dropping forward and hanging close to head. Raised when alert, on level with the top of the skull. The ear leather is thick, covered with soft short hair, and when measured, should reach the inner corner of the eye. Skull: Broad and large, with strongly defined occiput. Broad back skull. Stop: Deep and well defined. Muzzle: Broad, well filled and square when viewed from all sides. Proportions: Measurement from occiput to stop and stop to end of nose, equal or slightly shorter. Nose: Broad, well pigmented, with open nostrils. Black, except with blue/grey or blue/grey and tan dogs, the darkest shade of grey and brown dogs, the darkest shade of brown. Any other color to be severely faulted. Lips: Well developed, thick, with moderate flews and slightly pendulous lower lips. Bite: Complete scissor bite. Level bite acceptable. Essential that dentition fits tightly, to maintain square form of muzzle. Teeth: Canine teeth large, strong, broken teeth not to be faulted. Faults: Missing teeth, overshot, undershot bite.

**Neck, Topline and Body**—Neck: The neck is well muscled, moderately arched, and may have moderate dewlap. The neck, especially in dogs, is shrouded by a thick upstanding mane. Topline: Topline straight and level between withers and croup. Body: The chest is rather deep, of moderate breadth, with reasonable spring of rib. Brisket reaching to just below elbows. Underline with pronounced (but not exaggerated) tuck-up. The back is muscular with firmly muscled loin. There is no slope or angle to the croup. Tail: Medium to long, but not reaching below hock joint; well feathered. Set high on line with top of back. When alert or in motion, curled over back or to one side. Tails that are double curled or carried in an incomplete curl to be faulted.

**Forequarters**—Shoulders: Well laid back, muscular, strongly boned, with moderate angulation to match the rear angulation. Legs: Straight, with substantial bone and muscle, well covered with short, coarse hair, feathering, and with strong pasterns that have a slight slope. Feet: Cat feet. Fairly large, strong, compact, may have feathering between toes. Nails may be either black and/or white, regardless of coat color. A single dewclaw may be present on the front feet.

**Hindquarters**—Hindquarters: Powerful, muscular, with all parts being moderately angulated. Seen from behind, the hind legs and stifle are parallel. The hocks are strong, well let down (approximately one-third the overall length of the leg), and perpendicular. Feet: A single or double dewclaw may be present on the rear feet. Removal of rear dewclaws, if present, optional.

**Coat**—In general, dogs carry noticeably more coat than bitches. The quality of the coat is of greater importance than quantity. Double-coated, with fairly long, thick coarse guard hair, with heavy soft undercoat in cold weather which becomes rather sparse in warmer months. Hair is fine but hard, straight and stand-off; never silky, curly or wavy. Heavy undercoat, when present, rather woolly. Neck and shoulders heavily coated, especially in dogs, giving mane-like appearance. Tail and breeches densely coated and heavily feathered. The Tibetan Mastiff is shown naturally. Trimming is not acceptable except to provide a clean cut appearance of feet. Dogs are not to be penalized if shown with a summer coat.

**Color**—Black, brown, and blue/grey, all with or without tan markings, and various shades of gold. Tan ranges from a very rich shade through a lighter color. White markings on breast and feet acceptable. Tan markings may appear at any or all of the following areas: above eyes as spots, around eyes (including spectacle markings), on each side of the muzzle, on throat, on lower part of front forelegs and extending up the inside of the forelegs, on inside of rear legs showing down the front of the stifle and broadening out to the front of the rear legs from hock to toes, on breeches, and underside of tail. Undercoat, as well as furnishings on breeches and underside of tail, may be lighter shades of the dominant color. The undercoat on black and tan dogs also may be grey or tan. Other markings such as sabling, brindling, white on other areas of the body, or large white markings, to be faulted. All other coat colors, while accepted, are to be faulted.

**Gait**—The gait of a Tibetan Mastiff is powerful, steady and balanced, yet at the same time, light-footed. When viewed from the side, reach and drive should indicate maximum use of the dog's moderate angulation. Back remains level and firm. Sound and powerful movement more important than speed.

**Temperament**—The Tibetan Mastiff is a highly intelligent, independent, strong willed and rather reserved dog. He is aloof with strangers and highly protective of his charges and his property. In the ring he may exhibit reserve or lack of enthusiasm, but any sign of shyness is unacceptable and must be severely faulted as inappropriate for a guardian breed. Conversely, given its aloof nature, judges should also beware of putting a premium on showiness.

**Approved November 8, 2004**
**Effective January 1, 2005**

# LIVING WITH YOUR DOG

# Joining a Dog Club

*D*OG CLUBS BRING TOGETHER PEOPLE WITH A COMMON INTEREST IN RAISING, training, breeding, and competing with purebred dogs. Clubs are a popular place to socialize and exchange information with seasoned dog show folks.

Newcomers to the sport may be surprised by the number and variety of clubs. All told, nearly 5,000 clubs around the country currently hold AKC-licensed or sanctioned events each year. (The difference between licensed and sanctioned events is that points or *legs* toward a title are only offered at licensed events.) Some clubs, such as specialty clubs or national parent clubs, are devoted to the promotion of a single breed. In contrast, all-breed clubs welcome enthusiasts of every kind of registered purebred dog. Still other clubs are dedicated to the pursuit of a particular dog sport, such as Obedience, Tracking, Field Trials, Hunt Tests, Herding, Lure Coursing, Earthdog, or Agility.

Joining a dog club is a relatively simple process. In most cases, the prospective member needs to obtain two recommendations from current members in good standing. New members must agree to abide by the club's constitution, bylaws, and code of ethics, as well as all AKC rules. The application procedure varies from club to club. To find a club that fits your interest in dogs, you may find a geographical list of clubs at *akc.org*.

Many local all-breed clubs meet monthly. Some offer educational programs on topics such as grooming, breeding, or handling for the show ring. Once or twice each year they put on shows, trials, or AKC-sanctioned matches. Local clubs often participate in community activities to demonstrate responsible dog ownership to the general public. AKC all-breed clubs have Public Education Coordinators who provide educational material, and parent clubs can steer you toward responsible breeders and local specialty clubs in various parts of the country.

Each breed has a national parent club responsible for the important job of drafting and revising the breed standard, the document that describes the ideal dog of their breed. Parent clubs also hold specialty shows (shows at which only one breed is judged) and support the organization of independent specialty clubs throughout the country.

Many clubs offer basic companion-event classes (obedience, tracking, agility, and rally) that welcome nonmembers. They also organize trials where dogs can earn AKC titles. Similarly, field trial clubs hold events at which dogs can compete for prizes and points toward field championships. Field trial clubs may also hold noncompetitive AKC hunting tests to evaluate the pointing breeds, retrievers, and spaniels against written hunting standards under simulated hunting conditions.

Joining a dog club (or joining several) adds an extra dimension to owning any breed. It is highly recommended for anyone seeking deeper involvement in the world of purebred dogs.

# THE SPORT OF DOGS

*T*HOUSANDS OF COMPETITIVE EVENTS ARE HELD ANNUALLY UNDER AMERI-can Kennel Club rules. These events are divided into three realms: dog shows, companion events, and performance events. In each category, there are formal, licensed events (shows or trials at which points are awarded toward championships or titles) and informal events (match shows or practice events at which no points or titles are earned). Dogs can compete for titles, which are then officially recorded in the dog's permanent AKC record.

## DOG SHOWS

The signature event held under AKC rules is the dog show, or conformation event. After being examined by a judge, dogs are placed according to how well (in the judge's opinion) they measure up to their breed standard.

To be eligible to enter, an AKC-registered dog must be at least six months old on the day of the show and be of a breed for which classes are offered in the premium list (the list of breeds being shown, obtained from the show secretary of the club sponsoring the show, or from the show superintendent). Spayed or neutered dogs are ineligible, as are those with disqualifying faults as described in their breed standard.

There are three types of dog shows: specialty, group, and all-breed. Specialty shows are limited to dogs of one breed and group shows are limited to a particular AKC group. All-breed shows, as the name indicates, are for all AKC breeds.

Most show dogs are competing for points toward their championship. To become an official AKC champion of record, a dog must earn a total of 15 points. These points are awarded based on the number of dogs in *actual* competition—the more dogs, the more points. The number of dogs required for points varies with the breed, sex, and geographical location of the show. The AKC makes up a schedule of points each year to help equalize competition from breed to breed and area to area.

Dogs can earn from 1 to 5 points at a show. A win of 3, 4, or 5 points is called a *major.* The 15 points required for a championship must be won under at least three different judges, and must include two majors won under different judges.

There are six regular classes in which dogs seeking points may compete. (Dogs competing for points are frequently referred to as *class dogs.*) These classes are Puppy Dog (frequently subdivided into 6-to-9 Months and 9-to-12 Months); 12-to-18 Months; Novice (dogs that have no points toward their championship and have not won three first prizes in the Novice class or a first prize in any but the Puppy classes); Bred by Exhibitor (the dog must be owned or co-owned by any one of the breeders of record or a spouse and must be shown by one of the breeders or a member of their immediate family); American Bred; and Open.

There is no intersex competition in these classes; dogs compete against other dogs, and bitches against other bitches. Only one male (dog) and one female (bitch) of each breed can win points at a show.

Judging in every breed proceeds along the same lines. The judge begins with the Puppy Dog class. In each class the dogs are evaluated and placements are made for first, second, third, and fourth. Only the first-place winner in each class remains in competition; the others are eliminated.

After the judge has completed the Puppy Dogs, 12-to-18 Month Dogs, Novice Dogs, Bred-by-Exhibitor Dogs, American-Bred Dogs, and Open Dogs, the first-place winners from each class are brought back to compete against one another. This is called the Winners class. The dog selected best is the Winners Dog. He is the male who receives the points at the show. Next, the dog that placed second to the Winners Dog in his original class is brought into the ring to compete with the other class winners for Reserve Winners Dog. The Reserve Winners Dog will receive the points if for any reason the Winners Dog is disallowed by the AKC.

The same process is repeated in bitches, resulting in a Winners Bitch (the only bitch of the breed to receive points at the show) and a Reserve Winners Bitch.

Next, the Best of Breed class is judged. All the dogs and bitches that are already champions enter in the ring for this class, joined by the Winners Dog and the Winners Bitch. The judge examines all the entries and selects one Best of Breed. Then, between the Winners Dog and Winners Bitch, the judge selects a Best of Winners. If either the Winners Dog or the Winners Bitch is selected Best of Breed, it automatically becomes Best of Winners. (The Best of Winners gets the higher number of points, too. If the points at the show for the defeated Winner were higher than those of the Best of Winners, the Best now gets the same higher total.) The judge finishes the breed judging by selecting a Best of Opposite Sex to the Best of Breed.

At all-breed shows, this process of elimination takes place in every breed. Each Best of Breed winner then competes against other Best of Breed winners within its breed group (Hound, Sporting, etc.). In the group judging, the judge's job is to pick the dog that most embodies the standard for its breed. Four placements are awarded in each group, but only the first-place winner remains in competition. Finally, the seven group winners are brought into the ring and a Best in Show win-

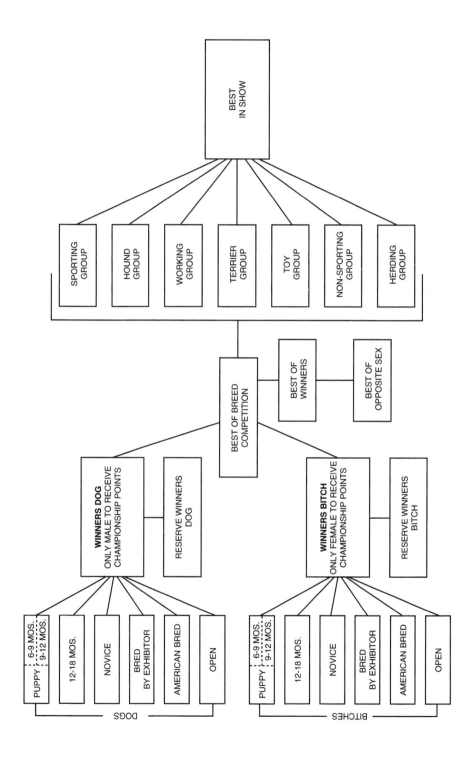

ner is selected. At the largest all-breed shows, more than 3,000 contestants are narrowed down to a single Best in Show winner.

Competing in shows is great fun for you and your dog. If you are interested in attending a show, you may find information in your local newspaper, at shops catering to pet owners, or at *akc.org*. A complete listing of nationwide shows is published each month in the AKC EVENTS CALENDAR, which accompanies a subscription to the AKC GAZETTE.

For advice on how to get your dog and yourself ready to show, the best place to turn is a dog club. Clubs that give shows often offer classes which teach the basics of handling show dogs. Many fine books on the subject are also available at bookstores or libraries. Some people prefer to have their dog shown by a professional handler, sometimes called an *agent*. Before you hire a professional handler, talk to several, evaluate their rate schedules, visit their facilities, and ask for references. Observe them both in and out of the ring. A professional handler is entrusted with your dog's care, so make sure you are entirely comfortable with the arrangement. (To find an AKC registered handler in your area, visit *akc.org*.)

# JUNIOR SHOWMANSHIP

AKC Junior Showmanship classes offer youngsters aged nine to eighteen the opportunity to develop their handling skills, practice good sportsmanship, and learn about dogs and dog shows.

Juniors are judged on their ability to present and handle their dogs within the same format and guidelines as those who compete in the conformation ring. The quality of the presentation, not the quality of the dog, is judged. Juniors are encouraged to develop their handling abilities, dress appropriately, conduct themselves in a proper manner, and present their dog in a well-groomed condition.

Junior Showmanship competitions are divided into Novice and Open classes. Novice classes are for juniors who have not won three first-place awards in a Novice class. It gives beginners a chance to gain experience and confidence. Open classes are for juniors with three or more first-place wins. Classes may also be subdivided by age.

Even though the dogs are not being judged, they must be eligible to compete in dog shows *or* companion events. The dog must be owned or co-owned by the junior, or a member of the junior's immediate family or household.

Junior Showmanship is not limited to conformation showing. More than ever before, young dog enthusiasts are competing in the full range of companion and performance events. By signing up for a free subscription to the e-newsletter "AKC Jr. News" at *akc.org*, you can learn more about juniors and their involvement in virtually every realm of AKC activity.

# COMPANION EVENTS

## Obedience

Obedience trials test a dog's ability to perform a set of exercises that are scored by a judge. Conformation is not a factor here; in fact, obedience trials are open to dogs that would be disqualified from the show ring, and spayed bitches and neutered dogs are welcome.

Any purebred dog over the age of six months and registered with the AKC can enter an obedience trial. Obedience is also open to breeds in the Miscellaneous class and dogs with an Indefinite Listing Privilege (ILP) number—purebred dogs without registered parents that, nevertheless, meet certain criteria. (For more information about ILP numbers, call the AKC at 919-233-9767 or visit *akc.org*.)

Training for obedience, or simply for a well-behaved companion dog, should begin early. For puppies two to five months old, puppy kindergarten classes that focus on basic skills are very useful. There are also basic training classes for five- to six-month-old dogs. Although many people begin training with very young puppies, it's never too late to start.

Once you've gained some experience, you can test your skills at informal obedience matches. Although you won't earn points toward your title, you will get a sense of the competition. Next, observe the participants at real trials and meet some people with valuable experience in the sport.

Competition in the obedience ring is divided into three levels, each more difficult than the previous one. At each level a competitor is working for an AKC Obedience title. The following are the three levels and titles:

- Novice—Companion Dog (CD)
- Open—Companion Dog Excellent (CDX)
- Utility—Utility Dog (UD)

To receive an obedience title, a dog must earn three legs in competition. To achieve a leg, a dog must score at least 170 points out of a possible 200 and get more than half the points available for each exercise. The exercises vary for each title.

Work at the Novice level includes the basic training that all dogs should receive to be good companions. Dogs need to demonstrate heeling both on and off lead at different speeds, coming when called, staying with a group of other dogs when instructed to do so, and standing for a simple physical examination.

Open, the second level, is similar to Novice but requires the dog to perform only off lead and for longer periods. There are also jumping and retrieving tasks. The final level, Utility, adds still more difficult exercises, and the dog must also perform scent-discrimination tests.

The best of the best may go on to earn more titles. A Utility Dog that earns qualifying scores in both the Open B and Utility B classes at ten different events becomes a Utility Dog Excellent (UDX). Utility Dogs that place first or second in Open B or Utility classes can earn points toward an Obedience Trial Champion (OTCH) title. (B classes are for experienced handlers; A classes are for beginners whose dogs have never received a title.)

## Tracking Tests

Tracking tests allow dogs to demonstrate their natural ability to recognize and follow human scent. This vigorous outdoor activity is great for canine athletes of all sizes. Unlike obedience trials that require a dog to qualify three times, a dog must complete only one track successfully to earn a title.

As in obedience, there are three levels of competition. A dog earns a Tracking Dog (TD) title by following a complex track laid by a person 30 minutes to two hours before the event. To earn a Tracking Dog Excellent (TDX) title, a dog must successfully follow a track that is older, longer, and less direct, while overcoming physical and scenting obstacles. Finally, a dog that can track through urban settings as well as through wilderness can earn a Variable Surface Tracking (VST) title. VST dogs demonstrate this ability by following a three- to five-hour-old track over a variety of surfaces, such as down a street, through a building, and across a lot. A dog that achieves all three titles TD/TDX/VST becomes a Champion Tracker (CT).

## Agility

Agility is open to all breeds. Dogs must be at least one year old to participate. The trials allow a dog to demonstrate the ability to negotiate a complex obstacle course that includes walking over a bridge, weaving in and out of a series of poles, jumping through and over objects, traversing tunnels, and pausing on command. There are different height categories for the jumps, so each dog can be tested fairly.

Agility is exciting for dogs, handlers, and spectators. Trials are held by AKC-licensed agility clubs, as well as many breed and obedience clubs. Many clubs also offer classes and less formal sanctioned trials for beginners. A list of clubs offering agility trials is available from the AKC Customer Service department or at akc.org.

There are three classes at an agility trial: Novice, Open, and Agility Excellent, with five different height divisions in each class. The course is the same for every class, but the scoring gets more and more demanding as you progress through the classes.

Credit toward AKC agility titles is earned only by qualifying in AKC-licensed and member club agility trials. In order to acquire a title, a dog must earn a qualifying score in its class at three different trials under two different judges. The maximum attainable score in any class is 100 points, and in order to earn a qualifying score a dog must receive 85 points or more and not be disqualified. The titles are Novice Agility (NA), Open Agility (OA), Agility Excellent (AX), and Master Agility Excellent (MX).

To earn the MX title, a dog must first have an AX, and then must receive qualifying scores in the Agility Excellent class at 10 licensed trials.

## Rally

The AKC Rally program was launched on January 1, 2005, and was an immediate hit with novice dog-sport enthusiasts and seasoned obedience trainers alike. Rally is an exciting family activity that emphasizes fun for dogs, owners, and spectators.

In rally, a dog-and-handler team negotiate a course of exercises according to sequentially numbered signs, in a manner similar to rally auto racing. The team works at its own pace, with the dog heeling from sign to sign.

Each sign contains a pictograph that illustrates a particular exercise. There are fifty exercise signs that judges can choose from to design courses unique to each trial. The number of required exercises can increase with each level of competition:

Novice
Advanced
Excellent

In Novice, all exercises are performed on leash. The Rally Advanced and Rally Excellent classes offer exercises that are more challenging, and these classes require that all exercises be performed off leash.

After saying "Forward" to start the run, the judge steps back and allows the dogs and handlers to work through the course, one team at a time. Scoring is on a 100-point scale; the time of the run is used as a tiebreaker.

Rally differs from traditional obedience competition in several ways, the most noticeable being that a handler may use hand signals, verbal encouragement, and generous applications of body language to urge their dog through the course. AKC-registered dogs of any breed may participate, and spayed or neutered dogs are eligible. Children are especially welcome, and many clubs offer special prizes for their top juniors.

# PERFORMANCE EVENTS

## Field Trials and Hunting Tests

Field trials and hunting tests are practical demonstrations of a dog's ability to perform the functions for which it was bred. Field trials are open to registered pointing breeds, retrievers, spaniels, Beagles, Basset Hounds, and Dachshunds that are more than six months old. Pointers, retrievers, and spaniels, including those with ILP numbers, are eligible for hunting tests. The AKC licenses or sanctions individual clubs that sponsor hunting tests and field trials conducted under AKC rules and regulations.

In hunting tests, the dog's ability to perform is judged against a standard of perfection established by the regulations. Dogs receiving qualifying scores at a number of tests achieve titles of Junior Hunter (JH), Senior Hunter (SH), and Master Hunter (MH). Each successive title requires greater skill. At field trials, dogs compete against one another for placements and points toward their championships. Successful dogs in the Sporting Group can earn a Field Championship (FC) or can earn an Amateur Field Championship (AFC). Basset Hounds and Dachshunds can earn only a Field Championship.

These field events are divided by type of dog (spaniels, retrievers, and so on) and sometimes are limited to specific breeds. Each type of event varies according to the breed's function as a hunting dog.

Beagles may compete in three types of trials: Brace, in which groups of two or three dogs are judged primarily on their accuracy in trailing a rabbit; Small Pack Option, in which the dogs are divided into packs of seven to pursue rabbits; and Large Pack trials, in which dogs are turned loose to find and track hares.

Basset Hound and Dachshund field trials are held separately, although they are run in a similar fashion to the Beagle Brace trials. Hunting tests are not available for these three hound breeds.

Pointing-breed field trials and hunting tests are open to Brittanys, English Setters, German Shorthaired Pointers, German Wirehaired Pointers, Pointers, Gordon Setters, Irish Setters, Spinoni Italiani, Vizslas, Weimaraners, and Wirehaired Pointing Griffons. Run in pairs around a course on which birds are liberated, the dogs demonstrate their ability to find birds, point staunchly, and retrieve downed birds.

Retrievers are tested on their ability to remember (*mark*) the location of downed birds and return those birds to their handlers. The hunting tests and field trials have different levels of difficulty and require dogs to mark multiple birds and, at higher levels, find unmarked birds (called *blind retrieves*). The eligible breeds are the Chesapeake Bay Retriever, Curly-Coated Retriever, Flat-Coated Retriever, Golden Retriever, Labrador Retriever, Nova Scotia Duck Tolling Retriever, and Irish Water Spaniel. Standard Poodles are eligible to participate in Retriever Hunting Tests.

Spaniels are judged on their natural and trained ability to hunt, flush, and retrieve game on both land and water. Clumber Spaniels, Cocker Spaniels, English Cocker Spaniels, English Springer Spaniels, Field Spaniels, Sussex Spaniels, and Welsh Springer Spaniels are eligible to compete. Field trials are available for Cocker Spaniels, English Cocker Spaniels, and English Springer Spaniels.

If you are interested in pursuing this type of competition, local dog clubs can lend support with training and advice. Once you've gotten started, you can try your hand at sanctioned events, which are practice events held by field or dog clubs. The next step would be to attend some actual tests and trials to observe and mingle with competitors.

## Herding Tests and Trials

AKC herding tests and trials are open to dogs of any registered Herding Group breed that are at least nine months old. Samoyeds and Rottweilers are also eligible. These events are designed to allow dogs to demonstrate their ability to herd livestock (sheep, cattle, goats, or ducks) under the direction of a handler.

In the herding test section, dogs can earn the titles of Herding Tested Dog (HT) and Pre-Trial Tested Dog (PT). The first title is awarded to dogs that show an inherent herding ability and the capacity to be trained in herding. A PT title is earned by dogs with some training in herding that can herd a small group of livestock through a simple course.

Trials offer four titles; the first three are Herding Started (HS), Herding Intermediate (HI), and Herding Excellent (HX). After earning an HX, dogs can then accumulate the necessary 15 championship points for the Herding Championship (HC). Such a dog is proficient in herding and capable of controlling even the most difficult livestock in diverse situations. The trials are run on three distinct courses, which differ in both physical appearance and style of herding.

## Lure Coursing

Lure coursing is to sighthounds what field trials are to scenthounds and sporting breeds: the chance for dogs to prove themselves doing what they were originally bred to do. For sighthounds, this means running down fleet-footed prey, sometimes over great distances. An exciting, fast-paced event, lure coursing keeps sighthounds physically and mentally fit.

In an AKC-licensed lure coursing event, the dogs follow an artificial lure around a course on an open field. Entrants must be at least one year old and be a member of the sighthound family: Afghan Hounds, Basenjis, Borzoi, Greyhounds, Ibizan Hounds, Irish Wolfhounds, Italian Greyhounds, Pharaoh Hounds, Rhodesian Ridgebacks, Salukis, Scottish Deerhounds, and Whippets. Competitors must be free of breed disqualifications; check the breed standard or the lure coursing regulations for more information.

Coursing dogs are scored on speed, enthusiasm, agility, endurance, and ability to follow the lure (a set of plastic bags). They can earn the title of Junior Courser (JC), Senior Courser (SC), Field Champion (FC), and Master Courser (MC). Many AKC-affiliated clubs offer noncompetitive lure coursing clinics for novices; a list is provided in the EVENTS CALENDAR. For a list of clubs approved for lure coursing events, visit *akc.org*.

## *Earthdog Tests*

Earthdog tests are for dogs that were originally bred to pursue quarry in dens or tunnels, called going to ground. Dachshunds and the smaller terriers—Miniature Schnauzers, and Australian, Bedlington, Border, Cairn, Cesky, Dandie Dinmont, Fox (Smooth and Wire), Glen of Imaal, Parson Russell, Lakeland, Manchester, Miniature Bull, Norfolk, Norwich, Scottish, Sealyham, Silky, Skye, Welsh, and West Highland White terriers—are eligible. Dogs must be at least six months old to enter.

The object of an earthdog test is to provide an opportunity for the dog to display the ability to follow game and work quarry (show interest in the game by barking, digging, and scratching). The quarry is either live (two adult rats, caged for their protection) or artificial, in which case it is located behind a barrier, properly scented and capable of movement.

Tests are run at four different levels. In Introduction to Quarry, the dog does not receive any qualifications or titles, but simply gets a taste of what it's like to be in a den and scent the prey. After passing this test, dogs advance gradually through the ranks. Titles are awarded for Junior Earthdog (JE), Senior Earthdog (SE), and Master Earthdog (ME). Each test requires a greater degree of skill in detecting and following a scent, gameness, and den savvy than the previous one. The distances from which a dog must locate the den, and the complexity of the tunnels it must maneuver in the dark, become increasingly more difficult.

For a list of clubs that are approved to hold earthdog tests, visit *akc.org*.

## *Coonhound Events*

The six Coonhound breeds that participate in these events are Treeing Walker Coonhound, Black and Tan Coonhound, Plott, American English Coonhound, Bluetick Coonhound, and Redbone Coonhound. Coonhound clubs offer "nite" hunts, field trials, water races, and bench shows. A national championship is held each year.

# CANINE GOOD CITIZEN

Administered by dog clubs and community-minded organizations throughout the United States, the AKC Canine Good Citizen® program is a fun, noncompetitive way to ensure that dogs are respected members of society. The program is based on ten tests, each designed to show that dogs can be well-behaved at home, in public, and around other dogs. All dogs, purebred and mixed-breed alike, are welcome to become AKC Canine Good Citizens.

It is not difficult to prepare for the AKC Canine Good Citizen test. In brief, the first test demonstrates that the dog will accept a friendly stranger. The second test demonstrates sitting politely while being petted by a friendly stranger. In the third test, the dog will permit an inspection and brief grooming by the stranger. The fourth test demonstrates that the handler is in control of the dog while out for a walk on a loose leash. The fifth test shows that the dog can move politely through a crowd. In the sixth test, the dog remains in place on a *sit* or *down* when commanded by the handler. The seventh test demonstrates that the dog comes when called. The dog must demonstrate polite behavior around other dogs in the eighth test. In the ninth test, the dog must react confidently to distractions. Finally, in the tenth test, the dog shows that it can maintain good manners while left on its own. All of the tests are evaluated on a pass/fail basis.

For more information about the AKC Canine Good Citizen test, call the AKC Customer Service department at 919-233-9767 or visit *akc.org*.

## AKC TITLES

| Prefix | Championship Titles |
| --- | --- |
| Ch. | Conformation Champion of Record |

**Performance Events**

| | |
| --- | --- |
| FC | Field Champion (field trials/lure coursing) |
| AFC | Amateur Field Trial Champion |
| NFC | National Field Champion |
| GDSC | Gun Dog Stake Champion |
| NAFC | National Amateur Field Champion |
| NGDC | National Gun Dog Champion |
| NOGDC | National Open Gun Dog Champion |
| RGDSC | Retrieving Gun Dog Stake Champion |
| HC | Herding Champion |
| DC | Dual Champion (Ch. and FC or HC) |
| TC | Triple Champion (DC plus OTCH, CT, *or* MACH) |

**Coonhound Events**

| | |
| --- | --- |
| CCH | Bench Show Champion |
| CGCH | Grand Champion |
| CGF | Grand Field Champion |
| CNC | Nite Champion |
| WNC | World Nite Champion |
| CGN | Grand Nite Champion |
| CSGN | Supreme Grand Nite Champion |

| CWC | Water Race Champion |
|---|---|
| CGW | Grand Water Race Champion |
| CSGW | Supreme Grand Water Race Champion |
| CSG | Supreme Grand Champion |
| CSGF | Supreme Grand Field Champion |
| CWSG | World Show Champion Grand Champion |

## Companion Events

| OTCH | Obedience Trial Champion |
|---|---|
| NOC | National Obedience Champion |
| CT | Champion Tracker (TD, TDX, and VST) |
| MACH | Master Agility Champion |
| VCCH | Versatile Companion Champion |

## SUFFIX TITLES

### Obedience

| CD | Companion Dog |
|---|---|
| UD | Utility Dog |
| CDX | Companion Dog Excellent |
| UDX | Utility Dog Excellent |

### Tracking

| TD | Tracking Dog |
|---|---|
| VST | Variable Surface Tracking Dog |
| TDX | Tracking Dog Excellent |

### Agility

| NA | Novice Agility |
|---|---|
| NAJ | Novice Agility Jumper |
| NAP | Novice Agility Preferred |
| AX | Agility Excellent |
| MX | Master Agility Excellent |
| MXP | Master Agility Excellent "B" Preferred |
| NAJ | Novice Jumpers with Weaves |
| NJP | Novice Jumpers with Weaves Preferred |
| AXJ | Excellent Agility Jumper |
| AXP | Agility Excellent "A" Preferred |
| AJP | Excellent Agility Jumpers with Weaves "A" Preferred |
| OA | Open Agility |
| OAJ | Open Agility Jumper |

| MX  | Master Agility Excellent |
|-----|--------------------------|
| OAJ | Open Jumpers with Weaves |
| OAP | Open Agility Preferred |
| OJP | Open Jumpers with Weaves Preferred |
| MXJ | Master Excellent Jumpers with Weaves |
| MJP | Master Excellent Jumpers with Weaves "B" Preferred |

## Rally

| RN  | Rally Novice |
|-----|--------------|
| RA  | Rally Advanced |
| RE  | Rally Excellent |
| RAE | Rally Advanced Excellent |

## Versatility Titles

| VCD1 | Versatile Companion Dog 1 (CD, NA, NAJ, TD or CD, NAP, NJP, TD) |
|------|----------------------------------------------------------------|
| VCD2 | Versatile Companion Dog 2 (CDX, OA, OAJ, TD or CDX, OAP, OJP, TD) |
| VCD3 | Versatile Companion Dog 3 (UD, AX, AXJ, TDX or UD, AX, AXJ, TDX) |
| VCD4 | Versatile Companion Dog 4 (UDX, MX, MXJ, VST or UDX, MXP, MJP, VST) |

## Earthdog

| JE | Junior Earthdog |
|----|-----------------|
| ME | Master Earthdog |
| SE | Senior Earthdog |

## Herding

| PT     | Pre-trial Tested |
|--------|------------------|
| HS     | Herding Started |
| HT     | Herding Tested |
| HSAdsc | Herding Started Course A (ducks, sheep, cattle) |
| HSBdsc | Herding Started Course B (ducks, sheep, cattle) |
| HSCs   | Herding Started Course C (sheep) |
| HI     | Herding Intermediate |
| HIAdsc | Herding Intermediate Course A (ducks, sheep, cattle) |
| HIBdsc | Herding Intermediate Course B (ducks, sheep, cattle) |
| HICs   | Herding Intermediate Course C (sheep) |
| HX     | Herding Excellent |
| HXAdsc | Herding Advanced Course A (ducks, sheep, cattle) |
| HXBdsc | Herding Advanced Course B (ducks, sheep, cattle) |
| HXCs   | Herding Advanced Course C (sheep) |

## Hunting Test

| | |
|---|---|
| JH | Junior Hunter |
| MH | Master Hunter |
| SH | Senior Hunter |

## Lure Coursing

| | |
|---|---|
| JC | Junior Courser |
| SC | Senior Courser |
| MC | Master Courser |
| LCX | Lure Courser Excellent |

# TRAINING

DOGS ARE INTELLIGENT, SOCIABLE ANIMALS THAT NATURALLY WANT TO PLEASE their owners. Training satisfies their need to know what we expect of them, and a well-trained dog feels happier and more secure. Training also teaches dogs discipline, and how to live in human society. Training unequivocally strengthens the bond between dogs and their owners, and is recommended for dogs of all sizes. It is especially important for the larger breeds.

From a practical standpoint, trained dogs are quiet, well-mannered, and trustworthy. They do not resist grooming or physical examinations, and they are welcome wherever they go in public. Training can also be very useful in an emergency. All in all, a well-behaved dog is a joy to own and a definite source of pride.

## BASIC PRINCIPLES

Like young children, dogs are curious and love to explore. They eagerly test their world in a variety of ways. Once your dog realizes you are the source of its needs and wants, your dog will experiment with different ways of attracting your attention until one or more brings results. The object is to channel these natural inclinations into paths that are socially acceptable, as well as useful and helpful.

From the time a puppy enters your life it is learning and adapting its behavior to you and its environment. Thoroughly pragmatic, dogs use modes of behavior that yield maximum results with minimum discomfort. Thus, if your dog learns that whining or refusing to eat results in attention, your dog will continue to whine and turn its nose up at dinner. If eliminating indoors brings less discomfort through discipline than the discomfort of waiting to go out, the dog will resist housebreaking. However, if your dog learns right from the start that *your* way of doing things results in praise and affection, while contrary ways result in firm, unvarying correction, it will choose the easier way. Making sure what you want is the easier and more desirable way is a fair definition of training.

The key words in training are *persistence, confidence,* and *consistency.* You should feel confident in yourself as a trainer, but your dog should also feel confident that you will consistently respond to a particular action with the same reaction. In training, this means certain actions are always prohibited and certain others are always encouraged. Inconsistency is the deadliest enemy of good training; it destroys the secure world in which all dogs, at any age, seek to live. A well-trained dog knows what behavior is acceptable and what is not, and this is only established by consistent reinforcement. A dog that is praised for every right action and corrected for every wrong one will soon learn acceptable behavior.

# PRAISE AND CORRECTION

The proper use of praise and correction is vital to successful training. Praise implies more than giving obvious approval when your dog has done something right. To maintain a positive relationship, praise should also be given after you have corrected or disciplined the dog. Many people err by prolonging their anger at a "naughty" dog or one that seems unable to absorb the message of a training session. It is important to realize that dogs have a very short memory; they forget what they did or did not do after a few minutes have passed, knowing only that you are displeased. Holding a grudge teaches your dog nothing, except that you are not very easy to get along with.

Praise should be given as soon after a correction as possible; just make sure the praise is for appropriate behavior. Do this no matter how many times you've made the identical correction. Giving a dog praise after a correction doesn't lessen the impact of the correction, but rather will reassure the dog and allow training to progress more smoothly. For example, if you catch your dog chewing on your shoe, give a correction, give the dog a chew toy, and then immediately praise the dog for chewing the right thing.

Corrections should always be mild and nonviolent. Your voice is your basic corrective tool, and the basic corrective command is "No!" This word should be delivered with clear authority and as much volume as you deem necessary. Try not to convey panic, anger, or annoyance. If your dog fails to respond appropriately to your commands, you are probably not being sufficiently authoritative. But remember, authority comes from the tone of your voice, not its volume.

There is tremendous variation from breed to breed in the degree of firmness necessary to get the proper response from a dog. Some breeds are far more strong-willed than others. A dog that has been allowed to develop unacceptable behavior and then is subjected to correction will require firmer correction than the dog that is never allowed to develop incorrect behavior in the first place.

Some behaviors, such as the basic obedience commands outlined in this chapter, must be taught in relatively structured, regular sessions. Other behaviors must be taught as you interact with your dog. For example, all young puppies experience a chewing phase. To deal with this behavior, make certain your puppy does not have access to inappropriate items when you are not around to supervise. When you are together, correct with a firm "No!" as soon as the puppy chews on your clothing, hands, or anything else that is inappropriate. Once the correction has been made, offer immediate praise. The dog must learn to accept correction for wrong behavior and receive abundant praise for doing what is right.

Most dogs respond well to a training collar (sometimes called a choke or slip collar), which is a metal chain with loops at each end. When used correctly, the choke collar allows the trainer to deliver an instantaneous correction without harming the dog. A complete discussion of this collar and its use is presented later in this chapter.

It is *never* advisable to hit or even threaten a dog, whether with a hand, newspaper, stick, or similar object. This tends to produce a hand-shy dog that cringes at the sight of any hand, raised or otherwise. The dog that expects the possibility of being struck whenever a hand is raised has good reason to try to avoid contact with humans.

Correcting a dog with a rolled-up newspaper slapped on the floor is such a widespread practice that it warrants additional discussion. Many people believe the noise of the blow, rather than its force, delivers an adequate correction by frightening the dog. This idea is wrong on three counts. *First, you cannot use fear to train a dog.* Second, deliberately teaching a dog to dread loud noises is unwise. What about noises such as thunder or firecrackers that are beyond your control? Do you want your dog to jump in fear at every noise? Third, it's not likely a rolled-up newspaper will be on hand at all times. Remember, the power of correction lies in immediate administration; its effect diminishes after even a few seconds.

You may notice that the word *punishment* does not appear in the discussion of training techniques. A dog is never punished; it is corrected. A fine point, perhaps, but in such fine points lies the difference between good and bad dog training.

Finally, never call a dog to you for correction or discipline. The canine mind makes direct and short-term connections, and the dog will link the action of coming to you with correction or discipline. Before long your dog may resist or refuse to come to you at all. If your dog has done something wrong at a distance, either go over to the dog for correction or wait for another opportunity. As in all training situations, it's a good idea to try to see things from your dog's perspective.

# HOUSEBREAKING

The importance of thorough housebreaking cannot be overemphasized, because anything less erodes the relationship between dog and owner. Some breeds are more difficult to housebreak than others, but all healthy dogs are able to learn this basic lesson.

There are two methods of housebreaking. One is accomplished directly, and the other uses paper training as an intermediate stage. Direct housebreaking is preferable by far, but it may be difficult if you do not have ready access to a yard or other place for the dog to use.

To housebreak a dog directly, follow a simple set of rules. The puppy must be allowed frequent access to the outdoors, and given a chance to urinate and defecate before being brought back inside. Once inside, you have two options. One is to restrict the puppy to a certain place in the house, such as the kitchen, while you keep a close eye on it. The other is to place the puppy in a comfortable but enclosed living and sleeping box, or crate, until you can supervise its activities. In either case, the puppy will be limited to a small area in which to play and sleep, an area that it will naturally be reluctant to soil.

When accidents happen, *mildly* chastise the puppy and immediately take it to a familiar outdoor place. Young puppies need to eliminate often, so be sure to go outside frequently in the early days—right after each feeding and anytime you suspect there's a need. The necessary outings will eventually be reduced, *but control develops slowly.*

If you think that crates are cruel, rest assured that they are not when used judiciously. Many dogs appreciate having a designated space of their own, and certainly it is kind to accomplish housebreaking quickly and efficiently. Most housebreaking problems originate with the softhearted owner who lets an untrained puppy have free run of the house. The puppy then falls into the habit of soiling the floors and furniture, and for years afterward, may be subjected to constant corrections. If you do use a crate, make sure it is big enough. A dog should be able to stand up and turn around comfortably in the crate. And never leave a dog in a crate all day. Give your puppy plenty of attention and playtime both in and out of the confinement area.

Some apartment dwellers have a harder time with housebreaking because they can't get outside as often as necessary. Therefore, they may opt to use paper training as an intermediate step to full housebreaking.

To paper train a dog, begin by covering the entire floor of one room (preferably a small room such as the kitchen) with several layers of newspaper and confine the puppy to that area. Replace soiled newspapers with fresh ones as necessary. After a day or two, leave a small corner of the room bare. If the puppy chooses the bare corner to urinate or defecate, give a mild correction and place the puppy on the newspaper. But remember, a correction is useful only if you catch the dog in the act. Never drag the puppy over to a soiled area and then scold it. Dogs are simply not able to understand what you are trying to teach them in that situation. They will not associate the correction with the housebreaking accident. If you cannot catch the puppy in the act, simply clean the mess and be patient with your dog.

As the puppy grasps the idea of the paper, gradually decrease the amount of covered floor until you are left with a papered space equivalent to two full newspaper sheets. Allow the puppy to use that area for a little while as you begin to reinforce the idea of eliminating outdoors. When the puppy seems to understand that the street is the proper place for elimination, remove the papers. During this transition time, watch carefully for any indication that the pup needs to go out, such as frantically searching for the papers, and respond immediately with a walk outside.

As with direct housebreaking, keep the puppy absolutely confined (in this case to the paper-training area) until the lesson is fully learned.

# USING A TRAINING COLLAR AND LEASH

Before you begin training your dog, you will need a training (choke or slip) collar and a lead. The choke collar is usually made of sturdy metal with a loop at each end. The correct size is determined by measuring around the largest part of the dog's head and adding one inch. The collar is formed by slipping the chain through one of the rings; the other ring will be used to attach the lead. Training leads are typically six feet long and made of leather or webbing a quarter inch to a full inch wide.

Because training is done with the dog on your left side, the choke collar is worn with the loose ring on the right side of the dog's neck. When placed correctly on the dog, the choke collar will look like the letter "p," and incorrectly will resemble the number "9." The correct use of the choke collar is to give a light, quick snap on the lead, which momentarily tightens the collar around the neck, followed by release. If the collar is positioned properly, it should immediately loosen.

Training collars are effective because they allow you to exert as much or as little control as necessary to get the dog's attention or to urge it into the right position or direction. A slight tug may be all that is required. Never use the training collar to exert constant pressure on the dog's neck. In the right hands, a training collar and lead are practical tools; in the wrong hands, they can be harmful or even cruel.

Before you begin training, gently introduce the collar and lead to the dog. Let it wear the collar for a day before trying anything further. When you feel the dog is accustomed to the lead, take your end and walk around, applying little or no pressure. Gradually, over a short period, increase your control until the dog learns the lead is not a threat. When you reach the point where you can persuade the dog to move in the general direction you want by making gentle snaps on the lead, you are ready to begin serious training.

# BASIC COMMANDS

Obedience training should begin at approximately four to six months, when the dog has sufficient powers of concentration to learn. As a rule of thumb, puppies that are still teething are generally too young for serious training. Conversely, *it's never too late to train an older dog.* Dogs are intelligent animals and can learn at any age.

Every civilized dog should know at least five basic commands: Heel, Sit, Stay, Down, and Come. These are the core exercises required for a Companion Dog degree in AKC Novice obedience competition, where they are regarded as the minimum requirements that make a dog a true companion. Even if you are not training for competition, one rule remains: The dog must learn to obey you instantly, with one and only one command. A sure sign of insufficient training is the repeated command, usually delivered in a steadily rising voice, which is only reluctantly obeyed by the dog, if at all.

Training sessions should take place regularly once or twice each day, starting with just five minutes and gradually increasing to no more than 30 minutes. Longer sessions will bore your dog (and you as well) and will actually devalue the training process. Your demeanor during training sessions should be businesslike, but don't forget to be friendly and offer frequent praise. Afterward, always take some time to play with your dog to ease the pressure and show that your relationship is amiable.

All movement exercises, such as Heel and Come, use commands that combine the dog's name with the desired action. When teaching stationary exercises, such as Sit and Stay, the trainer uses only the command. This is because when your dog is moving, hearing its name helps the dog focus on you. During a training session, a stationary dog should always be focused on you.

## Heel

Heeling is taught with the dog on your left side. Start to walk by calling the dog's name and commanding, "Fido, Heel!" Give the command just as you take the first step, starting with your left foot, and simultaneously give a light snap with the leash to persuade the dog to come along. Use only as much force as necessary to get the dog in motion. As you walk along, continue urging the dog to walk at your left side, with its neck and shoulder even with your left leg, by snapping the leash. Each time you snap, give the command "Heel!" and follow with praise. It need only be a few brief words, such as, "That's it, good dog!"

Since this is the first time the dog is being asked to perform on command, it will take a good deal of work before your pup understands what is going on. But if you are kind and patient, your dog will soon learn to perform with enthusiasm. It bears repeating that the secret of successful training is the correct use of the choke collar—the quick snap and release. Despite its name, the collar is not meant to choke a dog; *never exert a steady pull on the lead.* The collar is meant to get instant attention and correct when necessary, not harm the dog. The less often it is used and with the least amount of force, the better. Furthermore, you must remember to give praise after each snap. However mild your correction, each is a discomfort to the dog. If you praise immediately, it will remove the sting without removing the lesson.

Practice heeling in brief but lengthening sessions two or more times a day until you have to give only one command as you start walking and do not have to use the leash for corrections. Go through a variety of maneuvers, such as walking in circles and around corners, always keeping the dog at your side with snaps and praise, until you are confident that it is walking with you voluntarily. At that point you should be ready to start teaching the Sit exercise. But continue to regularly practice heeling as you work on other commands.

## Sit

An obedience-trained dog will sit facing straight forward at the handler's left side with its shoulder square to the handler's knee. The dog will sit automatically as soon as the handler stops moving.

To teach the Sit command, walk with the dog heeling at your left side. As you stop, give the command "Sit!" and simultaneously slide your left hand, palm down, fingers spread, toward the dog's rear and gently cup the rear into the sitting position as you bring your right hand straight up gently applying pressure to the training collar to raise the dog's head. Praise immediately every time your dog sits. Hold the dog in this position for a moment, then give the Heel command and resume walking. Again stop, give the Sit command, guide the dog into sitting position, and keep it seated a little longer.

Gradually, as the dog begins to understand, you will be able to abandon the hand and lead correction, and eventually abandon the command. The dog will sit automatically when you come to a stop, waiting either for you to start moving again or for a release through an established release word, such as "OK!"

Once the dog has learned to sit when you stop walking, you are ready to teach the Sit from any position. Put the collar and lead on and give the Sit command, guiding the dog into position as before. Concentrate on the Sit training until the dog will sit on command with no corrections, and then begin to introduce the Stay.

## Stay

A dog taught the Stay command will remain seated until released. To teach the Stay, place your dog in a sitting position with the lead on. Command "Stay!" as you place the palm of your left hand in front of the dog's muzzle and, starting with your right foot, take one step away. Use your release word to signal that the exercise is over, then praise your dog. The longest you should make the dog stay during the first few lessons is ten to twenty seconds. Very gradually increase the time and distance you step away, until the dog will stay in place for at least three minutes.

If the dog gets up, calmly walk over and place it in the Sit, give the Stay command again, and walk away.

When your dog understands the Sit-Stay, you are ready to teach the Stand-Stay. This exercise is particularly useful during grooming or veterinary examinations.

The Stand-Stay is taught from the Heel position. While heeling with the dog, slowly come to a halt and give the command, "Stand!" As you do so, use the lead to stop the dog's forward motion and prevent it from sitting by placing your left palm in front of your dog's right hind leg, at the top. Do not correct or scold the dog for trying to sit, since that's what you've been teaching up to this point. Simply start walking again with the Heel command, take a few more steps, stop, say "Stand!" and use your left hand more firmly to prevent the dog from sitting. Understandably the dog may be confused by the change in strategy, so praise reassuringly.

Continue practicing until the dog gets the idea that when you say "Stand!" the usual Heel and Sit routine does not apply. If it tries to sit, simply start heeling again with the accompanying command. Combine this training with normal Sits when you stop walking.

Now add the familiar Stay command and start practicing again. When the dog will stand firmly at your side until you start heeling again, you can begin leaving the dog in a Stand-Stay as you take a step or two away. If the dog attempts to move or follow you, give a firm "No!" and then repeat "Stay!" guiding it back into position with your hands and the lead. Step away again and move slowly until you are at the length of the leash. Stay there only a few seconds before returning to praise and release the dog.

Mix up the Sit-Stay and Stand-Stay commands during a training session so your dog clearly understands the difference. As training progresses, slowly increase the time you are away from the dog until you reach at least one minute while the dog remains in a Stand-Stay and three minutes while it holds the Sit-Stay. Then begin to move around the dog while it is sitting or standing. Still holding the lead, walk away and circle around the dog, being careful that the lead neither tugs nor drags across the dog's face. Continue until the dog will stay quietly and confidently for three minutes, whether or not you are in sight. Do not try to stop the dog's head from turning to watch you, but gently and firmly correct any break from position, then reinforce it with the command again and leave once more.

Remember to praise after every correction *and* when your dog does something right without correction. At the risk of taxing your patience, we have not written "praise" after every sentence in this section, but it should appear in your mind nonetheless. Praise is an integral part of your dog's learning process; there is no such thing as too much praise, only too little. Remember that your dog works to gain your praise and to please you.

## Down

To begin teaching your dog to lie down on command, start with the dog sitting in the Heel position. Kneel down on your right knee so that you are at the dog's level. Place your left hand on the dog's shoulders. Take your right hand and place it behind the dog's front legs. As you say the word "down" simultaneously apply gentle pressure to the dog's shoulders and scoop the dog's front legs out until the dog is in the down position. Stroke the dog's back for a few seconds to encourage it to stay down and relax. Once this is accomplished, praise the dog for being good.

Then use your release word and praise again. Command the dog to sit for another try. Continue until the dog will lie down on command without your assistance. After a few days, you should be able to stand erect and give only one "Down!" for your dog to lie at your side. From this point you can improvise until the dog goes down when you are several feet away. This lesson should be easier than before, because the dog already knows the meaning of "Stay!"

## Come

Coming when called may be the most important command your dog must learn. It is last on our training schedule because the dog must first know how to Heel and Sit.

While your dog is heeling at your side, take a sudden step backward and say, "Fido, come!" As you give the command, snap the lead to turn the dog around to its right and head back toward you. When the dog is facing you, keep walking backward, urging your dog to come toward you with continued gentle snaps of the leash as you repeat the command "Come!" Praise is particularly important during this confusing turn of events.

As the dog reaches you, stop and give the Sit command. It may be necessary to guide the dog into a sitting position directly in front of you, but there is a very good chance you won't have to. Tell the dog to Stay and walk around into the Heel position, then start up at heeling again for another try. Continue working this way until you need only step backward and give the command, with no urging from the leash, to get the dog to turn, walk to you, and sit. This is called a Recall.

From here, it's simple to progress to a Recall from a distance. Command the dog to sit, step away to the end of the leash, then give the "Come!" command. If the dog hesitates, a slight snap on the lead will tell the dog to get up, come to you, and sit again in front.

The key to the success of this method is that there is never a contest of brute strength between you and your dog. The dog is already in motion, heeling, when you first give the Come command, so there is no tugging on the lead to get the dog up from a Sit or Down before it understands what "Come!" means. Remember to praise every time your dog comes to you. And remember, *never* call your dog to you for punishment or scolding.

# BEYOND THE BASICS

Once your dog reliably responds to these five basic commands, you are ready for the final step: obedience without the control of the lead, also known as off-lead work. In preparation, you must be absolutely certain your dog will obey commands on lead without hesitation. Do this training inside the house, just in case. Seat the dog at your side as before. Next, remove the lead and start with the Heel command. Don't be surprised if your dog heels right along with you! If you have worked hard together during previous training sessions, your dog will have learned to reliably follow your commands.

Go through the whole routine—the Stands, Downs, Stays, and Recalls—just as if the leash were there. In most cases, if all has gone well before, all will go well now. If not, put the lead back on for correction whenever necessary. Work on any problems until the dog is performing properly, and then remove the lead and try again. It should work.

Some points to remember: At first, don't try the Recall off lead from too great a distance. Try it from six feet or so and slowly work up to greater distances. Like everything else in training, gradual progress is the key to success. Never work your dog off lead outside until you are *absolutely* sure it will come to you reliably every time you call.

With patience, consistency, and time, every owner can have a well-trained dog if they apply the methods outlined here. Training is not accomplished in a day, a week, or even a month, but it can be enjoyable if it is undertaken with the right attitude. The reward is having a dog that is under control and a true companion.

# GROOMING

$\mathscr{G}$ ROOMING BRINGS OUT THE NATURAL BEAUTY OF ANY DOG, WHETHER SHOW dog or pet. Coat care is the mainstay of grooming, but owners should also pay close attention to their dog's teeth, nails, eyes, ears, and anal sacs.

For best results, a regular grooming schedule should be established during puppyhood and maintained throughout the dog's life. This allows owners to quickly notice subtle changes in the dog's condition and get an early jump on eliminating common problems such as fleas or ticks.

## COAT CARE

The canine coat comes in many varieties. Proper grooming will depend on the dog's breed, coat texture, coat length, and purpose. Grooming a dog for competition, for instance, usually involves more time and effort than preparing to visit a friend.

In general, brushing several times each week keeps the average dog neat and clean. This removes dead hair and distributes natural skin oils. The coat should be brushed down to the skin, loosening and removing flakes of dandruff and stimulating blood circulation.

Longhaired dogs require more coat care than shorthaired dogs because they are more likely to develop mats, tangles, and other problems. To maintain their characteristic appearance for the show ring, wire-coated terriers must be plucked or stripped periodically—which means the dead hairs need to be carefully removed by hand or with a special grooming tool. Between strippings, the coat should be brushed and combed regularly. Wire-coated dogs that are not shown may be clipped for easier maintenance, although this may alter the coat texture.

Although you can groom a dog on the floor, a sturdy table or bench is better. The surface should be covered with a rubber mat or other nonslip material for secure footing. If you use a tabletop, never leave the dog unattended.

As for grooming equipment, it all depends on the type of dog and the desired result. Many groomers use a pin brush for longhaired breeds. These brushes have long, rounded stainless steel or chrome-plated bristles. Brushes with nylon or natural bristles are recommended for dogs with short, medium, or long coats. Slicker brushes, which come in sizes appropriate for small, medium, or large dogs, have bent wire teeth set close together and are useful for removing mats as well as dead hair. A palm pin brush—an oval rubber pad set with round-tipped pins—is used to brush out the facial hair and leg furnishings of terriers. A brush with soft, flexible rubber bristles can polish smooth coats and remove dead hair. In addition to these items, you can purchase clippers, stripping knives, hair dryers, and other equipment designed to keep a dog's coat in top condition. Be sure you understand the correct use of these products, because they can damage the dog's skin and hair if used improperly. Certain breeds require special grooming techniques, so you may need to consult your dog's breeder or a professional groomer for advice.

If you do not regularly groom your dog, several problems can develop. One is mats. Mats are solid masses of hair that form anywhere on the body, but they are most often found behind the ears and under the legs. Some mats can be gently teased apart with one or two teeth of a comb. Others must be removed with scissors. *This should be done with the greatest of care—it is extremely easy to cut the dog's skin.* For safety's sake, try working a comb underneath the mat and then snip between the mat and the comb.

When bathing is necessary, shampoos made especially for dogs are best. You can also use a mild soap, baby shampoo, or coconut-oil shampoo. Stand your dog in a tub or basin, and make sure the dog is secure. Take special care not to get water or shampoo too close to your dog's eyes and ears. You may choose to plug the ears with cotton and place a gentle ophthalmic ointment in the eyes. Longhaired dogs should be combed before bathing. Wet the dog with water, apply shampoo sparingly, and work up a good lather. Rinse well and wrap a towel around the dog before it starts to shake itself dry. Some brisk toweling will help dry the hair more quickly. Bathing can be done outdoors in fine summer weather, but keep a wet dog indoors on chilly or windy days until it is thoroughly dry. Brushing and combing should be done regularly thereafter to keep the dog as clean as possible.

How often you bathe your dog will depend on the climate as well as the dog's coat type and living situation (dogs that spend a lot of time outdoors or in a kennel will need to be bathed more often). Remember that too much bathing can remove the skin's natural oils and make the coat dry and harsh.

Many dog owners have to contend with burrs and other plant material that makes a mess of the coat. If you cannot avoid exercising the dog in areas known to contain these nuisances, remove them as quickly as they are found. Be sure to check between the dog's toes, under the legs, and around the ears and genitals after every outing.

Another common problem is skunk spray. The odor will be lessened considerably by bathing the dog in soap and water, followed by soaking the coat in tomato juice and then rinsing. You may have to repeat the process a few times. Be sure to discard the dog's collar, leash, or anything else that may have absorbed the skunk's scent.

If your dog's coat becomes contaminated with tar, sap, or paint, you may need to practice some creative trimming. You can also try soaking the affected areas in vegetable or mineral oil for twenty-four hours, then washing with soap and water. *Never* use gasoline, turpentine, kerosene, or any other chemical substance to remove anything from a dog's coat.

# NAILS

Regular exercise on rough ground helps wear some nails down to an appropriate length. If not, a dog's nails should be trimmed until they just clear the floor. Long nails can cause the foot to splay or spread. Even worse, they can curl under and pierce the skin. This happens most often with the dewclaws, the nails high on the foot, which are sometimes obscured by long hair. Dewclaws are often removed shortly after birth.

Nails should be trimmed with equipment specially designed for this purpose. Do not use ordinary scissors or your own toenail clippers. If you look carefully at a dog's nail, you will see a thin pink or red line inside. This is called the quick. Make the cut just before the quick. Trimming dark nails is admittedly more difficult, because the quick is not as easy to see. Gradually trim small pieces until the hook-like part is removed. Be prepared to stop any bleeding with a styptic pencil or cornstarch.

# EARS

The ears should be cleaned approximately every two weeks, depending upon the dog and whether it is prone to ear problems. In general, folded or hairy ears need to be cleaned more often than erect or basically bare ears. It's a good idea to inspect the ears regularly, checking for any unusual discharge or odor. Any suspicion of infection should be brought to the attention of a veterinarian.

For routine ear cleaning, wrap a damp towel or soft cloth around your finger and clean only the visible part of the outer ear. You can also use a cotton swab soaked in mineral oil. Every last bit of wax need not be removed, since a small amount naturally protects the ear canal. Do not try to clean out an infected ear; leave that to your veterinarian.

Some dogs grow profuse hair in their ears, which tends to block air circulation and contribute to infections. If your veterinarian has recommended plucking this hair, use your fingers or a tweezers and gently remove only the hairs that come out easily.

# EYE CARE

Some breeds have large, protruding eyes. Others have an abundance of hair around the eyes. These dogs are especially vulnerable to ocular irritation or injury, and their owners should be very vigilant about grooming. Hair should never be allowed to rub or touch the eyes, and the eyes should be monitored carefully for redness or unusual discharge, which should be brought immediately to the attention of a veterinarian. The eye area may be cleaned by gently wiping with a damp, soft cloth. Any hair clipping should be done with extreme caution.

# BRUSHING THE TEETH

Plaque and tartar can lead to painful periodontal (gum) disease and eventual tooth loss. If plaque—a soft white or yellow substance—is allowed to remain on the teeth, tartar can develop. Tartar is quite hard and must be removed by scaling, which is often done under anesthesia at a veterinary clinic.

To prevent oral disease, regular brushing—every two to three days—is highly recommended for all dogs. This may be done with a child's toothbrush and a small amount of canine toothpaste or a dab of paste made by mixing baking soda and water. (Do not use toothpaste designed for humans, since your dog cannot rinse after brushing.) A gauze pad wrapped around the finger can substitute for a toothbrush. Either way, the teeth should be scrubbed from crown to gum.

It is believed that dry food and hard chew-toys reduce the formation of tartar. However, this does not eliminate the need for additional teeth-cleaning or even periodic scaling. If the dog's gums bleed, appear reddened, or recede from the surface of the teeth, check with your veterinarian.

# ANAL SACS

Anal sacs are normal anatomical structures located on either side of the lower half of the canine anus. If you look carefully, you can probably see the tiny ducts through which a malodorous liquid exudes from these sacs. This natural substance is thought to help dogs mark their territory. Unfortunately, the sacs occasionally become impacted in some dogs, making them uncomfortable. A clear sign is when the dog drags its rear on the ground and licks its anus.

Impacted anal sacs need to be emptied; this can be done by you (with practice) or your veterinarian. If your efforts fail, however, you should seek professional help. Impacted anal sacs can become infected, which requires veterinary treatment. The discharge from an infected anal sac typically contains blood or pus, and the dog's anal area will be very sensitive.

To express the anal sacs, raise the dog's tail with one hand and hold a piece of gauze or tissue in the other hand. Grasp the skin outside the anal area with your thumb and forefinger in the eight and four o'clock positions. Then push in and squeeze very gently. The anal sac material should exude from the two ducts without undue pressure. Some people find it easier to express one gland at a time. This is done by placing a gloved and lubricated forefinger inside the rectum and then gently pressing the sac between the thumb and forefinger in a forward motion. It's best to have someone hold the dog still while you do this.

# RESPONSIBLE BREEDING

*B*REEDING DOGS HAS BEEN A PASSION FOR PEOPLE THROUGH MANY CEN-
turies. Part art, part science and total devotion, breeding will show you all
the best in the human-and-dog bond. It is exciting and challenging.

Breeding purebred dogs is also time consuming, expensive and, occasionally,
heartbreaking. If you go forward, your underlying purpose should be to improve
the breed—not just increase its numbers—and you must be prepared to accept full
responsibility for the puppies from the moment they are born until the day they die.

## BREEDING RESPONSIBLY

The AKC always welcomes responsible breeders to the world of purebred dogs.
What are some of the hallmarks of a truly responsible breeder?

**Responsible breeders are always studying.** Responsible breeders devote
hours to learning as much as they can about such things as their breed, other breed
specimens, health, behavior and training, and AKC rules. In short, they become canine experts. How can you go about becoming an expert?

First, study your breed standard. You'll find a copy of every official breed standard in this book. Many parent clubs offer more detailed information on the standard, such as amplifications, illustrated standards, and other written materials.

Attend dog events. By looking at lots of dogs in your breed and studying the
pedigrees of those you like, you will learn about different lines. For example, if you
want a dog that will excel in obedience competition, you may want to find a line
producing the attributes that contribute to jumping ability.

Become involved with dog clubs. Each breed has a national parent club, and
there are thousands of local clubs devoted to individual breeds (called specialty
clubs). If your interest lies in breeding a good dog for companion or performance
events, there are clubs devoted to those sports as well. All of these clubs sponsor educational programs and events designed to help you increase your expertise. The
AKC web site can help you locate these clubs.

Read, read, read! There are many books available about every aspect of the dog experience. There are books devoted to individual breeds, to many breeds, to health, to breeding and whelping, to genetics, to behavior and training, and on and on. There are magazines, too. The AKC GAZETTE contains informative articles on all of these topics. Most parent clubs also publish magazines or newsletters. For information on AKC materials or for a list of clubs, call the Customer Service Department at 919-233-9767 or visit *akc.org*.

**Responsible breeders know their dogs.** Every dog is the best dog in the world to its owner. But responsible breeders are able to step back from their love for their dogs and honestly evaluate the good and bad points. (In fact, many will tell you that their first dog, usually the one they loved the most, was the ugliest or clumsiest they ever owned!)

Why is such a detached point of view necessary? Breeding is a lot of work. Good breeders know that if they are going to exert all that effort, the result must be a better dog. To reach that goal, they need to recognize their dog's flaws and find a mate that can eliminate them. Thus, they need to use every educational tool at their disposal.

One such tool is the breeder of your dog. This person should have an extensive knowledge of their breeding stock and your dog's relatives; such information is invaluable. Use this resource!

The best way to make sure that you don't suffer from "kennel blindness" is to test your dog against others. If you want to breed a better specimen of the breed, enter dog shows. If you want to produce a great obedience dog, enter obedience trials. If you want a great hunter, enter field tests and trials. If your dog is a success in these events, you'll be more confident that you really can make a contribution to your dog's breed and to the world of purebred dogs.

**Responsible breeders condition their dogs.** Good puppies start long before the breeding ever takes place. Both parents need long-term care—what dog people call conditioning—to produce the best offspring. This means regular veterinary care, screening for genetic problems, both general (like eye problems or canine hip dysplasia) and those specific to your breed, pre-breeding tests and, of course, regular exercise and good nutrition.

Conditioning also means maintaining your dog's mental health. Anxious animals can experience fertility problems. And many breeders swear that the dam's temperament affects the puppies—good puppies come from good mothers. Consequently, they avoid breeding shy, unstable, or nasty dogs.

**Responsible breeders are devoted to their puppies.** A responsible breeder is more than just a perpetual student. Add on nursemaid, nutritionist, nursery school teacher, and child psychologist.

During the first couple of weeks the dam normally takes care of the puppies' needs, but you always have to be prepared for unusual situations such as a dam with no milk or an orphaned litter. Even when the dam is a good mother, you must provide a safe, very warm (at times as high as ninety degrees), dry place for the puppies and three or more times the normal amount of food and water for the dam.

Once the puppies begin to be weaned, they become loads of fun—and loads more work. All the normal cleanup, feeding, grooming, training, veterinary care, and playtime you put in for your dog needs to be multiplied by four or six or ten.

**Responsible breeders place puppies wisely.** It is your responsibility to make sure every single puppy goes to owners who will provide the kind of home for them for the next ten to fifteen years that you've provided in the first eight weeks. That means careful screening and asking lots of questions. It's like being an adoption counselor.

Having learned all you can about your breed, you now know all the pros and cons of ownership. Responsible breeders know that the negatives are just as important as the positives. They know that dogs requiring lots of coat care or training time may not be a good match for someone who's a workaholic. They know that tiny dogs may not fare well around a family of active small children. They know that a large, powerful dog may be too much for someone in frail health. They never sell dogs to people they believe will not be able to provide suitable homes.

Responsible breeders are also familiar with AKC rules and regulations concerning the sale and registration of AKC-registrable dogs. Before you even breed, you should contact the AKC to make sure you've got all the right paperwork, understand what you need to do, and are able to provide the right documents to your buyers.

There are also practical considerations. Breeding is not a profit-making activity. Some breeds are so popular that puppies may be easy to sell. Others are in such little demand that it can take months to find homes. Responsible breeders learn to ignore the financial realities in order to find just the right home for each puppy.

**Responsible breeders are responsible for life.** Perhaps the best part of being a breeder is having those great families you selected call you with news of puppy's first tooth, first vet visit, first birthday party, first dog event, first win. It's getting letters, holiday cards, and family portraits with your puppy smack in the middle. What's not to love about being a breeder at these times?

But now can come the difficult part. It's the fifteenth phone call asking how to cut toenails. It's the nice young couple getting a divorce and neither one can keep the puppy. It's the distraught owner calling from the vet with news of an unforeseen hereditary illness. It's the devastated mother telling you that the dog you encouraged them to train bit their child's friend.

Responsible breeders are there for all situations—both good and bad. They know that they were responsible for the birth of this puppy, and that also means they are responsible for the dog until the day it dies. They are willing to answer as many questions as they are asked, to provide resources and information, and are always concerned about their puppies. They are also willing to take a dog back at any point in its life. They never turn their back on a dog they've bred.

Oddly enough, responsible breeders know the best phone call is the one they receive twelve years later telling them that the dog died of old age, because they know they were responsible for bringing years of love and joy to someone else's family.

# GENETICS

Most dogs are chosen for breeding on the basis of their looks, but their genes are what really count. Genes are the fundamental units of inheritance. Each parent passes a set of their genes to their sons and daughters; which genes are actually expressed is left to chance.

Gene selection and mutation also influence the genetic outcome of a breeding. We guide the selection process by choosing a particular mating pair. This is the way the many diverse dog breeds developed from the domesticated wolf over thousands of years.

Genetic defects can occur in any breed and can affect any system in the body. Some genetic diseases may occur in many breeds (cataracts and deafness, for example); others occur in only one or a few breeds (such as Collie eye). Before you breed your first litter, you must learn all you can about the genetic problems that affect your breed.

Diseases that follow a *dominant* pattern of inheritance need only one abnormal gene. That is, if only one parent is affected, the condition will show up in each successive generation. Some individuals may be only mildly affected with the condition, making it difficult to detect. In such cases, the condition can mistakenly be thought to skip generations.

Diseases that follow a *recessive* pattern of inheritance occur in homozygous individuals, meaning dogs with two abnormal genes. Dogs with one mutant and one normal gene are heterozygous, and they are carriers of the condition. They appear normal but can pass the abnormal gene to their offspring. Recessive mutant genes can be passed through many generations before emerging in the offspring of two dogs that carry the same genetic mutation.

Polygenic disorders result from the cumulative action of a number of different genes. The exact number of genes involved and their individual functions are difficult to determine, and the pattern of inheritance tends to vary from family to family. Polygenic inheritance can sometimes mimic either dominant or recessive inheritance, and this feature may lead to erroneous conclusions regarding the type of underlying genetic abnormality.

Chromosomal anomalies—defects in chromosome number and structure—can also cause genetic diseases. Dogs normally have thirty-nine pairs of chromosomes (humans have twenty-three pairs) on which genes are located. Major abnormalities in chromosome number and structure can produce serious defects.

Whether you inbreed, linebreed, or outcross may have an effect on the incidence of genetic disease in the offspring. *Inbreeding* is the mating of two individuals that are related through one or more common ancestors. The closest form of inbreeding involves parent-child and brother-sister matings. *Linebreeding,* a form of inbreeding, usually involves mating more distantly related dogs. The rate of polygenic and recessively inherited diseases tends to increase with inbreeding because the chance that the two animals carry the same mutation is greater when the dogs are related. *Outcrossing* is the mating of two dogs of the same breed that are otherwise virtually unrelated.

# REPRODUCTIVE PHYSIOLOGY

Sexual maturity tends to occur earlier in small dogs and later in large dogs. On average, however, males become fertile after six months of age and reach full sexual maturity by twelve to fifteen months. Healthy stud dogs may remain sexually active and fertile to old age. Adult males are able to mate at any time.

Bitches have their first estrus (also known as *season* or *heat*) after six months of age, although it can occur as late as eighteen months to two years of age. Estrus recurs at intervals of approximately six months until late in life. During estrus, the female is fertile and will accept a male.

The bitch's cycle is divided into four periods:

**PROESTRUS**—The female attracts males, has a bloody vaginal discharge and her vulva is swollen. Proestrus lasts approximately nine days; the female, however, will not allow coitus at this time.

**ESTRUS**—During this period, which also lasts approximately nine days, the female will accept the male and is fertile. Ovulation usually occurs in the first 48 hours; however, this can vary greatly.

**DIESTRUS**—Lasting sixty to ninety days, diestrus is the period when the reproductive tract is under the control of the hormone progesterone. This occurs whether or not the bitch becomes pregnant. False pregnancy (*pseudocyesis*), a condition in which the bitch shows symptoms of being pregnant although she has not conceived, is occasionally seen during diestrus.

**ANESTRUS**—No sexual activity takes place. Anestrus lasts between three and four months.

# CONTRACEPTION

Various forms of contraception are available for the non-breeding dog. The most effective is surgical removal of the reproductive organs, i.e., spaying the female or castrating the male. For a less permanent solution, oral contraceptives for canines may be used until the time of breeding. These products must be used carefully and under the guidance of a veterinarian to avoid severe side effects.

Strict isolation of a bitch in estrus will also prevent pregnancy, but this sounds easier than it is. Dogs can be very persistent in their drive to reach a fertile female. Pregnancy termination can be achieved in cases of mismating, but the use of appropriate hormones carry certain risks that must be discussed with a veterinarian.

If you do decide to breed your bitch, it is advisable to skip at least the first heat; she is still maturing and should be spared the stress of pregnancy and lactation. Most breeders also avoid breeding a bitch twice in the same year or during consecutive heats, to allow sufficient time for recuperation between pregnancies.

# BREEDING

Breeding should always begin with excellent nutrition and management. The bitch should be in good condition, neither thin nor overweight. Some nutritionists believe that a steady weight increase for three weeks, beginning just before breeding, may increase fertility. However, this has not been proven.

A veterinarian should perform an examination at least one month before breeding, and update vaccinations if appropriate. The bitch should be tested and treated for internal and external parasites. Responsible breeders also test for brucellosis, an infectious bacterial disease that can cause sterility or spontaneous abortion between the forty-fifth and fifty-fifth days of pregnancy. Males should also be tested for brucellosis. To prevent transmission, these dogs should be kept apart from pregnant, whelping, or nursing bitches, and they should be tested for brucellosis at least twice a year.

Breeding management varies among individual breeders and breeds, but most dogs are first bred between the tenth and fourteenth day after the onset of proestrus. As long as the bitch will accept the male, mating every other day for a total of two or three matings is generally considered sufficient. However, signs of proestrus are not obvious in some bitches. To catch the peak fertile period, a veterinarian may need to perform hormone tests or examine vaginal smears under a microscope.

Bitches are usually less inhibited by new environments, and are therefore usually taken to the home of the stud dog for breeding. Breedings involving young males proceed smoother if they are paired with experienced bitches.

The male mounts the female from the rear and clasps her midsection with his front legs. Rapid pelvic thrusts follow, until intromission and ejaculation take place. After the pelvic thrusts cease, the male and female will not separate for ten to thirty minutes. Known as a tie, this results from a swollen section of the penis called the *bulbus glandis.* During the tie, the male may move around until he and the bitch are positioned rear to rear. Do not try to separate the dogs during the tie, because it can injure either or both animals. Sooner or later, they will part naturally.

Artificial insemination is a relatively simple procedure that can be used when natural breeding is impractical. It is performed by a veterinarian. Before breeding in this way, contact the AKC for information on properly registering the litter.

# PREGNANCY

Canine gestation lasts approximately sixty-three days. Signs of pregnancy include an increase in appetite, weight, and nipple size. A bitch with false pregnancy may also show these signs. Pregnancy can be definitively confirmed by a veterinarian through abdominal palpation, ultrasound, or X-rays. Special feeding requirements of the pregnant bitch are described in the Nutrition chapter. This is a good time, however, to talk with your veterinarian about how to care for the bitch throughout pregnancy and whelping, and what to do in case of an emergency.

A few days before the bitch is ready to give birth, she may stop eating and start building a "nest" where she plans to have her puppies. Unless you have already accustomed her to a whelping box, she may choose your closet or another place you may find inappropriate for a delivery room. It is a good idea to build a whelping box well in advance so the bitch has time to get used to it.

A good whelping box is roomy and has low sides, so you can easily reach in. It should also have a small shelf running halfway up along one or two sides so the pups have something to crawl under to avoid getting rolled on. The box should be located in a quiet, warm, dry, draft-free place. Many breeders line the box with newspapers until after delivery because paper can be changed quickly and easily when it becomes soiled. After whelping, newspapers are typically replaced with soft towels or something that provides better footing for the puppies.

The bitch's body temperature drops to ninety-nine degrees or less approximately twenty-four hours before the first stage of labor, when the cervix dilates and opens the birth canal for passage of the puppies. At this time she will pant, strain, appear restless, and perhaps vomit. Vomiting is normal at the onset of labor, but persistent vomiting may be a sign of illness.

# BIRTH

The next stage of labor involves abdominal straining as the puppies emerge. A normal, healthy bitch doesn't usually require human help during whelping, but you should be prepared to act in case of an emergency.

Each puppy emerges in its own sac. The bitch should promptly remove the sac, sever the umbilical cord, and lick the puppy to clean it and stimulate respiration. A placenta is delivered after each puppy, and the bitch may or may not attempt to eat it. Some people believe eating this tissue is good for the bitch; others disagree and believe it may cause a digestive upset. You may want to let your bitch eat one or two of the placentas, but not all of them.

Breeders should always keep track of how many placentas are delivered and ensure that the number matches the number of puppies, since a retained placenta may cause problems.

The breeder must take over if the bitch neglects to remove a sac or sever an umbilical cord. The sac membrane should be torn near the puppy's head and peeled backward until the puppy can be gently removed. Then mucus or fluids are removed from the puppy's mouth and nose, and circulation is stimulated by gentle rubbing with a towel. The umbilical cord can be tied with unwaxed dental floss, and cut on the far side of the tie about two inches from the abdomen. The cut end should be painted with iodine to prevent infection.

# WHEN TO CALL THE VETERINARIAN

If something goes wrong, don't hesitate to call the veterinarian for assistance. Signs of potential trouble include:

- indications of extreme pain
- strong contractions lasting for more than forty-five minutes without delivery of a pup
- more than three hours elapsing between puppies, with or without contractions
- trembling, shivering, or collapse
- passing a dark green or bloody fluid before the birth of the first puppy (after the first puppy, this is normal)
- if your bitch has not gone into labor by the sixty-fourth day of her last mating

It is an excellent idea to have a veterinarian check the bitch and her litter within a day of the delivery.

# NEWBORN PUPPIES

A newborn puppy cannot control its body temperature and must be kept in a warm environment. Chilling will stress the puppy and predispose it to infectious disease; overheating can kill it. The environmental temperature can be controlled with a well-insulated electric heating pad or a heat lamp. But make sure the puppies have a cooler place to crawl to if they become too warm.

The first milk produced by the bitch after whelping is called colostrum. Every puppy needs to ingest colostrum as early as possible after birth, and certainly during the first twenty-four hours of life. Colostrum contains a number of substances that are beneficial to the puppy, including immunoglobulins that protect newborns from the infectious diseases to which the mother is immune.

Occasionally, a bitch cannot or will not care for her puppies. In this case, it is the breeder's responsibility to see that they are fed, stimulated, and kept warm.

The immediate environmental temperature should be kept between eighty-five and ninety degrees for the first five days of life. From the seventh to the tenth day, the temperature can be gradually reduced to eighty degrees; by the end of the fourth week it can be brought down to seventy-five degrees.

Newborn puppies must be stimulated to defecate and urinate after each feeding. Ordinarily this would occur as the bitch licks her litter, but orphaned puppies need human intervention. Gently massage the puppy's anal region with a cotton ball that has been dipped in warm water. Observe the puppy's daily habits, and stimulate only as necessary. For information on formula and feeding techniques for hand rearing puppies, refer to the chapter on nutrition.

Gentle body massage is also beneficial for any hand-reared puppy. Massage stimulates the circulation and thoroughly awakens the puppy. Stroke the puppy's sides and back with a soft cloth. The best time for a massage seems to be when the puppies are waking up, while you're waiting for the formula to get warm. Simple grooming, performed only when necessary, should also take place at feeding time.

# WEANING

Puppies should begin the weaning process at about three weeks of age. It should be a gradual process. Start with a thin, bland cereal mixed with formula. Hand-fed puppies may be removed from the bottle by about four weeks, and ground meat or high-quality canned dog food may be offered in addition to the cereal-formula mixture.

By five weeks, gradually switch to a high-quality puppy food. Some breeders add ground meat, mixed with evaporated milk diluted with equal parts water. In addition to the meat and canned food, introduce a good commercial dry or moist puppy food into the feeding program. All changes in food or feeding schedules should be gradual, to allow the digestive system time to adjust.

# MORE TO LEARN

As you can see, breeding dogs is a complex, serious activity and should not be undertaken lightly. There's much to learn before you even begin, and much more that your dogs will teach you along the way.

# CANINE HEALTH
## AND FIRST AID

# A HEALTHY DOG

*K*EEPING A DOG HEALTHY AND CONTENT IS NEITHER AS EASY NOR AS DIF-
ficult as many people think. What it takes is an owner who is willing to
devote the necessary time and energy to exercise, train, groom, and attend to the
other needs of their pet. Conscientious dog care actually begins before you buy the
dog, by realistically evaluating the time you have to spend on a dog and opting for
a breed whose needs do not outstrip your resources. Good dog care is the dog
owner's responsibility. A healthy dog requires proper nutrition, regular grooming
and exercise sessions, training for good behavior, and plenty of love. And don't forget that even a well-cared-for, healthy dog needs to be examined and vaccinated
regularly by a veterinarian.

Although dogs can't come right out and announce how they feel, the alert
owner can always tell something is not quite right by changes in the dog's normal
appearance or behavior. This chapter describes signs of a healthy dog. Other chap-
ters on nutrition, grooming, and training help you maintain your dog's good health
and well-being.

Each dog is unique, with its own characteristics, appearance, and personality.
What may be normal for one dog may not be for another; only the dog's owner and
veterinarian know what is normal for any one particular dog. Get acquainted with
the way your dog acts and looks from day to day. Changes in appearance or behavior could be clues to possible illness. In general, however, the following describes
the physical state of a healthy dog.

## SKIN

Healthy skin is smooth and flexible, ranging from pale pink to brown or black.
Spotted skin is normal in dogs with spotted or solid-color coats. No scales, scabs,
growths, or areas of redness should be visible. Dogs have seasonal shedding cycles,
which may occasionally change. A healthy coat, however, is glossy and pliable, without dandruff, excessive oiliness, or areas of baldness.

Check to see that your dog does not have fleas, ticks, lice, or other external parasites by running your hand against the grain of the coat; some pests are stationary, while others, like fleas, may scurry away as soon as they are exposed. Signs of fleas include itching and the presence of small black and white specks on the skin, which are flea dirt or feces. It's a good idea to check the skin of longhaired dogs in several places.

# EYES

A healthy dog has bright, shiny eyes free of excessive watering or discharge. Eyelashes and hair should not rub against the eyeball; this is especially a concern for owners of longhaired breeds. Examine the moist pink inner lining of the eyelids (the *conjunctiva*) by placing your thumb near the edge of the eyelid and pulling gently upward or downward. This smooth membrane should not be inflamed, swollen, or have a yellow discharge. The whites of the eyes should not appear yellowish.

The dog's third eyelid, a light pink membrane, is located under the lower lid and is most easily visible in the inner corner of the eye. How much the third eyelid is visible on the surface of the eye varies from breed to breed. Get to know what is normal for your breed, so you will be able to spot any changes that could signal a problem.

# EARS

The outside of the ear flap is covered with hair similar to the rest of the body. The skin inside the dog's ears is light pink, clean, and lightly covered with hair. A small amount of yellow, brown, or black wax may be present in the ear canals, but an overabundance of this wax is abnormal. Healthy ears do not emit a bad smell, they are not red, swollen, itchy, or painful to the dog, and do not exude a discharge.

# MOUTH

To examine the inside of your dog's mouth, gently grasp the top of the muzzle with your fingers on one side and thumb on the other. Use the other hand to pull down on the lower jaw. Healthy gums will appear pink or pigmented (black or spotted) and will feel firm. The edges of healthy gums surround the teeth, which are free from soft white matter and hard white, yellow, or brown material. Your dog should not have unpleasant breath.

Young dogs have white, smooth teeth, which tend to darken a bit with age. The average puppy has twenty-three baby teeth with no molars. Normal adult dogs have forty-two permanent teeth, although some breeds have fewer because of the construction of their jaws. Once adult teeth have emerged, the baby teeth should not remain. These sometimes have to be removed by a veterinarian.

A dog may have a scissors bite (the upper front teeth tightly overlap the lower front teeth), a level bite, an overshot bite, or an undershot bite. The type of bite preferred in each breed is described in the breed's standard.

# NOSE

A dog's nose is normally cool and moist. Any secretions from the nose are clear and watery, not cloudy, yellow or green, thick, or foul-smelling. Black noses are most common, though a variety of colors and even spots can be normal. The nose should not be red or irritated—the possible result of an injury, disease, or sensitivity to sunlight.

Many people mistakenly believe that the condition of a dog's nose is the best indicator of its health. A sick dog, however, may have either a warm, dry nose or a cold, wet one, and owners are advised to use a rectal thermometer to correctly determine if the dog has a fever.

# TEMPERATURE

The normal temperature range for a dog, taken with a rectal thermometer, is from 101 to 102.5 degrees F (38.3 to 39.2 degrees C). It's important to keep the dog still while you are taking its temperature. This is best done while the dog is standing, but lying on its side will also work.

Begin by shaking down the thermometer and lubricating the bulb with petroleum jelly, or mineral or vegetable oil. Lift the dog's tail and gently slide the thermometer into the anus—the distance depends on the size of the dog. Half the thermometer may be required for a large dog, while an inch may do for a small one. Remove the thermometer after three minutes to read the temperature.

# PULSE

The heart rate of a healthy dog depends on its size and condition. Normally, the heart beats 50 to 130 times per minute in a resting dog. It is faster in puppies and small dogs, slower in large dogs or those in particularly good physical condition.

To feel a dog's heartbeat, place your fingertips or palm (never your thumb, because you have a pulse of your own in your thumb) against the left side of the dog's chest just behind the elbow, or place your ear against the chest over the heart. To feel the dog's pulse, gently press on the artery that lies on the inside of the thigh where the leg joins the body.

# ELIMINATION

Urine excreted by a healthy dog is yellow and clear. Most adult dogs move their bowels once or twice a day; the stools are well-formed and generally brown. The amount and color of stool produced by your dog will be affected by diet. Large amounts of odorous, loose, or unusually colored stools are abnormal.

It is most important to regard persistent diarrhea, difficult elimination, or a change in the frequency or amount of urination as signs of possible illness. Any of these signs should be brought to the attention of a veterinarian without delay.

# WEIGHT

Even if your dog appears fine in every other way, it can't receive a clean bill of health if it is underweight or, more commonly, overweight. Obesity is usually the result of overfeeding and can be easily corrected by changing the dog's diet. But a visit to the veterinarian is in order first, to rule out a hormonal imbalance or other physical problem.

An underweight dog, or one that refuses to eat, can have internal parasites or other serious health problems. Again, a visit to the veterinarian is the best way to deal with this problem.

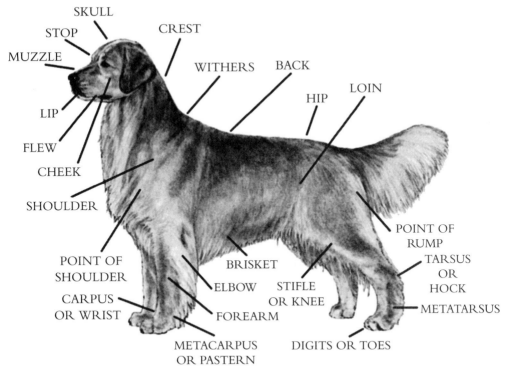

SKULL
STOP
MUZZLE
CREST
WITHERS
BACK
LOIN
HIP
LIP
FLEW
CHEEK
SHOULDER
POINT OF
RUMP
TARSUS
OR
HOCK
METATARSUS
POINT OF
SHOULDER
CARPUS
OR WRIST
BRISKET
ELBOW
STIFLE
OR KNEE
FOREARM
METACARPUS
OR PASTERN
DIGITS OR TOES

**External features of the dog**

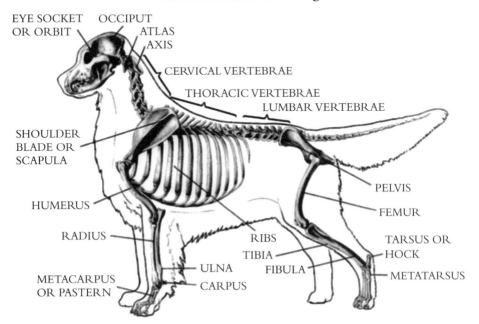

EYE SOCKET
OR ORBIT
OCCIPUT
ATLAS
AXIS
CERVICAL VERTEBRAE
THORACIC VERTEBRAE
LUMBAR VERTEBRAE
SHOULDER
BLADE OR
SCAPULA
PELVIS
HUMERUS
FEMUR
RADIUS
RIBS
TIBIA
TARSUS OR
HOCK
ULNA
FIBULA
METATARSUS
METACARPUS
OR PASTERN
CARPUS

**Bones of the dog**

# NUTRITION

*T*HE RIGHT AMOUNT OF NUTRITIOUS FOOD IS ESSENTIAL TO EVERY DOG'S health. Food provides the fuel to grow, maintain a healthy body, fight infection, and reproduce. Plenty of fresh water is equally important.

The right food contains balanced proportions of carbohydrates, protein, fats, vitamins, and minerals. High-quality dog foods offered by reputable companies can meet these needs, or a diet can be prepared at home, with help from a veterinarian. The correct proportion of each key ingredient and the amount to be fed depends on the individual. Is the dog young or old? Thin or fat? Active or sedentary? Does the dog spend most of its time indoors or outdoors, in a hot climate or a cold one? Is the dog a working dog? A pregnant bitch? Each of these cases presents its own nutritional needs.

Every dog in the household should have a separate food dish and access to fresh, clean water. The dishes and the utensils used to prepare food should be kept clean at all times. For best results, a regular feeding schedule should be maintained.

Puppies need more calories and essential nutrients than do adult dogs. Food quality is as important as quantity, especially just after weaning—usually at five to seven weeks old. Eggs, milk, meat, and cottage cheese are appropriate puppy foods because they are palatable, digestible, and contain plenty of high-quality protein. Foods with a very high fiber content are less desirable during the period of rapid growth. If a commercial dog food is offered, it should be formulated for puppies, or an adult food can be supplemented with the high-protein foods just mentioned. Be careful to consult your veterinarian on this issue to ensure the diet remains balanced.

Most young puppies are fed three times a day, although some breeders prefer four times daily for the first month and three thereafter. When a puppy reaches four to six months of age, two meals a day will be enough.

Perfectly healthy dogs occasionally skip a meal or eat less than normal. Unless the dog is showing signs of illness or its appetite doesn't pick up again soon, there is no cause for alarm. Be careful to avoid overfeeding young dogs because it can lead to a variety of medical problems. A puppy should be weighed weekly, and the growth rate should be compared with published charts for that breed. An average growth rate is preferable to a maximum one. Exercise is also important at this time. Small breeds often approach maturity at seven to ten months, at which time their total nutrient requirements gradually decrease. Larger dogs mature at a slower pace.

Always remember to provide fresh drinking water, even if your dog's food seems very wet. Between-meal snacks should be avoided, except for occasional treats used as rewards for good behavior.

# CALORIC REQUIREMENTS

The following chart is a general guide to the caloric requirements for an average adult dog. Your dog may need more or less food, depending on size, activity level, temperament, and metabolism. For example, a dog that works hard or spends a lot of time outside in a cold climate requires more energy from food than one that is basically sedentary or spends most of the time in a temperature-controlled apartment.

| DOG'S WEIGHT (LBS.) | KCAL NEEDED PER LB. OF BODY WEIGHT | DRY FOOD (OZ.) | SEMIMOIST (OZ.) | CANNED (OZ.) |
|---|---|---|---|---|
| 2 | 65 | 1.3 | 1.7 | 3.4 |
| 5 | 52 | 2.5 | 3.2 | 7.0 |
| 10 | 44 | 4.3 | 5.5 | 10.75 |
| 15 | 39 | 6.1 | 7.8 | 15.25 |
| 20 | 37 | 7.5 | 9.7 | 18.75 |
| 30 | 33 | 10.0 | 12.8 | 25.0 |
| 45 | 30 | 14.0 | 18.0 | 35.0 |
| 75 | 26 | 20.4 | 26.2 | 51.0 |
| 110 | 24 | 25.0 | 32.2 | 62.5 |

*(Caloric requirements for an adult maintenance diet. These are recommended daily food intakes of average adult dogs. Individuals may require one-quarter more or less than these averages.)*

There are three types of commercial dog foods: dry, semimoist, and canned. Assuming they are manufactured by reputable companies, all contain adequate amounts of carbohydrates, fats, protein, minerals, and vitamins. The selection of any diet, therefore, should depend on the nature of the dog, the performance desired by its owner, and the overall care of the dog. The adequacy of a particular diet may be judged by observing the dog. First, are the dog's stools very watery? Are they foamy, pale, or colored like the food? These indicate poor digestion. On the other hand, stools that are small, dark, and dense suggest good digestion. Next, look at the dog's coat. The proper diet helps it stay pliant, glossy, and clean-looking. Physical fitness is another important assessment, especially when deciding how much to feed. Reach over and run your hands along the dog's sides. If your dog is overweight (not an uncommon occurrence), you will not be able to feel the ribs.

# PREGNANT AND LACTATING BITCHES

A bitch should be in prime condition before she is bred. Pregnancy is not the right time to start rebuilding depleted body reserves, which may result in whelping complications. Any bitch that is part of a breeding program should be fed a complete, balanced diet slightly above her usual maintenance intake.

After the breeding has taken place, return to her usual amount and type of food. A bitch in good condition should continue into pregnancy with the same caloric intake that she had during adult maintenance. Her food intake should be increased only as her body weight increases, beginning about the last five weeks before whelping. Daily food intake should be increased gradually, so that at the time of whelping she may be eating 35 to 50 percent more than usual.

If you have been feeding your bitch a well-balanced, high-quality diet, you should not need to add anything during her pregnancy. However, some breeders advocate supplementation with a protein source such as evaporated milk, eggs, meat, or liver. These supplements should never represent more than 10 percent of the bitch's daily food intake. As her weight and food intake increase, begin offering small, frequent meals to spare her the discomfort that larger meals can cause, especially in a small dog.

Some bitches eat very little for the first day or two after whelping. Then their appetite and need for all nutrients rises sharply and peaks in about three weeks. During this entire period, adequate calcium, phosphorus, and vitamin D must be fed to avoid the onset of eclampsia. Optimal amounts of these nutrients are already present in a high-quality diet, so further supplementation should be unnecessary. Eclampsia causes nervousness, whimpering, unsteady gait, and spasms. Although very serious, it is readily cured by prompt veterinary treatment.

After whelping, the bitch ideally should be about the same weight as when she was bred, but not more than 5 to 10 percent heavier. For three weeks after whelping she will need two or three times more food than her normal maintenance diet, to help her provide nourishing milk to her puppies. This food should be divided into three or four meals. The composition of the food should be the same as it was during the last third of her pregnancy; only the amount per day should change.

Nursing puppies should be allowed to eat a little of their mother's food, as long as it has been well soaked or moistened, soon after they have normal sight and lo-comotion. As weaning progresses, begin limiting the bitch's food intake so that she will have fewer problems at time of complete weaning. On the first day of complete weaning do not offer the bitch any food at all, although plenty of water should always be available. On the second day, feed one-fourth of her normal maintenance diet; on the third day one-half; on the fourth day three-quarters, and then return completely to the diet she was fed before breeding. This will help decrease milk production and help prevent mammary gland problems.

Finally, even if you have followed the recommended feeding practices during pregnancy and lactation, the body reserves of many bitches become depleted during lactation. Therefore, carefully observe the bitch and be sure she is fed a high-quality diet, one that is easily digested and contains essential nutrients, until she has reached the same body condition and nutritional status that she enjoyed before breeding.

# HAND FEEDING NEWBORN PUPPIES

Newborn puppies must be hand fed if their mother is either unable or unwilling to nurse them. Cow's milk is a poor substitute for bitch's milk, which is more concentrated and has twice the level of protein, almost double the calories, and more than twice the calcium and phosphorus content. For feeding puppies, a commercial puppy formula is recommended; carefully follow the manufacturer's recommendations for feeding.

On the average, the following guidelines will help you decide how many calories a newborn puppy requires each day. A puppy may require one-quarter more or less than these guidelines, depending upon its individual needs.

| | |
|---|---|
| **FIRST WEEK:** | 60 to 70 calories per pound of body weight, per day. |
| **SECOND WEEK:** | 70 to 80 calories per pound of body weight, per day. |
| **THIRD WEEK:** | 80 to 90 calories per pound of body weight, per day. |
| **FOURTH WEEK:** | 90-plus calories per pound of body weight, per day. |

As an example, let's consider an average-sized, seven-day-old, ten-ounce puppy. This pup would need sixty calories times two-thirds of a pound, which is forty calories a day. If the commercial puppy formula supplies thirty calories per ounce, the puppy would need approximately one and a half ounces of formula per day. Remember that puppies grow very rapidly, so make sure you weigh them every day before you calculate how much to feed them.

You may need to start with slightly less formula at each feeding and gradually increase the amount as the puppy responds favorably to hand feeding. Steady weight gain and well-formed feces are the best evidence of satisfactory progress. If diarrhea develops, immediately reduce the puppy's intake to half the amount previously fed, then gradually increase it again to the recommended level. Diarrhea in newborns can be very dangerous, so consult a veterinarian for advice.

Never prepare more formula than is required for any one day—milk is a natural breeding ground for bacteria. Furthermore, maintain clean and sanitary conditions at all times. Divide the formula into the correct portions for each feeding and keep it refrigerated. Before feeding, warm the formula to about a hundred degrees Fahrenheit, or near body temperature. Using a bottle and nipple, hold the bottle at an angle to prevent air bubbles. The hole in the nipple can be enlarged slightly with a hot needle to let the milk ooze out slowly when the bottle is inverted. The puppy should suck vigorously, but should not nurse too rapidly. Consult a veterinarian if the puppies are not nursing well. You may need to resort to tube feeding, which is best taught by a health professional.

# OLDER DOGS

Activity level and metabolism rate slow down in older dogs, diminishing the amount of calories required for maintenance. To avoid obesity, the dog must therefore eat one-quarter to one-third less food. Older dogs still have the usual demands for essential nutrients, however, so a more nutritious diet may be required. Also, since the digestive process and food absorption take longer, you may need to feed smaller, more frequent meals.

Many older dogs suffer from kidney disease or other medical problems that respond to specialized diets. Check with your veterinarian to learn more about diets tailored to meet the needs of older dogs.

# COMMON ERRORS

Thanks to the availability of many palatable and nutritionally sound commercial dog foods, nutritional deficiencies are unusual in dogs today. Those rare instances of nutritional deficiency often result from misconceptions about feeding (offering an all-meat diet, for example) or oversupplementing a diet that is already well balanced. A common mistake is to add extra fats to increase the energy intake or to improve palatability. Too much fat will mean caloric needs are met before a dog has eaten enough protein, minerals, and vitamins necessary for good health.

Another common source of difficulty is oversupplementation with additional vitamins and minerals, such as calcium and vitamin D, during periods of growth and reproduction. An excess of minerals and vitamins, or imbalances among them, may cause problems that are more complex and difficult to diagnose or treat than simple deficiencies.

Most dogs love to chew on bones, but some bones can be hazardous to their health. Turkey, chicken, pork, or any bones liable to splinter should not be given to dogs because of the risk they pose. Their sharp, needle-like pieces can penetrate the mouth, stomach, or intestines, causing injury or even death. Large, hard bones such as knuckle or marrowbones are preferable, but be sure to boil them. Then make sure your dog only chews—not swallows—the bone.

# THE OVERWEIGHT DOG

Too much food and not enough exercise equals fat, an unhealthy situation in any animal. The first step in reducing your dog's weight is to check with a veterinarian to rule out a physical or metabolic problem. The next step is to put the dog on a strict diet. This means feeding slightly less than the number of calories it needs for daily maintenance (and no treats or table scraps) and increasing exercise. Special foods are available for this purpose; check with your veterinarian for more guidance. Weight loss should proceed slowly but steadily. To keep track of your dog's weight, stand on the bathroom scale with the dog in your arms, then weigh yourself alone and calculate the difference.

# Common Illnesses

$\mathcal{M}$ ANY MEDICAL PROBLEMS CAN BE PREVENTED WITH CONSCIENTIOUS CARE, but almost every dog, regardless of breed, will be ill at some point in life. Owners need to be alert for subtle signs of illness in their dog's body language. Any of the following signs, or any deviation from your dog's usual behavior or appearance, should be reported to a veterinarian.

- constipation
- straining to urinate
- increased urination
- shivering
- restlessness
- fever
- watery eyes
- labored breathing
- runny nose
- weight loss
- coughing
- increased water intake
- loss of appetite (or ravenous appetite without weight gain)
- weakness, lameness, or paralysis
- vomiting
- obvious pain or nervous symptoms

This chapter is intended to familiarize dog owners with the general characteristics of some common canine medical problems. It is important to realize, however, that there is no substitute for good professional care. If you suspect something is wrong with your dog, seek the advice of your veterinarian without delay. Time is often a deciding factor in the ability to halt the progression of disease and successfully treat it.

# THE SKIN

The skin is the largest organ and protects the internal organs and tissues from invasion, changing temperatures, and dehydration. It also synthesizes essential vitamins and provides a site where information about the external world can be processed through sensation. The following symptoms may indicate the presence of a skin problem:

- itching
- scabs
- swelling
- redness, soreness, or moistness
- hair loss
- purulent discharge
- scaling or dandruff
- discoloration
- lumps or bumps

**Abscess.** An abscess is a collection of pus under the skin. It is usually caused by a bite or puncture wound. The area is swollen, red, painful, and warm. Trapped fluid may be apparent. Some abscesses open and drain spontaneously; others must be lanced and cleaned out. Either way, an abscess should never be squeezed. As with other potentially serious conditions, see your veterinarian for treatment.

**Allergies.** Allergies to pollen, dust, mold, flea bites, flea collars, and food can cause itchy, red, irritated skin. Some allergic dogs develop hives, vomiting, diarrhea, runny nose, sneezing, or watery eyes. The allergen may be diagnosed by skin testing, food trials, or deductive reasoning. Once identified, the offending item must be avoided. If it is a food, it should be eliminated from the diet. If it is fleas, the dog must be kept parasite free. An infestation of fleas, lice, ticks, or mites is uncomfortable and unhealthy. A seriously allergic dog may need medical or hyposensitization therapy.

**Bacterial Infections.** Cuts, scrapes, and puncture wounds need adequate cleaning or suturing, depending upon their severity. An inflamed wound is red, swollen, warm, and painful. If it progressively worsens and starts to produce a pus-like discharge, it is probably infected and needs to be treated by a veterinarian.

**Calluses.** Calluses frequently occur in large dogs. They typically appear where skin rubs against hard or rough surfaces such as concrete. The affected skin thickens and becomes gray, wrinkled, and hairless. Most are found on the elbows, outer hocks, buttocks, and legs. Untreated calluses can develop into open sores. They may be prevented by providing soft bedding.

**Cushing's Syndrome.** Cushing's syndrome stems from an abnormality of the adrenal glands. The coat tends to thin out over the flanks and neck. The skin becomes scaly, dry, and dark. There may be an increase in thirst, appetite, and frequency of urination. Many dogs develop a potbellied appearance. Affected individuals are more susceptible to infections, especially of the skin, respiratory tract, and urinary tract. Treatment depends on the underlying cause; surgery or medical therapy may be warranted.

**Hot Spots.** Hot spots are a common problem, especially in heavy-coated breeds. These round patches of painful, moist, swollen skin develop abruptly and rapidly progress in size and severity. Tormented, dogs only worsen the problem by gnawing at the skin. Hot spots need to be clipped, cleaned, and medicated promptly. The source of the problem (fleas or impacted anal glands, for example) must be identified and resolved.

**Hypothyroidism.** The thyroid gland secretes hormones that control the body's metabolic rate. An insufficient supply of hormones means a lower metabolic level. The hypothyroid dog tends to gain weight, act sluggish, and chill easily. Hair is lost from the flanks and back, and there is increased pigmentation of the skin with scaling and seborrhea. Secondary bacterial infections of the skin are common. The ear canals may fill with thick, yellow, greasy material, which predisposes the dog to ear infections. Blood tests determine the level of thyroid function. If it is found to be low, thyroid hormone supplementation is recommended. Improvement is generally noted within three to four weeks, although the seborrhea and hair loss may take several months to clear up.

**Jaundice.** Jaundice—yellowing of the skin, eyes, gums, or ears—is a symptom rather than a disease. Leptospirosis, canine hepatitis, and other diseases that damage the liver can cause it, as well as disorders that involve red blood cell destruction. Jaundice is usually accompanied by other signs of illness, all of which mean the dog should be evaluated by a veterinarian.

**Pemphigus Vulgaris.** Pemphigus vulgaris is one of several autoimmune diseases in which cells destroy the body's own tissue as if it were a foreign substance. The tongue, gums, lips, eyelids, anus, vulva, nail beds, and nose of dogs with pemphigus vulgaris may develop ulcers, with erosions and crusting blisters.

**Ringworm.** Ringworm is actually a fungal infection. Hair loss is seen in association with circular, scaly lesions. These lesions can be localized, or they can involve large portions of the body. Crusty areas may develop, especially in young dogs. Ringworm, which is transmissible to humans, is diagnosed via skin scrapings and fungal cultures. Treatment may involve all household pets. The environment must be thoroughly cleaned to remove spores.

**Seborrhea.** Seborrheic skin is flaky or covered with greasy, yellow-brown scales. This problem is caused by abnormal skin cell production. Affected dogs often have a persistent, unpleasant odor. Seborrhea is usually incurable, but it can be controlled by regular bathing with a special shampoo.

**Tumors.** Tumors can form in, on, or under the dog's skin. In general, benign tumors grow slowly, are encapsulated, and do not seem to multiply or affect other parts of the body. Malignant tumors tend to appear suddenly, grow rapidly, and affect the surrounding tissues, perhaps breaking the skin and bleeding. A biopsy is always recommended. Owners should be alert for any new lumps or bumps, especially colored masses and moles that change in appearance or bleed. They should also be wary of sores that don't heal properly. All suspicious masses or skin changes should be promptly checked by a veterinarian.

**Warts.** Caused by a virus, warts (or papillomas) usually develop around the lips or in the mouths of young dogs. Warts on puppies often appear in groups; in older dogs, they tend to occur individually. Highly contagious, these round or cauliflower-like, gray, fibrous projections can vary in size from tiny to nearly two inches in diameter. Warts do not invade the skin or spread to other parts of the body. They usually clear up spontaneously, but if they cause discomfort or are slow to regress, surgical removal should be considered. Dogs that recover rarely become infected again.

# THE RESPIRATORY SYSTEM

The respiratory system consists of structures involved in breathing. It includes internal organs and muscles, such as the lungs and diaphragm, as well as the familiar nose and mouth. The signs that may indicate a respiratory problem are:

- coughing
- voice change or loss
- nasal discharge
- sneezing
- noisy or difficult breathing
- abnormal sounds within the chest

**Allergies.** Sneezing and coughing are occasional signs of an allergy. Dust, environmental chemicals, insect bites, and food are a few potential causes. Other signs include watery eyes, itching, vomiting, and diarrhea. The way to cope with your dog's allergy depends on its cause.

**Bronchitis.** Bronchitis can develop after a respiratory infection. The dog has a persistent dry, rough cough. It may retch after coughing or bring up foamy saliva. The temperature may be normal, but the dog will look sick. Good nursing care and appropriate medication usually restore a dog with bronchitis to good health.

**Cleft Palate.** A dog with a cleft palate has a hole between the oral and nasal cavities. This birth defect may interfere with proper nursing. Affected dogs typically have a nasal discharge.

**Collapsing Trachea.** Tracheal collapse occurs most often in small breeds. Affected dogs have episodes of noisy, labored breathing (especially during periods of excitement), and they tend to cough. This condition is rarely life-threatening, but surgery is occasionally warranted. Owners can help by maintaining the dog's proper weight and by attempting to keep the dog calm.

**Elongated Soft Palate.** Short-faced breeds are affected by this obstructive condition more frequently than other breeds. They tend to breathe noisily and have a nasal discharge. They also breathe through the mouth, make snorting noises, or snore during sleep. These problems are exacerbated by hot weather or physical exertion—conditions that require deep breathing.

**Foreign Body in the Nose.** Foreign material in the nose causes dogs to paw at their muzzles and sneeze violently. There may be nasal discharge or occasional bleeding. The item needs to be removed by a veterinarian as soon as possible, before it penetrates deeper into the body or causes more damage.

**Foreign Body in the Trachea.** Sudden, intense coughing may be caused by something in the windpipe such as vomitus or a foreign body. If coughing fails to clear the air passage, a veterinarian should be called immediately.

**Kennel Cough.** Kennel cough, or infectious canine tracheobronchitis, is thought to be caused by several viruses and a bacterium, *Bordatella Bronchiseptica*. Signs include an intermittent dry, hacking cough, sometimes accompanied by nasal discharge. Otherwise, most dogs with kennel cough do not seem seriously ill and most recover naturally in a few weeks. Any individual with kennel cough should be isolated from other dogs and kept in a warm, humid environment. Antibiotics may be prescribed to prevent complications.

**Laryngeal Paralysis.** Laryngeal paralysis affects large breeds during their middle to old age. The disease is typified by noisy breathing after exercise or excitement. Without surgical correction, laryngeal collapse is possible.

**Laryngitis.** Dogs that bark or cough excessively can develop a hoarse or faint voice. Resting the voice and treating the cough should resolve the laryngitis. A chronic case, however, should be analyzed by a veterinarian for a more serious source.

**Pneumonia.** Signs of pneumonia include coughing, rapid breathing, high fever, and a quick pulse. A dog may produce a rattling or bubbling noise within its chest. The cause may be viral, bacterial, allergic, or parasitic. To facilitate breathing, a dog with pneumonia may sit with head outstretched and elbows turned out. Although this is a serious illness, most dogs recover once they receive appropriate treatment.

**Rhinitis.** A dog with rhinitis, or nasal infection, produces a thick, green, rank-smelling discharge from the nose. Common causes are foreign bodies, masses, or infected maxillary teeth. Treatment depends on the source of the problem. Antibiotics or antifungals are typically necessary to resolve the problem.

**Stenotic Nares.** Another defect in short-nosed puppies is stenotic or narrowed nostrils. The nostrils collapse during inhalation and block the passage of air. A foamy nasal discharge is typical. When excited, dogs with stenotic nares will breathe through the mouth. Surgery may be required to enlarge the nostrils.

**Tumors.** Tumors of the respiratory tract can also cause noisy, difficult breathing or coughing. This is something a veterinarian must investigate and treat.

# THE MUSCULOSKELETAL SYSTEM

The musculoskeletal system supports, protects, and moves the dog's body. The bones also store fats and minerals, and provide a site for red blood cell production. Signs of a musculoskeletal problem include the following:

- limping
- pain
- unusual gait
- weakness
- stiffness
- swollen joints

**Arthritis.** Arthritis causes pain, lameness, and stiffness of the joints. It is not uncommon in old dogs. Large dogs are affected more often than small ones. Obesity aggravates the situation. Pain relievers, such as buffered aspirin, are often helpful. Moderate activity, soft bedding, and a warm, dry environment are recommended to sustain pliability in the joints.

**Disk Disease.** Normal disks act as shock-absorbing cushions between the vertebrae of the spine. When material from a disk protrudes or extrudes into the spinal cord area, however, the dog can experience considerable neck or back pain and possible neurological dysfunction. Signs include a stiff neck, leg weakness, and a gradual reduction of activity. Prolonged or severe pressure on the spinal cord can lead to paralysis and loss of bladder and bowel control. See a veterinarian immediately if these signs occur. Treatment may be medical or surgical.

**Dislocation.** Dislocated joints may make one limb appear shorter than its mate. Since most dislocations occur after a major trauma, the veterinarian will check for additional injuries and restore the joint. Sometimes this requires surgery.

**Fractures.** Most fractures result from trauma, such as being hit by a car. They are classified as *closed* or *open*. Open fractures are more serious because the ends of the bones break through the skin, causing extensive tissue damage and a potential for infection. All fractures need to be treated immediately by a veterinarian. Most are treated with splints, casts, or internal fixation devices such as screws, pins, plates, or wires. For more information about restraining an injured dog and temporarily splinting a broken limb, see the "Canine First Aid" chapter.

**Hip Dysplasia.** Hip dysplasia is a congenital, inherited defect. It occurs in all breeds and mixes, although it is most common in certain large breeds. In essence, the dysplastic dog has a malformed hip joint. Outward evidence of the abnormality can first appear at four to nine months, although some affected dogs seem normal until later in life. Signs include hip pain, a limp or swaying gait, hopping when running, and difficulty in rising. Arthritis of the hip joint commonly occurs. Managing a dysplastic dog includes maintaining the dog's proper weight, controlling its exercise, and keeping its environment warm and dry. Buffered aspirin or prescription drugs can help keep pain in check. If hip dysplasia is a problem in your breed, talk with your dog's breeder and veterinarian. You may want to have your dog's hips evaluated by radiologists.

**Lameness.** Weakness or pain due to trauma, nutritional imbalance, neurological disease, congenital defects, or infection can cause limping. The problem may be located by palpation or X-rays of the affected area. In the case of mild injury, healing may take place naturally within a few days. More serious problems (sprains, fractures, dislocations, and bone disease, for example) need prompt veterinary attention.

**Ruptured Cranial Cruciate Ligament.** The knee joint contains two crossed ligaments. One of them, the cranial cruciate ligament, can tear abruptly during exercise. The dog suddenly begins limping in pain. If the rupture is not repaired, the knee may become arthritic. Full use of the leg is usually restored when surgery is performed soon after the injury.

**Sprain.** A sprain occurs when ligaments suddenly stretch or tear slightly during activity. Although the joint is swollen and painful, it may heal within three to four days with strict rest. If not, or if the situation worsens, a veterinarian should check the dog's limb for a more serious problem such as a tear or rupture of the ligament.

# THE HEART

The heart is a pump that circulates blood throughout the body. Blood contains vital nutrients, including oxygen and the hormones that regulate body functions. Adequate blood circulation is necessary to eliminate waste products such as carbon dioxide. Poor cardiac performance compromises all other organ functions. The following are signs of a possible heart problem:

- coughing and shortness of breath
- stunted growth
- irregular and persistently fast heartbeat

- bluish gums
- lethargy and weakness
- distended abdomen and swollen limbs
- palpable vibrations over the heart
- fainting
- weight loss

**Cardiomyopathy.** Canine dilated (congested) cardiomyopathy is more common in large and giant breeds. It usually develops between the first and sixth year. The heart muscle weakens and degenerates, resulting in sluggish blood flow and generalized congestive heart failure. The heart becomes enlarged and is predisposed to irregularities in the heart rate. Signs of cardiomyopathy include fatigue, coughing, a distended abdomen, weight loss, swollen limbs, and collapse. Drugs may help prolong the dog's life, but they cannot reverse the change in the heart itself.

**Chronic Valvular Disease.** This disease causes the valves between the pumping chambers of the heart to thicken and seal improperly, allowing blood to leak backward. Little by little, the heart loses its ability to adequately pump blood. Heart failure may or may not occur. The dog may cough, have difficult or noisy breathing, and become restless at night. A heart murmur is usually detectable.

**Congestive Heart Failure.** Heart failure occurs when the heart is unable to deliver enough oxygenated blood to meet the body's needs. The term *congestive* applies when fluid accumulates in the lungs, causing coughing and shortness of breath. Dogs with congestive heart failure tire easily; some have a distended abdomen or swollen limbs. The veterinarian may hear abnormal heart sounds and fluid sounds within the lungs. X-ray images of the heart, an electrocardiogram, and an echocardiogram may be needed to fully diagnose the problem. Drugs can strengthen cardiac contractions and help the body excrete excess fluids. A special diet and limited exercise may be advised.

**Heartworm.** Microscopic heartworms enter a dog's bloodstream via a mosquito bite and develop in the dog's tissues. The parasites then travel through the venous circulation to the arteries of the lungs. Adult worms can grow to a foot long, physically obstructing blood flow and damaging the pulmonary arteries. Heart failure and severe lung damage occur in heavily infested dogs. Affected dogs tire easily, cough, and lose weight. Heartworm disease is detected by measuring the adult worm's antigen in a blood sample or by observing the microscopic parasites. Treatment is possible, but it is not without risk. All susceptible dogs should take preventive medication regularly to avoid infestation.

**Patent Ductus Arteriosus.** Fetal dogs have a short, broad vessel called the *ductus arteriosus,* which sends blood from the right ventricle to the aorta, thus bypassing the lungs. Shortly after birth this vessel should close naturally. When it doesn't, normal circulation is impaired. This congenital cardiovascular defect produces a distinctive murmur.

**Pulmonic Stenosis.** This defect is characterized by abnormal blood flow between the right ventricle and the pulmonary artery. The heart is forced to work harder than usual, which may result in heart failure. Dogs with pulmonic stenosis have conspicuous heart murmurs.

**Ventricular Septal Defects.** A ventricular septal defect is an abnormal opening in the muscular wall separating the two major pumping chambers of the heart. Most are small and have little effect on the general circulation. Those that are large, however, can cause signs of heart failure. The abnormal blood flow caused by this defect produces a heart murmur.

# THE GASTROINTESTINAL SYSTEM

The gastrointestinal system receives and processes food. It includes the entire passageway that begins with the mouth and ends with the anus. Symptoms of a potential gastrointestinal problem are the following:

- regurgitation
- distended, painful abdomen
- drooling
- excessive drinking and urination
- vomiting
- restlessness
- loss of appetite and weight
- blood or mucus in the stool
- flatulence
- jaundice
- anal irritation, scooting
- abnormally colored stools
- diarrhea
- constipation
- straining to defecate

**Bloat.** Bloat (acute gastric dilation or torsion) can rapidly kill an otherwise healthy dog. Large, deep-chested dogs are most often affected. Before they begin bloating, these dogs typically eat a big meal, drink lots of water, and exercise within two or three hours after eating. Their stomachs then fill with gas or fluids, swell, and may become twisted. *Bloat is a very serious, life-threatening situation. Death can occur in just a few hours if the dog is not treated by a veterinarian.* Signs of bloat include extreme restlessness, salivation, drooling, and unsuccessful attempts to vomit. The abdomen is severely distended. Depending on the duration of the condition, the dog may go into shock. Immediate intervention to decompress and reposition the stomach provides the best chance for survival. Owners of susceptible breeds may wish to feed small meals two or three times a day and restrict water intake and exercise after eating. If dry food is offered, it may be moistened first to help the dog to feel full faster and drink less water.

**Canine Hemorrhagic Gastroenteritis.** While the cause is uncertain, this disease is characterized by a sudden attack of bloody, foul-smelling diarrhea and vomiting, which can result in dehydration. This viral disease is probably spread by contact with infectious feces. A dog suspected of having gastroenteritis should be treated symptomatically for the diarrhea and vomiting without delay.

**Coccidiosis.** Coccidiosis is caused by a protozoal infection of the intestinal tract. A dog may have diarrhea, sometimes bloody, and appear poor in condition. It may cough and have a runny nose as well as discharge from the eyes. Puppies seem to be the hardest hit. Coccidiosis is diagnosed by examination of a stool sample. Owners are advised to keep the dog's living area clean and dry.

**Constipation.** Dogs that are normally regular and suddenly do not defecate for a day or two may be constipated. Constipation is caused by a variety of factors such as low dietary fiber or ingesting bones, grass, paper, or other indigestible substances. Dogs with impacted feces may seem listless, lose their appetite, or vomit. Even though they are constipated, they sometimes pass small amounts of blood-tinged or watery brown fecal material reminiscent of diarrhea. The feces of long-haired dogs can become trapped in the hair over the anus, blocking defecation. In still other cases, an enlarged prostate gland, colon problem, or perineal hernia can interfere with the dog's normal elimination process. Laxatives, enemas, or a change in diet may be necessary. The hindquarters of longhaired dogs must always be kept clean and free of mats.

**Diarrhea.** Diarrhea—loose, soft, often abundant stools—is common in dogs. Most cases of simple, mild diarrhea can be successfully treated at home. However, if diarrhea persists for more than twenty-four hours, contains blood, or is accompanied by vomiting, fever, or other signs of distress, call the veterinarian. Be ready to describe the color, consistency, and odor of the stool, as well as the frequency of elimination. As with vomiting, eating irritating and indigestible material is a common cause of diarrhea. Diarrhea can also follow an emotional upset such as a trip away from home. An abrupt change in diet or switching to unfamiliar water can also cause diarrhea. In addition, some dogs just can't tolerate certain foods. Other causes can include intestinal parasites or a viral or bacterial infection. Many of the diseases that cause vomiting also cause diarrhea. To resolve uncomplicated diarrhea at home, follow the recommendations outlined for vomiting. Continue for three days, even if the condition seems to have cleared up, and then return to a normal diet.

**Eating Stools (Coprophagy).** Some dogs are attracted to the taste of fecal material, an objectionable and unhealthy habit. A change of diet may solve the problem. Sprinkling meat tenderizer on the dog's food may also help by altering the taste of the feces. If all else fails, your veterinarian can provide you with something that imparts a bitter taste to the feces. A persistent case should be evaluated by a veterinarian to see whether there is an organic cause.

**Flatulence.** Various foods, including onions, beans, cauliflower, cabbage, and soybeans, can cause flatulence. So can a diet that includes a lot of milk or meat. If a change of menu does not improve the situation, a veterinarian may prescribe medication to control gas formation within the digestive tract.

**Giardiasis.** This disease is caused by *Giardia canis,* a microscopic intestinal parasite that lives in contaminated water. Dogs develop diarrhea, sometimes containing bloody mucus. A diagnosis of giardiasis is made by examining a stool sample.

**Pancreatic Insufficiency.** When the pancreas is unable to produce the necessary enzymes, food cannot be properly digested and absorbed. This is known as pancreatic exocrine insufficiency (PEI). A dog that usually has an enormous appetite starts losing weight. Stools are characteristically light in color and may appear soft or oily due to large amounts of undigested fats and proteins. Fecal material is typically produced in large quantity. Pancreatic exocrine insufficiency is treated with lifelong supplementation of pancreatic enzymes, with a low-fat, moderate-protein diet.

**Pancreatitis.** Acute pancreatitis tends to occur in young, adult, overweight dogs that eat fatty foods. The first signs of acute pancreatitis occur several hours after eating and include vomiting and diarrhea. A dog in this condition can become severely dehydrated, or even go into shock, and should be seen by a veterinarian as soon as possible.

**Proctitis.** Diarrhea, impacted anal glands, hard stools, insect bites, or worms can lead to a sore anal region. The dog may lick or bite or drag its hindquarters across the floor. The area should be cleaned and covered with a soothing ointment while the source of the problem is identified and eliminated.

**Regurgitation.** Unlike vomiting, regurgitation requires little or no effort— the food merely rolls up and out of the esophagus. Several conditions can cause regurgitation, including esophageal disease, obstruction, or generalized muscle disease.

**Swallowed Foreign Bodies.** Some swallowed objects pass harmlessly through the gastrointestinal tract. Others can block or puncture the stomach or intestines. A dog in trouble will vomit, retch, or cough, and may bleed or have abdominal pain. An esophageal blockage will cause a dog to drool, swallow painfully, and perhaps regurgitate food and water. Call a veterinarian for advice whenever something inappropriate has been swallowed. Surgery may be necessary to remove a potentially dangerous item.

**Vomiting.** Vomiting is a symptom rather than a disease. If your dog vomits once or twice but otherwise seems healthy, there is probably no need to worry. Frequent, forceful, or unusual vomiting (containing blood, fecal-type matter, worms, or foreign objects) or vomiting accompanied by other signs of illness (such as diarrhea, lethargy, weight loss, dull coat) should be checked by a veterinarian at once. Most cases of mild vomiting are caused by eating something inappropriate such as garbage or plants. After emptying their stomachs, many dogs produce a frothy, clear, or yellow liquid. If the vomiting is otherwise uncomplicated, you can try withholding food (small quantities of water are permissible) for twelve to twenty-four hours. Once the vomiting subsides, begin feeding the dog a bland diet—typical examples are baby food or a mixture of cooked rice and boiled hamburger. Give these foods in small portions for the first day. If the vomiting does not recur, feed bland food in normal portions the next day and then return to the dog's usual diet. Persistent or worsening vomiting should be brought to the veterinarian's attention. Vomiting can accompany infections, obstructions, tumors, pancreatitis, renal failure, liver failure, adrenal failure, and other serious illnesses.

# THE EYES

A dog's eyes serve the obvious purpose of vision, helping the dog interpret the physical world around it. Symptoms that may indicate an eye problem include the following:

- abnormal discharge
- excessive or inadequate tearing
- inflamed tissues
- vision loss
- unusual growths in or around the eye
- whiteness or opaqueness in the eye
- depressions on the surface of the eye
- swelling
- sensitivity to light
- fluttering of the iris

**Cataracts.** Cataracts are any opacity that occurs on the lens, an internal structure of the eye. They are very common in older dogs. Cataracts may be inherited (these occur at any age) or develop as a complication of diabetes. The degree of vision loss varies from individual to individual. Surgical removal of the lens can restore functional vision.

**Central Progressive Retinal Atrophy (CPRA).** Another inherited retinal disease, CPRA affects the pigment cells at the center of the retina, the area responsible for the dog's best vision. Because of this cellular destruction, the dog has difficulty seeing stationary objects. However, it can still see objects in motion because they are detected by cells in the peripheral areas of the retina (see PRA).

**Cherry Eye.** If the tear gland on the inner surface of the dog's nictitating membrane (third eyelid) becomes displaced, it can appear as a cherrylike growth in the inner corner of the eye. Antibiotics and anti-inflammatory drugs may help relieve very mild cases of cherry eye, but surgery is necessary to permanently repair most cases.

**Conjunctivitis.** Conjunctivitis is an inflammation of the smooth, pink tissue that lines the lids and covers part of the eyeball. Swelling and discharge are noted. A clear or watery discharge suggests an allergy, foreign body, or physical irritant such as a blast of wind. A puslike or colored discharge indicates the presence of bacterial infection. Conjunctivitis is treated by eliminating the cause and administering an ophthalmic antibiotic.

**Corneal Ulcer.** An ulcerated cornea often appears cloudy, and a depression in the corneal surface may be visible. The eye has a thin, watery discharge that becomes purulent. Ulcers are painful, so the eye is often closed. Many corneal ulcers begin as a small scratch or an irritation such as a misplaced eyelash. Ulcers should be treated as soon as possible to prevent serious complications.

**Distichiasis (extra eyelashes).** Some dogs have surplus or misplaced eyelashes on the inner edge of the lids. These hairs rub against the cornea and irritate the eye. Problematic eyelashes are often removed permanently through surgery.

**Ectropion.** Ectropion is the inverse of entropion; that is, the eyelid rolls away from the eye. Ectropion commonly occurs in dogs with loose facial skin. The condition is caused by heredity, injury, or loss of muscle tone. The eyes are insufficiently protected, so they are susceptible to irritation. Reconstructive surgery may be necessary.

**Entropion.** The eyelid of a dog with entropion rolls toward the eye, allowing the lashes to rub against and irritate the cornea. There is excessive tearing. The eye is at risk of infection or corneal ulceration. Surgical correction of entropion, which is usually a congenital and genetic defect, is required.

**Epiphora (watery eyes).** Excessive tearing stains the hair around the eyes and face, especially in white dogs, and can lead to local inflammation or infection. The cause may be eye pain or inadequate tear duct drainage. Removing the source of the irritation, treating the infection with antibiotics, or flushing the nasolacrimal drainage system can help.

**Glaucoma.** Glaucoma occurs when there is increased pressure inside the eye. This pressure destroys ocular tissue, particularly the retina and optic nerve. Complete or partial loss of vision can occur suddenly or gradually. Glaucoma is congenital or associated with other eye disease or damage. Early signs of glaucoma include redness of ocular tissue and squinting. In the late stages of glaucoma the dog may have a blank expression, enlarged pupils, and hazy, opaque corneas. Glaucoma requires immediate veterinary attention, at the earliest indication of a problem to prevent progression to blindness.

**Keratitis.** Keratitis is an inflammation of the cornea. A gradual loss of transparency is noted, until the cornea finally appears milky, bluish, or relatively opaque. The eyelids may be swollen, and the dog will squint. A watery or purulent ocular discharge can be seen. Keratitis can lead to partial or complete blindness, so have the dog treated as soon as signs are evident.

**Keratoconjunctivitis Sicca (dry eye).** Inadequate tear production can dry out and damage the cornea. This condition can be caused by a problem with the tear gland or as a side effect of some medications. Frequent administration of a lubricating solution, a tear-stimulating medication, or surgery to help the dog produce fluids that bathe the external eye, are possible remedies.

**Lens Luxation.** Dislocation of the lens can occur with glaucoma or as an inherited weakness of the intraocular tissues that hold the lens in place. One sign is fluttering of the iris. The lens can fall into other areas of the eyeball. Surgical removal of the lens may be necessary.

**Pannus.** Pannus, a form of keratitis, is most commonly observed in German Shepherd Dogs. A pink, fleshy membrane develops on the cornea. The eye may be watery and the eyelids are inflamed. Affected dogs are usually over two years old. Medical treatment and surgery are effective in controlling the disease, but there is no permanent cure.

**Progressive Retinal Atrophy (PRA).** PRA is a genetic disease in which the cells of the retina gradually degenerate, leading to blindness. Many breeds of dogs are affected. The age of onset varies with the breed and is usually breed specific. The first sign of disease may be loss of night vision. The dog may undergo a variety of behavioral changes, especially in situations where light is limited. There is no treatment for this disease (see CPRA).

**Prolapsed Eyeball.** A prolapsed eyeball has come out of its socket—a true emergency that can follow major trauma. Protect and moisten the eye as you seek immediate veterinary assistance, and be ready to treat the dog for shock. Do not try to force the eye back into place. This may increase swelling and cause greater damage. If you cannot get to a veterinarian right away, lubricate the eye with a few drops of olive or mineral oil and gently draw the lids outward and over the eyeball.

# THE EARS

The ears of dogs are finely tuned sensory organs that enable them to hear sounds we cannot. The following signs may indicate an ear problem:

- abnormal discharge
- abnormal wax accumulation
- scratching
- scabs or crusts

- swelling and tenderness
- hearing loss
- foul odor
- head tilt
- inflammation
- head shaking

**Deafness.** Deafness occurs because of trauma, congenital defects, infection, distemper, drugs, loud noises, or simply old age. Signs include difficulty in awakening the dog or failure to respond to a loud noise made outside the dog's field of vision. Some cases are curable, such as a bacterial infection of the middle or inner ear or a resectable tumor in the external ear canal. Deafness from trauma or loud noises may clear up with time. There is no cure or treatment for nerve deafness.

**External Ear Infection (Otitis Externa).** Infections of the external ear canal are common, especially in dogs with large, flaplike ears. These create a dark, moist environment suitable for fungal or bacterial growth. Soap, water, parasites, foreign bodies, or an excess of hair or wax in the ear can encourage an infection, as can allergies. Also, certain breeds are more prone to ear infections than are others. An infected ear is tender, red, swollen, and malodorous. An abundance of wax or discharge is often visible within the canal. A veterinarian should clean and treat the ear before the infection worsens. Chronic ear infections may be helped by surgery to improve drainage and air flow.

**Hematoma.** A hematoma is caused by bleeding between the cartilage and skin of the ear flap. These swollen areas tend to occur suddenly, often in conjunction with head shaking, and are especially common in dogs with long, hanging ears. Hematomas heal on their own, but the healing process often leaves the ear deformed. Many owners opt for surgery to remove the blood clot and restore a normal appearance to the ear.

**Parasites.** An infestation of otodectic or sarcoptic mites is extremely itchy. Affected dogs will repeatedly scratch and shake their head. In addition, dogs with sarcoptic mange will have red, crusty ear tips. Ticks may be found inside or on the ear. These should be removed carefully, making certain not to disturb the ear canal. The ears are also susceptible to annoying fly bites.

# THE MOUTH AND NECK

The structures within the mouth possess the ability to sense, defend, communicate, and obtain nutrition. The neck contains organs involved in respiration, subsistence, and vocalization. The following are signs that may indicate a mouth or neck problem:

- unusual drooling or discharge from the mouth
- pawing at the mouth
- bleeding
- head shaking
- dysphagia (difficulty in swallowing)
- scabs
- inflammation of the lips, mouth, tongue, gums, or throat
- appetite loss
- coughing
- gagging
- bad breath
- swelling beneath the eye
- unusual growths

**Burns.** Oral burns are not uncommon since dogs use their mouths to investigate their environment. Mild burns, such as those that result from chewing on an electrical cord, usually heal by themselves. Feeding a soft diet will help. If the burn is more serious or the tissue continues to look unhealthy, a veterinarian's help is necessary.

**Cheilitis.** Cheilitis is an inflammation of the lips and lip folds. Typical causes include an embedded thorn or burr, an injury, an infection of the mouth or ears, or even licking an infected area elsewhere on the body. Cheilitis is a particular problem in breeds with heavy jowls. Dogs will paw at the affected area. They may drool or stop eating, and the area smells foul. Crusts form at the edges of the lips over raw, sensitive skin. The affected area must be kept clean and dry. Antibiotics may be necessary.

**Drooling.** Drugs, poisons, local irritation or inflammation, nervousness or fear, infectious disease, or a problem with the salivary glands may cause abnormal drooling. Treatment depends upon identifying and correcting the cause of the problem.

**Foreign Bodies.** Foreign bodies in the mouth are not uncommon, especially splintered wood, which can penetrate the lips, gums, or palate or become wedged between the teeth or across the roof of the mouth. In fact, any sharp object can become embedded in a dog's mouth. Signs include gagging, coughing, drooling, and refusal to eat. Dogs may paw at their mouths or shake their heads. An infection can occur if the object is not removed promptly.

**Gingivitis and Periodontal Disease.** Gingivitis usually follows poor oral hygiene. The gums are red, swollen, and uncomfortable, and bleed easily. The breath is offensive. The problem worsens when food and bacteria collect between the teeth and gums, paving the way for periodontal disease. Brushing the dog's teeth regularly can help remove tartar and prevent gingivitis and periodontal disease. However, most dogs still need occasional dental scaling and possibly periodontal treatment in a veterinarian's office.

**Glossitis.** Glossitis, or inflammation of the tongue, may be associated with diseases elsewhere in the body. Excessive tartar on the teeth, foreign bodies, cuts, burns, or insect stings are also common causes. The dog drools and refuses food. The edges of the tongue may look red and swollen. In severe cases, the tongue may bleed or exude a thick, brown malodorous discharge.

**Oral Papillomatosis.** Oral papillomas are benign warts that appear individually or in groups in and around the mouth. They are most common in puppies. Although papillomas are not usually considered dangerous, they can interfere with eating or become infected, in which case they need veterinary treatment.

**Pharyngitis.** Pharyngitis may accompany a respiratory infection. The throat is inflamed, and dogs will cough, gag, and may lose their appetite or have a fever. In severe cases breathing is complicated by swollen lymph tissues in the back of the throat. Antibiotics and a soft diet during recuperation are usually recommended.

**Salivary Mucoceles.** Soft swellings under the jaw and on the neck could be due to a traumatized salivary gland and subsequent accumulation of saliva beneath the skin. See your veterinarian.

**Stomatitis.** A painful oral inflammation, stomatitis usually causes dogs to paw at their mouth, and shake their head. They drool, especially during meals, although many eat less or lose their appetite completely. They may drink more than usual. The gums are red, swollen, and tender and may bleed when touched (indications of gingivitis). The breath has an unpleasant odor and, in severe cases, there is a thick, brown oral discharge. Treatment depends upon the source of the inflammation—broken or diseased teeth, gingival disease, systemic illness, foreign bodies, or a tumor.

**Tonsillitis.** Tonsillitis usually affects young dogs and may be associated with a respiratory infection. As with pharyngitis the throat is sore, but fever is more pronounced. Short-faced breeds may be prone to chronic tonsillitis. Dogs are treated with antibiotics, but tonsillectomy may be recommended for patients with recurrent attacks or those whose tonsils interfere with normal breathing or swallowing.

# THE NERVOUS SYSTEM

The nervous system includes the brain, spinal cord, and peripheral nerves. It receives, conducts, and interprets sensory information and sends messages to muscles and other organs. The following are signs that may indicate a neurological problem:

- seizures
- lack of coordination
- sensory abnormalities
- bizarre behavior

- progressive weakness
- paralysis
- changes in muscle tone

**Rabies.** Rabies is transmitted by direct contact with the saliva of an infected animal, commonly a skunk, fox, bat, or raccoon. There is little chance of survival once the virus starts reproducing in the body. The first sign of disease is a marked personality change. The dog may seem overly affectionate or shy, or restless or aggressive. The pupils may be dilated, and the dog may be bothered by light. Rabid dogs progressively shun attention and finally resist handling. They may also vomit and have diarrhea or a fever.

Two types of rabies have been described: *furious* and *paralytic*. The *furious* dog bites at everything in sight. The facial muscles twitch, the teeth are bared, and movements are uncoordinated. The *paralytic* form causes loss of muscle control—the mouth drops open and the tongue hangs out. The dog may drool, cough, paw at the mouth, and experience a voice change. Eventually the dog loses coordination, collapses, becomes comatose, and dies. Dogs may have one form of the disease or a combination of both. There is no treatment for rabies in the dog. Regular vaccinations are imperative, for the protection of human and dog. The only test for rabies is through autopsy.

**Seizures.** During a typical seizure dogs will collapse, paddle their limbs, twitch, vocalize, urinate, or defecate. The dog returns to normal after the episode. Seizures are caused by viral, bacterial, and fungal infections of the brain or brain tumors, intoxication, and head trauma. Metabolic disease (such as low blood sugar) or an irregular heartbeat can also cause seizures. When a cause is unidentifiable, the dog is said to have *idiopathic epilepsy*. Certain breeds are thought to have a higher incidence of epilepsy than other breeds. Treatment with anti-epileptic drugs can prevent seizures or lessen their severity. Seizures are life-threatening when they are continuous or reoccur after only short breaks.

**Tetanus.** Tetanus is characterized by the gradual onset of generalized stiffness that often begins with spasms of the jaw and head muscles and progresses to a stiff, "sawhorse" gait. The dog has difficulty swallowing and the tail often becomes rigid. Spasms worsen until the dog breathes laboriously and seems exhausted. The tetanus bacteria lives in soil, feces, and putrefying material; it enters the body through injured tissue. A dog with tetanus requires hospitalization. Recuperation generally requires four weeks or longer.

**Tick Paralysis.** This disease occurs when dogs are poisoned by a toxin in the saliva of the wood tick. It may follow a heavy tick infestation. Although dogs do not seem to be in any pain, they grow progressively weaker. If the muscles of respiration are involved, the dog may suffocate.

**Tumors.** Tumors affecting the nervous system usually occur in older dogs, although they may appear in dogs of all ages. Signs depend on the site of the tumor.

# THE URINARY SYSTEM

The urinary system includes the kidneys, ureters, bladder, prostate (in male dogs), and urethra. The major organ is the kidney, which maintains the correct water and electrolyte balance and excretes the waste products of metabolism. The following signs may indicate a urinary problem:

- excessive drinking and urination
- inability to urinate
- hunched posture
- uncontrollable urination
- loss of weight and appetite
- straining to urinate
- blood or pus in the urine
- frequent urination in small amounts

**Bladder Infection (cystitis).** Cystitis is an infection of the bladder. It is common in both male and female dogs. Individuals with cystitis urinate frequently and there may be blood in the urine. Urination may appear difficult or painful. Bitches may also have a vaginal discharge and lick the vulva often. Antibiotics are needed.

**Bladder Stones.** Bladder stones are fairly common in both male and female dogs. Some breeds are more prone to this problem than others. Dalmatians, in particular, are predisposed to urate stone formation. Bladder stones cause a dog to strain while urinating and to urinate frequently in small amounts. The urine may have a strong odor and may contain blood. In male dogs, small stones can block the passage of urine through the urethra. The dog will strain but may not be able to produce any urine, or may dribble. Treatment is essential. Stones may need to be surgically removed, and medication or dietary changes can prevent new ones from forming.

**Chronic Kidney Failure.** Dogs in kidney failure cannot adequately clear the body of metabolic waste products. Chronic kidney failure, the most common form, can occur in any breed at any age. The first signs are excessive thirst and urination, weight and appetite loss, and vomiting. The kidney may already be considerably damaged by the time the problem is diagnosed. Waste products begin to accumulate in the blood, and the dog appears listless, weak, and depressed and may be dehydrated. Treatment and support may prolong what time the dog has left, but this disease is ultimately fatal. Recognizing kidney failure and obtaining proper veterinary help as soon as possible can help make treatment more effective.

**Congenital Kidney Defects (renal dysplasia, hypoplasia).** Some renal diseases arise from abnormal development of the kidneys. Signs include excessive thirst and urination, listlessness, depression, loss of appetite, and ammonia-like breath. Growth may be stunted. Treatment is similar to that for chronic renal failure.

**Prostate Infection (prostatitis).** A prostate infection typically causes difficult, painful urination in male dogs. They may be feverish and stand in a hunched-up manner. A penile discharge is often produced. Prostatitis is treated with appropriate antibiotics, but it can be a chronic problem.

# THE REPRODUCTIVE SYSTEM

The reproductive system includes organs that contribute to the production of offspring. The following signs may indicate a reproductive problem:

- abnormal genital discharge
- undescended testicles
- distended abdomen
- loss of appetite and energy
- excessive drinking and urination
- abortion or failure to conceive
- inflammation or pain in the genital or breast area
- unusual lumps in the genital or breast area

**Brucellosis.** Brucellosis, a bacterial disease, can cause sterility in either sex at any age. It can also cause abortion and failure to whelp in females, swollen or shrunken testicles in males, and enlarged lymph nodes in both sexes. Infected dogs may have a poor coat, seem slightly depressed, and have swollen, painful joints. However, dogs may show no signs of illness and still infect other individuals with whom they have contact. Brucellosis is commonly spread through sexual intercourse, aborted tissues, and vaginal excretions. When a bitch aborts, she and any other dogs in the kennel should be tested for brucellosis. Any male that has been associated with the infected female also needs to be examined.

**Canine Herpesvirus.** Signs of canine herpesvirus are usually so mild in adult dogs that the disease goes unnoticed, or a mild case of vaginitis may be observed in an adult bitch. The virus is fatal to newborn puppies, however, who become infected from their mother during birth or by exposure to infected saliva. Apparently healthy puppies suddenly die after only a brief period of illness, usually lasting less than twenty-four hours.

**Canine Venereal Granulomas.** This disease is characterized by soft tumors in the genital area of either sex. Intercourse or licking an infected individual seems to spread the disease. An infected bitch can pass the disease to her offspring. The tumors may heal spontaneously, or they can be removed.

**Infection of the Penis (balanoposthitis).** A small amount of discharge from the penis is normal for most adult, intact dogs. However, a dog that licks the prepuce often or has excessive, discolored, or foul-smelling discharge may have an infection. The penis may be intensely red and covered with small bumps. See your veterinarian for an accurate diagnosis and course of treatment.

**Inflammation of the Testicle (orchitis).** Orchitis may be caused by injury or disease, and can cause infertility. The inflamed testicles are firm, enlarged, and painful. The dog may walk strangely and prefer to sit on cold surfaces. Orchitis should be treated promptly, before the dog becomes infertile.

**Mammary Tumors.** Breast tumors are the most common type of tumor in intact bitches. Approximately half are benign. These small, firm lumps appear in the vicinity of the nipples, usually the rear nipples. They may start in groups that form a rapidly growing mass. Malignant mammary tumors tend to spread to the lymph nodes and the lungs. Early spaying (before the first heat) greatly reduces the risk of mammary tumors later in life. All bitches should have regular breast examinations, especially during middle and old age.

**Metritis.** Metritis is another serious uterine infection. Signs are similar to pyometra: depression, appetite loss, vomiting, diarrhea, and excessive thirst. A malodorous discharge from the vulva, when present, is reddish and watery or dark and purulent. The infection can occur during or after estrus, or postpartum. A retained placenta or fetus and the use of contaminated whelping instruments are some possible causes.

**Pyometra.** Pyometra is a potentially fatal uterine infection that occurs in unspayed females. The infected uterus fills with pus. If the pus manages to leak out the vulva, it is malodorous, thick, and bloody. The bitch typically stops eating, acts listless, and drinks and urinates more frequently. She may vomit and develop a fever. Medical treatment is occasionally attempted to save the bitch for future breeding, but surgical removal of the uterus is usually necessary.

**Undescended Testicles.** The canine testicles usually descend soon after birth. If both are not descended by six months, have the puppy examined by a veterinarian. Cryptorchid dogs—those with no descended testicles or only one testicle in the scrotum—run a higher risk of developing testicular tumors. These dogs should not be used for breeding, since the defect may be passed to the offspring.

**Vaginal Infection (vaginitis).** Signs include excessive licking of the vulva, which may be accompanied by an abnormal vaginal discharge that may stain the genital region. Vaginitis may also make a bitch unusually attractive to males. In young females, the infection may be characterized by painful urination and small amounts of discharge. Antibiotics and douches may be used to treat the condition.

# MULTISYSTEMIC PROBLEMS

Some diseases tend to affect several body systems simultaneously. A few of these multisystemic problems are represented here.

**Diabetes Mellitus.** Diabetes mellitus is characterized by uncontrolled levels of blood sugar. Diabetic dogs typically drink and urinate excessively. They also lose weight, although their appetite is good. They are at risk of developing cataracts. Some diabetic dogs become ketoacidotic, a serious complication that occurs when waste products accumulate in the blood. These dogs appear nauseated and they may vomit. Their breath may smell sweet. They become dehydrated, develop rapid, labored breathing, and can fall into a hyperglycemic coma. Intravenous fluids, insulin, and control of ketoacidosis are necessary. Many diabetic dogs lead long and happy lives through dietary control, exercise, and regular insulin injections to maintain a suitable blood glucose level. Spaying is recommended for intact females.

**Distemper.** Distemper is highly contagious and very dangerous to dogs. The first signs of this viral infection are loss of appetite, discharge from the nose and eyes, and a dry cough. The dog may also vomit or have diarrhea. Later, the dog may develop neurological symptoms. These include head shaking, drooling, and uncontrollable chewing motions. Twitching and seizures are other signs. The virus can also attack the skin of the feet and nose, causing these surfaces to harden. A dog may or may not recover during the first stage of distemper, but once the brain is affected the chances of recovery are poor. Distemper is a universal disease and remains a principal cause of sickness and death in unvaccinated dogs.

**Canine Hepatitis Virus.** Hepatitis usually spreads through contact with contaminated urine, stool, or saliva. The infected dog develops a fever, red eyes, and a discharge from the eyes, mouth, and nose. In severe cases the dog stops eating and becomes comatose. Within six to ten days after infection a dog either dies or quickly recovers. After recovery, some dogs show a temporary opacity of the eyes, known as *blue eyes.* To prevent infection, all dogs should receive a hepatitis vaccine. This is usually included with the combination vaccine given annually.

**Canine Parvovirus.** Parvovirus attacks rapidly reproducing cells of the bone marrow, lymph nodes, heart (in very young dogs), and gastrointestinal tract. The disease has two forms: the *enteric* or diarrheal form and the *myocardial* or cardiac form. Dogs affected with enteric parvovirus are depressed and lack appetite. Vomiting and diarrhea, frequently containing blood, follow. A fever is common, especially in young dogs. The onset and progression of the disease are rapid. A puppy may die suddenly, or die soon after showing initial signs. A puppy that has recovered from myocarditis can develop a chronic form of congestive heart failure, which may lead to premature death. Parvovirus spreads through contaminated feces, easily carried on the feet of humans or canines. Infected living quarters should be thoroughly washed with bleach solution. Sick dogs must be isolated. The only practical way to control parvovirus infection is with regular vaccinations.

**Leptospirosis.** A bacterial disease, leptospirosis is spread through contact with contaminated urine. Infected dogs are depressed and weak. Some show abdominal pain. They may drink and urinate frequently and in increased amounts. Painful ulcers form in the mouth or on the tongue, which may also develop a thick, brown coating. The whites of the eyes may appear red or jaundiced. Diarrhea, often bloody, and vomiting are also frequent symptoms. Death may occur five to ten days after signs appear. Recovery is slow because of damage to the digestive tract, liver, and kidneys. Because infected dogs can transmit leptospirosis to humans and other dogs, many veterinarians choose to vaccinate against a few variants of this disease.

**Toxoplasmosis.** Toxoplasmosis is a protozoal disease. Young animals are more commonly and seriously affected, but severe or fatal toxoplasmosis is rare. Signs of illness, when present, include coughing, labored breathing, fever, apathy, loss of appetite and weight, enteritis, and disturbances of the nervous system such as tremors, lack of coordination, and paralysis.

# CANINE FIRST AID

*F*IRST AID IS A PRACTICAL STEP TOWARD GAINING CONTROL IN AN EMERGENCY. Judiciously used, it can spare a dog further injury and pain. More significant, first aid can help save a dog's life.

For the most part, the following techniques are preliminary measures that owners should take *before* they reach their veterinarian. The telephone numbers of your veterinarian, local emergency clinic, and poison-control center should be kept nearby at all times. In an emergency, always call ahead to describe the nature of the problem and to alert the staff that you are on the way. If you are calling about poisoning, try to have whatever your dog ingested on hand.

## RESTRAINT

Pain may arouse the biting instinct in even the most trustworthy animal, so muzzling is recommended. You can use panty hose, cotton bandage material, a necktie, or a piece of rope—anything strong and about two feet long. Tie a loose knot in the middle, leaving a large loop. Slip the loop over the dog's nose and tighten the knot over the bridge of the nose. Bring the ends under the chin, tie a knot, and then draw the ends behind the ears and tie again. If the dog is short nosed, take one of the ends from behind the ears, pass it over the forehead, and slip it under the loop around the nose. Bring it back over the forehead and tie it firmly with the remaining end. Tie a muzzle firmly but not so tight that it interferes with breathing.

## TRANSPORTING AN INJURED DOG

Special handling is necessary to minimize the risk of further injury. An injured dog may be transported atop a suitably sized firm surface such as a plywood board.

A board is particularly useful for carrying large breeds. A blanket or large towel can serve as a stretcher for a dog of any size. Dogs weighing less than fifty pounds may be safely moved inside a sturdy box. Small dogs may also be wrapped gently in a blanket or towel and carried in your arms.

# ARTIFICIAL RESPIRATION

Artificial respiration helps supply oxygen to the dog that is not breathing. It requires breathing into the dog's mouth, so be cautious—even dogs in respiratory arrest can reflexively close their jaws without warning.

Lay the dog on its side. Open the dog's mouth and check for obstructions. Extend the tongue and look into the throat to make sure the passage is clear. Remove any mucus or blood from the mouth, then shut it and gently hold it closed.

Now inhale deeply. Completely cover the dog's nose with your mouth and exhale *gently*. Carefully force air into the lungs, and watch the dog's chest for expansion. Repeat every five to six seconds, or ten to twelve breaths a minute.

# HEART MASSAGE

Heart massage should be performed only if the dog's heart has stopped beating. It must be combined with artificial respiration to approximate a technique known as cardiopulmonary resuscitation (CPR). When performed properly, CPR can help restore breathing and cardiac function in an emergency. A basic course in CPR will help you better understand and perform this lifesaving technique.

Lay the dog on its right side, place your hands over the heart area on the dog's left side and press firmly about seventy times per minute. With small dogs, place one hand on either side of the chest wall near the elbows. Compress about seventy times per minute. The chest diameter should compress approximately 20 to 30 percent. Be careful not to break the ribs.

# BLEEDING

A pressure dressing is used to slow or stop external bleeding. Place several pieces of clean gauze over the wound and bandage snugly, applying pressure evenly. Watch for swelling below the pressure dressing, a sign that the bandage must be loosened or removed. If at all possible, avoid using elasticized tape or bandage material. When bandages are unavailable, you may place a pad or even a clean hand on the wound and press firmly.

Blood will spurt forcefully from a severed artery. If direct pressure fails to slow the rate of bleeding, a tourniquet may be necessary. Tourniquets must be used *very* carefully, or they can do more damage than good. A tourniquet may be fashioned out of a loop of rope, gauze, or cloth and should be placed on the extremity between the injury and the heart. Then, gently but firmly tighten the tourniquet until bleeding is visibly decreased at the wound site. The tourniquet must be loosened approximately every ten minutes to allow blood flow to the tissue.

# SHOCK

Shock is a general term for a condition characterized by collapse of the cardiovascular system. It occurs most often after major trauma, such as being hit by a car. Animals in shock are weak and depressed, and their pupils may be dilated. The pulse is weak and rapid. The gums are pale, and color is slow to return after they are pressed with a finger. (The gums of a healthy dog normally regain color within one to two seconds after pressure is applied.)

If you believe a dog is in shock, it is important to respond at once. Apply pressure to any bleeding wounds and keep the animal quiet and warm. Transport the dog to an emergency facility without delay.

# FRACTURES

To reduce the risk of further trauma, muzzle the dog and use a board or other secure method of transportation to reach a veterinarian. Move the dog as little as possible during the journey and try to support the broken limb at all times—a rolled-up magazine, cushion, or even a hand will help. If bone fragments are visible, place clean bandage material or cloth over the area until professional care is obtained.

# FISH HOOKS

A small fish hook caught in a relatively inoffensive place may be removed at home. Push the hook forward through the skin until the barb emerges, then clip it off with pliers or wire cutters. The other piece should then remove easily. Do not, however, attempt to remove a deeply embedded hook or one that is located on the face or feet. You must first muzzle the dog, and it may even be necessary to sedate the dog, because pushing the hook forward will be very painful.

If the problem involves a lure with multiple hooks, the dog may work at the lure and cause further injury. Cover the lure with a cloth or towel to protect yourself and the dog from the exposed barbs, and get to a veterinarian quickly.

Never attempt to retrieve a swallowed hook by pulling on the line. This can severely damage the esophagus or stomach, and increases the difficulty of removal. Cut the line as short as possible and seek immediate veterinary help.

# HEATSTROKE

Heatstroke causes fast, shallow breathing and a rapid heartbeat. The dog will run a very high temperature (104 degrees or above) and may be in shock. A dangerously overheated dog will probably die without prompt treatment. Immediately spray the dog with cool water; pack ice in the groin and around the head and neck; or wrap the dog in cold, wet towels. Seek professional care at once.

Most cases of heatstroke are preventable. Never leave a dog inside a closed car or poorly ventilated kennel on a hot day, and go easy with exercise in the summer. Dogs need fresh air, sufficient shade, and access to plenty of water during hot weather. Never leave your dog outside with no shelter from the sun or without clean water.

# POISONS

Signs of poisoning include trembling, weakness, drooling, vomiting, and loss of bowel control. Common sources of poisons are insecticides (products intended to kill fleas or ticks, for example, or garden bug sprays) and oral worming medications. These products should always be used according to a veterinarian's or manufacturer's instructions, and should never be combined without first seeking advice. If your dog exhibits any abnormal signs soon after treatment for parasites, remove the product, if possible, and consult a veterinarian immediately.

Rat poison and other oral rodenticides can produce internal bleeding. If vomiting is induced within a short time (less than thirty minutes) after ingesting most rat poisons, the chance of survival improves. Veterinary help is still necessary. Strychnine-based rodenticides are rapidly absorbed into the system and can cause convulsions and death in a short time.

Acids, alkalis, and petroleum products cause special problems. Vomiting is not advised in these cases, because the substance in the vomitus can damage the dog's esophagus. Immediately consult your veterinarian. If a veterinarian is not available, give an antacid (such as milk of magnesia or Pepto-Bismol) in case of acid poisoning—approximately two teaspoons per five pounds body weight is considered a safe dose. In case of alkali poisoning, a mixture of one part vinegar to four parts water may be given at the same dosage. Mineral or vegetable oil sometimes helps to protect the gastrointestinal tract in petroleum distillate poisoning. One tablespoon per five pounds body weight is a reasonably safe dose.

Antifreeze is another common poison. Severe kidney damage can occur after ingesting a very small quantity. Antifreeze spills should be cleaned up promptly, because they are very attractive to animals. If your dog licks even a very small amount, consult your veterinarian immediately.

Medications should always be kept out of reach of animals. Furthermore, human drugs—even common pain relievers such as aspirin or ibuprofin—should never be used without veterinary advice. In addition, chocolate and products with caffeine can be toxic to dogs.

# BURNS AND TOPICAL IRRITANTS

Minor burns may be treated by gently clipping away the hair, washing with a mild soap, and applying a topical antibiotic steroid ointment. Extensive burns require a veterinarian's attention. Apply ice or a cloth soaked in cold water, cover with a clean cloth, and transport the dog immediately.

Turpentine and gasoline are very irritating and potentially toxic chemical substances that should never be used to remove paint, tar, or grease from a dog's coat. Vegetable oil works quite well for this purpose. Treatment should be followed by bathing with a mild soap.

For a discussion of the condition called hot spots, see "The Skin" in the "Common Illnesses" section.

# DOGFIGHTS

Dogfights may erupt over territory, social hierarchy, or access to a bitch in heat. Most of these violent encounters end quickly when one dog indicates submission to the other.

Before you intervene, calmly (but rapidly) try to consider what will effectively separate the dogs without causing harm to you. This depends a great deal on the size and strength of the dogs, and on what you have on hand—a dousing with water, for example, can help stop a fight. You may have to let large dogs settle the dispute themselves. To lessen the turmoil, remove other dogs from the scene. If you decide to manually interrupt a fight between small dogs, be very careful—you may well get bitten, and even small teeth can do considerable damage.

Injuries sustained by dogs in a fight may look minor, but they can be misleading. Beneath small puncture wounds may be extensive damage to muscle and other tissues. Also, bite wounds are usually heavily contaminated with oral bacteria and are prone to infection. Flush fight wounds with water or hydrogen peroxide and seek veterinary attention as soon as possible.

# VOMITING AND DIARRHEA

Vomiting and diarrhea are signs of a problem involving the digestive system or other body systems. An immediate concern with persistent vomiting or diarrhea is dehydration, especially in very young and old dogs. For advice on treating simple diarrhea and vomiting, refer to the section in "Common Illnesses" on problems of the digestive system. If diarrhea or vomiting continues for more than twenty-four hours or if additional signs of illness are observed, get help from a veterinarian.

# SEIZURES

A seizure can cause a dog to collapse, paddle their limbs, twitch, vocalize, urinate, or defecate. Dogs must be protected from falling down stairs or striking their head or limbs against floors, walls, or furniture. Blankets or towels may be used to move the dog or cushion the body. Be careful when handling the head, because the dog might bite reflexively. Time the duration of the seizure and relay this information to the veterinarian.

# ADMINISTERING MEDICINE

**Pills.** Sometimes the easiest way to administer a pill is by mixing it with food. The pill is inserted into a small amount of soft food, such as peanut butter, or is crushed and mixed with something palatable, such as yogurt or canned dog food. It's easier if the dog is hungry, so it can be a good idea to administer pills right before a meal.

Some medications, however, should not be given with food, or they may not be scheduled to coincide with mealtimes. Also, some dogs have an uncanny way of detecting even the smallest adulteration to their food. In these cases, you must put the pill in the dog's mouth and make sure it is swallowed. Hold the pill in your right hand and stand on the dog's right side. Grasp the top of the muzzle with your left hand. Press the upper lips against the teeth and the dog's mouth will usually start to open. The lips will curl inward around the points of the teeth, protecting your fingers against injury if the dog attempts to close the jaw. Tilt the dog's head slightly upward.

Place the pill on top of the tongue, deep within the throat. Then withdraw your hand and gently hold the mouth closed. Keep the head elevated and tap the dog's nose or stroke the throat. Watch for signs of swallowing; some dogs lick their nose. If the pill is spit out, calmly but firmly repeat the process until you are successful. Feeding a small treat right after the dog has swallowed will help make sure the pill is swallowed, too.

**Liquids.** Liquid medication is best administered from an eyedropper, vial, or small bottle. Spoons are usually too awkward to be useful. Have someone hold the dog's head in a slightly elevated position. Insert two fingers inside the corner of the lips and pull outward away from the teeth. This forms a funnel-like pouch into which the medicine is poured. Most dogs will swallow the medication as it trickles between the teeth. You can also try tapping the nose or jiggling the pouch slightly.

If the dog clenches its jaw and prevents medication from entering the mouth, you can insert the handle of a spoon between the teeth. Once the dog starts swallowing, the rest of the medicine is usually taken without objection.

**Eye Medication.** To apply ophthalmic ointment, use your thumb or forefinger to roll the lower eyelid gently downward and squeeze the medicine into the space between the lid and eye.

For eye drops, grasp the muzzle with one hand and slightly elevate the head while holding the lower lid open. Use the other hand to hold open the upper lid and insert the medication.

Do not touch the open end of a bottle or tube to the eye. This can damage the eye and contaminate the medication.

**Ear Medication.** Tubes of ear ointment often have a long nozzle that can be inserted into the outer ear canal. Liquids can be administered by dropping the medication directly into the ear. Once the ear is medicated, grasp the cartilage below the opening and gently massage it up and down. A moist, sloshing sound indicates that the medication is being distributed inside the ear canal.

# GLOSSARY

**Abdomen:** The belly or undersurface between the chest and hindquarters.

**Abdomen, paunchy:** Loose, flabby abdominal walls, and especially a pendulous underline which, in extreme cases, combine to create a potbellied appearance, in contrast to a tucked-up abdomen.

**Abdomen, tucked-up:** See *Abdomen, paunchy; Tuck-up.*

**Acetabulum:** The cup-shaped portion of the sacrum that articulates with the head (proximal portion) of the femur. Anatomically important in evaluating hip dysplasia.

**Achilles tendon:** The longest and strongest tendon in the dog. Easily discernible in shorthaired breeds, such as the Greyhound and Whippet, the Achilles tendon forms an extension of the rearmost thigh muscle groups and anchors these muscles onto the fibular tarsal bone at the point of the hock.

**Achondroplasia:** A form of genetic dwarfism specifically characterized by arrested development of the long bones. A defect in most breeds and a requisite in others (e.g., Dachshund, Basset Hound).

**Action:** A term used to describe component functions of locomotion (e.g., "action of the hocks"); a synonym for gait in some standards.

**Agility trials:** An organized competition at which dogs negotiate a series of obstacles and jumps in three classes of increasing difficulty. Titles are earned at each level (Novice, Open, and Excellent) by qualifying a predetermined number of times.

**Agouti:** Used in the description of Huskies. This is the alternating bands of light and dark color along each hair in the coat.

**Aitches:** Taken from cattle terminology and interpreted to mean pelvic tubers.

**Albino:** A relatively rare, genetically recessive condition characterized by the inability to synthesize melanin, resulting in white hair and pink eyes.

**Almond eyes:** An elongated eye shape describing the tissue surrounding the eye itself. *Illustration p. 807.*

**Amble:** A relaxed, easy gait in which the legs on either side move almost, but not quite, as a pair. Often seen as the transition movement between the walk and other gaits.

**American-bred class:** A regular class for all dogs (except champions) six months of age whelped in the United States as a result of a mating that took place within the United States.

**Anal sacs:** Two sacs, located on each side of the rectum, just inside the rim of the anal sphincter.

**Anatomy, muscular:** The examination of the special structure of muscles, characterized by their power to contract when stimulated. There are three types of muscles: striated or skeletal muscles, smooth or visceral muscles, and specialized cardiac muscles.

**Anatomy, skeletal:** The examination of the skeleton, which is divided into two sections: the axial skeleton and the appendicular skeleton. The axial skeleton consists of mainly flat and irregular bones in the skull, spine, ribs, and pelvis; their purpose is to protect the vital organs. The appendicular skeleton consists of the fore and hind limbs; these bones provide support for the body and are used for locomotion.

**Anatomy, topographical:** The examination of the outward appearance and identification of the various regions of the dog's anatomy.

**Angulation:** The angles formed by the appendicular skeleton, including the forequarters [shoulders (scapula), upper arm (humerus), forearm (radius, ulna), wrist (carpus), pastern (metacarpus), toes (phalanges)], and hindquarters [hip, pelvis, thigh (femur), second thigh (tibia, fibula), hock (tarsus), rear pastern (metatarus), and toes (phalanges)].

**Ankle:** See *Hock*.

**Ankylosis:** The abnormal immobility and fusion of a joint.

**Anterior:** The front assembly of the body.

**Apex:** The occiput or the rear of the skull.

**Appearance, hard-bitten:** Giving a rugged and tough outward impression, such as that imparted by the Australian Cattle Dog and Australian Terrier.

**Appearance, Thoroughbred:** Resembling a high-quality, aristocratic-looking purebred animal in all respects.

**Apple head:** A domed topskull, rounded in all directions.

**Apron:** The longer hair below the neck on the chest; frill.

**Aquiline:** Curving like an eagle's beak.

**Arched loin:** Muscular development over the spine, *not* a roach.

**Arched skull:** Arches either from side to side or lengthwise from stop to occiput, as opposed to a domed skull.

**Arched toes:** Strong, well knuckled-up feet; cat feet.

**Arm:** The anatomical region between the shoulder and the elbow, including the humerus and associated tissues. Sometimes called the upper arm.

**Articulation:** The junction between two or more bones, typically held together by ligaments.

**Artificial insemination:** The introduction of semen into the female reproductive tract by artificial means.

**Axis:** The second vertebra of the neck. Also the center of rotation.

**Babbler:** A hound that gives tongue when not on the trail.

**Back:** The dorsal surface (topline) of the dog, usually extending from the withers.

**Back dropping through withers:** A topline similar to a hollow back but affecting only the front section immediately behind the withers.

**Back to back:** (1) *Conformation/Obedience:* Two events held by the same club on consecutive days with AKC approval. (2) *Performance:* Two events held on consecutive days at the same location, either by the same club or by two clubs.

**Backbone:** The spinal column.

**Backline:** See *Topline.*

**Badger:** A mixture of white, gray, brown, and black hairs.

**Bad mouth:** Crooked or misaligned teeth; bite overshot or undershot to a greater degree than the standard allows.

**Bait:** The food or object that an exhibitor uses to get a dog's attention or to have it look alert in the ring. The term bait or baiting can also be used to describe the action of getting the dog's attention using food or an object.

**Balance:** A condition wherein all proportions of a dog are in static and dynamic harmony.

**Banded hairs:** A type of hair evident only in the hard, wiry, outer coat. The top coat should be plucked, because clipping will remove the end color bands on each hair, resulting in a solid undesired mixture.

**Bandy legs:** Having a bend of leg outward. *Illustration p. 826.*

**Bar:** The arm or humerus.

**Bar on face:** See *Muzzle band.*

**Bare pastern:** A pastern devoid of long hair, as in the Afghan Hound.

**Barrel:** A rib (thoracic) region that is circular in cross section.

**Barrel hocks:** Hocks that turn out, causing the feet to toe in. Also called spread hocks.

**Barrelled vent:** A protruding anal sphincter.

**Basewide:** A wide footfall, caused by paddling movement, with the result that the body rocks from side to side. See *Paddling.*

**Bat ear:** An erect ear, rather broad at the base, rounded in outline at the top and with the orifice directed to the front (e.g., French Bulldog).

**Bay:** The prolonged bark or voice of the hunting hound.

**Bear ear:** A very rounded-tipped ear.

**Bearlike coat:** A double coat consisting of a harsh outer jacket coupled with a soft, dense, woolly undercoat.

**Beard:** Thick, long hair growth on the underjaw.

**Beauty spot:** A distinct spot, usually round, of colored hair, surrounded by the white blaze, on the topskull between the ears (e.g., Blenheim Spaniel, Boston Terrier). See *Lozenge*.

**Beaver:** See *Badger*.

**Bee-sting tail:** A tail relatively short, strong, straight, and tapering to a point.

**Beefy:** An overheavy development of the hindquarters.

**Belge:** A coat color of black and reddish brown mixture (e.g., Brussels Griffon).

**Belly:** The ventral (under) surface of the abdomen.

**Bell ear:** A big, wide ear.

**Belton:** A color pattern in English Setters (named after a village in Northumberland) characterized by either light or dark ticking or roaning, and including blue belton (black and white), tricolor (blue belton with tan patches), orange belton (orange and white), lemon belton (lemon and white), and liver belton (liver and white).

**Benched show:** A dog show at which the dogs are kept on assigned benches when not being shown in competition, thus facilitating the viewing and discussion of the breeds by attendees, exhibitors, and breeders.

**Best in Show:** The dog judged best of all breeds at a dog show.

**Best of Breed:** The dog selected by the judge as the best representative of a particular breed on that day.

**Best of Opposite Sex:** The best dog that is of the opposite sex to the Best of Breed winner.

**Best of Variety:** At an all-breed show, the award that is given in lieu of Best of Breed for those breeds divided by varieties. At specialty shows, the Best of Variety winners are judged in the Best of Breed competition. See *Variety*.

**Best of Winners:** The dog judged as best between the Winners Dog and Winners Bitch.

**Bevy:** A flock of birds.

**Bi-color:** Composed of two colors.

**Biddable:** Easily taught or controlled.

**Bilateral cryptorchid:** See *Cryptorchid*.

**Bird dog:** A sporting dog bred and trained to hunt game birds.

**Bird of prey eyes:** Light, yellowish eyes, usually harsh in outlook.

**Biscuit:** Grayish yellow color.

**Bitch:** A female canine.

**Bite:** The relative position of the upper and lower teeth when the jaws are closed, including scissors, level, undershot, or overshot. *Illustration p. 807*.

**Blade-bone, blade:** The shoulder blade or scapula.

**Blaireau:** See *Badger*.

**Blanket:** The color of the coat on the back and upper part of the sides, between the neck and the tail.

**Blaze:** A white stripe running up the center of the face, usually between the eyes.

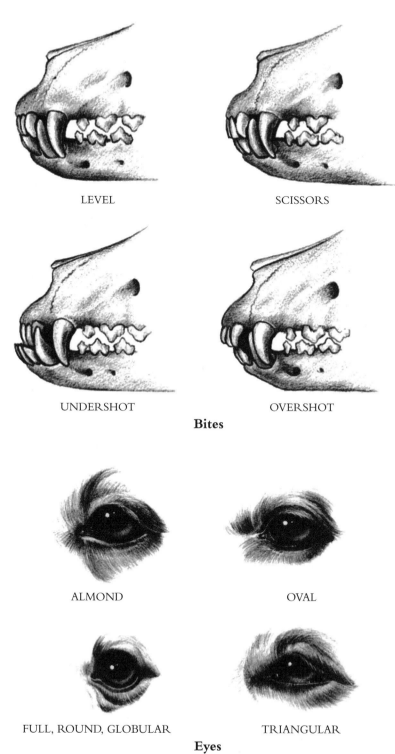

LEVEL

SCISSORS

UNDERSHOT

OVERSHOT

**Bites**

ALMOND

OVAL

FULL, ROUND, GLOBULAR

TRIANGULAR

**Eyes**

**Blenheim:** Used to define the color markings of a variety of the English Toy Spaniel and the Cavalier King Charles Spaniel (red and white).

**Blinker:** A dog that points a bird and then leaves it, or upon finding a bird avoids making a definite point.

**Blocky:** Square or cubelike shape of the head or body.

**Blooded:** A dog of good breeding; pedigreed.

**Bloom:** Prime condition. Often used to describe a dog's coat.

**Blue:** A genetic dilution of black coat color, due to the recessive dilution (dd) color locus, i.e., Bbdd or bbdd dogs will be blue.

**Blue merle:** A color pattern involving black blotches or streaks on a blue-gray background. See *Merle*.

**Bluies:** Colored portions of the coat with a distinct bluish or smoky cast. This coloring is associated with extremely light or blue eyes and liver or gray eye rims, nose, and lip pigment.

**Blunt muzzle:** The opposite of a pointed muzzle, cut off square, forming a right angle with the top of the muzzle.

**Blunt-tip ears:** A rounded-tip ear shape.

**Blunt triangle head:** A V-shaped head with square or rounded ends.

**Bobtail:** A naturally tailless dog or a dog with a tail docked very short. Often used as a nickname for the Old English Sheepdog.

**Bodied up:** Mature, well-developed.

**Body:** The anatomical section between the fore and hindquarters.

**Body, deep through the heart:** Good depth of chest.

**Body length:** Distance from the prosternum (anterior portion of the breastbone) to the posterior portion of the pelvic girdle, i.e., the ischial tuberosities.

**Body spots:** Patches of color, usually black, on the skin but not on the coat of dogs.

**Bone:** A type of connective tissue that forms the canine skeleton. Informally used to suggest the substance of limb bones in proportion to the overall size of a dog.

**Bone, good composition:** Clean, healthy, sound, and strong bone.

**Bone shape:** Reference to the shape of bone in cross section as taken through the forearm. The three types are flat, round, and oval.

**Bone, sound:** Properly structured bone of correct chemical composition, shape, strength, and density.

**Bossy:** The overdevelopment of the shoulder muscles.

**Bounce:** Movement characterized by a greater degree of buoyancy, elasticity, and springiness than usual.

**Bowed legs:** See *Barrel hocks* (rear); *Fiddle front* (front).

**Brace:** (1) Two of the same breed presented together as a pair. (2) To run dogs together in certain types of field events.

**Bracelets:** The name given to the rings of hair on the hind legs of the Poodle.

**Brachycephalic skull:** A broad skull base and short length, as in the Pug and Pekingese.

**Break:** The term used to describe changing coat color from puppies to adult stages. Also used to indicate the opposite of a continuous, smooth line (e.g., "a break in the topline").

**Break in ear:** The line of crease of the fold in a semidrop ear.

**Breastbone:** Also *Sternum;* a row of eight bones that form the floor of the chest.

**Bred-by-exhibitor class:** A regular class for dogs that are:
- Whelped in the U.S. or, if individually registered in the AKC Stud Book, whelped out of the U.S.
- Six months of age and over
- Not champions
- Owned or co-owned by one of its breeders (or the spouse of the breeder)
- Handled by one of its breeders or one of the breeder's immediate family (husband, wife, father, mother, son, daughter, brother, or sister)
- The breeder who handles the dog does not necessarily have to be the one who owns it.

**Breech:** The area designated by the inner thigh muscle groups around the buttocks.

**Breeching:** A fringe of longish hair at the posterior borders of the thigh regions.

**Breed:** A domestic race of dogs (selected and maintained by humans) with a common gene pool and a characterized appearance (phenotype) and function.

**Breed standards:** The set of breed descriptions originally laid down by the various parent breed clubs and accepted officially by international bodies.

**Breeder:** A person who breeds dogs. Under AKC rules, the breeder of a dog is the owner (or, if the dam was leased, the lessee) of the dam of the dog when the dam was bred.

**Breeding particulars:** Sire, dam, date of birth, sex, color, etc.

**Brindle:** A marking pattern used to describe many breeds, usually in conjunction with another color. Layering of black hairs in regions of lighter color (usually, fawn, brown, or gray) producing a tiger-striped pattern. Brindle is often used to describe Great Danes, Bulldogs, and Boxers. In Boxers, Reverse Brindle may occur, i.e., there is such a heavy concentration of black striping that the fawn background color barely, although clearly, shows through (appears black with fawn stripes). Color definitions may vary by breed.

**Brisket:** Usually refers to the sternum, but in some standards it refers to the entire thorax.

**Brisket, deep in brisket:** A reference to a chest well developed in depth.

**Bristle coat:** A coat that is short, bristly, wirehaired, and stiff.

**Broken coat:** A wiry, harsh, crisp coat, consisting of a harsh, wiry outer jacket plus a dense, softer undercoat.

**Broken color:** Self-color broken by white and another color.

**Broken down pastern:** See *Down in pastern.*

**Broken ear:** A deformed, misshapen ear caused by an injury or abnormal construction of the ear cartilage.

**Broken–haired:** A rough wire coat.

**Broken–up face:** A receding nose, together with a deep stop, wrinkle, and undershot jaw (e.g., Bulldog, Pekingese).

**Bronzing:** Tan coloration intermingled with black hairs.

**Brood bitch:** A female used for breeding.

**Brows:** The ridges formed above the eyes by frontal bone contours.

**Brush:** A bushy tail; a tail heavy with hair.

**Brush coat:** A natural, short coat, less than an inch, straight and off-standing, but lying flatter on the limbs.

**Brushing:** A gaiting fault occurring when parallel pasterns are so close that the legs brush in passing.

**Buff:** A color ranging from Irish Setter red to a light cream.

**Bulging eyes:** See *Protruding eyes.*

**Bullbaiting:** An ancient sport in which the dog baited or tormented the bull.

**Bull neck:** A heavy neck, well muscled.

**Burr:** The inside of the ear; the irregular formation visible within the cup.

**Butterfly nose:** A partially unpigmented nose; dark, spotted with flesh color.

**Buttocks:** The rump or hips.

**Button ear:** The ear flap folding forward, the tip lying close to the skull so as to cover the orifice.

**Bye:** At field trials, an odd dog remaining after the dogs entered in a stake have been paired in braces by a random drawing.

**Cabriole front:** See *Fiddle front.*

**Cafe au lait:** Usually used to describe Poodles, this color is typical of the French beverage of the same name, which is about equal parts of coffee and milk. It may be described as rich, well-saturated light brown.

**Calcaneus:** The uppermost extension of the large fibular tarsal bone in the hock joint. See *Achilles tendon.*

**Camel back:** An arched back.

**Canid:** A family (*Canidae*) of carnivorous animals, including dogs, wolves, coyotes, foxes, and jackals.

**Canine Eye Registry Foundation (CERF):** CERF maintains a registry of genetic eye diseases in dogs by cooperating with canine eye specialists, who certify that dogs are free of specific eye problems for one year from the date of the examination.

**Canines:** The two upper and two lower large, conical, pointed teeth behind the incisors and before the premolars. *Illustration p. 824.*

**Canker:** An infection of the external ear canal.

**Cannon bone:** From horse terminology, synonymous with the pastern or metacarpus.

**Canter:** A gait with three beats to each stride, two legs moving separately and two as a diagonal pair. Slower than the gallop and not as tiring.

**Canthus:** The usually well-developed third eyelid located at the inner angle of the palpebral fissure.

**Cap:** A darkly shaded color pattern on the skull of some breeds.

**Cape:** Profuse hair enveloping the shoulder region.

**Carnassial teeth:** The last or fourth premolars in the lower jaw, as well as the first molar in the upper jaw.

**Carpals, carpal joint:** The bones of the wrist.

**Carp back:** Another kind of roach back, similar to a camel back but with little or no initial drop behind the shoulders, and the arch tends to be not as high.

**Carpus:** See *Carpals.*

**Carrot tail:** A short, strong tail, thick at the root and tapering to the tip, carried straight up.

**Cat foot:** A round, compact foot, with well-arched toes, tightly bunched or close-cupped. *Illustration p. 820.*

**Caudal (coccygeal) vertebrae:** The only regionally variable number of vertebrae among breeds in the axial skeleton, lying posterior to the sacrum and defining the tail region.

**Cervical vertebrae:** The seven vertebrae of the neck, articulating anteriorly with the cranium and the thoracic vertebrae.

**Champion (Ch):** A prefix used with the name of a dog that has been recorded a Champion by the AKC as a result of defeating a specified number of dogs in specified competition at a series of AKC-licensed or member dog shows.

**Character:** The expression, individuality, and general appearance and deportment as considered typical of a breed.

**Cheeks:** The fleshy regions at the sides of the head.

**Cheek bumps:** Bulging or prominent cheek areas caused by incorrect bone formation and/or excessive muscle development.

**Cheeky:** Cheeks prominently rounded, thick, and protruding.

**Cherry nose:** See *Dudley nose.*

**Chest:** The part of the body or trunk that is enclosed by the ribs; the thoracic cavity.

**Chestnut:** Usually used to describe Irish Setters and Pharaoh Hounds, the color may be described as deep, heavily saturated, reddish brown (like the nut of the same name).

**Chevron pattern:** V-shaped markings.

**Chewing muscles:** The condyloid process at the top of each ramus that articulates with the temporal bones at the side of the skull to form the temporomandibular joint.

**Chin:** The lower portion of the muzzle.

**China eye:** A clear, flecked or spotted blue, light blue, or whitish eye.

**Chippendale front:** Named after the Chippendale chair. Forelegs out at elbows, pasterns close and feet turned out. See *Fiddle front. Illustration p. 821.*

**Chiseled:** Clean-cut in head, without bumpy or bulging outlines, particularly beneath the eyes.

**Choke collar:** A leather or chain collar fitted to the dog's neck in such a manner that the degree of tension exerted tightens or loosens it; slip collar.

**Chops:** Jowls or pendulous flesh of the lips and jaw.

**Choppy:** See *Mincing gait.*

**Chorea:** A nervous jerking caused by involuntary contractions of the muscles (may be caused by distemper or hepatitis).

**Claw:** Toenail.

**Clean:** Smooth, without excessive muscular or fleshy development.

**Clearing:** See *Break.*

**Cleft palate:** When the two bony halves of the hard palate fail to unite completely along the centerline, leaving a gap between them.

**Clip:** The method of trimming the coat in some breeds, notably the Poodle.

**Clipped keel:** Term used to describe an abnormally short sternum.

**Clipped tail:** See *Dock.*

**Clipping:** When pertaining to gait, the back foot striking the front foot.

**Cloddy:** Low, thickset, comparatively heavy.

**Close-coupled:** Comparatively short from last rib to the commencement of the hindquarters; occasionally used to characterize a comparative shortness from withers to hip bones.

**Close-knit foot:** See *Cat foot.*

**Close-lying coat:** A short, smooth-lying coat.

**Closed skull:** The complete formation of the bones in the center of the skull.

**Closed toe:** See *Cat foot.*

**Clown face:** Black/white and tan/white markings symmetrically divided by a longitudinal line down the center of the skull and foreface.

**Coach dog:** A dog that accompanies carriages as an ornamental appendage (e.g., Dalmatian).

**Coarse:** Lacking refinement.

**Coarse skull:** Excessive skull width, especially around the cheek area.

**Coat:** The dog's hair covering. Most breeds possess an outer coat and an undercoat.

**Cobby:** Short-bodied, compact.

**Coccygeal bone:** The tailbones.

**Cocked ears:** Semidrop, semiprick erect ears on which only the tip is bent forward.

**Cocked-up tail:** A tail raised at right angles to the backline, in terrier fashion, instead of being carried level with the back.

**Coconut matting:** A texture like the outside of a coconut; also the texture of the harsh, durable doormats used to scrape mud off shoes.

**Collar:** The markings around the neck, usually white; also a leather strap or chain for restraining or leading the dog, when the leash is attached.

**Collarette:** The slight ruff formation around the neck.

**Commisures:** The lip corners.

**Communal pad:** The metacarpal pad.

**Compact:** A term used to describe the firmly joined union of various body parts. Also used to describe a short- to medium-length coat, very close-lying, with a dense undercoat and giving a smooth outline.

**Compact toes:** See *Cat foot.*

**Concave neck:** See *Ewe neck.*

**Condition:** Health as shown by the coat, state of flesh, general appearance, and deportment.

**Cone-shaped head:** A triangular outline when viewed both from above and from the side.

**Conformation:** The form and structure, make, shape, and arrangement of the parts of the dog, as they conform to the breed standard.

**Congenital:** Present at birth; may have genetic or environmental causes.

**Conjunctiva:** The mucous membrane lining of both upper and lower eyelids.

**Corded coat:** A coat that hangs in even strands of varying length that is allowed and encouraged to grow into ringlets or dreadlocks.

**Corkscrew tail:** A spiral, curled tail.

**Corky:** Active, lively, alert.

**Corns:** The hard, horny, and callous material that forms on the soles of the foot.

**Couple:** Two hounds.

**Coupling:** The part of the body between the ribs and pelvis/hindquarters; the loin.

**Coursing:** The sport of chasing prey, with sighthounds, used to describe racing while chasing a target. See *Lure coursing.*

**Covering ground:** The distance traveled by a dog with each stride as it gaits.

**Cow-hocked:** Hocks turning in, accompanied by toeing out of the rear feet. *Illustration p. 826.*

**Cowlick:** A tuft, whirl, or twist of hair sticking up and facing in a direction different from that of the surrounding coat.

**Crabbing:** When a dog moves with his body at an angle to the line of travel. Also referred to as sidewinding.

**Cramped teeth:** An irregular, crowded alignment of teeth.

**Cranium:** The skull.

**Crank tail:** A tail carried down and resembling a crank in shape.

**Creaseless:** The absence of wrinkles and skin folds about the head.

**Crest:** The upper, arched portion of the neck.

**Crested neck:** A well-arched, well-developed neck.

**Crinkling coat:** A slightly wavy, harsh coat.

**Crisp coat:** A coat that is close and stiff.

**Crook:** Used to describe the forequarters assembly of some short-legged breeds with inward inclination of pasterns.

**Crook tail:** A malformed tail or crank tail.

**Cropping:** The cutting or trimming of ear leather to permit it to stand erect.

**Crossbreed:** A dog whose sire and dam are representatives of two different breeds.

**Crossing over:** An unsound gaiting action that starts with twisting elbows and ends with crisscrossing and toeing out. Also called knitting and purling, or weaving.

**Crouch:** An unnatural gathering up of the hindquarters due to excessive hind-limb angulation.

**Croup:** The region of the pelvic girdle, formed by the sacrum and surrounding tissue.

**Crown:** The dorsal (top) part of the head; topskull.

**Cryptorchid:** The adult male whose testicles are abnormally retained in the abdominal cavity. Bilateral cryptorchidism involves both sides—that is, neither testicle has descended into the scrotum. Unilateral cryptorchidism involves one side only—that is, one testicle is retained or hidden, and one descended.

**Cuffs:** The shorthaired pastern regions.

**Culotte:** The longer hair on the back of the upper thighs.

**Cup handle tail:** See *Pot-hook tail.*

**Cur:** A mongrel.

**Curled tail:** A tail that comes up and over the back. It can be a tight curl over the back only (Lhasa Apso or Norwegian Elkhound), a single curl falling over the loin with the tip toward the thigh (Finnish Spitz), or curled to one side (Samoyed). *Illustration p. 847.*

**Curly coat:** A coat in a mass of thick, tight curls.

**Curtain:** Portion of a dog's forelock hanging straight down over the eyes and at least partially covering them.

**Cushion:** Fullness or thickness of the upper lips, as in the Pekingese.

**Cut-up:** See *Tuck-up.*

**Cynology:** The study of canines.

**Dam:** The female parent of a dog.

**Dapple:** A mottled or variegated coat-color pattern. Dachshunds are dapple and Collies are merle, both determined by the dominant m gene or the m series of multiple alleles.

**Dead ear:** A sluggish, immobile ear poorly responsive to external stimuli, hound-like in appearance.

**Deadgrass:** Tan or dull straw color.

**Deep eyes:** See *Sunken eyes.*

**Dentition:** Forty-two adult teeth, including incisors (I), canines (C), premolars

(P), and molars (M). Formula for dogs is: upper jaw—6I/2C/8P/4M; lower jaw—6I/2C/8P/6M.

**Depth of chest:** An indication of the volume of space for heart and lungs, commonly referenced to the elbow, i.e., above, at the level of, or below.

**Derby:** A field trial competition for young, novice sporting dogs, usually between one and two years of age.

**Dewclaw:** An extra claw or functionless (vestigial) digit on the inside of the leg; a rudimentary fifth toe.

**Dewlap:** Loose, pendulous skin under the throat and neck.

**Diagonals:** The right front and left rear legs constitute the right diagonal; the left front and right rear constitute the left diagonal. In the trot, the diagonals move together.

**Diaphragm:** A muscular sheet that separates the thoracic and abdominal cavities.

**Digging terrier legs:** Correct shoulders, with short, sturdy, and well-boned legs, able to dig into the earth.

**Digit:** A synonym for toe.

**Dippy back:** See *Swayback*.

**Dish-faced:** A slight concavity of foreface when viewed in profile.

**Dishing:** A weaving gait.

**Disqualification:** A decision made by a judge or benched show committee following a determination that a dog has a condition that makes it ineligible for any further competition under the dog show rules or under the standard for its breed; an undesirable feature of a dog that results in such action.

**Distal bone:** A bone far away from the main structure of the dog, as in the end of the tail.

**Distemper teeth:** Teeth discolored or pitted as a result of distemper or other disease or deficiency.

**Distended pastern:** Knobby appearance when viewed from the front of the pastern joint.

**Distichiasis:** An extra row of eyelashes on the inner lid.

**Divergent hocks:** Hocks that turn out; barrel hocks.

**Dock:** To shorten the tail by cutting.

**Dog:** A male dog; also collectively to designate both male and female.

**Dog show:** A competitive exhibition for dogs at which the dogs are judged in accordance with an established standard of perfection for each breed.

**Dog show, conformation (licensed):** An event held under AKC rules at which championship points are awarded. May be for all breeds or groups or for a single breed (specialty show).

**Dolichocephalic:** A narrow skull base, coupled with great length, as in the Borzoi and Collie.

**Domed:** Evenly rounded in topskull; convex instead of flat.

**Domino:** A reverse facial mask pattern on some breeds.

**Dorsal:** The portion of the dog carried farthest from the substratum during normal locomotion, i.e., away from the ground.

**Double coat:** An outer coat resistant to weather and protective against brush and brambles, together with an inner coat of softer hair for warmth and waterproofing.

**Double-curl tail:** A tail curling over the back in a whirlpool shape. *Illustration p. 847.*

**Double-jointed:** Having joints capable of movement outside the normal parameters.

**Double-tracking:** Usually designates a wider pattern of movement. Having two distinct lines of travel: one for limbs on the left side, one for limbs on the right side.

**Down-faced:** Describes a muzzle inclining downward from the skull to the tip of the nose. Planes on top of the skull and planes on top of the muzzle are not parallel.

**Down in pastern:** A weak or faulty pastern (metacarpus) set at an incorrect angle. *Illustration p. 820, 821.*

**Draft:** The act of weight pulling; hauling.

**Drag:** A trail prepared by dragging a bag along the ground, usually impregnated with animal scent.

**Drawing:** The selection by lot of dogs to be run in pairs in a field trial stake.

**Drive:** A solid thrusting of the hindquarters, denoting sound locomotion.

**Droop:** Unusually excessive slope of the croup.

**Drop ear:** One of more than thirty terms used to characterize ears, wherein the leather is folded at least to some degree, contrasting with erect or prick ears.

**Dropped teeth:** A dental problem that usually affects the lower incisors, where they are set deeper into the gums.

**Dropper:** A bird dog cross.

**Drooping coat:** Coat that lacks body and undercoat.

**Drooping hindquarters:** Excessive slope of the croup region.

**Dry head:** See *Dry neck.*

**Dry neck:** The skin taut, neither loose nor wrinkled.

**Dual champion:** A dog that has won both a conformation show and a field trial championship.

**Dudley nose:** Flesh-colored nose.

**Ear:** The auditory organ consisting of three regions: inner ear, middle ear, and the pinna (or leather), which is supported by cartilage and which affects the expression of all breeds. *Illustration p. 824.*

**Ear carriage:** The combined visual effects of ear placement and position on the skull, coupled with usage.

**Ear flap:** Ear leather.

**Ears flare obliquely:** Ears that spread outward at the base.

**Ear leather:** The flap of the ear.

**Ears, set on:** The junction of the earlobe base and the skull, usually related to eye level and/or skull width. Can be set on high (ears joining the skull above the eye rim) or low set (ears joining below the eye level).

**East-west feet:** An incorrect positioning that causes the feet to turn outward.

**Eastern expression:** An Oriental expression caused by the combined effects of head structure, eye shape (slanted) and placement.

**Ectropion:** An inherited condition in which the lower eyelid rolls away from the eyeball. The opposite of entropion.

**Elastic pads:** Thick toe pads furnished with adequate amounts of cushioned elastic tissue to provide appropriate cushioning during movement.

**Elbow:** The joint in the front leg where the upper arm (humerus) meets the forearm (ulna).

**Elbows out:** Turning out or off from the body; not held close.

**Elliptical eyes:** Oblong eyes.

**Entire:** A dog whose reproductive system is complete and unaltered.

**Entropion:** A complex genetic condition that results in the turning in of the upper and lower eyelid, potentially resulting in corneal ulceration.

**Estrus:** Season; heat; part of the reproductive cycle during which ovulation occurs.

**Even bite:** The meeting of the upper and lower incisors with no overlap; level bite.

**Event:** A structured activity testing the conformation, training, or instinctive abilities of purebred dogs.

**Ewe neck:** A neck in which the topline is concave rather than convex.

**Expression:** The general appearance of all features of the head.

**Eyeteeth:** The upper canines.

**Eyes open:** Clear and distinct eyes.

**Face:** The front part of the head; the combination of nose, eyes, mouth, cheeks, and lips.

**Fall:** Hair overhanging the face.

**Fallow:** Pale cream to light fawn color, pale yellow, yellow-red.

**False rib:** The eleventh and twelfth ribs.

**Fancier:** A person especially interested and usually active in some phase of the sport of purebred dogs.

**Fangs:** See *Canines.*

**Farseeing eyes:** An expression dependent on the position, shape, and angle, the color of the iris is dark, and the eyes should be small.

**Fawn:** A brown, red-yellow with hue of medium brilliance.

**Feathering:** Longer fringe of hair on ears, legs, tail, or body.

**Femur:** The thighbone, extends from the hip to stifle.

**Ferret feet:** Similar to hare feet but with flatter toes.

**Fetlock:** The wrist or pastern area.

**Fibula:** One of the two bones of the leg (also the lower thigh, second thigh, or lower leg).

**Fiddle front:** Forelegs out at the elbows, pasterns close and feet turned out; French front. *Illustration p. 821.*

**Field trial:** A competition for certain Hounds and Sporting Breeds in which dogs are judged on their ability and style in finding or retrieving game or following a game trail.

**Filbert-shaped ear:** An ear in the shape of the hazelnut or filbert.

**Filled-up face:** Smooth facial contours, free of excessive muscular development.

**Fin:** A colloquial term for too profuse an arrangement of hair on the feet, as in the longhaired Dachshund.

**Fine bone:** Relating to the thickness, quality, and strength of the bone, which is slender and lightly constructed.

**Fisheye:** See *Walleye.*

**Flag:** Hair on tail that hangs down and forms a flag.

**Flag tail:** A long tail carried high; feathering on the tail.

**Flanged rib:** A ridge at or near the bottom on one or both sides, resulting from an inward curve in the downward slope. The result is a ridge or flange in all or part of the rib cage.

**Flank:** The side of the body between the last rib and the hip; the coupling.

**Flanks, drawn up:** Tucked-up flanks.

**Flare:** A blaze that widens as it approaches the topskull.

**Flared nostrils:** Wide, open nostrils, designed for maximum air intake.

**Flashings:** The white markings on the chest, neck, face, feet, or tail tip.

**Flat back:** A back that is horizontal as well as straight, without a dip or rise. See *Level back.*

**Flat croup:** A condition in which the area above and around the set-on of the tail is straight, has a high tailset, and no fall of the topline.

**Flat foot:** Toes that are straight and flat when viewed in profile, lacking arch. *Illustration p. 820.*

**Flat muscling:** Smooth, tight-lying muscle.

**Flat rib:** The opposite of barrel ribs. See *Slab-sided.*

**Flat skull:** In contrast to round or domed, flat in both directions across from ear to ear as well as from stop to occiput.

**Flat-sided:** Ribs insufficiently rounded as they approach the sternum or breastbone.

**Flat tail:** Broadening slightly in the center and tapering to a point.

**Flecking:** Spots or spotted markings of irregular shape.

**Flesh-colored nose:** An evenly colored nose, similar to the dudley nose. "Dudley" is used to describe a fault, whereas "flesh" is used in breed standards where pigmentation is acceptable.

**Fleshy cheeks:** A greater degree of cheek muscle than is desired.

**Fleshy ears:** Ears covered with thicker cartilage than is desired.

**Flews:** The pendulous lateral part of the upper lip, particularly at the inner corners. *Illustration p. 824.*

**Floating rib:** The last, or thirteenth, rib, which is not attached to the other ribs.

**Flop ear:** Normally erect ears that have flopped or dropped or fail to stand erect.

**Fluffy:** A coat of extreme length with exaggerated feathering on ears, chest, legs, and feet, underparts, and hindquarters. When this is a fault, trimming such a coat does not make it any more acceptable.

**Flush:** To drive birds from cover, to force them to take flight; to spring.

**Fluttering lips:** Loose, thin, excessively pendulous lips overhanging the lower jaw.

**Flying ears:** Any characteristic drop or semiprick ears that stand or "fly."

**Flying trot:** A fast gait in which all four feet are off the ground for a brief second during each half stride. Because of the long reach, the oncoming hind feet step beyond the imprint left by the front. Also called suspension trot.

**Folding ear:** A long, pendulous ear where the leading edge folds or rolls to give a draped appearance, as in the Otterhound standard.

**Foot:** The digits or toes, each consisting of three bones (phalanges) and a toenail or claw. The ventral surface is cushioned by pads of connective tissue. *Illustration p. 820.*

**Forearm:** The portion of the forelimb between the upper arm (humerus) and the wrist (carpus), including the radius and the ulna.

**Forechest:** A part of chest assembly in front of the forelegs.

**Forefeet:** Wrists, pasterns of the front feet, phalanges.

**Forelegs:** The front legs.

**Forepaw:** See *Forefeet.*

**Forequarters:** The combined front assembly from its uppermost component, the shoulder blade, down to the feet. *Illustration p. 821.*

**Forequarter angulation:** The angle formed by the shoulder blade (scapula) meeting the upper arm (humerus).

**Foreribs:** The front of the rib area.

**Foster mother:** A bitch used to nurse puppies that are not her own.

**Foul color:** A color or marking not characteristic of the breed.

**Fox brush:** See *Brush.*

**Foxlike feet:** Close and compact, with well-arched toes. The center toes are longer but not as long as on the hare foot.

**Foxy:** Sharp expression; pointed nose with short foreface.

**Free action:** Uninhibited, easy, elastic, strong, and untiring movement.

**Freighting size:** Built with power, the ability to draw a loaded sled.

**Frictionless gait:** Free, effortless, easy gait.

**Frill:** See *Apron.*

**Fringes:** See *Feathering.*

**Frogface:** An extending nose accompanied by a receding jaw, usually overshot.

PADS

BONES OF THE FOOT

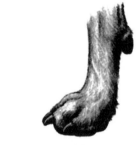

ROUND OR CAT FOOT

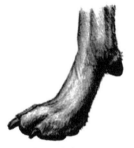

HARE FOOT

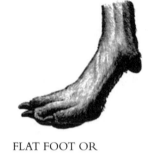

FLAT FOOT OR
DOWN IN PASTERN

SPLAY FOOT

**Feet**

NORMAL, STRAIGHT

TOO NARROW IN FRONT
AND EAST-WEST FEET

CHIPPENDALE OR
FIDDLE FRONT

OUT AT ELBOW AND
TOO WIDE IN FRONT

STRAIGHT FRONT

KNUCKLED OVER

DOWN IN PASTERN

**Forequarters**

**Front:** The forepart of the body as viewed head-on, i.e., forelegs, chest, brisket, and shoulder line. *Illustration p. 821.*

**Frontal bones:** The anterior bones of the cranium, forming the forehead.

**Frosting:** A process similar to graying at the temples, usually occurring about the muzzle.

**Furnishings:** The long hair on the extremities (including head and tail) of certain breeds.

**Furrow:** A slight indentation of the median line down the center of the skull to the stop.

**Fused toes:** Toes that are blended, joined together.

**Futurity Stakes:** A competition at dog shows or field trials for young dogs that have been nominated at or before birth.

**Gait:** The pattern of footsteps at various rates of speed, each pattern distinguished by a particular rhythm and footfall.

**Gallantly carried:** A tail carried in a brave fashion.

**Gallop:** The fastest of the dog gaits, has a four-beat rhythm and often an extra period of suspension during which the body is propelled through the air with all four feet off the ground.

**Galloping hound:** The long-legged sighthounds; reflects the fact that their natural gait in the field is a gallop.

**Game:** Wild birds or animals that are hunted; the desire to hunt.

**Gaskin:** The lower or second thigh.

**Gaunt head:** Emaciated, abnormally lean.

**Gay tail:** A tail carried above the horizontal level of the back. *Illustration p. 847.*

**Gazehound:** A Greyhound or other sight-hunting hound.

**Genealogy:** Recorded family descent; pedigree.

**Gestation:** A period of sixty-three days in the dog, from fertilization to whelping.

**Get:** Offspring.

**Giant breeds:** Classification of dog breeds, such as Great Dane, Mastiff, etc.; the much larger and heavier-than-average breeds.

**Girth:** The maximum measurement of the circumference just behind the withers.

**Giving tongue:** A sound made usually by hounds or terriers when working.

**Glass eye:** A fixed, blank, and uncomprehending expression.

**Glaucous:** Grayish blue.

**Glossy coat:** A shiny, lustrous coat, denoting health.

**Gnarled tail:** A badly twisted, malformed tail with enlarged joints.

**Go to ground:** When the quarry (prey) takes refuge below the ground; when dogs pursue their quarry underground.

**Goggle eyes:** See *Protruding eyes.*

**Gooseberry eye:** Light, hazel-colored eyes with a greenish tint.

**Goose neck:** An elongated, tubular-shaped neck. Also called *swan neck.*

**Goose rump:** A too steep or sloping croup.

**Goose step:** An accentuated lift of the forelimbs.

**Grizzle:** A mixture of black or red hairs with white hairs. Roan, frequently, a bluish gray or an iron gray.

**Groom:** To brush, comb, trim, or otherwise make a dog's coat neat.

**Groups:** The breeds as grouped into seven divisions by the AKC.

**Gruff expression:** A tough, hard-bitten appearance.

**Guard hairs:** The longer, smoother, stiffer hairs that grow through and normally conceal the undercoat.

**Gun-barrel front:** A true or straight front when viewed head-on.

**Gundog:** A dog trained to work with its master in finding live game and retrieving game that has been shot.

**Gun-shyness:** Fear of the sight or sound of a gun.

**Hackles:** Hairs on neck and back raised involuntarily in fright or anger.

**Hackney action:** A high lifting of the front feet accompanied by flexing of the wrist like that of a hackney horse.

**Hallmark:** A distinguishing breed characteristic, such as Keeshond spectacles.

**Halo:** The narrow circular ring of black pigment surrounding the eyes, as in the Bichon Frise standard.

**Hams:** The muscular development of the upper thigh.

**Hand-stripped:** When the hair is pulled out from the root by hand.

**Handler:** A person who handles a dog in the show ring, at a field trial, or obedience trial. See *Professional handler.*

**Hanging tongue:** A tongue that protrudes when the mouth is closed.

**Hard-driving action:** A powerful, jerky, rather exaggerated, and energy-consuming gait.

**Hard-mouthed:** Biting or leaving teeth marks on game that is retrieved.

**Hare foot:** A foot in which the two center digits are appreciably longer than the outside and inside toes of the foot and the arching of the toes is less marked, making the foot appear longer overall. *Illustration p. 820.*

**Harelip:** A congenital abnormality, resulting in irregular fissure formation at the junction of the two upper lip halves.

**Harlequin:** A patched or pied coloration, usually black or gray on white, as in Great Danes.

**Haunch bones:** The anterior-dorsal portion of the pelvic girdle (crest of the ilium); the hip bones.

**Haw:** A third eyelid or nictitating membrane on the medial (inside) corner of the eye.

**Head:** The anterior portion of the dog, including the muzzle and the cranium. *Illustration p. 824.*

**Head planes:** Viewed in profile, the contours of the dorsal (top) portion of the skull from the occiput to stop, and of the foreface from stop to tip of nose. Usually used in relation to one another, i.e., parallel, diverging, converging.

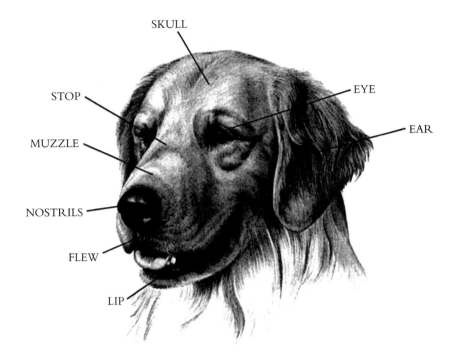

**External features of the dog's head**

SKULL

STOP

MUZZLE

NOSTRILS

FLEW

LIP

EYE

EAR

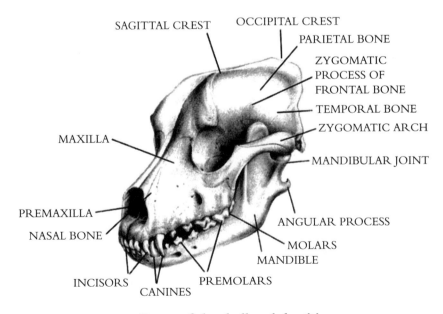

**Bones of the skull and dentition**

SAGITTAL CREST

OCCIPITAL CREST

PARIETAL BONE

ZYGOMATIC PROCESS OF FRONTAL BONE

TEMPORAL BONE

ZYGOMATIC ARCH

MANDIBULAR JOINT

MAXILLA

PREMAXILLA

NASAL BONE

ANGULAR PROCESS

MOLARS

MANDIBLE

INCISORS

CANINES

PREMOLARS

**Headfall:** See *Fall.*

**Heart-shaped ear:** Ear leather shaped like a heart.

**Heat:** The seasonal period of the female; estrus.

**Heavy-boned:** Relating to the thickness, quality, and strength of the bone; large, thick, and powerful.

**Heavy pads:** Thick toe pads on the bottom of the feet, with more than adequate amounts of elastic tissue to provide appropriate cushioning during movement.

**Hedge hunter:** A terrier that moves along the hedges and underbrush, as opposed to hunting in the holes or rocks.

**Heel:** See *Hock.* Also, a command to the dog to keep close behind its handler.

**Height:** The vertical measurement from the withers to the ground, also referred to as shoulder height. See *Withers.*

**Herding breeds:** A group of dogs whose main duty is to drive livestock from one place to another.

**Hie on:** A command to urge the dog on, used in hunting or in field trials.

**High-set ears:** Ears placed near the top of the skull above the level of the eye.

**High-standing:** Tall and upstanding, with plenty of leg.

**High-stationed:** A dog that has ground-to-brisket height greater than withers-to-brisket.

**High-stepping:** See *Hackney action.*

**Hindquarters:** The rear assembly of the dog (pelvis, thighs, hocks, pasterns, and rear feet). *Illustration p. 826.*

**Hindquarter angulation:** The angle formed by the upper thigh meeting the lower thigh. In most breeds, rear angulation should match front angulation.

**Hip:** The hip joint, located between the femoral head and the pelvic acetabulum.

**Hip dysplasia:** A developmental disease of the canine hip joint, occurring primarily in larger breeds.

**Hitching:** Moving in jerks, usually in the hindquarters.

**Hock:** The tarsus or collection of bones of the hind leg forming the joint between the second thigh and the metatarsus. This is the ankle in man. *Illustration p. 826.*

**Hock joint:** The joint on the hind limb located between the lower thigh and the rear pastern.

**Hocking out:** See *Spread hocks.*

**Hocks well let down:** Hock joints close to the ground; short hocks.

**Holders:** See *Canines.*

**Hollow back:** See *Saddle back.*

**Holt:** The lair of the fox or other animal in tree roots, banks, drains, or similar hideouts; lodge.

**Honorable scars:** Scars from injuries suffered as a result of work.

**Hooded ears:** Smallish ears with both lobe edges curving forward. The tips are directed more forward than at the base.

**Hook tail:** A tail that hangs down with an upward hook or swirl at the tip.

CORRECT, STRAIGHT, NORMAL

COW-HOCKED

BANDY OR WIDE

NARROW

NORMAL ANGULATED
HINDQUARTERS

STRAIGHT STIFLES

**Hindquarters and Hocks**

**Horizontal tail:** See *Bee-sting tail.*

**Horn:** The toenail.

**Horny pads:** Tough soles of the feet.

**Horse coat:** Extremely short in length, harsh, absolutely straight and off-standing on the body, and generally lying flatter on the limbs.

**Hound Breeds:** A group of dogs commonly used for hunting by scent or sight.

**Hound coat:** A coat that is hard, close, and medium in length, providing protection from the brush and brambles.

**Hound-fashion tail carriage:** A tail carried at approximately 90 degrees to the backline when the dog is in motion.

**Houndlike ears:** See *Drop ear.*

**Houndlike lips:** Well-developed, deep, pendulous flews.

**Hound-marked:** A coloration composed of white, tan, and black. The ground color is usually white and may be marked with tan and/or black patches on the head, back, leg, and tail. The extent and the exact location of such markings, however, differ in breeds and individuals.

**Hucklebones:** The top of the hip bones.

**Humerus:** The bone of the upper arm.

**Hump back:** See *Camel back.*

**Hunter:** A dog with the ideal anatomical construction and proportions to hunt, consisting of a relatively short body coupled with a maximum length of stride.

**Hunting tests:** Noncompetitive field events for flushing breeds, retrieving breeds, and pointing breeds.

**Hydrocephalus:** Water on the brain.

**Hyperextension of the hocks:** To extend so that the angle between the bones of a joint (hock) is greater than normal.

**Ilium:** One of the three bony components of the pelvic girdle.

**Inbreeding:** The mating of closely related dogs of the same breed.

**Incisors:** The six upper and six lower front teeth between the canines. Their point of contact forms the bite. *Illustration p. 824.*

**Indented stop:** See *Stop.*

**Inner thigh:** The portion of the upper thigh muscles located on the inside of the thighbone.

**Interbreeding:** The breeding together of dogs of different breeds.

**Interdigital:** Spaces between the toes.

**Inverted cross:** A color marking in the form of an upside-down cross.

**Intervertebral disks:** Soft cartilaginous structures located between the individual spinal vertebrae that allow smooth movement.

**Iris:** The colored membrane surrounding the pupil of the eye.

**Irregular bite:** A bite in which some or occasionally all the incisors have erupted abnormally.

**Isabella:** A fawn or light bay color, as in Doberman Pinschers.

**Ischial tuberosity:** The rearmost part of the pelvis.

**Ischium:** The rearmost extremity of the pelvic bone.

**Jabot:** The apron of the Schipperke; the area between the front legs.

**Jacket:** See *Coat.*

**Jasper:** Used as an alternative description of color patches; an opaque, usually red, brown, or yellow variety of quartz.

**Jewel eye:** See *Walleye.*

**Jowls:** The flesh of lips and jaws.

**Judge:** An official approved by the AKC to judge dogs in conformation, companion, or performance events.

**Junior Showmanship:** An AKC-sponsored class that evaluates the abilities of the young handler, not the quality of the dog.

**Keel:** The rounded outline of the lower chest, between the prosternum and the breastbone.

**Kink tail:** A deformity of the caudal vertebrae, producing a bent tail.

**Kiss marks:** Tan spots on the cheeks and over the eyes.

**Kissing spot:** The name given to the lozenge mark on the head of the Blenheim variety of the English Toy Spaniel and the Cavalier King Charles Spaniel.

**Knee:** See *Stifle.*

**Kneecap:** The patella bone. In a dog, part of the stifle.

**Knitting:** See *Crossing over.*

**Knuckled-up:** Strongly arched.

**Knuckling over:** Faulty structure of carpal (wrist) joint, incorrectly allowing it to flex forward. *Illustration p. 821.*

**Lachrymal gland:** The tear gland located at the inner corner of the eye.

**Landseer:** The black-and-white Newfoundland dog, so named in honor of artist Edwin Landseer, who painted such dogs.

**Languishing eyes:** An expression of appealing for sympathy.

**Lashing tail:** An active, powerful, moving tail.

**Lateral:** Pertaining to the side.

**Layback:** The angle of the shoulder blade, when viewed from the side (laterally).

**Lay-on:** The angle of the shoulder blade, when viewed from the front (medially).

**Lead:** A strap, cord, or chain attached to the collar or harness, used for restraining or for leading a dog; leash.

**Leather:** The flap of the ear; the outer ear supported by cartilage and surrounding tissue.

**Leggy:** Tall, not necessarily rangy, giving the appearance of being high off the ground.

**Lemon:** Used to describe Pointers, this color is a brilliant medium-saturated yellow.

**Leonine:** A term applied to the Chow Chow, meaning lionlike.

**Level back:** When the height at the withers is the same as the height over the top of the loins.

**Level bite:** When the front teeth (incisors) of the upper and lower jaws meet exactly edge to edge; pincher bite. *Illustration p. 807.*

**Level gait:** Moving without a rise or fall of the withers.

**License:** Formal permission granted by the AKC to a nonmember club to hold a dog show, obedience trial, or field trial.

**Ligament:** A fibrous tissue that connects bones.

**Light in loin:** Limited, not excessive loin development, creating a "waist."

**Line breeding:** Mating related dogs of the same breed, within the same line or family, to a common ancestor (e.g., a dog to his granddam or a bitch to her grandsire).

**Linty coat:** An unusually soft, downy texture.

**Lion color:** Tawny.

**Lippy:** Pendulous lip or lips that do not fit tightly.

**Lips:** The fleshy portions of the upper and lower jaws covering the teeth. *Illustration p. 824.*

**Lips tight and clean:** Lips fitting close to the jaw without any flew.

**Lithe body:** A supple, graceful form.

**Litter:** The puppy or puppies of one whelping.

**Liver:** A deep reddish brown color, produced by recessive (bb) alleles gene of the b (black) locus.

**Loaded shoulders:** An excessive development of the muscles associated with the shoulder blades (scapulae).

**Lobular ear:** See *Pendulous ear.*

**Loin:** The region of the body associated with the lumbar portion of the vertebrae (behind the ribs and before the pelvic girdle).

**Lolling tongue:** An overlong tongue; one that protrudes.

**Long back:** When the distance from the withers to the rump exceeds the height at the withers.

**Long in hock:** Also high in hock; when the rear pastern is greater in length than desired, the hock joints are far from the ground.

**Loose elbow:** See *Out at the elbows.*

**Loose shoulder:** See *Loose slung.*

**Loose slung:** A construction in which the attachment of the muscles at the shoulders is looser than is desirable.

**Loose tail:** A tail not fitted tightly over the back.

**Loosely coupled:** Having a weak and unusually long loin.

**Low at shoulders:** Flat withers, low in withers, set lower than rest of backline.

**Low-stationed:** A ground-to-brisket height less than that of withers-to-brisket.

**Lower arm:** The region encompassing the radius and ulna bones.

**Lower thigh:** See *Second thigh.*

**Lozenge:** The thumbprint spot situated on the skull between the ears, as in the English Toy Spaniel and the Cavalier King Charles Spaniel standard; a diamond shape, as in the Bloodhound standard.

**Lumbar:** An excessive amount of flesh.

**Lumbar vertebrae:** The seven vertebrae of the loin region, between the thoracic vertebrae and the sacrum.

**Lumbering:** An awkward gait.

**Lumpy shoulders:** See *Loaded shoulders.*

**Lung room:** Inferring chest dimensions sufficient to permit optimum lung and heart development.

**Lurcher:** A crossbred hound.

**Lure coursing:** Organized events for sight hounds, which chase an artificial lure over a course.

**Luxation:** The dislocation of an anatomical structure, i.e., lens or patella.

**Mahogany:** Used to describe several breeds, this color is a medium-saturated, dull, reddish brown.

**Major win:** A win that consists of 3, 4, or 5 points in conformation events and some performance events.

**Making a wheel:** The circling of the tail over the back that is characteristic of the Great Pyrenees when alerted.

**Malar bone:** See *Zygomatic arch.*

**Malocclusion:** An abnormality in the way the teeth come together.

**Mandible:** The lower jaw. *Illustration p. 824.*

**Mane:** Long and profuse hair on the top and sides of the neck.

**Mantle:** Dark-shaded portion of the coat on the shoulders, back, and sides.

**Manubrium:** The first sternebra of the chest; prosternum.

**Marble eye:** See *Walleye.*

**Marcel effect:** Regular, continuous waves in the coat, as in the American Water Spaniel.

**Marked flag:** Hair on the tail that hangs and forms a flag.

**Marked stop:** A noticeable stop.

**Markings:** Generally used in reference to white areas distributed on a colored background.

**Mask:** Dark shading on the foreface.

**Master hair:** Guard hair.

**Master of the hounds:** The person responsible for a pack of foxhounds and its affairs.

**Match show:** Usually an informal dog show at which no championship points or Obedience title legs are awarded.

**Mate:** To breed a dog and bitch.

**Measure out:** When the measured height at withers is determined to be outside the limits for that breed as set forth in the breed standard.

**Medial:** Toward the midline of the dog.

**Median line:** See *Furrow.*

**Melon pips:** See *Pips.*

**Merle:** A color pattern involving a dominant gene (the M or Merling Series) and characterized by dark blotches against a lighter background of the same pigment (e.g., blue merle in Collies and red dapple in Dachshunds).

**Merry tail:** A constantly wagging tail.

**Mesaticephalic:** A skull type with medium proportions of base width to overall skull length.

**Metacarpal pad:** The large communal pad located on the bottom rear of the front foot.

**Metacarpus:** The front pastern.

**Metatarsus:** Rear pastern.

**Milk teeth:** First teeth.

**Mincing gait:** Short, choppy, prancing movement, lacking power.

**Miscellaneous class:** Transitory class for breeds attempting to advance to full AKC recognition.

**Mismark:** (1) Coat or color. (2) A dog that has coat coloration or markings contrary to those described in a breed standard.

**Mobile ears:** Ears that can move. The ears can rest on the side of the head and when alert can rise upward to set on top of the skull.

**Modelling:** See *Chiseled.*

**Molars:** The posterior teeth of the dental arcade, with two on each side in the upper jaw and three on each side in the lower jaw in an adult with correct dentition (42 teeth). *Illustration p. 824.*

**Molera:** The incomplete, imperfect, or abnormal closure of the skull.

**Moles:** Markings on the cheeks. Also, a color ranging from dark gray to blue.

**Mongolian eyes:** See *Obliquely placed eyes.*

**Mongrel:** A dog whose parents are of two different breeds.

**Monorchid:** A dog that has one testicle retained or hidden in its abdominal cavity. See *Cryptorchid.*

**Mottled:** A pattern of dark roundish blotches superimposed on a lighter background.

**Moving close:** A gait in which the pasterns drop straight to the ground and move parallel to one another with little or no space between them; it is therefore said the dog is moving close in the rear. This type of action places severe strain on ligaments and muscles.

**Moving straight:** A balanced gaiting in which the angle of inclination begins at the shoulder, or hip joint, and the limbs remain relatively straight from these points to the pads of the feet, even as the legs flex or extend in reaching or thrusting.

**Muscle–bound:** Having excessive development of individual muscle groups, resulting in lumbering and cumbersome movement.

**Muscle tone:** The quality of muscular development.

**Musculature:** The disposition, development, and arrangement of muscles.

**Musculature wiry:** Referring to slender, strong, and sinewy muscular development.

**Music:** The baying of the hounds.

**Mustache:** Longish hair of varying texture arising from the lips and sides of the face, creating the appearance of a mustache.

**Mustard:** Usually used to describe Dandie Dinmont Terriers, this color is like the color of the spice, i.e., a dull, highly saturated, brown-yellow.

**Mute:** To run mute, to be silent on the trail; to trail without baying or barking.

**Muzzle:** The head in front of the eyes—nasal bones, nostrils, and jaws; foreface. Also, a strap or wire cage attached to the foreface to prevent the dog from biting or from picking up food. *Illustration p. 824.*

**Muzzle band:** White marking around the muzzle.

**Nape:** The junction of the base of the skull and the top of the neck.

**Narrow front:** A front in which the forearms, when seen head-on, stand closer to each other than is desired. *Illustration p. 821.*

**Narrow shoulder:** See *Narrow front.*

**Narrow thigh:** Insufficiently strong muscular development of the thigh regions.

**Nasal bone:** The bony section of the foreface forming the edge of the muzzle.

**Nasal septum:** The bony partition dividing the right and left nasal cavities.

**Naso-labial line:** The groove at the junction of the left and right upper lip halves.

**Natural ears:** Uncropped ears.

**Neck well set on:** Good neckline, merging gradually with the withers, forming a pleasing transition into topline.

**Neuter:** To castrate or spay.

**Nick:** A breeding that produces desirable puppies.

**Nictitating membrane:** See *Third eyelid.*

**Night blindness:** Poor sight at dusk or dawn, an early symptom of progressive retinal atrophy (PRA).

**Nite hunt:** Performance competition for coonhounds.

**Nonslip retriever:** A dog that walks at heel, marks the fall, and retrieves game on command; not expected to find or flush.

**Non-Sporting breeds:** A diverse group of multifunctional dogs not generally regarded to be game hunters.

**Nose:** Organ of olfaction. Also, the ability to detect by scent.

**Novice class:** (conformation) A regular class for dogs six months of age or over that have not, prior to the closing of entries for the show, won three first prizes in the Novice class, a first prize in Bred-by-Exhibitor, American-Bred, or Open classes, nor have one or more points toward their championship. (obedience) A class for dogs not less than six months that have not won the title Companion Dog (CD).

**Nuchal crest:** The top of the occiput.

**Obedience trial (licensed):** An event held under AKC rules at which a "leg" toward an obedience degree can be earned.

**Obliquely placed eyes:** Eyes with the outer corners higher than their inner ones.

**Oblique shoulders:** Shoulders well laid back.

**Oblong eyes:** An eye shape in which eyelid aperture appears longer than higher, with contours and corners gently rounded. See *Almond eyes.*

**Obtuse angles:** Angles exceeding 90 degrees but less than 180 degrees.

**Occipital protuberance:** A prominently raised occiput, characteristic of some sporting and hound breeds.

**Occiput:** The dorsal, posterior point of the skull. *Illustration p. 824.*

**Occlusion:** The meeting of the teeth when the mouth is closed.

**Off-square:** Slightly longer when measured from point of shoulder to point of buttocks, than height at withers.

**Olfactory abilities:** The sense of smell.

**Olfactory nerve:** One of the twelve cranial nerves of the dog.

**Olecranon process:** Point of elbow.

**Open bitch:** A bitch that can be bred.

**Open class:** (conformation) A class at dog shows in which all dogs of a breed, champions and imported dogs included, may compete. (obedience) A class for dogs that have won the Companion Dog title but have not won the title Companion Dog Excellent.

**Open coat:** A sparsely haired coat, where the fibers are usually widely separated from one another, usually off-standing and lacking in undercoat.

**Open foot:** See *Splayfoot.*

**Open hock:** See *Barrel hocks.*

**Orange belton:** See *Belton.*

**Orb:** The eyeball.

**Orbit:** The eye socket.

**Orifices:** The outer edges or openings.

**Ornamentation:** See *Furnishings.*

**Orthopedic Foundation for Animals (OFA):** An organization, established in 1966, that developed and maintains a registry of hip dysplasia in dogs. Dogs with OFA numbers are rated and certified free of canine hip dysplasia. This rating applies for the life of the dog.

**Otter tail:** Thick at the root, round and tapering, with the hair parted or divided on the underside. *Illustration p. 847.*

**Otter head:** A head shape resembling that of an otter.

**Out at the elbows:** Having elbows that turn out from the body, as opposed to being held close. *Illustration p. 821.*

**Out at shoulders:** Having shoulder blades loosely attached to the body, leaving the shoulders jutting out in relief and increasing the breadth of the front.

**Out of coat:** Long- and/or broken-coated dogs that have dropped their outer jackets or undercoat.

**Outcrossing:** The mating of unrelated individuals of the same breed.

**Oval chest:** A chest that is more deep than wide.

**Oval eyes:** See *Oblong eyes. Illustration p. 807.*

**Oval foot:** Spoon-shaped foot, similar to cat foot except both center toes are slightly longer.

**Oval skull:** Gentle, curving contours of the skull from ear to ear.

**Overbuilt back:** Having excessive development over the rump area, giving a padded appearance.

**Overfill:** The opposite quality of chiseling, may lack definition or elegance.

**Overhang:** A heavy or pronounced brow, as in the Pekingese.

**Overlapping:** See *Crossing over.*

**Overlay:** Mantle or blanket of dark color superimposed on a lighter background.

**Overreaching:** Fault in the trot caused by more angulation and drive from behind than from in front, so that the rear feet are forced to step to one side of the forefeet to avoid interfering or clipping.

**Overshot:** A bite in which the incisors of the upper jaw project beyond the incisors of the lower jaw, resulting in a space between the inner and outer surfaces.

**Pace:** A lateral gait that tends to promote a rolling motion of the body. The left foreleg and left hind leg advance in unison, then the right foreleg and right hind leg. See *Amble.*

**Pack:** Several hounds kept together in one kennel. A mixed pack is composed of dogs and bitches. Also used in reference to a Poodle with an English Saddle clip. The "pack" portion of the coat is situated over the loin and rump area.

**Padding:** A compensating action to offset constant concussion when a front with inadequate reach is subjected to overdrive from the rear; the front feet flip upward in a split-second delaying action to coordinate the stride of the forelegs with the longer stride from behind. Also refers to additional thickness of the lips.

**Paddling:** A gaiting fault, so named for its similarity to the swing and dip of a canoeist's paddle. Pinching in at the elbows and shoulder joints causes the front legs to swing forward in a stiff outward arc. Also referred to as "tied at the elbows."

**Pads:** Tough, shock-absorbing projections on the underside of the feet; soles. *Illustration p. 820.*

**Palate:** The partly bony, partly fleshy portion on the roof of the mouth separating the respiratory and digestive passages.

**Parallel planes:** See *Head planes.*

**Palpebral fissure:** The space between the eyelids when the eyes are open.

**Pancreatic degenerative atrophy:** A disease of the canine pancreas, which results in the inability to digest and absorb food.

**Pants:** See *Breeching* and *Trousers.*

**Paper foot:** A flat foot with thin pads.

**Parent club:** The national AKC club for a particular breed.

**Parrot mouth:** A much overshot bite.

**Parti-color:** Variegated with patches of two or more colors.

**Pastern:** The metacarpal bones of the front leg between the carpus and the foot and the metatarsal bones of the hind leg between the hock and the foot.

**Patchy tongue:** An incompletely pigmented tongue.

**Patella:** The kneecap.

**Peak:** See *Occiput.*

**Pedigree:** The written record of a dog's genealogy of three generations or more.

**Pelvic angulation:** The lay of the pelvis or pelvic slope.

**Pelvic girdle:** Two fused halves attached to the sides of the sacral vertebrae of the spinal column in the hindquarters.

**Pelvic shelf:** Buttocks extending beyond the tail, as in the Lakeland Terrier standard.

**Pelvis:** Hip bones, each consisting of three fused bones: an anterior ilium, a ventral pubis, and a posterior ischium, combined with the sacrum, forming the pelvic girdle.

**Pencilling:** Black lines dividing the tan on the toes.

**Pendant ear:** See *Drop ear.*

**Pendulous ear:** See *Drop ear.*

**Pendulous flews:** Full, loose-hanging upper lips.

**Peppering:** The admixture of white and black hairs, which, in association with some entirely black and some entirely white hairs, gives the "pepper and salt" appearance of some Schnauzer breeds.

**Philtrum:** The junction line of left and right upper lip and nostril halves.

**Pi-dog:** A crossbred, mongrel-type of dog, especially one of Eastern origin.

**Piebald:** See *Pied.*

**Pied:** Comparatively large patches of two or more colors; piebald, parti-colored, pinto.

**Pig eye:** Very small, close-set eyes.

**Pigeon-breast:** A narrow chest with a protruding breastbone.

**Pigeon-toed:** Toes pointing in toward the midline.

**Pigment:** The depth, intensity, and extent of color or markings.

**Pile:** Dense undercoat of soft hair.

**Pily coat:** A dense and harsh outer coat, coupled with a soft, furlike, and very close inner coat, as in the Dandie Dinmont Terrier.

**Pinched front:** A narrow front.

**Pinched muzzle:** See *Snipy.*

**Pinched together feet:** Toes that are closely set together; cat feet.

**Pink nose:** A lightly pigmented nose, in contrast to a black or brown nose.

**Pinto:** See *Pied.*

**Pipestopper tail:** A very short, upright tail.

**Pips:** The spots above the eyes of most black and tan breeds.

**Pitted teeth:** See *Distemper teeth.*

**Plaiting:** A crossing-over movement, also called knitting.

**Planes:** See *Head planes.*

**Pliant skin:** Skin that is flexible.

**Plucking:** Pulling out each hair from the root. Also called stripping, as in broken-coated terriers.

**Plume:** A long fringe of hair on the tail, covering part of the tail or the entire tail. *Illustration p. 847.*

**Point:** The immovable stance of the hunting dog, taken to indicate the presence and position of game.

**Point of shoulders:** See *Shoulder point.*

**Pointed muzzle:** A wedge-shaped muzzle that acutely tapers.

**Pointing breeds:** A term commonly applied to those sporting breeds that typically point birds.

**Points:** Color on face, ears, legs, and tail when correlated, usually white, black, or tan. Also, credits toward championship status.

**Poke:** To carry the neck stretched forward in an abnormally low, ungainly position, usually when moving.

**Pompon:** Rounded tuft of hair left on the end of the tail when the coat is clipped, as in the Poodle.

**Ponderous:** Very heavy or clumsy in either head or movement.

**Poodle clips:** For show-ring presentation, all varieties of Poodle may be exhibited only in the clips described in the standard.

**Poor flesh:** Poor muscle condition.

**Pop eye:** See *Protruding eyes.*

**Posterior:** The portion of the dog carried hindmost (or toward the rear) during normal locomotion.

**Posting:** A stance in which the front legs are extended too far forward and the rear legs are extended too far backward, which resembles the stance of a rocking horse.

**Pot-casse:** A bell-like tone to the bark, as in the Old English Sheepdog.

**Pot-hook tail:** A tail carried in an arch up and over the back, not lying flat on the back.

**Pouch:** Fold or loose skin overhanging the point of hock, as in the Basset Hound.

**Pounding:** A gaiting fault resulting when a dog's stride is shorter in front than in the rear, and the forefeet strike the ground hard before the rear stride is expended.

**Powderpuff:** The profusely haired variety of Chinese Crested.

**Prance:** A gait suggestive of a prancing horse; springy, bouncy.

**Predatory expression:** See *Bird of prey eyes.*

**Premium list:** An advance-notice brochure sent to prospective dog show exhibitors and containing details regarding a forthcoming show.

**Premolars:** The teeth that are located behind the canine teeth and in front of the molars. Most dogs have eight premolars on each side, four on the upper and four on the lower jaw. *Illustration p. 824.*

**Prepotency:** An unusually strong ability to transmit parental qualities to offspring.

**Prick ear:** Erect ear carriage, usually pointed at the tip.

**Professional handler:** A person who shows dogs for a fee.

**Professional trainer:** A person who trains hunting dogs and who handles dogs in field events.

**Primary teeth:** Milk teeth; puppy teeth.

**Progressive retinal atrophy (PRA):** An inherited disease that causes blindness. The retina is the light-sensitive membrane at the back of the eyeball.

**Prominent eyes:** See *Protruding eyes.*

**Propeller ears:** Ears that stick out sideways more or less horizontally, similar to flying ears.

**Propped stance:** A stance indicating defiance, where the forelegs are extended farther out than normal.

**Prosternum:** Point of the breastbone.

**Protruding eyes:** Round, full, bulging eyes.

**Provisional judge:** Title assigned to judges while they are being evaluated on their knowledge of designated breed(s) and/or level of obedience class in accordance with the current AKC judging approval system.

**Prow prominent:** A protruding sternum or forechest, as in the Flat-Coated Retriever.

**Puffs:** The circular bands of hair left on the forelegs of a clipped dog, such as a Poodle.

**Pump handle:** A long tail carried high.

**Put down:** To prepare a dog for the show ring. Also, a dog that did not place in competition.

**Puppy:** A dog under twelve months of age.

**Purebred:** A dog whose sire and dam belong to the same breed and are themselves of unmixed descent since recognition of the breed.

**Qualifying score:** *Obedience:* A qualifying score is comprised of scores of more than 50 percent of the available points in each exercise and a final score of 170 or more points, earned in a single regular class at a licensed or member obedience trial or sanctioned match. *Performance:* A generic term meaning that a dog has met, at least, the minimum standard necessary for qualifying in a class or test level at lure coursing, herding, earthdog, or hunting tests.

**Quality:** Refinement, fineness; a degree of excellence.

**Quarry:** Prey.

**Quarters:** Usually applied to the upper portion only, i.e., the pelvic and thigh regions. When "fore" or "hind" is added, it describes the whole section, including the legs.

**Quicksilver:** Able to make the abrupt turns, springing starts, and sudden stops required of a sheepherding dog.

**Racy:** Tall, of comparatively slight build.

**Radius:** One of the two bones of the forearm.

**Ram's head:** The skull and foreface contours appearing convex when viewed in profile.

**Ram's nose:** See *Roman nose*.

**Rangy:** Tall, long in body, high on leg, often lightly framed.

**Rat tail:** A tail with a thick root covered with soft curls and a tip devoid of hair or having the appearance of being clipped, as in the Irish Water Spaniel.

**Reach of front:** Length of forward stride taken by forelegs. *Illustration p. 839.*

**Rear pastern:** The metatarsus, the region of the hindquarters between the hock (tarsus) and the foot (digits).

**Receding skull:** One with diverging planes.

**Red sesame:** Red with sparse black overlay (e.g., Shiba Inu).

**Refinement:** Having bone and muscle in perfect proportion to the size of the dog.

**Register:** To record a dog's breeding particulars with the American Kennel Club.

**Reserve Winners:** The award given to the second place dog or bitch in the Winners class.

**Retrieve:** A hunting term. The act of bringing back shot game to the handler.

**Reverse scissors bite:** Having a somewhat longer lower jaw than upper jaw, causing the lower incisors to be positioned slightly in front of their upper counterparts.

**Ribbed-up:** Long ribs that angle back from the spinal column. A reference to a long rib cage.

**Rib cage:** The collection of paired ribs, cartilage, sternum, and associated tissue that define the thoracic region. In rib pairs 1 through 9 the cartilage articulates directly with the sternum ("true ribs"); in 10 through 12 the cartilage fuses with anterior cartilage ("false ribs"); and pair 13 is not attached ventrally ("floating ribs").

**Ridge:** A coat pattern, usually relatively long and narrow, formed by hair growing in the opposite direction to that of the surrounding hair, as in the Rhodesian Ridgeback.

**Ring tail:** A tail carried up and around almost in a circle.

**Ringed eyes:** An abnormal amount of clearly visible sclera surrounding the eye.

**GOOD MOVEMENT SIDE VIEW**

Showing good reach in front
and proper drive in rear

**POOR MOVEMENT SIDE VIEW**

**Roach back:** A convex curvature of the back, involving the thoracic and lumbar regions.

**Roan:** A fine mixture of colored hairs with white hairs: blue roan, orange roan, lemon roan, etc.

**Rocking horse:** Both front and rear legs extended out from body as in an old-fashioned rocking horse.

**Roll:** The fold of skin across the top of the nose. Also, gait caused by relative roundness of the rib cage coupled with short and bowed forearms, as in the Pekingese.

**Roll a coat:** A process in which the broken coat of a terrier is continually worked or plucked so that it does not have to be completely stripped.

**Rolled ears:** Ears that curl inward along the lower edge and tip.

**Rolling gait:** A swaying, ambling action of the hindquarters when moving.

**Roman nose:** A nose whose bridge is so comparatively high as to form a mildly convex line from forehead to nose tip; ram's nose.

**Root of muzzle:** The junction between the stop and the foreface.

**Root of the tail:** The base of the tail or the insertion.

**Ropy tail:** A tail normally feathered but now more or less devoid of hair; looking gnarled.

**Rose ear:** A small drop ear that folds over and back so as to reveal the burr.

**Rosette:** (1) A small tan patch on each side of the chest above the front legs. (2) A patch of hair over the loin of a Poodle trimmed in the Continental clip. (3) A pleated ribbon to resemble a rose, awarded at AKC events.

**Rotary motion:** A strong and purposeful gait, coupled with great thrust, causing the hocks and stifles to appear to move in a circular or rotary motion when viewed in profile.

**Round eye:** Eyes set in circular-shaped apertures. *Illustration p. 807.*

**Round foot:** See *Cat foot. Illustration p. 820.*

**Round neck:** A neck that is round in cross section, in contrast to a more elliptical shape.

**Rounded skull:** A topskull curved or arched in both directions from stop to occiput and from ear to ear, but not as exaggerated as in the domed skull.

**Rounding:** Cutting or trimming the ends of the ear leather, as in the English Foxhound, denoting membership in a hunting pack.

**Royal collar:** A well-developed, symmetrical, and evenly placed full white collar.

**Ruby:** A rich, mahogany red (e.g., English Toy Spaniel).

**Rudder:** The tail or stern.

**Ruff:** Thick, longer hair growth around the neck.

**Runty:** Small, weedy, stunted.

**Russet gold:** Reddish brown.

**Rust:** Used to describe several breeds, this color is a medium-brilliant reddish brown.

**Saber tail:** A tail carried in a semicircle.

**Sable:** A coat color produced by black-tipped hairs on a background of silver, gold, gray, fawn, or brown.

**Sacrum:** The region of the vertebral column that consists of three fused vertebrae that articulate with the pelvic girdle.

**Saddle:** A black marking over the back, like a saddle for a horse.

**Saddle back:** An overlong back, with a dip behind the withers.

**Sagback:** See *Swayback.*

**Saggy loin:** A weakness due to loins that are overlong and insufficiently well-muscled, causing the backline over the coupling area to sway.

**Sagittal crest:** The ridge of bone at the junction of the parietal bones, situated in the outer surface of the cranium. It runs lengthwise to and ends near the base of the skull, forming the occipital protuberance. *Illustration p. 824.*

**Sagittal suture:** The fusion of the frontal bones in the center of the skull, underlying the median line or furrow.

**Samoyed smile:** Specific expression brought about by the lips turning slightly upward at the corners of the mouth.

**Sawhorse stance:** Stance in which the long bones of the forearms or rear pasterns, or both, are not vertical to the ground when viewed from all angles.

**Scapula:** Shoulder blade.

**Scent:** The odor left by an animal on the trail (ground scent) or wafted through the air (airborne scent).

**Scimitar:** A saber tail in a more exaggerated curve.

**Scissors bite:** A bite in which the outer side (anterior portion) of the lower incisors touches the inner side (posterior portion) of the upper incisors. *Illustration p. 807.*

**Sclera:** The white membrane surrounding the cornea of the eye.

**Scrambled mouth:** Misaligned or scrambled incisors.

**Screw tail:** A naturally short tail twisted in a more or less spiral formation. *Illustration p. 847.*

**Scrotum:** The membranous pouch containing the testicles, located between the hind legs.

**Seal:** Used to describe Boston Terriers, this color appears black except that it has a red cast when viewed in the sun or bright light.

**Second joint:** The second vertebra of the tail from the point of the croup.

**Second thigh:** That part of the hindquarters from the stifle to the hock, corresponding to the human shin and calf. Lower thigh, including the tibia and fibula.

**Sectorial teeth:** The fourth premolar in the upper jaw and the first molar in the lower jaw.

**Sedge:** The color resembling dead grass, a dull tan.

**Self-color:** One color or whole color, except for lighter shadings.

**Self-marked:** A whole-colored dog with white or pale markings on chest, feet, and tail tip.

**Semi-hare foot:** Between oval and hare foot.

**Semiprick ears:** Ears carried erect with just the tips leaning forward.

**Septum:** The line extending vertically between the nostrils.

**Set-on:** A term applied to the junction of the skull and earlobe, or the junction of the tail and rump.

**Set up:** Posed so as to make the most of the dog's appearance for the show ring.

**Shagginess:** Rough, rugged, and hairy coat.

**Shambling walk:** To walk with a shuffle; lazy, uncoordinated.

**Shanks:** The thigh.

**Shark mouth:** A much overshot bite.

**Shawl:** An area of longer hair covering portions of a dog's forequarters; actually part mane, part ruff.

**Shelly:** A shallow, narrow body, lacking the correct amount of bone.

**Shepherd's crook tail:** A kink or U-shape at the end of the tail.

**Short back:** See *Close-coupled.*

**Short-coupled:** When the distance between the last rib and the beginning of the hindquarters is relatively short.

**Short head:** A muzzle excessively shortened and a skull both broad and square.

**Short stride:** Little reach and drive exhibited, and no extension of the legs.

**Short muzzle:** A stubby muzzle, shorter than half the total length of the skull.

**Shoulder blade:** The scapula; the large, flat, triangular bone just below the first and second thoracic vertebral spine.

**Shoulder joint:** A joint in the forequarters formed by the articulation of the shoulder blade and the arm.

**Shoulder point:** The formation of the scapula and humerus.

**Shuffling action:** A lazy, foot-dragging type of movement.

**Sickle-hocked:** The inability to straighten the hock joint on the backward reach of the hind leg. Hocks that cannot be perpendicular to the ground when the dog is standing.

**Sickle tail:** A tail carried out and up in a semicircle. *Illustration p. 847.*

**Sidewinding:** See *Crabbing.*

**Sighthound:** A hound that runs or courses game by sight rather than scent.

**Silver eye:** See *Walleye.*

*Sine qua non:* A Latin phrase meaning an essential element that has no equal, i.e., straight elbow, English Foxhound.

**Sinew:** Tendon; the bands of inelastic fibrous tissues formed at the termination of a muscle and attaching it to a bone.

**Sinewy:** Lean, hard condition, free from excessive muscle or fat.

**Single coat:** A dog that has no undercoat.

**Single-tracking:** Having all footprints fall on a single line of travel. When a dog breaks into a trot, its body is supported by only two legs at a time, which move as alternating diagonal pairs. To achieve balance, its legs angle inward toward a centerline beneath the body; the greater the speed, the closer they come to tracking on a single line.

**Sire:** The male parent of a dog.

**Skeleton:** Descriptively divided into axial (skull, vertebrae column, chest) and appendicular (forequarters, hindquarters) portions.

**Skewbald:** Irregular body patches of any color other than black, superimposed upon a white ground.

**Skully:** Thick and coarse through the skull.

**Slab-sided:** Flat ribs with too little spring from the spinal column.

**Slack back:** See *Swayback.*

**Slack loin:** A long, poorly muscled coupling.

**Slanting thighs:** Correctly sloping thighs.

**Sled dogs:** Dogs worked, usually in teams, to draw sleds.

**Slew feet:** Feet turned out.

**Slippage:** The outcome of patellar luxation or subluxation.

**Slipped hocks:** Popping hocks that bend forward or sideways or both, indicating joint and ligament instability.

**Slipped stifle:** Abnormality of the stifle; when the trochlear lips are insufficiently well-developed, the stifle leaves its normal position and lies on either the inside of the inner lip or on the outside of the outer lip.

**Slipper feet:** Long, oval feet.

**Sloping back:** The height measured at the withers exceeds that over the loins.

**Sloping pasterns:** The correct pastern position, between upright and down in pasterns.

**Sloping shoulder:** The shoulder blade set obliquely, or "laid back."

**Smooth coat:** Short hair, close-lying.

**Smudge nose:** See *Snow nose.*

**Snaky body:** See *Weaselness.*

**Snap tail:** Tail coming up and lying directly on the back, with the tip pointing toward the head. *Illustration p. 847.*

**Snatching hocks:** A gaiting fault indicated by a quick outward snatching of the hock as it passes the supporting leg and twists the rear pastern far in beneath the body. The action causes noticeable rocking in the rear quarters.

**Snipy:** A pointed, weak muzzle, lacking breadth and depth.

**Snow nose:** When a nose that is normally solid black acquires a pink streak in winter.

**Snowshoe feet:** Oval, firm, compact with well-knit, well-arched toes, and tough deeply cushioned pads. The feet are well furred, even between the toes, for protection.

**Socks:** White markings on colored animals from the feet and pasterns up to the wrists in the front and up to the hocks in the rear.

**Soft back:** See *Saddle back.*

**Soft feet:** See *Down in Pastern.*

**Soft mouth:** In hunting dogs, capable of retrieving game without causing physical damage to their prey.

**Soft palate:** On the roof of the mouth, a soft fleshy extension of the hard palate continuing backward toward the larynx.

**Somber expression:** A facial expression that occurs when the masking, instead of being restricted to the face, spreads onto the skull area, and rather than being clearly defined, blends indistinctly with the surrounding head color.

**Soundness:** The state of mental and physical health when all organs and faculties are complete and functioning normally, each in its rightful relation to the other.

**Spar:** To challenge the opposition cautiously. Often used to get some terrier breeds "on their toes."

**Spay:** To surgically remove a bitch's ovaries and uterus to prevent conception.

**Speak:** To bark.

**Speckling:** Flecking or ticking.

**Spectacles:** Shadings or dark markings over or around the eyes, or from eyes to ears coupled with expressive eyebrows, as in the Keeshond.

**Spike tail:** A straight, short tail that tapers rapidly along its length.

**Spinal column:** Vertebrae running from the neck to the end of the tail.

**Spindly:** Fine-boned.

**Spirally twisted tail:** A tail that is carried low with a spiral longitudinal twist at the end.

**Splashed:** Irregularly patched, color on white or white on color.

**Splashes:** In Boston Terriers, pied brindle spots on a white ground.

**Splayfoot:** A flat foot with toes spreading; open foot, open toed. *Illustration p. 820.*

**Split nose:** A line that extends from the lip and continues between the nostrils over the top of the nose.

**Split upper lip:** Incomplete union of the upper lip halves at their lower borders.

**Spoon ear:** See *Bat ear.*

**Spoon-shaped foot:** See *Oval foot.*

**Sporting Breeds:** A group of dogs developed for the hunting of feathered game.

**Spot:** The kissing spot on the Blenheim variety of the English Toy Spaniel and the Cavalier King Charles Spaniel, also a distinct patch of color on other parts of the body.

**Spotted:** Speckled, flecked, ticked.

**Spotted nose:** See *Butterfly nose.*

**Spread:** Width between the forelegs, when accentuated, as in the Bulldog.

**Spread hocks:** Hocks pointing outward.

**Spreading toes:** See *Splayfoot.*

**Spring:** See *Flush.*

**Spring of ribs:** The curvature of the ribs to create a cavity for the heart and lungs.

**Springy action:** A bouncing, buoyant motion.

**Square body:** A dog whose height from the withers to the ground equals its length from the forechest to the buttocks.

**Square muzzle:** See *Blunt muzzle.*

**Squirrel tail:** A tail carried up and curving more or less forward.

**Stack:** The posing of a dog in a natural position; pose. See *Set up.*

**Stag red:** Deep red (almost brown) with intermingling of black hairs (e.g., Miniature Pinscher).

**Stake:** The designation of a class, used in field trial competition.

**Stance:** A manner of standing.

**Standard:** A description of the ideal dog of each recognized breed, to serve as an ideal against which dogs are judged at shows.

**Stand-off coat:** A long or heavy coat that stands away from the body.

**Star:** A white mark on the forehead.

**Staring coat:** The hair dry, harsh, and sometimes curly at the tips.

**Station:** The comparative height from the ground, as in "high-stationed" and "low-stationed."

**Steep:** Used to denote incorrect angles of articulation. For example, a steep front describes a more upright shoulder placement than is preferred.

**Stern:** The tail.

**Sternebrae:** The bony components of the sternum or breastbone.

**Sternum:** See *Breastbone.*

**Stifle:** The joint of the hind leg between the thigh and the second thigh; the dog's knee.

**Stilted:** The choppy, up-and-down gait of a straight-hocked dog.

**Stippled:** A pattern of dots instead of lines, as in the harlequin Great Dane.

**Stockings:** An area of white covering most of the leg.

**Stop:** The step up from the muzzle to the back skull; indentation between the eyes where the nasal bones and cranium meet. *Illustration p. 824.*

**Stop effect:** A slight stop appearance produced by prominent eyebrows.

**Stopper pad:** The fleshy cushion on the front legs situated at the back of the wrist (carpus).

**Straddle:** A stance similar to a sawhorse position where the fore and hind limbs are extended away and out from the body's centerline.

**Straight back:** A back that runs in a straight line without dip or arch from withers to loin.

**Straight front:** True front; viewed head-on, the forearms run perpendicular to the ground as well as parallel to each other. *Illustration p. 821.*

**Straight-hocked:** Lacking appreciable angulation at the hock joints.

**Straight in pastern:** Little or no bend at the wrist.

**Straight shoulders:** The shoulder blades are straight up and down, as opposed to sloping or "well laid back." *Illustration p. 821.*

**Stripe:** See *Blaze.*

**Stripping:** A technique in which the hair is pulled by hand or with the aid of a stripping knife.

**Strong quarters:** Well-developed, powerfully muscled hindquarters.

**Stubby muzzle:** See *Short muzzle.*

**Stud book:** A record of the breeding particulars of dogs of recognized breeds.

**Stud dog:** A male dog used for breeding purposes.

**Stud Dog class:** A class where a stud dog is shown and judged with at least two of his offspring. Judging is based on the quality of the get, not the sire. (Show-giving club may permit more offspring to be shown. The upper limit must be stated in the premium list.)

**Stuffy neck:** A short, blocky, and inelegant neck. See *Bull neck.*

**Stump tail:** A tail naturally shorter than is desired.

**Subluxation:** A partial, incomplete, or slight dislocation.

**Substance:** Bone.

**Sunken eyes:** Eyes that are well recessed into the sockets.

**Sunken pastern:** See *Down in pastern.*

**Superciliary arches:** The ridge, projection, or prominence of the frontal bones of the skull over the eyes; the brow; supraorbital ridges.

**Superintendent:** An individual licensed by the AKC and hired by a club to be responsible for the mechanics of holding an event.

**Suspension trot:** See *Flying trot.*

**Swan neck:** See *Goose neck.*

**Swayback:** A concave curvature of the vertebral column between the withers and the hipbones.

**Sweepstakes:** A nonregular competition offered in conjunction with regular classes at specialty shows for puppies or veterans. Class divisions, requirements, and conditions are established by the show-giving club. No championship points are awarded.

**Swirl:** A slight upward turn of the tail; hook, sweep.

**Sword tail:** A tail that hangs down without deviation. When carried upward, it is synonymous with a flagpole tail.

**Symmetry:** The pleasing balance between all parts of the dog.

**Swirl tail:** See *Hook tail.*

**Tail carriage:** The manner of tail deportment, i.e., gay, sickle, curl. *Illustration p. 847.*

**Tail set:** How the base of the tail sets on the rump.

**Tailhead:** The beginning of the tail attachment to the croup.

**Tails**

**Tapering muzzle:** A wedge-shaped, pointed muzzle.

**Tapering tail:** A long, short-coated tail that tapers to a point.

**Tarsal bones:** The seven bones that make up the hock (tarsus).

**Tarsus:** The hock or the ankle.

**Tawny:** A light fawn color. See *Lion color.*

**Taut coat:** Skin that is sleek and stretched taut without any wrinkles, folds, or creases.

**Team:** A group, usually of four dogs, exhibited by one handler.

**Teapot curve curve tail:** See *Pot-hook tail.*

**Tear stain:** A dark brown stain running from the inner corner of the eye.

**Teeth eruption:** The process of teeth appearing through the gums.

**Temples:** Area just behind and slightly above the eyes.

**Tendon:** A band of inelastic tissue formed at the termination of a muscle, attaching it to the bone; sinew.

**Terrier breeds:** A group of dogs used originally for hunting vermin.

**Terrier expression:** A general outward head and facial appearance resembling a terrier; eyes small and deep set.

**Terrier front:** A straight front, as found on Fox Terriers.

**Testicles:** The male gonad that produces spermatozoa. AKC regulations specify that a male that does not have two normal testicles located in the scrotum may not compete at any show and will be disqualified, except that a castrated male may be entered in obedience trials, tracking tests, field trials (except Beagles), and as a stud dog in a Stud Dog class.

**Thick skull:** Coarse, excessive width, especially around the cheek area, due to thick, coarse bone.

**Thickset:** Having a burly body construction.

**Thigh:** The hindquarters from hip to stifle.

**Thigh bone:** The femur.

**Thin pads:** The opposite of well-cushioned pads.

**Third eyelid:** A semicartilaginous structure located at the eyes' inner corners.

**Thoracic vertebrae:** The thirteen vertebrae of the chest with which thirteen pairs of ribs articulate.

**Thorax:** The part of the body or trunk that is enclosed by the ribs.

**Thoroughbred appearance:** Resembling a high-quality, aristocratic-looking purebred horse.

**Throatiness:** An excess of loose skin under the throat.

**Throat latch:** The area of the head and neck junction immediately behind and below the lower jaw angles.

**Thumb marks:** Black spots on the region of the pastern.

**Tibia:** One of the two bones of the leg, i.e., the lower thigh, second thigh, or lower leg.

**Ticked:** Small, isolated areas of black hairs on a white ground.

**Tied at the elbows:** See *Paddling.*

**Tied in shoulders:** An anatomical construction that results in a firmer or more inelastic connection of the shoulder blade to the chest wall than is ideal.

**Tight-fitting jacket:** Taut skin and coat fitting without any sign of looseness or wrinkles.

**Tight-lipped jaws:** Outline created by relatively thin lips, closely following the bony jaw outline.

**Timber:** Colloquial expression for bone, usually leg bone.

**Title:** An award conferred on a dog for completing specific qualifications earned at AKC events or AKC-sponsored activities.

**Toeing in:** See *Pigeon-toed.*

**Tongue:** The barking or baying of hounds on the trail, as "to give tongue," to open or speak.

**Topcoat:** See *Coat.*

**Topknot:** A tuft of longer hair on top of the head.

**Topline:** The dog's outline from just behind the withers to the tail set.

**Topskull:** See *Crown.*

**Torso:** The body.

**Tottering gait:** A swaying, feeble, unsteady gait.

**Toy Breeds:** A group of dogs characterized by very small size.

**Toyishness:** The character of very small size.

**Trace:** A dark stripe down the back of the Pug.

**Tractable temperament:** Easily controlled. See *Biddable.*

**Trail:** To hunt by following ground scent.

**Trailing tail:** A tail carried straight out behind, where it is less apt to become tangled in the harness of a sled.

**Triangular eyes:** The eye set in surrounding tissue of triangular shape; three-cornered eye. *Illustration p. 807.*

**Triangular ears:** V-shaped ears.

**Trichiasis:** An abnormal direction or turning in of the eyelash.

**Tri-color:** Three color; white, black, and tan.

**Trim:** To groom the coat by plucking, clipping, or scissoring.

**Trimmings:** See *Furnishings.*

**Trot:** A rhythmic two-beat diagonal gait in which the feet at diagonally opposite ends of the body strike the ground together, i.e., right hind with left front and left hind with right front.

**Trousers:** Longish hair at the back of both the upper and lower thighs of some breeds.

**True front:** See *Straight front.*

**True ribs:** The first nine pairs of ribs.

**Trumpet:** The slight depression or hollow on either side of the skull just behind the orbit or eye socket, comparable with the temple in humans.

**Tuck–up:** Characterized by markedly shallower body depth at the loin; smaller waisted.

**Tufted tail:** A tail with a plume of hair at the end.

**Tulip ear:** An ear carried erect with edges curving forward and in.

**Turn–up:** An uplifted face.

**Turned over the back tail:** An exaggerated squirrel or snap tail, but making contact along the back.

**Tusks:** See *Canines.*

**Twisting hocks:** A gaiting fault in which the hock joints twist both ways as they flex or bear weight. Also called "rubber hocks."

**Twisted tail:** See *Spirally twisted tail.* Also, *Curled tail.*

**Two–angle head:** Diverging head planes when viewed in profile, in contrast to the desirable parallel head planes.

**Type:** The characteristic qualities distinguishing a breed; the embodiment of a standard's essentials.

**Ulna:** One of the two bones of the forearm.

**Umbrella:** Synonymous with the veil, but shorter.

**Unbalanced head:** Incorrect, uneven proportions of skull and foreface.

**Undercoat:** The short, soft, dense hair that supports the outer coat.

**Underline:** The combined contours of the brisket and the abdominal floor.

**Undershot:** The front teeth (incisors) of the lower jaw overlapping or projecting beyond the front teeth of the upper jaw when the mouth is closed. *Illustration p. 807.*

**Undulating:** To rise and fall regularly.

**Unilateral cryptorchid:** See *Cryptorchid.*

**Unsound:** A dog physically incapable of performing the functions for which it was bred.

**Ununited anconeal process:** An inherited defect at the elbow joint.

**Up–curve:** Referring to the shape of the underline.

**Up on leg:** See *High-stationed.*

**Upfaced:** The lower jaw is positioned upward.

**Upper arm:** The humerus or bone of the foreleg, between the shoulder blade and the forearm, and associated tissue.

**Upper thigh:** The area between the hip joint above and the stifle below.

**Upright ear:** See *Prick ear.*

**Upright pastern:** Steep pasterns; the longitudinal axis approaches the perpendicular. The opposite of "Down in pastern."

**Upright shoulders:** Steep in shoulders; straight in shoulders.

**Utilitarian:** Meant to be useful rather than beautiful.

**Utility class:** An obedience class for dogs who have won the title Companion Dog Excellent (CDX).

**Variety:** A division within a breed, based on size or coat type, approved by the AKC. Nine AKC breeds are divided into varieties: Cocker Spaniels, Beagles,

Dachshunds, Bull Terriers, Manchester Terriers, Chihuahuas, English Toy Spaniels, Poodles, and Collies.

**Varminty:** A keen, very bright, or piercing expression.

**Veil:** The portion of the dog's forelock hanging straight down over the eyes or partially covering them.

**Vent:** The anal opening.

**Ventral:** The belly; opposite of dorsal.

**Vertebra:** One of the bones of the spinal column.

**Vertebral column:** The bones of the central axis of the dog behind the skull, including cervical, thoracic, lumbar, sacral, and caudal vertebrae.

**Vine leaf ears:** Ear leather that is shaped to resemble a vine leaf.

**Waddling:** A clumsy, tottering, and restricted hindquarter motion.

**Waist:** The narrowing of the body over the loins.

**Walk:** A gaiting pattern in which three legs are supporting the body at all times, each foot lifting from the ground one at a time in regular sequence.

**Walleye:** An eye with a whitish iris; a blue eye, fisheye, pearl eye.

**Wasted motion:** An inefficient movement created by most movement faults.

**Weak hocks:** Hock joints that are not normal or are deformed.

**Weaselness:** A body shape that is long and lean, with short legs.

**Weather-resistant coat:** A coat that is resistant to wet, cold, freezing weather.

**Weaving gait:** See *Crossing over.*

**Webbed:** Connected by a membrane. Webbed feet are important for water-retrieving breeds such as the Chesapeake Bay Retriever and Newfoundland.

**Wedge-shaped head:** A V-shaped or triangular head when viewed from above or in profile.

**Weedy:** An insufficient amount of bone; light bone.

**Well-knit:** Body sections that are firmly joined by well-developed muscles.

**Well knuckled-up toes:** See *Cat foot.*

**Well laid back:** Well-angulated shoulders.

**Well let down:** The hock is well let down when the rear pasterns are short.

**Well padded toes:** Deeply cushioned toe pads.

**Well-proportioned:** Correct balance between various parts of the body.

**Wet neck:** Loose or superfluous skin; with dewlap.

**Wheaten:** Pale yellow or fawn color.

**Wheel back:** A marked arch of the thoracic and lumbar vertebrae; roached.

**Wheel tail:** See *Making a wheel.*

**Whip tail:** A tail carried out stiffly straight and pointed. *Illustration p. 847.*

**Whiskers:** The vibrissae or sensory organs (hair) on the sides of the muzzle.

**Whitelies:** White body color with red or dark markings, as in the Pembroke Welsh Corgi.

**Whorls:** A ridge of hair growing in a circular pattern, as in the Rhodesian Ridgeback.

**Wide thighs:** The maximum development of upper thigh muscles.

**Widow's peak:** A triangular marking on the hair of the forehead.

**Wildboar:** A mixture of black, brown, and gray.

**Wind:** To catch the scent of game.

**Winging:** A gaiting fault where one or both front feet twist outward as the limbs swing forward.

**Winners:** An award given at dog shows to the best dog (Winners Dog) and best bitch (Winners Bitch) competing in regular classes.

**Wirehair:** A coat of hard, crisp, wiry texture.

**Withers:** The region defined by the dorsal portions of the spinous processes of the first two thoracic vertebrae and flanked by the dorsal (uppermost) portions of the scapulae.

**Withers separation:** The space palpable between the scapulas vertebral borders at the withers region.

**Wolf claw:** A dewclaw on the hind leg.

**Work a coat:** A method of rolling or plucking the broken-coated terrier.

**Working breeds:** A group of dogs used to pull carts, guard property, and for search and rescue.

**Working condition:** An animal that is firm, well muscled, lean rather than plump.

**Wrinkle:** Loose, folding skin on forehead and foreface.

**Wrist:** The carpus; the joint between forearm and pastern on the front legs.

**Wry mouth:** An asymmetrical alignment of upper and lower jaws; cross bite.

**Xiphoid process:** The cartilage process of the sternum.

**Zygomatic arch:** A bony ridge extending posteriorly (and laterally) from beneath the eye orbit. Anatomically consists of two processes: zygomatic process of the maxilla and the maxillary process of the zygomatic bone. *Illustration p. 824.*

# INDEX